The 19th Century

1801-1900

Great Lives from History

The 19th Century

1801-1900

Volume 4
Friedrich Karl von Savigny - Émile Zola
Indexes

Editor
John Powell
Oklahoma Baptist University

Editor, First Edition
Frank N. Magill

SALEM PRESS
Pasadena, California   Hackensack, New Jersey

Editor in Chief: Dawn P. Dawson
Editorial Director: Christina J. Moose
Acquisitions Editor: Mark Rehn
Research Supervisor: Jeffry Jensen
Research Assistant: Rebecca Kuzins
Manuscript Editor: R. Kent Rasmussen

Indexer: Rowena Wildin Dehanke
Production Editor: Andrea E. Miller
Graphics and Design: James Hutson
Layout: Eddie Murillo
Photo Editor: Cynthia Breslin Beres
Editorial Assistant: Dana Garey

Cover photos: The Granger Collection, New York (Pictured left to right, top to bottom: Sitting Bull, Charles Darwin, Liliuokalani, Louisa May Alcott, Ludwig van Beethoven, Saʿīd ibn Sulṭān, Simón Bolívar, Cixi, Mark Twain)

∞ The paper used in these volumes conforms to the American National Standard for Permanence of Paper for Printed Library Materials, Z39.48-1992 (R1997).

Some of the essays in this work originally appeared in the following Salem Press sets: *Dictionary of World Biography* (© 1998-1999, edited by Frank N. Magill) and *Great Lives from History* (© 1987-1995, edited by Frank N. Magill). New material has been added.

Library of Congress Cataloging-in-Publication Data

Great lives from history. The 19th century, 1801-1900 / editor, John Powell.
    p. cm.
  "Editor, first edition, Frank N. Magill."
  Some of the essays in this work were originally published in Dictionary of world biography and the series of works collectively titled, Great lives from history, both edited by Frank N. Magill; with new material added.
  Includes bibliographical references and index.
  ISBN-13: 978-1-58765-292-9 (set : alk. paper)
  ISBN-10: 1-58765-292-7 (set : alk. paper)
  ISBN-13: 978-1-58765-296-7 (v. 4 : alk. paper)
  ISBN-10: 1-58765-296-X (v. 4 : alk. paper)
  [etc.]
  1. Biography—19th century. I. Powell, John, 1954- II. Magill, Frank Northen, 1907-1997 III. Dictionary of world biography. IV. Great lives from history. V. Title: 19th century, 1801-1900. VI. Title: Nineteenth century, 1801-1900.
  CT119.G69 2006
  920.009′034—dc22
                                2006020187

First Printing

CONTENTS

KEY TO PRONUNCIATION

Many of the names of personages covered in *Great Lives from History: The Nineteenth Century, 1801-1900* may be unfamiliar to students and general readers. For these unfamiliar names, guides to pronunciation have been provided upon first mention of the names in the text. These guidelines do not purport to achieve the subtleties of the languages in question but will offer readers a rough equivalent of how English speakers may approximate the proper pronunciation.

Vowel Sounds

Symbol	Spelled (Pronounced)
a	answer (AN-suhr), laugh (laf), sample (SAM-puhl), that (that)
ah	father (FAH-thur), hospital (HAHS-pih-tuhl)
aw	awful (AW-fuhl), caught (kawt)
ay	blaze (blayz), fade (fayd), waiter (WAYT-ur), weigh (way)
eh	bed (behd), head (hehd), said (sehd)
ee	believe (bee-LEEV), cedar (SEE-dur), leader (LEED-ur), liter (LEE-tur)
ew	boot (bewt), lose (lewz)
i	buy (bi), height (hit), lie (li), surprise (sur-PRIZ)
ih	bitter (BIH-tur), pill (pihl)
o	cotton (KO-tuhn), hot (hot)
oh	below (bee-LOH), coat (koht), note (noht), wholesome (HOHL-suhm)
oo	good (good), look (look)
ow	couch (kowch), how (how)
oy	boy (boy), coin (koyn)
uh	about (uh-BOWT), butter (BUH-tuhr), enough (ee-NUHF), other (UH-thur)

Consonant Sounds

Symbol	Spelled (Pronounced)
ch	beach (beech), chimp (chihmp)
g	beg (behg), disguise (dihs-GIZ), get (geht)
j	digit (DIH-juht), edge (ehj), jet (jeht)
k	cat (kat), kitten (KIH-tuhn), hex (hehks)
s	cellar (SEHL-ur), save (sayv), scent (sehnt)
sh	champagne (sham-PAYN), issue (IH-shew), shop (shop)
ur	birth (burth), disturb (dihs-TURB), earth (urth), letter (LEH-tur)
y	useful (YEWS-fuhl), young (yuhng)
z	business (BIHZ-nehs), zest (zehst)
zh	vision (VIH-zhuhn)

COMPLETE LIST OF CONTENTS

VOLUME I

Volume 2

VOLUME 3

VOLUME 4

LIST OF MAPS AND SIDEBARS

VOLUME I

VOLUME 2

VOLUME 3

VOLUME 4

THE WORLD IN 1801

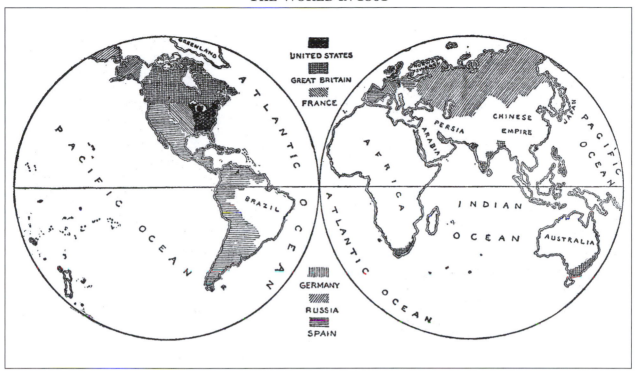

THE WORLD IN 1900

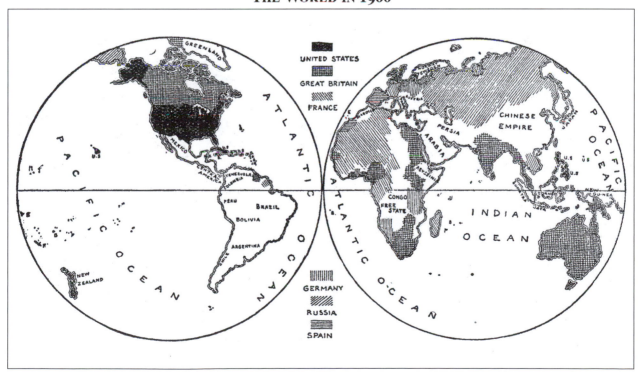

AFRICA AT THE END OF THE NINETEENTH CENTURY

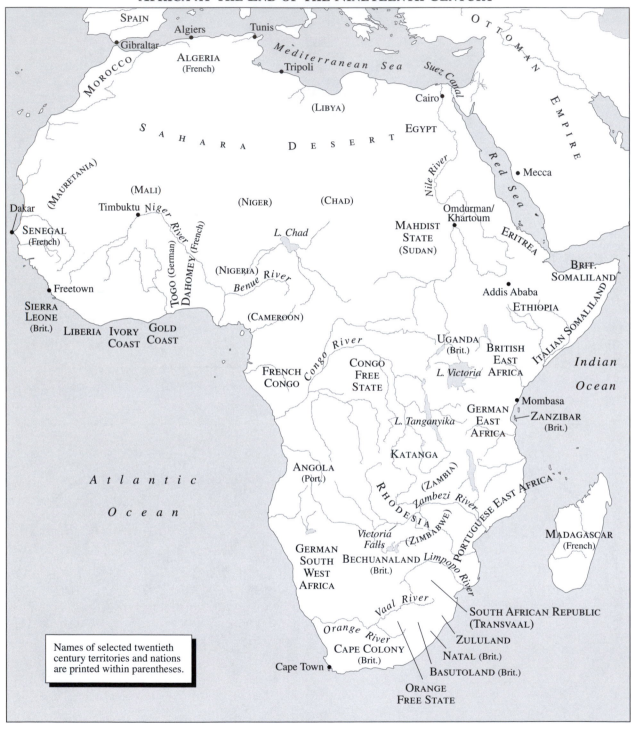

SPAIN

Gibraltar

Algiers

Tunis

MOROCCO

Mediterranean Sea

ALGERIA
(French)

Tripoli

Suez Canal

Cairo

(LIBYA)

EGYPT

OTTOMAN EMPIRE

S A H A R A   D E S E R T

Nile River

Red Sea

Mecca

(MAURETANIA)

(MALI)

Dakar

Timbuktu

Niger River

(NIGER)

(CHAD)

Omdurman/
Khartoum

SENEGAL
(French)

L. Chad

MAHDIST
STATE
(SUDAN)

ERITREA

BRIT.
SOMALILAND

TOGO (German)

DAHOMEY (French)

(NIGERIA)

Benue River

Addis Ababa

ETHIOPIA

ITALIAN SOMALILAND

Freetown

(CAMEROON)

SIERRA
LEONE
(Brit.)

LIBERIA

IVORY
COAST

GOLD
COAST

UGANDA
(Brit.)

BRITISH
EAST
AFRICA

*Indian
Ocean*

FRENCH
CONGO

Congo River

CONGO
FREE
STATE

L. Victoria

GERMAN
EAST
AFRICA

Mombasa

ZANZIBAR
(Brit.)

L. Tanganyika

Atlantic

Ocean

ANGOLA
(Port.)

KATANGA

RHODESIA

(ZAMBIA)

Zambezi River

PORTUGUESE EAST AFRICA

MADAGASCAR
(French)

*Victoria
Falls*

(ZIMBABWE)

GERMAN
SOUTH
WEST
AFRICA

BECHUANALAND
(Brit.)

Limpopo River

Vaal River

SOUTH AFRICAN REPUBLIC
(TRANSVAAL)

ZULULAND

NATAL (Brit.)

Orange River

CAPE COLONY
(Brit.)

BASUTOLAND (Brit.)

Cape Town

ORANGE
FREE STATE

Names of selected twentieth
century territories and nations
are printed within parentheses.

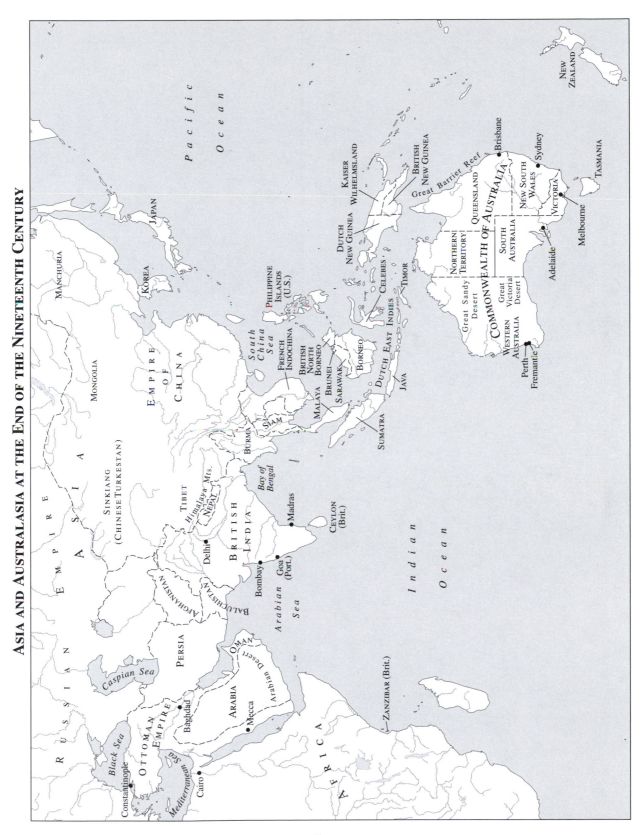

ASIA AND AUSTRALASIA AT THE END OF THE NINETEENTH CENTURY

EUROPE AT THE END OF THE NINETEENTH CENTURY

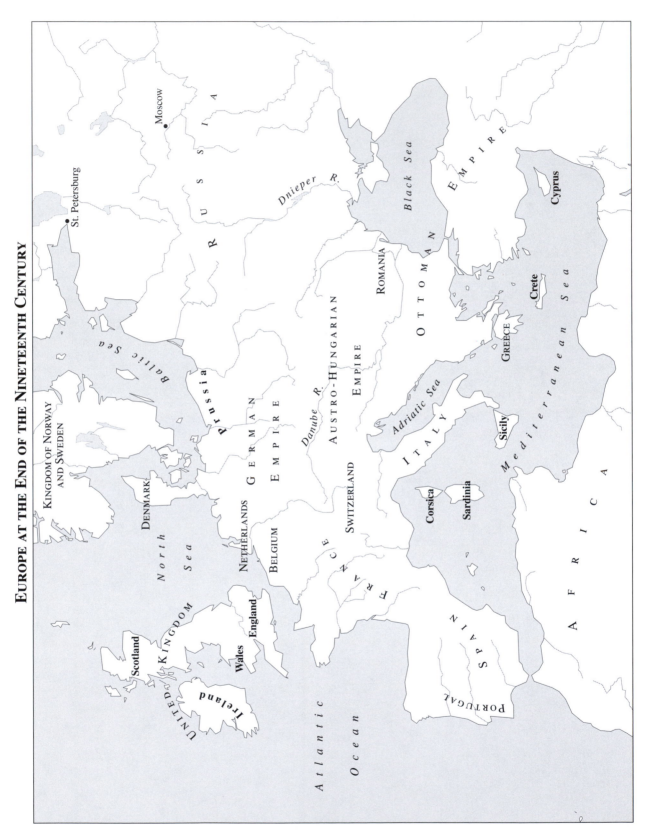

NORTH AMERICA AT THE END OF THE NINETEENTH CENTURY

Bering Sea

Bering Strait

Arctic Ocean

ALASKA

GREENLAND (Denmark)

Baffin Bay

KLONDIKE

D O M I N I O N   O F   C A N A D A

Hudson Bay

St. Lawrence River

NEWFOUNDLAND

Great Lakes

Washington

Oregon

Montana

North Dakota

Minnesota

Wisconsin

Michigan

Maine

Vermont

New Hampshire

Idaho

South Dakota

New York

Massachusetts

Rhode Island

Connecticut

Nevada

Wyoming

Nebraska

Iowa

Indiana Ohio

Illinois

Penn-sylvania

New Jersey

Delaware

California

Utah

Colorado River

Colorado

Kansas

Missouri

Ohio River

Maryland

Virginia

West Virginia

Arizona (terr.)

Rio Grande

New Mexico (terr.)

Oklahoma (terr.)

Arkansas

Kentucky

Tennessee

North Carolina

South Carolina

Mississippi River

Mississippi

Alabama

Georgia

Texas

Louisiana

Florida

M E X I C O

Gulf of Mexico

Pacific Ocean

Atlantic Ocean

CUBA

HAITI

PUERTO RICO

JAMAICA

DOMINICAN REPUBLIC

C E N T R A L   A M E R I C A

C a r i b b e a n   S e a

S O U T H   A M E R I C A

SOUTH AMERICA AT THE END OF THE NINETEENTH CENTURY

North Atlantic Ocean

Caracas

BRITISH GUIANA

DUTCH GUIANA

FRENCH GUIANA

VENEZUELA

Bogotá

COLOMBIA

Galápagos Islands

ECUADOR

Quito

Amazon River

Amazon Basin

BRAZIL

São Francisco River

PERU

Lima

Andes Mountains

La Paz

BOLIVIA

Sucre

South Pacific Ocean

PARAGUAY

Paraná River

Rio de Janeiro

CHILE

Santiago

ARGENTINA

Buenos Aires

Montevideo

URUGUAY

South Atlantic Ocean

Negro River

Falkland Islands (British)

Stanley

Cape Horn

South Georgia

The 19th Century

1801-1900

FRIEDRICH KARL VON SAVIGNY
German jurist and legal scholar

Savigny was a leading historian of Roman law. In the field of legal philosophy, he is considered generally to be either the founder or the leading exponent of the so-called historical or Romantic school of jurisprudence, which means that the content of a given body of law can only be understood through a process of historical research.

BORN: February 21, 1779; Frankfurt am Main (now in Germany)

DIED: October 25, 1861; Berlin, Prussia (now in Germany)

AREA OF ACHIEVEMENT: Law

EARLY LIFE

Thin, with thick dark hair and a kind and generous face, Friedrich Karl von Savigny (SAHV-ihn-yee) was descended from a wealthy Protestant noble family that had emigrated from Lorraine to Frankfurt. Their family name came from the castle of Savigny near Charmes in the Moselle valley.

Savigny was educated at the Universities of Göttingen, Jena, Leipzig, Halle, and Marburg; at Marburg, he studied under Philipp Friedrich Weiss, a specialist in medieval jurisprudence, and Anton Bauer, whose reputation was gained in activities keyed toward the reform of German criminal law. Receiving his degree in 1800, Savigny determined to spend his life in scholarly pursuits. Personally wealthy, he was probably the first of the ruling classes to take up teaching as a career, a field that, because of its low pay and accordingly poor social standing, had hitherto largely drawn its members from the lower-middle classes.

As privatdocent at Marburg, where Savigny lectured in criminal law and on the Pandects of the Roman law, he published *Das Recht des Besitzes* (1803; *Treatise on Possession: Or, The Jus Possessionis of the Civil Law*, 6th ed. 1848), which he allegedly wrote in seven months and which gained for him offers of two chairs, one at Greifswald and one at Heidelberg. Savigny also published in 1803 a brief article in a short-lived English periodical, *The Monthly Register*, in which, after an assessment of German universities at that time, he declared that only four of almost forty universities in Germany were of more than local importance. In 1804 Savigny married Kunigunde Brentano, so he declined both university offers in favor of a honeymoon that included searching the libraries of France and Germany for manuscripts that

would aid him in writing a proposed history of Roman law in the Middle Ages.

Savigny did, however, advise the government of Baden, one of the many independent German states, on the reorganization of the University of Heidelberg, which helped to make Heidelberg one of the important seats of learning in Europe. In 1808, Savigny went to the University of Landshut in Bavaria as professor of Roman law, and, in 1810, he not only took a significant share in the foundation of the University of Berlin but also was the first to be elected rector, or vice chancellor. He helped to organize the university on lines similar to those employed at Heidelberg, but with perhaps greater success. Savigny remained at the University of Berlin until March of 1842.

LIFE'S WORK

In 1817, Savigny became a member of the Department of Justice in the Prussian Privy Council and, in that same year, a member of a commission for organizing the Prussian provincial estates. In 1819, he became a member of the Berlin Court of Appeal and Cassation for the Rhine Provinces, in 1826 a member of the commission for revising the Prussian code, and in 1842 chairman of the newly established department for revision of statutes. In 1842, he was also appointed *Grosskanzler* (high chancellor), or head, of the juridical system in Prussia, a post he held until the revolutions of 1848, after which he devoted himself to his writing and research, holding no more government positions.

In 1806, Napoleon I promulgated the Code Napoleon, which provided a uniform body of rules for the French nation; many Germans looked upon this code enviously as an example of what should and could be done for the German people. In 1814, a professor of civil law at the University of Heidelberg, Anton Friedrich Justus Thibaut, wrote an article arguing that the law of the German people be codified both as a means of unifying the German states and as a means of applying a universally held logic or rule of reason to the law.

Savigny objected strenuously in his famous pamphlet *Vom Beruf unserer Zeit für Gesetzgebung und Rechtswissenschaft* (1814; *Of the Vocation of Our Age for Legislation and Jurisprudence*, 1831), theorizing that law, like language, arises out of the customs, traditions, needs, and spirit of a particular people or community (*Volkgeist*) and that law cannot be imposed on a people or community arbitrarily. Something that is logical and reasonable for the French or English mind may be entirely illogical for the German. Rather than arbitrarily impose a mass of legislation upon a people, one must research the particular history of that people to determine the law that suits it best.

This exaltation of customary law, as distinguished from law as a universal rule of reason, was derived from the worldview of the Romantics. It proved, whether intended so by Savigny, to be not only the glorification of things German but also a recognition of distinctions between one German state and another. Furthermore, this concept of Savigny argued against the codification of the law of any particular people at any particular time, because, according to Savigny, the law, wherever located, was always in the process of evolving and neither could nor should reach a point where codification was possible. In 1815, with Karl Friedrich Eichorn and Johann Friedrich Ludwig Göschen, he founded the *Zeitschrift für geschichtliche Rechtswissenschaft* (journal of historical jurisprudence), a periodical voicing the ideas of the historical school.

Savigny's theories, therefore, were the heart of the Romantic branch of the historical school of jurisprudence, which tended to dominate the German universities until his death and which were powerful enough to delay until 1900 the codification of German law— well after German unification in 1871. Nevertheless, despite Savigny's emphasis on the historical approach, he was not an advocate of natural law. In his *Juristische Methodenlehre, nach der Ausarbeitung des Jakob Grimm* (wr. 1802-1803, pb. 1951; legal methodology as elaborated by Jakob Grimm), delivered as a lecture at Marburg, Savigny voiced the view that the historical approach should be systematic, so that the result contributes to a clearly defined system of legal science.

A second aspect of Savigny's work dealt with the study and research of Roman law. His *Geschichte des römischen Rechts im Mittelalter* (1815-1831, 1834-1851; partial translation as *The History of Roman Law During the Middle Ages*, 1829) remains the definitive work on the subject. Although Roman law, which he admired, had been codified, Savigny tried to demonstrate that, despite the codifications, Roman law was actually administered as customary law, bringing it into conformity with the historical school of thought.

Apart from this, Savigny's scholarship eliminated much of the incongruity that had clouded the understanding of Roman law during the period from the fall of the Roman Empire until 1100 C.E. *System des heutigen*

römischen Rechts (1840-1849) presents in its eighth volume Savigny's theories of private international law and the first modern systematic presentation of this phase of the law. The eighth volume also shows that Savigny was acquainted with the work of Joseph Story, an associate justice of the U.S. Supreme Court. In 1850, Savigny published *Vermischte Schriften* (miscellaneous writings), a collection of various pieces on the law. *Das Obligationenrecht* (1851-1853; the law of contracts), which is a furtherance of *System des heutigen römischen Rechts*, emphasizes freedom of contract, which proved of great use after the unification of Germany in the rise of industrial capitalism prior to World War I.

Although Savigny opposed a codification of German law, he nevertheless approved the application of the Roman law code to Germany, avoiding this contradiction by stating that Roman law during the Middle Ages had been so generally applied to and used by the German people that it had become in many respects part of the German customary law and thereby reflective of the German *Volkgeist*. Savigny's thinking is weak in that codification is not necessarily an imposition of arbitrary law upon an unwilling people; it may be a mere memorial of a people's customary law, and codification may thus be a plateau in the natural evolution of a people's customary law. Further, as Julius Stone has noted, the *Volkgeist* doctrine

> probably exaggerated the role in legal development of popular consciousness as distinct from the consciousness of small groups, either of specialists or of a dominant class . . . [and] the element of conscious attitudes . . . which lies behind a people's relation with its law.

SIGNIFICANCE

Friedrich Karl von Savigny's contribution to law lies in his objection to codifications and in his scholarship in Roman law. He connected these two aspects of his work by maintaining that there had never really been a codification of Roman law but merely a development of customary law by an evolutionary process natural to the Roman people and the Roman Empire. This spirit of nationhood in the law was contrary to the nineteenth century efforts of the codifiers to press upon the German people an arbitrary set of laws unnatural to it.

At the time of his writing, Savigny was popular; those who wanted greater democracy were delighted with the concept that the people and not the nobility were the real makers of the law, and the nobility or aristocracy was happy to have found a way to avoid needed reforms. In the end, the results were not entirely salutary, for Savigny's emphasis on the *Volkgeist* tended to strengthen the concept of German mysticism, to glorify the superiority of German law, to stifle reforms, to inhibit the development of a badly needed code for a unified people, and perhaps even to set another stone in the edifice of corrupt nationalism. Savigny's major contribution to the law, it would appear, remains his scholarly work in laying open the field of Roman law, his insistence that the practice and theory of jurisprudence must be one and the same, his recognition of the evolutionary process in law, and his elevation of the profession of teaching and scholarship.

—Robert M. Spector

FURTHER READING

Allgemeine Deutsche Biographie. Leipzig, Germany: Duncker and Humblot, 1875-1912. The article on Savigny, in this fifty-six-volume biography of prominent Germans, presents a clear and sometimes provocative presentation of Savigny's life and doctrines. In German.

Jones, J. Walter. *Historical Introduction to the Theory of Law*. Reprint. New York: A. M. Kelley, 1969. Chapter 2 discusses the legal codes in France and Germany, Thibaut, and Savigny's criticism of the codes, together with excellent material on the pros and cons of the historical school of legal thought. The concepts of other legal historians of the period are brought to bear upon the historical school so that the reader obtains a fair view of the thinking on the subject during the nineteenth century.

Kantorowicz, Hermann U. "Savigny and the Historical School of Law." *Law Quarterly Review* 53 (July, 1937): 326-343. Presents some of the facts of Savigny's life but largely deals with the meaning of the historical school. Kantorowicz believes that it is Savigny's scholarship and research in Roman law that constitute his real contribution to legal science. The article, however, is difficult reading for the layperson.

Montmorency, James E. G. de. "Friedrich Karl von Savigny." In *Great Jurists of the World*, edited by John Macdonell and Edward Manson. Vol. 2. Boston: Little, Brown, 1914. Contains biographies of great jurists from Gaius through Rudolph von Ihering. In the selection on Savigny, Montmorency gives a general picture of Savigny's concepts of the historical school of law. Montmorency does not discuss the essential contradiction between Savigny's glorification of the evolutionary law of a particular people and his desire to impress Roman law upon the Germans, a point that is well discussed in the work by Stone, cited below.

Stone, Julius. *The Province and Function of Law*. Sydney, N.S.W.: Associated General, 1946. Chapter 18 is probably the best brief study of Savigny's ideas. Concisely presents Savigny's opposition to a code for Germany and gives a fine overview of his work in the Roman law of the Middle Ages in Europe and as applied to Europe in his own time. Also treats the essential conflict between Savigny's insistence on an evolutionary customary law, his demand for an acceptance of the codified Roman law, and his attempt to resolve the conflict.

Ziolkowski, Theodore. *Clio the Romantic Muse: Historicizing the Faculties in Germany*. Ithaca, N.Y.: Cornell University Press, 2004. Examines how a sense of history permeated German thought from 1790 to 1810, influencing the disciplines of law, philosophy, theology, and medicine. Includes biographical information on German scholars whose work exemplified this Romantic historicism, including chapters on Savigny and the historical school of law and the codification controversy.

SEE ALSO: Theodor Mommsen; Napoleon I; Joseph Story.

RELATED ARTICLE in *Great Events from History: The Nineteenth Century, 1801-1900:* 1824: Ranke Develops Systematic History.

GERHARD JOHANN DAVID VON SCHARNHORST
German military leader

*Scharnhorst's modernization of the Prussian army
made it the model for the European armies of the
nineteenth century. Among the reforms that he either
initiated or helped to push through were the
development of the general staff, the abolition of army
corporal punishment, a scheme for training large
numbers of recruits, and the overhaul of Prussian
tactical training.*

BORN: November 12, 1755; Bordenau, Lippe (now in
Germany)
DIED: June 28, 1813; Prague, Bohemia, Austrian
Empire (now in Czech Republic)
AREA OF ACHIEVEMENT: Military

EARLY LIFE

Gerhard Johann David von Scharnhorst (SHAHRN-
horst) was born in a small town in the principality of
Lippe, one of the sleepy, minor German states of the
time. The son of an independent small farmer, Scharnhorst was born a commoner whose connections to the aristocracy were limited to two uncles who sold fish and
other supplies to the kitchen of the Elector of Hanover.
Nevertheless, Scharnhorst's father had served in the artillery of the Hanoverian army as a sergeant major, and it
was a military career that the young boy would pursue.

Scharnhorst had the good fortune to be enrolled at the
Military Academy of the Count of Schaumburg-Lippe, a
cadet school that provided an education far above what
was commonly taught at such provincial institutions.
Commissioned as an officer-cadet in 1778 and made second lieutenant in the artillery in 1784, Scharnhorst, like
Napoleon I, took advantage of new openings in the military for men of the middle class. Recent inventions had
made the artillery technologically the most advanced
arm of the European armies, and its officers were necessarily chosen on a basis of proficiency rather than of noble birth.

Despite its incorporation of technological progress in
its military hardware, the army in which Scharnhorst
served was still grounded in the military philosophy of
the era that effectively ended with the American War of
Independence in 1776 and the advance of the armies of
the French Revolution after 1792. In both campaigns, the
old European armies, which relied on a small, perfectly
drilled body of professional soldiers able to move with
mathematical precision to the orders of its commander,
were beaten by an ill-trained but highly motivated mass

army that replaced chessboard strategies with a revolutionizing reliance on open fire and massive offensive
punches.

Since the European aristocrats had decided to fight
revolutionary France, Scharnhorst first fought on the bat-
tlefields of Belgium and distinguished himself both as a
courageous tactical leader and as a valuable chief of staff.
In order to share his new insights into modern warfare,
Scharnhorst took on the editorship of an influential military journal and began his lifelong career as a military
writer. The Hanoverian army, however, was not an adequate vehicle for Scharnhorst's ambitions, and the forty-
five-year-old major began to look for advancement elsewhere.

LIFE'S WORK

In 1801, Scharnhorst offered his services to King Frederick William III of Prussia; however, he attached three
conditions to his coming: He asked to be made lieutenant-
colonel, to be raised to the nobility, and to be allowed to
transform the Prussian army into a modern fighting force
that could therefore withstand the onslaught of France.
As further proof of his qualifications, the Hanoverian officer attached three essays on military topics.

In December, 1802, when Scharnhorst was actually
ennobled, the Prussian king had answered all of the
young man's requests and had made him director of the
War Academy in Berlin. Physically, Scharnhorst did not
quite fit one's idea of a Prussian staff officer: A portrait
by Friedrich Bury shows an intelligent face framed by
soft brown hair; Scharnhorst's expressive eyes gaze over
a long, fleshy nose, and his mouth seems to be trying to
suppress an ironic smile. His contemporaries noted an
absence of stiffness in Scharnhorst, and, on the parade
ground, his was not an impressive figure; when he addressed the troops, his voice failed to inspire them. On
the other hand, his writings were exceptionally clear,
witty, and persuasive. All in all, the Prussian king had obtained an officer who stood out of the crowd of his mostly
noble and aging colleagues.

From his first year in Prussian service, Scharnhorst
gathered around him an impressive body of students,
among whom was the young Carl von Clausewitz, whose
ideas would later revolutionize military thought. At the
same time, Scharnhorst communicated actively with fellow reformers in and out of the military; to create a forum
where the reform of the army could be discussed, he

founded the Military Society of Berlin in July, 1801. Soon, young and enlightened officers joined to express their ideas and to put them on paper in the society's publications.

Meanwhile, the triumphs of Napoleon began to draw the eyes of the Prussian reformers to his military machine. The movement and organization of large masses of soldiers required immense organizational support, and the French had designated that task to a still-rudimentary general staff. The idea caught on with the Prussians, and in 1803 the old quartermaster-general's staff was enlarged and reorganized. As a result, Scharnhorst was made general quartermaster-lieutenant for Western Germany (the Prussian possessions west of the river Elbe) and at once began to order such revolutionary activities as field trips for staff officers and peacetime reconnaissance and mapping of potential grounds of conflict.

War came in 1806, and Scharnhorst tested his theories of modern military leadership when he served as a staff aide to the charismatic General Gebhard Leberecht von Blücher; however, the two men could not save the generally poorly led Prussian army. Captured with Blücher and released later, Scharnhorst fought valiantly at Preussisch Eylau in the East, but his superiors failed to use this tactical gain in order to engineer a strategic reversal. In 1807, Prussia had to admit defeat and sign the Peace of Tilsit.

In the aftermath of defeat, the king appointed an Army Reform Commission, which, headed by Scharnhorst, would examine the wartime conduct of every Prussian officer. As a final result of these examinations, only two of the generals who had served in 1806-1807 would still be on active duty in 1813. Furthermore, the king ordered the institution of a Ministry of War. Scharnhorst was appointed head of its General War Department and thus was put in charge of overseeing the army as a whole.

In his new position, Scharnhorst began to draft energetic proposals for reform. Central to his thoughts was the idea of a standing army in which all male citizens would serve their nation for a certain time. An important step toward this goal was taken on October 9, 1807, when Scharnhorst's civilian counterpart, the great reformer Baron Heinrich vom und zum Stein, moved the king to proclaim the abolition of serfdom in Prussia as of November 11, 1810. By this, the people of Prussia were freed to serve the state rather than their landowners.

The French limit on Prussia's army, however, which was to be kept to forty-two thousand men, prohibited the building of a larger force of conscripts and volunteers. Here, Scharnhorst found an ingenious way out when he proposed his famous *Kruempersystem*, or "shrinkage system." According to this scheme, regular soldiers of a regiment were sent on leave, while fresh recruits took their place and received a quick but thorough training. Although the effect of this system has been overestimated, Prussia had at hand about sixty-five thousand trained soldiers in 1813, and some of the surplus came from the *Kruempersystem*.

Before the suspicious French effected his removal from the General War Department in 1810, Scharnhorst had also worked on the opening of the officer corps to members of the middle class. Meanwhile, for the common soldier, Scharnhorst was coinstrumental in abolishing humiliating forms of corporal punishment, such as scourging or "running the gauntlet." While he stayed with the emerging general staff, Scharnhorst gave the Prussian army its modern organization into brigades and divisions that would each consist of a combination of infantry, cavalry, and artillery. The need for modernized tactical training did not escape his view; the army training regulations of 1812 bear witness to his influence in their placing of a new emphasis on operational flexibility and common sense, fire power, and the formation of a strong attacking force. Soldiers were increasingly trained in the field and on the rifle range, while the parade ground became less important.

When France forced Prussia into war against Russia in 1811, Scharnhorst removed himself to a remote outpost in Silesia until fortunes changed and Prussia, now an ally of Russia, declared war on France on March 16, 1813. The new war brought to fruition all the reforms for which Scharnhorst and his colleagues had struggled. Universal service was proclaimed on February 9, and the idea of a militia was realized with the formation of the *Landwehr* and *Landsturm*. Volunteers rushed to the Prussian recruitment centers, and Scharnhorst found himself appointed chief of staff to General Blücher. Together, they engaged the French in two battles. At Grossgörschen, Scharnhorst received a foot wound that developed gangrene and ultimately killed him on June 28, 1813, while he was waiting in Prague on a mission to win Austria's entry into the war against France.

SIGNIFICANCE

At a crucial moment in Prussian history, Gerhard Johann David von Scharnhorst succeeded as a leading military reformer who laid the foundations for the survival and ultimate triumph of the Prussian army in the war with France after 1813. His idea of a well-organized citizen army backed by the logistical help of a general staff would find its ultimate expression in the victories of the Prussian armies in 1866 and 1871. Scharnhorst's ideas thus proved essential for the creation of the German Empire by Otto Bismarck and Kaiser William I.

Throughout his years in the service of the Prussian state, Scharnhorst stressed the importance of education and individual dignity and responsibility for all reforms. This emphasis links Scharnhorst's military work to the struggles of his civilian counterparts, reformers such as Stein and Prince Karl von Hardenberg; it also makes him exemplary of the zeitgeist of a new era in Prussia and Germany, which drew inspiration from thinkers such as Immanuel Kant and Georg Wilhelm Friedrich Hegel.

In his reforms, Scharnhorst was always led by a deep humanism as well as a sincere appreciation of the individual soldier. As a practicing Christian, Scharnhorst also rejected the idea that army and warfare fell completely within the private sphere of the ruler. Like his pupil Clausewitz, the great reformer firmly believed in a political, rather than a personal, purpose of a nation's defense forces.

—*R. C. Lutz*

FURTHER READING

Dupuy, T. N. *A Genius for War: The German Army and General Staff, 1807-1945.* Englewood Cliffs, N.J.: Prentice-Hall, 1977. Dupuy, a retired air force colonel, views Scharnhorst as a brilliant thinker who, together with an influential group of reformers, laid the groundwork for Prussia's emerging superiority in army organization and operational leadership. Very readable and richly illustrated. Contains useful maps.

Feuchtwanger, E. J. *Prussia: Myth and Reality.* Chicago: Henry Regnery, 1970. Covers the Prussian state from its origins to its abolition in 1947 and contains a valuable chapter on the reform era. Describes Scharnhorst's accomplishments in detail and places them in the context of a broad reform movement. Depicts the obstacles that were laid in the path of the reformers by opposing elements of the old establishment. Readable, with four maps.

Goerlitz, Walter. *History of the German General Staff, 1657-1945.* Edited and translated by Brian Battershaw. New York: Frederick A. Praeger, 1953. An extremely useful look at Scharnhorst in his role as a military reformer who would prove crucial to the development of the German war machine. Contains a personal view of the man, his general environment, and his supporters, friends, students, and opponents. Very readable; illustrated.

Kitchen, Martin. *A Military History of Germany from the Eighteenth Century to the Present Day.* Bloomington: Indiana University Press, 1975. Centers on the democratic aspects of Scharnhorst's reform work. Places him in the framework of Germany's military history. Gives some background information on the Prussian state and its army. Well written and persuasive.

Koch, H. W. *A History of Prussia.* New York: Longman, 1978. A detailed account of Scharnhorst's struggles with the Prussian establishment. Contains valuable extracts of Scharnhorst's writings in translation that are not generally available in English. Contains maps and tables. Somewhat scholarly and dry in its approach but useful for further studies.

White, Charles Edward. *The Enlightened Solider: Scharnhorst and the Militärische Gessellschaft in Berlin, 1801-1805.* New York: Praeger, 1989. The only English-language book focusing on Scharnhorst. White describes how Scharnhorst founded the *Militärische Gessellschaft* (Military Society) in Berlin, and how this society became a vehicle for transforming the Prussian army into a modern fighting force.

SEE ALSO: Otto von Bismarck; Gebhard Leberecht von Blücher; Carl von Clausewitz; August von Gneisenau; Karl von Hardenberg; Georg Wilhelm Friedrich Hegel; Napoleon I; Freiherr vom Stein.

RELATED ARTICLES in *Great Events from History: The Nineteenth Century, 1801-1900:* December 2, 1805: Battle of Austerlitz; October 16-19, 1813: Battle of Leipzig; June 18, 1815: Battle of Waterloo.

FRIEDRICH WILHELM JOSEPH VON SCHELLING
German philospher

Schelling contributed to the development of German Idealism and to the rise of German Romanticism. His later ontological and mythological speculations, though unpopular among his contemporaries such as G. W. F. Hegel, have influenced modern existentialism and philosophical anthropology.

BORN: January 27, 1775; Leonberg, Württemberg (now in Germany)
DIED: August 20, 1854; Bad Ragaz, Switzerland
AREA OF ACHIEVEMENT: Philosophy

EARLY LIFE

Friedrich Wilhelm Joseph Schelling (SHEHL-ihng) was the son of Joseph Friedrich Schelling, an erudite Lutheran pastor. In 1777, his family moved to Bebenhausen near Tübingen, where his father became a professor of Oriental languages at the theological seminary. Schelling was educated at the cloister school of Bebenhausen, apparently destined for the ministry by family tradition. A gifted child, he learned the classical languages by the age of eight.

From 1790 to 1792, Schelling attended the theological seminary at Tübingen, where he met Georg Wilhelm Friedrich Hegel and Friedrich Hölderlin, the great Romantic poet. The Tübingen Evangelical Theological Seminary, located in the buildings of an old Augustinian monastery, is idyllically set over the Neckar River on a cliff, ensconced in green hills, with a view of the snow-topped craggy Alps in the distance. Good friends while students at Tübingen, Schelling, Hegel, and Hölderlin were partisans of the French Revolution and spent many hours discussing philosophy: the pantheism of Baruch Spinoza, the pure concepts of Immanuel Kant, and the Idealist system of Johann Gottlieb Fichte.

For several years after finishing at Tübingen, Schelling was a tutor for the sons of a noble family in Leipzig. He was a precocious and passionate thinker and progressed more quickly in his career than the older Hegel. His first published philosophical work was *Über die Möglichkeit einer Form der Philosophie überhaupt* (1795; on the possibility and form of philosophy in general). This text was followed by *Vom Ich als Prinzip der Philosophie* (1795; of the ego as principle of philosophy) and the article "Philosophische Briefe über Dogmatismus und Kritizismus" (1796; philosophical letters on dogmatism and criticism).

The basic theme of these works is the Absolute, which Schelling interpreted not as God but as the Absolute ego. This ego is transcendental and eternal and can be experienced through direct intuition, which Schelling defined as an intellectual process. In 1798, at the exceptionally young age of twenty-three, Schelling became a professor of philosophy at the University of Jena, where Hegel taught as an unsalaried lecturer between 1801 and 1807, and where in October, 1806, Napoleon I defeated the Prussian army and thus conquered Prussia, the most powerful state in Germany.

LIFE'S WORK

Schelling's life's work as a philosopher and teacher began at the University of Jena, the academic center of Germany. At Jena, he became a colleague and friend of the famous Fichte, at the time Germany's leading philosopher. Fichte, who had been one of Schelling's idols, had read and strongly approved of Schelling's early philosophical work. Schelling and Hegel, both Idealist philosophers, coedited the *Kritisches Journal der Philosophie*. Even though Hegel was five years older than Schelling, he at this time was thought of as Schelling's disciple; his first book compared the philosophies of Schelling and Fichte.

Jena at this time was also the center of German Romanticism, and in nearby Weimar, Friedrich Schiller and Johann Wolfgang von Goethe, German dramatists and poets, were at the height of their careers. Schelling knew both and was profoundly influenced by the Romantic movement. German Romanticism, in turn, was influenced by Schelling's philosophy, which emphasized the importance of the individual and the values of art. German Romanticism and Schelling's Idealist philosophy are both characterized by the "inward path" to truth, the quest for the totality of experience, and the desire for unity and infinity. Schelling's career falls into two periods: the first, from 1795 to 1809, and the second, which was less productive but no less significant, from 1809 to 1854.

Schelling's peers at Jena—Goethe, Schiller, the Romanticists Friedrich and August Wilhelm Schlegel, the writer/critic Ludwig Tiech, and Hegel—constituted a close group of friends who strongly influenced one another's work. For convenience, Schelling's philosophy can be divided into four stages: the subjective Idealism or his work before Jena; the philosophy of nature;

the philosophy of identity; and the philosophy of opposition between negative and positive. The two middle stages belong to his first period of productivity, while the fourth stage belongs to his final period. The second stage, his most famous and influential, began with his *Ideen zu einer Philosophie der Nature* (1797; partial translation as *Introduction to the Philosophy of Nature*, 1871).

In opposition to Fichte's idea of the world as a product of ego, Schelling on the one hand argues that the world of nature is as important as the ego and on the other finds a common ground between the two in the essence of matter, which he defines as force. In his *Von der Weltseele, eine Hypothese der höheren Physik zur Erklärung des allgemeinen Organismus* (1798; on the world soul, a hypothesis of advanced physics for the interpretation of the general organism), Schelling argues that the interpretation of the unity of nature was the basic aim of science and thus that the object of scientific study was force, of which mechanical, chemical, electrical, and vital forces were merely different manifestations.

Friedrich Wilhelm Joseph von Schelling. (Library of Congress)

This theory is similar to the unified field theory sought by Albert Einstein and now being convincingly proposed by modern physicists such as John Hagelin. In 1799, Schelling published another book on natural philosophy, defining force as pure activity. He believed that nature realized itself in finite matter through an infinite self-referral that never reached completion. This theory he considered parallel to Immanuel Kant's idea of reason forever striving toward an unattainable absolute.

While in Jena, Schelling became engaged and eventually married under bizarre circumstances. Through his friendship with August Schlegel and his charming wife, Caroline, the daughter of a professor in Göttingen and one of the most intellectually gifted women in German Romanticism, Schelling became informally engaged to Auguste Böhmer, Caroline's sixteen-year-old daughter by a previous marriage. Auguste, however, died in 1800, and Schelling was later held partly responsible for having treated her illness on the basis of his amateur medical knowledge and his impetuous self-confidence—a common trait among the Romantics. This tragedy created a bond between Schelling and Caroline, who had already felt a mutual attraction. In 1803, through the aid of Goethe, Caroline obtained a divorce from Schlegel and married Schelling. The three remained friends in true Romantic style, but the intrigue surrounding the marriage renewed allegations of Schelling's role in Auguste's death, causing him to leave Jena and join the faculty at the University of Würzburg.

At the height of his second stage, Schelling published *System des transzendentalen Idealismus* (1800; *Introduction to Idealism*, 1871), his most mature and systematic philosophical statement, in which he attempts to unite his theory of nature with the theory of knowledge developed by Kant and Fichte. In defining human consciousness as pure self-activity in opposition to the not-self, Schelling built a theory involving three stages: a movement from sensation to perception, perception to reflection, and reflection to will. This movement connected knowledge and its object. Schelling believed that since concepts cannot exist without their objects, knowledge consists of a meeting of self, object, and process, or of knower, known, and process of knowing—a view also espoused by the Vedic philosophy of India. The transcendental idealism of this book was the one area in which Schelling influenced the mature philosophy of Hegel, especially his theory of the dialectic.

In 1806, Schelling was called to Munich to be an associate for the Academy of Sciences and the secretary of the Academy of Arts. Later, he became the secretary of the philosophical branch of the Academy of Sciences. These were government sinecure positions that gave Schelling extra time for research and allowed him to lecture in Stuttgart. Around this time, he became increasingly interested in aesthetic theory and lectures on the philosophy of art. He believed art to be an organic whole that was served by its parts and moved teleologically toward a specific purpose. This purpose was not pleasure, utility, knowledge, or morality but rather beauty, which Schelling defined as the infinite actualized within the finite. He held that human intelligence in philosophy is abstract and limited, whereas in art it awakens to itself and realizes its unbounded potential. Because it reconciles nature and history and is the aim of all intelligence, art is the highest philosophy.

Schelling's third stage of thought, the philosophy of identity, proposes that the production of reality arises not from the opposition of intelligence to nature but rather from the identity of all objects in the Absolute. The identity of nature and intelligence has its source in reason, defined as an infinite field. In describing Schelling's absolute theory of unity between subject and object, Hegel wittily compared it to the night, "in which all cows are black." Schelling's theory of absolute identity was a type of pantheism, holding nature to be inseparable, even if distinguishable, from God. Here Schelling derives from the mystic Jakob Böhme. Because the essence of God is will, He can be apprehended only by means of will—that is, in action—and not by means of mere rational comprehension.

During this period, Schelling published *Philosophische Untersuchungen über das Wesen der menschlichen Freiheit* (1809; *Of Human Freedom*, 1936), in which he distinguishes between two aspects of God: perfection and the ground of being. Evil is the ground that teaches humankind the difference between good and evil, and which is therefore a necessary stage in the development toward perfection.

In 1809, Caroline died prematurely. Schelling was so distraught he did not publish another book for the rest of his life and entered the final, existential phase of his career. He first propounded his positive philosophy of this period in *Die Weltalter* (1913, written in 1811-1813; partial translation as *The Ages of the World*, 1942), a work that consisted of three volumes, one of which is *Philosophie der Mythologie* (philosophy of mythology).

In *The Ages of the World*, Schelling describes the history of God as the divine principle expressed in human history, especially in religion and myth. God is the eternal nothing, the ungrounded basis necessary for the

ground to exist. By alienating himself from himself through his own oppositional nature, God the Absolute creates the possibility of his relative opposite, which Schelling defined as freedom. Freedom is both the cause of the fall from the Absolute and the trace of the Absolute after the fall. Whereas a negative philosophy developed the idea of God by means of reason alone, Schelling's positive philosophy developed this idea by reasoning backward from the existence of the created world to the existence of God as its creator.

SIGNIFICANCE

The two phases of Friedrich Wilhelm Joseph Schelling's career were distinctly different. His second, more despondent, phase consisted of his last philosophical period, stretching across forty-five years from 1809 to 1854, in which he saw his significance as a German Idealist decline. Failing to revive his influence against Hegelianism in Berlin in 1841, he became melancholic and pessimistic, a condition he tried to surmount by developing a system of metaphysics based on Christian revelation and a personal God. Hegel's great philosophical influence was denied to Schelling, whose early and middle periods—his philosophy of nature and philosophy of identity—fell between Fichte's Idealism and Hegel's system of the Absolute spirit.

Nevertheless, over the past century Schelling's independence and importance to philosophy have become more apparent. In its concern not only with the nature of reality but also with the fact of its very existence, Schelling's philosophy bears a strong, if suggestive, resemblance to modern existentialism. In *Philosophie der Mythologie*, Schelling ventures into the field of philosophical anthropology by arguing that humanity, as the embodiment of freedom and creative intelligence, is the essence of the world, which finds expression in myth-making and religion, humanity's most profound activities. He explored the moods of sadness associated with humanity's being in the world. Like Søren Kierkegaard, Friedrich Nietzsche, Martin Heidegger, and Jean-Paul Sartre, Schelling sought to express the ineffable poignancy of human existence, anticipating the notions of existential anxiety and psychoanalytic resistance to cure. Schelling, however, was convinced that despair was denied the last word on human existence by the revelation of God.

—*William S. Haney II*

FURTHER READING

Brown, Robert F. *The Later Philosophy of Schelling: The Influence of Boehme on the Works of 1809-1815*. London: Associated University Presses, 1977. A comprehensive analysis of Schelling's ontology and doctrine of God as influenced by Jakob Böhme's mysticism. Deals with philosophical and theological problems, such as the immutability of God, and the stages in which Schelling incorporates Böhme's ideas. Contains bibliography of German and English secondary texts.

Distaso, Leonardo V. *The Paradox of Existence: Philosophy and Aesthetics in the Young Schelling*. Boston: Kluwer Academic, 2004. Examines the development of Schelling's philosophy from 1794 to 1800, focusing on his ideas about the relationship of the Absolute to Finiteness.

Esposito, Joseph L. *Schelling's Idealism and Philosophy of Nature*. London: Associated University Presses, 1977. Analysis of Schelling's philosophy of nature and its influence on nineteenth century science. Also traces the influence of Schelling's Idealism in America and provides a modern vindication of objective Idealism against those who criticize Schelling for the lack of a guiding vision. Contains selected bibliography of secondary sources, mainly in German.

Marx, Werner. *The Philosophy of F. W. J. Schelling: History, System, and Freedom*. Translated by Thomas Nenon, with a foreword by A. Hofstadter. Bloomington: Indiana University Press, 1984. Explores Schelling's conception of history as the relationship between freedom and necessity, then compares this conception with the contemporary theory of history developed by J. Habermas, showing how the latter first renounces and then proceeds to incorporate the categories of the former. Also treats Schelling's self-intuition compared to Hegel's phenomenology and interprets Schelling's notion of human freedom.

Schelling, F. W. J. *The Ages of the World*. Translated with an introduction by Frederick de Wolfe Bolman. New York: AMS Press, 1942. Schelling's text is preceded by a seventy-nine-page introduction, in which Bolman analyzes the twofold nature of Schelling's philosophy, discusses reality and nature in his development through 1812 and his interests after 1812, and then interprets *The Ages of the World*. Ends with a synoptic outline taken from the original manuscript.

_____. *System of Transcendental Idealism*. Translated by Peter Heath, with an introduction by M. Vater. Charlottesville: University Press of Virginia, 1978. Schelling's most mature and complete philosophical statements and one of his few works translated into English. Concerns the relation between self and object in his transcendental Idealism. Good introduction that compares Schelling to Fichte, Hegel, and other philosophers and discusses the relationship between the self and consciousness.

White, Alan. *Schelling: An Introduction to the System of Freedom*. New Haven, Conn.: Yale University Press, 1983. White covers Schelling's entire fifty-year career in terms of the history of modern philosophy, lucidly arguing that Schelling attempted to produce a system of freedom. Schelling is shown to identify problems with freedom and evil not treated by Hegel. Contains selected annotated bibliography.

Wirth, Jason M. *The Conspiracy of Life: Meditations on Schelling and His Time*. Albany: State University of New York Press, 2003. Analysis of Schelling's philosophy, including his ideas about the crisis of truth, the primacy of the good, and the nature of time, art, and evil. Wirth maintains that Schelling was a belated contemporary of several twentieth century philosophers, such as Heidegger, Derrida, and Foucault.

_____, ed. *Schelling Now: Contemporary Readings*. Bloomington: Indiana University Press, 2005. Collection of essays examining Schelling's philosophy, including his ideas on religion and the quest for authenticity, his relationship to Kant, and his place among twentieth century philosophers.

SEE ALSO: Karl Ernst von Baer; Georg Wilhelm Friedrich Hegel; Aleksandr Herzen; Napoleon I.

RELATED ARTICLE in *Great Events from History: The Nineteenth Century, 1801-1900:* April, 1807: Hegel Publishes *The Phenomenology of Spirit*.

FRIEDRICH SCHLEIERMACHER
German religious leader

Schleiermacher helped Christian theology address the challenges and opportunities that were offered theological thought by modern historical consciousness. His most lasting contribution has been his theological system.

BORN: November 21, 1768; Breslau, Silesia, Prussia (now Wrocław, Poland)

DIED: February 12, 1834; Berlin, Prussia (now in Germany)

ALSO KNOWN AS: Friedrich Daniel Ernst Schleiermacher (full name)

AREA OF ACHIEVEMENT: Religion and theology

EARLY LIFE

As Friedrich Daniel Ernst Schleiermacher (SHLI-ee-MAH-ker) was growing up in Silesia, his parents entrusted his education to the Moravian Brethren at Niesky. This Moravian community espoused a form of Lutheran piety associated with Count Nikolaus Ludwig von Zinzendorf. They respected the primacy of the devotional life and particularly urged a devotion to Jesus over theological formulations. They also appreciated the disciplined life.

At Niesky, where the young Schleiermacher studied from 1783 to 1785, he followed a pietistic curriculum and also had his first taste of a humanistic education. First at Niesky and then at the Moravian theological school in Barby, he was engaged in the study of Latin and Greek. This Greek study was to prove to be the beginning of classical studies and eventually led to his great German translation of Plato. In these years, he came into contact with an impressive style of piety that continued to inform his life and thought. He withdrew from the seminary at Barby because he found little understanding among his teachers for his own honest struggles and doubts. His horizons were expanded beyond Moravian piety and his previous classical studies when, in 1787, he transferred to the University of Halle.

In Berlin in 1790, Schleiermacher passed his first theological examination, and shortly thereafter he accepted a position as a private tutor in the household of Count Dohna, in West Prussia. In 1793, he became a teacher in Berlin, and the following year he completed his second theological examination. In 1794, he also received ordination in the Reformed Church and entered its service as the assistant pastor in Landsberg. The tradition of Moravian piety, his classical studies, and his ordination for ministry in the Reformed Church all serve as the backdrop for Schleiermacher's life's work.

LIFE'S WORK

Schleiermacher's two most celebrated literary works are *Über die Religion: Reden an die Gebildeten unter ihren Verächtern* (1799; *On Religion: Speeches to Its Cultured Despisers*, 1892) and *Der christliche Glaube: Nach den Grundsätzen der evangelischen Kirche im Zusammenhange dargestellt* (1821-1822; *The Christian Faith*, 1928). Both works have their geographic place of origin in Berlin, yet they were written in two different periods of Schleiermacher's life and are separated by two decades.

On Religion was written after several years' experience as a preacher and after having worked on several philosophical treatises. The Reformed clergyman had been called to the Charité Hospital in Berlin as a chaplain and preacher. Close to the turn of the century, Schleiermacher was enjoying the cultural milieu of the new Berlin society and a circle of Berlin's Romantics, to whom he had been introduced through his friendship with the poet Friedrich Schlegel. This was the beginning of the first creative period in his career. It was especially the speeches collected in *On Religion* that first made Schleiermacher famous. His audience was a circle of nontheological friends, the cultured despisers of religion, the literary and philosophical circles of society in the capital city. For them, piety had been displaced by aesthetic intuition.

In the first speech, which Schleiermacher calls an apology or a defense, he draws the distinction between religion's trappings and religion itself. The young chaplain asks his friends why they have only been concerned with shells of religion rather than going to the kernel of the matter. That kernel concerns the "pious exaltation of the mind [*Gemüt*] in which . . . the whole world is dissolved in an immediate feeling of the Infinite and the Eternal." The second and longest speech develops the nature or essence of religion.

Schleiermacher's concern was that religion be certain of its own roots and its independence in its relationship to philosophy and to morality. Religion is not only knowing or rationalism. It is not simply doing or moralism. Religion starts and ends with history. History is the most general and the most profound revelation of the deepest and the most holy. What is the finest and dearest in history can only be received in the feeling of the religious mind. Religion has to do with receptivity; it has its life in gaining perspective or intuition and feeling (*Anschauung und Gefühl*). Perspective is oriented toward the *Universum*, which has to do not only with the universe of space but also with the spiritual or intellectual world and with the historical context of relationships.

The third speech collected in *On Religion* is about the cultivation or formation of religion. Piety lies beyond teaching. A teachable religion itself would be absurd. However, teaching can awaken piety in others. The fourth speech presents the relationship of religion and society and speaks of religious community, communication, and the church. The final speech discusses the God who became flesh, providing an overview of the phenomenological world of religion.

Following these speeches, in 1800 Schleiermacher published an ethical companion piece, *Monologen: Eine Neujahrsgabe* (*Schleiermacher's Soliloquies*, 1926). Taken together, *On Religion* and *Schleiermacher's Soliloquies* brought forth charges of pantheism. These charges, together with some concern about the young Schleiermacher's circle of friends in Berlin, led his elder and friend Friedrich Samuel Gottfried Sack to encourage a stay some distance from Berlin in Stolp. Schleiermacher thus left Berlin to serve as a court chaplain in Stolp from 1802 to 1804. He later accepted a call to Halle as preacher to the university, which included academic duties in a special appointment, which eventually became a regular appointment as professor. Schleiermacher's appointment made the theological faculty the first in Prussia to include both Lutheran and Reformed theologians.

When Schleiermacher returned to Berlin, he was a mature thinker, theologian, and philosopher. In 1809, he became preacher at Trinity Church, and in the same year he married Henriette von Willich, the widow of a friend who had died two years earlier. She brought two children into the marriage, and four other children issued from their union. By this time, the first edition of his translation of Plato's dialogues had appeared. The following fall he became a professor at the new university in Berlin, where he was to remain almost a quarter of a century. He was the first dean of the university's theological faculty, a position he occupied several times. He lectured in Christian ethics, church history, dogmatics, New Testament studies, and practical theology, as well as aesthetics, dialectics, ethics, hermeneutics, pedagogy, and psychology.

It was in the milieu of Berlin and his several responsibilities there that he conceived, composed, and published

Friedrich Schleiermacher. (Library of Congress)

his major work, *The Christian Faith*. The two-volume work has a significant title, which translated reads, "the Christian faith systematically set forth according to the principles of the Evangelical church." The last part of the title suggests that Schleiermacher was a church theologian who took history seriously. In his introduction to his magnum opus, Schleiermacher gives an explanation of dogmatics and its methods. After the introduction, he divided his work into two major parts. The first concerns the development of religious self-consciousness as it is presupposed by but also contained in Christian piety. It treats creation and preservation and also the attributes of God and the states of the world that correspond to creation and preservation. The original divine attributes are God's eternity, omnipresence, omnipotence, and omniscience.

The second part of *The Christian Faith* develops self-consciousness as it is determined by the antithesis of sin and grace. This part appears to move from an understanding of sin to Christology, through soteriology (theology dealing with salvation), ecclesiology, and eschatology (theology dealing with the Second Coming and Last Judgment). The theologies discussed in the second part are both more dialectical and more unified or coordinated than this simplified schema would suggest. For Schleiermacher, pious self-consciousness is determined by the consciousness of sin and grace. The consciousness of each person is developed within a system of three coordinates: the human being, the world, and God. Sin, both original and actual, is understood as the human condition. The state of the world is thus evil, while God's attributes are holiness and righteousness. The Christian is conscious of God's grace. The Holy Spirit is the means of grace, which arises out of God's love and wisdom.

Schleiermacher by and large held to the traditional dogmatic sequence of salvation history moving from Creation to the Last Judgment. His one departure from this traditional order comes in his treatment of the doctrine of God. Along with the doctrine of God's attributes (love, wisdom, omniscience, and the like), the doctrine of God usually appears at the beginning of dogmatics. In Schleiermacher's dogmatics, the doctrine of God's attributes is treated in three sections over the whole of the work, but there appears to be no doctrine of God. The human experience of reality is thus called to serve in characterizing God's attributes. Rather than being omitted in Schleiermacher's dogmatics, God is described in relation to humankind's experience of reality.

According to Schleiermacher's method, each part of *The Christian Faith* consists of an ingenious tripartite arrangement that discusses pious self-consciousness, theology or divinity, and cosmology or the world; yet, in each section, the sequence of these topics is different. The self, God, and the world are therefore treated three times before Schleiermacher comes to the conclusion of his work. For the conclusion of the work, Schleiermacher transposed the doctrine of the Trinity, traditionally in dogmatic literature at the beginning with the doctrine of God, to the climax of his dogmatics.

SIGNIFICANCE

Friedrich Schleiermacher is without a peer among modern theologians in the originality of his attempt to reconstruct the doctrine of God. His theology respects the fundamental distinctions between God and the world and between divinity and humanity, while affirming the interrelatedness of God, the self, and the world. In his life and thought, both piety and culture remained constant themes. He has rightly been recognized as the founder of modern theology.

Schleiermacher was not a theologian who disassociated himself from the preaching office of the church. Karl Barth has noted that Schleiermacher actively sought to present the most exposed, the most difficult and decisive theological position in the pulpit. That was true throughout his creative and mature life. Like Martin Luther and John Calvin before him, Schleiermacher gave himself year after year to the demands of both preaching and academic work.

—*Authur B. Holmes*

FURTHER READING

Barth, Karl. "Schleiermacher." In *Protestant Theology in the Nineteenth Century: Its Background and History*. Valley Forge, Pa.: Judson Press, 1973. An appreciation and critique of Schleiermacher's theology from Barth's own perspective as a theologian who provides an alternative to Schleiermacher. Contains a modest index of names.

Gadamer, Hans-Georg. *Truth and Method*. Edited and translated by Garrett Barden and John Cummings. New York: Continuum, 1975. This substantial work contains an analysis of Schleiermacher's hermeneutics and the questionableness of Romantic hermeneutics. Gadamer was a student of Martin Heidegger. Includes a helpful subject and name index.

Gerrish, B. A. "Continuity and Change: Friedrich Schleiermacher on the Task of Theology." In *Tradition and the Modern World: Reformed Theology in the Nineteenth Century*. Chicago: University of Chicago Press, 1978. Schleiermacher is discussed in the context of the Reformed tradition. Includes a good treatment of Emil Brunner's early work on Schleiermacher, which has never been translated.

_____. *A Prince of the Church: Schleiermacher and the Beginnings of Modern Theology*. Philadelphia: Fortress Press, 1984. A brief introductory study that places Schleiermacher's theology in a broad context.

Kelly, Thomas M. *Theology at the Void: The Retrieval of Experience*. Notre Dame, Ind.: University of Notre Dame Press, 2002. Examines how several philosophers have interpreted the experience of God, including Schleiermacher's belief that people experience God and use language to mediate this human experience.

Kelsey, Catherine L. *Thinking About Christ with Schleiermacher*. Louisville, Ky.: Westminster John Knox Press, 2003. An analysis of Schleiermacher's Christology, discussing how he organized various beliefs about Christ into a coherent system.

Niebuhr, Richard R. *Schleiermacher on Christ and Religion: A New Introduction.* New York: Charles Scribner's Sons, 1964. Treats the elements of Schleiermacher's style with fine discussions of his hermeneutical and historical background.

Redeker, Martin. *Schleiermacher: Life and Thought.* Translated by John Wallhausser. Philadelphia: Fortress Press, 1973. An excellent introduction by the editor of the German critical edition of *The Christian Faith.* Contains a good bibliography and a brief index of persons.

SEE ALSO: E. B. Pusey; Arthur Schopenhauer.
RELATED ARTICLE in *Great Events from History: The Nineteenth Century, 1801-1900:* 1835: Finney Lectures on "Revivals of Religion."

HEINRICH SCHLIEMANN
German archaeologist

A stunningly successful merchant in his early years, Schliemann began a new career in his middle age as an archaeologist. Relying on an unwavering faith in the ancient epics of Homer, he found and excavated Troy and unearthed the riches of Mycenae, and thus singlehandedly brought the splendors of the Greek Bronze Age to the attention of both amateurs and professionals.

BORN: January 6, 1822; Neu Bockow, Mecklenburg-Schwerin (now in Germany)
DIED: December 26, 1890; Naples, Italy
ALSO KNOWN AS: Julius Schliemann (birth name)
AREAS OF ACHIEVEMENT: Exploration, historiography

EARLY LIFE

Heinrich Schliemann was the fifth child in a large family. He was named Julius at birth, but he soon took the name of an older brother who had died ten weeks before he was born. Schliemann reports that by age seven he had already decided to find Troy upon seeing a woodcut of it in a history book that he received as a present from his father for Christmas in 1829. When he was nine years old, his mother died. It was also about this time that his father, Ernest, was disgraced for an affair with a maid and was temporarily suspended from his post as a Protestant clergyman. The scandal was an embarrassment and this, in addition to his mother's death, caused the family to break up.

Schliemann entered school, but in 1836 he was forced to leave to serve as an apprentice in a grocer's shop. It was during this period that he met a drunken miller, a former student, who recited Greek for Schliemann and intensified his love of Homer. Manual labor was difficult for Schliemann, who was of slight build and pale complexion. He soon departed to make his fortune in Venezuela, but a shipwreck caused him to land in Amsterdam, where he took a series of menial jobs. During this period, he began his lifelong habit of language study, based on a method of his own devising. He eventually learned some eighteen languages and claimed to learn them in periods ranging from six weeks to six months. In 1844, he joined a mercantile firm, and in 1846, his hard work and newly acquired fluency in Russian persuaded the firm to send him as its representative to Russia. There, Schliemann flourished, trading many items, but especially indigo, from his base in St. Petersburg, where he quickly established his own business.

Schliemann soon became a millionaire. In 1851, he embarked for the United States, ostensibly to help settle the affairs of his dead brother Ludwig but also to make investments in the booming West. He established a bank dealing in gold dust in Sacramento and earned large profits. By 1852, he was back in St. Petersburg, where he married Ekaterina Petrovna Lyschin. He was to have two children, Sergei and Nadezhda, but little happiness from this union. He profited greatly from the Crimean War and the American Civil War, and in 1863, in his early forties and at a stage at which most men look forward to settling down, he liquidated his business and began the second phase of his life.

LIFE'S WORK

In 1866, after a two-year world tour that included the Far East and resulted in the first of his eleven books, Schliemann enrolled in the Sorbonne, finally able to complete his education. He soon traveled again and once more visited the southern United States; yet most important for his future work were visits to several Greek sites that he would later excavate, including Ithaca, Mycenae, Tiryns, and Troy. He even dug, without permission, in the area of Troy in 1868, trying to disprove the theory that Burnarbashi held the remains of Homer's Troy. Schliemann was convinced that his choice, Hissarlik, was the true site of Troy.

Upon returning to St. Petersburg to find his estranged wife gone, along with their children, Schliemann left that city, never to return. In 1869, he received a doctorate from the University of Rostock for his publications to date and then returned to the United States to divorce under the state of Indiana's liberal laws. It was during this trip that Schliemann received American citizenship, and not in 1850 as he often related. He was proud of his citizenship and often signed himself "Henry Schliemann."

Even before Schliemann left the United States, he wrote a former tutor, now a Greek archbishop, asking him to find a wife suitable to help him pursue his dream of finding Troy. The archbishop suggested his cousin, Sophia Engastromenos, whom Schliemann courted cautiously. Impressed by her beauty and love of ancient learning, he married her on September 23, 1869. She, along with Troy, was to be an overriding passion in his life. The couple had two children, Andromache and Agamemnon.

In 1870, Schliemann began to dig at Hissarlik, again illegally, as his permit from the Turks was slow in coming. By 1871, he began legal excavations, but his excavation techniques were unquestionably inferior. He chose speed over care and eliminated higher strata without proper documentation in his zeal to get to the lowest levels. At times, he employed up to 150 men, and his equipment included jackscrews, chains, and windlasses to tear down walls that hindered his progress. In 1873, he found the famed "gold of Troy," a hoard of gold jewelry, which he smuggled out of the country. One crown alone was said to consist of 16,353 individual pieces. Widely displayed in a photograph of Sophia wearing them, the jewels were lost when Allied forces invaded Berlin at the end of World War II. Schliemann ended excavations in 1873 and published *Troja und seine Ruinen* (1875; *Troy and Its Remains*, 1875), whose bold claims of having found Priam's city brought strong criticism. Denied a permit for Troy by Turkish officials bristling at the loss of the treasure, he turned his sights elsewhere.

In 1874, Schliemann was already at Mycenae, where he dug illegally for five days before being stopped. There, he hoped to find Homer's "Mycenae rich in gold," the home of Agamemnon, Greek leader at Troy. As he waited for permission from the Greeks, however, he was well occupied. He first settled a suit by the Turks for the loss of the treasure and then traveled again, as he always did when between projects.

In 1876, Schliemann began at Mycenae and, with naïve faith in the ancient author Pausanias, excavated within the walls of the city, looking for the tombs of Agamemnon and Clytemnestra. He soon found five shaft graves that contained vast wealth (the gold alone weighed some thirty-three pounds). He was wrong in his dates, for these graves antedate the supposed dates of Agamemnon by some 250 to 300 years, but the excitement he caused was immense. Schliemann announced his finds in the media, and the public's imagination was immediately stirred. His subsequent book *Mycenæ* (1878) did not receive unanimous praise, because his tendency to make hasty judgments on incomplete evidence was antithetical to the staid approach of most classical scholars.

Never one to rest for long, Schliemann was off again for Troy, where he dug from 1879 to 1880. His book *Ilios* (1880) is more reasoned and careful than his previous

Heinrich Schliemann. (Library of Congress)

works and shows a greater respect for proper archaeological technique. It also contains the autobiographical essay that is the sole source for information on Schliemann's early life. In 1881, he excavated at Orchomenus, another city important in Homer's writings, and visited the ongoing excavations by the Germans at Olympia, where he was impressed by the modern and careful techniques being used.

In 1882, Schliemann was back at Troy, trying to understand its confusing stratigraphy, this time with the help of Wilhelm Dörpfeld, a young architect whom Schliemann had met at the Olympia excavations. The publication that resulted from this dig, *Troja* (1884), was a great improvement on his earlier works.

At this time Schliemann began to take an interest in the island of Crete, where he was convinced that he would find further prehistoric remains. With his astonishing skill for finding the right places to dig, he located the future site of Knossos, home of the Minoan civilization. The businessperson in him prevailed, however, as he never could agree to pay the asking price for the site. Later, this civilization would be unearthed by Sir Arthur Evans, a man who was much influenced by Schliemann and his finds.

Schliemann next turned to another site indicated by Homer, Tiryns. Just a few miles from Mycenae and the fabled home of Heracles, Tiryns was a strong citadel whose stone walls continue to be impressive. The publication of *Tiryns* (1885) served further to convince the world of the vibrancy of Bronze Age, or Mycenaean, culture. Schliemann traveled in 1886 and 1887, partly to rest and partly to recover his health that, never sound, had begun to deteriorate. In December of 1889, he returned to Troy in order to silence some of his critics. In 1890, on his way home to spend Christmas with his family in Greece, Schliemann's chronic earaches became worse. He underwent surgery in Halle in November, but in his haste to return to his family he left bed early, only to collapse on Christmas Day in Naples. Temporarily denied access to a hospital because of a lack of identification, Schliemann was taken instead to a police station. He died the next day, December 26, 1890, apparently as a result of the infection's spreading to his brain.

SIGNIFICANCE

Heinrich Schliemann was an uncompromising businessperson. He was also a passionate romantic who believed in Homer as others would believe in the Bible and who put a copy of Homer's *Iliad* to his son Agamemnon's forehead shortly after the child's birth. Schliemann was

cold and arrogant with his critics but could be tender to his wife and children. His early excavation techniques were undoubtedly appalling, and he destroyed much that was of value. However, it was he who found what others had failed to find, and he strove to improve his technique as he went along, often bringing experts such as Dörpfeld to his later excavations.

In some respects, it is Schliemann's energy that most impresses. He did not begin his archaeological career until he was in his forties, and he was largely self-taught. He financed his excavations himself, using profits from investments, which he continued to manage while he excavated and wrote ceaselessly.

Although other scholars produced theories from behind their desks, Schliemann went to Asia Minor with Homer in hand and found the site generally accepted today as Troy. Although others read Pausanias on Mycenae, Schliemann used his writings to unearth a civilization that had lain beneath the surface of the Greek soil for three thousand years. In the end, this was Schliemann's greatest accomplishment, for through his energy and excavations he changed forever the way the Western world viewed Homer and its own heritage.

—*Kenneth F. Kitchell, Jr.*

FURTHER READING

Brackman, Arnold C. *The Dream of Troy*. New York: Mason and Lipscomb, 1974. A novelistic biography recounting Schliemann's discovery of Troy. Vivid but not scholarly. Poorly reproduced illustrations.

Calder, William M., and David A. Traill, eds. *Myth, Scandal, and History*. Detroit: Wayne State University Press, 1986. Consists of five essays demythologizing Schliemann through critical examination of his record. Also includes an edition of his Mycenaean diary.

Cottrell, Leonard. *The Bull of Minos*. New York: Facts On File, 1953. A general book on Bronze Age Greece, with significant space devoted to Schliemann and his works. A good introduction for the reader who wants to learn something of the actual remains Schliemann unearthed as well as something about the man himself. Somewhat uncritical in its acceptance of Schliemann's versions of events.

Deuel, Leo. *Memoirs of Heinrich Schliemann*. New York: Harper & Row, 1977. Thorough analysis of Schliemann's life, with generous selections from his own works, letters, and diaries. Balanced, with careful criticism and analytical sections, full notes, and a bibliography.

Fitton, J. Lesley. *The Discovery of the Greek Bronze Age.* Cambridge, Mass.: Harvard University Press, 1996. Explores excavations by Schliemann and other archaeologists that led scholars to conclude that classical Greece had roots in the Bronze Age.

Moorehead, Caroline. *The Lost Treasures of Troy.* London: Weidenfeld & Nicolson, 1994. A history of the materials that Schliemann uncovered at Troy, describing how his finds were handled from their excavation through the early 1990's.

Payne, Robert. *The Gold of Troy: The Story of Heinrich Schliemann and the Buried Cities of Ancient Greece.* New York: Funk & Wagnalls, 1959. A readable and enjoyable biography, flawed only by its tendency to accept much of what Schliemann wrote at face value.

Poole, Lynn, and Gray Poole. *One Passion, Two Loves: The Story of Heinrich and Sophia Schliemann, Discoverers of Troy.* New York: Thomas Y. Crowell, 1966. A very enjoyable study of the later part of Schliemann's life, using previously unpublished letters.

Stone, Irving. *The Greek Treasure: A Biographical Novel of Henry and Sophia Schliemann.* Garden City, N.Y.: Doubleday, 1975. A biographical novel, based on careful study of the available Schliemann material, some of it used here for the first time.

SEE ALSO: Sir Richard Francis Burton; Sir Arthur Evans.

RELATED ARTICLES in *Great Events from History: The Nineteenth Century, 1801-1900:* 1803-1812: Elgin Ships Parthenon Marbles to England; 1839-1847: Layard Explores and Excavates Assyrian Ruins; November, 1839: Stephens Begins Uncovering Mayan Antiquities; April, 1870-1873: Schliemann Excavates Ancient Troy; March 23, 1900: Evans Discovers Crete's Minoan Civilization.

ARTHUR SCHOPENHAUER
German philosopher

As a philosopher in the tradition of Immanuel Kant, Schopenhauer developed a pessimistic system of philosophy based upon the primacy of will. He modified Kant's terminology and categories to accord primacy to will, regarding it as the inscrutable thing-in-itself.

BORN: February 22, 1788; Danzig, Prussia (now Gdańsk, Poland)
DIED: September 21, 1860; Frankfurt am Main (now in Germany)
AREA OF ACHIEVEMENT: Philosophy

EARLY LIFE
Arthur Schopenhauer (SHOH-pehn-HOW-er) was born in Danzig, a German city that was under the nominal control of Poland. His father, Heinrich, was an affluent merchant of Dutch aristocratic lineage, cosmopolitan in outlook and republican in politics. After Danzig lost its freedom to Prussia in 1793, he moved his family and business to Hamburg. Schopenhauer's mother, Johanna, also of Dutch descent, later became a successful romantic novelist.

Because Heinrich Schopenhauer planned a mercantile career for his son, Arthur's education emphasized modern languages, which came easily to him. At the age of nine, he was sent to Le Havre to learn French, the first of six foreign languages he mastered. In return for agreeing to enter a merchant firm as an apprentice, his father rewarded him with an extended tour—lasting nearly a year and a half—of England, Scotland, France, Switzerland, Austria, and Germany, an experience that strengthened his own cosmopolitan perspective and further developed his facility with languages.

As an apprentice and later a clerk, Schopenhauer found the work tedious and boring, and after the death of his father by drowning, presumed a suicide, in 1805, he altered his life's goals. With an inheritance adequate to assure independence and with encouragement from his mother, he entered grammar school at Gotha and then studied under tutors in Weimar, mastering Latin and Greek. At the age of twenty-one, he enrolled as a medical student in the University of Göttingen, changing to philosophy in his second year. His first influential teacher, G. E. Schulze, advised him to concentrate on Plato and Kant—the two thinkers who would exert the strongest impact on his philosophy.

In 1811, Schopenhauer attended lectures at the University of Berlin by Johann Gottlieb Fichte and Friedrich Schleiermacher; scathing responses in his notes set the tone of his lifelong contempt for German academic philosophy. When revolution against Napoleonic rule flared in Berlin, Schopenhauer fled to the village of Rudolstadt, where he wrote his dissertation for a doctorate from the University of Jena. In *Über die vierfache Wurzel des Satzes vom zureichende Grunde* (1813; *On the Fourfold Root of the Principle of Sufficient Reason*, 1889), he explores types of causation—physical, logical, mathematical, and moral.

After receiving his doctorate, Schopenhauer returned to Weimar to live in his mother's house, but the two could not agree. She found him moody, surly, and sarcastic; he found her vain and shallow. Disagreements and quarrels led her to dismiss him, and he left to establish his residence in Dresden in 1814, there to begin his major philosophical work. For the remaining twenty-four years of Johanna Schopenhauer's life, mother and son did not meet.

LIFE'S WORK

In Dresden, after completing a brief treatise on the nature of color, Schopenhauer was ready to begin serious preparation of his greatest philosophical work, *Die Welt als Wille und Vorstellung* (1819; *The World as Will and Idea*, 1883-1886). Its four books, with an appendix on Kantian philosophy, include the conceptual ideas that Schopenhauer developed and elaborated throughout his career as an independent philosopher. Book I explains the world, everything that the mind perceives, as representation, a mental construct of the subject. Through perception, reasoning, and reflection and by placing external reality within the mental categories of time, space, and causality, one understands how the world operates. However, one never understands reality as it exists, for the subjective remains an essential element of all perception.

The fundamental reality that eludes understanding is, as book 2 makes plain, the will, that Kantian thing-in-itself. Understood in its broadest sense, will exists in everything—as a life force and much more. In plants, it drives growth, change, and reproduction. In animals, it includes all of these as well as sensation, instinct, and limited intelligence. Only in human beings does the will become self-conscious, through reflection and analysis, though the will is by no means free in the usual sense. Every action is determined by motives—to Schopenhauer another name for causes—that predetermine one's choices. Thus, one may will to choose but not will to will. With its conscious and unconscious drives, will presses each person toward egoistic individualism; yet demands

Arthur Schopenhauer. (Library of Congress)

of the will, far from bringing peace, well-being, and gratification, lead only to additional struggle and exertion. As a consequence, unhappiness in life inevitably exceeds happiness.

As a respite from the imperious demands of the will, human beings find solace in the beauty that exists in nature and art, and the awakening of the aesthetic sense serves to tame the will by leading it toward disinterested contemplation. To enter a room and discover a table filled with food is to anticipate involvement, consumption, and interaction with others. To look at a painting of the same scene invites simply reflection and appreciation, removing any practical considerations from the will, thereby suspending its feverish activity.

However, the solace afforded by beauty is only temporary; in book 4, Schopenhauer explores saintliness, which implies denial and permanent taming of the will. By recognizing that others experience the same unrelenting strife that the will brings to himself, a person can develop compassion. Through the power of reflection, one can recognize one's own motives and, through studying motives, become aware of those previously unknown and unacknowledged. Thus, while he cannot achieve freedom of choice, human beings may acquire a negative capability of rejecting and taming the will. Renunciation, denial of the will, represents for Schopenhauer the path to Nirvana. The best attainable life is that followed by the Hindu *sanyasas* and the ascetic saints of early Christendom.

After publishing his magnum opus, Schopenhauer left for a vacation in Italy, confident that his work would be recognized as a true account of the philosophy foreshadowed by Kant and accepted as a solution to all outstanding problems of philosophy. Instead, the work was ignored both by the reading public and by academic philosophers. From Dresden, he moved to Berlin, where he expected to become a university professor. Appointed to lecture on philosophy at the university, he selected a schedule that competed with lectures by G. W. F. Hegel, then at the height of his popularity, whose optimistic system was the antithesis of Schopenhauer's. Unable to attract students, Schopenhauer spent more than a decade in reading and desultory wandering, though with Berlin as his primary residence. In 1833, he settled in Frankfurt, where he remained for the final years of his life.

There his life assumed a measure of regularity and simplicity. His modest wants were easily met on his inherited income. Although he gave serious consideration to marriage more than once during his lifetime, he rejected the idea, choosing casual relationships instead. He lived in a boardinghouse, took regular walks for exercise, and dined in company at the Englische Hof Hotel. His day began with work in the morning, followed by a brief diversion through playing the flute. In the afternoons, he stopped by the public library for reading and study; an omnivorous reader, he was widely knowledgeable in the arts and sciences and, like his father, read the London *Times* almost every day of his adult life. He was short of stature, with a thick neck—characteristics, he thought, of genius. His portraits show penetrating blue eyes; a lined, intelligent face; a prominent, forceful nose; and, in old age, two curled locks of white hair on either side of a bald head.

Schopenhauer produced a series of minor works as further elaboration of his system—an attack on academic philosophy, *Über den Willen in der Natur* (1836; *On the Will in Nature*, 1888), and *Die beiden Grundprobleme der Ethik* (1841; *The Basis of Morality*, 1903). After issuing a much-expanded second edition of his major work in 1844, he completed two volumes of essays and miscellaneous writings on a wide variety of subjects, *Parerga und Paralipomena* (1851; *Parerga and Parali-*

pomena, 1974). With its graceful if sometimes barbed style and its combination of brilliant insights and freely indulged speculation, it expanded the philosopher's reading public.

During his final decade, Schopenhauer experienced the fame and adulation he had long anticipated. A third edition of *The World as Will and Idea* appeared in 1859, this time owing to popular demand. His work was widely discussed and became the subject of university lectures throughout Europe. He began to attract followers, some drawn more by his lucid, jargon-free prose than by his ideas, and on his birthdays tributes poured in from admirers. Shortly before his death, he began to experience recurring chest pains; on the morning of September 21, 1860, he sat down to breakfast at his usual time. An hour later, his doctor, stopping by to check on him, found him still seated in the chair, dead.

SIGNIFICANCE

A philosopher in the tradition of Kant, Arthur Schopenhauer modified Kantian terms and categories to accord primacy to will, regarding it as the inscrutable thing-in-itself. Far from an optimistic view, his alteration implies a largely blind force striving for individual advancement and doomed to frustration and defeat. Confronted with this pessimistic reality, the reflective person seeks to tame the will through asceticism. In the *Upanishads*, his favorite bedtime reading, Schopenhauer discovered that Eastern religious thinkers had anticipated important ideas of his system, and he himself helped popularize Hindu and Buddhist thought in Europe.

Schopenhauer's successors have generally accepted portions of his system while rejecting others, and his influence has been almost as varied as his system. Friedrich Nietzsche followed him in granting primacy to the will but envisioned will as a constructive force for progress. Eduard von Hartmann attempted a synthesis of Schopenhauer and Hegel in his *Philosophie des Unbewussten* (1869; *Philosophy of the Unconscious*, 1931). Scholars have discovered a profound debt to Schopenhauer in Hans Vaihinger's *Die Philosophie des Als-Ob* (1911; *The Philosophy of "As If,"* 1924); Ludwig Wittgenstein was influenced by Schopenhauer as well. Sigmund Freud acknowledged that, in large measure, his theory of the unconscious was anticipated by the philosopher.

Because Schopenhauer gives aesthetics a prominent and honorable place in his system, it is not surprising to discover that he has influenced artistic creation significantly. Richard Wagner enthusiastically embraced

Schopenhauer's speculations on music, in part because he accorded music first place among the arts. Writers such as Leo Tolstoy in Russia; Thomas Mann in Germany; Guy de Maupassant, Émile Zola, and Marcel Proust in France; and Thomas Hardy, Joseph Conrad, and W. Somerset Maugham in Great Britain are, in varying degrees, indebted to Schopenhauer for their world view and for their pessimistic depiction of human life and character. One should note, however, that the enthusiasm for blind will at the base of twentieth century fascism is a perversion of Schopenhauer's thought. Passages in Schopenhauer that reflect racism, anti-Semitism, and misogyny, attitudes undeniably present in his work, should be placed within the context of his overall pessimism concerning human nature.

—Stanley Archer

FURTHER READING

Copleston, Frederick. *Arthur Schopenhauer, Philosopher of Pessimism*. London: Burns, Oates, and Washbourne, 1947. Examines Schopenhauer's system in the light of Roman Catholicism and religious thought. Calls attention to inconsistencies and contradictions but at the same time provides insightful summary and analysis of Schopenhauer's major ideas.

Fox, Michael, ed. *Schopenhauer: His Philosophical Achievement*. Brighton, England: Harvester Press, 1980. A collection of essays by distinguished scholars. The book is divided into three sections: general articles, giving overviews of Schopenhauer, articles dealing with basic philosophical issues, and comparative studies that relate Schopenhauer's ideas to other philosophers and explore intellectual debts.

Gardiner, Patrick. *Schopenhauer*. Baltimore: Penguin Books, 1963. A general but penetrating analysis of Schopenhauer's life and philosophy. Gardiner offers a balanced assessment of the philosopher's strengths and weaknesses, clarifying the intellectual debt to Kant but providing only brief consideration of Schopenhauer's influence on others.

Hamlyn, D. W. *Schopenhauer*. Boston: Routledge & Kegan Paul, 1980. A general survey of Schopenhauer's philosophy. Clarifies his terms, explains his epistemology, and offers extensive analysis of his philosophical debt to Kant.

Janaway, Christopher. *Schopenhauer: A Very Short Introduction*. New York: Oxford University Press, 2002. A concise overview of Schopenhauer's metaphysical system, concentrating on the original aspects of his thought. One in a series of books designed to provide user-friendly introductions to philosophy.

Magee, Bryan. *The Philosophy of Schopenhauer*. New York: Oxford University Press, 1983. A scholarly introduction to Schopenhauer's philosophical system. Explores the effects of his early life on his system and places his ideas in their philosophical tradition. Numerous appendixes trace his influence on others.

Mannion, Gerard. *Schopenhauer, Religion, and Morality: The Humble Path to Ethics*. Burlington, Vt.: Ashgate, 2003. Examines Schopenhauer's ideas, focusing on his moral philosophy and the relationship of his philosophy to theology and religion. Mannion concludes that Schopenhauer was not a nihilist or atheist who rejected religion, but a philosopher who reinterpreted religious ideas.

Wallace, William. *Life of Arthur Schopenhauer*. London: Walter Scott, 1890. A comprehensive overview of Schopenhauer's life, philosophical system, and influence. Biographical information draws heavily upon previous studies in German and offers an illuminating account of his daily life.

SEE ALSO: F. H. Bradley; Thomas Hardy; Georg Wilhelm Friedrich Hegel; Guy de Maupassant; Friedrich Nietzsche; Friedrich Schleiermacher; Leo Tolstoy; Richard Wagner; Émile Zola.

RELATED ARTICLES in *Great Events from History: The Nineteenth Century, 1801-1900:* 1819: Schopenhauer Publishes *The World as Will and Idea*; c. 1884-1924: Decadent Movement Flourishes.

OLIVE SCHREINER
South African novelist and essayist

*Schreiner wrote not only what is considered to be the first major novel to emerge from the British Empire—*The Story of an African Farm—*but also polemical essays that are regarded as pioneering feminist works and incisive critiques of colonialism.*

BORN: March 24, 1855; Wittebergen Mission Station, Cape Colony (now in South Africa)
DIED: December 10, 1920; Cape Town, South Africa
ALSO KNOWN AS: Olive Emilie Albertina Schreiner (full name); Ralph Iron (pseudonym)
AREAS OF ACHIEVEMENT: Literature, women's rights

EARLY LIFE

Olive Schreiner (SHRI-ner) was the ninth of twelve children of Methodist missionaries working in South Africa's Cape Colony. Her father, Gottlob Schreiner, was a German, and her mother, Rebecca Lyndall, was English. Olive was given three names, Olive Emilie Albertina, in honor of three previous siblings who had died in infancy.

Olive grew up in remote mission outposts in the Cape Colony. In 1861, her family moved to Healdtown when her father was appointed head of the Wesleyan Native Industrial Training Institution there. Four years later, he was dismissed from that position for violating mission rules on trading practices and entered private business but failed. The family's poor financial situation forced Olive to leave home at the age of twelve to work as a servant in the households of friends and relatives. From 1871 to 1880, she worked as a governess on isolated farms of Afrikaners. Early settlers of primarily Dutch descent, the Afrikaners were generally known as "Boers" after the Dutch word for farmer. Olive's experience of living among Afrikaner farmers would later help shape her fiction and color her attitude toward the South African (Boer) War of 1899-1902.

At an early age Olive questioned traditional religious beliefs to the dismay of her devout parents. She had no formal education apart from fragmented lessons given by her mother, but she found time while she worked as a governess to explore books by such great humanistic, scientific, and philosophical writers as Charles Darwin, Herbert Spencer, John Stuart Mill, Ralph Waldo Emerson, Thomas Carlyle, and many others. While educating herself during her ten years on Afrikaner farms, she also started writing fiction, and her finest novel, *The Story of an African Farm* (1883), grew out of that period. By 1881, she had saved enough money for passage to En-

gland. At the age of twenty-six, she left the Cape Colony with her manuscripts in hand.

LIFE'S WORK

Schreiner originally intended to study medicine in London, but her serious asthma intervened. Instead, she set out on a literary career, beginning in 1883 with publication of *The Story of an African Farm*. Appearing first under the very masculine pseudonym "Ralph Iron," the book met with success as well as controversy over its feminist views, didacticism, and religious skepticism. Because the novel was criticized for its loose structure and clumsy plot construction, Schreiner wrote a preface for the second edition, which bore her own name. She defended the novel by arguing that her writing method followed life just as it unfolds in unpredictable stages.

The book's reception gained Schreiner admission into liberal political and literary circles, where she met other young radicals, including Karl Marx's daughter, Eleanor Marx; Irish novelist George Moore; British writer and activist Henry Rider Haggard, who had worked in South Africa and was the author of the African novel *King Solomon's Mines* (1885); and Welsh poet Arthur Symons. In 1883, she met the noted psychologist and sexologist Havelock Ellis, with whom she formed a lifelong friendship. Their extensive correspondence would be published in 1992.

After leaving London, Schreiner traveled briefly in Italy, then returned to South Africa in 1889 and settled in the remote village of Matjesfontein for the sake of her health. No longer branded as the indigent daughter of a disgraced missionary, Schreiner had gained a considerable reputation in South Africa as the result of her literary success in England.

In 1894, Schreiner married Samuel Cron Cronwright, a gentleman farmer and businessperson. Undertaking an exceptional move for the time, he assumed her surname and was known thereafter as Cronwright-Schreiner. A year later, Schreiner bore a daughter who lived for only sixteen hours. The loss of her child was a devastating experience that affected Schreiner for the rest of her life. Meanwhile, her husband gave up his own work to assist her in her literary career. According to the devoted husband's biography, *The Life of Olive Schreiner* (1924), his efforts on Schreiner's behalf often caused him frustration because of Schreiner's mercurial moods, eccentricities, and lack of discipline. Schreiner also continued to suffer

THE STORY OF AN AFRICAN FARM

This preface from the second edition of the novel that Olive Schreiner first published under the pen name "Ralph Iron" in 1883 expresses some of her reactions to criticisms of her novel and reveals aspects of her writing methods.

I have to thank cordially the public and my critics for the reception they have given this little book.

Dealing with a subject that is far removed from the round of English daily life, it of necessity lacks the charm that hangs about the ideal representation of familiar things, and its reception has therefore been the more kindly.

A word of explanation is necessary. Two strangers appear on the scene, and some have fancied that in the second they have again the first, who returns in a new guise. Why this should be we cannot tell; unless there is a feeling that a man should not appear upon the scene, and then disappear, leaving behind him no more substantial trace than a mere book; that he should return later on as husband or lover, to fill some more important part than that of the mere stimulator of thought.

Human life may be painted according to two methods. There is the stage method. According to that each character is duly marshalled at first, and ticketed; we know with an immutable certainty that at the right crises each one will reappear and act his part, and, when the curtain falls, all will stand before it bowing. There is a sense of satisfaction in this, and of completeness. But there is another method—the method of the life we all lead. Here nothing can be prophesied. There is a strange coming and going of feet. Men appear, act and re-act upon each other, and pass away. When the crisis comes the man who would fit it does not return. When the curtain falls no one is ready. When the footlights are brightest they are blown out; and what the name of the play is no one knows. If there sits a spectator who knows, he sits so high that the players in the gaslight cannot hear his breathing. Life may be painted according to either method; but the methods are different. The canons of criticism that bear upon the one cut cruelly upon the other.

It has been suggested by a kind critic that he would better have liked the little book if it had been a history of wild adventure; of cattle driven into inaccessible kranzes by Bushmen; "of encounters with ravening lions, and hair-breadth escapes." This could not be. Such works are best written in Piccadilly or in the Strand: there the gifts of the creative imagination, untrammelled by contact with any fact, may spread their wings.

But, should one sit down to paint the scenes among which he has grown, he will find that the facts creep in upon him. Those brilliant phases and shapes which the imagination sees in far-off lands are not for him to portray. Sadly he must squeeze the colour from his brush, and dip it into the gray pigments around him. He must paint what lies before him.

—*R. Iron.*

Source: Olive Schreiner, *The Story of an African Farm* (new ed. London: Chapman and Hall, 1887).

from asthma and at times depended on narcotics for relief. Long periods of separation marked their stressful marriage.

In the polemical books and articles that Schreiner wrote over the years, she addressed a variety of causes and issues, including pacifism, socialism, imperialism, sexism, feminism, and racism. In 1897, she published a strongly political novel, *Peter Halket of Mashonaland*, that was a thinly veiled attack on the racial policies promoted by Cecil Rhodes's British South Africa Company, which had a royal charter to colonize what is now Zimbabwe. Although Schreiner was initially a friend and admirer of the empire builder, she stressed her sympathy for the exploited African population and indirectly accused Rhodes of advocating extermination of his company's African subjects.

In 1899, Schreiner's longtime partiality for Afrikaners led her to publish *An English South African's View of the Situation*, a pro-Afrikaner tract objecting to Great Britain's prosecution of the South African War. Because of her views, the British government placed her under martial law in 1900. Another work of Schreiner's that is still considered a significant feminist treatise, *Woman and Labour*, appeared in 1911. In that book, Schreiner argues that technology has robbed women of their work and a rightful place in the social structure, thereby turning them into parasites and passive sexual creatures. She pleads for a full understanding of the role women should play as equal partners with men.

Schreiner spent the years of World War I in London, where her health deteriorated. After the war, her husband, Cronwright-Schreiner, went to England to bring her back to Cape Town. On December 10, 1920, several months after she returned to South Africa, Schreiner died from a heart attack, at the age of sixty-five. At the time of her death, she left unfinished a novel that she had worked on for over forty years, *From Man to Man*. Cronwright-Schreiner edited this ambitious chronicle of two subjugated women and published it in 1926. Three years later, he published his edited version of Schreiner's unfinished novella *Undine*.

SIGNIFICANCE

Far ahead of her time, Olive Schreiner was a feminist trailblazer, a pioneering imperial critic, and an inventive novelist. Her views on the role of the new woman in society inspired some readers and offended others when her feminist writings first appeared, but during the half century after she died, her writings containing contentious proposals for equal status for women fell into oblivion. However, after the modern feminist movement gained momentum, Schreiner finally claimed her rightful place as a forerunner in the cause of women's rights. Numerous books and essays on her work by modern feminist critics underscore the importance of Schreiner's original contributions to the field.

After the dissolution of the British Empire, historians and literary theorists have devoted considerable energy to investigating colonial vestiges—the element of racism in particular. Schreiner initiated this discussion in her writings about South Africa's racial division and foresaw its catastrophic outcome. Although novels by other writers from the British Empire appeared before *The Story of an African Farm*, those works recorded colonial life in a realistic mode that imitated traditional British fiction. In sharp contrast, Schreiner devised a striking narrative technique to transform the colonial experience and the landscape itself into a metaphor that speaks for the human condition in all of its complexity. Her retelling of ordinary events on a remote farm in Africa is generally considered the first significant novel to come out of the far-flung empire.

—Robert Ross

FURTHER READING

Berkman, Joyce Avrech. *The Healing Imagination of Olive Schreiner: Beyond South African Colonialism.* Amherst: University of Massachusetts Press, 1989. Focuses on Schreiner's ideas, not on her life. Considers how political conflicts and intellectual currents formed her thinking and underscored her writing.

Burdett, Carolyn. *Olive Schreiner and the Progress of Feminism: Evolution, Gender, Empire.* New York: Palgrave, 2001. Places Schreiner's work within a historical context by tracing the complex relationship between gender and empire. Relates how the discussion of women's rights in England during the late nineteenth century and the South African War affected Schreiner's writing.

Chrisman, Laura. *Rereading the Imperial Romance: British Imperialism and South African Resistance in Haggard, Schreiner, and Plaatje.* Oxford, England: Oxford University Press, 2000. Investigates the historical experience of British imperialism in Africa through analyses of three writers who viewed imperialism in different ways. Sees Schreiner as focusing on the economic and materialistic aspects.

Clayton, Cherry. *Olive Schreiner.* New York: Twayne, 1997. Provides a succinct introduction to Schreiner's life and fiction, which is analyzed from a biographical standpoint.

Cronwright-Schreiner, Samuel Cron. *The Life of Olive Schreiner.* 1924. New York: Haskell House, 1973. Reprint of the biography of Schreiner by her husband that provides anecdotes about Schreiner's idiosyncrasies, firsthand accounts of incidents in her life, recollections of his devotion to her, and a broad analysis of her writing.

Heilman, Ann. *New Woman Strategies: Sarah Grand, Olive Schreiner, and Mona Caird.* Manchester, England: Manchester University Press, 2004. Explores how three women writers drew on, imitated, feminized, and altered the traditional literary devices, such as femininity, mythology, and allegory.

Horton, Susan. *Difficult Women, Artful Lives: Olive Schreiner and Isak Denisen—In and Out of Africa.* Baltimore: Johns Hopkins University Press, 1995. Examines the life and work of two unconventional women who wrote about Africa, placing their themes of race, gender and nationality strictly within the context of Africa.

Monsman, Gerald. *Olive Schreiner's Fiction: Landscape and Power.* New Brunswick, N.J.: Rutgers University Press, 1991. Provides a thorough and perceptive analysis of Schreiner's fiction to illustrate how she rendered the South African landscape to underscore the way colonialism exerted power over its subjects.

Stanley, Liz. *Imperialism, Labour and the New Woman: Olive Schreiner's Social Theory.* Durham, England: Sociology Press, 2002. Recapitulates Schreiner's role as the major feminist theorist of her time, through an original reading and critique of her political and feminist writings.

SEE ALSO: Thomas Carlyle; Charles Darwin; Sir Arthur Conan Doyle; Ralph Waldo Emerson; H. Rider Haggard; Paul Kruger; Karl Marx; John Stuart Mill; Cecil Rhodes; Herbert Spencer.

RELATED ARTICLES in *Great Events from History: The Nineteenth Century, 1801-1900:* August 13, 1814: Britain Acquires the Cape Colony; October 11, 1899-May 31, 1902: South African War.

FRANZ SCHUBERT
Austrian composer

Schubert created the Lied *(art song) and set models for subsequent ones in his more than six hundred* Lieder. *His larger instrumental works, in their freedom of form and enhanced key relationships, became models for the lyrical Romantic sonatas and symphonies of the later nineteenth century. The expressively songful character of his shorter piano pieces was equally influential.*

BORN: January 31, 1797; Himmelpfortgrund, near
    Vienna, Austria
DIED: November 19, 1828; Vienna, Austro-Hungarian
    Empire (now in Austria)
ALSO KNOWN AS: Franz Peter Schubert (full name)
AREA OF ACHIEVEMENT: Music

EARLY LIFE

Franz Schubert (SHEW-bert) was one of the five of fourteen children of a schoolmaster to survive infancy. Though the Schubert family was in humble circumstances, its members were highly musical, and Franz as a child learned violin from his father, piano from his older brother Ignaz, and singing and basic music theory from Michael Holzer, choirmaster of the parish church of Liechtenthal. At the age of nine, Franz was engaged as a boy soprano in the Imperial Chapel and was enrolled in its school, the Imperial and Royal Stadt-Konvikt (boarding school), where he was also a violinist in the student orchestra.

Schubert's earliest surviving compositions date from 1810. In 1811, he began keyboard studies with the court organist, Wenzel Ruzicka, and in the following year began studies in composition with Antonio Salieri, who had been Wolfgang Amadeus Mozart's rival and one of Ludwig van Beethoven's teachers. This year was critical in other ways for Schubert: His voice changed, thus preventing him from continuing in the chapel choir as a boy soprano, and his mother died. His father remarried in the following year.

Though Schubert's voice had changed, he remained a scholarship student at the Imperial and Royal Stadt-Konvikt. In 1813, he renounced his scholarship, probably because he would be required to devote his time to academic studies rather than to music, and instead entered the teacher training program at the St. Anna Normal School in 1814. He continued to participate in the Imperial and Royal Stadt-Konvikt's musical life and played in its orchestra, for which his first three symphonies were written. In 1814, he wrote string quartets for his family

ensemble, in which he played viola, and his first major compositions. He set to music the poem "Gretchen am Spinnrade" (Gretchen at the spinning wheel) from Johann Wolfgang von Goethe's *Faust: Eine Tragödie* (1808; *The Tragedy of Faust*, 1823). He also wrote the Mass in F Major for the parish church in Liechtenthal.

After passing the examination for teacher certification in 1814, Schubert was a part-time assistant in his father's school, preferring to devote most of his time to composition. He was exempted from military service because he was barely five feet tall (thus below the army's minimum height requirement); his friends called him *Schwammerl* (little mushroom) because of his stocky build and short stature.

Schubert met Therese Grob, a skilled amateur soprano, in 1814 and fell in love with her. In 1816, the relationship was ended, because Schubert could not afford to marry her after he was rejected for a post as music teacher at the Normal School in Laibach (modern Ljubljana, in Slovenia). From then on he was indifferent to women, seeking rather the company of congenial friends, many of whom he had known since his days at the Imperial and Royal Stadt-Konvikt and who were extremely helpful in getting his music performed or in writing texts that he set as songs. From the year 1816 come the fourth and fifth symphonies, a string quartet, the Mass in C Major, and more than one hundred songs. The following two years were relatively fallow.

LIFE'S WORK

Two works from 1819 mark Schubert's full musical maturity: the Piano Quintet in A Major (called *Trout* because the fourth movement is a set of variations on his song "Die Forelle," which means "trout") and a remarkably concise three-movement Piano Sonata in A Major. He also finished the first of his operas, *Die Zwillingsbrüder* (the twin brothers), which received six performances in the following year. Schubert made several ventures into opera during the following four years, all of which were unsuccessful because of the lack of dramatic interest in the librettos.

The year 1823 was critical for Schubert in other respects. He became seriously ill; most writers consider the ailment to have been syphilis, from which he recovered, although the secondary symptoms, especially headaches and gastritis, plagued him through the remainder of his life. However, he completed *Die Schöne Müllerin* (the fair maid of the mill), his first song cycle, so called because he set to music a group of poems by the same author, Wilhelm Müller, which were written around the central theme of a miller's apprentice who falls in love with his employer's daughter when she prefers a huntsman.

Schubert next concentrated on writing chamber music and songs. His main chamber works of this period are two great string quartets, in A minor and D minor; an octet for clarinet, bassoon, French horn, string quartet, and string bass in six movements; and several piano duets, written for the daughters of the Esterházy family when he spent the summer as a music teacher on their country estate of Zselis in Hungary (he had been there earlier in 1818). Schubert's immediately succeeding works include the Symphony in C Major, finished in 1826; a large-scale String Quartet in G Major, also completed in that year; and a large-scale Concert Rondo in B Minor for violin and piano.

The year 1827 saw two piano trios and the gloomy song cycle *Winterreise* (winter journey), in which Schubert again used poems by Müller. In *Winterreise*, a young man, rejected by his beloved, undertakes a journey on foot in midwinter in a vain effort to forget her and risks

losing his sanity. From this cycle comes one of Schubert's best-loved songs, "Der Lindenbaum" (the linden tree), which is virtually a folksong in German-speaking countries. The central theme of isolation and alienation displayed in this song cycle was a favorite one in Romantic literature.

The year 1828 saw Schubert's greatest achievement. Foreign journals were reviewing his music favorably, and foreign publishers were interested in his music. His public concert devoted entirely to his music was a great success. Many of his best compositions—the Fantasy in F Minor for piano duet, the String Quintet in C Major, the last three piano sonatas, the Mass in E-flat Major, and the group of songs published after his death as *Schwanengesang* (swan song)—stem from this, his final, year. He had even begun lessons in counterpoint with Simon Sechter, later to be the teacher of Anton Bruckner. In November, his health suddenly deteriorated; in slightly more than a week, he lapsed into a coma and died. His illness was diagnosed by his doctors as "nervous fever"; most modern scholars consider his fatal illness to have been typhoid fever, brought on by the unsanitary conditions of the suburb of Vienna where he was then living.

Many legends that have evolved about Schubert have been demolished by subsequent research. He was a prolific composer, but his supposed spontaneity was the result of much forethought and revision. For example, one of his most famous early songs, "Erlkönig" (the elf king), with a text by Goethe, was supposed to have been written in a single afternoon in 1815 and performed that evening. Schubert, however, revised "Erlkönig" six times before its publication as his Opus 1 in 1821. One of the tragedies of music is Schubert's abandonment of several major compositions before their completion. The most famous of these incomplete works is the "Unfinished" Symphony in B Minor (1822), in which Schubert wrote two outstanding symphonic movements and sketched a third movement as a scherzo, but not even sketches have survived for a finale.

Schubert's life of poverty has also been misunderstood. He rejected positions with regular hours, seeking one that would enable him to devote full time to composing. Such positions were bestowed on those with many years of musical achievement, and Schubert was passed over in favor of much older and more experienced men. He was relatively well paid by his publishers, but he spent money lavishly when he had it, not so much on himself as on the circle of friends with whom he lived and whom he accompanied on summer vacations in the mountains, where he did much of his composing.

Franz Schubert. (Library of Congress)

By Schubert's time, social conditions had changed: The nobility, ruined by the Napoleonic Wars, could not support a composer in the manner that Joseph Haydn or Ludwig van Beethoven had been aided, and the middle-class public could not provide a steady income. Schubert's main audience consisted of the friends who attended the so-called Schubertiads—evenings when Schubert and others played the piano and sang for a mostly male audience, who did much drinking and stayed as late as 3:00 A.M. He was beginning to achieve a wide reputation as a composer of merit during the last year of his life.

SIGNIFICANCE

Only a small amount of Franz Schubert's music was published during his lifetime—several songs and piano duets, but only one string quartet, four piano sonatas, and no orchestral music. His music was aimed more toward the middle-class drawing room than the concert hall, and Schubert himself was not a charismatic virtuoso performer such as Niccolò Paganini or Franz Liszt, who were able to attract well-paying crowds.

Schubert changed the course of music in many ways. Before him, composers who wrote songs undertook to provide a simple setting for a poem, with an almost rudimentary piano accompaniment that often was intended to be played by the singer, rather than to create an independent musical composition that would utilize the full resources of the piano and all the techniques of harmonic color and melodic expression in the way that Schubert did. In the sphere of the large instrumental work, Schubert provided an alternative to Beethoven, writing movements that were lyric and epic rather than heroic and dramatic. Schubert used the possibilities inherent in the widening of the tonal spectrum to expand the forms of his movements. The short, spontaneous piano piece was not original with Schubert, but he set the standard for subsequent works in this genre.

Schubert's influence on subsequent composers was not immediate but was especially strong on those who played major roles in making his music known throughout the nineteenth century: Robert Schumann, Franz Liszt, and Johannes Brahms. The full range of Schubert's genius has become appreciated only in modern times with the performance and recording of many of his large-scale works.

—*Rey M. Longyear*

FURTHER READING

Brown, Maurice J. E. "Schubert." In *The New Grove Dictionary of Music and Musicians*, edited by Stanley Sadie. London: Macmillan, 1980. Brown's critical studies of Schubert's music are distilled in this comprehensive article embracing both the composer's life and music.

_____. *Schubert: A Critical Biography*. New York: St. Martin's Press, 1958. The standard scholarly study of Schubert's work, with the focus on his music. Written for the person with musical understanding.

Deutsch, Otto Erich, ed. *Schubert: Memoirs by His Friends*. Translated by Rosamond Ley and John Nowell. London: A. & C. Black, 1958. Contains many firsthand accounts by those who knew Schubert personally and intimately.

Deutsch, Otto Erich, with Donald R. Wakeling. *The Schubert Reader: A Life of Franz Schubert in Letters and Documents*. New York: W. W. Norton, 1947. This documentary biography consists of English translations of the documents directly pertaining to Schubert, thus providing direct insight into the composer's life and the circumstances surrounding his work.

Einstein, Alfred. *Schubert: A Musical Portrait*. New York: Oxford University Press, 1951. This sensitive appreciation of Schubert's music by one of the giants of early twentieth century musical scholarship is well worth reading because of its valuable and penetrating insights into Schubert's music.

Gibbs, Christopher H. *The Life of Schubert*. New York: Cambridge University Press, 2000. Informative biography describing the relationship of Schubert's music to his life. Gibbs examines, and in some cases destroys, misconceptions about the composer.

_____, ed. *The Cambridge Companion to Schubert*. New York: Cambridge University Press, 1997. Collection of essays examining Schubert's life and music. Some of the essays analyze the various genres of his music, including operas, songs, and piano and chamber music; other essays describe his music in performance and the reception of his music in nineteenth century Europe.

Osborne, Charles. *Schubert and His Vienna*. New York: Alfred A. Knopf, 1985. A book for the general reader, with the emphasis on Schubert's life and environment rather than on his music. Provides a very readable introduction to Schubert, though the musical information is mostly praise rather than critical analysis.

Reed, John. *Schubert*. London: J. M. Dent & Sons, 1987. Provides excellent discussion of Schubert's life, with the music important though subordinate. Written in a style suited more for the general music lover than for the specialist scholar. Some musical background is necessary for a full appreciation of this volume.

SEE ALSO: Ludwig van Beethoven; Johannes Brahms; Anton Bruckner; Franz Liszt; Niccolò Paganini; Robert Schumann; Johann Strauss; Peter Ilich Tchaikovsky.

RELATED ARTICLE in *Great Events from History: The Nineteenth Century, 1801-1900:* April 7, 1805: Beethoven's *Eroica* Symphony Introduces the Romantic Age.

CLARA SCHUMANN
German musician

Schumann was one of the most admired musicians of her time. As a child piano prodigy she dazzled audiences all over Europe, and as an adult she promoted the work of her husband, composer Robert Schumann, by performing it in her own concerts. She was renowned for the integrity and breadth of her playing and was also a gifted composer.

BORN: September 13, 1819; Leipzig, Saxony (now in Germany)
DIED: May 20, 1896; Frankfurt, Germany
ALSO KNOWN AS: Clara Josephine Wieck (birth name)
AREA OF ACHIEVEMENT: Music

EARLY LIFE

Clara Schumann (SHEW-mahn) seemed destined from birth to become a piano virtuoso. Her father, Friedrich Wieck, a respected piano teacher in Leipzig, Germany, took her education and training in hand almost before she could walk. Her mother, who had been born Marianne Tromlitz, was a gifted musician with a performing and teaching career of her own. Having inherited considerable musical talent from both her parents, Clara responded well to the training she received. Her father trained her on the piano and in religion and languages, and she studied the violin, theory, composition, harmony, orchestration, and counterpoint under the best available teachers, not only in Leipzig, but also in Dresden and Berlin.

With her father as her manager, Clara embarked on a concert career at the age of nine and made her formal solo debut at the famed Leipzig Gewandhaus at the age of eleven. She appeared in Paris soon afterward and at the age of eighteen took Vienna by storm. She was admired by the leading musical celebrities of the day, including Niccolò Paganini, Louis Spohr, Frédéric Chopin, Franz Liszt, and Felix Mendelssohn. During all this time, Clara and her father together kept a diary. Clara also copied her father's letters, including those setting up her performances. These exercises taught her the business aspect of a musical career.

Along with her virtuoso playing, Clara wrote music for herself to play, as had Wolfgang Amadeus Mozart, Ludwig von Beethoven, and many other composers before her. At her debut as a solo performer she played one of her own works, and she continued throughout her youth to delight audiences with her compositions. One of her most remarkable childhood works is her Piano Concerto, Op. 7, which she began in 1832 at the age of thirteen and performed three years later in the Leipzig Gewandhaus.

LIFE'S WORK

In 1840, at the age of twenty-one, Clara married the composer Robert Schumann, whom she had known since childhood. Her father's strenuous opposition to their marriage gave rise to a now-legendary legal battle. At the time of her marriage, Clara had an international reputation as a virtuoso pianist. In contrast, her husband—though nine years older—was still relatively unknown, and Clara actively promoted his works by presenting them regularly in her own concerts. Robert did not usually accompany his wife on her concert tours because he, during the early years, did not care to be recognized only as "the husband of Clara."

Despite these problems, Clara's marriage to Robert Schumann was in many ways a partnership. Clara and Robert studied scores together, read poetry for possible song settings, and advised each other about their compositions. Clara also arranged a number of Robert's works for piano and acted as rehearsal pianist for orchestras that he conducted. Clara's concert tours took her to Austria, Belgium, Denmark, France, Germany, Switzerland, Russia and England and helped her husband's work become quickly known to the musical world. Because Robert did not play publicly himself and therefore could not

Clara Schumann. (The Granger Collection, New York)

the sculptor wanted to put Clara's image in front and Robert's in back, but Robert overrode him, arguing that the creative artist was more important than the performing artist. His profile was placed in the foreground. On the Schumann memorial, Clara is portrayed sitting on a step, gazing up at Robert's image in an attitude of loving admiration, almost worship. This deferential image of Clara persisted in the public mind for many years after her lifetime. There is some truth to it; she acquiesced because of her absolute devotion to Robert, and perhaps also because society accepted the idea that women were inferior to men.

Throughout her marriage—even during her pregnancies—Clara continued to perform, compose, and teach. Robert, however, suffered increasingly from mental illness. After he attempted suicide in 1854, at the age of forty-four, he was hospitalized for the rest of his life. After a hiatus following his death in July, 1856, Clara eventually resumed performing and teaching. However, she never again wrote music for public consumption during the remaining forty years of her own life. Dressed in black for mourning, she was revered as the serious elder stateswoman of her art. In order to support her seven living children, two of whom were very young, she spent long periods on tour, with the ironic result that she had to send her children to live with relatives or friends while she toured. Four of her children eventually predeceased her, two after long illnesses.

Ever devoted to her husband's memory and music, Clara spent much time and effort promoting both. She eventually brought out the authoritative complete edition of Robert Schumann's works, prepared an instructional edition of his piano compositions, and arranged many of his vocal works. This she accomplished with the help of her trusted friend Johannes Brahms and others.

The Schumanns met Brahms not long before Robert's hospitalization, when Brahms was a young composer just beginning what would become a distinguished career. Robert Schumann befriended the young man and was pleased to promote his work. Brahms remained loyal to the Schumanns and provided support to Clara after Robert's death. Although Clara's relationship with Brahms has drawn much speculation, there is no solid evidence to conclude that Clara regarded Brahms as anything but a cherished friend.

In 1878, Clara became the principal piano instructor at the Hoch Conservatory in Frankfurt and drew students from many countries. She performed in her last concert in 1891, and her work at the conservatory ended in 1892. On May 20, 1896, she died in Frankfurt.

perform his own music, Clara premiered almost every piece he wrote for piano, and virtually all his works for orchestra were introduced in concerts in which Clara appeared as solo pianist.

Robert encouraged Clara to continue to write music of her own, and her mature compositions fulfilled her early promise. Her Trio, Op. 17 (1846), for example, shows a masterly use of the sonata form and contrapuntal technique and is considered by many to be her finest work. There were also other facets to Robert's life, in addition to his compositions. He taught and conducted and managed the publication of both his and Clara's works. He was also a respected critic and the founding editor of the *Neue Zeitschrift für Musik*, a respected journal that still existed in the early twenty-first century.

The Schumanns supported each other in all their musical endeavors, but certain telling details in Clara's life suggest that all was not perfect. She lamented the fact that she could not practice while Robert was working and had to fit her needs around his. When a plaster relief sculpture portraying both their profiles was proposed,

SIGNIFICANCE

Clara Schumann's reputation as a teacher, and especially as a performer, endured after she died. However, her compositions were all but forgotten until the 1970's, when recordings of her works began to appear. Since then, her discography has grown to more than one hundred recordings, and printed editions of her work have also increased significantly.

Schumann was not a feminist as the term is used in the twenty-first century. She simply did the only things she was trained to do—give concerts, teach, and write music. After she reached the age of eighteen, she became her own manager, which required a certain amount of business acumen. During the early years of her marriage, before her husband became well known, hers was often the more dependable income for her family, even though she often had to subjugate her professional needs to those of her husband. After Robert's death she was the sole breadwinner for her family. One of her daughters later suggested in her autobiography that she and her siblings would have fared better had her mother been a more constant presence in their lives. That observation may simply be a reflection of the time in which it was written. However, it is true the very nature of Clara's work demanded that she make the same kinds of choices, compromises, and sacrifices that are made by many Western women in the twenty-first century.

—JoAnne M. Rogers

FURTHER READING

Galloway, Janice. *Clara: A Novel*. New York: Simon & Schuster, 2002. Fictional depiction of Clara Schumann's life that is accurate in many ways.

Litzmann, Berthold. *Clara Schumann: An Artist's Life, Based on Material Found in Diaries and Letters*. Translated and abridged from the 4th edition by Grace E. Hadow. New introduction by Elaine Brody. New York: Da Capo, 1979. An old work, which first appeared in 1902 and was later revised several times, that is the foundation of much of the later research on Clara Schumann.

Reich, Nancy B. *Clara Schumann: The Artist and the Woman*. Rev. ed. Ithaca, N.Y.: Cornell University Press, 2001. A landmark biography that strives to show Schumann as she was, rather than as she has been idealized.

Steegman, Monica. *Clara Schumann*. London: Haus, 2004. A concise biography that is both interesting and easy to read.

SEE ALSO: Ludwig van Beethoven; Johannes Brahms; Frédéric Chopin; Gustav Theodor Fechner; Franz Liszt; Felix Mendelssohn; Niccolò Paganini; Robert Schumann; Carl Maria von Weber.

RELATED ARTICLE in *Great Events from History: The Nineteenth Century, 1801-1900:* December 22, 1894: Debussy's *Prelude to the Afternoon of a Faun* Premieres.

ROBERT SCHUMANN
German composer

Schumann was important not only as a composer of music during the Romantic period but also as an editor of Neue Zeitschrift für Musik, *which did much to establish standards of musical criticism.*

BORN: June 8, 1810; Zwickau, Saxony (now in Germany)

DIED: July 29, 1856; Endenich, near Bonn, Prussia (now in Germany)

ALSO KNOWN AS: Robert Alexander Schumann (full name)

AREA OF ACHIEVEMENT: Music

EARLY LIFE

Robert Alexander Schumann (SHEW-mahn) was the youngest of five children—four sons and one daughter— of a publisher of scholarly books; his mother was the daughter of a surgeon. His father's publishing business was sufficiently prosperous for his parents to enroll him in a private preparatory school for his early education. Already, at his father's instigation, he was studying the piano, the instrument that would remain his favorite throughout his life. After the preparatory school, Schumann attended the Zwickau Lyceum, where he studied the classics as well as the piano. Literature and music, then, were both strong interests of the young Schumann and remained so throughout his life.

At the lyceum, Schumann played the piano in concerts, read widely in classical Greek and Roman authors, and studied such German writers as Friedrich von Schiller and Johann Wolfgang von Goethe. He even wrote some poetry, although when he attempted to recite from memory one of his poems before the student body, his mind went blank, and he stood in silent embarrassment on the stage. This incident may have contributed significantly to Schumann's aversion to public speaking throughout his life.

Schumann spent his formative years if not in affluence at least at a comfortable material level. In 1826, however, tragedy struck when his elder sister Emilie, who was afflicted with typhus fever and a terrible skin disease, committed suicide. August Schumann was crushed by this event and himself died a few weeks later. Schumann, too, was deeply affected by his sister's death and from that time forward could never bring himself to attend a funeral, not even his mother's. Schumann's mother, Johanna, and Gottlob Rudel, the guardian appointed to look after Robert's share of August's estate, agreed that the boy should pursue a legal career. With no one to support his own desires, Schumann acquiesced, although he knew that he would never lose his love of music. In an 1828 letter to a friend describing his feelings upon leaving the lyceum, he wrote, "Now the true inner man must come forward and show who he is."

Enrolling first at the University of Leipzig, Schumann found the study of law even more boring than he had feared. Influenced by a friend at Heidelberg, who wrote of the exciting university life there, Schumann persuaded his mother and Rudel that he should go to Heidelberg to continue his study. He was, however, anything but the model student, spending his time in taverns and restaurants instead of in the pursuit of his legal studies. He also spent much time with Anton Thibaut, a law professor much interested in music. Schumann spent many hours at Thibaut's home, making and enjoying music.

On July 30, 1830, Schumann wrote what he called the most important letter in his life: one to his mother, pleading that he be permitted to give up his legal studies and journey to Leipzig to study piano with Friedrich Wieck, who promised to turn the young Schumann into a great pianist. Johanna Schumann agreed, and at the age of twenty Robert Schumann began his musical career.

LIFE'S WORK
Schumann had met Wieck in Leipzig. A kind of self-made man, the latter's early life was the opposite of Schumann's. Poor, and often forced to rely on charity for food and for money to cover his education, he developed into an autocrat with a violent temper. Following his own system of instruction, he set himself up as a piano teacher. He saw the clear relationship between playing

Robert Schumann. (The Granger Collection, New York)

the piano and singing and trained his students to strive for a "singing touch" at the keyboard. His prize student was his own daughter Clara. Viewing her almost as an extension of himself, Wieck carefully molded and developed her talent to a level that made her something of a sensation across Europe. In 1832, when Schumann came to study with Wieck, Clara was thirteen years old. The relationship between them grew over the next several years from one of elder brother and younger sister to one of love.

On one occasion, when Wieck had taken Clara on a performing tour, Schumann, perhaps in an effort to find a technique to help him catch up with the talented Clara, fashioned a sling of sorts to keep one finger out of the way while the others were being exercised. Exactly what happened to his hand is not clear. Schumann himself only said that it was lamed. Some scholars suggest that no injury actually occurred and that Schumann may have suffered motor damage from an overdose of mercury, a substance then widely prescribed for syphilis. Whatever the cause, the effect was devastating to the young pianist. He tried numerous cures to no avail.

When Wieck discovered that the relationship between Schumann and Clara was becoming more than simply friendship, he flew into a rage, vowing that his daughter was destined to be a concert pianist, not a hausfrau. Love, however, was not to be daunted, and the two young people applied to the courts for permission to marry. The wedding took place on September 12, 1840, and the couple settled in Leipzig, an important musical center of the time.

An ardent admirer of Franz Schubert's piano music, Schumann, up to the time of his marriage, had written only for the piano. In 1840, however, he turned his creative efforts to *Lieder* (art songs), many of which were in celebration of his love for Clara. These *Lieder* show clearly Schumann's attention to form and reflect the same power of emotion and flow of melody as do Schubert's, although the harmonics are more complex. Schumann probably realized that such art songs gave him the opportunity to blend his feeling for poetry and his genius for melody. In these songs, as one might expect, the piano has a more significant role than it does in those of other composers of *Lieder*.

Schumann's gift with words was evidenced also in his editorship of *Neue Zeitschrift für Musik* (new journal for music), a magazine that served as an outlet for the writings of young Romantic musicians in Germany. Indeed, when Schumann first met Felix Mendelssohn in 1835, he was more noted for his work with this magazine than for his music, a situation that led Mendelssohn to see him first as a kind of dilettante. Schumann, on the other hand, had only the highest regard for Mendelssohn as a composer.

If 1840 could be called Schumann's year of songs, the next year could certainly be called the year of symphonies. Although he had flirted earlier with the idea of a symphony, he had never completed one. In 1841, he completed two. The First Symphony, whose initial idea came to Schumann from a poem about spring by Adolf Böttger, was completed in the remarkably short period of one month. Called the *Spring Symphony*, it is buoyant and fresh in its mood and is marked by a driving rhythmic energy. The Symphony in D Minor was also written in 1841, although it was not published until ten years later and is referred to as the Fourth Symphony. It was performed once in 1841, but because of the cold reception it received, Schumann withdrew it and put it aside until 1851, when he revised it. Schumann left no word as to what meaning lay behind the music of this symphony. It was no doubt Schumann's intention, according to Brian Schlotel, that it be received as absolute music.

Schumann spent the year 1842 working primarily on string quartets, three of which he dedicated to Mendelssohn. This same year, he accompanied Clara on a concert tour to Hamburg. Although her marriage no doubt lim-

ited her career as a concert pianist, Clara was ever ready to play her husband's compositions and to interpret them faithfully to her audiences. It was in a sense a perfect combination—Schumann's talent as a composer complemented by his wife's talent as a pianist.

In 1843, Schumann turned his efforts toward composing choral works, the most important of which was "Paradise and the Peri," a work for solo voices, chorus, and orchestra. Schumann conducted it himself December 4, 1843. Encouraged by the reception of this work, he composed a musical setting for Goethe's *Faust* (1790-1831). Also at about this time, Schumann suffered a second physical breakdown, the first, less serious, having occurred in 1842. This second breakdown was marked by constant trembling, a number of phobias, and auricular delusions, and it made serious work impossible. Hoping that a total change of scene would be helpful, the Schumanns moved to Dresden.

While at Dresden, Schumann completed the Piano Concerto in A Minor (1845), the famous C Major Symphony (1846), and his only opera, *Genoveva* (1848). The latter was an unsuccessful attempt to emulate Richard Wagner's German operas. In addition to composing, Schumann directed the Liedertafel, a male choral society. Neither of the Schumanns was particularly happy with the music scene in Dresden, and when the opportunity to become municipal director of music at Düsseldorf arrived, Schumann accepted. However, Schumann did not exhibit the same level of talent in conducting as he did in composing, and he was encouraged in 1852 to resign. After some argument, he finally left in 1853.

In 1850, Schumann completed his Symphony No. 3, the *Rhenish*, and also his Concerto for Cello and Orchestra. In the former, Schumann attempted to put into music his feelings about the Rhine, a river rich in scenery and legend. The full score of the symphony was completed in somewhat more than one month, and Schumann himself conducted it in Düsseldorf on February 6, 1851. Although his artistic talents and creative powers are apparent in this symphony, time for Schumann was running out. Within three years, in a period of utter depression, he attempted suicide by jumping into the river that had stimulated his imagination to compose the *Rhenish*. Although the suicide attempt was thwarted by some fishermen, death came soon enough. Schumann's last years were spent at Endenich, a hospital for the insane. With his limbs in terrible convulsions and with the sounds of music filling his head, Schumann died on July 29, 1856.

SIGNIFICANCE

Along with Frédéric Chopin, Felix Mendelssohn, Johannes Brahms, and Anton Bruckner, Robert Schumann composed works that reflect the artistic energies of the Romantic movement in music. Schumann was also instrumental in developing critical standards for music. His periodical *Neue Zeitschrift für Musik* served as an outlet for musical criticism and as a support for struggling composers of the time, including Chopin and Brahms.

Schumann's music itself reflects clearly the strong emotions and individualistic values of the Romantic period. Focusing early in his career on miniature pieces, Schumann exemplified the desire of Romantic composers to communicate directly and intensely with the listener. The year 1840 may be called Schumann's year of songs, many of which were inspired by his wife, Clara. These beautiful flowing melodies testify to Schumann's love of poetry and his desire to meld the literary with the musical.

Alternating periods of intense creative productivity with periods of deep depression, Schumann moved from miniatures and songs to larger works—symphonies, choral works, chamber music, piano concerti, and an opera. His four symphonies are generally considered the most significant contributions to that genre since Ludwig van Beethoven's works. Although sometimes criticized for their somewhat heavy and unimaginative orchestrations, Schumann's symphonies show his desire to experiment with both themes and form.

In his chamber music, Schumann made great use of the piano, sometimes to the consternation of some musicologists. Nevertheless, as John Gardner and others have pointed out, Schumann's influence ranged widely among his contemporaries and successors in that genre. After the piano took over from the harpsichord during the late eighteenth century, the door was open for Schumann to give the former its deserved place in chamber music.

Except for the Piano Concerto in A Minor, some musicologists view Schumann's concerti as representing a falling off of his creativity. Others argue, however, that Schumann, like other composers of the period, faced the challenge of "getting out from under" Beethoven and that his concerti are justified efforts in new directions of form and theme. He saw the concerto as a great art form, one that was to be treated not casually but nobly—but one that had to evolve if it were to remain vital.

Schumann completed his first symphony at the age of thirty, after having heard Schubert's Symphony in C Major in 1839. Certainly influenced by Beethoven's work in the symphony, Schumann nevertheless sought new forms in his own symphonies. Not generally considered a giant of symphonic composition, Schumann must still be viewed as having considerable importance in symphonic history. The same may be said for his choral music. Often neglected, this music came late in Schumann's life, when his mental problems increasingly interfered with his creative powers. Nevertheless, as Louis Halsey has argued, much of this music is of high quality. A man of restless personality and strong creative spirit, Schumann has been called the typical Romantic. Not a revolutionary to the same degree as Beethoven, he nevertheless made a significant contribution to music of the Romantic period.

—*Wilton Eckley*

FURTHER READING

Bedford, Herbert. *Robert Schumann: His Life and Work.* New York: Harper & Brothers, 1925. A readable biography that traces Schumann's career. Focuses on the cities in which Schumann lived and worked. Somewhat dated.

Brion, Marcel. *Schumann and the Romantic Age.* Translated by Geoffrey Sainsbury. New York: Macmillan, 1956. Places Schumann in the German Romantic tradition and examines his work against the background that influenced him. A good basic book on the composer.

Daverio, John. *Robert Schumann: Herald of a "New Poetic Age."* New York: Oxford University Press, 1997. Comprehensive biography depicting Schumann as a tragic figure who experienced periods of creativity followed by bouts of depression. Daverio connects Schumann's music to the events of his life and his passion for literature.

Jensen, Eric Frederick. *Schumann.* New York: Oxford University Press, 2001. Examination of Schumann's life and music, based in part on newly published journals and letters. The book alternates biographical chapters with chapters analyzing Schumann's music, describing how his life influenced his compositions.

Niecks, Frederick. *Robert Schumann.* London: J. M. Dent and Sons, 1925. A standard biography that presents a meticulous and exhaustive record of Schumann as a man and as a composer.

Ostwald, Peter. *Schumann: The Inner Voices of a Musical Genius.* Boston: Northeastern University Press, 1985. Written by a psychiatrist, this is a fascinating study of the degenerative forces that brought Schumann to his death in a mental hospital. Relates Schumann's music to his states of mind.

Schumann, Robert. *The Musical World of Robert Schumann*. Edited and translated by Henry Pleasants. New York: St. Martin's Press, 1965. Presents a chronological arrangement of Schumann's own writings on various composers of his time. A good view of Schumann the critic. Good for insights into various composers and their music.

Walker, Alan, ed. *Robert Schumann: The Man and His Music*. New York: Barnes & Noble Books, 1972. A study of Schumann through thirteen essays by music scholars. Covers Schumann's background as well as the various kinds of music he composed.

SEE ALSO: Ludwig van Beethoven; Georges Bizet; Johannes Brahms; Anton Bruckner; Frédéric Chopin; Gustav Theodor Fechner; Felix Mendelssohn; Franz Schubert; Clara Schumann; Richard Wagner; Carl Maria von Weber.

RELATED ARTICLES in *Great Events from History: The Nineteenth Century, 1801-1900:* April 7, 1805: Beethoven's *Eroica* Symphony Introduces the Romantic Age; December 22, 1894: Debussy's *Prelude to the Afternoon of a Faun* Premieres.

CARL SCHURZ
German-born American politician

Recognized as a leader of the German American community in the United States, Carl Schurz was a partisan of liberty who fled Germany after the revolutions of 1848 and made a career as a journalist and politician, serving as a Union general in the Civil War, a U.S. senator, and a secretary of the interior.

BORN: March 2, 1829; Liblar, Prussia (now in Germany)
DIED: May 14, 1906; New York, New York
AREA OF ACHIEVEMENT: Government and politics

EARLY LIFE

The son of Christian and Marianne (Jüssen) Schurz, Carl Schurz (shewrts) was born in one of the outbuildings of a moated castle in the Prussian Rhineland (Germany), where his grandfather worked for Baron Wolf von Metternich. His family was of humble origin but was respected in the local context of village life; his grandfather was the count's estate manager, one uncle was the mayor of a neighboring village, and his father was the Liblar schoolmaster. Schurz was reared a Roman Catholic, but with a strong dose of Enlightenment skepticism; as an adult, he considered himself a "freethinker."

As a boy, Schelling enjoyed the run of Metternich's estate, its formal gardens, its forests, and its farmlands. His parents noted his unusual intelligence and his musical skill and resolved to make sacrifices to give him a higher education. Thus he left his father's school in the village, going to preparatory school at neighboring Brühl and then at Cologne, several miles away. When he was

seventeen, the family moved to the nearest university town, Bonn, so that the boy could study there, even though his parents had suffered financial reverses that temporarily put his father in debtors' prison.

At Bonn, Schurz began to make a name for himself both in the politically liberal fraternal organizations and as a budding scholar, under the tutelage of the young Romantic Gottfried Kinkel. Then came the revolutionary fervor of 1848. Immediately, Schurz interrupted his formal education and turned to a life of political activity. Like many young men of his generation, he saw 1848 as the opportunity to achieve a unified German state with a liberal-democratic constitution. Too young to stand for election himself, he turned to journalism and popular agitation to support his goals.

Schurz's zeal for freedom and justice, his skills as a writer and speaker, and his tireless and combative commitment to his cause were characteristics that would distinguish him as a prominent American statesman years later. He joined the revolutionary army that fought against the old monarchies and barely escaped with his life when it was forced to surrender. In 1850, he returned to Prussia from exile in France and Switzerland in disguise and rescued Professor Kinkel from the prison to which the Prussians had condemned him. After spending a brief time in Paris and London, where he wooed and married Margarethe Meyer, daughter of a well-to-do Hamburg mercantile family, he decided to leave the Old World for America. If he could not be a citizen of a free Germany, he concluded, he would become a free citizen of the United States.

Carl Schurz. (The Granger Collection, New York)

The tall, slim young man with thick glasses affected the flowing hair and mustache of a Romantic liberal in 1848; as he matured, he was recognizable for his bushy beard and sharp features, so often caricatured by the New York editorial cartoonist Thomas Nast.

LIFE'S WORK

Schurz and his young wife arrived in the United States in 1852, staying first in Philadelphia and eventually settling in Watertown, Wisconsin, in 1855. As an immigrant, he was neither tired nor poor. His wife's dowry was enough to set him up in business. His fame as a daring fighter for freedom in Germany, his solid education, his gifts as a writer and speaker, and his political ambition combined to make him a well-known figure almost immediately. Although he rarely stood for election himself, his persuasiveness with German American voters made him a force to be reckoned with in the ethnic politics of that age.

Schurz led the Wisconsin delegation to the Republican National Convention in 1860. Though originally

pledged to William H. Seward, he became an avid supporter of Abraham Lincoln once he had received the nomination. Schurz traveled more than twenty-one thousand miles campaigning for Lincoln, speaking in both English and German, and was credited with swinging much of the German American vote away from its traditional inclination for the Democratic Party and into Lincoln's camp. In gratitude, Lincoln appointed him minister to Spain and, after the onset of the Civil War, brigadier and then major general in the Union army. Schurz's military career did little to enhance his reputation. He was only in his early thirties, and his high rank was clearly a result of political influence rather than demonstrated military skills. Schurz did his best, however, to contribute to the Union cause, seeing action at the Second Battle of Bull Run, Gettysburg, and Chancellorsville. Lincoln invited Schurz to report directly to him on the wartime situation, which Schurz did with great energy, pressing the president to emancipate the slaves.

After the war, Schurz settled in St. Louis as part owner and editor of the German-language *Westliche Post*. His wife never liked the American Midwest, however, and so she spent much of her time in Europe. While visiting his family in Germany in 1868, Schurz made a widely reported visit to Berlin, where the onetime revolutionary was warmly received by Otto von Bismarck, now prime minister of Prussia and chancellor of the emerging German Empire.

Schurz was critical of President Andrew Johnson but enthusiastically supported Ulysses S. Grant in the 1868 elections. German American forces were influential in Missouri politics, and the state legislature sent him to Washington, D.C., as a senator. After arriving there, he became disillusioned with the apparent corruption in the spoils system, and he turned his polemical skills to the issue of civil service reform. This challenge to the status quo alienated many of his party allies, and he was not returned to office in 1874. The Senate provided a platform for Schurz's oratorical skills, and he gained a national reputation as a spokesperson for reform and for the German American community. Because of his criticisms of United States politicians, some alleged that he was not a patriotic American. He responded with a turn of phrase that has become famous: "My country right or wrong: if right, to be kept right; and if wrong, to be set right."

No partisan loyalist, Schurz was active in founding the Liberal Republican Party, which supported Horace Greeley for president over Grant in 1872. With the election of 1876, however, he returned to the Republican Party, supporting Rutherford B. Hayes, and after Hayes's victory, Schurz was made secretary of the interior. He attempted to initiate environmental controls, particularly over forest lands, and to follow a humanitarian policy with respect to the Indians. His liberal idealism was unable to overcome deep-seated interests that opposed his policies. He left government office in 1881, never to serve again, and pursued his career as a journalist, author, and lecturer. He made New York his home, where he became editor in chief of the *Evening Post* and, eventually, *Harper's Weekly*.

As an independent, Schurz found himself among the "Mugwumps," who were more committed to his liberal ideals, especially civil service reform, than to any political party. Looking at his record, one sees a man who supported James A. Garfield (Republican) in 1880, Grover Cleveland (Democrat) in 1884, 1888, and 1892, William McKinley (Republican) in 1896, William Jennings Bryan (Democrat) in 1900, and Alton B. Parker (Democrat) in 1904. In an age when corruption was often an accepted part of the political process, Schurz remained free of its taint. His nineteenth century liberalism has been criticized as being narrow and doctrinaire, a laissez-faire philosophy that had little room for labor unions and social programs. However, his concepts of personal liberty, due process of law, and clean government surely put him in the mainstream of American political thought and action.

Schurz favored suffrage for black men—but not for women—and spoke out strongly against anti-Semitism. During the 1890's, he looked with dismay upon American diplomatic and military expansion and, polemically as ever, crusaded as an anti-imperialist. The onetime general loathed war and its accompanying atrocities; moreover, he seemed to fear that an active policy overseas by the United States might at some time lead to a conflict with the land of his birth, Germany. As a man in his sixties and seventies, he traveled and spoke as avidly against an American empire as he had once fought for Lincoln's election and freedom for the slaves. Though he no longer was

---

CLASSIFYING POST-CIVIL WAR SOUTHERNERS

After the conclusion of the Civil War, President Andrew Johnson commissioned Carl Schurz to tour the states of the defeated Confederacy and report on their condition. Schurz questioned hundreds of white southerners about their attitudes toward the postwar situation and in his report grouped southerners into these "four classes":

1. Those who, although having yielded submission to the national government only when obliged to do so, have a clear perception of the irreversible changes produced by the war, and honestly endeavor to accommodate themselves to the new order of things. Many of them are not free from traditional prejudice but open to conviction, and may be expected to act in good faith whatever they do. This class is composed, in its majority, of persons of mature age—planters, merchants, and professional men; some of them are active in the reconstruction movement, but boldness and energy are, with a few individual exceptions, not among their distinguishing qualities.

2. Those whose principal object is to have the States without delay restored to their position and influence in the Union and the people of the States to the absolute control of their home concerns. They are ready, in order to attain that object, to make any ostensible concession that will not prevent them from arranging things to suit their taste as soon as that object is attained. This class comprises a considerable number, probably a large majority, of the professional politicians who are extremely active in the reconstruction movement. They are loud in their praise of the President's reconstruction policy, and clamorous for the withdrawal of the federal troops and the abolition of the Freedmen's Bureau.

3. The incorrigibles, who still indulge in the swagger which was so customary before and during the war, and still hope for a time when the southern confederacy will achieve its independence. This class consists mostly of young men, and comprises the loiterers of the towns and the idlers of the country. They persecute Union men and negroes whenever they can do so with impunity, insist clamorously upon their "rights," and are extremely impatient of the presence of the federal soldiers. A good many of them have taken the oaths of allegiance and amnesty, and associated themselves with the second class in their political operations. This element is by no means unimportant; it is strong in numbers, deals in brave talk, addresses itself directly and incessantly to the passions and prejudices of the masses, and commands the admiration of the women.

4. The multitude of people who have no definite ideas about the circumstances under which they live and about the course they have to follow; whose intellects are weak, but whose prejudices and impulses are strong, and who are apt to be carried along by those who know how to appeal to the latter.

Source: Carl Schurz, *Report on the Condition of the South* (Washington, D.C., 1865).

alleged to be able to swing the German American vote in major elections, he was widely praised as that community's leader and was showered with honors. He died peacefully at his home in New York City at the age of seventy-seven.

SIGNIFICANCE

Schurz saw himself as "the main intermediary between German and American culture." He continued to be equally fluent in German and English, writing his widely read memoirs in both languages. He traveled back and forth many times between the United States and the old country, filled with pride for both. When accused of mixed loyalties, he responded that he loved equally his "old mother" and his "new bride." Stalwart and eloquent, he vigorously defended the cause of freedom, as he saw it, in Germany and in the United States.

Schurz's stubborn dedication to his principles and his combative temperament sometimes earned for him the enmity of political opponents. Surely not even all German Americans supported him on every issue. As a group, however, they were proud of his accomplishments, the most impressive of any German immigrant at that time, and they agreed with him that fondness for their country of origin did not diminish their patriotism as Americans. Schurz would have been deeply saddened by the political and diplomatic events of the first half of the twentieth century that brought the United States and Germany into conflict, but much heartened by the development of a firm alliance between America and a liberal-democratic Germany after 1945.

—*Gordon R. Mork*

FURTHER READING

Decker, Peter R. *"The Utes Must Go!" American Expansion and the Removal of a People.* Golden, Colo.: Fulcrum, 2004. Chronicles three centuries of Ute history, focusing on government policies that forced the tribe's removal from Colorado, New Mexico, and Wyoming. Includes information on Schurz's role in creating and enforcing these policies during his stint as secretary of the interior.

Easum, Chester V. *The Americanization of Carl Schurz.* Chicago: University of Chicago Press, 1929. A brief, older work, upon which further scholarship on Schurz has depended.

Fuess, Claude M. *Carl Schurz, Reformer: 1829-1906.* Edited by Allan Nevins. New York: Dodd, Mead, 1932. A gentlemanly biography by a scholar of German American parentage.

Schurz, Carl. *Intimate Letters of Carl Schurz: 1841-1869.* Edited and translated by Joseph Schafer. Madison: State Historical Society of Wisconsin, 1928. Hitherto unpublished letters, mostly to members of his family, which shed light on Schurz's career and personal life beyond that shown in the six-volume set cited below.

_____. *The Reminiscences of Carl Schurz.* 3 vols. Garden City, N.Y.: Doubleday, 1907-1908. An entertaining and enlightening view of Schurz as he saw himself, with insightful sketches of the great men he knew, especially Lincoln, Bismarck, and a long list of American political figures. A modern abridgment by Wayne Andrews (New York: Scribners, 1961) is available, with an introduction by Allan Nevins.

_____. *Speeches, Correspondence and Political Papers of Carl Schurz.* Edited by Frederic Bancroft. 6 vols. New York: G. P. Putnam's Sons, 1913. The vast array of Schurz's political output is set forth in this old, but well-edited, collection of his works.

Trefousse, Hans L. *Carl Schurz: A Biography.* Knoxville: University of Tennessee Press, 1982. A scholarly study of Schurz, based on exhaustive study of the printed and manuscript sources in the United States and in Europe, including some private letters to his companion in later life, Fanny Chapman. Excellent notes and bibliography.

Wallman, Charles J. *The German-Speaking Forty-eighters: Builders of Watertown, Wisconsin.* Madison, Wis.: Max Kade Institute for German American Studies, University of Wisconsin-Madison, 1990. Chronicles the experiences of Schurz and other emigrants who left Germany after the revolutions of 1848 and eventually settled in Watertown, Wisconsin.

SEE ALSO: Otto von Bismarck; Grover Cleveland; James A. Garfield; Ulysses S. Grant; Horace Greeley; Rutherford B. Hayes; Andrew Johnson; Abraham Lincoln; William McKinley; Metternich; Thomas Nast; William H. Seward.

RELATED ARTICLES in *Great Events from History: The Nineteenth Century, 1801-1900:* November 4, 1884: U.S. Election of 1884; February 8, 1887: General Allotment Act Erodes Indian Tribal Unity.

CHARLOTTE ANGAS SCOTT
English-born American mathematician

As the first professor of mathematics at Bryn Mawr College in Pennsylvania, Scott created an environment that encouraged a large number of women to work for higher degrees in mathematics. Her research and stature in the field of mathematics blazed a trail that was not matched by other women for many years.

BORN: June 8, 1858; Lincoln, England
DIED: November 10, 1931; Cambridge, England
AREA OF ACHIEVEMENT: Mathematics

EARLY LIFE

Charlotte Angas Scott was born in England, the second of seven children of Caleb and Eliza Ann Exley Scott. Her father was a pastor at a nonconformist (non-Anglican Protestant) church; when Charlotte was seven years old, he was elevated to the headship of Lancashire College. Charlotte was educated primarily at home, and her family could afford to provide her with a sequence of excellent tutors. In addition, the family often played mathematical games with her to provide an additional level of encouragement.

Charlotte's mathematical talents were sufficiently evident that she received a scholarship at Girton College, one of the newly created women's colleges at Cambridge University. At that time, women were not allowed to receive degrees from either Cambridge or Oxford University, the two most prestigious institutions of higher education in England. However, that limitation had not prevented the creation of women's colleges, in which female students could study, even if they could not receive degrees. The idea of offering higher education to women was then largely a subject of mockery. An example of public attitudes can be seen in W. S. Gilbert and Arthur Sullivan's musical play *Princess Ida* (1884). It took great resolution for women students to put up with antifeminist attitudes in education, but Charlotte Scott was a model of resolution.

Scott received her first—and largest—dose of public attention when she took the Tripos examination at Cambridge. This test took its name from a three-legged stool on which students had originally sat, but it had evolved into the most challenging mathematical exam in England. It was taken by students working for undergraduate degrees in mathematics—a highly select group. Women were allowed to take the exam, but their results were not reported along with those of the male students. When Scott took the exam, she earned a high score

equivalent to "eighth wrangler," but her name was omitted from the list of the results, according to university policy.

The Times of London, the most influential newspaper in Great Britain, took up Scott's case and transformed the question of reporting women's exam results into a national issue. The humorous weekly *Punch* pleaded her case, even though it was not known for holding progressive views. A campaign among the alumni of Cambridge University encouraged the university to change its policy by including women's exam results along with those of men. This change took place the year after Scott's success and was one of the first steps in the direction of allowing women to take degrees from the senior universities in England.

LIFE'S WORK

After her years as a student at Girton, Scott stayed on at Cambridge as a lecturer at the same college. Since the University of London did not have the same prohibition on women taking degrees that prevailed at Oxford and Cambridge, Scott earned an undergraduate degree there in 1882 and a doctorate in 1885, following in the footsteps of the relatively small number of women who had received advanced degrees in mathematics elsewhere in Europe. Her work was in the area of algebraic geometry, a subject that was at the forefront of mathematical research at the time. While she was at Cambridge, she had the chance to work with Arthur Cayley, one of the outstanding mathematicians in Europe and a founder of both modern algebra and its application to geometry.

The idea behind algebraic geometry is to use algebraic arguments to prove results about geometric objects. This process involves finding algebraic methods of describing curves and surfaces—which was usually done with equations. If one could work with the equations, one could apply the techniques of algebra rather than having to fall back on the principles of geometry, which sometimes were difficult to make precise. Many different types of geometry were being introduced into academic curricula during the late nineteenth century, and each came with a different range of algebraic techniques. Scott herself became especially well known for her applications of algebra to projective geometry, the branch in which curves are treated as identical when one can be projected onto the other.

During the year 1885, Bryn Mawr College opened in Bryn Mawr, Pennsylvania, to provide education of the highest quality, including graduate study, to women. The new college hired Scott to head its mathematics department, in part because she was one of the few women in the world with a doctorate in the subject. It is a tribute to her teaching skills that Bryn Mawr rapidly became a center for women pursuing doctorates in mathematics. During her tenure there, Bryn Mawr trailed only the University of Chicago and Cornell University in numbers of doctoral degrees in mathematics awarded to women. During that same period, of all U.S. doctorates awarded in mathematics, 14 percent went to women. By comparison, during the 1950's, only 5 percent of doctorates in mathematics went to women. Only in later years have the percentages of doctorates awarded to women exceeded the levels achieved by Scott at Bryn Mawr.

While she was teaching and supervising students at Bryn Mawr, Scott continued to do research. In 1894, she published a textbook with the ponderous title *An Introductory Account of Certain Modern Ideas and Methods in Plane Analytical Geometry* and later saw another edition through the press. The book was well received, and her gift for exposition was described as lucid.

During Scott's years at Bryn Mawr, she made annual pilgrimages back to England to be in a more active mathematical environment. However, she also promoted the professionalization of mathematics in the United States and was active in the newly formed New York Mathematical Society, the ancestor of the American Mathematical Society. She served on the council of the society on many occasions and served as its vice president in 1906. She was the first woman to hold that position, and she did not have a female successor for many decades. In recognition of her status, the first edition of *American Men of Science* (1906) included an entry for her.

Scott's views on education did not always make her life easy at Bryn Mawr. She disliked student behavior that she regarded as immoral, such as smoking and wearing makeup. On one occasion she took the president of the college to task for diluting the quality of women's education. However, she also made signal contributions to campus life, such as bringing the distinguished British mathematician and philosopher Bertrand Russell there to speak. Her teaching helped to put Bryn Mawr on the intellectual map in both England and the United States.

Scott taught at Bryn Mawr for forty years. By her last years there, ill health was interfering with her teaching as she became deaf and suffered from arthritis. When she retired to Cambridge, England, in 1925, she took up gar-

dening and also spent some of her time and money betting on horse racing. On November 10, 1931, she died at her Cambridge home, at the age of seventy-three.

SIGNIFICANCE

Charlotte Scott achieved her greatest prominence in the world at large while she was still a student. Her success on the Tripos exam indicated that women were at Cambridge for reasons other than to find husbands or make polemical statements. Her subsequent distinction as a mathematician made Cambridge University proud to have been her alma mater, even if it would not grant her a degree.

As a professional mathematician, Scott did not revolutionize the subjects in which she worked, but her solid accomplishments paved the way for women to achieve success in graduate work and beyond. She guaranteed that Bryn Mawr College would provide serious mathematical training for women, even if her insistence on high standards did not always make her an easy colleague. The fact that during the 1930's, Emmy Noether, the world's most eminent woman mathematician, left Germany because of the rise of Adolf Hitler and went to Bryn Mawr is a tribute to the mathematical environment that Charlotte Scott had created there.

—Thomas Drucker

FURTHER READING

Farquhar, Diane, and Lynn Mary-Rose. *Women Sum It Up*. Christchurch, New Zealand: Hazard Press, 1989. Study of female mathematicians that covers aspects of Scott's family background and personal life, rather than her mathematical career.

Gray, J. J. "Charlotte Angas Scott." In *Oxford Dictionary of National Biography*, edited by H. C. G. Matthew and Brian Harrison. Oxford, England: Oxford University Press, 2004. Mathematically well-informed summary of Scott's life against the background of the times.

Green, Judy, and Jeanne Laduke. "Contributors to American Mathematics." In *Women of Science: Righting the Record*, edited by G. Kass-Simon and Patricia Farnes. Bloomington: Indiana University Press, 1990. Recognizes Scott's work in encouraging women to higher education in mathematics.

Kenschaft, Patricia Clark. "Charlotte Angas Scott." In *Complexities: Women in Mathematics*, edited by Bettye Anne Case and Anne M. Leggett. Princeton, N.J.: Princeton University Press, 2005. One of several articles on Scott by Kenschaft; useful for filling in some cultural background.

Macaulay, F. S. "Dr. Charlotte Angas Scott." *Journal of the London Mathematical Society* 7 (1932): 230-240. The source on which most subsequent biographers draw, paying full attention to Scott's mathematical work.

SEE ALSO: Catharine Beecher; W. S. Gilbert and Arthur Sullivan; Sofya Kovalevskaya; Countess of Lovelace; Alice Freeman Palmer.
RELATED ARTICLE in *Great Events from History: The Nineteenth Century, 1801-1900:* September 26, 1865: Vassar College Opens.

DRED SCOTT
American slave

Perhaps the most famous slave in American history, Scott instigated a legal challenge to the definition of "citizenship" for black people in the United States. His challenge led to the Supreme Court's 1857 Dred Scott v. Sandford *decision, which became a step toward Civil War and the end of slavery.*

BORN: c. 1795; Southampton County, Virginia
DIED: September 17, 1858; St. Louis, Missouri
AREA OF ACHIEVEMENT: Social reform

EARLY LIFE

Dred Scott was born a slave in Virginia, and little information about him exists in the official record until he reached adulthood. He probably arrived in St. Louis, Missouri, in 1830 from Virginia and Alabama, accompanying his owner, Peter Blow, Blow's wife Elizabeth, and their children. The Blows had been farmers in Virginia and Alabama, but when they arrived in Missouri, they tried their hand as owners of a boardinghouse, which was only barely successful.

Scott is described in the record as being about five feet tall and dark skinned. He was illiterate. It is likely that Scott had been a slave to the Blows since his adolescence, if not his childhood, and the emotional connections Scott made with the sons of Peter and Elizabeth proved to be helpful to the Scott family later. During the series of trials that began with Scott's suit to be recognized as a citizen of the United States, a St. Louis newspaper reporter interviewed Scott and reported that, although he was illiterate, he was "not ignorant" and that it was clear that he had learned much from his travels. Scott had most likely led a life of hard work and little else. By 1832, however, both Peter and Elizabeth had died; thereafter, Scott entered the history books.

LIFE'S WORK

After Peter Blow's death, Scott was purchased by an army officer named John Emerson. Scott traveled with Emerson to Illinois when Emerson was transferred to an army base there in 1833. There is almost no written record of what Scott actually thought or felt about this major change in his life since neither Scott nor Emerson spoke or wrote about their experiences or their relationship with each other. Emerson had been born in Pennsylvania and had studied medicine there, and the two men were approximately the same age. Scott's primary duties centered on being Emerson's personal servant, but part of Scott's work also included clearing a parcel of land that Emerson had purchased in Iowa (then part of the Wisconsin Territory).

Sometime in 1836, Scott went with Emerson to Fort Snelling in an area that later became St. Paul, Minnesota, a region where slavery was prohibited by the Missouri Compromise. While he was in Minnesota, Scott married a woman named Harriet who was about half his age and who was also a slave in the territory. Scott's wife may have been purchased for him by Emerson, or she may have been given to him as a gift by a man who ran a trading post or worked as a liaison to American Indians in the territory. During their twenty-year marriage, Dred and Harriet Scott had four children: two sons who died in infancy and two daughters.

In 1837, Emerson transferred back to St. Louis, but he left the Scotts in Minnesota. Emerson had expected to send for the Scotts shortly after his return to Missouri, but he was almost immediately transferred again to Louisiana, where he married Eliza Irene Sandford, a woman about fifteen years his junior. Emerson then sent for the Scotts, who traveled to Louisiana unchaperoned and arrived as they had agreed by riverboat. By the time Scott and his wife packed and moved out of Minnesota to be reunited with Emerson, they had lived for one year or more on their own in free territory. This would eventually become the basis of their case in the Supreme Court.

About six months after their journey down the Mississippi River to Louisiana, the Scotts and the Emersons returned to Minnesota. The Scotts' first daughter was born during this trip, while they were still in free territory. They named her Eliza, after Emerson's wife. In December, 1843, Emerson died about one month after the birth of his own daughter. The chain of events ignited by his death changed the lives of Scott and his family and, perhaps, changed the course of American history as well.

In his will, Emerson bequeathed his earthly goods to his wife and, after her death, to his daughter. The will allowed Eliza to sell whatever she needed from the estate in order to support herself and her daughter. Eliza's brother, John Sandford, was named an executor for Emerson's will, although Eliza's father, Alexander Sandford, was administrator of record for the will in the state of Missouri. When her father died in 1848, Eliza took over the details of handling her husband's will. During the few years between the death of Emerson and the first court case brought by Dred and Harriet Scott, the couple traveled to Texas to work for Eliza's brother-in-law, who was also in military service. The Scotts returned to St. Louis in 1846, and shortly after their return, they put in motion the process that would eventually affect race, law, and politics in the United States.

Dred Scott. (Library of Congress)

Having lived as free people, the Scotts were no longer content to quietly accept their status as slaves. On April 6, 1846, they filed individual requests in the Missouri court to bring suit for their freedom based upon their long residence in free territory. These first requests were granted, and the Scotts then filed suit against Eliza for damages for "ill-treatment" and "false imprisonment" based upon the Scotts' contention that they were, in fact, free people. Because Scott was barely literate and a man of insubstantial means, it has been suggested that antislavery activists were at the bottom of this seminal case in an effort to mount a test case that would ignite the antislavery movement. However, the Scotts had observed the changing times and were also aware from their conversations with Peter Blow's son Taylor that other former slaves who had brought similar suits had been declared free based on the finding that taking a slave into free territory to reside amounted to an act of emancipation.

The basis of the case seemed clear-cut: Dred sued based on his long residence in Illinois and the Wisconsin Territory, while Harriet based her claim on her residence in the Wisconsin Territory. The cases filed later by the Scotts' daughters were based on the fact that the first daughter was actually born in free territory and the second daughter was born to a free mother. The Missouri court in St. Louis, following well-established precedent, found that the Scotts, based on their long residence in free territory, were indeed free.

In 1852, the Missouri Supreme Court disagreed and reversed the lower court's decision. The sons of Scott's former owner, Peter Blow, were sympathetic and helped Scott by contributing the fee for a new lawyer to represent the Scotts' appeal before the United States Circuit Court of Missouri. The motive for the Blows' long and steady support of Scott and his family seems to have been based on fond recollections of growing up with Scott, because Taylor Blow and his brother were strongly prosouthern in their politics. In any event, in 1854, the U.S. Circuit Court upheld the Missouri Supreme Court's finding that Dred and Harriet Scott should, and would, remain slaves. It was a remarkable coincidence of historical timing that brought the Scott case to the stage of national events; ultimately, the case had a significant impact on the hearts and minds of people around the world.

In 1855, Americans were concerned with the events in "Bloody Kansas" as settlers on both sides of the slavery question attempted to decide by violent means whether the Kansas-Nebraska Territory would be free or slave. Because of this, the *Dred Scott* case moved up on the docket of the Supreme Court. In early 1856, the matter of *Dred Scott v. Sandford* finally came up for argument in the Supreme Court, but jurisdictional and other technical matters were not resolved until December. After several months of debate, the Supreme Court voted 7 to 2 that Dred Scott was not a citizen of the United States. The language of Chief Justice Roger B. Taney's finding in the *Dred Scott* decision was clear:

> Can a negro, whose ancestors were imported . . . and sold as slaves, become a member of the political community . . . brought into existence by the Constitution of the United States, and as such become entitled to all the rights, and privileges . . . guaranteed by that instrument to the citizen?

The Taney Court's answer was a resounding "no," because they found that black people

> were not intended to be included, under the word "citizen" in the Constitution, can therefore claim none of the rights and privileges . . . that instrument provides. . . . On the contrary, they [are] . . . considered as a subordinate and inferior class of beings, who have been subjugated by the dominant race, and, whether emancipated or not, yet remained subject to their authority . . . [and were] so far inferior that they had no rights which the white man was bound to respect.

The response to the decision, delivered by Chief Justice Roger Taney and his associate justices to a standing-room-only crowd of newspaper writers and many others interested in the outcome of the case, was swift and divided along regional and political lines. Antislavery activists centered in the North denounced the finding as immoral, while many southerners expressed satisfaction with the decision.

The sons of Peter Blow refused to accept the judgment of the court and purchased Scott and his family, then freed them almost immediately. Dred and Harriet Scott continued to live and work in St. Louis, although the state required that they post a bond in the amount of $1,000 to ensure their good behavior. Again, Taylor stepped in to help, using his property as security for the Scotts' bonds. However, Scott's free status was short-lived: he died on February 17, 1858, and was buried in Calvary Cemetery in St. Louis.

SIGNIFICANCE
The life of Dred Scott had an ordinary beginning, and yet the flash point of pre-Civil War politics was the 1857 Supreme Court finding in *Dred Scott v. Sandford*, instigated by an illiterate, middle-aged black man who refused to accept slavery as his obligatory status in life. The Supreme Court found in *Dred Scott v. Sandford* that black people were not citizens of the United States and thus had no rights that white citizens were bound to respect. After the Civil War, in 1868, the Fourteenth Amendment to the Constitution, which ensured citizenship rights for black Americans, directly reversed this finding. Dred Scott, the man whose case against the Supreme Court was undoubtedly the catalyst to an organized fight against slavery, died in St. Louis, Missouri, before the citizenship of black Americans was clearly set out in the Constitution.

—*Dale Edwyna Smith*

FURTHER READING

Asim, Jabari. "Dred Scott Square." *Obsidian II: Black Literature in Review* 3 (Winter, 1988). Asim provides a poet's perspective on Scott.

Erlich, Walter. *They Have No Rights: Dred Scott's Struggle for Freedom*. Westport, Conn.: Greenwood Press, 1979. Erlich provides an overview of Scott's difficult battle for freedom.

Fehrenbacher, Don E. *Slavery, Law, and Politics: The Dred Scott Case in Historical Perspective*. New York: Oxford University Press, 1981. Fehrenbacher places the Scott case in the context of U.S. history in general and explores the ongoing implications of the Supreme Court's 1857 decision.

Finkelman, Paul. *Dred Scott v. Sandford: A Brief History with Documents*. Boston: Bedford, 1997. Finkelman's book contains detailed and useful documentation of the Scott case.

Kaufman, Kenneth C. *Dred Scott's Advocate: A Biography of Roswell M. Field*. Columbia: University of Missouri Press, 1996. Recounts the personal and professional life of Field, a St. Louis-based attorney who pled Scott's case before the U.S. Supreme Court.

SEE ALSO: James Buchanan; Roger Brooke Taney; Sojourner Truth; Harriet Tubman.

RELATED ARTICLES in *Great Events from History: The Nineteenth Century, 1801-1900:* March 6, 1857: *Dred Scott v. Sandford*; June 16-October 15, 1858: Lincoln-Douglas Debates; December 6, 1865: Thirteenth Amendment Is Ratified; March 28, 1898: *United States v. Wong Kim Ark.*

SIR GEORGE GILBERT SCOTT
English architect

Because of his designs for the Foreign Office, St. Pancras Hotel, and the Albert Memorial, as well as his restoration of many important medieval buildings throughout Great Britain, Scott became one of the most highly regarded architects in nineteenth century England.

BORN: July 13, 1811; Gawcott, Buckinghamshire, England
DIED: March 27, 1878; London, England
AREA OF ACHIEVEMENT: Architecture

EARLY LIFE

George Gilbert Scott was the fourth son of Thomas and Euphemia (née Lynch) Scott. Both his father, a curate at the church in Gawcott, England, and his mother, from a family with strong Wesleyan connections, held severe religious views and reared their large family in a strict and pious manner. Because of their mistrust of local High Church schools, Scott never received a formal education. Until the age of fifteen, he was taught at home by his father. Scott then demonstrated an interest in architecture, so his father sent him to an uncle for a year of preparatory schooling. In 1827, Scott was apprenticed to James Edmeston, a local architect with religious views similar to those of the Scott family. Scott always considered himself uneducated and regretted this lack of formal schooling throughout his life.

Scott's interest in medieval churches surfaced during this period under Edmeston, but the latter attempted to redirect his energies toward more practical designs and condemned Gothic architecture as too expensive and wasteful of building materials. In fact, Edmeston went so far as to write to Scott's father several times complaining that the young man wasted too much time sketching medieval buildings. In any case, Scott successfully completed his apprenticeship in 1831 and, after a two-month visit home, he moved to London and joined the firm of Grissell and Peto.

The next year, 1832, he moved to the firm of Henry Roberts, where he worked under the direction of Sir Robert Smirke. Scott would later look back at this period as unproductive and barren, years in which the emphasis on practical designs stifled his natural inclinations and originality. In 1834, following the death of his father, he associated himself with an architect who was drawing designs for workhouses that would be constructed under the New Poor Law. Scott saw this as an opportunity to

break free from the various practical masters who had thus far controlled the content of his work, and, in violation of certain rules of professional etiquette, he personally visited Poor Law boards throughout the country and pushed his own plans for the new workhouses. As a result, he obtained four contracts for workhouse construction, and, to handle this new work, he formed a partnership with W. B. Moffat, another former apprentice of Edmeston. Scott was finally on his own, and the famous firm of Scott and Moffat had been born.

On June 5, 1838, Scott was married to Caroline Oldrid, his second cousin. During their long marriage, they produced five sons, two of whom would later also pursue careers in architecture. Balding and stocky, Scott affected the long, bushy sideburns that were popular among Victorian men. Acquaintances noted that he was careless about his appearance and often arrived at important business meetings in rumpled and mismatched suits. However, behind this slightly eccentric facade lurked the clear, intelligent eyes and determined mouth of a young man who knew what he wanted and how to get it.

LIFE'S WORK

The partnership of Scott and Moffat endured until 1845, and, during its existence, the two men produced nearly fifty workhouses and orphanages. Scott also accepted commissions to construct churches in the towns of Birmingham, Shaftesbury, Hanwell, Turnham, Bridlington Quay, and Norbiton. Although church architecture would later become Scott's specialty, these early designs suffered from his concentration on workhouse construction and were generally undistinguished and rather clumsy.

During the early 1840's, Scott's latent talent for Gothic architecture was stimulated through his friendship with Augustus Northmore Pugin, a noted architect and a pioneer in the nineteenth century Gothic revival. Responding to Pugin's encouragement, Scott designed his first Gothic building, St. Giles in Camberwell, in 1840. Public response to this church was favorable and persuaded Scott to abandon his "practical" work in favor of more imaginative and romantic Gothic designs.

Scott's growing reputation as a Gothic architect received a tremendous boost in 1844 when he won an open competition to design the Lutheran Church of St. Nicholas in Hamburg, Germany. The success of this mock-fourteenth century structure led, in 1847, to an important commission to restore the Anglican cathedral in Ely. In preparation for this assignment, Scott visited France in order to observe the Gothic cathedrals at Amiens, Chartres, and elsewhere. This habit of visiting Gothic monuments on the Continent for inspiration for his work in Great Britain would become a regular feature of Scott's career.

Between 1845 and 1862, commissions literally poured into Scott's office. The design of new, and the restoration of old, churches constituted the vast majority of these assignments and included such excellent examples of neo-Gothic architecture as his creation of the cathedral of St. John in Newfoundland, Canada, and his restorations of cathedrals in Ripon, Salisbury, Lichfield, and Hereford. Perhaps his most famous work during this period was his restoration of the chapter house and monuments of Westminster Abbey in 1849. His careful research for this important project would later be incorporated into a book, *Gleanings from Westminster Abbey*, which Scott published in 1861. As a result of his growing fame, Scott was made an associate member of the Royal Academy in 1855 and was promoted to full membership in 1861.

In 1856, Scott entered a competition for the contract to rebuild the Foreign Office buildings. He proposed a French-inspired Gothic design for the buildings, and, in 1858, he was awarded the position of chief architect for the reconstruction project. Proponents of classical architecture, however, opposed his Gothic design and received support from such notable parliamentary leaders as Lord Palmerston. As a result, the House of Commons, after heated debates between supporters of the two architectural schools, ordered that an Italian classical design also be drawn up so that it could be compared with Scott's original Gothic proposal. Scott tried his best to maneuver around the order, but in 1861 he was forced to submit an Italian influenced design that satisfied both Palmerston and the House of Commons. Advocates of the Gothic school accused Scott of treason for this compromise, but the finished buildings nevertheless proved to be among the best in his career.

Scott's most prestigious commission came in 1864, when he won a court-sponsored competition to design a monument in memory of Queen Victoria's recently deceased husband, Prince Albert. The success of this memorial, a shrine containing a seated statue of the prince consort, led to other royal commissions, such as the restoration of Thomas, Cardinal Wolsey's chapel in Windsor Castle in 1869. In 1872, Scott was knighted as a reward for all of his work for the royal family.

A year after the Albert Memorial commission, in 1865, Scott designed perhaps his best work, St. Pancras Station in London. He regarded the completed building as the culmination of his search to achieve a Gothic style that would serve modern structural and aesthetic purposes. The station still stands as a monument to the Victorian Gothic revival that Scott did so much to launch and promote.

Although Scott worked busily until the end of his life, none of his work after 1865 equaled the quality of that of the 1850's and early 1860's. As befit his status as one of Great Britain's best-known architects, he spent much of his time during the late 1860's and 1870's engaging in honorary and educational activities. From 1873 to 1876, he served as president of the Royal Institute of British Architects. He also occupied the prestigious post of professor of architecture at the Royal Academy from 1868 to 1878. His lectures were published in 1879 as a two-volume work entitled *Lectures on the Rise and Development of Medieval Architecture*. In addition to these activities, Scott also devoted much time and energy to promoting the establishment of an Architectural Museum in London, a project that was realized shortly after his death. He died of a heart attack on March 27, 1878, at the age of sixty-six, and was buried in Westminster Abbey.

SIGNIFICANCE

Sir George Gilbert Scott had a prolific career. From 1847 until his death in 1878 he completed 732 projects, including twenty-nine cathedrals, 476 churches, twenty-five schools, twenty-three parsonages, fifty-eight monuments of varying size, twenty-five college chapels, twenty-six public buildings, forty-three mansions, and assorted other designs. He was the best known and most successful British architect during the mid-nineteenth century, and much of his work remains standing in the twenty-first century.

Even before Scott's death, a growing number of critics questioned both Scott's neo-Gothic style and the manner in which he conducted his restorations. His Gothic designs, as exemplified by his work on Westminster Abbey, are often eclectic and overblown. Scott all too frequently took the unique traits of medieval French, Italian, and German architecture and mixed them together in an apparently random fashion to produce his own "Gothic" designs. The result of this practice struck some contemporaries, and most modern students, as a rather gaudy and incoherent jumble, one that critics claim typified the Victorian Gothic revival.

Scott also remodeled buildings as he restored them. Rather than trying to recapture the original design, he frequently altered structural components, added ornamentation, and even changed the building materials. In many ways, he did not restore buildings at all; instead, he reconstructed them to conform with his vision of what Gothic architecture should be like. This practice, in fact, led to the formation in 1878 of the Society for the Protection of Ancient Buildings, an organization dedicated to preserving old structures from the revisionism of architects such as Scott.

Scott's reputation has suffered a tremendous decline since his death. He will always be recognized as one of the foremost advocates of the Gothic architectural revival of the mid-nineteenth century. Nevertheless, as the aesthetic quality and the historical integrity of this revival has been severely questioned by successive generations, Scott's place in the history of British architecture has steadily diminished.

—Christopher E. Guthrie

FURTHER READING

Bergdoll, Barry. *European Architecture, 1750-1890.* New York: Oxford University Press, 2000. This general survey of European architecture contains information about Scott, including his designs for the Law Courts and the Midland Grand Hotel at St. Pancras railway station.

Brooks, Chris, ed. *The Albert Memorial: Its History, Contexts, and Conservation.* New Haven, Conn.: Published for the Paul Mellon Centre for Studies in British Art by Yale University Press, 2000. Lavishly illustrated history of the memorial, including essays about Scott's conception, design, and construction.

Clarke, B. F. L. *Church Builders of the Nineteenth Century.* New York: Macmillan, 1938. Scott figures prominently in this generally positive assessment of the British Gothic revival.

Cole, David. *The Work of Sir George Gilbert Scott.* London: Architectural Press, 1980. The most complete work in print on Scott and his contribution to British architecture. The author's approach is generally sympathetic, and he stresses that an accurate appreciation of Scott's work can only be obtained by comparing it with that of his contemporaries, not by judging it by modern standards.

Ferriday, Peter, ed. *Victorian Architecture.* London: Jonathan Cape, 1963. A collection of essays, most written by the editor. The essay on the Gothic revival correctly emphasizes Scott's contribution but provides little in the way of biographical information.

Goodhart-Rendel, H. S. *English Architecture Since the Regency: An Interpretation.* London: Constable, 1953. This book includes only a few pages on Scott and his work, but it does provide an excellent summary of the various objections to the architect and the Gothic revival in general.

Hitchcock, Henry Russell. *Architecture: Nineteenth and Twentieth Centuries.* Baltimore: Penguin Books, 1958. This book includes a section on the British Gothic revival of the mid-Victorian period and provides a concise, though negative, interpretation of Scott's contribution to it.

Jordan, W. J. "Sir George Gilbert Scott, R.A.: Surveyor to Westminster Abbey, 1849-1878." *Architectural History* 23 (1980): 60-85. An excellent summary of Scott's career from midcentury until his death. In spite of the article's title, it goes beyond his work on Westminster Abbey and discusses his general role in the Gothic revival.

Scott, Sir George Gilbert. *Personal and Professional Recollections.* London: Sampson Low, Marston, Searle, and Rivington, 1879. A long, rambling autobiography that includes some insights into Scott's personal beliefs and an explanation of what he was trying to achieve. This book is also full of biographical details that are not available elsewhere.

SEE ALSO: Sir Charles Barry; John Nash; Lord Palmerston; George Edmund Street; Queen Victoria.

RELATED ARTICLE in *Great Events from History: The Nineteenth Century, 1801-1900:* 1884: New Guilds Promote the Arts and Crafts Movement.

SIR WALTER SCOTT
Scottish poet and novelist

Scott made three enduring contributions to literature—narrative poems, Scottish novels, and novels of chivalric romance—in each of which he produced works that delighted his contemporaries and proved to be of lasting popularity, and he is credited with being the creator of the historical novel.

BORN: August 15, 1771; Edinburgh, Scotland
DIED: September 21, 1832; Abbotsford, Scotland
ALSO KNOWN AS: First Baronet Scott
AREA OF ACHIEVEMENT: Literature

EARLY LIFE

Walter Scott counted among his ancestors many notable and colorful figures from Scottish history, and during his early years, after an attack of polio crippled his right leg, he spent hours listening to family stories and songs about their exploits. Even as a young boy, he collected these ballads and folktales, which vividly presented the past. He would later use this knowledge in the poems and novels that won great acclaim during his lifetime, and that endure to this day as classics of English literature.

After being educated at home, Scott was sent in 1778 to high school in Edinburgh. He impressed both his teachers and his peers with his intelligence, his good nature, and his ability to tell stories; he was less accomplished in his scholarship. In 1783, he entered the Old College, but his interest remained the study and pursuit of ballads. In 1786, he joined his father, who was a lawyer, as an apprentice and was called to the bar in July of 1792.

Scott made a competent though not outstanding lawyer, and his main interest continued to be literature, although he seemed to regard the writing profession as not quite suitable for a gentleman. Despite his doubts, however, he could not refrain from seeking out, collecting, and reciting the poetry of his native land. Almost inevitably, he tried his hand at composition.

In 1797, Scott visited the Lake Country, where he met Charlotte Mary Carpenter, daughter of a deceased French refugee. After a brief courtship, Scott's suit was approved by Charlotte's guardian, the marquis of Downshire, and the couple were married on Christmas Eve, 1797. Their union, comfortable rather than passionate, produced four children.

Through exercise to overcome his infirmity, Scott developed a powerful and robust physique; he was an avid horseman and walker, and graceful, despite his lameness. Scott's many portraits show a man of regular, rather than handsome, features, with keen, bright eyes. They also reveal the intelligence, good humor and compassion for which he was well known. Scott's contemporaries were universal in their admiration for him.

LIFE'S WORK

Scott's entry into the literary world was almost casual. After collecting the ballads of others, he began to compose some of his own. A government appointment with few duties gave him time to collect and write, and some of his earlier attempts were published in 1802 and 1803 in *The Minstrelsy of the Scottish Border*. Encouraged by the favorable attentions of friends and critics, Scott next wrote the *The Lay of the Last Minstrel*, which was published in early 1805.

This work was immediately popular and established Scott as a major literary figure. However, around this same time Scott entered into a long, complicated, and ultimately ruinous relationship with the printers and publishers John and James Ballantyne. Scott began loaning money to the Ballantynes in 1802; by 1805, he was a silent financial partner in the firm. This connection would eventually lead to fiscal disaster.

In the meantime, Scott continued his industrious and successful efforts. He edited a complete collection of John Dryden's poetry, wrote for the *Edinburgh Review*, and started writing *Waverley: Or, 'Tis Sixty Years Since* (1814). Putting aside the novel, however, he turned to another narrative poem, *Marmion: A Tale of Flodden Field*, which was published in 1808 with great success. In 1810, *The Lady of the Lake* followed and was equally well received.

In 1809, Scott joined with the Ballantynes in a publishing firm, John Ballantyne and Company. Scott advanced half of the capital himself, and perhaps provided the Ballantynes' portion as well. The unequal nature of this arrangement was to continue throughout the short life of the company. In 1813, the firm narrowly endured a serious crisis, surviving only through Scott's intercession with another publisher, Archibald Constable, whom he persuaded to purchase large amounts of debt-laden Ballantyne stock. Part of the problem lay in Scott's enthusiastic but injudicious support of other, less talented, authors, and part in the Ballantynes' business misadventures.

By 1810, all the considerable income from Scott's

writing was going to meet outstanding obligations. However, a threat appeared to that income. His next two books, *Rokeby* (1813) and *The Bridal of Triermain: Or, The Vale of St. John, in Three Cantos* (1813), sold reasonably well, but by no means as well as Scott's earlier works. Scott had probably exhausted himself in this particular genre and was faced with the growing competition from younger poets, such as George Gordon, Lord Byron. Scott's final attempts in historical narrative verse were *The Lord of the Isles* (1815) and *Harold the Dauntless* (1817). Neither poem was a major success, but by then Scott had found success in a genre of his own creation, the historical novel.

According to tradition, Scott rediscovered his manuscript of *Waverley* while looking for some fishing tackle and decided to finish it. It was published in July of 1814; six editions were printed the first year. Scott published this, and subsequent novels, anonymously; not until 1827 did he admit authorship, although it was widely known almost from the first.

Waverley was a new departure in British literature, a work that mingled fiction with historical fact, placing its imagined characters in the middle of real, dramatic events. Scott drew largely from the tales he had heard as a child, and *Waverley*, like the best of his novels, has an immediate, energetic quality that engages and excites the reader.

Scott now began a ten-year period of intense, almost unparalleled creativity; nine novels were finished within a five-year time span. *Guy Mannering* and *The Antiquary* appeared in 1815 and 1816, respectively, then the *Tales of My Landlord* series commenced in 1816 with the dual publication of *The Black Dwarf* and *Old Mortality*. *Rob Roy* (1817) and *The Heart of Midlothian* (1818) proved that the works were growing increasingly popular, as did another double publication, *The Bride of Lammermoor* and *A Legend of Montrose* (1819).

In 1819, Scott tried a new setting for his fiction, the Middle Ages. *Ivanhoe* (1819) was the first of a line of novels that drew, not on Scott's knowledge of his native land, but on his reading. The vivid characters and the forward, exciting thrust of the narrative made *Ivanhoe* immediately, and permanently, popular.

These were Scott's most successful years as a writer. His works were widely read and were bringing him a considerable income. He was constantly enlarging and expanding his home, Abbotsford, where he received many illustrious visitors and entertained the countryside in a fashion worthy of a Scots laird. He received a baronetcy from George IV in 1820, and the next year was ac-

Sir Walter Scott. (Library of Congress)

tive in the reception of the king in Edinburgh.

Scott continued to write, working the new vein of medieval romance. *The Monastery* (1820) and *The Abbot* (1820) fell short of the power and popular reception of *Ivanhoe*, but *Kenilworth* (1821) and *The Pirate* (1821) regained much of his earlier audience. In quick succession appeared *The Fortunes of Nigel* (1822), *Peveril of the Peak*, *Quentin Durward* (both published in 1823) and *St. Ronan's Well* (1823). The skill and ability Scott showed in these works varied considerably; he was clearly out of his element in tales of the gothic (*The Abbot*) or in the novel of society (*St. Ronan's Well*), but was adept at accounts of action and descriptions of the picturesque.

With the publication of *Redgauntlet* in 1824, however, Scott returned to the Scottish themes he knew so well. The novel is one of his finest, with memorable characters drawn from Scott's family and friends. In 1825, Scott brought out the dual set *Tales of the Crusaders*, containing the rather weak *The Betrothed*, and the much more successful *The Talisman*.

Scott's complicated relationship with the Ballantynes now brought about financial disaster. He had changed publishing houses from Ballantyne to Constable and Cadell, but considerable obligations were shared between his former publishers and Scott himself. Scott's continued expenses from Abbotsford further weakened his position. In 1826, after a long period of increasingly frantic negotiations, and amid general economic crisis, Scott and his publishers found that they faced bankruptcy. Scott declared himself personally responsible for the continuation of business and the settlement of all debts. The creditors' faith in Scott as an author and a man was shown by their prompt agreement to an arrangement that would permit Scott to take care of the debt without personal ruin or disgrace. Even as he returned to his writing desk, to work on a multivolume biography of Napoleon Bonaparte, fresh misfortunes dogged him. On May 15, 1826, his wife died. Although the couple had not been especially close, the loss was still keenly felt by Scott.

The Life of Napoleon Buonaparte was published in 1827, and Scott immediately began a new project, *Tales of a Grandfather*, which was to be a history of Scotland for children. It appeared in the winter of 1827 and was so successful that two more volumes appeared in 1828 and 1829. Plans were made for a uniform edition of the Waverley novels, with autobiographical prefaces by Scott; the edition proved a considerable success, and gave proof that Scott's better work remained popular with readers.

Such was not the case, however, with his later efforts. *The Fair Maid of Perth* (1828) and *Anne of Geierstein* (1829) showed an unmistakable decline in his abilities. His physical condition also declined, and in February, 1830, he suffered a stroke; another followed in November. During this time, he continued to work on a new novel, *Count Robert of Paris*, which was interrupted by a third, yet more serious attack in April of 1831. Upon his recovery, he completed *Count Robert of Paris* and his last novel, *Castle Dangerous*; these were published together in the fall of 1831.

Scott's friends now prevailed upon him to take a tour for his health. The government placed a naval frigate at his disposal to carry him to the Mediterranean. He toured Malta and Italy, where he viewed the tomb of the last of the Stuarts. He was traveling down the Rhine River when, on June 9, a severe attack left him paralyzed; he was carried back to Great Britain semiconscious. Upon his return to his beloved Abbotsford, he rallied briefly, but died on September 21, 1832.

SCOTT'S FICTION AND POETRY

LONG FICTION
1814	*Waverley: Or, 'Tis Sixty Years Since*
1815	*Guy Mannering*
1816	*The Antiquary*
1816	*The Black Dwarf*
1816	*Old Mortality*
1817	*Rob Roy*
1818	*The Heart of Midlothian*
1819	*The Bride of Lammermoor*
1819	*A Legend of Montrose*
1819	*Ivanhoe*
1820	*The Monastery*
1820	*The Abbot*
1821	*Kenilworth*
1821	*The Pirate*
1822	*The Fortunes of Nigel*
1823	*Peveril of the Peak*
1823	*Quentin Durward*
1823	*St. Ronan's Well*
1824	*Redgauntlet*
1825	*The Betrothed*
1825	*The Talisman*
1826	*Woodstock*
1827	*The Highland Widow*
1827	*The Two Drovers*
1827	*The Surgeon's Daughter*
1828	*The Fair Maid of Perth*
1829	*Anne of Geierstein*
1831	*Count Robert of Paris*
1831	*Castle Dangerous*
1976	*The Siege of Malta*

POETRY
1800	*The Eve of Saint John: A Border Ballad*
1805	*The Lay of the Last Minstrel*
1806	*Ballads and Lyrical Pieces*
1808	*Marmion: A Tale of Flodden Field*
1810	*The Lady of the Lake*
1811	*The Vision of Don Roderick*
1813	*Rokeby*
1813	*The Bridal of Triermain: Or, The Vale of St. John, in Three Cantos*
1815	*The Lord of the Isles*
1815	*The Field of Waterloo*
1815	*The Ettrick Garland: Being Two Excellent New Songs* (with James Hogg)
1817	*Harold the Dauntless*

SIGNIFICANCE

Sir Walter Scott's enduring contributions to literature fall into three categories: his narrative poems, his Scottish novels, and his novels of chivalric romance. In each of these three genres he produced works that not only delighted his contemporaries but also have shown themselves to be of lasting significance.

Scott himself was modest about the narrative poems, and there is much in them that is more narrative than poetic. However, at their best, works such as *The Lay of the Last Minstrel* or *The Lady of the Lake* have an undeniable power in rhythm and expression that makes them excellent examples of their particular genre.

Scott's gift for narrative best served him in his prose works, especially in the Scottish novels. In these books, he drew upon his own memories and experiences in the Scottish countryside, and from the tales and stories he had heard since his youth. Many readers find in *Waverley* or *Redgauntlet* merely exciting adventures, skillfully told, but Scott put more into his novels than that.

A passionate believer in community and tradition, Scott looked back on the Scottish past with sympathy and upon the present without illusion. He seems to have been acutely aware that the heroic age had passed, and that it had been replaced by one that was more prosaic. It is the tension between these two ideals, and the elegiac sadness for the older society that yet lingered in parts of the Highlands, that give additional resonance and power to the best of Scott's works.

As the virtual creator of the historical novel, Scott was responsible for an entirely new genre. Although some may point to anachronisms of detail or perspective in works such as *Ivanhoe*, more attention should be paid to Scott's renovation of history as a suitable topic for fiction. The historical novels have characters who lived in earlier times yet were understandable to contemporary readers. This was a new and often difficult task, and Scott succeeded in it more often than not.

Scott's place within the pantheon of English literature remains disputed. Some critics believe that he wrote too much and too hastily, and that his work suffered as a result. There is certainly some truth to this view, especially with Scott's later work, composed while he was in declining health and under intense pressure. Nevertheless, Scott's finest work can withstand this criticism, for his characters are vivid, his plots compelling, and his style vigorous. His work has weathered time and changes in critical fashions, and remains an essential part of our literary heritage.

—*Michael Witkoski*

FURTHER READING

Daiches, David. *Sir Walter Scott and His World*. London: Thames and Hudson, 1971. A well-written and extensively illustrated survey of Scott and his time. Daiches brings a considerable amount of knowledge to the reader in a clear, easily understood fashion.

Dekker, George G. *The Fictions of Romantic Tourism: Radcliffe, Scott, and Mary Shelley*. Stanford, Calif.: Stanford University Press, 2005. Scott and the other authors discussed in this book were avid tourists who saw their novels and tours as privileged spaces exempt from boring routine. Dekker describes how the authors brought tourism into their fiction and fiction into their tourism.

Gamer, Michael. *Romanticism and the Gothic: Genre, Reception, and Canon Formation*. New York: Cambridge University Press, 2000. Examines the links between Romantic and Gothic literature, describing why Romantic writers like Scott were drawn to Gothic novel conventions.

Johnson, Edgar. *Sir Walter Scott: The Great Unknown*. 2 vols. New York: Macmillan, 1970. A comprehensive biography of Scott that has become the modern definitive life. Johnson makes good use of the many sources and resources available and has an accurate perception of Scott's writings.

Lauber, John. *Sir Walter Scott*. New York: Twayne, 1966. A brief, introductory survey that concentrates on the work rather than the man. This study is excellent for the beginning student and helpful for the new reader of Scott's works. Contains a good basic bibliography.

Lockhart, John Gibson. *Memoirs of the Life of Sir Walter Scott*. 5 vols. Boston: Houghton Mifflin, 1901. Lockhart was Scott's son-in-law, and this work, first published in 1837-1838, is the seminal biography of Scott, containing much important information and almost as much mythology. Its firsthand material and documents make it essential for the serious student of Scott, but it must be read in conjunction with more recent, and less uncritical, studies.

Pearson, Hesketh. *Sir Walter Scott: His Life and Personality*. New York: Harper and Brothers, 1954. A brisk and readable work, but more in the nature of a popular biography than a serious study. The literary views are sometimes misleading.

Sutherland, John. *The Life of Sir Walter Scott: A Critical Biography*. Malden, Mass.: Blackwell, 1995. A critical yet balanced assessment of Scott's personality and literature that relates his life to his works.

SEE ALSO: Lord Byron; James Fenimore Cooper; Alexandre Dumas, *père*; Maria Edgeworth; George IV; Lord Jeffrey; Robert Louis Stevenson.

RELATED ARTICLE in *Great Events from History: The Nineteenth Century, 1801-1900:* 1814: Scott Publishes *Waverley*.

WINFIELD SCOTT
American military leader

The leading American commander during the Mexican War, Scott had a military career that lasted more than fifty years and left his mark in U.S. military·history by transforming the republic's feeble army into an efficient professional force.

BORN: June 13, 1786; Petersburg, Virginia
DIED: May 29, 1866; West Point, New York
ALSO KNOWN AS: Winfield Mason Scott (full name)
AREA OF ACHIEVEMENT: Military

EARLY LIFE

Winfield Mason Scott was the son of William Scott, a captain on the patriot side in the American Revolution who died in 1791, leaving only a modest inheritance and little in the way of a memory for the young boy. His mother, Ann Mason, was descended from an important Virginia family, and she spent her widowhood teaching her son the ways of the Virginia gentry until her death in 1803.

Young Scott was educated by private tutors in Petersburg and at the new capital at Richmond. At the age of nineteen, he enrolled at the College of William and Mary. He showed little aptitude for college work and left the Williamsburg school after a year without earning a degree. The young man decided on a career in the law, and in accordance with the custom of the day, studied law with an established attorney. When a war scare after 1807, however, caused Congress to vote funds to enlarge the United States Army in anticipation of war with Great Britain, Scott abandoned a legal career for the sword. In May, 1808, Scott became a captain in the regular army.

Scott was exceedingly tall by the standards of his day—six feet, five inches—and in his younger years, muscular but not fat. Photographs of the elderly Scott showing his three-hundred-pound bulk do not give an accurate picture of the young captain. Along with a striking figure, Winfield Scott bore a somewhat haughty manner. This was characteristic of many Virginia gentlemen of the time, but Scott was both especially quick to take offense at perceived snubs and insults and not shy about voicing his own opinions. Indeed, his lack of tact got him court-martialed during his first tour of duty at Natchez in the Mississippi Territory in 1810. Captain Scott openly proclaimed the former commanding officer, General James Wilkinson, a traitor in league with former vice president Aaron Burr. For this affront, Wilkinson had the young man disciplined for disrespect to a superior officer. Scott postponed marriage until the age of thirty; when he did wed, he chose Maria Mayo, the daughter of an important Richmond editor, for his bride.

LIFE'S WORK

The War of 1812 brought a host of young officers forward into national prominence. At the start of the war, the United States Army was commanded by men who had learned their military skills back in the Revolutionary War. Most of the commanders of the first year of the war were simply incompetent to fight a war on the offensive as called for by the leaders in Washington, and not until they were replaced by younger men did the war go more favorably for the Americans. The two great young generals who emerged in 1813 and 1814 were Andrew Jackson and Winfield Scott, a pair of men who later became bitter rivals.

The great task for an American commander in the War of 1812 (as in the revolution) was to solve the problem of making raw American troops stand up in the field to trained British regulars. Much of the American force consisted of state militiamen serving limited terms with little training. Too often in battle, the militia ran or refused to fight. Scott, more than any other commander on the Canadian front, managed to shape an army of militiamen and regulars into an effective fighting force. A measure of the success of his efforts may be seen by looking at the first and last battles on the Niagara Frontier, the stretch of land connecting Lake Erie to Lake Ontario and separating the United States from British North America.

In October, 1812, shortly after gaining the rank of lieutenant colonel in the United States Army, Scott participated in the Battle of Queenstown on the west bank of the Niagara River. The attack was a disaster for the Americans, as a large body of American militia refused

Winfield Scott. (Library of Congress)

to cross the river, claiming that their mission included only defense of New York and not the invasion of Canada. Scott's party, outnumbered and badly outfought, was captured by the British, and the young Virginian had to spend an enforced stretch in British captivity until he could be exchanged.

During the summer campaign of 1813 on the lakes, Scott distinguished himself by leading a successful assault on the British Fort George on the Niagara River and, later, by aiding in the burning of York (modern Toronto). The next spring—May, 1814—Scott was promoted to brigadier general and was given responsibility for training the men under the command of General Henry Dearborn for a campaign to clear the Niagara Frontier of British forces.

In July, Scott led American troops, both regulars and state militiamen, in the fierce Battles of Chippewa (opposite Buffalo) and Lundy's Lane (near Niagara Falls). The latter battle was perhaps the bloodiest of the war, with four hundred killed on both sides. The effect of the July fighting was to establish American control of the Niagara region and to show that Americans could stand up to British veterans who had fought successfully against Napoleon. At Lundy's Lane, Scott himself showed extraordinary personal courage: He had several horses shot

from under him and was hit twice by bullets, in the ribs and shoulder. He spent a month recovering in Buffalo before journeying to Philadelphia for further treatment, and at war's end Major General Scott was still recovering from his wounds.

In 1816, Scott journeyed to Europe not so much to sightsee as to interview veterans of the Napoleonic Wars. He came back filled with new ideas about how to train and lead a new American army and over the next thirty years put his ideas into practice. In 1817, he was called to New York City to head the Eastern Military District, a command he held until 1831. During these years, the general devoted himself to improving the training of troops, an effort that first saw print in his 1821 publication *General Regulations for the Army: Or, Military Institutes.* This writing consisted of rules for camp life and drill and reflected Scott's experiences in the War of 1812 and his European interviews. He later amplified his ideas on the use of the foot soldier in his *Infantry Tactics* (1835), a manual used by the army until the Civil War.

The 1830's were an extraordinarily busy time for the middle-aged Scott. He did more hard riding during this decade than any other. In the summer of 1832, President Jackson ordered him to take a regiment west to help in the suppression of the Sac rebellion led by Black Hawk. This was only one of a series of wars between Native Americans and white Americans prompted by Jackson's "removal" policy. The Sacs were defeated by Illinois and Wisconsin militiamen before Scott reached the Upper Mississippi country. The regiment was devastated by a cholera epidemic. Scott remained long enough to negotiate Black Hawk's surrender and the removal of the Indians west of the Mississippi. Next, the general traveled to Charleston, South Carolina, on a confidential mission for the president to survey the state of federal installations in the city and harbor in light of the threats made by the "nullifiers" in the Palmetto State. Scott made sure the hotheads in South Carolina knew that the federal government stood prepared to defend its property and the right to collect tariff duties.

After the successful defusing of the tariff showdown, Scott's next field assignment came in early 1836, when President Jackson sent him to Florida to put down the Seminole rebellion (again in response to Jackson's removal policy) led by Osceola. After six months with little success against the Indians, Scott was recalled to Washington and there faced a "court of inquiry" about his conduct in prosecuting the Florida war. Scott was enraged at this insult from the president but still managed to convince the court that his strategy of fortifying outposts in the swamps to launch small raids against the Indians was preferable to marching columns of hundreds of men back and forth in search of the Indians. The court cleared Scott of any malfeasance, and in the end, his strategy of counterguerrilla warfare against the Seminoles proved successful.

Almost as soon as the Washington charges were settled, Scott had to deal with a series of frontier crises. First, in January, 1838, he traveled to Buffalo to prevent the smuggling of American arms to Canada after the famous Caroline Affair. His apt diplomacy, surprising to some in a military man, helped ease a potential *causus belli* between the United States and Great Britain. Then, in May, Scott traveled to Tennessee to organize the army's handling of the removal of fifteen thousand Cherokees westward to the trans-Mississippi Indian Territory. Again, the army was needed to enforce a Jackson removal treaty, but the results were especially horrible as thousands of Indians suffered on what became known as the Trail of Tears. By the time the march was actually under way, however, Scott was otherwise engaged in more frontier diplomacy, this time at Detroit, where he sought to prevent a new border skirmish between the Americans and the British across the river.

With that task accomplished, the general ventured in winter across the northern United States to the Maine-New Brunswick border to prevent yet another border flare-up from exploding into war, this time in March, 1839, the so-called Aroostook War over the proper boundary along the St. John's River. While Scott was engaged in his journeys for peace, leaders of the Whig Party mentioned his name as a candidate to run for the presidency in 1840. Though he never became president, Winfield Scott hoped for the next twenty years to achieve that goal, and in 1852 he did get the Whig nomination but failed to convince the electorate.

In 1841, Scott finally became the senior officer in the United States Army and alternated his attention between military affairs and his political ambitions. His job was made harder in 1845 when a Democratic administration, hostile to Scott, came into office determined to engage in a war with Mexico. Scott was thought too old to command in the field the American detachment sent to acquire the Rio Grande territory in 1845 and 1846, and when this force did provoke a war, Scott's subordinate Zachary Taylor earned the glory at Monterrey and Buena Vista. President Polk found winning a peace harder than winning battles, however, and during the late fall of 1846 had to turn to Scott to lead a campaign to bring the Mexicans to surrender.

From March through September of 1847, Scott led one of the most brilliant campaigns in the history of the United States Army. Against a larger enemy fighting to defend its own capital, Scott captured Mexico City despite disease, despite the forces of Mexican general Antonio López de Santa Anna, and despite the sniping of various Democratic politicians (one of whom was on his staff by presidential order). The campaign began at Veracruz with an amphibious landing, the first such coordination between the army and navy in United States history. Scott laid siege to Veracruz for a week, bombarding the city daily and earning a reputation among the Mexicans as a barbarian because of the hundreds of women and children killed in the shelling.

Scott then began his march to Mexico City, first defeating the Mexican Army at the mountain heights of Cerro Gordo, where the enemy had hoped to bottle up the Americans. From April 19, 1847, through mid-May of the same year, Scott and his army advanced along the National Road toward Mexico City. When he got within fighting distance, the Mexicans asked to begin peace negotiations. Scott's army had decreased to five thousand men because of disease, and he used the summer months of negotiation to rebuild his army to fourteen thousand well-drilled men.

In August, when negotiations collapsed, Scott made his famous daring march south along Lake Chalco and flanked the Mexican forces, attacking Mexico City by the back door along the road from Acapulco. On August 20, Scott's men captured the mountain pass at Cherabusco, just four miles south of the capital. Again, the Mexicans asked to negotiate, and again the talks led nowhere. From September 8 through September 13, Scott carried out a series of feints against the Mexican forces and, at the climactic battle of Chapultepec, stormed into the city. His smaller army defeated the Mexican army of thirty thousand men.

The peace that followed was anticlimactic, and Scott became embroiled in charges and countercharges with Democratic officers in the army and politicians back in Washington. Although he was the acknowledged conqueror of Mexico, he was not universally seen as a hero, and he had to watch the junior Zachary Taylor receive the Whig nomination for the presidency in 1848. The difference in popular estimation between the two generals may be seen in their nicknames: Taylor was "Old Rough and Ready," Scott "Old Fuss and Feathers."

When Scott did finally run for the presidency in 1852, his opponent (and former subordinate in Mexico) Franklin Pierce trounced him, mainly because Scott's Whig

Party had self-destructed over a number of issues. Scott was honored for his services in 1853 and became lieutenant general of the army, a post he held until his retirement in October, 1861. He distinguished himself when the Civil War broke out, first by not succumbing to rebel blandishments to join the Confederacy and second by devising a plan that ultimately was carried out in defeating the rebels, the so-called Anaconda Plan. The plan bore that name because Scott envisioned a slow, squeezing attack against the South, first down the Mississippi, then a gradual frontal attack in Virginia, combined with a naval blockade to cut off the South's commerce. The strategy worked, though at a terrible cost that Scott could not foresee: 600,000 died. The old man spent much of the war working on his memoirs and, when he felt the end near, asked to be carried to West Point so that he could die at the Military Academy. Scott's death came on May 29, 1866.

SIGNIFICANCE

Winfield Scott came into the army when it was a tiny force and the nation was still a small, self-conscious republic; when he left the United States Army, it was on the verge of becoming the army of the "Coming of the Lord," the Union Army of two million soldiers that destroyed slavery and the rebel republic. The problem with which he wrestled as a military man was the same on the Niagara Frontier as in Mexico and would be, too, for the Union Army at the Battle of Bull Run: how to take an army of raw volunteers and make them an army capable of fighting European regulars. In other words, how could one ask amateurs to kill and be killed? This was a task at which George Washington had failed until the last year of the revolution, and it is to Scott's credit that he succeeded in 1814 and in 1847.

Most European observers had expected the Mexicans to win the war in 1846 precisely because Mexico had an army trained by Europeans and the Americans were still the same amalgamation of volunteers and militia that had performed so poorly in the War of 1812. Scott's solution to the problem of how to make obedient but innovative soldiers out of the manpower of a democratic society was to emphasize drill as well as humane treatment. During his commands after 1817, he sought to make the life of the common soldier more comfortable and less harsh, on the theory that men fought better when not brutalized by their own officers. The outcome at Lundy's Lane and Chapultepec shows that Scott indeed did adjust the hierarchical organization of military life to the democracy of the new republic.

—*James W. Oberly*

FURTHER READING

Bauer, Jack K. *The Mexican War: 1846-1848*. New York: Macmillan, 1974. This volume in the Wars of the United States series is useful for those interested in Scott as a strategist. It contains a good account of the Veracruz to Mexico City campaign, along with fine maps.

Eisenhower, John S. D. *Agent of Destiny: The Life and Times of General Winfield Scott*. New York: Free Press, 1997. Eisenhower, a military historian (and son of former president Dwight D. Eisenhower), provides a detailed account of Scott's military actions and the politics behind them. He portrays Scott as a courageous soldier and skilled military manager whose character was marred by ambition and vanity.

Johannsen, Robert. *To the Halls of Montezuma: The Mexican War in the American Imagination*. New York: Oxford University Press, 1985. Discusses how contemporaries saw the Mexican War and is especially perceptive about why Zachary Taylor became a hero and Scott did not.

Mahon, John K. *The War of 1812*. Gainesville: University of Florida Press, 1972. Gives Scott his due as part of the new generation of commanders who emerged in 1813. Helpful maps show the battles along the Niagara Frontier.

Peskin, Allan. *Winfield Scott and the Profession of Arms*. Kent, Ohio: Kent State University Press, 2003. Comprehensive biography portraying Scott as a visionary military manager who anticipated significant changes in technology and business principles and adapted U.S. Army practices in response to these changes.

Potter, David M. *The Impending Crisis: 1848-1861*. New York: Harper and Row, 1976. This political history of the coming of the Civil War treats Scott's election campaign of 1852 in the context of the breakup of the Whig Party. The author finds Scott a better general than a politician.

Scott, Winfield M. *Memoirs of Lieut.-General Scott*. 2 vols. New York: Sheldon, 1864. This is the essential starting point for Scott students. It is long-winded and touchy about points of honor, but Scott does get the final say against his critics. Scott's *Memoirs* are thin with regard to the subject's political career, emphasizing instead his military exploits.

Weigley, Russell F. *History of the United States Army*. New York: Macmillan, 1967. The author evaluates Scott both as a strategist in war and as a molder of the army. He sees Scott as an excessively vainglorious man, but still the builder of the professional officer corps.

SEE ALSO: Black Hawk; James Buchanan; Aaron Burr; Andrew Jackson; Osceola; Franklin Pierce; Antonio López de Santa Anna; Zachary Taylor.
RELATED ARTICLES in *Great Events from History: The Nineteenth Century, 1801-1900:* September 16, 1810-September 28, 1821: Mexican War of Independence; November 21, 1817-March 27, 1858: Seminole Wars; 1838-1839: Aroostook War; August 9, 1842: Webster-Ashburton Treaty Settles Maine's Canadian Border; February 2, 1848: Treaty of Guadalupe Hidalgo Ends Mexican War; May 30, 1854: Congress Passes Kansas-Nebraska Act; March 4, 1861: Lincoln Is Inaugurated President; July 21, 1861: First Battle of Bull Run.

EDWARD WYLLIS SCRIPPS
American publisher

Through delegating responsibility but maintaining control of his holdings, Scripps established a publishing empire that eventually included newspapers, the United Press Association, Acme Newsphotos, and the United Feature Syndicate. Late in life he cofounded the Scripps Institute of Oceanography, the Scripps Foundation for Research in Population Problems, and the Science News Service.

BORN: June 18, 1854; near Rushville, Illinois
DIED: March 12, 1926; at sea, off the coast of
　Monrovia, Liberia
AREA OF ACHIEVEMENT: Journalism

EARLY LIFE

Edward Wyllis Scripps was born on an Illinois farm, the son of James Mogg Scripps and Julia Osborne Scripps. He was the youngest of the thirteen children of his father's three wives. In a sense, Scripps was destined for a publishing career because his ancestors had been active in the field: William Armiger Scripps, his grandfather, had been the publisher of the *True Briton* and part owner of the *London Literary Gazette* in England, and his father had been a bookbinder in London, England, before he emigrated to the United States in 1844.

Because his mother, who was forty when he was born, disciplined him harshly and criticized him, Scripps became bitter toward her and turned to his half sister Ellen, who was eighteen years older than he, for affection, acceptance, and guidance. She became a surrogate mother and lifelong confidant, financial backer, and supporter. Her aversion to publicity, love of solitude, sense of responsibility, freedom from tradition and dogma, and range of intellectual interests all influenced Scripps. A loner and relative failure at school, he was, with Ellen's encouragement, a voracious early reader of the many books in his father's extensive library.

Scripps's half brother George, fifteen years his senior, was another ally who, despite the prevailing family notion that Scripps would amount to nothing, defended him. When George later joined Scripps and his brother James in the newspaper business, he usually sided with Scripps against James. James's relationship with Scripps was ambivalent. Although he recognized his half brother's talent, he was also jealous, more conservative than Scripps, and fearful of losing control. Squabbles, which sometimes became legal battles, were common in the Scripps family.

Before he joined James in Detroit, Michigan, in 1872, Scripps worked on his father's farm. Although he was a sickly child, he became quite healthy, probably because of the physical labor on the farm; however, he never liked the work and enjoyed his reputation as the "laziest boy in the county." Scripps was not really lazy. He hired boys his own age, rather than adults, to work on the farm, thereby saving money, and then increased their efficiency by encouraging them to race each other. This ability to seize an opportunity and get others to work efficiently for him also characterized his career in publishing and explained his willingness to hire good editors and then give them responsibility and incentives. Scripps did not believe in doing anything he could get someone else to do.

In 1872, when he was eighteen, Scripps had to decide what to do with his life. Because he had read so widely, he was drawn to a literary career, but the family newspaper tradition also attracted him. Because James was editor of the *Detroit Tribune*, he should have been assured of a place on his paper, but James, who remembered him as a sickly, argumentative youngster, refused to hire him. The only other career option for him was teaching, but when he met some of his pupils, a tough-looking group, he gave up his teaching plans.

LIFE'S WORK
Scripps's publishing career began in Detroit, where he was supposed to take a job in a drugstore that was being opened by one of his cousins. Scripps, however, went directly to the *Detroit Tribune*, where his half brother William, foreman of the job shop, employed him as an office boy in the counting room. When James and William left the *Detroit Tribune* and started a job-printing plant, Scripps went with them and gradually learned the printing business. When the *Detroit Tribune* burned to the ground, Scripps salvaged the lead from the type and earned about one thousand dollars.

Shortly afterward, James decided to found an old dream of his, a small, cheap (two cents), condensed newspaper rather than the large, conventional five-cent papers. The *Detroit Evening News* succeeded despite widespread predictions of failure. Instead of being a reporter, a job he was not qualified for, Scripps was a carrier boy, initially selling papers but quickly hiring others to do his job at less money until he had two thousand subscribers. He used a similar strategy, picking the right people as carrier boys, when he was put in charge of increasing circulation in outlying areas.

Not content with the business part of publishing, Scripps turned to writing. Because his brother would not give him a reporter's job, he had to offer his services for no pay. Through hard work and persistence he gradually, by rewriting other reporters' stories, honed his writing skills and became city editor. In this position he stressed "personal journalism," or exposé writing. When libel suits ensued, the family incorporated the paper in 1877, and Scripps used his one stock share (out of the fifty issued) to borrow money from family members to start other newspapers, which produced the stock to fund still more papers.

In 1879 Scripps traveled to Europe with George, and the trip became a pivotal point in Scripps's life. While abroad he decided that he would become wealthy, that environment and circumstances determined one's fate, and that he would establish his own paper in Cleveland, Ohio. While in the Colosseum in Rome, he also decided to create his own journalistic empire. Over James's protests, he became editor of the *Cleveland Penny Press*, a position from which he controlled the business manager, ostensibly equal in power. (In the future, Scripps editors would control the newspapers, while business managers sold advertising and subscriptions.) Despite some financial problems, the *Cleveland Penny Press* was as successful as the *Detroit Evening News*. With the *Cleveland Penny Press* Scripps established a policy that applied to all of his later papers: Report all the news and support the workers and the underdogs.

In Cleveland he defeated another giant in American newspaper publishing, Edwin Cowles, but when he started the *St. Louis Chronicle* in 1880, he was not as successful with Joseph Pulitzer, owner of the *St. Louis Post-*

Edward Wyllis Scripps. (Courtesy, Scripps Institution of Oceanography Archives)

Dispatch. When Scripps returned to Cleveland, he was accused of libel but won a "not guilty" verdict. Shaken by recent events, he went to Europe with Ellen and again resolved to take charge of his life, which had been marked by heavy drinking and womanizing. Upon his return to the United States in 1883, he focused his energies on the *Cincinnati Penny Post*, which became a voice against the corruption in Cincinnati, Ohio. By 1884 the *Cincinnati Penny Post* was in the black, and by 1885 its circulation exceeded that of the *Detroit Evening News*.

Following his secret marriage to Nackie Holtsinger on October 7, 1885, Scripps overcame the faults that had plagued him in the past. At this point he had also achieved his European resolutions of 1883. He was worth about $250,000 and had an annual income of $20,000. From his country home in West Chester, Ohio, he began to practice remote-control management. In 1887, during James's absence, Scripps was caught in a power struggle with John Sweeney, a favorite of James. Scripps won with the backing of George and a reluctant James and assumed, at the age of thirty-five, control of the four Scripps papers that became the Scripps League.

Scripps also established the New York Advertising Bureau to obtain national advertising for all four newspapers and the New York News Bureau to get news coverage in Washington, D.C., and abroad. However, once again there was trouble between James and Scripps, who lost the battle when George sided with James. Scripps was left with only the *Cincinnati Penny Post* and the *St. Louis Chronicle* under his control. Leaving Milton McRae (he called his two papers the Scripps-McRae League) in charge, he retreated to Southern California, where he built Miramar, a large estate near San Diego.

Scripps's fortunes turned in 1892 when George switched sides and added his *Cleveland Penny Press* to the Scripps-McRae League. When George died in 1900, James contested the will, which gave Scripps George's stock. When the dispute was settled, mostly in Scripps's favor, Scripps was able to expand the Scripps-McRae League and two other chains Scripps controlled. When he retired in 1908, his newspaper holdings included about two dozen papers. In addition, in 1907 he had created the United Press, which provided an alternative source of news to the Associated Press.

During his retirement, Scripps oversaw his journalistic empire, though he left the day-to-day operations to his editors and to McRae. By 1907, however, a growing rift between Scripps and McRae led to McRae's removal from the business. Scripps's son Jim subsequently became the business manager of the firm and served in that

capacity until he, too, became the target of Scripps's displeasure and was removed from power in 1919, when Scripps came out of retirement. In 1922 Scripps put his son Robert and Roy Howard in charge of a new newspaper conglomerate, Scripps-Howard, which added still more newspapers. Scripps then retired again and retreated to the *Ohio*, his yacht, on which he died on March 12, 1926.

SIGNIFICANCE

Scripps was one of the giants of the newspaper industry. Like William Randolph Hearst, Pulitzer, and Cowles, he established a journalistic empire that endured. With his "penny" newspapers he helped bring all the news to the lower classes, and his papers were independent rather than public relations organs for political parties. Despite his own capitalistic success, his sympathies were with the workers, the underdogs, and the forces that opposed political corruption. He believed in the right of labor to organize and bargain collectively, even though his own profit margins were diminished by such activities. In fact, Scripps was more than willing, especially after 1908, to disclose his values and beliefs; in his "disquisitions" and letters, usually dictated, he commented on a wide range of topics, including biographical anecdotes (although not always reliable) and newspaper policies.

It was these policies that accounted for his success. From the beginning, he was an idea person who started things, found able people and gave them the freedom to finish what he had started, and then moved on to new projects. That is why his editors rather than his business managers ran the papers. If their papers, which were owned by Scripps, were successful, the editors could acquire stock in them, thus providing them with real financial incentives. Scripps always insisted on keeping at least 51 percent of each paper, however, and thereby retained control of the entire chain. It was this desire for autocratic rule, even if exercised by remote control from Miramar or one of his yachts, that brought him into conflict with members of his family, especially James and Jim, and with his trusted associates when their ideas clashed with his. Seldom has a man so indelibly put his stamp on a business enterprise he founded.

—*Thomas L. Erskine*

FURTHER READING

Baldasty, Gerald J. *E. W. Scripps and the Business of Newspapers*. Urbana: University of Illinois Press, 1999. Biography focusing on the development of Scripps's newspaper chain.

Casserly, Jack. *Scripps: The Divided Dynasty.* New York: Donald I. Fine, 1993. After an initial chapter on Scripps, the remainder of the book is devoted to Scripps family squabbles and the life and career of Edward Scripps, Scripps's grandson. Contains the Scripps family tree.

Cochran, Negley D. *E. W. Scripps.* 1933. Reprint. Westport, Conn.: Greenwood Press, 1961. An early appreciative biography of Scripps, including many details about the newspapers he founded.

Gilson, Gardner. *Lusty Scripps: The Life of E. W. Scripps, 1854-1926.* 1932. Reprint. St. Clair Shores, Mich.: 1971. Extensive early biography of Scripps, including material on Scripps's publishing ancestors.

Knight, Oliver, ed. *I Protest: Selected Disquisitions of E. W. Scripps.* Madison: University of Wisconsin Press, 1966. Contains comments on the nature of the "disquisitions," a succinct but helpful biography, and many well-edited disquisitions arranged in thematic groups, including several on journalism.

McCabe, Charles R., ed. *Damned Old Crank: A Self-Portrait of E. W. Scripps Drawn from His Unpublished Writings.* 1951. Reprint. Westport, Conn.: Greenwood Press, 1971. A series of Scripps's writings, arranged chronologically, that span his life; the essays concern his "bad habits," business anecdotes, family quarrels, and journalistic insights. The selections were chosen by a family member.

Schaelchlin, Patricia A. *The Newspaper Barons: A Biography of the Scripps Family.* Foreword by Neil Morgan. San Diego, Calif.: San Diego Historical Society, 2003. Biography of the Scripps family, tracing the history of the family's newspaper empire.

Trimble, Vance H. *The Astonishing Mr. Scripps: The Turbulent Life of America's Penny Press Lord.* Ames: Iowa State University Press, 1992. The most complete biography of Scripps. Trimble had access to Scripps's voluminous correspondence and his disquisitions; consequently, much of the biography is in Scripps's own words.

SEE ALSO: James Gordon Bennett; George Brown; Horace Greeley; Joseph Pulitzer.

RELATED ARTICLES in *Great Events from History: The Nineteenth Century, 1801-1900:* September 3, 1833: Birth of the Penny Press; 1895: Rise of Yellow Journalism; 1895-1898: Hearst-Pulitzer Circulation War.

RICHARD JOHN SEDDON
Prime minister of New Zealand (1893-1906)

The first New Zealand prime minister who was not considered a "gentleman," Seddon completely dominated the fledgling nation's politics between 1893 and 1906. Astute, domineering, and incredibly popular, Seddon laid the foundation of the first social democratic, egalitarian welfare state in the world.

BORN: June 22, 1845; Eccleston, St. Helens, Lancashire, England
DIED: June 10, 1906; on board SS *Oswestry Grange*, off Sydney, Australia
ALSO KNOWN AS: King Dick
AREA OF ACHIEVEMENT: Government and politics

EARLY LIFE

Richard John Seddon (SEHD-n) was the second son of Thomas Seddon, the headmaster of Eccleston Hill Grammar School, and his Scottish wife, Jane Lindsay of Annan, Dumfriesshire. His mother, who had lost a leg as a child and whose willpower and intellect Richard inherited along with his father's powerful physique and stentorian voice, was schoolmistress of the local denominational school. Seddon's school record was undistinguished. Unmanageable, unruly, and disinterested, he was sent at the age of twelve to his grandfather's farm at Bickerstaffe. This was a disaster, and in 1859, when he was fourteen, he was apprenticed to a firm of engineers at St. Helens.

Although a competent workman, Seddon was sacked for agitating for better pay; he then moved to the Vauxhall works at Liverpool, where he obtained his Board of Trade engineer's certificate. Trade depression and restlessness compelled him to emigrate to the goldfields of Australia in 1863. He worked first at the government railway workshops at Williamstown, Melbourne, and returned to that job after he failed to find gold at Bendigo. In Williamstown, Seddon became a corporal in the local Volunteer Artillery Corps and a noted boxer and athlete. Already, he was a young man of great strength, on one occasion walking the length of a two-hundred-foot-long workshop with fifty-six-pound weights attached to each foot and two others strapped to each hand. A further twenty-eight-pound weight he held in his teeth.

Seddon became engaged to Louisa Jane Spotswood, the daughter of a former Geelong ferryman whose family, after distinguished service in the East India Company, had gone down in the world. On hearing that alluvial gold had been discovered on the west coast of New Zealand, Seddon joined the rush and arrived at Hokitika on March 1, 1866. A diligent prospector and member of mining parties, he put his Australian experience to work in constructing Californian-type water races, dams, and sluices. By 1866, he was a storekeeper and butcher at Big Dam, Waimea, where in 1872 he opened a saloon, adjacent to his store. Seddon walked around the diggings with a five-gallon keg of beer strapped on his back, refreshing miners and expounding his political views. He knew most people on the goldfields and never lost his great political talent for remembering names and distributing patronage.

At this time in his life, Seddon was a huge, broad-shouldered man with heavy features, fair hair, and piercing blue eyes—an unmistakable personality in a small world of rough-and-ready miners. He had already returned to Geelong and married Louisa, by whom he had three sons and six daughters. His family life was contented, simple, and loving. One son later became a member of Parliament and another was killed in action in France in 1918.

Seddon began his political career in 1870, when he was elected to the Arahura Road Board. Service on the Westland Provincial Council followed. He obtained a growing reputation as a miners' advocate whose intimate knowledge of mining legislation and of local needs carried him into the New Zealand parliament in 1879. In 1876, he had shifted his Queen's Hotel and store to the Kumara goldfields, was bankrupted but recovered, and was regarded as a clever, loquacious local politician.

In the New Zealand parliament, Seddon joined a small band of radicals who unswervingly supported Sir George Grey, his political mentor. Seddon's early career in the New Zealand parliament was relatively undistinguished, although he did, after seven years, manage to get the gold duty abolished. It was in Parliament that he developed his great capacity for stonewalling, his antipathy to Chinese miners (which he shared with his Australian and Californian brethren), and his complete mastery of parliamentary procedures and tactics. A rough diamond, the like of whom the New Zealand parliament had

seldom seen, a man whose aitches were misplaced or not used at all, Seddon was nevertheless the complete, new, working individual's politician, giving long speeches packed with detail in which "his words came in a full flood, rushing along with a great sound like many waters."

In 1890, this humanist, radical, vigorous bush lawyer and complete politician was returned as a member of a group that in 1891, as the new Liberal-Labour government, embarked on the most thorough series of social democratic reforms in New Zealand history.

LIFE'S WORK

Seddon became minister for public works, mines, and defense in the John Ballance ministry. Working nearly eighteen hours a day, he quickly mastered the routines of his department and, after establishing a new system of railways and roads construction on the cooperative principle, embarked, as the "Jolly Minister," on a continuous series of travels throughout New Zealand. This developed into a royal progress, during which Seddon attended countless banquets, saw innumerable delegations, and distributed largess in the form of patronage, roads, and railways. At the same time, the Liberal ministry was embarking on the greatest program of reforms in New Zealand history. Under the lands minister John Mackenzie, large estates were acquired for settlement and distribution to small farmers on favorable terms and cheap loans from the state.

Under William Pember Reeves, the minister for labor and education, the world's first Industrial Conciliation and Arbitration Act, designed to avoid clashes between capital and labor and to regulate every aspect of labor relations, was introduced. A redistributive land and income tax was introduced and the ability of the Legislative Council to reject radical legislation was smashed when the colonial secretary acknowledged the right of Ballance to nominate enough councillors to allow the passage of his legislation.

Ballance was already a dying man when Seddon became acting premier and leader of the House in 1892. He had no special claims to succeed Ballance, especially as Sir Robert Stout was the acknowledged leader of the radical Liberals and Reeves the most creative and intelligent member of the cabinet. Seddon, believing that possession was nine-tenths of the law, completely outmaneuvered them both and became premier on May 1, 1893, after New Zealand's most extreme cabinet crisis. As Seddon himself said, "When the Captain was called away, the First Mate took his place." From then until his death, Seddon reigned supreme in New Zealand politics. Indeed, after 1900, he secured increasing majorities at the elections, although his dominance over mediocre cabinet colleagues created a vacuum that the Liberals could not fill after his death.

Although Seddon never matched the great range of reforms of 1891-1893, his speedy response in saving the Bank of New Zealand during the financial crisis of 1894, by giving it a state guarantee and making the government supreme in public finance, laid the foundation for monetary policies more in tune with his humane feelings. In restraining those who wanted to prohibit the sale of liquor by introducing local option polls, he outflanked the most powerful social protest movement of the time. Though an early enemy of woman suffrage, he facilitated the measures by which New Zealand became the first nation in the world (after the American states of Wyoming and Utah) to grant the vote to women.

Seddon's great triumph came with the passing of the world's first Old Age Pensions Act in 1898. This guaranteed New Zealand's preeminence as the world's social democratic laboratory. The act was extended in 1905, and further measures safeguarded women's and children's lives while at the same time access to state secondary and technical education was granted. The state involved itself in virtually all aspects of New Zealand life.

Fabian socialists Sidney and Beatrice Webb visited New Zealand in 1898 and, with a combination of English condescension and fascination, observed Seddon at the height of his power. They had seen him in England at the Jubilee as "a gross, illiterate and forceful man . . . incurably rough in manner and sometimes rather the worse for liquor." However, on his native ground, the New Zealand parliament, he was a gentleman with tremendous courage and unbelievable industry; he kept three secretaries busy at dictation at once, and was "shrewd, quick, genial—but intensely vulgar—tolerant and blunt." Devoted almost entirely to politics and politicians, he was a great practical "doer" whom the common people adored as he responded, "like a player upon a pianner," to their every need and wish. In short, the Webbs compared him with a successful American city boss, which was rather unfair. Their further assessment that he resembled a talented popular senator from the western United States was nearer the mark.

After attending Queen Victoria's Diamond Jubilee celebrations in London in 1897, Seddon took up the imperial mantle that Grey had worn. He maintained his complete grip on New Zealand politics and his place in the hearts of the people, whose material circumstances rose as New Zealand recovered from the ravages of the world depression. Already, on September 15, 1893, Grey had telegraphed Seddon that his "position is a capital training for higher things—all the great questions between England and her colonies, and the United States are coming on in the greatest way the world has ever known."

Seddon visited Great Britain again for the coronation of King Edward VII in 1902. He became a privy councillor of Great Britain and pressed for more formal ties between the various parts of the empire. His visits reinforced his horror at the evils of industrialism, and he constantly reiterated his creed that New Zealand was "God's own country." He attempted to annex Samoa, New Caledonia, Fiji, and the Cook Islands, but only succeeded in persuading the British Colonial Office to allow New Zealand to control the latter. Seddon even saw President William McKinley but got short shrift when he requested that the United States allow New Zealand to control the Hawaiian Islands.

Under Seddon's leadership, New Zealand became in 1899 an enthusiastic participant in the South African War, sending six thousand troops and much unsolicited and bombastic advice. Seddon visited South Africa on his way to the coronation and renewed his unsuccessful attempts to make the British Empire economically and militarily self-sufficient and contained. Indeed, it was after a hectic visit to Australia seeking preference for New Zealand goods after New Zealand had declined to join the Australian Federation that the 280-pound Seddon clutched his heart and died with his head resting on his wife's shoulder. He died on board the SS *Oswestry Grange* on June 10, 1906. His body was embalmed, and he was buried at Wellington, New Zealand, amid scenes of mourning and a sense of loss that was both genuine and universal.

SIGNIFICANCE

Through his long career, Richard John Seddon displayed political skills of a high order. A tremendously hard-working premier, he carried a load of additional portfolios ranging from treasury to Maori affairs that would have killed lesser men. He never faltered; indeed, his popularity increased with his tenure of office. He placed New Zealand on the map with his social legislation, and his reforms lasted. He managed prosperity well; as a conservative said, "I would sooner have Seddon with prosperity than anyone else without." He left his country prosperous and contented and for a brief time strutted on the imperial stage during the glittering height of the British Empire. Above all, he left the lot of the common people much improved. He divined and reflected their aspirations for modest property and for economic security. As he said soon before his death,

> All legislation which I have brought to bear upon the human side of life is the legislation which counts most with me. . . . There is much talk of men being Radicals, Conservatives, Socialists, and Liberals. I am none of these. I am a humanist. I desire to improve the conditions of the people, to inspire them with hope, to provide for their comfort, and to improve them socially, morally, and politically.

—Duncan Waterson

FURTHER READING

Burdon, Randal Mathews. *King Dick: A Biography of Richard John Seddon*. Christchurch, England: Whitcombe and Tombs, 1955. Although more than fifty years old, this thorough, vigorous, and critical biography remains the standard reference. It should be supplemented by more recent interpretations summarized in the relevant chapters of *The Oxford History of New Zealand*. Burdon also wrote the entry for Seddon in A. H. McLintock's *The Encyclopaedia of New Zealand*, Vol. 3 (Wellington: Government Printer, 1966).

Drummond, James. *The Life and Work of Richard John Seddon*. Christchurch, England: Whitcombe and Tombs, 1906. Completed by a journalist soon after Seddon's death, this eulogistic panegyric nevertheless conveys some of the spirit of the times and the popular (and populist) appeal of "King Dick."

Reeves, William Pember. *State Experiments in Australia and New Zealand*. 2 vols. London: Alexander Morning, 1902. The classic account, still not superseded, of the state initiatives taken by reforming liberal governments in Australia and New Zealand. Particularly useful on the Ballance and Seddon administrations. Reeves, a Fabian socialist, was Seddon's minister for labor and education until 1896, when he became agent-general for New Zealand in London after failing to stop the Seddon surge to political dominance. His history of New Zealand, *The Long White Cloud* (3d ed. London: Allen and Unwin, 1924), is still worth consulting for its cool appraisal of Seddon and his ministry. Reeves himself coined the sobriquet "King Dick," the title of chapter 24, still the most lively and perceptive profile of Seddon.

Ross, Angus. *New Zealand Aspirations in the Pacific in the Nineteenth Century*. Oxford, England: Clarendon Press, 1964. Chapters 14 and 15, "Seddon's Imperialism I and II," analyze in a scholarly and seminal fashion Seddon's attempts to fulfill New Zealand's imperial dream of a "mini-empire" in the Southwest Pacific.

Siegfried, André. *Democracy in New Zealand*. Translated by E. V. Burns. London: G. Bell, 1914. The Tocqueville of the Antipodes, Siegfried's shrewd and rational French insights encapsulate Seddon's colonial milieu.

Sinclair, Sir Keith. *William Pember Reeves: New Zealand Fabian*. Oxford, England: Clarendon Press, 1965. An intriguing biography of one of the few intellectuals in New Zealand politics. Chapter 11, "The Captain Called Away," is especially useful, as are the numerous quotations and descriptions of Seddon from Reeves's unpublished papers.

Webb, Beatrice, and Sidney Webb. *Visit to New Zealand in 1898: Beatrice Webb's Diary with Entries by Sidney Webb*. Wellington, New Zealand: Price, Milburn, 1959. A valuable portrait of Seddon in political action by two English Fabians.

SEE ALSO: Sir George Grey; William McKinley; Meri Te Tai Mangakahia; Queen Victoria; Sir Julius Vogel; Edward Gibbon Wakefield.

RELATED ARTICLE in *Great Events from History: The Nineteenth Century, 1801-1900:* September 19, 1893: New Zealand Women Win Voting Rights.

ANAÏS SÉGALAS
French writer

One of the major French women writers of her time, Ségalas wrote a wide variety of poetry, drama, fictional prose, and criticism over a literary career that spanned six decades and reflected changing currents in French history.

BORN: September 21, 1814; Paris, France
DIED: August 31, 1893; Paris, France
ALSO KNOWN AS: Anne-Caroline Ménard (birth name); Anaïs Ménard Ségalas
AREA OF ACHIEVEMENT: Literature

EARLY LIFE

Anaïs Ménard Ségalas (ah-na-hees may-nahr say-gah-lahs) was born Anne-Caroline Ménard, the daughter of Charles Ménard, a cloth merchant in northern France's Picardy region, and Anne-Bonne Portier, a Creole from the Caribbean nation of Haiti. Her father, aloof and significantly older than her mother, led an austere life as a staunch vegetarian. With his 1825 publication of *L'Ami des bêtes* (animal lover), her father made known his personal conviction that human beings had no right to use animals for their own sustenance.

Anaïs was raised primarily by her sensitive, doting mother, who openly shared her love of verse with her precocious child, and displayed her own poetic talent at the age of seven. When she was eight, she wrote a birthday ode for her father, and at the age of ten, she wrote a vaudeville play. In her explorations of her father's library, Anaïs developed a passion for poetry and discovered the geniuses of French classical theater—Molière, Jean Racine, and Pierre Corneille.

When Anaïs was only thirteen years old, she became betrothed to Victor Ségalas, a Basque barrister who enjoyed a distinguished record at the royal court in Paris. Two years later, she married him. Intent on cultivating her poetic gift, she exchanged a solemn vow with her new husband, who agreed not to stand in the way of her literary aspirations. She exhibited an early feminist sensibility by continuing to demand equality in her marriage and her right to pursue her own career.

Anaïs had already published some of her work in the widely read literary publication *Le Cabinet de Lecture* (reading room) and in a collection of verse titled *Psyché* in 1829. In 1831, she made her grand poetic debut with *Les Algériennes, poésies* (Algerians, poems), a volume that she wrote in response to the French conquest of Algiers in 1830. She thus launched a richly diverse writing

career that would continue with extensive forays into poetry, theater, prose, and literary criticism—for which she garnered a place among the creative minds of her time.

LIFE'S WORK

During the nineteenth century, European bourgeois women were seen as figures of propriety whose place was in the home, and they were expected to devote themselves to cultivating good manners. Anaïs Ségalas did not fit into the mold. She was a fascinating and complex woman, an accomplished equestrian with a spirit of adventure who nevertheless refused to travel outside Paris. She successfully combined her roles as wife, mother, and writer, which she did not consider incompatible. It was through poetry, however, that she developed what she understood as woman's civilizing role to inculcate virtue. The critical reception of her work as a writing mother in particular suggests that she amply fulfilled her stated mission. She dedicated her critically acclaimed 1844 collection, *Enfantines: Poésies à ma fille* (childlike: poems for my daughter), to her only child, Bertile, a daughter who had been born the year before. That book, which underscored maternal duty and love, made Ségalas's reputation as the poet of mothers, children, and family.

Unlike other women authors of her day, such as George Sand and the countess Marie d'Agoult, Anaïs Ségalas did not join the growing ranks of opponents of the oppression of women in a patriarchal society. In fact, in prefatory comments to another important volume of her poetry, *La Femme* (1847), she denied any connection with the increasingly militant feminist socialists of the 1840's. Upholding the traditional assignment of separate spheres for men and women, she pointedly distanced herself from the Bluestockings, as women writers who ceased to appear womanly were disparagingly called. Indeed, much of her poetic expression stressing women's civic duty and social importance as mothers was inspired by the fervent Roman Catholic faith that she demonstrated throughout her life.

Nineteenth century biographers and literary critics followed Ségalas's dramatic writings with varying degrees of interest and admiration. Among her plays that made it to Paris stages were *Loge de l'Opéra* (opera box) and *Trembleur* (trembler). Her own critical reviews of theater also brought her notice. However, her later poetic and prose writings that intersect with salient moments in French colonial history inexplicably drew little attention. The strong reception of her *Algériennes* in 1831, like that of *Les Oiseaux de passage* (birds of passage) in 1836, suggests that issues of slavery and race that had seized her poetic imagination also appealed to the early nineteenth century public.

In Ségalas's poetic response to the great moral debate about the emancipation of slaves that gathered force during the 1820's and reached a feverish pitch in France during the 1840's, she expressed empathy for the plight of black peoples who desired to join the rest of the human race. Her long narrative poem "La Créole (L'esclavage)" (creole woman [slavery]), which she published in *La Femme* in 1847—the year before France's abolition of slavery in its colonies—implored French Creole women in the Caribbean to assume the work of civilization and prepare former slaves to become French citizens.

The colonial world again captured Ségalas's fertile imagination and led to her exotic work *Récits des Antilles: Le Bois de la soufrière* (tales from the Antilles: the forest of the volcano) in 1884, at the same time France was calling for major colonial expansion into Africa and Asia. Echoing a political stance that mirrored the racist culture of late-nineteenth century France, Ségalas's Parisian narrator in that work saw little progress long after emancipation in the "new world," where the shadow of slavery and inherited prejudice still haunted the Creole population.

During the last years of her life, Ségalas created a literary salon over which she presided with her daughter and continued to create new works. She remained keenly aware of what topics interested her public and fashioned her place in French literary history. She died in Paris, on August 31, 1893, during her seventy-ninth year.

SIGNIFICANCE

Anaïs Ségalas's writings offer modern readers glimpses into the life of a mind of a politically conservative and yet deeply creative bourgeois woman cultivated in a century that made the high art of poetry the prerogative of the male sex. Nineteenth century literary critics generally included Ségalas among the ranks of accomplished women, highlighting her writing about women as mothers with no overtly feminist agenda. In 1917, the Académie Française established the Prix Anaïs Ségalas, which acknowledged both her life's work and the work of other strong women authors who became its recipients.

Some of Ségalas's most important works coincided with major turning points in France's colonial enterprises. The fact that she was a Parisian with a Creole heritage has been brought to light in a modern critical edition of her popular *Récits des Antilles: Le Bois de la Soufrière* and select poems. Hers is an achievement all the more striking at a distance from which one can measure the conditions under which she produced volumes of poems, plays, short stories, and novels that often went through multiple editions.

—*Adrianna M. Paliyenko*

FURTHER READING

Czyba, Luce. "Anaïs Ségalas." In *Femmes Poètes du XIXe siècle: Une Anthologie*, edited by Christine Planté. Lyon, France: Presses universitaires de Lyon, 1998. A modern feminist assessment of the literary and sociological import of Ségalas's writings.

Delaville, Camille. *Mes contemporaines.* 1st series. Preface by Henri des Houx. Paris: P. Sévin, 1887. An account of Ségalas in the latter years of her life by one of her contemporaries.

Desplantes, François, and Paul Pouthier. *Les Femmes de lettres en France, 1890.* Geneva, Switzerland: Slatkine Reprints, 1970. A late-nineteenth century anthology of women of letters that accords Ségalas an honorable place.

Doumic, René. *La Vie and les mœurs.* Paris: Perrin, 1895. A late-nineteenth century account of Ségalas's celebrity.

Finch, Alison. *Women's Writing in Nineteenth-Century France.* New York: Cambridge University Press, 2000. Survey of French literature that contains several references to Ségalas.

Mirecourt, Eugène de. *Madame Anaïs Ségalas: précédée d'une lettre à M. Alphonse Karr.* Paris: Havard, 1856. A comprehensive account of Ségalas's early life and critical reception of her writings through the 1840's.

Ségalas, Anaïs. *Récits des Antilles: Le Bois de la Soufrière, suivis d'un choix de poèmes.* Edited by Adrianna M. Paliyenko. Paris: L'Harmattan, 2004. A modern critical edition of Ségalas's popular late-nineteenth century novel that retrospectively measures the effects of the French abolition of slavery.

Sullerot, Évelyne. *Histoire de la presse féminine en France des origines à 1848.* Paris: Armand Colin, 1966. A brief historical account of the Christian nineteenth century feminist circles with which Ségalas associated.

SEE ALSO: Guy de Maupassant; George Sand; Flora Tristan.

RELATED ARTICLE in *Great Events from History: The Nineteenth Century, 1801-1900:* October 1-December 15, 1856: Flaubert Publishes *Madame Bovary*.

IGNAZ PHILIPP SEMMELWEIS
Hungarian physician

Semmelweis was the first medical professional to recognize the infectious nature of puerperal fever (childbed fever). His use of antiseptic techniques in obstetric practice greatly reduced deaths from the fever and paved the way for the development of modern surgery.

BORN: July 1, 1818; Buda, Hungary, Austrian Empire (now Budapest, Hungary)
DIED: August 13, 1865; Vienna, Austrian Empire (now in Austria)
AREA OF ACHIEVEMENT: Medicine

EARLY LIFE

Ignaz Philipp Semmelweis (ZEHM-el-vis) was the fifth of ten children of József Semmelweis, a prosperous grocer, and Terézia Müller, the daughter of a coach manufacturer, one of the richest men in Buda, Hungary. Semmelweis's father belonged to a German ethnic group and had moved to Buda from Kismarton, becoming a citizen in 1806. During the early nineteenth century, the influence of the German and Serbian elements was so great in Buda that the busy center of commerce had lost much of its Hungarian, Magyar, character.

The trading class, including the Semmelweis family, spoke a German dialect, Buda Swabian, at home and in commerce. Although most people in this class spoke Hungarian fluently, few were able to read and write it correctly. The teaching of Hungarian was compulsory in the secondary schools, but formal instruction was still, for the most part, in Latin and German. Consequently, Semmelweis experienced language difficulties throughout his lifetime. His clumsy German dialect made him the butt of jokes in Vienna, where he was to spend the most important part of his life, and his confessed antipathy to writing made him reluctant to publish his discoveries and respond to his critics.

Little is known about Semmelweis's childhood. Described by his contemporaries as a happy, honest, and industrious child, Semmelweis attended the Royal University Catholic Grammar School, one of the best schools in Hungary, where he placed second in a class of sixty. After a two-year arts course at the University of Pest, he began the study of law in 1837 in Vienna. The University of Vienna and its affiliating general hospital, the Allgemeines Krankenhaus, were world centers for the study of medicine. After attending an autopsy with friends who were medical students, Semmelweis abandoned the study of law for medicine. He studied medicine in Vienna for a year, continued his studies from 1839 to 1840 at the University of Pest, and returned to Vienna to complete his studies and receive his medical degree in 1844 at the age of twenty-six.

Three rising young professors who were to make medical history befriended and influenced Semmelweis: Josef Škoda, professor of internal medicine, Karl von Rokitansky, the pathologist who directed the Institute for Pathological Anatomy of the medical school, and Ferdinand von Hebra, the first professor of dermatology at the University of Vienna. Under these professors, the carefree young Semmelweis became a serious and disciplined doctor.

LIFE'S WORK

Semmelweis decided to specialize in obstetrics and gynecology, working in the obstetric and surgical clinics of the Allgemeines Krankenhaus. During the two years he had to wait for the position that he had been promised, he obtained his master's degree in obstetrics and doctor's degree in surgery, visited the obstetric clinic daily, frequented Škoda's lectures, and dissected with Rokitansky. Semmelweis was appointed first assistant lecturer to Professor Johann Klein in July of 1846.

The obstetric clinic was divided into ward 1, where medical students were instructed, and ward 2, where midwives were taught. Semmelweis was assigned to ward 1, where Klein was in charge. Before going to the clinic each day, Semmelweis performed autopsies on obstetric and gynecological cases. Postmortem dissection followed every death in the hospital. Ward duties included examining every patient in labor, conducting daily teaching rounds, assisting with operations, and instructing the medical students through autopsies and clinical practice.

Sensitive and compassionate by nature, Semmelweis was appalled by the mortality rate from childbed fever, or puerperal fever (from puerperium, the six weeks following childbirth), which ranged as high as 25 to 30 percent. Although the disease had been known since ancient times, it did not become a scourge until the beginning of the seventeenth century, when lying-in hospitals were established to care for the poor. It rarely occurred outside the hospitals. Between 1653 and 1863, there were two hundred so-called epidemics of puerperal fever in Europe.

The disease was variously attributed to atmospheric influences, overcrowding, poor ventilation, the onset of lactation, anxiety, bowel inflammation, deterioration of the blood, suppression of the discharge from the uterus, and a host of other causes. By the end of the eighteenth century, many English physicians had come to believe it was a specific acute infectious disease peculiar to pregnant women, transmitted in the same way as smallpox or scarlet fever, through direct or indirect contact. To prevent epidemics, doctors isolated the patient, used disinfectants, and maintained clean and well-ventilated wards. Thus, they were able to prevent the spread of the disease, while not completely understanding its nature. Oliver Wendell Holmes, Harvard anatomist and professor, subscribed to this contagion theory and in 1843 was the first to discuss the danger of attending women in labor after performing autopsies.

Although most obstetricians in Europe believed that puerperal fever was unpreventable, Semmelweis was ob-

Ignaz Philipp Semmelweis. (The Granger Collection, New York)

sessed by the desire to discover the cause of the disease. He systematically eliminated each hypothesis. Except for the fact that medical students were taught in ward 1 and midwifery students were taught in ward 2, the two wards were identical; they were both filthy, poorly ventilated, and crowded. Admissions to each ward occurred on alternate days. However, the death rate in ward 1 was two to three times higher than in ward 2. Semmelweis concluded that puerperal fever could not be an epidemic of infectious disease because an epidemic would affect the two wards indiscriminately, occur outside the hospital, and exhibit seasonal variations.

Through careful analysis of statistical data from 1789 on, Semmelweis determined that the fatality rate was lower during periods when there was less interference with the birth process, fewer examinations, or fewer dissections. Gradually he came to suspect a connection between puerperal fever and the students' common practice of examining patients without careful handwashing after dissection. However, his preoccupation with a problem that Klein considered inevitable and the collection of statistics that put the clinic in a bad light alienated his superior, and on October 20, 1846, Semmelweis's appointment was discontinued.

Semmelweis was reinstated in his position on March 20, 1847, and returned to work from a holiday, only to learn that his friend Jakob Kolletschka had died in his absence from blood poisoning from a septic wound incurred during an autopsy. The findings at Kolletschka's autopsy were identical to those of the puerperal patients and their babies. By May, 1847, Semmelweis was sure that matter from the cadavers caused puerperal fever. The mortality in the second ward was low because midwifery students did not do postmortem examinations. Semmelweis decided that hands could only be considered clean if they no longer smelled of the cadavers.

Semmelweis instituted a strict policy of handwashing in chlorinated lime and using a nailbrush before each examination. Mortality rates in his ward dropped from 18.27 in April, 1847, to 0.19 by the end of the year. There were no deaths in March and August of 1848, but mortality rates increased when students were careless and when a woman with cancer of the uterus and another woman with an infected knee were admitted. Semmelweis now realized that infection could be airborne and transmitted from any infected source as well as from the examining hand soiled from cadavers. He prescribed handwashing between examination of individual patients.

Semmelweis encountered resistance to his methods. Klein did not understand him, resented his innovations, and became his bitter enemy. Medical students and nurses resented having to wash their hands. The rest of the world misunderstood his theory. Because he refused to publish, his friend Hebra published an editorial in December, 1847, in the journal of the Medical Society of Vienna about Semmelweis's discovery. Hebra clearly indicated that discharge from living organisms as well as cadaveric infection could cause puerperal fever but made the mistake of calling it an epidemic disease.

A second article by Hebra, stressing the spread of puerperal infection from postmortem dissection, appeared in the journal in April, 1848, but this time he failed to allude to Semmelweis's discovery that the disease could be transmitted by material from living bodies as well as from cadavers. This created a serious misunderstanding of Semmelweis's theory. Physicians who did not practice postmortem dissection rejected the theory outright.

Meanwhile, Europe was in political turmoil and Semmelweis's Hungarian patriotism further offended Klein. When his appointment ended in March, 1849, Klein refused to renew it. Semmelweis tried to regain his post. When it was finally offered to him, there were restrictions he believed too degrading to accept. Before leaving Vienna for the last time, in May, 1850, he presented his discovery to the Medical Society of Vienna in a lecture, "The Origin of Puerperal Fever."

For the following six years, Semmelweis was in charge of the obstetrics department at the St. Rochus Hospital in Pest. There, he reduced the mortality rate from puerperal fever to less than 1 percent, compared with 10 percent to 15 percent in Vienna during the same period. He became professor of obstetrics at the University of Pest in 1855, developed a successful private practice, married in 1857, and had five children. His theory was accepted in Budapest, but the hostility of Vienna and the world community of obstetricians filled him with agony and bitterness.

In 1861, he finally published his life's work, *Die Ätiologie, der Begriff, und die Prophylaxis des Kindbettfiebers* (*The Cause, Concept, and Prophylaxis of Childbed Fever*, 1941). Prominent obstetricians and medical societies ignored or rejected his work, and he responded in scathing open letters that alienated even his friends. In 1865, fifteen years after leaving Vienna, Semmelweis developed signs of mental illness, and on August 13, died in a mental home in Vienna. Ironically, the cause of death was blood poisoning from an injury sustained during an operation he had performed. The truth of his doctrine was not accepted in Europe for at least two decades after his death.

SIGNIFICANCE

It is difficult to appreciate Ignaz Philipp Semmelweis's contribution to medical science from the perspective of the present, as so many advances have become commonplace; so many truths that were bitterly resisted have become self-evident. Working before Louis Pasteur's research in 1857 led to the germ theory and laid the foundation for advances in modern medicine, Semmelweis recognized the infectious nature of puerperal fever and realized that it was not a specific disease per se but could be caused by contact with any infected material through either direct or indirect means.

Many physicians of Semmelweis's day working in different countries recognized aspects of the truth about puerperal fever. There are similarities in the work of Semmelweis, Holmes, and Joseph Lister, so the debate about who deserves the most credit in the history of antisepsis may never be resolved. Semmelweis, however, was the first to recognize that the disease was a form of blood poisoning, and he applied antisepsis in surgery as well as in obstetrics fifteen years before Lister.

Semmelweis was a great scientist who combined the powers of clinical observation, expert knowledge of pathology and obstetrics, and scientific honesty. He refused to accept the prevailing dogma of his day but persevered in his determination to understand the cause of the disease and the means of preventing it. He developed a theory about the cause of puerperal fever, tested it, and developed a means of preventing the disease. He was the first person in medical science to prove his theory using statistics.

It was Semmelweis's great misfortune that all but a few of his contemporaries rejected his theory, which resulted in the needless sacrifice of countless lives. Great discoveries have seldom been accepted without a struggle, but there can be no doubt that he contributed to his own tragedy. He antagonized his critics by his abrasive manner, and he refused to publish. If he had published when he was in Vienna with the help of Škoda and Hebra, his ideas might have been received more favorably.

—*Edna B. Quinn*

FURTHER READING

Antall, József, and Géza Szebellédy. *Pictures from the History of Medicine: The Semmelweis Medical Historical Museum, Budapest*. Budapest, Hungary: Corvina Press, 1973. A collection of color photographs of portraits and artifacts from the Semmelweis Museum. Narrative includes a brief overview of Semmelweis's life and contributions and a history of the museum, which is the house where he was born.

Carter, K. Codell, and Barbara R. Carter. *Childbed Fever: A Scientific Biography of Ignaz Semmelweis, with a New Introduction by the Authors*. New Brunswick, N.J.: Transaction, 2005. The Carters' book, originally published in 1994, describes birthing conditions in the Vienna hospital where Semmelweis worked and his attempts to eradicate the disease.

Céline, Louis-Ferdinand. *Mea Culpa and the Life and Work of Semmelweis*. Translated by Robert Allerton Parker. Boston: Little, Brown, 1937. Reprint. New York: Howard Fertig, 1979. A subjective, romantic, and passionate tribute to Semmelweis, written by a French novelist.

Dormandy, Thomas. *Moments of Truth: Four Creators of Modern Medicine*. Hoboken, N.J.: Wiley, 2003. Semmelweis is one of the four nineteenth century physicians and scientists whose efforts to improve the quality of medicine are described in this book.

Gortvay, György, and Imre Zoltán. *Semmelweis: His Life and Work*. Translated by Eva Rona. Budapest, Hungary: Akademiai Kiadó, 1968. A comprehensive and definitive biography, translated from Hungarian for the Federation of Hungarian Medical Societies' celebration of Semmelweis's birth. Incorporates the latest research to correct errors in previous biographies and includes a chronological list of events in the life of Semmelweis, along with numerous illustrations.

Nuland, Sherwin B. *The Doctors' Plagues: Germs, Childbed Fever, and the Strange Story of Ignaz Semmelweis*. New York: W. W. Norton, 2003. Recounts how Semmelweis uncovered the origins of childbed fever and the controversy his discovery created.

Semmelweis, Ignaz. *The Etiology, Concept, and Prophylaxis of Childbed Fever*. Translated by K. Codell Carter. Madison: University of Wisconsin Press, 1983. Semmelweis's classic contribution to medical literature. Includes statistical proofs and logical arguments. Redundant, awkward style.

Slaughter, Frank G. *Semmelweis, the Conqueror of Childbed Fever*. Reprint. New York: Collier Books, 1961. A readily available and beautifully written biography of Semmelweis, with imaginative speculations. Helpful orientation to historical and scientific context of Semmelweis's life and work. Contains a few insignificant errors from previous biographers.

SEE ALSO: Emil von Behring; Oliver Wendell Holmes; Baron Kelvin; Joseph Lister; William Thomas Green Morton; Louis Pasteur.

RELATED ARTICLES in *Great Events from History: The Nineteenth Century, 1801-1900:* May, 1847: Semmelweis Develops Antiseptic Procedures; 1867: Lister Publishes His Theory on Antiseptic Surgery.

SEQUOYAH
Native American scholar

Sequoyah single-handedly devised a Cherokee syllabary that allowed his tribal nation to become literate in their own indigenous language—a first for American Indian cultures located north of the advanced pre-Columbian civilizations of Mexico and Central America.

BORN: c. 1770; Taskigi, near Fort Loudon (now in Tennessee)

DIED: August, 1843; near San Fernando, Tamaulipas, Mexico

ALSO KNOWN AS: Sequoia; Sikwaji; Siwayi; Sogwili; George Gist; George Guess; George Guest

AREA OF ACHIEVEMENT: Linguistics

EARLY LIFE

Solid factual information on the life of Sequoyah (seh-KWOY-ah) is sparse, and some anecdotes tend toward myth making. There is uncertainty about both the date of his birth and the time and circumstances of his death. Various sources also render his American Indian name as Sikwaji, Siwayi, or Sogwili, meaning "sparrow" or "principal bird." Furthermore, his Euro-American name is cited as George Gist, Guess, or Guest. However, standard accounts generally adhere to the following sketch of Sequoyah's early life and later accomplishments.

Sequoyah was born in a Cherokee village on the Tennessee River in what became Tennessee. The original Cherokee homeland was a large and scenic mountainous region encompassing northern Georgia, southern Tennessee, northern Alabama, and corners of the Carolinas. Most sources assert that his father was a white trader named Nathanial Gist who deserted Sequoyah's mother, Wurteh, a full-blooded Cherokee. The youngster and his mother moved to near Williston, Alabama, when he was twelve years old. Later he pursued various occupations or trades, working as a farmer, a blacksmith, a silversmith, a hunter, and a fur trader. Moreover, he also displayed considerable artistic talent in sketching animals and nature scenes.

Along with other Cherokee volunteers, Sequoyah served for several months during 1813 and 1814 under the command of General Andrew Jackson in a war against a rebellious faction of Muskogee Creek traditionalists. In 1815, he married a woman known as Sally, the first of five wives. Sometime before this period, his name began to appear in documentary sources as George Guess, probably a misspelling of Gist. In spite of his mixed heritage and assumed name, he neither spoke nor read English, having grown up in a traditional Cherokee community with no formal education. In 1818, Sequoyah moved westward with a group of over two hundred Cherokees who settled in northwestern Arkansas. About one thousand of their countrymen had preceded them to the area a few years earlier. These groups, known as the Western Cherokees or Old Settlers, increased in

numbers and later moved into adjacent areas of present-day Texas and Oklahoma.

LIFE'S WORK

Sequoyah is internationally acclaimed as a Native American genius who succeeded in creating a system of writing for Cherokee speakers. Work on this great task began almost one decade before his westward migration. Contact with white people and observation of their customs led to his fascination with the uses of writing. The letters and notes that he saw white people using ("the talking leaves") represented an advanced means of communication with such obvious advantages as transmission of knowledge and information over long distances. Convinced that he could produce a written Cherokee language, he threw himself into what would become a twelve-year obsession. Another contributing factor may have been a hunting accident or war wound that left him lame in one leg. Forced to assume a less active lifestyle, the former hunter and warrior now devoted nearly all of his time and energy to the ambitious project.

At first scratching symbols on bark and wood and later using pen, ink, and paper, Sequoyah experimented by trial and error with various methods of developing a script. His initial efforts centered on using symbols or pictures for every word in the language. After creating about two thousand characters, he rejected this approach as too cumbersome and difficult to memorize. Following other futile attempts, he finally seized on the idea of breaking up words into the various syllables or sounds that formed them. This involved the rigorous and patient task of identifying all sounds used in Cherokee speech, then assigning a symbol to each. Because certain sounds or syllables in one word are repeated in many others, the number of required characters was greatly reduced. Constant refinement eventually lessened the number of symbols in his emerging syllabary to eighty-six. Sequoyah created some of these characters himself. Others were Greek and Roman letters copied at random from written materials that he could not understand.

Sequoyah faced ridicule from some Cherokees who viewed his obsession as a foolish waste of time and violent opposition from others who linked it with sorcery. In 1821, after

Sequoyah. (Library of Congress)

having taught his system to a daughter and a few family friends, he temporarily returned to the East, where he put finishing touches to his work and met with the Cherokee National Council, which officially approved the new syllabary.

The simple and ingenuous nature of this remarkable discovery was soon evident. This syllabary of sounds was different from an alphabet of letters used in spelling words. Although it contained many more characters than the twenty-six-letter English alphabet, the syllabary could rapidly be mastered. By memorizing the eighty-six characters for every sound in their native speech, Cherokees could become literate within days or weeks. In contrast, it took three to four years for Cherokee pupils to learn to read and write English in the schools established by missionaries. Furthermore, with a completely phonetic system, spelling was not a problem. Soon thousands mastered the syllabary without the use of schools or textbooks. In a few years, nearly all members of this Native American tribal nation were literate in their own language.

The Cherokee national leadership, which was struggling to retain possession of the homeland in the face of increasing pressure by avaricious local white settlers to dispossess the tribe, took advantage of this transformation to mass literacy. Tribal leaders who adopted a constitution and legal system similar to that of the United States believed that by appropriating many features of the dominant Euro-American culture, the Cherokees would be accorded the right to remain on their lands. The nation soon acquired a printing press with type set in the new Cherokee script. Publications included Christian literature and a tribal newspaper, *The Cherokee Phoenix*. Cherokee laws were codified, legislative acts were printed, and business transactions were recorded in ledger books. Literacy also bound the eastern and western Cherokees closer together.

Sequoyah's accomplishments were not limited to his miraculous syllabary. He is also credited with creating a new Cherokee numbering system. Heretofore, the Cherokees had used "mental" numbers up to one hundred without means of adding, subtracting, multiplying, or dividing. The new process provided for nearly infinite totals and employed signs and formulas for calculating.

Now a prominent figure among the Cherokees, Sequoyah returned to Arkansas in late 1822 and served as diplomat and mediator. In 1827, he accompanied a delegation of Western Cherokees to Washington, D.C., for the purpose of securing their land, personal property, and treaty rights from the illegal activities of white settlers. The result was the 1828 treaty that exchanged Cherokee holdings in Arkansas for new lands a little farther west.

Thereafter, Sequoyah resided in the Indian Territory. His cabin was located near Salisaw in what is now Sequoyah County of eastern Oklahoma.

The spring of 1839 witnessed the traumatic arrival of more than thirteen thousand eastern Cherokees. The newcomers were victims of a controversial removal policy that forced over seventy thousand Native Americans of the "Five Civilized Tribes" (Cherokees, Chickasaws, Choctaws, Creeks, and Seminoles) from their sacred homelands in the South. The genocidal Cherokee experience, known as the Trail of Tears, cost about four thousand lives. Outnumbered two to one, the Old Settlers did not wish to relinquish any governing control to the eastern faction.

Especially dangerous was the intense ill feeling between the newcomers and a small group that had arrived around 1836 after signing a controversial removal treaty with the United States in defiance of the legitimate Cherokee government and 90 percent of their countrymen. Sequoyah took a more flexible position in opposition to that of many other Western Cherokees and assisted in obtaining a unified Cherokee government in the summer of 1839. At this same time, he also persuaded about fifteen hundred Cherokee refugees from Texas, survivors of a murderous assault by a Texan military unit, to forego revenge and settle permanently with their countrymen in Indian Territory.

Sequoyah's intellectually curious nature persisted into old age. In 1842, he left on an expedition to trace the location of a mysterious group of Cherokees who were believed to have migrated to the Southwest around the time of the Revolutionary War. He was never heard from again. In 1845, a party sent to look for him reported that Sequoyah had died in August, 1843, and was buried near the village of San Fernando in the northern Mexican state of Tamaulipas. The account, however, remained unconfirmed, and his body was never found.

Because of his international fame, Sequoyah received various honors during his lifetime and after his death. In 1841, the Cherokee National Council awarded him a silver medallion and granted him a small life pension. In 1911, the state of Oklahoma had the famous Cherokee's statue placed in Statuary Hall of the Capitol Building in Washington, D.C. Finally, the species of towering giant redwood trees along the northern California coast is named Sequoia in his honor.

SIGNIFICANCE

If the story of Sequoyah is accurate, he stands alone as the only person in world history to single-handedly create a complete alphabet, a process that took other cultures, including the white races, centuries to develop in a collaborative effort. It should also be noted that Cherokee is one of the most complex Native American languages. For this reason, the Moravians and other missionary groups failed in earlier attempts to create a Cherokee alphabet. Although the astounding and difficult nature of this breakthrough by an uneducated individual has prompted some to doubt the truth of his discovery, no one has disproved it.

The scarcity of solid sources on this interesting American Indian intellectual, as well as the political-ideological bias of his biographers, has contributed to widely differing interpretations and speculation about his role and significance. Sequoyah is a cultural hero to both Caucasians and his own people. White supporters of past government policies to assimilate tribal people proclaim his great accomplishment as that of uplifting a tribal nation to the Euro-American level of civilization.

On the other hand, Cherokees used the syllabary to record and thereby preserve many ancient tribal traditions and rites that the U.S. government policy sought to eradicate in the name of civilization and progress. These include medical lore, healing ceremonies, ball games, and the use of magic. Regardless of differing interpretations, many agree that Sequoyah's remarkable creation aided the beleaguered Cherokee people by stimulating national pride and providing another means to fight injustice, and later to rebound from defeat, during this difficult period of their history.

—David A. Crain

FURTHER READING

Bird, Traveler. *Tell Them They Lie: The Sequoyah Myth.* Los Angeles: Westernlore, 1971. This revisionist account is by a descendent of Sequoyah who argues that a Cherokee alphabet predated Sequoyah. The book depicts him as representative of an old tradition of warrior-scribes, a fiery traditionalist, and resistance leader against U.S. cultural imperialism rather than one who sought to facilitate assimilation.
Foreman, Grant. *Sequoyah.* Norman: University of Oklahoma Press, 1938. Foreman's book is regarded by some as the standard biography of this creative and famous Cherokee. It relies heavily on archival records and descriptive views of individuals who encountered Sequoyah.
Foster, George E. *Se-quo-yah: The American Cadmus and Modern Moses.* 1885. Reprint. New York: AMS Press, 1979. This is a classic example of the late nineteenth century assimilationist outlook of Christian reformers who influenced federal American Indian policy. Foster glorifies Sequoyah as the great educator of his nation who led the Cherokees to the promised land of U.S. civilization.
Hoig, Stan. *Sequoyah: The Cherokee Genius.* Oklahoma City: Oklahoma Historical Society, 1995. Comprehensive biography of Sequoyah.
Kilpatrick, Jack F. *Sequoyah: Of Earth and Intellect.* Austin, Tex.: Encino Press, 1965. The author, a Cherokee whose wife is a descendent of Sequoyah, presents a fairly standard account of his subject's impressive life and accomplishments. The book employs a few documentary sources not found in Foreman's book.
Waters, Frank. *Brave Are My People: Indian Heroes Not Forgotten.* Santa Fe, N.Mex.: Clear Light Publishers, 1993. Contains a brief biographical sketch of Sequoyah based on secondary sources that provides a standard heroic treatment of the subject.
Woodward, Grace Steele. *The Cherokees.* Norman: University of Oklahoma Press, 1963. Woodward focuses largely on the early nineteenth century period during which Sequoyah was an active force in Cherokee history. The book is useful for grasping the relevant background events, but the interesting and readable narrative account sometimes becomes polemical in its advocacy of the Cherokee national cause.

SEE ALSO: Andrew Jackson; John Ross; Noah Webster.
RELATED ARTICLES in *Great Events from History: The Nineteenth Century, 1801-1900:* February 21, 1828: *Cherokee Phoenix* Begins Publication; 1830-1842: Trail of Tears; May 28, 1830: Congress Passes Indian Removal Act; March 18, 1831, and March 3, 1832: Cherokee Cases.

SAINT ELIZABETH SETON
American educator

Through her resourceful, independent, and pioneering spirit, Elizabeth Seton had a profound influence on nineteenth century American education, laying the foundations of the Roman Catholic Church's parochial school system.

BORN: August 28, 1774; New York, New York
DIED: January 4, 1821; Emmitsburg, Maryland
ALSO KNOWN AS: Elizabeth Ann Bayley (birth name); Elizabeth Ann Bayley Seton (full name)
AREA OF ACHIEVEMENT: Education

EARLY LIFE

Elizabeth Bayley Seton (SEE-t-n) was the daughter of Dr. Richard Bayley, an eminent surgeon and professor of anatomy at King's College (later Columbia University). Her mother, Catherine Charlton Bayley, was the daughter of the rector of an Episcopalian church in New York. Little else is known of her, and she died when Elizabeth was three. Bayley remarried, but Elizabeth never formed a close bond with her stepmother. As a child, Elizabeth was a lively, exuberant girl. She was educated at a private school, excelling in French and enjoying dancing and music. She also had a strong introspective tendency and a profoundly religious temperament. Her early upbringing was unsettled; her father was dedicated to his work and gave her little close attention (although there is no doubt of his love for her), and she and her seven half brothers and half sisters were frequently sent to stay with relatives in New Rochelle.

As a young woman, Elizabeth was under medium height, but she was well proportioned and graceful; her features had a pleasing symmetry, and her dark, lively eyes attracted attention. She radiated intelligence and charm. In 1794, at the age of nineteen, she married William Magee Seton, the son of a prominent New York businessperson. It was by all accounts a successful and happy marriage, and between 1795 and 1802, Elizabeth Seton gave birth to two sons and three daughters.

Seton was not to have a conventionally serene and prosperous life. Forced by circumstances to mature early, responsibility for the welfare of others became a constant feature of her life. The death of her father-in-law in 1798 left her in charge of six more young children, and the death of her own father in 1801 was another severe blow. In the meantime, William Seton's business affairs had foundered, and the family was faced with

a financial crisis, which was complicated by a steady deterioration in her husband's health. Doctors recommended a sea voyage, and in 1803 William, Elizabeth, and their eldest daughter, Anna, sailed for Italy. William survived the voyage but died in Pisa, Italy, just after the family had been released from quarantine at Leghorn.

It was while in Italy, where Seton stayed for three months following her husband's death, that she first came into contact with Roman Catholicism. This contact was through her friendship with the Filicchi family, particularly the two brothers, Philip and Antonio. Her interest in religion, which had never been far from the surface, had earlier been stimulated by Henry Hobart, the gifted Episcopalian minister who preached at Trinity Church in New York. Now she felt the attraction of Catholicism, and her stay in Italy initiated a period of intense inner turbulence, the issue of which was to have momentous consequences.

LIFE'S WORK

On her return to New York in 1804, Seton was torn between the Catholic faith that she now wished to embrace and the innumerable ties that held her to the Protestant religion into which she had been born. For a year, she struggled to make a decision, corresponding with the Filicchis, John Carroll, the bishop of Baltimore, and Bishop John Cheverus of Boston, while also receiving the opposite counsel of Henry Hobart. Finally, on March 14, 1805, she publicly professed her allegiance to the Roman Catholic faith and began to attend St. Peter's Church, the only Roman Catholic Church in New York City. Thus began a period of three years in which her new faith was tested to its utmost. She had exchanged social position and respectability, the security of being in the majority, for a minority faith composed mainly of poor immigrants. Her family and friends reacted with coolness to her decision, turning to dismay when Seton's sister-in-law, Cecilia Seton, became a convert to Catholicism in 1806.

Seton's most pressing need at this time was to establish a secure home for her young family. She took part in a scheme to establish a small school at which she would be an assistant teacher, but the enterprise failed. Following this failure, with financial support from her friend John Wilkes, Seton established a boardinghouse for boys. This, however, was also a short-lived venture.

By 1808, at the instigation of Father William Du-bourg, the president of St. Mary's College at Baltimore, she had left New York for Baltimore to take charge of a boarding school for girls located in Paca Street, next to St. Mary's Chapel. The school got off to a slow start, with only two pupils, rising to ten by the end of the year. During this period of one year, Elizabeth's vocation was becoming clear to her; she wanted to form a religious community. By March of the following year, in consultation with her friends and advisers, she had agreed to move to the village of Emmitsburg, about fifty miles from Baltimore. The new settlement was to be financed by Samuel Cooper, a Catholic convert. Seton took vows of poverty, chastity, and obedience, was adopted as the head of the community, and became known as Mother Seton.

On June 21, 1809, accompanied by her eldest daughter and three other women, Seton traveled to Emmitsburg. The Sisters of Charity of St. Joseph had been formed. Father Dubourg became the first superior, and the new community adopted a slightly modified version of the constitution and rules of the French community, the Daughters of Charity of St. Vincent de Paul. By December, sixteen women were living in a simple cottage known as the Stone House, which was the community's first home. There were only five rooms, one of which was set aside as a temporary chapel, and it was with some relief that the sisters moved into their more spacious permanent home, known as the White House, in February, 1810.

From this point onward, growth was rapid. By the summer, there were forty pupils at the school, many from well-to-do families, and by 1813, the number of sisters had increased to eighteen. The curriculum consisted mainly of reading, writing, spelling, grammar, geography, and arithmetic. Music, language, and needlework were also taught. Mother Seton played some part in teaching, but as the school became established, she spent more time in administration and supervision. The success of the school was a result of the effective inculcation of piety and strict morality, reinforced by firm but compassionate discipline. It is through her work at Emmitsburg that Mother Seton is rightly known as the founder of the Catholic parochial school system in the United States. She worked indefatigably—encouraging, consoling, admonishing, mothering, and organizing. She translated religious texts from the French, prepared meditations, gave spiritual instruction, kept a journal, and still had time to carry on a lively correspondence.

Mother Seton continued to be surrounded by the illnesses and deaths of those she loved. Her half sister Har-

Saint Elizabeth Seton. (Library of Congress)

riet died in 1809, and Cecilia Seton followed four months later. The death of her eldest daughter, Anna Maria, in 1812, affected her more deeply than any other. However, her strength of character, serenity, and resilience were never more apparent than in adversity. Her ability to rise above sorrows and maintain her devotion to her calling ensured the survival and growth of the community in the difficult early years.

Within a short period, the community was expanding. By 1814, the St. Joseph orphanage in Philadelphia had applied to the Sisters of Charity for the services of a matron and two sisters, and in the following year, four other sisters were sent to Mount Saint Mary's College in Emmitsburg. In 1817, the first establishment of the Sisters of Charity was founded in New York City, originally as an orphanage, but like the earlier community in Philadelphia, quickly expanding into a school. Plans were made for schools in Baltimore, and the first of these was established in 1821. Mother Seton, however, did not live to see it. After several years of declining health, she died on January 4, 1821, at the age of forty-six.

SIGNIFICANCE

Born two years before the declaration of the republic, Elizabeth Seton grew up in a land that was alive with a newfound sense of freedom, of its own vast potential. She, too, was an American pioneer, although her expertise was not in the claiming and cultivation of land but in the edification and training of the young and in the schooling of souls. In addition to her profound contribution to nineteenth century education, she offered comfort, support, and hope to an untold number of people who came under her care. She combined the American virtues of innovation, self-sufficiency, and independence with the spiritual values of humility and service. Neither mystic nor theologian, she was a practical woman who emphasized simplicity and efficiency in daily affairs, both spiritual and material.

It had always been clear to those who came into contact with Seton that she was a woman of exceptional spiritual stature. Some recognized, with prophetic accuracy, that she would make her mark on history. As early as 1809, before Seton had even moved to Baltimore, Bishop John Cheverus envisaged "numerous choirs" of her order spreading throughout the United States, and she herself expected "to be the mother of many daughters." At her death, her confessor, Father Simon Bruté, instructed the Sisters of Charity to preserve every scrap of her writing for posterity. After her death, her communities quickly spread across the land: to Cincinnati, Ohio, in 1829; to Halifax, Nova Scotia, in 1849. By 1859, a community had been formed in Newark, New Jersey, and by 1870, Greensburg, Pennsylvania, had been added to the list.

It was not until 1907, however, that the cause for Seton's canonization was introduced. In 1959, her life was declared heroic, and she received the title of Venerable. Two miraculous cures, which had taken place in 1935 and 1952, were attributed to her intercession, and beatification followed in 1963. In 1975, Pope Paul VI proclaimed her a saint. The poor widow who had endured many trials, the convert who had founded a holy order, had become, 154 years after her death, the first American-born saint of the Roman Catholic Church.

—*Bryan Aubrey*

FURTHER READING

Celeste, Marie, ed. *Elizabeth Ann Seton: A Woman of Prayer. Meditations, Reflections, Prayers, and Poems Taken from Her Writings.* New York: Alba House, 1993. Reprint. Lanham, Md.: University Press of America, 2000. Contains some of Seton's prayers, poems, and other writings that express her religious beliefs and her personal relationship with God.

Dirvin, Joseph I. *Mrs. Seton: Foundress of the American Sisters of Charity.* Rev. ed. New York: Farrar, Straus and Giroux, 1975. One of the three biographies that were reissued to mark the occasion of Mother Seton's canonization. Strongly Catholic in tone yet also scholarly and well documented, it presents a warm, sympathetic portrait that captures the essential, simple goodness of the woman as she went about her daily affairs.

Feeney, Leonard. *Mother Seton: Saint Elizabeth of New York.* Rev. ed. Cambridge, Mass.: Ravengate Press, 1975. Concise biography that will appeal to Catholic readers. Others may find themselves alienated by the author's stylistic eccentricities and his conservative religious point of view, which tends to intrude upon his subject.

Heidish, Marcy. *Miracles: A Novel About Mother Seton, the First American Saint.* New York: New American Library, 1984. Notable for the ingenious device of using as narrator a fictionalized version of a priest who sat on the tribunal investigating one of the miraculous cures attributed to Mother Seton. His job is to be devil's advocate. The flaw in the novel is that the down-to-earth, skeptical priest, full of doubt and wry humor, becomes far more interesting than the heroine.

Hoare, Mary Regis. *Virgin Soil.* Boston: Christopher Publishing House, 1942. Detailed examination of the American Catholic parochial school system, and convincing argument for Elizabeth Seton as its founder.

Kelly, Ellin M., ed. *The Seton Years, 1774-1821.* Vol. 1 in *Numerous Choirs: A Chronicle of Elizabeth Bayley Seton and Her Spiritual Daughters.* Evansville, Ind.: Mater Dei Provincialate, 1981. Useful primarily for the long extracts from Seton's letters and journals, which form the core of the narrative and give vivid insight into her mind. Arranged in strict chronological order, with as little editorial comment as clarity permits.

McCann, Mary Agnes. *The History of Mother Seton's Daughters: The Sisters of Charity of Cincinnati, Ohio, 1809-1917.* 3 vols. New York: Longmans, Green, 1917. The story of the first ninety years of the Cincinnati community. The chief interest centers on the stormy episode in 1850, when the Cincinnati Sisters refused to join the other communities in affiliating themselves to the French Sisters of Charity of St. Vincent de Paul (see volume 2).

Melville, Annabelle M. *Elizabeth Bayley Seton: 1774-1821*. New York: Charles Scribner's Sons, 1976. Definitive biography, scholarly and objective, free of the hagiographic tone of many other biographies.

SEE ALSO: Frances Xavier Cabrini; James Gibbons; Leo XIII; Charles Wilkes.
RELATED ARTICLE in *Great Events from History: The Nineteenth Century, 1801-1900:* October 9, 1845: Newman Becomes a Roman Catholic.

GEORGES SEURAT
French painter

Seurat was one of the most perceptive imagists of the modern city during the late nineteenth century. His great curiosity about new developments in technology and the sciences transformed his art into one based increasingly upon scientific and pseudoscientific theories, something valued highly by twentieth century modern movements. His work may be seen also as a prophecy of surface abstraction and grand decoration.

BORN: December 2, 1859; Paris, France
DIED: March 29, 1891; Paris, France
AREA OF ACHIEVEMENT: Art

EARLY LIFE

Georges Seurat (sew-rah) was the son of Chrysostome-Antoine Seurat, a legal official who retired at the age of forty-two and lived apart from his wife, Ernestine, and their three children. Seurat saw his father each week at dinner at his mother's apartment on the boulevard de Magenta in Paris. His parents' marriage has been described as advantageous, respectably bourgeois, and comfortable but dreary.

Seurat shared his mother's strong and regular features as well as the precision and diligence with which she applied herself undemonstratively to tasks at hand. With his father, Seurat shared a quiet, serious, even distant mien. Very little is known of Seurat's childhood, and he was difficult to get to know as a man. Most reminiscences from his friends or colleagues are consistent in their inability to penetrate the artist's personality. It is debatable, however, whether Seurat's private nature was abnormal. In his dedication to work, he was serious to the point of humorlessness, touchy, and even irritable.

Seurat, who drew well as a child, was encouraged in art especially by a maternal uncle, Paul Hausmonte-Faivre. The novice artist drew objects from his environment that caught his interest; by age fifteen, Seurat's interest in art had become an obsession, and he withdrew

from a regular school to enroll in a local drawing school. At this municipal school from 1875 to 1877, he moved through a demanding and classically based curriculum, which stressed endless hours of drawing human anatomy from engravings, from casts of antique sculpture, and from live models. Seurat's academy drawings reveal that he apparently preferred disciplined and sober images from symmetrically ordered compositions with a minimum of gesture and dramatic movement. He thus studied the work of Jean-Auguste-Dominique Ingres and Hans Holbein the Younger.

Seurat's next stage of training came on entering the prestigious École des Beaux-Arts in 1878; he was admitted to the painting class of Henri Lehmann, a disciple of Ingres. Seurat may have appreciated Lehmann's disciplined drawings more than his paintings, and Seurat's academic training may have failed to stimulate a healthy interest in color. The years 1875-1879 witnessed Seurat's growth primarily in draftsmanship, careful techniques, sophisticated design, and an identification with imagery carrying moral overtones, all lessons carried over into his mature work.

LIFE'S WORK

Following a year of compulsory military service, Seurat returned to Paris in November of 1880 and in a short time settled into a studio not far from the site where he had studied with Lehmann. Seurat left the École des Beaux-Arts after barely a year for reasons still unclear, but by 1880-1883 he was again submitting work to the Salon. During this same period, Seurat devoted himself to challenges in drawing and in so doing developed a mature style. His drawing and painting methods became parallel manifestations of a desire to regularize Impressionist painting methods and record everyday urban life with the nobility of classical art in the museums.

With Impressionism as a starting point, Seurat restricted himself to drawing in black and white, usually with charcoal, chalk, or conte crayons, moving away from an emphasis on line and contour toward softer, broader marks that acknowledged mass, the subtleties of atmosphere, and a concentration upon light. This approach yielded effects both academic and vanguard. The drawings reveal by 1883 a strong traditional handling of form through tonal contrast. However, the regularized all-over treatment, the neutral stance toward imagery, and the increasing concern with scientific theory had little in common with accepted academic practices at the time.

A masterful approach was evident by 1883 in Seurat's drawings; at that time, he felt sufficiently confident to develop a major painting, one upon which he hoped to establish a reputation. His confidence was based upon intense practice in drawing over three years plus much exploration in painting methods and in color theory. A thorough familiarity with Eugène Chevreul's theories of simultaneous complementary contrasts of colors and a reading of Ogden Rood's *Modern Chromatics* (1879) helped him immeasurably to realize optical mixing in both painting studies and finished drawings.

The first painting to benefit from this theoretical and technical input was the large work *A Bathing Place, Asnieres* (1883-1884). In the preparatory works and the final painting, French citizens swim, go boating, or rest as they enjoy a noon-hour break from work in the industries of a northern Paris suburb. Here the artist calculated and toiled to synthesize the variables and immediacy of Impressionist works by Claude Monet, Pierre-Auguste Renoir, and others.

The Salon jury of 1884 did not find *A Bathing Place, Asnieres* museum-worthy, but fortunately for Seurat a number of other rejected artists that year formed the Société des Artistes Indépendants, which sponsored uncensored, unjuried shows and accepted Seurat's painting. Seurat was encouraged but remained frustrated and threw himself into an even more ambitious painting, *A Sunday on the Grand Jatte*, painted 1884-1886, and with dimensions nearly the same as *A Bathing Place, Asnieres*.

The monumental painting depicts nearly life-size middle-class Parisians enjoying a work-free day on a slender island in the river Seine, where, dressed in current fashions, many promenade or sit quietly. Compositionally speaking, the lengthening shadows of mid-afternoon help unify the complex placement of figures. Many of the strollers are arranged in silhouetted profile, and almost no figures venture a spontaneous movement. Thus, there is a sense of the illogical leisure of mannequins instead of humans occupying a charmed environ-

ment. This mechanical aesthetic was no accident. In *A Sunday on the Grande Jatte*, Seurat methodically constructed a painting that extends the Impressionist treatment of subject but does not emulate the Impressionists' pursuit of transitory effects. It became a landmark work because it necessitated a new critical language and, as it happened, a new movement. Upon viewing the painting at the last Impressionist group show in 1886, art critic and friend to Seurat Félix Fénéon proposed the term Neo-Impressionism.

Furthermore, *A Sunday on the Grande Jatte* possessed a radical appearance, composed as it was of thousands and perhaps millions of tiny dots painted with impressive control and evenness. The technique employed became known as pointillism because of the use of points or dots of unmixed pigments. However, pointillism, arresting in its own right, was not the most important part of Seurat's program. The artist was investigating new quasi-scientific painting theories devised by critics Chevreul, Charles Blanc, and John Ruskin, as well as developments in commercial printing.

That intense study resulted in the concept of divisionism, a theory that advocated breaking down colors into separate components and applying them almost mechanically to a primed canvas in almost microscopic amounts, whereupon an optical mix occurred for spectators. The resultant optical mix was thought to be superior in luminosity to effects possible from traditional palettes wherein colors were mixed as tints or hues before application to a canvas. The immediate difference for Seurat was a painted approximation of the vibrating subtleties of reflected light, for example, as found in the partial tones of shadows in nature.

Not to be overlooked too was a concurrent advancement in color printings—the chromotypogravure, which intrigued Seurat, already fascinated by technology. The chromotypogravure replicated colors via screens or regular systems of dots and, as in Seurat's pointillism, produced an atmospheric mass and subtle gradations instead of lines or sharp contrasts of form.

Pointillism and divisionism, which regularized the painted effects of Impressionism, would have been satisfying accomplishments in themselves for some progressive painters of the 1880's, but not for Seurat. Upon finishing *A Sunday on the Grande Jatte*, which was also rejected at the Paris Salon, he took up a different challenge, that of systematizing the means of expressing emotional effects in paintings through carefully predetermined amounts of colors and types of light. Regularizing emotions in paintings was not new in France. There were plenty of precedents from Nicolas Poussin in the seventeenth century to Jacques-Louis David during the late eighteenth century. Seurat's new preoccupation, though, was based mostly on the publications of Charles Henry, a contemporary psychologist and aesthetician. Henry sought a scientific way to regularize connections between the formal elements of painting—colors, tones, or lines—and their impact upon viewers' emotional responses.

Such formulas appeared in Seurat's next well-planned painting, *Une Parade de cirque* of 1888. Known generally as *La Parade* (the side show), it focused on the midway of an urban circus. The scene, lit by gas jets, may be a nocturne, but more is dark in *La Parade* than the atmosphere. This entertainment scene is not joyous, despite a milling crowd and performing musicians. Solemnity and dutiful actions seem the rule and are reinforced by a muted surface system of dark blue and red dots. The painting is a balanced geometrical artifice underscored by the application of the ancient Greek guide, called the golden section, believed to establish beautiful proportions.

A number of marine subjects painted at or near Honfleur, Grandcamp, Port-en-Bessin, and Gravelines represent the artist's other painting interests from 1885 to 1891. These paintings parallel the works discussed in this essay technically and compositionally, and, though perhaps less provocative, they are no less brilliant in conception or execution.

Only days before the Salon des Indépendants opened in 1891, Seurat became ill, possibly from infectious angina or acute meningitis. Quickly moved from inadequate lodging to his mother's apartment, also in Paris, he lapsed into delirium and died there on March 29.

SIGNIFICANCE

Precocious as a youth, Georges Seurat was the master of his intentions for art by 1880. He could not know it at the time, but his career would be over in only eleven years. Deliberate in technique and a theoretician besides, his mature oeuvre included fewer than twenty major paintings, yet Seurat is considered one of the most influential of the late nineteenth century painters in France.

Seurat modernized classical configurations and exhausted orthodox formulas, after which he ventured into uncharted waters and speculated upon radical approaches to picture-making. Indeed, art viewers during his life and since usually imagine that technique or process was his dominant concern. Much of Seurat's conceptual direction was governed by careful reading of art theory, litera-

ture, physics, and pioneering works in psychology. Furthermore, despite the appearance of Cartesian order and asymmetrical balance invoked through the golden section of the ancient Greeks, Seurat's paintings by 1886 reflect an exploration of the new Symbolist movement, a movement decidedly subjective.

Seurat's primary subject, interwoven among fields of dots, was the modern city and the activities of its various classes of people, in particular the middle class at its leisure. In so doing, he transformed pedestrian information into a dignified and clarified expression, befitting the traditional art of the museums while simultaneously reflecting an enthusiasm for science and technology.

—*Tom Dewey II*

FURTHER READING

Broude, Norma. "New Light on Seurat's 'Dot': Its Relation to Photomechanical Color Printing in France in the 1880's." *Art Bulletin* 56 (December, 1974): 581-589. In a valuable piece of scholarship, Broude explores the parameters of the pointillist technique. In doing so, she draws quite helpful connections between Seurat's method, begun about 1885, and a new commercial printing technique involving chromotypogravure. There are also connections to an equally new attempt at color photography called the autochrome process. Those technologies fascinated Seurat because he was searching for an optically induced half-tone value system.

Dorra, Henri, and John Rewald. *Seurat*. Paris: Les Beaux-arts, 1959. Noteworthy are letters between Seurat and the Symbolist art theorist Fénéon, a perceptive and well-documented chapter titled "The Evolution of Seurat's Style," a chronological list of exhibitions in which Seurat's paintings have been shown, a lengthy bibliography, plus indexes of patrons and collectors as well as Seurat's art listed by title and subject.

Düchting, Hajo. *Georges Seurat, 1859-1891: The Master of Pointillism*. English translation by Michael Hulse. Cologne, Germany: Taschen, 2000. A survey of Seurat's life and work.

Goldwater, Robert J. "Some Aspects of the Development of Seurat's Style." *Art Bulletin* 23 (March, 1941): 117-130. Concentrates upon stylistic developments in the last five years of the artist's career, plus relationships between Seurat's career and those of his contemporaries. Goldwater emphasizes that Seurat was highly interested in various currents of his time, both in art and in other professions, to the degree that he was as much influenced by contemporary developments as he influenced others.

Herbert, Robert L. *Seurat: Drawings and Paintings.* New Haven, Conn.: Yale University Press, 2001. Examines the full range of Seurat's work, concentrating on the personal and social meaning of his individual paintings and drawings.

_____. *Seurat and the Making of "La Grande Jatte."* Chicago: Art Institute of Chicago in association with University of California Press, 2004. Describes the genesis, creation, artistic technique, reception, and other information about Seurat's well-known painting *A Sunday on the Grande Jatte*. The book accompanied an exhibition of the painting and related drawings and oil paintings.

Prak, Niels Luning. "Seurat's Surface Pattern and Subject Matter." *Art Bulletin* 53 (September, 1971): 367-378. This fine article addresses some of Seurat's intentions for the surface characteristics of his mature style, chief among which were the transformation of observed fact into rigorous abstract pattern. That, according to Prak, was achieved eventually by the painter through continual simplification of figures, continuity of forms (either defined or suggested), and the application of Blanc's theories to painting.

Thomson, Richard. *Seurat.* Salem, N.H.: Salem House, 1985. A good monograph that benefits from international research. Its standard chronological approach is enriched by rarely seen drawings and painted studies and a penetrating text, which correctly explores Seurat's absorption in current art and scientific theory.

SEE ALSO: Jacques-Louis David; Vincent van Gogh; Jean-Auguste-Dominique Ingres; Camille Pissarro; Pierre-Auguste Renoir; John Ruskin.

RELATED ARTICLES in *Great Events from History: The Nineteenth Century, 1801-1900:* April 15, 1874: First Impressionist Exhibition; Late 1870's: Post-Impressionist Movement Begins; 1892-1895: Toulouse-Lautrec Paints *At the Moulin Rouge*.

WILLIAM H. SEWARD
American politician and diplomat

After John Quincy Adams, Seward had the broadest vision of any secretary of state in U.S. history. As an antislavery leader who helped to found the Republican Party during the 1850's, he unsuccessfully challenged Abraham Lincoln for the presidential nomination in 1860 but went on to achieve his greatest triumphs as secretary of state and is remembered principally for his role in the U.S. acquisition of Alaska.

BORN: May 16, 1801; Florida, New York
DIED: October 10, 1872; Auburn, New York
ALSO KNOWN AS: William Henry Seward (full name)
AREAS OF ACHIEVEMENT: Government and politics, diplomacy

EARLY LIFE

The ancestors of William Henry Seward came to America from England during the early eighteenth century. His parents, Samuel and Mary Seward, reared five children. Young Seward was influenced mainly by his father, who valued discipline and wealth. At the age of fifteen, Seward left home for Union College in Schenectady, New York. A financial dispute with his father led him to leave Union College for Georgia, where he taught school (and observed slavery at first hand) for a short time. Returning to New York State, he completed his studies at Union College. He then worked for two law firms before being admitted to the bar in 1822. The following year, Seward moved to Auburn, near Syracuse, where he joined the law firm of Judge Elijah Miller. Judge Miller provided him not only a job but also a bride, for Seward married the judge's daughter, Frances, in 1824.

For men such as Seward, Auburn proved to be a great source of political opportunity. By the mid-1820's, Seward had already become active in the National Republican Party, which supported John Quincy Adams, and he then became active in the Antimasonic Party, which not only challenged the "secret government" of the Masons but also advocated protective tariffs and government support for the construction of roads, canals, and railroads. It was as an Antimason that Seward launched his public career.

Seward won a seat in the state senate, and he increasingly became a favorite of the leading political organizer of his party, Thurlow Weed (also of Auburn). The two men became close friends and established a lifelong political relationship that soon brought Seward to national prominence. Weed first carried Seward into the new

Whig Party as it emerged during the winter of 1833-1834, then engineered Seward's nomination for governor. Although Seward lost when he first ran for the office in 1834, he triumphed four years later.

By the time he became governor, Seward had proven himself to be highly ambitious, often unprincipled, and tough. He stood for the Whig economic program of tariffs, internal improvements, and the national bank, and took a daring position in support of temperance, prison reform, and the abolition of jail sentences for debtors. On race issues, however, he was inconsistent. Although he detested slavery, he opposed, with equal vehemence, granting the right to vote to blacks. However, he recognized that the controversy over slavery might offer him political opportunities, and he grabbed them during the next twenty-five years.

LIFE'S WORK

Portraits of Seward show a handsome man about five feet, six inches tall, with a graceful, thin face marked by an aquiline nose, a ruddy complexion, and wavy, red hair. Early photographs of Seward are not as flattering: The lines in his face are less graceful, his look less direct. This discrepancy can be observed also in his political ca-

William H. Seward. (The Granger Collection, New York)

reer, for Seward often offered less than met the eye. As governor, he became well known for his opposition to slavery and his support for the education of Catholic immigrant children in the face of nativist Protestant objections, and he continued to advocate high tariffs and internal improvements. However, he took none of these positions without first having carefully assessed their potential impact on his career. When the Whigs in New York suffered reverses during the mid- and late-1840's, they turned to Seward as their best chance to regain a seat in the U.S. Senate. Their plan succeeded. In 1849, the Auburn lawyer moved to Washington, D.C.

The next twenty years witnessed the zenith of Seward's political career. Opposing the Compromise of 1850 because it did not end the expansion of slavery, Seward delivered his most famous speech. He argued before the Senate that there existed "a higher law than the Constitution" that prohibited the movement of slavery into free territory. This speech, which was reprinted thousands of times during the following decade, turned Seward into one of the leading symbols of the antislavery movement, a hero to northerners, a demagogue to southerners. Moreover, Seward's "higher law" speech guaranteed that when the Whig Party disintegrated during the period between 1852 and 1854, Seward would be called upon to lead the Republican Party, which replaced it. Seward in New York, Abraham Lincoln in Illinois, and Salmon Chase in Ohio all came to lead the new party that was both sectional (not national) and fundamentally opposed to the expansion of slavery into the territory acquired by the United States following the Mexican War.

Both Seward's friends and his foes exaggerated his opposition to slavery, for he was first and foremost a nationalist—and, as such, hardly a radical within the abolitionist cause. Slavery, he believed, would impede national development, but he was against so rapid and wrenching a transition away from slavery as might lead to war and destroy the Union. Seward favored gradual, not immediate, abolition. He advocated compensation for slaveholders who freed their slaves. A conservative and traditionalist, unlike many abolitionists, he continued to praise the Constitution.

The fact that Seward was a nationalist also explains his support of federal funding of internal improvements, tariffs, and development of the West. He remained suspicious of executive power, although not when it was used to assert the national interest against foreign competitors. Seward believed that, eventually, the United States would extend its boundaries from coast to coast and would encompass Canada and Mexico and Alaska (which he helped to purchase from Russia in 1867). As a nationalist, he believed, as did his hero John Quincy Adams, that Providence intended for the United States to dominate the Western Hemisphere. He believed that the political and moral contradictions of slavery would discredit this mission.

Seward viewed the systems of the nation's free and slave states and territories as incompatible. This incompatibility would, he claimed in an 1858 speech, lead to "an irrepressible conflict," meaning that the United States would eventually have to extend either the free or the slave system to all of its borders. Lincoln shared this conviction, and the likelihood that either Lincoln or Seward would become the Republican Party nominee for president in 1860 led many influential southerners to advocate secession.

Seward desperately wanted to become president, but, for a number of reasons, he failed to receive his party's nomination. The "irrepressible conflict" speech had become so notorious that many Republicans feared that its author could not win the election. Furthermore, Seward's long-standing support for Catholic education, stemming back to the New York education quarrels of the 1840's, left nativists in his party dissatisfied. (As for Thurlow Weed, another likely candidate that year of 1860, he was simply outmaneuvered by the opposition— a rare but important occurrence in his political career.) Thus, the Republican Party named Abraham Lincoln its candidate for the presidency. Seward's defeat was a bitter blow, yet—although he genuinely believed Lincoln to be less qualified than himself—Seward loyally supported Lincoln in the general election. Lincoln rewarded this loyalty, offering Seward the post of secretary of state following his electoral victory.

During the next eight years, Seward proved himself to be among the nation's most outstanding State Department chiefs, though it was not immediately apparent. He began his work in a provocative manner. He proposed that Lincoln, in effect, serve as a figurehead president while Seward assume the real powers of the presidency. He threatened war against England and France in order to motivate the South to return to the Union in a burst of nationalistic fervor. He insulted the British at a moment when the Union needed foreign support against the challenge of the Confederacy.

If Seward's early diplomacy appeared belligerent, however, he quickly mended his ways. From the beginning of the Civil War in 1861, Seward's major task was to minimize foreign support for the Confederacy. The South not only sought diplomatic recognition from the

Europeans; it also sought military aid in the form of loans and equipment, especially naval craft that could challenge the Union blockade of Southern ports.

Preoccupied with military and political matters, Lincoln gave Seward a free hand in the diplomatic arena. Seward played it well. When a Union naval captain plucked two Confederate officials off the *Trent*, a British frigate, officials in London threatened war. Seward avoided conflict in an adroit maneuver in which the British, for the first time since the American Revolution, accepted the American view of neutral rights on the high seas. In like manner, Seward, through a combination of bluff, public appeal, and skillful negotiation, discouraged both the British and the French from aiding the Confederacy either diplomatically or materially.

Seward's skill was evident in more than simply wartime diplomacy. He shrewdly unveiled the Monroe Doctrine when the French installed a puppet regime in Mexico, and he effectively laid the foundation for American financial claims against London stemming from damage inflicted on Union shipping by a Confederate cruiser, the *Alabama*, constructed in Great Britain. More important, his vision of an American continental empire culminated in his imaginative purchase of Alaska in 1867. "Seward's Folly," his critics called the acquisition, but even an unfriendly Congress recognized its potential value.

The plot to kill Lincoln also targeted Seward, who was severely wounded. He recovered to serve President Andrew Johnson as secretary of state, generally endorsing Johnson's Reconstruction policy. The fact is that Seward remained willing to subordinate black rights to what he believed to be the main task, that of the reconciliation of the North and the South. Nevertheless, it was foreign policy, not Reconstruction politics, for which he would be remembered. Retiring from public life in 1869 and returning to Auburn, he died three years later, October 10, 1872.

SIGNIFICANCE

William Seward's career touched upon virtually all the major issues of the pre-Civil War era. He became one of the country's leading Whig (and later Republican) leaders in part because he thoroughly supported the main Whig principles: nationalism, a limit on executive power, strict support for the Constitution, a high tariff to fund internal improvements, and low land prices in order to stimulate westward expansion. However, it was antislavery that, above all, shaped his career. Seward became a leading opponent of the expansion of slavery, and he nearly rode this issue into the presidency.

What Seward lacked, however, was conviction. Seward never conveyed Lincoln's sense that slavery was a genuine American tragedy. To an extent, Seward was victimized by his evident ambition. He was not fully trusted, in large measure because he was not fully trustworthy. Too often he subordinated political principle to personal interest, a weakness that limited his effectiveness with allies and foes alike. Nevertheless, Seward's skepticism about principle allowed him to compromise where compromise was necessary and made him a particularly effective diplomat. Next to John Quincy Adams, he had the broadest vision of any secretary of state in American history. He was a practical man, a man of action rather than an intellectual. Whatever the flaws in his character, his record speaks for itself.

—Gary B. Ostrower

FURTHER READING

Adams, Ephraim D. *Great Britain and the American Civil War*. 2 vols. New York: Longmans, Green, 1925. Adams, while sympathetic toward the British, nevertheless provides a fair and detailed account of Seward's first four years as secretary of state.

Case, Lynn M., and Warren F. Spencer. *The United States and France: Civil War Diplomacy*. Philadelphia: University of Pennsylvania Press, 1970. An excellent survey of Seward's foreign policy from a Continental perspective. Seward is viewed with grudging respect.

Ferriss, Norman B. *Desperate Diplomacy: William H. Seward's Foreign Policy, 1861*. Knoxville: University of Tennessee Press, 1976. A sympathetic account of Seward's diplomacy, with a focus on the *Trent* affair.

_____. *The Trent Affair: A Diplomatic Crisis*. Knoxville: University of Tennessee Press, 1977. A thorough but dull account of the crisis that nearly brought Great Britain and the United States to war in 1861.

Paolino, Ernest N. *The Foundations of American Empire: William Henry Seward and U.S. Foreign Policy*. Ithaca, N.Y.: Cornell University Press, 1973. The author views Seward as defining a commercial imperial mission for the United States. Curiously, the book ignores the Civil War.

Seward, William H. *William H. Seward: An Autobiography from 1801-1834, With a Memoir of His Life, and Selections from His Letters*. 3 vols. Edited by Frederick Seward. New York: Derby and Miller, 1877. The editor was Seward's son. This volume provides a look at Seward's entire life from his own perspective.

Taylor, John M. *William Henry Seward: Lincoln's Right Hand*. New York: HarperCollins, 1991. Balanced, straightforward biography, focusing on Seward's relationship with Lincoln. Describes Seward's handling of the Trent affair and John Wilkes Booth's assault on Seward the night Booth assassinated Lincoln.

Van Deusen, Glyndon G. *William Henry Seward*. New York: Oxford University Press, 1967. The best one-volume biography. Van Deusen is sympathetic to but rarely uncritical of Seward, whom he views as a man both unprincipled and practical.

Warren, Gordon H. *Foundation of Discontent: The Trent Affair and Freedom of the Seas*. Boston: Northeastern University Press, 1981. This work is less kind to Seward than the work of Ferriss. It is very helpful in clarifying the complex legal issues of the affair.

SEE ALSO: John Quincy Adams; Salmon P. Chase; Millard Fillmore; Horace Greeley; Andrew Johnson; Abraham Lincoln; Charles Sumner.

RELATED ARTICLES in *Great Events from History: The Nineteenth Century, 1801-1900:* 1820's-1830's: Free Public School Movement; 1840's-1850's: American Era of "Old" Immigration; January 29-September 20, 1850: Compromise of 1850; September 18, 1850: Second Fugitive Slave Law; July 6, 1854: Birth of the Republican Party; November 6, 1860: Lincoln Is Elected U.S. President; March 4, 1861: Lincoln Is Inaugurated President; January 1, 1863: Lincoln Issues the Emancipation Proclamation; April 9 and 14, 1865: Surrender at Appomattox and Assassination of Lincoln; March 30, 1867: Russia Sells Alaska to the United States; July 28, 1868: Burlingame Treaty.

SHAKA

South African military leader

Shaka revolutionized the military and political organization of the Zulu and their neighboring peoples, transforming the systems from the traditional to what might have developed into a modern nation-state, had not European imperialism intervened. His achievements enabled the Zulu to resist European conquest until the late nineteenth century and preserved Zulu national identity.

BORN: c. 1787; Mtetwa Empire (now in South Africa)
DIED: September 22, 1828; Zulu Empire (now in South Africa)
ALSO KNOWN AS: Shaka Zulu; Chaka; Tshaka
AREAS OF ACHIEVEMENT: Government and politics, warfare and conquest

EARLY LIFE

Shaka (SHAH-kah) was the illegitimate child of a young Zulu chieftain and a woman from a clan with whom his father, Senzangakhona, could not have chosen a wife because of kinship restrictions. His parents attempted unsuccessfully a contrived marriage, but Shaka and his mother, Nandi, were soon exiled from his father's homestead. They went to live with his mother's clan, a branch of the Mthetwa people, but there Shaka found himself ostracized and humiliated by the boys in his age group.

Even before attaining puberty, Shaka displayed the personality that was to mold his career. He was a reclusive, brooding child, deeply attached to his mother, prone to outbursts of consuming violence. It has been reported that he once nearly killed two older boys who had taunted him. When his father's community offered reconciliation and membership in his adolescent age group, Shaka angrily rejected the offer in public, embarrassing his father and deepening the feud between the two clans of Shaka's parents.

There is nothing to indicate that Shaka received any more than the traditional education provided for all Zulu youths in adolescence. That would have amounted to indoctrination into tribal customs and pragmatic knowledge of the environment. Oral tradition depicts Shaka as a youth driven to reckless bravery, a superior athlete and warrior whose talents only fed the jealousy of his peers.

LIFE'S WORK

At the age of twenty-one, Shaka joined the fighting ranks of the great Mthetwa chief, Dingiswayo. A remarkable leader in his own right, Dingiswayo had conquered some thirty tribes, including the Zulu, and had attempted to discourage the incessant feuding among his subjects, much of it caused by the food and land shortages resulting from a prolonged drought in the region during the late eighteenth century. Dingiswayo organized trading expeditions to the tiny European outpost on the coast of Southern Africa and formulated the beginnings of a centralized kingdom.

Life as a soldier offered Shaka the opportunity to display his genius for military innovation. Traditionally, combat in Southern Africa had been decided by the two opposing groups deploying themselves some fifty yards apart and hurling javelins and spears across the intervening distance until one side or the other retired. Shaka, dissatisfied with these tactics, adopted the *assegai*, a short stabbing sword, as his weapon, thus requiring hand-to-hand combat with enemies. There is some evidence that Shaka was familiar enough with advanced forms of iron-smelting technology to comprehend that, properly forged, these blades could be made much harder and more destructive than the less elaborate iron weapons normally used by his people.

Shaka also developed more disciplined tactics than previously used in the region. He disdained the loose array of warriors characteristic of javelin combat in favor of a close-order deployment, wherein a solid line of animal-skin shields confronted the enemy. Two "horns" of infantry extended from this central formation to outflank enemy forces. Reserves to the rear of the formation stood ready to rush into any weakness created in the enemy lines. Shaka's regiment won victory after victory against confused opponents. His new tactics changed warfare from limited skirmishing to a modern bloodletting that often terrorized potential opponents into submission.

Shaka's father, meanwhile, had maneuvered himself into the Zulu chieftancy. Upon his death in 1816, a grateful Dingiswayo had Shaka installed as the Zulu leader. Two years later, Zwide, the chief of a rival tribe and would-be usurper, assassinated Dingiswayo. Shaka set out to wreak vengeance. Luring Zwide's much larger force into a valley where no provisions could be found and foregoing the final battle until his opponents were weak from hunger, Shaka's men devastated Zwide's forces.

Shaka now displayed an insight even more remarkable than those that punctuated his military career. He dispatched the survivors of Zwide's army to his rear guard and, following their retraining in Zulu military tactics, incorporated them into his army. The lands vacated by Zwide's fighters and their families were colonized by Zulu. Shaka evidently perceived that, in order to build a large army and empire, the tribal structure of Southern Africa had to be broken down. The notion of awarding land to successful and loyal soldiers, in a country where most land had been held more or less in common, carried the seeds of social and economic revolution.

Within six years after the death of Dingiswayo, Shaka's empire embraced tens of thousands of square miles. He could muster an army of 100,000 men. From the giant village at Bulawayo, Shaka ruled over an entity without precedent in Southern Africa. European traders and diplomats made their way to Bulawayo to seek alliances and privileges.

It was a fleeting moment. Shaka's military regimen was harsh beyond reason, a product of his own troubled mind. He demanded celibacy of his troops, granting the right to marry only to those who excelled in battle. His officers clubbed to death any recruit too fainthearted to bear the pain and deprivation of forced marches and ordeals. His new military tactics were like a plague loosed on the land, virtually depopulating the country around Bulawayo and forcing his columns to march hundreds of miles for new recruits and conquests. Shaka ruled as an absolute monarch, and a tyrannical one at that. His periodic fits of rage often led to the execution of hundreds of innocent bystanders. Soldiers who were only suspected of cowardice were killed at once. European guests at Bulawayo reported that Shaka almost daily chose soldiers or courtiers, at whim, for execution.

Throughout Shaka's career, his penchant for violence seems to have been most pronounced in connection with the original injustice meted out to his mother. Shortly after becoming chief of the Zulu, Shaka hunted down those who had ostracized him and his mother and had them impaled on stakes. The occasion of his mother's death—by natural causes—caused a violent outburst. In Bulawayo alone, seven thousand people were killed over the next two days. Shaka's officers summarily butchered anyone who did not meet arbitrary standards for adequate display of grief. Shaka ordered his empire into a bizarre year of mourning for his mother. Under pain of death, married couples were to abstain from sexual relations. No cows or goats were to be milked, no crops planted. Shaka's army embarked on a new round of conquests, in some cases hundreds of miles from Bulawayo.

Such demands pushed even the most loyal of Shaka's followers beyond their limits. Food shortages and dis-

ease quickly began to take their toll. In 1828, when Shaka ordered his army to attack the Portuguese settlement at Delagoa Bay, his brothers, Dingane and Mhlangane, assassinated him. Dingane then killed Mhlangane, assumed the throne, recalled the exhausted army, and revoked some of Shaka's most irrational edicts.

SIGNIFICANCE

Given Shaka's extraordinary behavior, especially in the last years of his life, historians have been prone to characterize him in psychological terms. Shaka has been labeled a psychotic and a manic-depressive. Because he left no male heir—he often observed that a son would try to kill him for the throne—and because he demanded nudity and celibacy among his soldiers, some historians suspect latent homosexuality. Perhaps any leader of Shaka's dimensions might be cast in psychological types. Preferably, however, one should understand Shaka as a true innovator, perhaps a genius, let loose in a society and environment typified by violence, natural upheaval, and the beginnings of contact with the outside world.

Most historians concur that Shaka lived in a South Africa wherein the population was approaching the limits of agricultural productivity; land, therefore, was already coming to be viewed as a scarce resource and a basis of political power. The great droughts and famines that seem to have ravaged South Africa in the eighteenth century, together with the more limited but still novel sociopolitical achievements of his predecessor Dingiswayo, made Shaka's world one of turbulence and frayed traditions. As is evident from the frequent appearance of potential usurpers and ambitious chiefs among Shaka's opponents, there were many who might have undertaken the task of building an empire. Shaka succeeded because of his unique mentality.

Shaka's achievement also passes a crucial historical test: It survived and flourished long after the death of its creator. Despite the level of violence that seems to have attended it, Shaka created a Zulu protostate that remained intact for the rest of the nineteenth century. Only the British, using the latest in automatic weapons, finally managed to subdue the Zulu in 1879. Consciousness of a Zulu national identity remains a strong mobilizing force in the struggle for authority and land in the modern Republic of South Africa.

—*Ronald W. Davis*

FURTHER READING

Ballard, Charles. "Drought and Economic Distress: South Africa in the 1800's." *Journal of Interdisciplinary History* 17 (1986): 359-378. Discusses how favorable conditions in the eighteenth century fostered growth of Nguni population and herds, while drought during the early nineteenth century forced rapid migration and accelerated development of the absolutist state of Shaka by forcing Zulu into military service.

Gluckman, Max. "The Rise of a Zulu Empire." *Scientific American* 202 (April, 1960): 157-168. Gives an excellent summary of major events, and speculates on Shaka's possible psychological condition.

Hamilton, Carolyn. *Terrific Majesty: The Powers of Shaka Zulu and the Limits of Historical Invention.* Cambridge, Mass.: Harvard University Press, 1998. The author analyzes why Shaka has acquired iconic status, examining how his image has changed over time.

Inskeep, R. R. *The Peopling of Southern Africa.* New York: Barnes & Noble Books, 1979. A study of the factors influencing population movements in Southern Africa and methods of reconstructing these patterns.

Kets de Vries, Manfred F. R. *Lessons on Leadership by Terror: Finding Shaka Zulu in the Attic.* Northampton, Mass.: Edward Elgar, 2004. The author views Shaka as a symbol of despotism, and examines his rule to better understand how and why people in positions of leadership abuse their power.

Marks, Shula. "Firearms in Southern Africa: A Survey." *Journal of African History* 12 (1971): 517-530. Suggests that, although the Zulu acquired firearms early in the eighteenth century, they were little used for military purposes until it became necessary to defend against the British. Underscores the importance of Shaka's military innovations in using indigenous weapons and tactics.

Ritter, E. A. *Shaka Zulu: The Rise of a Zulu Empire.* New York: G. P. Putnam's Sons, 1955. A classic account of the career of Shaka. Some passages take the style of a historical novel, but the work is essentially accurate.

Roberts, Brian. *The Zulu Kings.* New York: Charles Scribner's Sons, 1975. A popular but useful and innovative account of the rise of Shaka. Stresses Shaka's concept of a territorial power base as a revolutionary development in African political thought.

Selby, John. *Shaka's Heirs.* London: George Allen & Unwin, 1971. Provides an extended discussion of Shaka's career and of those who attempted to emulate him in the Zulu environment that the warrior king had altered forever.

Taylor, Stephen. *Shaka's Children: A History of the Zulu People.* London: HarperCollins, 1995. Traces the rise of Shaka and the Zulu nation, providing information about current Zulu nationalism and the tribe's relationship with whites and other South African tribes.

Wylie, Dan. *Savage Delight: White Myths of Shaka.* Pietermaritzburg, South Africa: University of Natal Press, 2000. Examines how, and why, white writers from the 1830's to the present have mythologized Shaka.

SEE ALSO: Lobengula.

RELATED ARTICLES in *Great Events from History: The Nineteenth Century, 1801-1900:* August 13, 1814: Britain Acquires the Cape Colony; c. 1817-1828: Zulu Expansion.

ANNA HOWARD SHAW
English-born American social reformer

The first American woman to hold divinity and medical degrees simultaneously, Shaw was a central figure in the crusades for political equality and women's rights.

BORN: February 14, 1847; Newcastle upon Tyne, Northumberland, England
DIED: July 2, 1919; Moylan, Pennsylvania
AREAS OF ACHIEVEMENT: Women's rights, social reform

EARLY LIFE

As the sixth child of a fragile and despondent mother and a restless and irresponsible father, Anna Howard Shaw was not a likely prospect for fame or fortune. At the age of four, she moved with her family to the United States, settling in New Bedford, Massachusetts. Shortly before the Civil War, the Shaw family moved to the Michigan frontier. Anna spent her early teens cutting firewood, digging wells, caring for her sickly mother, and generally overseeing the Shaw household while her father and older brothers were away at war.

Anna pitied her mother, viewing her as a weak, lonely woman, overburdened with meaningless household chores, embittered by her plight yet unwilling or unable to escape her oppression. As a youth, Anna dreamed that she would be different. After years of indecision, Anna marshaled the courage to defy family tradition and pursue a formal education. At the age of twenty-four, despite the protests of her father, she left home to attend a high school in Big Rapids.

While in Big Rapids, Shaw met the Reverend Marianna Thompson. Inspired by this new and unusual role model, Shaw decided that she also would prepare for the ministry. Embarrassed at her decision, yet knowing that his disapproval would not stop her, her father attempted to dissuade Anna by offering to send her to the University of Michigan if she agreed to abandon her ministerial ambitions. By now a young woman with growing self-confidence, Shaw rejected her father's offer, secured a Methodist preaching license, and enrolled at Albion College, a Methodist school in southern Michigan.

Without financial or emotional backing from her family, Shaw supported herself during her two years at Albion with occasional preaching and public temperance speaking. Buoyed by her success, Shaw left Michigan for the School of Theology of Boston University, becoming only the second female to enroll at the institution. After being graduated in 1878, she secured a pastorate in East Dennis, Massachusetts. In 1880, Shaw pursued full ordination within the Methodist Episcopal Church. Denied such ordination, she entered into fellowship with the smaller Methodist Protestant denomination, and, amid great controversy, she was ordained as an elder in October of 1880.

Having successfully entered one profession dominated by men, Shaw embarked in 1883 on a second "for men only" profession. Without giving up her pastorate, Shaw began part-time work toward a medical degree. After completing her studies in 1886, Shaw became the first American woman to hold divinity and medical degrees simultaneously.

Despite her accomplishments, Shaw during the 1880's was undergoing a midlife crisis. Sympathetic from her youth to the plight of the disadvantaged, Shaw had entered the ministry in hopes of elevating the discouraged from their spiritual poverty. Convinced later that she must do more to relieve human suffering, she returned to medical school, and, after her graduation, requested a temporary leave from the pastoral ministry in order to serve as a paramedic in the slums of South Boston. While ministering to the emotional and physical needs of women prostitutes, Shaw concluded that the solutions to many of their problems were political. Ministers and physicians could treat the symptoms, but legislatures responding to the demands of an enlightened electorate were needed to eliminate the root causes of social injustice, poverty, and sickness.

LIFE'S WORK

At the age of thirty-nine, Anna Howard Shaw left the preaching and healing ministry for another career. Joining first the Massachusetts Suffrage Association and later the American Woman Suffrage Association (AWSA), Shaw became a full-time organizer and lecturer for the causes of suffrage and temperance. At the urging of Frances Willard, a fellow Methodist preacher and president of the Woman's Christian Temperance Union (WCTU), Shaw accepted the chair of the Franchise Department of the WCTU. Her task was to work for woman suffrage and then to use the ballot to gain "home protection" and temperance legislation.

In 1888, Shaw was selected as a delegate to represent both the WCTU and the AWSA at the first meeting of the International Council of Women. While at the gathering in Washington, D.C., Shaw met Susan B. Anthony, the renowned leader of the more radical National Woman Suffrage Association (NWSA). Anthony, who at this time was looking for recruits to groom for leadership within the NWSA, was immediately impressed with Shaw's potential. As a sturdy, spunky young woman, Shaw had the stamina for travel; as a single person, Shaw had total control of her time; as an extemporaneous preacher, Shaw had impressive oratorical skills; and as a respected religious figure, Shaw had a reputation that would soften the NWSA's "irreligious and radical" public image.

During the convention, Anthony made Shaw her special project, flattering her and reprimanding her for not efficiently using her gifts for the cause. Unlike Willard and other "social feminists," Anthony viewed suffrage less as a means to an end than as a fundamental right that must not be denied. As a single-issue woman, Anthony challenged Shaw not to waste her talents on temperance, but to commit herself totally to full suffrage. In response

to Anthony's challenge, Shaw shifted her allegiance from the AWSA to the NWSA and promised Anthony that suffrage would become her consuming goal.

The emerging Anthony-Shaw friendship had a profound impact on the suffrage movement. In 1889, Shaw helped to persuade the AWSA to merge with Anthony's and Elizabeth Cady Stanton's NWSA, creating for the first time in two decades a semblance of organizational unity within the movement. Three years later, Anthony accepted the presidency of the unified National-American Woman Suffrage Association (NAWSA) and secured for Shaw the vice presidency.

The Anthony-Shaw tandem was inseparable—collaborating, traveling, even living together. An odd-looking couple, good-naturedly called by friends "the ruler and the rubber-ball," Anthony and Shaw were strikingly different in appearance, style, and talent: Anthony was tall and thin, an unconventional, religious agnostic

A CHILDHOOD MYSTERY WOMAN

My second friendship, and one which had a strong influence on my after-life, was formed in Lawrence. I was not more than ten years old when I met this new friend, but the memory of her in after-years, and the impression she had made on my susceptible young mind, led me first into the ministry, next into medicine, and finally into suffrage-work. Living next door to us, on Prospect Hill, was a beautiful and mysterious woman.... To me she was a princess in a fairy-tale, for she rode a white horse and wore a blue velvet riding-habit with a blue velvet hat and a picturesquely drooping white plume....

Very soon she noticed me. Possibly she saw the adoration in my childish eyes. She began to nod and smile at me, and then to speak to me, but at first I was almost afraid to answer her. There were stories now among the children that the house was haunted, and that by night a ghost walked there and in the grounds....

One day the mysterious lady bent and kissed me. Then, straightening up, she looked at me queerly and said: "Go and tell your mother I did that."... While my mother was considering the problem the situation presented, for she knew the character of the house next door, a note was handed in to her—a very pathetic little note from my mysterious lady, asking my mother to let me come and see her. Long afterward mother showed it to me. It ended with the words: "She will see no one but me. No harm shall come to her. Trust me."

That night my parents talked the matter over and decided to let me go. Probably they felt that the slave next door was as much to be pitied as the escaped-negro slaves they so often harbored in our home. I made my visit, which was the first of many, and a strange friendship began and developed between the woman of the town and the little girl she loved....

Once, when we had become very good friends indeed and my early shyness had departed, I found courage to ask her where the ghost was—the ghost that haunted her house. I can still see the look in her eyes as they met mine. She told me the ghost lived in her heart, and that she did not like to talk about it, and that we must not speak of it again. After that I never mentioned it, but I was more deeply interested than ever, for a ghost that lived in a heart was a new kind of ghost to me at that time, though I have met many of them since then. During all our intercourse my mother never entered the house next door, nor did my mysterious lady enter our home; but she constantly sent my mother secret gifts for the poor and the sick of the neighborhood, and she was always the first to offer help for those who were in trouble. Many years afterward mother told me she was the most generous woman she had ever known, and that she had a rarely beautiful nature. Our departure for Michigan broke up the friendship, but I have never forgotten her; and whenever, in my later work as minister, physician, and suffragist, I have been able to help women of the class to which she belonged, I have mentally offered that help for credit in the tragic ledger of her life, in which the clean and the blotted pages were so strange a contrast.

Source: Anna Howard Shaw, *The Story of a Pioneer* (New York, 1915), chapter 1.

and organizational genius; Shaw, a roly-poly Methodist preacher with a quick wit and golden tongue. Despite, or perhaps because of their differences, they were able to extend each other's outreach and effectiveness.

Exploiting her religious reputation and church contacts, Shaw introduced Anthony into mainline Protestant circles previous closed to Anthony and "her girls." Anthony, in return, taught the inexperienced Shaw how to devise and execute a strategy for suffrage victory. Grooming Shaw for executive leadership, Anthony prodded Shaw to follow a strategy of moderate agitation, always pressing forward the cause of suffrage, yet never alienating the masses with unnecessary conflict. More traditional than Anthony, Shaw accepted her master teacher's pragmatism. By the time of Anthony's death in 1906, Shaw had learned her lessons well.

Between 1904 and 1915, Shaw served as president of the NAWSA. During this era, the organization grew from 17,000 to 200,000 members and superintended suffrage victories in eight additional states. As the organization grew, however, it also became more divided. The success of the militant suffragettes in England pressured Shaw to abandon the methods she had learned under Anthony for more militant tactics such as campaigning against the political party in power rather than individual candidates unfriendly to suffrage, picketing the White House, calling hunger strikes, and pressing for immediate suffrage elections, even if there was no prospect for victory. Although Shaw grew to accept "passive resistance," she refused to abandon her mentor's game plan. "I am, and always have been," Shaw asserted in 1914, "unalterably opposed to militancy, believing that nothing of permanent value has ever been secured by it that could not have been more easily obtained by peaceful methods."

Although Shaw's policy of moderation raised her stature among the rank and file of the NAWSA, it also cost her respect among the more aggressive members within her executive committee. In December, 1915, at the age of 68, Shaw stepped down as president of the NAWSA, a position she had held longer than any other woman, and accepted the lifetime honorary position of president emeritus. Although official NAWSA publications attempted to cover up the internal feud, and most members never realized the depth of the disharmony, Shaw's resignation was not voluntary. Leaving the administrative details to the returning president, Carrie Chapman Catt, Shaw began working full-time at what she did best—traveling, lecturing, and evangelizing for the suffrage cause.

In May, 1917, President Woodrow Wilson asked Shaw to head the Woman's Committee of the Council of National Defense. Always an American patriot, and, like Wilson, mesmerized by the prospect of making the world safe for democracy, Shaw left the suffrage circuit to accept the appointment. For two years, she worked to mobilize American women to contribute to the war effort. Following victory in Europe, Shaw resigned as chair of the Woman's Committee. In appreciation for her war service, President Wilson awarded her the Distinguished Service Medal of Honor, an award never before bestowed upon an American woman.

Shaw's retirement from public service, however, was short-lived, for soon she returned to the lecture circuit—this time to win support for the League of Nations. Although her spirit was willing, the ailing Shaw was unable to withstand the strain of another campaign. Succumbing to pneumonia, Shaw died in her home in Moylan, Pennsylvania, on July 2, 1919.

SIGNIFICANCE

A Methodist clergywoman who was persuaded that Jesus Christ embodied the best attributes of both man and woman, that in Christ there was neither male nor female, and that full suffrage would adorn the coming millennial Kingdom, Anna Howard Shaw was an eternal optimist who never doubted that suffrage victory would be won. Claiming the motto Truth loses many battles, but always wins the war, Shaw spoke and acted as if the impossible was already a reality. For Shaw, full suffrage, like the coming Kingdom, could be delayed but not denied.

Shaw's religious reputation and noted nonmilitancy made her an ideal candidate to lead the counterattack against those who opposed suffrage rights for women. In virtually every address, Shaw hammered at the "ridiculous" arguments of those who insisted that woman suffrage would destroy the home, the church, and the nation. Early in the campaign, her opponents often challenged Shaw to public debates. By 1913, however, the National Anti-Suffrage Association adopted a policy of prohibiting any of its speakers from debating Shaw. Their cause, they believed, was better served by ignoring rather than challenging the Methodist suffrage evangelist.

Following her death, newspaper editors, regardless of their stand on the woman question, united in their testimonials to Shaw. The *New Haven Register* eulogized Shaw as "the best beloved and most versatile of the suffrage leaders"; *The Nation* labeled her as "the ideal type of reformer [to represent] the despair of the anti-suffragists because she was so normal and sane, so sound and so effective"; the *Philadelphia Press* praised the "sense, moderation and dignity in her methods which won and held respect even of those who opposed her cause"; and the more conservative *Atlanta Constitution* characterized Shaw as follows: "Though an ardent suffragist, her sense of justice was so impressed upon her records that anti-suffragists and suffragists alike trusted her." Such tributes from both suffrage friends and foes suggest that the woman widely known as the "Demosthenes of the suffrage movement" had become by the time of her death a national heroine. Despite these accolades, however, Shaw has been largely neglected by historians, and she remains the only central leader of the suffrage movement without a full-length biography.

—Terry D. Bilhartz

FURTHER READING

Flexner, Eleanor. *Century of Struggle: The Woman's Rights Movement in the United States.* Rev. ed. Cambridge, Mass.: Belknap Press of Harvard University, 1975. A revision of an original 1959 publication, this overview remains the standard textbook on the women's rights movement.

Linkugel, Wil A. *Anna Howard Shaw: Suffrage Orator and Social Reformer.* New York: Greenwood Press, 1991. This introduction to Shaw includes a collection of her speeches and is an extension of Linkugel's 1960 doctoral dissertation "The Speeches of Anna Howard Shaw."

Pellauer, Mary D. *Toward a Tradition of Feminist Theology: The Religious Thought of Elizabeth Cady Stanton, Susan B. Anthony, and Anna H. Shaw.* Brooklyn, N.Y.: Carlson, 1991. A monograph within the Chicago Studies in the History of American Women series, this volume analyzes Shaw's feminist theology and compares it with the theologies of other leading feminists of the period.

Shaw, Anna Howard. *The Story of a Pioneer.* New York: Harper & Brothers, 1915. In the absence of a full-length biography, this readable autobiography remains the best general introduction to the life of this suffrage crusader.

Spencer, Ralph W. "Anna Howard Shaw." *Methodist History* 13, no. 2 (January, 1975). This article, which is derived from Spencer's 1972 doctoral dissertation, sketches Shaw's career, emphasizing her Methodist contacts and experiences.

Zink-Sawyer, Beverly Ann. *From Preachers to Suffragists: Woman's Rights and Religious Conviction in the Lives of Three Nineteenth-Century American Clergywomen.* Louisville, Ky.: Westminster John Knox Press, 2003. Examines the lives of Shaw and two other clergywomen—Olympia Brown and Antoinette Louise Brown Blackwell—whose involvement in the women's rights movement was an extension of their call to the ministry.

SEE ALSO: Susan B. Anthony; Elizabeth Cady Stanton; Frances Willard.

RELATED ARTICLE in *Great Events from History: The Nineteenth Century, 1801-1900:* May, 1869: Woman Suffrage Associations Begin Forming.

MARY WOLLSTONECRAFT SHELLEY
English novelist

As an innovative and politically subversive writer of novels, tales, and stories—including the classic Frankenstein, *Shelley was a significant contributor to the history of women's writing and the development of prose fiction.*

BORN: August 30, 1797; London, England
DIED: February 1, 1851; London, England
ALSO KNOWN AS: Mary Godwin (birth name)
AREA OF ACHIEVEMENT: Literature

EARLY LIFE

Mary Wollstonecraft Shelley was the daughter of the celebrated feminist writer Mary Wollstonecraft and the radical philosopher William Godwin. Ten days after she was born, her mother died of puerperal fever, and for four years William raised his daughter and her half sister Fanny (Wollstonecraft's daughter with Gilbert Imlay) alone. From infancy, Mary was in the company not only of her philosopher father but also of his friends, among them the poet Samuel Taylor Coleridge and the essayists Mary and Charles Lamb.

Godwin apparently felt unfit to raise his daughters alone, and when he married Mary Jane Clairmont in 1801, he cited as one motivation his need for assistance with educating Mary and Fanny. Mary seems to have disliked her new stepmother, and whatever the truth of Clairmont's feelings about her stepdaughter, Mary certainly believed that her stepmother—who tended to privilege her own daughter, Jane—resented the bond between William and his daughter. As Mary grew into adolescence, she turned to a study of her mother's writings, often reading in the solitude of Wollstonecraft's grave in Saint Pancras churchyard. She read and absorbed not only Wollstonecraft's works but also William's 1798 memoir of his late wife; thus, before she reached adulthood, Mary was immersed in her parents' radical political beliefs and became aware that society frowned on those who espoused such views.

In 1812, English poet Percy Bysshe Shelley introduced himself to William, whom he admired; before long, Percy was a regular visitor at the Godwin establishment. Percy's frequent visits notwithstanding, Mary probably met him briefly only once or twice before 1814, when she returned from a lengthy visit to Scotland. Percy was a married man, but he and young Mary were drawn to each other. Within months of their first real meeting, and despite the disapproval of the Godwins, Mary and Percy eloped to France. With them was Jane Clairmont. The trio traveled through Europe for six weeks, after which they returned to England. The Godwins and the Shelleys were hostile to the irregular relationship that had developed between Mary and Percy, so the couple had to live on their own in a series of lodgings, often moving to evade their creditors.

LIFE'S WORK

Mary and Percy were together for nearly eight years, but they were unable to marry until 1816, when Percy's first wife, Harriet, committed suicide. That year was important to Mary Shelley for another reason: In June she began to write *Frankenstein*, which she completed the next year. The Shelleys' unconventional lifestyle left them vulnerable to criticism and social ostracism, and eventually, in 1818, they left England once again to escape the hostility and settled in Italy.

For Mary, the Italian years were eventful. She studied Italian and Spanish with her husband and learned Greek with the help of an aristocratic émigré. Percy also tutored Mary in Latin, and within two years she was collaborating with him on translations. Mary's efforts were not limited to the acquisition of language skills. She completed two works of fiction—the novella *Mathilda* (1818), the historical novel *Valperga: Or, The Life of Castruccio, Prince of Lucca* (written between 1818 and 1821), and possibly the short piece "Valerius: The Reanimated Roman." During those years, she also wrote two mythological dramas—*Proserpine* (1922) and *Midas* (1922)—in blank verse.

The Shelley marriage was not without problems. Although heir to a fortune, Percy only had an allowance while his father lived, and the young couple's financial worries followed them to Italy. Two of their four children died (their first child lived only eleven days). In addition, Mary succumbed to bouts of depression, possibly exacerbated by her husband's infatuations with other women, including Jane Clairmont—now called Claire—whose presence in the Shelley home was problematic. Having given up her daughter by George Gordon, Lord Byron, Claire embroiled the Shelleys in her quarrels with Byron about custody of the child. During the Shelleys' last year together, the marriage was in trouble, and the two were virtually estranged from one another. To compound their difficulties, in June, 1822, Mary suffered a miscarriage and nearly died, and her depression deepened.

Percy drowned in July, 1822, in a storm off the Italian coast, leaving Mary a penniless widow at twenty-four with a two-year-old son, Percy Florence. The poetry that she wrote in the months after her husband's death reveals the depth of her grief and her feelings of guilt about their estrangement in the year before the accident. After remaining in Italy for one year after her husband's death, Mary was forced to return to England by her financial difficulties and by the need to ensure her son's future as the Shelley heir. She spent the remaining twenty-nine years of her life working as a professional writer to support herself, her son, and her aging father and stepmother.

When Mary, having buried her husband's ashes in Rome, returned to England in 1823 to begin her professional writing career, she was already a published author. In addition to *Mounseer Nongtongpaw* (a satiric poem published in 1812, when she was fifteen) and *Frankenstein* (1818), she and Percy had published *History of a Six Weeks' Tour Through a Part of France, Switzerland, Germany, and Holland* (1817). *Valperga* (1823) was published shortly after her arrival in England.

Mary Wollstonecraft Shelley. (Library of Congress)

During a forty-year writing career, Mary produced a considerable body of literary work in a number of different genres: six novels and one novella; nineteen pieces of short fiction; travel narratives; short nonfiction articles in a variety of periodicals and other publications; biographies of scientific and literary figures in France, Italy, Spain, and Portugal; poetry; and drama. In addition, she edited and wrote introductions for two editions of Percy's poems as well as a collection of his essays and letters. She also published translations of works originally written in German and Italian. In the context of literary history, Mary's most important works are her novels and her nonfiction prose works.

Mary Shelley's most significant contribution to the history of the English novel are *Frankenstein* (1818), *The Last Man* (1826), and possibly *Valperga*. Her three other novels—*The Fortunes of Perkin Warbeck* (1830), *Lodore* (1835), and *Falkner* (1837)—were written much later, during the years when her literary efforts were focused on making money, and they are not as polished; nevertheless, these later novels are important elements of Shelley's oeuvre and should not be discounted.

Frankenstein, Shelley's best and most famous novel, was published when its author was only twenty-one. According to Shelley's journal, the novel was inspired by two 1816 events—a ghost-story-writing contest and a discussion of the possibility of employing electricity to "galvanize" a manufactured humanoid—that culminated in a nightmare from which Shelley awoke to begin *Frankenstein*. Although frequently classified as "horror fiction," *Frankenstein* is a more serious work than the popular label suggests. The novel is not only a provocative interrogation of scientific method but also an exploration of the nature of loneliness and the role of environment in shaping an individual's psyche.

Shelley's short fiction exists in the form of one novella—*Mathilda*—and several short stories, many of which were published in *The Keepsake*, a popular annual publication with silk or leather covers, gilt edges, engravings, and poetry and stories from popular authors. Much has been said about the autobiographical elements that appear in Shelley's short fiction, but her novella and tales can also be read as explorations of narrative form or as treatments of the tensions between the domestic sphere and the public sphere.

Although many agree that Shelley's most significant works are her novels, she also produced an important body of nonfiction of three distinct types: travel narrative, biography, and literary criticism and review. Between 1823 and 1844, she contributed to several major

FRANKENSTEIN MEETS HIS CREATION

The different accidents of life are not so changeable as the feelings of human nature. I had worked hard for nearly two years, for the sole purpose of infusing life into an inanimate body. For this I had deprived myself of rest and health. I had desired it with an ardour that far exceeded moderation; but now that I had finished, the beauty of the dream vanished, and breathless horror and disgust filled my heart. Unable to endure the aspect of the being I had created, I rushed out of the room and continued a long time traversing my bed-chamber, unable to compose my mind to sleep. At length lassitude succeeded to the tumult I had before endured, and I threw myself on the bed in my clothes, endeavouring to seek a few moments of forgetfulness. But it was in vain; I slept, indeed, but I was disturbed by the wildest dreams. I thought I saw Elizabeth, in the bloom of health, walking in the streets of Ingolstadt. Delighted and surprised, I embraced her, but as I imprinted the first kiss on her lips, they became livid with the hue of death; her features appeared to change, and I thought that I held the corpse of my dead mother in my arms; a shroud enveloped her form, and I saw the grave-worms crawling in the folds of the flannel. I started from my sleep with horror; a cold dew covered my forehead, my teeth chattered, and every limb became convulsed; when, by the dim and yellow light of the moon, as it forced its way through the window shutters, I beheld the wretch—the miserable monster whom I had created. He held up the curtain of the bed; and his eyes, if eyes they may be called, were fixed on me. His jaws opened, and he muttered some inarticulate sounds, while a grin wrinkled his cheeks. He might have spoken, but I did not hear; one hand was stretched out, seemingly to detain me, but I escaped and rushed downstairs. I took refuge in the courtyard belonging to the house which I inhabited, where I remained during the rest of the night, walking up and down in the greatest agitation, listening attentively, catching and fearing each sound as if it were to announce the approach of the demoniacal corpse to which I had so miserably given life.

Oh! No mortal could support the horror of that countenance. A mummy again endued with animation could not be so hideous as that wretch. I had gazed on him while unfinished; he was ugly then, but when those muscles and joints were rendered capable of motion, it became a thing such as even Dante could not have conceived. . . .

Source: Mary Wollstonecraft Shelley, *Frankenstein: Or, The Modern Prometheus* (London, 1818), chapter 5.

and some shorter pieces, including *Memoirs of William Godwin* in the 1831 edition of Godwin's *Caleb Williams*.

Although not strictly biography, Mary Shelley's prefaces and notes to the editions of Percy Shelley's work are key elements in the development of the Percy Shelley legend. Through her careful selection and arrangement of the works to be included in the editions, she constructs a distinctive version of Percy, one that privileges his talents and virtues and glosses over his radicalism. At the same time, Mary's prefaces and notes make up part of her literary criticism in that her commentary on Percy's poetry incorporates her ideas on the nature and functions of poetry and on poetic genres. Like Mary's annotations for the editions of her husband's poetry, her book reviews and essays on literary subjects are significant for their influence on the substance and shape of literary taste in nineteenth century England.

SIGNIFICANCE

Although known primarily as a novelist and founding mother of the science fiction genre, Mary Shelley's literary contributions are much more extensive than her popular reputation suggests. As a book reviewer and author of short prose for various literary journals and periodicals, she was one of the first modern professional literary critics. In her role as an early arbiter of popular literary taste, she and her fellow critics were influential in creating a literary canon that privileged English literary works.

Throughout her life, Shelley was conscious of her heritage as the daughter not only of William Godwin but also, and more especially, of Mary Wollstonecraft; Percy Shelley encouraged her to prove herself worthy of her family history. From her study of her mother's work, Mary Shelley absorbed ideas about independence and sexual freedom for women; from her father she received a progressive education embodying the ideals of the

periodicals, including the *Westminster Review*, *The Liberal*, and *London Magazine*, and completed several books. Her travel writing, which includes several short essays as well as *Six Weeks' Tour* and *Rambles in Germany and Italy* (1844), explores several ideas, including the distinction between a tourist and a traveler and the nature and manifestation of taste. Shelley's biographical work includes the three-volume *Lives of the Most Eminent Literary and Scientific Men of Italy, Spain, and Portugal* (1835-1837) and the two-volume *Lives of the Most Eminent Literary and Scientific Men of France* (1839),

French Revolution. However, Mary Shelley was also very much a product of her culture and time, and her work reflects the tensions she must have felt as she attempted to negotiate a compromise between the ideals of her early education and the conventions of nineteenth century English society.

—E. D. Huntley

FURTHER READING

Fisch, Audrey A., Anne K. Mellor, and Esther H. Schor, eds. *The Other Mary Shelley: Beyond Frankenstein.* New York: Oxford University Press, 1993. This is a valuable collection of critical essays that illuminate Shelley's major and less well-known works. The essays by Corbett, Favret, Paley, and Schor are particularly recommended.

Garrett, Martin. *Mary Shelley.* New York: Oxford University Press, 2003. This text provides a general overview for young-adult readers new to Shelley's work, discusses Shelley's early, formative years, and includes a rich collection of illustrations, with excerpts from diaries and letters. Part of the British Library Writers' Lives series.

Mellor, Anne K. *Mary Shelley: Her Life, Her Fiction, Her Monsters.* New York: Routledge, 1988. Mellor discusses Shelley's major works. Among other things, the book provides a discussion of *Frankenstein* in the context of early nineteenth century science and illuminates Percy Shelley's contributions to his wife's novel.

Poovey, Mary. *The Proper Lady and the Woman Writer: Ideology as Style in the Works of Mary Wollstonecraft, Mary Shelley, and Jane Austen.* Chicago: University of Chicago Press, 1984. Poovey places Shelley in the context of her contemporaries in late eighteenth and early nineteenth century England. Includes a particularly valuable discussion of Shelley's revisions of *Frankenstein* for the 1831 edition of that novel.

Schor, Esther, ed. *The Cambridge Companion to Mary Shelley.* New York: Cambridge University Press, 2003. Collection of essays analyzing Shelley's novels and other writing, including her work as an editor, travel writer, biographer, and cultural critic.

Seymour, Miranda. *Mary Shelley.* New York: Grove Press, 2000. Well-defined portrait of Shelley, who emerges as an intelligent and sometimes cantankerous woman.

Smith, Johanna. *Mary Shelley.* New York: Twayne, 1996. Smith provides an excellent and detailed overview of Shelley's writings arranged by genre and focusing on the political and cultural milieu in which Shelley lived and wrote.

Spark, Muriel. *Mary Shelley: A Biography.* New York: Dutton, 1987. Considered by many to be one of the best short biographies of Shelley, this crucial book reestablished Shelley as a serious writer whose work is worthy of critical attention.

St. Clair, William. *The Godwins and the Shelleys: A Biography of a Family.* Baltimore: Johns Hopkins University Press, 1989. A useful introduction to the radical tradition that shaped Shelley's life and career. Although the book provides a great deal more information on William Godwin than on the other principals, his life and activities provide the context for his daughter's development as a writer.

Sunstein, Emily. *Mary Shelley: Romance and Reality.* Boston: Little, Brown. 1989. Sunstein's book is the most complete biography of Shelley. The appendix provides detailed listings of works definitively identified as Shelley's as well as works that might be attributed to her; chapter notes explicitly identify key primary sources of information about Shelley's life and work.

Williams, John. *Mary Shelley: A Literary Life.* New York: St. Martin's Press, 2000. Comprehensive overview of Shelley's life and work, providing analysis of her seven novels, short stories, and other writings.

SEE ALSO: Lord Byron; Samuel Taylor Coleridge; Percy Bysshe Shelley.

RELATED ARTICLES in *Great Events from History: The Nineteenth Century, 1801-1900:* 1814: Scott Publishes *Waverley*; December, 1816: Rise of the Cockney School; 1842: Tennyson Publishes "Morte d'Arthur."

PERCY BYSSHE SHELLEY
English poet

In his zeal to renew the human spirit and to reform society, Shelley produced an impassioned, philosophically complex poetry suffused with prophetic vision.

BORN: August 4, 1792; Field Place, near Horsham, Sussex, England
DIED: July 8, 1822; at sea off Viareggio, Lucca (now in Italy)
AREA OF ACHIEVEMENT: Literature

EARLY LIFE

Percy Bysshe Shelley was the eldest of seven children of Timothy Shelley, a socially prominent country squire and sometime member of Parliament, and the former Elizabeth Pilford. Although there were eventually problems between the politically radical poet and his comparatively conventional father, Shelley's early homelife was both emotionally and physically comfortable. Shelley received an excellent education, first with a local clergyman, the Reverend Evan Edwards, and later at Sion House Academy (1802-1804), Eton (1804-1810), and, for a short time, Oxford (1810-1811). Supplementing this formal instruction with omnivorous reading, Shelley was rivaled for erudition among the English Romantic poets only by Samuel Taylor Coleridge. In addition to his extensive knowledge of literature, philosophy, and science, young Shelley purportedly dabbled in the occult, attempting on at least one occasion, according to some biographers, to communicate with the devil. The attempt was unsuccessful.

With abundant curly hair and facial features that might more accurately be described as pretty than handsome, the bookish Shelley was the object of much adolescent bullying during his days at Sion House and Eton, a circumstance that helps to explain his lifelong hatred of oppression. Part of this persecution was the result of the traditional hazing of underclassmen by upperclassmen and part an expression of the scorn directed against apparent weakness and actual eccentricity by the strong and the conventional. Because of the victimization he experienced directly and because of the more serious social and political inequities that he read about and witnessed, Shelley was a rebel against irresponsible power and unreflecting obedience to authority from early in his life, seeing in selfish strength and mindless conformity twin props to injustice.

Despite his zeal to change the world, Shelley's first publications were not manifestations of his rebelliousness but of his fascination with gothic horror. While still in his teens, he wrote and published a pair of gothic novels, *Zastrozzi: A Romance* (1810) and *St. Irvyne: Or, The Rosicrucian* (1810), neither of which made an impression on the reading public. A collaboration with his sister Elizabeth, *Original Poetry by Victor and Cazire* (1810), also contained much gothic material, including several pages plagiarized from the anonymous ballad collection *Tales of Terror* (1801).

After his matriculation at Oxford in April of 1810 and his acquaintance with fellow undergraduate Thomas Jefferson Hogg, Shelley's gothic urge gave way to iconoclasm, with dire consequences for his future. Having worked together on a handful of trifling compositions, Shelley and Hogg delivered to the printer toward the end of 1810 an unsigned tract entitled *The Necessity of Atheism*. Shelley sent copies to various English ecclesiastics and to virtually all the Oxford faculty, and after their authorship had been discovered, he and Hogg were expelled from the university, still largely a theological institution, on March 25, 1811.

Shelley moved about restlessly during the next few months, spending part of his time in London, where he renewed his acquaintance with sixteen-year-old Harriet Westbrook, a friend of his sister. Convinced that Harriet was a victim of authoritarian persecution, the impulsive Shelley fled with her to Edinburgh, where the two were married on August 28, 1811. Although the marriage was one of the great mistakes of Shelley's life, it was, at first, reasonably happy despite the disapproval of Shelley's father, already furious over the Oxford fiasco. Harriet accompanied the peripatetic Shelley from Edinburgh to York to Keswick to Dublin. When his pamphleteering and speechmaking among the Irish failed to stir their zeal for freedom, Shelley and Harriet moved temporarily to Wales and then to Lynmouth, Devon, where his political agitation brought him under government surveillance. In September of 1812, after a short return to Wales, Shelley, just turned twenty, traveled with his young wife back to London.

LIFE'S WORK

Shelley's purpose in going to London was to raise funds for a Welsh land-reclamation project, but its more important consequence was the formation of friendships with the publisher Thomas Hookham, who would soon print Shelley's first important poem, *Queen Mab: A Philosophical Poem* (1813), the poet Thomas Love Peacock, who would eventually inspire the brilliant "A Defence of Poetry," and the political philosopher William Godwin. Godwin, with whom Shelley had been corresponding since January, was the writer of *An Inquiry Concerning the Principles of Political Justice* (1793), the primary source of Shelley's egalitarian political thought.

After another short stay in Wales, during which much of *Queen Mab* was written and an attempt made on Shelley's life by a mysterious assailant, the Shelleys moved again to Ireland and from there back to London, where *Queen Mab* was printed—for private circulation among England's political radicals—in May of 1813. Heavily influenced by Godwinism, the poem attacks monarchy, capitalism, marriage, and other aspects of European civilization as Shelley knew it with a fervor that discouraged public distribution of the poem in reactionary England. In fact, when an unauthorized edition of the poem was released in 1821, its publisher was quickly imprisoned for his temerity.

The years immediately following the printing of *Queen Mab* were a period of chaos in Shelley's personal life, and for this reason, they were comparatively less productive than the extraordinary times still to come. Gradually realizing his incompatibility with Harriet, who had borne him a daughter in June of 1813 and would bear him a son in November of 1814, Shelley fell in love with the brilliant young Mary Godwin, much to the consternation of her generally freethinking father. The couple fled to France in July of 1814, returning to England in September. The scandal inspired by their elopement and by the birth of their daughter in February of 1815, a child who died within a month, increased their ostracism from respectable English society.

Sir Bysshe Shelley, the poet's grandfather, died in early January of 1815, and in June, Timothy Shelley, almost certainly to minimize complications in the transfer of estate properties, granted the wayward Percy a one-thousand-pound yearly allowance, 20 percent of which was to go to Harriet. Freed at last from severe financial problems, Percy and Mary rented accommodations in the vicinity of Bishopsgate, where Shelley worked intensely on *Alastor: Or, The Spirit of Solitude, and Other Poems*. When it appeared in February of 1816, a few days after the birth to Mary of William Shelley, the book included its author's name, the first of Shelley's works to do so. Its title poem is a symbolic narrative of a young poet's destruction when he undertakes an impossible quest for a

self-generated ideal. The poem seems at least partially to be a warning to the idealistic Shelley himself.

Mary and Percy, along with Mary's half sister Claire Clairmont, began their second trip to the Continent in May of 1816. They arrived at Lake Geneva soon thereafter, where they hoped to encounter Lord Byron, with whom Claire had recently become involved and whose daughter, Allegra, she would bear in the following year. Despite the clash between Byron's dark cynicism and Shelley's customary idealism, the two poets got on well together, and while the Alps were inspiring Byron's gloomy *The Prisoner of Chillon* and portions of *Childe Harold's Pilgrimage* (1812-1818), Shelley was composing the "Hymn to Intellectual Beauty" and *Mont Blanc* (1817). Suggesting a transformed Wordsworthianism, Shelley's two poems imply a nonanthropomorphic something whose power lies behind all things but who can be known only indirectly through one's own power of creative intellect.

Following the Shelleys' return to England on September 8, 1816, two tragedies occurred that haunted the poet for the remainder of his life. On October 9, Fanny Imlay, another of Mary's half sisters, took a fatal dose of laudanum, and on November 9, Harriet jumped into the Serpentine. Her body was recovered on December 10. Percy and Mary were married on December 30, but this attempt to make their relationship socially acceptable failed. Shelley was declared an unsuitable father for his two children, and their care was entrusted to a Dr. and Mrs. Hume.

Despite the emotional trauma of this period, Shelley became acquainted with Leigh Hunt, the liberal editor of *The Examiner*, literary parodist Horace Smith, essayist Charles Lamb, critic William Hazlitt, and poet John Keats. He also achieved a reconciliation of sorts with his father-in-law, Godwin. His London friends, new and old, provided ample companionship for the Shelleys during visits to their latest home, this time in Great Marlowe, where they lived from February of 1817 until February of the following year and where their daughter Clara was born on September 2.

Through this period, neither Shelley nor his wife neglected their writing. While Mary completed *Frankenstein* (1818), inspired by an evening of ghost stories at Byron's villa on Lake Geneva the previous August, Percy wrote two political tracts, *A Proposal for Putting Reform to the Vote Throughout the Kingdom* (1817) and *An Address to the People on the Death of the Princess Charlotte* (1817?), as well as the longest of his poems, *The Revolt of Islam* (1818). Originally published as *Laon*

SHELLEY'S "HYMN TO INTELLECTUAL BEAUTY"

The awful shadow of some unseen Power
Floats though unseen among us; visiting
This various world with as inconstant wing
As summer winds that creep from flower to flower;
Like moonbeams that behind some piny mountain shower,
It visits with inconstant glance
Each human heart and countenance;
Like hues and harmonies of evening,
Like clouds in starlight widely spread,
Like memory of music fled,
Like aught that for its grace may be
Dear, and yet dearer for its mystery.

Spirit of BEAUTY, that dost consecrate
With thine own hues all thou dost shine upon
Of human thought or form, where art thou gone?
Why dost thou pass away and leave our state,
This dim vast vale of tears, vacant and desolate?
Ask why the sunlight not for ever
Weaves rainbows o'er yon mountain-river,
Why aught should fail and fade that once is shown,
Why fear and dream and death and birth
Cast on the daylight of this earth
Such gloom, why man has such a scope
For love and hate, despondency and hope?

No voice from some sublimer world hath ever
To sage or poet these responses given:
Therefore the names of Demon, Ghost, and Heaven,
Remain the records of their vain endeavour:
Frail spells whose utter'd charm might not avail to sever,
From all we hear and all we see,
Doubt, chance and mutability.
Thy light alone like mist o'er mountains driven,
Or music by the night-wind sent
Through strings of some still instrument,
Or moonlight on a midnight stream,
Gives grace and truth to life's unquiet dream.

Love, Hope, and Self-esteem, like clouds depart
And come, for some uncertain moments lent.
Man were immortal and omnipotent,
Didst thou, unknown and awful as thou art,
Keep with thy glorious train firm state within his heart.
Thou messenger of sympathies,

That wax and wane in lovers' eyes;
Thou, that to human thought art nourishment,
Like darkness to a dying flame!
Depart not as thy shadow came,
Depart not—lest the grave should be,
Like life and fear, a dark reality.

While yet a boy I sought for ghosts, and sped
Through many a listening chamber, cave and ruin,
And starlight wood, with fearful steps pursuing
Hopes of high talk with the departed dead.
I call'd on poisonous names with which our youth is fed;
I was not heard; I saw them not;
When musing deeply on the lot
Of life, at that sweet time when winds are wooing
All vital things that wake to bring
News of birds and blossoming,
Sudden, thy shadow fell on me;
I shriek'd, and clasp'd my hands in ecstasy!

I vow'd that I would dedicate my powers
To thee and thine: have I not kept the vow?
With beating heart and streaming eyes, even now
I call the phantoms of a thousand hours
Each from his voiceless grave: they have in vision'd bowers
Of studious zeal or love's delight
Outwatch'd with me the envious night:
They know that never joy illum'd my brow
Unlink'd with hope that thou wouldst free
This world from its dark slavery,
That thou, O awful LOVELINESS,
Wouldst give whate'er these words cannot express.

The day becomes more solemn and serene
When noon is past; there is a harmony
In autumn, and a lustre in its sky,
Which through the summer is not heard or seen,
As if it could not be, as if it had not been!
Thus let thy power, which like the truth
Of nature on my passive youth
Descended, to my onward life supply
Its calm, to one who worships thee,
And every form containing thee,
Whom, SPIRIT fair, thy spells did bind
To fear himself, and love all human kind.

and Cythna (1817), *The Revolt of Islam* tells the story of a revolution carried out without malice and eventually defeated by the ruthless reactionary forces of oppression. The poem implies, as does much of Shelley's work, that the task of reforming the world will meet with many temporary defeats before its final triumph and that true revolutionaries must operate out of a spirit of love rather than a spirit of hatred, even if death is the reward of such virtue.

On March 11, 1818, the Shelleys left England for the third time, an exile from which the poet would never return. After traveling overland to Milan, Shelley corresponded tactfully with George Gordon, Lord Byron about Byron's infant daughter Allegra, but the aristocratic poet, involved in a period of monumental debauchery in Venice and wanting to avoid Claire at all costs, refused to claim his daughter. He eventually agreed to take her from the hands of her nurse Elise, but the hopes of Claire and the Shelleys that Allegra would win her father over and become a beloved member of the Byron family were never realized. She would die of typhus on April 20, 1822, in a convent nursery near Ravenna, Italy, where Byron had placed her.

After leaving Milan, the Shelleys took up residence in Leghorn for a month, followed by a two-month stay in the Appenines. Percy was working on a translation of Plato's *Symposium* at about this time and was completing *Rosalind and Helen* (1819), a poetic narrative of the trials and triumphs of love. A reunion of Shelley and Byron at Venice in late summer provided material for *Julian and Maddalo: A Conversation* (1824), primarily a poetic dialogue between a Shelleyan idealist and a Byronic cynic. Most of the poem was written at a villa in Este lent to the Shelleys by Byron, as were much of the "Lines Written Among the Euganean Hills," a topographic poem about personal and social regeneration, and the first act of Shelley's great poetic drama *Prometheus Unbound* (1820). *Prometheus Unbound* was ultimately to become Shelley's deepest statement on the transforming power of love and forgiveness in a world dominated by vengeful hatred.

Shelley himself was in need of forgiveness during the Este period. Having been forced by a lie to Byron to ask Mary to make a precipitate journey to Este, Shelley inadvertently caused the death of his frail daughter Clara, barely a year old. Under the stress of travel, Clara developed dysentery and died at Venice on September 24, 1818. The grief-stricken Mary never entirely forgot this apparent lapse in her husband's concern for his family's welfare.

On November 5, 1818, the Shelleys left Este and, after visiting Rome, lived for several weeks in Naples. They then returned to Rome, where Shelley wrote the second and third acts of *Prometheus Unbound* and began *The Cenci* (1819), which he finished in August at Leghorn. If *Prometheus Unbound* is Shelley's profoundest statement on the power of love to save and purify, *The Cenci*, a drama influenced by Jacobean tragedy, is his strongest delineation of the power of hatred to corrupt. The play narrates the downfall of Beatrice Cenci, whose participation in a plot to kill the father who has raped her destroys her soul in a way that her father's crime alone could never have done.

The move to Leghorn during the composition of *The Cenci*, at least partially a reaction to the latest unhappy episode in the Shelleys' lives, the death of their son William in Rome on June 7, 1819, also produced *The Masque of Anarchy*, an allegory of political oppression inspired by the slaughter of peaceful demonstrators for reform in Manchester on August 16, 1819, the infamous Peterloo Massacre. Although intended for quick publication in Leigh Hunt's *The Examiner*, the poem was so volatile that it was not presented to the public until 1832.

From Leghorn, the restless Shelleys moved to Florence, settling in during October of 1819. On November 12, Mary gave birth to Percy Florence Shelley, her only child to survive to adulthood. Also at Florence, Percy finished *Peter Bell the Third*, a Wordsworthian parody that remained unpublished until 1839, and the final act of *Prometheus Unbound*. Eventually published in the *Prometheus Unbound* volume was another of the poems of the Florence period, the magnificent "Ode to the West Wind," Shelley's visionary statement of the revolutionary's faith that a new and better world will arise when a corrupt world falls into ruin.

The Shelleys' next move was to Pisa, where they lived during much of the first half of 1820. They then spent several weeks of the summer at Leghorn, moving from there to the Baths of San Giuliano and returning to Pisa on October 31. The poems of this period include several more of those that appeared in the *Prometheus Unbound* volume, among them "The Sensitive Plant," "The Cloud," and "To a Skylark." All three poems explore humankind's mingled compatibility and incompatibility with the sublunary natural world. Two other products of 1820 were *Oedipus Tyrannus: Or, Swellfoot the Tyrant*, a farcical drama satirizing contemporary English politics, and *The Witch of Atlas*, a seriocomic allegory of the presence of divine beauty in the realm of mutability. *Oedipus Tyrannus* was anonymously published in 1820 and was immediately suppressed, while *The Witch of Atlas* appeared in the *Posthumous Poems of Percy Bysshe Shelley* (1824).

The last two years of Shelley's life, spent mainly at Pisa, were among his most productive. Buoyed by the companionship of such friends as Thomas Medwin, Edward and Jane Williams, Lord Byron, and Edward Trelawny, all members at one time or another of the famous Pisan Circle, Shelley wrote both inspired poetry and inspired prose. In January and February of 1821, after visiting Teresa Viviani in the Convent of St. Anna, where her father had sent her until he could find her an appropriate husband, Shelley composed *Epipsychidion* (1821), a poem of the psyche's yearning for its ideal mate. The poem was published anonymously in May of 1821.

In February and March of the same year, in answer to Thomas Love Peacock's "The Four Ages of Poetry," Shelley wrote "A Defence of Poetry," an eloquent essay on the poet's function as prophetic visionary, but that work did not appear in print until 1840. In May and June, after hearing of the death of Keats, he produced *Adonais: An Elegy on the Death of John Keats* (1821), among the finest of all English elegies and a passionate affirmation of the immortality of artistic genius. In October, he wrote *Hellas: A Lyrical Drama*, a poetic drama inspired by the War of Greek Independence and dedicated to Prince Alexander Mavrocordato, a Pisan friend who had left to fight on the side of the revolutionaries. Published in February of 1822, *Hellas* was the last of Shelley's works to appear during his lifetime.

In the final months before his death, Shelley was working on the drama *Charles the First* (1824) and on the dark dream vision *The Triumph of Life* (1824). He finished neither. Occupying many of his hours during this period, too, was a daredevil fascination with sailing. Many of his poems include comparisons of the imaginative soul to a boat moving across an expansive sea, and though Shelley had never learned to swim, the dangerous freedom of the open ocean possessed an irresistible appeal for him. With a cabin boy, Charles Vivian, and his friend Edward Williams, Shelley set sail during threatening weather on July 8, 1822, for San Terenzo from Leghorn in his new boat, the *Don Juan*. The bodies of the three washed ashore several days later. Shelley was not yet thirty years old.

SIGNIFICANCE

Shelley was a poet for whom the millennial promise of the French Revolution had not been realized but might still be achieved. He despised the reactionary politics of the postrevolutionary period and worked tirelessly to inspire that transformation of the human soul that might prepare the way for the era of freedom, peace, and love that he so deeply desired. He saw the poet as reforming prophet, capable of energizing the human spirit by giving it glimpses of perfect, eternal truth. He yearned for the ideal and desperately hoped for the salvation of the mundane.

Since his death in Italy at the age of twenty-nine, Shelley has been viewed as the symbolic embodiment of youthful rebellion and unvanquished benevolence for generations of liberal reformers, Although they have not produced a world equal to his vision of a new Golden Age, they have achieved, often under his direct influence, some of his most cherished goals.

—Robert H. O'Connor

FURTHER READING

Baker, Carlos. *Shelley's Major Poetry: The Fabric of a Vision*. Princeton, N.J.: Princeton University Press, 1948. A pioneering and eminently successful attempt to present a unified reading of Shelley's most important poems. Weaving intellectual biography together with extensive analyses of individual works, Baker treats Shelley as a philosophical visionary.

Bieri, James. *Percy Bysshe Shelley: A Biography. Youth's Unextinguished Fire, 1792-1816*. Newark: University of Delaware Press, 2004.

_____. *Percy Bysshe Shelley: A Biography. Exile of an Unfulfilled Renown, 1816-1822*. Newark: University of Delaware Press, 2005. This two-volume biography presents new insights into Shelley's family relationships and life. Bieri, a psychologist, explains the relationship between Shelley's complex personality and his poetry.

Blunden, Edmund. *Shelley: A Life Story*. London: Oxford University Press, 1965. A readable, intelligent biography of medium length. Excellent for gaining an understanding of the historical context of Shelley's life and work.

Curran, Stuart. "Percy Bysshe Shelley." In *The English Romantic Poets: A Review of Research and Criticism*, edited by Frank Jordan. New York: Modern Language Association of America, 1985. A description and evaluation of scholarly work on Shelley. A standard source for any serious student of the poet.

_____. *Shelley's Annus Mirabilis: The Maturing of an Epic Vision*. San Marino, Calif.: Huntington Library, 1975. A discussion by one of the century's foremost Shelley scholars of the writings produced from late 1818 to early 1820. Curran's premise is that Shelley fully embraced the vocation of poet during this key period and dedicated himself to the arduous task of creating a poetic vision worthy of standing beside those of the epic visionaries of the past. The breadth of Shelley's sources is voluminously documented.

Holmes, Richard. *Shelley: The Pursuit*. New York: New York Review Books, 2003. An excellent biography, originally published in 1974, that meticulously re-creates the details of Shelley's life. In contrast to some biographers who depict Shelley as bland and ethereal, Holmes describes the poet as "a darker and more earthy, crueler and more capable figure."

Reiman, Donald H. *Percy Bysshe Shelley*. New York: Twayne, 1969. An excellent condensed analysis of Shelley's life and writings. Includes a useful three-page chronology of major events and a six-page selected bibliography. Especially worthwhile for the beginning student.

Shelley, Percy Bysshe. *Shelley's Poetry and Prose: Authoritative Texts and Criticism*. Edited by Donald H.

Reiman and Sharon B. Powers. New York: W. W. Norton, 1977. Authoritatively edited texts of nearly all Shelley's important works, with informative notes and a generous selection of essays by the critics.

Wasserman, Earl R. *Shelley: A Critical Reading*. Baltimore: Johns Hopkins University Press, 1971. A book of uneven brilliance that lacks the unity and consistency of Baker's volume but is highly original and strongly recommended for the advanced student looking for intellectual challenge.

White, Newman Ivey. *Shelley*. 2 vols. New York: Alfred A. Knopf, 1947. Despite its date of publication, this compendiously detailed study remains the standard scholarly biography. Extensively endnoted and indexed.

SEE ALSO: Lord Byron; Samuel Taylor Coleridge; John Keats; Mary Wollstonecraft Shelley; William Wordsworth.

RELATED ARTICLE in *Great Events from History: The Nineteenth Century, 1801-1900:* December, 1816: Rise of the Cockney School.

WILLIAM TECUMSEH SHERMAN
American military leader

Sherman was one of the architects of the Union victory in the Civil War and a significant contributor to the development of modern warfare. He was also a leader in the late nineteenth century Indian wars in the American West.

BORN: February 8, 1820; Lancaster, Ohio
DIED: February 14, 1891; New York, New York
ALSO KNOWN AS: Tecumseh Sherman (birth name); Cump; Uncle Billy
AREA OF ACHIEVEMENT: Military

EARLY LIFE

William Tecumseh Sherman was born Tecumseh Sherman. His father, Charles R. Sherman, was a lawyer and Ohio supreme court justice. His mother, Mary Hoyt, was a graduate of an eastern school for women. They migrated from Connecticut to Ohio in 1811 and produced there a family of eleven children, including later senator and federal cabinet member John Sherman. Tecumseh (Cump) was their sixth child.

When Tecumseh was nine years old, his father died suddenly, and his family was broken up. He was taken up

the street to live with the family of Thomas Ewing, later a U.S. senator and a cabinet member. There he was baptized in the Roman Catholic Church and received the Christian name William to go with his Indian one. From that moment he was William Tecumseh Sherman. Ewing never adopted him but always treated him like a son.

Sherman had a happy childhood, enjoying his friends and relatives and often participating in innocent pranks. He received the best education Lancaster had to offer and, at the age of sixteen, Ewing arranged a West Point appointment for him. Sherman endured the military academy boredom and was graduated sixth in his 1840 class.

During these early years, Sherman came to admire his foster father and adopt many of his Whig Party attitudes. At the same time, he always felt a need to prove himself capable of survival without Ewing's help. At West Point, he accepted the aristocratic concept of the superiority of the professional soldier over the volunteer. Sherman came to view his military friends as his family and throughout his life always felt most comfortable around them.

Upon his graduation, Sherman received a commission in the artillery and assignment to Florida, where he participated in the Second Seminole War. Though combat was rare, he came to see the Indians at first hand and developed the mixture of admiration and repugnance toward them that he was to hold all of his life. In March, 1842, he was sent to Fort Morgan, in Mobile Bay, where he first experienced the pleasures of polite society. His June 1, 1842, transfer to Fort Moultrie, near Charleston, allowed him to continue his socializing, of which he soon tired. For four years, he lived a boring existence, brightened only by his passion for painting, a furlough back to Ohio highlighted by his first trip down the Mississippi River, and investigative duty in the area of his later march on Atlanta. He also became engaged to Ellen Ewing, his foster sister, with whom he had corresponded since his 1836 departure for West Point. Sherman never painted much after he left Fort Moultrie in South Carolina, but all these other experiences were to have a profound effect on his later life.

When the Mexican War erupted, Sherman hoped to participate in the fighting. He was instead sent to Pittsburgh on recruiting duty. He chafed under his bad luck and jumped at the chance to travel around the Horn to California. By the time he arrived, however, the war there was over, and he found himself adjutant to Colonel Richard B. Mason, spending long hours battling correspondence, not Mexicans. He became depressed. The 1849 discovery of gold provided him with new excitement, and he absorbed all he could of the gold fever, though the inflation almost ruined him. In 1850, he was sent East with messages for General Winfield Scott, and on May 1 he married Ellen Ewing. Their wedding was an important Washington social event, as Thomas Ewing was then a member of President Zachary Taylor's cabinet.

During the decade of the 1850's, Sherman fathered six children and tried unsuccessfully to support them. From 1850 to 1853, he served in the Army Commissary Service in St. Louis and New Orleans, at which time he resigned his commission to open a branch bank in San Francisco for some St. Louis friends. The pressures of banking in the boom and bust California economy, his chronic asthma, and a homesick wife who wanted to return to her father's house caused Sherman to spend the years from 1853 to 1857 in recurring depression. When the bank closed in 1857, he took on as personal debts the unsuccessful investments he had made for army friends.

Sherman carried that financial burden to New York, where he opened another branch bank only to see it fail during the Panic of 1857. He was crushed; no matter what he tried, he met failure. Instead of establishing inde-

William Tecumseh Sherman. (Library of Congress)

pendence from his foster father, he repeatedly had to look to him for support. Thomas Ewing continued to hope that Sherman would agree to manage his salt interests in Ohio, but Sherman refused. Instead, he went to Kansas as part of a law and real estate business, along with two Ewing sons.

The business failed, and Sherman desperately tried to return to the army for his economic (and psychological) salvation. There were no openings, but an officer friend told him about a new Louisiana military seminary looking for a superintendent. Sherman applied and became founder of what became modern Louisiana State University. When secession came, duty persuaded him he had to leave the job and the people he had come to love. He believed that he had to sacrifice his economic well-being for the sake of the Union.

LIFE'S WORK

After leaving Louisiana in February, 1861, Sherman became angry over alleged northern nonchalance toward southern secession. He found a position with a St. Louis street railway company, determined to remain aloof from the national crisis until he could see a change. Thomas

Ewing and John Sherman urged him to reenter the Union army, and, through their efforts, he was named a colonel of the Thirteenth Infantry Regiment in May, 1861. He stood over six feet tall, with long legs and arms, piercing blue eyes, sandy red hair that seemed always to be mussed, a grizzly reddish beard, and a generally unkempt appearance. He spoke rapidly and often, his mind able to reach conclusions before his charmed listeners understood his premises.

Before he could serve with the Thirteenth Infantry, he was appointed to a staff position under Winfield Scott and, in July, 1861, commanded a brigade at Bull Run. He saw that fiasco as further proof that the North was not taking the war seriously enough.

Sherman was happy to leave chaotic Washington for Kentucky to help Fort Sumter hero Robert Anderson organize the Union war effort there. Upon arrival, he quickly convinced himself that the Confederate forces were much larger than his were and that it was only a matter of time before they would overrun him. He sank into depression and lashed out at newspaper reporters for allegedly publicizing his weaknesses. At his own request, he was transferred to Missouri in November, 1861, where his outspoken negativity convinced many that he was unbalanced. He took a twenty-day leave in December, 1861, and was mortified to see his sanity unfairly questioned in the press. When he returned to duty and was given command over a training facility in Missouri, his depression deepened and he even contemplated suicide. The Union war effort and his own career seemed hopeless.

Sherman's transfer to Paducah, Kentucky, in February, 1862, and his association with the successful Ulysses S. Grant slowly lifted his spirits. He distinguished himself as a division commander in the bloody Battle of Shiloh in April, 1862, and he then defended Grant and other generals against press and political criticism of their roles in the battle. When he was promoted to major general of volunteers and took part in Henry W. Halleck's capture of Corinth in May, 1862, he began to believe that the Union effort had hope and he could play an important role in any success.

In July, 1862, Grant appointed Sherman to the post of military governor of recently captured Memphis. Sherman was able to use both his banking and military experience to govern that hotbed of secession sentiment. It was there that the activities of Confederate guerrillas caused him to see at first hand that the war was not simply a contest between professional soldiers. The general populace had to be controlled if the Union effort was to

be successful. When guerrillas fired on a boat in the Mississippi River, Sherman leveled a nearby town. He had long recognized the determination of the Southern populace, and he now began to see that only a destruction of this stubborn intensity would resolve the conflict in the Union's favor. He would utilize this insight at the appropriate time.

In December, 1862, Sherman led an unsuccessful assault on the heights above Vicksburg. When the press resuscitated the insanity charge against him, he court-martialed a reporter, the only such event in American history. The trial, though it might have been an excellent exposition of the almost inevitable conflict between the military and the press in wartime, proved to be little more than a conflict of personality. It settled little.

Sherman was part of Grant's enormous army that captured Vicksburg in July, 1863, and he was made brigadier general in the regular army as a reward. He became commander of the Army of the Tennessee when Grant became supreme commander in the West; he participated in the successful November lifting of the Confederate siege at Chattanooga. In January, 1864, he commanded the Meridian, Mississippi, expedition, which showed him yet again the effectiveness of the destructive activity he was later to use during his March to the Sea.

In the spring of 1864, Grant moved East to become general-in-chief of all Union armies, and Sherman took command over Western forces. On May 5, 1864, Grant attacked Lee in Virginia, and Sherman took on Joseph E. Johnston in Georgia. After first organizing railroads to supply his troops, Sherman battled Johnston throughout the spring and summer of 1864, slowly but inexorably pushing the Confederates from the Chattanooga region toward Atlanta. Jefferson Davis became nervous at Johnston's constant retreat and replaced him with offensive-minded John Bell Hood. The new Confederate commander attacked Sherman and was defeated. Atlanta fell in September, in time to influence the reelection of Abraham Lincoln that November.

Sherman then showed the Confederates that war had indeed become total. He ordered the civilian evacuation of Atlanta. When his order was met with shocked protests, he responded: "War is cruelty, and you cannot refine it." He did not: In November, he began his March to the Sea, revolutionizing warfare by cutting himself off from his base of supplies, living off the countryside, and destroying goods and property. His aim was to convince the Confederates that their war effort was doomed. He became the founder of psychological warfare. On December 21, 1864, his army reached Savannah and made contact with the Atlantic fleet. His presentation of the Georgia city to Lincoln as a Christmas present electrified the North.

On February 1, 1865, Sherman began his march through the Carolinas. On April 17, Johnston and his Confederate forces surrendered at Durham Station, North Carolina. Sherman, who had retained his affection for Southerners throughout the war and had only conducted his total warfare as the most efficient way to end the hostilities quickly, demonstrated his feelings in the peace agreement he made with Johnston. He negotiated political matters, neglected to insist that slavery was over, and, in general, wrote an agreement favorable to the South. In Washington, the administration, just then reeling from the assassination of Lincoln, was shocked. Secretary of War Edwin Stanton and General Henry W. Halleck led the opposition to the agreement, and Sherman was forced to change it, suffering sharp criticism from both the public and the press.

With the war over, Sherman became commander of troops in the West. He fought the Indians and helped construct the transcontinental railroad. When Grant became president in 1869, Sherman became commanding general, a position he held until his retirement in 1883. His tenure was filled with controversy as he battled secretaries of war and Congress over his authority, his salary, and sufficient appropriation for the troops. When he published his memoirs in 1875, the blunt directness of those two volumes created a controversy, including a bitter exchange with Jefferson Davis.

From his retirement in 1883 until his death in 1891, Sherman kept busy attending veterans' reunions and the theater, while also becoming a popular after-dinner speaker. In 1884, he categorically refused to run for the presidency, establishing a standard that allegedly reluctant office seekers have been measured against ever since. In 1886, he and his family moved from St. Louis to New York. On February 14, 1891, he died from pneumonia.

SIGNIFICANCE

William Tecumseh Sherman was one of the leaders of the successful Union war effort that prevented the disruption of the United States. He helped introduce the nation and the world to the concept of total war, his Civil War activities serving as a harbinger of the kind of conflict to be fought in the twentieth century. He devised his mode of warfare as a way to end the hostilities quickly, but it helped prolong southern animosity toward the North into the twentieth century. However, when

Sherman toured the South in 1879, he received a friendly greeting.

Sherman's life, apart from his Civil War years, is important in itself. Before the war, he attended West Point with many of the other military leaders of the Mexican and Civil wars. He served in the army in Florida during the Second Seminole War. In California, he composed a report to President James K. Polk that announced the discovery of gold and helped set off the famous gold rush of 1849. During the 1850's, as a banker, he was one of San Francisco's leading businesspeople during its formative years. In 1860, he helped found what is modern Louisiana State University. After the war, Sherman's tenure as general-in-chief of the United States Army from 1869 to 1883 allowed him to influence the direction of such events as the Indian Wars, Reconstruction, and the disputed election of 1876. Thus, Sherman influenced the development of American society throughout his life. He was one of the major figures of the nineteenth century.

—John F. Marszalek

FURTHER READING

Athearn, Robert G. *William Tecumseh Sherman and the Settlement of the West*. Norman: University of Oklahoma Press, 1956. A thorough study of Sherman's participation in the postwar Indian troubles and his role in the construction of the transcontinental railroad. Sherman was neither as harsh toward the Indians as the West desired nor as lenient as the East wished. He believed that the completion of the railroad would force the hostile Indians onto reservations.

Bailey, Anne J. *War and Ruin: William T. Sherman and the Savannah Campaign*. Wilmington, Del.: Scholarly Resources, 2003. Chronicles Sherman's March to the Sea, from its inception in Atlanta to its culmination in Savannah, describing its impact upon Georgians. Bailey contends that the physical damage was less severe than the psychological horror inflicted by the march; the campaign depleted Southerners' morale and spurred Confederate defeat.

Barrett, John G. *Sherman's March Through the Carolinas*. Chapel Hill: University of North Carolina Press, 1956. A detailed military history of Sherman's final campaign through North and South Carolina. Sherman reluctantly put his concept of total war into practice during this march from Savannah, Georgia, to Raleigh, North Carolina. His army inflicted special punishment on South Carolina because the soldiers blamed the Palmetto State for starting the war.

Glatthaar, Joseph T. *The March to the Sea and Beyond: Sherman's Troops in the Savannah and Carolinas Campaigns*. New York: New York University Press, 1985. An excellent analysis of the makeup and attitudes of the common soldier in Sherman's army during his marches. The author analyzes the soldiers' views about their cause, black Southerners, white Southerners, camp life, and pillaging.

Kennett, Lee. *Sherman: A Soldier's Life*. New York: HarperCollins, 2001. Generally sympathetic biography, focusing on Sherman's military career, including descriptions of his military training and Civil War battles.

Lewis, Lloyd. *Sherman: Fighting Prophet*. New York: Harcourt, Brace, 1932. Though dated and written without the benefit of all the now available Sherman documentation, this is still a valuable and very readable biography. It puts special emphasis on Thomas Ewing's influence on his foster son. The vast bulk of the book details the Civil War years; coverage of the postwar years is brief.

Liddell Hart, Basil H. *Sherman: Soldier, Realist, American*. New York: Harcourt, Brace, 1958. A fine study of Sherman's Civil War military activities by a leading military historian. The author states that Sherman was far ahead of his time and that later generations of military men might have profited from his example had they paid attention.

Marszalek, John F. *Sherman's Other War: The General and the Civil War Press*. Memphis, Tenn.: Memphis State University Press, 1981. A thorough account of Sherman's battles with reporters during the war, this study also contains an extended analysis of his personality during this period. Argues that Sherman fought the press in a constitutional battle formed more by personality than by First Amendment principles.

Merrill, James M. *William Tecumseh Sherman*. Skokie, Ill.: Rand McNally, 1971. A detailed popular biography that has the benefit of the major Sherman manuscript collections. It discusses all aspects of Sherman's life but is especially valuable for its coverage of his postwar years.

Sherman, William T. *Memoirs of General William T. Sherman*, 2 vols. New York: D. Appleton, 1875. Reprint. Introduction by William S. McFeely. New York: Da Capo Press, 1984. Sherman's controversial and absorbing account of his life from 1846 to the end of the Civil War, originally published in 1875. This is an essential source for gaining an understanding of Sherman's perception of the battles in which he participated and the leaders with and against whom he fought.

SEE ALSO: George A. Custer; Jefferson Davis; Ulysses S. Grant; Abraham Lincoln; James K. Polk; Winfield Scott; Edwin M. Stanton; Zachary Taylor; Tecumseh.

RELATED ARTICLES in *Great Events from History: The Nineteenth Century, 1801-1900:* July 1, 1863-November 25, 1863: Battles of Gettysburg, Vicksburg, and Chattanooga; November 15, 1864-April 18, 1865: Sherman Marches Through Georgia and the Carolinas; December 21, 1866: Fetterman Massacre; November 27, 1868: Washita River Massacre; c. 1871-1883: Great American Buffalo Slaughter; June 27, 1874-June 2, 1875: Red River War.

HENRY SIDGWICK
English educator

A proponent of higher education for women and an advocate of research into paranormal phenomena, Sidgwick attempted in philosophy to reconcile an intuitive approach to morality with that of utilitarianism. His reasoned defense of the resulting ethical method produced one of the most significant works on ethics in English, the capstone of nineteenth century British moral philosophy.

BORN: May 31, 1838; Skipton, Yorkshire, England
DIED: August 28, 1900; Terling, Essex, England
AREAS OF ACHIEVEMENT: Philosophy, education, women's rights

EARLY LIFE

Henry Sidgwick was the son of William and Mary (Crofts) Sidgwick, both from northern England. His father, an Anglican clergyman and headmaster of the Skipton, Yorkshire, grammar school, died in 1841. Henry's early life was characterized by frequent moves (which apparently brought on a kind of stammer that never left him), but in 1852 Henry was sent to Rugby School; the rest of the family, his mother and three other surviving children, settled in Rugby the following year.

Sidgwick was strongly influenced in his early life by one of his Rugby masters, Edward White Benson, a cousin nine years older than he. Benson soon joined the Sidgwick household; he would later marry Sidgwick's sister, Mary, and would be the archbishop of Canterbury from 1883 until the year of his death. The precocious Henry came to idolize his cousin and followed his advice by enrolling at Trinity College, Cambridge, after his graduation from Rugby in 1855. Cambridge was to be his home for the rest of his life.

Sidgwick's early university experience brought a host of academic awards, and as an undergraduate he was elected to the Apostles Society. The Apostles were dedicated to the pursuit of truth, wherever it might be found, and Sidgwick found himself taken by the spirit of honest inquiry into religion, society, and philosophy. He would devote his life to the great philosophical questions, seeking always for honesty and truth to triumph over rhetoric. Indeed, Sidgwick's writing is characterized by a kind of zealous balance, the author being at pains to give each aspect of an argument or counterargument its due.

Some readers of Sidgwick have taken this balancing effort as a fault and have yearned for the simple dogmatic

statement that Sidgwick was loathe to make. He was not a system builder in philosophy; his was the task of honest elucidation and tentative judgment.

In curious contrast to the stodgy feel of his major works, Sidgwick the man was a witty conversationalist (using his stammer at times as a dramatic device) and a lover of poetry. Small in stature, his large silken beard flapping in the breeze as he ran along the streets of Cambridge to his lectures, he was vigorous, sturdy, and good-humored. The academic life suited him perfectly.

LIFE'S WORK

Sidgwick was twenty-one in 1859. In that year, his sister married Edward Benson; Henry himself was elected a fellow of Trinity and appointed to an assistant tutorship in classics and thus began his career as a teacher and writer. It was a time of ferment in the intellectual world; that same year, *On the Origin of Species by Means of Natural Selection* by Charles Darwin first saw publication, as did *On Liberty* by John Stuart Mill. Mill became a major influence on Sidgwick, though the two often took differing philosophical positions. Through his contact with the Apostles, Sidgwick became convinced that the truth of Christianity was an open question. The influence of Benson's Anglican orthodoxy had begun to wane.

Sidgwick did not lightly dismiss the Christian story, yet even an intense study of the ancient Semitic texts left him unsatisfied. He realized that he was dealing with philosophical issues: If the miracle stories from the Scriptures were true, then reports of miracles from all ages must be considered, but then the accuracy of science itself (which admits of no supernatural interventions in its descriptions of the regularities of the world) is called into question. It appeared to Sidgwick that the probability of a real miracle was much less than the likelihood that witnesses were erroneous, untruthful, or credulous. "I still hunger and thirst after orthodoxy," he wrote, "but I am, I trust, firm not to barter my intellectual birthright for a mess of mystical pottage." However, Sidgwick, never given to fanaticism, produced no anti-Christian propaganda. He recognized the value of the faith for others, but honesty compelled him to a skeptical view of Christianity. He would wrestle with the idea of theism for the rest of his life.

Sidgwick's honesty became a cause célèbre in 1869 when he resigned his Fellowship at Cambridge rather than continue to subscribe to the Thirty-nine Articles of the Church of England, which was required by law for the post. Though by 1869 affirmation of the Anglican doctrines was an empty formality in academic circles, it is characteristic of Sidgwick that he took the matter seriously. It is further a recognition of his abilities as an instructor that, far from being relieved of his duties, Sidgwick was appointed to a special post at Cambridge that did not require doctrinal subscription and reappointed as a fellow when such tests were abolished in 1871. In 1872, he was passed over for the Knightsbridge Professorship of Moral Philosophy but was elected to the post in 1883 after the death of the incumbent. Sidgwick continued teaching at Cambridge, in one post or another, until his death, with only occasional lectures elsewhere. (Several collections of his lectures were published posthumously.)

Sidgwick began his academic duties as a lecturer in the classics, but his interests soon encompassed moral and political philosophy, economics, and epistemology. His most enduring contribution came in *The Methods of Ethics*, first published in 1874, which ran to seven editions (the last, published after his death, came in 1907).

The Methods of Ethics does not seek to build a theoretical system of ethics but rather to discover if some coherence can be brought to the moral judgments actually made by men and women and if two apparently conflicting sources of moral imperatives can be reconciled. One source, intuitionism, was exemplified by the "common sense" philosophy of Thomas Reid, who made conscience the self-evident supreme authority in moral choices, and William Whewell, who allowed for a progressive intuition of moral concepts. Ethics must be based on principles derived by reason (the so-called moral faculty) and not on some calculation of the consequences of an action. This, the second source, is utilitarianism (or "universal hedonism"), which calls those actions right that produce the greatest happiness for the greatest number. Its varied exemplars included William Paley, who disavowed some inherent moral sense, Jeremy Bentham, associated with political reform movements and a secular approach to ethics, and John Stuart Mill, who deprecated intuitionism as merely the consecration of deep-seated prejudices.

Sidgwick agreed with the intuitionists that the common moral judgments of humankind could only be ordered by some self-evident first principle, but he attempted to demonstrate that this first principle was none other than the utilitarian dictum. Thus, moral choices are actually made on the basis of the self-evident principle of maximizing the good. However, there were really two kinds of utilitarianism: universal hedonism (or rational benevolence), which strived to maximize the universal, or societal, good, and egoism (or prudence), which strived for maximizing the agent's good. When these two forms of utilitarianism are in conflict (when, for example, an agent must choose to save either himself or his fellows), can a rational choice be made between them? Is it possible to determine the cases in which egoism should take precedence over altruism?

For Sidgwick the answer was no. Without bringing in additional assumptions (for example, that God exists and will ultimately reward the altruistic choice), it is impossible to pronounce egoism or altruism the more rational way. Sidgwick was left with a kind of fundamental dualism of the practical reason, needing some cosmic postulate in which to ground ethical choice. However, God's existence is far from self-evident, and the mere desire that virtue be rewarded is not proof that it will be. Here *The Methods of Ethics* concludes, leaving for others the task of placing ethics in a larger context and so avoiding Sidgwick's dilemma.

Sidgwick's interest in psychic phenomena paralleled his quest for some evidence that might justify belief in another realm of existence and so provide the "cosmic postulate" for practical ethics. He had become interested in the paranormal when he was twenty-one; in 1882, in response to a sustained fascination with the subject, Sidgwick became the first president of the newly formed Society for Psychical Research. Though he would often observe purported mind readers or those with "second sight," Sidgwick's greatest contribution was in validating the very existence of such an organization. As he put it, "My highest ambition in psychical research is to produce evidence which will drive my opponents to doubt my honesty or veracity."

Sidgwick married Eleanor Mildred Balfour, the sister of Arthur James Balfour, in 1876; as a couple, they became deeply involved in probing supposed psychic events. Eleanor was perhaps the more credulous; she was convinced that telepathy was a reality, while her husband was never quite certain.

Sidgwick was certain that speculative philosophy did not excuse him from practical responsibilities. He had long been interested in the education of women and, after reading *On the Subjection of Women* (1869) by Mill, laid plans for giving university lectures to women. Victorian thought generally assumed women were by nature unable to reach higher learning, but Sidgwick eventually saw the opening of Newnham Hall for Women, as part of Cambridge, in the year of his marriage. In 1892, Eleanor Sidgwick became president of the college. Childless, the Sidgwicks lived there the rest of their lives.

Sidgwick was a prolific writer. An essay for the *Encyclopaedia Britannica* in 1878 was issued in 1886 as *Outline of the History of Ethics*. In 1883, he published *Principles of Political Economy*; *Elements of Politics* followed in 1891. His life was terminated by cancer on August 28, 1900. He had requested that these words should accompany the simple burial service: "Let us commend to the love of God with silent prayer the soul of a sinful man who partly tried to do his duty."

SIGNIFICANCE

Henry Sidgwick believed he had failed to develop a coherent ethics without reliance on some cosmic postulate that would guarantee a reward for the selfless. Others would attempt to place ethics within the context of evolutionary thought, and still others would ground ethics on metaphysics (idealism, for example). Nevertheless, Sidgwick's masterwork, *The Methods of Ethics*, was a hallmark in Victorian philosophy not for its originality but for its clarity and exquisitely precise exploration of reason in ethical decision making. Sidgwick concluded that reason alone could not resolve the conflict facing beings who had an ego life and at the same time a life in community. He had shown in his history of ethics that the Greek idea of the Good involved both pleasure and virtue (or duty); now the two had become separated, with reason powerless to mediate between individual pleasure and one's duty to society.

Sidgwick has been characterized as the last of the classical utilitarians; in his work he prepared the way for new approaches to ethics by marshaling the data of common sense and articulating how far the principle of universal hedonism could be taken. He embodied in his life, as well as in his writing, the qualities of caution, good sense, an irenic spirit, balance, and the conviction of the supreme importance of moral choices.

—Dan Barnett

FURTHER READING

Blanshard, Brand. "Henry Sidgwick." In *Four Reasonable Men*. Middletown, Conn.: Wesleyan University Press, 1984. Popular study of Sidgwick, bordering at times on hagiography, by a rationalist philosopher. Blanshard is impressed by Sidgwick's quiet reasonableness on the printed page and in life.

James, D. G. *Henry Sidgwick: Science and Faith in Victorian England*. London: Oxford University Press, 1971. A short study of Sidgwick, full of prickly observations about his constant uncertainty and incurable irresolution. Part of the Riddell Memorial Lectures series, the volume remains unfinished because of the untimely death of James, formerly the vice chancellor of the University of Southampton. An entire lecture is devoted to Sidgwick and the poet Arthur Hugh Clough.

Schneewind, J. B. *Sidgwick's Ethics and Victorian Moral Philosophy*. Oxford, England: Oxford University Press, 1977. A major technical study of *The Methods of Ethics*, attempting to place it in the context of Victorian philosophical movements. This volume, which has extensive bibliographies, is useful as a guide to each section of *The Methods of Ethics*. Clearly written, for the most part.

Schultz, Bart. *Henry Sidgwick: Eye of the Universe, An Intellectual Biography*. New York: Cambridge University Press, 2004. Comprehensive biography of Sidgwick, offering an accessible explanation of his philosophy within the context of Victorian Britain.

_____, ed. *Essays on Henry Sidgwick*. New York: Cambridge University Press, 1992. The essays, originally presented at a conference held in 1990, analyze various aspects of Sidgwick's philosophy, including its contemporary relevance, its relationship to nineteenth century British ethical thought, and Sidgwick's concept of rational egoism.

Sidgwick, Arthur, and Eleanor M. Sidgwick. *Henry Sidgwick: A Memoir*. London: Macmillan, 1906. The standard reference for Sidgwick's life, compiled by his brother and Henry's widow. Arranged chronologically, the book contains excerpts from correspondence and diaries and includes a comprehensive bibliography of Sidgwick's writings. The section on Sidgwick as a teacher contains numerous appreciations.

Sidgwick, Henry. *The Methods of Ethics*. 7th ed. London: Macmillan, 1907. Reprint. Indianapolis: Hackett, 1981. Sidgwick's masterwork, complete with analytical table of contents, comprehensive index, and an autobiographical fragment written by Sidgwick later in his life. Difficult to follow for the uninitiated.

_____. *Outline of the History of Ethics for English Readers*. 6th ed. London: Macmillan, 1931. Reprint. New York: St. Martin's Press, 1967. The book contains the enlarged text of Sidgwick's original article for the *Encyclopaedia Britannica*. A final chapter on the work of Sidgwick himself has been added by Alban Widgery of Duke University.

SEE ALSO: Dorothea Beale; Charles Darwin; Dame Millicent Garrett Fawcett; Mary Putnam Jacobi; John Stuart Mill.
RELATED ARTICLES in *Great Events from History: The*

Nineteenth Century, 1801-1900: 19th century: Development of Working-Class Libraries; 1820's-1830's: Free Public School Movement; 1828-1842: Arnold Reforms Rugby School.

THE SIEMENS FAMILY
German inventors

The four Siemens brothers are noted for their many seminal contributions to applied technology in nineteenth century electrical and steel industries, including telegraphy, the electric dynamo, and the open-hearth steel furnace.

WERNER SIEMENS

BORN: December 13, 1816; Lenthe, Prussia (now in Germany)
DIED: December 6, 1892; Berlin, Germany
ALSO KNOWN AS: Ernst Werner von Siemens (full name)

WILLIAM SIEMENS

BORN: April 4, 1823; Lenthe, Prussia (now in Germany)
DIED: November 19, 1883; London, England
ALSO KNOWN AS: Karl Wilhelm Siemens (birth name); Charles William Siemens; Sir William Siemens

FRIEDRICH SIEMENS

BORN: December 8, 1826; Lübeck, Prussia (now in Germany)
DIED: May 24, 1904; Berlin, Germany

KARL SIEMENS

BORN: March 3, 1829; Lübeck, Prussia (now in Germany)
DIED: March 21, 1906; St. Petersburg, Russia
AREA OF ACHIEVEMENT: Science and technology

EARLY LIVES

Four brothers among the thirteen children of Christian Ferdinand and Eleonore Deichmann Siemens and many of the brothers' sons became famous as inventors, scientists, and engineers, whose applied technology led to the creation of significant advances in electrical and steel industries, especially in telegraphy, the dynamo, the electric railways, and in the open-hearth steel furnace. Their father was a farm manager of large Prussian estates; he died in 1840, only a year after their mother had died.

The eldest son, Ernst Werner, while serving in the Prussian artillery at the age of twenty-three, assumed the guardianship of his seven younger brothers and successfully guided them into technological schools and profitable positions across nineteenth century Europe. Two brothers and one sister died in childhood; one brother became a farmer; and another became a glass manufacturer. Werner, William (earlier named Karl Wilhelm), Friedrich, and Karl were all born in Prussia (modern west Germany). These four made enormous contributions to modern technology and manufacturing in their lifetimes.

Werner and some of his brothers attended St. Catherine's School in Lübeck. Upon completion of grammar school there, Werner enlisted in the Prussian army in order to enter the Berlin Artillery and Engineering School. Upon graduation in 1837, he was promoted from ensign to second lieutenant in the Third Artillery Brigade and was stationed at Magdeburg. He took William along to study at the Trade and Commerce School there while he continued in the military service. Transferred to Wittenberg in 1840, Werner experimented with electrolysis and succeeded in developing a process for gold plating by galvanic current and was granted a five-year patent for it in 1842. By selling his rights to a jewelry firm, he began a lifelong income from his inventions.

William Siemens emigrated to England in 1843 and became a naturalized citizen in 1859. A prolific inventor, he was granted 113 English patents; as a shrewd businessperson, moreover, he accumulated a large fortune. Karl Siemens had studied at Lübeck and at Berlin before joining his brother Werner in his endeavors. He became the most cultivated and diplomatic member of the family, having a keen sense of business management. Werner wrote of him: "Karl was the true connecting link between us four brothers, who indeed differed radically from one another, but were bound together for lifelong common work by an all-abiding fraternal love." Friedrich Siemens had gone to sea from Lübeck in sailing ships but returned to work with Werner and then with William in England. Werner declared him "the born inventor" with a "characteristic of steady, spontaneous, uninfluenced thinking and self-training [which] gave him a peculiarly meditative air and his performances a pronounced originality."

LIVES' WORK

One of the great technological achievements of the Siemens brothers was the development of instruments and the establishment of international firms under their control for the European and Asian telegraph systems. First to utilize the substance called gutta-percha for covering underground telegraph wires, Werner created a screw press that extruded the substance around the wire while hot and cooled it into a seamless insulated covering that could carry electrical current underground or underwater. Then, he joined forces with a young physical mechanic, Johann Georg Halske, forming the firm of Siemens and Halske in Berlin, to perfect his invention of a self-interrupting dial telegraph instrument. Werner resigned from the military service in 1847, the year of his dial invention, and began manufacturing telegraph cable and equipment to fulfill contracts from Prussia and Russia to lay long lines between key cities, which soon outmoded all optical semaphore systems along military or railroad routes.

By the 1850's, Werner's firm had constructed the line from Berlin to Frankfurt am Main, and that success led to contracts with his brother William to lay submarine cables across the Atlantic, with his brother Karl to lay lines out of St. Petersburg for Russia, and to connect the famous London to Calcutta, or Indo-European, telegraph line that opened in 1870. The rare combination of inventive skill, manufacturing capability, and useful diplomatic-political connections enriched the firms of the Siemens brothers and their shareholders.

As the London agent for his brothers' European firm of Siemens and Halske, William spent much of his career advancing the realm of the electric telegraph. In 1874, he laid the first Atlantic cable from England to the United States from a special ship he designed, the *Faraday*. For his distinguished achievements, he won medals at industrial exhibitions and the presidency of many English engineering and metals associations. In 1862, he was elected a Fellow of the Royal Society of London, the oldest scientific society, founded in 1662. In 1883, seven months before his death, he was knighted by Queen Victoria for his services. He had married Anna Gordon in 1859; they had no children, and she died in 1901.

Karl developed the Russian branch of the German firm and directed most of the construction of the international telegraph lines and cables that the family firms won contracts to build. Later, he became a Finnish-Russian citizen in order to do business in Russia; he married and lived in St. Petersburg for many years and was raised to the hereditary Russian nobility in 1895. After Werner's death, Karl became head of Siemens and Halske (Johann Georg Halske withdrew from the partnership in 1867).

Perhaps the most significant invention of the Siemens brothers was the construction of the regenerative furnace for the emerging steel industry. Friedrich pioneered the work of the firm on the application of the regenerative principle into the smelting of steel in conjunction with the French engineer Pierre-Émile Martin to create the famous Siemens-Martin open-hearth furnace. In England in 1856, Sir Henry Bessemer had patented a forced-air process for the smelting of steel; in the United States, William Kelly had devised a "pneumatic process" as early as 1849 but belatedly received an American patent in 1857. Friedrich and William applied their regenerative principle to the smelting furnaces with much larger capacities for molten metal, glass, and special materials. In 1864, in cooperation with Martin, they developed the so-called Siemens-Martin process, which works on the heat-storage principle.

In conventional furnaces, air and the combustible gases are introduced cold into the furnace, and the hot waste gases escape via smokestacks. In the regenerative process, the heat of the waste gases is captured for use in preheating the air and the combustible gases. Two or four refractory brick chambers are next to the smelting unit, and, in alternating fashion, the hot waste gases are passed through the chambers, which have large thermal storage capacity. Then, valves close and new air and gases are preheated as they are introduced through the hot chambers and fed into the furnace. This process creates much higher temperatures for smelting, permits the use of low-grade gases, and saves on fuel costs.

For twelve years, from 1847 to 1859, William, in England, had tried unsuccessfully to apply this regenerative principle to steam engines. In 1856, Friedrich obtained a patent for the idea of using a waste heat condenser for industrial furnaces. In France, Martin had made steel by wrought iron, or cast iron, in a similar regenerative open-hearth furnace. Martin and the Siemenses combined their efforts in the Siemens-Martin process, which utilized iron ore directly from the mines. Eventually, the open-hearth process became immensely profitable as the recycling of scrap iron was implemented. First adopted for commercial steel manufacture in 1865, by 1896 the tonnage of steel from England's Siemens-Martin furnaces had surpassed the production of all Bessemer furnaces.

A third field of invention and manufacture evolved from Werner's invention of the "dynamo-electric machine," which he demonstrated in 1866. Almost at the same time, Charles Wheatstone in England and Samuel Alfred Varley in France had exhibited similar apparatuses and contested the priority of Werner's claim. Eventually Werner gained recognition when he demonstrated his invention and published an account of the principle behind it. Again, it was the firm of Siemens and Halske that was quickly able to apply the new dynamo in practical applications and then manufacture the electrical apparatus.

Nearly 250 dynamos were manufactured each year by Siemens and Halske during the 1880's. The number reached five hundred by 1892, as street and home lighting came of age, as did electrical motors for streetcars, railways, and factories. Siemens and Halske proceeded to develop the first electric tramway in 1881 in Lichterfelde with an overhead bow collector touching the trolley line. Siemens's arc lamps illuminated the Berlin Potsdamer Platz in 1882; the brothers demonstrated their first electric lift or elevator at the Mannheim Industrial Exhibition in 1880, and in 1892 produced their first electricity meter, called a "saber meter."

SIGNIFICANCE

Werner and Sir William Siemens were the outstanding geniuses among the Siemens brothers; Friedrich and Karl Siemens extended the technology developed by the firm of Siemens and Halske into telegraph and electric systems sold, installed, and maintained by the company across the Western world. The family was instrumental in advancing the theoretical and technological fields of nineteenth century electronics with hundreds of patents granted to them and to members of their pioneering firm.

The Siemens brothers were significant leaders in German, English, and Russian enterprises of telegraphy, telephones, and electrical systems that served to promote the advancement of knowledge, the speedy transmission of information, and the shipment of people and material via electrical railways across Europe and Asia. Their several contributions to the manufacturing of steel, copper, and glass into less expensive materials for modern life immensely contributed to the Industrial Revolution after the great Crystal Palace Exposition of London in

1851, when Siemens and Halske were awarded the Council Medal, the first of hundreds to be won by the brothers.

—Paul F. Erwin

FURTHER READING

Derry, T. K., and Trevor I. Williams. *A Short History of Technology from the Earliest Times to A.D. 1900.* New York: Oxford University Press, 1961. This text is a sequel to the five-volume *A History of Technology,* begun by Charles Singer. Good coverage of the Industrial Revolution. A chapter entitled "Coal and the Metals" covers developments in the making of inexpensive steel. Comparative tables showing the chronological events of technological achievements in Great Britain, Europe, and the United States along with bibliographies for each chapter enhance this introductory study.

Feldenkirchen, Wilfried. *Werner von Siemens: Inventor and International Entrepreneur.* Columbus: Ohio State University Press, 1994. This first book in a three-volume history of the Siemens Corporation focuses on Werner's business career, describing how he and his brothers achieved their vision of a multinational electric technology company.

Karwatka, Dennis. "Technology's Past." *Tech Directions* 56, no. 10 (May/June, 1997): 12. Profile of Werner Siemens, describing his family background, technological innovations, and the company he founded.

Pole, William. *The Life of Sir William Siemens.* London: John Murray, 1888. The authorized biographer of the Siemens brother who had made England his home. It was produced by a popular biographer of that era with the help of family and friends, who provided personal papers and recollections.

Siemens, Charles William. *The Scientific Works of C. William Siemens.* 3 vols. Edited by E. F. Bamber. London: John Murray, 1889. These papers, including his addresses, lectures, and papers read before scientific societies, provide closer detail of his inventions and business ventures.

Siemens, Georg. *History of the House of Siemens.* 2 vols. Freiberg, Germany: Karl Alber, 1957. This set describes the development of inventions by the various Siemens brothers and the practical applications of them via the business enterprises in Europe and elsewhere. Much of the business story relates the efforts of William and Werner (volume 1). The tragic chapters on the two world wars include the technological advancements in telephony, telegraphy, and electrical fields to the year 1945 (volume 2).

Siemens, Werner von. *Inventor and Entrepreneur: Recollections of Werner von Siemens.* Translated by W. C. Coupland. 2d ed. London: Lund Humphries, 1966. This autobiographical work provides one of the best stories of the gifted Siemens family and modestly relates Werner's own great achievements as inventor and businessperson. His story centers on the telegraph and electrical systems that his firm, Siemens and Halske, had established in many nations.

Singer, Charles, et al., eds. *The Late Nineteenth Century, 1850 to 1900.* Vol. 5 in *A History of Technology.*

Oxford, England: Clarendon Press, 1954-1958. Although the Bessemer process had pioneered the making of steel, the Siemens-Martin open-hearth method ultimately outproduced it in the twentieth century. This volume presents the most readable introduction of both means of steel manufacturing.

SEE ALSO: Sir Henry Bessemer; William Fothergill Cooke and Charles Wheatstone; Alfred Krupp; Queen Victoria.

RELATED ARTICLE in *Great Events from History: The Nineteenth Century, 1801-1900:* May 1-October 30, 1893: Chicago World's Fair.

SITTING BULL
Native American leader

One of the outstanding icons of nineteenth century Indian defiance of American expansion, Sitting Bull led his Lakota (Sioux) people from their zenith in the middle of the nineteenth century to the decline of their culture in the face of superior technology and numbers of the whites.

BORN: March, 1831; near the Grand River, Dakota Territory (now in South Dakota)

DIED: December 15, 1890; Standing Rock Agency, South Dakota

ALSO KNOWN AS: Tatanka Iyotanka (birth name)

AREAS OF ACHIEVEMENT: Government and politics, warfare and conquest

EARLY LIFE

Sitting Bull was born Tatanka Iyotanka in a village a few miles below where Bullhead, South Dakota, now stands. During his first fourteen years, his Lakota (Sioux) friends called him Slow, a name he earned because of his deliberate manner and the awkward movement of his sturdy body. The youth grew to manhood as a member of the Hunkpapa tribe, one of seven among the Teton Lakota, the westernmost division of the Sioux Confederation. His people thrived as a nomadic hunter-warrior society. As an infant strapped to a baby-board, he was carried by his mother as the tribe roamed the northern Plains hunting buffalo. At five years, he rode behind his mother on her horse and helped as best he could around the camp. By the age of ten, he rode his own pony, wrapping his legs around the curved belly of the animal (a practice

that caused him to be slightly bowlegged for the remainder of his years). He learned to hunt small game with bow and arrows and to gather berries. He reveled in the games and races, swimming and wrestling with the other boys. His was an active and vigorous life, and he loved it.

The warrior dimension of Lakota male life came more into focus as the boy grew. The Tetons concentrated most of their wrath on the Crow and Assiniboin Indians at first, and the whites at a later time. The hub of Lakota society centered on gaining prestige through heroic acts in battle. Counting coups by touching an enemy with a highly decorated stick was top priority. The Lakota lad learned his lessons well, and, at the age of fourteen, he joined a mounted war party. He picked out one of the enemy, and, with a burst of enthusiasm and courage, he charged the rival warrior and struck him with his coup stick. After the battle, word of this heroic deed spread throughout the Hunkpapa village. The boy had reached a milestone in his development; for the remainder of his life, he enjoyed telling the story of his first coup. Around the campfire that night, his proud father, Jumping Bull, gave his son a new name. He called him Sitting Bull after the beast that the Lakota respected so much for its tenacity. A buffalo bull was the essence of strength, and a "sitting bull" was one that held his ground and could not be pushed aside.

In 1857, Sitting Bull became a chief of the Hunkpapa. He had ably demonstrated his abilities as a warrior, and his common sense and his leadership traits showed promise of a bright future for him. Although his physical appearance was commonplace, he was convincing in argument, stubborn, and quick to grasp a situation. These traits gained for him the respect of his people as a warrior and as a statesman.

LIFE'S WORK

Sitting Bull's leadership qualities were often put to the test in his dealings with the whites. During the 1860's, he skirmished with the whites along the Powder River in Wyoming. He learned of their method of fighting, and he was impressed with their weapons. In 1867, white commissioners journeyed to Lakota country to forge a peace treaty. They also hoped to gain Lakota agreement to limit their living area to present-day western South Dakota. While his Jesuit friend Father Pierre De Smet worked to gain peace, Sitting Bull refused to give up his cherished hunting lands to the west and south and declined to sign the Treaty of 1868. Other Lakota, however, made their marks on the "white man's paper," and the treaty became official.

Developments during the 1870's confirmed Sitting Bull's distrust of the white men's motives. Railroad officials surveyed the northern Plains during the early 1870's in preparation for building a transcontinental railroad that would disrupt Lakota hunting lands. In 1874, the army surveyed the Black Hills, part of the Great Sioux Reservation as set up by the treaty, and, in the next year, thousands of miners invaded this sacred part of the Sioux reserve when they learned of the discovery of gold there. The tree-covered hills and sparkling streams and lakes were the home of Lakota gods and a sacred place in their scheme of life. The whites had violated the treaty and disregarded the rights of the Lakota. Sitting Bull refused to remain on the assigned reservation any longer and led his followers west, into Montana, where there were still buffalo to hunt and the opportunity remained to live by the old traditions.

As many other Lakota became disgruntled with white treatment, they, too, looked to Sitting Bull's camp to the west as a haven from the greedy whites. In this sense, he became the symbol of Lakota freedom and resistance to the whites, and his camp grew with increasing numbers of angry Lakota.

The showdown between Lakota and whites came in 1876. The U.S. government had ordered the Lakota to return to their reservations by February of 1876, but few Indians abided by this order. The government thus turned the "Sioux problem" over to the army with instructions to force the Indians back to the agencies. In the summer of 1876, General Alfred H. Terry led a strong expedition against Sitting Bull's camp. The Indian chief had a pre-

monition of things to come when he dreamed of blue-clad men falling into his camp. Soon, he would learn the significance of this portent. A detachment of cavalry from Terry's column under the command of Lieutenant Colonel George A. Custer attacked Sitting Bull's camp. The forty-five-year-old chief rallied his men, and they defeated Custer, killing more than three hundred soldiers, including their leader.

Although the Lakota had won the Battle of the Little Bighorn, they decided that it was time to leave the area and divide up into smaller groups in order to avoid capture. Many additional soldiers were ordered into the northern Plains, and they spent the remainder of the summer and fall chasing and harassing the fleeing Lakota. While other groups of Lakota eventually returned to their agencies, Sitting Bull led his people to Canada, where

Sitting Bull. (The Granger Collection, New York)

they resided until 1881. Even though the Canadian officials refused to feed the Lakota, the latter were able to
subsist in their usual manner of hunting and gathering
until 1881, when the buffalo were almost gone. Because
of homesickness and a lack of food, Sitting Bull finally
surrendered to United States officials, who kept him prisoner at Fort Randall for two years.

By 1883, Sitting Bull had returned to his people at
Standing Rock Agency in Dakota Territory and soon became involved in unexpected activities. In that same
year, the Northern Pacific Railroad sponsored a last great
buffalo hunt for various dignitaries, and Sitting Bull participated. In the next year, he agreed to tour fifteen cities
with Colonel Alvaren Allen's Western show. Sitting
Bull was portrayed as the Slayer of General Custer, but
the stubborn Indian chief found this label inaccurate and
distasteful. In 1885, Sitting Bull signed with Buffalo Bill
Cody's Wild West Show and traveled in the eastern
United States and Canada during the summer. He sold
autographed photographs of himself and eventually gave
away most of the money he made to poor white children
who begged for money in order to eat. At the end of the
season, the popular Buffalo Bill gave his Indian friend a
gray circus horse and large white sombrero as a remem-
brance of their summer together.

During the latter part of the decade, Sitting Bull returned to Standing Rock, where he settled into reservation life. The Hunkpapa still cherished him as their
leader, much to the dismay of agent James McLaughlin,
who sought to break the old chief's hold over his people.

In 1890, Wovoka, a Paiute Indian prophet from Nevada, began to preach a message that most Indians
prayed was true. He dreamed that he had died and gone to
Heaven. There, he found all the deceased Indians, thousands of buffalo, and no whites. The Indian prophet
taught that, in order to achieve a return to the old ways of
life, the Indians had only to dance the Ghost Dance regularly until the second coming of the Messiah, who would
be in the form of an Indian. The Ghost Dance spread
rapidly throughout much of the West, and soon Lakota
were following Wovoka's teachings. Sitting Bull had his
doubts about the new religion, but he realized that it disturbed the whites and in particular agent McLaughlin,
and so he encouraged his people to dance.

The events that followed brought about the death of
Sitting Bull as well as the military and psychological defeat of the Lakota. Cautious Indian officials deplored the
fact that the Lakota were dancing again. Sitting Bull, the
symbol of the old culture, was still their leader, and they
decided to arrest him. McLaughlin chose Lakota Indians
who served in the Agency Police Force to apprehend Sitting Bull. They came to his hut to seize him during the
night of December 15, 1890, and a scuffle broke out. The
fifty-nine-year-old chief was one of the first to be killed.
In the dust and confusion of the struggle, fourteen others
died. Several days later, other Lakota who had left their
reservation were stopped at Wounded Knee Creek, and a
scuffle again broke out with the white soldiers, who were
trying to disarm them and to force them back to the
agency. When the fighting was over on that cold December day, 153 Lakota had died and the dream of a return to
the old way of life was lost forever.

SIGNIFICANCE

Sitting Bull, the proud leader of the Hunkpapa, had died
along with many of his people. He had served his people
well as a feared warrior and respected chief. He had
fought against Indians and whites, including sixty-three
coups against unfortunate Indians. The whites had suffered their worst defeat when they attacked his village.
Although the old chief was unable to fight, he proved his
inspirational mettle to the people. During his last years,
he continued to serve as a model for his followers, although in a losing cause.

Technology and the overwhelming white population
were forces that even the stubborn Lakota leader could
not subdue. Gone were the days of nomadic camp life,
horseback riding, and buffalo hunting. Also gone were
the memories of courtships and polygamous marriages:
White Americans hoped to convert the Lakota tribesmen
into Christian yeoman farmers. By 1890, the frontier
phase of American history had passed, and citizens confronted the problems of immigration from southern and
eastern Europe, the growing urbanization, and the massive industrialization that would make the United States
a world leader. The Lakota life that was so well adapted
to the Plains environment was gone forever.

—*John W. Bailey*

FURTHER READING

Adams, Alexander B. *Sitting Bull: An Epic of the Plains*.
New York: G. P. Putnam's Sons, 1973. A richly detailed popular account of Sitting Bull's life, with a
good description of the various divisions and tribes of
the Lakota.

Anderson, Gary Clayton. *Sitting Bull and the Paradox of
Lakota Nationhood*. New York: Longman, Addison
Wesley, 1996. Biography focusing on the challenges
Sitting Bull faced in leading the Lakota people.

Bailey, John W. *Pacifying the Plains: General Alfred
Terry and the Decline of the Sioux, 1866-1890*. West-

port, Conn.: Greenwood Press, 1979. Follows Sitting Bull's career in the period after the Civil War, with particular emphasis on his role as the leader of the nonreservation Lakota and their conflict with the military during the 1870's.

Johnson, Dorothy M. *Warrior for a Lost Nation: A Biography of Sitting Bull*. Philadelphia: Westminster Press, 1969. A readable book based upon limited research. Includes Sitting Bull's pictographs or calendar of winter counts that recorded his feats in battle.

Utley, Robert M. *The Lance and the Shield: The Life and Times of Sitting Bull*. New York: Ballantine Books, 1994. A definitive biography that portrays Sitting Bull as a complex leader.

_____. *The Last Days of the Sioux Nation*. New Haven, Conn.: Yale University Press, 1963. An excellent book that focuses on the death of Sitting Bull and the Wounded Knee battle of 1890. The author illustrates how the Lakota suffered a military and psychological conquest that saw their demise after the failure of the Ghost Dance.

Vestal, Stanley. *Sitting Bull: Champion of the Sioux, a Biography*. Boston: Houghton Mifflin, 1932. Rev. ed. Norman: University of Oklahoma Press, 1957. The most reliable biography of Sitting Bull, based upon oral and documentary research. The author was closely associated with the Plains Indians since his boyhood and proved to be a careful student of their culture.

SEE ALSO: William Cody; Crazy Horse; George A. Custer; Geronimo; Annie Oakley; Red Cloud.

RELATED ARTICLES in *Great Events from History: The Nineteenth Century, 1801-1900:* 1876-1877: Sioux War; June 25, 1876: Battle of the Little Bighorn; 1890: U.S. Census Bureau Announces Closing of the Frontier; December 29, 1890: Wounded Knee Massacre.

SAMUEL SLATER
American industrialist

During the early years of America's modern economic history, Slater almost single-handedly established the basis upon which the country's industrial development would be built by effectively founding textile manufacturing in New England.

BORN: June 9, 1768; near Belper, Derbyshire, England
DIED: April 21, 1835; Webster, Massachusetts
AREA OF ACHIEVEMENT: Business

EARLY LIFE
The fifth child and second son of William Slater, a yeoman farmer, and Elizabeth Fox Slater, Samuel Slater was educated in the village school of Master Thomas Jackson. When he was fourteen, his father was killed in a farming accident, and Slater apprenticed himself to Jedediah Strutt, one of the early English textile manufacturers and a collaborator with Richard Arkwright in the development of textile-manufacturing machinery. Strutt was like a second father to Slater, and he rewarded the boy for the design of a device for distributing yarn more effectively on the spindle.

During the late eighteenth century, England enjoyed a virtual monopoly in advanced textile manufacturing technology. This monopoly was guarded by laws that prescribed heavy penalties for exporting technical information or for emigration of textile workers. At the same time, state governments in the United States were offering substantial incentives for the development of technology for the industrial exploitation of American cotton and wool, and while Slater was still indentured, Pennsylvania granted a bounty of a hundred pounds for a carding machine, even though it was only partially successful.

Slater therefore was determined to go to America. Before he was twenty-one he was given responsibility for assembling the equipment at one of Strutt's new mills, and this experience and the memorized details of everything he had learned in his apprenticeship were the only assets he carried to the newly formed United States when he emigrated in September, 1789, disguised as a farm laborer to escape detection as a textile worker breaking the laws of England.

Arriving in November, 1789, Slater found work for a brief time in New York City in the small factory of the New York Manufacturing Company, which was producing yarn with inferior equipment. Meanwhile, he made contact with Moses Brown of Providence, whose mill was machine-spinning cotton with defective equipment, and offered to duplicate the machinery of Richard Arkwright. Brown introduced him to his kinsman, Sylvanus

Brown, and Slater agreed to build yarn-making equipment at the latter's mill in Pawtucket, Rhode Island. He was only twenty-one.

LIFE'S WORK

Establishing a partnership with William Almy and Smith Brown, two kinsmen of Moses Brown, Slater, at a wage of a dollar a day, built the first efficient yarn-making equipment in the United States, duplicating the basic elements of Arkwright's system—the carder and the water-frame spinner—and the Almy-Brown mill began using it to spin yarn on December 20, 1790, producing relatively small quantities because Slater was forced to use Surinam cotton, which was finer and more carefully cleaned than cotton from the American South. Three years later, however, Eli Whitney's invention of the cotton gin made possible the mass production of cotton thread and cloth from domestic supplies. In staffing the mill, Slater followed the practice, which apparently had proven efficient in England, of employing children under the age of twelve to operate the machinery. This machinery was built of oak and iron parts forged by Oziel Wilkinson, whose daughter Hannah became Slater's wife on October 2, 1791.

Samuel Slater. (Library of Congress)

In 1793, the firm of Almy, Brown and Slater built what came to be called the Old Slater Mill in Pawtucket, and spinning began there on July 12, 1793. Slater continued his partnership with Almy and Brown, even though they opened another mill on their own in 1799 and ran it in competition with Slater, using without compensation the methods he had perfected. Then, forming a partnership with relatives of his wife, he built at Rehobath the first mill in Massachusetts to use the Arkwright system, the so-called White Mill, which began production in 1801.

By this time, Slater was using power looms and was hiring experienced English textile workers to tend them, including his brother John, who arrived in America in 1803 with plans for the "mule," invented in 1779 by Samuel Crompton for making muslin. Slater was still employing children, but he had established a reputation for fair dealing. He lent new employees money to establish themselves, and from the beginning he provided a Sunday school that taught his juvenile employees reading, writing, and arithmetic. In fact, Slater for a time taught in this school himself, and ultimately he created a day school for mill children, usually paying the teachers' salaries himself.

In 1806, the town of Slaterville, Rhode Island, was established, built around a mill that Slater had built there in partnership with Almy, Brown, and John Slater. By the time that American industry was suffering a recession because of the Embargo Act of 1807 and the Non-Intercourse Act of 1809, Slater's mills were surviving because of careful domestic marketing of yarn, and in 1812 he built yet another mill at Oxford, Massachusetts. When the New England mills suffered a severe depression in the aftermath of the Napoleonic Wars because of the flood of cheap English goods into American markets, Slater suffered severe losses, but the Protective Tariff of 1816 soon restored the industry.

On October 2, 1812, Hannah Slater died, leaving her husband with six small sons to rear. In November, 1817, he married a widow, Esther Parkinson. He involved his sons, if they were interested, in the operation of his mills, even in their adolescence. For example, his son John at the age of thirteen was his father's representative at the Oxford mill. Only one of the four sons who survived their father, Horatio Nelson Slater, lived to old age.

In 1814, in partnership with Edward Howard, Slater established a second mill at Oxford for the manufacture of woolen cloth, and when Howard sold his interest to Slater in 1829, the latter established Slater and Sons with his sons George, John, and Nelson. In time, this firm became the Dudley Manufacturing Company, and the company towns of Oxford and Dudley were merged in 1832 as the town of Webster, which Slater so named because of his admiration of Daniel Webster. Webster, Massachusetts, was home to Slater for the rest of his life.

Slater's establishment of mills continued through the prosperity of the 1820's. In 1823 at Jewett City, Connecticut, he formed S. and J. Slater with his brother, selling out his share to John in 1831. In 1825, with five partners, he acquired a mill at Amoskeag, near Manchester, New Hampshire. There he built a second mill, a sawmill, a cornmill, and a dam for water power, and established the Amoskeag Manufacturing Company. Up to this time, all of Slater's mills had been powered by water, but in 1827 he built at Providence the first steam-power textile factory in Rhode Island and one of the first in the country. In all, between 1790, when he formed his first partnership with Almy and Brown, and 1827, Slater formed thirteen partnerships. In addition, he maintained a farm, engaged in a variety of philanthropic enterprises, and helped to incorporate and was for fifteen years president of the Manufacturers' Bank of Pawtucket.

The economic slump that began in 1829 was accompanied by the onset of the ill health that plagued Slater's last years. He once said that in his first thirty years in America he worked sixteen hours a day. In his last years, in ill health, he was struggling to maintain his industrial enterprises in the face of poor economic conditions. He died at Webster, Massachusetts, on April 21, 1835, recognized throughout the country as what President Andrew Jackson called him when he greeted him at Pawtucket in 1833: the father of American manufactures.

SIGNIFICANCE

At a remarkably young age, Samuel Slater almost single-handedly created the American textile industry and established the basis of American industrialism. Less an inventor than a man who built upon the inventions of others, he possessed considerable mechanical aptitude; his commercial success, however, derived mostly from his great cleverness in establishing factories, organizing production, taking advantage of the latest mechanical developments, and discovering the most effective methods of marketing his product. His single most important contribution to the growth of American industry was his establishment of a system of manufacture broken down into steps so simple that even children could perform them. This was of crucial importance during the early development of American industry because of the chronic

shortage of skilled manpower in that period. With Eli Whitney, who inaugurated the system of manufacturing interchangeable parts rather than complete, custom-made assemblies, Slater stands as one of the two most influential figures in the first years of the American industrial revolution.

—*Robert L. Berner*

FURTHER READING

Bagnall, William R. *Samuel Slater and the Early Development of Cotton Manufacturing in the United States.* Middletown, Conn.: J. S. Steward, 1890. Except for an obscure biography published in the year following Slater's death, this is the only nineteenth century biography. Superseded by Cameron.

Blake, John. "Samuel Slater." In *Lives of American Merchants*, by Freeman Hunt. New York: Hunt's Merchant's Magazine, 1856. A brief nineteenth century account of Slater's life and achievements.

Burlingame, Roger. "The Spinning Hero: Samuel Slater." *North American Review* 246 (Autumn, 1938): 150-161. A brief and somewhat superficial tribute to Slater's achievements by a distinguished historian of American industry.

Cameron, E. H. *Samuel Slater, Father of American Manufacturers.* Freeport, Maine: Bond Wheelwright Company, 1960. The only modern full-length biography, written with the assistance of H. N. Slater, Samuel Slater's great-grandson, and based in part on the research and unpublished manuscript of Frederick L. Lewton.

Gordon, John Steele. *The Business of America.* New York: Walker, 2001. This collection of Gordon's columns from *American Heritage* magazine includes the article "Technology Transfer," describing how Slater brought the textile industry from Great Britain to the United States during the late eighteenth century.

Lewton, Frederick L. "Samuel Slater and the Oldest Cotton Machinery in America." In *Smithsonian Report for 1936*. Washington, D.C.: Smithsonian Institution Press, 1936. Lewton devoted a large part of his life to research on Slater and was the primary modern authority on the technical aspects of Slater's equipment. Cameron based his biography on Lewton's unpublished manuscript. The oldest Slater machinery is in the Smithsonian museum. This is a semitechnical description of it.

Tucker, Barbara M. *Samuel Slater and the Origins of the American Textile Industry.* Ithaca, N.Y.: Cornell University Press, 1984. Largely a case study of Slater's factory system from 1790 to 1860. Examines Slater's management methods in relation to the English system in which he was trained and the innovations made necessary by American conditions. Valuable for an understanding of Slater as a factory master, but thin on biographical detail.

Welles, Arnold. "Father of Our Factory System." *American Heritage* 9 (April, 1958): 34-39, 90-92. A brief account of Slater's life and accomplishments, with useful and enlightening illustrations from the prints of the period.

SEE ALSO: Andrew Jackson; Daniel Webster.

RELATED ARTICLE in *Great Events from History: The Nineteenth Century, 1801-1900:* September 10, 1846: Howe Patents His Sewing Machine.

JEDEDIAH SMITH
American frontiersman

One of the greatest, and certainly the most adventurous, of American mountain men, Smith charted trails through the Rockies that helped open the West to settlement by the pioneers who followed the fur traders.

BORN: January 6, 1799; Jericho (now Bainbridge), New York

DIED: May 27, 1831; near Cimmaron River en route to Santa Fe, New Mexico

ALSO KNOWN AS: Jedediah Strong Smith (full name)

AREA OF ACHIEVEMENT: Exploration

EARLY LIFE

Jedediah Strong Smith was born into a New York family that moved a number of times as the frontier pushed farther west. His family appears to have been thoroughly middle class and respectable, and he received a good education and was well read. Family tradition, in fact, credits a book, the 1814 publication by Nicholas Biddle of *History of the Expedition of Captains Lewis and Clark*, with firing the young Smith's imagination and making him determined to see the places Merriwether Lewis and William Clark described in their journals. By 1822 he and his family had made their way to Missouri. There he signed on with the Rocky Mountain Fur Company, recently organized by William Ashley and Andrew Henry. Smith became one of the original Ashley Men, the individual fur trappers and traders that set off into the wilderness under Ashley's command.

LIFE'S WORK

Ashley, a Missouri businessperson, and Henry, an experienced fur trapper, originated the annual trappers' rendezvous in the intermountain regions of the West. The Rocky Mountain Fur Company would pack supplies and trade goods for the mountain men in to a central location, such as a site on the Green River in Wyoming, and pack the furs out, eliminating the lengthy trek to St. Louis for individual trappers and traders. Ashley's plan met resistance from the Arikara, a Native American tribe whose members had become accustomed to serving as the middlemen between white fur traders and other tribes on the upper Missouri, but Ashley simply relocated his base of operations and effectively cut the Arikara out of the fur business. Other trading companies quickly copied the idea and, before overtrapping ended the fur trade, hundreds of mountain men would gather for the midsummer rendezvous to dispose of the furs taken in the previous year and to stock up on supplies for the coming winter.

Unlike the stereotypical image of the uncouth mountain man, generally portrayed in popular culture as hard-drinking and vulgar in language and behavior, Smith was a devout Christian, neither drank nor smoked, and was consistently serious in his demeanor. Even when personally in danger or in pain, he remained calm, never allowing his men to see his concern or fear. On his second expedition, a grizzly bear attacked and mauled Smith. The bear smashed Smith's ribs and tore at his scalp. The bear left Smith alive, but with his scalp literally dangling by an ear. He coolly instructed one of his companions, Jim Clyman, to reattach the loose skin using needle and thread. Clyman stitched the scalp back in place as best he could but was convinced that repairing the ear was hopeless. Smith told him to try anyway. Clyman did. After a two-week convalescence, Smith resumed command of the party.

Contemporaries of Smith described him both as highly respectable and as an inspiration to those around him. When called upon to say a few words over the grave of John Gardner, a recently deceased fellow fur trader,

Smith's eulogy moved observers to comment that Smith left no doubt in anyone's mind that their friend had found salvation. Coupled with his legendary physical courage, it is not surprising Smith quickly established himself both as a leader and as an explorer.

Smith spent his first winter in the mountains along the Musselshell River in present-day Montana. The following summer, 1823, Ashley directed Smith to take a group of men and find a Native American tribe known as the Crow with the object of establishing trade relations with them. Smith's party succeeded in making contact with the Crow people and spent the winter with them. Members of the Crow tribe described to Smith the Green River area in what is now the state of Wyoming. The Green was reputed to be an area rich in furs and thus far unexploited by other traders, and Smith and his men resolved to explore the region.

During the spring of 1824 Smith and his party rediscovered South Pass, a passageway through the Rocky Mountains, and successfully traversed it with both wagons and livestock, proving that such travel was possible. Previous parties had relied completely on pack animals to carry supplies and trade goods. South Pass had been utilized before by white men, in 1814, but the route had been forgotten. Other trails, such as the one over Lemhi Pass used by the Lewis and Clark Expedition, were impassable with wagons and were just barely passable with horses and mules. The trail that Smith blazed through Wyoming in 1824 later became an integral part of the Oregon Trail, the path that thousands of pioneers would take to reach the Pacific Northwest.

Smith and the men with him spent the following year trapping and trading in Wyoming and Idaho. Following the first trappers' rendezvous, he returned to St. Louis with William Ashley and the company's furs. Andrew Henry had decided to retire from the fur trade, so Ashley asked Smith to replace Henry as his partner.

Smith returned to the mountains ahead of Ashley and his main party the following spring to arrange for the trappers' rendezvous. At the rendezvous, Ashley negotiated the sale of his share of the company to Smith and two new partners, David Jackson and William Sublette. Ashley—in exchange for a promissory note signed July 18, 1826, which committed Jackson, Smith, and Sublette to pay "not less than seven thousand dollars nor more than fifteen thousand dollars" for merchandise—agreed to arrange for the shipment of trade goods to the location of the following year's rendezvous. After the rendezvous ended, Ashley returned to St. Louis while Smith, Jack-

son, and Sublette divided their party into smaller groups for the fall hunt.

Smith, accompanied by seventeen men, decided to explore the region south of the Great Salt Lake and to assess its potential for the fur trade. Smith and his men traveled the length of Utah, following first a tributary of the Colorado River and then the Colorado itself, pushed on into what is present-day northern Arizona, and then crossed the Mojave Desert into California, eventually reaching the Spanish mission at San Gabriel near present-day San Diego. The 1776 Spanish Dominguez-Escalante Expedition had attempted this route across the desert but had failed to complete it. The bulk of Smith's party remained on the Stanislaus River in California in the spring of 1827 while Smith and two men attempted to find a route back to northern Utah through the Sierra Nevada. They succeeded and, striking northeast across Nevada, became the first white men to cross the Great Salt Lake Desert as they returned to Utah for the trappers' rendezvous at Sweet (now Bear) Lake.

Smith, as was common practice among many American explorers, fur traders, and mountain men, kept extensive journals. His harrowing description of the journey across the Salt Lake Desert—replete with phrases such as "I durst not tell my men of the desolate prospect ahead" and "We dug holes in the sand and laid down in them for the purpose of cooling our heated bodies"—makes it clear that even Smith had his doubts regarding their survival. Nonetheless, having survived the trek across not merely one but several arid deserts, Smith continued his explorations. He arrived at the rendezvous July 3, having traveled through most of the American Southwest during the previous year, only two days later than he had promised Ashley in 1826 that he would be there. Scarcely two weeks after completing his harrowing journey from California, he was again heading south and west, motivated, as he said in his journal, "by the love of novelty."

Having left a significant number of his men in California in the spring of 1827, Smith retraced his route to the Pacific Ocean in the fall of that year. Highly suspicious of Smith's motives, the Spanish governor threatened the Americans with jail. Officials softened their stance and did allow Smith and his men to spend the winter of 1827-1828 in the San Francisco Bay area, but they made it clear that they did not want the Americans to linger any longer than necessary.

In the spring, the party proceeded north to present-day Oregon, and Smith became the first white man to travel from California to Oregon by an overland route. The

Kelawatset Indians of the region proved hostile, however, and killed the majority of Smith's men in an attack. Smith and three other survivors managed to reach Fort Vancouver, where they were aided by British trappers. After spending the winter of 1828-1829 at Fort Vancouver, Smith returned to the Flathead region for the 1829 trappers' rendezvous. Briefly reunited with his partners, Jackson and Sublette, Smith then led a large force of men into the Blackfoot country of Montana and Wyoming for the fall hunt.

The Indians of the northwest were becoming increasingly unfriendly, worsening the risks to both trappers and traders, so in 1830 Sublette, Smith, and Jackson decided to sell their trapping interests to the Rocky Mountain Fur Company. They returned to St. Louis and became involved in the growing trade with Santa Fe. Smith himself planned to give up the wandering life and settle down in St. Louis. His mother had died recently, and he felt a strong sense of obligation to his family. By 1830 he had spent eight years in almost constant travel and exploration. Perhaps the novelty of new places was finally losing some of its allure.

Smith purchased both a farmhouse and a town house, hired servants, and talked about preparing his complete journals and maps for publication. However, he allowed himself to be persuaded to make one last trip. In the spring of 1831 he agreed to lead a trading expedition to Santa Fe to help the buyers of his fur company procure supplies. A band of Comanche apparently surprised and killed Smith while he was scouting ahead of the main party in search of drinking water near the Cimmaron River along the Santa Fe Trail. The planned editing and publication of his complete journals never took place, and most of his papers were lost following his death.

SIGNIFICANCE

Although numerous American explorers charted sections of the continent, few covered as much territory or saw as wide a variety of terrain as Smith, nor did their travels have as significant an impact on later settlement. Smith's journal, written on his trek from the Green River in Wyoming to Arizona and then on to the Pacific coast, contains the first descriptions by Americans of both the wonders of the Grand Canyon and the magnificent redwood groves of California. His trek across the South Pass of the Rockies, a five-hundred-mile journey with pack wagons and livestock, opened a trail that would be utilized by thousands of pioneers en route to Oregon. Similarly, his trek across the Great Salt Lake Desert and Ne-

vada blazed a more direct route to California. It later served as the route first for the Pony Express and then for U.S. Highway 50.

—*Nancy Farm Mannikko*

FURTHER READING

Allen, John Logan. *Jedediah Smith and the Mountain Men of the American West*. Introduction by Michael Collins. New York: Chelsea House, 1991. This biography written for a juvenile audience chronicles the exploits of the early nineteenth century mountain men who opened trails through the American West. Bibliographical references and index.

Brooks, George R., ed. *Southwest Expedition of Jedediah S. Smith: His Personal Account of the Journey to California, 1826-1827*. Lincoln: University of Nebraska Press, 1990. Smith's journey across the Mojave and the Great Salt Lake Desert, in his own words.

Dale, Harrison Clifford. *The Explorations of William H. Ashley and Jedediah Smith, 1822-1829*. Lincoln: University of Nebraska Press, 1991. Originally published as *The Ashley-Smith Explorations and the Discovery of a Central Route to the Pacific, 1822-1829*, in 1941. Includes original journals edited by Dale. Excellent history that summarizes the travels of both Ashley and Smith and sets them in a historical context.

Davis, Lee. "Tracking Jedediah Smith Through Hupa Territory." *The American Indian Quarterly* 13 (Fall, 1989): 369. Provides vivid details about one segment of Smith's travels. Davis, by looking at one aspect of Smith's explorations in detail, helps to flesh out the more general accounts of his travels.

Morgan, Dale L. *Jedediah Smith and the Opening of the West*. Lincoln: University of Nebraska Press, 1994. A good basic biography of Smith, containing a portrait.

Neihardt, John Gneisenau. *The Splendid Wayfaring: Jedediah Smith and the Ashley-Henry Men, 1822-1831*. Lincoln: University of Nebraska Press, 1990. Fascinating examination of Smith and his fellow fur traders and trappers and their mythic status in American history.

Smith, Jedediah Strong. *The Southwest Expedition of Jedediah S. Smith: His Personal Account of the Journey to California, 1826-1827*. Edited by George R. Brooks. 1977. Reprint. Lincoln: University of Nebraska Press, 1989. These accounts, by the explorer himself, are supplemented by a bibliography and an index.

Sullivan, Maurice S. *The Travels of Jedediah Smith*. Lincoln: University of Nebraska Press, 1992. Originally published in 1934 using materials from Smith's surviving journals, this book has long been considered the definitive reference on Smith's life and travels.

SEE ALSO: Nicholas Biddle; Kit Carson; Meriwether Lewis and William Clark; Zebulon Pike; Sacagawea.
RELATED ARTICLE in *Great Events from History: The Nineteenth Century, 1801-1900:* 1822-1831: Jedediah Smith Explores the Far West.

JOSEPH SMITH
American religious leader

The founder of the Church of Jesus Christ of Latter-day Saints—an indigenous American religion that was the fastest-growing religion in the United States at the turn of the twenty-first century—Smith developed a novel exegesis of the traditional Protestant Bible and provided new scriptures, including the Book of Mormon.

BORN: December 23, 1805; Sharon, Vermont
DIED: June 27, 1844; Carthage, Illinois
ALSO KNOWN AS: Joseph Smith, Jr. (birth name)
AREAS OF ACHIEVEMENT: Church government, religion and theology

EARLY LIFE

Joseph Smith was the third son of Joseph Smith, Sr., and Lucy Mack Smith. The Smiths were a hardworking but impoverished farm family of New England stock. Through the first ten years of his life, his family moved from one rocky New England farm to another, unable to achieve the financial success that would enable them to settle and become established members of the community. In 1816, the Smiths joined the stream of migrants leaving New England for the trans-Appalachian West. They settled in upstate New York, eventually purchasing a farm near Palmyra.

The Smiths, in moving to Palmyra, had arrived at one of the focal points for the religious revivals that convulsed the nation during the first three decades of the nineteenth century. In the fervor of religious controversy, mainstream denominations splintered and sects multiplied, especially in upstate New York, which was known as the "burnt over district," because it had been repeatedly scorched by the fires of the spirit. There, shouting evangelists from the mainstream denominations competed with prophets of a forthcoming millennium and communitarian groups such as the Shakers. Others, disgusted by revivalism and competition between denominations, longed for Christian unity

through a restoration of the primitive Church of apostolic times.

The Smiths, like other poor farmers during the 1820's, suffered from the precarious conditions caused by the developing American economy. Young Smith, with only limited schooling, worked as a laborer on his father's mortgaged farm. Upstate New York was dotted with Indian mounds. Like many others in the area, Joseph sometimes searched for buried treasure. In 1826, he was brought to trial as a disorderly person and impostor in connection with these "money-digging" activities.

LIFE'S WORK

Smith's outward life was that of any other farmer's son. In 1827, he married Emma Hale and seemed to have embarked upon an ordinary life, marred only by his lack of financial security. However, Smith's life was far from ordinary. In 1830, he emerged as a prophet and began to build the Church of Jesus Christ of Latter-day Saints.

The series of extraordinary events that transformed Smith into the Mormon prophet began when he was fourteen. As he later told his followers, he had gone into the forest to pray for guidance as to which of the competing denominations and sects he should join. The Lord and Christ Jesus appeared to him and told him that all the denominations were in error.

The revelations that led to the formation of the Mormon Church began in 1823, when, according to Smith, he was visited by the Angel Moroni. The angel guided Smith to a buried stone box, which contained a book written on gold plates and a set of spectaclelike stones that, when worn, enabled Smith to read the book. In September, 1827, Smith was allowed to take the plates home and began translating the book, dictating the text to various scribes from behind a curtain. When the translation was completed, the plates were given back to the angel. In 1830, the Book of Mormon was published.

The Book of Mormon tells the story of a pre-Columbian settlement of Hebrews in America. They are visited

Joseph Smith. (Library of Congress)

by Christ after his crucifixion. He establishes his church in America. After two hundred years, this church and the Hebrew civilization in America are destroyed in a war between the Hebrew tribes, the Nephites and the Lamanites. One of the Nephite survivors, Moroni, buries golden plates containing a history of his people in a hill in upstate New York, where they could be recovered and used to restore Christ's church in America.

With the publication of the Book of Mormon, Smith, then twenty-four, began to attract a nucleus of believers. In 1834, the Church of Jesus Christ of Latter-day Saints was organized. Believers were to be guided by the Bible, the Book of Mormon, and subsequent revelations announced by Smith. The new church grew rapidly, and the Saints gathered into communities to be near their prophet, who promised that a Mormon city, a new Zion, would soon be built on the western frontier in Missouri. Mormons moved into Missouri to prepare the way, while Smith and the Church's leadership moved from New York to a Mormon community in Kirtland, Ohio.

The Mormons' clannishness and religious unorthodoxy aroused hostility among the old settlers in Mis-

souri. In addition, the Mormons were nonslaveholding Yankees, moving into a slave state. A small-scale war broke out between the old settlers and the Mormons. Smith himself was arrested in 1838 and convicted of treason by a Missouri court. Sentenced to death, he managed to escape to Illinois.

There, Smith and the other Mormon refugees, joined by new converts from Great Britain, began to build a model city on the banks of the Mississippi. Incorporated in 1840, Nauvoo became one of the wonders of the American West. Mormons moved there by the thousands, and construction began on a massive temple.

Smith was the acknowledged leader of the city's spiritual and political life. He was prophet and "lieutenant general" of a Mormon legion of two thousand troops. Still a young man in his thirties, Smith impressed visitors with his vibrant personality. Tall, handsome, with light-brown hair, blue eyes, and a sharp, prominent nose, Smith was a commanding presence in Nauvoo. He also wielded considerable political power in Illinois. Nauvoo's city charter made it almost independent of state authority. However, the Mormons, by voting as a bloc, could swing Illinois state elections. The Mormons' power made their neighbors suspicious and afraid; their fears were not allayed when, in 1844, Smith announced his intention to run for the presidency, hoping to focus the public's attention on the injustices to which his people had been subjected.

Smith's control over the Church also made some of his followers uneasy, as did the rumors (later proven true) that the prophet had privately authorized plural marriage, or polygamy. In 1844, Mormon dissidents set up a press, intending to publicize their discontent. Smith ordered the press destroyed. He was arrested by the state of Illinois, charged with treason, and incarcerated in the Carthage, Illinois, jail. On June 27, 1844, a mob attacked the jail, and Smith was killed.

In death, Smith became a martyr. His church continued to grow and prosper, establishing a center in Utah and eventually becoming a respected American denomination with millions of converts throughout the world.

SIGNIFICANCE
Historians have argued that Smith founded the only truly native American religion, and that his theology reflected both the optimism and the anxiety of early nineteenth century United States. The new church was especially appealing to Americans who were tired of sectarian squabbles, because it offered a restoration of apostolic and priestly authority. The Latter-day Saints could cut

WITNESSES TO THE BOOK OF MORMON

The Church of Jesus Christ of Latter-day Saints regards the Book of Mormon as a sacred text containing the history of ancient immigrants from the Middle East to the New World. Joseph Smith claimed to have translated the book from golden plates that were revealed to him by an angel and later carried back to heaven. Apart from Smith himself, only eleven people publicly claimed to have seen the golden plates. Their signed testimonies are printed in the introductory pages of every edition of the Book of Mormon. The credibility of these eleven witnesses has faced many challenges, but the value of their testimony can be judged, in part, through close examination of what they actually are saying.

THE TESTIMONY OF THREE WITNESSES

Be it known unto all nations, kindreds, tongues, and people, unto whom this work shall come: That we, through the grace of God the Father, and our Lord Jesus Christ, have seen the plates which contain this record, which is a record of the people of Nephi, and also of the Lamanites, their brethren, and also of the people of Jared, who came from the tower of which hath been spoken. And we also know that they have been translated by the gift and power of God, for his voice hath declared it unto us; wherefore we know of a surety that the work is true. And we also testify that we have seen the engravings which are upon the plates; and they have been shown unto us by the power of God, and not of man. And we declare with words of soberness, that an angel of God came down from heaven, and he brought and laid before our eyes, that we beheld and saw the plates, and the engravings thereon; and we know that it is by the grace of God the Father, and our Lord Jesus Christ, that we beheld and bear record that these things are true. And it is marvelous in our eyes. Nevertheless, the voice of the Lord commanded us that we should bear record of it; wherefore, to be obedient unto the commandments of God, we bear testimony of these things. And we know that if we are faithful in Christ, we shall rid our garments of the blood of all men, and be found spotless before the judgment-seat of Christ, and shall dwell with him eternally in the heavens. And the honor be to the Father, and to the Son, and to the Holy Ghost, which is one God. Amen.

—Oliver Cowdery
David Whitmer
Martin Harris

THE TESTIMONY OF EIGHT WITNESSES

Be it known unto all nations, kindreds, tongues, and people, unto whom this work shall come: That Joseph Smith, Jun., the translator of this work, has shown unto us the plates of which hath been spoken, which have the appearance of gold; and as many of the leaves as the said Smith has translated we did handle with our hands; and we also saw the engravings thereon, all of which has the appearance of ancient work, and of curious workmanship. And this we bear record with words of soberness, that the said Smith has shown unto us, for we have seen and hefted, and know of a surety that the said Smith has got the plates of which we have spoken. And we give our names unto the world, to witness unto the world that which we have seen. And we lie not, God bearing witness of it.

—Christian Whitmer
Jacob Whitmer
Peter Whitmer, Jun.
John Whitmer
Hiram Page
Joseph Smith, Sen.
Hyrum Smith
Samuel H. Smith

Source: The Book of Mormon, translated by Joseph Smith, Jr. (Salt Lake City, Utah: Church of Jesus Christ of Latter-day Saints, 1920).

through endless debates as to which church was right and promise Christian unity. The Church also appealed to those offended by the emotionalism of the revivals. Finally, the new church tapped into the stream of millennialism then current in American religious thought, promising the establishment of the kingdom of God on earth, the building of the new Zion in the United States.

Smith's church also appealed to Americans who disliked the intensely competitive economy and society characteristic of the United States during the 1830's. For every individual who achieved success, there were thousands like the Smiths who barely scraped by, lacking money and status. The early Mormons experimented with communally held property; although these experiments were not successful, the Church continued to offer a ready-made community that promised economic security to all members. In addition, the structure of the Church itself provided positions of authority and respect for all male believers.

Smith's views on the afterlife can be seen as the quintessence of American optimism. After a life spent progressing in the service of the Church, Mormon men could continue to progress after death and would themselves become gods. Non-Mormons would be relegated to a lesser Heaven, but very few people would actually be doomed.

Smith thus founded a highly successful church that offered stability and security as well as progress to people living in an era of rapid change. For his followers, he was also an inspired prophet who had provided them with new scriptures authenticated by divine revelation.

—*Jeanette Keith*

FURTHER READING

Arrington, Leonard J., and Davis Bitton. *The Mormon Experience: A History of the Latter-day Saints.* New York: Alfred A. Knopf, 1979. A sympathetic but objective Church history by two Mormon historians, placing Smith in the context of his times. The first section deals with Smith and the early days of the Church.

Bailyn, Bernard, et al. "Dissent: The Mormons as a Test Case." In *The Great Republic: A History of the American People*, edited by David Brion Davis. Lexington, Mass.: D. C. Heath, 1977. A brief but highly informative analysis of the Mormons as dissenters from the economic, social, and sexual norms of nineteenth century America.

Barrett, Ivan J. *Joseph Smith and the Restoration: A History of the Church to 1846.* Provo, Utah: Brigham Young University Press, 1967. Written for Mormons and published by the press of a Mormon university, this book is hardly objective but does offer an interesting and detailed chronicle of Smith's life as seen by his followers.

Brodie, Fawn M. *No Man Knows My History: The Life of Joseph Smith, the Mormon Prophet.* New York: Alfred A. Knopf, 1946. The most famous biography of Joseph Smith. According to Brodie, Smith was a likable phony who made up the Book of Mormon as part of a money-making scheme. In later life, surrounded by people who believed in him as a prophet, he became what he had pretended to be. A revised 1971 edition of the work contains a psychoanalytic interpretation of Smith's actions, concluding that he may not have been a deliberate fraud, but rather an impostor, using fantasy to resolve his own identity conflict.

Bushman, Richard L. *Believing History: Latter-day Saint Essays.* Edited by Reid L. Neilson and Jed Woodworth. New York: Columbia University Press, 2004. Part 3 of this collection of essays, "Joseph Smith and Culture," contains eight essays analyzing various aspects of Smith's life, ideas, and influence within the Mormon Church.

_____. *Joseph Smith and the Beginnings of Mormonism.* Urbana: University of Illinois Press, 1984. Mormon historian Bushman recounts the history of the Mormon movement prior to 1831, focusing on Smith and his family and describing events as participants perceived them.

_____. *Joseph Smith: Rough Stone Rolling.* New York: Alfred A. Knopf, 2005. Expanded biography that examines Smith's entire life in detail, using all available sources.

Flander, Robert B. *Nauvoo: Kingdom on the Mississippi.* Urbana: University of Illinois Press, 1965. This history of the Mormon model city explores Smith's role as city planner and town leader.

Hansen, Klaus J. *Mormonism and the American Experience.* Chicago: University of Chicago Press, 1981. In this volume in the University of Chicago's History of American Religion series, Hansen discusses the origins of the Mormon Church, summarizing most of the theories historians and psychologists have propounded about Smith, and analyzes Smith's theology and its applications in the history of the Latter-day Saints.

Remini, Robert V. *Joseph Smith.* New York: Viking Press, 2002. An accessible biography, recounting Smith's life and creation of a new religion. Remini traces the origins of Mormonism to early nineteenth century religious evangelism.

SEE ALSO: Alexander Campbell; Mary Baker Eddy; Brigham Young.

RELATED ARTICLES in *Great Events from History: The Nineteenth Century, 1801-1900:* April 6, 1830: Smith Founds the Mormon Church; February 4, 1846: Mormons Begin Migration to Utah.

MARY SOMERVILLE
Scottish scientist and writer

After preparing a celebrated translation and explanation of Pierre-Simon Laplace's Traité de mécanique celeste, *Somerville became a central figure in British and American scientific networks, and her widely read books helped define the disciplines within the physical sciences.*

BORN: December 26, 1780; Jedburgh, Roxburghshire, Scotland
DIED: November 29, 1872; Naples, Italy
ALSO KNOWN AS: Mary Fairfax (birth name); Mary Greig
AREAS OF ACHIEVEMENT: Mathematics, science and technology

EARLY LIFE

Mary Somerville was born Mary Fairfax, the fifth of seven children, only four of whom survived to adulthood. Her Scottish mother, Margaret Charters, was the second wife of her father, William George Fairfax, an English admiral who fought with James Wolfe at Quebec during the Seven Years' War of 1756-1763. Although Mary attended boarding school for one year at the age of ten, her parents believed that women should develop domestic skills and not pursue formal education. When she was a teenager, however, she became intrigued by mathematics problems she found in a women's magazine and began to teach herself. An uncle encouraged her, and she was able to obtain John Bonnycastle's *An Introduction to Algebra* (1782) and Euclid's *Elements of Geometry* when she was fifteen.

In 1804, Mary married a cousin, Samuel Greig, a captain in the Russian navy who was stationed in London, where Mary gave birth to two sons, in 1805 and 1806. She was unable to continue her studies during that period, but after Greig died in 1807, she returned to her birthplace in Scotland, Jedburgh, and began to educate herself openly. She was assisted by professors from the nearby University of Edinburgh, such as John Playfair

and John Leslie. She also became a friend of Henry Brougham and other founders of the *Edinburgh Review*, with whom she shared her Whiggish political views. Her most significant mentor was William Wallace, who became the professor of mathematics at Edinburgh after Playfair died in 1819.

Mary also gained support from her second husband, William Somerville, a first cousin whom she married in 1812. A surgeon and fellow of the Royal Society, William studied geology and mineralogy with Mary. Mary also read French mathematics and astronomy under Wallace's tutelage and studied Greek and botany.

In 1814, one of Mary's first sons died. The following year she had another son, who died the same year. She and William also had three daughters together: Margaret (born in 1813), Mary (1815), and Martha (1817). In 1816, William moved the family to London, where he took up a position as principal inspector for the Army Medical Board. After his job was lost to government budget-cutting in 1817, he worked only occasionally. He and Mary used his free time to visit Jean-Baptiste Biot, François Arago, Pierre-Simon Laplace, and other scholars in Paris. In 1819, William was appointed director of the Royal Military Hospital in Chelsea, where he remained until 1836.

LIFE'S WORK

Although Mary believed too much study was responsible for her ten-year-old daughter Margaret's death in 1823, she continued her own studies and prepared her first scientific paper, on the relationship between sunlight and magnetism. William communicated it to the *Philosophical Transactions of the Royal Society* in 1826. Although Mary's conclusions in that paper proved to be incorrect, her friends encouraged her to continue with public presentations.

In 1827, Henry Brougham asked Mary to translate Laplace's *Traité de mécanique celeste* (5 vols., 1798-1827), a treatise demonstrating that the solar system was self-regulating, as was predicted by Isaac Newton's gravitational theory. After consulting with Augustus de Morgan and Charles Babbage, she added to her translation a "preliminary dissertation" that explained the mathematics readers needed to understand Laplace's ideas. Her introduction also set Laplace's work in historical context and presented some of her own mathematical work. Her translation, with her commentary, was published as *The Mechanism of the Heavens* in 1831. The book was immediately pirated in the United States; translated into French, German, and Italian; and adopted as a textbook at the University of Cambridge in 1837.

In 1834, Mary followed this work with the two-volume *On the Connexion of the Physical Sciences*. This book's explanation of interconnections among astronomy, physics, magnetism, meteorology, and physical geography secured her fame as an expositor. The English physicist David Brewster praised her book's argument—although he was unsure women would read it—and the Scottish physicist James Clerk Maxwell later described it as a seminal work of the nineteenth century. During that same year, Mary was elected to honorary memberships in the Royal Irish Academy and the Société de Physique et d'Histoire Naturelle of Geneva. In 1835, she was elected an honorary member of the Royal Astronomical Society, and the Royal Society commissioned a bust of her for its main hall. To encourage others to synthesize and explain science, British prime minister Robert Peel awarded Mary an annual pension of two hundred pounds—an amount increased to three hundred pounds in 1837. Meanwhile, ten editions of *On the Connexion of the Physical Sciences* appeared during the first four decades after its original publication.

Mary's husband William was frequently ill, and both Mary and William had substantial financial obligations to their relatives. The family's poor financial situation prompted the family to reside in Italy, where the cost of living was much lower, almost continuously after 1838. In 1836, Mary wrote a paper for the French Academy of Science that was delivered by François Arago. In 1845, she wrote a paper for the Royal Society that was delivered by John Herschel.

Through these years, Mary maintained her scientific friendships, which also included Charles Lyell and Alexander von Humboldt. In 1848, she published *Physical Geography*. This book covered the same subject as a book by Humboldt but was organized differently. Her division of geography into physical regions, rather than nations, and her description of the inhabitants of earth, sea, and air made the book a popular text. She also relied on

Lyell's uniformitarian geology and assigned a central role to solar energy. Although her acceptance of the theory of an old Earth led to denunciations from the House of Commons and the Church of England, *Physical Geography* went through seven editions.

Despite the controversy her book raised, Mary continued to receive honors. In 1857, she was elected to the American Geographical and Statistical Society, and the Italian Geographical Society made her a member in 1870. Meanwhile, she made significant revisions in some of her books as they were republished, but she never incorporated Charles Darwin's theory of evolution by natural selection into *Physical Geography*.

Mary supported woman suffrage and signed a petition in 1862 that urged the University of London to permit women to sit for degrees. She finished her last book, *On Molecular and Microscopic Science*, in 1869. During that same year, she was elected to the American Philosophical Society and presented with the Royal Geographical Society's Victoria Gold Medal and the Victor Emmanuel Gold Medal of the Geographical Society of Florence. She received at least twenty-five awards in all, of which a dozen came from Italian organizations.

Mary's last decades were saddened by the deaths of her husband in 1860 and her only surviving son, Woronzow Greig, in 1865. Greig had become a lawyer and had been elected to the Royal Society in 1853. Although Mary's daughters, Martha and Mary, outlived her, they never married. Mary Somerville died in Florence, Italy, on November 29, 1872, one month short of her ninety-second birthday. After her death, an island in the Arctic Ocean was named for her in recognition of her interest in polar exploration, and Oxford University's Somerville College was named after her when it opened in 1879.

SIGNIFICANCE

Mary Somerville was viewed as the leading woman scientist of her era. She was part of the last generation that was able to understand all of the scientific knowledge then extant. Male intellectuals treated her as an equal; they praised her publications and accepted her definitions of the physical sciences. Because no clear boundaries between professional and amateur scientists then existed, Mary was able to study independently and participate in scientific culture alongside premier scientists, just as men did who learned science informally. Indeed, both provincial and foreign scientists considered it essential to call on Mary when they visited Europe after 1830.

Like most women of her time, Mary Somerville believed that women were incapable of making truly original discoveries. Although male scientists appreciated her work, they offered her only honorary memberships in their learned societies. Curiously, gender-based perceptions of Somerville also reversed during her lifetime. After she died in 1872, women eulogized her as a scientific pioneer, while men developed a sentimental view of her as a symbolic curiosity. Later scholars have wrestled with interpreting the meaning of her roles and contributions.

—*Amy Ackerberg-Hastings*

FURTHER READING

Chapman, Allan. *Mary Somerville and the World of Science*. Bath, England: Canopus, 2004. A brief but lively introduction to Somerville's life that summarizes her background and writings, putting them into the wider context of nineteenth century science.

Neeley, Katherine A. *Mary Somerville: Science, Illumination, and the Female Mind*. Cambridge, England: Cambridge University Press, 2001. Although vague on chronology and dates, Neeley's book takes a provocative approach by treating Somerville's activities and the ways in which others celebrated her as a metaphor for the illumination of science.

Patterson, Elizabeth Chambers. *Mary Somerville and the Cultivation of Science*. Boston: Martinus Nijhoff, 1983. Patterson catalogued Somerville's manuscripts and produced the most thorough account of her life's work and influences.

Sanderson, Marie. "Mary Somerville: Her Work in Physical Geography." *Geographical Review* 64 (1974): 410-420. Somerville's contributions to meteorology and climatology are described and assessed in the context of her famous male scientific friends.

Sheffield, Suzanne Le-May. *Women and Science: Social Impact and Interaction*. Santa Barbara, Calif.: ABC-CLIO, 2004. A pioneering attempt at a general study of women's education and participation in science. Somerville is covered in the section on women scientists in the men's world.

Somerville, Martha. *Personal Recollections, From Early Life to Old Age, of Mary Somerville*. Boston: Roberts Brothers, 1874. Somerville's autobiography, published posthumously and edited by her daughter to omit scientific details and people deemed uninteresting.

SEE ALSO: Charles Babbage; Henry Brougham; Charles Darwin; Sophie Germain; Alexander von Humboldt; Sofya Kovalevskaya; Pierre-Simon Laplace; Countess of Lovelace; Sir Charles Lyell; Sir Robert Peel; Henri Poincaré; Charlotte Angas Scott.

RELATED ARTICLES in *Great Events from History: The Nineteenth Century, 1801-1900:* 1899: Hilbert Publishes *The Foundations of Geometry*; 1900: Lebesgue Develops New Integration Theory.

JOHN HANNING SPEKE
English explorer

A central figure in the nineteenth century European search for the source of the Nile River, Speke traveled extensively in East Africa and is credited with being the first European to see and report on Lake Victoria.

BORN: May 4, 1827; Orleigh Court, near Bideford, Devon, England
DIED: September 15, 1864; Neston Park, Corsham, Wiltshire, England
AREA OF ACHIEVEMENT: Exploration

EARLY LIFE

John Hanning Speke (speek) was the son of William Speke, a retired army officer, and Georgiana Hanning Elizabeth Speke, who came from a family of wealthy merchants. Relatively little is known of Speke's early years. He showed an interest in zoology from a tender age but was a restless boy who cared little for school. Whenever possible, he was out in the fields and woods, and it is from these youthful days that a lifelong interest in natural history and sport dates.

In 1844, the same year his father came into possession of the family estate at Jordans (many sources wrongly suggest that this was Speke's birthplace), he received assignment as a second lieutenant in the Forty-sixth Bengal Native Infantry Regiment, in the Indian Army. This assignment followed completion of his studies at Blackheath New Preparatory School in London.

April 24, 1844, may be said to be the day when Speke was vested with the responsibilities of manhood. On this day the seventeen-year-old lad was examined and passed as an entering officer cadet for Indian army service. Speke's preferment was in all likelihood largely a result of his mother's influence with the duke of Wellington. He had already passed the required medical examinations prior to his final application, so he was able to begin active service almost immediately. On May 3, 1844, he boarded ship and four months later was in India. The Asian subcontinent and its life apparently suited him well. He demonstrated some facility with languages, and by the end of his second year of service, he had passed an examination in Hindustani. He also had ample opportunity to indulge his love of hunting and made many forays into the plains and the Himalaya Mountains in search of sport.

John Hanning Speke. (Library of Congress)

Speke saw active service in the Second Sikh War when he served as a subaltern officer in the "fighting brigade" of General Colin Campbell's division, and on October 8, 1850, he was promoted to the rank of lieutenant. It was also at this point that he first began to think of African exploration, although at the time collecting specimens of the continent's animal life weighed more heavily in his mind than geographical discovery. For the time, though, any such journey was only a dream. He still had five years' service remaining before he would become eligible for an extended furlough.

Meanwhile, he scrupulously saved his money and underwent conscious training in preparation for African exploration. Each year he made excursions into the mountains of Tibet, he developed his skills as a surveyor and cartographer, and he became an excellent hunter and marksman. Speke actually cared little for the dull routine of army life, as he later confessed, and he clearly was a man in search of adventure. This obsession would drive him all of his life, as he constantly sought to conquer that which was mysterious or unknown. This trait, coupled with his interest in nature, was vital in his choosing the arduous life of an explorer.

Thanks to the favor of his superiors, he was able to obtain regular extended leaves, and late in 1854, he had the opportunity for which he had so long waited. He was to join a fellow Indian army officer, Richard Francis Burton, in exploring Somaliland. He and Burton had met on shooting outings in India, and their common interest in Africa had drawn them together. From this juncture onward, for the remaining ten years of his life, Speke would be almost completely preoccupied with African discovery.

LIFE'S WORK

The Somaliland undertaking proved an abortive one. While camped on the coast, the party was attacked, with Speke being badly wounded and briefly held captive. The attack also planted the seeds of discord between Burton and Speke, for in the confusion Burton believed that his companion had not responded to the native attack as readily or bravely as he should. However, realizing that Speke had "suffered in person and purse," Burton invited him to join another expedition. This journey began in December, 1856, with its primary objective being the discovery of the mysterious sources of the Nile River.

The pair, rather than taking the standard approach of moving upriver along the Nile, traveled overland from the East African coast opposite Zanzibar. Together they discovered Lake Tanganyika, which would ultimately prove to be the source of the Congo River, although Burton thought it might be their objective. On the return journey, while Burton remained in camp at Kazeh (modern Tabora, Tanzania) investigating some of the social and sexual customs that so fascinated him, Speke made a flying march to the north.

Speke's objective was a lake that local reports said stretched to the ends of the earth, and on July 30, 1858, he first sighted the vast body of water that he instinctively knew was the Nile's source. He named it Lake Victoria, after his sovereign, but because of time considerations and the fact that he was nearly blind from ophthalmia, Speke had no opportunity for a proper reconnaissance of the lake. Nevertheless, he returned to Kazeh proclaiming that he had discovered the Nile's source, a conclusion that Burton ridiculed. Henceforth there would be bitter discord between the two, although they had little choice but to retain at least the vestiges of friendship during the perilous return journey to Zanzibar.

After returning to England, Speke immediately claimed credit as the discoverer of the Nile's source, and his theories attracted widespread attention. He had preceded Burton back to England, and when the leader of the East African expedition returned a few weeks later, he found, to his regret, that Speke was the "lion of the day." The Royal Geographical Society, with the encouragement of Sir Roderick Impey Murchison, had decided to finance a new expedition for the purpose of obtaining proof of Speke's claims. Accompanied by James Augustus Grant, another acquaintance from his Indian army days, Speke returned to East Africa in 1860.

Despite facing an incredible variety of obstacles, ranging from incipient warfare among tribes living along the route to recurrent demands for *hongo* (passage fees), the expedition made its way to the important lake kingdoms of Buganda and Karagwe. While Grant stayed behind at the latter location (ostensibly because of a leg injury but probably owing to Speke's egotistical reluctance to share any fame that might come from his discoveries), Speke marched eastward to the Nile. On July 21, 1862, he reached the river and followed it upstream until he reached the falls at the north end of Lake Victoria. This massive outflow of water he named the Ripon Falls, in honor of the president of the Royal Geographical Society, Lord Ripon.

At this juncture, his task seemed simple enough. All that remained was to collect Grant and proceed downriver until the expedition reached a known point on the Nile. This proved impossible, though, thanks to objections raised by tribes living along the river. The necessity

of taking a detour away from the Nile as he moved downriver left Speke's claims open to dispute, and it would not be until 1890, long after his death, that his contentions would be proved completely correct. Nevertheless, after overcoming a series of vexing impediments placed in their way by African chieftains, Speke and Grant managed to resume their travels downriver. Falling in with a company of Arab slave and ivory traders, they reached Gondokoro, the last outpost of European civilization, on February 15, 1863.

There they met Samuel White Baker and his mistress (later to become his wife), Florence von Sass. After a few days with this extraordinary couple, they proceeded onward in their journey back to England. After returning home, Speke and Grant were welcomed in tumultuous fashion, although challenges from Burton and others regarding the accuracy of Speke's geography produced considerable controversy. The matter occasioned widespread debate in newspapers, learned circles, and among the general public. Eventually, it was agreed that Burton and Speke would debate on the subject before a meeting of the British Association for the Advancement of Science, with the noted missionary/explorer Dr. David Livingstone acting as moderator.

The debate was scheduled for September 16, 1864, but it never took place. As a packed house listened in shocked silence, it was announced that Speke had shot himself while out hunting partridges the previous afternoon. The dramatic nature of his death added to the controversy surrounding the entire matter of the Nile's source, and the subject would be one of contention and uncertainty in Africanist and geographical circles for another generation. The nature of Speke's death, which was officially ruled accidental but which many believed, with some justice, was suicide, simply added a further element of poignancy. Only in 1890, after the travels of Baker, Henry Morton Stanley, and others had added to knowledge of the Nile's headwaters, was the problem completely solved. In the end, Speke's claim to precedence as discoverer of the Nile's source was fully vindicated.

SIGNIFICANCE

John Hanning Speke's fame rests entirely on his African travels, and his discovery of Lake Victoria was, as another African explorer, Sir Harry H. Johnston, has said, the greatest geographical discovery since North America. His work, along with that of Livingstone, Burton, Stanley, and other African explorers, excited great public interest in Africa and thereby eventually fueled the flames of imperialism. In a sense, African discovery provided the foundation upon which the scramble for colonial possessions on the continent was built, and Speke did much to create the widespread interest in all things African that characterized the mid-Victorian era.

There can be no doubt that Speke was a contentious individual, but his single-minded mania for discovery loomed large in his success as an explorer. His legacy is one of having solved an age-old mystery and in so doing directing European attention to Africa in an unprecedented fashion. He remains in many ways an elusive figure, thanks to a paucity of surviving personal papers and a rather secretive nature, but recent research suggests that his was a complex personality, as was indeed generally the case with African explorers.

—*James A. Casada*

FURTHER READING

Bridges, Roy C. "Negotiating a Way to the Nile." In *Africa and Its Explorers*, edited by Robert I. Rotberg. Cambridge, Mass.: Harvard University Press, 1970. A useful overview of Speke's explorations set against the wider scope of nineteenth century African discovery.

Maitland, Alexander. *Speke*. London: Constable, 1971. The only full-length biography of Speke yet written, this work is flawed by inadequate research and an overemphasis on psychoanalysis. Nevertheless, it is the best available account of Speke's life.

Moorehead, Alan. *The White Nile*. New York: Perennial, 1960. Reprint. 2000. Covers Speke's and Burton's exploration of Zanzibar, Speke's subsequent exploration of other parts of Africa, and his discovery of the Nile's source.

Speke, John Hanning. *Journal of the Discovery of the Source of the Nile*. Edinburgh: William Blackwood, 1863. Speke's personal account of his final African journey.

SEE ALSO: Sir Richard Francis Burton; Mary Kingsley; David Livingstone; Henry Morton Stanley; Duke of Wellington.

RELATED ARTICLES in *Great Events from History: The Nineteenth Century, 1801-1900:* November 17, 1853: Livingstone Sees the Victoria Falls; 1873-1880: Exploration of Africa's Congo Basin.

HERBERT SPENCER
English philosopher

Best known as the leading social Darwinist of the nineteenth century, Spencer was a wide-ranging thinker who epitomized the scientific mentality of his age. He coined the phrase "survival of the fittest" and attempted to build a comprehensive philosophical synthesis based on evolution.

BORN: April 27, 1820; Derby, Derbyshire, England
DIED: December 8, 1903; Brighton, Sussex, England
AREA OF ACHIEVEMENT: Philosophy

EARLY LIFE

An only child, Herbert Spencer was educated until the age of ten by his father, a private tutor. His unorthodox father, a Dissenter, and the lack of peers molded the young Spencer into an intellectual introvert. He was reared amid discussions of the great political and philosophical issues of the day, and his father's associates consisted primarily of Quakers and Unitarians. Spencer received further education, mostly in mathematics and mechanics, from his uncle, Thomas Spencer, who

headed a school near Bath. The enormous learning that he later demonstrated was acquired principally through his own efforts.

Declining an offer from his uncle to send him to Cambridge, in 1837 Spencer took a job as a civil engineer with the London and Birmingham railway company. He worked for a number of different railways, traveled widely, introduced several technical innovations, and advanced in his career. He had, however, developed a deep interest in politics, and in 1841 he left his engineering career and returned to Derby to live on his savings while writing political commentary.

Initially, Spencer dabbled in radical politics rather unselectively, but some of his early pieces in the *Nonconformist* reveal that his narrow view of the role of the state had already developed. In 1843, he moved to London, where he believed he could advance his literary career. He did poorly, selling only a few items, most of them on phrenology. Soon, his funds depleted, he returned to his engineering work. He quickly became disillusioned with the world of business, and he left it in 1846, exposing railway fraud in an essay in the *Edinburgh Review*.

At the age of twenty-six, Spencer had largely failed in engineering, politics, and journalism. He was both lonely and alone in his increasingly deep meditations. His dedication to philosophical inquiry and his serious reading precluded a social life, and he never married. His dark brown hair was beginning to recede, and in later life he was partially bald, a feature he sought to counter by wearing his hair long on the sides, with bushy sideburns. His face was calm, but pale, and in general his slight figure suggested frailness and delicacy. He was an excellent conversationalist but somewhat abrupt and quite fixed in his opinions.

LIFE'S WORK

In 1848, Spencer's career took a turn for the better when his schoolmaster uncle assisted him in securing a position in London as subeditor of *The Economist*. With this position, Spencer had not only a modest level of financial security but also the spare time to work on the great philosophical project he had been contemplating. At *The Economist* Spencer found like-minded individualists, and his laissez-faire attitude hardened into the rigidness for which he would become famous.

The serious writing effort on which Spencer had been working for some time was completed in the summer of 1850 and published the following year under the title *Social Statics*. With his job and his book, Spencer enjoyed a wider social life, but he continued his father's traditions of nonconformity and he enjoyed being something of an eccentric who flaunted convention. In 1853, the death of his uncle, who had aided him so greatly, brought him a legacy, which was small but sufficient for him to leave *The Economist* and live independently as an author. During that same year, however, he suffered the first of a series of physical and nervous ailments that plagued him for the rest of his life. He traveled widely in search of better health, argued with his friends, remained lonely and unhappy, and became a confirmed hypochondriac.

Spencer continued, however, to write prolifically. In 1855, he published *The Principles of Psychology*, and in 1860 he announced his plan to produce a ten-volume work with the general title *The Synthetic Philosophy*. He suffered a serious nervous breakdown and treated himself with opium, but the work was finally completed in

Herbert Spencer. (Library of Congress)

1896. He financed his work by selling subscriptions, with the subscribers receiving installments of about ninety pages every three months. Some interest in the work was expressed in Great Britain, but it was support from the United States that actually gave Spencer the financial wherewithal to complete his work. An inheritance from his father, along with the proceeds from the sale of his books, allowed him to live comfortably for the rest of his life. He died on December 8, 1903, and the remains of his cremation are at Highgate Cemetery.

At the basis of Spencer's philosophy lay two fundamentals: first, the tremendous importance given to science that was characteristic of his age; second, the sanctity of political and economic laissez-faire that he acquired from his Dissenter and radical background. In fact, Spencer combined these two to make laissez-faire a natural law. He was not, however, the only one to do this. Both science and the idea of laissez-faire were dominant during the mid-nineteenth century, as was the idea of progress, also important to him. Spencer, however, was the foremost spokesperson of these ideas, and he set them forth in his volumes in a way that convinced his contemporaries.

Spencer was the only philosopher of his time to attempt a synthesis of all thought—based on science and especially evolution—that included philosophies of education, biology, psychology, sociology, and ethics, as well as politics. Such a comprehensive system was possible only to the nineteenth century mind, which embraced science in such an enthusiastic and general fashion. Most of Spencer's proofs rested on mere analogies, usually biological, and by the time of his death such generalizations were outdated in a world that had become highly technical and specialized. Having been the most popular thinker of his time, especially in the United States, Spencer fell from favor as rapidly as he had risen, and by the early years of the twentieth century he was largely forgotten, dismissed by philosophers as not being sufficiently philosophical and by scientists as being too much the generalist. Spencerian thought, however, remains well worth studying, not only for what it suggests about the nineteenth century mind but also for what it reveals about the origins of the modern social sciences.

Spencer is always linked, and rightly so, to Darwinian evolution, but it is not merely as a disciple of Charles Darwin that he is important. The evolutionary perspective was current before Darwin produced his famous *On the Origin of Species by Means of Natural Selection* in 1859. Geological evidence supported evolution, and Spencer was aware of these investigations and had been moved to that view by his own observations during excavations for railways. Moreover, his own writings on competition in business influenced Darwin, and while Darwin's work revolutionized Spencer's thinking, as it did that of so many others, it was Spencer who coined the term "survival of the fittest." Spencer, it should be noted, never became a complete Darwinist; for example, he continued to hold to the pre-Darwinian notion of the inheritability of acquired characteristics. It was Spencer, though, who was the most energetic in applying the principles of evolution and natural selection to society, and in doing so he became the archetypal social Darwinist.

The great work, *The Synthetic Philosophy*, that Spencer announced in 1860 took nearly forty years to complete and is divided into several separately titled parts. *First Principles* appeared in 1862 and is typically metaphysical with its insistence on the existence of an ultimate Unknowable, which could be appreciated but never understood, and typically scientific with its assertion on evolution as the motor of all development, change, and progress. *The Principles of Biology*, a work of two volumes published in 1864 and 1867, was both a survey of developmental physiology and an assertion of the iron law of evolution in the movement from lower to higher forms. He followed his evolutionary theme in the reworking of *The Principles of Psychology* (originally

published in 1855), which appeared in a second edition in 1870 and 1872, by insisting that consciousness, too, had gone through successive stages.

Spencer's most influential thesis came in *The Principles of Sociology*, which appeared in three volumes from 1876 to 1896. Here, he provided his organic view of society, that is, that a society is like an organism. In making this analogy, Spencer introduced the study of structure and function into the field of sociology, as well as proving the value of comparative analysis. He also stated in the strongest terms his extreme individualism and negative view of government. From such attitudes has come the tradition that Spencer was rather brutal and pessimistic. In fact, he viewed progress as a natural process, but progress involved the elimination of the weak and unfit.

The last portion of Spencer's great synthesis was *The Principles of Ethics*, of which one volume was published in 1892 and the other in 1893, and here he took the lessons from nature to create a moral code. In the preface to the last volume of *The Principles of Ethics*, he included a note indicating that evolution had not been the absolute principle, at least in ethics, that he had hoped. In addition to these works, he completed an autobiography in 1889 (published in 1904), and in 1902, a year before his death, he was nominated for the Nobel Prize for Literature.

SIGNIFICANCE

Enormously popular in his day, by the middle of the twentieth century Herbert Spencer was entirely neglected by serious scholars, except to be mentioned as the classic proponent of social Darwinism, an honor that served only to strengthen his negative image. Nevertheless, Spencer made important contributions in the study of society, particularly in the areas of social evolution and the problem of the individual versus the state. If nothing else, his version of natural selection, which he expressed in the phrase "survival of the fittest," has secured for him a permanent historical significance.

—*Roy Talbert, Jr.*

FURTHER READING

Duncan, David. *The Life and Letters of Herbert Spencer.* London: Methuen, 1908. Useful because of the primary sources included.

Elliot, Hugh. *Herbert Spencer.* London: Constable, 1917. Interesting because of the early date and because it clearly shows that Spencer's decline had already begun.

Hofstadter, Richard. *Social Darwinism in American Thought.* Rev. ed. Boston: Beacon Press, 1955. An excellent examination of Spencer's considerable influence in the United States.

Kennedy, James G. *Herbert Spencer*. Boston: Twayne, 1978. A brief but useful and available survey of Spencer's life and thought.

McCann, Charles R. *Individualism and the Social Order: The Social Element in Liberal Thought*. London: Routledge, 2004. Analyzes the role of community and society in the social thought of Spencer and other liberal philosophers of the nineteenth and twentieth centuries.

MacRae, Donald G., ed. *The Man Versus the State*. Baltimore: Penguin Books, 1969. An excellent essay assessing Spencer's importance regarding individualism vis-à-vis big government; introduces eight pieces by Spencer.

Peel, J. D. Y. *Herbert Spencer: The Evolution of a Sociologist*. New York: Basic Books, 1971. Excellent on Spencer's contributions to sociology.

Spencer, Herbert. *An Autobiography*. 2 vols. New York: D. Appleton, 1904.

_____. *Herbert Spencer on Education*. Edited by Andreas M. Kazamias. New York: Columbia University Press, 1966. With a lengthy introduction, these selections from Spencer's writings focus on one of his least-known areas of concern.

Turner, Jonathan H. *Herbert Spencer: A Renewed Appreciation*. Beverly Hills, Calif.: Sage, 1985. A sympathetic view, citing Spencer's contributions to modern sociological methodology and theory.

Weinstein, D. *Equal Freedom and Utility: Herbert Spencer's Liberal Utilitarianism*. New York: Cambridge University Press, 1998. Examines Spencer's role in creating a liberal utilitarian moral and political philosophy, exploring his ideas on social evolution, freedom, moral rights, and other issues.

Wiltshire, David. *The Social and Political Thought of Herbert Spencer*. Oxford, England: Oxford University Press, 1978. A good biographical overview that concentrates on political theory.

SEE ALSO: Charles Darwin; Ernst Haeckel.

RELATED ARTICLES in *Great Events from History: The Nineteenth Century, 1801-1900:* September 2, 1843: Wilson Launches *The Economist*; 1862: Spencer Introduces Principles of Social Darwinism; 1871: Darwin Publishes *The Descent of Man*; 1883: Galton Defines "Eugenics."

MIKHAIL MIKHAYLOVICH SPERANSKY
Russian administrator

A career bureaucrat, Speransky sought to liberalize and modernize the Russian government by limiting the power of the autocracy, reforming local government, and codifying Russian law.

BORN: January 12, 1772; Cherkutino, Russia
DIED: February 23, 1839; St. Petersburg, Russia
ALSO KNOWN AS: Count Speransky
AREAS OF ACHIEVEMENT: Government and politics, law

EARLY LIFE

Of peasant origins, Mikhail Mikhaylovich Speransky (spyeh-RAHN-skee) was born in a small provincial Russian village northeast of Moscow. His family was impoverished and poorly educated and lacked even a family surname. In fact, Speransky did not acquire his name until he began his formal education at the age of twelve, when he entered the ecclesiastical academy at the provincial capital of Vladimir. He was already a promising student, and his intellectual skills and academic accomplishments brought him immediate recognition.

In 1790, Speransky was accepted for advanced study at the prestigious Alexander-Nevsky Seminary in St. Petersburg, once more distinguishing himself in his academic pursuits. In addition to the traditional seminary curriculum, Speransky acquired a thorough foundation in the rationalist and materialist thought of the Enlightenment and philosophe writers, which would influence him for the rest of his life.

Following his graduation in 1792, Speransky was offered a part-time teaching post at the academy, and in 1795 he was appointed instructor of philosophy and prefect (dean). After rejecting the proffered appointment, Speransky entered the service of Prince A. B. Kuratin, an influential member of the imperial court. For the next year, Speransky continued his study of French Enlightenment thought and encountered the philosophy of Immanuel Kant as well. In 1796, Kuratin was appointed by Emperor Paul I as procurator-general of the senate, which was similar to being prime minister of the government. Kuratin then used his influence to secure for Speransky a position in the government bureaucracy at the beginning of 1797.

By the end of 1798, Speransky had ascended into the upper levels of the bureaucratic Table of Ranks. In the process, he acquired increased responsibilities and hereditary noble status, both of which reflected his growing importance and influence within the bureaucracy and St. Petersburg society. He became acquainted with the concepts of English political philosophy and its emphasis on conservative social corporateness and institutional reform, which now attracted the previously Francophile nobility following the excesses of the French Revolution. It was at one of these encounters that Speransky met his future wife, Elizabeth Stephens. They were married in 1798 and in 1799 produced a daughter, also Elizabeth. His wife died shortly after their daughter's birth. Speransky, already aloof and introverted by nature, became even more withdrawn as he used his career as a means to overcome his personal grief.

LIFE'S WORK
In 1801, a new czar, Alexander I, ascended the Russian throne. With him came the hope on the part of many younger Russians that his vague sympathies toward liberalism and reform could be translated into reality. For Speransky, it brought the notice of the new czar and his appointment to the newly formed Ministry of Interior. Attaching himself to the fringes of the "unofficial committee," Speransky spent the years between 1802 and 1808 creating the intellectual foundations required for the restructuring of the Russian political and social order. In his deliberations, he drew upon the philosophical ideals of the Enlightenment, the political concepts of the English system, and his own understanding of Russian historical development.

From the outset, Speransky recognized that the key to any broad reform within Russia was the reform of the autocracy itself. As constituted by the reforms of Peter I and consolidated by Catherine II in the previous century, the autocracy was the only legitimate source of authority within the Russian political system and could not be prevented from exercising that authority in a capricious and arbitrary manner.

To Speransky, this situation represented the epitome of political lawlessness, which could not be tolerated in a rational and enlightened society. Not only was such lawlessness destructive to the stability, cohesion, and order of the society in general, but also in Russia's case it was

the primary cause of its political, economic, and social backwardness. Moreover, it prevented Russia from throwing off the burdens of that backwardness by obstructing modernization through meaningful reforms. The only enlightened means to overcome this lawlessness on the part of the ruler, Speransky argued, was the establishment of the rule of law to which all within the society were subject. In this way, rules could be established to govern the relationship between the ruler and the ruled, while also formulating the context in which authority would be exercised by the ruler.

Although Speransky formulated the essential elements of his rule of law concept in 1801-1802 and 1803 for "Mémoire sur la legislation fondamentale en général," summarized by V. I. Semevskii as "Pervi politicheskii traktat Speranskogo" (1907; on the fundamental laws of the state) and "Zapiska ob ustroistve sudebnykhi i pravitel' stvennykh uchrezhdenii v Rossii" (1905; report on the establishment of judiciary and government institutions in Russia), the opportunity to present his formulations to Alexander did not occur until 1809. By the time it did, Alexander's earlier sympathies had dissipated.

The czar rejected Speransky's constitutional plan (known also as the Plan of 1809) as an unacceptable limitation of authority of the autocracy. Speransky's influence at the imperial court began to wane. By 1812, a variety of factors conspired to drive him from power. The cruelest blow, however, came from Alexander himself, who sent his former administrative secretary and assistant into exile, first at Nizhni Novgorod on the upper Volga River and then to Perm in western Siberia near the Ural Mountains. He remained there in disgrace until 1816.

In 1816, the exiled Speransky was permitted to return to government service as a provincial official in the remote province of Penza, near Perm. There he began the difficult task of reforming the chaotic Siberian local government. Pleased with his success, Alexander then appointed Speransky governor-general of Penza in 1819 so that he could implement his Penza reforms throughout Siberia. In 1821, Alexander recalled Speransky to St. Petersburg and appointed him to the State Council for the purpose of reorganizing the system of local government in Russia along the Siberian model. By 1825, Speransky succeeded in establishing a system that would serve Russia for the remainder of the nineteenth century.

Speransky now turned his attention to judicial and legal reform. All agreed that the Russian judicial system, like that of local government previously, was in shambles. The obvious solution was a new codification of Russian laws to replace the Sobornoye Ulozheniye 1649

(code of 1649), which had never been effectively updated. By 1832, Speransky published the *Plonoye
sobraniye zakanov Rossiyskoy imperii* or PSZ (1830;
complete collection of the laws of the Russian Empire),
which represented the codification of all laws enacted
between 1649 and 1832. Speransky also compiled and
published the *Svod Zakanov* (1832-1839; digest of laws),
incorporating all legislation still in force in 1832. Together they served as the ultimate source of legal authority in Russia until 1917. When Speransky died in 1839,
he was a much honored and respected statesman.

SIGNIFICANCE

Ironically, the impact of Mikhail Mikhaylovich Speransky's career as a reformer is twofold. His early reforms
demonstrated that there were individuals in Russia who
were concerned about the direction of Russian development during the first half of the nineteenth century. Many
of them, like Speransky, concluded that Russia's only
hope for future salvation was through the dissolution of
the autocracy and the establishment of some form of constitutional government.

The fact that Speransky's own constitutional proposals foundered on the rock of autocracy and were thus
stillborn did not alter that outlook. Others soon emerged
to assume the mantle of leadership in the struggle against
the autocracy. One such group, the Decembrists, incorporated many of the ideas from Speransky's Plan of 1809
into their political programs for reform in 1825. Although they also failed in the attainment of their goals, it
became clear that the struggle against the autocracy
would continue until it accepted the end of its absolutism. Had the autocracy been willing to implement the
constitutional reforms put forth by Speransky in 1809,
limited as they were, it might have survived the challenges against it after 1870. The fact that it did not do so
only postponed the fate that it suffered in 1917.

This leads to the second aspect of Speransky's reforms that must be considered. For the most part, it involves the nature of his work after 1816, which significantly enhanced the efficiency and effectiveness of
government administration in Russia. The great irony is
that while Speransky's earlier reforms contributed to efforts to reform the autocracy, his later reforms made it
possible for the autocracy to resist those efforts and to
survive during the remainder of the nineteenth century.

—*David K. McQuilkin*

FURTHER READING

Christian, David. "The Political Ideals of Michael Speransky." *The Slavonic and East European Review* 54
(1976): 192-213. A scholarly and historiographical
examination of Speransky's political ideals. Belongs
to the school of interpretation that argues that Speransky was a radical liberal reformer and thus rejects
Marc Raeff's *Rechtstadt* interpretation (see below).
Excellent footnotes incorporating considerable bibliographical material.

Gooding, John. "The Liberalism of Michael Speransky."
The Slavonic and East European Review 64 (1986):
401-424. Thorough criticism of Speransky's writings, with Gooding supporting the conclusions of
Christian's article (see above). Includes extensive
footnotes that encompass a wide range of bibliographical materials.

Jenkins, Michael. "Mikhail Speransky." *History Today*
20 (1970): 404-409. A short and popularized account
of Speransky's career designed primarily for high
school students.

Raeff, Marc. *Michael Speransky: Statesman of Imperial
Russia, 1772-1839*. The Hague: Martinus Nijhoff,
1957. The most comprehensive, analytic, and scholarly biographical treatment of Speransky in the English language. Contains exhaustive notes, a bibliography, and indexes that guide the student to every
facet of Speransky's life and activities as well as that
of general Russian history between 1772 and 1839.

_____. *Siberia and the Reformers of 1822*. Seattle:
University of Washington Press, 1956. A comprehensive and scholarly treatment of Speransky's Siberian
reforms of 1816-1821 and their impact on the shaping
of his reform of local government in Russia after
1822. Extensive notes, a bibliography, and indexes.

_____, ed. *Plans for Political Reform in Imperial Rus-
sia, 1730-1905*. Englewood Cliffs, N.J.: Prentice-
Hall, 1966. This collection of original sources includes documents on government reform (1802) and
the codification of state law by Speransky (1809).

Whisenhunt, William Benton. *In Search of Legality:
Mikhail M. Speranskii and the Codification of Russian Law*. Boulder, Colo.: East European Monographs:
New York: Distributed by Columbia University Press,
2001. A thorough examination of Speransky's attempts to codify Russian law during the 1820's and
1830's.

SEE ALSO: Alexander I; Alexander II.
RELATED ARTICLE in *Great Events from History: The
Nineteenth Century, 1801-1900:* December 26, 1825:
Decembrist Revolt.

LELAND STANFORD
American railroad builder and politician

As president of the Central Pacific Railroad, Stanford guided the project that produced the nation's first transcontinental railroad; he also founded California's Stanford University.

BORN: March 9, 1824; Watervliet, New York
DIED: June 20, 1893; Palo Alto, California
ALSO KNOWN AS: Amasa Leland Stanford (full name)
AREAS OF ACHIEVEMENT: Business, education

EARLY LIFE

Amasa Leland Stanford was the son of a versatile Yankee who combined farming, innkeeping, and contracting on local road and canal projects. In 1836, Josiah Stanford moved the family to a farm on the Albany-Schenectady turnpike, where the young Stanford and his five brothers observed the westward migration pass directly in front of their home. This Western exodus and his father's contracting business greatly influenced Stanford and helped to inspire him in his later railroad pioneering ventures.

Educated in local public schools and by itinerant tutors, Stanford enrolled, at the age of seventeen, in the small and racially integrated Institute of Science and Industry in Whitesborough, New York. Unhappy with its limited curriculum, he soon transferred to another school near Utica, New York, before settling at the Methodist Cazenovia Seminary near Syracuse. There, he became an active member of the debate society; became interested in the Whig politics of his hero, Henry Clay, the spokesperson of a national program of internal improvements; and kept up a steady correspondence with his father on the latter's newfound interest in railroads. By the spring of 1845, Stanford quit school to apprentice at an Albany law firm and was admitted to the bar in 1848.

In the same year and with his law credentials now established, Stanford left Albany and traveled West, first to Chicago and then, by year's end, to Port Washington, Wisconsin, almost twenty miles due north of Milwaukee. In the nation's newest state, Stanford prospered and earned more than a thousand dollars in his first year on the frontier. He continued his earlier political interests and ran unsuccessfully as a Whig candidate for county district attorney. He then returned to Albany briefly in 1850 to marry Jane Lathrop, the daughter of a substantial Albany merchant, whom he had met in his law apprentice days. They returned to Port Washington, where he practiced law for another two years before becoming restless and dissatisfied with his profession.

In 1852, Stanford left Wisconsin, determined to start again in gold rush California. Again returning to Albany before the journey west, he encountered unrelenting opposition from his wife's father, who forbade her from accompanying her husband to the wilds of California. Bowing to his father-in-law's demands, Stanford sailed from New York City without his wife in June, 1852. Thirty-eight days later, after a passage through the Nicaraguan isthmus, Stanford arrived in San Francisco on July 12 and quickly moved on to Sacramento, the gateway to the gold country.

All five of the Stanford brothers had already preceded him to California and had established themselves in a loose-knit network of mercantile ventures. The Stanford clan understood early that more gold could be extracted through storekeeping than through gold-panning. Indeed, one of the brothers, Charles, had returned to Albany to serve as purchasing agent for the Stanford family's expanding commercial enterprises in California. Stanford soon opened a store of his own, first in the town of Cold Springs, then in the boomtown of Michigan Bluff, which, in 1853, had grown from a population of thirty to two thousand. Because of his previous law experience, Stanford was soon elected the town's justice of the peace, his only elective office until his 1861 gubernatorial victory.`

In 1855, upon the death of his father-in-law, Stanford was finally able to bring his wife to California. In the fall of that year, they relocated to Sacramento and built a store valued at fourteen thousand dollars. Now fond of the substantial, he had quit the goldfields for good. He was no longer a storekeeper but a prosperous merchant who was supplementing his income by numerous profitable investments in mining ventures.

As a gentleman of property and standing, Stanford next turned to politics. In the 1856 presidential election year, Stanford became an active organizer for the infant Republican Party. As a delegate to the party's first statewide convention, he endorsed its demand for the building of a Pacific transcontinental railroad. In the spring of 1857, he was an unsuccessful candidate for Sacramento city alderman and in the fall lost a race for state treasurer. Despite these defeats, Stanford had firmly established himself in Republican Party circles and was nominated for governor in 1859. The Democratic Party dominated California politics, and Stanford won less than 10 percent of the votes. National events, however, were rapidly changing the state's political picture. By 1861, the California Republican Convention, now greatly encouraged by Abraham Lincoln's election, nominated Stanford again. The fall gubernatorial election closely paralleled the presidential race of the previous year, and Stanford was elected by defeating a badly divided Democratic Party.

LIFE'S WORK

Inaugurated governor in January, 1862, Stanford began to merge his two new careers, politics and railroading. Since June of the previous year, Stanford had been president of the newly formed Central Pacific Railroad of California. Indeed, while he discharged his gubernatorial duties faithfully and ably throughout his two-year term, he remained, by his own definition, a businessperson who was primarily committed to the transcontinental railroad enterprise that became his life's work. He may have worn two hats, but railroading was his overarching passion.

Stanford's association with the Central Pacific Railroad can be traced to his Whig political roots and his longtime interest in internal improvements. It took Theodore Dehone Judah, however, a Connecticut-born engineer, to help transform Stanford's dreams into tangible realities. Judah had already built New York's Niagara Gorge Railroad, and by the late 1850's he had devoted his life to the building of a transcontinental railroad. When San Francisco investors turned him down, he was given an enthusiastic reception by Sacramento businesspeople, including Stanford. In addition to Stanford, Judah recruited three other principal investors: Charles Crocker, Mark Hopkins, and Collis Huntington. Each of the associates was a prosperous Sacramento merchant, all were about the same age, all but Huntington were native New Yorkers, and all had been active in the California Republican Party. In June, 1861, these four (soon known as the Big Four) became the railroad's directors, with Stanford the president.

The Big Four's first priority was electing Stanford governor. As Judah advised, "A good deal depends upon the election of Stanford, for the prestige of electing a Republican ticket will go a great way toward getting what we want." With Stanford as governor, it became easier to attract potential investors and to secure favorable action from the state legislature. According to Huntington, the company's vice president, "President Stanford promoted, the California legislature passed, and Governor Stanford signed seven acts of benevolence toward the Central Pacific"—one of which was a $500,000 subsidy, which was passed in the wake of some personal lobbying on the floor of the legislature by the governor.

Stanford was equally successful in his dealings with Washington. Regarding California gold as central to the financial health of the nation in the midst of the Civil War, Congress and President Lincoln probably needed little persuasion in aiding Stanford's transcontinental railroad. On July 1, 1862, only six months after he had become governor, a federal bill to float loans to the Central Pacific became law. The terms provided both outright land grants and mortgage bonds in the form of long-term loans.

Stanford's venture began on a shoestring. On paper, the Central Pacific Railroad was capitalized at $8,500,000, with each share selling at one hundred dollars. The reality, however, was far different. Only fifteen hundred shares were actually sold, and the associates purchased 40 percent of the stock for a

Leland Stanford. (Courtesy, San Francisco Public Library)

mere 10 percent down. Stanford, then, began his mete-oric rise to fortune, fame, and philanthropy with a fifteen-hundred-dollar investment.

Finally, in October, 1863, the Central Pacific began to lay its first tracks, and Stanford had already resolved not to seek reelection but to devote his entire energy to the building of the railroad. His most important contribution during this period involved the creation of a separate "dummy" company, the so-called Contract and Finance Company, which, in turn, "sold" its construction services and its equipment back to itself under the name of the Central Pacific Railroad. This financial sleight-of-hand allowed the associates to juggle the books successfully and to transfer funds from one account to the other, as well as to hide their own personal profits. As the sole owners of the "Contract and Finance Company," the Big Four reaped huge profits that far exceeded comparable investments by the other investors, who could only pur-chase stock in the railroad.

Stanford, however, frequently found time to travel into the field and to rough it with the workers. He pro-posed that snowsheds be constructed in the Sierra to pro-tect the tracks and the work crews. By 1869, thirty-nine miles of sheds had been built at a cost of two million dol-lars, a vivid demonstration of the massive undertaking that Stanford was leading. Finally, with a reliable and sufficient source of funding secured and a steady supply of materials guaranteed, Stanford's Central Pacific Rail-road cut through and over the Sierra Nevada, raced through the high desert of the state of Nevada, and joined the Union Pacific Railroad at Promontory Point (near Ogden), Utah, on May 10, 1869. With Stanford (the only member of the Big Four present) to drive (and to miss) the ceremonial golden spike, the nation's first transconti-nental railroad had been completed.

This was not the end for Stanford and his associates, but rather the beginning of a comprehensive and near-monopolistic railroad system in California and the Southwest. In 1867, Stanford engineered the buyout of the Western Pacific, a prospective competitor. This was soon followed by a successful raid on the Southern Pa-cific Railway, which had received a charter to run from San Francisco south to San Diego and on to New Or-leans. Before the Southern Pacific could begin to operate as an independent entity, however, Stanford and the Cen-tral Pacific acquired control of it, probably sometime be-tween March and September, 1868. By 1884, twenty separate lines had been consolidated and reorganized into the Southern Pacific Corporation. Stanford and the associates had knitted together a system that managed

five thousand miles of track and controlled 85 percent of California's railroads.

Presiding over the empire, however, did take an in-creasing toll on Stanford. In May, 1880, near Hanford, eight men were killed in the Battle Mussel Slough in the course of eviction proceedings. Despite public opinion to the contrary, Stanford took the hard line and helped to precipitate the bloody confrontation. Ever more defen-sive in the next few years, Stanford lashed out against the reformers who called for railroad regulation and ada-mantly refused to answer questions that touched on brib-ery and influence-peddling posed by the state's railroad commissioners, whom he abhorred. Moreover, the South-ern Pacific was incorporated in the state of Kentucky to protect the company from the ever-increasing hostility of California juries.

The financial complexities of the Central Pacific-Southern Pacific combine have always been shrouded in mystery. Nobody who knew of the inside workings would ever talk; nobody on the outside could ever get in. From an initial investment of fifteen hundred dollars in cash, each of the associates earned thirteen million dol-lars from the Central Pacific alone. When he died in 1893, Stanford, who had already given away money lav-ishly, was still worth at least thirty million dollars and was one of the richest men in the United States.

With such an immense fortune, Stanford did not stint on the good life. His sumptuously decorated fifty-room mansion atop San Francisco's Nob Hill, with its precious wood paneling, was palatial. As befit a man of means, Stanford was able to live the life of a country squire. He purchased nearly eight thousand acres of land south of San Francisco that he called the Palo Alto Farm. He raised championship trotters there and became an international expert on their breeding and training. His farm was uni-versally considered the best of its kind in the world.

Stanford's interest in horses also led to the world's first motion-picture experiments at the Palo Alto estate. In the hope of discovering whether a trotter had all four feet off the ground at some point during its gait, Stan-ford hired the noted English photographer Eadweard Muybridge and planned much of the experiment him-self. Stanford was a pioneer in the California vinoculture, and his Vina Winery, set amid an immense fifty-five-thousand-acre spread, was the largest and most modern in the world. For all the money and attention he lavished on this endeavor, however, the results were little better than mediocre.

By the 1880's, travel became a way of life with the Stanfords, who frequently took the grand tours of Europe. On one such excursion, their only (indeed, almost revered) child, Leland, Jr., died of typhoid fever in March, 1884, in Florence, Italy. Grief-stricken, the Stanfords resolved to build a university in memory of their son on their Palo Alto property. Active from the beginning in every phase of the establishment of the university, from architecture to curriculum, Stanford was a solicitous and affectionate overseer of the enterprise. Stanford University, one of the few private coeducational universities, was opened on October 1, 1891, and in some ways, Stanford considered it his most significant achievement.

Although still active in planning the university and continuing as president of the Southern Pacific system, Stanford unexpectedly entered politics when the Republican-dominated California legislature elected him to the U.S. Senate in January, 1885. He served a relatively undistinguished eight years in that body and was a conservative spokesman for an unregulated economy. On occasion, however, Stanford demonstrated that he could transcend the limitations of his Darwinistic philosophy. He introduced a radical federal loan program for debt-ridden farmers and supported an innovative national funding proposal for education. In the last decade of his life, Stanford was, by far, the most popular of the Big Four. He died at his Palo Alto home on the evening of June 20, 1893.

SIGNIFICANCE

Stanford was quintessentially an American "type." Born of pure Yankee stock, he joined the Western migration to the frontier and rose to become a millionaire and the richest man in the Senate. He did not possess an extraordinarily brilliant or analytical mind, like an Andrew Carnegie, for example, but he did possess a wealth of diligence and patience, and an unerring eye for the main chance. He was productively restless and was adroit enough to seize opportunities that were wide open in California. In its early days, the state broke far more men than it made, and it is a tribute to Stanford that he survived the test.

Stanford was not wholly of the Central Pacific-Southern Pacific system, but he was the paramount leader of the Big Four. Of all the associates, he was the one best able to work with all segments of the population. He was the glue that kept this hard-driving clique together. His single-mindedness during his two-year gubernatorial term probably saved the endeavor. At the same time, and for the same reason, this unswerving commitment to his transcontinental railroad interrupted his political career. As governor, Stanford did exercise undue influence on the California legislature, and throughout the years,

his railroad system did exercise an octopus-like grip on the entire state.

At a time when a transcontinental system was a national imperative, beyond the means of any individual or private group, Stanford helped to discover how to harness the financial resources of government. In the process, he did, indeed, become wealthy, but the public gained, too. Certainly, San Francisco became and remained the hub of the West, because it was at the center of Stanford's transportation network. For all of its rapaciousness, the system did offer reliable service. This enriched California agriculture, the state's source of wealth after the gold rush had played out.

Stanford was not quite a robber baron. His workers were loyal and were well paid. He was a collector of things (houses, horses, jewels, art), but he did not flaunt them. He was a man of great wealth but also a man of philanthropy. He was, finally, a new kind of American capitalist, who, in the absence of regulatory legislation and income tax, tested the outer limits of private enterprise. Stanford both lived in and helped define an age. Rules had not been made to temper the acquisitive men of his generation. His life was proof that he made the most of all of his opportunities; his life was also proof that more legislation was needed to hold men of business more accountable to the general public.

—*LeRoy J. Votto*

FURTHER READING

Ambrose, Stephen E. *Nothing Like It in the World: The Men Who Built the Transcontinental Railroad, 1863-1869.* New York: Simon & Schuster, 2000. This history of the transcontinental railroad offers a great deal of information about the role of Stanford and his associates in building the Central Pacific Railroad.

Bancroft, Hubert Howe. *History of the Life of Leland Stanford: A Character Study.* Oakland, Calif.: Biobooks, 1952. Published posthumously, this work is valuable because it was written by the dean of Western historians, who knew Stanford personally. Valuable primary sources, especially on the founding of Stanford University.

Bean, Walton E. *California: An Interpretive History.* 2d ed. New York: McGraw-Hill, 1973. A magnificent study of California that skillfully combines narrative and interpretation. Provides the context in which to place Stanford.

Brown, Dee. *Hear the Lonesome Whistle Blow: Railroads in the West.* New York: Holt, Rinehart and Winston, 1977. Good analysis of the effects the transcontinentals had on Native Americans and on the ecology of the West. Very strong on how the various systems helped to transform life and society in the West.

Clark, George T. *Leland Stanford: War Governor of California, Railroad Builder and Founder of Stanford University*. Stanford, Calif.: Stanford University Press, 1931. Written by the director emeritus of the Stanford library, the work is an adulatory biography. Very strong on the founding of the university.

Griswold, Wesley S. *A Work of Giants: Building the First Transcontinental Railroad*. New York: McGraw-Hill, 1962. A gripping popular account, especially strong on the engineering marvels; also helpful in comparing the Union Pacific with the Central Pacific. Also strong on describing the personalities of both systems.

Lewis, Oscar. *The Big Four: The Story of Huntington, Stanford, Hopkins, and Crocker*. New York: Alfred A. Knopf, 1938. Written with verve, this is a generally critical account of Stanford and associates; contains excellent character sketches of each of the partners and Theodore Judah.

Norris, Frank. *The Octopus: A Story of California*. New York: Doubleday, Page, 1901. Reprint. Edited by Kenneth S. Lynn. Boston: Houghton Mifflin, 1958. The first of a projected trilogy on the growing, selling, and use of wheat, this novel is an account of the struggle between the wheat growers of California and Stanford's Southern Pacific.

Tutorow, Norman E. *The Governor: The Life and Legacy of Leland Stanford, a California Colossus*. With the special research and editorial assistance of Evelyn "Evie" LaNora Tutorow. 2 vols. Spokane, Wash.: Arthur H. Clark, 2004.

_____. *Leland Stanford: Man of Many Careers*. Menlo Park, Calif.: Pacific Coast, 1971. Tutorow initially wrote a relatively brief, and definitive, biography of Stanford; more than thirty years later, he published a more extensive and detailed two-volume biography. Both books are impressive in their research, offering indispensable accounts for any extensive consideration of Leland Stanford.

SEE ALSO: Andrew Carnegie; Henry Clay; Abraham Lincoln; Frederick Law Olmsted.

RELATED ARTICLES in *Great Events from History: The Nineteenth Century, 1801-1900:* May 10, 1869: First Transcontinental Railroad Is Completed; 1878: Muybridge Photographs a Galloping Horse.

HENRY MORTON STANLEY
British American explorer

Best known for finding the missionary explorer David Livingstone in 1871, Stanley was the first explorer to chart a number of the great lakes in Central Africa and to follow the Congo River to its mouth. His explorations opened much of Africa to European commerce and colonization.

BORN: January 28, 1841; Denbigh, Denbighshire, Wales
DIED: May 10, 1904; London, England
ALSO KNOWN AS: John Rowlands (birth name); Sir Henry Morton Stanley; Bula Matari
AREA OF ACHIEVEMENT: Exploration

EARLY LIFE

The illegitimate child of nineteen-year-old Elizabeth Perry, Henry Morton Stanley was born in Wales and was christened John Rowlands, thus receiving the same name as his probable father, a twenty-six-year-old farmer. At the age of four, he entered the local grammar school, but two years later he was placed in St. Asaph Union Workhouse, where he received most of his formal education.

Stanley applied himself diligently to his studies, exhibiting a trait that would endure throughout his life. Though he was a man of action who could act impetuously, his successes in Africa owed much to the care with which he prepared his expeditions. A journalist who visited Stanley's apartment in 1874 noted that "the chairs, tables, sofas and settees, nay even the very floor itself—are laden with books, newspapers, manuscripts and maps" over which Stanley pored until late every night, making careful notes about weather, topography, and needed supplies.

Stanley also demonstrated his penchant for rashness at St. Asaph, for, according to his autobiography (1909), he ran away at the age of fifteen after knocking his teacher unconscious. He fled first to a cousin, Moses Owen, for whom he worked briefly as a teacher while receiving the last of his own classroom instruction. Owen's mother disliked her nephew, so after nine months Stanley had to leave his post as student-tutor. Instead, he earned a precarious living as a shepherd and bartender at Treneirchion, Wales, before crossing the border to Liverpool. From this port, in December, 1858, he sailed as a cabin boy aboard the *Windermere*, bound for New Orleans.

After arriving in the United States, Stanley again ran away from a desperate situation, jumping ship even though he was a stranger without prospects for employment. Luck favored him, though, and he was adopted by a generous cotton broker, Henry Hope Stanley, whose name he took; the "Morton" was a later addition. After clerking in New Orleans and Cypress Bend, Arkansas, Stanley enlisted in the Arkansas Greys when the Civil War began. Captured by Union forces at the Battle of Shiloh in April, 1862, he shifted his allegiance rather than languish in a prison camp. This phase of his military career ended quickly when he received a medical discharge less than a month after joining an Illinois regiment. He would make one further attempt to serve, signing with the federal navy on July 19, 1864. After seeing action off the coast of North Carolina, he jumped ship on February 10, 1865; Stanley was apparently born to command but not to serve.

A perpetual victim of wanderlust, in June, 1865, Stanley agreed to work as a freelance writer for the Missouri *Democrat* (in St. Louis) to report on the Colorado gold rush. Over the next two years, this love of travel would carry him from the American West to the Middle East and back to his native Denbigh before he returned to Missouri.

LIFE'S WORK

Shortly after returning to the United States, Stanley seized an opportunity to travel once more. England was preparing to invade Abyssinia, and Stanley offered to cover the story for the New York *Herald*. Its owner, James Gordon Bennett, agreed—provided that Stanley would pay all of his own expenses. Stanley accepted these terms. Through bribery, skill, and luck, he was the first to report the British victory at the Battle of Magdala, thus securing a permanent spot on the staff of Bennett's paper.

Two years later, Bennett selected his young European correspondent for the mission that would make Stanley's name a household word and forever change the map of Africa. Dr. David Livingstone, missionary and geographer, had first gone to Africa in 1841. In 1866, he set out to find the source of the Nile River but soon disappeared. As concern for his safety mounted, Bennett asked Stanley to find and resupply the missing explorer.

Henry Morton Stanley. (Library of Congress)

Bennett's concern, though, was more journalistic than humanitarian; he recognized what Stanley's story would do for the circulation of the *Herald*. To be sure that the newspaper would have good copy regardless of the outcome of the rescue effort, Bennett first sent Stanley to cover the opening of the Suez Canal, on November 17, 1869, and to file a series of reports on the Middle East. Thus, Stanley could not begin his search for Livingstone until early 1871.

On November 10, 1871, after overcoming bad weather, disease, and hostile communities, Stanley found the man he was seeking, greeting him with the words that would soon echo throughout Europe and America: "Dr. Livingstone, I presume?" Stanley had given the *Herald* its story, and he had saved Livingstone, whose supplies were almost exhausted and who was suffering from dysentery. Livingstone tried to persuade Stanley to join him in his quest for the source of the Nile, while Stanley argued that Livingstone should return to England. Neither convinced the other, but Stanley was clearly captivated by the missionary and by Africa. Even though he was ea-

"DR. LIVINGSTONE, I PRESUME?"

Henry Morton Stanley crossed what is now mainland Tanzania, from the east coast to the village of Ujiji on the east shore of Lake Tanganyika, where he found David Livingstone on November 10, 1871. He described this meeting in chapter 9 of his best-selling book, How I Found Livingstone. *The encounter is one of the most famous incidents in the European exploration of Africa.*

We were now about three hundred yards from the village of Ujiji, and the crowds are dense about me. Suddenly I hear a voice on my right say,

"Good morning, sir!"

Startled at hearing this greeting in the midst of such a crowd of black people, I turn sharply around in search of the man, and see him at my side, with the blackest of faces, but animated and joyous—a man dressed in a long white shirt, with a turban of American sheeting around his woolly head, and I ask:

"Who the mischief are you?"

"I am Susi, the servant of Dr. Livingstone," said he, smiling, and showing a gleaming row of teeth.

"What! Is Dr. Livingstone here?"

"Yes, sir."

"In this village?"

"Yes, sir."

"Are you sure?"

"Sure, sure, sir. Why, I leave him just now."

"Good morning, sir," said another voice.

"Hallo," said I, "is this another one?"

"Yes, sir."

"Well, what is your name?"

"My name is Chumah, sir."

"What! are you Chumah, the friend of Wekotani?"

"Yes, sir."

"And is the Doctor well?"

" Not very well, sir."

"Where has he been so long?"

"In Manyuema."

"Now, you Susi, run, and tell the Doctor I am coming."

"Yes, sir," and off he darted like a madman.

But by this time we were within two hundred yards of the village, and the multitude was getting denser, and almost preventing our march. Flags and streamers were out; Arabs and Wangwana were pushing their way through the natives in order to greet us, for according to their account, we belonged to them. But the great wonder of all was, "How did you come from Unyanyembe?"

Soon Susi came running back, and asked me my name; he had told the Doctor I was coming, but the Doctor was too surprised to believe him, and when the Doctor asked him my name, Susi was rather staggered.

But, during Susi's absence, the news had been conveyed to the Doctor that it was surely a white man that was coming, whose guns were firing, and whose flag could be seen; and the great Arab magnates of Ujiji—Mohammed bin Sali, Sayd bin Majid, Abid bin Suliman, Mohammed bin Gharib, and others—had gathered together before the Doctor's house, and the Doctor had come out from his veranda to discuss the matter and await my arrival.

In the meantime, the head of the Expedition had halted, and the kirangozi was out of the ranks, holding his flag aloft, and Selim said to me, "I see the Doctor, sir. Oh, what an old man! He has got a white beard." And I—what would I not have given for a bit of friendly wilderness, where, unseen, I might vent my joy in some mad freak, such as idiotically biting my hand; turning a somersault, or slashing at trees, in order to allay those exciting feelings that were well-nigh uncontrollable. My heart beats fast, but I must not let my face betray my emotions, lest it shall detract from the dignity of a white man appearing under such extraordinary circumstances.

So I did that which I thought was most dignified. I pushed back the crowds, and, passing from the rear, walked down a living avenue of people, until I came in front of the semicircle of Arabs, before which stood the "white man with the grey beard."

As I advanced slowly towards him I noticed he was pale, that he looked wearied and wan, that he had grey whiskers and moustache, that he wore a bluish cloth cap with a faded gold band on a red ground round it, and that he had on a red-sleeved waistcoat, and a pair of grey tweed trousers.

I would have run to him, only I was a coward in the presence of such a mob—would have embraced him, but that I did not know how he would receive me; so I did what moral cowardice and false pride suggested was the best thing—walked deliberately to him, took off my hat, and said:

"Dr. Livingstone, I presume?"

"Yes," said he, with a kind, cordial smile, lifting his cap slightly.

I replaced my hat on my head, and he replaced his cap, and we both grasped hands. I then said aloud:

"I thank God, Doctor, I have been permitted to see you."

He answered, "I feel thankful that I am here to welcome you."

Source: Henry Morton Stanley, *How I Found Livingstone* (abridged edition, London, 1873), chapter 9.

ger to tell his story to the Western world, Stanley tarried at Ujiji on Lake Tanganyika until March 14, 1872.

Back in London, Stanley described his life as a "whirl of cabs, soirées, dinners, dress-clothes and gloves." He was added to Madame Tussaud's waxworks; Queen Victoria sent him a jeweled snuffbox bearing the inscription:

> Presented by Her Majesty, Queen Victoria to Henry Morton Stanley, Esq. in recognition of the prudence and zeal displayed by him in opening communication with Doctor Livingstone and thus relieving the general anxiety felt in regard to the fate of that distinguished Traveller.

The queen also granted Stanley an audience at Dunrobin Castle.

Not everyone was equally enthusiastic over Stanley's achievement, particularly since he pointed out that neither the Royal Geographical Society nor the British government had done much to help Livingstone. Stanley was accused of fabricating the whole account and of forging the Livingstone letters and diary he brought back with him. In August, 1872, he bitterly described the treatment he had received from the Royal Geographical Society and the British upper classes:

> First they would sneer at the fact of an American having gone to Central Africa—then they sneered at the idea of his being successful. . . . My story is called "sensational" and unreal etc. I assure you that I think after decently burying Livingstone in forgetfulness they hate to be told he is yet alive.

When Stanley offered to accompany the belatedly organized relief expedition under the auspices of the Royal Geographical Society, he was rebuffed. Nevertheless, the society could not ignore the general sentiment concerning Stanley's success, and on October 31, 1872, it reluctantly awarded him its highest honor, the Victoria Gold Medal.

In the midst of speeches, dinners, honors, and receptions, Stanley found time to write two books about his recent adventures, *How I Found Livingstone* (1872) and *My Kalulu* (1873). The latter, a fictionalized adventure tale for youngsters, did not do well, but *How I Found Livingstone* was an immense success, selling more than seventy thousand copies.

Finding and resupplying Livingstone had captured the popular imagination; as Sir Clements Robert Markham observed, however, "The fellow has done no geography." The same could not be said of Stanley's next ex-

pedition. On November 17, 1874, he plunged into the African jungle again, determined to cross the continent from east to west, locate the source of the Nile, and chart the unknown equatorial regions.

Such a feat offered great rewards and equally large challenges. The weather could be oppressively hot, and torrential rains could quickly turn a campsite into a sea of mud. The Africans who carried the supplies often proved unreliable; they would desert or, worse, mutiny. Dysentery, malaria, and typhus took a heavy toll: Stanley was the only white man in the party to survive the journey. Hostile tribes posed yet another danger; in a single battle at Vinyata, twenty-one people were killed by Nyaturu warriors. Within three months, Stanley had lost more than half of his original caravan.

The jungle exacted a price from Stanley himself also. In 1874 in London, he had weighed 178 pounds; since he was only five feet, five inches tall, his figure was portly. However, he carried himself with military erectness, and photographs show arching brows above clear, gray eyes, a firm mouth, and flowing mustache. By the time he reached Ujiji on Lake Tanganyika early in 1876, he weighed only 118 pounds, and his black, wavy hair was streaked with gray.

Already, though, he had become the first white man to navigate and chart Lake Victoria, and he had discovered Lake George. Still greater achievements lay ahead. From Lake Tanganyika, he headed north along the Lualaba River, taking a route no European had ever followed and one that even Africans feared, for the river was lined with cannibals. By choosing to go north rather than south, Stanley was to "do" geography indeed, for he not only discovered Stanley Falls and Stanley Pool, but also was to demonstrate conclusively that the Lualaba was part of the Congo rather than the Nile. Moreover, he would become the first European to travel the length of the Congo, for waterfalls and rapids blocked the way from the west, and previously the jungle had denied access from the east.

Again Stanley's feats aroused the interest of the Western world. Gold medals flowed in from learned societies in Europe and the United States; both houses of Congress gave Stanley a unanimous vote of thanks. Léon Gambetta of France summarized the popular sentiment of the day when he declared,

> Not only, sir, have you opened up a new continent to our view, but you have given an impulse to scientific and philanthropic enterprise which will have a material effect on the progress of the world.

Such, in fact, were Stanley's aims. He hoped to end the slave trade in Central Africa, Christianize the Africans and improve their material lot through commerce with the West. Events were to prove these plans illusory, for Stanley's explorations were to open the western half of the continent to Arab slave traders and equally exploitative European empire builders.

Stanley was still largely unaware of this perversion of his dreams when he agreed to return to the Congo for the Comité d'Études du Haut Congo, organized by King Leopold II of Belgium. He would have preferred British support, but England was not interested. When Lieutenant Verney Lovett Cameron attempted to annex part of the Congo for the British Empire, Parliament refused the offer. Working for Leopold, Stanley earned his nickname, Bula Matari, "smasher of stones." Between 1879 and 1882, he surpassed the king's expectations, founding Leopoldville, building a three-hundred-mile wagon road from the Atlantic to Stanley Pool, and creating a small fleet to navigate the upper Congo River beyond. Because of these efforts, Belgium would receive 900,000 square miles in the center of the continent.

In November, 1886, Stanley began a lecture tour in the United States to recount his recent adventures, about which he had also written a book, *The Congo and the Founding of Its Free State* (1885). The work was sufficiently popular to be translated into seventeen languages. He was quickly recalled for his final trip to Africa, though, this time to rescue Emin Pasha (born Eduard Carl Schmitzev), a German posing as a Turk. This mysterious figure had been appointed governor of the Equatorial Province in southern Sudan and had remained loyal to England after the followers of Muhammed Ahmed (the Mahdi) had overrun Khartoum and killed General Charles George Gordon, the British governor (1885).

For some reason, Stanley chose to approach Emin Pasha from the west. If he expected that the roads, stations, and fleet he had set up along the Congo would speed his journey, he was mistaken, for much of what he had established was already reverting to jungle. The march was in many ways a disaster. More than half the members of the expedition died along the way, and rumors of Stanley's death also circulated. On December 21, 1887, however, Parliament learned that Stanley had accomplished his mission of resupplying Emin, and the House of Commons rose in a body to give him an ovation in absentia.

Of all Stanley's forays into Africa, this last had the least enduring significance. Emin was better supplied than Stanley with everything but ammunition, and even this relief was not sufficient to prevent his being forced to flee shortly afterward. However, Stanley was again the hero of the day. Already in Zanzibar, Stanley found piles of telegrams from world leaders. He had promised his publisher a book about the expedition, so he stayed in Cairo because he knew that in Europe he would be kept too busy to complete it. Meanwhile, in Berlin audiences watched a play about his adventures in Africa. In Reykjavík, people sang "Aurora Borealis" about his feats. Mugs and plates bearing Stanley's picture appeared in London shops, as did song sheets with titles such as "Stanley's Rescue" and "The Victor's Return." A lecture tour in the United States brought Stanley sixty thousand dollars; a similar round of talks in England added another ten thousand dollars.

The workhouse boy from Wales had become rich. He also finally found a wife. Twice before, he had been jilted, and in 1886, Dorothy Tennant had rejected his proposal. Now she changed her mind, and on July 12, 1890, they were married in Westminster Abbey. The ceremony assumed the scale of a coronation. The Abbey was filled with the prominent and the powerful, including William Ewart Gladstone, the Lord Chancellor, and the Speaker of the House of Commons. So popular was the event that five thousand people had to be turned away from the overcrowded church.

At his wife's urging, in 1892 Stanley gave up his American citizenship, which he had taken in 1885 to protect his royalties from piracy. Shortly afterward, he stood for Parliament; though he lost his first bid, he succeeded in 1895 and served for five years. To a man of action, the House of Commons held little fascination, however, and he complained of its "asphyxiating atmosphere." Honors continued to pour in; in 1899, he was awarded the Grand Cross of the Bath, thus becoming Sir Henry Morton Stanley, and the Atheneum, the most prestigious club in London, elected him a member.

Stanley still longed for action and Africa, but his four expeditions had aged him. In 1900, he retired to Surrey, where his wife named a local stream the Congo and a small lake Stanley Pool. These were the closest he would come to the places that had made him famous. He died in London on May 10, 1904.

SIGNIFICANCE

Henry Morton Stanley had hoped to be buried in Westminster Abbey near Livingstone, with whom his name had been so closely linked. Although his funeral did occur there, he was denied burial in the historical shrine because by 1904 his name had also become associated with the Congo Free State, a synonym for atrocities.

"I was sent for a special work," Stanley had written in his autobiography, a work he had defined as "the redemption of the splendid central basin of the continent by sound and legitimate commerce." Through his explorations and his writings, he had opened up that area to reveal its richness to the Western world. His call for missionaries during the 1870's had brought such a response from England that Uganda became a British colony. He not only drew up the borders of the Congo Free State, later to become the Belgian Congo, but also ensured British involvement in the Sudan and eastern Africa through his various expeditions. As a journalist and explorer, he never failed to accomplish the missions on which he was sent. Whether he thereby effected Africa's redemption or damnation, though, remains an open question more than a century after he shed the first rays of light on Africa's heart of darkness.

—*Joseph Rosenblum*

FURTHER READING

Anstruther, Ian. *Dr. Livingstone, I Presume?* New York: E. P. Dutton, 1957. A detailed account of Stanley's early years and his rescue of Dr. Livingstone. Though the book touches briefly on Stanley's later achievements, it essentially ends in 1874.

Dugand, Martin. *Into Africa: The Epic Adventures of Stanley and Livingstone.* New York: Doubleday, 2003. In alternating chapters, Dugand traces both men's journeys into Africa. Provides a detailed recreation of their expeditions; contrasts their personalities and thoughts about Africa.

Farwell, Byron. *Man Who Presumed: A Biography of Henry M. Stanley.* New York: Holt, Rinehart and Winston, 1957. A good biography for the general reader. Farwell adds no new information, but his account is clearly written and entertaining.

Gallop, Alan. *Mr. Stanley, I Presume? The Life and Explorations of Henry Morton Stanley.* Thrupp, Stroud, Gloucestershire, England: Sutton, 2004. Frank and scholarly account of Stanley's life and personality.

Hall, Richard. *Stanley: An Adventurer Explored.* Boston: Houghton Mifflin, 1975. The most detailed biography, revealing many previously unknown details about Stanley's early life. Maps and photographs supplement the well-written text.

Newman, James L. *Imperial Footprints: Henry Morton Stanley's African Journeys.* Washington, D.C.: Brassey's, 2004. Re-creates Stanley's seven African journeys, describing his reasons for making the expeditions, what happened en route, and the results of his trips.

Severin, Timothy. "The Making of an American Lion." *American Heritage* 25 (February, 1974): 4-11, 82-85. Stanley was passing himself off as an American two decades before he assumed United States citizenship. Severin tells Stanley's story from the American perspective, concentrating on his early life in this country and the ecstatic American response to his achievements.

Smith, Ian R. *The Emin Pasha Relief Expedition, 1886-1890.* Oxford, England: Oxford University Press, 1972. A scholarly examination of Stanley's last African adventure. Draws on previously unpublished material to place the expedition in the context of European imperialism. Also recounts the harrowing experiences of both the Advance and Rear Columns trying to reach Emin Pasha.

Tames, Richard Lawrence Ames. *Henry Morton Stanley.* Aylesbury, England: Shire, 1973. In less than fifty pages, Tames provides a good overview of Stanley's career. The brief text is richly illustrated to reveal both the man and his milieu.

SEE ALSO: James Gordon Bennett; Sir Richard Francis Burton; Léon Gambetta; William Ewart Gladstone; Charles George Gordon; Leopold II; David Livingstone; John Hanning Speke; Tippu Tib; Queen Victoria.

RELATED ARTICLES in *Great Events from History: The Nineteenth Century, 1801-1900:* 1873-1880: Exploration of Africa's Congo Basin; November 15, 1884-February 26, 1885: Berlin Conference Lays Groundwork for the Partition of Africa.

EDWIN M. STANTON
American politician

Combining excellent administrative skills with attention to detail, Stanton as U.S. secretary of war made a major contribution to Union victory during the Civil War.

BORN: December 19, 1814; Steubenville, Ohio
DIED: December 24, 1869; Washington, D.C.
ALSO KNOWN AS: Edwin McMasters Stanton (full name)
AREA OF ACHIEVEMENT: Government and politics

EARLY LIFE

Edwin McMasters Stanton was the eldest child of a physician descended from a Quaker family. When he was thirteen, his father died, and he had to leave school to help support his family. He worked in a local bookstore and continued his education during his spare time. Impressed by the young man's ambition, his guardian and mother's attorney, Daniel L. Collier, lent him money in 1831 so that he could attend Kenyon College at Gambier, Ohio.

A year after entering Kenyon College, worsening family finances forced Stanton to withdraw from school. His former employer contracted with Stanton to manage a bookstore in Columbus, Ohio. After a disagreement with his employer, Stanton asked Collier for loans to study law in Columbus. Collier, however, suggested that Stanton return to Steubenville to study with him. Stanton passed the bar in 1836 and practiced in Cadiz, Ohio, as a partner of an established attorney and also formed an association with Judge Benjamin Tappan. In 1838, Stanton returned to Steubenville to oversee the practice of senator-elect Tappan.

Stanton proved to be an extremely hardworking attorney. He spent hours preparing cases and consequently was often better prepared than his colleagues. By 1840, Stanton had established himself as a lawyer, had managed to repay all of his debts to Collier, and for the first time was providing a financially secure environment for his family. He married Mary Lamson of Columbus on December 31, 1836. Stanton and his wife shared a love for contemporary literature and often spent evenings reading aloud and discussing current events. The Stantons had two children, Lucy Lamson and Edwin Lamson. The death of Lucy was a terrible blow to the Stantons, and in March, 1844, the death of his wife nearly drove Stanton insane. In 1846, his brother Darwin, whom Stanton had put through medical school, committed suicide.

These personal tragedies completely changed Stanton's personality. He had been sickly as a child and, because of his health and his need to work, was isolated from others. Even so, he had a pleasant demeanor and enjoyed socializing, but now he became withdrawn and suffered from a deep depression. He disliked social events and was often rude and quarrelsome. He exhibited these traits for the remainder of his life.

Lonely and unhappy, Stanton decided to seek new opportunities in Pittsburgh, Pennsylvania, in the fall of 1847. He maintained residency in Ohio, however, and kept in touch with state affairs. His law practice bloomed in Pittsburgh, and he achieved national recognition. He represented the state of Pennsylvania against the Wheeling and Belmont Bridge Company, a company in Wheeling, Virginia, which had obtained permission from the state of Ohio to build a suspension bridge across the Ohio River. The proposed bridge, too low to permit existing steamboats to cross under the structure, would cut off Pittsburgh from river commerce. Pennsylvania sued either to stop construction of the bridge or to force the company to build a higher bridge. Stanton proved his point when he hired a steamboat to run at full speed under the bridge. When the steamboat's smokestack and superstructure were destroyed, Stanton won a favorable judgment.

The bridge case brought Stanton numerous clients, and he also worked as a junior counsel in the patent infringement case of *McCormick v. Manny*. Stanton's client, John H. Manny, lost, but Stanton performed ably in the case. During the trial, he met Abraham Lincoln briefly for the first time.

On June 25, 1856, Stanton married Ellen Hutchinson of Pittsburgh, and moved to Washington, D.C., to devote his time to practicing before the U.S. Supreme Court. Stanton found happiness with his new wife, and they had four children, but he never recovered the more congenial demeanor so manifest during earlier days. The ambitious attorney did well in the new environment. In 1858, Stanton was selected as a special United States attorney to represent the government in numerous fraudulent land claims in California arising from land deeded to individuals before the Mexican war. He spent most of the year in California laboring to reconstruct the necessary records. Stanton's attention to detail allowed him to win a number of victories and saved the government millions of dollars.

Although Stanton devoted his energies to civil law, he also proved himself to be an able criminal lawyer. Daniel E. Sickles, a New York congressman, scandalized the country in February, 1859, when he murdered Philip B. Key. United States Attorney for the District of Columbia and son of Francis Scott Key, best known as the author of "The Star-Spangled Banner," Key had been carrying on an affair with Sickles's wife, and the congressman acted while in a rage. Stanton and his associates used the plea of temporary insanity for the first time in the United States. The jury acquitted Sickles, and Stanton's fame grew.

LIFE'S WORK

Stanton had not been actively engaged in politics before the Civil War. He was a Jacksonian Democrat who opposed slavery. He accepted the *Dred Scott* decision, however, and believed that constitutional provisions regarding slavery had to be enforced. He disliked southern Democrats and fervently supported the Union as the crisis atmosphere grew in 1859 and 1860. After Lincoln's election in November, 1860, the nation faced a crisis of immense magnitude. Stanton believed in the Union and on December 20 agreed to serve in President James Bu-

chanan's cabinet as attorney general for the short time before Lincoln assumed office. Stanton worked hard to preserve the Union and to stiffen Buchanan's resolve to keep the country together. Stanton joined others in the cabinet in opposing the abandonment of Fort Sumter, South Carolina, and kept an eye on individuals he believed were plotting against the government.

Stanton distrusted Lincoln's administration during the early months of the Civil War. Highly critical of Lincoln, Stanton became a friend and adviser of Major General George B. McClellan after he took command of the Army of the Potomac and then became general in chief.

Lincoln needed a new manager for the War Department capable of handling the massive mobilization of men and resources needed to fight to preserve the fractured Union. Secretary of War Simon Cameron, however, had turned out to be both inept and corrupt. It is not clear why Lincoln decided to appoint Stanton, but the Republican president needed support from War Democrats. For whatever reason, on January 15, 1862, Stanton was confirmed as secretary of war; the War Department and the United States Army had found a master.

Stanton acted immediately by reorganizing the War Department, hiring new and better qualified personnel, and carefully investigating existing contracts. Contractors were pressured to deliver needed supplies, but supplies had to arrive on time and be of proper quality. He often worked far into the night, and he expected the same of his subordinates. Stanton efficiently managed a large-scale enterprise, and the Union armies never lost a battle for lack of supplies or equipment.

The war secretary also understood the importance of communications and transportation. Acting through Congress, he took over telegraph and railroad lines essential to carrying on the war. Stanton created a military telegraph system operated by the civilian-controlled War Department, not the army. Consequently, all information flowed through Stanton's office, enabling him to manage the flow of news and to censor anything of value to the South. The press criticized Stanton for censorship, but his actions were a sound and necessary wartime measure.

The railroad was equally important to the war effort. On one occasion, Stanton moved two army corps from the eastern theater to Chattanooga, Tennessee, complete with arms, equipment, and supplies, in less than a week. Government control of the railroads in military areas proved to be a key factor in the war. Stanton established a railroad building program to repair and build new rail lines at an unprecedented rate. The war secretary clearly understood the technology of modern war.

Edwin M. Stanton. (Library of Congress)

In his early months as secretary, Stanton maintained a close relationship with McClellan. The general and Lincoln, however, had never agreed on strategy. Stanton soon realized that McClellan was a brilliant organizer but no fighter. The secretary's views may also have been colored by his improving relationship with Lincoln. The president wanted a fighting general who understood the political and military realities of the war. In August, 1862, Stanton worked to remove McClellan from command, although the general was briefly returned to duty during the fall.

Both Stanton and Lincoln sought a general who acted rather than one who simply asked for more men and supplies. Consequently, both often interfered with military operations early in the war when they thought generals were not doing enough. They maintained civilian control of the war effort in the face of a real danger that armies and generals might become too powerful and gain the upper hand in government.

In 1863, Major General Ulysses S. Grant, with his victories at Vicksburg and Chattanooga, emerged as the general both Lincoln and Stanton had sought. In March, 1864, Lincoln appointed Grant to the newly created rank of lieutenant general and gave him command of the entire one-million-man Union army. Grant found no cause to complain about Stanton. Stanton did all in his power to procure what Grant needed, but Grant never asked for more than could be realistically delivered. The combination of Stanton, Lincoln, and Grant brought Union victory when General Robert E. Lee surrendered to Grant at Appomattox Courthouse on April 9, 1865.

Stanton was shattered by Lincoln's assassination on April 14. The two men had developed a close working relationship, making it possible to wage an immense war. Stanton's anger never really abated, and he sought and prosecuted the assassins with a vengeance.

Grant's terms to Lee had been generous, but within political limits set by Lincoln. Major General William Tecumseh Sherman, however, fearing a bloodbath in the wake of Lincoln's death, negotiated a much broader surrender agreement with Confederate general Joseph E. Johnston in North Carolina two weeks after Appomattox. Sherman's terms enraged Stanton, who leaked them in garbled terms to the press and who privately accused Sherman of disloyalty. Sherman had certainly exceeded his authority, and after a cabinet meeting, Grant went to North Carolina and quietly supervised new terms. Sherman never forgave Stanton for his behavior. Ironically, both men probably acted out of grief over Lincoln's death.

President Andrew Johnson asked Stanton to stay in his cabinet. During the war he had left the Democratic Party, and by 1865 he fully sympathized with the Radical Republicans. Johnson's view of Reconstruction turned out to be far different from that of the Radical Republicans and of Stanton. The war secretary from the summer of 1865 onward differed with the president, wanting harsher terms imposed on the South. He approved of the Freedmen's Bureau and the Civil Rights Act of 1866, although both were enacted over Johnson's veto. He supported the Military Reconstruction Act, which passed over Johnson's veto on March 2, 1867, and assisted Radicals in formulating additional Reconstruction legislation that summer.

Johnson decided to remove Stanton from office early in August and demanded Stanton's resignation. The war secretary refused, however, on the grounds that the Tenure of Office Act gave Congress control over his removal. He used this pretext even though he himself believed that the act was unconstitutional. Johnson then suspended Stanton, making Grant secretary of war *ad interim*, until Congress could act. When the Senate refused Johnson's request, Stanton returned to office, and Johnson decided to remove him anyway. Impeachment proceedings against the president followed, failing by one vote on May 26, 1868. At that point, Stanton stepped down.

The tension-filled years had damaged his health, and he never fully recovered. Stanton had abandoned his law practice to serve his country and, without the energy to reestablish it, faced serious financial difficulties. When Grant assumed the presidency, he gave Stanton an appointment to the U.S. Supreme Court, which was quickly confirmed by the Senate. Stanton, however, died before taking office, on December 24, 1869.

SIGNIFICANCE

Stanton faced many adversities early in life. He struggled to get an education because of his family responsibilities. Even so, he appears to have been a cheerful and congenial youth with a taste for literature and political discussion.

Stanton's great ability as an attorney gave him national prominence. By 1859, Stanton was on the road to great wealth with an annual income in excess of forty thousand dollars. Personal tragedies, however, altered Stanton's personality. The death of his first child followed by the death of his first wife and the suicide of his younger brother had a profound effect on the man. He had always been demanding, but with personal tragedy he became rude and quarrelsome, and his relations with others remained cold and distant.

Stanton gave up wealth and security for public office, apparently with patriotic motives. A Democrat who opposed slavery, he fervently supported the Union. He joined Buchanan's cabinet in its waning months to help keep the nation together. With the onset of the Civil War, while critical of the Republican Party, he supported the Union. Stanton proved to be an able secretary of war and thus a key to Union victory. The ability to act quickly while at the same time paying attention to the smallest detail made him a good administrator. He expected the best from subordinates and replaced those who did not measure up. Along with Lincoln, he ensured the maintenance of civilian control over an enormous army during a revolutionary time.

After the war, Stanton opposed readmission of the South to the Union without guarantee of full freedom to the former slaves. Stanton disagreed with Johnson's lenient Reconstruction policy. He fought hard to retain his position in the government for the simple reason that he believed himself to be right and Johnson to be wrong. Too much blood had been shed for him to do otherwise. A truly remarkable man, Stanton certainly deserves to be remembered as one of the great war secretaries, perhaps even the greatest.

—David L. Wilson

FURTHER READING

Flower, Frank Abial. *Edwin McMasters Stanton: The Autocrat of Rebellion, Emancipation, and Reconstruction*. New York: Saalfield, 1905. A laudatory biography that has some value because of the author's access to papers no longer available.

Gorham, George C. *Life and Public Service of Edwin M. Stanton*. 2 vols. Boston: Houghton Mifflin, 1899. Gorham was commissioned by Stanton's family to prepare this biography. The author also had access to family papers that have since been scattered.

Hearn, Chester G. *Ellet's Brigade: The Strangest Outfit of All*. Baton Rouge: Louisiana State University Press, 2000. Recounts how engineer Charles Ellet, Jr., commanded the Ram Fleet, a unique Civil War unit that was ignored by the army and navy yet won a major battle for Union forces in 1862. Explains Stanton's role in authorizing and organizing the fleet.

Hyman, Harold M. "Johnson, Stanton, and Grant: A Reconsideration of the Army's Role in the Events Leading to Impeachment." *American Historical Review* 66 (October, 1960): 85-100. This is an excellent discussion of the clash between Stanton and Johnson.

Perret, Geoffrey. *Lincoln's War: The Untold Story of America's Greatest President as Commander in Chief*. New York: Random House, 2004. This book about Lincoln's leadership during the Civil War includes information about Stanton, including the two men's relationship, Stanton's working style, and Stanton's abolitionist sentiments.

Pratt, Fletcher. *Stanton: Lincoln's Secretary of War*. New York: W. W. Norton, 1953. A readable treatment of Stanton, but unequal to Thomas and Hyman.

Thomas, Benjamin P., and Harold M. Hyman. *Stanton: The Life and Times of Lincoln's Secretary of War*. New York: Alfred A. Knopf, 1962. A beautifully written biography based on massive research. It is unlikely that a more balanced treatment will appear.

United States War Department. *The War of the Rebellion: A Compilation of the Official Records of the Union and Confederate Armies*. 128 vols. Washington, D.C.: Government Printing Office, 1880-1901. These volumes contain the essential documents covering Stanton's work in wartime.

SEE ALSO: James Buchanan; Ulysses S. Grant; Andrew Johnson; Francis Scott Key; Robert E. Lee; Abraham Lincoln; Dred Scott; William Tecumseh Sherman; Tecumseh.

RELATED ARTICLES in *Great Events from History: The Nineteenth Century, 1801-1900:* January 1, 1863: Lincoln Issues the Emancipation Proclamation; March 3, 1863: Union Enacts the First National Draft Law; April 9 and 14, 1865: Surrender at Appomattox and Assassination of Lincoln; February 24-May 26, 1868: Impeachment of Andrew Johnson.

ELIZABETH CADY STANTON
American social reformer

Stanton was one of the founders of the organized women's rights movement in the United States and served as one of its chief leaders during the second half of the nineteenth century.

BORN: November 12, 1815; Johnstown, New York
DIED: October 26, 1902; New York, New York
ALSO KNOWN AS: Elizabeth Cady (birth name)
AREA OF ACHIEVEMENT: Women's rights

EARLY LIFE
Elizabeth Cady Stanton was born Elizabeth Cady, the fourth of the six children of Daniel and Margaret Cady who survived childhood. Through her mother she was descended from a wealthy family, the Livingstons, who were part of the political elite of New York. Her mother's father, James Livingston, was an officer in George Washington's army during the American Revolution and a member of the New York state legislature. Elizabeth's father, Daniel Cady, was a successful lawyer who served in the New York state legislature and the U.S. House of Representatives, and, after 1847, he was a member of the New York State Supreme Court. Daniel Cady was a conservative in his political views and became an active member of the Federalist Party. Elizabeth's parents were strict Presbyterians who held firmly to traditional Calvinist doctrines of predestination and the depravity of human nature. As a child, Elizabeth found this version of religion frightening, even to the point of having nightmares that the Devil was attempting to possess her.

Several events in Elizabeth's childhood helped awaken her to the realization that women held a subordinate position in American society. Her father wanted very much to have a son, but each of Elizabeth's three brothers died young. At the death of his third son, Daniel Cady openly lamented to Elizabeth that she was not a boy. Part of the impetus for Elizabeth's refusal to accept a traditional female sex role may have stemmed from her attempt to be the son her father so fervently desired. A second instance that brought a new awareness of the disadvantage of being female occurred in her father's law office. Hearing of a case in which a female friend sought unsuccessfully to reclaim property she had purchased with her own money, but of which she had been deprived because of a state law transferring a woman's property to her husband when she married, Elizabeth became so up-

set that she attempted to cut the relevant pages out of her father's law books.

Even as a child, Elizabeth displayed intellectual ability considerably beyond that of the average youth. Believing that becoming a learned person was essential if she were to be equal to boys, she began the study of Greek at the age of eleven, later winning a prize at the Johnstown Academy for her achievements in this area. In spite of her outstanding academic record, she was not allowed to enroll at Union College, which admitted only boys, and had to be content with a girls' boarding school, Troy Female Seminary, which she attended from 1830 to 1833. Although most girls' boarding schools at this time were primarily finishing schools, concentrating on developing their students' social skills, Troy was unusual in that it attempted to provide academic training comparable to that which colleges provided men. The seminary encouraged its students to be self-reliant and provided careful training in writing skills, which Elizabeth later believed to have contributed to her success as an author.

After graduation from Troy Female Seminary, Elizabeth did not seek a career and at this point displayed little evidence that she would become a reformer. Even in this period, however, she occasionally displayed those qualities of independence and a militant opposition to efforts to place women in a subordinate position that marked her later life. She became the head of a young women's association that raised funds to enable an aspiring minister to attend seminary. When the recipient of their funds was invited to deliver a special sermon and chose to speak on women's inferiority, Elizabeth rose from her seat in the front pew and led the other young women out of the church in a gesture of protest.

During the 1830's, Elizabeth was increasingly drawn into the abolitionist reform effort by her cousin Gerrit Smith. Her cousin's home was a station on the Underground Railroad, and the accounts of their experiences by fugitive slaves made a lasting impression on Elizabeth. It was while attending an antislavery meeting that Elizabeth met the man who eventually became her husband. Henry Stanton was a member of the executive committee that directed the activities of the American Anti-Slavery Society. He was a gifted public speaker who had risked his life on several occasions by speaking against slavery to hostile crowds. When he proposed marriage to Elizabeth, her parents were totally opposed, because they considered abolitionists to be fanatics.

Marriage to Henry was an important turning point in Elizabeth's life, for he was not wealthy, and she knew that the social elite of New York would never accept them as long as he remained an abolitionist. Nevertheless—and even though her parents remained opposed and did not attend her wedding—Elizabeth married Henry in May, 1840. In two important respects, the marriage ceremony reflected her emerging feminist consciousness: At her request, the traditional bride's promise to obey her husband was deleted from the wedding vows, and, while adding her husband's name, she retained her own name.

Life's Work

Almost immediately after their marriage, Elizabeth and Henry left for London to attend an international anti-slavery convention. This proved to be a traumatic experience for her. Many male delegates feared that association with feminism would harm the abolitionist cause and opposed allowing women to be delegates. The first major issue discussed at the conference was whether women delegates should be allowed to participate on an equal basis with men. It was eventually decided that women should not be allowed to sit on the convention floor with men and should not be permitted to speak at the conference. Stanton was deeply angered by the treatment accorded women and resolved to organize a women's rights convention when she returned to the United States. Although eight years passed before that conference was held, her treatment at the London convention was directly responsible for convincing her that women must join together in an organized effort if they were to progress toward equality.

After their return to New York, Stanton became immersed in domestic activities. She had seven children between 1842 and 1859, and her husband considered it her responsibility to rear them. Partly because Henry was often away from home, sometimes for as long as eight months, Stanton was frequently depressed and resented the burdens of housework and child rearing. In her speeches and writings in later years, she often stressed birth control as of central importance in improving the position of married women; it is likely that her remarks at least partially reflected her own experiences.

After discovering that other women shared her sense of discontent, Stanton organized a women's rights convention at Seneca Falls, New York, at which women's grievances could be expressed. It was intended to be a local event, and she did not expect a large turnout. Nevertheless, more than three hundred persons came for the convention, including a number of prominent reformers from nearby Rochester. Stanton wrote the key document discussed by the convention, a list of women's grievances that she called the Declaration of Sentiments.

The declaration was modeled after the Declaration of Independence and drew upon the same natural-rights arguments to justify an end to discrimination based on sex . The list of grievances was lengthy and covered a wide spectrum: the admission of women to institutions of higher education, the right to enter professions such as law and medicine, the right of employed married women to retain their earnings, and an end to the double standard of sexual morality. Resolutions on these points received the unanimous support of those at the convention. A resolution proposing woman suffrage, however, proved far more controversial and passed by only a bare majority. Even Stanton's husband, Henry, opposed the suffrage resolution. After the convention, Stanton's father attempted to persuade her to remove her name from the list of those who had signed the Declaration of Sentiments, but she refused to do so. Her decision to persevere was an important turning point in her emer-

Elizabeth Cady Stanton. (Library of Congress)

EARLY EXPOSURE TO THE LAW

In her autobiography, Elizabeth Cady Stanton recalls how she became aware of the gross unfairness to women of statutory laws, about which she read in her father's law office when she was young.

As my father's office joined the house, I spent there much of my time, when out of school, listening to the clients stating their cases, talking with the students, and reading the laws in regard to woman. In our Scotch neighborhood many men still retained the old feudal ideas of women and property. Fathers, at their death, would will the bulk of their property to the eldest son, with the proviso that the mother was to have a home with him. Hence it was not unusual for the mother, who had brought all the property into the family, to be made an unhappy dependent on the bounty of an uncongenial daughter-in-law and a dissipated son. The tears and complaints of the women who came to my father for legal advice touched my heart and early drew my attention to the injustice and cruelty of the laws. As the practice of the law was my father's business, I could not exactly understand why he could not alleviate the sufferings of these women. So, in order to enlighten me, he would take down his books and show me the inexorable statutes. The students, observing my interest, would amuse themselves by reading to me all the worst laws they could find, over which I would laugh and cry by turns. One Christmas morning I went into the office to show them, among other of my presents, a new coral necklace and bracelets. They all admired the jewelry and then began to tease me with hypothetical cases of future ownership. "Now," said Henry Bayard, "if in due time you should be my wife, those ornaments would be mine; I could take them and lock them up, and you could never wear them except with my permission. I could even exchange them for a box of cigars, and you could watch them evaporate in smoke."

With this constant bantering from students and the sad complaints of the women, my mind was sorely perplexed. So when, from time to time, my attention was called to these odious laws, I would mark them with a pencil, and becoming more and more convinced of the necessity of taking some active measures against these unjust provisions, I resolved to seize the first opportunity, when alone in the office, to cut every one of them out of the books; supposing my father and his library were the beginning and the end of the law. However, this mutilation of his volumes was never accomplished, for dear old Flora Campbell, to whom I confided my plan for the amelioration of the wrongs of my unhappy sex, warned my father of what I proposed to do. Without letting me know that he had discovered my secret, he explained to me one evening how laws were made, the large number of lawyers and libraries there were all over the State, and that if his library should burn up it would make no difference in woman's condition. "When you are grown up, and able to prepare a speech," said he, "you must go down to Albany and talk to the legislators; tell them all you have seen in this office—the sufferings of these Scotchwomen, robbed of their inheritance and left dependent on their unworthy sons, and, if you can persuade them to pass new laws, the old ones will be a dead letter." Thus was the future object of my life foreshadowed and my duty plainly outlined by him who was most opposed to my public career when, in due time, I entered upon it.

Source: Elizabeth Cady Stanton, *Eighty Years and More: Reminiscences, 1815-1897* (New York, 1898), chapter 2.

gence as a nationally prominent feminist reformer.

During the years after the Seneca Falls convention, Stanton continued her activities on behalf of women's rights but was also active in other reform movements. In 1852, angry because the New York State temperance organization discriminated against women, she helped found the Women's State Temperance Society of New York. Her advocacy of temperance reflected a belief that excessive drinking by men often had serious consequences for women.

Because of the brutality often exhibited by drunken men toward their wives, Stanton urged that the grounds for divorce be expanded to include consistent heavy drinking. The majority of the women members were too conservative to consider Stanton's suggestion that the grounds for divorce be liberalized, and when they refused to reelect her as president, she withdrew from the organization. She also remained active in the abolitionist movement, urging the immediate emancipation of slaves, and opposed Abraham Lincoln's candidacy for the presidency in 1860 on the grounds that he was too moderate on the slavery issue and might compromise with the South. When, after the war, constitutional amendments were proposed extending the suffrage and civil rights to blacks, Stanton campaigned to have the amendments extended to women. Opposition to this step by her abolitionist friends contributed to its failure and drove a wedge between them; this was widened when she, in turn, argued against the Fourteenth and Fifteenth amendments because she feared the newly enfranchised black men would be hostile to woman suffrage.

In 1851, Stanton met Susan B. Anthony and initiated a friendship that had an important influence on the American feminist movement in the second half of the nineteenth century. Stanton persuaded Anthony to become involved in the campaign for women's rights, and the two worked closely on behalf of that cause for the next forty years. Stanton was a talented writer and public speaker but disliked the administrative work necessary to conduct a major campaign. Anthony excelled at such work, however, and thus the two formed an effective team. Although Anthony later received more public recognition for her role in bringing about woman suffrage, she was the junior partner in the relationship and acknowledged that Stanton was the true founder of the organized women's rights movement in the United States.

With the assistance of Anthony, Stanton promoted the cause of woman suffrage in a variety of ways. In 1866, she ran for Congress as an independent in order to test the constitutional right of a woman to hold public office. In the following year, she conducted an extensive campaign in Kansas, speaking throughout the state on behalf of a state constitutional amendment on woman suffrage.

In 1871, Stanton and Anthony made a speaking tour around the West, seeking to stimulate support for woman suffrage. In 1878, Stanton was responsible for the introduction of a woman suffrage amendment to the Constitution in Congress, a measure that was reintroduced in each subsequent Congress until it was passed in 1920. She appeared in Congress almost every year until late in her life to speak on behalf of the woman suffrage amendment. Perhaps her most important contribution to that movement was the major part she played in establishing and directing the National Woman Suffrage Association. Stanton and Anthony formed the NWSA in 1869, and Stanton served as its president until 1890, when it merged with the rival American Woman Suffrage Association. A prolific writer, Stanton joined with Anthony in coediting three volumes of *History of Woman Suffrage* (1881-1886), an invaluable source on the American woman suffrage movement.

Although woman suffrage was her major concern, Stanton never restricted her reforming efforts to one issue. She frequently shocked female audiences by her ideas on marriage and divorce. This caused friction between her and Anthony, who maintained that the cause of woman suffrage was being harmed by associating it with radical proposals for easier divorce. Stanton also alarmed Anthony with her criticisms of the Church. She believed that the Church was a major force maintaining the subordinate position of women, and from 1878, Stanton endeavored to persuade the NWSA to take a public stand against this.

Unsuccessful in that effort, Stanton then attempted to establish a committee of women to prepare a revised version of the Bible that would eliminate its sexist language. Eventually she proceeded on her own to write an extensive commentary on the biblical passages that directly discussed the status of women. Published in 1895 as *The Woman's Bible*, it defended women against the claim that they were responsible for Original Sin because of Eve's behavior in the Garden of Eden. Stanton was deeply hurt when the work was repudiated by other woman suffrage leaders, who feared that it would lead the public to dismiss the suffrage movement as irreligious.

Although her eyes began to fail during the last years of her life (she was completely blind by the time of her death), Stanton continued to write on women's issues until her death, on October 26, 1902, in New York City. She continued to enjoy life during old age, but her last years were marred by the breakdown of her friendship with Anthony and the efforts of woman suffrage leaders to distance themselves from her because of their belief that *The Woman's Bible* would prove harmful to their cause.

SIGNIFICANCE

The position of women in American society has changed considerably since the mid-nineteenth century, and Stanton was one of the central figures helping to bring about that change. As the founder of the organized women's rights movement in the United States and its recognized leader during the second half of the nineteenth century, she was a vital figure in an important and continuing reform movement. Although often remembered primarily in connection with the woman suffrage issue, she viewed suffrage as a means by which reforms could be instituted in other areas affecting women rather than an end in itself. Although she held important offices in women's organizations, Stanton was equally important as a publicist whose writings articulated the reasons that feminists wished to alter relationships between the sexes. Her writings on these issues were so extensive that it would be appropriate to consider her the chief theorist or intellectual of the late nineteenth century women's rights movement.

Since her death, Stanton's contribution to the American women's suffrage movement has been overshadowed by that of Anthony. This is in part because many of the women's suffrage activists in the generation immediately after Stanton's death did not share her views on issues other than suffrage. The revival of feminism in the United States since 1960, however, has brought a renewed interest in her life and work, partly because she did emphasize that the nonpolitical forces that kept women in a subordinate position were as important as those that were political.

—*Harold L. Smith*

FURTHER READING

Banner, Lois. *Elizabeth Cady Stanton: A Radical for Women's Rights.* Boston: Little, Brown, 1980. The best single volume on Stanton's life and thought. It presents her as the philosopher of the feminist movement and is especially helpful on her theories.

DuBois, Ellen Carol, ed. *Elizabeth Cady Stanton, Susan B. Anthony: Correspondence, Writings, Speeches.* New York: Schocken Books, 1981. This is an excellent collection of the correspondence between Stanton and Anthony, which also includes many of Stanton's more important speeches and articles. The critical commentary by DuBois is helpful in placing the documents in context.

Flexner, Eleanor. *Century of Struggle: The Woman's Rights Movement in the United States.* Cambridge, Mass.: Harvard University Press, 1959. Widely regarded as the best history of the campaign for woman suffrage. It includes some references to Stanton but focuses on the movement itself rather than on its leaders.

Forster, Margaret. "Elizabeth Cady Stanton, 1815-1902." In *Significant Sisters.* New York: Oxford University Press, 1984. A well-written chapter in a book about prominent feminists. It makes extensive use of Stanton's letters and other original sources in conveying a vivid sense of her personality.

Griffith, Elisabeth. *In Her Own Right: The Life of Elizabeth Cady Stanton.* New York: Oxford University Press, 1984. A detailed account of Stanton's life based upon extensive research in primary sources. It is a psychological study that excels in discussing Stanton's private life.

Kern, Kathi. *Mrs. Stanton's Bible.* Ithaca, N.Y.: Cornell University Press, 2001. Examines Stanton's nonsexist Bible, published in 1895. Kern argues Stanton's biblical commentary alienated her from less radical feminists and may have delayed passage of the woman suffrage amendment.

Lutz, Alma. *Created Equal: A Biography of Elizabeth Cady Stanton.* New York: John Day, 1940. This was the first scholarly biography of Stanton. It is a clear, objective, narrative account that concentrates more on her political activities than on her thought.

Stanton, Elizabeth Cady. *Eighty Years and More: Reminiscences, 1815-1897.* London: T. Fisher Unwin, 1898. Reprint. New York: Schocken Books, 1971. Written near the end of her life, Stanton's autobiography provides the fullest account of her life from her own point of view. Although invaluable for its firsthand information, it is brief on some events in her life and omits others entirely, and thus must be supplemented by other sources.

Wellman, Judith. *The Road to Seneca Falls: Elizabeth Cady Stanton and the First Women's Rights Convention.* Urbana: University of Illinois Press, 2004. Chronicles the events that took place during the historic women's rights meeting, describing how abolitionism, radical Quakerism, and the campaign for legal reform shaped the convention's proceedings—and Stanton's life.

SEE ALSO: Susan B. Anthony; Amelia Bloomer; Matilda Joslyn Gage; Sarah and Angelina Grimké; Abraham Lincoln; Lucretia Mott.

RELATED ARTICLES in *Great Events from History: The Nineteenth Century, 1801-1900:* 1820's-1850's: Social Reform Movement; December 3, 1847: Douglass Launches *The North Star*; July 19-20, 1848: Seneca Falls Convention; May 28-29, 1851: Akron Woman's Rights Convention; May 10, 1866: Suffragists Protest the Fourteenth Amendment; May, 1869: Woman Suffrage Associations Begin Forming; December, 1869: Wyoming Gives Women the Vote; July 4, 1876: Declaration of the Rights of Women; February 17-18, 1890: Women's Rights Associations Unite.

FREIHERR VOM STEIN
German politician

Stein was the architect of an early nineteenth century reform movement in Prussia that altered the authoritarian nature of the Prussian state in the direction of modern liberalism and resulted in fundamental changes in Prussian institutions.

BORN: October 26, 1757; Nassau, Holy Roman Empire (now in Germany)

DIED: June 29, 1831; Cappenberg, Prussia (now in Germany)

ALSO KNOWN AS: Heinrich Friedrick Karl vom und zum Stein (full name)

AREA OF ACHIEVEMENT: Government and politics

EARLY LIFE

Heinrich Friedrich Karl vom und zum Stein (shtin) was the ninth of ten children of Karl Philipp Freiherr vom Stein and Langwerth vom Stein (née von Simmern). The vom Stein family was of the Imperial Knighthood and had been independent proprietors within the Holy Roman Empire for more than seven hundred years when Karl (as he was called by his family and friends) was born in his ancestral home at Nassau on October 26, 1757. His father had entered the bureaucracy of the neighboring state of Mainz, where he eventually rose to the rank of privy councillor.

Stein's parents impressed upon him that as a representative of his caste he had the patriotic duty to devote his life to the service of the community. With that end in mind, he was matriculated at the age of sixteen at the University of Göttingen to study law and political science preparatory to entering government service. Although Göttingen was experiencing perhaps its most dynamic era of literary ferment during Stein's stay there, he was relatively unaffected by it. He concentrated on the study of history and of constitutional and legal theory, which apparently deepened the patriotic feelings imbued in him by his parents and strengthened his determination to enter government service.

Stein's original inclination was to enter the still-extant but ineffective government machinery of the Holy Roman Empire. After leaving Göttingen, he traveled to the Imperial Chamber at Wetzlar, the Imperial Court Council in Vienna, and the Imperial Diet at Regensburg in order to gain an understanding of the political and administrative structure of the empire.

Apparently disillusioned by the largely figurehead nature of imperial administration, Stein accepted an appointment to the Prussian bureaucracy under Frederick William II in 1780 at the age of twenty-three. Some of his biographers have suggested that even at this early age, Stein had already concluded that the best hope of unifying all the German people into a strong political entity, with liberal institutions and a constitution, lay with Prussia.

LIFE'S WORK

For the next sixteen years, Stein held progressively more responsible positions within the Prussian government, primarily in mining operations and in the provincial administration in Prussian Westphalia. This experience gave him an intimate knowledge of the workings of local government and led to his appointment in 1796 as head of all the Prussian Rhenish and Westphalian administrative districts. His success in this capacity and other endeavors resulted in his appointment in 1804 as minister of economic affairs for the royal government in Berlin. There Stein rapidly developed the conviction that the Prussian governmental and social systems would have to be drastically reformed and modernized if Prussia were to survive what Stein perceived as an inevitable clash with the burgeoning Napoleonic empire. Stein's vocal insistence on reform resulted, in 1807, in his dismissal by Frederick William III shortly after the disastrous Prussian defeat by Napoleon I at the Battles of Jena and Auerstedt.

Stein's forced retirement to his family estate at Nassau gave him time to systematize and set down on paper his ideas concerning the reforms necessary to modernize and rejuvenate the Prussian state. In his famous *Nassauer Denkschrift* (1807; Nassau memorandum), Stein argued that if the Prussian state was to survive, its citizens must be allowed to participate in the management of its affairs. He further suggested in his memorandum that only self-government could instill into the Prussian people the patriotism and community spirit that would allow Prussia to survive in an increasingly dangerous world. Stein's lifelong study of British history and his admiration for the British parliamentary system undoubtedly contributed to his advocacy of the establishment of a similar system in Prussia.

During Stein's unwilling retirement, Napoleon forced Frederick William to sign the Treaty of Tilsit. The terms of the treaty considerably diminished the size and autonomy of the Prussian state and convinced many

Prussians in the bureaucracy and the army of the necessity of sweeping reforms in the governmental apparatus. Napoleon insisted on the dismissal of Frederick William's foreign minister, Karl von Hardenberg, and the appointment of Stein in his place. Frederick William confirmed Stein as prime minister of Prussia on October 4, 1807.

Stein took advantage of a wave of patriotism and widespread demand for reform engendered by the twin debacles of Jena and Tilsit to force Frederick William to accede to the first of the great changes in Prussian government, administration, and society later known collectively as the Prussian Reform movement. The first, and in many ways the most far-reaching, of the reforms was promulgated on October 19, 1807, as the Law Concerning the Emancipated Possession and the Free Use of Landed Property and the Personal Relationships of the Inhabitants of the Land. This law emancipated the Prussian serfs from feudal obligations and enabled the Prussian aristocracy to sell their land to non-nobles. In addition, the law enabled all Prussians to follow the vocation of their choice. The law was a decisive step toward the destruction of the old caste relationships of Prussian society and the creation of civic and legal equality.

One year later, Stein was responsible for the creation of effective local self-government for the towns and cities of Germany through the issuance of the *Städteordnung* (municipal ordinances). He then turned his attention to modernizing the national government. He replaced the old, secretive councillor administration with departmental ministries of foreign affairs, internal affairs, finance, justice, and war, each with responsibility and authority for the whole of the Prussian kingdom. He also reorganized provincial administration along more efficient lines. Whether Stein would have succeeded in introducing in Prussia the national parliament, which he so admired in the English system, will never be known. Napoleon forced Frederick William to dismiss him from office on November 24, 1808, after French spies intercepted a letter Stein sent to a friend criticizing the French emperor and his policies toward Prussia.

Stein took refuge until 1812 in Austria, where he continued to correspond with his successor Hardenberg and with other men in the bureaucracy and the army of Prussia who were carrying the banner of reform. In 1812, he answered a summons by Alexander I of Russia to come to St. Petersburg as a political adviser. He was instrumental in that capacity in negotiating the Russo-Prussian alliance in 1813, after Napoleon's 1812 invasion of Russia ended in catastrophe.

Stein then provided moral leadership for the German states during the war of liberation, which ended with Napoleon's final defeat and exile in 1815. During that period, Stein also continued to influence those men in Prussia who pursued progressive reform, men such as Johann Gottlieb Fichte, August von Gneisenau, Ernst Arndt, Heinrich von Kleist, and Wilhelm and Alexander von Humboldt. At the Congress of Vienna, Stein championed the cause of the political unification of the German states but was not satisfied with the final form that unification took. He regarded the Germanic Confederation that resulted from the deliberations at Vienna as little more than the ghost of the recently deceased Holy Roman Empire.

After the Congress of Vienna, Stein retired to his estate of Cappenberg, Westphalia, where he devoted the remainder of his life to the writing of history and to the publication of the works of other historians on the subject of German history. He died in his home on June 29, 1831.

SIGNIFICANCE

Freiherr vom Stein was a pivotal figure in the transformation of Prussian government from an absolute monarchy toward liberalism and constitutionalism. He was, along with Hardenberg, one of the champions of the concept that such changes must be instituted peacefully and slowly from above, or else they will be brought about violently and quickly, and with unforeseeable consequences, from below, as in the French Revolution. His conviction that the reforms must be made was based less on a concern for individual liberty and human rights than on a desire to prevent German institutions from being overwhelmed by the French. He realized that the powerful forces of nationalism and liberalism unleashed by the French Revolution of 1789 could not be withstood without unleashing similar forces in Germany. He hoped to control those forces while retaining the virtues of older Prussian society.

The unfinished nature of his reforms had far-reaching consequences for the development of Prussian and German society: The serfs were freed, but without land; the former serfs were reduced to the status of migrant agricultural laborers, many of whom migrated to the cities and became the nucleus of the proletariat, which turned to Marxism and trade unionism in later decades and caused much turmoil in imperial Germany. Equality before the law was established, but without constitutional guarantees; the widespread and unsatisfied desire among the Prussian intellectual community and the bourgeoisie for a constitution and a parliament culminated with the revolutions of 1848. The principle of participatory government was established, but without a medium through which it could be practiced. The essentially conservative approach to reform adopted by Stein created a tradition in Prussia of expecting the government to effect necessary reform in societal institutions that prevailed into the twentieth century.

—Paul Madden

FURTHER READING

Gray, Marion W. *Prussia in Transition: Society and Politics Under the Stein Reform Ministry of 1808.* Philadelphia: American Philosophical Society, 1986. This book, a reprint of an article from *Transactions of the American Philosophical Society*, is primarily concerned with the milieu in which Stein's reforms took place and the effects of the reforms on Prussian society, rather than with Stein himself. An excellent introduction to the era of the Prussian Reform movement.

Holborn, Hajo. *A History of Modern Germany, 1648-1840.* New York: Alfred A. Knopf, 1964. Holborn's book contains several chapters on the Prussian Reform movement and provides sketches of the most important movement leaders, including Stein. The book places the reform movement and the reformers in their proper perspective within German history.

Meinecke, Friedrich. *The Age of German Liberation, 1795-1815.* Translated by Peter Peret and Helmuth Fischer. Berkeley: University of California Press, 1977. One of the best accounts of the period, providing a good overview of Stein's life and work. Mei-necke argues that Stein and the other reformers successfully provided the transition between absolutism and representative government that made possible the unification of Germany half a century later.

Seeley, John Robert. *Life and Times of Stein: Or, Germany and Prussia in the Napoleonic Age.* New York: Greenwood Press, 1968. Seeley's book is the only full-length biography of Stein in English. It is perhaps overly laudatory. In the main, it agrees with Meinecke's evaluation of Stein and his reforms.

Simon, Walter. *The Failure of the Prussian Reform Movement.* Ithaca, N.Y.: Cornell University Press, 1955. Simon is critical of both the reforms and the reformers, including Stein, of whom he writes at great length. Simon argues that the failure of the reforms to establish a unified German state with a constitutional, parliamentary form of government led directly to the development of an authoritarian German empire after 1871 and ultimately to the Third Reich.

SEE ALSO: Alexander I; Gebhard Leberecht von Blücher; August von Gneisenau; Karl von Hardenberg; Alexander von Humboldt; Heinrich von Kleist; Justus von Liebig; Napoleon I; Barthold Georg Niebuhr; Gerhard Johann David von Scharnhorst.

RELATED ARTICLES in *Great Events from History: The Nineteenth Century, 1801-1900:* June 8-9, 1815: Organization of the German Confederation; January 1, 1834: German States Join to Form Customs Union; March 3-November 3, 1848: Prussian Revolution of 1848.

JAKOB STEINER
Swiss mathematician

One of the greatest geometers of the first half of the nineteenth century, Steiner wrote books and dozens of articles on geometry that established him as a chief authority on isoperimetric geometry and as the founder of modern synthetic geometry in Germany.

BORN: March 18, 1796; Utzentorf, Canton of Bern, Switzerland
DIED: April 1, 1863; Bern, Switzerland
AREA OF ACHIEVEMENT: Mathematics

EARLY LIFE

Jakob Steiner (SHTI-ner) was born into a family of thrifty, humble, and hardworking Swiss farmers. Though the youngest of five children, he contributed from a very early age to the family income, the family expecting nothing more than the most modest intellectual development. Consequently, he remained illiterate until he was fourteen and continued farm work until he was nineteen. According to his later recollections, before he had any formal education he developed an astounding capacity for spatial conceptualization.

Contrary to the desires of his father, Jakob entered the school of the Swiss educational reformer Johann Pestalozzi at Yverdon. Out of conformity with Swiss educational precepts, Pestalozzi continued stressing the pedagogical importance of individual training and direct experience for his students. Before Pestalozzi's institution failed, Steiner had become a teaching assistant. Thereafter, Steiner entered Heidelberg University, where he pursued numerical perceptions in connection with imaginative spatial concepts. From 1818 until 1821, while earning a living as a teacher, Steiner worked with one of the institution's leading geometers, whose lectures and ideas he profoundly disdained. Notwithstanding, Steiner obtained his doctorate from Heidelberg, thereafter accepting a teaching position as a tutor at a private school.

The eldest son of the famed German statesman and philologist Wilhelm von Humboldt was one of Steiner's pupils. Steiner's acquaintance with the distinguished Humboldt family altered his fortunes. The Humboldts introduced him to Berlin's premier mathematicians, and Steiner was encouraged to accept a teaching post at a Berlin vocational institution during the next decade. Eventually the University of Berlin created an endowed chair, which Steiner was to fill—indeed, he had, since 1834, been a member of the Berlin Academy on the basis of his previous mathematical, or geometrical, writings.

LIFE'S WORK

Steiner's mathematical publications commenced in 1826, while he still tutored at his vocational school. This creative production coincided with the founding by August Leopold Crelle of what became one of the nineteenth century's most famous mathematical publications, *Journal für die reine und angewandte Mathematik* (the journal for pure and applied mathematics). Professionally, Steiner expanded his reputation in 1832 with his *Systematische Entwicklung der Abhängigkeit Geometrischer Gestalten* (systematic evolution of the mutual dependence of geometrical forms), a planned introduction to a five-part series never to be completed.

Steiner's work does not readily reduce to layman's terms. It is projective geometry, built upon synthetic constructions. Geometry's basic forms are based on planes. Projective geometry moves from the fundamental plane to lines, planar pencils of lines to pencils of planes, bundles of lines, bundles of planes—and then into space itself, steadily generating higher geometric forms. For Steiner, one form in this projective hierarchy related with the others.

It was not the originality of Steiner's work that was dominant, although the questions he raised were then novel considering geometers' principal preoccupations. Steiner's own view was that "the writings of the present day have tried to reveal the organism by which the sundry phenomena of the external world are bound to one another." What he sought to determine was how "order enters into chaos," how all parts of the external world fit naturally into one another, and how related parts join to form well-defined groups. Specifically, it was the brilliantly stated and systematic treatment Steiner lent to his inquiries that gained for him his reputation.

The unique and justly famed French École Polytechnique, with its unparalleled training of France's intellectual elite and special concentration of intensive mathematical training, had long before Steiner's day divided geometry into two branches: the analytical and the synthetic, or projective. During the early seventeenth century, René Descartes had explained how numbers could be utilized to describe points in a plane or in space algebraically. Steiner, however, concentrated on the other branch: projective geometry, which did not usually resort to the measurements or lengths of angles.

Steiner learned something from Johann Pestalozzi and his eccentric preoccupation with right triangles, and as a pedagogue Steiner, like Pestalozzi, encouraged his students' independent and rigorously logical search for learning. As might be expected, Steiner avoided figures to illustrate his lectures. His own intuitions were so much a part of his character, he sought both in teaching and writing to use them. He did not neglect his own disciplined scholarship. He read exhaustively the works of his European counterparts, staying on the cutting edge of his investigations.

Mathematical authorities agree that in midcareer Steiner still fell short of his goals by rejecting the achievements of some of his predecessors and contemporaries. For example, he lost the chance to employ signs drawn from Karl August Möbius's synthetic geometry and therefore the opportunity for the full deployment of his imagination. It is small wonder that Steiner sometimes wrote of "the shadow land of geometry."

Steiner's practical ambitions, related to, but lying near or on the margin of his geometrical scholarship, were not as shadowy. Perhaps this was understandable, for in class-conscious Berlin and the German academic world, his social origins were not advantageous. His special professorship or chair created for him at Berlin University was partly an effort to avoid this implicit embarrassment. Moreover, the timing of his publications was partly calculated to advance him toward the directorship of Berlin's planned Polytechnic Institute. Hence, in 1833 he published a short work, *Die geometrischen Konstructionen, ausgeführt mittelst der geraden Linie und eines festen Kreises* (*Geometrical Constructions with a Ruler, Given a Fixed Circle with Its Center*, 1950), which was intended for high schools and for practical purposes. Indeed, following his appointment to his Berlin chair, he never completed what he promised would be a comprehensive work.

Steiner apparently was not surprised when analytical geometricians discovered that his own results could often be verified analytically. It was not so much that Steiner disdained others' analyses. Rather, he was headed in a different direction of inquiry, and he believed that analysis prevented geometricians from seeing things as they actually are. Like other projective geometers, he thought that because projective geometry could advance so swiftly from a few fundamental concepts to significant statements, he, like them, eschewed the formidable axiomatic studies that were the hallmark of Euclidean geometry. Most mathematicians argued against him, however, that despite Steiner's disclaimers, there was no royal road to a new geometry. No matter how logical, clear, and intuitive Steiner's projective geometry was, most geometricians actually wanted to see—metrically and analytically—what the projectivists were describing. Geometry was, for its nineteenth century scholars, simply too full of irrationals to make its results completely tenable.

SIGNIFICANCE

Jakob Steiner was not the originator of projective or synthetic geometry. Nevertheless, his contributions were substantial and significant in the revival and advancement of synthetic geometry. This was the result of his clearly presented intuitions and his marvelous systematization of his projections. Before the close of his career, moreover, he had both trained others through the clarity of his lectures and writings and encouraged other geometricians such as Julius Plücker, Karl Weierstrass, and Karl von Staudt to resolve problems that had eluded or defeated him. These geometricians, through their own citations and references to his work, spread his name further throughout the European mathematical community. In addition, Steiner left a substantial body of published works.

By the 1850's, his health declined and the eccentricities of an always contentious character increased. He journeyed from spa to spa seeking the rejuvenation of his health. He died on April 1, 1863, at such a spa in Bern, Switzerland. However, his repute and the respect of geometricians for his revitalization of synthetic geometry and its conundrums outlasted him.

—Clifton K. Yearley

FURTHER READING

Courant, Richard, and Herbert Robbins. *What Is Mathematics? An Elementary Approach to Ideas and Methods.* Revised by Ian Stewart. 2d ed. New York: Oxford University Press, 1996. This overview of mathematical history, aimed at readers with some knowledge of the subject, contains information about Steiner's geometric constructions and "Steiner's problem."

Klein, Felix. *Development of Mathematics in the Nineteenth Century.* Translated by M. Ackerman. Brookline, Mass.: Math-Sci Press, 1979. Klein's work is indispensable, as little of Steiner's writing has been translated into English. Filled with technical mathematical signs, symbols, and equations, it nevertheless contains much that is understandable to lay readers. His expositions include biographical material on all mathematicians treated, with Steiner prominently among them, as well as good contextual explanations of their objectives, problems, and results. Contains ample illustrations.

Kline, Morris. *Mathematical Thought from Ancient to Modern Times*. New York: Oxford University Press, 1972. A layperson's survey, which largely ignores Steiner but places his work in a broad comprehensible framework. Contains illustrations, a good select bibliography, and an index.

Newman, James R., ed. *The World of Mathematics: A Small Library of the Literature of Mathematics from A'h-mosé*, the Scribe, to Albert Einstein. 4 vols. New York: Simon & Schuster, 1956. Volume 2 of this work is pertinent to Steiner's context and to defining aspects of his work. Illustrations help nonspecialists appreciate the nature of some synthetic, isoperimetric geometrical problems and their attempted solutions. A fine explication of certain projective geometrical investigations. There are bibliographical citations scattered throughout and a select bibliography and usable index at the end of the second volume.

Porter, Thomas Isaac. "A History of the Classical Isoperimetric Problem." In *Contributions to the Calculus of Variations, 1931-1932: Theses Submitted to the Department of Mathematics of the University of Chicago*. Chicago: University of Chicago Press, 1933. Rather than a raw thesis, this essay is an excellent survey of the synthetic geometrical problems Steiner, among others, tackled. Illustrated and readily understandable for those lacking special math training. Includes a substantial, if somewhat dated, bibliography.

Torretti, Roberto. *Philosophy of Geometry from Riemann to Poincaré*. Boston: Reidel, 1978. This important study is critical for a sound understanding by specialists as well as nonspecialists of a creative period in the development of both German and French mathematics, once again placing Steiner in a somewhat different historical context from that of the works cited above. It has some illustrations, a select bibliography, and an index.

SEE ALSO: Carl Friedrich Gauss; Nikolay Ivanovich Lobachevsky; Henri Poincaré.

RELATED ARTICLE in *Great Events from History: The Nineteenth Century, 1801-1900:* 1899: Hilbert Publishes *The Foundations of Geometry*.

CHARLES PROTEUS STEINMETZ
American engineer and inventor

Steinmetz helped lay the engineering foundations for the large-scale use of electric power through his technical achievements, his role as an educator and inspirer of other engineers, and his creation of research and engineering institutions. In the process, he came to personify electrical engineering to a public that understood little of its technical details.

BORN: April 9, 1865; Breslau, Prussia (now Wrocław, Poland)
DIED: October 26, 1923; Schenectady, New York
ALSO KNOWN AS: Karl August Rudolf Steinmetz (birth name)
AREAS OF ACHIEVEMENT: Engineering, education

EARLY LIFE
Charles Proteus Steinmetz (STIN-mets) was born Carl August Steinmetz in a German city that is now part of Poland. His father, Carl Heinrich Steinmetz, the son of a German Lutheran father and Polish Catholic mother, worked as a clerk and lithographer with the state railways and was a congenital hunchback who passed that disability on to his only son. His mother, born Caroline Neubert, was the daughter of a well-to-do Breslau family of German Lutherans. She died when Carl August was only a few months old.

Reared mainly by his grandmother, Steinmetz had a pleasant and comfortable childhood. His combination of strong intelligence and a weak body directed him to a university education. He enrolled at the University of Breslau as a student of philosophy, specializing in mathematics. The friend who drew him into mathematics, Henry Lux, also drew him into socialism. Steinmetz joined a group of Social Democrats espousing the ideal of Ferdinand LaSalle, who opposed Karl Marx by arguing that socialism could be achieved without revolution, a theme that Steinmetz would develop throughout his life.

Steinmetz's involvement in both mathematical study and socialism came to a critical point in 1888. Still without a degree, Steinmetz was completing a dissertation based on the geometrical ideas of the German mathematician Bernhard Riemann when he assumed the editorship of the local Social Democratic newspaper. It had already drawn the attention of the police with its anti-government, though nonviolent, editorial policy. According to Steinmetz's later recollections, he left the country in 1888 with the police looking for him and the threat of possible prosecution hanging over him.

Steinmetz spent a year in Zurich, Switzerland, where he took the only engineering courses of his career at Federal University but again departed without a degree. He had begun writing technical articles about the new field of electricity; the most promising place to make a career in that field was the United States, where capital and opportunities for electrification were abundant and engineering talent was scarce. With a prosperous friend, Oscar Asmussen, he sailed to New York.

LIFE'S WORK

Steinmetz's entry into New York Harbor in June, 1889, past the new Statue of Liberty, was in the best Emma Lazarus tradition: Tired and weak (Steinmetz was suffering from a bad cold in addition to his disability), a member of a huddled mass yearning to breathe free, he was still a socialist on the lam, penniless and in shabby clothes, and he spent two days at Ellis Island, where he was nearly rejected for entry into the country. However, he also had assets: the friendship of the wealthy Asmussen and a letter of introduction to an earlier political refugee, Rudolf Eickemeyer, who had long since established himself at Yonkers, New York, as a successful manufacturer of hat machinery and Civil War revolvers. Steinmetz was set with a job as the one-man research and development staff supporting Eickemeyer's efforts to diversify into the new business of electric motors.

Within only two years, Steinmetz rose to the top of the American electrical engineering profession. His distinctive appearance—his twisted form, less than five feet tall, his neat if grizzled beard and ever-present cigar—became well known first among engineers and soon among that segment of the public that was interested in science and technology. He then changed his name to Charles Proteus Steinmetz, reflecting his confidence in his own powers and his sense that he had made a new life for himself in America. In 1890, he introduced to engineers his law of hysteresis, a formula for predicting the energy lost through magnetizing and demagnetizing the electromagnets used in electrical equipment. This was no academic exercise but a crucial tool for designing gener-

Charles Proteus Steinmetz. (Library of Congress)

ators, motors, and transformers. His accomplishment was repeated in 1893 with his second major contribution to electrical engineering, the use of "imaginary" numbers in electrical calculations, which made it possible to determine the characteristics of complex electrical machines by calculation rather than trial and error.

The unexpectedness of Steinmetz's rise and the importance of his purely technical work, however, should not be overrated. His patron, Eickemeyer, was a fine inventor who had developed an important new type of electric motor before Steinmetz came along as well as instruments that made it easy for Steinmetz to study hysteresis. The "law" was actually an empirical special case of more general findings arrived at earlier by a British physicist; the imaginary number applications had been anticipated by a Harvard professor. Steinmetz's greatness lay in communicating these ideas, educating a generation of engineers about them, and inspiring others to use mathematics to solve practical problems. Meanwhile, the electrical inventions of Eickemeyer's company caught the eye of a giant company created in 1892 to dominate the electrical manufacturing business, the General Electric

Company. It followed its consistent policy of buying up competing companies and absorbing good engineers in the bargain by purchasing Eickemeyer's company and rights to Steinmetz's services in 1893.

General Electric sent Steinmetz to its second biggest plant, in Lynn, Massachusetts, to serve as a calculator of the electrical characteristics of its products and systems. He was unhappy there, but a reorganization in 1893 sent him to a more congenial setting in Schenectady, New York, where there were plenty of German immigrants and trained engineers. Soon, he was Schenectady's best-known citizen. Defying his physical weakness, he rode a bicycle, skied, and paddled a canoe. He filled his home laboratory with sparking and glowing electrical apparatus as well as a crow and collections of orchids, cacti, and lizards. His weekly poker games drew General Electric executives and engineers, and his summer cabin drew young protégés. He befriended in particular a young engineer, Joseph Hayden, whom he adopted, and his family. On the job, he moved beyond engineering calculations to consulting.

As General Electric's chief consulting engineer, he provided problem solving and advice for all of the company's departments. He gained fame as an oracle, but a closer look shows that he was not particularly adept at putting his finger on key trends. For example, he did not recognize the system of polyphase alternating current as the key to modern electrification, and he badly underestimated the industry's ability to develop high-voltage transmission systems. He made some two hundred patented inventions, but only one of them, a new type of streetlight, had any substantial commercial success. In the narrow realms of invention and consulting, his impact on the electrical art was not as great as that of such now-obscure contemporaries as his General Electric colleagues William LeRoy Emmet and Ernst Alexanderson, his Westinghouse rival Benjamin Garver Lamme, or the independents Nikola Tesla and William Stanley.

It was as educator and inspirational motivator that he truly shone. He wrote twelve books, including the classic *Theory and Calculation of Alternating Current Phenomena* (1897), an often-reprinted textbook. He published more than two hundred articles, in everything from mass periodicals to the *Physical Review*. While still an employee at General Electric, he accepted a professorship in electrical engineering at Schenectady's Union College and created a first-rate department that he then turned over to one of his protégés, Ernest Berg.

Steinmetz received an honorary degree from Harvard in 1899, and its accompanying citation for him as "the

foremost expert in applied electricity of this country and therefore the world" captures in its hyperbole and chauvinism some of the reasons for which America embraced Steinmetz as a public figure. He enjoyed and used the publicity. For example, he used his eminence to sponsor within General Electric the first industrial laboratory devoted in part to true scientific research (1900) and one of industry's best engineering laboratories (1907).

Steinmetz had completed his major technical work by 1910 (a later and highly publicized experiment in making lightning in the laboratory was a useful engineering exercise that does not rank with his earlier work). His interest in socialism, dormant since the 1890's, revived. He became a leader of the local Socialist Party that took over Schenectady's city government in 1912. In the posts as head of the Board of Education, head of the Parks Commission, and president of the Common Council, he led efforts to build schools and parks that greatly improved the quality of life in that city.

Steinmetz still espoused evolutionary socialism, but now it was colored by his industrial experience. His major statement of that view, the book *America and the New Epoch* (1916), emphasized cooperation and organization as the keys to socialism. The large corporation and its methods would gradually blend with the state and turn it into a cooperative commonwealth run by experts who were above politics.

This brand of corporate socialism may have disappointed his more doctrinaire colleagues. He and other members of the reformist wing were briefly expelled from the party, though he was taken back and ran in 1922, unsuccessfully, on the Socialist Party ticket for the post of state engineer. Steinmetz showed that he had not adopted reform socialism out of cowardice or a need to conform. From the sinking of the *Lusitania* in 1915 until American entry into World War I in 1917, he argued the proneutrality case with a vigor dangerous for one so obviously of German descent. After the war, he also voiced a number of unpopular or extreme positions in newspaper articles and interviews. His predictions and advocacies ranged over electric vehicles, the capabilities of the varied European "races," the coming energy crises and biological revolutions, and a widely publicized exchange of letters with Vladimir Ilich Lenin about the electrification of the Soviet Union. Never of strong constitution, he died after a brief illness in Schenectady in 1923.

SIGNIFICANCE
Steinmetz was a brilliant engineer and inventor, but his emergence as the individual embodying the profession

of electrical engineering for the American public during the early twentieth century was attributable to more than his brilliance. Electricity was a glamorous new technology with a theory inaccessible to the public. People needed to personify it, and the novelty of a small, misshapen man commanding lightning caught their fancy. He was indeed a leader in the application to electrical engineering of new methods of applied mathematics and organized research, but the same could be said of a half-dozen contemporaries whose names remained unknown. His true greatness was as an educator, explainer, and motivator. Those strengths, along with his distinctive appearance, an immigrant background personifying the melting-pot myth, an adherence to a personal and nonradical brand of socialism, and (especially posthumously) the support of the publicity machine of his long-time employer, the General Electric Company, won for him renown that went far beyond technology.

—George Wise

FURTHER READING

Alger, Philip, and Ernest Caldecott, eds. *Steinmetz the Philosopher*. Schenectady, N.Y.: Mohawk Development, 1965. A valuable collection of Steinmetz's essays on political, social, and educational topics. Perhaps best summed up by one essay's title: "The Bolsheviks *Won't* Get You if You *Do* Watch Out."

Hammond, John Winthrop. *Charles Proteus Steinmetz: A Biography*. New York: Century, 1924. The most comprehensive summary of Steinmetz's life, written by a General Electric publicity writer who worked with him at Schenectady. Uncritical in its admiration for the subject. Makes little attempt to put either the technical work or the political and social ideas in perspective. A combination of useful primary material and mythmaking.

Kline, Ronald R. *Steinmetz: Engineer and Socialist*. Baltimore: Johns Hopkins University Press, 1992. Intellectual biography that attempts to deconstruct some of the mythology surrounding Steinmetz.

Lavine, Sigmund A. *Steinmetz: Maker of Lighting*. New York: Dodd, Mead, 1952. Another recycling of the Hammond material.

Leonard, Jonathan Norton. *Loki: The Life of Charles Proteus Steinmetz*. Garden City, N.Y.: Doubleday, 1929. This account by a science journalist is somewhat livelier than Hammond's book, but it contains little additional information, beyond puncturing one or two myths. (Steinmetz worked for a salary, not as myth would have it, in exchange for a checkbook given him by General Electric.)

Miller, John Anderson. *Modern Jupiter*. New York: American Society of Mechanical Engineers, 1952. Again, the Hammond material and approach, but supplemented somewhat by material made available by the Steinmetz heirs and a former assistant. Though the author is an engineer, he does little to clarify Steinmetz's technical role. Perhaps because he is an engineer, he does little to clarify Steinmetz's socialism.

Steinmetz, Charles Proteus. *America and the New Epoch*. New York: Harper and Brothers, 1916. Steinmetz here made his fullest exposition of his brand of socialism. Argues that the era of competition is dead and that the era of cooperation has succeeded it. Corporations and government must blend together to form a corporatist state ruled by large organizations where the distinction between public and private has vanished.

SEE ALSO: Michael Faraday; Emma Lazarus; Karl Marx; Nikola Tesla.

RELATED ARTICLES in *Great Events from History: The Nineteenth Century, 1801-1900:* October, 1831: Faraday Converts Magnetic Force into Electricity; December 15, 1900: General Electric Opens Research Laboratory.

STENDHAL
French novelist

Stendhal combined the themes of Romanticism with the style of realism. His insistence on telling the truth about emotions in simple, stark terms resulted in novels that, although not popular during his lifetime, have become classics.

BORN: January 23, 1783; Grenoble, France
DIED: March 23, 1842; Paris, France
ALSO KNOWN AS: Marie-Henri Beyle (birth name)
AREA OF ACHIEVEMENT: Literature

EARLY LIFE

Stendhal (stahn-dahl) was the pen name of Marie-Henri Beyle. Information about his life is voluminous, but almost all of it is suspect, as most of it comes from his own autobiographical works—*Vie de Henry Brulard* (1890, 1949; *The Life of Henry Brulard*, 1925) and *Souvenirs d'égotisme* (1892, 1950; *Memoirs of an Egotist*, 1949). These works are faithful accounts of Stendhal's feelings about the events of his life, but they are not necessarily faithful accounts of the events themselves.

Stendhal's father, Chérubin Beyle, was a lawyer and, according to Stendhal, acquisitive and stern. His mother, Henriette Gagnon Beyle, to whom he was exceptionally close, was gay and urbane. The loss of his mother in 1790 was a devastating blow. His Aunt Séraphie Gagnon took over the task of rearing the seven-year-old Marie-Henri, but he found her a sour-tempered disciplinarian. Their relationship was never warm. His grandfather, Henri Gagnon, provided not only a cheerful refuge from his father and Aunt Séraphie but also an introduction to the intellectual world of the Enlightenment. The young Marie-Henri found little companionship outside his family. He was kept away from the other children of the community, whom his father and aunt regarded as common. His tutor, the Abbé Jean-François Raillane, was cold and old-fashioned. One of the many things Beyle liked about the French Revolution was that in 1794 Raillane had to flee from it.

One of the many reforms generated by the revolution was the creation of local schools. Such an institution opened in Grenoble in 1796, and Beyle was enrolled. It was his first opportunity to mix freely with people his own age. His performance was poor during his first year. He soon fell head over heels in love with a theater performer, Virginie Kubly, and although they never actually met, she was his first passion. Romantic turmoil would never again be long absent from his life. By 1799, he had

the opportunity to study mathematics at the École Polytechnique in Paris.

Beyle, however, never enrolled at the school. With the fascination of a small-town boy in the big city, he began to explore Paris. Within a month, he was seriously ill and was rescued by cousins named Daru, who gave him a place to stay and an introduction to society. Later, they obtained for him a position as clerk at the Ministry of War. Although Beyle's health returned, his illness caused him to lose much of his hair. From this time on, he wore a wig, and as he was stout, with short legs and a large head, he always felt physically inadequate. His luminous eyes were his only striking feature.

Beyle's position as a clerk proved depressing, but in May, 1800, he was invited to join his cousins in Italy. En route, he visited Jean-Jacques Rousseau's birthplace in Geneva and then joined Napoleon I's army, which was passing through the St. Bernard Pass to surprise the Austrians. Milan entranced Beyle. He began learning Italian and was smitten by Angela Pietragrua, whose bureaucrat husband tolerated her many liaisons. Sexually uninitiated and still very shy, he was unsuccessful with Angela but contracted syphilis from a prostitute. Symptoms, apparently from this disease, recurred for the remainder of his life. In September, Pierre Daru was able to get his young cousin a provisional commission as sublieutenant in the cavalry. His posts in small rural villages proved boring, and Beyle soon finagled a staff position. Daru was angered because his name was used without his permission, and after a few months Beyle was ordered back to his regiment. He returned on October 26, 1801, only to fall ill; taking a medical leave, he set out for Grenoble.

Beyle enjoyed his new status in his hometown and prolonged his leave, occupying his time by studying the philosophy of the Sensationalists. Beyle came to deny that human beings were rational, but although he rejected free will, he did conclude that self-aware humans could change their fate by living deliberately. Intellectually, he was growing up, and his long yearning for action was giving way to analysis. He resigned his commission and resolved to pursue a career of letters. Following yet another unrequited infatuation, he set off for Paris in April, 1802, to become a playwright.

LIFE'S WORK

For the next two years Beyle lived the life of a scholar in Paris, reading William Shakespeare, John Locke,

Thomas Hobbes, and especially Antoine Destutt de Tracy, whose rationalism he found appealing. He tried unsuccessfully to write drama in verse and lived on a small allowance from his father, who was glad to have his son out of the army.

While taking acting lessons, Beyle fell in love with Mélanie Guilbert, a starlet of twenty-four and an unwed mother. In April, 1805, he agreed to accompany her to Marseilles, where she had a job and he had an opportunity to go into business with his friend Fortuné Mante. These plans soon fell apart. In the spring of 1806, he returned to Grenoble and began to seek the favor of Pierre Daru again. In October, he went to Brunswick with Pierre's brother Martial, who was to be intendant there. Beyle spent the next two years as a civil servant in Brunswick, bored but successful.

Beyle was now a favorite of Pierre Daru and a good friend of his wife, Alexandrine, who with good grace and no ill will rebuffed a clumsy effort at seduction. On August 1, 1810, Beyle was appointed auditor of the Council of State. He was soon living sumptuously and beyond his means. He also began an affair with Angélina Bereyter, a member of the Opéra-Bouffe of the Théâtre Italien. Al-

though the two remained together until 1814, the attraction for him was essentially physical.

After a leave in 1811, during which he toured his beloved Italy and renewed his courtship of Angélina Bereyter—successfully this time—Beyle asked to be reassigned to active military duty. He was sent off as a courier in the summer of 1812 and found himself following the army to Moscow. When Napoleon ordered retreat, Beyle was appointed commissioner of war supplies and ordered to organize supplies at Smolensk, Mohilar, and Vitebsk. With the retreat becoming little more than a rout, he could not continue his mission beyond the first city, and after much hardship and danger as he joined the flight, he got back to Paris on January 31, 1813. He was justly proud of his conduct but ready to be done with war.

In the spring, however, he was ordered back to duty and, surprisingly revitalized, was a witness to the Battle of Bautzen in May. He then fell ill, probably from typhus, but recuperated and was back in Milan in early September. His military experiences proved invaluable for later writing, when he became one of the first to portray battle realistically from the individual's perspective. At the end of the year, he returned to Paris, hoping to write comic plays and find a permanent situation in Italy. Instead, he was ordered to help prepare for the defense of Dauphiné. The strain was too much, and he was soon ill again. He took leave but, lacking income, had to give up his luxurious lifestyle. Eager to establish himself as an author, he published, at his own expense, a biographical study of the composers Joseph Haydn, Wolfgang Amadeus Mozart, and Pietro Métastasio in 1815, but the book was mostly plagiarized. He was fortunate that his love of secrecy and aliases had led him not to use his own name.

Unable to find a job, Beyle returned to Milan, where he tried to live on his army pension and renewed his relationship with Angela Pietragrua. Needing money, he devoted himself to writing, publishing two books in 1817, *Histoire de la peinture de Italie* (1817) and *Rome, Naples, et Florence en 1817* (1817, 1826; *Rome, Naples, and Florence in 1817*, 1818). The former was in part plagiarized, and the original parts were personal, emotional reactions to the work of various painters. The latter was a sort of travelogue with commentary and was a minor success.

That work was also Beyle's first use of the name "Stendhal," taken from a small German town and used to obscure the identity of an author critical of the handling of Italy at the Congress of Vienna. It was to become Beyle's most common pseudonym and the one under which he became famous. Pleased by having had some

Stendhal. (Library of Congress)

success, Stendhal started the first of two efforts to write a study of Napoleon. Neither of these was ever finished, and the manuscripts were published only after his death. They do make clear the author's view of the young Napoleon as the heir of the revolution, of the empire as a betrayal of the revolutionary ideals, and of the restored Bourbon government as contemptible.

On March 4, 1818, Stendhal met Mathilde, Viscontini Dembowski, whom he always called Métilde. Wildly in love, he pursued her for three years, only to be repeatedly rejected. In 1821, penniless and again suffering from venereal disease, he returned to Paris. The relationship with Métilde resulted in *De l'amour* (1822; *Maxims of Love*, 1906), in which he offered a combination of objective analysis and confession. He was developing his characteristic style, combining the rationalism of the Enlightenment with the emotional outpourings of the Romantics.

Stendhal made his home in Paris for the next decade, visiting England twice and Italy once during those years. In 1823, he published part 1 of *Racine et Shakespeare* (1823, 1825; *Racine and Shakespeare*, 1962). This work catapulted Stendhal from the rank of minor author into a prominent place among those battling over aesthetic standards. Stendhal's firm assertion that there are no permanent criteria for beauty put him clearly in the ranks of the Romantics. Shakespeare was his example of a playwright who rejected the traditions and took his art into glorious new realms. Stendhal continued his role of Romanticism's champion with *Vie de Rossini* (1823; *Memoirs of Rossini*, 1824), which defends Romantic music.

As Stendhal's fame grew, so did his acquaintants among the literati of Paris; among his associates were Honoré de Balzac, Benjamin Constant, Alfred de Musset, Alphonse de Lamartine, and Adolphe Thiers. His love during the mid-1820's was Countess Clémentine (Menti) Curial, but though they remained friends, she ended the affair in 1826. Stendhal responded by writing *Armance* (1827; English translation, 1928), his first novel. Although generally regarded as a failure, *Armance*, which concerned the frustrations of love dampened by impotence, allowed Stendhal to express his sense of alienation and launched him on a career of writing fiction.

At the end of the decade, Stendhal, realizing that his greatest success had come with travel books, added *Promenades dans Rome* (1829; *A Roman Journal*, 1957), which became a popular guidebook to the city. He also had several brief love affairs. Suddenly, in 1830, Stendhal's years of struggle culminated in a work of genius. *Le Rouge et le noir* (*The Red and the Black*, 1898) was a brilliant blending of styles: first- and third-person perspectives, Romantic self-revelation, and classical external analysis. Stendhal achieved a remarkable shifting of perspectives among characters and narrator without losing simplicity or sacrificing the clarity of the story.

Even as Stendhal was producing *The Red and the Black*, France was undergoing the July Revolution, and with the establishment of the more liberal government of Louis-Philippe, the author hoped that he might again find a place in government service. He requested a job as consul in Italy and was posted to Trieste, only to be rejected by the Austrian government, which controlled that city, as a radical—his political comments in his travel books had not been forgotten. In February, 1831, he was

STENDHAL'S MAJOR WORKS	
LONG FICTION	
1827	*Armance* (English translation, 1928)
1830	*Le Rouge et le noir* (*The Red and the Black*, 1898)
1839	*La Chartreuse de Parme* (*The Charterhouse of Parma*, 1895)
1855	*Lucien Leuwen* (English translation, 1950)
1889	*Lamiel* (English translation, 1929)
NONFICTION	
1815	*Vies de Haydn, de Mozart et de Métastase* (*The Lives of Haydn and Mozart, with Observations on Métastase*, 1817)
1817, 1826	*Rome, Naples et Florence en 1817* (*Rome, Naples, and Florence, in 1817*, 1818)
1822	*De l'amour* (*Maxims of Love*, 1906)
1823	*Vie de Rossini* (*Memoirs of Rossini*, 1824; also as *Life of Rossini*, 1956)
1823, 1825	*Racine et Shakespeare* (*Racine and Shakespeare*, 1962)
1829	*Promenades dans Rome* (*A Roman Journal*, 1957)
1838	*Mémoires d'un touriste* (*Memoirs of a Tourist*, 1962)
1838	*Voyage dans le midi de la France* (*Travels in the South of France*, 1971)
1888	*Journal*
1890	*Vie de Henry Brulard* (*The Life of Henry Brulard*, 1925)
1892	*Souvenirs d'égotisme* (*Memoirs of an Egotist*, 1949)

named consul at Civitavecchia on the Tyrrhenian Sea, near Rome.

During his service at Civitavecchia, Stendhal wrote his two previously mentioned autobiographical pieces and the unfinished novel *Lucien Leuwen* (1855, 1894, 1926-1927; English translation, 1950). His writing was interrupted by intermittent ill health, and in March, 1836, he returned to Paris, where he remained for three productive years. His most important work of this period was *La Chartreuse de Parme* (1839; *The Charterhouse of Parma*, 1895), which he expanded from one of his Italian short stories in about two months. The hero, Fabrice del Dongo, is more like the youthful Stendhal in being innocent and idealistic than was Julien Sorel of *The Red and the Black*, who is crafty and self-serving. Both characters, however, are examples of men who rise from relatively obscure beginnings and whose careers conclude on the executioner's scaffold.

In June of 1839, Stendhal reluctantly began his return to Civitavecchia, taking three months to make the trip. In the fall, he began a new novel, *Lamiel* (1889, 1971; English translation, 1929). Although typically Stendhalian in describing the struggle of an ambitious youth to find success and love, it is unusual in that the youth is, in this case, female. As a result of increasing problems with vertigo and, in March, 1841, an attack of apoplexy, Stendhal could not complete this novel. On October 21, 1841, he left for France, where, after attending a rally, he died of a stroke during a walk on March 23, 1842.

SIGNIFICANCE

As a novelist, Stendhal broke new ground by his skillful combination of classical style and Romantic themes. All of his important works are consciously autobiographical, though they are much more concerned with accurate descriptions of feeling than of events. Despite the emphasis on the personal, the prose style remains simple and analytical, much more like that of the philosophes than the Romantics. With his ability to tell a story from shifting points of view, displaying the emotions of various characters, Stendhal was establishing a new novel form that would be a hallmark of the twentieth century.

Stendhal also contributed to social history. His travel works, such as *Mémoires d'un touriste* (1838; partial translation in *Memoirs of a Tourist*, 1962), offer not only travel notes but also social and political commentary. Such eyewitness accounts are always valuable, but when the witness has the sensitivity of a Stendhal, their value is

much enhanced. Thus, his writings are still read as both history and literature.

—*Fred R. van Hartesveldt*

FURTHER READING

Alter, Robert, with Carol Cosman. *A Lion for Love: A Critical Biography of Stendhal*. New York: Basic Books, 1979. The emphasis of this volume is criticism, and its authors do an excellent job of presenting their analysis of Stendhal in a historical context. Not the book to read, however, for a clear chronological description of his life.

Atherton, John. *Stendhal*. London: Bowes & Bowes, 1965. A short but effectively done biography. Atherton's comments are insightful and well grounded in research.

Bloom, Harold, ed. *Stendhal*. New York: Chelsea House, 1989. An introduction to Stendhal's work, designed for literature students. Includes an introductory essay by Bloom, critical analyses of Stendhal's work, and a bibliography.

Brombert, Victor H. *Stendhal: Fiction and the Themes of Freedom*. New York: Random House, 1968. Although a work of criticism, this book contains much biographical information, and it gives a useful analysis of the themes in Stendhal's fiction. Ties his work into what is known of the nineteenth century novel.

Keates, Jonathan. *Stendhal*. New York: Carroll & Graf, 1997. Well-written, straightforward narrative account of Stendhal's life.

May, Gita. *Stendhal and the Age of Napoleon*. New York: Columbia University Press, 1977. An excellent, full biography that provides a detailed chronological account of Stendhal's life. The best straightforward biography available.

Strickland, Geoffrey. *Stendhal: The Education of a Novelist*. New York: Cambridge University Press, 1974. An attempt to analyze the forces that shaped Stendhal and to show how those forces influenced his work. It is both biographical and critical, and although it could not replace a traditional biography, it does provide much useful analysis with a biographical foundation.

SEE ALSO: Honoré de Balzac; Napoleon I; Hippolyte Taine; Adolphe Thiers.

RELATED ARTICLES in *Great Events from History: The Nineteenth Century, 1801-1900:* March 3, 1830: Hugo's *Hernani* Incites Rioting; October 1-December 15, 1856: Flaubert Publishes *Madame Bovary*.

ALEXANDER H. STEPHENS
American politician

Called "Little Aleck" by his colleagues because he weighed only one hundred pounds, Stephens served in the U.S. Congress until the eve of the Civil War and then became vice president of the Confederate States of America. After the war, he returned to the U.S. Congress and served as governor of Georgia.

BORN: February 11, 1812; Wilkes County, Georgia
DIED: March 4, 1883; Atlanta, Georgia
ALSO KNOWN AS: Alexander Hamilton Stephens (full name); Little Aleck
AREA OF ACHIEVEMENT: Government and politics

EARLY LIFE

Alexander Hamilton Stephens was born in the Georgia Piedmont about fifteen miles southwest of Washington, Georgia. He was the third child of Andrew B. and Mary Stephens. Soon after his birth, his mother died. Alexander inherited his mother's poor health and was plagued by illnesses throughout his life. In 1813 his father married Matilda Lindsey, the daughter of a Revolutionary War veteran. Alexander did not get along well with his stepmother, but he was close to his father, who was a skilled craftsperson and teacher.

From 1820 through 1824, Alexander attended his father's school. In 1826, Andrew Stephens died at the age of forty-four, and Alexander was sent to Warren County, Georgia, to live with his uncle, Aaron Grier. At first he attended a Roman Catholic school, but in 1827 he entered an academy in Washington, Georgia, to study Latin and geography. While there he lived at the home of Alexander Hamilton Webster, a Presbyterian minister. Alexander's admiration of Webster led to his adoption of Hamilton as his own middle name. In 1828 he entered Franklin College in Athens, Georgia, and he graduated first in his class in 1832 at the age of twenty.

Following his graduation from college, Stephens took a teaching position in Madison, Georgia; however, he left that position after only four months. He then worked as a tutor for the children of a doctor in Liberty County in southeastern Georgia. In January, 1834, he moved to Crawfordville, Georgia, and began to study law. In July of that year he passed the bar and, at the age of twenty-two, began to practice law in Crawfordville.

LIFE'S WORK

In 1836 Stephens began his political career in Taliaferro County, Georgia, when he was elected by a two-to-one margin to the Georgia House of Representatives. He served in that position until 1841. He then left politics to concentrate on his law practice but returned two years later and was elected to the state senate, where he served for two years. During his six years in the Georgia legislature, Stephens learned how to respond to his constituents and mastered the skills of legislative tactics, parliamentary procedure, and party strategy.

In 1843 Stephens was selected by the Whig Party to run against the Democratic candidate, James H. Starke, for the U.S. House of Representatives. In a statewide campaign, Stephens, defending the Whig program of tariffs, distribution, and a national bank, defeated Starke by a vote of 38,051 to 35,001. He then began a political career in the U.S. House of Representatives that lasted until 1859. In Congress, Stephens supported the annexation of Texas in 1845, not solely for the purpose of extending slavery but also to increase southern political power in the Union. However, while Stephens condemned the slave trade, he defended slavery by arguing that it would always be necessary wherever white and black people lived together in comparable numbers. Stephens supported both the Compromise of 1850 and the Kansas-Nebraska Act of 1854, both of which attempted to establish criteria for the extension of slavery into the territories.

After the Whig Party disintegrated during the 1850's, Stephens reluctantly joined the Democratic Party. During intraparty battles between 1857 and 1860, Stephens defended Senator Stephen A. Douglas and popular sovereignty and consistently opposed secession. In 1859 Stephens made a speech in which he advocated reopening the African slave trade, a position that few southerners supported. His argument was based on the idea that if there was an expansion of the slave states admitted to the Union, it would be necessary to secure more slaves to occupy these new states. If the prohibition against the slave trade continued, the South would have to abandon its race with the North for colonizing new states.

Following the election of Abraham Lincoln as president in 1860, Stephens argued in a speech before the Georgia legislature that Georgia should remain loyal to the Union. He believed that Lincoln's election had been constitutional and that there was not sufficient grounds to secede from the Union. Furthermore, if the South seceded it would be committing the aggression. He argued that the South should wait for the North to commit an act of aggression against the region before trying to secede. Stephens's position, however, was largely rejected.

On January 16, 1861, a convention was held in Milledgeville, Georgia, to consider the question of secession. Stephens was offered the presidency of the convention, but he declined. He argued against secession once again, saying that the point of resistance should be the point of aggression. He felt that a united South could obtain a redress of grievances in the Union and said that he would vote against secession because no existing cause warranted it. Despite Stephens's plea, the ordinance of secession passed by an overwhelming majority.

Shortly thereafter, Stephens was selected as a delegate from Georgia to go to Montgomery, Alabama, for a convention of the seceded states, where he served on a committee that drafted the Constitution for the Confederacy. The document was remarkably similar to the U.S. Constitution except for the provisions that recognized and protected slavery. Included in the document was a provision supported by Stephens and his moderate allies that would allow the admission of nonslave states to the Confederacy.

The convention also chose former U.S. senator Jefferson Davis of Mississippi as president of the Confederacy and Stephens as vice president. On February 11, 1861, Stephens took the oath of office as vice president of the Confederacy on his forty-ninth birthday. Soon thereafter, Davis asked Stephens to lead a Confederate commission to go to Washington, D.C., to negotiate with the United States for the transfer of forts at Charleston, South Carolina, and Pensacola, Florida. Stephens refused since he saw such efforts as futile.

Despite the fact that they held the top two positions in the Confederacy, the relationship between Davis and Stephens quickly cooled. Two measures passed by the first Confederate Congress, a conscription law and an act authorizing the suspension of the writ of habeas corpus in the Confederacy, were strongly opposed by Stephens. He argued that such measures were despotic and threatened constitutional liberty. In February, 1865, Stephens headed the Confederate commission to a peace conference at Hampton Roads, Virginia. This effort failed.

Following the end of the Civil War, Stephens was arrested in Crawfordville. On May 25, 1865, he was sent to prison at Fort Warren in Boston Harbor. One month after he was imprisoned, Stephens applied directly to President Andrew Johnson for a pardon. In his letter to President Johnson, he reviewed his political career, his support of states' rights and the Constitution, and his opposition to secession. Johnson felt it was important that Stephens and other moderates who would support Johnson's plan for Reconstruction should be at home instead of in jail. In October, 1865, Johnson granted Stephens a pardon. Stephens met with Johnson in Washington, D.C., after his release and pledged support for Johnson's policy for Reconstruction. He then returned home to Crawfordville, Georgia, and became involved in politics.

Alexander H. Stephens. (Library of Congress)

In 1866 Stephens was elected to the U.S. Senate; however, he was denied his seat because Georgia had not properly reconstructed according to congressional guidelines. Stephens then wrote a two-volume work titled *A Constitutional View of the Late War Between the States* (1868-1870) in which he presented the South's position on states' rights and secession. He argued that the South had failed in its efforts in part because of the Confederacy's attempt to centralize power.

During this period Stephens also argued that the Democratic Party should oppose Reconstruction, the Fourteenth and Fifteenth Amendments, and test oaths to determine eligibility for office in the post-Civil War South. To accept these things would be a repudiation of secession and states' rights. However, between 1868 and 1870, Georgia was subject to Radical Reconstruction. During this era, the Ku Klux Klan was organized in Georgia, and the Klan functioned as the military arm of the Democratic Party, attacking the freedmen and their white supporters. Despite Stephens's states' rights beliefs, he rejected the activities of the Ku Klux Klan because it went outside the law.

Stephens's view of the role of African Americans also changed after the Civil War. He proposed a system of representation for the new Georgia Constitution based on class. He argued that at first the freedmen should have their franchise restricted or should be required to have white representatives; however, he felt that political rights ought to be granted to them for the South's own future good, that provisions for the education of African Americans should be granted immediately, and that school attendance should be compulsory.

In December, 1868, Stephens was offered the position of chair of history and political science at the University of Georgia, but he declined it because of poor health. He returned to political life in 1873 when he was elected to the U.S. Congress, where he remained until 1882; however, his focus on constitutional issues had ceased to be relevant to a country that was concerned with economic growth. He returned to Georgia in 1882 and ran for governor despite his poor health. On October 4, 1882, Stephens was elected governor by over sixty thousand votes, carrying 130 out of 137 counties. In February, 1883, Stephens went to Savannah, Georgia, to speak at the city's sesquicentennial celebration. Exposure to the cold and damp air, however, resulted in his final illness. On March 4, 1883, Stephens, the Georgia statesman and political leader, died after serving only 119 days as governor.

SIGNIFICANCE

Despite his small stature and poor health, Alexander Stephens was one of the dominant figures in Georgia politics during the nineteenth century. His political life seemed to be a series of contradictions. Politically, he went from being a Whig to a Democrat. He was a strong supporter of states' rights, but, as the South moved toward secession, Stephens stressed the virtues of the Union and became a reluctant supporter of the Confederacy. While he served as vice president of the Confederacy, Stephens found himself in conflict with President Jefferson Davis over the relationship between the Confederacy and its members. He strongly opposed the centralization of power even though the Confederacy was involved in a war.

Some historians view Stephens as an impractical idealist; others view him as a man who lived by his principles. Despite the contradictions in his life, Stephens remained enormously popular in the state of Georgia throughout his life. His election as governor in 1882, with over 60 percent of the vote, illustrated that Little Aleck's popularity with the people of Georgia was a constant in a personal life filled with contradictions.

—*William V. Moore*

FURTHER READING

Brumgardt, John A. "The Confederate Career of Alexander H. Stephens." *Civil War History* 28 (March, 1981): 64-81. A sympathetic analysis of Stephens's philosophy and conflicts with Jefferson Davis during the Civil War.

Davis, William C. *The Union That Shaped the Confederacy: Robert Toombs and Alexander H. Stephens.* Lawrence: University Press of Kansas, 2001. Documents Stephens's friendship with Toombs, the secretary of the Confederacy. The two men served in the Georgia legislature and U.S. Congress; during the war, they were members of the Confederate government, rebelling against the leadership of Jefferson Davis. Meticulously researched account by an expert in Civil War history.

Rabun, James Z. "Alexander Stephens and Jefferson Davis." *American Historical Review* 58 (January, 1953): 290-321. An analysis of the two major leaders of the Confederacy. This article analyzes the differences and conflicts between the two men and how they symbolized the differences that existed in the Confederacy itself.

Richardson, E. Ramsey. *Little Aleck: A Life of Alexander H. Stephens, the Fighting Vice-President of the Con-*

federacy. Indianapolis: Bobbs-Merrill, 1932. A biography of Stephens that presents a sympathetic interpretation of his life and accomplishments.

Scholt, Thomas E. *Alexander H. Stephens of Georgia*. Baton Rouge: Louisiana State University Press, 1988. The most comprehensive biography of Stephens's personal and political career.

Stephens, Alexander H. *Recollections of Alexander H. Stephens: His Diary Kept When a Prisoner at Fort Warren, Boston Harbor, 1865*. Reprint. Edited by Myrta L. Avary. Baton Rouge: Louisiana State University Press, 1998. A reprint of a 1910 volume, it includes reflections on his prison life and reminiscences.

See also: Jefferson Davis; Stephen A. Douglas; Andrew Johnson; Robert E. Lee; Abraham Lincoln.

Related articles in *Great Events from History: The Nineteenth Century, 1801-1900:* May 30, 1854: Congress Passes Kansas-Nebraska Act; February 8, 1861: Establishment of the Confederate States of America; December 8, 1863-April 24, 1877: Reconstruction of the South; April 9 and 14, 1865: Surrender at Appomattox and Assassination of Lincoln.

George Stephenson
English engineer

Stephenson was one of the great pioneers in railroad development. By constructing and equipping the Stockton and Darlington and the Liverpool and Manchester railways, he demonstrated the economic practicality of the steam railway, guaranteeing its rapid development as Great Britain's basic transportation system.

Born: June 9, 1781; Wylam, Northumberland, England
Died: August 12, 1848; Tapton, near Chesterfield, Derbyshire, England
Area of achievement: Engineering

Early Life

George Stephenson was born and raised along the banks of the River Tyne. Because the economy of his native Tyneside was based on coal, he grew up surrounded by technological elements used extensively in coal mining that were later to be brought together in the railway industry. Coal from the mines often reached the coal-carrying ships on the Tyne by means of tramways, where wagons rolled on wooden rails. On the level, horses were used to pull the wagons. On the downgrade, gravity sufficed. Large stationary steam engines pumped water from the mines and operated the winding gear that lifted coal and miners from the depths. Steam engines had been introduced into England by Thomas Savery and Thomas Newcomen toward the beginning of the eighteenth century and had been greatly improved by James Watt during the 1760's.

Stephenson's father worked as an engineer with steam machinery at a succession of Tyneside pits. The younger Stephenson embarked on a similar career when, barely out of childhood, he joined his father as an assistant fireman. He received no formal schooling and was still illiterate at the age of eighteen. Educational credentials were of no concern, however, to the miners and mine owners of the Tyneside. Their interests were in the extraction and shipment of coal, efficiently and, if possible, safely. Stephenson rapidly proved to have the skills and instincts of a natural mechanic.

Engaged as a maintenance man for the Grand Allies, a consortium of Northumbrian mine owners, Stephenson quickly earned a reputation as one who could fix or improve a machine after briefly watching its operation, absorbing its principles in his own mind even though he was generally unable to explain those principles adequately to others. At the age of thirty, in 1811, his success in refining a hitherto unsuccessful steam pump, so that a constantly flooded coal pit could for the first time be worked, attracted more than local attention. Four years later, in the autumn of 1815, a brief spate of experimentation led to Stephenson's creation of a safety lamp for use by coal miners, a lamp that would not ignite mine gases and cause disastrous underground explosions.

Stephenson's lamp emerged almost simultaneously with that of Sir Humphry Davy. Apparently, the unschooled Northumbrian and the respected scientist had independently hit upon the same principle at the same time. Stephenson's work for the mines led also to his participation in improvements in the transport of coal. In 1814, Stephenson's first locomotive, the *Blucher*, went into operation, a cumbersome, slow, and inefficient machine, not a major improvement on other Northumbrian locomotives, which had begun to supplement horses and fixed engines in the Tyneside coal fields. Stephenson's older brother was driver of the *Blucher* and—indicative of the still-early stage of locomotive evolution—his sister-in-law was once called upon to push the *Blucher* when it stalled. In 1816, Stephenson patented a new type of rail assembly for use on coal tramways, because as motive power became heavier, the permanent way required analogous improvement.

LIFE'S WORK

Stephenson might have remained a locally respected but obscure mechanical jack-of-all-trades on the Tyneside had he not attracted the attention of Edward Pease, the Quaker proprietor of coal mines in County Durham, thirty-five miles south of Stephenson's Tyneside. The County Durham coalfield had suffered historically, as contrasted with that of the Tyneside, because of its inadequate access to deep water. Pease and his circle hoped to overcome that handicap by constructing a canal or tram-

George Stephenson. (Library of Congress)

way connecting the mines west of Darlington with tidal water at Stockton.

On April 19, 1821, Pease and Stephenson met at Darlington, and from that consultation came Stephenson's appointment as engineer of the Stockton and Darlington Railway. Stephenson surveyed the twenty-five-mile line and supervised its construction. His son Robert, born in 1803, assisted in the survey and in June, 1823, was put in charge of Robert Stephenson and Company, of Newcastle, a firm established by the two Stephensons and the Pease family to build locomotives that would supply some of the power for the Stockton and Darlington.

The new railway, opened on September 27, 1825, was a hybrid operation. Horses pulled some trains, locomotives others. Although there was some passenger traffic, the road was designed primarily for coal, and several inclined planes sped the coal wagons on their way toward the sea by gravity. The Stockton and Darlington was an immediate success, financially as well as mechanically. Investors, engineers, and journalists from throughout Great Britain and the Continent as well made tours of inspection, returning home to spread the news of Stephenson's triumph.

Even before the opening of the Stockton and Darlington, Stephenson had been engaged by Liverpool investors as engineer of the Liverpool and Manchester. Heavy traffic in that vital corridor, raw cotton from America passing through the port of Liverpool to the textile factories at Manchester, and manufactured cloth making the return journey from Manchester had been monopolized by the Bridgewater Canal, which supplied service that shippers considered both unreliable and expensive.

Plans for a rival means of transport had been around for years, but it took the evident progress on the Stockton and Darlington to convert talk into action. Stephenson, working from earlier surveys and relatively cursory fieldwork of his own, presented plans to a parliamentary committee in March, 1825, only to discover, for the first time in his life, the existence of substantial opposition to his plans. The canal interests joined with local landowners to contest the Liverpool and Manchester's application for permission to acquire land by eminent domain, and opposing counsel found it easy to make Stephenson sound incompetent and his plans inadequate.

Stephenson's engineering genius lay in his ability to get things built and operating and in his confidence in that ability. His paper plans were faulty—to the consternation of conventionally trained engineers—because he fully intended to resolve real problems on the ground when construction was under way. That approach had always been his method and, with Stephenson, it worked. Speaking in a heavy Northumbrian dialect almost incomprehensible to the parliamentarians in London, and saddled with admittedly defective specifications, Stephenson was unable to defend his project, and it was rejected by the parliamentary committee.

The Liverpool promoters reacted to Stephenson's humiliation by engaging three professionally trained engineers, George and John Rennie and Charles Vignoles. It was they who won parliamentary approval for the Liverpool and Manchester in the parliamentary session of 1826. Men of that stripe, with the right accents and paper qualifications, including membership in the Institute of Civil Engineers, presented a striking contrast to Stephenson.

Intellectually insecure, Stephenson throughout his career remained defensively hostile toward his better-connected competitors. Even physically, the contrast between Stephenson and men such as the Rennies was obvious. Tall, muscular, and ruddy-cheeked, Stephenson looked like a man accustomed to hard labor out-of-doors. The proprietors, well aware of the contrasts, had nevertheless not lost their basic faith in Stephenson, who was again put in charge of the project once the parliamentary hurdle had been surmounted. The Liverpool and Manchester was built under Stephenson's close personal supervision. Not only was Stephenson the engineer of the thirty-mile line, which included the massive cut at Olive Mount at the Liverpool end and the difficult construction across the unstable bog at Chat Moss toward Manchester, but also the Stephensons supplied the company's motive power.

Before trials held on the line at Rainhill in 1829, there had been some question as to whether the line would be operated by horse or by locomotive. The development, primarily by Robert Stephenson, of a much speedier and more efficient locomotive, the *Rocket*, which won the Rainhill competition against four other machines, settled the question of railway power definitively in favor of the steam locomotive. When the Liverpool and Manchester was opened on September 15, 1830, the railway had come of age, and Stephenson was the man most prominently associated with it in the public mind.

Even before the completion and striking financial success of the Liverpool and Manchester, serious plans for its extension were in hand. Stephenson was appointed engineer of the southern portion of the Grand Junction, a line designed to connect the Liverpool and Manchester with Birmingham, but once again sloppy paperwork revealed deficiencies in his survey and the Grand Junction passed out of his control.

Stephenson supervised construction of the Manchester and Leeds, which made the first rail crossing of the Pennines by means of a tunnel more than a mile and a half long, and of the lines that were to become the core of the giant Midland Railway: the Birmingham and Derby, the North Midland, and the York and North Midland. Their completion, in 1840, resulted in a complete although circuitous connection between London and York. It fell to his son, Robert, to direct construction of the London and Birmingham, completed in 1838, and the routes north from York. With the opening of Robert Stephenson's Royal Border Bridge at Berwick in 1850, two years after George Stephenson's death, a through route was established between London and Edinburgh, only twenty years after the opening of the Liverpool and Manchester.

SIGNIFICANCE

Dr. Dionysius Lardner, a publicist sometimes more addicted to rhetoric than to facts, awarded to George Stephenson in 1836 the title "Father of the Locomotive," a claim impossible to defend. Locomotives, in common with many other important inventions, were not the product of one mind. If anyone deserved that title, it is probably Richard Trevithick, the Cornish mining engineer. In the Stephenson family, Robert's contribution to development of the locomotive is greater than that of his father.

Stephenson's achievements in mechanical engineering, although certainly not minimal, are greatly surpassed by his contributions in civil engineering, the survey and construction of economically profitable railway lines without which there would have been no scope for the locomotive. Stephenson strove always to construct a nearly level line in order to enable the locomotive to use its power for speed rather than for climbing. Consequently, a Stephenson line is marked by cuts, great earthen fills, tunnels, and occasional circuitry—anything to avoid grades. Although some of Stephenson's successors were less willing to sacrifice directness for levelness, Stephenson's designs established a norm for subsequent British railway-building practice.

An even greater contribution is tied to Stephenson's insistence on use everywhere of a "standard" gauge between parallel rails, although the question of gauge also points to limitations characteristics of Stephenson. He adopted his "standard" gauge (four feet, eight and a half inches) without apparent calculation, merely using the gauge customarily found on Northumbrian tramroads. There was no technological justification for selection of the basic measurement that governed all future construction of railway lines and rolling stock. When first identified by Stephenson, his gauge was four feet, eight inches. The extra half inch appears to have crept in through usage, an indication of Stephenson's rough-and-ready methods.

Stephenson's insistence on a standard gauge was central to his early recognition of the potential of a unified national railway system. Only with a standard gauge would it be possible for railway equipment to run freely throughout Great Britain. By contrast, Isambard Kingdom Brunel, engineer of the Great Western Railway, a man of greater technological brilliance, used a seven-foot gauge, indicative of Brunel's lack of concern about the significance of the resultant inability to interchange traffic with other lines. Fixed firmly in Stephenson's mind was a vision of the kind of integrated national rail network that in fact emerged, and that to Victorian Britain became as vital and basic as the automobile was to become for the late twentieth century world.

—John Ranlett

FURTHER READING

Carlson, Robert E. *The Liverpool and Manchester Railway Project, 1821-1831*. New York: Augustus M. Kelley, 1969. A detailed study of the project through which Stephenson gained and held the public eye.

Jeaffreson, J. C., and William Pole. *The Life of Robert Stephenson*. 2 vols. London: Longman, Green, Longman, Roberts and Green, 1864. The standard nineteenth century biography of Robert Stephenson, carefully composed but less readable, and therefore less influential, than Samuel Smiles's work on George Stephenson.

McGowan, Christopher. *Rail, Steam, and Speed: The "Rocket" and the Birth of Steam Locomotion*. New York: Columbia University Press, 2004. An account of the 1829 Rainhill Trials—the competition between five locomotives to power the Liverpool and Manchester Railway. Describes the technology employed by Stephenson and his son, Robert, in the design of "Rocket," the locomotive that won the competition, and the Stephensons' subsequent influence on British railway development.

Perkin, Harold. *The Age of the Railway*. London: Panther, 1970. This is a well-documented study, by a social historian, of the impact of the railway on Victorian society. Chapter 3, "The Men Who Made the Railways," contains material on Stephenson.

Rees, Gareth. *Early Railway Prints: British Railways from 1825 to 1850*. Ithaca, N.Y.: Cornell University Press, 1980. Contains ninety-five contemporary plates, thirty-one in color, offering a vivid visual impression of British railways in the period of Stephenson. Included are sixteen views of the Liverpool and Manchester Railway.

Robbins, Michael. *The Railway Age in Britain and Its Impact on the World*. Baltimore: Penguin Books, 1965. A highly readable short account of the building of the British railways and their place in the Victorian scene. Chapter 3 is entitled "George Stephenson and the Great Builders."

Rolt, L. T. C. *The Railway Revolution: George and Robert Stephenson*. New York: St. Martin's Press, 1962. The major modern biography, working from the premise that the two Stephensons were complementary figures, neither of whom can be adequately understood in isolation from the other. Based on both published and manuscript materials and including maps of Stephenson lines and drawings of Stephenson locomotives.

Simmons, Jack. *The Railway in England and Wales, 1830-1914: The System and Its Working*. Leicester: Leicester University Press, 1978. An excellent modern introduction to the English railway, containing numerous references to Stephenson's contributions.

Smiles, Samuel. *Life of George Stephenson*. London: John Murray, 1864. The classic biography, of major importance in solidifying Stephenson's reputation as a Victorian hero. Occasionally attributes to George Stephenson work that was in fact that of his son.

Worth, Martin. *Sweat and Inspiration: Pioneers of the Industrial Age*. Stroud, Gloucestershire, England: Sutton, 1999. This book, which accompanied a British Broadcasting Company radio series about engineers, includes information on Stephenson's construction of the Stockton and Darlington Railway.

SEE ALSO: Isambard Kingdom Brunel; Sir Humphry Davy; Richard Trevithick.
RELATED ARTICLE in *Great Events from History: The Nineteenth Century, 1801-1900:* November 10, 1852: Canada's Grand Trunk Railway Is Incorporated.

THADDEUS STEVENS
American politician

Although greatly disliked, both during his lifetime and by some later historians, Stevens was the leading American congressional advocate of a just policy for former slaves, and he had a larger commitment to equality for all people.

BORN: April 4, 1792; Danville, Vermont
DIED: August 11, 1868; Washington, D.C.
AREAS OF ACHIEVEMENT: Government and politics, social reform

EARLY LIFE

Born with a clubfoot, Thaddeus Stevens was the last of four children of Sally and Joshua Stevens. His mother, who had the greatest influence on his personality, was a Baptist. Her Calvinism, evangelism, and piety contributed to his later devotion to principle and duty. She worked, saved money, and taught young Stevens. She wanted her son to have the finest available education, and she succeeded. Stevens's father, Joshua, was a generally unsuccessful shoemaker. The family was poor. Thaddeus was close to his mother since she provided most of his elementary education. She discouraged him from playing or associating with the local boys because of his physical disability.

Under his mother's guidance, Stevens learned to read the Bible at a young age. Intellectually, he was not disadvantaged. Although he had various run-ins with those in authority, at the age of twenty-two he was graduated from Dartmouth College. He was a shy young man who nevertheless often spoke his mind on issues and situations throughout his long life. Undoubtedly, his verbal skills were compensation for his physical disability; his wit and scorn became legendary.

In 1814, Stevens moved to York, Pennsylvania, to begin his law practice. He soon moved to the village of Gettysburg and became a leading lawyer in the area and a partner in the James D. Paxton Iron Works. Stevens served on the Gettysburg town council. His earlier political activity was with the Federalist Party, but as that party declined, Stevens became a leader in the Anti-Masonic movement because he distrusted the influence of secret societies in a republic. He believed that secret societies were elitist and created aristocracies of special privilege for their membership. Though the Anti-Masons generally became Whigs, Stevens was never popular with that party's leadership despite his strong opposition to Andrew Jackson and his policies. From his first political ex-

perience, Stevens was a strong nationalist whose program included the belief that government could create opportunities for all men. He never retreated from that general belief.

In 1833, Stevens was elected to the Pennsylvania house of representatives. During the next ten years, Stevens was politically active. He opposed any propositions based on class distinctions or any discrimination based on race or color. For example, Stevens in 1835 saved the principle of free public schools for all in Pennsylvania by defeating a proposed charity or pauper-school law. He also supported state aid to higher education. Stevens was a member of the Board of Canal Commissions, a powerful state planning agency. Unfortunately, his party, the Whigs, greatly influenced by Stevens's leadership, lost the dispute over control of the state house of representatives known as the Buckshot War. Discouraged, after another election, Stevens retired from party politics. He also needed to repair his personal fortune; his ironworks had put Stevens more than $200,000 in debt. By 1842, Stevens was practicing law in Lancaster, Pennsylvania. He was fifty years old, and his prospects appeared to be limited; he was, however, on the eve of his greatest contribution to American history.

LIFE'S WORK

From 1848 to 1853, Stevens served in the House of Representatives as a Whig. His strong opposition to the Fugitive Slave Law, as part of the Compromise of 1850, contributed to his defeat. He returned to Lancaster, working to save his failing iron business. An important figure in the creation of the Republican Party in Pennsylvania, he was returned to the House in 1858, where he served until his death ten years later.

Despite his age and poor health, Stevens played a major role in the dramatic Civil War decade. He opposed any concession to the threat of secession from the southern states. Early in the war, Stevens clearly stated his belief that the rebel states, by their behavior, had placed themselves beyond the pale of the Constitution; therefore Congress would determine their future status in any program of reconstruction.

In 1861, he became the chairman of the Ways and Means Committee and helped formulate the government's fiscal policy during the war, supporting the distribution of greenbacks, for example. Unlike many of his fellow Americans, Stevens recognized that slavery and the Union's fate were intermingled. He argued that any slave used in any military capacity should be freed, and he urged confiscation of all property used for insurrectionary purposes. Despite his contemporary and historical reputation for harshness, he never advocated execution for any rebel leaders. In fact, he opposed capital punishment. Nevertheless, he pushed for a punitive program against the Confederacy.

On March 28, 1864, he introduced the Thirteenth Amendment in Congress. As chairman of the House group of the Joint Committee on Reconstruction, he was a key member of the Radical Republicans. He contributed to the writing of the Fourteenth Amendment, and he supported it as part of the Reconstruction Act. He broke with President Andrew Johnson over his veto of the Freedmen's Bureau Bill. The alienation increased as Johnson pardoned more and more Confederates. On March 19, 1867, Stevens introduced a bill to confiscate all public land in the South, including individual rebel property. He wanted "forty acres and a mule" for every freedman and planned to use the money from the sale of rebel lands to finance military pensions and to retire the national debt. The bill was not passed. A milder form of Reconstruction prevailed.

Although he personally doubted its success, Thaddeus Stevens introduced the resolution for the impeachment of President Andrew Johnson. He was chairman of the managers who argued for impeachment before the Senate, but his failing health limited his contribution to the proceedings. The vote for removal failed by one vote. As a practical matter, the president now controlled Reconstruction.

Exhausted by his age and his activities, Stevens died on August 11, 1868, in Washington, D.C. As a matter of honor, the Republicans in his district kept his name on the ballot in the fall election.

SIGNIFICANCE

Praised and cursed during his lifetime and after, Stevens nevertheless was one of the few politicians to see how slavery and the Union were combined. A strong abolitionist, Stevens believed that the federal government should ensure civil rights and just economic opportunities for freedmen. Although in the minority during his lifetime because of prevalent racism and because of his contemporaries' belief in limited government, Stevens's ideas were later vindicated by historical developments. Without any reservation, Thaddeus Stevens was an egalitarian. He recognized that class and class origins were

key elements in determining a person's chances in life. He believed that government could balance the equitable opportunities between the rich and the poor. In his own way, Stevens's ideas anticipated the creation of the modern welfare state. Because the cemeteries of Lancaster were for whites only, Stevens, on his deathbed, ordered that he be buried in a black graveyard. In death as in life, Thaddeus Stevens continued questioning the status quo and thereby became one of the greatest American reformers.

—Donald K. Pickens

FURTHER READING

Belz, Herman. *Emancipation and Equal Rights: Politics and Constitutionalism in the Civil War Era*. New York: W. W. Norton, 1978. Good overview of the complex issues facing the United States during the Civil War.

Brodie, Fawn M. *Thaddeus Stevens, Scourge of the South*. New York: W. W. Norton, 1966. The most balanced biography. The author still views Stevens's motivation in terms of punishment and hostility.

Current, Richard N. *Old Thad Stevens: A Story of Ambition*. Madison: University of Wisconsin Press, 1942. Highly critical. Stevens is depicted as ambitious for power and is held responsible for many evils, including the rise of big business.

Foner, Eric. *Free Soil, Free Labor, Free Men: The Ideology of the Republican Party Before the Civil War*. New York: Oxford University Press, 1970. A basic study for understanding the varied ideologies that influenced Stevens's life and thought.

Korngold, Ralph. *Thaddeus Stevens: A Being Darkly Wise and Rudely Great*. New York: Harcourt, Brace, 1955. In this biography, Stevens is heroic in stature, pure in motive. Tends to overstate his many achievements.

McCall, Samuel W. *Thaddeus Stevens*. Boston: Houghton Mifflin, 1899. The best of the biographies written in the nineteenth century. It dwells on the public life of Stevens.

McPherson, James M. *Ordeal by Fire: The Civil War and Reconstruction*. New York: Alfred A. Knopf, 1982. With a massive bibliography, broad chronological scope, and illuminating details, this book is the best available volume on the subject.

Trefousse, Hans L. *The Radical Republicans: Lincoln's Vanguard for Racial Justice*. New York: Alfred A. Knopf, 1970. In a revision of the traditional argument, this book claims that Radicals led Lincoln to positions that he was inclined to take in the first place but had regarded as politically risky.

_____. *Thaddeus Stevens: Nineteenth-Century Egalitarian*. Chapel Hill: University of North Carolina Press, 1997. Balanced and comprehensive biography, portraying Stevens as an egalitarian, powerful orator, and adamant opponent of slavery who was unable to realize his political goals and personal ambitions.

Vaughn, William P. *The Antimasonic Party in the United States: 1826-1843*. Lexington: University Press of Kentucky, 1983. An insightful history of political Anti-Masonry. Balanced. Explains why an egalitarian such as Stevens could be attracted to such a cause.

SEE ALSO: Caleb Cushing; Horace Greeley; Andrew Jackson; Andrew Johnson; Abraham Lincoln.

RELATED ARTICLES in *Great Events from History: The Nineteenth Century, 1801-1900:* 1820's-1830's: Free Public School Movement; December 2, 1840: U.S. Election of 1840; February 25, 1863-June 3, 1864: Congress Passes the National Bank Acts; December 8, 1863-April 24, 1877: Reconstruction of the South; March 3, 1865: Congress Creates the Freedmen's Bureau; April 9, 1866: Civil Rights Act of 1866; February 24-May 26, 1868: Impeachment of Andrew Johnson; July 9, 1868: Fourteenth Amendment Is Ratified.

ROBERT LOUIS STEVENSON
Scottish novelist

The author of thirty-two books during his brief lifetime, Stevenson created enduring classics in the field of children's literature as well as several popular adult works, including The Strange Case of Dr. Jekyll and Mr. Hyde, *which has exerted a powerful influence on Western cultural imagination.*

BORN: November 13, 1850; Edinburgh, Scotland
DIED: December 3, 1894; Vailima, near Apia, Samoa
ALSO KNOWN AS: Robert Louis Balfour Stevenson (full name)
AREA OF ACHIEVEMENT: Literature

EARLY LIFE

Scotland was not only the country of Robert Louis Balfour Stevenson's birth but was also the history-laden nation he later often revisited in both his nomadic life and his adventure romances. As the son and only child of Thomas Stevenson, a lighthouse engineer in Edinburgh, Robert was expected to adopt his father's profession. However, he was more interested in the sea and travel in general than in the coast. In fact, from his teenage years until his death, Stevenson's travels were so extensive that no biographer has been able to give a full account of them. His journeys began when his mother took him, as a young man, on periodic visits to the European continent for the sake of his health, which was compromised throughout his life by lingering pulmonary disorders.

Despite a lackluster performance as a student and numerous interruptions in his education caused by illness, Stevenson eventually completed a law degree at the University of Edinburgh in 1875. Nevertheless, his heart was set on travel and writing. Although Stevenson was sincere in these avocations, they also expressed resistance to his Scottish family's expectations in particular and to Victorian respectability in general.

This implicit rebellion against convention informed Stevenson's early substitution of "Louis" for his baptismal name "Lewis," his agnosticism, his profligate behavior as a university student, and his flamboyant adult public image. To his disapproving parents and friends, rebelliousness seemed at first to account for Stevenson's sudden departure for California, where on May 19, 1880, he married Fanny Van de Grift Osbourne, a divorcée ten years his senior who had two children. This sensational marriage was a good match for Stevenson, who subsequently created his most enduring work. Up to this point he had published various discursive travelogues such as *An Inland Voyage* (1878), a record of a canoe journey in Belgium and France; *Edinburgh: Picturesque Notes* (1878), a book of prose and pictorial sketches of his quaint birthplace; and *Travels with a Donkey in the Cévennes* (1879), an account of a ten-day French mountain walking tour taken with a donkey named Modestine. These books attracted some interest when they first appeared, but none of them could have established Stevenson's reputation.

LIFE'S WORK

Treasure Island (1881-1882) and *The Strange Case of Dr. Jekyll and Mr. Hyde* (1886) are Stevenson's most enduring books. *Treasure Island*, based on a watercolor map created to amuse Stevenson's stepson Lloyd Os-

Robert Louis Stevenson. (Library of Congress)

bourne, was not an immediate success when it was serialized in *Young Folks* between July, 1881, and June, 1882. It became a best seller as a book one year later. This morally ambiguous, dreamlike romance, with its larger-than-life villain Long John Silver as observed by young Jim Hawkins, was popular with juvenile and adult readers alike, including Stevenson's father. As a classic of children's literature, *Treasure Island* has not been out of print since its publication and has often been exploited in sequels by later authors as well as retold in stage, film, radio, comic-book, and television versions.

The Strange Case of Dr. Jekyll and Mr. Hyde has likewise remained in print for more than a century and has been similarly adapted to various media. A morally ambiguous, nightmarish romance of a dual personality divided against itself between base desires and noble ideals, this book was at first undertaken by Stevenson as a shilling shocker, a sensational type of fiction to be marketed cheaply for mass readership. With his wife's advice, however, Stevenson reshaped the work into a stunning Hawthorneian allegory of good and evil that

became an instant best seller in Britain and the United States (where pirated editions were prevalent). The fact that the two main character types in this romance have made an indelible impression on Western cultural imagination is evident in the frequency of allusions to Jekyll and Hyde in both ordinary and professional speech.

These two books of absent or equivocated moral message reflect the psychological terrain established during Stevenson's early life, during which he personally challenged familial and social expectations. If *Treasure Island* is a boy's daydream and *The Strange Case of Dr. Jekyll and Mr. Hyde* is a man's nightmare, both share a rebellious fantasy of gratifying the self's desires without guilt. Jim Hawkins's flight to a pirate world of vicious self-indulgence is related to Hyde's relish for wanton dissipation and violence. Such an observation provides a glimpse into an underground motive behind Stevenson's creativity, not his conscious intention. Concerning intention, Stevenson's expressed primary goal was to entertain and, on occasion, to instruct. *The Strange Case of Dr. Jekyll and Mr. Hyde*, it could be reasonably argued in terms of Stevenson's intentional allegorical design, therapeutically urges its readers to embrace community as the cornerstone of a healthy personal identity.

Stevenson's physical health lapsed in the interval between these two books. Confined to bed in a dark room as a result of a bronchial hemorrhage, he wrote most of *A Child's Garden of Verses* (1885), an enormously popular work of poetry that satisfied his immediate financial exigencies. Stevenson, who uncomfortably depended upon the largess of his father, always felt harassed by the need for money. As a result and in spite of being an invalid, Stevenson maintained an extraordinary productivity even from his sickbed. While ill, he wrote, among other books, *Kidnapped* (1886), a historical romance featuring an adolescent Scottish Lowlander; *The Black Arrow* (1888), a juvenile novel set during the War of the Roses; and *The Master of Ballantrae* (1889), a psychological tale of a fatal rivalry between two Scottish brothers.

Concern for his relentlessly precarious health led Stevenson to accept an offer by Scribners, his American publisher, to write a book about the Pacific islands. Setting sail in June, 1888, he and his family visited, among other places, Tahiti, Oahu, and the Hawaiian Islands. Within the next two years, they voyaged to Australia, the Gilbert and Marshall Islands, and Samoa, where he built a home on a four-hundred-acre estate he named Vailima. The welfare of the Samoans, particularly a concern over their economic exploitation by colonists, became a fervid cause for Stevenson, who in turn was fondly nick-named *Tusitala* (storyteller) by the islanders.

Stevenson delighted in narrating original tales to his admiring Samoan audience, such as the clever "The Isle of Voices." This tale, with a moral about living life as if it were a work of art, is included with the well-known "The

---

STEVENSON'S MAJOR WORKS

LONG FICTION

1881-1882	*Treasure Island* (serial), 1883 (book)
1886	*The Strange Case of Dr. Jekyll and Mr. Hyde*
1886	*Kidnapped*
1888	*The Black Arrow*
1889	*The Master of Ballantrae*
1889	*The Wrong Box*
1892	*The Wrecker* (with Lloyd Osbourne)
1893	*Catriona* (also known as *David Balfour*)
1894	*The Ebb-Tide* (with Osbourne)
1896	*Weir of Hermiston* (unfinished)

SHORT FICTION

1882	*The New Arabian Nights*
1885	*More New Arabian Nights*
1887	*The Merry Men, and Other Tales and Fables*
1893	*Island Nights' Entertainments*

POETRY

1882	*Moral Emblems*
1885	*A Child's Garden of Verses*
1887	*Underwoods*
1890	*Ballads*
1896	*Songs of Travel, and Other Verses*

NONFICTION

1878	*An Inland Voyage*
1878	*Edinburgh: Picturesque Notes*
1879	*Travels with a Donkey in the Cévennes*
1881	*Virginibus Puerisque*
1882	*Familiar Studies of Men and Books*
1883	*The Silverado Squatters: Sketches from a Californian Mountain*
1887	*Memories and Portraits*
1890	*The South Seas: A Record of Three Cruises*
1892	*Across the Plains*
1892	*A Footnote to History*
1895	*Amateur Emigrant*
1895	*Vailima Letters*
1896	*In the South Seas*
1899	*The Letters of Robert Louis Stevenson to His Family and Friends* (2 volumes), 1911 (4 volumes)
1988	*The Lantern-Bearers, and Other Essays*

Bottle Imp" and the critically acclaimed "The Beach of Falesá" in *Island Nights' Entertainments* (1893). Stevenson also rapidly completed *Catriona* (1893), also known as *David Balfour*, as a sequel to *Kidnapped*, which some readers thought needed such a conclusion. *Catriona* contains Stevenson's most ambitious attempt to depict female characters, and he spoke of it as his best book. It was, however, never as popular as several of his earlier writings, and later critics preferred two non-juvenile works (written in collaboration with his Lloyd Osbourne) composed during this late period of his brief career: *The Wrecker* (1892), a suspenseful tale involving a shipwreck, massacre, and treasure; and *The Ebb-Tide* (1894), a dark account of three island outcasts that anticipated Joseph Conrad's early fiction.

Weir of Hermiston (1896), a posthumously published work left as an incomplete manuscript when Stevenson died of a cerebral hemorrhage on December 3, 1894, at the age of forty-four, was soon acclaimed as Stevenson's potential masterpiece. The novel, dictated to his stepdaughter Isabel Osbourne Strong, combines Stevenson's most effective characterization and his inveterate affection for Scottish history. Whether Stevenson had finally matched or surpassed the achievement of his predecessor Sir Walter Scott, the writer to whom he had been compared throughout his career, did not matter to his friends in Samoa. In honor of their beloved *Tusitala*, grieving Samoans cut, with extreme difficulty, a steep pathway to the summit of Mount Vaea, where Stevenson was buried as he had requested.

SIGNIFICANCE

Since his death, as during his lifetime, Stevenson's reputation as a writer has been as divided in sentiment as his books are divided between an insistence on disciplined conscience and a celebration of uninhibited imagination—in other words, between Victorian mores and amoral aesthetics, austere realism and carefree romance. Whereas his poetry, travelogues, and essays have little currency, Stevenson's fiction endures among a wide audience. His contemporary reviewers, anticipating later literary critics, may have found much to fault in his fiction, but for over a century, general readers, young and old, have found much to admire.

The romance form of the novel preferred by Stevenson and other writers of his time has fallen into disfavor and is often regarded as escapist literature suitable for children. *Treasure Island* and *Kidnapped* indeed remain classics of children's literature despite their lack of a clear moral center. *The Strange Case of Dr. Jekyll and Mr. Hyde* endures as a widely recognized fixture in Western culture despite Stevenson's low estimation of it. *The Ebb-Tide* and "The Beach of Falesá" have been favored with increased attention in literary studies, whereas "The Suicide Club" (from *The New Arabian Nights*, 1882), "The Body Snatcher" and "Markheim" (from *The Merry Men, and Other Tales and Fables*, 1887), and "The Bottle Imp" prevail as perennial choices for anthologies marketed to a general audience.

The compass of Stevenson's influence on other writers is as extensive as were his many travels. To observe the impact of *Treasure Island* on H. Rider Haggard's *King Solomon's Mines* (1885) and Sir James Barrie's *Peter Pan* (1904), and of *Kidnapped* on John Buchan's *The Thirty-nine Steps* (1915) is merely to single out three phenomenal best sellers indebted to Stevenson's work. The fact that Stevenson's fiction continues to entertain countless readers is ample testimony to his achievement.

—*William J. Scheick*

FURTHER READING

Bell, Ian. *Robert Louis Stevenson: Dreams of Exile*. Edinburgh: Mainstream Press, 1992. Interprets Stevenson's life as an ongoing effort to reconcile various opposite inclinations, including his ambivalent attitude toward Scotland.

Callow, Philip. *Louis: A Life of Robert Louis Stevenson*. Chicago: Ivan R. Dee, 2001. Relatively brief and admiring account of Stevenson's life, aimed at general readers.

Daiches, David. *Robert Louis Stevenson and His World*. London: Thames and Hudson, 1973. A profusely illustrated overview of Stevenson's life and work that is especially suitable for young adults.

Eigner, Edwin M. *Robert Louis Stevenson and the Romantic Tradition*. Princeton, N.J.: Princeton University Press, 1966. A reliable, accessible discussion of the sources and implications of the Romantic features of Stevenson's writings.

Gray, William. *Robert Louis Stevenson: A Literary Life*. New York: Palgrave Macmillan, 2004. Focuses on Stevenson's writing, placing it within the geographical, cultural, and political contexts that shaped it.

Hennessy, James Pope. *Robert Louis Stevenson*. London: Jonathan Cape, 1974. A dramatic retelling of Stevenson's life with particular attention devoted to details of human interest.

McLynn, Frank. *Robert Louis Stevenson: A Biography*. New York: Random House, 1994. Definitive biography, chronicling the events of Stevenson's life and their influence upon his writing. McLynn argues that Stevenson was Scotland's greatest writer, and a major influence upon Joseph Conrad, Oscar Wilde, and William Butler Yeats.

Maixner, Paul, ed. *Robert Louis Stevenson: The Critical Heritage*. London: Routledge & Kegan Paul, 1981. A valuable collection of reviews of Stevenson's books published between 1878 and 1894.

Nollen, Scott Allen. *Robert Louis Stevenson: Life, Literature and the Silver Screen*. Jefferson, N.C.: McFarland, 1994. Documents and analyzes the history of radio, film, and television adaptations of Stevenson's stories.

Stevenson, Robert Louis. *The Letters of Robert Louis Stevenson*. 8 vols. Edited by Bradford A. Booth and Ernest Mehew. New Haven, Conn.: Yale University Press, 1994-1995. Offers a treasure trove of Stevenson's opinions that generally tell the story of Stevenson's life better than any biographer.

SEE ALSO: H. Rider Haggard; Sir Walter Scott; Mark Twain.

RELATED ARTICLE in *Great Events from History: The Nineteenth Century, 1801-1900:* July, 1881-1883: Stevenson Publishes *Treasure Island*.

LUCY STONE
American social reformer

A gifted orator and activist for the abolitionist movement, Stone was the first woman to speak out full time for women's rights, and she devoted her life to the struggle for woman suffrage and equal rights.

BORN: August 13, 1818; Coy's Hill, near West Brookfield, Massachusetts

DIED: October 18, 1893; Dorchester, near Boston, Massachusetts

AREAS OF ACHIEVEMENT: Social reform, women's rights

EARLY LIFE

Lucy Stone was born into a family whose ancestors were among New England's first European settlers. Her father, Francis Stone, tanned hides and served as the community's teacher until her birth, at which time he settled into farming. At home he commanded absolute authority, and discipline was swift, marked with severe whippings and humiliation. Lucy's mother, Hannah Matthews Stone, was an obedient, hardworking housewife. Despite this outward docility, Lucy saw in her mother a quiet anger and resentment against male domination as prescribed by fundamental Christian ideology. Her father's control and her mother's grudging submission were such powerful influences that as a child Lucy swore never to marry or accept such a contemptible station in life.

Stone's developing objection to the status of women compelled her to pursue a solid education and, in the process, to learn Greek so that she could verify the accuracy of biblical translations regarding a woman's position in society. At the age of sixteen, she was hired to teach at a local school with a salary of four dollars per month. The salary itself enraged Stone because male teachers with the same credentials earned four times the money.

When not teaching, Stone continued her studies at the local seminary for girls until 1843, when, at the age of twenty-five, she entered Oberlin College in Ohio, the only college that admitted female students and one that also supported the emancipation of slaves. Abolitionism was not new to Stone. She had avidly read William Lloyd Garrison's *The Liberator* since it began publication, and she considered herself a "Garrisonian"—supporting a more radical antislavery stance than Oberlin College itself.

While a student at Oberlin, Stone taught former slaves, worked in the school cafeteria, learned Greek, founded the college's first women's debating society, and delivered her first public speech on women's rights and slave emancipation. Considered too radical by her peers and a potential troublemaker by the college, she nevertheless earned respect for her determination, intelligence, and ability to argue an issue soundly and convincingly. Following her graduation in 1847, she was hired by the Massachusetts Anti-Slave Society as a public speaker—a position considered socially improper for a woman.

LIFE'S WORK

Against her parents' wishes, Lucy Stone delivered her first public address on slave emancipation and women's rights in the summer of 1847. Stone possessed strong conviction, sound logic, and an eloquence in oratory that compelled even the most ardent opponent of women's rights to listen respectfully. Stone made frequent public lectures during that year, and most of these speeches concentrated on issues of women's rights.

By the end of the decade, New England had become the center of a growing social reform movement in the nation, and Stone was quickly emerging as one of the movement's most competent and committed proponents. She advocated the strict control of alcoholic beverages, arguing that liquor destroyed the fabric of the home and emboldened men to abuse their wives. She criticized Christianity for relegating women to a position of social inferiority and for not taking a stronger antislave position. She championed a woman's right to own property, to receive an advanced education, and to be granted equal status before the law. Without doubt, her arguments were sharply criticized by the male-dominated social order of the era, but the women who filled her lecture halls and whispered encouragement strengthened Stone's resolve to continue speaking for equality. She made women's rights her principal topic and was noted as the first woman speaker to do so. For her near solitary public position, she became known as the "morning star" of the women's rights movement.

Lucy Stone was the primary organizer of the First National Woman's Rights Convention, held in Worcester, Massachusetts, on October 23, 1850. More than one thousand participants listened to speakers such as Sojourner Truth, Sarah Tyndall, Frederick Douglass, and Stone present their calls for equality for women. Although the Seneca Falls Convention of 1848 was the first such gathering, it had drawn a limited local audience of reformers. The 1850 convention, however, placed the issue of women's rights before a national audience and set into motion an annual conference largely directed by Stone, who, at her own expense, published a report of the conference proceedings.

Stone's hectic lecture schedule took her across much of the nation pressing state assemblies for equal rights for women. In 1853, she endorsed a woman suffrage petition presented to the Massachusetts Constitutional Convention in Boston. From there, she spoke in Cincinnati, Pittsburgh, St. Louis, Louisville, and several other cities. Her presentations included specific points regarding women's equality in marriage—perhaps because of her developing relationship with Henry Blackwell, to whom she was married in May, 1855.

The Civil War interrupted Stone's public lecturing. Also, the birth of her daughter refocused Stone's attention to child rearing and would have taken her from the lecture circuit even if the war had not erupted. Moreover, she started having severe headaches that occasionally confined her to bed for days.

Despite these interruptions, Stone resumed her active public life following the war. Increasingly, she emphasized woman suffrage in her speeches—a right she believed was central to women's equality. She argued for suffrage in a series of lectures throughout New England and New York, coauthored a petition for Congress to consider women's right to vote, and helped organize a convention that led to the founding of the American Equal Rights Association.

In March, 1867, Stone argued for black and woman suffrage before the New Jersey legislature, stating that every person capable of rational choice was entitled to the right to vote. Democracy required equal suffrage. When a woman is denied the vote, she added, the very principle of democracy itself is violated. If women were indeed the natural possessors of morality, she concluded, then extension of the franchise would automatically bring a humane attitude to legislation. She spread her views throughout the North and again lobbied Congress, was instrumental in the formation of the New England Suffrage Association, and helped organize the New Jersey Woman Suffrage Association.

The fact that women were not included in the Fifteenth Amendment only intensified Stone's battle for equal rights. Throughout 1869, she labored to publish *Woman's Journal*, with seven thousand copies of the first edition sold in early January, 1870. Voting rights was the primary focus of each edition, and this first issue

Lucy Stone. (Library of Congress)

highlighted Wyoming's new woman suffrage law. The *Journal* also addressed a variety of women's issues and concerns such as education, health, marriage, work, and the rearing of children.

Stone took residence on the floor above the *Journal*'s office and from there worked to gain advertisers, subscribers, and news stories. She spent hours managing the office, handling financial matters, and arranging for printing and distribution. Despite the hectic and consuming work, she maintained a lecture schedule that took her into Pennsylvania, Vermont, New York, and throughout Massachusetts. At the same time, she continued her active involvement in the American Equal Rights Association and in the creation of an amendment to grant woman suffrage nationally.

The 1870's were no less busy for Stone. Persons who could not vote, she consistently argued, were defenseless in society. Power rested in the ballot box, and once women received the franchise the ills of society would be remedied. To bring added pressure on state legislatures, Stone looked for untapped sources of support. The suffrage movement had relied upon a minority of women—those who were well educated, skilled at public speaking and organization, and not intimidated by the male population or by accepted norms for proper female behavior.

During the late 1870's, Stone sought to include middle-class women by making the push for suffrage a socially acceptable position among women themselves. The formation of women's clubs in communities across the nation would afford women the opportunity to discuss the issue of suffrage and to chart a course of action locally to advance the cause. With clubs becoming fashionable outlets for middle-class women, Stone believed suffrage specifically, and the demand for equal rights in general, could be pressed forcefully by a new body of supporters. She imagined the widespread effect of such political action in every town and anticipated the strength such clubs could use in lobbying state legislatures. In one month she recruited almost eleven hundred women into local clubs.

At the same time, Stone criticized government efforts to provide protective legislation for women in the workplace, arguing that gender-based laws guaranteed unequal treatment for women, even if the intention of the legislation was positive. In addition, through the *Woman's Journal*, she championed better working conditions for all individuals, an end to inhumane conditions in reform schools, and the elimination of government and business corruption, and she protested vigorously existing federal policy regarding American Indians. Before the decade ended, *Woman's Journal* was distributed in every state and in thirty-nine foreign countries.

Despite declining health throughout the 1880's, Stone remained as active as possible. In May, 1893, she attended the World's Congress of Representative Women at the World's Columbian Exposition in Chicago. More than 150,000 people from twenty-seven nations assembled for a week-long convention. Among the slated speakers was Lucy Stone. Weak and frail, she took the podium and delivered her address entitled "The Progress of Fifty Years." She traced the course of the women's rights movement over five decades, praised the women who had unselfishly devoted themselves to the struggle, and clearly detailed the much improved status of women in contemporary America. She ended the speech with a reminder—much more work was needed, and the movement must continue until full equality was achieved.

Stone's speech in Chicago was her last. Five months later, on October 18, she died with her daughter Alice at her side.

SIGNIFICANCE

Symbolic of her expectations and demands for equality in marriage, Stone retained her maiden name and never did she refer to herself as Mrs. Blackwell, preferring in-

stead Lucy Stone, wife of Henry Blackwell. Taking the husband's name amounted to the loss of a woman's identity, she argued. She further insisted that once married, a woman's property should remain hers, and the same should be true for the product of her labor and the guardianship of the children. According to Stone, a husband's control over a wife's property amounted to nothing short of legal theft. Moreover, nonconsensual sex was the equivalent of marital rape, she stated. She further demanded the abolition of the entire system of legal codes and customs that placed women under the care, protection, and exclusive control of their husbands. Personal independence and equal human rights, she maintained, could never be relinquished by a woman because of marriage, and the law should recognize the institution as an equal partnership.

Stone's arguments were certainly advanced for the era in which she lived. More often than not she was considered too extreme in her views. Typically, male listeners were outraged by Stone's speeches, and women found her ideas correct but impossible to attain. Despite the cool, and sometimes even hostile, response given her by the general public, Stone persisted in demanding equal rights in marriage.

In commemoration of Lucy Stone's life's work, university dormitories, city parks, and public schools were named in her honor. The suffrage movement persisted until passage of the Twentieth Amendment in 1919 that granted woman suffrage. The *Woman's Journal* continued publication until 1931 and, with each issue, echoed Stone's demand for gender equality.

—*Kenneth William Townsend*

FURTHER READING

Blackwell, Alice Stone. *Lucy Stone: Pioneer of Woman's Rights.* 2d ed. Norwood, Mass.: Alice Stone Blackwell Committee, 1930. Reprint. Charlottesville: University Press of Virginia, 2001. Alice Stone Blackwell, Lucy Stone's daughter, presents an insightful and personal view of her mother's personal and public life.

Hays, Elinor Rice. *Morning Star: A Biography of Lucy Stone, 1818-1893.* New York: Harcourt, Brace & World, 1961. Hays portrays Stone as a solid, committed champion of women's rights and the emancipation of slaves—a model for contemporary feminists and reformers.

Kerr, Andrea Moore. *Lucy Stone: Speaking Out for Equality.* New Brunswick, N.J.: Rutgers University Press, 1992. Kerr presents a thorough and well-researched biography of Lucy Stone, and she ranks Stone as one of the most powerful women reformers of the nineteenth century.

Lasser, Carol, and Marlene Merrill, eds. *Friends and Sisters: Letters Between Lucy Stone and Antoinette Brown Blackwell, 1846-93.* Chicago: University of Illinois Press, 1987. Lucy Stone's personal thoughts, views on women's rights, and half-century friendship with Antoinette Brown Blackwell, the first woman ordained into the Protestant ministry, are revealed through their private letters to each other.

Million, Joelle. *Woman's Voice, Woman's Place: Lucy Stone and the Birth of the Woman's Rights Movement.* Westport, Conn.: Praeger, 2003. Million recounts the events of Stone's personal life and her significant role in the antebellum women's rights movement.

Woloch, Nancy. *Women and the American Experience.* New York: Alfred A. Knopf, 1984. This publication surveys the history of women in America from the early seventeenth century through the late 1970's and places Lucy Stone in the broader context of the suffrage movement.

SEE ALSO: Susan B. Anthony; Frederick Douglass; Abby Kelley Foster; William Lloyd Garrison; Thomas Wentworth Higginson; Lucretia Mott; Sojourner Truth.

RELATED ARTICLES in *Great Events from History: The Nineteenth Century, 1801-1900:* 1820's-1850's: Social Reform Movement; May 28-29, 1851: Akron Woman's Rights Convention; May 12, 1857: New York Infirmary for Indigent Women and Children Opens; December 6, 1865: Thirteenth Amendment Is Ratified; May 10, 1866: Suffragists Protest the Fourteenth Amendment; May, 1869: Woman Suffrage Associations Begin Forming; June 17-18, 1873: Anthony Is Tried for Voting; February 17-18, 1890: Women's Rights Associations Unite.

JOSEPH STORY
American jurist

During more than three decades as a U.S. Supreme Court justice, Story was an ally of Chief Justice John Marshall, with whom he contributed to the early formation of constitutional law in the United States, particularly in determining the appellate role of the Court in civil cases.

BORN: September 18, 1779; Marblehead, Massachusetts
DIED: September 10, 1845; Cambridge, Massachusetts
AREA OF ACHIEVEMENT: Law

EARLY LIFE
Joseph Story was the first son of Mehitable Pedrick and Elisha Story. His father, a physician, had participated in the Boston Tea Party, had joined the Sons of Liberty, and had confronted the British at Lexington, Concord, and Bunker Hill. Brought up in a family that was profoundly religious but inclined to liberal theological doctrine, firmly patriotic and Republican, Story was prepared for Harvard at the Marblehead Academy, a private school, where he learned the rudiments of a classical education.

In 1794, Story entered the Cambridge institution. He was ambitious, studious, articulate, and committed to intellectual pursuit. Working his way through a curriculum that included the obligatory Greek and Latin, Euclidian geometry and trigonometry, history, and theology, there was yet time to read the works of William Shakespeare, Johann Wolfgang von Goethe in translation, and Jean-Jacques Rousseau; to converse with his classmate, William Ellery Channing, the later founder of New England Unitarianism; and to write poetry. He was graduated from Harvard, second to Channing, in 1798 and immediately became a law apprentice to Samuel Sewall, a Federalist congressman and later a Massachusetts Supreme Court justice, and, for a short time, to Samuel Putnam in Salem, Massachusetts.

Story was twenty-two years old when he was admitted to the Essex County bar; three years later, he married Mary Lynd Oliver, only to be temporarily traumatized by her death in June, 1805 (he remarried in 1808), and the subsequent demise of his father two months later. However, he rapidly became the leading practitioner before the Essex County Court of Common Pleas, derived a lucrative income from his legal talents and associations, was elected as a Jeffersonian Republican to the Massachusetts legislature, and found time to write the first of a plethora of law volumes. In the Massachusetts General Court (the technical name for the state assembly), he sponsored new legislation to structure and increase judicial salaries, to enhance the authority of the courts, and to create an equity tribunal. His brief career as a congressman in 1808 earned for him the enmity of President Thomas Jefferson, for although he defended the Embargo Act at its inception, Story later urged its repeal, convinced that the prohibition on international trade would destroy New England's commercial economy.

Story's most important case was *Fletcher v. Peck*. In February, 1810, he argued the position of Massachusetts speculators in Georgia lands before the U.S. Supreme Court. Although there was no doubt that the 1795 grant by the state legislature was stained with widespread corruption, and although Chief Justice John Marshall deplored the circumstances of the land deal, he held for the Court that the rescinding act of the Georgia assembly offended the contract clause of the Constitution. It was the first time that the Supreme Court exercised judicial review over state legislation.

LIFE'S WORK

Story was soon to become a colleague of the justices before whom he appeared in the Georgia litigation. On November 11, 1811, two months after his thirty-second birthday, despite Jefferson's misgivings, he was appointed by President James Madison as an associate justice of the U.S. Supreme Court. He was the youngest man ever to be seated on the high tribunal.

Throughout his thirty-three years on the Supreme Court, Story justified the confidence that Madison had bestowed upon him. He witnessed the War of 1812, the controversy over Missouri's entrance to the Union as a slave state, the emergence of an industrial economy, the election of Andrew Jackson, and, in 1835, the appointment of Marshall's successor, Roger B. Taney. His opinions were almost uniformly learned, closely argued, and logically consistent.

Along with Marshall, his friend and colleague, Story was strongly nationalistic and intent on energizing and facilitating the development of a national economy. In *Martin v. Hunter's Lessee* in 1816, he responded to Virginia's challenge to the Supreme Court's appellate jurisdiction by arguing that uniformity of decisions and of application of the constitutional imperatives necessitated review of state laws and judicial opinions. He collaborated with Marshall in framing the great nationalistic rulings in *McCulloch v. Maryland* (1819) and *Gibbons v. Ogden* (1824). In his concurring opinion in *Dartmouth College v. Woodward* (1819), he explicitly extended the immunity of charters from legislative annulment to business corporations. Later, in 1837, in *Charles River*

Bridge v. Warren Bridge, he wrote a measured but trenchant dissent to Taney's opinion that public charters were to be interpreted narrowly in favor of the state.

Story was persuaded that economic investment would decline if American businesspeople came to the conclusion that state grants and charters were at the mercy of legislative whim and that debts could easily be dissolved by retroactive bankruptcy acts. He strove to create a climate in which individual entrepreneurs could use their skills and inventive genius to exploit the vast economic potential of the American continent. He pursued this objective not only in more prominent cases but also in some forty legal opinions relating to patents, favoring inventors and promoting technological advancement.

At the same time, there were others on the Marshall and Taney courts who believed that bankruptcy laws cushioned the danger of making financial mistakes and encouraged risk-taking. They contended that state-granted monopolies would breed complacency, discourage technological innovation, and slow economic progress. Their differences with Marshall and Story were not over the goals of economic policy but over the strategies of achievement.

The Marshall Court was committed to the protection of private property rights. On the surface, it maintained an aura of unanimity in cases involving slavery and the foreign slave trade. However, underneath, the justices' personal views of the South's "peculiar institution" diverged from Story's hatred of slavery to Bushrod Washington's public defense of his ownership of human beings. In December, 1819, in the midst of the Missouri Controversy, Story made a long and passionate address at the Salem town meeting, denouncing the extension of slavery as contrary to the spirit of the Declaration of Independence and the Constitution.

In the case of *La Jeune Eugénie* (1822), which Story heard and decided while acting as a circuit judge in Boston, he depicted the nightmarish slave trade, and although he remanded the ship to the French consul, he declared that the nefarious traffic was against international law. Later, in 1841, in the *Amistad* case, he ruled that the captive Africans who had mutinied on board the ship, killed its officers, and attempted to sail back to Africa were free men who were justified in taking extraordinary measures to regain their liberty.

Story's most difficult opinion on slavery came a year later, in *Prigg v. Pennsylvania*. The case involved the constitutional right of slaveholders to recapture fugitives escaping across state lines. Committed to the supremacy of federal law and torn by his personal antipathy toward slavery, the associate justice effected a compromise, upholding the constitutionality of the Fugitive Slave Act of 1793 but at the same time declaring that individual states had no legal obligation to assist in its enforcement.

The *Prigg v. Pennsylvania* decision was excoriated by abolitionists, applauded by southerners, and criticized in dissent by Chief Justice Taney as rendering the Fugitive Slave Act inoperative. Although Story was deeply aggrieved by the abolitionist reaction, he was no stranger to popular and legal controversy. In *Cherokee Nation v. Georgia* in 1831, in a rare instance in which he parted company with Marshall and joined with Smith Thompson in dissent, he argued that the southwestern tribe was entitled to federal protection from state oppression. A year later, in *Worchester v. Georgia* (1832), he saw his views vindicated as the chief justice decided that Georgia law interfered with Cherokee treaty rights and could not withstand constitutional scrutiny.

Story's record on slavery and the American Indian in part manifested an empathy with oppressed minorities. However, he was fearful of the democratic spirit of the Jacksonians. He was concerned that the excess and disorder of unruly majorities threatened the fabric of the Union. He became increasingly isolated on a court dominated by Jacksonian appointment; although he respected Taney and was a personal friend of the Ohioan John McLean, he was dismayed by the political atmosphere of the Court and by his perceived defects in its legal scholarship. His dissent rate on major constitutional issues relating to slavery, the commerce clause, and the status of corporations rose to 50 percent; in no important case did he produce an opinion favoring southern interests.

Story believed that law was a science. Along with his erudite opinions, from 1805 to 1845, he published eleven law digests, treatises, and commentaries on such varied subjects as equity jurisprudence, agency, and conflict of laws. Perhaps the most important was the *Commentaries on the Constitution of the United States* (1833). Dedicated to Marshall, the *Commentaries* reviewed the legal history of the United States, beginning with the colonial charters, covering the Articles of Confederation, and concluding with a close examination of the Constitution. The book is nationalistic in perspective, sometimes combative in tone, and almost always elaborate in style. Story's history was biased; his strictures on Jefferson and other exponents of states' rights were polemical. However, the work was popular, went through several editions, was cited in later Supreme Court decisions, and was still in use at the end of the nineteenth century.

The *Commentaries* reflected an effort to educate the American people. From the judicial bench and the author's desk, Story also went into the classroom to teach a generation of aspiring lawyers. Appointed as Dane Professor of Law at Harvard in 1829, he was in part responsible for the development of its legal reputation; he sold at below cost his own library to enhance its holdings and brought prominent politicians and lawyers such as Daniel Webster and John Quincy Adams to his classes. His lectures, sprinkled with personal experience and vivid digressions, combined case law and legal history, comparative jurisprudence, and treatise literature; they were intended to produce a system geared to the needs of American society. His students included the abolitionist Wendell Phillips, the writer Richard Henry Dana, and the senator Charles P. Sumner.

Although the law was his passion, Story planned to resign his seat on the Supreme Court in the fall of 1845. He had been ill in 1842 and ill again until the spring of 1843. He felt alienated from his colleagues on the Court; he was shocked and disgruntled by the defeat of Henry Clay and the election of yet another Democrat, James K. Polk, to the presidency in 1844. He wanted to devote his efforts to full-time teaching at Harvard Law School and to writing his memoirs and a tenth commentary on admiralty. He died on September 10, 1845, probably the victim of a heart attack, his last circuit court opinion lying on his desk.

SIGNIFICANCE

An 1828 portrait of the associate justice depicts Story in judicial robes, given to baldness, with magnetic blue eyes and a round face radiating firmness and energy. It was an appropriate characterization. Story, as had Marshall and his other colleagues, had a unique opportunity to shape American law and to interpret the language of the Constitution. There were few precedents; the English common law was often too rigid to meet the exigencies of the new American environment of bustling commerce and incipient industrialization. Story seized the opportunity to strengthen the federal government by expanding its powers at the expense of the states and by furthering an economic policy that would protect and promote the activities of American entrepreneurs.

Story's heroes were George Washington and John Marshall; his villains, Thomas Jefferson and Andrew Jackson. His predilections were conservative and antidemocratic. Although his influence and reputation waned in a nation of rapid change and later egalitarian orientation, his contributions to American nationalism, to the rational study of law, and to legal education are incalculable.

—*David L. Sterling*

FURTHER READING

Baxter, Maurice G. *The Steamboat Monopoly: Gibbons v. Ogden, 1824.* New York: Alfred A. Knopf, 1970. A narrative and assessment of the case in which the Marshall Court had its first opportunity to interpret the commerce clause of the Constitution.

Beveridge, Albert J. *The Life of John Marshall.* 4 vols. Boston: Houghton Mifflin, 1916-1919. The classic biography of the chief justice, in four volumes, elegantly written, but marred by a consistent anti-Jefferson and pro-Marshall bias. The last two volumes go beyond Marshall's life and constitute a history of the Court over which Marshall presided.

Cable, Mary. *Black Odyssey: The Case of the Slaveship Amistad.* New York: Viking Press, 1972. A short history of the Supreme Court's slave-trade opinion, known by contemporaries as the Case of the African Captives. The book focuses on the background and incarceration of the kidnapped Africans in a Boston jail and the arguments before the Supreme Court of Francis Scott Key for the Spanish claimants and John Quincy Adams for the detained Africans and on their subsequent return home.

Dunne, Gerald T. *Justice Joseph Story and the Rise of the Supreme Court.* New York: Simon & Schuster, 1970. A nontechnical and well-written introduction to the life of the associate justice and to the cases and decisions in which he participated.

Newmyer, R. Kent. *Supreme Court Justice Joseph Story: Statesman of the Old Republic.* Chapel Hill: University of North Carolina Press, 1985. The most comprehensive and analytic review of Story's public life. Argues that his judicial record and his roles as legal educator and publicist can best be understood in the context of a Republican culture originating with the American Revolution.

_____. *The Supreme Court Under Marshall and Taney.* Northbrook, Ill.: AHM, 1968. A survey of the pre-Civil War Supreme Court that emphasizes the continuity of decisions under the leadership of Marshall and that of his successor.

Story, William W., ed. *Life and Letters of Joseph Story, Associate Justice of the Supreme Court of the United States, and Dane Professor of Law at Harvard University.* 2 vols. Union, N.J.: Lawbook Exchange, 2000. Originally published in 1851, the book contains some of Story's letters and treatises, selected by his son, William. The letters describe Story's childhood and youth, education, legal career, and judicial and professorial life. Also includes Story's influential treatise, *Commentaries on the Constitution.*

Swisher, Carl Brent. *Roger B. Taney.* New York: Macmillan, 1935. The standard analysis of the judicial philosophy of Taney and his court. In part, attempts to refurbish Taney's reputation in relation to the notorious 1857 *Dred Scott v. Sandford* decision.

SEE ALSO: John Quincy Adams; William Ellery Channing; Henry Clay; Andrew Jackson; John Marshall; Wendell Phillips; James K. Polk; Roger Brooke Taney; Daniel Webster.

RELATED ARTICLES in *Great Events from History: The Nineteenth Century, 1801-1900:* March 16, 1810: *Fletcher v. Peck*; March 6, 1819: *McCulloch v. Maryland*; March 2, 1824: *Gibbons v. Ogden*; March 18, 1831, and March 3, 1832: Cherokee Cases.

HARRIET BEECHER STOWE
American novelist

Stowe was the author of Uncle Tom's Cabin, *which almost certainly had the greatest social and political impact on the United States of any book ever published. In attacking slavery as a threat to the Christian family, her novel helped to abolish that institution, and many people credit it with helping to bring on the Civil War.*

BORN: June 14, 1811; Litchfield, Connecticut
DIED: July 1, 1896; Hartford, Connecticut
ALSO KNOWN AS: Harriet Elizabeth Beecher (birth name); Catherine Stowe (pseudonym)
AREAS OF ACHIEVEMENT: Social reform, women's rights

EARLY LIFE

Harriet Beecher Stowe was the daughter of Lyman Beecher, a stern New England Calvinist preacher whose image of a God who predestined humans to heaven or hell left a mark on his children, and one of her brothers was Henry Ward Beecher, the famous Brooklyn preacher. The fact that Harriet's mother died when she was four made her father's influence even more important. By the age of six and a half, the young "Hattie," as she was known to her family, had memorized more than two dozen hymns and several long chapters in the Bible. As an adult, however, she would substitute for her father's dogmas a religion of hope that stressed the love and compassion of Christ rather than the divine judgment that her father preached. Some people hold that she "feminized" her father's religion. Throughout her life, she retained a strong sense of religious mission and zeal for social improvement.

At the age of twelve, Harriet moved to Hartford to live with her older sister Catharine, a purposeful woman who had started the Hartford Female Seminary. Harriet attended Catharine's school and stayed on as a teacher and guardian of young children. In 1832, she moved with her family to Cincinnati, Ohio, where her father had been offered the post as president of the new Lane Theological Seminary. Three years after arriving in Cincinnati (in January, 1836), Harriet Beecher married Calvin Stowe, a Lane professor.

These years in the West prepared Stowe for her later career. She had eight children between 1836 and 1850, and if she and Calvin had not alternated taking "rest cures" in Vermont over the years, she might have had more. In 1834, Harriet won a fifty-dollar prize for "A New England Sketch," which was published in the *Western Monthly Magazine*. From that point on, the members of her family saw her as a person of literary promise, even though she claimed that this activity was only a way of supplementing the always meager family income. In 1842, Calvin wrote to his wife, "[My] dear, you must be a literary woman. It is written in the book of fate."

While in Cincinnati, Harriet also experienced the intense emotions aroused by the slavery issue during these years. On one visit to a Kentucky plantation, she saw slaves whom she later used as models for some of the characters in *Uncle Tom's Cabin*. In 1836, a local mob attacked the print shop of an abolitionist in the city, and the struggle between the abolitionists and the moderates at Lane eventually drove her father to retire and her husband to take a job at Bowdoin College in Maine in 1850.

LIFE'S WORK

When President Abraham Lincoln met Harriet Beecher Stowe in the fall of 1862, he greeted her as "the little lady who made this big war." He was not alone in believing that the publication of Stowe's *Uncle Tom's Cabin* (1852) had been a crucial event in arousing the antislavery sentiments that led to the outbreak of the American Civil War in 1861. Although *Uncle Tom's Cabin* was not the best novel of the nineteenth century, it certainly had the greatest impact. *Uncle Tom's Cabin* sold 300,000 copies the year it was published, and Stowe's great work helped to end slavery by personalizing that "peculiar institution." Slavery was wrong, the novel argued, because it was un-Christian. More specifically, slavery tore children from their mothers and thus threatened the existence of the Christian family. It has been said that *Uncle Tom's Cabin* was "a great revival sermon," more effective than those of her father. Harriet herself later wrote that the book was written by "the Lord Himself. . . . I was but an instrument in his hands."

Each of the main characters in this melodramatic novel displayed virtues and vices that were important to Stowe. The main character, Tom, was sold by a kind master, Mr. Shelby, to a second one, Augustine St. Clare, who had ambiguous feelings about slavery and planned to free Tom. Before he could do so, St. Clare was killed and Tom was sold to a singularly evil man, Simon Legree, who finally beat Tom to death when the slave refused to tell him the hiding place of two slaves who were planning to escape.

Aside from Tom, the strongest characters in the novel were female. The slave Eliza, also sold by Mr. Shelby, escaped with her son (who would have been taken from her) by jumping across ice floes on the Ohio River. She and her husband George were finally reunited in Canada. Little Eva, the saintly and sickly child of Augustine St. Clare, was a Christlike figure who persuaded her father to free Tom before she herself died. Mary Bird, the wife of an Ohio senator, shamed her husband into helping Eliza when she sought comfort at their home. Senator Bird violated the Fugitive Slave Law of 1850— which he had helped to pass and which required northerners to return escaped slaves—by helping Eliza. Ophelia, a cousin of Augustine St. Clare who came from Vermont to help him care for his invalid wife and child, was the model of a well-organized homemaker who was especially proud of her neat kitchen. Another courageous female was the slave Cassy, who quietly poisoned her newborn with opium after she had had two other children sold away from her.

It was no accident that so many of the heroes in *Uncle Tom's Cabin* were women motivated by a Christian love of neighbor or that the most dramatic events in the novel focused on the way slavery destroyed families. *Uncle Tom's Cabin* was particularly effective in arousing antislavery sentiment and particularly infuriating to southern defenders of slavery, precisely because it dramatically attacked one of the strongest arguments of slaveholders, the religious one that saw slavery as an essential part of the patriarchal system of authority established by God and sanctioned by Scripture. For Stowe, Christianity began at home with a strong family. Any institution that undermined the family was necessarily unchristian.

In many ways, Harriet Beecher Stowe was a lay preacher whose writings were sermons. Like some other nineteenth century advocates of women's rights, Stowe believed that women were morally superior to men. She did not believe that women should govern the country or replace men in the world of business, but rather that they should set a moral example for society through their control of the "domestic sphere," where they could influence society by shaping the lives of their children. Stowe advocated greater equality between the men's sphere and the women's sphere. Women deserved greater respect because most of them—slave or free—were mothers, and therefore they had a greater understanding of both love and the "sacredness of the family" than men did.

In some of her later novels, especially *Pink and White Tyranny: A Society Novel, My Wife and I* (both 1871), and *We and Our Neighbors* (1875), Stowe continued to argue that women could improve the world by being guardians of morals in the home. She was not a "radical" advocate of full social equality for women, and she was critical of reformers such as Elizabeth Cady Stanton and Susan B. Anthony. Despite her active professional career as a writer, which made her the principal wage earner in the family after 1853, Stowe continued to maintain that she wrote only to supplement the family income. She also continued to write novels in which strong women— for example, Mary Scudder in *The Minister's Wooing* (1859) and Mara in *The Pearl of Orr's Island* (1862)— acted as female ministers who taught their families the path to salvation from the well-ordered kitchen that was, in effect, a domestic pulpit.

This complex woman continued to publish until she was nearly seventy. Although *Uncle Tom's Cabin* had a greater impact on American history than any other single novel, Harriet Beecher Stowe's literary reputation rests on those novels that portrayed life in the New England villages of her youth: *The Pearl of Orr's Island, Oldtown Folks* (1869), and *Poganuc People: Their Loves and*

Harriet Beecher Stowe. (Library of Congress)

Lives (1878). Although peopled by stern Calvinist ministers and wise, compassionate women, these works were not consciously written to correct a social injustice, as was *Uncle Tom's Cabin*. In 1873, Stowe used some of her income to buy a large home in Hartford, Connecticut, where she and Calvin spent their last years. Calvin died in 1886, ten years before his sometimes controversial wife.

INTRODUCING UNCLE TOM

Harriet Beecher Stowe's Uncle Tom makes his first appearance in the fourth chapter of Uncle Tom's Cabin, *after a detailed description of the cabin in which he and his wife, Chloe, live.*

The cabin of Uncle Tom was a small log building, close adjoining to "the house," as the negro *par excellence* designates his master's dwelling. In front it had a neat garden-patch, where, every summer, strawberries, raspberries, and a variety of fruits and vegetables, flourished under careful tending. The whole front of it was covered by a large scarlet bignonia and a native multiflora rose, which, entwisting and interlacing, left scarce a vestige of the rough logs to be seen. Here, also, in summer, various brilliant annuals, such as marigolds, petunias, four-o'clocks, found an indulgent corner in which to unfold their splendors, and were the delight and pride of Aunt Chloe's heart.

Let us enter the dwelling. The evening meal at the house is over, and Aunt Chloe, who presided over its preparation as head cook, has left to inferior officers in the kitchen the business of clearing away and washing dishes, and come out into her own snug territories, to "get her ole man's supper"; therefore, doubt not that it is her you see by the fire, presiding with anxious interest over certain frizzling items in a stew-pan, and anon with grave consideration lifting the cover of a bake-kettle, from whence steam forth indubitable intimations of "something good." A round, black, shining face is hers, so glossy as to suggest the idea that she might have been washed over with white of eggs, like one of her own tea rusks. Her whole plump countenance beams with satisfaction and contentment from under her well-starched checked turban, bearing on it, however, if we must confess it, a little of that tinge of self-consciousness which becomes the first cook of the neighborhood, as Aunt Chloe was universally held and acknowledged to be. . . .

A table, somewhat rheumatic in its limbs, was drawn out in front of the fire, and covered with a cloth, displaying cups and saucers of a decidedly brilliant pattern, with other symptoms of an approaching meal. At this table was seated Uncle Tom, Mr. Shelby's best hand, who, as he is to be the hero of our story, we must daguerreotype for our readers. He was a large, broad-chested, powerfully-made man, of a full glossy black, and a face whose truly African features were characterized by an expression of grave and steady good sense, united with much kindliness and benevolence. There was something about his whole air self-respecting and dignified, yet united with a confiding and humble simplicity.

He was very busily intent at this moment on a slate lying before him, on which he was carefully and slowly endeavoring to accomplish a copy of some letters, in which operation he was overlooked by young Mas'r George, a smart, bright boy of thirteen, who appeared fully to realize the dignity of his position as instructor. . . .

Source: Harriet Beecher Stowe, *Uncle Tom's Cabin* (New York, 1852), chapter 4.

SIGNIFICANCE

Harriet Beecher Stowe will always be remembered primarily as the author of *Uncle Tom's Cabin*, which helped to end slavery in the United States and to spark the bloodiest war in American history. During the 1850's and 1860's, she remained one of the most popular American writers. Many of her works were first serialized in the *Atlantic Monthly* and then published as books, which earned her a steady and comfortable income.

Historians now recognize that Harriet Beecher Stowe's contribution to American history goes beyond these accomplishments. Although one cannot view this traditionally religious woman as a modern feminist, she did play an important role in women's history. Writing was one of the few "respectable" careers open to women in nineteenth century America, because women could write at home and legitimately argue that their work was necessary to supplement family income. It is somewhat ironic that Stowe's fiction, which powerfully affected the course of events outside the "domestic sphere," was written to earn greater respect for women as leaders of the home and family. It is also interesting that a century after Stowe's reputation was at its peak, Betty Friedan's pathbreaking book *The Feminine Mystique* (1963) would attack the central idea of Harriet Beecher Stowe: that women's primary role should be to lead and shape the home and family.

It is a tribute to Harriet Beecher Stowe that Friedan's work was necessary. Stowe softened the harsh Calvinism of her father by emphasizing a religion of love more congenial to women; she also defended a separate "sphere" for female activity in American life. It can be argued that both of these things were necessary to raise the status of women in America. That, in turn, made it easier for other women to demand later the greater freedom that women enjoy in the United States a century after Stowe's death.

—*Ken Wolf*

FURTHER READING

Adams, John R. *Harriet Beecher Stowe*. New York: Twayne, 1963. This short biography emphasizes the connection between Stowe's personality and her writings. Adams sees Stowe as a subservient person who finally declared her independence from domestic restrictions by writing *Uncle Tom's Cabin*.

Ammons, Elizabeth, ed. *Critical Essays on Harriet Beecher Stowe*. Boston: G. K. Hall, 1980. This useful collection contains essays on Stowe by literary critics and modern feminist scholars. Dorothy Berkson's essay "Millennial Politics and the Feminine Fiction of Harriet Beecher Stowe" is particularly good.

Crozier, Alice. *The Novels of Harriet Beecher Stowe*. New York: Oxford University Press, 1969. This study provides the best synopses of Stowe's works. The author stresses Stowe's religious motivation and notes that most of her novels were widely read and respected by educated readers of her day.

Degler, Carl N. *At Odds: Women and the Family in America from the Revolution to the Present*. New York: Oxford University Press, 1980. The passages on Stowe show a self-reliant woman who was equal to her husband in many ways. She managed her own financial affairs, was more interested in her writing than in routine domestic chores, and even gave her husband advice on how to control his sexual urges.

Douglas, Ann. *The Feminization of American Culture*. New York: Doubleday, 1988. The introduction to this work and a later section on Stowe show how she feminized the religion of the Calvinist preachers of her father's generation. Douglas sees Stowe's contribution to American life as an ambiguous one that both helped and hindered her twentieth century sisters.

Hedrick, Joan D. *Harriet Beecher Stowe: A Life*. New York: Oxford University Press, 1994. Definitive biography, using new materials, such as letters and diaries, to offer a fresh perspective on Stowe's life and work. Winner of a 1995 Pulitzer Prize.

Stowe, Harriet Beecher. *Uncle Tom's Cabin*. New York: Bantam Books, 1981. This famous work, often mentioned in textbooks but less often read, offers the best way to acquire an understanding of what was important to Stowe—and to many of her female readers in nineteenth century America. Many editions are available.

White, Barbara A. *The Beecher Sisters*. New Haven, Conn.: Yale University Press, 2003. Recounts the lives of Harriet and her sisters, Catharine and Isabella. Catharine founded the Hartford Female Seminary and published numerous books on religion and women's education; Isabella was active in the women's rights movement. Focuses on Isabella, who has never before been the subject of a biography.

Wilson, Robert Forrest. *Crusader in Crinoline: The Life of Harriet Beecher Stowe*. Reprint. Westport, Conn.: Greenwood Press, 1972. This lengthy biography, originally published in 1941, remains the best single source for a full account of Stowe's life. It must be supplemented with some of the newer studies cited previously.

SEE ALSO: Susan B. Anthony; Henry Ward Beecher; Sarah and Angelina Grimké; Sarah Josepha Hale; Sarah Orne Jewett; Abraham Lincoln; Elizabeth Cady Stanton; Bertha von Suttner.

RELATED ARTICLES in *Great Events from History: The Nineteenth Century, 1801-1900:* September 18, 1850: Second Fugitive Slave Law; 1852: Stowe Publishes *Uncle Tom's Cabin*.

JOHANN STRAUSS
Austrian composer

Strauss built upon the musical achievements of his father and Austrian dance composer Joseph Lanner to raise the waltz to its highest level of development, a point at which it passed from dance music to symphonic music. His achievements in the operetta were less dramatic, for only two of his operettas have received lasting acclaim.

BORN: October 25, 1825; Vienna, Austria
DIED: June 3, 1899; Vienna, Austria
ALSO KNOWN AS: Johann Strauss the Younger; Waltz King
AREA OF ACHIEVEMENT: Music

EARLY LIFE

Johann Strauss (shtrows) was the eldest child of Johann and Anna (Streim) Strauss, both of whom were musically accomplished. Indeed, the father's reputation as a composer, performer, and conductor of waltzes was already established when the younger Strauss was born. The younger Strauss early demonstrated his musical gift when, at the age of six, he played a waltz tune on the piano. Despite the considerable musical talent of all of his sons, the elder Strauss forbade them to pursue their interests, allowing them to play only the piano, not the violin, the instrument essential to waltz composition. Strauss's mother, however, not only preserved his first composition but also successfully circumvented her husband's prohibition against the violin lessons. The conspiracy between son and mother, who provided one of her husband's violins and the money for the lessons, was eventually discovered by the elder Strauss, who destroyed the violin and beat his son.

Although his father had enrolled him in the prestigious Schottengymnasium for four years and the Polytechnikum, where he studied business, for an additional two years, Strauss was able to escape the banking career that his father intended for him when the elder Strauss left his family for Emily Trampusch in 1842. Strauss had secretly studied the violin under Franz Amon, whose position as conductor of one of the Strauss orchestras made him familiar with the elder Strauss's gestures and mannerisms, which the younger Strauss imitated. When Strauss could openly pursue his musical career, he continued his violin studies with Anton Kohlmann, ballet master and violinist at the Kärnthnertortheater, and studied music theory with Joseph Drechsler, organist and composer of church music. Under Drechsler's tutelage

and prodding, Strauss composed a church cantata, though Strauss's real interest was in waltz composition.

Because of his father's stubborn opposition, Strauss encountered many obstacles when he attempted to stage his first concert. The elder Strauss, by suggesting that he would musically boycott any ballroom allowing his son to perform, effectively closed the Viennese musical world to his son. Strauss accordingly went outside the inner city and staged his first concert at Dommayer's Casino at Heitzing, a suburb of Vienna, on October 15, 1844. Despite the somewhat hostile crowd—his father's business manager, Carl Hirsche, had provided tickets to rowdies to disrupt the concert, which consisted of Strauss's own waltz compositions—the *Sinngedichte* (poems of the senses) earned nineteen encores. One reviewer wrote, "Good evening, Father Strauss! Good morning to you, Strauss Junior!"

After his son's triumphant debut, the elder Strauss offered his son a position as concertmaster and assistant conductor, but the offer was refused. The two men effected a reconciliation of sorts, but their essential differences surfaced in 1848, when civil war erupted. The conservative elder Strauss sided with the Royalists, and his son sided with the rebels. Though neither Strauss's political commitment was strong, the change from waltzes to marches did produce some notable music. When the revolt was brutally crushed and Francis Joseph became emperor, the younger Strauss incurred royal displeasure, but his father's fate was worse: a decline in personal popularity, unprofitable tours, depression, and in 1849 death from scarlet fever. With his father's death, the son began a career that would establish him as "the Waltz King."

LIFE'S WORK

After his father's death, Strauss assumed control of his father's orchestra and at his first concert, on October 11, 1849, played Mozart's *Requiem*, thereby winning the loyalty of the Viennese, some of whom had resented his challenge to his father. He also partly atoned for his political "error" of 1848 by his 1854 performance of his popular *Annen-Polka* at the ball prior to Francis Joseph's marriage to Elisabeth von Wittelsbach. During the 1850's, the waltz craze captivated Vienna, and the prolific Strauss produced scores of new waltzes to meet the increasing demand. Although many of the compositions were named for professional associations and societies—the astute Strauss knew how to market his

Johann Strauss. (Library of Congress)

product—only one, the *Acceleration Waltz* (written for the students of the Vienna engineering school), involved a marriage of title and music.

So popular were Strauss's waltzes and so exhausting was his conducting schedule (he conducted daily, and often more than one of his orchestras) that in 1853 he had to convalesce in the Alps. It was this hectic pace that resulted in his drafting his brother Joseph, who was an engineer, as a conductor. (Strauss later persuaded his brother Eduard to assume a similar role.) Because he had been freed from sole responsibility for the family business, Strauss could tour and perform abroad as his father had done. In 1854, he signed a contract to perform yearly in Russia at the resort of Pavlovsk, and he toured Europe with an orchestra between 1856 and 1886.

Aside from his abortive relationship with Olga Smirnitzki, whom he had met in Pavlovsk, Strauss had only casual liaisons with women until 1862, when he met and married Jetty Treffz, an older woman who had been mistress to Baron Moritz Todesco. In a sense, Jetty replaced Anna Strauss. Released in 1864 from all contractual obligations as conductor of the family orchestral business, Strauss turned to composition at the mansion he and Jetty

had bought at Heitzing. The 1860's were marked by Strauss's greatest waltzes, *Tales from the Vienna Woods* and *The Blue Danube*, though the latter, which was originally written for performance with a choral group, was initially a failure, primarily because of the lyrics. When it was later played in Paris as a purely orchestral performance, it was so well received that it became the musical motif of the International Exhibition of 1867.

Strauss's triumph in Paris resulted in an invitation to England in 1867, where he won more critical acclaim. His most notable tour, however, occurred in 1872, when he was paid $100,000 to appear at the World's Peace Jubilee in Boston. There, before an outdoor audience of 100,000 people, he conducted, with the help of many assistant conductors, an orchestra of 1,087 instruments. This musical extravaganza, later repeated on a more modest scale in New York, appalled Strauss, who nevertheless thereby became the richest musician of his time.

Even though the waltz was virtually synonymous with Strauss and Vienna, another musical form began gaining favor among the Viennese. Jacques Offenbach had popularized the operetta, a kind of parodic opera with a socially subversive message. Jetty and Maximilian Steiner, impresario of the Theatre an der Wien, persuaded Strauss to apply his talent to the operetta. Had he remembered the fate of *The Blue Danube*, Strauss might well have foreseen that music without a suitable libretto was doomed to failure. In addition, Strauss seemed an unlikely composer for operetta because he had had practically no exposure to theater and consequently knew little about dramatic composition; he was simply more comfortable with music than with language. On the other hand, he already had found the constraints of the waltz formats incompatible with his developing symphonic interests.

The first operetta was not staged because of casting problems; the next two, with mediocre librettos, were comparative failures with brief runs. However, *Die Fledermaus* (1874; the bat), his third effort, proved to be an enormous success, though its farcical content was at odds with a depressed Vienna, which had just suffered a stock market crash. The operetta, involving a masked ball and a confusion of characters, was adapted from a play and had a good plot; the libretto by Richard Genée and Karl Hafner was exceptional. In fact, *Die Fledermaus* marked the zenith of Strauss's career in operetta, and, though he wrote several more, he did not return to the form until 1885, when *Der Zigeunerbaron* (the gypsy baron) was staged. Like *Die Fledermaus*, *Der Zigeunerbaron* succeeded because the music and the libretto, which was by Ignaz Schnitzer, were complementary rather than at odds.

During the eleven years between his operetta successes, Strauss's life changed dramatically. Jetty, the inspiration for his more serious music and his operetta efforts, died in 1877. After a disastrous five-year marriage to Angelica Dietrich, who was thirty-three years his junior, he married in 1887 Adele Deutsch Strauss, a young widow, with whom he spent his remaining years. In order to divorce Angelica and marry Adele, he had to become a Protestant, surrender his Austrian citizenship, and become a citizen of the Duchy of Saxe-Coburg-Gotha.

Strauss's marriage and his developing friendship with Johannes Brahms made Strauss's last years contented ones. He continued to write operettas, as well as some orchestral waltzes. One of his most notable waltzes was the *Kaiserwaltzer* (1888; emperor waltz), written in celebration of Francis Joseph's forty-year reign. This piece is both waltz and march, suggesting the emperor's glory, and has been regarded as more tone poem than dance. Such was the identification between "the Waltz King" and Francis Joseph that Strauss's death on June 3, 1899, was regarded as the end of a political as well as a musical era.

Significance

The Strauss family's virtual control of the music business in Vienna paralleled the dominance of the Habsburg dynasty, which in the nineteenth century enjoyed one of its most opulent and successful periods. The waltz and the beauty and harmony it represented became a kind of opium of the people, and the Habsburg prosperity created a mood receptive to it. The acknowledged "Waltz King" was the younger Johann Strauss, arguably one of the most Viennese of composers.

Strauss found in the waltz the almost perfect vehicle for his own personality, which had its dark side. Beneath the sweeping vitality and lush sweetness of the waltz was a wistful melancholy especially suited to Strauss. The waltz, however, became a prison for him as he attempted to force his musical inspiration into the tyranny of monotonous three-quarter time. As he developed, absorbing not only the waltz influence from his father and Joseph Lanner but also the more liberating influence of Franz Liszt and Richard Wagner, he was drawn toward the symphonic and away from the demands of the dance industry. His waltzes accordingly changed; the introduction and coda became almost as long as the waltz proper.

For his operettas, Strauss used the work of Jacques Offenbach and Franz von Suppé as the foundation for his

own efforts. In his *Der Zigeunerbaron*, however, he transcended his predecessors and actually gave the operetta a new direction that was followed by others, including Franz Lehár. Strauss, in effect, brought both nineteenth century music forms to their artistic heights, but neither form was to survive the cultural and political upheaval that also accounted for the Habsburgs' demise. Strauss embodied the nineteenth century, and his grave, opposite Schubert's and next to Brahms's in the Central Cemetery in Vienna, testifies to his stature not only in Austria but also in the universal world of music.

—Thomas L. Erskine

Further Reading

Crittenden, Camille. *Johann Strauss and Vienna: Operetta and the Politics of Popular Culture*. New York: Cambridge University Press, 2000. Crittenden describes how, and why, Strauss's operettas expressed Viennese pride and anxiety during the late nineteenth century. Provides a general overview of Viennese operetta, analyzes the interaction between Strauss's operettas and their audience, and discusses Strauss's role as a national icon during his lifetime and the twentieth century.

Fantel, Hans. *The Waltz Kings: Johann Strauss, Father and Son, and Their Romantic Age*. New York: William Morrow, 1972. Although Fantel provides biographies of the two Strausses, he stresses the relationship of music to politics so that the reader has a broad cultural and political context for tracing the evolution of the waltz. The well-written, informal text is well indexed, and Fantel provides a good bibliography, particularly of the extramusical context, and a list of the compositions of father and son.

Gartenberg, Egon. *Johann Strauss: The End of an Era*. University Park: Pennsylvania State University Press, 1974. Places Austria in a broader European political context and provides an interesting account of the predecessors of the waltz. Gartenberg analyzes *Die Fledermaus* in detail and explains why Strauss's operettas, with two exceptions, did not succeed critically. Profusely illustrated, well indexed, and documented; contains bibliographies concerning the Strauss family, as well as the literature and music of the period, the Habsburg dynasty, and the political context.

Jacob, Heinrich E. *Johann Strauss, Father and Son: A Century of Light Music*. Freeport, N.Y.: Books for Libraries Press, 1939. Jacob stresses the conditions in Vienna that facilitated the development of the waltz, relates Strauss's waltzes to other contemporary music, and devotes much attention to the operettas. Although the focus is on the Strauss family, Jacob does discuss the heirs, notably Franz Lehár, to the Strauss tradition.

Pastene, Jerome. *Three-Quarter Time: The Life and Music of the Strauss Family of Vienna.* Westport, Conn.: Greenwood Press, 1971. Pastene divides his book into three parts: Johann Strauss, the father; Johann Strauss, the son; and the other Strauss sons and Lehár. Pastene, himself a conductor, provides lengthy analyses of several major works and also includes a catalog by opus numbers and the works by the four members of the Strauss musical dynasty.

Wechsberg, Joseph. *The Waltz Emperors: The Life and Times and Music of the Strauss Family.* New York: G. P. Putnam's Sons, 1973. Wechsberg discusses the origins of the waltz, defines the era of the waltz as beginning with Joseph Lanner and ending with Strauss's death in 1899, finds Strauss's best waltzes really symphonic music, and explores the psychological side of his subject. The book is profusely illustrated (many of the illustrations are in color) with memorabilia and lithographs.

See also: Johannes Brahms; Fanny Elssler; Engelbert Humperdinck; Franz Liszt; Maximilian; Jacques Offenbach; Richard Wagner.

Related article in *Great Events from History: The Nineteenth Century, 1801-1900:* August 13-17, 1876: First Performance of Wagner's Ring Cycle.

George Edmund Street
English architect

An exceptionally productive and influential architect, Street designed and built the Law Courts in London and was a leading builder of churches in England and Europe during the Gothic Revival.

Born: June 20, 1824; Woodford, Essex, England
Died: December 18, 1881; London, England
Area of achievement: Architecture

Early Life

George Edmund Street was the third son of Thomas Street, a solicitor in London with an office in Philpot Lane. His forebears came from the Worcestershire area of England. George's mother was Mary Anne Millington, Mr. Street's second wife. In 1830, Thomas Street moved his family from London to Camberwell. There, George attended a local school at Mitcham and went on to the Camberwell Collegiate School, from which he was graduated in 1839. Shortly thereafter, in 1840, George went to work for his father at the Philpot Lane office. George did not seem suited for a solicitor's work, however, and he was unhappy there. A few months later, Thomas Street died suddenly, and his office was closed.

George, then unemployed, in the next few months came under the influence of his older brother Thomas, who was an avid sketcher. George began to take up drawing himself and found that he had some talent for it. For a short time he took drawing lessons from Thomas Haseler, a painter, and through this teacher's influence and his mother's encouragement, in 1841 George became a pupil under the architect Owen B. Carter of Winchester. Because formal schools of architecture were in short supply in Victorian England, most future architects learned their profession by apprenticing themselves to an established architect, as George Street did.

In 1844, young Street, having shown enthusiasm for ecclesiastical building, moved to the office of George Gilbert Scott as an assistant. Scott kept Street in his employ for five years but, seeing the young man's potential, also let him begin to work for his own clients, although still from Scott's office.

Life's Work

By 1849, Street had completed architectural work on several churches, including the restoration of St. Peter's in Plymouth. He was now fully prepared to open his own architect's office. Early in his new career, Street, through his church restorations, came to know Samuel Wilberforce, the bishop of Oxford. The bishop was so impressed with Street's hard work and careful planning that he appointed him the diocesan architect. As a result, Street moved to a new home at Wantage, from which he could conduct his work on churches in Oxfordshire.

Street was also a frequent traveler at this time. He first roamed the English countryside with his brother Thomas, sketching church buildings. In 1850 and 1851, he made the first of his foreign tours and especially studied the famous churches of France and Germany.

George Edmund Street. (Library of Congress)

In May of 1852, Street moved his practice to a larger office in Oxford and acquired two pupils, Edmund Sedding and Philip Webb, both of whom would later become noted architects. In 1853, Street was awarded two large contracts: one for a theological college at Cuddesdon for the Anglican Church, and the other for the East Grinstead Sisters' institution. The latter work he did without financial compensation, because his sympathy with the sisters' work was strong.

In 1853, Street completed a very important tour on the Continent. He visited northern Italy, especially to study ancient church architecture. While on all of his tours, Street was a hard worker; he was determined to examine as many buildings as possible each day. In order to achieve this goal, he would tour and sketch all day and then board a train where he would sleep at night while en route to his next destination. All the hours of research that Street expended in Italy paid off well. Besides finding some inspiration for his own architecture, he collected notes for his influential book *Brick and Marble in the Middle Ages: Notes of a Tour in the North of Italy* (1855). Similarly, in 1854, Street toured the churches of northern Germany and wrote several papers on his research there.

When French churchmen planned to build a new cathedral at Lille in 1855, they held an open competition to find the best architect for the work. Such competitions were frequent in Victorian England and Europe. They encouraged many architects to submit designs for new buildings; then the best design was awarded the commission for the project. Runners-up were sometimes given awards as well. Street placed second in the contest at Lille, France.

In 1856, when the British government held an architects' competition for the planning of a new government office building, more than two hundred architects took part. Street's design was one of only seventeen that won premiums. His design was in the Gothic style, of which he was an enthusiastic advocate. England, in the middle of the nineteenth century, was experiencing a Gothic revival, in which the most favored architectural style was to copy and adapt thirteenth century designs for current buildings. Most of Street's work was done in the Gothic style, and he is considered, along with his mentor Sir George Gilbert Scott, to be one of the greatest Gothicists of Victorian England.

According to one estimate, about 80 percent of Street's completed buildings are churches or church-related structures. Some of Street's most powerful and memorable churches include St. Mary Magdalene's in Paddington, St. John's in Torquay, All Saints' in Clifton, and St. James the Less in Westminster. A review of these buildings helps to explain Street's style and his success. St. Mary Magdalene's shows some details of design that point to an influence from northern Italian Gothic. An innovation by Street at All Saints' was the wide nave with its aisles being narrower than usual in the English tradition of church building; these elements were incorporated by the architect to benefit large congregations. Of this group of churches by Street, the most famous, however, is St. James the Less.

St. James the Less was basically a Gothic-style church, but it also had picturesque aspects. The picturesque style of architecture emphasized the harmony of buildings with their surroundings (which was especially popular in England during the early nineteenth century). This particular church also shows Street's Continental influences at work. In 1862, when St. James the Less was completed, architectural critics especially noted its foreign aspects. The touches on this church reflect designs from northern Italy and were appreciated by the critics, who believed that they enhanced the beauty of the building. A tower 134 feet in height is the most breathtaking aspect of St. James the Less. It is of Italian design and a departure from the slender steeples of previous Victorian English churches. Street also personally designed the interior of St. James; he planned the tile work that appeared in the aisles, as well as the pillar carvings that depict Christ's miracles. In this area of fine design in architecture, Street was considered a master with an artist's touch. He also was effective in blending various architectural styles.

Despite a considerable amount of church work throughout the 1860's, Street found time to continue his tours in Europe. Between 1861 and 1863, he completed three study trips to Spain. The result was his fine book *Some Account of Gothic Architecture in Spain* (1865); in addition to writing this text, Street also provided his own drawings for its illustrations.

In 1866, Street entered a famous and controversial competition for a new public building in London. This was the contest to design the new Law Courts to be located on the Strand. This particular architectural competition provoked controversy because Street was awarded the contract even though he did not officially win the competition. A committee of lawyers, for whose use the Law Courts was intended, liked best the designs of Alfred Waterhouse. The assigned architectural judges thought that Street should design the building itself and that Edward M. Barry should do the interior decoration (a split contract). Finally, in June of 1868, Street alone was commissioned to build the Law Courts, only after much discussion.

Street had some obstacles to surmount in finishing the Law Courts: He was dealing with government officials who kept a strict and parsimonious budget, he was not the favorite architect of the lawyers, and the building itself was an enormously large project. Street would draft in ink and by hand some three thousand designs for the exterior and the interior of the Law Courts. He was also still heavily involved in ecclesiastical building all through the 1860's and 1870's, while work on the Law Courts progressed.

The Law Courts, completed the year after Street died, received some harsh criticism from the lawyers who used them, as well as from Street's fellow architects. Although the building's complex yet enriching exterior designs form an exquisite picturesque grouping along the Strand, some critics believed that the exterior was too diverse, appearing as several buildings rather than as one unit. Also, lawyers complained that the acoustics inside were of poor quality, making their work more difficult. One feature almost everyone admired was the majestic great vaulted hall of 230 feet by 82 feet that Street made

the focal point of the building's interior. This dignified hall was an example of the Victorian Gothic style at its best.

Street worked for the dioceses of York, Winchester, and Ripon during the 1860's and 1870's, in addition to the Oxford diocese. He undertook many church restorations, most notably the cathedral at Bristol, where he rebuilt the nave. In 1871, he also restored York Minster and Carlisle churches; at the latter he was required to rehabilitate a fratry that dated to the fifteenth century. After Street built his own home in 1873 at Holmbury in Surrey, he became active in the local parish. As a result, he designed and built, at his own expense, the church of St. Mary in Holmbury.

Along with all this strenuous work, Street also suffered from personal tragedies during the 1870's. His wife, Mariquita Proctor Street, to whom he had been married on June 17, 1852, died in 1874. Their marriage had produced a son in 1855, Augustus Edmund Street, who worked with and later succeeded his father in their architectural office. On January 11, 1876, Street married Jessie Holland, but sadly, she died that same year. He remained a widower for the rest of his life. After suffering two paralyzing strokes, Street died in London on December 18, 1881, at the age of fifty-seven.

SIGNIFICANCE

George Edmund Street enjoyed a highly productive and influential career as an architect. He was an innovator in church design and made a strong impression in English Victorian architectural circles. He was a forceful member of the Ecclesiological Society, a frequent contributor to its journal, *The Ecclesiologist*, and a celebrated lecturer on matters of decoration, style, and taste in architecture. He was elected to the prestigious Royal Society in 1871 and served as its president during the year before his death.

Street also enjoyed a career as a church builder throughout Europe. He designed and constructed churches for American communities in Paris and in Rome and for English communities in Genoa, Lausanne, Mürren, and Rome. In 1878, in recognition of his outstanding designs on display at the Paris Exhibition, Street was awarded the Knighthood of the Legion of Honor in France. He was also given membership in the Royal Academy at Vienna, Austria.

Only one year before his death, Street had the honor of being appointed as professor of architecture at the Royal Academy in England. He also made a lasting impact on the several students he had trained in his office; the group included Philip Webb, J. D. and Edmund Sedding (brothers), Norman Shaw, and William Morris (the founder of the Arts and Crafts movement in England).

For all of his many accomplishments in building and his lasting contributions to English architecture and decoration, George Edmund Street is immortalized in a statue by H. H. Armstead in the Law Courts. He is depicted as a long-legged craftsperson, seated, engaged in supervising a task. Street here has a long face with a high forehead, further highlighted by his baldness. He also sports a long, full beard. He gazes down, engrossed in his work as he was in life.

—Patricia E. Sweeney

FURTHER READING

Dixon, Roger, and Stefan Muthesius. *Victorian Architecture*. New York: Oxford University Press, 1978. A good survey of Victorian architecture. Street is covered in detail in a section on church building. The 250 illustrations include many building plans and photographs from the Victorian era. An appendix lists the individual works of more than three hundred architects.

Eastlake, Charles. *A History of the Gothic Revival in England*. London: Longmans, Green, 1872. Eastlake discusses in detail the phenomenon of the Gothic architectural style in Victorian England. He reviews Street's place in the revival and his churches at length. An appendix contains a chart of famous buildings (and their outstanding features) by several architects, including Street. A very useful book.

Fergusson, James. *History of the Modern Styles of Architecture*. London: John Murray, 1891. Fergusson was a contemporary of Street and a harsh critic of the design of the Law Courts. The information on Street is found in the second volume of this two-volume set. Street's fine work on churches is also highlighted.

Richards, J. M. *The National Trust Book of English Architecture*. New York: W. W. Norton, 1981. In this handsome volume intended for the general reader, Richards discusses Street's church designs to some extent but focuses more attention on the Law Courts competition. Includes many black-and-white photographs, as well as color plates, all of excellent quality. A glossary is included.

Stalley, Roger, ed. *George Edmund Street and the Restoration of Christ Church Cathedral, Dublin*. Dublin: Four Courts Press, 2000. Street was especially proud of his restoration of the medieval Christ Church Cathedral, believing he saved the building from further deterioration. Stalley examines what Street meant by "restoration," and how contemporary Dubliners responded to the project.

Street, Arthur Edmund. *Memoir of George Edmund Street, R.A., 1824-1881*. London: John Murray, 1888. The author was the architect's son; this account provides both a discussion of his father's career and a list of his works. Six lectures that George Street gave as a professor form an appendix.

Summerson, John. *Victorian Architecture: Four Studies in Evaluation*. New York: Columbia University Press, 1970. This volume is based on a series of four lectures delivered in 1968. By way of introduction, Summerson describes the nature of Victorian architecture in general. He analyzes in detail the style and design of St. James the Less, Street's famous church in London. Includes many black-and-white photographs, featuring interiors as well as exteriors.

Watkin, David. *English Architecture: A Concise History*. London: Thames and Hudson, 1979. A well-illustrated text, in which Watkin gives a precise account of Street's career and buildings. He also explains the various architectural influences found in Street's works. Watkin places Street in perspective as a major British church builder. A good bibliography is included.

SEE ALSO: Sir Charles Barry; William Morris; John Nash; Sir George Gilbert Scott.

RELATED ARTICLE in *Great Events from History: The Nineteenth Century, 1801-1900:* 1884: New Guilds Promote the Arts and Crafts Movement.

ANTONIO JOSÉ DE SUCRE
South American military leader and nationalist leader

Although little remembered outside South America, Sucre was one of the foremost military and political leaders in that continent's struggle to achieve independence from European rule, and he played an important role in the creation of modern Venezuela, Colombia, Ecuador, Peru, and Bolivia.

BORN: February 3, 1795; Cumaná, New Granada (now Venezuela)

DIED: June 4, 1830; in the Berruecos Mountains, Gran Colombia (now on the border of Ecuador and Colombia)

ALSO KNOWN AS: Antonio José de Sucre Alcalá (full name)

AREA OF ACHIEVEMENT: Military

EARLY LIFE

Antonio José de Sucre (SEW-krah) was a member of the fourth generation of his family to reside in Cumaná, a port city located on the far eastern coast of present-day Venezuela. His great-grandfather, Carlos de Sucre, re-established the family in northern South America after having served as an official of the Spanish crown in Cartagena and Havana. Carlos's son, Antonio, married a descendant of a conquistador family and served as a colonel in the royal Spanish infantry. Vicente, son of Antonio, served first as a lieutenant of the Spanish army and, after the independence movement began, as a colonel in the newly formed revolutionary army. Vicente fathered a large family. Antonio José was his seventh son.

The Spanish Empire collapsed in 1808, one of the victims of French emperor Napoleon Bonaparte's expansionist policies. This event accelerated the aspirations of independence that had developed among the Creole element within the Spanish colonies. The Creoles were the Spaniards born in the Americas. They felt that they had been relegated to a second-class status by the Spanish crown. Positions of power and importance were reserved for the *Peninsulares*—those Spaniards born in the mother country.

Young Sucre supported this movement for liberation and subsequently devoted his entire life to its service. As early as his sixteenth birthday, he followed the tradition of his family and became a soldier. After a brief stint at a Caracas military school, he returned home, joined the rebel army, and was given command of a company of engineers. From 1813 to 1817, he fought in a series of campaigns against royalist forces. Sucre's military ac-complishments earned him the rank of general in the rebel army at the early age of twenty-three.

LIFE'S WORK

In 1819, Sucre met Simón Bolívar, a fellow Venezuelan who would go down in the annals of Latin American history as the "Liberator." The two formed a lifelong friendship, and Sucre would prove to be Bolívar's most loyal and trusted supporter in the many military campaigns that followed in Colombia, Venezuela, Ecuador, Peru, and Bolivia.

Sucre had earned a good reputation as a military leader in the liberation of both Venezuela and Colombia from the Spanish crown. The struggle against the royalist forces had been bloody, with both sides killing prisoners even after surrender. Two of Sucre's own brothers were shot while being held as prisoners of war, and a third was assassinated while a patient in a hospital. Moreover, the campaigns were made doubly difficult by fratricidal fights within the ranks of the rebels themselves, a situation that would continue throughout the struggle for independence.

However, it was for his accomplishments under the direction of Bolívar in the emancipation of Ecuador, Peru, and Bolivia that Sucre acquired his greatest fame. Bolívar sent his young charge into Ecuador to emancipate that country, which was no small compliment to Sucre, because Bolívar had planned to lead the campaign himself. Sucre proved his military ability. Although he was operating in unfamiliar territory—the mountains of the Andes—and commanding an army of his own for the first time, he defeated the royalist forces, first at Yaguachi and then at Mount Pichincha on the outskirts of Quito. He broke the pattern of killing prisoners by offering the royalists free passage from the area if they surrendered the city itself. The Spaniards accepted the offer and left Quito. The power of the Spaniards in Ecuador had ended. Bolívar promoted Sucre to major general and made him governor of Quito.

Hardly had Sucre commenced the task of organizing Ecuador when Bolívar sent him on a new assignment to Lima to command the Colombian forces in the area and to protect the newly won territory from reconquest by a new Spanish army. The task was further complicated by infighting among the Peruvian officials themselves, as well as by Peruvian, Chilean, and Argentine military commanders who failed to achieve agreement on how to meet the new threat.

Sucre persisted despite the problems within the rebel camp. On December 7, 1824, he met the opposing Spanish commander, Viceroy José de La Serna y Hinojosa, in a battle on the Plain of Ayacucho, some eleven thousand feet above sea level. This would be the deciding battle for control of Peru. La Serna, thinking that he had the patriot forces trapped, launched what turned out to be a disastrous attack on Sucre's well-positioned forces. Despite a royalist force that was one and one-half times as large as his own, Sucre's superior battlefield tactics won the day. He accomplished this goal in just one hour of intense fighting. The royalists lost twice as many men in the battle as did Sucre. The Spanish prisoners that were taken, including Viceroy La Serna himself, outnumbered the patriots' own total forces. Ayacucho was to be Sucre's greatest military victory. He was named grand marshal of Ayacucho as a result. The Spanish hold on South America was broken forever.

Sucre's next task involved securing the independence of Upper Peru. He marched into the province in January of 1825. Bolívar charged him with restoring order to an area that was in a state of virtual anarchy. Sucre had to assume the role of governor and establish a framework for a stable political structure. The new grand marshal had protested to Bolívar on more than one occasion that such a task was beyond him, that he was a soldier and lacked the necessary formal education to carry on such work. Nevertheless, Bolívar completely trusted his loyal subordinate and prevailed upon him to undertake the task.

The hero of Ayacucho faced an initial problem in the matter of jurisdiction of the area that he had entered. Upper Peru had been assigned to Buenos Aires, not Peru, so he had, technically at least, entered foreign territory. Nevertheless, Sucre took up the task of organizing the newly acquired territory. He issued a decree that dictated the formation of a representative assembly of local citizens to adopt a form of government satisfactory to the constituency, including a guarantee of provincial autonomy if they desired it. Bolívar criticized his old comrade-in-arms for this action, stating that it inferred the right to sovereignty by the Upper Peruvians rather than simply provincial status. Sucre refused to back down in the matter and proceeded with plans to create a truly representative democracy rather than one dominated solely by the upper class. Bolívar reluctantly sanctioned the formation of the assembly and placed Upper Peru under Sucre's political authority on a temporary basis.

The assembly convened, named the new country Bolivia in honor of Bolívar, and called on Sucre to assume

the role of supreme ruler in Bolívar's absence. Sucre agreed with some hesitation. As he had so often stated publicly, he did not like political life. Shortly thereafter, Bolívar himself visited the new country and promised to use his influence with the Peruvian legislature to promote Bolivian independence. He recommended a series of democratic reforms as well, leaving their implementation to Sucre after his departure.

Sucre then began the challenging process of developing an administrative structure for the country. He introduced a tentative constitution, established ministries, laid out boundaries for departments, and secured, by treaty with Peru, an outlet for Bolivia to the Pacific Ocean. This vital corridor was seized by Chile later during the subsequent War of the Pacific.

Sucre organized a judicial system separate from the political establishment. He introduced a merit system for government employees and a postal program with regular communications to both Lima and Buenos Aires. The marshal also encouraged private enterprise by setting up a favorable economic climate for the country's mining industry.

After completing this initial labor for the new country, Sucre sought to be relieved from further responsibility. Instead, the new congress prevailed on him to accept

Antonio José de Sucre. (Library of Congress)

the office of the country's first president, in spite of Sucre's personal preferences to the contrary. On October 9, 1826, he took the oath of office. Sucre's two-year term turned out to be a difficult one. Bolivia proved hard to govern, given the continuous unrest that was generated among its various political factions. Sucre himself suffered a serious wound to his right arm in quelling an incipient revolt launched by a group of discontented soldiers stationed at Chuquisaca. The damage was so severe that Bolivia's first president remained politically crippled throughout the remainder of his life. He was required, at one point, to defend the new country against an incursion by his former allies, the Peruvians. Sucre left office in 1828 with evident relief.

Now a former soldier and a former politician, Sucre returned to Quito, Ecuador, married Doña Mariana Carcelón y Larrea, marquise of Solanda, and entered into private life. His new spouse, a wealthy heir, owned substantial estates in and around Quito. Sucre contented himself with their management. His daughter, Teresa, was born the following year. He continued to maintain regular correspondence with his old Venezuelan comrade Bolívar, expressing sorrow at the political turmoil that existed throughout the countries that they had played such a major role in liberating.

The fratricide that plagued the independence movement throughout the campaigns against the Spaniards continued into the period of nation-building that followed. Sucre himself turned out to be a victim of this tragedy when, on June 4, 1830, while on his way through the Berruecos Mountains of Ecuador bound for Quito, the thirty-five-year-old grand marshal of Ayacucho was ambushed and assassinated. His death was charged to a political rival, José María Obando, commander of the army in nearby Pasto, although the latter never paid for the crime. Sucre lies buried today in the cathedral at Quito, Ecuador.

SIGNIFICANCE

Although Antonio José de Sucre played a subordinate role to the more famous liberator, Simón Bolívar, he was instrumental in the accomplishment of many of Bolívar's military successes. He was a talented soldier who lacked the charisma of his famous leader, but he accomplished much with his quiet, determined, and skilled leadership. His tenure as the first president of Bolivia gave that new country a set of laws and a politi-

cal structure that launched it on the road to permanent statehood.

—*Carl Henry Marcoux*

FURTHER READING

Harvey, Robert. *Liberators: Latin America's Struggle for Independence, 1810-1830.* Woodstock, N.Y.: Overlook Press, 2000. Chronicles the battle for independence in South America, focusing on Sucre and other liberation leaders.

Hoover, John P. *Admirable Warrior: Marshal Sucre, Fighter for South American Independence.* Detroit: Blaine-Ethridge, 1977. This is a well-written, uncomplicated biography of Sucre by an author who saw his subject as an unselfish patriot in the cause of the South American liberation from Spain.

Lopez Contreras, Eleazar. *Synopsis of the Military Life of Sucre.* New York: H. R. Elliot, 1942. This brief biography by a former fellow Venezuelan general emphasizes the military aspects of Sucre's career.

Lynch, John. *The Spanish American Revolutions, 1808-1826.* 2d ed. New York: W. W. Norton, 1986. Lynch gives an overview of all the South American battles for independence, providing a background for the independence movement to which Sucre committed his life.

Robertson, William Spence. *Rise of the Spanish-American Republics.* New York: Free Press, 1946. Chapter 8 is devoted solely to a detailed biography of Sucre.

Rodríguez O, Jaime E. *The Independence of Spanish America.* New York: Cambridge University Press, 1998. Covers the wars for independence in Mexico and South America between 1808 and 1826, including information about Sucre's role in the independence movement.

Sherwell, Guillermo A. *Antonio José Sucre, Hero and Martyr of American Independence.* Washington, D.C.: Byron and Adams, 1924. Sherwell's flattering biography emphasizes the positive characteristics of Sucre: his honesty, fairness, and humility, even when he led armies of thousands and held a country's presidency.

SEE ALSO: Simón Bolívar; Bernardo O'Higgins; José de San Martín.

RELATED ARTICLES in *Great Events from History: The Nineteenth Century, 1801-1900:* January 18, 1817-July 28, 1821: San Martín's Military Campaigns; September 7, 1822: Brazil Becomes Independent.

LOUIS SULLIVAN
American architect

Remembered as the primary creator of the modern skyscraper, Sullivan was a pioneer in the artful design of tall buildings and in the development of distinctly American architecture.

BORN: September 3, 1856; Boston, Massachusetts
DIED: April 14, 1924; Chicago, Illinois
ALSO KNOWN AS: Louis Henry Sullivan (full name)
AREA OF ACHIEVEMENT: Architecture

EARLY LIFE

Louis Henry Sullivan was the son of Adrienne List Sullivan, who had been born in Geneva, Switzerland, to a Swiss mother and a German father. Her family emigrated to Boston in 1851, where she met the man who was to become Louis's father, an Irish immigrant dancing master named Patrick Sullivan. During his infancy, Louis and his parents shared a house with his mother's family, in part from financial necessity. Louis formed a strong attachment to his grandparents, particularly to his grandfather, a former teacher.

When the two families separated in 1861, the Sullivans took up residence briefly at the seaside in Folly Cove, Massachusetts. There, Sullivan developed a great love of the sea that would remain with him into maturity. Louis was reluctant to leave the life of rambling on the rocky coast to start school in Boston in 1862, and there is some evidence that it was his strong rebellion against first grade at the Brimmer School that prompted his parents to send him to live again with his grandparents, who had since moved to the country themselves. There, Louis continued to find classroom learning tedious but enjoyed wandering the countryside and learning from his grandfather, who was tolerant of his questions and of absenteeism from school.

Rebelliousness toward formal education, faith in his own interests and instincts, and a conviction that learning was better accomplished through observation of nature and close interaction with a master would characterize the rest of Sullivan's educational career. By the age of twelve, he was already so fixed in his ambition to become an architect that he chose not to accompany his parents when they moved to Chicago, but rather to live with his grandparents near Boston, where he believed he could get a superior education.

Without completing high school, Sullivan gained admission to the Massachusetts Institute of Technology at the age of sixteen, but within the year he became disillu-

sioned with the rigidity and classicism of the architecture program there and sought more practical training, working for the Philadelphia architect Frank Furness. Sullivan's later work showed the influence of both Furness, who was noted for his ability to subsume detail into an overall composition, and the Philadelphia Functionalists, architects of commercial buildings who emphasized structure and height; nevertheless, Sullivan moved on quickly to Chicago, where he worked in the office of another prominent architectural master of the day, William Le Baron Jenney.

In 1874, Sullivan made another, characteristically brief, attempt to gain academic training in architecture. Against stiff competition, he won admission to the prestigious École des Beaux Arts in Paris, only to remain enrolled for less than a year. Despite its brevity, this experience shaped his method of working throughout his life; it was at the École des Beaux Arts that Sullivan learned the "esquisse," or sketch, method of design, whereby the architect, after carefully considering a problem, prepares a rapid drawing that becomes the fixed basis for all future work on the project. Sullivan used this technique throughout his career, on one occasion completing the initial sketch for one of his most famous works, the Wainwright Building, in less than three minutes.

LIFE'S WORK

The period of Sullivan's most important contributions to American architecture began in 1883 when he formed a partnership with the German-born Dankmar Adler, a structural engineer. Sullivan had begun collaborating with Adler on a freelance basis after his return to Chicago in 1875. Only four years earlier, Chicago had been devastated by the great fire, so there was much architectural work to be had. The partners concurred in their preference for designing public buildings, and as the men gained fame, these became an ever-increasing proportion of their commissions, ultimately adding up to at least two-thirds of their completed works.

Adler, who had both technical genius and the ability to work with clients, was the perfect complement to the artistic and sometimes temperamental Sullivan. The most illustrious product of their collaboration was the massive Auditorium Building, erected between 1886 and 1890 at a cost of three million dollars to house the Chicago Opera Festival. The building took up an entire city block and rose to seventeen stories in a massive tower. When the building was completed, Adler and Sullivan took up offices in the top two floors of the tower, and it was there that the young Frank Lloyd Wright worked as personal assistant to Sullivan until 1893, at which time the two men had a falling out over Wright's taking on freelance design work, in defiance of the terms of his contract with Adler and Sullivan. Despite the ill will on which they parted, Wright acknowledged Sullivan as his master in his autobiography.

Adler and Sullivan's success with the Auditorium Building led to other commissions, and in increasing numbers, these were outside Chicago. Adler, because of his expertise in acoustics, was invited to consult on the design of Carnegie Hall in New York City, and the firm was hired to build a new opera house in Pueblo, Colorado. In 1890, they were asked to design the Wainwright Building in St. Louis, an office tower that first illustrated Sullivan's ability to give the tall building an artful and coherent structure.

In 1895, the firm dissolved with Adler's retirement from architecture to work for an elevator company and earn a regular salary, a step necessitated by a period of

economic depression in the country that left Sullivan and Adler with few design commissions. The two men parted with some hard feelings that were intensified by Sullivan's claiming sole credit for the last building they designed, perhaps the most magnificent of their skyscrapers, the Guaranty Building in Buffalo, New York.

The last twenty years of Sullivan's life were spent in increasing hardship, isolation, and embitterment; his marriage at the age of forty-two to a much younger woman ended after ten years. In the midst of another national depression that left him with little work, Sullivan was forced to sell most of his possessions in order to make a settlement with his estranged wife. Included in the sale was the vacation home he had designed for himself on the sea at Ocean Springs, Mississippi; the house was revolutionary in its simple, horizontal design that took maximum advantage of the ocean setting, while offering protection from summer heat. At this retreat, Sullivan had designed elaborate rose gardens and again displayed the love of nature and the sea that he had first manifested as a boy.

In his last years, Sullivan's only commissions were for a series of eight small banks in midwestern cities. Although they were not immediately recognized as masterpieces, these structures display the balance of contradictory impulses that is characteristic of Sullivan's genius. They are brick structures whose simple mass is offset by intricate decoration, concentrated at points of interest, highlighting either the entrance or the flat roof line. At this time, Sullivan also expressed his aesthetic philosophy in writing, completing his *The Autobiography of an Idea* only days before his death on April 14, 1924.

SIGNIFICANCE

Sullivan worked in a period of aesthetic ferment, at a time when American artists were attempting to discover a national style and to break free from European tradition. Sullivan, who believed that the architect should be "a poet and an interpreter of the national life of his time," expressed his democratic convictions in his preference for designing public buildings, in his inviting and encompassing entrances—most notably the famous golden doors of the Transportation Building that he designed for the Columbian Exposition—and in his use of humble native plants such as corn husks, weeds, and grasses in his design motifs.

The development of steel frame construction and of the elevator made the construction of skyscrapers a possibility and introduced a range of new design difficulties, notably how to make such buildings light and how to or-

Louis Sullivan. (The Granger Collection, New York)

ganize their facades so as to create aesthetic wholes rather than agglomerations, which Sullivan was the first to master. He pioneered in the treatment of the exterior of such buildings as a skin through which their structure could be perceived, and he applied his famous principle, "form follows function," to the design of the facade of the skyscraper, arguing that it should reflect the functional tripartite division of such buildings into an entry level or base, a stack of office tiers, and an attic that would house machinery. Sullivan's theory of the skyscraper was articulated not only in his most successful buildings, such as the Guaranty Building in Buffalo, but also in his influential essay, "The Tall Office Building Artistically Considered."

During the first half of the twentieth century, Sullivan was largely respected for his modernism. The increasing simplicity of his overall designs was praised, while his profuse surface ornamentation was largely ignored, or was considered to be a regrettable remnant of nineteenth century taste. During the 1970's, however, with the reawakening of interest in Art Nouveau and the contemporary British Arts and Crafts Movement, reassessment of Sullivan's contribution also began, and an appreciation for the contradictory elements of his work arose.

—*Patricia Sharpe*

FURTHER READING

Bush-Brown, Albert. *Louis Sullivan*. New York: George Braziller, 1960. A brief but informative overview of Sullivan's life and work containing many excellent illustrations, showing interior and exterior views of many of his most famous buildings.

Kaufman, Edgar, Jr., ed. *Louis Sullivan and the Architecture of Free Enterprise*. Chicago: Art Institute, 1956. The exhibition catalog includes illustrations and a discussion of many of Sullivan's major works.

Manieri Elia, Mario. *Louis Henry Sullivan*. Translated by Anthony Shugaar and Caroline Green. New York: Princeton Architectural Press, 1996. Overview of Sullivan's life and work, placing his buildings within a historical and theoretical context. Contains black-and-white drawings, plans, and photographs.

Menocal, Narciso G. *Architecture as Nature: The Transcendental Idea of Louis Sullivan*. Madison: University of Wisconsin Press, 1981. This study of the ideas underlying Sullivan's design work, written by an architectural historian, emphasizes his connections to nineteenth century American thought.

Morrison, Hugh. *Louis Sullivan: Prophet of Modern Architecture*. Introduction and revised list of buildings by Timothy Samuelson. New York: W. W. Norton, 2001. Originally published in 1935, this groundbreaking work was the first full-length biography of Sullivan. It focuses on the historical and intellectual context in which Sullivan's work was accomplished.

Sprague, Paul E. *The Drawings of Louis Henry Sullivan: A Catalogue of the Frank Lloyd Wright Collection at the Avery Architectural Library*. Princeton, N.J.: Princeton University Press, 1978. This catalog emphasizes Sullivan's skill as a draftsman and facilitates study of his design methods.

Sullivan, Louis Henry. *The Autobiography of an Idea*. New York: American Institute of Architects, 1924. This embittered intellectual autobiography, written in the third person late in the architect's life, is as revealing in its omissions as it is in its often unreliable narrative of events.

_____. *Kindergarten Chats*. In *The Interstate Architect and Builder*, 2-3 (February 16, 1901-February 8, 1902). Reprint. New York: Dover Press, 1980. This extended Socratic dialogue on architecture conducted with a younger colleague, reputedly modeled on Frank Lloyd Wright, was originally published in fifty-two installments.

Twombly, Robert. *Louis Sullivan: His Life and Work*. New York: Viking Press, 1986. This well-researched study corrects misinformation provided in Sullivan's autobiography and in books by other writers. It emphasizes Sullivan's achievements in the context of American architectural history.

Van Zanten, David. *Sullivan's City: The Meaning of Ornament for Louis Sullivan*. Photographs by Cervin Robinson. New York: W. W. Norton, 2000. Focuses on the evolution of Sullivan's use of ornamentation from his earliest skyscrapers to his later buildings.

Wright, Frank Lloyd. *An Autobiography*. New York: Duell, Sloan and Pearce, 1943. In chapter 2, Wright recounts his experiences working as Sullivan's assistant.

SEE ALSO: Charles Bulfinch; Daniel Hudson Burnham; James Buchanan Eads; Henry Hobson Richardson.

RELATED ARTICLES in *Great Events from History: The Nineteenth Century, 1801-1900:* March 31, 1889: Eiffel Tower Is Dedicated; May 1-October 30, 1893: Chicago World's Fair.

CHARLES SUMNER
American politician

Through the quarter of a century that he served in the U.S. Senate, Sumner was the most significant proponent in high public office of equal rights and equal opportunities for black Americans.

BORN: January 6, 1811; Boston, Massachusetts
DIED: March 11, 1874; Washington, D.C.
AREAS OF ACHIEVEMENT: Government and politics, social reform

EARLY LIFE

The son of a puritanical father, a Boston lawyer and politician, and his severe, distant mother, who was preoccupied with rearing his eight younger brothers and sisters, Charles Sumner received little affection from his parents. Shy and inhibited, young Sumner avoided outdoor games in favor of solitude and books. After studying at the Boston Latin School during the early 1820's, he attended Harvard College, from which he was graduated in 1830 at the age of nineteen. At six feet, two inches in height, weighing only 120 pounds, Sumner was ungainly, amiable, studious, humorless, and nervous near women.

Sumner was graduated from the Harvard Law School in 1834, but, temperamentally unsuited to his father's profession, he was unable to establish a successful practice. In December, 1837, he abruptly left Boston for Europe, where he spent three years in travel, living mostly on borrowed money. Letters of introduction from friends of his father procured for him invitations to visit eminent jurists, writers, and political leaders in Great Britain and France, many of whom were favorably impressed by the young New Englander's good manners and eager idealism.

Arriving home in May, 1840, Sumner gloried in his sudden prominence as one of the few Americans during that era who had enjoyed social success in Europe. He volubly recapitulated his triumphs in Boston drawing rooms while his law practice languished. As his celebrity diminished during the early 1840's, however, Sumner became increasingly moody, suspicious, and sensitive. In 1844, he suffered a breakdown.

LIFE'S WORK

The crisis eventually passed. Ardent involvement in social reform movements was Sumner's therapy for recovering from his depression. Embracing the cause of prison reform, he soon divided the local penal improvement society into warring factions when he tried to replace its

longtime secretary with his friend Francis Lieber. As a member of the Peace Society, he used an Independence Day address in 1845 not only to denounce all wars but also to attack personally the uniformed militia members in his audience. Such exhibitions of tactless self-righteousness soon made Sumner a social outcast in Boston. Nevertheless, the pugnacious eloquence with which he assailed established institutions brought him many admirers outside his immediate circle.

In time, Sumner confined his attempts at social regeneration almost exclusively to the antislavery movement. By the mid-1840's, he had begun to give speeches and publish articles condemning the South's peculiar institution as a national evil, which Congress ought eventually to abolish. Following the admission of Texas to the Union in 1845, Sumner joined a group of "Young Whigs" in Massachusetts, including Charles F. Adams, Richard H. Dana, Jr., John G. Palfrey, and Henry Wilson, who challenged the Boston Whig oligarchy, led by Congressman Robert Winthrop and Senator Daniel Webster, for collaborating in the aggrandizements of southern slaveholders. Joining for the first time in party politics, Sumner helped edit the antislavery newspaper published by this group. His bitter denunciations of the Mexican War further alienated the Boston Brahmins but drew praise from northern abolitionists and peace advocates, who characterized their new spokesperson's relentless vituperation as high moral courage.

After the Mexican War, Sumner became a candidate for Congress on the ticket of the Free-Soil Party, but he lost the 1848 election to Winthrop by a large margin. Two years later, running for the same office, he received less than five hundred votes. Once again, he seemed a failure.

Early in 1851, however, a coalition of Democrats and Free-Soil Party members in the Massachusetts legislature elected Sumner to the U.S. Senate. Cautious at first, he did not make the first of many Senate speeches against slavery until August 26, 1852. Soon, however, he was trading denunciations and insults with spokespeople for the slaveholding aristocracy, while other northern senators spoke circumspectly or remained silent. His combativeness produced a surge of sentiment in his favor throughout the North, while he became a hated symbol of radical abolitionism in the South. In 1855, seeking political allies, he joined the Massachusetts Republican Party, recently established.

Sumner's most famous Senate speech, which was delivered on May 19, 1856, was entitled "The Crime Against Kansas." For three hours, he denounced what he called Stephen Douglas's swindle, the Kansas-Nebraska Act of 1854, and berated both its author and his former Senate seatmate, Andrew P. Butler of South Carolina. Continuing his indictment on the following day, he labeled Douglas a loathsome animal, and he called Butler a liar and a madman. On May 22, South Carolina congressman Preston Brooks, avenging the wrong to his kinsman Butler, used his cane to beat Sumner senseless on the Senate floor.

Rendered an invalid by his wounds, Sumner became a martyr in the North, his empty seat in the Senate a convenient symbol for Massachusetts Republicans in the 1856 presidential election campaign. John C. Frémont led their ticket to a statewide sweep, and Sumner was overwhelmingly reelected to the U.S. Senate in January, 1857.

For the next three years, Sumner made only rare appearances in the halls of Congress. Most of that time he spent in Europe, alternating between ineffectual treatments by physicians and extensive touring and social engagements. Not until June 4, 1860, did he feel well enough to deliver a substantial speech in the Senate. Entitled "Barbarism of Slavery," it was his main contribution to Abraham Lincoln's successful presidential campaign, an effusion of vituperation against the slaveholders whom Sumner held responsible for his difficulties, both physical and emotional.

To the southern threat of secession, Sumner retorted that there could be no compromise with slavery. For a time he hoped that the withdrawal of southerners from Congress would make possible the acquisition by the United States of Canada. As for the cotton states, he was quite willing to let them depart. As his former friends and benefactors Senator William H. Seward of New York and Congressman Charles F. Adams of Massachusetts struggled along with others to construct a principled compromise designed to avert civil war, Sumner accused them of obliquity and labeled them Ishmaelites. He was willing to relinquish territory, he said, but he would never barter principle. He tried to prevent the appointment of Adams as Lincoln's minister to Great Britain and to undermine Seward's direction of U.S. foreign policy as secretary of state. Indeed, he worked covertly for the next two years to cause Seward's ouster from the cabinet in order to obtain the State Department for himself, but Lincoln greatly valued the services of the New Yorker and refused to give him up.

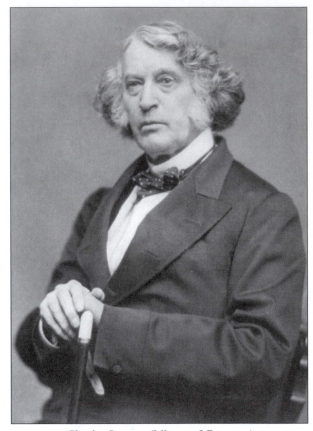

Charles Sumner. (Library of Congress)

For the next eleven years, Sumner served as chairman of the Senate Foreign Relations Committee. He believed that his should be the decisive voice on U.S. foreign policy. Using spies in the State Department such as the eccentric Adam Gurowski, denouncing Seward to foreign diplomats and journalists in Washington, and criticizing him to highly placed correspondents abroad, Sumner worked surreptitiously to appease the antidemocratic governments of European nations. His object was to avoid foreign complications, but his methods actually exacerbated them.

An example of this was the *Trent* affair. When the British government, in December, 1861, sent an ultimatum requiring the release of four Confederate envoys seized by a federal naval captain from a British mail steamer, the *Trent*, Sumner pleaded with President Lincoln to hold out for international arbitration of the question, an approach that would probably have brought Great Britain and France into the Civil War on the side of the slave states. Lincoln, following Seward's counsel, instead authorized the release of the captives.

Trying to rouse support in Massachusetts during 1862 for his reelection to a third term in the Senate, Sumner continually pressed the president to proclaim the entire abolition of slavery. Lincoln, trying to hold the border slave states in the Union, insisted that the object of the war was to restore the Union, not to free the slaves. Nevertheless, in February, 1862, Sumner publicly propounded the doctrine of state suicide, asserting that the seceding states had forfeited their sovereignty within the Union and must become conquered provinces. It was past time, he declared, for the confiscation of southern property, especially of slaves, by the federal military authorities. When Lincoln issued his preliminary emancipation proclamation in September, Sumner claimed that the president was finally following his lead.

In the Senate during the last two years of the Civil War, Sumner was increasingly isolated even from the other radicals of his own party. In relentless pursuit of freedom and equal rights for black Americans, he regularly castigated rather than attempted to cajole his colleagues, and despite being cultivated assiduously by both the president and Mrs. Lincoln, he regularly criticized the chief executive in his conversations and correspondence for being lethargic, disorganized, and ineffectual. He refused to support Lincoln for renomination in 1864 and only reluctantly campaigned for him against General George B. McClellan, the Democratic nominee, as the lesser of two evils.

Because of his alienation from most of the other senators, Sumner played a minor role in constructing the apparatus of postwar reconstruction, including the passage of the Thirteenth, Fourteenth, and Fifteenth Amendments to the Constitution. He was kept off the Joint Committee on Reconstruction and was barred from the committee set up to supervise the Freedmen's Bureau and the enforcement of civil rights legislation in the South. He continually exasperated his fellow radicals by carping at their efforts but rarely suggesting practical alternatives. As always, he stressed principles, not means.

In October, 1866, four months after the death of his mother, Sumner married Alice Mason Hooper, the widowed daughter-in-law of a Massachusetts congressman. The senator was fifty-five; his new wife was still in her twenties. The marriage soon foundered. Mrs. Sumner sought younger male companionship and humiliated her husband by flaunting her liaison. Eight months after the wedding, the couple separated, and the senator never spoke to his wife again. In 1873, he divorced her.

Almost from the start of Andrew Johnson's presidency, Sumner excoriated him as a disgrace to the office. By early 1868, the Massachusetts senator was a determined exponent of impeachment, accusing Johnson of treason against the United States. When the effort to remove the chief executive from office fell short by a single vote in the Senate, Sumner bitterly denounced those who cast ballots against Johnson's deposition. Soon thereafter, he began campaigning for Ulysses S. Grant for president, in the process successfully seeking his own reelection to a fourth term.

While Johnson was still president, Sumner supported ratification of the Alaska purchase treaty negotiated by Secretary of State Seward. His opposition would have been fatal to that project, as it was to Seward's treaties to annex the Danish West Indies (later known as the Virgin Islands) and to purchase territory in the Dominican Republic for an American naval base. Sumner's committee also rejected the Johnson-Clarendon convention with Great Britain, negotiated on Seward's instructions in an attempt to ease dangerous tensions growing out of the Fenian crisis and out of the refusal of the British government thus far to arbitrate American claims for damages incurred at the hands of British subjects during the Civil War. Sumner declared in a Senate speech on April 13, 1869, that because British aid to the Confederates had caused the war to be doubled in duration, the English owed the American people damages of two billion dollars.

For a while, Sumner was able to dictate U.S. foreign policy to Seward's successor, the inexperienced Hamilton Fish. As the senator with the longest continuous service, he even exercised influence, for the first time, over domestic legislation. This stopped, however, after he repeatedly blocked bills and appointments favored by Grant, culminating his obstructiveness by getting the Senate to kill a treaty to annex the Dominican Republic (the president's principal foreign policy objective). The angry chief executive retaliated by dismissing Sumner's friend John L. Motley as minister to England. When Sumner threatened a peaceful settlement of the Civil War Alabama claims by calling for the transfer of Canada to the United States as his price for support of an arbitration award, Fish and Grant were able to get him ousted as chairman of the Foreign Relations Committee.

On May 31, 1872, a vitriolic Sumner delivered a four-hour speech, "Republicanism Versus Grantism," charging the president with nepotism and corruption, hoping thereby to help block Grant's renomination for a second term. The Republican National Convention at Philadelphia nevertheless endorsed the president by acclamation. Sumner then backed Horace Greeley, the Democratic and liberal Republican candidate for the presidency. Grant's easy victory, accompanied by the rise of the venal Benjamin F. Butler to political supremacy in Massachusetts, signaled the nadir of Sumner's influence in his home state. His health declined rapidly. Facing an uphill battle for reelection in 1874, virtually isolated and widely ridiculed in the Senate, having through many years driven away most of his friends and political allies by egotistical outbursts against them, and worried about heavy debts incurred during buying binges, Sumner lived his final months as a solitary invalid, his attacks of angina pectoris increasing in frequency and intensity, until on March 11, 1874, his heart finally stopped.

Significance

Sumner served in the U.S. Senate for more than twenty-three years. However, he was never a universally respected leader in that body, nor is his name attached to any portion of the landmark legislation of his epoch. Whether his party was in or out of power, his role was invariably that of obstructionist. For this he was well suited: His diligence in preparing elaborate, didactic assaults on the purposes and programs of others, his power of invective, and his uncompromising adherence to his own ideas brought him a strong following among reformers of the North, who admired his fidelity to principles of human rights and who were not subjected personally to his vehemence.

The widely repeated story, the main author of which was Sumner himself, that he played a decisive role in keeping the United States from armed conflict with Great Britain and France during the Civil War is untrue. His greatest service to the nation was that of keeping relentless pressure on other politicians for almost a quarter of a century to include black Americans under the protection of the Bill of Rights.

—Norman B. Ferris

Further Reading

Blue, Frederick J. *Charles Sumner and the Conscience of the North*. Arlington Heights, Ill.: Harlan Davidson, 1994. Analyzes the achievements and shortcomings of Sumner's battle to abolish slavery, portraying Sumner as a voice of conscience who persistently reminded nineteenth century Americans about the realities of racism.

Donald, David. *Charles Sumner and the Coming of the Civil War*. New York: Alfred A. Knopf, 1960. Based on extensive research, this is the most thorough treatment of Sumner's life prior to the inception of the Civil War. Although Donald is appreciative of his subject, he is more objective than most earlier writers.

_____. *Charles Sumner and the Rights of Man*. New York: Alfred A. Knopf, 1970. The fullest account available of Sumner's career during the period of the Civil War and Reconstruction, this is the concluding volume of Donald's highly praised modern biography.

Pierce, Edward L. *Memoir and Letters of Charles Sumner*. 4 vols. Boston: Roberts Brothers, 1877-1893. Typically Victorian, this study comprises extracts from documents, held together with uncritical commentary and reminiscences of the subject by people disposed to speak only well of him.

Schurz, Carl. *Charles Sumner: An Essay*. Edited by Arthur Reed Hogue. Urbana: University of Illinois Press, 1951. This long eulogy of Sumner by a younger contemporary should be read skeptically but with appreciation of some shrewd insights.

Storey, Moorfield. *Charles Sumner*. Boston: Houghton Mifflin, 1900. A brief laudatory account in the famous "American Statesman" series. Though biased and not always factually reliable, it is probably the best available introduction to Sumner.

Sumner, Charles. *Charles Sumner: His Complete Works*. Boston: Lee and Shepard, 1900. Collection of speeches carefully edited in later years by their author. To obtain a closer approximation of what Sumner actually said, a careful researcher will consult contemporary newspapers, the *Congressional Globe*, and, if possible, Sumner's manuscripts.

_____. *The Selected Letters of Charles Sumner*. Edited by Beverly Wilson Palmer. 2 vols. Boston: Northeastern University Press, 1990. The first volume contains letters from 1830 through 1859, while the second volume includes correspondence from 1859 to 1874.

Taylor, Anne-Marie. *Young Charles Sumner and the Legacy of the American Enlightenment, 1811-1851*. Amherst: University of Massachusetts Press, 2001. Focuses on Sumner's first forty years, before he took public office, to demonstrate the evolution of his character and thought. Taylor maintains Sumner was not a self-righteous fanatic, but was motivated by the Enlightenment principles upon which his young nation was founded.

See also: Dorothea Dix; Stephen A. Douglas; John C. Frémont; Ulysses S. Grant; Horace Greeley; Samuel Gridley Howe; Andrew Johnson; Abraham Lincoln;

William H. Seward; Taddeus Stevens; Daniel Webster.

RELATED ARTICLES in *Great Events from History: The Nineteenth Century, 1801-1900:* May 30, 1854: Congress Passes Kansas-Nebraska Act; January 1, 1863: Lincoln Issues the Emancipation Proclamation;

March 30, 1867: Russia Sells Alaska to the United States; February 24-May 26, 1868: Impeachment of Andrew Johnson; July 9, 1868: Fourteenth Amendment Is Ratified; May 8, 1871: Treaty of Washington Settles U.S. Claims vs. Britain; October 15, 1883: Civil Rights Cases.

BERTHA VON SUTTNER
Austrian writer and religious leader

Suttner inspired and organized peace movements and was instrumental in persuading Alfred Nobel to establish the Peace Prize that became named for him. Her novel Lay Down Your Arms *was a clarion call for disarmament.*

BORN: June 9, 1843; Prague, Bohemia, Austro-Hungarian Empire (now in Czech Republic)
DIED: June 21, 1914; Vienna, Austro-Hungarian Empire (now in Austria)
ALSO KNOWN AS: Bertha Félicie Sophia, Countess Kinsky of Wchinitz and Wettau (birth name); Baroness von Suttner; Countess Kinsky; Berta Oulot (pseudonym)
AREAS OF ACHIEVEMENT: Literature, social reform

EARLY LIFE

Bertha von Suttner was born Countess Kinsky into an old noble Polish family with a long and distinguished military tradition. Her father, Field Marshal Count Joseph Kinsky, died before she was born. On her mother's side, Kinsky was related to the poet Joseph von Korner. While she was in her teens, she dreamed of a career as an opera singer; she was encouraged in this, but, after a short while, she realized that her talent was insufficient. A precocious child, she read Plato's works and those of Alexander von Humboldt, a great German scientist, before she was sixteen. From her governesses she learned French and English. Later, she taught herself Italian. Kinsky must have been a beautiful girl. When she was only thirteen years old, a prince wanted to marry her, and in letters she is invariably mentioned as a lovely girl. She was an only and lonely child, and until the age of twelve she had no playmates. This experience reinforced her inclination to live in a world of dreams and fantasies.

After her father's death, her mother was left with a modest income, but the expenses of Kinsky's singing lessons and her mother's compulsive gambling at the

fashionable casinos diminished their limited funds. At the age of thirty, Kinsky took a job as a governess with the family of Baron and Baroness von Suttner. Though their youngest son, Arthur, at twenty-three years of age, was seven years younger than Kinsky, the two fell in love. Their romance was eagerly fostered by the girls of the family; they were fond of Bertha and were fascinated by the development of romantic love. It was quite otherwise with the parents. When the romance was discovered, the highly incensed baroness did not lose any time in finding a new, distant position for Kinsky.

This new position was with Alfred Nobel, the inventor of dynamite, who lived, at the time, in Paris. A bachelor at the age of forty-three, he was looking for a secretary-housekeeper who was also familiar with languages. In his advertisement he wrote, "A very wealthy, cultured, elderly gentleman, living in Paris, desires to find a lady, also of mature years, familiar with languages, as secretary and manager of his household." Despite her youth, Kinsky undoubtedly fit all the other requirements, for she was hired right away. A week later Nobel had to return to Sweden; the king had summoned him. Kinsky too was called away from Paris. Upon receipt of a telegram from Arthur confessing that he could not live without her, Kinsky hurried to Vienna. There, in great secrecy, they married.

For their honeymoon, which according to Kinsky lasted nine years, they went to the Caucasus in Russia. The invitation had come from a prince, who was one of their friends. Their stay was a curious blend of being both guests and employees of their hosts. At first the prince had hopes of finding employment for Arthur. When that failed, Arthur was employed as an architect and overseer while Bertha gave music and language lessons. When the day's work was done, they changed their work clothes for evening dresses and tuxedos and mingled on equal footing with the local aristocracy. Arthur started to write articles that were published in the Austrian newspapers.

Whether out of envy or the desire to imitate—she herself wrote that she could not decide that—Bertha too began to write. Her first published work was a light piece, an essay of the type known as a *feuilleton*, and it was signed with a pseudonym, but still it gave her confidence. Filled with the assurance that they could make a living as writers, they were ready to return home. In May, 1885, after nine years, they said farewell to the Caucasus.

LIFE'S WORK

Upon their return, Bertha and Arthur were forgiven for their secret marriage, and they rejoined Arthur's family. Published two years before their return, Bertha's book *Inventarium einer Seele* (1883; inventory of a soul) gave her entrée into literary circles. She soon added two important works to her oeuvre: *Daniela Dormes* (1886) and *Das Maschinenzeitalter: Zukunftsvorlesungen über unsere Zeit* (1889). *Daniela Dormes* in many ways is more a discussion than a novel. In it, however, one can discern Suttner's philosophical and moral views: She is sympathetic to the plight of the Jews, and she believes in Darwinism as a social force. *Das Maschinenzeitalter* is a look into the future. Suttner commented that she wrote the book to rid herself of the gloom with which the present filled her. The book was replete with scientific and philosophical themes; in scientific circles there was so much prejudice against the capacity of women as thinkers that a book signed with a woman's name would not have been read, so Suttner used the pseudonym "Jemand" (anyone).

The turning point of Suttner's life was approaching. With the money earned by *Das Maschinenzeitalter*, she and her husband decided to go to Paris. There they again met Nobel, and through him they also met the intellectual and social elite of the city. It was in Paris that Suttner first heard about the existence in London of a society called the International Peace and Arbitration Society. From that moment, she decided to promote it with all her efforts. She realized that her talent lay in writing; she also realized that in order to reach as many people as possible, the novel form would be best.

As a published author, Suttner assumed that the publication of *Die Waffen nieder!* (1889; *Lay Down Your Arms*, 1892) would not be a problem. The topic, however, was considered so dangerous that many publishers refused it. Suttner would have liked to have had the book run as a serial in a periodical, but this was refused. A publisher finally accepted the work but demanded that certain parts be cut and others be rewritten. The publisher also wanted to change the title to a less provocative one. Suttner refused. To the astonishment of the publisher, *Lay Down Your Arms* became a best seller; it was translated into dozens of languages. She received plaudits from Nobel and Leo Tolstoy, among others. Tolstoy compared the book to Harriet Beecher Stowe's *Uncle Tom's Cabin* (1852) and commented that he hoped that just as Stowe's work had influenced the abolition of slavery, so should *Lay Down Your Arms* influence the abolition of war.

Bertha von Suttner. (Library of Congress)

The success of the book soon engulfed Suttner in a series of peace activities. In 1891, she was elected president of the Austrian Peace Society, and she represented her country at a congress of international peace movements in Rome. The same year, she met a journalist, Alfred Hermann Fried, who also was later to receive a Nobel Peace Prize. The two founded a monthly periodical that bore the same title as Suttner's book. During the next eight years, this monthly was a powerful instrument in keeping the peace movement before the eyes of the world. Suttner also was occupied with the preparations for the First Hague Peace Conference. The conference aroused great expectations.

The czar of Russia, Nicholas II, had called upon world leaders to discuss efforts toward universal peace. This call was hailed by the champions of peace as a gigantic step toward its achievement. Until that time, pacifists had been considered as dreamers and utopians. This condescending attitude hurt their cause as much as the hostile attitude of the militarists. Jean-Henri Dunant, the founder of the Red Cross, commented that now, "whatever may happen, the world will not shriek, 'Utopia!'" "Utopians," as Suttner noted, was the favorite circumlocution for "crazy fellows."

At the conference, France was represented by a former prime minister and Great Britain by Julian Pauncefote, the British ambassador to the United States. One of the honorary presidents of the conference was Andrew D. White, the American ambassador to Germany. Among all these glittering personalities, Suttner was feted, admired, and listened to. Ivan Bloch, a Russian journalist, was instrumental in the endeavor to change world opinion to accept disarmament and peace as a real possibility and not merely as a utopian dream. Bloch's book *Budushchaia voina* (1898; partial translation as *The Future of War, in Its Technical, Economic, and Political Relations*, 1899) was widely regarded as being partially responsible for the idea of a peace conference. His thesis was that with the advanced technology of arms and armies the idea that one could wage war without destroying society was "utopian." Before going to the conference, Bloch had a long interview with the czar.

Suttner also fought against anti-Semitism. Her husband perhaps played a more important role in this fight, but she was his coworker. Anti-Semitism was virulent in the Austro-Hungarian Empire. Indeed, one of Adolf Hitler's chief idols was the anti-Semitic mayor of Vienna. Arthur founded the Union to Combat Anti-Semitism.

In December, 1902, Arthur died. In order to bear her grief, Suttner threw herself into furthering the cause of peace. She wrote, she attended meetings, and she went to conferences. In 1904, she went on a speaking tour in the United States. She met President Theodore Roosevelt, who assured her that universal peace was coming. She was impressed by Philadelphia and its Quaker inhabitants, friends of peace. On her return to Europe, she was greatly encouraged by the way many dominions of the British Empire were about to be given Commonwealth status. She saw a promising future for other states, particularly for her homeland, where the old age of the emperor made people aware of changes that would follow his death. In 1905, she received the Nobel Peace Prize.

In the summer of 1914, an International Peace Conference was scheduled to be held in Vienna. In the last week of June of that year, however, a shot rang out in a provincial city in an obscure province of the Austro-Hungarian Empire. It killed the heir to the throne of the empire as well as his wife. Soon there were millions and millions of other victims; World War I had erupted. Suttner was spared the knowledge of war—she died of stomach cancer a week before the assassinations in Sarajevo.

SIGNIFICANCE

Bertha von Suttner united in herself two traits that are rarely found together: idealism and realism. It was her idealism that led to her faith in a world without war. Hundreds before her had that same dream, but Suttner also had the clear-sightedness, the practical sense, and the knowledge of the way the world is directed by statesmen and leaders.

In Suttner's work, she was helped by her husband, who shared her ideas and was also a writer of some note. Even greater help came to her in the form of the zeitgeist. At the turn of the century, a host of great writers, philosophers, and statesmen were advocating the idea of a peaceful world. The idea was there—in search of a leader. Suttner took the role. The peace conferences she organized, the speaking tours she embarked upon, her book with its noble challenge, and the periodical she helped found all had the effect of making and keeping the world aware that the fight for peace can be as vigorous as its opposite. When Suttner was received by the crowned heads of Great Britain, Sweden, Norway, and the Netherlands, and when she conferred with a former president and the president of the United States, it was not only a personal triumph but also a victory for the cause of peace. The Nobel Peace Prize and the annual peace conferences that followed the First Hague Peace Conference are testimony to her influence.

—*George Javor*

FURTHER READING

Braker, Regina. *Weapons of Women Writers: Bertha von Suttner's "Die Waffen nieder!" as Political Literature in the Tradition of Harriet Beecher Stowe's "Uncle Tom's Cabin."* New York: Peter Lang, 1995. Examines similarities between *Uncle Tom's Cabin* and *Lay Down Your Arms.* Describes how Suttner and Stowe were influenced by author Leo Tolstoy's ideas about art, and how both authors sought the role of moral messenger.

Davis, Calvin DeArmond. *The United States and the First Hague Peace Conference.* Ithaca, N.Y.: Cornell University Press, 1962. An excellent account of the First Hague Peace Conference with particular emphasis on American participation. Offers a scholarly, lucid presentation of the problems of establishing a Permanent Court of Arbitration.

Hamann, Brigette. *Bertha von Suttner: A Life for Peace.* Translated by Ann Dubsky, with an introduction by Irwin Abrams. Syracuse, N.Y.: Syracuse University Press, 1996. Traces Suttner's life and involvement in the peace movement within the context of social and political conditions in Austria on the eve of World War I. Hamann makes use of diaries, letters, and other previously unpublished materials.

Kemp, Beatrix. *Woman for Peace: The Life of Bertha von Suttner.* Translated by R. W. Last. London: Oswald Wolff, 1972. Kemp had access to the Library of the United Nations in Geneva, where most of the material pertaining to Suttner's work is now collected. Occasionally laudatory, this nevertheless critical work provides an illuminating look at Suttner's life and work. The accounts of her lecture tours and the text of her speech in San Francisco in 1912 are valuable. Complete bibliography and index.

Playne, Caroline E. *Bertha von Suttner and the Struggle to Avert the World War.* London: Allen & Unwin, 1936. The author knew Suttner personally and participated with her in two International Peace Conferences. Contains good anecdotal material. The style is somewhat pedestrian, but the eyewitness accounts are useful. Index, no bibliography.

Suttner, Bertha von. *Memoirs of Bertha von Suttner: The Records of an Eventful Life.* Boston: Ginn, 1910. Suttner kept a diary, so her memoirs are quite detailed. She gives outstanding sketches of statesmen, writers, and leaders of nations. Index.

Wiener, P. B. "Bertha von Suttner and the Political Novel." In *Essays in German Language, Culture, and Society*, edited by Siegbert S. Prawer et al. London: University of London, 1969. A useful and enlightening essay on the essence of the political novel, with special regard to the difference between the political novel and the social novel. Provides a good analysis of Suttner's main work, *Lay Down Your Arms*, and compares it to other antiwar novels. The notes following the articles are alone more valuable than many a longer article.

SEE ALSO: Jean-Henri Dunant; Alexander von Humboldt; Alfred Nobel; Harriet Beecher Stowe; Leo Tolstoy.

JOSEPH WILSON SWAN
English inventor

Swan's invention and business leadership helped launch the electric lighting industry. He pioneered in artificial fibers. His technical contributions enriched a wide range of other fields, from photography to batteries to tanning.

BORN: October 31, 1828; Sunderland, Durham, England
DIED: May 27, 1914; Warlingham, Surrey, England
ALSO KNOWN AS: Sir Joseph Wilson Swan
AREAS OF ACHIEVEMENT: Science and technology, business

EARLY LIFE

Joseph Wilson Swan was the son of John and Isabella Cameron Swan, who were both descended from Scottish families that had settled in England during the middle of the eighteenth century. His father built up a comfortable business selling iron fittings for ships, such as anchors and chains. He was, however, easygoing, generous, and unbusinesslike and lost much of his wealth by backing his own unsuccessful ventures and inventions.

While the family money lasted, Joseph was educated at a dame school and a local boarding school, but his real education came from everyday life in the bustling Tyneside region of England, then one of the world's leading centers for the iron industry, shipbuilding, the mining and use of coal, and a wide range of supporting industries. Highlights of this education included some excursions to an uncle's rope works and a demonstration by a family friend of a static-electricity machine.

Departure from school at the age of fourteen served to further Swan's education. He was apprenticed to two Sunderland druggists, both of whom died before three years of his six-year term were up. He then moved on to work as a full-fledged chemist for a friend, John Mawson, a chemist and druggist, first in Sunderland and later in Newcastle. While working with Mawson, Swan found enough spare time to experiment, improvising equipment using the flasks and bottles in the pharmacy. He made coils and condensers and tried out simple electrical experiments. "He was a great enthusiast," a coworker recalled:

> It was only after the day's work was over that he was able to experiment, for he had no proper laboratory. . . .

His experiments were always carried out not only with skill and forethought, but with the least possible risk of failure.

LIFE'S WORK

This low-risk, incremental approach to invention characterized Swan's life's work. He later concluded that his particular strength as an inventor was not in conceiving wholly new things but in "looking at anything being done in the nature of a handicraft or process and finding a better way of doing it." At the age of seventeen, he began to apply this strength to the electric light, an invention already more than thirty years old but not yet in practical use. By 1848, he had developed his own version of one of the principal types already proposed, an incandescent carbon conductor glowing in a glass-enclosed vacuum. Swan's main improvement was to use a strip of carbonized paper in place of a graphite rod for the conductor. Electricity, however, was too expensive to make the lamp economical, and the vacuum he could produce was not good enough to give it a long life, so he turned to other areas.

Swan's employer, Mawson, a prosperous businessperson, devout Methodist, and public servant, ushered Swan into Newcastle's inner circle of religious dissenters and political liberals. Swan also became a leader of the local literary and philosophical society. His associations thus brought Swan local business, public, and scientific backing as he emerged as an inventor.

The first photograph he saw, in a Sunderland shop window in about 1850, launched him on a series of photography inventions. By 1856, he had improved the formula for making collodion, a key ingredient in photographic plates, and Mawson built a factory to manufacture it. By 1864, Swan had improved the process of photographic printing, taken up the manufacture of specialty chemicals, and earned one of the world's first patents on the process of chrome tanning.

Swan's chemical inventions won for him prizes at the Paris Exposition of 1867. In that year, however, he was to suffer two personal tragedies. First Mawson died in an explosion. Then Frances White Swan, whom he had married in 1862 and who had borne him four children, died suddenly of a fever contracted in childbirth. It was well into the 1870's before Swan had stabilized his family and business life. He was married to his late wife's sister,

Hannah White, who bore him five more children, and found new partners for the pharmaceutical and chemical firm of Swan and Mawson. In 1877, electricity generation and vacuum technology had advanced far enough to justify another attempt at the electric light. Swan hired Charles Stearn, a bank clerk turned vacuum experimenter, to assist him in experiments on producing light by the incandescence of carbon.

By February, 1878, he was probably closer to this goal than any of his several worldwide rivals when he demonstrated publicly at Newcastle a light based on the now-familiar combination of carbon conductor and evacuated glass bulb. At that time, his great American rival, Thomas Edison, was still concentrating on unworkable schemes involving platinum conductors turned on and off frequently by thermostats.

However, Swan's was not yet a practical lamp. He stalled at this point for the next several months. Meanwhile, Edison made two crucial decisions: to return to carbon, perhaps inspired in part by Swan's success, which was reported in the technical press, and to use a hair-thin, high-resistance filament as his conductor, rather than the thicker, lower-resistance rods or strips used by Swan and others. Early in 1880, after Edison had publicly unveiled his filament, Swan followed with a similar design. He proceeded to make several improvements to filament manufacture. The judgment of historians is that he emerged a close but distinct second to Edison as inventor of the practical incandescent lamp.

In 1881, backed by Newcastle investors, Swan incorporated the Swan Electric Light Company, a successful venture for the manufacture and sale of incandescent lamps. This led to a patent suit by Edison, in which, if brought to trial, Swan foresaw, "the word 'filament' [would be] strongly insisted on." Forestalling a trial, the parties compromised, and in 1884 the Edison and Swan United Electric Company was formed. For several years thereafter, it dominated Great Britain's electric light manufacturing business.

Swan moved on to other areas of invention, developing an improved form of the lead acid storage battery and carrying out work on copper brazing and the fuel cell. The best known of his later inventions were spin-offs of his light bulb work. Seeking to perfect the filament during the mid-1880's, he decided that the best results would come from making a carbon structure with uniform properties. Assisted by Leigh S. Powell, Swan found a practical solvent for gun-cotton (nitrocellulose) and squeezed the resulting paste through a die to make fine, uniform threads. Swan soon recognized that they

had possibilities as fabrics as well as filaments. Hannah Swan knitted some into lace, which was exhibited in 1885 under the name "artificial silk." This was a milestone on the path to the invention of rayon and the development of the artificial fiber industry. Swan himself, however, left the exploitation of this invention to others.

During the late 1880's, he widened his interest to carry out scientific researches on the electrodeposition of copper and the stress in materials produced by high electric fields. The quality of his research won for him election as a fellow of the Royal Society in 1894. He earned many other honors, including the presidencies of the Institution of Electrical Engineers, the Society for Chemical Industry, and the Faraday Society. Swan was knighted in 1904. In 1908, he retired to Warlingham on the North Downs of Surrey.

The leisure of his later years allowed full expression of the personal qualities that he had displayed throughout his life: fairness, an open mind, modesty, gentleness, and courtesy. All rested, however, as an associate recalled, on "a tranquil undercurrent of dignity and power." Dark, slim, and serious in his youth, he matured into a plump patriarch with a long white beard and sparkling eyes, a writer of lively letters with occasional bursts of poetic imagination. He was a rigid teetotaler, an optimist, a liberal in politics, and a great believer in the progressive influence of science, always emphasizing that the value of science was greater than any material improvement. He died peacefully at Warlingham on May 27, 1914.

SIGNIFICANCE

Joseph Wilson Swan was born into the nineteenth century world of the heroic inventor-craftspeople immortalized by Samuel Smiles. He survived to see a world of giant corporations and government- and industry-sponsored laboratories. His own work linked the two eras. His inventing showed a sure sense for picking the field that was ripe for a major step and a sure hand at experiment and improvement.

Swan's efforts in electric lighting and artificial fibers stopped just short of total success but placed him among the top few major contributors in each area. Unlike his great rival Edison, he was not a footloose independent entrepreneur and self-promoter. Instead, he invented from a secure base in an established industrial community. He was welcome in the university laboratory, the scientific society's meeting hall, the government hearing room, or the businessperson's office, and his activities foreshadowed the formalizing of such ties into the academic-industrial-government science-and-technology complex of the twenty-first century. However, Swan operated with a nineteenth century optimist's independence and dignity that inventors of any era could well emulate.

—George Wise

FURTHER READING

Bazerman, Charles. *The Languages of Edison's Light.* Cambridge, Mass.: MIT Press, 1999. Describes how Edison and his colleagues created a system of symbols and communication to describe the new invention of electric lighting. Includes information about Swan.

Chirnside, R. C. "Sir Joseph Swan and the Invention of the Electric Lamp." *Electronics and Power*, February, 1979, 95-100. Discusses Swan's contribution to electric lighting technology, and the Edison-Swan rivalry.

_____. *Sir Joseph Wilson Swan, FRS, Pharmacist, Chemist, Electrical Engineer.* Newcastle-on-Tyne, England: Newcastle-on-Tyne Philosophical Society, 1979. Discussion by a chemist of Swan's work in the context of Newcastle science and technology, adding technical background not available in the inventor's biography.

Clouth, Diane. *Joseph Wilson Swan, 1828-1914.* Gateshead, England: Tyne-and-Wear Archives, 1979. Well-illustrated history of Swan's achievements and local developments; gives a good sense of the context of Swan's life and work.

Dyson, James. *A History of Great Inventions.* New York: Carroll & Graf, 2001. Chapter 4, "1830-1899: Electricity on the Move," mentions Swan in its overview of nineteenth century inventions.

Flatow, Ira. *The Fascinating Stories Behind the Great Inventions That Changed Our Lives.* New York: HarperCollins, 1992. Chapter 3, "Whose Light Bulb? Edison in a New Light," includes information about Swan's contributions to the invention of electric lighting.

Swan, Mary E., and Kenneth R. Swan. *Sir Joseph Wilson Swan, FRS, Inventor and Scientist.* London: Ernest Benn, 1928. Well-written biography by two of Swan's children. Contains many valuable personal details and clear, nontechnical descriptions of his major inventions.

Wise, George. "Swan's Way." *IEEE Spectrum* 19 (April, 1982): 66-72. Describes Swan's inventive style, especially in contrast with that of his rival Edison, and indicates how those differences in style led to Edison's victory in the electric lamp race, but also to Swan's harmonious and productive total career.

SEE ALSO: Thomas Alva Edison; Michael Faraday; Sir William Robert Grove; The Siemens Family; Nikola Tesla; George Westinghouse.

RELATED ARTICLES in *Great Events from History: The Nineteenth Century, 1801-1900:* October 21, 1879: Edison Demonstrates the Incandescent Lamp; May 1-October 30, 1893: Chicago World's Fair.

TADANO MAKUZU
Japanese social reformer and philosopher

Tadano Makuzu's far-reaching and perceptive philosophical analysis of the nature of gender conflict and the problems of Japanese society earned her the grudging respect of male scholars during an age in which the open participation of women in Japanese political and philosophical debate was rare. She was also a major writer and joined the debate about Christianity in Japan.

BORN: 1763; Edo (now Tokyo), Japan
DIED: July 26, 1825; Sendai, Japan
ALSO KNOWN AS: Makuzu (pseudonym); Kudō Ayako
AREAS OF ACHIEVEMENT: Women's rights, literature

EARLY LIFE

When Tadano Makuzu (tah-dah-no mah-koo-tsoo) was born, she received the given name of Ayako and had the family name of Kudō. She later chose Makuzu as her pen name and added Tadano, which was her second husband's family name. She became most commonly known as Tadano Makuzu and signed her works simply as Makuzu. She was born into the lower aristocracy of Edo. Her father, Kudō Heisuke, served as physician to the daimyo, or lord, of Sendai. Heisuke himself was the adopted son of Kudō Jōan, a former masterless samurai or *rōnin*, who had also been the physician of the Sendai daimyo. Ayako's mother was the daughter of another physician of the Sendai daimyo, Kuwabara Takatomo. The oldest surviving child of her family, Ayako had two brothers and four sisters.

Ayako was born with a large mole below her right eye, which according to Japanese customary belief was an omen for a life of tears. However, Ayako's childhood was happy. Her father appreciated her keen intelligence and did not exclude her from the intellectual, philosophical, and political discussions in his house, which also served as the base of his medical practice and as a medical school.

In 1778, when Ayako was fifteen, she became an attendant of Princess Akiko, the daughter of the Sendai daimyo. In 1785, her father's opposition to the new senior councillor of the shogun, Matsudaira Sadanobu—the de facto ruler of Japan—placed his family in peril. In 1787, when Ayako returned from serving Princess Akiko, she was twenty-four years old, and her father despaired of her prospects for marriage. However, when he forced her to marry an old and sick samurai two years

later, she rebelled. Her incessant tears soon ended the marriage, and she returned home.

Over the enusing decade, Ayako saw much misfortune. One of her brothers, two of her sisters, and her mother died. In 1795, her father was placed under house arrest. After her father himself remarried, he arranged a new marriage for her. In 1797, when Ayako was thirty-four years of age, she married the widowed samurai Tadano Iga Tsurayoshi. Her new husband had to work in Edo. During the winter, Ayako traveled alone to her husband's family home in Sendai, a place about two hundred miles north of Edo—a city that she would never see again. She later called her trip her journey into hell.

During the spring of 1798, Ayako's husband rejoined her in Sendai, where Ayako was caring for three new stepsons. Her husband, with whom she had never had any children of her own, returned to Edo later in the year and would afterward visit Sendai only rarely. Meanwhile, in 1800, Ayako's father died; seven years later, she lost her only remaining brother. The Kudō family then adopted a new male heir, who sold everything that had belonged to Ayako's father. Finally, in 1812, Ayako learned that her husband had died in Edo. By then she was beginning to write and was becoming known as Makuzu.

LIFE'S WORK

In 1812, Makuzu finished her autobiography, *Mukashibanashi* (stories from the past). Not published until 1925, this work revealed a great deal about the living conditions of lower aristocratic Japanese families during the late eighteenth and early nineteenth centuries. Makuzu's reminiscences of her relatives and commentaries on own character make for lively reading. She gave a sympathetic account of her mother and wrote admiringly of her father. The narrative ends with the tragedy of her husband's death, when Makuzu was forty-nine years old and had another thirteen years to live.

Next turning her attention to the northern Japanese country around Sendai, Makuzu wrote two collections of essays and poems about the people, landscape, and folklore of her new home. *Isozutai* (1891; along the coast) and *Ōshūbanashi* (1891; stories from ōshū) were likely written in 1817, when she was about fifty-three. Her keen but sympathetic observations reveal much about life in a region outside Edo, which was the center of Japanese political and commercial life.

Makuzu initially felt despair at the collapse of the Kudō family fortune. After two visions in which the Buddhist goddess of mercy, Kannon. and a male Buddha appeared to her, she believed she had reached enlightenment. The visions instructed her to continue her philosophical writing, even though the fact that she was a woman meant she would face an uphill battle. Makuzu ostensibly declared that she was merely continuing the legacy of her father; however, she was, in fact, creating her own legacy.

Makuzu's most important work was *Hitori kangai* (1994; *Solitary Thoughts*, 2001). Written between January, 1818, and January, 1819, it reflected Makuzu's philosophical insights at their sharpest. Central to her philosophy was a defiant challenge to male authorities, including the ancient Chinese philosopher Confucius, who had held that women, like servants, should not be taken seriously. The very fact of Makuzu's writing proved such views wrong, and she won grudging respect from her male intellectual counterparts.

Insisting that personal, family and national life should obey what Makuzu called the natural rhythm of heaven and earth, she rejected social and economic politics that unbalanced human lives. Anticipating the work of the Austrian founder of psychoanalysis, Sigmund Freud, and the French philosopher Jacques Lacan, Makuzu commented on male castration anxiety as being irrelevant from the point of view of a woman. She reasoned, as Lacan would more than a century later, that men subordinate women because they consider them lacking a phallus.

Makuzu's *Solitary Thoughts* promoted education for women, even though Makuzu wrote that education might make them miserable in a patriarchal world. She preferred Japanese texts over Chinese texts and especially disliked Confucian classics. In the field of social economics, she stressed that human society was built upon struggle, anticipating the English naturalist Charles Darwin's ideas of the survival of the fittest. *Solitary Thoughts* contained the shocking observation that townsmen and artisans hated the samurai class for their idleness and sought to exploit them financially to gain revenge. Her economic writings reflected a certain innocence of the laws of supply and demand, as when she questioned why merchants would raise their prices during times of need.

To engage in intellectual discourse, Makuzu sent a manuscript of *Solitary Thoughts* to the philosopher Takizawa Bakin in late March, 1819. Bakin was initially put off by what he considered her female audacity; however, he was positively surprised by the intellectual quality of her writing. Afterward, the two corresponded. Later in 1819, Bakin finished their discourse with a detailed, paragraph-by-paragraph criticism of *Solitary Thoughts*, rejecting many of Makuzu's ideas as anti-Confucian. He then said that he was too busy now to continue their correspondence.

After 1819, Makuzu appears to have ceased writing. She wrote her arguments for rejecting Christianity as a Western system of thought that was likely to disrupt imperial Japanese order in undated essays that were first published in 1994 in her collected works. She was apparently ill, with her writing hand in pain, and was suffering from growing nearsightedness. She thus may have stopped writing for physical reasons.

In 1825, Bakin sent a written apology to Makuzu, belatedly praising *Solitary Thoughts* for its vigorous spirit. However, his letter arrived too late to reach her. Tadano Makuzu died in Sendai on July 26, 1825, at the age of about sixty-two.

SIGNIFICANCE

Most of Makuzu's writings survived only in manuscript form. The essays and poems she wrote about Sendai were later appreciated for their local color during the Meiji era (1868-1912), when the emperor's powers were restored and Japanese nationalism flourished. Her autobiography's publication in 1925 attracted critical attention and was especially treasured by Japanese women writers and thinkers of the modern era.

Makuzu's major confrontational work, *Solitary Thoughts*, was kept alive by Bakin's 1819 commentary and his 1825 apology. Most of the manuscript that Makuzu had sent to him was copied in 1848, and the copy was rediscovered in 1980. Characteristically, however, the copyist dropped strong passionate pro-woman and anti-Confucian passages. Makuzu's original manuscript does not survive, but the missing portions were restored from Bakin's critical notes. The last known manuscript containing the first chapter of *Solitary Thoughts* burned in Tokyo's great fire of 1923.

In 1936, Eiko Nakayama published *Tadano Makuzu* (no English translation), a biography containing the opening chapter of *Solitary Thoughts*. Toward the end of the twentieth century, Japanese women scholars developed a strong interest in publishing all of *Solitary Thoughts*—a goal finally achieved in 1994. An English translation followed in 2001.

Tadano Makuzu's determination to follow her self-described journey into hell in 1797 by becoming a passionate and original writer was crowned with success. during the early twenty-first century, with her work finally fully accessible, the power of her arguments and the weight of her sympathetic yet critical analysis of the society of her times and the difficult role of intelligent women in the late Tokugawa shogunate met with international critical interest. To Japanese readers, her autobiography is a classic.

—*R. C. Lutz*

FURTHER READING
Fister, Patricia. *Japanese Women Artists, 1600-1900.* Lawrence, Kans.: Spencer Museum of Art, 1988. Briefly mentions Tadano Makuzu and her unusual confrontation of the male scholarly establishment in the context of the difficulties experienced by Japanese women artists of Makuzu's age.
Gramlich-Oka, Bettina. "Kirishitan kô by Tadano Makuzu: A Late Tokugawa Woman's Warnings."

Bulletin of Portuguese-Japanese Studies 8 (2004): 65-92. Analyzes Makuzu's negative view of Christianity, as expressed in her undated philosophical essay, and argues that Makuzu influenced shogunate politics—a remarkable achievement for a woman of her times.
_____. "Tadano Makuzu and Her *Hitori Kangae*." *Monumenta Nipponica* 56, no. 1 (Spring, 2001): 1-20. Comprehensive review of the life and work of Makuzu that explores the range of her major philosophical text, a translation of which follows the article and is continued in the next number of the journal. Analyzes her intellectual relationship with Bakin and discusses the survival of her manuscript.

SEE ALSO: Charles Darwin; Ho Xuan Huong.
RELATED ARTICLE in *Great Events from History: The Nineteenth Century, 1801-1900:* March 31, 1854: Perry Opens Japan to Western Trade.

TÁHIRIH
Persian religious reformer and poet

Táhirih cast off the conventions of her day to help spread the ideas of Sayyid ʿAlī Muḥammad Shīrāzī, the founder of Bābīism. Renowned as both a poet and a revolutionary, she has inspired feminist activists and dissidents since her execution.

BORN: c. 1814-1820; Qazvin, Persia (now in Iran)
DIED: 1852; Tehran, Persia (now in Iran)
ALSO KNOWN AS: Fāṭima Baraghani (birth name); Táhira; Táhirah; Qurrat al-ʿAyn; Janab-i Táhirih; Fāṭima Khanum Baraghani Qazvini; Zarrin Taj
AREA OF ACHIEVEMENT: Religion and theology

EARLY LIFE
Táhirih (TAH-heh-reh) was born Fāṭima Baraghani, the oldest daughter of a famous Muslim jurist, Hajji Mullā Muḥammad Salih Baraghani. She was educated in a standard Islamic curriculum.

As a young woman, Táhirih was married to Mullā Muḥammad, the son of her uncle, and together they had three sons and one daughter. While staying with her uncle in the holy city of Karbala in Iraq, she, her sister, and her brother-in-law joined the Shaykhī sect, which was then under the guidance of Sayyid Kazim Rashti. Her decision provoked fierce hostility from her husband

and would eventually lead to her divorce from him. In the meantime, while staying in Karbala, she received instruction from Sayyid Rashti, who was so impressed by a treatise that she wrote on Shaykhī doctrine that he gave her the nickname Qurrat al-ʿAyn (solace of the eyes).

LIFE'S WORK
On May 22, 1844, Sayyid ʿAlī Muḥammad announced that he was the successor to Sayyid Rashti and declared himself the Bāb (gate, or intermediary) between the Hidden Imam and the populace. Sometime after this, Táhirih and a group of Shaykhī disciples arrived in Shīrāz from Karbala. Thirteen of them met the Bāb and converted to his teachings. At the time, Táhirih herself had already won a reputation in Karbala as an outstanding but radical cleric. While still in Qazvin, she sent a letter to the Bāb, and on its basis alone, he made her the leader in his group of premier disciples known as the Letters of the Living. According to Bābī doctrine, this select group and its founder constituted the first "Unity" of a series of believers. The Bāb came to regard the Letters of the Living as incarnations of Shīʿism's most holy figures, and they were sent out to disseminate the claims of the Bāb to Shaykhī communities in the areas they visited.

In 1845, the Persian government placed the Báb under house arrest in Shīrāz and heavily restricted his activities. Responsibility for proselytizing then fell upon the Báb's small core of believers, and the exposition of Bábí doctrine was increasingly performed by the Letters of the Living and select religious scholars in the provinces. While other disciples led insurrections in Māzandarān, Neyrīz, and Zanjān, the task fell to Táhirih in Karbala and Baghdad.

The Letters of the Living were regarded as messianic figures by followers of the Bábí faith. In keeping with the quasi-divine status accorded to them, Táhirih claimed to be an incarnation of the Prophet Muḥammad's daughter Fāṭima, the most important female figure in Islam, and a focus of Shīʿi veneration. Even among the Letters of the Living, Táhirih's status was unique. Some followers called her the "point of divine knowledge," after their former leader Sayyid Kazim Rashti. While residing in Rashti's home in Karbala, Táhirih assumed supreme control of the Shaykhī-Bábí community in the region.

Táhirih's claim to be an incarnation of Fāṭima led to the first crisis of authority in the Bábí movement. A local religious leader, Mullā Aḥmad Khurāsānī, and his followers opposed her unprecedented status and challenged the role of the Letters of the Living in the Bábí community of Iraq. Táhirih's unconventional behavior and radical pronouncements led to increasing conflicts in the area.

Although the Báb promoted adherence to Islamic piety in his early writings, Táhirih seized upon his more zealous ideals, stressing his overriding authority and the advent of a new age. Her behavior and speech extolled the importance of inner realities at the expense of conformity to proscribed external practices. In the classes she taught to Bábí men, she flouted Islamic convention by appearing without a veil. In addition, she challenged the sacristy of the Muslim ritual calendar by celebrating the birth of the Báb during the early days of month of Muḥarram. Her letters suggest that her abrogation of Islam was incited by the receipt of a letter from the Báb calling on her to "enter the gate of innovation." This notion is corroborated by a contemporary account stating that with the Báb's explicit permission, Táhirih proclaimed existing Islamic laws and observances null and void.

Táhirih's radical actions naturally provoked controversy within the Bábí community. Although some followers of the Báb wrote to ask him to stop her, it appears that he supported her unconditionally. In the meantime, other followers began to follow Táhirih's example, fueling further conflict that eventually spread beyond the Bábí community. Sometime in 1846 or 1847, Táhirih was arrested in Karbala and forced to leave the city for Baghdad. After being held under house arrest in the home of Sheikh Maḥmūd al-Ālūsī, she was expelled from Iraq on orders sent from Ottoman headquarters in Constantinople. She returned to Qazvin later in the same year, but not before stopping in the Iranian cities of Hamadan and Kirmanshah to proselytize.

Controversies surrounding Táhirih's behavior and the growing power of Bábí missionaries in Iran led to serious resistance against the sect there. Soon after Táhirih's return to Qazvin, three Bábís attacked her uncle, Hajji Mullā Muḥammad Taqi Baraghani, the leading cleric of the town. Three days after his death, large numbers of Bábís were arrested and several were sentenced to death in retaliation for the cleric's murder. Matters escalated in early 1848, when the Báb proclaimed himself the Hidden Imam and called for the abolition of Shariʾa, the Islamic law.

Because Táhirih was widely suspected of complicity in her uncle's death, it was no longer possible for her to remain in Qazvin, so she left for Tehran. She then traveled to Māzandarān to attend a major gathering of Bábí leaders at Badasht. There, she figured prominently in the conference's key events. According to contemporary accounts, she preached constantly, often without wearing a veil. In 1850, she was arrested and brought to Tehran, where she was detained as a prisoner. After an attempt on the life of the Persian ruler, Nāṣir al-Dīn Shāh, in 1852 by three Bábís, Táhirih and at least twenty-seven other Bábís were put to death in Tehran.

SIGNIFICANCE

Táhirih was famous both inside and outside the Bábí movement for her beauty, eloquence, and dedication to her cause. She is also remembered for a series of mystical poems that she composed to articulate her devotion. Perhaps more significantly, accounts of her fortitude in the face of a cruel and painful execution contributed to her reputation as a courageous revolutionary.

Among the Letters of the Living, Táhirih played a particularly significant role in defining and disseminating Bábí doctrine in Shīʿism's most holy city of Karbala. She assumed supreme control of the Shaykhī-Bábí community there, and it appears that she was responsible for introducing ideas from Shaykhīʿism into Bábīsm. In particular, she stressed the importance of inner realities at the expense of outward practice—a view that was made literal in her choice to appear unveiled. Táhirih's unprecedented role in both religious and public life established a potent model for feminist action and political dissent. Her life continues to provide inspiration for feminist groups in Iran and elsewhere into the twenty-first century.

—Anna Sloan

FURTHER READING

Afaqi, Sabir and Jan Teofil Jasion. *Táhirih in History: Perspectives on Qurratu'l-'Ayn from East and West.* Vol. 16 in *Studies in the Babi and Baha'i Religions.* Los Angeles: Kalimat Press, 2004. A compilation of historical work written on Táhirih since the nineteenth century, including Baha'i sources by 'Abdu'l-Bahá and Shoghi Effendi; essays by scholars in India and Pakistan; and scholarship by Western writers, such as E. G. Browne, A. L. M. Nicolas, Abbas Amanat, and Farzaneh Milani.

Banani, Amin, ed. *Táhirih: A Portrait in Poetry: Selected Poems of Qurratu'l-'Ayn.* Los Angeles: Kalimat Press, 2004. A collection of Táhirih's poems, published in the original Persian with English translations by Jascha Kessler and Anthony A. Lee. Its introduction discusses Táhirih in the context of the literary history of Persia.

Root, Martha L. *Táhirih the Pure.* Rev. ed. Los Angeles: Kalimat Press, 2000. A brief recounting of Táhirih's life and martyrdom, with a selection of her poems.

Stumpel, Isabel. "Tahira Qurrat al-'Ain." In *Iran im 19 Jahrhundert und die Entstehung der Baha'i-Religion,* edited by Johann Christoph Burgel and Isabel Schayani. Hildesheim, Germany: Olms, 1998. German-language study of the history and personality of Táhirih, focusing on her role in the formation of the Bābī community.

SEE ALSO: The Bāb; Bahā'ullāh; Jamāl al-Dīn al-Afghānī.

RELATED ARTICLE in *Great Events from History: The Nineteenth Century, 1801-1900:* 19th century: Arabic Literary Renaissance.

HIPPOLYTE TAINE
French writer

As a critic and historian of the arts and society, Taine dominated much of the intellectual life in France in the last half of the nineteenth century. His work was influential in England and the United States, but much of his history and literary theory fell into disrepute during the twentieth century. However, his method and his appreciation of literary works continue to engage critics and historians.

BORN: April 21, 1828; Vouziers, France
DIED: March 5, 1893; Paris, France
ALSO KNOWN AS: Hippolyte-Adolphe Taine (full name)
AREAS OF ACHIEVEMENT: Literature, art

EARLY LIFE

Hippolyte-Adolphe Taine (tehn) was twelve years old when his father, an established attorney, died. Left with a modest inheritance and scholarly inclinations, the young man was sent to a boarding school in Paris. He loved learning and soon revealed a mind superior to both his fellow students and his teachers. Deeply influenced by the philosopher Baruch Spinoza, Taine had lost his religious faith by the age of fifteen. He took a naturalistic view of the world, in which the human intellect and nature are viewed as parts of a single process. History, if it was examined carefully, revealed a total structure that functioned on the same principles as nature. Consequently, societies grew and declined in an organic manner, as did natural phenomena, and the historian or philosopher could find the laws of society, history, literature, or any human endeavor in the same way that scientists found such laws to operate in nature.

It was Taine's devotion to Spinoza that led to his failing the *agrégation* (a series of examinations at the École Normale Supérieure) in 1851. His conservative examiners found his elucidation of Spinoza's moral system to be "absurd." In effect, Taine was flouting their most fundamental conceptions about free will and morality, for he argued that human beings were largely the products of their race, their time, and their environment. Taine seemed to attack the concept of individuality and of moral responsibility, apparently abandoning the notion that human beings created their own world in favor of a belief in determinism.

If Taine's early academic career was hampered by his unorthodox views, his lectures on literature and art soon brought him attention both in France and abroad. He was the harbinger of the great naturalistic novelists of the nineteenth century such as Émile Zola, who took as their subject matter the way a culture shapes human character. Taine was one of the first men of letters to study science rigorously and to develop a human psychology based on his courses in physiology, botany, zoology, and anatomy. His work was greeted with enormous enthusiasm, because it promised to put the study of history, literature, and culture as a whole on an objective basis and free it from the arbitrary prejudices of the critic.

LIFE'S WORK

The publication of Taine's *Histoire de la littérature anglaise* (1863-1864; *History of English Literature*, 1871) solidified his reputation as the leading philosophical critic of his age. Rather than simply present summary descriptions of the great English authors' lives and works, Taine propounded the notion that English literary history was not solely the record of individual achievements. Rather, it had a shape and a structure that could be elucidated, so that each author became a part of a tradition and could be seen as the product of his environment and his age. Literature was no more an accident, or mercly the manifestation of an individual mind, than were the elements of nature.

In collections of essays and lectures in the next ten years and in his travels across Europe, Taine promoted a methodology based, he believed, on the rigor of scientific principles. In a lecture on the nature of art (first given in Paris in 1864 and published in English translation in 1875), Taine established the rules of his method. According to Taine, one must first study the artist's body of work and become familiar with the artist's characteristic themes and techniques. Then one must examine the artistic tradition out of which the artist develops, taking note of how the artist's work is illustrative of that tradition. Finally, it is necessary to explore the social climate, the intellectual influences, the race, the language, and the customs of the world the artist inhabits. Taken in total, this method, in Taine's view, yields a comprehensive, unbiased view of art.

Taine's view of art is historical: "Arts appear and disappear along with certain accompanying social and intellectual conditions," he asserts in his lecture on the nature of art. The implication of his argument is that artistic genius is an intensified example of environmental influences. The artist is the finest expression of the whole cul-

Hippolyte Taine. (Library of Congress)

ture but not a creation unto himself. All that makes William Shakespeare distinctive can be found in his contemporaries, Taine argues, but only Shakespeare expresses the exquisite combination and modulation of those elements that make a great artist. Returning to science as his guiding principle, Taine concludes: "The productions of the human mind, like those of animated nature, can only be explained by their *milieu*." Such a statement, in his estimation, was a law he had discovered in his study of art, not an idea he foisted upon it. He offers his readers "facts," for science "imposes no precepts, but ascertains and verifies laws."

It must be remembered that Taine was writing at a time when eminent Victorian figures such as Thomas Carlyle were advancing a "great man" theory of history. The legacy of Romanticism had been to exult in individualism and to see society coalescing about the figures of extraordinary men. On the contrary, Taine contends, a writer such as Honoré de Balzac is great precisely because he creates a literature of characters who typify their times, their culture, and their race. Balzac's *La Comédie humaine* (1829-1848; *The Human Comedy*, 1885-1893, 1896), his series of novels on French life, are the best history of his era because he is so attuned to the way in which his characters are manifestations of their society. Similarly, Stendhal repays study because he is so intimately aware of how individual psychology is linked to the history of his times. His characters are motivated by historical conditions; there is a logic to their imaginations that springs from their milieu.

In the last twenty years of his life, Taine shifted from an interest in art and philosophy to the writing of a history of contemporary France. Never deeply engaged by political issues, he nevertheless felt the need (given his historical frame of mind) to discover the roots of his culture. Because he believed that societies grow organically, and thus that individuals and events are all connected to one another, he devised a multivolume history beginning with the ancien régime (the era before the revolution) and ending in his own day.

The French Revolution bothered Taine because it seemed more like a disruption than a continuation of history. The year 1789 was when France was radically changed from a society that evolved from a tradition to a new country that established a government according to universal, abstract principles. Taine did not believe that such principles existed, except insofar as they might be seen evolving in history. His profoundly conservative cast of mind could not allow for a catastrophic event that suddenly transforms the structure of a society. In his view, such an upheaval is doomed to failure.

Taine is not nostalgic about the past. Indeed his history of France documents the desperate situation of the people in the twenty-five years preceding the revolution. He does not deny the need for change, but he deplores the anarchy and violence of the revolution. Napoleon I restored order but at the cost of destroying liberty among various social classes. Having to deal with the failed revolutions of his own time (the upheaval of 1848, the Paris Commune of 1871), Taine was not sanguine about the way his countrymen effected change. His rather vague solution was to counsel a sympathetic understanding of the place of all classes and elements of society.

SIGNIFICANCE

Except for his literary essays, Hippolyte-Adolphe Taine is little read in the twenty-first century. His notions of science are outdated and suspect, and he is unable to see that the vaunted objectivity of his methodology is no such thing. When Taine's history of France is examined, it is clear that it is as subjective and determined by his biases as any other history would be. Taine would not have been surprised by this judgment, because he believed that human beings were the products of their times. How-

ever, he did fail to see the contradictions in his own methodology, that his brand of conservatism was temperamental and could not be explained only in terms of his time, place, and tradition.

It has been noted that Taine's reputation since his death has steadily declined. However, subsequent critics and historians owe Taine an enormous debt. For example, Taine reversed the excesses of Romanticism, with its lionizing of the individual, and perceived important facts about the relationship between the individual and society that naturalistic novelists explored with considerable brilliance. Nearly every critic who has covered the subjects and the periods that were at Taine's command has felt compelled to deal with his ideas—if only to refute them. Finally, Taine merits study as one of the last men of letters who tried to integrate his insights into many different fields of study: psychology, literary criticism, aesthetics, art, philosophy, and history. In an era of specialization, his work is still an admirable example of the effort to grasp intellectual life in its entirety.

—*Carl Rollyson*

FURTHER READING

Eustis, Alvin A. *Hippolyte Taine and the Classical Genius*. Berkeley: University of California Press, 1951. A well-written scholarly monograph that concentrates on Taine's debt to classical writers and scholarship. Information is presented succinctly and judiciously. The bibliography remains useful.

Gargan, Edward T., ed. Introduction to *The Origins of Contemporary France*, by Hippolyte-Adolphe Taine. Chicago: University of Chicago Press, 1974. Gargan's long introduction provides important biographical information on Taine and a shrewd analysis of his position as a historian.

Kahn, Sholom J. *Science and Aesthetic Judgement: A Study in Taine's Critical Method*. London: Routledge & Kegan Paul, 1953. An important monograph for specialists, this book will prove somewhat difficult for students not already familiar with several of Taine's texts. Nevertheless, this is an essential study of Taine's philosophy and methodology.

Nias, Hilary. *The Artificial Self: The Psychology of Hippolyte Taine*. Oxford, England: Legenda, 1999. Drawing on Taine's unpublished manuscripts and letters, Nias characterizes Taine as a model European intellectual of the second half of the nineteenth century. She describes how Taine was influenced by Darwinism, new scientific discoveries, and Impressionism to acquire a self-disgusted, tentative, and ironic mentality, similar to the mentality he described in his psychological writings.

Weinstein, Leo. *Hippolyte Taine*. Boston: Twayne, 1972. The only comprehensive introduction in English to Taine's life and work. Chapters on his life, philosophy, method, and psychology; career as a literary and art critic; and role as a historian of France give a thorough summary and critique of Taine's achievements and influence. Notes, an annotated bibliography, and an index make this an indispensable study.

Wellek, René. *A History of Modern Criticism, 1750-1950*. Vol. 4. New Haven, Conn.: Yale University Press, 1965. One of the most important sources for tracing the history of literary criticism and Taine's place within it. Wellek discusses the significance of Taine's *History of English Literature* and the way the critic deals with matters of style.

SEE ALSO: Honoré de Balzac; Thomas Carlyle; Auguste Comte; Napoleon I; Stendhal; Émile Zola.

RELATED ARTICLE in *Great Events from History: The Nineteenth Century, 1801-1900:* c. 1865: Naturalist Movement Begins.

THOMAS TALBOT
Irish-born Canadian pioneer

A retired British army officer, Talbot played a major role in promoting the settlement of what is now Ontario during the early nineteenth century by bringing in new immigrants, overseeing their development of the land and infrastructure, and administering a region that grew to encompass twenty-seven townships on the north shore of Lake Erie.

BORN: July 19, 1771; Malahide, Dublin County, Ireland

DIED: February 5, 1853; London, Upper Canada (now in Ontario, Canada)

AREAS OF ACHIEVEMENT: Geography, military

EARLY LIFE

Thomas Talbot (TAL-buht) was born near Dublin into an old family of the Anglo-Irish aristocracy. Following the military tradition of his family, he obtained an appointment as an ensign in the Sixty-sixth Regiment of Foot shortly before his twelfth birthday. Before turning twenty, he spent two years in Dublin as an aide to the Marquis of Buckingham, who was then the British viceroy for Ireland. In that role he became intimate with the highest circles of European nobility, and his courtly manners became polished to a high gloss.

After Lord Buckingham's resignation, Thomas rejoined his regiment and did garrison duty in the newly acquired British colony of Lower Canada, which later became Quebec. Through the good offices of Lord Buckingham, he soon became an aide to John Graves Simcoe, the first lieutenant governor of Upper Canada (now Ontario). He joined Simcoe as soon as the latter arrived

from England in November of 1791. In addition to using his excellent manners to entertain the lieutenant governor's wife, Talbot was employed as a personal messenger to Native Americans and British representatives in the United States on matters too delicate and secret to be written down.

In June of 1794 Talbot was promoted to a captaincy in the Eighty-fifth Regiment of Foot, and he left the Simcoes. Upon his return to Europe, he fought against the French in Holland and Germany, did garrison duty on Gibralter, and attained the rank of colonel. When he returned to Great Britain, his life seemed to be progressing nicely, but something happened to change its course. Perhaps, he was disappointed in love or frustrated by the pace of his career advancement. No one knows for sure, but some disillusionment with the society of the Old World seems to have persuaded him to go in a new direction. On Christmas day of 1800, he sold his army commission for five thousand guineas and set sail again for the uncharted wilderness of Upper Canada.

LIFE'S WORK

In recognition of his military accomplishments, Talbot was entitled to a five-thousand-acre land grant, which he claimed near Long Point, an Upper Canada location about forty miles distant from the nearest settlements. Under arrangements he made with the government of Upper Canada, he was to receive additional land for each new settler that he set up on his original grant. Talbot originally planned to grow hemp in the fertile soil of his land for sale to the British War Department. However, other crops and activities proved more profitable, and that part of his original plan was never realized.

Talbot's first project, after establishing his own home, was to build several grist- and sawmills to process the grains and lumber that were plentiful in the area into marketable commodities. He also obtained a concession from the government to build a road along the north shore of Lake Erie. He accomplished that task by distributing land to settlers along the route on the condition that they extend the road through their own property during the first two years of their occupancy. If they failed to complete that obligation, or to make other agreed-upon improvements, they were to be removed from the land. Following this scheme, Talbot's territory gradually opened to further development and his original grant was greatly expanded.

Progress was slow at first, however, as Talbot was able to settle only four families on his grant by the end of 1805. At this time, the total population of the settlement, including Talbot's own employees, numbered only about one hundred. Some people suspected that Talbot had invented some of his first recorded settlers in order to extend his territory and preserve his monopoly in Dunwich and Aldborough Counties. During the long course of his operation, Talbot often assumed an aristocratic prerogative, took government powers into his own hands, and did things his own way. In the vast majority of instances, the results were positive, so the government adjusted its policy to follow his lead.

One issue that became controversial was the timing of fee collections from settlers. At first, Talbot collected fees as prescribed by the government, when the settlers first arrived on their plots. After they paid, however, they typically felt entitled to stay regardless of progress of work on their property. Talbot found it more effective to wait until the required work was finished and the settlers were applying for their official ownership papers before collecting their fees. Thus, when settlers failed do the required work within the set times, they had no sense of entitlement to the land, and Talbot could more easily evict them, freeing their plots for others to develop. This approach minimized the problem of absentee ownership, which was a major impediment to settling the territory.

Talbot held many important positions in his settlement and wielded almost complete authority. He was a justice of the peace, a commissioner of oaths, a commissioner for hemp purchasing, the head of the local militia, a trustee for local schools, a roads commissioner, and a magistrate. After a lull in immigration during the War of 1812, settlers began pouring into Talbot's settlement,

which was estimated to have 1,315 families by the end of 1817. However, his personal fortunes had suffered during the war, and he found himself in financial difficulties that lasted well into the 1820's. In 1824, he finally received some compensation for his losses during the war, and he was also awarded an annual pension of four hundred pounds for his long service to the colony. By 1829, the population of his settlement was estimated at some thirty thousand people. However, by the mid-1830's, Talbot was running out of land to distribute.

An eccentric bachelor, Talbot became increasingly cantankerous as he grew older. He kept only sketchy and idiosyncratic records of his complicated operations. When he started his settlement, he got into the habit of recording everything in pencil so that settlers who failed to improve their land could be easily erased from his books. After an altercation with a demanding Scottish highlander, he started dealing with settlers through a small, sliding window, which opened onto his porch. People learned not to bother him after supper because he devoted the hours before bedtime to meditations over brandy.

In February, 1838, the lieutenant governor of Upper Canada relieved Talbot of his unique agency. Long after his official dismissal, Talbot continued to be involved in the affairs of his settlement, and government authorities did not get possession of the township maps on which he had recorded the locations of his settlers' plots until after his death in 1853.

SIGNIFICANCE

Thomas Talbot was an unusual combination of elitist aristocrat and rugged individualist. His firm conviction of his own innate superiority did not translate into the expectation that other people should take care of him. Quite the opposite, he felt a superior obligation to serve others. He left the attractions of high society in Europe to live simply and without ostentation in the Canadian wilderness and took delight in doing the most menial domestic tasks for himself and others.

On the other hand, Talbot's political ideology was extremely conservative and he fought hard against the reformers and republicans of his day. He was, for example, deeply depressed by the passage of the Reform Bill in England in 1832. He referred to Methodist reform groups that challenged exclusive government support for the Church of England and promoted temperance as "Damned Cold Water Drinking Societies, where they meet at night to communicate their poisonous and seditious schemes. . . ."

Aside from personal issues, Talbot's main motivation for his settlement activity was to perform service to the British Empire. He made many trips home and used his old family connections to promote the needs of his settlement over the heads of local colonial officials. Local officials agreed with most of Talbot's practices but not always his tactics. Great Britain's top priority in Canada after the American Revolution was to fill its remaining North American colonies with loyal British subjects. This approach was seen as the best way to contain the crude democracy of the United States, which threatened to spill over from the south.

—*Steven Lehman*

FURTHER READING

Craig, Gerald M. *Upper Canada: The Formative Years*. Toronto: McClelland and Stewart, 1963. Describes the settlement of what is now the province of Ontario from 1784 to 1841 under the colonial oligarchy known as the Family Compact.

Ermatinger, Edward. *The Life of Colonel Talbot and the Talbot Settlement*. Belleville, Ontario: Mika Silk Screening, 1972. An account by a Talbot contemporary that was first published in 1859.

Gray, Charlotte. *Sisters in the Wilderness: The Lives of Susanna Moodie and Catherine Parr Traill*. Toronto: Penguin, 1999. A descriptive account of the day-to-day challenges of life in Upper Canada in the early nineteenth century.

Hamil, Frederick Coyne. *Lake Erie Baron: The Story of Colonel Thomas Talbot*. Toronto: Macmillan, 1955. Despite its age, still the most complete biography of Talbot that is available.

McNairn, Jeffrey L. *The Capacity to Judge: Public Opinion and Deliberative Democracy in Upper Canada, 1791-1854*. Toronto: University of Toronto Press, 2000. Traces the debate over "responsible government" that framed the settlement issue and most others during this era.

SEE ALSO: Susanna Moodie; Louis Riel; David Thompson; Catharine Parr Traill.

RELATED ARTICLES in *Great Events from History: The Nineteenth Century, 1801-1900:* 1829-1836: Irish Immigration to Canada; February 10, 1841: Upper and Lower Canada Unite; August 9, 1842: Webster-Ashburton Treaty Settles Maine's Canadian Border.

TALLEYRAND
French diplomat

Talleyrand directed the foreign relations of France during a time of changing principles and changing regimes—the Directory, the Consulate, the empire, and the Restoration Monarchy—trying to adjust his French patriotism with the establishment of a stable balance of power that formed the basis of European relations for a century.

BORN: February 2, 1754; Paris, France
DIED: May 17, 1838; Paris, France
ALSO KNOWN AS: Charles-Maurice de Talleyrand-Périgord (full name); Prince de Bénévent
AREAS OF ACHIEVEMENT: Government and politics, diplomacy

EARLY LIFE

Talleyrand's family came from an old and highly distinguished line of sovereign counts, but at the time he was born the family had lost a considerable amount of its former importance. His parents were courtiers whose business, attending the offspring of Louis XV, gave them little time to spend with their most recent addition. Talleyrand was sent to a wet nurse, a poor woman who lived in the Saint-Jacques district. Although such surrogate mothering was a common practice, with Talleyrand it was excessive: The parents did not see their son for the next four years. While he had been in his nurse's care for only several months, he fell from a chest of drawers, breaking his right foot. The injury did not receive proper medical attention and the bones knit badly, leaving him with a clubfoot. For the rest of his life he was unable to walk without a cane or a brace.

When Talleyrand was three, his older brother died, leaving him heir to the family title and estates. He would have become a soldier, but his injury made this impossible. The family therefore decided to have him forfeit his rights in favor of his younger brother, Archambaud, and become a churchman. After elementary school, he attended the seminary of Saint Sulpice. From there, he went to the Sorbonne, receiving, in 1774, a degree in theology. He took his first vows in April, 1775. Several months later, as the Abbé de Périgord, he attended the royal coronation of Louis XVI at the Cathedral of Rheims.

Talleyrand's noble lineage gave him entrée to the court and its opportunities. In September, 1775, he was confirmed as the abbot of Saint-Rémy in Rheims, a sinecure that paid him eighteen thousand livres a year. Henceforth, his rise in the church hierarchy was rapid: In 1779, he became a deacon and a priest; in 1880, he became an agent-general of the Assembly of the Clergy to manage ecclesiastical property; in 1789, he became the bishop of Autun. He also managed to pick up other properties in Champagne and Poitou. All of his benefices combined gave the thirty-four-year-old prelate a personal income of about 100,000 livres a year. With such resources he could now live the good life, far from ecclesiastical duties in provincial cities.

In church matters Talleyrand had a reputation as a defender of tradition and privilege, but his private life was otherwise. He preferred to spend his time in Paris, frequenting the salons, conversing with such men as Voltaire, Comte de Mirabeau, and Charles Alexandre de Calonne, and seducing women. His sexual successes were the subject of much gossip, admiration, and amusement.

Despite absenteeism from his official obligations—Talleyrand visited his bishopric only once, for a period of thirty days—he became Autun's clerical delegate to the meeting of the Estates General held at Versailles in May, 1789. The petition of grievance, or cahier, which he brought with him, and which he helped to write, called for the establishment of local representative government, for the abolition of feudal privilege, and for the creation of a national assembly to curb the power of royal despotism. He favored putting the estates of the Church at the disposition of the nation; when the time came, he provided the rationale for reconciling such expropriation with the sacredness of private property. Talleyrand argued that these church lands had been the property of the nation all along, maintaining the entire body of the faithful in a Catholic land could be the nation itself. His knowledge of Church administration was invaluable in helping to destroy the organization's power.

Talleyrand also gave legitimacy to the civil constitution of the clergy by celebrating Mass on the Feast of the Federation, July 14, 1790, at the Champ de Mars on the first anniversary of the taking of the Bastille. He helped consecrate recently elected bishops to replace those who had refused to pledge their loyalty to the new order. Shortly afterward, in February, 1791, he renounced his priestly vows and returned to the status of layman, whereupon he was excommunicated by the pope.

LIFE'S WORK

Talleyrand's first attempt at national diplomacy, a métier that became his main profession the rest of his life, came in 1792. Because of the self-denying ordinance, he was unable to run for election to the new parliament created by the old constituent assembly. Instead, he managed to be sent on a mission to London to try to secure British neutrality in the event of the outbreak of hostilities between France and Austria. The mission was not successful; the British wanted to maintain their free hand as the holder of the balance of power and rejected any commitments. Talleyrand nevertheless continued his diplomatic efforts. He returned to London on two other occasions—in January and May of 1792—but the results were equally disappointing.

At home Talleyrand watched with dismay the increasingly radical direction of politics. During his third visit to the British capital, France was at war with both Austria and Prussia. The early defeats led to the outbreak of domestic violence that led to the September Massacres,

Talleyrand. (Library of Congress)

which made life dangerous for all men of Talleyrand's antecedents. With the coming of the Reign of Terror, he fled to Great Britain, then was forced to leave for the United States, where for a time he lived in Philadelphia. He did not like American hospitality. In his opinion the climate was too hot or too cold, there was a dreadful lack of culture, and the food was inedible.

Not until 1796 did he return to France, the new government of the Directory giving him permission. He found that in his absence he had been elected to the newly formed Institute of Arts and Sciences. He renewed old acquaintances, through which he came to the attention of the powerful director, Vicomte Paul de Barras, who had him named minister of foreign affairs in July, 1797. At this time France was in an expansionist mood, believing its destiny lay in extending its boundaries to the Alps and the Rhine and in liberating Europe's suppressed peoples from the yoke of feudalism and despotism. Its mission was to carry out a crusade for universal freedom.

Such ambitions did not seem unreasonable to nationalists, even though, as long as France was committed to such goals, there would be constant war. None who held high office at this time could have publicly believed otherwise, least of all a minister of foreign affairs. Talleyrand wanted to make France respected and feared, but he believed war to be wasteful and absurd. He wanted to end the current hostilities with Austria and Great Britain, but the victory had to contribute to the stabilization of Europe by not destroying the balance of power. It must also contribute to French prosperity.

To these ends Talleyrand put forth a scheme to establish French preponderance in the eastern Mediterranean by mounting an expedition to Egypt. The Turkish Empire was in dissolution and, by seizing its choicest parts, France could expand its commercial interests and hold bargaining counters to bring about peace with the British. Ever mindful of his own interests, Talleyrand began cultivating a friendship with Napoleon I, who also favored the Egyptian campaign. Both were contemptuous of the current political system that they believed was contributing to French defeat and weakness.

In July, 1799, sensing that the end of the Directory was near, Talleyrand resigned his post and retired to private life. When Napoleon returned from Egypt in October of that year, Talleyrand joined a conspiracy to bring the general to power. For his support, Napoleon made Talleyrand foreign minister. The two seemed to agree on the essentials of French foreign policy and upon the necessity of creating a European equilibrium that could assure the security and prestige of France.

Talleyrand presided over the reorganization of Germany. He helped to arrange compensation for princes dispossessed of their territories on the west bank of the Rhine by giving them church lands in other parts of Germany. These transactions satisfied the time-honored principle of compensations, but they also made Talleyrand tremendously wealthy. In fact, the foreign minister was one of the greediest men of France in an age renowned for corruption. He saw nothing wrong in demanding kickbacks for his services to enable him to live in the style befitting his station. Such venality often made it difficult to ascertain the dividing line between personal and public advantage.

The height of his professionalism undoubtedly came with the signature of the Peace of Amiens, on March 25, 1802. In this treaty the British had to acknowledge effective French control of the Netherlands, Belgium, the left bank of the Rhine, and northern Italy. The British, especially in recognizing French power in the lowlands, abandoned a policy that they once regarded as essential for their security. Thus, after a decade of wars, France emerged as the most powerful state in Europe. Talleyrand boasted that his country now enjoyed such power, glory, and influence that even the most ambitious person could desire nothing more for his country.

Napoleon, however, was not the sort of master ever to be satisfied. While his foreign minister struggled to make the Peace of Amiens the basis of a new European equilibrium, Napoleon was planning ever larger conquests. Relations between the two men began to chill, but Talleyrand continued to share in Napoleon's glory. He could be an embarrassingly servile sycophant when it suited his purposes. When it at last became obvious that Talleyrand could no longer reconcile his sense of moderation and longing for personal survival with such a willful conqueror, he resigned. This event occurred in 1807, after the signing of the Treaty of Tilsit with Russia that recognized the division of Europe into two spheres: the Russian in the East and the French in the West. Talleyrand, having accumulated sufficient worldly goods to live in royal style—he was the master of the vast feudal estate of Valençay and of a superb town house in Paris on the Place de la Concorde—became the reigning prince of Benevento but again left before the fall of a regime.

Napoleon was vexed at his minister's desertion but continued to use him for special tasks. In these tasks Talleyrand proved less than reliable. At the summit conference at Erfurt with Alexander I, Talleyrand secretly urged the Russian czar to stand firm and not let Napoleon destroy Austria. After helping Napoleon arrange the overthrow of the Spanish Bourbons, Talleyrand turned against the venture and conspired with Police Minister Joseph Fouché to have Napoleon overthrown, replacing him with Napoleon's brother-in-law, Joachim Murat. Napoleon discovered who was behind the scheme and denounced Talleyrand, on January 28, 1809, before a restricted meeting of the council of state.

Talleyrand lived in retirement until 1814, when, with the Napoleonic empire in ruins, he helped arrange the Bourbon Restoration. Talleyrand insisted that this be conditional upon the establishment of constitutional government. Talleyrand again became minister of foreign affairs. He was largely responsible for the Treaty of Paris, which concluded peace between France and the allies. He was also the principal French representative at the Congress of Vienna—arranged by the British, Russians, Prussians, and Austrians— which restored an equilibrium to a Europe ravaged by a quarter of a century of war.

Talleyrand retired once more, this time unwillingly, in September, 1815. Fifteen years later, however, with the advent of the July Monarchy, he was again offered the foreign ministry. He chose instead to go to London as an ambassador. He stayed in this post the next four years, participating in the negotiations that established an independent Belgium. In his long career he had served under seven different regimes and had intrigued against more than half of them; as he later noted, however, these betrayals had the support of a majority of his fellow countrymen. Upon his deathbed, he insisted that he receive extreme unction on the knuckles of his clenched fists rather than on his palms as befitting a bishop of the Roman Catholic Church.

SIGNIFICANCE

Talleyrand embraced the assumptions existent since the Treaty of Westphalia (1648) that foreign policy was essentially nonideological and that states could preserve their independence by preserving a proper balance of power. This moderate approach made him favor creating an entente with the entrenched powers against the revisionist powers, which meant assisting Great Britain and Austria curb Russia and Prussia, as he did at the Congress of Vienna. He characteristically exaggerated his role at that summit meeting, but his performance there was consistent with the principles by which he believed the affairs of nations should be conducted. He told the representatives of the great powers:

> The first need of Europe is to banish forever the opinion that right can be acquired by conquest alone, and to cause the revival of that sacred principle of legitimacy from which all order and stability spring.

Through skillful exploitation of the differences among the allies, Talleyrand managed to put France on a more equal footing with them, helping to increase the respectability of the French monarchy as a force for order, moderation, and conservatism.

Although frequently vilified for his material and sexual excesses, Talleyrand is a Freudian's delight with his loveless mother, his disinheritance, and his love-hate relationship with Catholicism. Talleyrand stands forth as the quintessential diplomat, one who realized that international politics is the art of the possible. He realized, too, that national security is not dependent on the survival of the fittest but on the mutual acceptance by great powers of their limitations and on the need to temper their rivalries and ambitions to preserve the security of one another.

—*Wm. Laird Kleine-Ahlbrandt*

FURTHER READING

Brinton, Crane. *The Lives of Talleyrand*. New York: W. W. Norton, 1936. If Brinton's biography were not so engaging, intelligent, and analytically erudite, it would be dismissed as a rank apology. Indeed, Brinton seems to go out of his way to make allowances for Talleyrand, but his presentation of Talleyrand as the consummate moderate diplomat is nevertheless convincing.

Cooper, Duff. *Talleyrand*. New York: Harper & Row, 1932. This Tory politician makes no great discourse on Talleyrand's skills or vices, presenting him simply as an eminently sensible Frenchman, a practical, peace-loving man free from the vice of nationalism and horrified by the spirit of conquest—in a sense, one of the first Europeans.

Dwyer, Philip G. *Talleyrand*. London: Longman, 2002. Dwyer portrays Talleyrand as a pragmatic politician who was willing to mediate between various factions to achieve a compromise. Part of the Profiles in Power series.

Ferrero, Guglielmo. *The Reconstruction of Europe: Talleyrand and the Congress of Vienna, 1814-1815*. Translated by Theodore R. Jaeckel. New York: G. P. Putnam's Sons, 1941. Ferrero credits three men with the creation of a new and stable order out of the ruins of the Napoleonic empire: Czar Alexander I, King

Louis XVIII, and Talleyrand, who "seems to have the right of precedence over all the statesmen who have appeared in the Western world since the Revolution." Ferrero attributes Talleyrand's predisposition to revolt against all regimes and powers to the childhood accident that left him disabled.

Greenbaum, Louis S. *Talleyrand, Statesman and Priest: The Agent-General of the Clergy and the Church of France at the End of the Old Regime.* Washington, D.C.: Catholic University of America Press, 1970. Primarily an examination of the administrative history of the French Catholic Church in the last third of the eighteenth century. Greenbaum also shows how such an organization became the school for statesmanship in forging the political career of Talleyrand.

Orieux, Jean. *Talleyrand: The Art of Survival.* Translated by Patricia Wolf. New York: Alfred A. Knopf, 1974. Comprehensive treatment that borrows heavily from the definitive biography in French by Georges Lacour-Gayet. Written in a catechistic style, the work portrays Talleyrand as a great custodian and transmitter of civilization, one "ever willing to meet the demands of the future for the sake of survival and the preservation of mankind's achievement."

Talleyrand-Périgord, Charles Maurice de. *Memoirs of the Prince de Talleyrand.* Edited by the Duc de Broglie. Translated by Raphaël Ledos de Beaufort and Mrs. Angus Hall. 5 vols. New York: G. P. Putnam's Sons, 1891-1892. A standard primary source. The first two volumes are somewhat sketchy in documentation. There is some compensation in the fullness of the official correspondence concerning the Congress of Vienna and the London Conference.

SEE ALSO: Alexander I; Viscount Castlereagh; Eugène Delacroix; Metternich; Napoleon I.

RELATED ARTICLES in *Great Events from History: The Nineteenth Century, 1801-1900:* September 25, 1804: Twelfth Amendment Is Ratified; April 11, 1814-July 29, 1830: France's Bourbon Dynasty Is Restored; September 15, 1814-June 11, 1815: Congress of Vienna; November 20, 1815: Second Peace of Paris.

ROGER BROOKE TANEY
American jurist

During his long tenure as chief justice of the United States, Taney used his considerable talents to adjust the law to the new egalitarian political and economic currents and states' rights concerns of Jacksonian democracy, while preserving the essentials of both property rights and the authority of the federal government. In dealing with the volatile issue of the expansion of slavery in the territories, Taney also sought moderation until the Dred Scott *case, when he unsuccessfully attempted to resolve judicially what Congress and the president were unable to decide legislatively.*

BORN: March 17, 1777; Calvert County, Maryland
DIED: October 12, 1864; Washington, D.C.
AREA OF ACHIEVEMENT: Law

EARLY LIFE

Roger Brooke Taney was the third of seven children of Michael Taney, a member of old Maryland planter family of some wealth who had been educated in Europe. His mother, née Monica Brooke, was the daughter of another distinguished Maryland planter family. Michael Taney, though hot-tempered and impatient, loved his children and took great interest in their upbringing. Monica Taney was a pious and gentle person of little education, always willing to give help to anyone in need, including slaves. Roger Taney apparently learned from her solicitude for American blacks.

Taney attended a local school, then a boarding school, and then for several years he and the other Taney children studied at home under David English, a tutor and graduate of Princeton hired by their father. At the age of fifteen, Taney was sent off to Dickinson College in Carlisle, Pennsylvania, where he studied and lived with the difficult but brilliant Dr. Charles Nisbit, president of the college. In the spring of 1795, Taney passed the oral examination required for graduation and was voted valedictorian by his classmates. It was an honor he had wanted but did not relish achieving. Public speaking was difficult for Taney throughout his life, upsetting his somewhat delicate health and often leaving him worn out and ill for days. Taney was a thin, flat-chested youth with thick black hair, solemn eyes, and a face that showed much character but was not handsome. Like his mother, he was painfully shy, but those who learned to know him found a warm and friendly personality with an engaging and penetrating intellect. Taney had a gift for stating the difficult in clear, simple language, which served him well in his profession.

From 1796 to 1799, Taney clerked in the office of a prominent Annapolis judge. During this time, he made friends with Francis Scott Key, later famous for his poem "The Star-Spangled Banner." After being admitted to the bar in 1799, Taney tried practicing in several locations, but because of insufficient business, he moved to Frederick, Maryland, in March of 1801, where he remained for the next twenty years. Frederick was a small town of three thousand, but there were old family friends and relatives in the vicinity.

Taney accepted all types of cases and was soon the most prominent lawyer in the area. In 1803, he was a candidate for the Maryland state legislature, but lost. During this time, he courted Anne Key, sister of his friend Francis Scott Key, who lived nearby at Terra Ruba, the Key family estate. By 1805, he was secure enough financially to propose, and they were married on January 6, 1806. Anne Taney was a kind and tranquil person who soothed Taney when his nerves were frayed, nursed him when his health was bad, and was a great comfort to him all their married life. Six daughters and a son, who died in infancy, were born to the Taneys.

Although a respectable stalwart in Maryland Federalist circles, Taney leaned toward more flexible democratic ideals, a tendency that the War of 1812 accentuated. He led a dissenting prowar faction nicknamed the "Coodies." His popularity with the voters increased as a result, and he was elected to the Maryland senate in 1816, serving until 1821. During these years, partly as a result of his southern plantation heritage, Taney opposed the second Bank of the United States, particularly after the economic slump of 1819, which was widely blamed on the bank. He welcomed the bank's power to provide regulation of state banks but opposed what he perceived as its excessive power and privilege.

Taney also became involved in projects to aid black Americans. He was no abolitionist but did believe that slavery was an unfortunate institution and should be ended someday. He supported the African colonization movement for free blacks and measures to protect free blacks from unscrupulous slavers who would kidnap them for sale as slaves in the lower South, freed his own slaves, and was always kind and attentive to their interests. However, while he agreed that slavery must be ended, he believed that the change must be undertaken slowly and solely by the actions of the individual states. He was deeply concerned all his life that the federal government would intrude and end slavery abruptly and destroy the South.

By 1823, when Taney was forty-six, he had acquired a statewide legal reputation and an increasing amount of business requiring him to be in Baltimore. To advance his career, he sold his practice and home and moved to Baltimore. Taney's success, however, was atypical. In an era in which public speaking was judged by style and the ability to quote from great literature, he spoke without gestures or emphasis, in a low voice, simply, earnestly, and without apparent artfulness. The effect, coming from the frail, stooped figure in black, ill-fitting clothes, with a long, solemn face, was considerable. He had many wealthy clients, and by 1827, he was so well known that the governor selected him for the prestigious post of state attorney general. He held the post and continued his private practice until 1831.

LIFE'S WORK

After the collapse of the Federalist Party and the adoption of many Federalist ideas by the Jeffersonians during the Era of Good Feelings, Taney drifted into the Democratic Party. In 1824, he supported the election of Andrew Jackson but was not active in the campaign. His former Federalist associates, who had not forgiven Taney for leading the Coodies, generally supported John Quincy Adams and his program, which favored commercial and financial interests over agriculture. Taney could not agree with them and by 1826 headed the Maryland Central Committee to elect Jackson in the 1828 election. When a scandal involving Jackson's secretary of war, John Henry Eaton, split Jackson's cabinet, Secretary of State Martin Van Buren maneuvered to get the entire cabinet to resign and President Jackson to appoint a new one. The United States attorney generalship was offered to Taney, who accepted. It did not pay well, and Taney had not wanted a position with the government, but he decided that he should accept.

Taney gained national prominence and notoriety in Jackson's cabinet over his role in the Bank War. When a law was passed in Congress renewing the charter of the second Bank of the United States, Taney recommended that Jackson veto it; Jackson agreed, and Taney wrote the constitutional portion of Jackson's veto message. Taney was convinced that the bank meant to put state banks out of business and dominate the American economy. Jackson had similar suspicions. The probank interests in Congress, which were primarily members of the Whig Party, were furious with Taney and in June of 1834 refused to confirm him as secretary of the treasury when Jackson appointed him to that post.

Taney returned to Baltimore to resume his law practice. Jackson kept seeking his advice and offering him various official positions, which Taney refused until he was offered an associate justice position on the Supreme Court. In January of 1835, the Whigs in the Senate once again blocked Taney's confirmation. In July of 1835, Chief Justice John Marshall died, and President Jackson, determined to find a place in government for Taney, nominated him as Marshall's successor. After the fall election, a new, more favorable Congress was sitting, and this time Taney was confirmed, on March 15, 1836.

As chief justice of the United States, Taney brought change to the Supreme Court. When riding circuit, he ended the custom of giving long lectures to grand juries on the philosophy of American law and government. Federalist judges had often turned such lectures into political speeches against the Democratic Party. He also ended the custom of wearing small clothes (knee breeches) under judicial robes and wore ordinary trousers instead.

In *Charles River Bridge v. Warren Bridge* (1837), his first important constitutional case, Taney gave notice of a change of emphasis from the supremacy of national law toward states' rights. The case involved the constitutional provision barring states from altering the obligations in a contract. The Marshall Court had interpreted this clause strictly to protect property rights, including even implied obligations. Taney was not hostile to property rights or the contract clause of the Constitution but thought Marshall's interpretation too extreme and believed that an implied obligation should not prohibit state legislatures from exercising their best judgment on behalf of the general welfare and to promote progress.

In other cases, Taney made it clear that the Marshall doctrine on the supremacy of national law to control interstate commerce would not be destroyed, only amended to allow some state involvement. Although Taney distrusted the power of great aggregations of wealth in corporate form and believed that the state needed some authority to police such power, he also recognized the advantages to the American economy of the corporations' success and the need for the Court to protect their interests in the American economic system.

Taney was not the dominating figure on the Court that Marshall had been. It was not because he lacked the brilliance, but because he chose to operate in a more colle-

gial fashion and because the Taney Court had a greater diversity of political philosophy than did Marshall's. It sometimes proved impossible for the Court to arrive at a consensus. It is perhaps the mark of his ability that he achieved agreement as often as he did in times that were racked by sectionalism and the changes brought by the beginnings of the Industrial Revolution.

The most troublesome issue for the Supreme Court was slavery. The issue reached the Court in the form of questions concerning nonpayment for slaves brought illegally into a state, whether slaves who had overpowered a ship's crew and sailed to a northern port were free men or still slaves to be returned to their owners, and free black sailors on English ships who were locked up while their ship was docked in Charleston.

These cases were slowly dragging the Supreme Court into the sectional conflicts over slavery when the case of *Prigg v. Pennsylvania* (1842) came before the Court and sped up the process. Justice Joseph Story, writing for the majority, which did not include Taney, declared a Pennsylvania law unconstitutional because it interfered with a federal power. The state law would make free persons of slaves who could reach the state's territory, which conflicted with the national government's responsibility to see fugitive slaves returned to their proper owners. Story went on, however, to declare that federal power over the matter was exclusive. Taney disagreed because he did not want to discourage those states willing to help, nor did he like the implications for Congress.

Soon, many northern states made it illegal for their state and local officials to give any aid to federal officers attempting to enforce the federal Fugitive Slave Law. The southern states then asked Congress to consider the problem and enact a stronger law, the very action Taney had feared. Any congressional attempt to cope with the problem could only increase North-South friction. Taney was aware that if the friction increased too much, the South would be likely to attempt secession. He believed that if slavery remained strictly a state issue, a North-South confrontation could be avoided, and the South would then have the time necessary to end it slowly, without massive disruption. This appears to be the motivation behind his generally misunderstood and infamous *Dred Scott* decision.

There had been several attempts to get the Supreme Court to rule on the federal government's power to prohibit the expansion of slavery into the territories. The issue came squarely before the Court in 1857 in the *Dred Scott* case. The specific issue was whether Dred Scott, a slave, had been made a free man when his master took him first to a free state and then to a territory free of slavery because of the Missouri Compromise. There was enormous political pressure put on the Court to resolve what neither the president nor Congress wanted to touch.

At first, the Court tried to dodge the issue and decide the case on the narrow grounds that in returning voluntarily with his master to Missouri, Dred Scott reconfirmed his status as a slave, and, because slaves had no right to sue in court, the Supreme Court had no jurisdiction. This would have meant a low-key opinion. Justice Louis McLean, however, hoping to be nominated by the newly formed Republican Party for president, insisted on writing a dissenting opinion to advertise his position that Congress had the authority to decide whether slavery could exist in a territory and that the Missouri Compromise was constitutional.

Taney felt impelled by McLean's improvident action to answer for the Court's majority. Taney reasoned that the South's and the Union's security required that the Court declare that slaves were property and not persons, that property could not sue in court, that Congress had no authority to allow a kind of property—in this case slaves—in one part of the American territories while making it illegal in the rest of the territories, that this meant the Missouri Compromise was unconstitutional, and that Congress was obliged by the Constitution to protect all forms of property in all parts of the territories equally. Because the Constitution recognized the institution of slavery and the Court was bound by the Constitution, no other decision on these issues was possible.

The uproar in the North over the Court's decision, however, was enormous. The seven majority justices were bitterly vilified as the vicious minions of slavocracy, especially Taney. The abolitionists, the Free-Soilers, and the Republicans perceived the Missouri Compromise as a proof of the power of Congress over slavery in the territories, and its constitutionality was central to their case against the expansion of slavery in the territories. The *Dred Scott* decision left their whole political platform in a constitutional shambles. Taney did not reply to his critics, and his friends were unable and unequal to the task. The prestige of the Court collapsed, and the federal government was now virtually helpless to resolve the conflict over slavery in a manner acceptable to both North and South. Taney was impressed and encouraged by President Abraham Lincoln's conciliatory inaugural address, but the South greeted it with secession.

Taney was an old, sick man when the Civil War began, and his last years were difficult; his wife had died in 1855, few members of the Lincoln administration had anything but scorn for him, and the press continued to vilify his decisions. He continued, though, to insist that the Constitution be honored even in war. When he issued a writ of *habeas corpus* to force the army to release John Merryman, a prominent Marylander arrested for suspected secessionist activities, he was in fact declaring President Lincoln's suspension of the writ unconstitutional. When the matter was finally decided by a Republican Court after Taney's death, Taney was fully vindicated and an important new rule of law was established.

Taney made other attempts to restrain the federal government's exercise of arbitrary power, and each time, he was attacked by the press and rebuffed by the executive branch of the government. Nevertheless, he continued and also drafted opinions on important constitutional principles likely to come up in cases before the Court. In the fall of 1864, a chronic intestinal disorder from which he had suffered for some years became acute and violently painful. With his mind clear until the end and two of his daughters by him, he died October 12, at 10:00 P.M. As he had requested, the funeral service was a quiet and modest affair, all the more so because most Republican cabinet officers refused to attend.

SIGNIFICANCE

Taney was a man of modest tastes, but his intellect and strength of character made of him a judicial statesman of the highest order. Before *Dred Scott*, even his critics respected him, and some, such as Henry Clay, even came to admire him. As chief justice, he first dedicated himself to restraining the concentrations of financial, commercial, and industrial power that threatened to dominate and plunder the agricultural majority. He was neither radical nor doctrinaire in his judicial philosophy. The Marshall Court's doctrines protecting inalienable rights were not destroyed and even became stronger in being adapted to the changing economic conditions of the Industrial Revolution.

As the sectional conflict over slavery increased, Taney perceived its potential threat to the South and to the Union. He hoped to keep Congress from assuming any authority over slavery to avoid tempting the North to force its views on the South. Should the North attempt coercion, Taney could conceive of only two possible results: Either the North would succeed and the South be destroyed, or the South would choose secession and rupture with the Union. Both alternatives could be avoided if the slave states were allowed the time necessary to find their own means of ending their peculiar institution, a development to which he was sympathetic and that he considered inevitable.

The *Dred Scott* decision became the means by which Taney attempted to carry out these ideas, but only after Justice McLean insisted on publishing his contrary beliefs. Here Taney may have made an error in strategy. It might have been better for the Court to ignore McLean and keep to the original narrowly based decision. It is unlikely, however, that it would have made any difference. The political moderates who had achieved the compromises of 1820 and 1850 had been too far reduced in number by 1857 to support the Court's solution.

—Richard L. Hillard

FURTHER READING

Baxter, Maurice G. *One and Inseparable: Daniel Webster and the Union*. Cambridge, Mass.: Harvard University Press, 1984. A superb biography of one of Taney's most formidable political opponents, who frequently argued cases before the Supreme Court during much of Taney's time as chief justice. Provides an original view of Taney's years on the Court.

Fehrenbacher, Don E. *The Dred Scott Case: Its Significance in American Law and Politics*. New York: Oxford University Press, 1978. This excellent example of historical writing is a serious and detailed scholarly account of the *Dred Scott* case, with considerable attention given to the whole range of issues facing the United States on the eve of the Civil War.

Friedman, Lawrence M. *A History of American Law*. New York: Simon & Schuster, 1973. A readable yet scholarly history of American law from colonial times to 1900, with a short epilogue on the twentieth century. Mentions the impact of the Taney Court, but there is little about Taney personally.

Horwitz, Morton J. *The Transformation of American Law, 1780-1860*. Cambridge, Mass.: Harvard University Press, 1977. Probably the best single volume on the history of American law of the era yet written. Emphasis is on the transformation of English law in the colonies into a modern national legal system and how this transformation aided economic development. Mentions Taney only briefly.

Huebner, Timothy S. *The Taney Court: Justices, Rulings, and Legacy*. Santa Barbara, Calif.: ABC-CLIO, 2003. An examination of Taney's twenty-eight-year tenure on the Supreme Court, including historical background, biographical sketches of the justices, and analyses of the Court's major decisions and legacy.

Hyman, Harold M., and William Wiecek. *Equal Justice Under Law: Constitutional Development, 1835-1875*. New York: Harper and Row, 1982. A thorough and scholarly treatment of constitutional history from 1835 to 1875. The early chapters include discussions of the decisions of the Taney Court.

Kelly, Alfred H., Winfred A. Harbison, and Herman Belz. *The American Constitution: Its Origins and Development*. 6th ed. New York: W. W. Norton, 1983. An excellent single-volume constitutional history of the United States. Emphasis on cultural and historical influences. Includes mention of Taney and the Supreme Court's decisions during his tenure as chief justice, but covers little of his personal life.

Kutler, Stanley I. *Privilege and Creative Destruction: The Charles River Bridge Case*. Philadelphia: J. B. Lippincott, 1971. An excellent short discussion of the *Charles River Bridge* case, its background, and Taney's reasons for the decision. Little concern for Taney's personal life.

Newmyer, R. Kent. *The Supreme Court Under Marshall and Taney*. New York: Thomas Y. Crowell, 1968. A succinct but thorough and perceptive study of the Taney Court in the context of the people and events of the times. The Taney chapters concentrate on his tenure as chief justice.

Rehnquist, Warren H. *The Supreme Court*. New ed. New York: Knopf, 2001. Chief Justice Rehnquist provides a history of the Court and its most significant decisions, including the *Dred Scott* case. The book also includes biographical information about Taney.

Swisher, Carl Brent. *Roger B. Taney*. New York: Macmillan, 1935. This is the only scholarly biography of Taney, and, although dated, it is very well done and useful. The author explains Taney's constitutional principles within the context of his experience and heritage.

SEE ALSO: John Quincy Adams; Salmon P. Chase; Henry Clay; Andrew Jackson; Francis Scott Key; Abraham Lincoln; John Marshall; Dred Scott; Joseph Story; Martin Van Buren.

RELATED ARTICLES in *Great Events from History: The Nineteenth Century, 1801-1900:* July 10, 1832: Jackson Vetoes Rechartering of the Bank of the United States; August 1, 1846: Establishment of Independent U.S. Treasury; March 6, 1857: *Dred Scott v. Sandford*; March 4, 1861: Lincoln Is Inaugurated President.

ZACHARY TAYLOR
President of the United States (1849-1950)

After climaxing a nearly forty-year military career with major victories in the Mexican War, Taylor used his popularity as a war hero to win office as twelfth president of the United States but served only a little more than one year before he died.

BORN: November 24, 1784; Orange County, Virginia
DIED: July 9, 1850; Washington, D.C.
ALSO KNOWN AS: Old Rough and Ready
AREAS OF ACHIEVEMENT: Military, government and politics

EARLY LIFE

Born at a kinsman's Virginia country home, Zachary Taylor was the third of eight children of Richard and Sarah Dabney Strother Taylor, both members of prominent Virginia families. His father had been a lieutenant colonel in a Virginia regiment during the American Revolution; his paternal grandfather, also named Zachary Taylor, was a wealthy planter and surveyor general of Virginia.

During 1769 and 1770, Richard Taylor surveyed land in central Kentucky and around the falls of the Ohio at the modern city of Louisville. In the spring of 1785, shortly after Zachary's birth, Richard Taylor moved his family to Jefferson County, Kentucky, where he carved out a farm known as Springfield, near Louisville. As a youth, Zachary studied under Kean O'Hara, who would become one of Kentucky's leading early nineteenth century educators, and Elisha Ayer, an itinerant Connecticut teacher. He also assisted his father with farm work.

In 1806, possessing a youthful passion for a military career, Taylor got a brief taste of army life as a volunteer in the Kentuckian militia. His long career as an officer did not commence until June, 1808, however, when he received a commission as first lieutenant in the United States Army from Secretary of War Henry Dearborn. Appointed to the Seventh Infantry Regiment, he spent several months on recruiting duty in Kentucky, followed by temporary command of Fort Pickering, near modern Memphis, Tennessee, before reporting to General James Wilkinson at New Orleans in June, 1809. A short time later, he contracted yellow fever and returned to Louisville to recover. While at home, he met Margaret Mackall Smith, whom he married on June 21, 1810. They had six children, four of whom lived to maturity. Their daughter Sarah Knox Taylor was the first wife of Confederate

president Jefferson Davis. Richard Taylor, their only son, became a lieutenant general in the Confederate army.

After his recovery and marriage, Taylor was promoted to captain and assigned to General William Henry Harrison, territorial governor of Indiana. In April, 1812, just before the War of 1812, Captain Taylor assumed command of Fort Harrison, near Terre Haute, which he successfully defended against an attack by some four hundred Indians the following September. Promoted to the rank of brevet major, he commanded several frontier posts during the second war with England.

In early 1815, Taylor won promotion to the full rank of major, but when the army was disbanded, he was reduced to his prewar rank of captain. Deciding to pursue private business, he declined reassignment, resigned his commission, and returned to his family's Kentucky farm.

Now thirty years old, Taylor epitomized neither the country gentleman nor the military hero. Five feet, eight inches in height, he was muscular and broad-shouldered with disproportionately long arms. He had an oval face, a wide, somewhat slanting brow, and prominent cheekbones. His long nose and hazel eyes gave him an eaglelike appearance.

LIFE'S WORK

Zachary Taylor was devoted to the soil, but his passion for military service was even stronger. Thus, in 1816, when President James Madison offered to reinstate him at his previous rank of major, Taylor accepted. His initial assignment was command of Fort Howard, near Green Bay, Wisconsin, where he remained for two years. After a furlough in Kentucky, he received a promotion to lieutenant colonel in 1819 and was assigned to the Fourth Infantry at New Orleans. A series of commands and special assignments followed over the next twelve years.

In 1822, Taylor built Fort Jesup, Louisiana, and the following year, he served as commandant of Baton Rouge. In 1824, he was appointed superintendent general of the recruiting service at Cincinnati and Louisville and served until 1826, when he reported to Washington, D.C., to serve on a board chaired by General Winfield Scott to study militia organization. In May, 1828, Taylor assumed command of Fort Snelling, in the unorganized Minnesota territory. Fourteen months later, he took command of Fort Crawford at Prairie du Chien in the Michigan Territory, now part of Wisconsin. There he remained until mid-1830.

In April, 1832, Taylor was promoted to colonel. Meanwhile, the Black Hawk War had erupted in Illinois. Colonel Taylor, on leave in Kentucky after recovering from an illness, sped to Galena, Illinois, and in May took charge of the First Infantry Regiment, under command of General Henry Atkinson. Three months later, Taylor participated in the decisive Battle of Bad Axe on the Mississippi River, north of Prairie du Chien. Black Hawk escaped the battlefield but was captured in late August. Taylor received custody of the defeated war chief and turned him over to Second Lieutenant Jefferson Davis, who escorted Black Hawk to Jefferson Barracks, Missouri.

With the end of the Black Hawk War, Taylor resumed command of Fort Crawford, where he remained until November, 1836. During this duty, he demonstrated a strong interest in the education of both white and Indian children and attempted to control the harsh practices of whiskey merchants and fur traders in their dealings with the tribes in the region. Upon relinquishing his command at Fort Crawford, the colonel reported to Jefferson Barracks and took charge of the right wing of the army's Western Department under General Edmund P. Gaines. In this capacity, Taylor exercised military authority over the entire Northwest.

Taylor's new command lasted less than eight months. In July, 1837, Taylor received instructions to take elements of the First Infantry from Forts Snelling and Crawford to Tampa Bay, Florida, where General Thomas S. Jesup was bogged down in the Second Seminole War. While the colonel was en route, Jesup violated a temporary truce and captured Seminole leader Osceola and about two hundred of his followers—but hundreds more waited deep in the Everglades.

Taylor and his troops arrived in Florida in the fall, and the colonel took command in the field. In early December, 1837, after weeks of preparation, Taylor left Fort Gardiner with a force of more than one thousand regular and volunteer troops. Pursuing the Seminoles into the vicinity

of Lake Okeechobee, Taylor made contact with a large force on Christmas Day. In a fierce battle that cost the lives of several of his top officers, Taylor routed the Seminoles and drove them from the field. The victory won for Taylor a promotion to brevet brigadier general, and a short time later, he replaced General Jesup as commander of the Florida theater.

General Taylor remained in Florida for two more years before assuming command at Baton Rouge. The following year, Taylor succeeded General Matthew Arbuckle as commander of the Second Department, Western Division, headquartered at Fort Smith, Arkansas. There he remained until May, 1844, when he returned to Fort Jesup to assume command of the First Department. In June, 1845, after the United States annexed Texas, he received orders to move his troops to Corpus Christi, on the Nueces River, to protect the new state in case of attack by Mexico. The following January, President James K. Polk ordered Taylor to move to the Rio Grande, occupying territory whose possession was a source of dispute. In late March, Taylor established a position opposite the Mexican town of Matamoros. A month later, several American soldiers were killed in a skirmish with Mexican troops. On May 13, 1846, Congress declared war on Mexico.

U.S. RELATIONS WITH EUROPE

Zachary Taylor's single year as president of the United States happened to fall during the immediate aftermath of a year of violent political upheavals throughout Europe. In his only state of the union address, he commented on his administration's efforts to stay out of European politics.

I have scrupulously avoided any interference in the wars and contentions which have recently distracted Europe. During the late conflict between Austria and Hungary there seemed to be a prospect that the latter might become an independent nation. However faint that prospect at the time appeared, I thought it my duty, in accordance with the general sentiment of the American people, who deeply sympathized with the Magyar patriots, to stand prepared, upon the contingency of the establishment by her of a permanent government, to be the first to welcome independent Hungary into the family of nations. For this purpose I invested an agent then in Europe with power to declare our willingness promptly to recognize her independence in the event of her ability to sustain it. The powerful intervention of Russia in the contest extinguished the hopes of the struggling Magyars. The United States did not at any time interfere in the contest, but the feelings of the nation were strongly enlisted in the cause, and by the sufferings of a brave people, who had made a gallant, though unsuccessful, effort to be free. . . .

Source: Zachary Taylor, "State of the Union Address," December 4, 1849.

Taylor, however, did not wait for the declaration of war. On May 8, he engaged and defeated a much larger Mexican force at Palo Alto. The next day, he defeated the Mexicans again at Resaca de la Palma. As a result, Polk promoted him to major general and gave him command of the Army of the Rio Grande. More victories followed as he captured Monterrey in September and crushed a force under General Antonio López de Santa Anna at Buena Vista in February, 1847.

With the end of the Mexican War, Taylor returned to the United States, receiving a hero's welcome at New Orleans in December, 1847. A short time later, he retired to his home in Baton Rouge and began tending to the affairs of Cypress Grove, the Mississippi plantation he had acquired a few years earlier. His retirement was brief. In 1848, the Whig Party, starved for victory, nominated the military hero for president and secured his election over Democrat Lewis Cass and Free-Soiler Martin Van Buren.

Although a slaveholder, President Taylor was a staunch Unionist. Faced with the volatile issue of slavery in the territories acquired from Mexico, he supported California's admission as a free state in 1849 and the organization of New Mexico and Utah without consideration of the slavery issue. When Congress convened in January, 1850, Senator Henry Clay proposed a series of compromise resolutions designed to defuse these and related issues, including a Texas-New Mexico border dispute, the fugitive slave question, and the future of the slave trade in Washington, D.C.

While Congress debated the Compromise of 1850, delegates from nine southern states met in Nashville in June to consider the defense of southern rights and their section's future within the Union. Moderate voices prevailed, but more radical "Fire-eaters" raised the specter of secession. Taylor, however, continued to resist any compromise that would promote the expansion of slavery and promised to meet disunionist threats with force.

The political deadlock remained on July 4, when Taylor attended a ceremony related to construction of the Washington Monument. He became overheated and, according to tradition, tried to cool off by consuming large quantities of cherries and iced milk. During that same evening he contracted gastroenteritis, from which he died on July 9.

SIGNIFICANCE

In many respects, Zachary Taylor symbolized both the aspirations and the anxieties of the American people during the mid-nineteenth century. In a period pervaded by

the spirit of manifest destiny, his victories in the Mexican War contributed to the nation's acquisition of a vast new territory, including the future states of California, New Mexico, Arizona, Nevada, and Utah. Only four days before his death, President Taylor signed the Clayton-Bulwer Treaty with England, the first diplomatic step toward construction of the Panama Canal.

As president, however, the victor of Buena Vista had to deal with the practical consequences of manifest destiny. As both a Unionist and a plantation owner with more than one hundred slaves, he embodied the conflicting social and economic forces that confronted the nation during the decade before the Civil War, especially citizens of the border states and Upper South. In Taylor's case, Unionist sentiments formed during four decades in the nation's military service triumphed over his own economic interests. During the decade that followed his death, however, a growing number of his fellow southerners resolved the conflict between slavery and Union in the opposite direction. When the election of Abraham Lincoln as president in 1860 convinced many southerners that they no longer could protect their "peculiar institution" within the Union, they chose secession. They elected as their president Zachary Taylor's friend and former son-in-law, Jefferson Davis.

—*Carl E. Kramer*

FURTHER READING

Bauer, K. Jack. *Zachary Taylor: Soldier, Planter, Statesman of the Old Southwest*. Baton Rouge: Louisiana State University Press, 1985. This well-researched, well-written volume is the first account of Taylor's life to appear since 1951. Particularly useful for the general reader, Bauer's work gives a balanced view of Taylor's early life, military career, and brief presidency.

DeVoto, Bernard A. *The Year of Decision, 1846*. Boston: Little, Brown, 1943. Taylor fares poorly in this spectacular, almost theatrical saga of America's westward march. From the Mexican War to the Mormon emigration to Utah, DeVoto captures the profound national emotions that undergirded manifest destiny.

Hamilton, Holman. *Zachary Taylor: Soldier of the Republic*. Indianapolis: Bobbs-Merrill, 1941. Volume 1 of Hamilton's magisterial biography, this remains the best single book on Taylor's early life and military career. Thoroughly researched and highly readable, it is sympathetic yet balanced, especially in regard to Taylor's dealings with his military and political rivals.

_____. *Zachary Taylor: Soldier in the White House.* Indianapolis: Bobbs-Merrill, 1951. A worthy companion to the preceding volume, this book explores the brief but important tenure of the nation's last slaveholding president. Thoroughly researched, it demonstrates that Taylor was a much more active president than is commonly believed.

Potter, David M. *The Impending Crisis, 1848-1861.* Completed and edited by Don E. Fehrenbacher. New York: Harper and Row, 1976. Taylor is one of the many important figures who appear in this excellent narrative of the political events leading from the Mexican War to the outbreak of the Civil War. An outstanding contextual volume, it synthesizes the vast literature dealing with the complex issues of slavery, expansionism, and sectional politics.

Singletary, Otis A. *The Mexican War.* Chicago: University of Chicago Press, 1960. This concise treatment of the war that climaxed American continental expansion is both historically sound and quite readable. Its emphasis is on military events and political intrigues at the expense of diplomatic relations between the United States and Mexico.

Smith, Elbert B. *The Presidencies of Zachary Taylor and Millard Fillmore.* Lawrence: University Press of Kansas, 1988. Smith maintains that Taylor and Fillmore are misrepresented and underrated presidents who acted responsibly by supporting the Compromise of 1850.

Weinberg, Albert K. *Manifest Destiny: A Study of Nationalist Expansionism in American History.* Baltimore: Johns Hopkins University Press, 1935. Zachary Taylor's name does not appear in this analytical study of American expansion from the Louisiana Purchase to the Spanish-American War, but the book is essential to understanding the policy motives behind the military ventures in which he participated.

Winders, Richard Bruce. *Mr. Polk's Army: The American Military Experience in the Mexican War.* College Station: Texas A&M University Press, 1997. Using diaries, journals, and reminiscences, Winders recounts the daily life of soldiers who fought the war, analyzing the cultural, social, and political aspects of the army. He also contrasts the leadership styles of Generals Taylor and Winfield Scott.

SEE ALSO: Black Hawk; Henry Clay; Jefferson Davis; Ulysses S. Grant; William Henry Harrison; Abraham Lincoln; Osceola; James K. Polk; Antonio López de Santa Anna; Winfield Scott; Martin Van Buren.

RELATED ARTICLES in *Great Events from History: The Nineteenth Century, 1801-1900:* September 16, 1810-September 28, 1821: Mexican War of Independence; November 21, 1817-March 27, 1858: Seminole Wars; May 8, 1846: Battle of Palo Alto; February 2, 1848: Treaty of Guadalupe Hidalgo Ends Mexican War; January 29-September 20, 1850: Compromise of 1850.

PETER ILICH TCHAIKOVSKY
Russian composer

Tchaikovsky has remained one of the most popular Western composers since his death. His soaring melodies, expressive supporting harmonies, and lush orchestration have made his concertos and later symphonies the epitome of late Romantic musical opulence.

BORN: May 7, 1840; Votkinsk, Vyatka Province, Russia
DIED: November 6, 1893; St. Petersburg, Russia
AREA OF ACHIEVEMENT: Music

EARLY LIFE
The son of a mining engineer, Peter Ilich Tchaikovsky (chi-KAHF-skee) received a good education as a child through his French governess, Fanny Dürbach, and his piano teacher, Mariya Palchikova. In 1848, his father retired and moved to St. Petersburg, where Tchaikovsky entered the preparatory program of the School of Jurisprudence in 1850, graduating nine years later. His mother, from whom he inherited his sensitivity, died in 1854. Tchaikovsky remained close to his father and siblings, five brothers and a sister, especially to his younger twin brothers, Anatoly and Modest.

Tchaikovsky accepted a position as a clerk in the Ministry of Justice in 1859, and in 1861 he began studies at the Russian Musical Society, which was transformed into the St. Petersburg Conservatory in 1862 under Anton Rubinstein. Tchaikovsky resigned his government position in the following year to become a full-time student at the conservatory, studying composition and orchestration with Rubinstein. He was graduated, with a silver medal in composition, in 1865. In the following year, he began his duties as a teacher of harmony at the newly founded conservatory in Moscow, headed by Anton Rubinstein's brother Nikolay.

LIFE'S WORK

Tchaikovsky's musical development was late in comparison with that of such composers as Ludwig van Beethoven, Franz Schubert, Robert Schumann, or Frédéric Chopin: The main compositions from his twenties are the song "None but the Lonely Heart," which contains the quintessential Tchaikovskyan melody in accompaniment to a text written by Johann Wolfgang von Goethe, and the uneven First Symphony in G Minor, subtitled *Winter Daydreams*. The first version of *Romeo and Juliet*, a fantasy overture based on William Shakespeare's tragedy, was finished in 1869, although the final version was not completed until 1880; this is the first of his orchestral works to be part of the standard repertory.

The works of Tchaikovsky's thirties include the second, third, and fourth symphonies; three string quartets (the first contains the famous "Andante cantabile," based on a Ukrainian folk song that Tchaikovsky collected on a summer holiday in Kamenka in 1865); the first piano concerto (the introduction to the first movement is perhaps Tchaikovsky's best-known melody); and a violin concerto. The piano concerto received its premiere in the United States. Also from these years is his finest opera, *Yevgeny Onyegin* (Eugene Onegin), based on the poem by Alexander Pushkin; it is a psychological drama rather than a grand opera or mythological drama and showed that there was an alternative path to Richard Wagner's music dramas in the serious musical theater. Other major works include his orchestral fantasy *Francesca da Rimini* and the ballet *Swan Lake*.

The 1870's were the years in which Tchaikovsky began to establish his international musical reputation, but they were tragic for him personally. In 1868, he met the Belgian soprano Désirée Artôt, four years his senior, and began a courtship that was terminated first by his doubts about marriage and then by her sudden marriage to another singer in the touring opera company of which she was a member. In 1877, he married Antonina Milyukova, a young woman whom he scarcely knew; biographers have speculated that his real reason for his marriage was to quiet the rumors of homosexuality, which may have been manifested during his student days at the School of Jurisprudence. The marriage to Milyukova

Peter Ilich Tchaikovsky. (Library of Congress)

was a disaster, never consummated, and it eventually ended in divorce in 1881 after she bore another man's illegitimate child.

Further rumors about homosexual affairs at the Moscow Conservatory may have caused Tchaikovsky to resign his professorship there at the end of 1878. A more likely explanation is that Tchaikovsky came increasingly to resent the demands that teaching made on the time he wished to devote to composition. The advent of a mysterious patroness, Nadezhda von Meck, who provided him with a generous subsidy on the condition that they never meet (although they exchanged a voluminous correspondence), gave Tchaikovsky financial independence for twelve years.

The six years afterward were less productive ones for the composer. The main works of this relatively fallow period were the opera *Orleanskaya Dyeva*, after Friedrich Schiller's drama *Die Jungfrau von Orleans* (1801; *The Maid of Orleans*, 1835), a fanciful historical drama about Joan of Arc; the Piano Trio in A Minor, an elegy for Nikolay Rubinstein; and the serenade for string orchestra.

Tchaikovsky was not a member of the circle of composers around Mily Alekseyevich Balakirev, the *Moguchkaya Kuchka* (mighty handful), which included Modest Mussorgsky and Nikolay Rimsky-Korsakov, but he did receive advice from Balakirev on *Romeo and Juliet* and on the work marking Tchaikovsky's creative renewal, the program symphony *Manfred*, based on a poem by George Gordon, Lord Byron, featuring the wanderings and unfulfilled love of an alienated outsider.

Tchaikovsky finished the work in 1885; it belongs to that small group of literary program symphonies that includes Hector Berlioz's *Symphonie fantastique* and *Harold in Italy* and Franz Liszt's *Faust Symphony*. The four movements depict, respectively, Manfred's wanderings and his memories of his beloved Astarte; Manfred's encounter with the witch of the Alps; a pastoral slow movement where Manfred encounters the inhabitants of the Swiss mountains; and a final movement first depicting the court of the demon Ahriman, then featuring Manfred's forgiveness by Astarte and his peaceful death. The work is Tchaikovsky's orchestral masterpiece, but it is not performed frequently because of its length and technical difficulty.

Among the other works marking Tchaikovsky's creative renewal are the Fifth Symphony, his most popular work, in which he follows the technique of *Manfred* in having a "motto theme" appear in all four movements of the work in various transformations; the pleasant string sextet "Souvenir of Florence"; and his other major opera, *Pikovaya dama* (*The Queen of Spades*), based on a story by Alexander Pushkin as adapted by Tchaikovsky's brother Modest. Despite its macabre topic, the opera has been one of Tchaikovsky's most popular.

Tchaikovsky's last few years were marked by outward success and constant travel, but deep inner conflicts. He was the first major European composer to visit the United States, conducting his music in April and May of 1891 (especially the first piano concerto) in New York, Baltimore, and Philadelphia and visiting Washington, D.C., and Niagara Falls. He was pleased at the acclaim and hospitality he received, but he was torn with homesickness for Russia.

During the following year, Tchaikovsky received an honorary doctor of music degree from the University of Cambridge in England. His outward honors were canceled in his mind by fits of despair, fears that his creativity was exhausted and that he was repeating himself musically, and compulsive travel marked by spells of homesickness during which he would cancel concerts to return to Russia. His two main last works, however, reveal the disparity in his creative impulses: The Sixth Symphony (called, after his death, the *Pathétique* by his brother Modest), with its unusual form, ends with a despairing slow movement; while the ballet *Shchelkunchik* (*The Nutcracker*, based on a tale by E. T. A. Hoffmann), has delighted children at Christmas for decades—the suite extracted from the ballet is Tchaikovsky's most frequently performed composition.

The circumstances of Tchaikovsky's death in November, 1893, shortly after the first performance of the Sixth Symphony, are still a matter of controversy. The traditional account is that either by accident or by design (if one accepts the "suicidal" thoughts expressed in the last movement of the Sixth Symphony) he drank a glass of unboiled water during a cholera epidemic in St. Petersburg in late 1893. Alexandra Orlova brought to the West the story that she had heard from an elderly member of the Russian Museum staff, who claimed that the drink was actually poison and was taken to escape the possibility of a scandal brought on by a homosexual encounter. More recently a less lurid theory has been advanced: Tchaikovsky did ingest contaminated food or water during the cholera epidemic, but his doctor misdiagnosed his ailment until it was too late to institute a regimen of proper treatment.

SIGNIFICANCE

Tchaikovsky composed effectively in virtually every musical genre of the late nineteenth century: symphony, opera, ballet, art song, concerto, chamber music, and even church music (his Russian Orthodox Church music, especially the Vespers of 1882, includes some of the finest examples of the genre), though his solo piano music is the least effective of his works. He worshiped Wolfgang Amadeus Mozart's music and esteemed his French contemporaries—such as Georges Bizet, Léo Delibes, and Camille Saint-Saëns—over such German composers as Richard Wagner and Johannes Brahms, whose music he particularly disliked (Brahms reciprocated this feeling).

Tchaikovsky's musical development is more comparable to the spiral (as his brother Modest suggested) than to the straight-line development of a Beethoven or Schubert. Particularly striking elements of his style are his soaring melodies, his effective use of the orchestra, his rich supporting harmony (which in many respects recalls the devices of Liszt), and his experiments with musical form. Though not particularly close to the Russian nationalist composers, he could use Russian folk songs as effectively as any of them, as best seen in the finale of his Second Symphony.

Tchaikovsky's extensive travels in the West and his formal training in Western compositional techniques at the St. Petersburg Conservatory have given rise to the mistaken idea that he was Western rather than Russian in his musical orientation, yet he considered himself Russian above all, and he is still honored as a national treasure in the Soviet Union. Tchaikovsky has been faulted by critics for his piling of climax upon climax in an almost frenzied and hysterical manner (the development section of the first movement of the Fourth Symphony, for example), his compositional technique of seeming to stitch blocks of music together, and an almost blatant vulgarity (the finale of the Fifth Symphony), but Beethoven, Giuseppe Verdi, and Gustav Mahler similarly have been accused of vulgarity.

Tchaikovsky set the standard for the large-scale epic symphony, bravura concerto, and dramatic ballet among Russian and Soviet composers, and he is often the composer through whom many young persons are first attracted to art music. He remains one of the few composers for whom programs devoted entirely to his music attract a sizable audience. His popularity among the general musical audience shows no sign of waning, and recent critical studies have elevated his stature to that of one of the major composers of the late nineteenth century.

—Rey M. Longyear

FURTHER READING

Abraham, Gerald, ed. *The Music of Tchaikovsky*. New York: W. W. Norton, 1946. A series of ten essays by specialists on various aspects of Tchaikovsky's life and work. Edward Lockspeiser's account of "Tchaikovsky the Man" is of special interest for the general reader, though all the essays are oriented more toward music lovers than musical scholars.

Brown, David. "Pyotr Il'yich Tchaikovsky." In *Russian Masters 1: Glinka, Borodin, Balakirev, Musorgsky, Tchaikovsky*. New York: W. W. Norton, 1986. The entry is essentially Brown's article on Tchaikovsky's life and works in *The New Grove* dictionary with additions. The article provides the best short survey of the composer's life and works, though it is flawed by the author's uncritical acceptance of a lurid account of Tchaikovsky's suicide. The list of works and bibliography are especially complete.

_____. *Tchaikovsky*. 4 vols. New York: Norton, 1978-1992. The most complete account of the composer's life, with critical analyses of his musical works. Brown provides a meticulously detailed narrative of

Tchaikovsky's life and musical development; he concludes that the composer killed himself rather than reveal his homosexuality.

Holden, Anthony. *Tchaikovsky: A Biography*. New York: Random House, 1995. Good introduction to Tchaikovsky's life, placing more emphasis on his homosexuality than some previous accounts. Holden argues the composer lived in fear of being "outed" as a homosexual and committed suicide to keep his sexual orientation a secret.

Kearney, Leslie, ed. *Tchaikovsky and His World*. Princeton, N.J.: Princeton University Press, 1998. Collection of scholarly essays examining Tchaikovsky's life and work, including a discussion of how his homosexuality affected his music and excerpts of his letters to his brothers.

Poznansky, Alexander. *Tchaikovsky's Last Days: A Documentary Study*. New York: Oxford University Press, 1996. Examines the last twenty days of the composer's life, refuting the view of Holden (see above) and other biographers who maintain Tchaikovsky committed suicide rather than be "outed" as a homosexual.

_____, ed. *Tchaikovsky Through Others' Eyes*, Compiled, edited, and with an introduction by Alexander Poznansky. Translations from Russian by Ralph C. Burr, Jr., and Robert Bird. Bloomington: Indiana University Press, 1999. Collection of memoirs, diary entries, and interviews written and conducted by Tchaikovsky's contemporaries, detailing the public and private lives of the composer.

Wiley, Roland John. *Tchaikovsky's Ballets*. New York: Oxford University Press, 1985. This study examines the music of Tchaikovsky's three grand ballets— *Swan Lake*, *Sleeping Beauty*, and *The Nutcracker*— and also investigates the circumstances surrounding their composition, their original and subsequent productions, and their audiences.

Yoffe, Elkhonon, ed. *Tchaikovsky in America: The Composer's Visit in 1891*. Translated by Lidya Yoffe. New York: Oxford University Press, 1986. Copious excerpts from Tchaikovsky's diaries, correspondence, and news accounts of the time of Tchaikovsky's visits to New York, Baltimore, and Philadelphia in 1891, and the abortive ventures to bring him to the United States for subsequent tours.

SEE ALSO: Ludwig van Beethoven; Hector Berlioz; Georges Bizet; Johannes Brahms; Frédéric Chopin; Léo Delibes; Edvard Grieg; Franz Liszt; Modest

Mussorgsky; Alexander Pushkin; Nikolay Rimsky-Korsakov; Franz Schubert; Robert Schumann; Giuseppe Verdi; Richard Wagner.

TECUMSEH
Native American leader

Leading Indians of the Old Northwest in a united defense against the intrusion of white settlers, Tecumseh contributed significantly to the development of pan-Indianism in American history.

BORN: March, 1768; Old Piqua, western Ohio
DIED: October 5, 1813; Thames River, southeastern Canada
AREA OF ACHIEVEMENT: Warfare and conquest

EARLY LIFE

Born in a Shawnee village in what is now western Ohio, Tecumseh (teh-KAHM-seh) was the son of a Creek Indian woman. Her Shawnee husband, Puckeshinwa, had met her earlier, while staying with Creek Indians in Alabama. When Tecumseh was still a very young boy, Virginians began pushing into Kentucky onto lands used extensively for hunting by the Shawnee. The Indians resisted, and in 1774, Virginia governor Lord John Dunmore led troops into the area. Puckeshinwa died in one of the subsequent battles, leaving support of his family in the hands of relatives and in those of a war chief named Blackfish from a nearby village.

During the American Revolution, the Shawnee again went to war against whites. In 1779, local Kentuckians wrongly accused several Shawnee, including a popular leader known as Cornstalk, of some recent killings and senselessly killed them. The intense fighting that followed eventually led about a thousand members of the tribe to move for a time to southeastern Missouri. Tecumseh's mother, Methoataske, was one of the migrants, but Tecumseh and his seven brothers and sisters did not accompany her. Instead, other family members took the children. Tecumseh moved in with his sister Tecumpease and her husband and eventually developed a close relationship with his older sibling.

The muscular young Tecumseh also became popular among his peers, distinguishing himself in games and in shooting skills. At the age of fifteen, Tecumseh experienced his first battle. American pioneers again started flooding onto Shawnee lands near the end of the American Revolution, many of them crossing the Appalachian Mountains and then descending the Ohio River in flatboats. In 1783, the young warrior accompanied his brother Chiksika on a war party in an effort to stop the flatboat traffic.

After winning independence, Americans considered themselves the owners of lands formerly claimed by Great Britain, including the Old Northwest (the area bordered by the Appalachian Mountains on the east, the Mississippi River on the west, the Ohio River on the south, and Canada on the north, comprising the modern states of Ohio, Indiana, Illinois, Wisconsin, and Michigan). Kentuckians attacked Shawnee villages in 1786 after blaming that group for raids actually launched by the Mingoes and Cherokee in opposition to settlement west of the Appalachians. The Shawnee hit back, with Tecumseh frequently taking part in the fighting. In 1787, he joined a war party led by his brother that went south and helped Cherokee attack settlements in Tennessee and southern Kentucky. Chiksika was killed in the action. The death of his brother greatly intensified Tecumseh's hatred for the expansionistic whites, and he stayed in the area for the next two years, seeking vengeance.

With Chiksika no longer in a position of leadership, Tecumseh was able to assert himself. Five feet, ten inches tall, with a powerful physical presence and a dynamic speaking ability, he quickly gained a large following, especially among the younger, more antiwhite members of his tribe. By the time the group of Shawnee warriors returned to the Old Northwest in 1790, Tecumseh had emerged as a popular war chief. In addition to his outstanding skills in warfare, however, he also gained a reputation for being kind and good-humored. He frequently demonstrated compassion for those who were weakest or least privileged and an aversion to the torture or murder of prisoners. These qualities made him exceptional at a time when indiscriminate brutality was common on both sides in frontier warfare.

LIFE'S WORK

Upon his return to the Old Northwest, Tecumseh found his antiwhite sentiments increasingly in tune with those

RELATED ARTICLE in *Great Events from History: The Nineteenth Century, 1801-1900:* January 27, 1895: Tchaikovsky's *Swan Lake* Is Staged in St. Petersburg.

of many Indians in the region. Settlers had been pouring into the southeastern Ohio River Valley, and the frontier again erupted into violence. During the early 1790's, the U.S. government sent armies in on two occasions in attempts to counter Indian resistance, but in both cases, tribes united to hand the whites embarrassing defeats. Together with the prodding of the British to the north in Canada, these victories encouraged tribes to join in a common political front to negotiate a permanent Indian state in the Old Northwest. Differences among the groups, however, prevented success in the effort. The United States then tried a third time for a military solution, sending an army under Major General Anthony Wayne. This time the results were different, with the Americans claiming victory in the 1794 Battle of Fallen Timbers. The next year, some of the defeated Indians signed the Treaty of Greenville, giving up more than two-thirds of what became Ohio.

Tecumseh fought well in the last two of the three famous battles for control of the Old Northwest and thus added to his growing reputation. He refused to accept the outcome of the Treaty of Greenville, however, and soon was recognized as the dominant leader of those Indians who resolved to put an end to any further white incursions into the region. Over the next decade, Tecumseh

Tecumseh. (Library of Congress)

and his followers traveled and lived throughout Ohio and Indiana.

In 1805, one of Tecumseh's brothers, who had failed at nearly everything he had attempted, claimed to have died, to have been taken to the Master of Life, and to have been appointed to lead his people to salvation. He renounced liquor and launched a fundamentalist spiritual movement that encouraged Indians to reject white influence and return to traditional values. He promised believers that the happier times of the past would be restored. He was known as Tenskwatawa, or the Prophet, and after Tecumseh's conversion to the new faith, the two brothers moved first to Greenville in western Ohio and eventually to Tippecanoe Creek in Indiana. There, in a village that would be named Prophetstown, Indians from throughout the Old Northwest came to live and join the movement, including Wyandot, Kickapoo, Potawatomi, Miami, Wea, and Delaware.

American officials such as William Henry Harrison, the governor of the Indiana Territory, watched events with apprehension. Harrison was well known for making treaties with individual tribes and winning much land for the government at low prices and through means that were not always ethical. In fact, his practices had deepened the antiwhite attitudes of many younger Indians who resented the loss of homelands and led them to join the Prophet's movement. Then, in 1809, Harrison gathered chiefs friendly to the government and persuaded them to cede more than three million acres of land in the Treaty of Fort Wayne. This event quickly elevated the status and position of Tecumseh, who had been developing a position that rejected the legitimacy of recent controversial treaties. Land was commonly owned by all tribes, according to the Shawnee war chief, and could not be sold individually.

Tecumseh traveled throughout the Old Northwest and even into the South, trying to win support for a political and military confederacy that would join many tribes under his leadership to stop white expansion. Then, just as Tecumseh was experiencing some success, Governor Harrison took advantage of his absence from Prophetstown and in November of 1811 marched an army to within two miles of the Indian village. Tenskwatawa had been left in charge and decided to take the initiative and attack first. The subsequent Battle of Tippecanoe was not a dramatic Indian defeat, but the defenders withdrew and allowed the whites to destroy Prophetstown.

Eventually, Tecumseh returned home, broke with his brother in anger over the way he had handled the situation, and struggled to put his broken movement back together. The coordinated attack that Tecumseh had hoped would stop the onrush of settlers became a series of random raids across the frontier. Many Americans blamed the British for the violence because they supplied the Indians with arms. This became one of several events that contributed to the outbreak of the War of 1812 against Great Britain. Tecumseh and many of his followers joined the British because the former mother country had tried several times to control American expansion and thus offered Indians the best hope for retaining their homelands. Tecumseh fought in a number of battles and was eventually killed in Canada on October 5, 1813, at the Battle of the Thames.

SIGNIFICANCE

In the last half of the eighteenth century, white expansion undermined the livelihood and lifestyle of Indians in the Old Northwest. Settlers destroyed game, treaties (many of them fraudulent or at least questionable) eroded the Indian land base, and alcohol disrupted social arrangements. Tribes grew dependent on European trade goods and eventually were used as pawns in the rivalries between the European superpowers over dominance in North America. The result was an almost constant state of war. This, in turn, elevated the importance of war chiefs among groups such as the Shawnee, who traditionally had separate political leadership for war and for peace.

As a war chief, Tecumseh emerged into a position of leadership in this environment. The movement that he would lead started as a primarily spiritual one under his brother, the Prophet. Tecumseh secularized and politicized the movement as Indians, under intense pressure to give up their lands, were increasingly attracted to his vision for stemming the tide of white advance. He encouraged Native American groups to forget their traditional hostilities toward one another and join in a common military and political effort.

Tecumseh's position has been called Indian nationalism, or pan-Indianism, and has been one of the most significant developments in the long term of Indian history. Identification on the basis of being Indian with less emphasis on tribal divisions remains a strong force in Native American affairs during the late twentieth century. Other Indian leaders before Tecumseh had attempted intertribal alliances, but on more limited scales and without much success. Even though he was a brilliant strategist, Tecumseh's movement ultimately failed in its immediate objectives as well. However, he undoubtedly contrib-

uted as much toward the evolution of pan-Indianism as any other single historical figure.

Tecumseh has enjoyed more admiration and respect, even among his contemporary foes, than any other Native American leader. As a result, he has attained an unparalleled status in legend and mythology. Evidence of this can be seen not only in the many biographies written about him but also in the many spurious or exaggerated stories about his life that have gained popularity and fooled even some of the best historians who have written about him.

—Larry W. Burt

FURTHER READING

Antal, Sandy. *A Wampum Denied: Procter's War of 1812*. East Lansing: Michigan State University Press, 1997. Chronicles the battle on the Detroit frontier, led by British commander Henry Procter, during the War of 1812. Details Tecumseh's role in assisting the British.

Edmunds, R. David. *The Shawnee Prophet*. Lincoln: University of Nebraska Press, 1983. Focuses on Tenskwatawa but contains much information on Tecumseh. Demonstrates how the stories of the two famous brothers are intertwined and have to be considered together and also describes the social and political milieu in which their movement thrived.

_____. *Tecumseh and the Quest for Indian Leadership*. Boston: Little, Brown, 1984. One of the best complete biographies of Tecumseh. Scholarly, yet relatively brief and very readable. It is also one of the most balanced accounts, discussing in a concluding chapter many of the myths surrounding the Shawnee leader's life to which other historians have fallen victim.

Josephy, Alvin M., Jr. "Tecumseh, the Greatest Indian." In *The Patriot Chiefs*. New York: Penguin Books, 1961. Reliable and well written, this stands as the best short summary of Tecumseh and his importance in history, although the author presents a slightly more romanticized version of the leader's life than most of the good later scholarship.

Klinck, Carl F., ed. *Tecumseh: Fact and Fiction in Early Records*. Englewood Cliffs, N.J.: Prentice-Hall, 1961. This useful anthology presents a variety of perspectives on Tecumseh's significance and on some of the controversies about his life through selections of both primary and secondary resource materials.

Sugden, John. *Tecumseh: A Life*. New York: Henry Holt, 1998. Definitive biography of Tecumseh, placing his life within the context of Shawnee and general Native American history. Sugden details Tecumseh's failed attempts to create a pan-Indian resistance movement.

_____. *Tecumseh's Last Stand*. Norman: University of Oklahoma Press, 1985. A very good treatment of a narrow range of Tecumseh's life. It begins in the summer of 1813 and discusses in great detail his role in the War of 1812. It also deals with some of the later controversies, such as who actually killed Tecumseh and where he was buried.

Tucker, Glenn. *Tecumseh: Vision of Glory*. Indianapolis: Bobbs-Merrill, 1956. A long and basically reliable bi-

ography, but it stands as perhaps the best example of the common tendency to overromanticize Tecumseh and accept too many of the questionable myths that shroud his life.

SEE ALSO: Sir Isaac Brock; William Henry Harrison; Red Cloud.

RELATED ARTICLES in *Great Events from History: The Nineteenth Century, 1801-1900:* April, 1808: Tenskwatawa Founds Prophetstown; November 7, 1811: Battle of Tippecanoe; July 27, 1813-August 9, 1814: Creek War; October 5, 1813: Battle of the Thames.

THOMAS TELFORD
Scottish engineer

By building an extraordinary number of bridges, canals, harbors, roads, and waterways, Telford became one of the great engineers of his day and helped to establish the profession of civil engineering in Great Britain.

BORN: August 9, 1757; Westerkirk, Eskdale, Dumfriesshire, Scotland
DIED: September 2, 1834; London, England
AREA OF ACHIEVEMENT: Engineering

EARLY LIFE

Thomas Telford was the son of a man who died several months after his birth. Afterward, his mother was soon put out of the cottage that had been provided as part of her deceased husband's salary and moved to a small cottage where she and her son occupied one of the two rooms. She was devoted to her son, although she did not have the means to support him. However, her brother paid the fee for Thomas to attend the parish school in Westerkirk. There the boy received some rudimentary education and made several lifelong friends.

As a very young child, Thomas helped to support himself by bird scaring, cow herding, and sheepherding. The latter took him away from home for weeks at a time. While spending long nights in the countryside, his intense love for nature and his native country grew. Before leaving the Eskdale Valley in his early twenties, he wrote a poem in its honor in which he referred to feeling "Nature's love" and rejected the "artificial joy" of urban life.

In Telford's day the primary education received by a

boy was through an apprenticeship to a master of a craft. At the age of fourteen, his formal schooling complete, Telford was apprenticed to a stonemason who mistreated him. "Laughing Tam" was good-natured but also well able to protect himself, and after several months he left his apprenticeship rather than stay with a cruel master. A cousin came to the rescue by arranging for an apprenticeship with another stonemason. Although he worked in a country village, a large-scale program of improvement was under way there that afforded him opportunities to learn his craft well as both apprentice and journeyman mason.

Telford informally continued his education throughout this period. A woman heard of his eagerness to learn and opened her small library to him. He reveled in reading John Milton's *Paradise Lost* (1667, 1674) and any other available books. Poetry and prose remained the loves of his life, to which he turned after long, hard days of labor. Many of Telford's poems were published anonymously, including one in memory of Robert Burns.

Thomas Telford was a tall, well-built man with brown, curly hair and lively, twinkling brown eyes. He was among the most sociable of men and was always quick to laugh and make others laugh with his anecdotes. Despite the ready laugh, however, little is known of this private man, who never married or shared himself freely with others.

Opportunities for work and career advancement in eighteenth century Scotland were extremely limited, so many Scots flocked to England, outposts in the British Empire, and America. After working for a year in Edinburgh, Telford joined the exodus. In January, 1782, at the age of twenty-four, with a borrowed pair of breeches and a horse that was to be delivered, he set out for London.

LIFE'S WORK

In London, the newcomer was soon at work building Somerset House at the end of Waterloo Bridge. Forty years later, as the world-renowned resident of the Institution of Civil Engineers, he would proudly point out the masonry that he had laid with his own hands. While laying these stones, he wrote of his ambition to a friend back in Eskdale:

> At present I am laying schemes [plans] of a pretty extensive kind. . . . My innate vanity is too apt to say when looking on the Common drudges—as well as other places—Born to command ten thousand slaves like you.

Thus, while still a stonemason, Telford already thought as a master. He formed a friendship with the best workman among his fellow workers and thought of ways for the two of them to make their fortunes. At night he read books on architecture and wrote his friend that

> knowledge is my most ardent pursuit, a thousand things occur that would pass unnoticed by good, easy people who are contented with drudging on in the beaten path, but I am not contented unless I can reason every particular.

Although his original business plans fell through, Telford continued his hard work and studies and found other opportunities. At his next job, he assumed the role of supervisor.

The great patron of Telford's early career was Sir William Pulteney, who had originally come from the stonemason's home country. When Pulteney began a significant building program in Shrewsbury, he entrusted Thomas with much of the work. Telford was soon called "young Pulteney" by the local inhabitants and greatly enhanced his reputation by defying public opinion when he predicted the collapse of a medieval church several days before it occurred. Though Telford had only good things to say about Pulteney, this wealthy man was also extraordinarily frugal and could not have been an easy employer.

The only breach between the two men occurred in 1791, when, under the reformist influence of the French Revolution, Telford occasioned a riot in Scotland by sending a copy of Thomas Paine's *The Rights of Man* (1791-1792) under Pulteney's postage frank. Telford, who subsequently had little concern for politics except as they affected his projects, lost his interest in radical political change after this unsettling experience. He joined the secret, fraternal society of the Freemasons, which provided a safe outlet for his rationalistic inclinations.

Telford's first great project was the Ellesmere Canal, which connected the Mersey, Dee, and Severn Rivers. The aqueduct at Pont Cysyllte was an unprecedented engineering triumph that Sir Walter Scott described as a magnificent work of art. Telford's innovative spirit is reflected in his pioneering the use of iron in the building of bridges. Although others built the first iron bridges, Telford gained public acceptance for them.

During this same period, he did a significant amount of dock, harbor, and pier building and was soon involved in building an enormous number of roads and bridges in the Highlands of Scotland. This region was suffering

Thomas Telford. (Smithsonian Institution)

from the decline of the clan system and severe depopulation as sheep replaced men on the hillsides. The government was alarmed, because it feared that this great source of military recruits would soon dry up and that much of Scotland would become an economic desert. Another problem was that the sea-lanes around Scotland were so treacherous that when two ships left Newcastle on the same day, one bound for India via the English Channel and the other for Liverpool via the Scottish seas, Bombay was reached before Liverpool. Thus was born Telford's greatest challenge: the Caledonian Canal.

This extraordinary engineering triumph had been envisioned by James Watt and John Rennie but was completed by Telford. The construction went on from 1803 to 1822 and beyond, at great cost and in the face of enormous obstacles. Regrettably, the canal was not an economic success, as it cost twice as much as predicted, the size of ships increased beyond the capacity of its locks, governmental tariff policies destroyed its economic base, and the steamship and steam railroads made it obsolete.

Telford took his first sea voyage in 1808 when he traveled to Sweden to begin work on the Gotha Canal. This remarkable canal was built between 1809 and 1833 in the most inclement weather. It was primarily the work of Count Baltzar Bogislaus von Platen, who relied heavily on Telford and who honored him with a Swedish grant of nobility that the Scot, characteristically, failed to use in England. Telford returned to Britain soon after completing the canal and devoted much of his enormous energy to building roads and bridges in northern Wales. The Menai suspension bridge was one of his greatest achievements. Another was the setting of concrete under water.

Robert Southey, the poet laureate, after taking a six-week trip with the engineer in 1819, wrote "Telford's is a happy life, everywhere making roads, building bridges, forming canals, and creating harbours [sic]." It was a nomadic existence; Telford traveled so often and widely that he did not have a permanent residence until late in his life. Wherever he went, he enjoyed warm and friendly relationships. Part of the secret of his success was his intimate knowledge of the capabilities and habits of common workers. He had a great disdain for theoretical engineers and chose his able assistants from among his workers. He was an excellent judge of men and had a marked preference for hiring Lowland Scots. His administrative skills were excellent, as witnessed by his ability to oversee a large variety of complex, long-term projects simultaneously. His reputation for fairness, honesty, and good judgment was such that he served as the final arbiter in disputes.

Telford's ability to deal effectively with people is evident in his maintaining support for long-term, costly projects, despite the difficulties of dealing with governmental bureaucrats, to whom he referred as "insects." He was one of a number of men bringing a heightened respect to the emerging profession of civil engineering. Road building, which his great rival John Rennie disdained, was accepted by him as a worthy area of activity. Indeed, Telford, the "Colossus of Roads," unlike his contemporary John McAdams, built in the Roman manner, which lasts for centuries and even millennia. His status with engineers was such that when he joined the struggling Institution of Civil Engineers in 1820 as its first president, it became the center of the profession in Great Britain. Telford was honored with membership in the Royal Society, and in 1828 a royal charter was granted to the society he headed. He raised its intellectual level by establishing the rule that all members give an annual professional paper.

Thomas Telford's final years brought difficulties as well as honors. He was alone, having never married; in declining health; and increasingly deaf. Furthermore, the railroad mania was breeding a new group of engineers who could not understand the Scot's lack of enthusiasm for this revolutionizing mode of transportation. Though he saw the steam engine as a practical mode of transportation, Telford believed too strongly in the principle of the open road not to have doubts about the monopolistic practice of building private railroads. Though he was associated with the building of some railroads, his loyalty to canal owners also deterred him from active participation. As a result, a railroad-obsessed generation of engineers unjustly remembered him as a reactionary opponent of the technology of the future.

Telford's lifelong love of literature was reflected in his generous bequests to the English poet Southey, to the Scottish poet Thomas Campbell, and to the establishment of several libraries in Scotland. His beloved Institution for Civil Engineering and other friends received the rest of his worldly goods.

SIGNIFICANCE

Thomas Telford epitomized the ideal of the self-made man who helped to create the economic infrastructure of industrial society. He considered the poverty of his birth to be an advantage as he worked his own way up from humble stonemason in rural Scotland to the greatest engineer of his day in London. His jovial public personality hid both his enormous professional ambition and the complexity of his private self.

Telford was a driven man. His contemporaries saw him as the "Colossus of Roads" who relentlessly built bridges, canals, harbors, roads, and waterways. The importance of the improved transportation and communications that he wrought cannot be exaggerated. Britons, especially the Scottish and Welsh, were brought within a single cultural and economic network.

The Menai Bridge in Wales and the Caledonian Canal in Scotland were monuments to his art and dedication as an engineer. The economic failure of the Caledonian Canal was caused by factors well beyond his control, because no one could foresee the manner in which the steamship and steam railroad would transform transportation. The engineer's reputation suffered severely because of his lack of enthusiasm for the railroad.

Telford made a great contribution to the rise of the profession of civil engineer. He did this in a number of ways. He set an extraordinary example, in Rickman's words, "as a soldier, always in active service," and in the enormous volume of his work and its importance for Great Britain's development. Finally, he lent his name to the presidency of the Institution of Civil Engineers and his considerable efforts to make the association a success.

Telford's legacy is visible in the numerous roads and bridges that he built that are still in service, withstanding loads that were unimaginable two centuries ago, when he designed them. It is also present in the permanence of the Institution of Civil Engineers. In 1968, Telford's special contributions were recognized when an entire industrial district was named Telford in his honor.

—*Paul H. Elovitz*

FURTHER READING

Burton, Anthony. *Thomas Telford*. London: Aurum Press, 1999. Comprehensive account of Telford's life and diverse engineering achievements. Includes black-and-white illustrations.

Gibb, Alexander. *The Story of Telford: The Rise of Civil Engineering*. London: Alexander MacLehose, 1935. This volume provides a fairly complete, chronological record of Telford's work. Though the diversity of his projects is hard to follow at times, the book is still an invaluable source. The list of Telford's engineering works at the end is most helpful.

Hadfield, Charles. *Thomas Telford's Temptation: Telford and William Jessop's Reputation*. Cleobury Mortimer, Shropshire, England: M & M Baldwin, 1993. Jessop, an engineer who assisted Telford in building the Ellesmere and Caledonian canals, is hardly mentioned in Telford's autobiography. This book examines the roles the two men played in constructing the canals and Telford's role in writing their history.

Pearce, Rhoda M. *Thomas Telford: An Illustrated Life of Thomas Telford, 1757-1834*. 2d ed. Aylesbury, England: Shire, 1977. This forty-eight-page survey is worth examining.

Quartermaine, Jaime, Barrie Trinder, and Rick Turner. *Thomas Telford's Holyhead Road: The A5 in North Wales*. York, England: Council for British Archaeology, 2003. Surveys the Welsh section of Telford's London-to-Holyhead road, citing archaeological and historical information to describe his road building plan.

Rolt, L. T. C. *Thomas Telford*. London: Longmans, Green, 1958. Reprint. Harmondsworth, England: Penguin Books, 1985. This is a short, readable, and comprehensive biography of the founder of civil engineering. Readers should begin their study with this volume, unless Telford's autobiography is available to them.

Smiles, Samuel. *Thomas Telford*. Vol. 2 in *Lives of the Engineers*. London: John Murray, 1862. Reprint. New York: Augustus M. Kelley, 1968. This Victorian biographer loved to record the history of the self-made man. Telford was a perfect subject for him, and though the book is marred by a worshipful approach and a failure to examine some of the oral history it recorded, it is still readable and of value.

Telford, Thomas. *Life of Thomas Telford, Civil Engineer, Written by Himself*. Edited by John Rickman. London: James and Luke G. Hansard, 1838. Telford's longtime friend compiled this lengthy account of his labors and the beautiful companion atlas of his works. However, it offers no real insight into Telford the man. There is little published material on his private life.

SEE ALSO: Isambard Kingdom Brunel; Marc Isambard Brunel; James Buchanan Eads; Gustave Eiffel; Ferdinand de Lesseps; John Augustus Roebling; Sir Walter Scott.

RELATED ARTICLE in *Great Events from History: The Nineteenth Century, 1801-1900*: July 29, 1825: Stockton and Darlington Railway Opens.

ALFRED, LORD TENNYSON
English poet

Generally considered to be the quintessential Victorian poet, Tennyson grappled with grief in the midst of the most profound theological crisis in the history of the modern world, caused by the emergent theory of evolution. His poetry of spiritual struggle and affirmation captured the soul of his generation.

BORN: August 6, 1809; Somersby, Lincolnshire, England
DIED: October 6, 1892; Aldworth, near Haslemere, Sussex, England
ALSO KNOWN AS: Alfred Tennyson (birth name); Alfred Tennyson, First Baron Tennyson of Aldworth and Freshwater
AREA OF ACHIEVEMENT: Literature

EARLY LIFE

Alfred Tennyson was the fourth of George Tennyson's twelve children. His mother, née Elizabeth Fytche, was an easygoing and indulgent woman who encouraged her children's literary efforts. At the rectory, young Alfred had access to his father's twenty-five-hundred-volume scholarly library, which included books on theology, philosophy, history, classical and Asian literature, and science.

Although Tennyson was educated formally first at a village school and later at a boys' school in Louth, the majority of his preuniversity instruction was received at home under his father's supervision. George Tennyson was an intellectually gifted and well-educated man whose intelligence and learning were undermined by his emotional instability. Alfred Tennyson's tempestuous and insecure home life during childhood fostered periods of despondency that were severe enough to affect adversely his physical health throughout his lifetime. However, despite having to undertake numerous water cures for a variety of ailments that were indiscriminately identified as gout, Tennyson lived a long and productive life. Although the instability of his early years contributed to his unhappiness, it also deepened his sensitivity to the spiritual turmoil of his generation.

Six months before Tennyson began his studies at Cambridge University in 1827, a volume entitled *Poems by Two Brothers* was published by a Lincolnshire bookseller. It was in fact a collection by three brothers; half of the poems it contained were written by Alfred Tennyson, while the other poems were contributed by his elder brothers Frederick and Charles. The volume received little notice, but it did allow Tennyson to enter university with some confidence in his poetic ability.

Tennyson's physical appearance, as it was described upon his arrival at Cambridge, communicated a greater confidence than he felt. Standing more than six feet tall, he towered above his fellows, and his broad chest and massive head were imposing. His swarthy handsomeness, deep brown eyes, and long, dark, unkempt hair gave him a mysterious, romantic air. Severe shortsightedness lent him a remote gaze that was often mistaken for aloofness. His poor eyesight also contributed to his social ineptness on occasions when he would either scrutinize his companions at an awkwardly close range or else, insecure without visual cues, withdraw from general conversation entirely.

At Cambridge, in 1829, Tennyson made the most important acquaintance of his life. Arthur Henry Hallam, who had been a fellow competitor for the Chancellor's Gold Medal for English verse, which Tennyson won with his poem "Timbuctoo," became not only his closest friend but also his literary advocate. He encouraged Tennyson to publish his first notable collection of poetry, *Poems, Chiefly Lyrical*, in 1830 and anonymously gave it a favorable commentary in *The Englishman's Magazine* in 1831. In his review, Hallam defined Tennyson's style in terms that modern critics have described as an anticipation of Symbolist poetics. Tennyson's enduring dislike of magazine criticism began with a scathing review of *Poems, Chiefly Lyrical* in *Blackwood's Magazine* in 1832. Because of his fear of poor reviews, Tennyson was hesitant to publish new poems, a tendency that remained with him throughout his career. However, this fear also drove him to scrupulous revision, which often improved his work.

LIFE'S WORK

Tennyson was recalled to Somersby immediately before his father's death in March, 1831, and he never returned to the university to complete his degree. The following year, at Hallam's urging, he assembled the manuscript of a volume entitled *Poems* (1832). It included a number of pieces often found in modern anthologies: "The Lady of Shalott," "Œnone," "The Palace of Art," and "The Lotos-Eaters." *Poems* was unfavorably received when it was first published, but in 1835, the philosopher John Stuart Mill wrote a review praising Tennyson's use of scenery to symbolize feeling. Mill's encouragement ar-

Alfred, Lord Tennyson. (Courtesy, The University of Texas at Austin)

rived too late, however, to offer much comfort; when it appeared, Tennyson was still grieving Hallam's untimely death in the summer of 1833.

Tennyson composed some of his finest poems in the period following his friend's death, particularly the exquisite elegiac stanzas that were to make up the commemorative poem *In Memoriam* (1850). Lacking Hallam's energetic support, the young poet failed to publish a new volume of poetry until 1842. Between Hallam's death in 1833 and the publication of *In Memoriam* in 1850, only two books appeared: *Poems* (1842) and *The Princess* (1847).

Tennyson's 1842 volume incorporated revised versions of the best work he had published in 1833 along with some new poems including "Ulysses," "Break, Break, Break," and his early Arthurian piece, "Morte d'Arthur." *The Princess*, a long narrative poem, presents a rather superficial treatment of the serious Victorian issue of women's education. The conflict between a prince and a princess, whose engagement is broken when the princess decides to found a women's university, dissolves when she sees the error of her politics and returns to fulfill her promise of marriage. The resolution is

achieved principally through the songs, which focus on the personal rather than the political implications of the couple's relationship. Despite its poetic imperfections, *The Princess* was a popular success.

In Memoriam established Tennyson's growing reputation as a lyric poet. The volume's short poems, in the distinctive *abba* stanza form, are arranged not by date of composition but by their place in the psychological pattern of grieving. The tone of the poems moves from frustration and anger at the indifference of Nature to humankind's fate toward a celebration of human love. The publication of *In Memoriam* opened new opportunities in Tennyson's personal life. The trial edition that he sent to Emily Selwood in 1849 helped to revive their broken engagement, and in 1850, after fourteen years' delay, they were married. The success of *In Memoriam* also brought royal recognition; at the end of the year, Queen Victoria made Tennyson poet laureate. Shortly before his death, the monarch awarded him a barony.

After 1850, Tennyson published many short poems, which appeared first in literary magazines and later in collected volumes. He also wrote several unsuccessful plays. His major works in this period were two long poems, *Maud and Other Poems* (1855) and *Idylls of the King* (1859-1885). Tennyson's first attempt at a narratively conceived poem since *The Princess, Maud* tells of a young man driven mad by thwarted love who kills his lover's brother in a duel. His act of murder and Maud's subsequent death plunge the hero into even greater despair until he redeems himself through self-sacrifice in a patriotic war. The story unfolds not in a conventional narrative but in a series of lyrics that express the hero's subjective responses to external events. The innovative style perplexed the critics, whose reviews were generally hostile. Tennyson forever maintained that *Maud* was his favorite poem, despite its miserable reception, and he became notorious for reading it aloud to company at every opportunity.

Idylls of the King is based on Sir Thomas Malory's medieval account of the Arthurian knights in his *Le Morte D'Arthur* (1485). Tennyson had first dealt with the topic in his own "Morte d'Arthur," published in *Poems*. Revised and renamed "The Passing of Arthur," it eventually appeared as the conclusion of twelve "idylls," which make up Tennyson's complete Arthurian cycle. *Idylls of the King* is a complex and occasionally brilliant narrative poem that has stimulated a remarkable amount of scholarly criticism since the mid-1960's. Although the contemporary critical response was ambivalent at best, *Idylls of the King* met with wide popular acclaim.

TENNYSON'S "THE LOTOS-EATERS"

"Courage!" he said, and pointed toward the land,
"This mounting wave will roll us shoreward soon."
In the afternoon they came unto a land
In which it seemed always afternoon.
All round the coast the languid air did swoon,
Breathing like one that hath a weary dream.
Full-faced above the valley stood the moon;
And like a downward smoke, the slender stream
Along the cliff to fall and pause and fall did seem.

A land of streams! some, like a downward smoke,
Slow-dropping veils of thinnest lawn, did go;
And some thro' wavering lights and shadows broke,
Rolling a slumbrous sheet of foam below.
They saw the gleaming river seaward flow
From the inner land: far off, three mountain-tops,
Three silent pinnacles of aged snow,
Stood sunset-flush'd: and, dew'd with showery drops,
Up-clomb the shadowy pine above the woven copse.

The charmed sunset linger'd low adown
In the red West: thro' mountain clefts the dale
Was seen far inland, and the yellow down
Border'd with palm, and many a winding vale
And meadow, set with slender galingale;
A land where all things always seem'd the same!
And round about the keel with faces pale,
Dark faces pale against that rosy flame,
The mild-eyed melancholy Lotos-eaters came.

Branches they bore of that enchanted stem,
Laden with flower and fruit, whereof they gave
To each, but whoso did receive of them,
And taste, to him the gushing of the wave
Far far away did seem to mourn and rave
On alien shores; and if his fellow spake,
His voice was thin, as voices from the grave;
And deep-asleep he seem'd, yet all awake,
And music in his ears his beating heart did make.

They sat them down upon the yellow sand,
Between the sun and moon upon the shore;
And sweet it was to dream of Fatherland,
Of child, and wife, and slave; but evermore
Most weary seem'd the sea, weary the oar,
Weary the wandering fields of barren foam.
Then some one said, "We will return no more";
And all at once they sang, "Our island home
Is far beyond the wave; we will no longer roam."

Source: Electronic text from The Wondering Minstrels, www.cs.rice.edu/
~ssiyer/minstrels/poems. Accessed on October 12, 2005.

SIGNIFICANCE

The self-absorbed lyricism of Alfred, Lord Tennyson's early poems, tempered by the conservative fears of social upheaval that preoccupied the poet later in life, evolved into a poetry that dealt with the important issues of his time by drawing them into a personal focus. What John Stuart Mill discussed in a philosophical treatise, *On the Subjection of Women* (1869), for example, Tennyson explored through the relations between a prince and his intellectually ambitious princess. Although Tennyson's emphasis in *The Princess* on an ideal of domestic harmony that ignores the complex socioeconomic forces that shape political reality may seem myopic and naïve to a modern reader, the use of an intimate focus in *In Memoriam* is very effective. It was in personal terms that nineteenth century individuals were best able to comprehend the chaos that scientific discovery and growing industrialization had made of their worldview.

The Princess, Tennyson's first serious attempt to reconcile the social and didactic with the personal and emotive claims of poetry, earned for him not only popularity but also the financial security to proceed with his long-postponed marriage. The stellar success of *In Memoriam* three years later thrust Tennyson into a degree of fame and fortune that swelled with the interest of an increasingly literate middle-class population at home and the growing enthusiasm of his audience in the United States.

In the wake of two equally hostile poetic sensibilities (*fin de siècle* aestheticism, which denigrated the moral dimension of art, and early twentieth century modernism, which abhorred subjectivity), Tennyson's reputation suffered an unfortunate reversal. Not until the middle of the twentieth century, when modern American scholars such as W. D. Paden and Edgar F. Shannon reevaluated Tennyson's achievement, did the great Victorian begin to regain literary respectability. Since the publication of Jerome H. Buckley's seminal study in 1960, excellent modern editions have appeared along with a host of scholarly, biographical, and critical works that have reclaimed Tennyson for the twentieth century.

—Beverley Allix

FURTHER READING

Buckley, Jerome H. *Tennyson: The Growth of a Poet*. Cambridge, Mass.: Harvard University Press, 1960. Buckley examines the external influences of the Victorian moral, social, intellectual, and scientific climate in the light of the personal details of the poet's biography to chart the growth of Tennyson's poetic sensibility.

Jump, John, ed. *Tennyson: The Critical Heritage*. New York: Barnes and Noble Books, 1967. Reprints thirty-five reviews of Tennyson's works. A useful documentary companion to Edgar F. Shannon's book.

Levi, Peter. *Tennyson*. New York: C. Scribner's Sons, 1993. A scholarly and generally admiring biography, examining Tennyson's life, writings, and literary influences.

Martin, Robert Bernard. *Tennyson: The Unquiet Heart*. New York: Oxford University Press, 1980. Martin's readable study draws on a wealth of published Tennyson biographies and criticism as well as unpublished letters and manuscripts.

Palmer, D. J., ed. *Tennyson*. London: Bell and Sons, 1973. A collection of essays, three of which are particularly interesting: "Tennyson: A Reader's Guide" gives a historical bibliographic survey of Tennyson scholarship and criticism; "Tennyson and His Public 1827-59" and "Tennyson and Victorian Social Values" provide social and literary context.

Ricks, Christopher. *Tennyson*. New York: Macmillan, 1972. The modern editor of Tennyson's poems offers a critical biography that makes use of previously inaccessible manuscripts and biographical material.

Shannon, Edgar F. *Tennyson and the Reviewers: A Study of His Literary Reputation and of the Influence of the Critics upon His Poetry, 1827-51*. Cambridge, Mass.: Harvard University Press, 1952. An examination of the dynamic relationship between Tennyson's poetry and the reviews.

Shaw, W. D. *Tennyson's Style*. Ithaca, N.Y.: Cornell University Press, 1976. An excellent study of Tennyson's poetry in the context of literary tradition in general and of Romantic and Victorian poetic theory and practice in particular.

Tennyson, Alfred. *The Poems of Tennyson*. Edited by Christopher Ricks. London: Longman, 1969. The most complete and scholarly edition of Tennyson's poems. It includes one early play, *The Devil and the Lady* (wr. c. 1823) but excludes the later plays. Ricks draws on the Eversley edition, which contains Tennyson's own annotations, and on numerous unpublished manuscripts.

Tennyson, Sir Charles. *Alfred Tennyson*. New York: Macmillan, 1949. Written by Tennyson's grandson, this is the first authoritative formal biography of Tennyson. In addition to Tennyson's life and personality, the book deals with the poet's social, political, intellectual, and religious milieu.

Tennyson, Hallam, Lord. *Alfred Lord Tennyson: A Memoir*. 2 vols. New York: Macmillan, 1897. Reprint. New York: Greenwood Press, 1969. A rather biased and overprotective biography by the poet's eldest son. Despite its lack of objectivity, it is an excellent biographical sourcebook. All subsequent biographers have relied on its materials.

Thorn, Michael. *Tennyson*. New York: St. Martin's Press, 1993. Comprehensive biography, linking Tennyson and his work to the Victorian era. Thorn disagrees with some critics who claim Tennyson created his best work in his youth; he analyzes and points out the merits of Tennyson's later works.

SEE ALSO: Matthew Arnold; Henry Irving; William Charles Macready; John Stuart Mill; Christina Rossetti; Ellen Terry; Queen Victoria.

RELATED ARTICLES in *Great Events from History: The Nineteenth Century, 1801-1900*: 1842: Tennyson Publishes "Morte d'Arthur"; November 5, 1850: Tennyson Becomes England's Poet Laureate; 1878-1899: Irving Manages London's Lyceum Theatre.

ELLEN TERRY
English actor

*As the leading female Shakespearean actor and one of
the most liberated women of her time, Terry left an
indelible impression on the artistic and social worlds
of Victorian England.*

BORN: February 27, 1847; Coventry, Warwickshire,
England
DIED: July 21, 1928; Smallhythe, Kent, England
ALSO KNOWN AS: Alice Ellen Terry (full name); Dame
Alice Ellen Terry
AREA OF ACHIEVEMENT: Theater

EARLY LIFE

Alice Ellen Terry was, as the theatrical cliché has it, very
nearly "born in a costume trunk." One of eleven children
of the roving players Ben and Sarah Terry, she was delivered in a theatrical rooming house in Warwickshire, England, while her parents were on tour. Her early years
were spent in the then marginally respectable world of
the theater. She literally grew up backstage, and, because she never received any serious formal education,
the theater served as her schoolroom. From the beginning, young Ellen was overshadowed by her older sister Kate, whose promise as an actor won for her a contract with the legendary actor-manager Edmund Kean in
1852. It was at Kean's Princess's Theatre in London that
the nine-year-old Ellen made her theatrical debut in the
role of Prince Mamillius in William Shakespeare's *The
Winter's Tale* (pr. c. 1610-1611). The Keans, especially
the disciplinarian Mrs. Kean, were an important influence on Ellen, teaching her lessons about acting and
about theatrical protocol that would serve her well in
later years.

Though Kate was clearly the burgeoning star of the
family, Ellen had gained considerable exposure during
her family's years with the prestigious Kean troupe, and
in 1861 she joined the London-based troupe of Albina de
Rhona, under whose auspices she appeared in some ten
plays, most of them forgotten melodramas. In 1862, Ellen joined the Bristol stock company that employed
Kate, and the Terry sisters quickly became local celebrities, attracting the attention of fans and critics alike.
Among the latter was Edward William Godwin, an aspiring architect and theatrical designer. Ellen was strongly
attracted to the married, twenty-eight-year-old Godwin,
and to what he represented: culture, sophistication, and
bohemianism.

Terry was a busy actor who, still in her teens, was methodically learning her trade and attracting favorable attention. In the space of a year she appeared in Shakespeare's *Othello* (pr. 1604) and *Much Ado About Nothing*
(pr. c. 1598-1599), in Richard Brinsley Sheridan's *The
Rivals* (pr., pb. 1775), and in Tom Taylor's 1858 play
Our American Cousin (which was to achieve notoriety as
the play Abraham Lincoln was watching when he was assassinated in 1865). It was playwright Taylor who introduced Ellen to the painter George Frederick Watts, a
temperamental and talented portraitist and a member of
the increasingly important Pre-Raphaelite school of poets and painters. Struck by the picturesqueness of the
Terry sisters, Watts used them as models for his beautiful
The Sisters. He was the first painter to immortalize Ellen
Terry, and she later served as a model for some of his
best paintings, including *Choosing, Ellen Terry*, and
Ophelia, Ellen posing as Shakespeare's doomed heroine
in the latter.

On February 20, 1864, the sixteen-year-old Terry
married the forty-six-year-old Watts, and the marriage
seems to have been disastrous from the first. Terry's desire for stability and respectability in what had been a
peripatetic and uncertain life is somewhat understandable; less understandable is Watts's motivation for marrying a girl thirty years his junior. An inept lover and a
hopeless neurotic, Watts immediately tried to educate
Terry in the ways of polite society, and the formerly carefree, high-spirited girl was miserable. The constant
stream of celebrities through the Watts home—including
the poets Robert Browning and Alfred, Lord Tennyson,
and the politicians Benjamin Disraeli and William Ewart
Gladstone—only slightly alleviated Terry's boredom
and frustration at being seen and not heard.

After ten months, Terry left Watts and returned to her
parents, a social outcast. Reluctantly, she began to act
again, though for two years she was still overshadowed
by her sister's now undisputed stardom. In 1867, Terry
joined the acting company at the New Queen's Theatre,
where she met a young actor named Henry Irving and
played opposite him in a bastardization of Shakespeare's
The Taming of the Shrew (pr. c. 1593-1594). Somewhere
along the line, however, Edward Godwin reentered her
life, and in October, 1868, Terry ran off with him, leaving no word of her whereabouts with her family and leading them to believe that she had met with foul play. The
mystery was soon solved, and it was discovered that she

and Godwin had taken up residence together in the village of Wheathampstead, thirty-five miles from London. She stayed with Godwin for some seven years and bore him two children: Edith in December, 1869, and Edward in January, 1872. The world would later know the boy as Gordon Craig.

LIFE'S WORK

Little is known of Terry's years with Godwin, though for a time, at least, they seem to have been happy. This was the most settled and domestic period that Terry would ever know, and she took great pleasure in keeping the house, tending the children, and welcoming her lover home after his daily commute from London. Terry and Godwin shared many interests, the most important of which was the theater. Terry learned to aid Godwin in his stage designs, and together they read the works of Shakespeare. In time, Godwin designed and built a house for his family, and together he and Terry planted and tended a garden. Their rural idyll came to an end, however, when finances forced Terry to return to the stage. Though undeniably a major architectural and artistic talent, Godwin had no head for business, and by the winter of 1873-1874

Ellen Terry. (Library of Congress)

the bill collectors were pounding at the door. The playwright Charles Reade, an old family friend, offered Terry a part in his current play, *The Wandering Heir* (1872), and in February, 1874, Terry returned to the stage after an absence of some five years.

Bolstered both by favorable reviews and by the need for money, Terry performed in several more plays with Reade before accepting an offer from a Mrs. Bancroft, the actor-manager of the Prince of Wales Theatre, to play Portia in Shakespeare's *The Merchant of Venice* (pr. c. 1596-1597). Though her career was straining her relationship with Godwin, he was enlisted to supervise the scenery and costumes for the production, and the results were magnificent. Godwin's design work, however, was dominated by Terry's performance: When the play opened in April, 1875, Terry became an overnight sensation. Her first major Shakespearean role had made her a major star, and she had acquired a legion of fans who came to see her perform even in the less distinguished plays that followed the closing of *The Merchant of Venice*.

Terry's relationship with Godwin, however, could not bear the strain. In March, 1876, he was married to one of his students. Terry, in turn, was married to the actor Charles Wardell in November, 1877, soon after her divorce from Watts became final.

During that same year, Terry moved to the Royal Court Theatre, where she scored a huge success in *Olivia*, an adaptation of Oliver Goldsmith's novel *The Vicar of Wakefield* (1764) written especially for her by W. G. Wills. In 1878, theatrical history was made when the same Henry Irving with whom Terry had acted eleven years before invited her to play opposite him in a new production of *Hamlet* (pr. c. 1600-1601) at the Lyceum Theatre. This was the great age of the theatrical actor-manager who not only acted in plays but also oversaw nearly every facet of their production, from costume design to music to provincial tours. With his closest rival, Sir Herbert Beerbohm Tree, Irving reigned over this era, combining artistic sensibility with an unparalleled flair for public relations. He and Terry were to remain together for some twenty years, during which they undertook nearly every major Shakespearean play and transformed the Lyceum into a theatrical legend.

During those years, Terry maintained a schedule that would fell most modern performers. Besides performing at the Lyceum in London, she and Irving regularly toured the British provinces and together made seven grueling but profitable tours of the United States. In addition, she still had family responsibilities. By 1881, she and

Charles Wardell had legally separated, and Terry acted as both mother and father to her children. Her correspondence shows that she was a caring parent to both "Edy" and "Teddy," but it is clear that her son was the love of her life.

From early childhood, he displayed the talent and temperament of the born artist, often appearing in plays with his mother but possessing in greater measure his father's talent for the graphic arts. As Gordon Craig, he would change the history of theatrical design, but his personal life was always a shambles. Financially and personally irresponsible, he was forever relying on his mother's name and on her money to establish him in one business venture after another, and to extricate him from a lifetime of trouble. Though he often neglected her, Terry adored him to the end of her life, acting as a doting grandmother to his many illegitimate children, including one by the dancer Isadora Duncan.

In spite of a short-lived third marriage late in her life, Terry's only other enduring professional and personal commitment was to Irving, though whether the two were ever really romantically involved is unknown. Certainly she spent more time with him than with anyone else, both on stage and off stage. Besides the plays of Shakespeare, the two scored major triumphs in Wills's adaptation of Johann Wolfgang von Goethe's *Faust*, in Tennyson's *The Cup*, and in revivals of *Olivia*.

As famous in the United States as in their native England, the pair became the stuff of myth, anticipating such great twentieth century acting duos as Alfred Lunt and Lynn Fontanne, and Hume Cronyn and Jessica Tandy. Unlike modern performers, however, who characteristically star in a play for a Broadway season and then, perhaps, tour with it for a year, Terry and Irving never abandoned their great roles. Less haughty than modern theater, the theater of the Victorian era demanded that actors maintain a repertoire of tried-and-

---

TAKING ADVICE FROM AUTHORS

In her autobiography, Ellen Terry recalled how valuable the advice of Charles Reade was to her acting career.

The relation between author and actor is a very important element in the life of the stage. It is the way with some dramatists to despise those who interpret their plays, to accuse us of ruining their creations, to suffer disappointment and rage because we do not, or cannot, carry out their ideas. . . .

The first author with whom I had to deal, at a critical point in my progress as an actress, was Charles Reade, and he helped me enormously. He might, and often did, make twelve suggestions that were wrong; but against them he would make one that was so right that its value was immeasurable and unforgettable.

It is through the dissatisfaction of a man like Charles Reade that an actress *learns*—that is, if she is not conceited. Conceit is an insuperable obstacle to all progress. On the other hand, it is of little use to take criticism in a slavish spirit and to act on it without understanding it. Charles Reade constantly wrote and said things to me which were not absolutely just criticism; but they directed my attention to the true cause of the faults which he found in my performance, and put me on the way to mending them. . . .

The difficulty that [Reade] was now urging me to knock down was one of *pace*, and I am afraid that in all my stage life subsequently I never quite succeeded in kicking it or walking over its prostrate body!

Looking backward, I remember many times when I failed in rapidity of utterance, and was "pumped" at moments when swiftness was essential. Pace is the soul of comedy, and to elaborate lines at the expense of pace is disastrous. Curiously enough, I have met and envied this gift of pace in actors who were not conspicuously talented in other respects, and no Rosalind that I have ever seen has had enough of it. Of course, it is not a question of swift utterance only, but of swift thinking. I am able to think more swiftly on the stage now than at the time Charles Reade wrote to me, and I only wish I were young enough to take advantage of it. But youth thinks *slowly*, as a rule.

Vary the pace. Charles Reade was never tired of saying this, and, indeed, it is one of the foundations of all good acting. . . .

Source: Ellen Terry, *The Story of My Life* (New York, 1908), chapter 5.

---

true hits that, in the event of another play's failure, could be revived at short notice and with a minimum of rehearsal. Such performers as Terry, Irving, and their great contemporaries Sarah Bernhardt, Eleanora Duse, Edwin Booth, and Joseph Jefferson carried around in their heads dozens of parts, ranging from the English and Continental classics to long-forgotten popular melodramas. Irving had just finished an engagement with one of these latter, *The Bells* (1871), when he died on October 13, 1905.

The reverence and dignity accorded Irving at the time of his death bespoke the respectability that he had brought to the profession of acting, a lower-class business when he and Terry had first begun. Terry, too, garnered honors late in her career. In 1906, her friends and admirers staged a benefit to celebrate her fiftieth anniversary on the stage, and among the participants were actors Mrs. Patrick Campbell and Lillie Langtry, opera star Enrico Caruso, composer Sir Arthur Sullivan, mystery writer Sir Arthur Conan Doyle, and poet and novelist Rudyard Kipling. From 1910 to 1921, she undertook a series of lecture tours and was everywhere received as a royal personage. In 1925, she was accorded the honor that had long eluded her: She was created Dame Grand Cross of the Most Excellent Order of the British Empire by King George V and Queen Mary. Ever open to new experiences, the elderly Terry appeared in several silent films, though the cinema was clearly not her medium. She died of a stroke on July 21, 1928, in her beloved cottage at Smallhythe.

SIGNIFICANCE

During her long life, Ellen Terry attracted the attention of many celebrities. Although yet an obscure young bride, she befriended Great Britain's poet laureate, Alfred, Lord Tennyson, and was photographed by Lewis Carroll, the author of *Alice's Adventures in Wonderland* (1865), who adored her. She was painted not only by her husband, G. F. Watts, but also by John Singer Sargent, the most acclaimed portraitist of his age. The painter William Holman Hunt designed her first bridal gown. She counted among her fans painter James McNeill Whistler and poet Algernon Charles Swinburne. Poet, playwright, and novelist Oscar Wilde wrote sonnets for her, and J. M. Barrie, the author of *Peter Pan* (pr. 1904, pb. 1928), wrote a play for her. For many years she carried on an intimate correspondence with George Bernard Shaw, who also wrote a play for her. Isadora Duncan confided in her as she would have in a mother, and her women friends included the legendary actors Lillie Langtry, Sarah Bernhardt, and Eleanora Duse.

Little wonder, then, that Ellen Terry is credited with helping to create the modern star system, in which performers are lauded not only for their performances but also for their personalities. She was one of the first female actors to endorse a commercial product, and one of the first to start a fashion trend when she appeared in *Olivia* for the first time during the 1870's. In her unaffected and "natural" style of acting and in her unconventional personal life, Terry was in every way an original, representing as she did a sharp departure from the histrionics of the early nineteenth century stage and from the restrictive morals of Victorian England.

—*J. D. Daubs*

FURTHER READING

Craig, Edward Gordon. *Ellen Terry and Her Secret Self*. London: Sampson Low, Marston, 1931. Terry's son's reminiscences of his mother tell as much about him as they do about her, but they are continually interesting, providing anecdotes and impressions that one can find nowhere else. A colorful memoir by a spoiled child who became an important personage in his own right.

Irving, Laurence. *Henry Irving: The Actor and His World*. London: Faber and Faber, 1951. Any study of Terry must include a biography of Irving, and this one, though written by the great actor-manager's grandson, is surprisingly thorough and well documented. A definitive biography.

McDonald, Russ. *Look to the Lady: Sarah Siddons, Ellen Terry, and Judi Dench on the Shakespearean Stage*. Athens: University of Georgia Press, 2005. Examines the lives, careers, and acting techniques of Terry and two other actors who were renowned for their interpretations of Shakespeare's heroines.

Manvell, Roger. *Ellen Terry*. New York: G. P. Putnam's Sons, 1968. The closest thing to a definitive biography, this study is exhaustive and carefully researched.

Prideaux, Tom. *Love or Nothing: The Life and Times of Ellen Terry*. New York: Charles Scribner's Sons, 1975. Written by a distinguished popular journalist, this book is chatty, personal, and interpretive. Recommended for the general reader.

St. John, Christopher, ed. *Ellen Terry and Bernard Shaw: A Correspondence*. New York: G. P. Putnam's Sons, 1932. A fascinating record of the relationship between two luminaries. These letters show Terry's private side to have been as compelling and charismatic as her stage performances.

Saintsbury, H. A., and Cecil Palmer, eds. *We Saw Him Act: A Symposium on the Art of Sir Henry Irving*. New York: Benjamin Blom, 1939. Reprint. 1969. This eccentric and lively collection of essays on Irving's stage career contains innumerable references to Terry. Essential to understanding the chemistry between Terry and Irving.

Shearer, Moira. *Ellen Terry*. Stroud, Gloucestershire, England: Sutton, 1998. A brief overview of Terry's life and career, describing how she earned her reputation as the greatest female actor in Victorian Britain.

Terry, Ellen. *Ellen Terry's Memoirs*. New York: G. P. Putnam's Sons, 1932. First published as *The Story of My Life* in 1908. Like any autobiography, this book is not to be trusted as fact, but it provides otherwise unattainable insights into Terry's dedication, humor, and humanity.

SEE ALSO: Sarah Bernhardt; Edwin Booth; Lewis Carroll; Benjamin Disraeli; William Ewart Gladstone; William Holman Hunt; Henry Irving; Edmund Kean; Rudyard Kipling; Lillie Langtry; John Singer Sargent; Alfred, Lord Tennyson; James McNeill Whistler; Oscar Wilde.

RELATED ARTICLE in *Great Events from History: The Nineteenth Century, 1801-1900:* 1878-1899: Irving Manages London's Lyceum Theatre.

NIKOLA TESLA
Croatian-born American inventor

With his brilliant, intuitive insight and endless creative imagination, Telsa laid the foundations for many of the technological developments of the twentieth century, and his development of alternating current continues to affect the daily lives of the entire world into the twenty-first century.

BORN: July 9, 1856; Smiljan, Austro-Hungarian Empire (now in Croatia)
DIED: January 7, 1943; New York, New York
AREA OF ACHIEVEMENT: Engineering

EARLY LIFE

Nikola Tesla (TEHS-lah) was the son of an Orthodox Croatian priest. His mother, in spite of her lack of formal education, was a remarkably capable woman who invented numerous household devices and developed a prodigious memory for epic poetry. Tesla was later to attribute his own powers to her influence. When he was six, the family moved to the city of Gospic, and Tesla excelled at the local school, particularly in languages and mathematics. From his earliest years he showed a remarkable aptitude for solving mechanical problems and the rigid self-discipline and unshakable self-confidence that were to lead him to success. As a boy, he also possessed a delicate constitution and frequently suffered from ill health.

In 1875, Tesla entered the Austrian Polytechnic School in Graz, where he studied compulsively, sometimes for twenty hours a day. Even at this young age he was occupied with the problem of the feasibility of using alternating current for the distribution of electrical energy. His solution, when it came, was to revolutionize the world of electrical engineering.

Financial difficulties forced Tesla to leave the Polytechnic at the end of his second year. His mother raised the money for him to travel to Prague, where he continued his studies, although he was not officially enrolled in any university. For the most part, Tesla was self-taught.

In 1881, he traveled to Budapest and found a lowly position in the Central Telegraph Office. While in Hungary he suffered from one of the nervous disorders that were to be a regular feature of his life, but following his recovery came a significant moment. One evening he was walking toward the sunset reciting a passage from Johann Wolfgang von Goethe's *Faust*, when the principle of the rotating magnetic field came to him in a sudden flash of realization, and he knew that he had the solution to the problem of the alternating current system. At this time, however, he had neither time nor means to build the machine he could see so clearly in his mind.

In 1882, he moved to Paris, where he secured a job with the Continental Edison Company. Two years later, in 1884, armed with a splendid recommendation from the manager of the company, a former associate of Thomas Alva Edison, Tesla sailed for the richer pastures of America, arriving in New York in June of that year. The stage was set for Tesla's brilliant and extraordinary career.

LIFE'S WORK

Edison was impressed by Tesla and offered him a job. The two great inventors were vastly different in method and personality, however, and were not destined to have a long working relationship. Tesla resigned over a disagreement about financial compensation for his redesign of Edison's dynamos. Tesla's reputation had been growing, however, and a group of financiers offered him a company under his own name, for which Tesla developed an improved and more economical arc lamp. However, he was given little control over the company, and there was no scope for his large ambitions. He soon resigned. For the next year, his life was difficult, and he was forced to take any job that came along in order to stay alive.

By 1887, his luck changed, and so began a decade of high achievement and recognition. A. K. Brown, of the Western Union Telegraph Company, became interested in Tesla's ideas concerning alternating current, and this quickly led to the formation of the Tesla Electric Company. In the same year Tesla filed his first alternating current patents, and in 1888 he was invited to address the American Institute of Electrical Engineers. He made such an impact that another inventor and industrialist, George Westinghouse, showed keen interest. Westinghouse soon negotiated a contract with Tesla for his polyphase system of alternating current dynamos, a system that would allow power to be economically distributed over large distances. This gave rise to a bitter rivalry between Westinghouse, armed with Tesla's system, and Edison, whose company was committed to using the direct current system; it became known as the "battle of the currents."

By the early 1890's, Tesla had developed a worldwide reputation as a brilliant inventor. He was invited to Europe, where he lectured to prestigious scientific societies, including the Royal Society of Great Britain. He made an impressive figure. Standing six and one-half feet tall, of slender build, with blue eyes and black hair, and always immaculately dressed, he was the complete showman. During his lectures he would conduct spectacular electrical demonstrations, keeping his audience enthralled with his almost unlimited vision of the possibilities of electrical power.

By 1893, the battle of the currents was all but over. Tesla's system had provided the power for the spectacular Chicago World's Fair in 1893, the first electrical fair in history, and in the same year the Niagara Falls Commission announced that it had awarded a contract to build three generators at Niagara Falls to Westinghouse's firm. The project proved to be one of the great engineering feats of the age.

These were highly productive years for Tesla; he worked on a variety of different projects at once and also led a lively social life in New York alongside the wealthy and famous. He built the Tesla coil, an air-core transformer designed to produce high voltages at high frequencies; he discovered the healing possibilities in high-frequency currents applied to the human body; he invented the carbon button lamp, the shadowgraph (forerunner of the X ray), and a new reciprocating dynamo, which proved to be the inspiration for the modern electric clock. In a lecture in 1893, he described the principle of radio broadcasting, a number of years before Guglielmo Marconi's practical demonstrations; in 1898 he demonstrated the first radio-controlled robot boat. In many of his ideas, Tesla was ahead of his time. He pioneered the basic principles of radar, which were not

Nikola Tesla.

to be developed for another thirty years. He wanted to create artificial lightning to control the world's weather, and he developed a new science called telegeodynamics, which he said could be used to locate ore deposits.

Restlessly spinning new ideas, he then entered on a major project, the building of a laboratory at Colorado Springs, which was to develop his vision of a worldwide broadcasting system. There he built the largest Tesla coil ever, a twelve-million-volt machine capable of producing artificial lightning that soared up to 135 feet in the air. His spectacular experiments aroused a great deal of local curiosity, and his much-publicized belief that he had received signals from another planet earned for him considerable ridicule.

In 1900, Tesla closed the laboratory and returned to New York. By the following year he had obtained the backing of the financier J. P. Morgan, for the construction of a transmitter for the world broadcasting system on a site Tesla named Wardenclyffe, on Long Island, New York. The combination of labor troubles and Morgan's withdrawal of financial support, however, resulted in the failure of the project.

After the failure of Wardenclyffe, Tesla's scientific reputation came under attack. His opponents portrayed him as an impractical dreamer, and the high point of his career was over. Despite the criticism, Tesla's inventive spirit remained undimmed. In 1906, he turned to designing a new turbine, which he thought could drive an ocean liner across the Atlantic in three days, but he lacked funds to translate the theory into practice.

In 1915, it was rumored that he and Edison had won the Nobel Prize, but in what appears to have been a last-minute change of mind by the Nobel committee, the prize was awarded elsewhere. Tesla's disappointment was only partially allayed when in 1917 he was awarded the prestigious Edison Medal from the American Institute of Electrical Engineers.

In his last years Tesla was increasingly afflicted by phobias and neuroses and lived virtually as a recluse. He had never accumulated wealth from his inventions, and he was now saved from poverty only by an honorarium of seven thousand dollars per annum from the Tesla Institute in Belgrade, which had been founded in 1935.

At the age of eighty-six, Tesla died alone, on January 7, 1943, in his hotel room in New York. At his funeral in the Cathedral of St. John the Divine in New York, two thousand people were in attendance, and tributes from many of the world's great scientists poured in to honor the man who had, so to speak, set the world alight.

SIGNIFICANCE

The last quarter of the nineteenth century was the great age of invention and industrial expansion in the United States. Circumstances were highly favorable for growth. There were wide markets, and labor, raw materials, and capital were freely available. There were few political or social barriers to free enterprise, and farsighted entrepreneurs were quick to see commercial possibilities in the breakthroughs being made in science and technology. The rewards were great for those who were prepared to take the risks. Machines and mass production revolutionized home, factory, and office: electric lighting, telephones, cameras, adding machines, and typewriters all became commonplace.

Circumstances were particularly favorable for the growth of the electrical manufacturing industry. Tesla, who was one of the estimated fourteen million European immigrants who arrived in America in the last two generations of the nineteenth century, arrived at the right place at the right time. There is no doubt that he had found his

natural home. Although a Serb by birth, he was perfectly attuned to the American spirit. He was, he said, "at heart an American before I thought of coming here to live." All of his life he prized the American citizenship he had been awarded in 1891.

Tesla's legacy is everywhere apparent. His greatest discovery, the alternating current motor, laid the foundation for the power system used throughout the industrialized world. The Tesla coil is widely used in television and radio sets, and scientists still eagerly explore Teslian concepts. The Tesla turbine, for example, was still being investigated and developed nearly half a century after his death. The publication in 1978 of Tesla's research notes from Colorado Springs aroused a fresh wave of interest, although because Tesla could always visualize his designs and possessed a photographic memory, his written records are usually incomplete.

In 1975, Tesla was inducted into the National Inventors Hall of Fame, a fitting honor for the man whose brilliant skill and indefatigable labor harnessed the basic forces of nature for the betterment of the human condition.

—*Bryan Aubrey*

FURTHER READING

Cheney, Margaret. *Tesla: Man Out of Time*. Englewood Cliffs, N.J.: Prentice-Hall, 1981. Admiring, competent, readable biography. Especially good on the numerous ways in which Tesla anticipated modern technologies. Interesting chapter on the fate of Tesla's papers after his death.

Hall, Stephen H. "Tesla: A Scientific Saint, Wizard or Carnival Sideman?" *Smithsonian* 17 (June, 1986): 120-134. Lively article, ranging over Tesla's achievements, his eccentricities, and the controversies that surround the extent of his contributions to science.

Hunt, Inez, and Wanetta W. Draper. *Lightning in His Hand: The Life Story of Nikola Tesla*. Denver: Sage, 1964. Not as detailed as Cheney (see above), but soundly researched, sympathetic to Tesla's achievements. Uses Tesla correspondence not available to O'Neill (see below).

Jonnes, Jill. *Empires of Light: Edison, Tesla, Westinghouse, and the Race to Electrify the World*. New York: Random House, 2003. Explains how the three inventors sought to create businesses that would provide safe, reliable electricity. Jonnes describes the inventions and careers of Tesla, Edison, and Westinghouse, and relates how they worked with bankers, lawyers, and financiers to create electrical "empires."

O'Neill, John J. *Prodigal Genius: The Life of Nikola Tesla*. New York: Ives Washburn, 1944. Earliest biography. O'Neill was science editor of the New York *Herald Tribune* and Tesla's friend. Lively and anecdotal; presents a fascinating portrait of the man. Has been partially superseded by the greater information available to later biographers.

Seifer, Marc J. *Wizard: The Life and Times of Nikola Tesla: Biography of a Genius*. Secaucus, N.J.: Carol, 1996. Exhaustively researched, definitive biography, describing Tesla's experiences as an entrepreneur, experimental physicist, and inventor. Traces Tesla's life, describing how the once flamboyant and nouveau-riche inventor ended his life in eccentricity and poverty.

Tesla, Nikola. *Nikola Tesla: Lectures, Patents, Articles*. Edited by Vojin Popović, Radoslav Horvat, and Nikola Nikolić. Belgrade, Yugoslavia: Nikola Tesla Museum, 1956. Contains five of the most important of Tesla's lectures, including an explanation of the induction motor. Also includes more than eighty patents, scientific and technical articles, and Tesla's views about how electricity will solve world problems.

SEE ALSO: William Fothergill Cooke and Charles Wheatstone; Thomas Alva Edison; Michael Faraday; Sir William Robert Grove; James Clerk Maxwell; Charles Proteus Steinmetz; George Westinghouse.

RELATED ARTICLES in *Great Events from History: The Nineteenth Century, 1801-1900:* October, 1831: Faraday Converts Magnetic Force into Electricity; October 21, 1879: Edison Demonstrates the Incandescent Lamp.

TEWODROS II
Emperor of Ethiopia (r. 1855-1868)

After rising from obscurity to become emperor of Ethiopia, Tewodros tried to restore order and unify a country that had suffered from decades of feudal anarchy. He ultimately failed, but his vision inspired his successors to work for national reform and reconstruction of the empire.

BORN: c. 1818; Qwara, Ethiopia
DIED: April 13, 1868; Magdela, Ethiopia
ALSO KNOWN AS: Lij Kassa Hailu (birth name); Lij Kassa Haylu; Kassa; Kasa; Lij Kassa; Theodore II
AREAS OF ACHIEVEMENT: Government and politics, warfare and conquest

EARLY LIFE

Ethiopia's Emperor Tewodros II (teh-WOH-drohs) was born Kassa Hailu, the son of a minor nobleman in northwestern Ethiopia. After losing his father at an early age, he grew up with his mother in poverty. As a young man he entered into the service of an uncle who was the governor of a frontier province. When his uncle died, he returned to his birthplace of Qwara and started a new career as leader of a bandit group, a favorite occupation for ambitious young men in war-torn Ethiopia during the early nineteenth century.

Contemporary accounts of Kassa portray him as a sort of Robin Hood figure with a keen sense of social justice who used his exploits as a bandit to benefit the local population. He also built a reputation for bravery and good leadership and was able to attract a large following within a few years. By the mid-1840's, Kassa's fame had spread so wide as to attract the attention of the great lords in the country. The most prominent of these, Ras Ali, sought to win Kassa over to his side by giving him his daughter in marriage and confirming him as governor of Qwara. This, however, did little to curb Kassa's ambition. He continuously clashed with Ali and fought with neighboring lords, strengthening his army and expanding his domain at their expense.

LIFE'S WORK

By 1850, Kassa had emerged as one of the most powerful contenders for power. He continued to enjoy successive victories against the major regional lords who had dominated Ethiopian politics over the previous several decades, including Ras Ali. In February, 1855, he defeated Dejazmach Wube of Semien, the last remaining warlord, thereby bringing to an end the Era of Princes (*Zemene Mesafint*), during which political decentralization and feudal warfare had gripped Ethiopia for nearly a century.

On February 11, 1855, Kassa had himself crowned as "King of Kings" of Ethiopia under the throne name of Tewodros II. His choice of regnal name reflected his vision and ambition. Popular Ethiopian prophecy foretold the coming of a king called Tewodros who, after a period of great suffering, would restore the ancient glory of the Ethiopian Empire and establish a millennium of peace and just administration. Tewodros believed himself called upon to lift Ethiopia from the abyss of the Era of Princes and attributed his spectacular rise to power to divine intervention.

Immediately after his coronation, Tewodros declared his desire to unify Ethiopia and reform its administration. To that end, he set out to create a modern army that would be disciplined and integrated into a national force under his command. He also initiated a movement toward a modern form of government in which he sought to replace traditional feudal chiefs with salaried, loyal, and competent administrators. However, he lacked the resources to implement his reform plans and also faced other formidable obstacles. Entrenched feudal interest groups strongly resisted his efforts to reform the system on which their livelihood depended.

Uprisings led by disgruntled members of the nobility flared up almost everywhere throughout the empire. The embattled Tewodros was forced to spend inordinate amounts of time and resources to suppress rebellions. The Ethiopian Orthodox Church on which he relied for ideological support turned against him when he sought to limit its control over land. With the clergy turned against him, Tewodros found himself increasingly estranged from his own people. Frustrated by his failure to realize any of his visions, he resorted to increasingly harsh measures to deal with his detractors and merely multiplied his enemies.

Other challenges to Tewodros's position came from his relations with European powers. He greatly admired the technological advances of European nations and counted on their support for his planned modernization, hoping that fellow Christian nations would come to the aid of a Christian African state that was surrounded by hostile Muslim neighbors. He wrote letters to several European rulers soliciting their support, but his overtures were rebuffed in all the European capitals. Tewodros saw their rejection as a personal affront. He was particularly enraged by Great Britain's failure even to reply to a letter he sent to Queen Victoria in 1862 and had the British consul and several other Europeans in his country arrested. His relations with Great Britain reached a crisis level in 1866, when he imprisoned members of the British diplomatic mission sent to secure the release of the diplomats he had detained earlier.

The British government could not continue to ignore this affront to its prestige. Many in British political cir-

cles worried that Britain's reputation would suffer in the Middle East and Asia if Tewodros continued to defy its government. By 1867, all diplomatic efforts to resolve the hostage issue had failed, and the British government decided on military intervention to secure the release of the captives and restore British honor. An expeditionary force of thirteen thousand British and Indian soldiers, who were equipped with the latest weapons, was organized in India sent to Northeast Africa under the command of General Robert Napier. In early 1868, this massive expedition reached the African coast and began to work its way inland, toward the Ethiopian capital. Including soldiers, auxiliary workers, and camp followers, the total force numbered sixty-two thousand people, and it was supported by thirty-six thousand animals.

The British expeditionary force had to cross some four hundred miles of rugged terrain to reach Magdela, the mountain fortress in which Tewodros was holding his European captives. However, the terrain was the only serious challenge that the expedition faced. By the time it arrived at Magdela, Tewodros had virtually lost control of his empire. The entire region through which the British expedition passed had already fallen into the hands of Tewodros's enemies, who were happy to cooperate with the British in return for promises of arms and other support.

The expedition reached Magdela in early April without meeting any serious resistance. On April 10, 1868, Napier scored an easy victory over the handful of soldiers that constituted Tewodros's remaining army. Realizing the hopelessness of his situation on April 13, Tewodros released the captives and committed suicide a few minutes before British forces stormed his fortress.

SIGNIFICANCE

Tewodros's reign marked the opening of a new era of Ethiopian history. Although he did not succeed in realizing his objectives during his lifetime, he resurrected the ideal of a strong unitary state so effectively that Ethiopia never reverted back to its previous decentralization and feudal disorder. Almost all of the strong political actors that arose after Tewodros aspired to continue his work of centralization. His two immediate successors, Emperors Yohannes IV and Menelik II, followed the path that he had charted. Both succeeded to a large extent in building a highly centralized and effective Ethiopian state. Tewodros was also the first monarch with a concept of modernization and set the stage for the incorporation of European technology in his country, the only sub-Saharan native African state not to fall under European colonialism.

—*Shumet Sishagne*

FURTHER READING

Abir, Mordecai. *Ethiopia: The Era of the Princes—The Challenge of Islam and the Re-Unification of the Christian Empire, 1769-1855*. New York: Praeger, 1968. A well-researched book that provides excellent background information on the rise of Emperor Tewodros.

Bates, Darrell. *The Abyssinian Difficulty: The Emperor Theodorus and the Magdala Campaign, 1867-1868*. Oxford, England: Oxford University Press, 1979. An excellent account of the rise to power of Emperor Tewodros and the challenges he faced, with a detailed description of the British campaign against him.

Beyene, Tadesse, et al., eds. *Kasa and Kasa: The Lives, Times and Images of Tewodros II and Yohannes IV, 1855-1889*. Addis Ababa, Ethiopia: Institute of Ethiopian Studies, Addis Ababa University, 1990. A critical evaluation of the reigns of Tewodros and his successor, examining Tewodros's policy of reform and modernization and its legacy in modern Ethiopian thought.

Crummey, Donald. "Tewodros as Reformer and Modernizer." *Journal of African History* 10, no. 3 (1969). An excellent analysis that connects Tewodros's polit-ical troubles and his ideas of reform and modernization.

Debterā Zaneb. *The Chronicle of King Theodore of Abyssinia*. Translated and edited by Enno Littmann. Princeton, N.J.: Princeton University Library, 1902. Account of Tewodros's reign by his private secretary, who was an eyewitness to many of the events described in the chronicle. This is one of the best local sources on the personality of Tewodros and the challenges he faced.

Plowden, Walter. *Travels in Abyssinia and the Galla Country with an Account of a Mission to Ras Ali in 1848*. London: Longmans, Green, 1868. Plowden was one of the few Europeans who followed the career of Tewodros closely. His book about Ethiopia is now difficult to find, but it is a credible work based on Plowden's intimate knowledge of the country and personal access to Tewodros.

Rubenson, Sven. *King of Kings: Tewodros of Ethiopia*. Addis Ababa: Haile Selassie I University Press, 1966. The most authoritative account of the life and career of Emperor Tewodros.

SEE ALSO: Cetshwayo; Lobengula; Menelik II; Samory Touré; Shaka; Queen Victoria.

RELATED ARTICLES in *Great Events from History: The Nineteenth Century, 1801-1900:* April, 1868: British Expedition to Ethiopia; September 13, 1882: Battle of Tel el Kebir.

WILLIAM MAKEPEACE THACKERAY
English novelist

Thackeray wrote two fictional masterpieces, Vanity Fair *and* Henry Esmond, Esq.*, along with many other books and essays that rank him among the leading writers of mid-Victorian England.*

BORN: July 18, 1811; Calcutta, India
DIED: December 24, 1863; London, England
ALSO KNOWN AS: Ikey Solomons, Jr. (pseudonym); M. A. Titmarsh (pseudonym); George Savage Fitz-Boodle (pseudonym)
AREA OF ACHIEVEMENT: Literature

EARLY LIFE

William Makepeace Thackeray (THAHK-er-ee) was the only child of Richmond Makepeace Thackeray and his wife, Anne Becher Thackeray. He was born in India, where his English father worked for the East India Company. When William was four, his father died, leaving an estate worth about seventeen thousand pounds—an immense sum in the early nineteenth century. In December, 1816, William was sent back to England for schooling, while his mother remained in India to marry her first love, Captain Henry Carmichael-Smyth. William was not reunited with his mother until July, 1820.

In January, 1822, Thackeray entered London's Charterhouse School, where he remained for six years before matriculating at Trinity College, Cambridge in February, 1829. Sixteen months later, he left Cambridge without a degree but with gambling debts amounting to fifteen hundred pounds. Thackeray's first publications were

William Makepeace Thackeray. (Courtesy, The University of Texas at Austin)

several poems that appeared the *Western Luminary*, a Devon newspaper, in 1828. During his brief tenure at the university he helped start a literary magazine called *The Snob*. After it collapsed, he contributed to the *Gownsman*.

Seeking a career after leaving Cambridge, Thackeray entered the Middle Temple (London) in June, 1831, to study law but left the following year, once again without a degree. (He was called to the bar in 1848 but never practiced law.) In May, 1833, he used some of his inheritance to buy the *National Standard and Journal of Literature, Science, Music, Theatricals, and the Fine Arts*, to which he contributed as Paris correspondent. Bank failures in India in late 1833 essentially wiped out his inheritance from his father and left him in serious need of earning a living for the first time. He returned to London in the hope of saving his recently acquired magazine, but it failed in February, 1834.

LIFE'S WORK

With his inheritance mostly gone and his magazine dead, the twenty-three-year-old Thackeray returned to Paris, where he hoped to become an artist. There he married

seventeen-year-old Isabella Shawe on August 20, 1836. His wife's mother would later serve as the model for many an unpleasant mother-in-law in Thackeray's fiction. To support his wife, Thackeray began writing for the *Constitutional and Public Ledger*. After it failed in July, 1837, he turned to other magazines and wrote about ninety pieces for periodicals through the end of 1840. During the period between January, 1841, and January, 1847, he was even more prolific, producing 386 magazine articles and three books.

Among Thackeray's first books was his first novel, *The Luck of Barry Lyndon*, which was serialized in *Fraser's Magazine* in 1844; it was not well received and did not appear in book form until 1852-1853. *Barry Lyndon*, as the book is better known, is modeled on the eighteenth century English author Henry Fielding's *The Life of Mr. Jonathan Wild* (1743) and satirizes both the vogue for novels about rogues and a society that admired success above morality. During that period, Thackeray was also reviewing books for the *Morning Chronicle* and writing both fictional and nonfiction pieces for *Fraser's Magazine*, the *New Monthly Magazine*, and *Punch*.

Thackeray's literary apprenticeship ended in January, 1847, with the beginning of the serialization of *Vanity Fair*, which was published in book form the following year with Thackeray's own illustrations. In his journalism Thackeray satirized materialism and pretension, which are the subjects of this novel as well. Set in England during the Napoleonic era, *Vanity Fair* offers a detailed portrait of the age; its subtitle in serialization was "Pen and Pencil Sketches of English Society." The work presents a set of unforgettable if not necessarily likable characters; in book form it bore the subtitle, "A Novel Without a Hero." Again imitating Henry Fielding, Thackeray as narrator inserts sardonic comments in the course of his work.

Thackeray's next novel introduced Arthur Pendennis, the eponymous hero modeled on the author. *Pendennis* (1848-1850) presents a critical portrait of contemporary England as its protagonist gains insights and maturity. As the author's alter ego, Pendennis would also serve as narrator for *The Newcomes* (1853-1855), Thackeray's most popular novel during his lifetime, and *The Adventures of Philip* (1861-1862). Although the success of *Vanity Fair* ended Thackeray's pressing financial needs, over the next four years he wrote nearly 250 pieces for various magazines. Although most critics and readers regard *Vanity Fair* as Thackeray's greatest achievement, *Henry Esmond, Esq.* (1852) is a close rival and was more highly regarded by his contemporaries.

Thackeray was an admirer of the eighteenth century, and in 1851 he began lecturing on the comic writers of the period. His lectures were collected in *The English Humourists of the Eighteenth Century* (1853), and a second set of lectures about the eighteenth century appeared as *The Four Georges: Sketches of Manners, Morals, Court and Town Life* (1860). *Henry Esmond Esq.*, set in the reign of Queen Anne (1701-1714), might share that subtitle, offering a lively picture of the age. The first edition was printed in eighteenth century Caslon typeface and incorporated some eighteenth century spellings. Esmond retires to Virginia at the end of this work; *The Virginians* (1857-1859), set during the American Revolution, was a less successful sequel.

When the *Cornhill Magazine* began in January, 1860, Thackeray became its first editor. In that capacity, he attracted to the magazine the leading writers of the day, including Anthony Trollope and poet laureate Alfred, Lord Tennyson. He also used that magazine to serialize his own final fictional works, *Lovel the Widower* (1860), *The Adventures of Philip*, and the unfinished *Denis Duval* (1863). Only the last of these, set in late eighteenth century England, presents Thackeray at his best. At the same time he was writing occasional essays for the magazine, "The Roundabout Papers," which are replete with wit and astute observation.

In 1860, Thackeray bought a Queen Anne-style house at 2 Palace Green, Kensington, London. It was a fitting choice, given his admiration of the eighteenth century and its writers. There he died of a stroke on December 24, 1863. He was buried in London's Kensal Green cemetery, and his bust stands in Poet's Corner in London's Westminster Abbey.

SIGNIFICANCE

William Makepeace Thackeray's reputation rests primarily on two novels, *Vanity Fair* and *Henry Esmond, Esq.* which rival the best works of his contemporaries Charles Dickens, George Eliot, and Anthony Trollope. In those two book he succeeded in achieving his goal of producing realistic fiction that showed the form and pressure of the era and at the same time pointed a moral. In his lecture on Richard Steele, he declared:

> Out of the fictitious book I get the expression of the life of the time; of the manners, of the movement, the dress, the pleasures, the laughter, the ridicules of society—the old times live again, and I travel in the old country of England.

The same may be said of Thackeray's work. As a youth he enjoyed eighteenth century British authors as well as the historical fiction of the early nineteenth century Sir Walter Scott. He even wrote a sequel to *Ivanhoe* (1819): *Rebecca and Rowena* (1850). It is not coincidental that both of his best novels are historical fiction.

In his own day, Thackeray was regarded primarily as a satirist, and *Vanity Fair*'s social commentary applies as much to the Victorian age in which it was written as to the Napoleonic age in which it is set. Much of Thackeray's other writing has not worn as well, focusing as it does on issues of his day. However, some of his other work, such as the sketches collected in *The Book of Snobs* (1848) can still amuse. That particular book not only provides astute judgments of his contemporaries but also contains sound observations about the role of the writer and the function of literature. Even in his own day Thackeray did not enjoy the

---

THACKERAY'S NOVELS	
1839-1840	*Catherine: A Story* (as Ikey Solomons, Jr.)
1841	*The History of Samuel Titmarsh and the Great Hoggarty Diamond* (published as *The Great Hoggarty Diamond* in 1848)
1844	*The Luck of Barry Lyndon: A Romance of the Last Century*
1847-1848	*Vanity Fair: A Novel Without a Hero*
1848-1850	*The History of Pendennis: His Fortunes and Misfortunes, His Friends and His Greatest Enemy*
1850	*Rebecca and Rowena: A Romance upon Romance* (as M. A. Titmarsh)
1852	*The History of Henry Esmond, Esquire, a Colonel in the Service of Her Majesty Q. Ann*
1853-1855	*The Newcomes: Memoirs of a Most Respectable Family*
1857-1859	*The Virginians: A Tale of the Last Century*
1860	*Lovel the Widower*
1861-1862	*The Adventures of Philip on His Way Through the World, Shewing Who Robbed Him, Who Helped Him, and Who Passed Him By*
1864	*Denis Duval*

same popularity as his contemporary Charles Dickens. When Dickens died, his estate was estimated at something under eighty thousand pounds—four times that of Thackeray's estate. Moreover, Thackeray's reputation has not worn as well as that of Dickens or George Eliot (who regarded him as the leading writer of the time). Nevertheless, his best writing rivals that of any of his contemporaries.

—*Joseph Rosenblum*

FURTHER READING

Harden, Edgar F. *Thackeray the Writer*. New York: St. Martin's Press, 1998-2000. 2 vols. A study of Thackeray's literary career, beginning in 1833, with individual chapters devoted to each of the major novels. Written for the general reader.

Shillingsburg, Peter L. *Pegasus in Harness: Victorian Publishing and W. M. Thackeray*. Charlottesville: University Press of Virginia, 1992. Examines Thackeray's relationships with his various publishers in Great Britain and America, with financial and bibliographic information about his writings.

_____. *William Makepeace Thackeray: A Literary Life*. New York: Palgrave, 2001. Not a full-fledged biography but a good introduction that relates the writings of Thackeray to his life.

Taylor, D. J. *Thackeray*. London: Chatto & Windus, 1999. Drawing on Thackeray's letters, other contemporary documents, and subsequent scholarship, Taylor provides an admiring and detailed account of the author's life.

Thackeray, William Makepeace. *Vanity Fair: Authoritative Text, Backgrounds, and Contents, Criticism*. Edited by Peter Shillingsburg. New York: W. W. Norton, 1994. Authoritative edition of Thackeray's most widely read novel that offers extensive annotations and many related writings that illuminate Thackeray's life and authorship.

SEE ALSO: Charles Dickens; George Eliot; Daniel and Alexander Macmillan; John Ruskin; Sir Walter Scott; Anthony Trollope.

RELATED ARTICLES in *Great Events from History: The Nineteenth Century, 1801-1900:* March, 1852-September, 1853: Dickens Publishes *Bleak House*; July 26, 1858: Rothschild Is First Jewish Member of British Parliament.

SYLVANUS THAYER
American educator

Known as the founder of West Point, Thayer is remembered for reorganizing the administration and curriculum of the U.S. Military Academy and for firmly establishing a scientific and theory-based system of engineering education in the United States.

BORN: June 9, 1785; Braintree, Massachusetts
DIED: September 7, 1872; Braintree, Massachusetts
AREAS OF ACHIEVEMENT: Education, engineering, military

EARLY LIFE

The son of a wealthy Massachusetts farmer, Sylvanus Thayer (thahr) initially embarked on a classical education at Dartmouth College in Hanover, New Hampshire, which he attended from 1803 to 1807. While at Dartmouth, however, Thayer became an avid student of Napoleon Bonaparte and his campaigns and developed such a strong interest in a military vocation that he sought and obtained an appointment as a cadet to the U.S. Military

Academy at West Point, New York, in 1807. Graduated from the academy in 1808 after only one year of attendance, he was commissioned a second lieutenant of the Army Corps of Engineers. Although the threat of war with England after the Chesapeake affair undoubtedly accelerated his graduation, Thayer had impressed his instructors as being a capable student who took his chosen profession of military engineering seriously.

Still stationed at West Point upon graduation, Thayer spent the next four years engineering coastal fortifications in New York and New England, a reflection of the poor condition of U.S. coastal defenses and of the sudden importance of the academy and its engineer graduates to the defense of the nation. While at West Point during this period, Thayer was additionally assigned as an instructor of mathematics at the academy, an indication of his interest in education. He also continued his professional development as a military engineer through active membership in the U.S. Military Philosophical Society, demonstrating what would become a lifelong commitment to military engineering and engineering education.

With the advent of the War of 1812, Thayer, now a first lieutenant, left West Point and began active campaigning first as chief engineer to General Henry Dearborn on the Niagara frontier in 1812 and then as engineer to General Wade Hampton along Lake Champlain in 1813. Promoted to captain of engineers in October, 1813, Thayer was assigned to improve the harbor defenses of Norfolk, Virginia, during 1814 under the command of General Moses Porter. From his wartime service, Thayer gained an appreciation of the U.S. Army's great need for professionally educated and disciplined officers.

At the war's end, Thayer, holding the rank of brevet major for his service at Norfolk, again found himself stationed at West Point and once again able to pursue his study of military and civil engineering. With Napoleon's escape from Elba and the beginning of the Hundred Days, the final campaign of the Napoleonic Wars in Europe, Thayer requested a furlough in order to study military developments in France. However, Brigadier General Gardner Swift, chief of engineers, instead ordered Thayer to Europe on active duty on a trip that historian Todd Shallat has termed "a crucial event in American engineering."

LIFE'S WORK

Recognizing in the aftermath of the War of 1812 that it was imperative for the U.S. Army and its academy to stay abreast of contemporary European military theory and practice, Thayer and Colonel William McRee, a fellow West Point graduate and engineer, left for France in the spring of 1815. They spent the next two years observing allied military operations, studying French fortifications, studying procedures at the French artillery school at Metz, and, most important, conferring with instructors at France's premier military engineering school, the École Polytechnique. When Thayer and McRee were recalled to the United States in early 1817 to assume other duties, they brought with them campaign maps, engineering charts, scientific instruments, and nearly one thousand military, scientific, and engineering texts for use at the academy.

On July 17, 1817, Major Thayer became the U.S. Military Academy's third superintendent, a post that he would hold for sixteen years and one for which he would become known as the "Father of West Point." Although the academy had formally been in existence since 1802, there were still no definitive systems of administration or

instruction in place, deficiencies recognized by both the civilian and the military leadership.

With poor discipline rampant in the corps of cadets, a lack of consistent academic instruction and supervision, and meager technical facilities, little had actually changed at West Point since Thayer had been a cadet. Thayer, who had a thorough knowledge and an appreciation of French engineering and methods of instruction and who was highly regarded for his keen analytical mind and organizing abilities, was the perfect choice for superintendent. With a strong commitment to the Army and to military engineering, and with the complete support of both Brigadier General Swift and the new secretary of war, John C. Calhoun, Thayer began an institutional reform of the U.S. Military Academy that has endured essentially unchanged to the present day.

Thayer's comprehensive reforms of the academy were both administrative and curricular in nature. With regard to the former, the "Thayer System," as it came to be known, bore the strong imprint of the French École Polytechnique and embodied a reorganization of academy life that included weekly examinations, weekly recitations, the ranking of cadets according to their academic performance, the institution of small-group instruction in sections composed of students with similar academic rankings, and the assignment of cadets to branches of the service according to their academic performance. The rigor of the new curriculum became renowned among American educators. George Ticknor, a Dartmouth College classmate of Thayer and a future president of Harvard University, was not alone when he voiced the opinion that the cadets at the academy were

> a body of *Students*, constantly devoted to an intellectual discipline much more severe than their military discipline—who are much more thoroughly taught . . . than any of the young men, who are sent to any of our colleges.

Like the academy's new administrative procedures, the technical curriculum that Thayer established borrowed a great deal from French military education. First and foremost, French became a mandatory subject at the academy because Thayer felt it to be the language of military science and engineering and because the majority of the academy's textbooks were in French. In addition, four of the seven professors actually were French. However, the true substance of Thayer's academic reforms lay in the science and mathematics courses that became the foundation of the academic curriculum.

By adding regular offerings of engineering, natural philosophy (science), and mathematics to the curriculum and then weighting them more than traditional subjects such as military tactics and French, Thayer established a science- and theory-based system of education at the academy. The technical education received by academy graduates was so comprehensive that it remained unmatched by any other college or university in North America until after the Civil War. The prominence of army engineers in civil engineering projects, particularly railroad and canal building, was so great that it is clear that academy-trained engineers were at least as important to the antebellum United States as the professional officer corps it provided to ensure the nation's defense (the primary reason for the academy's existence).

Although Thayer resigned as superintendent of the U.S. Military Academy in 1833 after a dispute with President Andrew Jackson over Jackson's interference with Thayer's disciplining of cadets, the academy continued to bear Thayer's imprint long afterward. Part of Thayer's success as superintendent was based on his being an able administrator and his talent for picking the right people for the right jobs. Several professors who were handpicked by Thayer during the 1820's and 1830's continued their professorships well into the 1870's, lending a definite continuity of Thayer's vision of West Point and of military service to successive generations of army officers.

Thayer himself returned to field duty with the Army Corps of Engineers and was primarily responsible for the harbor defenses of Boston, Massachusetts. He later served as the president of the Army's Board of Engineers. After taking a medical leave because of failing health in 1858, Thayer finally retired from the Army as a colonel of engineers and a brevet brigadier general in 1863. Even then, he continued his interests in education and engineering by endowing a private academy and founding a library in his hometown of Braintree, Massachusetts, and contributing to the establishment of a school of architecture and civil engineering (now known as the Thayer School of Engineering) at his first alma mater, Dartmouth College.

SIGNIFICANCE

During the sixteen years that Sylvanus Thayer presided as superintendent of the U.S. Military Academy at West Point, he instituted reforms that caused the academy to graduate disciplined, well-educated officers for the U.S. Army. The small corps of West Point graduates performed well during the mass mobilizations of the Mexi-

can and Civil Wars and in leading and administering a tiny peacetime army spread across a constantly expanding United States. Although the Army still had organizational problems throughout the nineteenth century, Thayer's reforms at West Point helped prevent the military disasters of the War of 1812 from reoccurring. After 1817, academy graduates proved to be true professional soldiers, putting the U.S. Military Academy at West Point on an equal footing with its European counterparts.

Thayer's establishment of a rigorous, scientific curriculum at the U.S. Military Academy also contributed to the creation of a technical institution that was unequaled during the antebellum period. West Point-trained civil, railroad, and mining engineers, on active duty and as civilians, were commonly regarded as the premier builders and technical advisors of the early republic and made substantial contributions to the economic growth and technological expansion of the United States during the nineteenth century. Academy graduates proved to have an impact on the social, cultural, and technical life of the United States in far greater proportion than their numbers would suggest. Ultimately, the "Thayer System" at West Point helped standardize engineering and scientific education in the United States by providing a model for other academic institutions to emulate.

—*J. C. Larrabee*

FURTHER READING

Ambrose, Steven A. *Duty, Honor, Country: A History of West Point*. Baltimore: Johns Hopkins University Press, 1967. A history of the U.S. Military Academy at West Point that concentrates on the service of famous graduates. Thayer's importance as the founder of West Point is emphasized.

Crackel, Theodore J. *West Point: A Bicentennial History*. Lawrence: University Press of Kansas, 2002. This history includes a chapter entitled "Sylvanus Thayer, Father of the Military Academy, 1817-1833."

Hill, Forest G. *Roads, Rails, and Waterways: The Army Engineers and Early Transportation*. Norman: University of Oklahoma Press, 1957. Covers the importance of army civil engineers to the internal improvement of the antebellum United States. The first chapter covers the formation of U.S. Military Academy at West Point and the development of the "Thayer System."

Morrison, James L., Jr. *The Best School in the World: West Point: The Pre-Civil War Years, 1833-1866*. Akron, Ohio: Kent State University Press, 1986. Morrison covers the history of the U.S. Military Academy from Thayer's resignation as superintendent in 1833 to the removal of the academy from the Army Corps of Engineers' jurisdiction in 1866. Several chapters highlight the legacy of Thayer's educational and administrative reforms.

Pappas, George S. *To the Point: The United States Military Academy, 1802-1902*. Westport, Conn.: Praeger, 1993. This history of the academy's early years emphasizes Thayer's efforts to make the institution a high-caliber military academy and engineering school.

Shallat, Todd A. *Structures in the Stream: Water, Science, and the Rise of the U.S. Army Corps of Engineers*. Austin: University of Texas Press, 1994. Though intended as a broader social history of the Army Corps of Engineers and its management of water projects, chapters highlight the impact of European engineering traditions on the development

of scientific engineering in the United States and Thayer's persistent advocacy of the French system of education at the École Polytechnique.

Tyack, David. *George Ticknor and the Boston Brahmins*. New York: Oxford University Press, 1967. Tyack focuses on George Ticknor and his educational reforms at Harvard University but briefly describes Thayer's reforms at the U.S. Military Academy from the perspective of a civilian and a humanist. Ticknor, a Dartmouth classmate of Thayer, regarded the academy at West Point under Thayer's tutelage as a model for collegiate education in the United States.

SEE ALSO: John C. Calhoun; Andrew Jackson.

RELATED ARTICLES in *Great Events from History: The Nineteenth Century, 1801-1900:* March 16, 1802: U.S. Military Academy Is Established; July 2, 1862: Lincoln Signs the Morrill Land Grant Act.

ADOLPHE THIERS
French politician

Thiers was a central figure among the moderate French politicians of the early nineteenth century who created the July Monarchy of 1830 and, forty years later, the Third Republic. He also wrote important multivolume histories of the revolutionary and Napoleonic eras.

BORN: April 15, 1797; Marseilles, France
DIED: September 3, 1877; Saint-Germaine-en-Laye, near Paris, France
ALSO KNOWN AS: Marie-Joseph-Louis-Adolphe Thiers (full name)
AREA OF ACHIEVEMENT: Government and politics

EARLY LIFE

Marie-Joseph-Louis-Adolphe Thiers (tyahr) was born a month before his parents married. Four months later his ne'er-do-well father, Louis, disappeared and was not heard from again until his son was successful enough to provide financial support. Meanwhile, Adolphe was reared in poverty by his mother, Marie-Madeleine (née Amic), and her mother. The experience left him with a lifelong inclination to seek some support and approval of his actions from older women.

With the help of relatives, Thiers received a proper education, and in November, 1815, he began a three-year

tenure in law school at Aix-en-Provence. Thiers became a member of the bar in November, 1818, but times were hard for young lawyers. Thiers, short, almost gnomish, with a reedy voice, lacked the presence to get even his share of cases. He filled his time and pockets by competing for literary prizes offered by regional academies, but his real livelihood was provided by his mother. Prospects were few, and, urged by his friend François Mignet, Thiers decided to try his hand as a writer in Paris. He left his family and a woman who seems to have expected marriage.

In November, 1821, after a brief stint in a secretarial position, Thiers joined the staff of the liberal newspaper the *Constitutionnel*; three months later, he signed a contract to write a history of the French Revolution. Bourbon Royalism was in the political ascendancy, and the liberals were happy to have new recruits, so Thiers rose quickly.

By the mid-1820's, Thiers's reputation as a journalist was established, and the ten-volume *Histoire de la révolution française* (1823-1827; *The History of the French Revolution*, 1838) proved him to be a historian of note. He was moving in prominent circles, such as that of the banker Jacques Laffitte, where, along with his future rival François Guizot, he met the legendary Talleyrand. Political discussion was intense, and Thiers's hostility to the Bourbons and the aristocracy was growing. Although, like most liberals of the era, Thiers embraced the Enlightenment's faith in reason, commitment to civil rights, and religious skepticism, he still favored constitutional monarchy rather than a republic.

LIFE'S WORK

In January, 1830, Thiers, Mignet, and Armand Carrel inaugurated the *National*, which became Thiers's chief organ of persuasion for a number of years. The paper was a leading voice in the criticisms of the government of Charles X, and when the king's efforts to strengthen royal authority provoked open resistance in July, its offices were a center of revolutionary activity. Although he had spoken for moderation, faced with revolt, Thiers helped to write a proclamation claiming credit for the *National* in calling France to arms. He worked diligently to get a constitutional monarchy created under Louis-Philippe, the duke of Orléans. That was formally accomplished on August 9.

In the first month of the new regime, Thiers was given several senior-level government appointments and resigned from his journalistic connections. He would serve in six governments over the next decade. Thiers, however, had too little property to qualify. The Dosne family sold him a house in Paris on good terms, and Thiers was elected deputy for Aix-en-Provence and appointed parliamentary undersecretary for the Ministry of Finance.

Practical experience influenced Thiers's views of government, and by the spring of 1832 he had shifted from the Party of Movement to the Party of Resistance. The death of the premier, Casimir Périer, led to a new government with Thiers as minister of the interior. His delicate task was to control the duchess of Berry, who was leading efforts for a legitimist uprising in the name of her dead husband. She was interned without trial and, conveniently for Thiers, proved to be illegitimately pregnant. The duchess was allowed to leave the country quietly. In January, 1833, Thiers shifted to the Ministry of Commerce and Public Works, and in June he was elected to the French Academy.

The next November, the thirty-six-year-old Thiers married Élise Dosne, who had turned fifteen the day before the wedding. The dowry was 300,000 francs plus, unofficially, the money remaining due on his house, which was simply never paid. The relationship between Thiers and Élise was never close, but Thiers became part of his wife's family, who gained political and economic influence from the connection. Madame Dosne, Thiers's

Adolphe Thiers. (Library of Congress)

mother-in-law, served for many years as the older woman Thiers needed for emotional support.

Thiers's political influence continued to grow, and by early 1834 he and Guizot were the dominant figures in the government. In the spring, unrest among workers, encouraged by the left-wing press, led to efforts at censorship and arrests for union activities. On April 13, barricades were erected in Paris, and Thiers, as minister of the interior, sent troops that crushed the uprising. Thiers's reputation was marred for the rest of his career, however, because of deaths that became known as the Massacre in the Rue Transnonain. The Left never forgot Thiers's involvement.

Elections in June resulted in extended political infighting among the leading politicians, but Thiers remained at the Ministry of the Interior. In February, 1836, the government, then under the duke of Broglie, was defeated, and on February 22 Thiers became the premier. Knowing that his majority was undependable, he kept the chamber busy with noncontroversial internal improvements, while he pursued an active foreign policy in hopes of boosting his standing. After clashing with the king about support for a pro-French liberal government in Spain, Thiers was out of office in September.

Thiers was active in opposition until January, 1840, when, having organized the defeat of the current government, he left Louis-Philippe little choice but to ask him to form a government. Drawing in the Left with patronage and winning the support of the moderate conservatives who were eager for stability, Thiers had what appeared to be a solid administration. He had, however, inherited Middle Eastern trouble. A territorial dispute dating to the Greek revolt of the 1820's had been simmering between Muḥammad ʿAlī Pasha of Egypt and his overlord, the sultan.

Thiers, the historian, tied Egypt's troubles to Napoleon I and also was interested in French expansion in North Africa. Thiers backed the Egyptian against all the other powers, believing that Mehemet could get hereditary possession of Egypt and life possession of Syria as a minimum concession. Eventually, the other powers acted without consulting France, and the Egyptians collapsed in the face of a token force. Anti-French feeling spread all over Europe, and by October, 1840, Louis-Philippe, who had never been willing to do more than talk to help Mehemet, replaced Thiers with a government run by Guizot. Although he did not suspect it at the time, Thiers was beginning thirty years as a member of the opposition.

Although he remained active in the chamber, Thiers devoted much time to writing. In 1839, he had signed a contract for a history of the consulate and the empire, receiving 500,000 francs for the first ten volumes. He traveled to Napoleonic battle sites and worked in French archives as he began to write this history. In December of 1840, he was elected to the Académie des Sciences, Morales, et Politiques.

In 1842 and 1846, Guizot was reelected, but there was more and more unrest. In February, 1848, a campaign of protest banquets came to a head when the government attempted to block one scheduled for a working-class district in Paris. Frightened by the ensuing demonstration, Guizot resigned. Frantic maneuvering to reestablish government led to a brief attempt by Thiers to take control, but, when told he was too unpopular, he stepped aside. In the end, the king abdicated in favor of his grandson. That proved unacceptable—Thiers made no effort to support the arrangement—and the Second Republic emerged. Openly reluctant about participating, Thiers was defeated in the first series of elections for the new National Assembly. In May, however, he won in four separate by-elections.

After he was in office, Thiers began to fight for a bicameral legislature, which was rejected, and in opposition to the right to work. He argued that the country could not afford the national workshops, employing 1.5 to 2 million workers, started by the revolutionaries. He established his economic ideas in *Du droit de propriété* (1848). He grudgingly approved the election of Louis-Napoleon Bonaparte as president, but refused, out of loyalty to the Orleanist family and reluctance to face the many problems of the new government, to preside at the first cabinet.

Over the next few years, Thiers devoted himself to conservative party politics, helping with a successful election campaign in the spring of 1849. He helped develop the very conservative Falloux Law, reforming education and a new electoral law reducing the electorate by almost one-third. In debating the latter, he spoke of the dangers of the "vile mob," a phrase that would haunt him. Thiers openly broke with Louis-Napoleon in 1851 over control of the military, but a prosperous economy and a reputation for stable government kept the prince-president's popularity high.

When in December, 1851, Louis-Napoleon made himself Emperor Napoleon III, Thiers and seventeen other deputies were among ten thousand opponents exiled or transported. Thiers settled in Switzerland until August, 1852, when the exile was lifted, and worked on his history of the consulate and empire. Over his life, Thiers produced some thirty volumes of political history. He also wrote his memoirs.

By 1863, Thiers had finished the last volume of his twenty-volume *Histoire du consulat et de l'empire* (1845-1862; *History of the Consulate and the Empire of France Under Napoleon*, 1845-1862) and was open for new employment. Napoleon's popularity was in decline and the republicans were gaining popularity. Thiers was persuaded to run in the following year's elections. He won a Parisian seat, getting workers' votes despite his anti-Left reputation. He promptly embarked on a campaign, championing individual freedoms. With the emperor seeking to regain lost support, liberalization was steadily achieved.

The July, 1870, confrontation with Prussia over the question of a Hohenzollern (a royal German family) candidate for the Spanish throne found Thiers arguing for peace. Although he was the subject of jeers when the Franco-Prussian War erupted, the rapid and overwhelming Prussian victory—Napoleon was captured at Sedan, and Paris was besieged by mid-September—vindicated him. Thiers refused to be in the government of national defense, but he accepted a diplomatic mission, visiting London, St. Petersburg, Vienna, and Florence in a vain quest for support. He did manage to arrange for armistice talks.

Thiers's goal was to hold elections and, having established a new government, to make peace on the best possible terms, though France was not in a good bargaining position. He was opposed by Léon Gambetta, leader of the republican Left. Thiers prevailed, and elections were held February 8, 1871, with Thiers's supporters winning a clear victory. The new assembly elected Thiers, almost unanimously, as chief of the executive power of the French republic. In the peace treaty with Prussia, France lost Alsace-Lorraine and was saddled with a 5,000-million-franc indemnity. One of Thiers's biggest successes as head of the new Third Republic was raising two large loans and getting that indemnity paid without undermining the national economy.

The withdrawal of the Prussians had left left-wing militants in control of Paris. When the new national government tried to assert control, civil war erupted. Thiers had to raise an army and defeat the Paris Commune, keep the Prussians from taking advantage of the trouble, and hold public support. Although the city had to be shelled and brutality was common, the city was recaptured, and, because the action was prompt and uncompromising, the Prussians found little opportunity to fish in troubled waters. There was left-wing sentiment especially in the cities, but few were willing to chance a renewal of the horrors of 1793. In the end, Thiers triumphed.

In August, 1871, Thiers was appointed president of the republic, a post he held until May, 1873. During his tenure, he presided over the establishment of a conservative republic. He fought unsuccessfully for protectionism and blocked efforts to establish an income tax. He also resisted the adoption of the Prussian system of universal military service. Thiers had become convinced that a republic was the only workable system for a conservative France. His loss of power was largely the result of urging the right to abandon its dream of monarchy and accept the republic. This cost him support, and he was unable to control a confrontation between conservatives and radicals. He had to resign. Thiers spent his last four years active in opposition politics and, on September 3, 1877, after a choking fit at lunch, lapsed into a coma and died.

SIGNIFICANCE

Adolphe Thiers's life can hardly be separated from nineteenth century French politics. He devoted his energies to public service, political journalism, and political history. His biography is really the political history of nineteenth century France, for he was intimately involved in all the major changes of that century. He had made his name in time to influence the Revolution of 1830—he produced more than one hundred articles for the *National* in the first six months of that year—and became part of the new government. Thiers's skills, however, were most effective in opposition—as practical politician, journalist, or historian. Thiers spent almost his entire career out of power. The conversational debating style he developed to overcome his naturally weak voice was effective, and he was a formidable parliamentary foe.

During the middle of the century, Thiers wrote history and championed political moderation in the chambers, his reputation for knowledge and stability growing. In retrospect, his rise to power in the crisis of 1870 seems almost inevitable. Not only was he already respected, but also his resistance to the wave of nationalism that led to the war won for him even more kudos. Not only did he deal effectively with making peace but also he proceeded to oversee the creation of a conservative republican regime that lasted until it was destroyed by the Nazi conquest of World War II.

—Fred R. van Hartesveldt

FURTHER READING

Albrecht-Carrié, René. *Adolphe Thiers: Or, The Triumph of the Bourgeoisie*. New York: Twayne, 1977. A short, straightforward biography by a very good historian. Does a good job of showing Thiers to be a part of the rise of the middle class to dominance during the nineteenth century.

Allison, John M. S. *Thiers and the French Monarchy*. Boston: Houghton Mifflin, 1926. A major study involving Thiers's career. The main theme is the monarchy, but, given Thiers's intimate involvement with that institution, he plays a major part in the book.

Bury, J. P. T. *France, 1814-1940*. London: Methuen, 1949. A classic survey introduction to French political history. An excellent source for brief accounts of Thiers's activities, but more important for providing context in which those activities must be seen to be understood.

Bury, J. P. T., and R. P. Tombs. *Thiers, 1797-1877: A Political Life*. London: Allen & Unwin, 1986. Excellent biography with the emphasis on Thiers's public life. The authors portray their subject as a centrist who evolved from constitutional monarchist to republican over the course of his career.

Fortescue, William. *The Third Republic in France, 1870-1940: Conflicts and Continuities.* London: Routledge, 2000. Information about Thiers is included in chapters 1 and 2, which cover the emergence of the Third Republic and the political climate in the republic's earliest years.

Horne, Alistair. *The Fall of Paris: The Siege and the Commune, 1870-71.* New York: St. Martin's Press, 1965. A superbly written account of the collapse of the Second Empire and the emergence of the Third Republic. The author's treatment of these events as part of the same larger development is effective and informative. Both the style and the approach lend themselves to the nonspecialist.

Mayer, Jean-Marie, and Madeleine Rebérioux. *The Third Republic from Its Origins to the Great War, 1871-1914.* Vol. 4 in *The Cambridge History of Modern France.* Translated by J. R. Foster. New York: Cambridge University Press, 1984. Chapter 1, "The End of the Notables, 1871-1879," covers the rise and fall of "Thiers's Republic."

SEE ALSO: Léon Gambetta; Napoleon I; Napoleon III; Arthur Rimbaud; Talleyrand.

RELATED ARTICLES in *Great Events from History: The Nineteenth Century, 1801-1900:* July 29, 1830: July Revolution Deposes Charles X; February 13, 1871-1875: Third French Republic Is Established; March 18-May 28, 1871: Paris Commune.

THEODORE THOMAS
Prussian-born American musician

A professional musician from childhood, Thomas pioneered the role of virtuoso conductor, markedly raising standards of orchestral performance in both light and serious works. With the Chicago Orchestra, he also perfected the means of supporting and maintaining ensembles of the highest quality. He was virtually the founder of the modern American symphony orchestra.

BORN: October 11, 1835; Esens, East Friesland, Prussia (now in Germany)
DIED: January 4, 1905; Chicago, Illinois
ALSO KNOWN AS: Theodore Christian Friedrich Thomas (full name)
AREA OF ACHIEVEMENT: Music

EARLY LIFE

Theodore Christian Friedrich Thomas was the son of Johann August Thomas, the master of music for the Prussian town of Esens. Surrounded by music and musicians from birth, young Theodore quickly established himself as a prodigy. As a child he could read any music set before him by the town's musicians and was an accomplished violinist by the time he was ten and his family emigrated to New York City.

At first, the Thomas family scarcely prospered; son as well as father found it necessary to play in a variety of theater orchestras, dancing schools, and even saloons to support the household. In 1848, they traveled to Portsmouth, Virginia, for steady employment; Theodore, thirteen years old, was nominally in the United States Navy, in whose band he was playing second horn. A year later, Theodore resigned; he would reminisce at the end of his life that his father had so increased his income that the son's contribution was no longer needed. The fourteen-year-old fiddler then took off by himself on a tour of the American South, playing concerts wherever he could drum up an audience and attending to every detail, from putting up posters to selling tickets. It should not be imagined that he did nothing but play unaccompanied violin, however, for whenever the materials presented themselves, he formed ad hoc ensembles. His wanderlust satisfied for the time being, he returned to New York City in 1850.

Thomas had virtually no formal schooling in the United States. His performing jobs usually kept him up well past midnight, and there were no laws either forbidding child labor or compelling attendance at school. Nevertheless, he grew up to be not only cultivated but also a genuine intellectual. In part, this achievement reflected the high culture of his parents, as well as his keen receptivity to the many plays, poems, and librettos he encountered in his many musical jobs. What he did not pick up from the orchestra pit, he supplied by self-directed reading.

Between 1850 and 1860, Thomas established himself as one of the finest violinists in the booming cultural milieu of New York City. In 1854, the New York Philharmonic Society elected him to membership; in the same year, he accepted a position in a small orchestra, touring the United States with what surely was the leading concert attraction of the season, Adelina Patti, soprano; Maurice Strakosch, piano; and Ole Bull, violin. It should be pointed out that orchestras were then ephemeral things, summoned into being by managers of theaters, opera houses, choral societies, or concert tours. National and international concert circuits were also relatively new, especially in the United States. Even the most famous musical celebrities normally toured in groups, to provide their audiences with the greatest possible variety of musical delights.

In 1855, at the age of twenty, Thomas accepted the invitation of William Mason to play first violin in his string quartet. Mason, the son of the pioneering New England musician Lowell Mason, had recently returned from studying music in Europe, culminating in piano lessons with Franz Liszt in Weimar. He and the quartet became the nucleus for a series of chamber-music concerts that would last until 1870. Thomas soon assumed so much responsibility and radiated so much leadership that the series became known as the Mason-Thomas concerts. During the early years, guest artists, especially vocalists, abounded, and each program would contain a single weighty work otherwise surrounded by short, melodious, and popular numbers. Within the first year, however, the quartet was playing Ludwig van Beethoven's Opus 130, a work that can daunt all but the most serious audiences. In their later years, however, Mason and Thomas offered nothing but major works by major composers.

Thomas first led an orchestra in 1860, taking over an opera performance on short notice because the regular conductor was unhappy about his pay being in arrears. In 1862, the Brooklyn Philharmonic hired Thomas as coconductor. He was sole conductor there from 1866, and that proved to be his longest employment, ending only in 1891, when he moved to Chicago. More significant for the future, however, were the concerts of 1862 that Thomas organized and conducted himself in New York City.

Thomas had long since determined that most conductors merely kept time, that most orchestras had such shifting and unreliable personnel and so little rehearsal time that no really fine performances could possibly be drawn from them. Furthermore, the musicians themselves, needing to pursue jobs whenever and wherever they could, were unable to enforce standards of quality even when they planned concerts through their own

guilds or unions. The Philharmonic Society, founded in 1842, was such a guild and retained that organization into the early twentieth century. The orchestra hired its conductors, usually from among the membership; such conductors were always fine musicians, but they had no disciplinary powers whatever.

Thomas was determined to change all this; in the course of his lifetime, he succeeded. By 1864, established both as a virtuoso violinist and a rising conductor, Thomas married Minna Rhodes; in subsequent years, they had three sons and two daughters, the marriage ending with Minna's death in 1889. As a young man, he was strikingly handsome, slender, and of medium height, with a well-trimmed dark mustache, penetrating eyes, and the look of a sensitive artist. As an older man, he was no longer slender, and the mustache became bushy, while his aura of authority continued to grow.

LIFE'S WORK
In 1864, Thomas began his series of Symphony Soirees, in competition with the New York Philharmonic Concerts, but since each organization presented only six programs a year, the small but growing concert audience in

Theodore Thomas. (Library of Congress)

New York City was hardly overtaxed. Seeking more work for himself and his players, he began, in 1865, his long series of "summer garden" concerts, chiefly in New York, but also on tour and, from 1877 onward, often in Chicago. The touring began in 1869 and, in conjunction with the popular summer concerts, gave the Theodore Thomas Orchestra something like full-time employment. This was unique in the United States at the time; indeed, only the remaining court and church orchestras of Europe then provided full-time work for classically trained players.

The Theodore Thomas Orchestra grew from thirty to sixty players in its years of touring and summer concerts; it was never of the size and force of modern virtuoso orchestras, and it played chiefly the sort of light concert music that survives in the programs of the Boston Pops and its imitators. However, Thomas was still preparing the way for the future great orchestras of the United States by the quality of his ensemble, which profited from his devoted leadership and from the unprecedented advantage of staying together, month after month and year after year. Although his programming assumed an unsophisticated audience, he managed to include at least one serious work in each concert, thereby gradually educating the public.

In 1873, Thomas began a new phase of his career by taking his orchestra to the first Cincinnati May Festival. He was musical director of the whole undertaking and continued as such through the sixteenth festival in 1904, just before his death. The United States had seen several music festivals already, but they had tended mainly toward massive accumulations of singers, players, and fireworks, rather than aiming at the highest possible expressions of musical art.

The idea of concentrating large ensembles and audiences for a few intense days of music-making, especially when the weather is neither paralyzingly cold nor suffocatingly hot, has always made sense. Although Thomas's music festivals had plenty of symphonies, concertos, and concert arias, they were built around large-scale works for soloists, chorus, and orchestra. The oratorio, perfected by George Frideric Handel in eighteenth century England, became one of the most popular musical forms in nineteenth century Germany, Britain, and the United States. The music festival gave Thomas an unprecedented opportunity to raise public taste, so he tried to promote similar festivals in other leading cities. He succeeded in several, including Pittsburgh, San Francisco, St. Louis, Chicago, and New York, but after one or two festivals these cities failed to maintain the required level of commitment; only the Cincinnati Festival became permanent.

The exposition held in Philadelphia in 1876 proved that Thomas had become the most celebrated musician in the United States, for he was chosen to direct its music. In the end, he overreached himself, planning more concerts than the public could support, but even with cancellations and unpaid debts, the Centennial Exposition advanced both Thomas's career and his sacred cause of serious music. He commissioned several works by such American composers as John Knowles Paine and Dudley Buck and invited leading performers from all over the world. However, there was one more source of discord. Thomas encouraged the Women's Committee to raise the unprecedented sum of five thousand dollars for an original piece of music by the great Richard Wagner. That curious genius applied more energy to getting himself paid than to executing his commission; the work he submitted was inferior in quality to the contribution of the Americans, or indeed to anything Wagner himself had composed since his student days.

In 1877, Thomas accepted the post of conductor of the New York Philharmonic, on the understanding that he would continue to give a separate series of concerts with his own orchestra. This appointment also continued, with brief interruptions, until his move to Chicago. He tried a permanent move in 1878, accepting the leadership of the Cincinnati Conservatory of Music. Autocrat that he was, however, he soon resigned: The trustees of the organization would not grant him the power he deemed necessary to produce good musicians. Based again in New York, with increasingly long guest appearances elsewhere, he continued strengthening his position through the 1880's, though he barely survived the collapse of the American Opera Company. That was an attempt to present modern operas in English translation with American-trained singers; altogether worthy in plan, it was inadequately financed and poorly managed. It was also in competition with the new Metropolitan Opera, where young Walter Damrosch was successfully presenting the music dramas of Richard Wagner with European-trained singers.

Still the best-known and most widely respected conductor in the United States and financially secure after the final liquidation of the opera company, Thomas nevertheless suffered from severe depression in 1889. Minna died after a long and painful illness. Losing the resiliency of youth, he disbanded the orchestra, which depended on touring for most of its engagements. Artistically, he was exasperated with what he called scratch orchestras, by which he meant ensembles whose personnel he could not choose and shape to his own high standards.

In May, 1890, Thomas married Rose Fay, a woman of great musical and literary culture. Her brother, Charles Norman Fay, a utilities executive in Chicago, then organized what Thomas most desired: a permanent association, underwritten by wealthy citizens, to guarantee the budget of an orchestra over which he would have absolute artistic control. Here was the model for virtually all the major orchestras of the United States. The New York Philharmonic had typically played six concerts each season; the Chicago Orchestra (later the Chicago Symphony Orchestra) played twenty.

However, problems remained. Chicago's great World's Fair of 1893 tempted Thomas, its music director, to another surfeit of newly commissioned works, guest orchestras and choruses, and famous soloists. After some unpleasant carping caused by merely allowing Ignacy Jan Paderewski to play his own Steinway piano (technically barred from the fairgrounds because Steinway and Sons had declined to exhibit in Chicago), Thomas resigned. Nevertheless, as in 1876, the programs of classical music in Chicago set new standards of scope and virtuosity.

Thomas led the Chicago Orchestra through fourteen seasons; only the Boston Symphony Orchestra, founded in 1881 by Henry Lee Higginson and run on idealistic and autocratic principles similar to those of Thomas, could rival it for the quality of programs and execution. The conductor, however, had one more goal to accomplish. The Auditorium Theater, that landmark of American architecture, was far too vast and cavernous for Thomas's taste. Also, he had to share it with several other organizations. With the help of his friend Daniel Hudson Burnham, he planned and built Orchestra Hall. Tragically, Thomas died after a brief illness in January, 1905, within a month of playing his first concert, with his own orchestra, in his own hall.

SIGNIFICANCE

When Theodore Thomas began his conducting career during the 1860's, there was no such thing as a famous orchestral conductor in the United States and scarcely a permanent symphony orchestra. Through tours, festivals, considerate programming, persistence, and even through writing essays on the appreciation of good music, he contributed more than anyone else to the emergence of virtuoso orchestras in the United States. Entirely trained in this country, he was a genuine cosmo-

polite, eager to promote genius wherever it appeared. He was a great musician, and he helped make music a great force for cooperation and civility.

—*Robert McColley*

FURTHER READING

Bowen, José Antonio, and David Mermelstein. "The American Tradition." In *The Cambridge Companion to Conducting*, edited by José Antonio Bowen. New York: Cambridge University Press, 2003. This historical survey of American conductors includes information about Thomas.

Burg, David F. *Chicago's White City of 1893*. Lexington: University Press of Kentucky, 1976. Discusses Thomas's second venture in planning music for a world's fair.

Carter, Richard. "The New World Symphony." *Humanities* 20, no. 5 (September/October, 1999): 52. A history of the Chicago Symphony Orchestra, focusing on Thomas and successive conductors.

Davis, Ronald L. *A History of Music in American Life*. 3 vols. Huntington, N.Y.: R. E. Krieger, 1980-1982. Presents a balanced view of all aspects of American musical life. The second volume treats the era of Theodore Thomas.

Mueller, John H. *The American Symphony Orchestra: A Social History of Musical Taste*. Bloomington: Indiana University Press, 1951. Takes a broad, detailed, and scholarly view of its subject.

Otis, Philo Adams. *The Chicago Symphony Orchestra: Its Organization, Growth and Development, 1891-1924*. Chicago: Clayton F. Summy, 1925. A valuable compendium of facts by a long-term participant in the musical life of Chicago.

Russell, Charles Edward. *The American Orchestra and Theodore Thomas*. Garden City, N.Y.: Doubleday, Page, 1927. Entertainingly traces Thomas's role in the development of major orchestras and star conductors.

Thomas, Rose Ray. *Memoirs of Theodore Thomas*. New York: Moffat, Yard, 1911. Contains the fullest treatment of the conductor's life. Written by his second wife, it is reverent and idealistic in tone.

Thomas, Theodore. *Theodore Thomas: A Musical Autobiography*. Edited by George P. Upton. 2 vols. Chicago: A. C. McClurg, 1906. Falls into several sections. Thomas avoided personal anecdotes and any form of gossip; his essay in the autobiography chiefly outlines his career and expresses his musical ideals. His friend and longtime admirer, George P. Upton, partly makes up the want of personal details in his appreciative essay. The second volume, lovingly gathered from Thomas's papers by the editor, sets forth the concert programs of more than forty years; it is uniquely valuable as a record of musical performances. The reprint (New York: Da Capo Press, 1965) omits this second volume.

Upton, George P. *Musical Memories: My Recollections of Celebrities of the Half Century, 1850-1900*. Chicago: A. C. McClurg, 1908. Contains many reminiscences of Thomas while re-creating the artistic world

in which he played so significant a part. Upton was music critic of the *Chicago Tribune* for more than forty years.

SEE ALSO: Ludwig van Beethoven; Daniel Hudson Burnham; Franz Liszt; Johann Strauss; Richard Wagner.

RELATED ARTICLE in *Great Events from History: The Nineteenth Century, 1801-1900:* May 7, 1824: First Performance of Beethoven's Ninth Symphony.

DAVID THOMPSON
English explorer of Canada

Thompson traveled through most of northern and western Canada and was the first person accurately to survey river courses, trading post locations, and the U.S.-Canadian border. He also drew the first accurate maps of western Canada and recorded the customs and cultures of the indigenous Canadian peoples.

BORN: April 30, 1770; London, England
DIED: February 10, 1857; Longueuil, near Montreal, Lower Canada (now in Quebec, Canada)
AREAS OF ACHIEVEMENT: Geography, exploration

EARLY LIFE

David Thompson was the son of Welsh immigrants to London, where he was born. After he was educated in a London charity school in navigational mathematics, he was apprenticed to the Hudson's Bay Company in May, 1784. As a company apprentice, he was responsible for maintaining account books and general clerical work first at Fort Churchill, in what is now Manitoba. He later worked at York Factory fur trading posts in British Canada.

In 1786, the Hudson's Bay Company transferred Thompson to Cumberland House (Saskatchewan), where he joined a thirteen-man expedition to construct a new company post along the South Saskatchewan River. Between 1786 and 1790, he served at several company posts as both clerk and trader, and learned both the Cree and Peigan languages. In 1788, he severely injured his leg. During his recovery, he lost sight in his right eye. However, during his long recuperation at Cumberland House, he made good use of his time by studying mathematics, astronomy, and surveying under the company surveyor Philip Turnor.

LIFE'S WORK

Although Thompson's physical ailments disqualified him from accompanying a survey team to Lake Athabasca (Northwest Territories) in the spring of 1790, he wrote to Hudson's Bay Company officials in London and requested a personal set of survey and observational equipment. While fulfilling his duties as a clerk, Thompson began collecting data for his future maps of the Canadian interior. In the fall of 1792, after the arrival of his new survey equipment, he was ordered on his first survey expedition into the Lake Athabasca region. He was assigned to produce an accurate chart of the region between the Nelson and Churchill Rivers, and find—it was hoped—a more direct river route to the fur-rich Athabasca region. Hudson's Bay Company officials regarded Thompson's mission as urgent because of the growing competition between their London-based company and the newly founded Montreal-based Northwest Company.

Thompson's work in the Canadian west reflected the intense commercial competition for furs, alliances with native communities, and the quicker river routes to untapped fur-bearing regions. For his surveying work of 1792-1794, Thompson was promoted to official surveyor of the Hudson's Bay Company in May, 1794. However, Thompson grew increasing dissatisfied with company management. In an autobiographical narrative that he composed shortly before his death in 1857, he cited the company's lack of exploratory vigor and concern with sheer profit as reasons for leaving it to join the Northwest Company in May, 1797.

Thompson's abandonment of the Hudson's Bay Company for the Northwest Company left lingering bitterness toward him by British officials. However,

Thompson was about to embark on the most productive and challenging period of his career. In the summer of 1797, the Northwest Company assigned him to survey the proposed international boundary between British Canada and the United States. In particular, Thompson was to guarantee that his company's trading posts were north of the forty-ninth parallel.

During Thompson's year-long mission, he proposed that the origin of the contested Mississippi River was at Turtle Lake (Minnesota), well south of the newly delineated border. That conclusion barred British-Canadian traders legal access to the Mississippi River. Thompson's 1797-1798 expedition provided the basis for his first maps of central Canada and the Lake Superior littoral. Through the remainder of 1798-1799, he charted river routes from Northwest Company posts in Saskatchewan to Lake Athabasca.

On his return to the company post at Grand Portage, on what is now the Minnesota-Ontario border, in the spring of 1799, Thompson married Charlotte Small, a Meti woman who was the daughter of a company manager. Thompson and his wife eventually had a total of thirteen children, five of whom were born at various Northwest Company trading posts. Unlike many other European men who married native women, Thompson remained committed to his wife and children through the rest of his life.

The expansion of the fur trade toward the Rocky Mountains and the attempt to find a navigable river route to the Pacific Ocean occupied the remainder of Thompson's career with the Northwest Company. The purchase of the Louisiana Territory by the United States in 1803 and the success of the Meriwether Lewis and William Clark expedition in 1804-1806 further pressed Thompson's company to secure a river route to the Pacific, ahead of American and Hudson's Bay Company claims.

In July, 1808, another Northwest Company employee, Simon Fraser, charted a route to the Pacific. However, his river route proved dangerous, as it was filled with rapids and waterfalls. Moreover, the company's situation on Fraser's route was complicated by the fact that the company had been trading with the Peigan people, who wanted to retain their status as middleman traders between the company and the Pacific coastal tribes. Consequently, the Peigans were less displeased with the prospect of more European traders entering their territory.

Thompson's exploratory expeditions in western Canada from 1806 to 1812 were shaped by the need to find a less problematic river route to the Pacific. After several years of attempting to locate and survey the headwaters of the Columbia River, the Northwest Company sent Thompson on an urgent mission to find it. His exploring party was delayed, and nearly captured, by Peigan war parties, but Thompson finally reached the Pacific Ocean via the Columbia River in July, 1811. Unfortunately for the Northwest Company, Thompson found a trading post of the American Pacific Fur Company already established at the mouth of the river.

Although disappointed that his discovery was spoiled by the presence of the American traders, he later recorded his personal satisfaction in surveying and charting the Canadian interior from Lake Superior to the Pacific Ocean. The Pacific expedition was Thompson's last for the Northwest Company. He, his wife and five children traveled back to Montreal, where Thompson settled into semiretirement with an annual pension of one hundred pounds from the company. During this period, he began organizing and completing accurate maps for the company and completed his first map in 1814.

After the War of 1812, Thompson was hired by British government officials to complete surveys of the U.S.-Canadian border. His survey of 1817-1827 fixed the modern border but also reportedly caused bitterness among British-Canadian officials who thought he had been too accommodating with the American survey crews, who has wanted him to make sure that British-Canadian trading posts were on the northern side of the border. Resentment against Thompson, first for leaving Hudson's Bay Company in 1797 and for his border survey of 1817-1827, may have been a partial reason for both his later financial problems and his long-overdue recognition for his contributions to Canadian history.

The last decades of Thompson's life were beset by financial difficulties and poor health. With the bankruptcy of the Northwest Company in 1825, Thompson lost his pension. His maps of the Canadian interior found few buyers, and for several years he supported his family with surveys of townships and proposed canal routes. By 1840, Thompson was so indebted that it was reported he had to sell his survey equipment. In 1845, he and his wife moved into the home of one of their daughters at Longueuil, near Montreal.

Now seventy-five years old, Thompson saw his health rapidly decline but finally began to organize his journals and travel notes for publication. In 1851, he went completely blind and never finished journals. His death in Longueuil on February 10, 1857, attracted little public attention.

SIGNIFICANCE

David Thompson remained almost forgotten in history until 1916, when Canadian historian Joseph Burr Tyrrell published *David Thompson's Narrative of His Explorations in Western America, 1784-1812*. His exploratory and cartographic work for the Hudson's Bay and Northwest Companies affected British imperial expansion in North America and the fur trade—both of which needed accurate geographic knowledge. Thompson's maps of the Canadian interior were the most accurate for their period and demonstrate the increasing technical and mathematical skills required in the cartographic sciences.

In addition to their value as collections of geographical data, Thompson's journals are rich ethnographic portraits of Canada's indigenous peoples, their customs, stories, and spiritual beliefs. His respect for, and interest in, Native Canadians moreover highlights the codependence and cross-cultural contacts between Europeans and Native Americans in economic, exploratory, and imperial endeavors.

Although Thompson undertook his explorations and surveys around the same time as the famous Lewis and Clark expedition, he received little attention in Canada until the early twentieth century, when Canadian nationalists and historians "resurrected" him to exemplify Canadian national spirit and pride during and after World War I.

—*Tyler T. Crogg*

FURTHER READING

Jenish, D'Arcy. *Epic Wanderer: David Thompson and the Mapping of the Canadian West*. Toronto: Doubleday Canada, 2003. A popular historian, Jenish uses Thompson's journals, notebooks, and other materials to chronicle his life and explorations.

Lavender, David. *Winner Take All: The Trans-Canada Canoe Trail*. New York: McGraw-Hill, 1977. A broad narrative of French and British explorations of western Canada and its links with the fur trade. Chapter 21 covers Thompson's expeditions.

Nisbet, Jack. *The Mapmaker's Eye: David Thompson on the Columbia Plateau*. Pullman: Washington State University Press, 2005. A chronicle of Thompson's life and expeditions, focusing on his travels in the Columbia River country.

Pole, Graeme. *David Thompson: The Epic Expeditions of a Great Canadian Explorer*. Canmore, Alta.: Altitude Publishing Canada, 2003. Recounts Thompson's expeditions during his twenty-eight years in the fur trade.

Rich, E. E. *The Fur Trade and Northwest to 1857*. Toronto: McClelland and Stewart, 1967. A broad socioeconomic and political narrative and analysis of the Franco-British fur trade system and its shaping of modern Canadian history. Excellent chapters on the Hudson's Bay Company and Northwest Companies.

Thompson, David. *David Thompson's Narrative of His Explorations in Western America, 1784-1812*. Edited by J. B. Tyrrell. Toronto: Champlain Society, 1916. Reprint, 1968. An edited collection of Thompson's unfinished autobiographical travelogue. Several of Thompson's maps and drawings are included in the volume, as are a separate envelope of his smaller regional Canadian maps. Occasionally inaccurate details, dates, or locations should not take away from the nearly encyclopedic amount of information on indigenous Canadian peoples and the Canadian environment.

SEE ALSO: Meriwether Lewis and William Clark; Susanna Moodie; Zebulon Pike; Thomas Talbot; Catharine Parr Traill.

RELATED ARTICLE in *Great Events from History: The Nineteenth Century, 1801-1900:* May 14, 1804-September 23, 1806: Lewis and Clark Expedition.

HENRY DAVID THOREAU
American philosopher

As essayist, naturalist, social critic, and editor, Thoreau has come to be recognized as a major figure in the Transcendentalist movement and is now one of the most widely studied, read, and respected American authors of the nineteenth century.

BORN: July 12, 1817; Concord, Massachusetts
DIED: May 6, 1862; Concord, Massachusetts
AREA OF ACHIEVEMENT: Literature

EARLY LIFE

David Henry Thoreau (THOH-roh), who, characteristically, chose to reverse the order of his first and middle names, traveled widely in his imagination but spent most of his forty-four years in the remarkable New England town of Concord, Massachusetts, in which he was born. His mother, née Cynthia Dunbar, was a forceful, socially conscious woman of Scottish ancestry. His father, John Thoreau, came of French Huguenot stock; a reticent man, he was not successful in business until he became a pioneer manufacturer of lead pencils. Henry was close to his older brother John, whose death in 1842 affected him deeply. His sister Helen died in 1849, but his other sister, Sophia, survived him to serve as the guardian of his reputation.

After his graduation from Harvard, Thoreau taught briefly in a Concord school, but he resigned rather than be required to flog his pupils. From 1838 to 1841, he ran his own, relatively progressive, school in Concord, teaching Latin, Greek, and science. He spent 1843 in Staten Island, as a tutor in the household of Ralph Waldo Emerson's brother William. He also worked at various times as a house painter, carpenter, mason, surveyor, and pencil maker. During the years he lived with Ralph Waldo Emerson and his wife, Thoreau served as a kind of handyman. He also helped Emerson edit the Transcendentalist magazine *The Dial*.

Thoreau gave his first public lecture in the Concord Lyceum in 1838, and he continued intermittently as a lecturer for the remainder of his life. He was uncompromising toward his audience, particularly on the subject of slavery, and the reaction to his presentations was mixed. At Emerson's instigation, Thoreau began to keep a journal, which, published posthumously, serves as a valuable source for his experiences, observations, and reflections.

At five foot seven, he was slightly taller than average for his time, with longish hair and a prominent nose. He was striking, though not especially handsome, in appearance, and he made no effort to dress stylishly. Thoreau's only proposal of marriage, to a seventeen-year-old woman in 1840, was rejected, and he recoiled in horror from another woman's offer to him. He died, an equable bachelor, of the tuberculosis that first struck him in 1836 and that afflicted several members of his family.

LIFE'S WORK

From August 31 to September 13, 1839, during a break from their school, Thoreau and his brother John traveled by canoe along the Concord and Merrimack Rivers. Over the course of a decade, Thoreau transformed their experiences into *A Week on the Concord and Merrimack Rivers* (1849), one of only two Thoreau books published during his lifetime. A short work, *A Week on the Concord and Merrimack Rivers* reshapes a fourteen-day excursion into a Saturday-Friday rhythm. In addition to recording the flora, fauna, and people that Thoreau encountered along the way, the book is a miscellany of poems and essays on a variety of topics, including friendship, local history, fishing, Christianity, Oriental religion, quackery, and Geoffrey Chaucer. Thoreau published one thousand copies of the work at his own expense, and he noted in his journal that 706 of them remained unsold in his attic.

On July 4, 1845, Thoreau moved into a cabin that he had built on land belonging to Emerson, along the shores of Walden Pond, two miles from Concord. He lived there, alone, for more than two years, until September 6, 1847, but in his account of his stay, the experience is translated into the natural cycle of a single year. Because of the indifferent response to *A Week on the Concord and Merrimack Rivers*, Thoreau did not rush into print with his second book. Instead, between 1846, when he first began writing it, and 1854, when he finally published it, he reshaped his material through journal entries, essays, poems, lectures, and more than half a dozen successive manuscript drafts.

The result of Thoreau's efforts, *Walden: Or, Life in the Woods* (1854), is his supreme achievement and one of the most accomplished works in American literature. Written in a baroque, epigrammatic style, *Walden* is not simply the record of one man's eccentric sojourn in a sylvan setting; it is an allegory of the deliberate life, a crafty provocation to its readers to awaken from the torpor and the quiet desperation of their lives. Thoreau describes his solitary existence beside Walden Pond as an experiment, and so, too, is his prose reenactment.

I went to the woods because I wished to live deliberately, to front only the essential facts of life, and see if I could not learn what it had to teach, and not, when I came to die, discover that I had not lived. . . . I wanted to live deep and suck out all the marrow of life, to live so sturdily and Spartan-like as to put to rout all that was not life, to cut a broad swath and shave close, to drive life into a corner, and reduce it to its lowest terms, and, if it proved to be mean, why then to get the whole and genuine meanness of it, and publish its meanness to the world; or if it were sublime, to know it by experience, and be able to give a true account of it in my next excursion.

Thoreau is intent on clearing his life of the unnecessary encumbrances that materialism and a lack of self-reliance encourage. His book, which concludes with the exuberance of spring revivifying the pond, would have readers undergo a similar process of purifying enlightenment. *Walden* demands a careful reader, one alert enough not to dismiss it as a naïve effusion over nature, one sensitive to its author's extravagant, incendiary wit compounded of puns, paradoxes, and hyperboles.

In July, 1846, Thoreau spent one night in the Concord jail because of his refusal to pay a local poll tax. In a lecture first delivered in January, 1848, he explained his actions as a refusal to collaborate in the injustices of a government whose conduct of the Mexican War and whose perpetuation of the institution of slavery he stubbornly opposed. First published under the title "Resistance to Civil Government," the essay into which it evolved is best known as "Civil Disobedience" and is Thoreau's best-known essay. It proclaims the primacy of the individual and insists that if governmental policy cannot pass the muster of conscience, it ought to be resisted.

In 1857, Thoreau met abolitionist John Brown and was enormously impressed. He had earlier lectured in opposition to slavery, but Brown's arrest, following his raid on Harpers Ferry, Virginia, to incite a slave insurrection, inspired Thoreau to write his impassioned "A Plea for Captain John Brown." Though Thoreau's strenuous defense of Brown's actions did not save Brown from execution, the essay was probably the most widely read Thoreau work during his lifetime. "Slavery in Massachusetts," which he had written in 1854, calls for the state to secede from the nation and the individual from the state rather than acquiesce in an oppressive system. Published in William Lloyd Garrison's *The Liberator*, "Slavery in Massachusetts" also had a relatively large readership.

Though he was more closely tied to Concord than were any of its other major authors, Thoreau undertook a few brief excursions elsewhere—to Maine, Cape Cod, New Hampshire, Quebec, and Minnesota. These trips provided material for several works that were not published in their entireties until after his death. *Cape Cod* (1865), for example, is a cheerful report on the environment and the local lore of what was then an exotic region. *The Maine Woods* (1864) is a fairly straightforward and perceptive description of the people, plants, and animals in the northeastern frontier of the United States. Thoreau's final excursion came on May 6, 1862, in the family home in Concord; according to his sister Sophia, his last sentence was: "Now comes good sailing."

SIGNIFICANCE

Thoreau was a friend of several of the most important New England authors of the mid-nineteenth century, among them Ralph Waldo Emerson, Nathaniel Hawthorne, and Bronson Alcott. He was not widely known

Henry David Thoreau. (Library of Congress)

ON CIVIL DISOBEDIENCE

I heartily accept the motto, "That government is best which governs least"; and I should like to see it acted up to more rapidly and systematically. Carried out, it finally amounts to this, which also I believe—"That government is best which governs not at all"; and when men are prepared for it, that will be the kind of government which they will have. Government is at best but an expedient; but most governments are usually, and all governments are sometimes, inexpedient. The objections which have been brought against a standing army, and they are many and weighty, and deserve to prevail, may also at last be brought against a standing government. The standing army is only an arm of the standing government. The government itself, which is only the mode which the people have chosen to execute their will, is equally liable to be abused and perverted before the people can act through it. Witness the present Mexican war, the work of comparatively a few individuals using the standing government as their tool; for, in the outset, the people would not have consented to this measure.

Source: Henry David Thoreau, "Civil Disobedience."

outside the Concord circle during his lifetime, however, and within it he was generally condescended to as someone who had never accomplished anything beyond a local interest. Both *A Week on the Concord and Merrimack Rivers* and *Walden* were out of print by the time of his final illness. However, those two books were reprinted within weeks of his death, and five volumes of Thoreau's unpublished writings were brought out during the early 1860's. His reputation began to expand, first as a nature writer. Despite his crusty insistence, in *Walden* and in the pugnacious essay "Life Without Principle," that he refused to be exemplary of anything but fierce independence, he even attracted disciples.

Late in the nineteenth century, Thoreau attracted the admiration of British critics, particularly Laborites, as a social critic. Early in the twentieth century, Mahatma Gandhi was so impressed by "Civil Disobedience" that he published it as a pamphlet. Gandhi credited Thoreau's ideas on nonviolent resistance to illegitimate authority as being a principal inspiration behind the movement for Indian independence. In the United States, Martin Luther King, Jr., was a fervent champion of Thoreau's political ideas. "Civil Disobedience" has continued to be invoked not only by opponents of racism but also by those objecting to nuclear armaments and nuclear power. More than one protester has spent more than one night in jail, convinced that he or she was a genuine Thoreauvian.

The ascendancy of Thoreau's literary reputation was more gradual, but, with more than two hundred editions

of *Walden* in existence and his face on a postage stamp, the recluse of Walden Pond is now one of the foremost celebrities of American literature, as widely studied, read, and respected as any other author of his time. He has even eclipsed his Transcendentalist mentor Emerson in popularity. *Walden* is acknowledged as Thoreau's masterpiece, and it is read not as a series of naïve nature descriptions but as a complex and sophisticated literary performance. The delights of its dazzling style have drawn attention to the craftsmanship of many of his other writings.

Despite Thoreau's posthumous apotheosis as master of observation, of political principles, and of the English language, he remains a difficult writer. His rich prose is elusively allusive and often deliberately abrasive. Those who would keep pace with the brisk movement of his prickly mind are those who have learned, and earned, the serenity of self-reliance.

—*Steven G. Kellman*

FURTHER READING

Bloom, Harold, ed. *Henry David Thoreau*. Philadelphia: Chelsea House, 2003. Aimed at literature students, the book features a biography of Thoreau and analysis of his writing, including essays by Ralph Waldo Emerson and Thoreau biographer Walter Harding.

Glick, Wendell, ed. *The Recognition of Henry David Thoreau: Selected Criticism Since 1848*. Ann Arbor: University of Michigan Press, 1969. An anthology of historical commentaries documenting the growth in Thoreau's reputation—from obscurity and condescension to veneration.

Hahn, Stephen. *On Thoreau*. Belmont, Calif.: Wadsworth/Thomson Learning, 2000. A brief overview of Thoreau's ideas designed to introduce students and other readers to his work.

Harding, Walter. *The Days of Henry Thoreau: A Biography*. New York: Alfred A. Knopf, 1965. The standard full-scale biography by the most respected specialist in the field.

_____, ed. *Thoreau: Man of Concord*. New York: Holt, Rinehart and Winston, 1960. A compilation of recollections of Thoreau by dozens of his contemporaries, it provides testimony to the life within its nineteenth century contexts.

Lebeaux, Richard. *Thoreau's Seasons.* Amherst: University of Massachusetts Press, 1984. An application of psychologist Erik Erikson's theory of personality development to Thoreau's life from his Walden Pond experiment until his death.

Matthiessen, Francis O. *American Renaissance: Art and Expression in the Age of Emerson and Whitman.* New York: Oxford University Press, 1941. With extensive chapters on each of its major figures, this is the pioneering study of the Transcendentalist movement, the one that set the agenda for future studies of the period.

Porte, Joel. *Consciousness and Culture: Emerson and Thoreau Reviewed.* New Haven, Conn.: Yale University Press, 2004. A study of Thoreau and Emerson as writers, portraying them as complementary literary geniuses whose ideas moved provincial New England readers into a broader international culture.

Richardson, Robert D., Jr. *Henry Thoreau: A Life of the Mind.* Berkeley: University of California Press, 1986.

A biography, concentrating on Thoreau's intellectual development from age twenty until his death.

Shanley, J. Lyndon. *The Making of Walden.* Chicago: University of Chicago Press, 1957. A fascinating analysis of the stages in the composition of Thoreau's most celebrated work; it demonstrates that, far from a spontaneous record of actual experiences, *Walden* was in fact a carefully contrived work of art.

Wagenknecht, Edward. *Henry David Thoreau: What Manner of Man?* Amherst: University of Massachusetts Press, 1981. A brief, literate overview of the major themes in Thoreau's life. Wagenknecht proceeds topically rather than chronologically.

SEE ALSO: Louis Agassiz; Bronson Alcott; Louisa May Alcott; John Brown; Ralph Waldo Emerson; Margaret Fuller; William Lloyd Garrison; Nathaniel Hawthorne; Theodore Parker; Elizabeth Palmer Peabody; Walt Whitman.

RELATED ARTICLE in *Great Events from History: The Nineteenth Century, 1801-1900:* 1836: Transcendental Movement Arises in New England.

TIPPU TIB
East African trader

One of the leading slave and ivory traders of the nineteenth century, Tippu Tib built a commercial empire in East and Central Africa and unwittingly contributed to his own downfall by assisting European missionaries and explorers, whose work promoted the European imperial expansion that pushed him out of his own domains.

BORN: c. 1837; Zanzibar, East Africa (now in Tanzania)
DIED: June 14, 1905; Zanzibar, East Africa
ALSO KNOWN AS: Hamid bin Muhammed el Mujerbi (birth name); Muhammed Bin Hamid; Tippu Tip
AREAS OF ACHIEVEMENT: Business, warfare and conquest, geography

EARLY LIFE
Tippu Tib was born Hamid bin Muhammed. His father, Muhammed bin Juna, had 112 children by his three Arab wives and his harem of seventy African concubines, but Hamid was his first-born Arab son and for that reason was the most likely heir to his father's vast financial enterprise. Due to a nervous twitch, Hamid was also destined to be known by his nickname Tippu Tib, from an Arab expression meaning "one who blinks." Later, however, he preferred to say that his nickname came from the sound made by rifles fired by the armed retainers in his trading caravans.

Although Tippu Tib's birthplace of Zanzibar was a tiny island, it was the center of the East African slave trade. Most of its population of Swahilis, Arabs, Indians, and African slaves were directly or indirectly involved in the slave trade. His father amassed considerable wealth trading in slaves and ivory operating from his mainland base of Tabora and moving his trade goods through Zanzibar.

Hamid spent his childhood attending Islamic school at a mosque, where he studied the Qur'ān while developing basic literacy skills. He developed elegance in manners and refinement in speech. Most observers who later recorded firsthand meetings with Tippu Tip alluded to these characteristics as well as to his strong character and courage. He never drank or smoked, believing that those vices would interfere with his endless search for elephant tusks and slaves. Observers also noted Tippu Tip's dark skin and African features were unusual for a child who originated from a pure Arab mother and an Arab father. However, Tippu Tip's strong African features were the genetic legacy of a great-great-grandmother who had been an African.

The turning point in Tippu Tip's education came at the age of twenty-two, when he accompanied his father on a one-thousand-mile journey to obtain ivory and slaves to be sold in Zanzibari markets. On that trip, he observed the constant battles among tribes for cattle and slaves and the tribute in ivory that his father received for not attacking villages and offering villages protection against other enemies. He also noted how easy it was for successful traders to get loans from Indian banking houses to outfit caravan expeditions. Although bankers earned as much as 2,000 to 3,000 percent on their investments, the organizers of the expeditions themselves made great profits. Although smallpox almost ended Tippu Tip's life on his first trading journey, the lessons he learned on the trip would pay dividends after his father went into semiretirement in 1859, and he ventured forth on his first caravan expedition.

LIFE'S WORK

In 1859, when Tippu Tib was about twenty-two, he undertook his first independent expedition. He was not content to follow his father's conservative caravan route through territory traveled by other Arab traders. Instead, he pushed farther west, through present Tanzania into northern Katanga, in what is now the eastern Congo, in search of more profitable goods. That journey established the pattern that would lead to his eventual domination of trade over a region nearly half the area of Europe. His system was to attack the most powerful chief in a region and then force neighboring chiefs to trade with him on favorable terms to pay tribute to him in ivory and slaves. Tippu Tip also offered small communities protection against their enemies, in return for which they had to pay him taxes when he returned.

Tippu Tip's first independent trading expedition lasted a full year and reaped enormous profits. In 1865, he mounted an even larger caravan and in 1867, one larger still. On his third expedition, which lasted two years, he met the famous Scottish missionary/explorer David Livingstone, who was camped southwest of Lake Tanganyika near the village of Ponda. A friendship developed between the two men that each described in his published diaries. Tippu Tip had some of his guards accompany Livingstone on his journey to Lake Mweru.

Livingstone was not the only European missionary or explorer whom Tippu Tip would assist. On another caravan journey in August, 1874, he met the English explorer Vernon Lovett Cameron, who had been sent by the British Geological Society to assist Livingstone. Tippu Tib took Cameron to his base in Kasongo. In October, 1876, Tippu Tip met the British-American explorer Henry M. Stanley at the Lualaba River. Stanley paid Tippu Tib a large fee to permit his own caravan to accompany Tippu Tip's caravan as it penetrated deep into the Congo. Stanley intended to reach the Congo River, carefully noting unknown territories along the way, and ultimately reached the Atlantic Ocean. That journey proved particularly profitable for Tippu Tib, who was pleased to encounter forest-dwelling peoples who hunted elephants for their meat and had little use for the animals' tusks. Tippu Tib used more than two thousand porters to carry the tusks he collected back to the East Coast.

Tippu Tip and Stanley parted company on December 27, 1876, but Stanley did not forget the wealthy and powerful trader. In 1887, Stanley persuaded the Belgian king Leopold II to appoint Tippu Tip governor of the Stanley Falls district in the Congo Free State that he was creating. Before accepting the appointment, Tippu Tib accompanied Stanley on a steamship journey to Cape Town in South Africa. It was Tippu Tip's first experience of seeing a European-controlled city; he could not have predicted that his native Zanzibar would soon become a European-dominated island. For the moment, the Congo governorship must have appeared to him to be a golden opportunity, as it enabled him to continue conducting his trading business from a secure position of power that allowed him to increase the volume of his trade.

Tippu Tip's fall began in 1890, when the new sultan of Zanzibar, Khalifa, ordered him to return from Stanley Falls to face trial on charges that he had breached an agreement with Stanley to send troops and supplies during an expedition. Khalifa's predecessor, Sultan Barghash, had maintained a degree of independence from British influence and had had good relations with Tippu Tip. However, Great Britain was controlling Zanzibar by 1890. Moreover, the Belgian administrators of King Leopold's Congo Free State were eager to clear the Congo of Arab influences.

In clash with Belgian troops on the River Luama, to the west of Lake Tanganyika, in October, 1893, Tippu Tip's forces were defeated, and he lost all his holdings in the Congo. He also lost his his oldest son, Sef, the heir apparent to his trading empire. However, he did not lose extensive holdings in Zanzibar and the mainland coast.

After being forced into retirement, Tippu Tip told his life story to the German professor Heinrich Brode, who published the story in 1903. Tippu Tip died in his Zanzibar mansion on June 14, 1905, at the age of about sixty-eight. At the time of his death, his native Zanzibar was a British protectorate, and what is now mainland Tanzania was a German colony called German East Africa colony (later renamed Tanganyika).

SIGNIFICANCE

Tippu Tip was the most famous East African slave trader of the nineteenth century. He employed large and well-armed caravans to create a trading empire that stretched from the Luba River in the south to the great westward bend of the Upper Congo River. Many of the people within that region paid taxes to him in return for protection from rival tribes. Tippu Tib's trade in ivory and slaves made him almost fantastically wealthy and contributed to Zanzibar's notoriety as a major slave-trading center at a time when Western European nations were working to end the African slave trade.

Tippu Tib's search for ever-greater profits drove him deeper and deeper into little-known areas of the Congo, and he made a major a contribution to negatively disrupting the traditional lives and culture of the societies that he encountered. His path crossed the paths of some of the greatest European explorers of the time, and his assistance helped some of them succeed in their quests. Ironically, the success of the explorers whom he assisted also contributed to his own downfall by helping to advance European influence in East and Central Africa and bring to bear greater world pressure to end the traffic in human beings on which his own wealth was largely based.

—*Irwin Halfond*

FURTHER READING

Farrant, Leda. *Tippu Tip and the East African Slave Trade*. New York: St. Martin's Press, 1975. Based on primary sources, this is still the major study of Tippu Tib's life, work, and times. Includes a genealogy of Tippu Tib's family.

Grant, Kevin. *A Civilized Savagery: Britain and the New Slaveries in Africa, 1884-1926*. Philadelphia: Taylor & Francis, 2004. A scholarly study, based on archival sources, of attempts by the British government and evangelical churches to end slavery and forced-labor practices.

Monahan, Merry P. *The Sound of Guns: A Biography of Tippu Tip*. San Francisco: San Francisco State College, 1972. An interesting biographical study of Tippu Tib and analysis of his role as a slave trader.

Tippu Tip. *Tippu Tip: The Story of His Career in Zanzibar and Central Africa—Narrated from His Own Accounts by Heinrich Brode*. Translated by H. Havelock. Old Castle, Ireland: Gallery Publications, 2000. New edition of book first published in German in 1903. Dictated by Tippu Tib during his retirement and filled with interesting detail, Tippu Tib's life is explained and rationalized by the slave merchant himself.

SEE ALSO: Sir Richard Francis Burton; Leopold II; David Livingstone; Saʿīd ibn Sulṭān; Henry Morton Stanley.

RELATED ARTICLES in *Great Events from History: The Nineteenth Century, 1801-1900:* 1848-1889: Exploration of East Africa; 1873-1897: Zanzibar Outlaws Slavery.

ALEXIS DE TOCQUEVILLE
French traveler and historian

A political and social analyst, Tocqueville was the earliest, the greatest, and surely the most percipient observer of the initial growth and increasing persuasiveness of democracy in all areas of American culture. His book Democracy in America *is regarded as the classic treatment of its subject throughout the Western world.*

BORN: July 29, 1805; Paris, France
DIED: April 16, 1859; Cannes, France
ALSO KNOWN AS: Alexis-Henri-Charles-Maurice Clérel, comte de Tocqueville (full name)
AREAS OF ACHIEVEMENT: Exploration, literature

EARLY LIFE

Alexis-Henri-Charles-Maurice Clérel, comte de Tocqueville (tohk-veel) was born in Paris a few years after his aristocratic parents had been released from their imprisonment by revolutionary forces for their close relations with the collapsed monarchy of Louis XVI and for their outspoken support of it before revolutionary tribunals. His father, Hervé, subsequently became a prefect (governor) in various states under the restored monarchy of Charles X. His mother never fully recovered from her treatment during the revolution. Living on family properties at Verneuil, Tocqueville was first tutored by Abbé Lesueur, the Catholic priest who had taught his father and a man whom Tocqueville would remember affectionately for having instilled in him a belief in the Christian principles that he would abandon for a time but would return to in later life.

In his adolescence, the young Tocqueville spent six years in Metz and completed his studies brilliantly at the local *lycée*. A perceptive, if not an omnivorous, reader profoundly impressed by the writings of René Descartes, Tocqueville gave up his strict Catholicism for a more critical Christian Deism, that is, a belief in human reason, rather than God, as the operative force in humankind's affairs. Emotionally and intellectually more at ease with tangible matters that were susceptible to precise analysis than with theories, Tocqueville embarked on law studies, which he completed in 1825. Almost immediately, he and his brother Edward took an extended tour of Italy and Sicily, the importance of which emerged in the voluminous and detailed journals he kept. What he perceived were not so much the invariable landscapes as evidences of social structure, the shape of which he deduced by the structure of the applicable political systems and laws.

Perhaps because he was only twenty-two years old, he imaginatively compared his keen observations on the Italian scene with his knowledge of French and British institutions.

Meanwhile, in 1827, he was offered a career that both his family background and his own predilections seemed to favor. By royal patent from Charles X, Tocqueville was appointed to a Versailles judgeship in the department of Seine and Oise, literally within the shadow of the king's residence. Fearful that the routines of his office might render him incapable of judging great movements or of guiding great undertakings, Tocqueville, nevertheless, devoted himself to his duties. Later, Charles X, the king who had appointed him, chose abdication in the face of the Revolution of 1830. At war with himself for having to swear allegiance to the new monarch, Louis-Philippe, whose values he repudiated, Tocqueville still remained in service long enough to request from the minister of interior in 1831 leave to investigate the penal system in the United States.

LIFE'S WORK

Accompanied by another French magistrate who was both a colleague and a friend, Gustave de Beaumont, a man who later served as a deputy to the National Assembly and as the French ambassador to London and Vienna and was a writer-scholar of distinction in his own right, Tocqueville invented the pretext of studying the American penal system in order to tackle the larger task that he had set for himself—a thorough, on-site investigation of what then was the world's first and only completely democratic society: the United States. Only twenty-six years old, Tocqueville appeared less robust than the country that would absorb his attention. Portraits accent long arms and a short, thin, and frail body. Beneath locks of brown hair, his delicate, aristocratic face was dominated by large, intelligent brown eyes. He and Beaumont embarked for New York in April, 1831.

Returning to France in 1832, Tocqueville and Beaumont finished their study of the American penal system. It was published in 1833 as *Du système pénitentiaire aux États-Unis et de son application en France* (*On the Penitentiary System in the United States and Its Application in France*, 1833). This official obligation resolved, Tocqueville left his judicial post, moved into a modest Paris apartment, and began what he later described as the happiest two years of his life, writing his two-volume *De la démocratie en Amérique* (1835, 1840; *Democracy in America*, 1835, 1840). This work was proclaimed the classic treatment of its subject throughout the Western world and ensured Tocqueville's fame as a political observer and political philosopher, and, later, as a sociologist.

While writing the third volume of *Democracy in America*, Tocqueville in 1837 sought election as a deputy from his native constituency, La Manche. Failing in 1837, he succeeded in 1839, serving in the Chamber of Deputies continuously until 1851 and almost always in opposition to the government of Louis-Philippe. From 1842 to 1848, practicing his belief that a healthy state was founded upon vigorous local government, he served on the local general council. Although he never perceived himself as a political leader, he nevertheless reinforced his convictions by public service.

Meanwhile, he was among the few who prophesied the coming of the revolutions of 1848, which ended the Second Republic, replacing it with the plebiscite government of Louis Napoleon, who was soon to proclaim the Second Empire and his rule as Napoleon III. Though he had voted against Napoleon, Tocqueville was reelected to a new national assembly and on June 2, 1849, was appointed France's foreign minister. Once again, his acceptance of the post was intended to keep the republican spirit alive, certain as he was that Napoleon intended to bury it. Over the next few months as foreign minister—he resigned on October 31, 1849—he dealt with the Austrian-Piedmontese conflict, the Turkish question, problems with the Roman Catholic Church, and Swiss rights of asylum, each an important problem at the time.

Exhausted when he left office, he served on yet another parliamentary commission studying the question of Napoleon's reeligibility as president—an issue resolved dramatically by the president's own coup d'état of December 2, 1851. It was amid such events, the latter of which shocked Tocqueville as well as most of Europe's informed opinion, that he began writing *Souvenirs de Alexis de Tocqueville* (1893; *The Recollections of Alexis de Tocqueville*, 1896, 1949) in June, 1850. Although many scholars regard it as his greatest book, a classic historical, sociological, and political analysis of the antecedents, personalities, and events of the revolutions of 1848 in France, Tocqueville had not intended it for publication.

With the completion of *The Recollections of Alexis de Tocqueville*, Tocqueville was already embarked on his *L'Ancien Régime et la révolution* (1856; *The Old Régime and the Revolution*, 1856), in which, after five years of exhaustive archival research, he demonstrated that the centralization of power in France was not a consequence of the Revolution of 1789 but rather had been proceeding for centuries. This extension of power, pursued by an alienated and obsolete aristocracy and running counter to gains in popular power and popular enthusiasm for equality and freedom, helped make revolution almost inevitable. This was Tocqueville's last work. Lying ill for several weeks at his family estate at Cannes, he confessed, regretted that he had not been a more ardent disciple of Catholicism, and died on April 16, 1859.

SIGNIFICANCE

Alexis de Tocqueville's principal moral and intellectual concern was with freedom. He was not a liberal, however, any more than he was a democrat. Liberalism skirted on unbridled individualism, democracy on an egalitarian reductionism, a tendency to put everyone on an equal but low level. Rather, in Tocqueville's view, all freedom begins with recognition that humankind is the creature of a larger collectivity, a creature of God. Lacking this appreciation, no one can really call himself free. From that basic premise—and it suffuses all of Tocqueville's major works—he strove through his extraordi-

---

SLAVERY'S IMPACT ON THE SOUTH

In his observations on American society and government, Alexis de Tocqueville looked closely at the impact of slavery, which was still widely used throughout the southern states. Here he comments on slavery in Virginia's history.

The colony was scarcely established when slavery was introduced, and this was the main circumstance which has exercised so prodigious an influence on the character, the laws, and all the future prospects of the South. Slavery, as we shall afterwards show, dishonors labor; it introduces idleness into society, and with idleness, ignorance and pride, luxury and distress. It enervates the powers of the mind, and benumbs the activity of man. The influence of slavery, united to the English character, explains the manners and the social condition of the Southern States.

Source: Alexis de Tocqueville, *Democracy in America*, translated by Henry Reeve (Cambridge, Mass., 1863), book 1, chapter 1.

nary powers of observation and research to develop a political philosophy that struck a balance between people's rights and their duties. Although capable of dealing in abstractions in these matters, he nevertheless felt comfortable only when fitting them into historical and substantive cultural contexts, whether his immediate interests were structural, that is, sociological, or lay in the measurement and movement of power, that is, political.

Being neither a liberal nor a democrat but a French aristocrat who recognized that the authority of aristocracies in France and Great Britain had been shattered—and in the United States, he believed, had never existed—lent Tocqueville's work its much-admired objectivity. His major studies were offered primarily for the consideration of Frenchmen. While democratization had proceeded much further in the United States, France, he believed, also confronted the same conditions. Although manifested dramatically in political upheavals and revolutions, both historical tendencies (toward popular power and toward centralized power), he believed, were centuries in the making. The question for his day was, Would the age-old centralizing process that he discerned, when joined with the almost inevitable centralizing power of majoritarian and egalitarian democracy, lead to tyranny—though a tyranny of, or in the name of, the masses?

Tocqueville sensed what the twentieth century has proved—most authoritarian states have justified themselves as being democratic, as governing in the name of the people. Democrats, it seemed on his evidence, were assuming the political and administrative roles of aristocracies. In the face of the egalitarian surge, however, the centralization of power was broadening, not declining, hence the interference of the state increasingly menaced the integrity of the individual's freedom.

Thirteen years older than Karl Marx, Tocqueville wrote of the importance of classes in history, while utterly rejecting what later became Marx's determinism respecting their roles. Unearthing the interrelations among a people's perceived and historical experiences, their manners and mores, and the configuration of their political institutions, his works place him among the other great men who analyzed the nature of society, beginning with Aristotle and proceeding through modern times.

—*Clifton K. Yearley*

FURTHER READING

Drolet, Michael. *Tocqueville, Democracy, and Social Reform*. New York: Palgrave Macmillan, 2003. Tocqueville investigated and wrote about numerous social issues, including prison reform, pauperism, and the problems of abandoned children. This book examines the intellectual and social context of his social reform literature and how that literature relates to his better-known work.

Herr, Richard. *Tocqueville and the Old Regime*. Princeton, N.J.: Princeton University Press, 1962. The author, a specialist in modern French history, deals with the incompleteness and apparent inconsistencies of Tocqueville's *The Old Régime and the Revolution*. An informative and well-written work with a selective bibliography and a useful index.

Laski, Harold J. "Alexis de Tocqueville and Democracy." In *The Social and Political Ideas of Some Representative Thinkers of the Victorian Age*, edited by F. J. C. Hearnshaw. London: G. G. Harrap, 1933. Laski, a distinguished British liberal-left political analyst and a force behind the extension of the British welfare state, cogently examines Tocqueville's views on social democracy and their relevance to modern democracies.

Mayer, Jacob Peter. *Alexis de Tocqueville: A Biographical Study in Political Science*. New York: Harper & Brothers, 1960. Mayer is one of the foremost authorities on Tocqueville, having researched, translated, revised, and completed many of Tocqueville's works. This is a delightfully informative and clearly written overview intended for general readers.

Mayer, Jacob Peter, and A. P. Kerr. Introduction to *Recollections*, by Alexis de Tocqueville. Translated by George Lawrence. Garden City, N.Y.: Doubleday, 1970. This is the best edition of what many regard as Tocqueville's finest work. Mayer and Kerr, experts on Tocqueville, provide an informative introductory essay, many footnotes, a select bibliography, and an extensive index.

Pierson, George W. *Tocqueville and Beaumont in America*. New York: Oxford University Press, 1938. This remains the definitive study of Tocqueville's months in the United States. A thorough evaluation of the settings through which these two friends passed, the people they met, and the sources they employed for their study of the American penal system and, in Tocqueville's case, for his great study of democracy. Traces Tocqueville's intellectual development with an eye to clarifying all of his writings. Clearly written and understandable to general readers.

Tocqueville, Alexis de. *Democracy in America by Alexis de Tocqueville*. Edited by Phillips Bradley. 2 vols. New York: Alfred A. Knopf, 1945. This is a revised version of the first English translation and includes informative notes, historical essays, useful bibliographies, and extensive indexes in each volume. The author claims that Tocqueville's work remains one of the most magisterial analyses ever produced on the principle of the sovereignty of the people, its cultural roots, and its evolving political effects.

Wolin, Sheldon S. *Tocqueville Between Worlds: The Making of a Political and Theoretical Life*. Princeton, N.J.: Princeton University Press, 2001. Wolin, a prominent political philosopher, focuses on Tocqueville's active political life, tracing the development of his theories about democracy and other political issues.

Zetterbaum, Marvin. *Tocqueville and the Problem of Democracy*. Stanford, Calif.: Stanford University Press, 1967. An examination of Tocqueville's proposition that democracy was inevitable and therefore that democracy had to be made safe for the world. The author's view is that the "inevitability thesis" distracted readers from Tocqueville's central concern about perfecting democracy and of harmonizing the demands of justice with those of excellence. However brief, this is an enlightening study, clearly written and intended for the general reader.

SEE ALSO: Karl Marx; Napoleon III.

RELATED ARTICLES in *Great Events from History: The Nineteenth Century, 1801-1900:* May, 1831-February, 1832: Tocqueville Visits America; February 22-June, 1848: Paris Revolution of 1848; 1859: Mill Publishes *On Liberty*.

LEO TOLSTOY
Russian novelist

During the first half of his long and active life, Tolstoy brought universal fame to Russian literature through his fiction. In later years, he achieved worldwide renown as a pacifist, social activist, and moralist. He is equally significant as a novelist and moral philosopher.

BORN: September 9, 1828; Yasnaya Polyana, Russia
DIED: November 20, 1910; Astapovo, Russia
ALSO KNOWN AS: Count Leo Nikolayevich Tolstoy (full name); Lev Tolstoy; Leo Tolstoi
AREA OF ACHIEVEMENT: Literature

EARLY LIFE

Leo Tolstoy traced his aristocratic origins back to the founding of the Russian state in the ninth century. His ancestors, at times faithful servants, at times opponents of the Crown, amassed fame as well as respectable wealth over the centuries. Thus Tolstoy, though orphaned at the age of eight, grew up in comfort under the care of relatives at the various Tolstoy residences. He subsequently shaped a vague memory of his mother, who died when he was two, into an idealized portrait of the perfect woman and featured such a paragon in many of his major works. His first published narrative, *Detstvo* (1852; *Childhood*, 1862), re-creates a boy's tender relationship with and painful loss of his mother.

A flamboyant lifestyle, filled with carousing and gambling, prevented Tolstoy from completing university study, but he revealed an early talent for writing and meticulously recorded daily details, from purest thoughts to debauched acts, in his diaries. He continued keeping such journals until old age, providing future literary historians with rich source material for every stage of his life. His elder siblings and relations, dismayed at the young count's irresolution and wantonness, sent him in 1851 to the Caucasus, where Russia was engaged in sporadic military operations with hostile local peoples.

Tolstoy's subsequent participation in the Crimean War put an end to the unstable years of his youth. Active service during the siege of Sevastopol motivated him to set down his impressions of the carnage in a series of sketches, "Sevastopol v dekabre," "Sevastopol v maye," and "Sevastopol v avguste" (1854-1856; collected in translation as *Sebastopol*, 1887). His original and above all truthful accounts pleased a public that had grown tired of the prevailing vainglorious, deceitful war reports. So convincingly did Tolstoy chronicle the horror of battlefield life and communicate his disillusionment with war that czarist censors moved to alter his exposés. Tolstoy's later devotion to nonviolence stems from these experiences. His perceptions about the ineptitude of military commanders juxtaposed to the courage and common sense of foot soldiers resurface in his major work, *Voyna i mir* (1865-1869; *War and Peace*, 1886). Moreover, his dispute with the authorities over his forthright reporting set the stage for a lifelong confrontation with the imperial autocracy.

LIFE'S WORK

Tolstoy's long literary career followed several distinct directions. The labors of his younger years belong to the field of aesthetic literature, though he embarked on that course only after lengthy deliberation. When he returned to St. Petersburg in 1855 following military service, high society lionized the young hero and for a time drew him back into the swirl of its carefree amusements. His strong didactic bent and quarrelsome nature did not, however, endear him to the literary establishment. He soon antagonized writers on all sides of the social and political spectrum and in the end thought it best to develop his talents without the help of contemporaries.

The deaths of two brothers and an execution witnessed in Paris in 1857 led Tolstoy to approach life in a more serious vein. He opened and directed a school for peasant children on his estate, using pedagogical methods that he himself established, and entered into lively journalistic polemics with other educators over his scheme of placing moral teachings above the acquisition of knowledge. These and other controversial public exchanges brought renewed government interference that impelled Tolstoy to turn to less antagonistic activity. In 1862, he married Sophia Behrs, sixteen years his junior, became a country gentleman, and settled down to a life of writing.

The 1860's were almost wholly devoted to the composition of the epic *War and Peace*, which went through so many revisions and changes of focus, even as it was being serialized, that no clearly definitive version of the novel exists. Among the diverse issues embedded in the finished product are Tolstoy's own interpretation of the Napoleonic Wars, a richly drawn panorama of early nineteenth century Russian upper-class society supplemented by many biographical details, a firm conviction that the values of close-knit family life are far superior to social rituals, and a wealth of sundry philosophical observations. *War and Peace* owes its immense success to the author's vast descriptive talents, which manage to neutralize his lifelong tendency to sermonize.

Reflections on the importance of stable domestic existence also dominate Tolstoy's second major work, *Anna Karenina* (1875-1877; English translation, 1886), in which he chronicles the fates of three aristocratic families and demonstrates that the title figure's insistence on personal happiness to the detriment of family duty engenders tragedy for all concerned. The novel also develops Tolstoy's pet notion that Russian peasant mores are morally superior to high society's ideals. Ideas about the meaning of death and the validity of suicide also represent an important strain in *Anna Karenina*, reflecting Tolstoy's own frequent contact with death, as he lost several children and other close relatives during the 1870's during the composition of the novel. The themes of these two major works are echoed in the many shorter pieces produced by the prolific Tolstoy during the same period.

The late 1870's represented a watershed for Tolstoy, a time when a prolonged spiritual crisis forced him to evaluate both his privileged life and his literary endeavors. A drastic reorientation evolved from this period of introspection. No longer able to justify his considerable wealth in the face of millions of illiterate, destitute peasants and laborers, Tolstoy resolved to make amends by placing his talent and means at the disposal of the poor. In consequence, he actively challenged what he perceived to be the hypocrisy of Russia's ruling institutions. Because the Russian Orthodox Church worked closely with

Leo Tolstoy. (Library of Congress)

the conservative czarist government to maintain the status quo, it too became a target of Tolstoy's dissatisfactions.

After publication of the strongly anticlerical *Voskreseniye* (1899; *Resurrection*, 1899), Tolstoy found himself excommunicated, an action he dismissed lightly, having over the years developed a personal Christianity that became the basis of much of his nonfictional writing. His spiritual anxieties and search for an acceptable faith are chronicled in *Ispoved* (1884; *A Confession*, 1885). Both Tolstoy's literary style and his subject matter underwent extreme changes during this time. The works became shorter, using more succinct and simpler language, and became decidedly more opinionated.

Tolstoy's fiction largely gave way to social and philosophical commentary, and even the remaining fictional pieces were intricately shaped to transmit his moral messages. Thus, *Smert' Ivana Il'icha* (1886; *The Death of Ivan Ilyich*, 1887) presents Tolstoy's view of the proper attitude toward death and dying, and the play *Vlast tmy* (1887; *The Power of Darkness*, 1888) warns of the grim consequences engendered by evil thoughts and deeds. Tolstoy justified the political nature of this type of fiction by challenging the very morality of aesthetic detachment. Because even his polemical commentaries adhered to respectable literary standards, he never lost his readership. On the contrary, people of all persuasions debated his works with interest, even fascination.

Tolstoy's efforts to use his name and fortune in support of favorite causes gave rise to severe disharmony within the Tolstoy family. For long years, the spouses battled over property and copyright privileges. These quarrels led Tolstoy to replace his earlier emphasis on family unity with issues of personal salvation and questions of ethics. He returned to the theme of family in one of his most controversial narratives, *Kreytserova sonata* (1889; *The Kreutzer Sonata*, 1890). In this work he denies that marriage is a valid social institution by defining its main purpose as the gratification of lust, detrimental to women and destructive of personal integrity. The major character, Pozdnyshev, murders his wife in a bout of jealousy and proposes the abolition of

TOLSTOY'S FICTION	
LONG FICTION	
1852	*Detstvo* (*Childhood*, 1862)
1854	*Otrochestvo* (*Boyhood*, 1886)
1857	*Yunost'* (*Youth*, 1886)
1859	*Semeynoye schast'ye* (*Family Happiness*, 1888)
1863	*Kazaki* (*The Cossacks*, 1872)
1865-1869	*Voyna i mir* (*War and Peace*, 1886)
1875-1877	*Anna Karenina* (English translation, 1886)
1886	*Smert' Ivana Il'icha* (*The Death of Ivan Ilyich*, 1887)
1889	*Kreytserova sonata* (*The Kreutzer Sonata*, 1890)
1899	*Voskreseniye* (*Resurrection*, 1899)
1911	*Khadzi-Murat* (*Hadji Murad*, 1911)
SHORT FICTION	
1855-1856	*Sevastopolskiye rasskazy* (*Sebastopol*, 1887)
1940	*The Kreutzer Sonata, The Devil, and Other Tales*
1943	*Notes of a Madman, and Other Stories*
1947	*Tolstoy Tales*

all sexual acts, even at the expense of humanity's extinction.

Not all Tolstoy's later views express such absolute negatives, but most of his mature output was disputations in nature. For example, his treatise *Chto takoye iskusstvo?* (1898; *What Is Art?*, 1898) sets forth his revised opinion on the nature and role of literature. He dismisses most art, including his own earlier writings, as immoral and undemocratic, suggesting instead that all art forms be morally instructive and executed in simple, guileless fashion accessible to the multitudes.

Throughout his long life, Tolstoy continued to espouse peaceful settlement of international conflicts. In time, his advocacy of nonresistance made him into a prominent spokesman against war and the death penalty. His regard for the impoverished masses and his many controversial stands brought him worldwide fame. The image of the revered, bearded, aged "repentant nobleman," holding court and expounding his position on national and global topics while dressed in homemade rural attire, drew diverse crowds from far and wide. His very renown prevented an angry czarist government from treating him harshly.

To prevent the total dissolution of his domestic bonds, Tolstoy permitted the family to remain at the imposing country estate, but he himself withdrew to a humble corner of it to observe a rigorously modest lifestyle. At the age of eighty-two, he decided to cut even these ties and secretly left home to live henceforth entirely according to

Tolstoy, Leo   THE NINETEENTH CENTURY

his convictions. Illness almost immediately forced him to abandon the train journey, and he died at the station-master's house a week later, surrounded by dignitaries and reporters. He lies buried in a distant corner of his estate. His simple, unadorned grave and the mansion, converted into a Tolstoy museum after the Russian Revolution, are a favorite stop for countless visitors and tourists.

SIGNIFICANCE

Leo Tolstoy's impact as both artist and moralist continues undiminished into the twenty-first century. His fictional works, especially his earlier ones, retain a charm that is proof of his enormous descriptive powers. However, even these works express personal preferences and values, which the author elucidates at every opportunity. Thus it is, in the final analysis, Tolstoy the teacher, moralist, and public commentator who dominates. Through his doctrine of nonresistance, which he based on the words of Jesus and through which he resisted many inequities of the state, he set examples for similar movements in India under Mohandas Gandhi and the United States under Martin Luther King, Jr.

Although Tolstoy's pronouncements on behalf of the poor often assume an overly shrill tone, he backed these convictions with solid action. Not only did his income and efforts facilitate great humanitarian projects, from famine relief to resettlement of religious dissenters, but he also himself found no peace until he had adjusted his lifestyle to fit the humblest. His deliberations on death and ideas on how to cope with it cut through the stilted social conventions of his time to find universal appreciation and application in the twentieth century.

Closely linked to Tolstoy's thoughts about death and dying was his quest for a new religious attitude. By examining the doctrines and practices of the Russian Orthodox Church as well as other religions and finding them incompatible with Jesus' words, he pointed to alternative approaches, advocating a way of life based on the Gospels, not church dogma. In this, too, he anticipated certain twentieth century movements toward a personal fundamentalism.

Tolstoy also generated opposition. His dogmatic and frequently cantankerous method of conveying his beliefs alienated many potential adherents. In the manner of all prophets, he brooked no contradiction of his scheme of universal ethical improvement. Even so, his many achievements and contributions as major writer, social activist, and moral philosopher remain universally acknowledged.

—*Margot K. Frank*

FURTHER READING

Benson, Ruth Crego. *Women in Tolstoy: The Ideal and the Erotic*. Urbana: University of Illinois Press, 1973. Concentrates on Tolstoy's changing vision of the role and importance of family life. Suggests that Tolstoy struggled most of his life with a dichotomous view of women, regarding them in strictly black-and-white terms, as saints or sinners. Analyzes the female characters in the major and several minor works in terms of such a double view. An interesting and provocative piece of feminist criticism.

Bloom, Harold, ed. *Leo Tolstoy*. New York: Chelsea House, 1986. A collection of critical essays, encompassing the years 1920-1983. The views expressed provide a good sampling of the wide range of opinions about Tolstoy prevalent among Western critics. Many of these critics assign a prominent place in literary history to Tolstoy, comparing him to, among others, Homer and Johann Wolfgang von Goethe. Some of the articles deal with specific works; others define Tolstoy's contributions to nineteenth century European intellectual movements.

De Courcel, Martine. *Tolstoy: The Ultimate Reconciliation*. Translated by Peter Levi. New York: Charles Scribner's Sons, 1987. A detailed biography, annotated with selected bibliography, which relies heavily on the notebooks and diaries of Tolstoy and those of his wife, Sophia. Concentrates on Tolstoy's domestic life but has extensive references to his general public activity. Posits the unique notion that Tolstoy left home at the end of his life to return to aesthetic literature.

Greenwood, E. B. *Tolstoy: The Comprehensive Vision*. New York: St. Martin's Press, 1975. Greenwood maintains Tolstoy's diverse strivings can be attributed to his belief that art and life could be brought together under one philosophical tenet. Greenwood detects a search for such a unified vision in most of the major writings, stressing Tolstoy's contribution to philosophy and religion.

Moss, Walter. *Russia in the Age of Alexander II, Tolstoy, and Dostoevsky*. London: Anthem Press, 2002. Chronicles the reign of Czar Alexander II, interweaving these events with information about the lives and ideas of Tolstoy, Dostoevski, and other writers and thinkers from the "golden age" of Russian literature. Provides valuable background for understanding Tolstoy's life.

Mounce, H. O. *Tolstoy on Aesthetics: "What Is Art?"* Burlington, Vt.: Ashgate, 2001. An analysis of Tolstoy's aesthetic theories. Mounce describes Tolstoy's aesthetic concerns and explains how these concerns relate to contemporary ideas about the value and importance of art.

Orwin, Donna Tussing, ed. *The Cambridge Companion to Tolstoy*. New York: Cambridge University Press, 2002. Collection of essays, including critical analyses of *War and Peace* and *Anna Karenina*; discussions of Tolstoy as an artist, public figure, and writer of popular literature; and examinations of Tolstoy's aesthetics, development of style and theme, and treatment of women, sexuality, and the family.

Rowe, William W. *Leo Tolstoy*. Boston: Twayne, 1986. Concise introduction to Tolstoy's life and work, with special emphasis on the major novels and later didactic writings. Briefly discusses most of Tolstoy's major concerns. Excellent treatment of individual characters in the major novels.

Simmons, Ernest J. *Tolstoy*. London: Routledge & Kegan Paul, 1973. Extensive chronological account of Tolstoy's public activities. Includes social and cultural background on Russia during Tolstoy's time and discusses the importance of Tolstoy's theories on religion, society, morality, and literature. Adds comments on Tolstoy's relevance to the twentieth century and his international stature.

Tolstaia, Andreevna S. *The Diaries of Sophia Tolstoy*. Edited by O. A. Golinenko et al. Translated by Cathy Porter with an introduction by R. F. Christian. New York: Random House, 1985. This massive personal record of Tolstoy's wife, detailing their life together, spans the years 1862-1910. Sophia Tolstoy kept an almost daily account of her husband's opinions, doubts, and plans concerning his literary activity, social ventures, and relationships with other writers and thinkers. The diaries often portray Tolstoy in an unfavorable light, because the spouses were temperamentally incompatible, and she chafed under his domination. However, she collaborated closely with Tolstoy for many decades, and her notes give a fascinating and intimate view of the Tolstoy family and the extent to which this family served as background for many of the literary episodes.

Wilson, A. N. *Tolstoy*. New York: W. W. Norton, 1988. A long but immensely readable biography, breezy, insightful, and opinionated, by a prolific and highly regarded British novelist. Illustrated; includes a useful chronology of Tolstoy's life and times as well as notes, bibliography, and index.

SEE ALSO: Anton Chekhov; Fyodor Dostoevski; Nikolai Gogol; Mikhail Lermontov; Alexander Pushkin; Ivan Turgenev.

RELATED ARTICLE in *Great Events from History: The Nineteenth Century, 1801-1900:* December, 1849: Dostoevski Is Exiled to Siberia.

HENRI DE TOULOUSE-LAUTREC
French painter

Through the creation of more than seven hundred paintings, sketches, lithographs, and posters, Toulouse-Lautrec vividly recorded the people and activities of Paris in the last decades of the nineteenth century and elevated color lithography and the poster to major art forms.

BORN: November 24, 1864; Albi, France
DIED: September 9, 1901; Château de Malromé, France
ALSO KNOWN AS: Henri Marie Raymond de Toulouse-Lautrec Monfa (full name)
AREA OF ACHIEVEMENT: Art

EARLY LIFE
Henri Marie Raymond de Toulouse-Lautrec Monfa (tew-lewz-loh-trek mahn-fah) was born into an aristo-cratic family whose lineage went back to the time of Charlemagne. In separate falls when he was an adolescent, he broke the femurs of both legs. Throughout his life his legs remained small, while his upper body grew normally. He always required a cane to support his four-foot, six-inch frame. After these accidents, he was not able to dance or to ride, the usual activities of his social class. During his convalescence, his mother and a family friend, René Princeteau, a deaf-mute artist of equestrian scenes, encouraged him to paint.

Though tentative in technique, his early pictures, *Soldier Saddling His Horse*, *Trotting Horseman*, *Amazon*, and *White Horse Gazelle*, are full of life and quite accomplished. They manifest an unfiltered naïveté and are all the more striking for their deliberate use of bold color combinations.

In 1882, Toulouse-Lautrec became a pupil of Léon-Joseph-Florentin Bonnat and, in 1883-1887, of Fernand Cormon. Both academicists, they taught Toulouse-Lautrec the principles of composition. His work was thenceforth more controlled. A visit home in 1883 produced the somewhat Impressionistic oil *The Artist's Mother at Breakfast*.

In 1885, when he was nearly twenty-one years of age and financially independent, Toulouse-Lautrec opened a studio in Montmartre in the building where Edgar Degas had his studio. Degas became his artistic idol, though in 1894 Degas would harshly accuse Toulouse-Lautrec of imitation. His first lithograph was a song-sheet cover in 1887 for Aristide Bruant, who gave Toulouse-Lautrec his first public showing on the walls of his café, Le Mirliton. Toulouse-Lautrec's pastel portrait of Vincent van Gogh, whom he had met at Cormon's in 1886, belongs to the same year.

In 1887, Toulouse-Lautrec painted *Portrait of the Artist's Mother Reading*. At first it seems Impressionistic, but, in fact, the subject is not treated as the focus of light; thrust in the foreground, her presence dominates the painting. For Toulouse-Lautrec, "Nothing exists but the figure. . . . Landscape is only accessory."

LIFE'S WORK

Toulouse-Lautrec's art is set against the period known as fin de siècle or la belle époque. Toulouse-Lautrec, who saw beauty in the ugly and heroism in the underside of Paris, reflects both terms. He called himself a historian of life, which he viewed without pity, false moralizing, or self-righteousness. His pictures are precious historical documents and rival novels and histories in describing the life and moral outlook of his generation.

Impressionism influenced Toulouse-Lautrec's work, yet he more precisely falls in the French drawing tradition of Jacques-Louis David, Jean August Dominique Ingres, and Degas. He did not use shimmering, all-enveloping light as did the Impressionists. He emphasized line, pattern, and pure, unmodeled color without chiaroscuro, as in Japanese art and the then-current Nabi movement. His colors, as are his subjects, are theatrical and often harsh. In his love of line, he differed from other post-Impressionists, such as van Gogh and Paul Gauguin, who stressed mass and solidity. By a few deft strokes of line, he penetrated his subjects' essential character. Toulouse-Lautrec's gift, as was Degas', was to capture figures from contemporary scenes in characteristic poses at unguarded moments, always with some caricature. As his friends noted, he would passionately pur-

Henri de Toulouse-Lautrec.

sue his subjects in the prime of their careers, then drop them.

In 1888, under the spell of Degas, Toulouse-Lautrec began to illustrate the lowest classes of Paris. Montmartre was its focus since the opening of the café Le Chat Noir in 1881. His first important painting was *Le Cirque Fernando: Circus Rider*, done in the flat style of the Japanese prints he collected. Like Gauguin, whom he had recently met, he preferred a bold distortion of perspective to the Impressionists' sense of light.

By this time, Toulouse-Lautrec drew for the leading illustrated journals, *Courrier Français*, *Paris Illustré*, *Figaro Illustré*, and *Rire*. He did this not for money—Toulouse-Lautrec never needed art to make a living—but for recognition. In 1888, too, Toulouse-Lautrec first submitted work for the annual Brussels exhibition of the avant garde XX (the twenty) group. The next year saw his major oils, *Au bal du Moulin de la Galette* and *The Girl with Red Hair*. The Moulin de la Galette was one of Toulouse-Lautrec's café haunts.

The Moulin Rouge's opening ushered the gay nineties into Paris. This café became the in place for Paris society, including Toulouse-Lautrec and his cousin and companion, Gabriel Tapié de Céleyran. It was the venue of his best-known pieces. His painting *Au Moulin Rouge: La Danse* (1890) graced the foyer of the café. It is his first depiction of the dancer La Goulue (the glutton: the stage name of Louise Weber) and her partner, Valentin le Désossé. In 1891, the Moulin Rouge commissioned Toulouse-Lautrec's first poster to advertise the same dancers. He created a sensation by flaunting La Goulue's scandalous white muslim drawers. The poster both launched her career and gave the artist wider recognition. Désossé dominates the foreground in stark profile, while Toulouse-Lautrec and his friends are silhouetted in back. In the same year, *La Goulue au Moulin Rouge* featured her famous deep décolletage.

Toulouse-Lautrec's thirty-one posters are consciously flat, asymmetrical, and decorative; figures are often cropped at the border. His "line, flair, and daring layout" were immediately praised in the press. Jules Chéret, the greatest poster artist of his day, named Toulouse-Lautrec as his successor. Toulouse-Lautrec's prints were better for his painting skills, but the fluidity and economy of stroke of the lithographic medium added to the descriptive capability of his paintings. He did many identical pictures in both mediums.

Toulouse-Lautrec's friendship with the rising star Jane Avril is marked by numerous representations of her over several years. Avril admired his art and may have been in love with him. *Jane Avril Entering Moulin Rouge*, *Jane Avril Leaving Moulin Rouge*, and *Jane Avril Dancing at Moulin Rouge* appeared in 1892. In the last, Toulouse-Lautrec used oils in a sketchy manner to render the dancer's movements. Avril is absorbed in her dancing, her isolation emphasized by the couple in the background who pay her no attention.

In 1892 came a masterpiece, *Au Moulin Rouge*. In a framework of diagonals appear the artist himself, his cousin Tapié de Céleyran, La Goulue, other friends at the table in the foreground, and the mysterious green-faced lady partially cropped off at the right. In 1892, two posters of Bruant in his familiar black coat and red scarf made the entrepreneur's profile known throughout Paris.

A Corner of the Moulin de la Galette of the same year is a minor masterpiece. Human forms are set in overlap-

ping planes. The isolation of these denizens of the demimonde is established by the fact that no one's gaze engages that of another person.

In 1893, Toulouse-Lautrec's poster *Jane Avril at the Jardin de Paris* again "put her in the limelight," said the journal *Fin de Siècle* on September 3. Another poster, *Jane Avril at Divan Japonais*, announced a new café that opened auspiciously, attracting crowds to hear the songs of Yvette Guilbert, but closed soon after. Avril is in the foreground while Guilbert is shown performing but with her head cropped out of the frame. Toulouse-Lautrec's frequent use of cropping as well as his ability to focus on one area, allowing all else to appear marginal or distorted, reflects his awareness of the new medium of photography, which was then influencing the art world. On the psychological level, too, Toulouse-Lautrec recorded his subjects as a camera, with emotional detachment.

Also in 1893, Toulouse-Lautrec did a painting and poster, *Loie Fuller at the Folies Bergère*, of an American to whom he was briefly attracted for her whirling, serpentine "fire dance." His paintings won the approval of Degas and an invitation to join and exhibit for the Independents, a prestigious society of engravers.

Around 1893, Toulouse-Lautrec's interest turned to faces, especially as highlighted by the gas-flares of theaters, rather than the human form as a whole (now often merely sketched in). In this year, his theater prints for *L'Escarmouche* appeared, as did eleven litho-portraits of Paris show-people for a *Café-Concert* album and a poster for the book *Au pied de l'échafaud* (1893; at the foot of the scaffold), which was the memoir of Abbé Jean-Baptiste Faure, the chaplain to thirty-eight condemned men. The silhouetted spectators behind the condemned man's harshly lit face are reminiscent of the first Moulin Rouge poster.

Already in 1892, Toulouse-Lautrec had painted prostitutes, most notably *Woman with Black Boa*, whose hard smile betrayed a calculating coldness. Two years later, he set up his studio in the newest and finest brothel, remained there for several months, and produced fifty oils and hundreds of drawings. The last and unquestioned masterpiece of this group names the brothel: *The Salon des Moulins*. Early in that year, Toulouse-Lautrec's poster for a new book, *Babylone d'Allemagne*, "papered every wall in Paris," according to *Fin de Siècle* of February 18, 1894.

Toulouse-Lautrec also did lithographs for the *Revue Blanche*. His chief occupation for nine months, however, was the album of sixteen lithographs of Guilbert performing her risqué half-spoken chansons. The album had caused a scandal for its deification of a mere café diva. Critics called Guilbert the ugly made uglier. She herself complained at Toulouse-Lautrec's unflattering caricatures of her red hair, uptilted nose, and thin lips but still autographed the hundred copies. In addition, a charcoal and an oil of Guilbert displayed her odd, angular appearance and her trademarks: a low-cut gown and long black gloves.

In London in 1895, Toulouse-Lautrec sketched Oscar Wilde at his celebrated trial. In Paris, his large (five-foot square) oil entitled *Marcelle Lender Dancing the Boléro in "Chilperic"* and several drawings of her back reveal his then current female interest. An album, *Thirty Lithographs*, contained bust-only studies of Jeanne Granier, Lucien Guitry, Jeanne Hading, Sarah Bernhardt, and other stars of the stage. In this same year came his oil of *La Clownesse, Cha-U-Kao*, whose name derives from *chahut-chaos*, a wild dance popular at the Moulin Rouge; *La Danse de La Goulue*; and a portrait of cabaret singer May Belfort. The girl in *La Toilette* (1896) may have belonged to the dancers at Les Moulins. Herein Toulouse-Lautrec returned to a more modeled style. Important works in this year include an oil and a poster *Mademoiselle Eglantine's Troupe* dancing the can-can. Eleven prints of life in the brothels appeared in the women's journal *Elles*. Toulouse-Lautrec showed that these girls, portrayed conversing with clients and serving them chamomile tea, were not uniformly lewd but had "exquisite feelings unknown to virtuous women."

An exhibition of lithographs at Maurice Joyant's Paris gallery first engendered a still-prevalent pejorative interpretation of Toulouse-Lautrec's life and art. The critic A. Hepp wrote, "The odd, deformed and limping man was evident in the works." Edmond Goncourt added, "All his drawings seem to reflect his own caricature-like deformity."

Certainly, Toulouse-Lautrec's deformity affected his outlook. An alternative view, however, recognizes that Honoré Daumier, Édouard Manet, Degas, and others had already established the lower classes as a subject of art. Thus, though Toulouse-Lautrec often joked about his appearance, was sensitive to others' comments, and felt less exceptional in the rough society that he portrayed, he was not morbidly alone in drawing on that society for his work. Rather, he was accepted in that company for his coarse wit and generosity as a congenial, nonthreatening presence.

Toulouse-Lautrec's drawings of lesbians in 1897 raised the forbidden to the level of art by their compassionate detachment. He was drinking heavily and reached a nadir early in 1899. On March 17, an alcoholic and suffering from venereal disease, he entered St. James Clinic at Neuilly-sur-Seine, on the outskirts of Paris, where he remained until May 20. While in the clinic, he nevertheless contributed twenty-two animal prints to the *Histoires Naturelles* of his friend Jules Renard and did a series of circus scenes from memory. After his release he recuperated by the sea, traveled, and painted *The Englishwoman at the "Star," Le Havre* in 1899. There then followed (1899-1901) a series of lithographs on the world of the racetracks, of which the best known is *The Jockey*, in color. He painted *La Modiste* in 1900.

After seven months with his mother at Malromé in 1900, he returned to Paris in 1901. His last painting is the unfinished *Examination Board*, in which the figures are not outlined but solidly modeled. The examinee is his cousin Tapié de Céleyran. His last months were spent at Malromé, where he died in September, 1901.

SIGNIFICANCE

Henri de Toulouse-Lautrec was a post-Impressionist who, in altering what he saw in order to increase its impact on the observer, presaged the more subjective twentieth century German expressionism. His influence can be seen in the work of Edvard Munch, Pablo Picasso, and Henri Matisse. Amid the emergence of new movements in art such as pointillism, symbolism, and primitivism, he ascribed to no school. His most original achievements were in color lithography and poster art. Toulouse-Lautrec preeminently lived the French writers' slogan, that an artist must be of his time.

—*Daniel C. Scavone*

FURTHER READING

Canaday, John. *Mainstreams of Modern Art*. 2d ed. New York: Holt, Rinehart and Winston, 1981. Chapter 22 contains a brilliant appreciation of Toulouse-Lautrec, placing him in the larger context of fin de siècle art.

Cooper, Douglas. *Henri de Toulouse-Lautrec*. New York: Harry N. Abrams, 1952. A short biography. Includes twenty-six illustrations, ten in color; available in most museum shops.

Fermigier, André. *Toulouse-Lautrec*. Translated by Paul Stevenson. New York: Frederick A. Praeger, 1969. The best and most accessible biography; includes more than two hundred illustrations.

Frey, Julia. *Toulouse-Lautrec: A Life*. New York: Viking Press, 1994. Readable and comprehensive chronicle of Toulouse-Lautrec's life. Frey attributes Toulouse-Lautrec's self-destructiveness to family conflict and his despair over his dwarfism. Includes eighty-four photographs and fifty color plates of the artist's work.

Thompson, Richard, Philip Dennis Cate, and Mary Weaver Chapin. *Toulouse-Lautrec and Montmartre.* Princeton, N.J.: Princeton University Press, 2005. Catalog of an art exhibit presented at the National Gallery of Art and the Art Institute of Chicago in 2005. The exhibit, and catalog, focus on Toulouse-Lautrec's portrayal of Montmartre, placing his posters, drawings, and paintings within the context of the area's art scene and nightlife between 1885 and 1901. The book includes 370 color plates, reproducing works by Toulouse-Lautrec, and by Picasso, van Gogh, Degas, and other artists whom Toulouse-Lautrec influenced.

Toulouse-Lautrec, Henri de. *The Posters of Toulouse-Lautrec.* Edited with an introduction by Edouard Julien. Boston: Boston Book and Art Shop, 1966. A short text, but fine color copies of all thirty-one posters.

_____. *Toulouse-Lautrec.* Text by John Nash. New York: Funk & Wagnalls, 1978. A volume in the Great Artists series, this concise biography rebuts the theory that Toulouse-Lautrec's deformity embittered his life and influenced his choice of subjects. Sixteen color illustrations with excellent commentaries.

_____. *Toulouse-Lautrec: His Complete Lithographs and Dry Points.* Edited by Jean Adhémar. New York: Harry N. Abrams, 1965. A thorough biography emphasizing his lithography and posters. Complete in its reproduction of 350 lithographs.

SEE ALSO: Sarah Bernhardt; Jacques-Louis David; Edgar Degas; Paul Gauguin; Vincent van Gogh; Hiroshige; Édouard Manet; Oscar Wilde.

RELATED ARTICLES in *Great Events from History: The Nineteenth Century, 1801-1900:* April 15, 1874: First Impressionist Exhibition; Late 1870's: Post-Impressionist Movement Begins; 1892-1895: Toulouse-Lautrec Paints *At the Moulin Rouge.*

CATHARINE PARR TRAILL
English-born Canadian writer and naturalist

One of several nineteenth century Canadian women who published influential works on their adopted homeland, Traill wrote popular books about adjusting to frontier life and Canadian natural history that helped to attract immigrants to the colony. She also described the traditions of indigenous peoples and the medicinal qualities of wild plants, while painting clear pictures of the rigors of life in the backwoods.

BORN: January 9, 1802; London, England
DIED: August 28, 1899; Lakefield, Ontario, Canada
ALSO KNOWN AS: Catharine Parr Strickland (birth name); Catherine Parr Traill
AREAS OF ACHIEVEMENT: Literature, biology

EARLY LIFE
Catharine Parr Traill was born Catharine Parr Strickland, the daughter of Thomas Strickland, a prosperous English businessperson who invested in property and industry, and his wife, Elizabeth Strickland. She was named after Henry VIII's sixth wife, Catherine Parr, with whom the family claimed an ancestral tie. Catharine was born in London but spent most of her childhood in rural Suffolk, on the east coast of England.

Of the family's six daughters, four—including Catharine—would eventually become published authors. Like other bright women of eighteenth and early nineteenth century Great Britain, such as Elizabeth Carter and Joanna Baillie, Catharine and her sisters were educated through their father's library, in which they read the works of John Locke, John Milton, and William Shakespeare, while their two brothers were sent to the Norwich Grammar School. When their parents left home to visit the boys, the sisters often amused themselves by staging scenes from Shakespearean plays. *Hamlet*'s Ophelia and *The Tempest*'s Ariel were among Catharine's favorite roles. She was a gentle and whimsical child who mediated among family members when quarrels arose.

Catharine's interest in botany and natural history was sparked by her belief that divine agency could be seen in the works of creation. Her father encouraged her to develop a skill in carefully observing and classifying natural objects. Each of the Strickland girls was given a small garden of her own to tend, and the girls roamed the Suffolk countryside searching for shells, amber, and wildflowers. Even as a child, Catharine spent hours collecting, pressing, mounting, and labeling her finds. Thomas

Strickland ensured that his daughters knew the scientific name of each plant they found. It was a great blow to the family when he died unexpectedly in 1818. Catharine was only sixteen years old at the time.

LIFE'S WORK

Thomas Strickland's death led to the beginning of Catharine's publishing career. When the family guardian, a man named Morgan, discovered some of Catharine's short stories, he submitted them to a publisher at St. Paul's Churchyard, London. The stories were immediately published as *The Tell Tale: An Original Collection of Moral and Amusing Stories* (1818).

Catharine and her sisters realized they could support their family through their writing, but their early publications helped sustain their own basic needs at Reydon Hall, their family home, and paid their brothers' educational fees. During the 1820's, Catharine and her sister Susanna became involved with the British abolitionist movement through their contact with Methodist and Quaker fellowships. Catharine published *Prejudice Re-*

proved: Or, The History of a Negro Toy-Seller in 1826. Susanna transcribed a slave narrative titled *The History of Mary Prince* (1831). Catharine and Susanna's early work is didactic, framed to provide readers with messages regarding personal or social ethics. Catharine published approximately eleven books in the period between 1818 and her marriage in 1832.

Catharine is best known for the guidebooks she published after she married Thomas Traill and moved to Upper Canada in 1832. Her Canadian titles include *The Backwoods of Canada* (1836), *Canadian Crusoes: A Tale of the Rice Lake Plains* (1852), *The Female Emigrant's Guide* (1854), *Canadian Wildflowers* (1868), *Studies of Plant Life in Canada: Or, Gleaning from Forest, Lake and Plain* (1885), *Pearls and Pebbles: Or, Notes of an Old Naturalist* (1894), and *Cot and Cradle Stories* (1895). As the titles of her books testify, she fell deeply in love with the Canadian people and landscape. She was set on making the best of the grueling life in the backwoods, but her sister Susanna Strickland Moodie, who also moved to Upper Canada with her husband, wrote with a different sensibility. Susanna's *Roughing It in the Bush: Or, Life in Canada* (1852) is written in a wry and satirical manner that is absent from Catharine's sincere mixture of friendly advice and natural history.

In *The Backwoods of Canada*, Catharine depicts the Chippewa people empathetically and the wildlife carefully. Catharine writes:

> I can yet make myself very happy and contented in this country. If its volume of history is as yet blank, that of Nature is open, and eloquently marked by the finger of God; and from its pages I can easily extract a thousand sources of amusement.

The influence of poet William Wordsworth is clearly evident in Catharine's prose. She adhered to Wordsworth's emphasis on the function of God's creation as a book of moral instruction. Her careful descriptions of trees—from maples to pines—and animals—from beavers to black-

---

BLACKBIRDS

This passage from The Backwoods of Canada *illustrates Catharine Parr Traill's ability to blend poetic imagery with scientific detail.*

The blackbird is perhaps our best songster, according to my taste; full as fine as our English blackbird, and much handsomer in its plumage, which is a glossy, changeable, greenish black. The upper part of the wing of the male bird of full growth is of a lively orange; this is not apparent in the younger birds, nor in the female, which is slightly speckled.

Towards the middle of the summer, when the grain begins to ripen, these birds assemble in large flocks: the management of their marauding parties appears to be superintended by the elders of the family. When they are about to descend upon a field of oats or wheat, two or three mount guard as sentinels, and on the approach of danger, cry *Geck-geck-geck*; this precaution seems a work of supererogation, as they are so saucy that they will hardly be frightened away; and if they rise it is only to alight on the same field at a little distance, or fly up to the trees, where their look-out posts are.

They have a peculiarly melancholy call-note at times, which sounds exactly like the sudden twang of a harp-string, vibrating for a second or two on the ear. This, I am inclined to think, they use to collect their distant comrades, as I have never observed it when they were all in full assembly, but when a few were sitting in some tree near the lake's edge. I have called them the *"harpers"* from this peculiar note. . . .

Source: Catharine Parr Traill, *The Backwoods of Canada: Being Letters from the Wife of an Emigrant Officer, Illustrative of the Domestic Economy of British America* (London: C. Knight, 1836), Letter 13.

---

birds—surpass those of Wordsworth in their documentary detail and blend poetic imagery with an almost scientific exactitude.

Catharine found solace in continuing to write accounts of her natural surroundings during years through which she and her husband suffered financial hardship. Thomas was a melancholic man not suited to the rigors of farming. He originally received a plot of free farmland because of his position as a military officer, but he and Catharine sold that land in 1839 and would move five times before Thomas's death in 1859. These were difficult years for Catharine. She lost two babies, and her remaining children were often sick. Nevertheless, nine of her eleven children survived into adulthood. After she was widowed, she moved back to the countryside north of Peterborough and lived with her oldest daughter, Katherine.

During her later years, Catharine acquired a public reputation as an expert on Canadian botany. This reputation was bolstered by her publication of *Canadian Wildflowers* in 1868. The book consisted of hand-painted lithographs by her niece Agnes Fitzgibbon, Susanna Moodie's daughter, and botanical descriptions by Catharine. Catharine continued to write for publication into her ninety-eighth year. She died in her sleep on August 28, 1899.

SIGNIFICANCE

Catharine Parr Traill is often remembered as the older sister of Susanna Moodie. However, interest has been growing in Catharine's unique contributions to early Canadian literary life, which were as significant as her sister's. Indeed, Catharine published more prolifically than Susanna. Catharine is now praised for her intimate knowledge of Canada's northern landscape, wildlife, and indigenous peoples, recorded in her published accounts of settler life. She was the first person to identify and name many Canadian wildflowers and plants, and her catalogs of pressed plants and flowers are currently held in the Museum of Nature in Ottawa, Ontario. She also documented the traditions of the Chippewa people, including their clothing, songs, and use of native plants for healing the sick.

During Traill's lifetime, her publications gained her invitations to meet two governors-general of Canada. She also formed friendships with influential scientists such as Sanford Fleming. In recognition of her role as a gifted early Canadian writer, Trent University in Peterborough, Ontario, named its Traill College after her.

—*Natasha Duquette*

FURTHER READING

Ballstadt, Carl, Elizabeth Hopkins, and Michael Peterman, eds. *I Bless You in My Heart: Selected Correspondence of Catharine Parr Traill*. Toronto: University of Toronto Press, 1996. The letters are grouped into three periods of approximately thirty years each, beginning in 1830 and ending in 1899. Each section is prefaced with a short introduction. A useful chronology of Traill's life appears at the front of the book.

Eaton, Sara. *Lady of the Backwoods: A Biography of Catharine Parr Traill*. Toronto: McClelland and Stewart, 1969. This short and entertaining biography is written in an anecdotal style. It is deceptively simple in form but contains many fascinating details.

Fowler, Marian. *The Embroidered Tent: Five Gentlewomen in Early Canada: Elizabeth Simcoe, Catharine Parr Traill, Susanna Moodie, Anna Jameson, Lady Dufferin*. Toronto: House of Anansi Press, 1982. In this critical biography Fowler sets Traill among her contemporaries. Fowler's argument is that women's experiences of settler life caused them to negotiate between the feminine propriety of household crafts and the masculine rigor of backwoods survival.

Gray, Charlotte. *Sisters in the Wilderness: The Lives of Susanna Moodie and Catharine Parr Traill*. Toronto: Penguin Books, 1999. This is an excellent overview of the life of Catharine set in relation to that of her sister Susanna. The text is complemented with maps of Suffolk and of the Canadian backcountry, as well as miniatures of Thomas Traill, Catharine and Susanna, and a photograph of Catharine's lifelong friend Frances Stewart.

Traill, Catharine Parr. *The Backwoods of Canada*. Edited by Michael Peterman. Ottawa: Carleton University Press, 1997. This is the work for which Traill is best known, and it is often compared to her sister Susanna's *Roughing It in the Bush*. In his new edition, Peterman includes a nineteenth century map of Upper Canada and the title page from the second issue of the book's first edition. Three letters written by Catharine appear as appendixes. Electronic texts of the original edition of *The Backwoods of Canada* and several other books by Traill are freely available on Project Gutenberg at www.gutenberg.org.

SEE ALSO: Anna Jameson; Susanna Moodie; Thomas Talbot; David Thompson; William Wordsworth.
RELATED ARTICLE in *Great Events from History: The Nineteenth Century, 1801-1900:* February 10, 1841: Upper and Lower Canada Unite.

RICHARD TREVITHICK
English engineer

Trevithick developed the high-pressure steam engine, whose invention lies not merely in its efficiency but in the fact that it made steam engines applicable for many uses. He is remembered as the founder of the locomotive engine, as his engines were used for road and rail locomotives, for powering dredgers and steamships, and in agricultural threshing machines.

BORN: April 13, 1771; Illogan, Cornwall, England
DIED: April 22, 1833; Dartford, Kent, England
AREA OF ACHIEVEMENT: Engineering

EARLY LIFE

Richard Trevithick (TREHV-ih-thihk) was born in Cornwall, one of the most remote parts of England, more than 250 miles from London. The Cornish were a fiercely independent group, unrelated racially to the English, and with a language of their own similar to Gaelic, Welsh, and Breton. Although that language had gone out of general use about one hundred years before Trevithick's birth, there remained heavy remnants of Cornish in the everyday language of the miners among whom he grew up. The countryside of west Cornwall around his birthplace of Illogan is wild and poor. During the 1770's, there were only two occupations that could sustain a family—fishing and mining—a harsh factor that is immortalized in the county's coat of arms. Until 1870, Cornwall was the world's greatest source of copper and tin but subject to frequent periods of boom and depression.

Richard Trevithick was the only son of Richard Trevithick, manager of several mines until his death in 1797. The elder Trevithick was a friend of the preacher John Wesley and himself became a Methodist class leader. The young Trevithick did not enjoy his encounter with formal education at Camborne School. He often played the truant. He was, however, an impressive athlete. At six feet, two inches tall, with prodigious strength, he became one of the most powerful Cornish wrestlers of his day, and stories abound concerning his lifting strength.

In addition, after Trevithick grew up listening to his father, who was a noted pumping engineer; to William Murdock, James Watt's chief assistant and a resident at Redruth from 1780 to 1799; and to William Bull, the leading exponent of a rival Cornish school of engineers, he developed an inventive genius. As early as 1795, the young Cornishman received payments for improvements he made in steam-engine fuel consumption. By

1797, he was engineer at Ding Dong mine near Penzance. During that same year, Trevithick married Jane Harvey, the daughter of John Harvey, who was the owner of the famous Hayle foundry.

Trevithick was in many respects a most impressive man. With his broad shoulders, great height, massive head, and bright blue eyes, he was imposing indeed. In his ideas and projects, he was courageous and ingenious. By all accounts, he could be fierce but was also tenderhearted, impetuous but too easily discouraged. He constantly worked facing a shortage of capital. Trevithick was essentially an experimenter, not a businessperson, and for this he was to pay dearly.

LIFE'S WORK

Cornish mines were often old and very deep. From the early part of the eighteenth century, steam engines were used to pump out the water collecting in the bottom of the shafts. The old Newcomen engines were modified by Cornish engineers, but the appearance, in 1777, of the new engine developed by Matthew Boulton and James Watt soon made the Cornish among the firm's first and best customers. There were, however, two problems. The first was that the Watt engine was under patent, which made its purchase expensive. The second was that to power the engine, one needed coal. Cornwall had no coal deposits and thus had to import, again at great expense. By 1800, Cornish engineers were engaged in a bitter fight with Boulton and Watt, evading patent rights with minor improvements and trying to come up with an alternative, more efficient engine of their own.

In this, Trevithick succeeded. He invented a high-pressure steam engine that could pump water at a level of forty to fifty pounds per square inch, in contrast to the five to ten pounds of the Watt engine, and that he later developed to work at 145 pounds per square inch. Naturally, Watt disliked this rival, more efficient development and tried all he could to get a law passed in Parliament banning Trevithick's engine as a danger to the public. In addition to this large engine for pumping water from the mines, Trevithick, in the same year, designed and built a small steam-winding engine for the Wheal Hope mine to power the transit of miners between surface and mine galleries and to raise ore and refuse. It was known as the "Puffer Whim," after the noise it made. It was this engine, the first human-made compact and portable source of power, that Trevithick patented in

1802 and that formed the basis of his efforts in road and rail locomotion. By 1804, Trevithick had made and sold fifty such engines.

As early as 1796 and 1798, Trevithick had made models of a steam locomotive. After his invention of the Puffer Whim, he set about designing and building a steam carriage for road use. On Christmas Eve, 1801, at Beacon Hill near Camborne, the first road test was carried out. Trevithick's steam carriage carried several passengers up the hill at four miles per hour and sped along at eight to nine miles per hour along the flat. It was Great Britain's earliest self-propelled road vehicle.

During the following month, January, 1802, Trevithick and his cousin Andrew Vivian, who supplied the money, set off for London to exhibit the machine and to solicit interest. Trevithick was interviewed by the president of the Royal Society and the famous scientist Sir Humphry Davy, both Cornishmen, and at least two trips of several miles each were undertaken by the steam carriage around suburban London in heavy traffic. The results were mixed. On the second trip, a pothole momentarily wrested control of the vehicle from its inexperienced driver, and it plowed into a wall. Trevithick suddenly canceled the public exhibitions, upset by the lack of publicity and, no doubt, discouraged by the fact that the roads of Great Britain were so bad that general adoption of his vehicle was impractical.

Not completely daunted, Trevithick took a job at the Pen-y-darran ironworks in South Wales. There, in 1803, he invented a rail locomotive. It later pulled ten tons of iron, seventy men, and five wagons at five miles per hour for nine and a half miles. However, misfortune again prevented Trevithick's triumph from achieving national recognition. The locomotive and its load proved to be too heavy for the tramway. Many of the tramplates broke under the strain, as did several of the hooks linking the wagons. After a few runs, the owners, not wanting the expense of replacing the track, converted the locomotive into a stationary pump. In 1805, Trevithick applied his engine for use in a dredger in the Thames estuary. By 1808, he designed a lighter, simpler locomotive, the "Catch-Me-Who-Can," which ran on an oval track near the site of Euston Square in north London. Passengers rode for one shilling each. Once again, bad luck dogged him, and, after a rail broke and the locomotive left the track, the venture, which had never been a financial success, was aborted.

The next year, 1809, Trevithick was consulted on the practicality of a tunnel under the Thames. His experimental driftway was three-quarters complete when he seems to have tunneled too near the riverbed. The passage was flooded and his efforts abandoned.

In 1811, Trevithick went bankrupt. The same year saw him collaborate with the London engineer Matthew Murray on a high-pressure steam engine and boiler for *L'Actif*, a captured French privateer that was being outfitted as a packet boat. The engine was later used on the *Courier*, which made one of the first sea voyages by steam along the English coast. The following year, 1812, Trevithick turned his attention to agriculture. He experimented with a steam plow and constructed a powered threshing machine that proved an unqualified success but was not adopted. In the same year, he developed a cylindrical boiler that was widely used as a steam-supplier for stationary engines until 1844.

By 1814, Trevithick became absorbed with a plan to engineer the famous mines of Peru on Cornish principles. Nine of his engines were shipped out to Lima with several of his associates as engineers. It was a complete success, and in 1816, Trevithick himself gave up all of his prospects in England and set sail. He arrived in Lima in early 1817 and was received royally. After he surmounted countless difficulties and had made and lost several fortunes, Peru's war of independence broke out. His machines were destroyed, and he was pressed into the army. He invented a new gun. Forced by all the upheavals to leave Peru, Trevithick reached Cartagena on the Isthmus of Panama after several mishaps, nearly drowning, nearly starving, having done some prospecting in Costa Rica, and having lost everything. There, in 1827, he chanced to meet Robert Stephenson, the young railway engineer who was returning home from the mines of Colombia to help his father, George, save his business. Stephenson lent Trevithick fifty pounds to get home. They were shipwrecked before they reached New York.

Back in England, Trevithick lived the remainder of his life in poverty, constantly inventing. His last patent, for the use of superheated steam, was granted in 1832. The previous year, he had been invited to speak before a parliamentary committee that was investigating the use of steam vehicles on roads. He made a sad picture. As the historian of early British motorcars wrote:

> One gets the feeling that Trevithick, old, ill, *passé*, and concerned mainly with talking about his latest steam engine design, was trundled in as a polite gesture to an ancient and revered national monument, who could hardly be ignored on such an occasion—certainly he was little questioned.

Trevithick died a pauper in Dartford, Kent. No stone marks his grave. He was outlived by his wife and six children. Two of his sons themselves became notable engineers.

SIGNIFICANCE

Richard Trevithick's life was dogged by misfortune and his lack of commercial incentive. He was much more concerned with finding new and better ways to apply his inventions than with developing a business around them. He constantly ran out of money and, mainly for that reason, the value of his inventions was often not widely known or appreciated.

It was often several years after his inventions were made that they were taken up by others who were accorded the credit. The Cornish Engine, which gained a worldwide reputation in the nineteenth century, was developed from Trevithick's high-pressure steam engine of 1800 and his cylindrical boiler of 1812. His work on a road locomotive was rediscovered during the 1820's and 1830's by several engineers. The rail locomotive he built in 1804 at Pen-y-darran was reproduced by his assistant, John Steele, the following year at Wylam Colliery near Newcastle and served as a basis for George Stephenson's experiments a decade and more later.

Later in the nineteenth century, Trevithick was acclaimed "the real inventor of the locomotive" and "one of the greatest mechanical benefactors of our country." In 1888, a memorial window to Trevithick was erected in Westminster Abbey, a Trevithick medal was enacted by the Institution of Civil Engineers, and an engineering scholarship was endowed in his name at Manchester. Trevithick, the wayward inventor, still suffers from lack of recognition when compared with Watt or the Stephensons. In inventive genius, he was every bit their equal.

—*Stephen Burwood*

FURTHER READING

Burton, Anthony. *Richard Trevithick: The Man and His Machine*. London: Aurum Press, 2000. Popular biography, placing Trevithick within the context of Cornwall's history and economy, explaining how the area's mining industry spurred development of the steam engine.

Dickenson, H., and A. Titley. *Richard Trevithick: The Engineer and the Man*. Cambridge, England: Cambridge University Press, 1934. A good account of the man and his importance in the history of engineering. Sober, but sometimes overly critical of the man's personal faults. An excellent starting place.

Landes, David S. *The Unbound Prometheus: Technological Change and Industrial Development in Western Europe from 1750 to the Present*. Cambridge, England: Cambridge University Press, 1969. Widely regarded as a classic explanation of how and why Europe industrialized.

Mantoux, Paul. *The Industrial Revolution in the Eighteenth Century*. Rev. ed. Chicago: University of Chicago Press, 1983. A brilliant, clearly written, comprehensive account by a famous French historian, it provides the background necessary to understanding why England was the first country to witness an industrial revolution.

Nicholson, T. R. *The Birth of the British Motor Car, 1769-1897*. 3 vols. London: Macmillan, 1982. Contains much material on Trevithick either missing elsewhere or lightly passed over. Very useful for a sense of the scope of Trevithick's genius.

Pike, Fredrick B. *The Modern History of Peru*. New York: Praeger, 1967. Chapters 2 and 3 explain the troubled times in which Trevithick chose to work in Peru, providing a good description of the intricacies of revolutionary upheaval.

Ransom, P. J. G. *Locomotion: Two Centuries of Train Travel*. Stroud, Gloucestershire, England: Sutton, 2001. Ransom begins this railroad history with Trevithick's invention of the Pen-y-darran locomotive.

Rolt, R. T. C. *Victorian Engineering*. London: Allen Lane, 1970. Excellent in establishing the place in engineering history held by Cornwall, the bitter rivalry that developed between the Cornish engineers and the Boulton and Watt Company, and Trevithick's most influential role in the development of steam engines.

Ross, David. *The Willing Servant: A History of the Steam Engine*. Stroud, Gloucestershire, England: Tempus, 2004. A history of the steam engine and its impact on society. Ross begins his chronicle with Trevithick's invention of the first steam engine during the early nineteenth century.

Smiles, Samuel. *The Locomotive: George and Robert Stephenson*. Vol. 5 in *Lives of the Engineers*. London: John Murray, 1879. By the famous author of *Self-Help* (1859), the book contains much valuable information on the early attempts at road locomotives, including much of interest on Trevithick, including his penniless meeting with Robert Stephenson in a Central American seaport in 1827 and their subsequent shipwreck.

Turner, R., and S. L. Goulden. *Great Engineers and Pioneers in Technology*. Vol. 1. New York: St. Martin's

Press, 1981. Although the biographical entry devoted to Trevithick is necessarily short, a perusal of those of his contemporaries and of the next generation of engineers reveals the man's outstanding importance.

SEE ALSO: Isambard Kingdom Brunel; Sir Humphry Davy; George Stephenson; George Westinghouse.

RELATED ARTICLES in *Great Events from History: The Nineteenth Century, 1801-1900:* March 24, 1802: Trevithick Patents the High-Pressure Steam Engine; May 22-June 20, 1819: *Savannah* Is the First Steamship to Cross the Atlantic; January 31, 1858: Brunel Launches the SS *Great Eastern.*

FLORA TRISTAN
French writer and social reformer

During a life cut short by a murderous former husband, Tristan championed the causes of women's and workers' rights by documenting social conditions in Europe and Peru and calling for the international organization of labor.

BORN: April 7, 1803; Paris, France
DIED: November 14, 1844; Bordeaux, France
ALSO KNOWN AS: Flore-Célestine-Thérèse-Henriette Tristan y Moscozo (birth name)
AREAS OF ACHIEVEMENT: Women's rights, literature

EARLY LIFE

The circumstances of the birth of Flora Tristan (floor-ah tris-tuhn) to a large extent shaped her life. Her parents, a Peruvian-born Spanish nobleman named Don Mariano de Tristan y Moscozo and a French woman named Anne-Pierre Laisnay, met in Spain, where her father was serving in the Spanish army. They were married by a Roman Catholic priest but never registered their union with the civil authorities, as then required by law in Spain. Thus, while their marriage was sanctified by the church, it was legally irregular, if not illegitimate. The marital status of Flora's parents would affect the circumstances of the births and future prospects of her and her siblings.

Flora spent her years in Paris, where the future South American liberator Simón Bolívar was a frequent guest in her family's home. The sudden death of her father in 1807 changed the family's circumstances drastically. Because of the legal irregularity of his marriage, his wealthy Peruvian family refused to recognize his widow or children, including a son born posthumously, as the rightful heirs to his fortune. Flora's mother and siblings were forced to make their way outside Paris, and it is doubtful the young Flora received a full education. Sometime during her adolescence, she and her mother returned to Paris, where Flora became a lithographic

colorist in the workshop of André Chazal. Flora soon married her employer. She later claimed that she had been forced into the marriage by her mother.

Flora and her husband had two sons and a daughter in rapid succession, but their marriage was anything but happy. They were prone to violent arguments and frequent separations, during which Flora fled from her husband to her mother's home, even while pregnant with her third child. In 1832, she was granted a legal separation from her husband.

LIFE'S WORK

As a wife estranged from her husband at a time when divorce was prohibited, Flora had no clear place in patriarchal society but still had to make her way on her own. In 1833, she embarked on a journey to Peru in an effort to lay claim to her paternal inheritance. Her hopes of finding her rightful place were dashed, however. Her Uncle Pio, the titular head of her father's family, welcomed her with open arms as his brother's daughter but refused to acknowledge her as a legitimate heir.

Flora later recounted the details of her travels in her best-known literary work, *Pérégrinations d'une paria* (*Peregrinations of a Pariah*, 1986), an autobiographical work first published in French in 1838. She used the book to take her status as an unmarried outcast and forge it into a new and unconventional identity, deploying the term "pariah" as an affirmation of her difference and independence. Meanwhile, her detailed descriptions of people she encountered and their living conditions became the hallmark of her writing style, often characterized as sociological and ethnographic.

Flora's return to France in 1834 marked the beginning of her careers as a journalist and later as a professional writer, as well as a social critic and reformer. Thanks to the small allowance she had gleaned from her Peruvian family and her own earnings, she was now able to sup-

---

TRISTAN'S MAJOR WORKS

1835 *Nécessité de faire bon accueil aux femmes étrangeres* (on the need to provide hospitality for women travelers)

1838 *Pérégrinations d'une paria* (*Peregrinations of a Pariah*, 1986)

1838 *Méphis, ou le prolétaire* (Mephis, or the proletarian)

1840 *Promenades dans Londres* (*Flora Tristan's London Journal*, 1980)

1843 *L'Union ouvrière* (*The Worker's Union*, 1983)

1973 *Le Tour de France: État actuel de la classe ouvrière sous l'aspect moral, intellectuel, et matériel* (*Flora Tristan's Diary, 1843-1844*, 2002)

---

port herself, and she produced two polemic works during the period directly following her journey to Peru. In 1835, she published a pamphlet, *Nécessité de faire bon accueil aux femmes étrangères* (on the need to provide hospitality for women travelers), in which she underscored the need for societies to welcome women from other countries by establishing programs to help them integrate into their new surroundings.

Meanwhile, Tristan was being harassed by Chazal, but he eventually permitted her to take custody of their youngest child, their daughter Aline. In 1837, Flora sent a letter petitioning the French Chamber of Deputies to reinstitute divorce in France. Her early polemical works set the stage for an increasing social activism on her part, and they reflect her experience of the special burdens placed on women and children in societies that kept unyielding laws and social conventions.

Publication of Flora's *Pérégrinations* in 1838 brought her instant celebrity, but at significant cost. Enraged at her accusations against him, her estranged husband confronted her on a public street near her home in Paris and shot her. The bullets from Chazal's pistol narrowly missed Flora's heart and lodged in her chest. Chazal was charged with attempted murder, and a sensational trial ensued. Chazal was sentenced to twenty years at hard labor, and soon thereafter Flora won the right to use her patronym, Tristan, as her legal name. However, she would suffer physically until her premature death from her bullet wounds. In the aftermath of the scandal, her uncle in Peru was so angered by her depiction of the Tristan family in her book that he cut off all financial support to her. It was only after Flora's death that her daughter Aline Gauguin, along with her young son, the future painter Paul Gauguin, would find a family welcome in Peru.

Méphis, or le prolétaire (1838; Mephis, or the proletarian), the melodramatic fiction that Tristan wrote during her convalescence, was met with harsh criticism, in large part because its protagonist, an artist turned social activist, was a thinly disguised vehicle for Tristan's own criticism of the class system and the Roman Catholic clergy. As a work of fiction, *Méphis* lacks structure and verisimilitude, but it does reveal the writer's preoccupation with many forms of injustice.

In 1840, Tristan returned to her most successful genre with *Promenades dans Londres* (*Flora Tristan's London Journal*, 1980), a work in which she documented various aspects of British society. Her work on England was more systematic than her work on Peru, because the express purpose of her travels was research. Her topics included women's education, the living conditions of the Irish in London slums, conditions in urban factories and the mental asylum at Bedlam, and the British parliament.

Tristan next turned to her native France and produced *L'Union ouvrière* (*The Worker's Union*, 1983), a manifesto issuing the first call for the organization of labor both nationally and internationally. Her agenda included the foundation of an association uniting all of the laboring classes, workers and artisans alike; a fund for the union's programs; and the establishment of centers for the education of children and care of the aged. Tristan also dedicated an entire chapter of the book to working-class women, addressing them on the realities of their lives.

Because some of her ideas resembled those of utopian socialists who preceded and influenced her, Tristan is often categorized among them. However, she herself focused on the *practical* implementation of her ideas during her own lifetime at the national, rather than local, level. She set out on a journey through France, following the traditional journeyman's practice of traveling throughout the country before earning the rank of master tradesman. She went from industrial city to industrial city, attempting to enlist workers in her union and to garner support from all quarters, including municipal officials and clergymen, and even business owners. She also made it a point to speak with women from the working classes wherever she went.

Tristan found a number of patrons for her workers union among France's literati, but workers often proved less open to her project and remained entrenched in older artisan movements. Even when working-class leaders recognized the value of organizing labor, they were skeptical of Tristan's ability to accomplish real reform.

As Tristan traveled—often while sick, exhausted, and discouraged—she was frequently harassed by police suspicious of her project. Her notes and journal entries from this period became the posthumously published book *Le Tour de France* (1973), a rich portrait of life in urban France during the nineteenth century. Ill and exhausted, Tristan finally succumbed to typhoid fever in Bordeaux on November 14, 1844. She never completed her "tour de France."

SIGNIFICANCE

Flora Tristan's posthumously published journal, *Le Tour de France*, was not a polished volume, but rather the raw material intended for a future study. It included not only detailed observations but also harsh judgments formed on the spur of the moment, as well as commentaries on Tristan's own state of mind, be it exultant or disheartened. Tristan's journal is also colored by her use of religious metaphors, which she used to characterize her mission as messianic, while comparing herself to a Christ figure. The journal lacks the objective tone of previous works, such as *Pérégrinations* and *Promenades dans Londres*, but offers powerful testimony about the condition of the French working classes.

Tristan was among the first French women openly to protest against the status of women under the early nineteenth century Napoleonic Code. She documented Peruvian, British, and French society; called for reforms to better the lives of women and workers; and was the first French socialist to propose a workable plan for the organization of French labor.

—*Mary Rice-DeFosse*

FURTHER READING

Cross, Máire Fedelma. *The Letter in Flora Tristan's Politics, 1835-1844*. New York: Palgrave Macmillan, 2004. Explores Tristan's politics through her dialogue with contemporaries in her correspondence.

Cross, Máire, and Tim Gary. *The Feminism of Flora Tristan*. Providence, R.I.: Berg, 1992. Traces the development of Tristan's feminist thought.

Grogan, Susan. *Flora Tristan: Life Stories*. London: Routledge, 1998. A study of the author's self-representation in a variety of roles related to her social context.

Strumingher, Laura. *The Odyssey of Flora Tristan*. New York: Peter Lang, 1988. A complete and well-researched biography.

SEE ALSO: Simón Bolívar; Paul Gauguin; Clorinda Matto de Turner; Pierre-Joseph Proudhon.

RELATED ARTICLE in *Great Events from History: The Nineteenth Century, 1801-1900:* 1839: Blanc Publishes *The Organization of Labour*.

ANTHONY TROLLOPE
English novelist

In forty-seven well-crafted novels, Trollope depicted the social and political life of his times through characters involved in such institutions as the Church of England and Parliament.

BORN: April 24, 1815; London, England
DIED: December 6, 1882; London, England
AREA OF ACHIEVEMENT: Literature

EARLY LIFE

Anthony Trollope (TRAHL-uhp) was the son of the writer Frances (Fanny) Milton Trollope and Thomas Anthony Trollope, a barrister. Shortly after his birth, the family, including five older children, moved from London to a farm in Harrow-on-the-Hill, sixteen miles outside London. His father hoped to work the farm and commute to London for his law practice. He never prospered at either endeavor and lived in the hope of inheriting the fortune of a bachelor uncle, only to see him marry and start a family of his own late in life. This disappointment would later inspire Anthony Trollope to create fictional characters who feel they have been treated harshly by life.

Anthony began his education at Harrow in 1823 but was brutally bullied by its older students and later attended Winchester, where his older brother Tom beat him daily. Because of the family's declining fortunes, Anthony's mother, Fanny Trollope, decided to go to the United States in 1827, partly in order to help her son Henry set up a business in Cincinnati.

When Anthony's father could no longer keep up his Winchester school fees, Anthony returned to Harrow as a charity student. In 1831, Fanny returned from America and wrote a travel book about her experiences. Her vivid attack on the idea of democracy made her famous overnight. Although she was already in her fifties, she published more than forty additional travel books and novels. Nevertheless, her new fame did not spare the family from having to flee to Belgium because of her husband's debts.

Unable to acquire a scholarship to Cambridge or Oxford, Anthony obtained a clerical position with the government post office in 1834 through his mother's influence. His father died during the following year. Anthony had been a generally poor student during his school days, but he now spent his evenings reading the great works of English literature. He hated his post office work and, after a serious illness in 1840, decided he had to change his life. In 1841, he was posted to Ireland as an inspector of postmasters' accounts and lived there on and off through the next seventeen years.

LIFE'S WORK

In 1842, when Trollope was twenty-seven, he met twenty-year-old Rose Heseltine, who was traveling with her family. He married her twenty months later. Their first son, Henry, was born in 1846, followed by Fred in

Anthony Trollope. (Library of Congress)

1847. Meanwhile, spurred by the need to prove himself and support his family, Trollope wrote his first novel, *The Macdermots of Ballycloran* (1847), which was inspired by his Irish experiences. Although his mother did not think him clever enough to be a novelist—unlike his brother Tom—she gave him an introduction to a publisher. After his first two published novels sold poorly, his publisher advised him to give up writing.

Trollope's next novels, a play, and an Irish travel guide were all rejected, and he failed to achieve advancement in the post office, even after successfully promoting the use of pillar boxes for depositing mail. Trollope persevered with his writing, although it was hindered by his work, which involved extensive traveling by horseback as well as constant reassignments to new responsibilities in Ireland, England, Scotland, Wales, and even the Channel Islands.

Trollope's published his next major novel, *The Warden*, in 1855. Inspired by a new posting in England's West Country and his familiarity with the clerical life through several relatives, this first of Trollope's Barchester tales used the power struggles of a group of clergymen to satirize gently the political reformers of the day. Subsequent Barchester novels also employ ecclesiastical settings as microcosms of much larger social and political issues. Although *The Warden* is now considered a classic, it sold poorly, and his publisher rejected its sequel, *Barchester Towers* (1857).

Trollope's third Barchester novel, *Doctor Thorne* (1858), was his first success and began his long associations with the publisher Chapman & Hall and with Mudie's Select Library, a famous subscription library whose book selections were central to literary success in Victorian London. As critics became aware of Anthony Trollope as something more than merely Fanny Trollope's son, they complained about his voluminous output, which continued at a rate of at least one book a year until his death.

This new success allowed Trollope and his family to travel to the West Indies, which became the inspiration for his most highly regarded travel book, *The West Indies and the Spanish Main* (1859), and to New York. Upon their return to England, they purchased Waltham House in Waltham Cross, their first permanent home. Trollope began contributing stories and essays to such leading periodicals as *Cornhill Magazine*. After the success of *Framley Parsonage* (1860-1861), he was considered the star among the *Cornhill* contributors. He also became a friend of other literary figures, such as Robert Browning, George Eliot, John Everett Millais, and William Makepeace Thackeray, as well as the Prince of Wales.

Trollope was a florid-faced, cigar-smoking, heavy-drinking, and often loud man whom many people found vulgar and annoying. However, his boisterousness and lack of physical charms did not keep him from developing a platonic relationship with Kate Field, whom he met at his brother Tom's house in Florence in 1860. An attractive twenty-two-year-old American actor and writer, Field is best known for her friendships with English writers and her promotion of Alexander Graham Bell's new invention, the telephone. Trollope and Field remained devoted friends until his death, despite his lack of sympathy for her feminist views. Meanwhile, his long-delayed literary success and his new friendships gave him a sense of belonging for the first time, even though he suffered from bouts of depression. He wondered how his life might have been different if he had married someone like Kate.

In addition to his Barchester novels, Trollope is also known for the Palliser series, which begins with *Can You Forgive Her?* (1864-1865) and features the rising politician Plantagenet Palliser, his headstrong wife, Lady Glencora, and the impulsive Irish politician Phineas Finn.

TROLLOPE'S NOVELS	
1847	*The Macdermots of Ballycloran*
1848	*The Kellys and the O'Kellys*
1855-1867	Barchester Novels (*)
1855	*The Warden**
1857	*Barchester Towers**
1858	*The Three Clerks*
1858	*Doctor Thorne**
1859	*The Bertrams*
1860	*Castle Richmond*
1860-1861	*Framley Parsonage**
1861-1862	*Orley Farm*
1862-1864	*The Small House at Allington**
1863	*Rachel Ray*
1864-1865	*Can You Forgive Her?*
1865	*Miss Mackenzie*
1865-1866	*The Belton Estate*
1866-1867	*The Claverings*
1867	*The Last Chronicle of Barset**
1867-1869	*Phineas Finn: The Irish Member*
1868-1869	*He Knew He Was Right*
1869-1870	*The Vicar of Bulhampton*
1871-1873	*The Eustace Diamonds*
1873-1874	*Phineas Redux*
1874-1875	*The Way We Live Now*
1875-1876	*The Prime Minister*
1876-1877	*The American Senator*
1877-1878	*Is He Popenjoy?*
1878-1879	*John Caldigate*
1879-1880	*The Duke's Children*
1880	*Dr. Wortle's School*
1881	*Ayala's Angel*
1881-1882	*The Fixed Period*
1882-1883	*The Landleaguers*
1882-1883	*Mr. Scarborough's Family*

Trollope used this series of novels to satirize contemporary politics more openly than in his Barchester novels. Sympathetic to the Irish cause, he was perturbed by the British government's moribund policies toward Ireland. Although he was a liberal, like his fictional Palliser, he had the conservative views of the English gentleman he aspired to be. As with his mother, his travels in America introduced him to the notion of the "tyranny of democracy."

Trollope also created several outstanding non-series novels. *He Knew He Was Right* (1868-1869), presenting a young husband consumed by an irrational jealousy, is perhaps his most psychological work. *The Way We Live Now* (1875), depicting the fall of a ruthless financier, is his most complex satire, looking at moral and spiritual bankruptcy in several strata of society.

Trollope finally resigned from the post office in 1867, by which time he was earning much more money from his writings than from his job. He was also distressed at he continued lack of advancement, despite having made such contributions as organizing London into postal districts. In 1868, he stood for a seat in Parliament representing Beverley but finished last. During his election campaign, he was a passionate debater on the issue of fox hunting, which was one of his greatest pleasures.

In 1876, Trollope hurried to finish his autobiography because he believed that death was near. However, he lived to write fourteen more books, including a biography of William Makepeace Thackeray. He died in London on December 6, 1882, a few days after suffering a stroke. He was sixty-seven years old at the time of his death. His wife, Rose, lived until 1917.

SIGNIFICANCE

In addition to creating a large body of work that continues to be read and enjoyed, Trollope stands out from other Victorian writers, notably Charles Dickens, by striving to create realistic and well-rounded characters. For example, his Palliser and Lady Glencora display credible mixtures of good and bad qualities, strengths and weaknesses. Trollope is especially notable for making even his villains sympathetic. His unscrupulous adventurer Ferdinand Lopez, in *The Prime Minister* (1875-1876), uses everyone with whom he comes into contact, yet he sincerely loves his wife, even though he has married her for the wrong reasons. Thus, Lopez's suicide comes as a jolt to readers. Despite his aversion to Field's feminism and perhaps inspired by her, Trollope created several strong and independent female characters. For example, in *Phineas Redux* (1873-1874), Madame Max Goesler is so determined to have Finn that she proposes marriage to the hesitant politician herself.

Trollope is also notable for his creative energy and his devotion to his craft. Always up at 5:30 A.M., he wrote for three hours before breakfast and leaving for his post office duties. Given that he worked at a full-time job through most of his writing career, his literary productivity is amazing. He would frequently begin a new novel the day after completing another.

Trollope's contemporary reputation began to wane somewhat after his death because of the relatively weak quality of his final books, but his vivid characters and his acute social commentary were rediscovered in the twentieth century. A number of biographies, critical evaluations, and televised dramatizations of his novels have helped keep his works before the public.

—*Michael Adams*

FURTHER READING

Durey, Jill Felicity. *Trollope and the Church of England*. Basingstoke: Palgrave, 2002. Considers the treatment of ninety-seven clerical characters in Trollope's fiction.

Glendinning, Victoria. *Anthony Trollope*. New York: Alfred A. Knopf, 1993. This first biography to view Trollope from a woman's perspective shows the influence of his mother, Fanny; his wife, Rose; and Kate Field on his writing.

Marwick, Margaret. *Trollope and Women*. London: Hambledon Press, 1997. Discussing the treatment of women in thirty of Trollope's novels, Marwick finds subtle references to their sexual desires.

Nardin, Jane. *Trollope and Victorian Moral Philosophy*. Athens: Ohio University Press, 1996. Examines Trollope's combination of skepticism and moral principle.

Sadleir, Michael. *Trollope: A Commentary*. London: Constable, 1927. The first penetrating study of Anthony Trollope based in part upon interviews with his son Henry Trollope.

Super, R. H. *Trollope in the Post Office*. Ann Arbor: University of Michigan Press, 1981. Most detailed account of Trollope's career in the government post office.

Trollope, Anthony. *An Autobiography*. Edinburgh: Blackwood, 1883. Autobiography that emphasizes Trollope's working habits.

Turner, Mark W. *Trollope and the Magazines: Gendered Issues in Mid-Victorian Britain*. New York: St. Martin's Press, 2000. This analysis of Trollope's contributions to periodicals considers their demographics.

SEE ALSO: Alexander Graham Bell; Mary Elizabeth Braddon; Samuel Butler; Charles Dickens; George Eliot; Thomas Hardy; William Makepeace Thackeray; Frances Trollope; Charlotte Mary Yonge.

RELATED ARTICLES in *Great Events from History: The Nineteenth Century, 1801-1900:* 1814: Scott Publishes *Waverley*; March, 1852-September, 1853: Dickens Publishes *Bleak House*; July, 1881-1883: Stevenson Publishes *Treasure Island*.

FRANCES TROLLOPE
English writer

One of the most widely read authors of her time, Trollope played a major role in shaping English literature by popularizing the use of fiction-writing techniques in travel books. She also wrote the first novels to decry slavery and evangelical excess, promote the rights of women, and expose social injustice.

BORN: March 10, 1779; Bristol, England
DIED: October 6, 1863; Florence, Italy
ALSO KNOWN AS: Frances Milton (birth name); Frances Milton Trollope; Fanny Trollope
AREAS OF ACHIEVEMENT: Literature, women's rights

EARLY LIFE

Frances Trollope (TRAHL-uhp) was born Frances Milton, the daughter and third child of the Reverend William Milton and Mary Milton (née Grisley), three of whose six children died in infancy. Nicknamed Fanny, she grew up with an older sister, Mary, and younger brother, Henry. After her mother died around 1784, her father raised the children and served as clerk of holy orders at a Bristol church. Oxford-educated and an avid inventor, he also designed coaches and a tidal bypass system.

Typical of the English girls of her time, Fanny did not receive a formal education. She took lessons in music and art, and gained fluency in Latin, French, and Italian. She may have attended a school for girls, but no records of her doing so exist. In 1801, when Fanny was twenty-two, her father remarried and became the vicar of Heckfield. Fanny and her sister moved to their brother's house in London two years later. Bright and outspoken, Fanny enjoyed a busy social life and attended many cultural performances.

In 1808, when Fanny was twenty-nine, she met Thomas Anthony Trollope, a thirty-five-year-old barrister. She married him on May 23, 1809, and Fanny bore seven children in nine years. Tom arrived in 1810, followed by Henry in 1811, Arthur in 1812, Emily in 1813 (died the same day), Anthony (the noted novelist) in 1815, Cecilia in 1816, and another Emily in 1818.

From 1809 through 1815, the family lived in London and employed many servants. After Fanny's husband began suffering migraine headaches and fits of rage, they moved to Julians Manor on a leased farm in Harrow. Fanny's drawing room there became the center of the town's social activity, with political radicals often in attendance. By 1824, her husband's migraines had forced him to give up practicing law. During that same year, Fanny's son Arthur died of tuberculosis. Deeply in debt, the family moved to a dilapidated farmhouse in 1827.

LIFE'S WORK

In November, 1827, Fanny Trollope accepted the invitation of British abolitionist Frances Wright and sailed to America with her daughters, her son Henry, the French artist and exiled political refugee Auguste Hervieu, and two servants. Their intended destination was Nashoba, Wright's utopian community in Tennessee. On their arrival there, they discovered a malaria-infested outpost with little food or sanitation. Trollope borrowed three hundred dollars and went to Cincinnati.

Faced with bills and no income, Trollope teamed with Hervieu and others to produce *The Invisible Girl* at the Western Museum in April, 1828. The show attracted large crowds and ran eight weeks. Three months later, they staged another profitable performance based on Dante Alighieri's *Divine Comedy* (1321). Buoyed by these successes, Trollope built a cultural center using money inherited from her father. Trollope despised many American social practices, most notably the public separation of men and women, and envisioned a center in which the sexes could mingle. The finished structure, mockingly called "Trollope's Folly," employed a cacophony of architectural styles. The venture flopped, and she lost her entire investment.

In March, 1830, Trollope moved with her children to Washington, D.C. Sixteen months later, they returned to England with Hervieu. Trollope had relied financially on Hervieu during nearly her entire stay in America, and he paid for her passage home.

Trollope kept detailed notebooks during her time in America, and within months of her return she published a manuscript detailing her experiences. *Domestic Manners of the Americans*, her unflattering portrayal of American social structures, appeared in 1832. The book's American readers expressed outrage, and English critics maligned it as vulgar, but it sold well in both countries. Trollope's second book, *The Refugee in America: A Novel*, also came out in 1832. Driven by financial necessity, she wrote every morning from 4 A.M. until breakfast, then undertook her familial duties. She

THOMAS JEFFERSON, THE "HEARTLESS LIBERTINE"

Fanny Trollope suffered through many unpleasant experiences during her several years in the United States, and her rancor toward that country and its institutions often shows in the book she wrote about her time there. This passage about former president Thomas Jefferson shows why many Americans were outraged by her book and why some British critics called the book vulgar.

Few names are held in higher estimation in America, than that of Jefferson; it is the touchstone of the democratic party, and all seem to agree that he was one of the greatest of men; yet I have heard his name coupled with deeds which would make the sons of Europe shudder. The facts I allude to are spoken openly by all, not whispered privately by a few; and in a country where religion is the tea-table talk, and its strict observance a fashionable distinction, these facts are recorded, and listened to, without horror, nay, without emotion.

Mr. Jefferson is said to have been the father of children by almost all his numerous gang of female slaves. These wretched offspring were also the lawful slaves of their father, and worked in his house and plantations as such; in particular, it is recorded that it was his especial pleasure to be waited upon by them at table, and the hospitable orgies for which his Monticello was so celebrated, were incomplete, unless the goblet he quaffed were tendered by the trembling hand of his own slavish offspring.

I once heard it stated by a democratical adorer of this great man, that when, as it sometimes happened, his children by Quadroon slaves were white enough to escape suspicion of their origin, he did not pursue them if they attempted to escape, saying laughingly, "Let the rogues get off, if they can; I will not hinder them." This was stated in a large party, as a proof of his kind and noble nature, and was received by all with approving smiles.

If I know anything of right or wrong, if virtue and vice be indeed something more than words, then was this great American an unprincipled tyrant, and most heartless libertine.

Source: Frances Trollope, *Domestic Manners of the Americans* (London: Whittaker, Treacher, 1832), chapter 7.

---

the first novel to protest slavery in America, in 1836, sixteen years before Harriet Beecher Stowe's *Uncle Tom's Cabin* appeared in the United States. Among Trollope's other social commentaries, *The Vicar of Wrexhill* (1837) exposed the religious excess of the evangelical church. Critics judged that topic a scandalous one for a woman writer, and the book became one of her best sellers. *The Life and Adventures of Michael Armstrong, the Factory Boy* decried child labor practices in northern England. It appeared in serial installments beginning in February, 1839. Eight years later, the Factory Act of 1847 forbade the employment old in textile mills of children under eight years of age.

Despite her commercial success, Trollope repeatedly teetered on the brink of financial collapse and suffered several heartbreaking losses. Creditors seized the family farm in 1834, and the family fled to Belgium to keep her husband out of debtor's prison. Later during that same year, her son Henry died in Bruges, and her husband died the following October. In January, 1836, Trollope and her daughter Emily moved to a village near London. Emily died a month later.

followed this schedule throughout her entire working life.

Trollope was fifty-three years old when she published her first book. Over the next twenty-five years, she wrote 115 successful books, including works of travel, commentaries, and gothic, detective, romance, and humorous novels. She tackled socially charged subjects, such as slavery and patriarchy, and satirized the London social scene. Her settings often mirror the places and people she knew, and reflect the manners and styles of her day. She is now best known for her travel books. However, after publishing her sixth travel book, *Vienna and the Austrians* (1838), she decided that travel costs absorbed too much of her profits and turned to novels.

Trollope published *The Life and Adventures of Jonathan Jefferson Whitlaw: Or, Scenes of the Mississippi,*

Trollope's fiction appealed to common tastes, and her free-spirited behavior kept her name in the headlines. Through a twenty-year period that began in the 1830's, her novels consistently ranked among the most popular in Britain. By 1839, she commanded eight hundred pounds per manuscript—a large sum equivalent to about four thousand dollars in the United States at that time. Nevertheless, Trollope was still struggling with her debts in 1840, when she was at the age of sixty-one. In 1842, she built a home in Penrith, near her daughter Cecilia in northern England, but vacated the property in 1843 because the cold weather and lack of a social life did not suit her.

By 1852, Trollope was living in Florence, Italy, in the home of her son Tom and his wife. She published her last book, the third volume of *Fashionable Life: Or, Paris and London*, in 1856. On October 6, 1863, she died peacefully during her sleep in Florence.

SIGNIFICANCE

Frances Trollope was one of the most popular and influential English writers of her time. Her first novel, *Domestic Manners of the Americans*, gained such renown that "trollope" became slang for an ill-mannered person. It also popularized the use of personal opinion and lively characterization in travel writing. Trollope's influence can also be seen in the work of such better-known contemporary writers as Charles Dickens and her own son Anthony Trollope. Dickens praised Trollope's observations about America and visited her in Italy. Her son became a highly regarded author and freely borrowed plots and characters from her work.

Fanny Trollope undermined sexist conventions and advanced the cause of women writers. She produced socially and politically themed novels on a par with those of male authors and portrayed friendships among women in a positive light. As the only female novelist of her time to have two books serialized concurrently, she demonstrated that women possess the drive required to meet the special demands of serial publishing.

Trollope's popularity declined as Victorian morals became stricter. After 1883, her books were not reprinted. However, around the turn of the twenty-first century, several new biographies of Trollope recognized the important role she played in shaping modern literature. Scholars also attribute the renewed interest to the vigor with which she advocated social change.

—*Rose Reifsnyder*

FURTHER READING

Ayres, Brenda, ed. *Frances Trollope and the Novel of Social Change*. London: Greenwood Press, 2002. This collection of essays provides a discussion of Trollope's work in terms of its subject matter and includes chapters on her personal history and literary importance.

Neville-Sington, Pamela. *Fanny Trollope, The Life and Adventures of a Clever Woman*. New York: Viking Press, 1998. A thoroughly researched account of Trollope's life and travels, the book includes thirty illustrations and a bibliography of Trollope's books.

Ransom, Teresa. *Fanny Trollope: A Remarkable Life*. New York: St. Martin's Press, 1995. This book provides a detailed account of Trollope's travels, family life, and writings. Along with black-and-white family photos and reproductions of sketches originally printed in her books, it includes a family tree and a chronological bibliography of Trollope's books. The postscript excerpts her obituaries and summarizes the lives of her children and grandchildren.

Simmons, James C. *Star-Spangled Eden, Nineteenth Century America Through the Eyes of Dickens, Wilde, Frances Trollope, Frank Harris, and Other British Travelers*. New York: Carroll & Graf, 2000. The first chapter in this compilation of essays discusses the influence of Jacksonian America on Trollope and her writing.

Trollope, Frances. *Domestic Manners of the Americans*. Reprint. New York: Dover, 2003. Inexpensive reprint of Trollope's most important book, whose text is also freely available in electronic format on Project Gutenberg (www.gutenberg.org).

SEE ALSO: Charles Dickens; Anna Jameson; Mary Kingsley; Harriet Beecher Stowe; Anthony Trollope; Frances Wright.

RELATED ARTICLES in *Great Events from History: The Nineteenth Century, 1801-1900:* 1814: Scott Publishes *Waverley*; May, 1831-February, 1832: Tocqueville Visits America; March, 1852-September, 1853: Dickens Publishes *Bleak House*; July, 1881-1883: Stevenson Publishes *Treasure Island*.

SOJOURNER TRUTH
American social reformer

A featured speaker at abolitionist meetings before the Civil War, Truth worked initially to expose the immorality of the practice of slavery and later to ensure the welfare of emancipated African Americans.

BORN: c. 1797; Hurley, Ulster County, New York
DIED: November 26, 1883; Battle Creek, Michigan
ALSO KNOWN AS: Isabella Baumfree (birth name);
  Isabella Van Wagener
AREA OF ACHIEVEMENT: Social reform

EARLY LIFE

Sojourner Truth was born into slavery in New York as Isabella Baumfree. Her parents were slaves owned by Colonel Johannes Hardenbergh, a prosperous farmer of Dutch descent. Her father, James, a tall man said to be "straight as a tree" (for which he received the Dutch surname of "Baumfree"), was of African and possibly American Indian descent. Her mother, Betsey, also known as "Mau Mau Bett," was of African lineage; through family and biblical stories, she instilled in Isabella and her ten siblings the value of family and spirituality. She assured Isabella she could always talk to God when there was no one else to turn to. Formal education was not available, but Isabella developed a self-reliance and strength in her young years that would preserve her through severe testing and make her work in social reform possible. Her childhood also provided the background from which the vivid and memorable anecdotes used in her lectures would later spring.

Isabella herself was sold at the age of nine. Although she was a diligent worker, she was beaten for her inability to communicate with her owners, the Neelys (Isabella spoke a Dutch dialect). Next, she was sold to the Schryvers, who owned a tavern. During her time with the Schryvers, her mother died, and her father soon followed. Eventually, Isabella was sold to the Dumonts, where she worked part time as a field hand and helped in the kitchen. At this time, Isabella's greatest wish was to please; sometimes, she would stay up half the night working to gain favor with her master.

When grown, Isabella fell in love with Robert, a slave from a neighboring farm, but they were forbidden to marry because Robert's master disapproved of the match. After the couple continued to meet secretly, Robert was severely beaten and made to marry another woman. Isabella, in turn, was given in marriage to another Dumont slave named Tom. She still had the youngest two of their five children with her as the date for her emancipation approached in 1827 (New York legislators had decreed that all slaves above the age of twenty-eight in that year would be emancipated; previous laws had freed slaves born after 1799).

The year 1827 marked a turning point in the life of Isabella Baumfree. Dumont had promised Isabella and her husband their freedom in 1826 and a log cabin in which to live in exchange for her hard work and faithfulness as a slave. Despite sustaining an injury to her hand, Isabella worked harder than ever for that year in order to fulfill her part of the bargain. When the time came for Dumont to deliver, however, he refused, knowing that he needed her labor in order to overcome losses from crop failure. Furthermore, he illegally sold Isabella's son Peter out of state after she escaped his farm.

Isabella sought help after her escape. Quaker friends sent her to live with Isaac and Maria Van Wagener. It was during this period that Isabella took her first successful political action, suing for the recovery of her son by entering a plea before the Grand Jury of Kingston, and winning; Quakers helped Isabella raise money to retrieve Peter, and they were reunited. The fact that the Van Wageners insisted on being called by their names, rather than by "master," impressed Isabella, because she had always perceived slaveholders as being innately better than slaves.

Isabella's religious conversion followed, as did the beginning of her life as Sojourner Truth. Truth recounts her conversion as suddenly being overcome by the feeling she was loved, and feeling love for everyone else—even people who had abused her. She also sensed the presence of someone between her and God (Jesus), and realized her mission in life was to preach the injustice of slavery until it had disappeared for good.

Truth moved to New York City in 1829 and worked there as a maid until 1843, when she left to begin her career as a lecturer for the abolition of slavery and human rights. Truth, who said she conversed with God as with another person, claimed that God himself had now given her the name of "Sojourner" because she was to be a traveler and "Truth" because that was what she was to spread throughout the land. This name change signaled Truth's break with her former identity as a laborer, a slave bearing her master's name, and marked the beginning of her lifelong dedication to the fight to recognize the rights of all human beings.

LIFE'S WORK

During the twenty-five years that followed, Sojourner Truth traveled thousands of miles, lecturing in twenty-one states and in the District of Columbia. She would routinely set up the white sash given to her by abolitionist women with texts written across it "proclaiming liberty throughout the land," begin singing, then preach about the injustice of slavery as people gathered around her. By the 1840's, Truth had become a popular figure and known to be an impressive speaker, six feet tall, clad in gray dress with a turbanlike scarf covering her head, and armed with a mind quick and courageous enough to adapt to, disarm, and delight audiences that were especially hostile to African Americans and women who supported abolition or women's rights.

Many lecturers left the United States at this time, rather than face proslavery mobs who frequently threatened lives and broke up meetings. Truth also inspired a famous work of art by the American sculptor William Wetmore Story, entitled *The Libyan Sibyl*; the statue, of marble, resulted in part from the description given to the sculptor by Harriet Beecher Stowe, and was known for its majesty and mysterious quality.

Truth lived for many years in Northampton, Massachusetts, where she had happened onto the Garrisonian abolitionists during her travels. The Garrisonians held

Sojourner Truth. (Courtesy, The University of Texas at Austin)

the brotherhood and sisterhood of all people sacred; thus, slavery was a violation against God, and the fight against it became a holy war. The group was resolved to overthrow the system of slavery through education and persuasion, and Truth demonstrated this after Frederick Douglass's declaration in a public meeting that the only way for African Americans to gain their freedom was by force, when she asked, "Frederick, is God dead?"

The Garrisonians believed that women were men's equals, and in this way were allied with the women's movement. In 1850, Truth attended the Worcester, Massachusetts, Woman's Rights Convention and participated in the Woman's Rights Convention in Ohio in May of 1851. In the refrain (also the title) of her famous speech, "Ain't I a Woman?," Truth addressed the white women present who wanted rights for women, but at the same time believed African American women to be inferior because of their race. Truth also related her own lifelong history of backbreaking labor, refuting the conventional ideal of women as being unaccustomed to labor or confrontation. Most notably, she addressed biblically based claims of the natural intellectual inferiority of women, countering them with biblical facts. For example, she noted that while men based their claims of superiority upon the fact that Christ was a man, Christ himself was the product of God and a woman, leaving men out of the picture altogether.

Truth's narrative was first written down in 1850 by Olive Gilbert, a white abolitionist. Gilbert's rendering offers vivid stories of Truth's early life and transformation into revivalist and abolitionist, including humorous anecdotes and instances of Truth's effective handling of audiences, but also masks much of her renowned enthusiasm and directness—especially where this directness clashes with the ideal of womanhood during her time. An example of Truth's direct approach that is not included in Gilbert's text is Truth's response to male hecklers who asked if she were a man or a woman; she bared her breasts in proof—not to her own embarrassment, but rather to their collective shame.

A second edition of Truth's narrative, published in 1878, included news articles and correspondence regarding Truth, as well as samples from her "Book of Life"—a book she carried with her, filled with signatures of authors, senators, politicians, and friends—including President Abraham Lincoln, whom she visited in Washington, D.C., in 1864. During the Civil War, Truth nursed soldiers, bringing them food and gifts, funding her work by lecturing, singing, and selling her own photograph on

SOJOURNER TRUTH'S SEARCH FOR HER SON

In Narrative of Sojourner Truth, *a book based on her testimony to Olive Gilbert, Truth recalls her reaction to the news that her young son Peter had been illegally sold. The narrative variously refers to Truth as "Isabel," "Isabella," and "Bell."*

A little previous to Isabel's leaving her old master, he had sold her child, a boy of five years, to a Dr. Gedney, who took him with him as far as New York city, on his way to England; but finding the boy too small for his service, he sent him back to his brother, Solomon Gedney. This man disposed of him to his sister's husband, a wealthy planter, by the name of Fowler, who took him to his own home in Alabama.

This illegal and fraudulent transaction had been perpetrated some months before Isabella knew of it, as she was now living at Mr. Van Wagener's. The law expressly prohibited the sale of any slave out of the State—and all minors were to be free at twenty-one years of age; and Mr. Dumont had sold Peter with the express understanding, that he was soon to return to the State of New York, and be emancipated at the specified time.

When Isabel heard that her son had been sold South, she immediately started on foot and alone, to find the man who had thus dared, in the face of all law, human and divine, to sell her child out of the State; and if possible, to bring him to account for the deed.

Arriving at New Paltz, she went directly to her former mistress, Dumont, complaining bitterly of the removal of her son. Her mistress heard her through, and then replied—"Ugh! a fine fuss to make about a little nigger! Why, haven't you as many of 'em left as you can see to, and take care of? A pity 'tis, the niggers are not all in Guinea!! Making such a halloo-balloo about the neighborhood; and all for a paltry nigger!!!" Isabella heard her through, and after a moment's hesitation, answered, in tones of deep determination—"I'll have my child again." "Have your child again!" repeated her mistress—her tones big with contempt, and scorning the absurd idea of her getting him. "How can you get him? And what have you to support him with, if you could? Have you any money?" "No," answered Bell, "I have no money, but God has enough, or what's better! And I'll have my child again." These words were pronounced in the most slow, solemn, and determined measure and manner. And in speaking of it, she says, "Oh my God! I know'd I'd have him agin. I was sure God would help me to get him. Why, I felt so tall within—I felt as if the power of a nation was with me!"

Source: Olive Gilbert, *The Narrative of Sojourner Truth* (Boston, 1850).

1863, Truth stayed in Washington, D.C., to work with newly freed slaves whose children were being kidnapped and taken to Maryland—still a slave state—organizing posses and persuading mothers to swear out warrants, as she once had done, finding homes and jobs in the northern states for many others. Truth also produced fifty petitions at her own expense in 1870 (when she was nearly eighty years old) asking Congress for land in the western United States that could be used to resettle freed people who were elderly, homeless, or unemployed.

Truth believed strongly that unemployment robbed people of dignity and humanity; crime was becoming a problem among the homeless and unemployed. Truth endorsed a general plan to Christianize, educate, and provide land for freedmen, as well as prohibit the drinking of rum, another source of demoralization. Truth attempted to convince politicians that since the future of her people was at stake, money used to imprison vagabond children could be better used to give them homes, churches, and schools. Truth also believed that children would fare better if women were allowed political rights.

Truth died in Battle Creek, Michigan, in November of 1883, after almost a century of struggle for social reform. Her funeral was attended by more than a thousand people, and a marble monument was erected there in her honor in 1947.

which was written: "I sell the shadow to support the substance." She also became a freedom rider on the streetcars that she rode to take care of the soldiers. On one occasion after successfully fighting to remove the Jim Crow cars (cars reserved for African Americans, but often used by whites), Truth drew a crowd while voicing her desire for a ride, which was at last granted, and rode further than she needed to make her point definite.

After the Emancipation Proclamation was signed, in

SIGNIFICANCE

At a time when the cooperation between white abolitionists and African Americans was limited, as was the alliance between the woman suffrage movement and the abolitionists, Sojourner Truth was a figure that brought all factions together by her skills as a public speaker and by her common sense. She worked with acumen to claim and actively gain rights for all human beings, starting with those who were enslaved, but not excluding women, the poor, the homeless, and the unemployed. Truth believed that all people could be enlightened about their actions and choose to behave better if they were educated by others, and persistently acted upon these beliefs.

Truth's written narrative is one of many narratives presented to the public by abolitionists as proof against proslavery advocates' claims that African Americans were content with slavery and incapable of caring for themselves. Her speeches were also an effective weapon against slavery and were especially successful in drawing crowds to antislavery meetings and opening eyes to the injustice and irrationality of slavery. Like other freed slaves, Truth was a primary witness who could testify to the real suffering of slaves as well as demonstrate to proslavery crowds that, contrary to popular belief, African Americans were thinking, feeling human beings. Sojourner Truth is considered, along with Harriet Tubman, to be one of the two most influential African American women of the nineteenth century. W. E. B. Du Bois conveyed the importance of her contribution best when he described Truth as "one of the seven who made American slavery impossible."

—Jennifer McLeod

FURTHER READING

Campbell, Karlyn Kohrs. "Style and Content in the Rhetoric of Early Afro-American Feminists." *Quarterly Journal of Speech* 72 (November, 1986): 434-445. Campbell discusses the difficulties African American women abolitionists faced as public speakers, which Truth was successful in combating through the power of metaphor and personal experience in speaking.

Dick, Robert C. *Black Protest: Issues and Tactics*. Westport, Conn.: Greenwood Press, 1974. Dick describes Truth's work as an African American antislavery lecturer, demonstrating her charisma, humor, and strength, as well as discussing the significance of slave narratives, both written and oral, in the antislavery movement.

Fauset, Arthur Huff. *Sojourner Truth: God's Faithful Pilgrim*. New York: Russell & Russell, 1971. This is yet another rendition of the narrative of Sojourner Truth as told to Olive Gilbert (see below), made into factual fiction by Fauset. The narrator focuses on Truth's religious devotion and strength, as does Gilbert.

Fitch, Suzanne Pullon, and Roseann M. Mandziuk. *So-journer Truth as Orator: Wit, Story, and Song*. Westport, Conn.: Greenwood Press, 1997. An analysis of Truth's oratory, placing it within a historical context and describing its rhetorical strategies. Includes some of Truth's speeches, songs, and public letters.

Gilbert, Olive. *Narrative of Sojourner Truth*. Edited by Margaret Washington. New York: Vintage Books, 1993. In the introduction to this edition of the *Narrative of Sojourner Truth*, editor Margaret Washington explores the Dutch culture in relation to slavery, the elements of culture and community in interpreting the effects of slavery upon African Americans, and the issue of gender in relation to the authorship of the narrative.

_____. *Narrative of Sojourner Truth, a Bondswoman of Olden Time: With a History of Her Labors and Correspondence Drawn from Her "Book of Life."* New York: Oxford University Press, 1991. Introduced by Jeffrey C. Stewart, the prefacing material to Olive Gilbert's rendering (originally published in 1850) outlines Truth's contribution to African American women's literature beginning with Phillis Wheatley. This book is part of a series aiming to resurrect the literature of African American women by uncovering the genre's nineteenth century roots.

McKissack, Patricia C., and Fredrick McKissack. *Sojourner Truth: Ain't I a Woman?* New York: Scholastic, 1992. This juvenile biography provides a straightforward introduction to Sojourner Truth, clarifying the details of her early life in slavery, explaining her connection with early abolitionists, and providing insights into her efforts on behalf of women's rights. Includes a bibliography of sources for further study.

Painter, Nell Irvin. *Sojourner Truth: A Life, a Symbol*. New York: W. W. Norton, 1996. Comprehensive biography that challenges the authenticity of historical sources regarding Truth's life. Painter places Truth's life in the proper social context by creating a clear picture of African American life in New York City.

SEE ALSO: John Brown; Frederick Douglass; Abby Kelley Foster; Abraham Lincoln; Harriet Beecher Stowe; Harriet Tubman.

RELATED ARTICLES in *Great Events from History: The Nineteenth Century, 1801-1900:* December, 1833: American Anti-Slavery Society Is Founded; May 28-29, 1851: Akron Woman's Rights Convention.

TU DUC
Emperor of Vietnam (r. 1847-1883)

One of the best-educated emperors of the Nguyen Dynasty, Tu Duc worked to modernize Vietnam, improve education, and maintain his nation's independence from Western powers. However, his edicts directly led to the loss of Vietnam's independence.

BORN: September 22, 1829; Hue, Vietnam
DIED: July 9, 1883; Hue, Vietnam
ALSO KNOWN AS: Nguyen Phuoc Hoang Nham (birth name)
AREA OF ACHIEVEMENT: Government and politics

EARLY LIFE

Tu Duc (tew dewc) was born Nguyen Phuoc Hoang Nham, the youngest son of Vietnam's Emperor Thieu Tri. The emperor was considered to be the Son of Heaven, whose mandate was above law, and as a divine leader, he was often hidden from view. As a child of the emperor, Nguyen Phuoc Hoang Nham was also kept hidden from public view. He was a sickly child through some portion of his youth, as he suffered from smallpox.

Nguyen Phuoc Hoang Nham spent a large portion of time during his youth studying the arts and humanities. Emperors were required to uphold Confucian ideals because they were the supposed to promote "social happiness" and uphold the structure of Confucian society, which had four classes: Confucian scholars (*Si*), landlords (*Nong*), artisans (*Cong*), and merchants (*Thuong*). Nguyen Phuoc Hoang Nham was also expected to uphold Confucian ideals and was well versed in them. He excelled at the written and verbal, and showed an immense interest in poetry, philosophy, and history.

Under the principle of primogeniture, Nguyen Phuoc Hoang Nham was not in line to ascend his father's throne; that was the destiny of his oldest brother, Hong Bao. However, Thieu Tri decided to do away with primogeniture and declared Nguyen Phuoc Hoang Nham his heir. When he died in 1847, eighteen-year-old Nguyen Phuoc Hoang Nham became Emperor Tu Duc.

LIFE'S WORK

Nguyen Phuoc Hoang Nham ascended the throne as Tu Duc with some question of his legitimacy because his succession violated the old principle of primogeniture. In order to secure his legitimacy immediately, he sought China's recognition and support. On September 10, 1849, he welcomed a Chinese delegate with great fan-

fare, a tactic that spurred some resentment among the Vietnamese people.

Tu Duc also encountered opposition from his brother Hong Bao, who had been passed over for the throne. At first, his brother supported his accession, but three years later he and his supporters revolted. One of Hong Bao's supporters revealed the details of a planned coup, and Hong Bao was swiftly arrested and sentenced to execution. Dowager Tu Du, the mother of both Tu Duc and Hong Bao, ordered Hong Bao's sentence reduced to life in prison, but Hong Bao later took his own life in a prison cell.

In 1864, Tu Duc began building a mausoleum for himself on the Perfume River, an action that created discontent. Doan Trung, the son-in-law of Tu Duc's uncle Prince Tung Thien Vuong, took advantage of the discontent by planning another coup, this time to place Hong Bao's son on the throne. On September 8, 1866, members of Doan Trung's party took a blood oath and descended on Tu Duc's palace. The rebels easily entered the palace and approached Tu Duc's quarters. However, unfortunately for Doan Trung, one of his followers read an unfavorable horoscope and left the party to warn the emperor's guards. As Doan Trung laid siege to the imperial quarters, troops arrived to protect the palace, and Doan Trung and his party were arrested. All the plotters were executed immediately, except for Doan Trung, who was tortured. When he refused to confess, every member of his entire famiy—except his wife, a cousin of the emperor—was beheaded.

In addition to these rebellions, Tu Duc faced uprisings from supporters of the Le Dynasty, which had formerly ruled Vietnam, in 1854, 1861 and 1862. In an effort to stop these rebellions, he sent Nguyen Tri Phuong to suppress all anti-Nguyen movements. Nguyen Tri Phuong accomplished that task with the defeat of Ta Van Phung in 1864.

Tu Duc was also concerned about what he regarded as the infiltration of his country by Christian missionaries, who threatened to disrupt Vietnamese life and undermine his status as the Son of Heaven. His concern was heightened by the fact that a Roman Catholic priest had been involved in the Hong Bao coup. He followed his father's example by persecuting missionaries in order to drive them out of Vietnam. In 1848, near the beginning of his reign, he issued an edict that demanded Christian peasants to renounce their faith or faced being labeled heretics. Tu Duc gave members of the upper classes one month to renounce their Christian faith, under the threat of losing their rank and facing possible exile. After he issued these edicts, Christian-led rebellions arose in the northern provinces. A 1855 rebellion in Tongking moved Tu Duc to inflict harsher punishments on Christians and to execute Spanish and French missionaries.

Tu Duc's decision came at an inopportune time. The French government was then moving to colonize Southeast Asia, and the execution of European missionaries in Vietnam increased public support for imperial expansion. In 1856, the French government demanded that Vietnam permit religious freedom and open trade, but Tu Duc refused. He continued his anti-Christian policies. In 1858, his execution of the Spanish missionary Monsignor Díaz provoked the Spanish and French governments to take military action. Vietnam was then plunged into the French Indochina War, which it could not win.

Several times during the ensuing war, which lasted from 1858 until 1863, Tu Duc misinterpreted French actions with the result that each time Vietnam lost more territory. Often the French had to retreat because their troops were not physically prepared for the tropics, and Tu Duc repeatedly took their retreats as a sign of weakness. Early in the war Tu Duc won some victories by taking advantage of French inability to fight in heavy jungle. Despite France's overwhelming advantages in modern weaponry and manpower, the Vietnamese stopped the French from advancing from Da Nang into Hue, the imperial capital, in 1858. However, that level of success was not repeated, and Tu Duc consistently lost territory as he refused to heed to French demands. In 1862, he was forced to sign the Treaty of Saigon, by which he relinquished his southern provinces and Cambodia to French control.

Despite the treaty, the Vietnamese still did not want France in their country, and several anti-French rebellions encouraged Tu Duc to send an embassy to Paris in 1863 to negotiate a new settlement. He wanted to buy back his southern provinces, known as Cochin-China, and offered to make Cochin-China a French protectorate, give the French special trade rights and commercial access, and pay an annual tribute to France. The French emperor, Napoleon III, initially accepted the offer, which was an important victory for Tu Duc, but later changed his mind.

The French presence in Vietnam also created other problems for Tu Duc. His persecution of Christians nur-tured pro-French sentiments among Roman Catholic Vietnamese, and as France gained territory in Vietnam, uprisings in Tongking against him increased. In 1865, he sent a large force to Bac Bo in Tongking to crush a Christian-supported rebellion. However, that tactic only increased pro-French feelings, and soon Vietnamese Catholics began working for the French. At the same time, many peasants began to view Tu Duc as unworthy of his throne. Not only was he proving unable to protect their country from the French, but the country also experienced a high incidence of natural disasters and a cholera epidemic that killed more than one million people in 1865.

Although he was steadily losing public support and had no reason to think that he could be a match for French forces, Tu Duc continued to seek ways to overthrow the French. In 1873, when a French trader named Dupuis attempted to carry his wares up the Red River, Tu Duc declared his behavior a violation of the Treaty of Saigon. However, instead of carrying out their treaty responsibilities by removing Dupius, the French sought to open all rivers in Vietnam to trade. In 1874, Tu Duc was forced to sign another treaty that opened the Red River. However, he had no intention of honoring that treaty and continued persecuting Christians.

As a last option, Tu Duc renewed Vietnam's vassal relationship with China. This move was a violation of the Treaty of Saigon that the French seized as an opportunity to take complete control of Vietnam. Tu Duc enlisted the bandit group Black Flags to disturb French commercial interests, but that move proved to be a terrible mistake. France then swiftly descended on Hanoi. It captured the city in 1882 and then extended conquests outward. On July 9, 1883, as the French were occupying his country, Tu Duc died in Hue.

SIGNIFICANCE

Some scholars have suggested that if Tu Duc had been emperor without having to face the threat of French imperialism, he might have become a great ruler. However, his fervid desire to banish European influence from Vietnam was untimely and had drastic consequences. His policy of persecution was influenced by the Hong Bao revolt, and his refusal to abandon his policies ultimately led to the downfall of Vietnam. Although his policies were intended to drive out Western sway, they only hardened French resolve to control Vietnam. France already had economic interests in Vietnam, but the persecution and murder of French missionaries created French public support of an invasion of Vietnam.

Ultimately, Tu Duc's policies not only provoked the French but also alienated his own people, particularly Christian Vietnamese. The result of his policies was that Vietnam lost its independence for the first time in nine hundred years.

—*Tina Powell*

FURTHER READING
Chapuis, Oscar. *A History of Vietnam*. Westport, Conn.: Greenwood Press, 1995. General history of Vietnam that places Tu Duc's reign in a larger context.
_____. *The Last Emperors of Vietnam: From Tu Duc to Bao Dai*. Westport, Conn.: Greenwood Press, 2000. Chronicles France's relationship with Vietnam and neighboring countries from the seizure of Cochin-China during Tu Duc's reign until the French defeat at Dien Bien Phu in 1954.
Karnow, Stanley. *Vietnam: A History*. 2d ed. New York: Viking Press, 1997. One of the most widely available English works on Vietnam. Includes a useful chronology.
Sardesai, D. R. *Vietnam: Past and Present*. Boulder, Colo.: Westview Press, 2005. A detailed discussion of the history of Vietnam with an emphasis on colonial expansion, the colonial period, and the rise of nationalism in Vietnam.
Tate, D. J. M. *The Making of Modern South-East Asia: The European Conquest*. Kuala Lumpur: Oxford University Press, 1977. Detailed discussion of Tu Duc's policies and actions regarding the French and how they directly affected Franco-Vietnamese relations.

SEE ALSO: Gia Long; Ho Xuan Huong; Napoleon III.
RELATED ARTICLES in *Great Events from History: The Nineteenth Century, 1801-1900:* August, 1858: France and Spain Invade Vietnam; April, 1882-1885: French Indochina War.

HARRIET TUBMAN
American social reformer

Tubman was one of the towering figures in the American abolitionist movement. A fugitive slave herself, she earned the nickname of "Moses" of her people for rescuing numerous slaves from bondage and leading them to freedom through the Underground Railroad that she helped to create.

BORN: c. 1820; Bucktown, Dorchester County, Maryland
DIED: March 10, 1913; Auburn, New York
ALSO KNOWN AS: Araminta Ross (birth name); Harriet Ross Tubman; Moses
AREA OF ACHIEVEMENT: Social reform

EARLY LIFE
Harriet Tubman was born into slavery on the eastern shore of Maryland. She was the daughter of two slaves, Benjamin Ross and Harriet Green, one of ten or eleven of the couple's children. Her ancestors had been brought to the United States from Africa sometime during the early eighteenth century. Her master, Edward Brodas, named her Araminta, but she quickly took on her mother's name and came to be known as Harriet.

Harriet's slave status quickly became obvious to her. As a young child, she saw two of her sisters carried away in chains. She received no schooling, and by the age of five she was already at work as a baby-sitter and maid. Her mistress worked her as a maid during the day and then demanded that she remain alert to the baby's cries at night. Once when Harriet dozed off and the baby's crying awakened the mistress, the woman pummeled the young slave about her face and neck.

At the age of six, Harriet was hired out to a new master who taught her how to trap muskrats and how to weave. Once, he caught her taking a sugar cube from his table, and she had to run away to avoid punishment. When she returned, tired and hungry, after several days' absence, she was whipped. The remainder of her childhood was spent in various other occupations. She worked again as a nursemaid and later split and hauled wood, part of the time working with her father. She was also a field hand. None of her various masters seemed happy with her work, and she was frequently in trouble.

When Harriet was twelve or thirteen, she suffered an accident that was to affect her for the rest of her life. An overseer became angry at another slave for leaving his work and demanded that Harriet help in his whipping. She refused and instead tried to help the man escape. In his anger, the overseer picked up a two-pound weight and threw it at the fleeing slave. His aim proved faulty, however, and he struck Harriet on the head, knocking her unconscious. For the rest of her life, she suffered a form of sleeping sickness brought on by the blow, often falling asleep involuntarily. These spells only increased her reputation as a poor worker.

In 1844, Harriet's mother forced her to marry a free black man named John Tubman. She lived with him for five years but had no children. While discussing her husband's free status, Harriet became curious about her own background. In 1845, her inquiries turned up the fact that her mother had actually been emancipated some years previously, but a former master had hidden this fact from her. This revelation caused Tubman to look at her enslavement in an even more critical light.

The year 1849 proved to be the turning point in Harriet's life. Her master at this time was a young, sickly white man who was under the care of an adult guardian. When the young man died in 1849, the rumor spread that the guardian planned to sell all of his slaves. Tubman decided to run away. Her husband refused to join her, but two of her brothers went along. They quickly lost their nerve, however, and Tubman was forced to travel the one hundred miles or so out of Maryland, through Delaware, to Philadelphia on her own. Along the way, she found aid from sympathetic blacks and white people. When she reached free soil, she had mixed feelings. She was excited about reaching freedom but was sad that her family members were still chattel. She determined somehow to free them. Her life of slavery was over; a new career was soon to begin.

LIFE'S WORK

When Tubman reached Philadelphia, she met William Still, a black man reputed to be the chief "conductor" on what was referred to as the Underground Railroad. This collection of abolitionists, Quakers, and other sympathetic black and white people had established a series of houses, barns, caves, passageways, and the like for fugitive slaves to use as they made their way north to freedom. This so-called Underground Railroad was not nearly as well organized as myth would have it, but there is no denying that numerous individuals helped the fugitives escape. Tubman had already experienced some of this help during her own escape, and now she learned more about the system from Still and another close ally, the Quaker Thomas Garrett of Wilmington, Delaware.

Tubman first had to find work in a hotel to earn a livelihood, and thus she began the pattern she was to follow from then on. She was never a paid agent, so she had to do manual labor of various sorts to pay her own way and

Harriet Tubman. (Library of Congress)

help finance her slave-rescuing activities. (Sometimes, abolitionists did give her some financial support for particular excursions.) In December, 1850, she made the first of some twenty trips back into slavery. She went to Baltimore and brought out her sister and two children. In 1851, she rescued a brother and his family. When she returned for her husband in the fall of that year, she found him remarried and uninterested in joining her.

Through the rest of the 1850's Tubman engaged in her slave-stealing activities, rescuing somewhere between sixty and three hundred people. Her work was complicated by the recently enacted Fugitive Slave Law of the Compromise of 1850, which made it no longer safe for runaways to remain in the North. She began to take her fugitives into Canada, from 1851 to 1857 considering St. Catharines, Ontario, her home. From there, she made eleven trips into slave territory. Her most spectacular rescue, and the most personally satisfying one, was her success in bringing out her parents in 1857 in a specially contrived wagon. Her raids were so successful, in fact, that frightened Maryland slaveholders held a meeting in 1858 and put a price of forty thousand dollars on her head.

Tubman's success was the result of intelligence, planning, determination, a mystical faith in God, and courage. She carried drugs to anesthetize babies. She used a pistol to embolden fugitives on the verge of losing their nerve, giving them the choice of continuing or dying on the spot. She used cryptic messages to announce her arrival and sang songs with hidden messages to implement her plans. On one occasion, she and her fugitives boarded a southbound train on the supposition that no slave hunter would suspect a black person traveling in that direction. Another time, she saw a former master approaching her and loosed some chickens as a diversionary tactic to get by him unnoticed. She sometimes physically carried fugitives; she encouraged; she prayed; she bullied. As she later explained: "I never ran my train off the track and I never lost a passenger." She was convinced that God had chosen her for her work and protected her in its execution.

During the 1850's, Tubman's fame spread among the abolitionists. She traveled to New England, where she came to know Ralph Waldo Emerson, Frederick Douglass, Gerrit Smith, and Thomas W. Higginson. William Henry Seward, though hardly an abolitionist, befriended her also and in 1857 sold her a house in his hometown, Auburn, New York, where she took up residence with her aged parents.

In 1859, when Tubman spoke to the Fourth of July meeting of the Massachusetts Anti-Slavery Society, she so mesmerized its secretary that he forgot to take notes and had to apologize to the membership for the lapse. However, others whom Tubman met during these years left descriptions of her. She was short, of dark color, medium build, with missing upper front teeth. She dressed simply, reminding one observer of her slave past and another of her Quaker acquaintances. By most standards, she was not an attractive woman, and the fact that she often fell asleep as soon as she sat down gave the impression of fragility rather than the strength that she actually possessed.

During the late 1850's, Tubman met John Brown when he was touring black communities in Canada look-

ing for recruits to join in his attempt to capture the federal arsenal at Harpers Ferry and begin a massive slave uprising. Tubman approved of his slave-insurrection plan, and only an unknown illness at a crucial time prevented her from completing her recruiting mission. She considered him the personification of Jesus Christ because of his willingness to die for black people in slavery. Brown was similarly impressed with her, introducing her to Wendell Phillips as "General" Tubman. At another time, he offered the quintessential nineteenth century sexist praise, referring to her repeatedly as a man.

In the spring of 1860, while Tubman was on her way to an anti-slavery meeting in Boston, she passed through Troy, New York. She found to her dismay that federal marshals had discovered a fugitive and were preparing to take him back to slavery. Tubman helped lead the city's opposition. She grabbed hold of the fugitive and, though her clothes were nearly ripped from her, she held on. After further struggle and several near misses, she successfully gained for the fugitive his freedom. Later that year she made her last trip into Maryland, but by that time the nation was on the verge of war and her abolitionist friends were concerned for her safety. They now escorted her into Canada, where she had led so many fugitives previously. Her slave-rescuing days were over.

Tubman remained in St. Catharines only briefly. In the spring of 1861, she returned to the United States and apparently followed General Benjamin Butler's Massachusetts troops as they marched southward to defend Washington. In May, 1862, armed with a letter from the governor of Massachusetts, she went to General David Hunter's command in South Carolina to help in the war effort. At first she served as a nurse, gaining renown for her ability to cure disease among those under her care. Later she became a spy, given authority to organize and command a black scout and spy unit. She participated in several raids, leading the successful July, 1863, Combahee River expedition. Later she watched black troops attack Fort Wagner near Charleston. In 1864, she became concerned over the health of her parents and traveled to Auburn, returning to Virginia near the end of the war to work briefly at a hospital in Fortress Monroe.

On her way home from Virginia, Tubman learned that slavery's end had not created a promised land for the newly freed people. The conductor on the railroad refused to honor her nurse's pass and called her a racist name. Despite her strenuous protests, he and three other men threw her bodily into the baggage car.

Tubman returned to Auburn, where she spent the rest of her life. She began a home for aged African Americans in her own house, married Civil War veteran Nelson Davis in 1869 (John Tubman having died several years previously), and helped Sarah Bradford write an autobiographical book entitled *Scenes in the Life of Harriet Tubman* (1869). The publication of this book allowed her to complete the purchase of her house, but she remained in difficult financial straits all of her life. Beginning during the late 1860's, with Seward's support, she requested federal payment for her Civil War service. Nothing happened until 1897, when she received a pension of twenty dollars a month.

During these post-Civil War years, Tubman was also active in the temperance and the women's rights movements, working with Susan B. Anthony and other feminists. Her fame had early spread overseas, and upon the publication of her autobiography, Queen Victoria sent her a gift and invited her to visit England.

Harriet Tubman died in Auburn on March 10, 1913. She received a full military funeral conducted by the Grand Army of the Republic. The following year, the city of Auburn dedicated a memorial to her on the county courthouse lawn. Booker T. Washington was the main speaker for the event. In 1978, when the United States Postal Service inaugurated its "Black Heritage U.S.A." stamp series, Tubman was the first person honored.

SIGNIFICANCE

In a world that saw the slaveholder as dominant and the slave powerless, in a society that believed in white superiority and black inferiority, in a time when men were movers and women's place was in the home, Tubman was a contradiction. She showed slaveholders that they were not all-powerful; she showed slaves that enslavement might not have to be permanent. She demonstrated to a racist and sexist age the truth of black and female capability. She was a "Moses" leading people from slavery into freedom.

Though Tubman's symbolic effect was significant, her actual success was limited. She affected slaves only in a border area, and no more than sixty to three hundred of them. She did not rescue any slaves in the Deep South, their chances of running away made impossible by the simple fact of distance. However, even there she had an effect. If slavery was insecure anywhere, it was threatened everywhere. Runaways in Maryland were perceived to be a threat to Mississippi slaveholders as they were to those in Maryland. The bounty for her capture demonstrated better than any words just how upsetting her activities were.

Tubman represented the ideals of freedom and the willingness to endanger one's life for others. This small woman, who never learned to read and write and thus never read the Declaration of Independence, nevertheless exemplified this document in a most profound way.

—John F. Marszalek

FURTHER READING

Bradford, Sarah E. H. *Harriet Tubman: The Moses of Her People*. Introduction by Butler A. Jones. New York: G. R. Lockwood and Son, 1886. Reprint. New York: Corinth Books, 1961. A republication of the 1886 expanded version of the 1869 original book, this is the basic source for information on Harriet Tubman's life. Bradford interviewed Tubman and also included comments about her by a number of leading nineteenth century Americans. In many ways, this is Tubman's autobiography.

Clinton, Catherine. *Harriet Tubman: The Road to Freedom*. New York: Little, Brown, 2004. One of two comprehensive, adult biographies of Tubman published in 2004 (see Larson below). Clinton's meticulously detailed book places Tubman's life within the context of the nineteenth century American south.

Conrad, Earl. *Harriet Tubman*. Washington, D.C.: Associated Publishers, 1943. This is the best biography available and is much more detailed than the Bradford book because Conrad added data not included in the earlier account. This book concentrates on the ten-year period from 1849 to 1859 and cites Tubman as a symbol of the many other nameless fugitives who fled to freedom.

Heidish, Marcy. *A Woman Called Moses*. Boston: Houghton Mifflin, 1976. A historical novel grounded firmly in historical fact. The reader receives an accurate feeling for Tubman, particularly because the book is written in the first person and emphasis is placed on the forces that shaped and directed her.

Humez, Jean M. *Harriet Tubman: The Life and the Life Stories*. Madison: University of Wisconsin Press, 2003. A collection of primary source materials, including letters, diaries, memorials, and speeches, that provide a description of Tubman's life and personality. The materials document Tubman's relationships with abolitionist John Brown, Abraham Lincoln, Frederick Douglass, Sojourner Truth, and others.

Larson, Kate Clifford. *Bound for the Promised Land: Harriet Tubman, Portrait of an American Hero*. New York: Ballantine, 2004. Comprehensive account of Tubman's life, based in part on new sources, including court records, contemporary newspapers, wills, and letters.

SEE ALSO: Susan B. Anthony; John Brown; Frederick Douglass; Ralph Waldo Emerson; Thomas Wentworth Higginson; Wendell Phillips; Sojourner Truth; Queen Victoria; Booker T. Washington.

RELATED ARTICLES in *Great Events from History: The Nineteenth Century, 1801-1900:* December, 1833: American Anti-Slavery Society Is Founded; October 14, 1834: Blair Patents His First Seed Planter; c. 1850-1860: Underground Railroad Flourishes; September 18, 1850: Second Fugitive Slave Law; December 6, 1865: Thirteenth Amendment Is Ratified.

SIR CHARLES TUPPER
Canadian politician

While he was premier of Nova Scotia, Tupper played a major role in the creation of the Canadian confederation; he later held major cabinet posts in the national government, headed the Conservative Party, and briefly served as national prime minister.

BORN: July 2, 1821; Amherst, Nova Scotia (now in Canada)
DIED: October, 30, 1915; Bexleyheath, Kent, England
ALSO KNOWN AS: First Baronet Tupper
AREAS OF ACHIEVEMENT: Government and politics, medicine

EARLY LIFE

Charles Tupper was the son of a Baptist minister whose grandfather had moved from New England to Nova Scotia in 1763 after the expulsion of the Acadians. Charles was educated at home and at local schools until he was old enough to enroll at the University of Edinburgh, which offered the best available medical training. After obtaining a medical degree in 1843, he opened a successful practice in Amherst, Nova Scotia, where he earned a reputation as a diligent physician. On one occasion, for example, he stayed up all night long administering half-hourly glasses of champagne to the sick wife of a political opponent. He served as first president of the Canadian Medical Association, from 1867 to 1870. Meanwhile, he married Frances Amelia Morse in 1846. Their marriage lasted sixty-six years and produced one daughter and three sons who survived to maturity.

In 1855, Tupper won election to the Nova Scotia assembly as a Conservative, defeating Joseph Howe, the leading Liberal. Tupper became the major spokesperson for his party, vigorously attacking the Liberal government. Conservatives won an overwhelming victory in 1863; when the party leader became a judge in May 1864, Tupper succeeded him as Nova Scotia's premier.

LIFE'S WORK

During his 1863 campaign, Tupper called for expanding Nova Scotia's railway net and improving public education. As premier the following year, he awarded contracts extending the railways and passed a Free School Act establishing a state-controlled system of nondenominational common schools. When too few districts provided sufficient funds for the schools, he imposed compulsory taxation in 1865. He rejected public funding of sectarian schools but reached an agreement with the Roman Catholic archbishop allowing grants to church schools that followed the prescribed government curriculum and limited religious instruction to after school hours.

As early as 1860, Tupper had advocated uniting Great Britain's North American colonies. As a step toward that goal after he became premier, he proposed a conference to discuss unifying the Maritime colonies. The September, 1864, meeting at Charlottetown, Prince Edward Island, attracted deputations from Upper (Ontario) and Lower (Quebec) Canada who persuaded the delegates to reconvene in Quebec in October to plan a wider union. The Quebec conferees agreed on seventy-two resolutions that were forwarded to a London meeting. Those resolutions became the basis of the 1867 British North America Act, which served as Canada's constitution until 1982.

Tupper himself participated in all three conferences, and his leadership persuaded reluctant Nova Scotians to join the new confederation. On July 1, 1867, a British royal proclamation established the Dominion of Canada, which then comprised Ontario, Quebec, New Brunswick, and Nova Scotia (Prince Edward Island did not join until 1873). With the purchase of the Hudson's Bay Company's Northwest Territories in 1870 and the accession of British Columbia in 1871, the Dominion stretched from coast to coast and into the Arctic, making Canada one of the largest countries on earth.

In meetings held during and shortly after the U.S. Civil War, Tupper and other delegates were determined to avoid mistakes made by the United States. Proud to be monarchists and pleased to be subjects of Queen Victoria and part of the British Empire, they rejected the American concept of a federal republic. Canada was to be ruled by a strong, English-style central parliament. Tupper blamed the federal structure and the idea of states' rights in the U.S. Constitution for the disaster of the Civil War. He wanted Canada to be a complete union that reduced provinces to municipal status but knew that that idea would not be accepted, so he settled for the alternative of a highly centralized federal union. The Quebec conference deliberately designated the Canadian Parliament as supreme, with provincial assemblies playing a distinctly subordinate role. However, later amendments and court interpretations shifted the balance of power more toward the provinces than Tupper envisaged.

In 1867, when Canada's first prime minister, John A. Macdonald, had difficulty balancing his first cabinet among the various factions seeking representation, Tupper voluntarily withdrew from consideration in favor of an Irish Catholic from Nova Scotia. However, he joined the cabinet in June, 1870, as president of the Privy Council and in July, 1872, moved to the Ministry of Revenue. As minister of customs for nine months in 1873, he installed the British system of weights and measures as the Canadian standard.

From 1874 to 1878, when the Conservatives were out of power, Tupper resumed his medical practice and burnished his party credentials by campaigning for Conservative candidates across Canada. He became chief parliamentary critic of the ruling Liberal government, rejecting its free-trade policy and demanding an all-Canadian rail route to the Pacific. Such was his growing prominence that Tupper seemed to be Macdonald's heir apparent as head of the Conservatives.

When Macdonald resumed power in 1878, Tupper became his minister of public works. After Macdonald's ministry was divided during the following year, Tupper kept the department of railways and canals. He arranged vital grants and loans for the Canadian Pacific Railway Company, helping create an all-Canadian coast-to-coast railway. He also arranged subsidies for railways in Quebec, Ontario, and the Maritime Provinces, and spent large amounts improving the St. Lawrence River channel and Great Lakes canals. Canadian Pacific board members were grateful for his help. After he left the cabinet to become Canada's high commissioner in London, they awarded him one hundred thousand dollars in stock in 1884.

While serving as high commissioner in London from 1883 to 1896, Tupper did not abstain from partisan politics. In 1887, he returned to Canada at Macdonald's request to head the Ministry of Finance and lead the Conservative election campaign—all the while remaining high commissioner. In 1888, he served as Canadian representative on a British commission negotiating a fisheries treaty with the United States that was so favorable to Canada that the U.S. Senate rejected it.

Meanwhile, Tupper was knighted in 1879 and was created a hereditary baronet in 1888, in recognition of his diplomatic service. In May, 1888, he left the cabinet and returned to London to resume his duties as high commissioner.

After John Macdonald died in 1891, he was succeeded as prime minister by John Abbott (1891-1892), John Thompson (1892-1894), and Mackenzie Bowell (1894-1896). None of these men proved able to resolve conflicts among Conservatives over a dispute about Manitoba schools. Primarily French-speaking Roman Catholics in Manitoba had been promised their own state-supported schools when the province was founded. However, in 1890, a Protestant-dominated provincial government abolished funding for sectarian schools. A cabinet revolt against the inept leadership of Prime Minister Bowell brought Tupper back from England as party leader in February, 1896. Tupper believed that a promise had been made to Catholics that the federal government should implement; however, he could not pass a bill to that effect.

On May 1, 1896, Tupper became prime minister. He confidently called an election for June 23, expecting that Quebec voters would obey the Roman Catholic hierarchy's instructions to vote Conservative and believing Protestant voters in other provinces would reject Wilfred Laurier, a Roman Catholic who was running as the Liberal candidate. He proved to be mistaken in both assumptions. Laurier won decisively, forcing Tupper to resign on July 8. Tupper remained opposition leader until the 1900 election, which Laurier again won. Tupper himself lost the election for his parliamentary seat in Nova Scotia. It was his first loss in Nova Scotia since entering the provincial legislature in 1855, so he resigned his party leadership and returned to England, where he lived the rest of his life. On October, 30, 1915, he died in Bexleyheath, Kent.

SIGNIFICANCE

Tupper's brief service as Canada's prime minister was

his least consequential political act. It is notable primarily because his ten-week tenure was the shortest in the history of the office. By contrast, as premier of Nova Scotia he founded the province's system of free schools and improved its railway system. As federal minister of railways and canals, he played a creative part in the expansion of Canada's transportation facilities and was indispensable in completing an all-Canadian coast-to-coast railway.

An ardent partisan, Tupper created many political enemies, and accusations of corruption dogged him throughout his career, but there is no evidence that he ever engaged in illegal activity. However, nineteenth century views on conflicts of interest affecting office-holders were vague, and Tupper used information and contacts acquired through his political activities to become wealthy, exemplifying that era's comparatively low ethical standards.

Tupper's most constructive and significant role was as a founder of the Canadian confederation. He helped draft Canada's first constitution and persuaded Nova Scotians, despite their reluctance to abandon provincial independence, to join in establishing the dominion.

—*Milton Berman*

FURTHER READING

Longley, James Wilberforce. *Sir Charles Tupper*. Toronto: Oxford University Press, 1926. The only full-scale biography of Tupper, very sympathetic to its subject.

Martin, Ged. *Britain and the Origins of Canadian Confederation, 1837-1867*. Vancouver: University of British Columbia Press, 1995. Describes how British sympathy and support aided the achievement of Canadian Confederation.

Murray, Jock, and Janet Murray. *Sir Charles Tupper: Fighting Doctor to Father of Confederation*. Markham, Ont.: Associated Medical Services, Fitzhenry & Whiteside, 1999. Favorable biography that contains information on Tupper's work as a physician and his contributions to Canadian medicine, as well as his political career.

Seary, Victor Perrin. *Sir Charles Tupper*. Toronto: Ryerson Press, 1930. A brief and favorable sketch by an admirer of Tupper.

Silver, Arthur I. *The French-Canadian Idea of Confederation, 1864-1900*. 2d ed. Toronto: University of Toronto Press, 1997. Explores the evolution of French-Canadian views of confederation.

Vaughan, Frederick. *The Canadian Federalist Experiment: From Defiant Monarchy to Reluctant Republic*. Montreal: McGill-Queen's University Press, 2003. Stresses the monarchist orientation of Confederation leaders and their desire to avoid resembling the United States.

SEE ALSO: Sir John Alexander Macdonald; Alexander Mackenzie; Queen Victoria.

RELATED ARTICLES in *Great Events from History: The Nineteenth Century, 1801-1900:* July 1, 1867: British North America Act; November 5, 1873-October 9, 1878: Canada's Mackenzie Era; September, 1878: Macdonald Returns as Canada's Prime Minister; July 20, 1896-September 21, 1911: Laurier Era in Canada.

IVAN TURGENEV
Russian novelist

One of the great Russian novelists of the nineteenth century, Turgenev combined the lyrical with the realistic in fiction that had a powerful influence on social conditions in his own time and on later writers such as Anton Chekhov and Henry James, who truly ushered in the modern period in literature.

BORN: November 9, 1818; Orel, Russia
DIED: September 3, 1883; Bougival, France
ALSO KNOWN AS: Ivan Sergeyevich Turgenev (full name)
AREA OF ACHIEVEMENT: Literature

EARLY LIFE

Ivan Turgenev (TEWR-gyah-nyehf) was the son of Varvara Petrovna, a wealthy landowner, and Sergey Turgenev, a Russian cavalry officer. According to Turgenev's own comments, he was an enthusiastic reader at an early age, reading not only the fiction and poetry of Russian writers but also the English fiction of Charles Dickens.

Turgenev's family moved to Moscow in 1827, and in 1833 he entered the University of Moscow, which he attended for one year, when, upon another family move to St. Petersburg, he entered the university there. He was graduated in 1837 and went to Berlin, where he was enrolled at the University of Berlin, studying philosophy for three years. Upon returning to St. Petersburg in 1841 and failing to find an academic position, he secured a minor post with the Ministry of the Interior. While traveling in Europe in 1843, he met Pauline Viardot, a French singer, who became his lifelong love and inspiration.

Turgenev retired from the civil service in 1845 and began to devote himself full time to writing poetry. Because his mother disapproved of this decision as well as of his infatuation with Viardot, a married woman, she cut off his allowance. Turgenev followed Viardot, who tolerated his infatuation, to Europe to be near her. He returned to Russia in 1850 because of his mother's serious illness. When she died, he was left the heir of a substantial fortune and was thus able to follow his literary interests, which at this time he successfully shifted from poetry to fiction. In 1847, he had begun the writing of the short stories that, in 1852, were to be published as one of his greatest works, *Zapiski okhotnika* (*Russian Life in the Interior*, 1855; better known as *A Sportsman's Sketches*, 1932).

LIFE'S WORK

When *A Sportsman's Sketches* were being published in periodical form, they created a social uproar in Russia, for they presented the serf as more than a mere slave and, in fact, as often more human and genuine than the landowners themselves. Because the stories were seen as a protest against the serf system, the authorities began to watch Turgenev closely. In 1852, when he wrote an enthusiastic obituary notice on the death of his fellow writer Nikolai Gogol, he met further disapproval; the authorities banished him to his country estate, where he was forced to stay for a year and a half.

When he returned to St. Petersburg, after the publication of *A Sportsman's Sketches* in book form, he found himself to be the leading light of St. Petersburg literary culture. *A Sportsman's Sketches* has often been considered historically important for the influence it had on the abolition of the serf system in Russia; in fact, the book has even been compared in this regard to Harriet Beecher Stowe's *Uncle Tom's Cabin: Or, Life Among the Lowly* (1852). However, the aesthetic and critical importance of the stories, the reason many of them continue to be read, lies in their unique blend of the lyrical and the realistic. Such stories as "Bezhin Meadow" and "The Country Doctor," two of the most familiar in the collection, create a dreamlike and sometimes surrealistic world, even as they manage to remain solidly grounded in phenomenal experience. As a short-story writer, Turgenev historically stands somewhere between the folktale fantasy of Nikolai Gogol and the nightmare reality of Franz Kafka.

For the next few years after the success of *A Sportsman's Sketches*, Turgenev, who felt inspired by travel, was forced to stay at home because of the Crimean War. Moreover, many biographers suggest that he was in a deep depression because of the impossibility of his tireless love for Viardot. As a result, he published little during this period, with the exception of his short novel *Rudin* (*Dmitri Roudine*, 1873; better known as *Rudin*, 1947), which appeared in 1856. In a drastic shift—which may have resulted partly from his freedom to travel and partly from his acceptance of the Viardot situation—within the next five years Turgenev alternated between traveling on the Continent and writing some of his most respected works, including the novels *Dvoryanskoye gnezdo* (1859; *Liza*, 1869; better known as *A House of Gentlefolk*, 1894) and *Nakanune* (1860; *On the Eve*,

TURGENEV'S MAJOR FICTION

SHORT FICTION

1852　*Zapiski okhotnika* (*Russian Life in the Interior*, 1855; also known as *A Sportsman's Sketches*, 1932)

LONG FICTION

1856　*Rudin* (*Dimitri Roudine*, 1873; better known as *Rudin*, 1947)

1858　*Asya* (English translation, 1877)

1859　*Dvoryanskoye gnezdo* (*Liza*, 1869; also as *A Nobleman's Nest*, 1903; better known as *A House of Gentlefolk*, 1894)

1860　*Nakanune* (*On the Eve*, 1871)

1860　*Pervaya lyubov* (*First Love*, 1884)

1862　*Ottsy i deti* (*Fathers and Sons*, 1867)

1867　*Dym* (*Smoke*, 1868)

1872　*Veshniye vody* (*Spring Floods*, 1874; better known as *The Torrents of Spring*, 1897)

1877　*Nov* (*Virgin Soil*, 1877)

1871), the novella *Pervaya lyubov* (1860; *First Love*, 1884), and the essay "Gamlet i Don Kikhot" (1860; "Hamlet and Don Quixote," 1930). He also finished his best-known novel, *Ottsy i deti* (*Fathers and Sons*, 1867), in 1861 and had it published the following year.

Fathers and Sons is built around what Turgenev perceived as an emerging type of man in Russia, a type that he named "nihilist," a term to which Turgenev's novel gave great currency at mid-century. The character Bazarov in Turgenev's novel is one who rejects religion, art, and the Russian class system and emphasizes instead scientific empiricism. Turgenev was vilified by Russian intellectuals and praised by the Russian secret police for this depiction, for the novel was misinterpreted as supporting the conservative "fathers," while casting doubt on the radical "sons." Turgenev, in a defense of his work, argued that by "nihilist" he really meant "revolutionary," and that his work was directed against the gentry as the leading class. As a result, Russian critics began to see the work as the herald of the coming revolution.

In addition to frequently coming in conflict with either the authorities or the radical dissenters, Turgenev's life was also often plagued by conflict with his literary relationships. He was friends with such great Russian writers as Ivan Goncharov and Leo Tolstoy but had bitter quarrels with both of them. Goncharov accused him of plagiarizing from an unpublished manuscript, and Tolstoy accused him of moral illness because of his liaison with Viardot. The quarrel with Tolstoy, which occurred at a dinner party and involved a disagreement about helping the poor, almost resulted in a duel and lasted for seventeen years. A few years later, he also had quarrels with Fyodor Dostoevski because of a debt Dostoevski owed Turgenev.

In 1863, when the Viardots went to live in Baden-Baden, Germany, Turgenev visited them there, where he was received as an old family friend, a role he seemed willing to play, if only for the opportunity to be near Pauline. Indeed, his desire to be near her was so great that he also moved to Baden-Baden. From all indications, his life there was happy and his health was good, in spite of the fact that his relationship with the beloved Pauline was less than he desired. Enjoying a life of hunting and social leisure, however, Turgenev did little work; *Dym* (1867; *Smoke*, 1868) is the only novel that he wrote during his eight years in the German resort.

Turgenev's life always seemed dominated by his attachment to Viardot; when she moved once again, Turgenev followed, first to London and then to Bougival, France, where Turgenev and the Viardots bought a summer home jointly in 1874. In France, Turgenev began a close relationship with several prominent writers, including Gustave Flaubert, George Sand, Émile Zola, Edmond de Goncourt, and others. Once more, Turgenev seemed preoccupied with matters that kept him from his writing. The only important works he published during this period were two novellas, one of which was *Veshniye vody* (1872; *Spring Floods*, 1874; better known as *The Torrents of Spring*, 1897).

Turgenev began working on his last, and his longest, novel, *Nov* (*Virgin Soil*, 1877), in 1876. This story of love and revolution, published in 1877, was not well received by Russian critics; conservative commentators thought it criticized Russia too much, while radical critics thought the revolutionary characters were not true to life. However, the work was enthusiastically read outside Russia, being immediately translated into many different languages and receiving rave reviews from influential critics.

Turgenev fell ill in early 1882 and moved to the summer home he owned with the Viardots in Bougival in June of that year. Although he was in much pain, his illness was not properly diagnosed as spinal cancer, and Turgenev did not believe his life was in danger. On September 3, 1883, after having dictated a story critical of the Russian aristocracy, Turgenev died surrounded by his family and friends. In a funeral that amounted to national mourning, he was buried in St. Petersburg in Volkov cemetery.

SIGNIFICANCE

Ivan Turgenev always declared himself a realist whose every line was inspired by something that he actually observed. When his works were published, their importance lay less in their artistic and aesthetic qualities than in their documentation of the social realities of Russian life. Indeed, such works as *A Sportsman's Sketches* were said to have been at least a partial cause for the abolition of the serf system, much as *Uncle Tom's Cabin* had an effect on the abolition of the system of slavery in the United States. Turgenev's later works are also remembered for their depiction of a world that was doomed to die with the Russian Revolution.

When Turgenev is studied in the twenty-first century, it is not for his social realism, but rather for what has been termed his poetic realism. It is his stories and his novellas, in which reality is presented as often lyrical and dreamlike, rather than his novels, in which he sought to present reality concretely and socially, that have won for him a permanent place in the history of modern literature. The influence of his short-story style on those writers who ushered in the modern period, such as Anton Chekhov, Henry James, and later Sherwood Anderson and others, is his most important literary legacy.

—*Charles E. May*

FURTHER READING

Bloom, Harold, ed. *Ivan Turgenev*. Philadelphia: Chelsea House, 2003. Collection of essays about Turgenev's life and work, including comparison of his writing to that of Ernest Hemingway and Nathaniel Hawthorne, and an introduction written by Bloom. One of the titles in the Modern Critical Views series.

Freeborn, Richard. *Turgenev: The Novelist's Novelist*. New York: Oxford University Press, 1960. A general study of Turgenev's novels, both in terms of their place in nineteenth century Russian literature and culture and in terms of Henry James's view that Turgenev was a "novelist's novelist." Freeborn primarily discusses Turgenev's four major novels: *Rudin*, *A House of Gentlefolk*, *On the Eve*, and *Fathers and Sons*.

Magarshack, David. *Turgenev: A Life*. London: Faber & Faber, 1954. A detailed but highly readable account of Turgenev's life. Along with Yarmolinsky's biography cited below, it is the most frequently referred to work on Turgenev. The work attempts to account for the relationship of Turgenev's art to his life and is particularly helpful in discussing the role that Turgenev's dramas played in the development of his art.

Pritchett, V. S. *The Gentle Barbarian: The Life and Work of Turgenev*. New York: Random House, 1977. This popular study is quite accessible to the general reader but is largely based on the previous biographies of Magarshack and Yarmolinsky. Although little is new here, it is characterized by Pritchett's lucid style and his critical understanding of Turgenev's fiction. Pritchett uses details from Turgenev's life to increase the reader's understanding of his novels and short stories.

Ripp, Victor. *Turgenev's Russia: From "Notes of a Hunter" to "Fathers and Sons."* Ithaca, N.Y.: Cornell University Press, 1980. This critical study deals only with Turgenev's fiction between *A Sportsman's Sketches* and *Fathers and Sons* and therefore does not deal with his drama. It is valuable in clarifying Turgenev's place in nineteenth century Russian literature and thought and in delineating the important cultural issues that inform his fiction.

Schapiro, Leonard. *Turgenev: His Life and Times*. New York: Random House, 1978. This biography makes use of materials about Turgenev's life and work previously available only in Russian and materials about his relationship with Viardot previously available only in French. This is purely a biographical study and makes no efforts to analyze Turgenev's work.

Yarmolinsky, Avrahm. *Turgenev: The Man, His Art, and His Age*. Rev. ed. New York: Orion Press, 1959. This is a revision of Yarmolinsky's authoritative biography of 1926. Not only is it valuable in providing a detailed account of Turgenev's life and artistic development, but it also discusses his intellectual and artistic development and his contribution to an understanding of nineteenth century Russian culture.

SEE ALSO: Anton Chekhov; Charles Dickens; Fyodor Dostoevski; Gustave Flaubert; Nikolai Gogol; Henry James; Guy de Maupassant; George Sand; Harriet Beecher Stowe; Leo Tolstoy; Émile Zola.

RELATED ARTICLE in *Great Events from History: The Nineteenth Century, 1801-1900:* December, 1849: Dostoevski Is Exiled to Siberia.

J. M. W. TURNER
English painter

The outstanding revolutionary painter of landscapes, Turner was a Romantic. With the vast complexity of his work, he has been called the Shakespeare of English art. He was an artist far ahead of his time and remains without equal in depicting the sea in all of its moods.

BORN: April 23, 1775; London, England
DIED: December 19, 1851; London, England
ALSO KNOWN AS: Joseph Mallord William Turner
   (full name)
AREA OF ACHIEVEMENT: Art

EARLY LIFE

Joseph Mallord William Turner was the son of a barber and a wigmaker. His mother, Mary Marshall, was some six years older than his father, William. Although he is said to have been the eldest son in the family, there are no extant references to other children, except for a sister three years younger, Mary Ann, who died when Turner was eleven.

Turner's mother was apparently subject to fits of manic rage. When she was in her early sixties, she was committed to Bethlehem Hospital for the Insane in December, 1800—by neighbors, not by family members—and died there in April, 1804. Biographers have frequently attributed Turner's problems with women and his fascination with nature in its most violent phases to his mother's influence. As he left no journals or autobiography, his own thoughts on this subject, as on others, remain unknown. Only his words in reported conversations are available.

Turner's father, who, Turner said, never praised him except for saving a shilling, exhibited his son's drawings in the shop window and boasted that his son would become a painter. After the death of Mary Turner, William Turner served as his son's factotum until his death in 1829 at the age of eighty-five.

From childhood, Turner was completely absorbed with capturing on paper what his eye saw and his mind perceived and imagined. His relations considered him inarticulate and found him ungrateful because he failed to write thank-you notes. As a child, he knew the urban life of London, the shipping on the Thames, the open sea at Margate (the subject of some of his earliest and last drawings), and the rural scene at Brentford, where he stayed with an uncle and attended the Free School as a day boarder in 1786.

Turner took lessons from Thomas Malton, a watercolor painter of architectural studies, and in December of 1789, he was admitted as a student at the Royal Academy school, where he studied for four years. His first exhibit at the Royal Academy was a watercolor in 1790, and in March, 1793, he was awarded the "Greater Silver Pallet" for landscape painting by the Society of Arts. He was employed by Dr. Thomas Monro to copy drawings by John Robert Cozens and other artists during the evenings. He exhibited his first oil painting—*Fishermen at Sea*—at the Royal Academy in 1796. In 1799, Turner was elected an associate of the school and left his parents' home, taking lodgings in Harley Street. In 1802, Turner was elected a full member of the Royal Academy at the youngest age possible.

Turner was a very short man, so short that when walking and holding a presumably not large fish by its gills, its tail dragged on the ground, as did the bottom of Turner's frock coat. When prevailed upon to paint his self-portrait, Turner worried that his work would be devalued because of his appearance. He was a man of phenomenal energy and industry, routinely hiking twenty-five miles a day to sketch; who carried secrecy to extremes; and who was devoted to a small number of friends, including W. F. Wells and Walter Fawkes.

In 1799, Turner met Sarah Danby, a young widow with four children; although they were never married, they had two daughters, Evelina and Georgianna. Because Turner never spoke of his relationships with women—his mother; his sister; Sarah Danby; her niece, Hannah Danby; Sophia Booth, the second widow with whom he lived (1834 until his death)—his personal life is subject to much speculation. Nothing is known of Sarah Danby's death, but it is likely that Turner's relationship with her lasted into the 1820's. In Turner's will of 1829, he provided for each of his two daughters, for Sarah Danby, and for Hannah Danby. Assumptions abound, but probably names disappear from his subsequent wills simply because Turner outlived those individuals.

The only contemporary biography—by G. W. Thornbury, recognized as quite unreliable—portrayed Turner as a miser and accused him of "wallowing in Wapping" (the brothel district). Although Turner was indeed concerned with money— which he saw as his only means of pursuing his artistic ambition—there is evidence that he was frequently generous and in no way mean-spirited, much less vulgar, despite his Cockney accent. He did

J. M. W. Turner. (Library of Congress)

go to Wapping to collect rents. If his figure drawings came from Wapping, this will never be known for certain, because his champion, John Ruskin, destroyed these drawings, which he pronounced obscene, after Turner's death.

LIFE'S WORK

Turner's life's work, his art, was his life: No separation is possible. If his relationships with women remain a mystery, it is nevertheless clear that his life was consumed by his practice of his art. When he died, he left to his nation, on condition that a gallery be built to house his work, three hundred oil paintings and twenty thousand watercolors and drawings, which did not include the hundreds of oils and watercolors already in private collections. There are also more than two hundred bound sketchbooks in the British Museum.

Turner became an expert architectural and topographical draftsman, and there is an underlying sense of structure even in his late abstract work. He sketched from nature all of his life and intently studied the work of others. It was as if he had to conquer the artistic method and

achievement of every previous artist in order to find his own mode of expression. After his election to membership in the Royal Academy, Turner made his first trip to France and Switzerland (he had already made many sketching tours in England and Wales). His paintings have been cataloged in terms of his trips to Europe that he continued up to the age of seventy.

There are 318 oil paintings in the Turner bequest and more than two hundred in private collections. Martin Butlin and Evelyn Joll divide his paintings into five periods: 1793-1802, before Turner went abroad; 1803-1819, before he made his first trip to Italy; 1819-1829, before he made his second trip to Italy; works painted in Rome, 1828-1829; and 1829-1851, his later works—with the second and fifth the largest groups. Turner's work was viewed with increasing bewilderment. *The Fifth Plague of Egypt* was Turner's first historical subject and was well received. *Calais Pier, Sun Rising Through Vapour*, and *The Battle of Trafalgar* elicited negative comment. *Snow Storm: Hannibal and His Army Crossing the Alps* was well received and exemplifies Turner's very different approach to historical painting with nature playing the dominant role. *Dido Building Carthage* and *Sun Rising Through Vapour* were finally offered to the National Gallery in Turner's will, on the condition that they be hung permanently next to two of Claude Lorrain's paintings.

Turner remained ever cognizant of his duty to the Royal Academy, which he viewed as the mother of all British artists. He put aside his inclination to withdraw into his work to meet all of his responsibilities as a member. He was proud of his appointment as a professor of perspective in 1807—frequently signing his work RA, PP. He did not, however, deliver any lectures until 1811, when he had completed lengthy study and nearly two hundred large drawings and diagrams to demonstrate his points. His lectures were unintelligible; often he seemed to be laughing at some private joke. He did not resign his position until 1837, although his last lectures were in 1828. His work sold consistently, much of it on commission, first at the Royal Academy and later in his own galleries.

Turner valued poetry and read widely, appending words from James Thomson, Mark Akenside, Edward Young, and John Milton to his paintings. Beginning in 1812, he used lines from his own unpublished poem, "Fallacies of Hope," which are of interest only because they are Turner's. He did illustrations for Sir Walter Scott, and in 1834, his illustrations of Lord Byron's poems were exhibited. However, with all of Turner's travel on the Continent, he never learned French, German, or Italian, for words were never his medium. He was apparently completely unaware of the political upheaval around him, but he knew the conditions of the roads.

The *Liber Studiorum* (1807-1819) constitutes a text without words on the expressive power and scope inherent in landscape art. W. F. Wells, one of Turner's best friends, persuaded him to begin these engravings in 1806; the first volume was published in 1807 and the last in 1819. Turner published these engravings at his own expense and marked each of the seventy-one plates in one of six ways: as pastoral, epic or elevated pastoral, marine, architectural, mountainous, or historical. These engravings are in mezzotint on copper and printed in dark brown. The *Liber Studiorum* is an unequaled compendium of landscape styles.

Turner was sufficiently self-reliant that the harsh, sometimes venomous, criticism of his work did not deter him. Sir George Beaumont and *Blackwood's Magazine* remained hostile, and Turner was accused of having an optical disease and was frequently pronounced insane. He rarely said anything critical about his fellow artists and never made any attempt to respond to negative criticism. When the young middle-class John Ruskin met the sixty-year-old bohemian artist for the first time and called him the Great Angel of the Apocalypse, Turner was considerably taken aback.

Turner was no purist in method, but would use any means to achieve the truth he sought. Although he used constant sketches as a basis for his drawings, watercolors, engravings, and paintings, his finished works were not intended to represent the optical truth of the moment in terms of light or weather (Claude Monet found Turner antipathetic), but rather his own inspiration. His two oils of the fire in 1834 at the Houses of Parliament are visionary, not realistic. Turner placed his Juliet in Venice rather than Verona because he was in love with the former city (*Juliet and Her Nurse*). In *The Fighting Temeraire Tugged to Her Last Berth to Be Broken Up* and *Rain, Steam, and Speed—The Great Western Railway*, Turner shows his fascination with humankind's battle to control nature, however pessimistic he might have been about the future of humanity. The imagery in *Slavers Throwing Overboard the Dead and Dying*, *Peace: Burial at Sea*, and *Death on a Pale Horse* is indubitably powerful and without equal in British art.

Toward the end of Turner's life, when he was living with Sophia Booth in a house he had purchased in her name (and was letting people in the area call him Puggy or Admiral Booth), he lost his teeth, and a false set would

not help. He subsisted on two quarts of milk and an equal amount of rum a day.

In his will, Turner bequeathed his finished work to the nation on condition that a gallery be built and gave most of his large fortune to what was to be a charity to support poor male artists of legitimate British issue. Because his father's relatives contested the will and his executors failed to protest, the latter never happened. No distinction was ever made between his finished and his unfinished work— which he might not have wanted anyone to see—and the National Gallery received all of his work. Turner did want his work to be seen as a whole, so the meaning would be clear, but it was not until 1987 that the Turner Gallery next to the Tate opened its doors.

SIGNIFICANCE

J. M. W. Turner may indeed be likened to William Shakespeare, for the richness of his exploration of humankind's relationship with the environment is beyond measure. Only by mastering the difficulties of landscape could he free himself of society's views and express himself. He was a poetic, not a scientific, painter. He was seeking a reality of his imagination, even though he drew from nature. After Turner, landscape painting could never again be regarded as inferior. In his late and abstract oils of an estate, Petworth, which he never exhibited, he had completely merged his technique in watercolor with his technique in oil. He perceived reality as constantly changing, as light and energy, and he saw light as color.

Although his landscapes have people, they are not the most prominent part of the works: He presents his human figures as he draws his viewers into his work, by his vortices. In attempting to present a comprehensive view of the world, he involved in his art the interaction of nature and humanity. He drew from mythology, history, poetry, contemporary events, and his own private poetry, the subjects for his work. The apocryphal best he could say about art was that it was "a rum business." Although he took enormous artistic license, his grasp of water, land, trees, mountains, masonry, ships, leaves, and fish was exact. However, only in Turner's time is his *The Angel Standing in the Sun* even conceivable. What he offers finally is a vision of enchantment.

Because of his scope, Turner is difficult to comprehend as an artist; the label Romantic does not suffice any more than Elizabethan suffices for Shakespeare. It has been said that no other artist captured the landscape of Switzerland as Turner did. It has also been said, more remarkably in view of Italian art, that no other artist captured the light of Venice as Turner did. Elizabeth Rigby wrote that Turner "does what he will—others do what they can." If Turner country is not to be located in any one geographical place, surely it is because Turner's artistic vision is both rare and universal.

—Carol Bishop

FURTHER READING

Butlin, Martin, and Evelyn Joll. *The Paintings of J. M. W. Turner.* 2 vols. New Haven, Conn.: Yale University Press, 1977. Discusses each of Turner's oil paintings—its origin, exhibition history, contemporary reviews—providing rare reproductions. Invaluable.

Hamilton, James. *Turner.* New York: Random House, 2003. Hamilton uses material contained in Turner's sketchbook to describe the artist's life and work, concluding that Turner owed his fame to opportunism as much as to talent.

Heffernan, James A. W. *The Re-Creation of Landscape: A Study of Wordsworth, Coleridge, Constable, and Turner.* Hanover, N.H.: University Press of New England, 1985. Argues that the literature of the two poets is not definable in terms of dynamic temporality nor the work of the two artists in terms of spatial fixity. Cogent and important.

Herrmann, Luke. *Turner: Paintings, Watercolors, Prints and Drawings.* London: Phaidon Press, 1975. Valuable data on the artist and his work, with reproductions and notes by a Turner scholar.

Joll, Evelyn, Martin Butlin, and Luke Herrmann, eds. *The Oxford Companion to J. M. W. Turner.* Oxford, England: Oxford University Press, 2001. Contains more than 760 alphabetically arranged entries examining all aspects of Turner's private and public lives, including his working methods, his influence on other artists, and the subjects and settings depicted in his art. Some entries are essay length, providing a good deal more than basic "ready reference" material.

Lindsay, Jack. *Turner: The Man and His Art.* New York: Franklin Watts, 1985. Provides valuable data on Turner's life and place in English landscape art.

Paulson, Ronald. *Literary Landscape: Turner and Constable.* New Haven, Conn.: Yale University Press, 1982. A valuable discussion of the relation between landscape images and literary texts and Turner's use of literary references, as opposed to John Constable's suppression of the same.

Rosenblum, Robert. *Modern Painting and the Northern Romantic Tradition: Friedrich to Rothko.* New York: Harper and Row, 1975. Traces a tradition from Romantics, such as Turner, to Vincent van Gogh and Edvard Munch during the late nineteenth century, to German expressionism and twentieth century abstract painters, such as Piet Mondrian.

Shanes, Eric. *Turner: The Life and Masterworks.* Rev., expanded and updated 3d ed. New York: Parkstone, 2004. An updated catalog from an exhibition of Turner's watercolors, presented at the Royal Academy of Arts in London. Several essays describe the importance of Turner's watercolors within the context of his entire body of work, and how his watercolors influenced other painters. Also includes two hundred colored reproductions.

Turner, J. M. W. *Collected Correspondence of J. M. W. Turner.* Edited by John Gage. Oxford, England: Clarendon Press, 1980. A thorough presentation of 342 of Turner's generally brief letters.

Walker, John. *Joseph Mallord William Turner.* New York: Harry N. Abrams, 1976. The most complete single volume on Turner, essential to any study of this artist.

SEE ALSO: Lord Byron; John Constable; Winslow Homer; John Ruskin; Sir Walter Scott.

RELATED ARTICLE in *Great Events from History: The Nineteenth Century, 1801-1900:* Fall, 1848: Pre-Raphaelite Brotherhood Begins.

NAT TURNER
American slave rebellion leader

Turner led the largest slave revolt in the history of the United States. As a slave preacher, he linked religion, liberation, and black militancy, thus providing a model for many future black liberation movements.

BORN: October 2, 1800; Southampton County, Virginia
DIED: November 11, 1831; Jerusalem, Virginia
ALSO KNOWN AS: Nathaniel Turner (birth name)
AREA OF ACHIEVEMENT: Social reform

EARLY LIFE

Nat Turner was born a slave on the Benjamin Turner plantation in Southampton, Virginia. His mother was African born, and his father escaped from slavery to the North when Turner was a young child. From the beginning, Turner was perceived as a remarkable child by both his family and his white owner. Born into a slave culture that mixed elements of African tradition with Christianity, Turner exhibited birthmarks that, according to African custom, marked him as a person with spiritual gifts and power. He was treated accordingly by his relatives and the local slave community.

Turner's owner saw his early intelligence and encouraged him to learn to read and write. Turner's paternal grandmother was extremely religious and provided religious education. Turner attended services and received religious education at Benjamin Turner's Methodist meeting house, where the slaves were encouraged to worship with their master and his family. Turner, from his childhood, read the Bible regularly and engaged in prayer and meditation, coming to believe that he had a special calling. His religious study and his visions convinced him that Christianity affirmed the equality and dignity of all people and that slavery was a sin against God and his teachings.

By the 1820's, Turner had already acquired a reputation among other slaves in terms of his intelligence and spiritual gifts. He also began to have regular religious visions. Most important was his report of an encounter with a spirit that approached him and spoke the Biblical verse, "Seek ye the Kingdom of Heaven and all this shall be added unto you" (Luke 12:31). Turner interpreted this as a sign that he had a special religious mission. Later, in 1821, he escaped after a dispute with his master; however, after thirty days and another vision, he returned to his enslavement.

Turner believed that personal escape was an evasion of the greater mission to which he had been called. After this, his mystical experiences increased in number and intensity as he began to find signs in the heavens and in hieroglyphic figures that he discovered on leaves. During this time, he took on the role of a Baptist preacher. His reputation as a preacher spread, and he was allowed some freedom in traveling about, reportedly journeying as far as Hartford County, North Carolina, in 1828. His power as a preacher was so great that even some white people were impressed by his message, including a plantation overseer, Ethelred T. Brantley, who, despite disapproval from the white community, was baptized by Turner.

During this time period, Turner had a vision that was to shape future events. He saw a battle in the air between black and white spirits in which streams of blood flowed. Later, in May of 1828, he was informed by the spirit that, like Christ, he was to wage a "fight against the Serpent" and that he would receive the appropriate sign when the battle was to begin. Drawing heavily on the judgment motifs of the Old Testament prophets and the biblical apocalyptic visions of a battle that is described as the final war between good and evil, Turner came to understand himself as a messianic figure who was called to initiate an upcoming battle between good and evil that would end with the freeing of the slaves.

LIFE'S WORK

The sign that Turner was seeking and the events that gained Turner historical notoriety began with a solar eclipse in February, 1831. Turner saw this as the sign that the battle would soon begin. He began planning a slave revolt with four other slaves—Henry Porter, Hank Travis, Nelson Williams, and Sam Francis—that was to begin on July 4. The plan was to kill local slave owners, seize their weapons, rally other slaves to their cause, and then march on the county seat, Jerusalem, Virginia, and seize weapons from an armory. The hope was that by then, a well-armed slave army would be formed to engage in a final battle to end slavery. On July 4, however, Turner fell ill, and the attack was postponed.

Turner waited for another sign. It came in August, 1831. For three days—the "Three Blue Days of 1831"—the sun over North Carolina and Virginia had a strange blue cast. In response, on August 21 Turner called together his group of followers, which now numbered eight. They gathered for an evening meal, finalized their plans, and then, just after midnight on August 22, put the plan into action. They first went to the house of Turner's current owner, John Travis, and, armed with a hatchet and broadax, killed Travis, his wife, and their children—six people in all. They gathered some guns and ammunition and moved from farm to farm in the region. By Tuesday morning, August 23, the group with Turner numbered about seventy, and they had killed fifty-seven white people, over half of which were women and children, in the twenty-mile area of the Boykins district of Southampton.

As the rebels moved down the road from Cross Keys to Jerusalem, they met their first resistance in the form of a white militia under the command of Captains Alexander Peete and James Bryant. After some initial success, Turner's group was subsequently scattered. Soldiers from Fort Monroe and white militia from surrounding areas were dispatched to put down the rebellion. Many of the slave insurgents were quickly captured. White people retaliated with a terrorist campaign against black people in the area, both slave and free. As many as two hundred black people may have been murdered; many of them were lynched, and many were tortured. The massacre would have become worse had not General Eppes intervened and dismissed the militia groups.

Turner escaped and lived in the woods near Cabin Pond, eluding capture for six weeks. He was discovered by a white man, Benjamin Phipps, on Sunday, October 30, hiding in a hole he had dug under a fallen tree. He was taken to Jerusalem on November 1, convicted during a five-day trial, and hanged on November 11. During the time he was in prison, he made lengthy verbal confessions to his attorney, Thomas R. Gray, which were subsequently published and became the primary source of information about Turner and his planned revolt. When asked at his sentencing whether he had more to say, Turner showed no remorse, but only replied, "Was not Christ crucified?" Fifty-three black people, including Turner, were arrested. Twenty-one were acquitted, twelve were transported out of state, and nineteen others, in addition to Turner, were hanged.

At the time of Turner's revolt, antislavery sentiment had become strong in the North and some parts of the South. David Walker's *Appeal to the Coloured Citizens of the World*, which advocated the violent overthrow of slavery, had been published in 1829, and William Lloyd Garrison was already actively involved in advocating the abolition of slavery through political action. The Southampton rebellion intensified the debate and tended to harden positions on both sides. As a response to the revolt, legislation was passed throughout the South that set new penalties for teaching slaves to read, limited the rights of slaves to preach, and placed limits on the rights of slaves to gather for religious services. The education of free black people was also severely limited as many of the informal black schools were closed. Many free black people were pressured to move North.

TURNER'S MOTIVES

After Nat Turner was arrested, he was interviewed at length, and the resulting transcript was published as The Confessions of Nat Turner *(a title that William Styron used for a novel about Turner in 1967). In response to a question about the reason for his slave rebellion, he gave this reply.*

Sir,—You have asked me to give a history of the motives which induced me to undertake the late insurrection, as you call it—To do so I must go back to the days of my infancy, and even before I was born. I was thirty-one years of age the 2d of October last, and born the property of Benj. Turner, of this county. In my childhood a circumstance occurred which made an indelible impression on my mind, and laid the ground work of that enthusiasm, which has terminated so fatally to many, both white and black, and for which I am about to atone at the gallows. It is here necessary to relate this circumstance—trifling as it may seem, it was the commencement of that belief which has grown with time, and even now, sir, in this dungeon, helpless and forsaken as I am, I cannot divest myself of. Being at play with other children, when three or four years old, I was telling them something, which my mother overhearing, said it had happened before I was born—I stuck to my story, however, and related somethings which went, in her opinion, to confirm it—others being called on were greatly astonished, knowing that these things had happened, and caused them to say in my hearing, I surely would be a prophet, as the Lord had shewn me things that had happened before my birth. And my father and mother strengthened me in this my first impression, saying in my presence, I was intended for some great purpose, which they had always thought from certain marks on my head and breast—[a parcel of excrescences which I believe are not at all uncommon, particularly among negroes, as I have seen several with the same. . . .]

Source: Nat Turner, *The Confessions of Nat Turner* (Baltimore, 1831).

The debate surrounding the rebellion emerged again during the 1960's with the publication of William Styron's fictionalized account of the life of Turner, *The Confessions of Nat Turner* (1966). According to African American critics, the book portrays Turner as a crazed fanatic and a precursor of the black militants who were gaining prominence during the 1960's and thus is a veiled criticism of black radicalism. African American scholars responded to the book with a period of intense historical research and inquiry to present a more accurate portrayal of Turner.

SIGNIFICANCE

Nat Turner's notoriety came as a result of his leading the largest slave revolt in the history of the United States. More important, however, Turner was a black religious leader who embodied a central theme of the black religious tradition in the United States. Like those who would follow, including Martin Luther King, Jr., and Malcolm X, he proclaimed that the God of the Old Testament was a god that set slaves free and demanded social justice, a god who exacted judgment on societies that were not just and who required people to take action to rectify social injustice. Turner's actions also highlight the fact that slaves did not passively accept slavery but acted to obtain their freedom and equal rights. Turner's confessions have been an important historical source that demonstrates the continued influence of African traditions on slave culture and African American religion.

The historical debates surrounding the portrayal of Turner are significant in understanding the racial divide that exists in the United States. The focus on the brutality of Turner's revolt in the debate following the rebellion and in later portrayals by people such as Styron shows the refusal of white America to understand the context of black radicalism. Turner's revolt was a demand for freedom and rights, a response to a system that bought and sold people, separated families, and arbitrarily tortured and executed slaves. To understand the violence of some forms of black radicalism, it is necessary to understand the violence of the system to which it is a response.

—*Charles L. Kammer*

FURTHER READING

Aptheker, Herbert. *American Negro Slave Revolts*. New York: International, 1943. Aptheker places Turner's revolt in the historical context of other slave revolts during this time period.

Clarke, John Henry, ed. *William Styron's Nat Turner: Ten Black Writers Respond*. Westport, Conn.: Green-wood Press, 1968. A response to Styron's novel by a variety of black scholars who are attempting to counteract what they see as a distorted portrayal of Turner.

Duff, John B., ed. *The Nat Turner Rebellion: The Historical Event and the Modern Debate*. New York: Harper and Row, 1971. A recounting of the ongoing debate about the interpretation of Turner and his rebellion.

Foner, Eric, ed. *Great Lives Observed: Nat Turner*. Englewood Cliffs, N.J.: Prentice-Hall, 1971. Collection of historical documents, representing reactions to, and changing interpretations of, Turner in a variety of historical time periods.

French, Scot. *The Rebellious Slave: Nat Turner in American Memory*. Boston: Houghton Mifflin, 2004. Analyzes Turner's legacy by examining how he has been depicted in popular culture. Describes how Turner's image has changed from the immediate aftermath of his rebellion to more recent debates.

Greenberg, Kenneth S., ed. *The Confessions of Nat Turner and Related Documents*. New York: St. Martin's Press, 1996. Includes the text of Turner's confessions to Thomas R. Gray and other historical documents from the time period.

_____. *Nat Turner: A Slave Rebellion in History and Memory*. New York: Oxford University Press, 2003. Collection of essays about Turner, including an exploration of his relationship with the black community in Southampton County, Virginia, and the role of women in his insurrection. Includes an interview with William Styron and an essay written by Herbert Aptheker in 1937.

Oates, Stephen B. *The Fires of Jubilee: Nat Turner's Fierce Rebellion*. New York: Harper and Row, 1975. Oates provides a detailed historical account of the life of Turner, the rebellion, and the debates and legislation that ensued.

Styron, William. *The Confessions of Nat Turner: A Novel*. New York: Random House, 1966. A controversial but popular fictionalized account of Turner's life and the rebellion, written by a white southern author.

Tragle, Henry Irving, ed. *The Southampton Slave Revolt of 1831: A Compilation of Source Material*. Amherst: University of Massachusetts Press, 1971. A comprehensive collection of historical reports and accounts of the revolt and the ensuing debate.

Wilmore, Gayraud. *Black Religion and Black Radicalism: An Interpretation of the Religious History of Afro-American People*. Maryknoll, N.Y.: Orbis

Books, 1983. Wilmore places Turner's life and self-understanding in the context of African American religious traditions.

SEE ALSO: John Brown; William Lloyd Garrison; Dred Scott.

RELATED ARTICLES in *Great Events from History: The Nineteenth Century, 1801-1900:* c. 1830-1865: Southerners Advance Proslavery Arguments; August 21, 1831: Turner Launches Slave Insurrection; July 2, 1839: *Amistad* Slave Revolt; July, 1859: Last Slave Ship Docks at Mobile.

MARK TWAIN
American writer

Twain gave the world one of its enduring children's classics, The Adventures of Tom Sawyer, *and in its sequel,* Adventures of Huckleberry Finn, *gave America the prototypical initiation novel. However, as he approached the end of his life, his humor and nostalgia for the past increasingly gave way to his pessimism about humanity's technological progress.*

BORN: November 30, 1835; Florida, Missouri
DIED: April 21, 1910; Redding, Connecticut
ALSO KNOWN AS: Samuel Langhorne Clemens (birth name); Samuel L. Clemens
AREA OF ACHIEVEMENT: Literature

EARLY LIFE

Samuel Langhorne Clemens was the sixth of seven children of Jane (née Jane Lampton) and John Marshall Clemens. His ancestors on both sides were mostly English and Irish who had lived in Virginia and Kentucky. Although both sides of his family claimed distinguished English ancestors, those aristocratic ties were never clearly identified, and the Clemens family was anything but affluent when Samuel was born. Nevertheless, Samuel's father was a cultivated, educated man (he had studied law) who was determined to be successful financially. Consequently, because there appeared to be more opportunity, in 1839 the elder Clemens moved his family to Hannibal, located on the banks of the Mississippi.

John Clemens's financial dreams never materialized, and he died in 1847, when Samuel was eleven. Partly by default and partly because of her personality, Jane Clemens became a central influence in Samuel's life. In fact, the similarities between his mother and Olivia Langdon, his wife, were so pronounced that one could speculate that his mother's influence subconsciously affected his choice of a wife.

Shortly after his father's death, Samuel, probably for financial reasons, was apprenticed to a local printer, and his newspaper career was launched. In 1850, he went to work for his older brother, Orion, on the Hannibal *Western Union*, and until 1857, he worked as a typesetter for various newspapers. During this period, he also wrote sketches and published his first story. His newspaper career was fortuitously interrupted in 1857, when he learned to be a steamboat pilot on the Mississippi. Those experiences formed the basis for his *Life on the Mississippi* (1883) and also deepened the influence that the Mississippi had on the body of his work. In 1862, he first used the pen name "Mark Twain," taken from the river boatmen's cry to indicate two fathoms of safe water. When the outbreak of the Civil War brought his piloting career to an end, Twain served briefly with some Confederate "irregulars," but he gladly accepted Orion's offer to accompany him to Nevada, where Orion served as "secretary" to that territory.

During his Nevada years, Twain unsuccessfully prospected for gold and silver and successfully returned to the newspaper world, writing for the *Virginia City Territorial Enterprise*, where he developed, partly through emulating humorist Artemus Ward, his lecturing persona. In 1864, he moved to San Francisco, where he continued his newspaper work on the *Morning Call* and also contributed work to the *Californian*, a literary magazine. Among his California works was "The Celebrated Jumping Frog of Calaveras County," a short story that catapulted him to national prominence and established him as a spokesperson for the vanishing American frontier. After a trip to Hawaii, about which he wrote and lectured, he left California in 1866 and went east to New York City.

LIFE'S WORK

Twain's decision to go east was a significant one. Despite his "frontier" humor and southern speech, he became an easterner who looked nostalgically to the South for his literary landscape and to the West for his values.

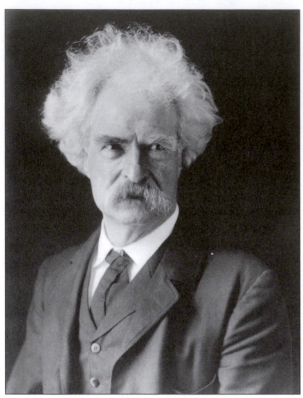

Mark Twain. (Library of Congress)

In effect, Twain was split between the progressive, materialistic East of the future and the reactionary, individualistic Southwest of the past. Even Twain's appearance seemed a contradiction: A handsome man given to elegant clothes (white suits became his trademark in his later years), he was also a cigar smoker and whiskey drinker who never became "genteel" in manner. Far from subscribing to the notion of "art for art's sake," he made writing his business and was ambitious both financially and socially. In fact, it was the split between art and business that produced works that appear inconsistent, contradictory, and careless. The pressure to make money did cause him to produce inferior work, as Twain himself acknowledged.

Shortly after moving to New York, Twain met Henry Ward Beecher, a prominent preacher and brother to Harriet Beecher Stowe, the author of *Uncle Tom's Cabin* (1852). When he learned that Beecher's congregation was planning a Mediterranean steamboat excursion to Europe and the Holy Land, he persuaded the *Alta California* to finance his trip in exchange for providing the newspaper with travel letters, which were popular at the time. The revised travel accounts eventually became *The*

Innocents Abroad (1869), a book that enabled him to abandon his newspaper work and to devote his full attention to writing. The trip was also significant because it resulted in his marriage, in 1870, to Olivia Langdon, whose brother had met Twain on the voyage and had showed the author Olivia's picture. During their thirty-three years of marriage, Olivia was the ideal wife and confidante, but she also served as an unofficial "editor" whose moral views tempered Twain's writing.

After his marriage, Twain embarked on what was to become a typical divided course of action: He began to write *Roughing It* (1872), and he acquired part ownership of the Buffalo *Express*, the first of a series of unsuccessful business ventures. Another pattern was also established during the early years of the marriage: depression caused by sickness and death. Olivia's father died in 1870; Olivia herself was sick and gave birth prematurely to their first child, Langdon, who died in 1872. Despite these setbacks, Twain moved his family to Hartford, Connecticut, where he built an impressive mansion, a symbol of his ambition and materialism.

Twain's Hartford years were his most productive artistically and financially. In 1873, he published, in collaboration with his Hartford neighbor, Charles Dudley Warner, *The Gilded Age*, his first attempt at an extended work of fiction. After successfully adapting the novel to the stage (1874), he published *The Adventures of Tom Sawyer* in 1876 and, in 1880, published another travel book, *A Tramp Abroad*. In 1882, *The Prince and the Pauper* appeared, and in 1884, *Adventures of Huckleberry Finn*, his most artistic and significant novel, was published. Within a month, *Adventures of Huckleberry Finn* was embroiled in censorship problems that continued to plague the novel, but the novel also quickly became a best seller and has become one of the most widely read and taught novels in American literature.

Adventures of Huckleberry Finn was the first publication of the Charles L. Webster and Company, which Twain formed after having problems with his previous publishers. Like his father, Twain believed that he had business acumen, and the financial success of *Adventures of Huckleberry Finn* and *The Personal Memoirs of U. S. Grant* (1885-1886), which Twain's company published, confirmed his belief that he was both a financial and artistic genius. In 1886, an overconfident Twain, who optimistically believed in technology and in the promise of a typesetting machine, acquired half ownership of the Paige Typesetter; in 1889, he purchased all rights to the machine.

By the time Twain ended his futile speculation in the ill-fated invention during the early 1890's, he had accumulated debts of $100,000. In an effort to economize, he closed his Hartford house in 1891 and moved to Europe, but he was bankrupt by 1894. Even his substantial earnings from the publication of *A Connecticut Yankee in King Arthur's Court* (1889) and *Tom Sawyer Abroad* (1894) could not compensate for the financial strain caused by his obsession with the typesetting machine.

To his credit, Twain did not attempt to take advantage of bankruptcy laws and instead set about paying off his debts by undertaking an exhausting round-the-world lecture tour in 1895 and by continuing to publish books: *Personal Recollections of Joan of Arc* (1896), *Tom Sawyer, Detective* (1896), and *Following the Equator* (1897), a travel account prompted by his 1895 lecture tour. These sales, coupled with a lucrative contract with Harper and Row for rights to his collected works, enabled Twain to pay off his debts in full by January of 1898. Although he recovered financially, Twain suffered several setbacks from which he never fully recovered. While he was in England in 1896, his favorite daughter died of meningitis; his already frail wife died in 1904, after suffering from physical and mental problems; his daughter Clara married and settled in Europe in 1909; and Jean, his other daughter, died scarcely two months after Clara's marriage.

Despite the misfortunes that plagued him after 1898, Twain continued to write prolifically, but most of this material, because of its nihilistic philosophy, was not published until after his death. Olivia, who was concerned about his image and who served as his literary editor/censor, opposed the publication of the deterministic tract *What Is Man?* (1906). "The Mysterious Stranger" stories, which occupied Twain for several years and took a variety of forms, were not published in any form until 1916, when Albert Bigelow Paine, Twain's official biographer, and a Harper's editor conflated Twain's

---

AN ECCENTRIC AUTOBIOGRAPHY

Although Mark Twain wrote and dictated nearly one-half million words of autobiographical reminiscences, he never assembled a coherent autobiography. At least six editions of his autobiographical writings have been published, but none is close to complete, and several follow their editors' own arrangements. The only publication of any of the material that Twain personally supervised was a series of twenty-five "chapters" in the North American Review. *The opening paragraphs of the first chapter, which he dictated in March, 1906, explain his eccentric plan:*

I intend that this autobiography shall become a model for all future autobiographies when it is published, after my death, and I also intend that it shall be read and admired a good many centuries because of its form and method whereby the past and the present are constantly brought face to face, resulting in contrasts which newly fire up the interest of all along, like contact of flint with steel. Moreover, this autobiography of mine does not select from my life its showy episodes, but deals mainly in the common experiences which go to make up the life of the average human being, because these episodes are of a sort which he is familiar with in his own life, and in which he sees his own life reflected and set down in print. The usual, conventional autobiographer seems to particularly hunt out those occasions in his career when he came into contact with celebrated persons, whereas his contacts with the uncelebrated were just as interesting to him, and would be to his reader, and were vastly more numerous than his collisions with the famous.

[William Dean] Howells was here yesterday afternoon, and I told him the whole scheme of this autobiography and its apparently systemless system— only apparently systemless, for it is not that. It is a deliberate system, and the law of the system is that I shall talk about the matter which for the moment interests me, and cast it aside and talk about something else the moment its interest for me is exhausted. It is a system which follows no charted course and is not going to follow any such course. It is a system which is a complete and purposed jumble—a course which begins nowhere, follows no specified route, and can never reach an end while I am alive, for the reason that if I should talk to the stenographer two hours a day for a hundred years, I should still never be able to set down a tenth part of the things which have interested me in my lifetime. I told Howells that this autobiography of mine would live a couple of thousand years without any effort and would then take a fresh start and live the rest of the time.

He said he believed it would, and asked me if I meant to make a library of it. I said that that was my design; but that, if I should live long enough, the set of volumes could not be contained merely in a city, it would require a State, and that there would not be any multi-billionaire alive, perhaps, at any time during its existence who would be able to buy a full set, except on the instalment plan. . . .

Source: Mark Twain, "Chapters from My Autobiography—I." *North American Review* 183, no. 598 (September 7, 1906), pp. 321-322.

versions and published their reconstruction as Twain's own work. The fact that the 1916 publication was, in effect, an editorial fraud was not publicly known until decades later.

Twain, who had been left quite alone by Clara's marriage and the deaths of his wife and other children, died April 21, 1910, long before the American public had been made aware of the "literary Lincoln's" darker side.

SIGNIFICANCE

In many ways, Mark Twain was as contradictory a person as his real name and pen name suggest. The adoption of the pen name indicates, to some extent, a person not content with himself but determined to forge a new personality, to create a new person—in effect, not unlike James Gatz/Jay Gatsby, to be both creator and creature. Like Gatsby, too, Twain was caught up in the American dream of material success, social ascent, and technological progress; unlike Gatsby, however, he came to satirize and scorn many of the values to which he subscribed.

For most Americans, Mark Twain is indelibly associated with Huckleberry Finn, the youthful protagonist who "lights out for the Territory" rather than return to the "civilization" represented by Aunt Sally. However, *Adventures of Huckleberry Finn* contains another juvenile persona who only "plays" at nonconformity and rebellion: Tom Sawyer. There is as much Tom Sawyer in Twain as there is Huckleberry Finn. Even *Adventures of Huckleberry Finn* is more than it appears to be, juvenile fiction in the vein of *The Adventures of Tom Sawyer*; it is also an initiation novel that depicts a boy's adventures and his inner growth, presents the conflict between appearance and reality, and satirizes southern gentility and aristocratic pretension. Because *Adventures of Huckleberry Finn* is such an enjoyable story, however, many readers ignored the Colonel Sherburn incident, with its scathing indictment of humankind. For many readers, Mark Twain was the lecturer-writer of juvenile fiction and travel books, a humorous teller of frontier tales.

Twain's humor was considerably blacker than the general public—which lionized him—believed. In some ways, his humor was similar to Ambrose Bierce's, but that similarity was overlooked by a public that dubbed the latter "Bitter Bierce." As his ambitious entrepreneurial schemes failed and his loved ones died, Twain became increasingly pessimistic about people and about institutions, and his later works are marked by pessimism, determinism, and nihilism.

Although Twain was nostalgic about the innocence of children, the children in *The Mysterious Stranger* are light-years away from Tom and Huck. *A Connecticut Yankee in King Arthur's Court* provides yet another example of public unwillingness to confront the complexity that was Twain. Twain's novel satirizes the institutions, particularly chivalry and the Church, of medieval England, which is juxtaposed to turn-of-the-century America, represented by Hank Morgan, a believer in progress and technology. Morgan's well-intentioned technology, however, ultimately produces only death. When Twain's novel was adapted to film, it was bowdlerized into a musical starring Bing Crosby.

Twain was very much a product of his age. As a spokesperson for an already vanishing frontier, he lampooned the pretense and the institutions of the East while he yearned for the lost values of youth and individualism. These nineteenth century values were in conflict with the twentieth century technology he first embraced and then, like Henry Adams, came to despise.

—*Thomas L. Erskine*

FURTHER READING

Burns, Ken, Dayton Duncan, and Geoffrey C. Ward. *Mark Twain: An Illustrated Biography.* Alfred A. Knopf, 2001. Lavishly illustrated companion volume to a four-hour PBS television documentary on Twain.

Camfield, Gregg, ed. *The Oxford Companion to Mark Twain.* New York: Oxford University Press, 2003. Collection of alphabetically arranged essays on a wide variety of subjects by Camfield and several guest contributors.

Emerson, Everett. *Mark Twain: A Literary Life.* Philadelphia: University of Pennsylvania Press, 2000. Biography of Twain emphasizing the chronological development of his literary work, with useful discussions of individual writings.

Fishkin, Shelley Fisher. *Lighting Out for the Territory: Reflections on Mark Twain and American Culture.* New York: Oxford University Press, 1997. Personal explorations of the complex interactions between Twain's literary heritage and modern American culture, with particular attention to Hannibal's slave history.

_____. *Was Huck Black? Mark Twain and African-American Voices.* New York: Oxford University Press, 1993. Controversial study that examines African American cultural influence on *Huckleberry Finn*, particularly in Huck's spoken language.

_____, ed. *A Historical Guide to Mark Twain.* New York: Oxford University Press, 2002. Collection of original articles on such topics as religion, commerce, race, gender, social class, and imperialism. Includes a bibliographical essay.

Horn, Jason Gary. *Mark Twain: A Descriptive Guide to Biographical Sources.* Lanham, Md.: Scarecrow Press, 1999. Useful and comparatively up-to-date summary of the most important works on Twain. Emphasis is on biographical sources, but works of literary criticism are covered as well.

Kaplan, Fred. *The Singular Mark Twain: A Biography.* New York: Doubleday, 2003. Revisionist biography that seeks to merge the "Mark Twain" and "Samuel Clemens" personas into a singular whole. Describes Twain's personality, foibles, and evolution as a writer.

Kaplan, Justin. *Mr. Clemens and Mark Twain: A Biography.* New York: Simon and Schuster, 1966. Pulitzer Prize-winning biography that covers Twain's life from the time he left piloting on the Mississippi to his death. Remains the starting point for any serious study of Twain.

LeMaster, J. R., and James D. Wilson, eds. *The Mark Twain Encyclopedia.* New York: Garland, 1993. Containing signed articles written by nearly two hundred scholars, this comprehensive reference differs from Rasmussen's *Mark Twain A to Z* in focusing more on literary topics.

Ober, K. Patrick. *Mark Twain and Medicine: "Any Mummery Will Cure."* Columbia: University of Missouri Press, 2003. Physician's study of the role of medicine in Twain's life and writings that reveals many other dimensions of Twain's life.

Rasmussen, R. Kent. *Mark Twain A to Z.* New York: Facts On File, 1995. Comprehensive reference on Twain's life and writings with detailed entries on most of the people, places, and events that figured in Twain's complex life. A substantially expanded and revised edition was scheduled to be published in 2006 as *Critical Companion to Mark Twain.*

_____. *Mark Twain for Kids.* Chicago: Chicago Review Press, 2004. Well-illustrated biography containing educational activities. Written for younger readers, but older readers will find it a clear and useful summary of Twain's life.

SEE ALSO: Henry Adams; Horatio Alger; Henry Ward Beecher; Ambrose Bierce; Joel Chandler Harris; Henry James; Robert Louis Stevenson; Harriet Beecher Stowe.

RELATED ARTICLE in *Great Events from History: The Nineteenth Century, 1801-1900:* December, 1884-February, 1885: Twain Publishes *Adventures of Huckleberry Finn.*

WILLIAM MARCY TWEED
American politician

Tweed's name is synonymous with corruption and dishonesty in urban government. Through the power waged by his Tammany Hall political machine, New York City and its citizens were systematically bilked of millions of dollars in taxes meant for civic projects. Tweed was eventually brought down by his own greed and the combined efforts of a reform coalition of prominent citizens, ordinary people, The New York Times, *and political cartoonist Thomas Nast.*

BORN: April 3, 1823; New York, New York
DIED: April 12, 1878; New York, New York
ALSO KNOWN AS: Boss Tweed
AREA OF ACHIEVEMENT: Government and politics

EARLY LIFE

William Marcy Tweed was the son of Richard and Eliza Tweed. His great-grandfather, a blacksmith, had emi-

grated to America from Scotland around 1750. His father was a maker of chairs, and William left school at eleven to apprentice in that trade. At thirteen, he apprenticed with a saddler, leaving to spend a brief stint at a private school in New Jersey to learn bookkeeping. He became a junior clerk at a New York mercantile firm before advancing to a position as head bookkeeper at the small brush manufactory in which his father had invested. At nineteen, he became an officer in the company, and at twenty-one, he married Mary Jane Skaden, the daughter of the factory's principal investor.

The young Tweed, an energetic, powerfully built, ruddy-faced, jovial man, six feet tall and a robust three hundred pounds, may have found the business of making brushes a dull undertaking, for he soon discovered an outlet much more to his liking: volunteer firefighting. By 1850, he had become foreman of a company he had helped to organize, the celebrated Americus No. 611. He was then twenty-seven years old. In the latter half of the nineteenth century in America, volunteer firefighting organizations were one of the ways for ambitious young men to get ahead in politics. Powerful "Big 611," easily identified by the Bengal tiger symbol painted on the company's fire engine, propelled its leader into the public eye; he was soon running for the position of alderman in his home ward under the auspices of the Democratic Party. He lost by a small margin, but he won his next race easily owing to a split in the Whig vote engendered by a third candidate—a friend of Tweed who was persuaded to do him a favor. The year was 1852, and Tweed was learning how to succeed in politics.

LIFE'S WORK

He was learning fast and from the best—the New York City Common Council was widely and cynically known at that time as The Forty Thieves—and the brush factory was soon abandoned for more lucrative pastures. He was an urban political animal, in his element in city politics, a truth realized when he served for two unmemorable years (1853-1855) in the U.S. House of Representatives in Washington, D.C., something he would not repeat again. From then on, he would stick to running for the

William Marcy Tweed. (Library of Congress)

state senate and city aldermanic positions. In 1856, however, he lost his next race for alderman. Undaunted, and now drawn into the Tammany faction with Peter B. Sweeny and Richard B. Connolly in opposition to Mayor Fernando Wood, he was picked to be head of a new, bipartisan, popularly elected board of supervisors formed to check election fraud. It became, instead, another opportunity for graft and corruption.

Other appointed and elected offices beckoned in quick succession, and Tweed became commissioner of schools, deputy street commissioner, a New York state senator (1867-1871), and chairman of the New York state finance committee. On the Tammany Hall front, he was elected sachem in 1857 and by 1859 was clearly the most influential man in the organization. (He appropriated the Bengal tiger from the volunteer fire company to stand as a symbol of the society, alongside the head of Tammany, a Native American.) He dominated the 1860 state Democratic convention and was thus able to secure several choice spots for his friends and allies. Owing to his influence, Sweeny was elected district attorney in 1857 and Connolly county clerk; George G. Barnard was elected to the office of recorder and later to the New York State Supreme Court. Another crony, A. Oakey Hall, succeeded Sweeny as district attorney in 1860. Although Tweed himself was defeated in a run for the office of sheriff in 1861, the election was not a total loss, as his enemy Fernando Wood was also defeated in the mayoral race.

Undeterred by his lack of legal expertise, Tweed had himself certified by his friend Barnard as a lawyer, and he further enriched his coffers by opening a law office in 1860. He extorted large payoffs for his services from companies desirous of doing business with New York such as the Erie Railroad. In 1864, he bought control of the New York Printing Company, which shortly thereafter became the official printer for the city; other businesses were also coerced into having to deal with the company. His next acquisition, the manufacturing Stationers' Company, was a way for him to sell supplies to the city at graft-inflated prices. The greatest boondoggle of all, the new county courthouse (later to be known as the Tweed Courthouse), was built with stone and marble from a Massachusetts quarry owned by Tweed. The courthouse, expected to cost half a million dollars, wound up costing the city's taxpayers approximately $13 million, most of it winding up in Tweed's capacious pockets.

Now a millionaire as well as a sachem of Tammany Hall, Tweed began to move in much more exalted circles. In 1867, he bought a large residence uptown in

THE NINETEENTH CENTURY

Tweed, William Marcy

Murray Hill, off Fifth Avenue. He was now hobnobbing with neighbors such as the banker J. P. Morgan. He became a partner of the notorious financier/robber barons Jay Gould and James Fisk and became a director of several important utility companies and financial institutions. Gould and Fisk paid him off handsomely, in stock and a board directorship, for enabling them to get the Erie Classification Bill through the state legislature in order to legalize fraudulent railroad stock issued by their firm.

By the time Tweed secured the post of grand sachem of Tammany Hall in 1868, his power in New York was absolute. The "Tweed Ring," a confederation of like-minded crooks and ward heelers with whom "Boss" Tweed surrounded himself, were the rulers of all they surveyed. The ebullient Tweed shared his ill-gotten gains with his ring, increasing the proportion of their graft intake from 50 percent of all bills rendered to the city in 1869 to an astounding 85 percent shortly thereafter. Proceeds were divided by Tweed, the city comptroller, the county chairman, and the mayor. They also had a separate fund used exclusively for bribery.

Tweed moved into an even larger house on Forty-third Street and Fifth Avenue and maintained a stable and carriage house on 40th Street. By the early 1870's, he had been named to the boards of the Harlem Gas Company, the Brooklyn Bridge Company, and the Third Avenue Railway Company and was president of the Guardian Savings Bank. He also organized the Tenth National Bank to control city monies and his ever-increasing personal fortune.

Incredibly, a number of New York City's respected leaders were duped for a long period as to Tweed's criminal character. The city charter of 1870, which further cemented the Tweed Ring's hold on New York, was actually supported by honest and upstanding luminaries such as philanthropist Peter Cooper and newspaper publisher Horace Greeley. Retribution, however, was on its way.

The talented political cartoonist Thomas Nast launched the first volley against the Tweed Ring in 1869 with a series of caricatures that ran in *Harper's Weekly*—among them the memorable "Let Us Prey," which depicted Tweed and his cronies as fat vultures feeding off the city. The Tammany Tiger became a familiar symbol in Nast's drawings; he did not let up his barrage until 1872. In the fall of 1870, *The New York Times* ran an editorial concerning the massive cost overruns on the county courthouse. Some months later, in the spring of 1871, whistle-blowers within the Tammany organization supplied hard proofs of widespread swindling and

corruption to George Jones, publisher of *The New York Times*.

Although the Tweed Ring attempted to bribe the newspaper so that the story would not see print, it appeared in July of that year; soon thereafter, an indignant group of citizens met at the Cooper Union to form a committee to take back their city. Democratic state chairman Samuel Jones Tilden filed an affidavit citing Tweed and his ring's misdeeds, and the affidavit became the basis of a civil suit for recovery of the city's money.

Despite this notoriety, the serious threat of imminent arrest, and his summary expulsion from the Tammany Society, Tweed was reelected to the state senate. By December, 1871, however, his astonishing luck had run out, and he was arrested in a criminal action. (Others in his ring, taking no chances, had already fled abroad.) It took two trials to convict Tweed; in late 1873, he was fined $12,750 and sentenced to twelve years in prison. He nevertheless managed to get his sentence reduced on appeals to one year and paid only $250 in fines.

Tweed was rearrested in early 1875 in a civil action brought by New York State to recover $6 million of what had been stolen. Unable to secure the $3 million in bail set by the state, he escaped from his prison cell later that year, fleeing first to Florida, then Cuba, and from there to Spain. A Nast cartoon printed in *Harper's Weekly* on July 1, 1876, led to his arrest in Spain, and he was returned to the United States during the late fall of that year. The warrant issued in New York for his arrest described him thus at the end of his career:

> [F]ifty-five years of age, about five-feet eleven inches high, will weigh about two hundred and eighty pounds, very portly, ruddy complexion, has rather large, coarse, prominent features and large prominent nose; rather small blue or grey eyes, grey hair, from originally auburn color, head nearly bald on top from forehead back to crown, and bare part of ruddy color; head projecting toward the crown. His beard may be removed or dyed, and he may wear a wig or be otherwise disguised....

Unable to pay the judgment that had been levied against him in the civil action, in which he was convicted in absentia of 204 out of 240 counts, he was confined to jail. His subsequent lengthy and detailed testimony confessing his guilt, an attempt to be pardoned for his crimes, did not work. He died of pneumonia in the Ludlow Street prison on April 12, 1878. At his side was his manservant, who had opted to accompany him to jail; everyone else, including his family, had long since deserted him.

SIGNIFICANCE

William Marcy Tweed has come to stand for all that is bad in American urban politics. He helped to spawn a particularly grotesque breed of individual—the bloated, powerful political boss—whose like has appeared again and again on the local and national scene; few such successors, however, have even begun to approach the phenomenal levels of graft achieved by the Tweed Ring and its leader. In the twentieth century, Mayor Richard Daley of Chicago and Carmine De Sapio of New York City were old-time political bosses in the spirit—if not the intense corruption—of Boss Tweed. Modern historians estimate that the Tweed Ring stole betweeen $30 million and $200 million from the city of New York, but a final, definitive figure will probably never be known.

The tragedy of William Marcy Tweed was that he had tremendous leadership and organizational skills, which, combined with a genial personality, could have served him well and long if he had chosen to follow an honest career in government. He did have good instincts when it came to running a municipal government, and some of what he did was positive and humanitarian. He was responsible for the widening of Broadway and for the preservation of the Central Park site that became the Metropolitan Museum of Art; and he helped new immigrants to the city—at a time when they were disdained and overlooked by most New Yorkers—by seeing to it that they had food, clothing, and shelter.

Tweed also helped set up the Manhattan Eye and Ear Hospital; opened orphanages, almshouses, and public baths; sought funding for parochial schools; and worked to increase state aid to private charities. He also was behind the effort to obtain a greater degree of home rule for New York City. Although it has been argued that these public services were mere sops granted to the poor in an attempt to gain even more political power, some scholars do not agree with such an assessment.

The scope of the corruption, fraud, and graft of Tweed and the Tweed Ring, however, remains unparalleled in urban government, and their unrestrained feeding at the public trough is what history most vividly remembers. For his years of systematically cheating the city and manipulating public trust, Tweed has continued to be vilified as one of the nineteenth century's most reprehensible men. On his death, New York City mayor Smith Ely refused to fly the city hall flag at half-staff; that verdict still stands.

—Jo Manning

FURTHER READING

Ackerman, Kenneth D. *Boss Tweed: The Rise and Fall of the Corrupt Pol Who Conceived the Soul of Modern New York*. New York: Carroll & Graf, 2005. Popular, balanced chronicle of Tweed's rise and fall, tracing his successful organization of working-class and immigrant voters, and his eventual downfall and disgrace.

Allen, Oliver E. *The Tiger: The Rise and Fall of Tammany Hall*. Reading, Mass.: Addison-Wesley, 1993. A look at the times and political machine that spawned Boss Tweed.

Bales, William A. *Tiger in the Streets*. New York: Dodd, Mead, 1962. A straightforward account of Tweed's life and career.

Callow, Alexander B., Jr. *The Tweed Ring*. New York: Oxford University Press, 1966. Detailed, thoroughly documented history of Tweed and the men he handpicked to defraud the city of New York.

Hershkowitz, Leo. *Tweed's New York: Another Look*. Garden City, N.Y.: Doubleday, 1977. A reevaluation of Tweed's impact on New York City.

Mandelbaum, Seymour J. *Boss Tweed's New York*. New York: John Wiley & Sons, 1965. Gives credit to Tweed for exerting strong leadership at a time of chaos and change in the growing metropolis of New York City.

Werner, Morris R. *Tammany Hall*. Garden City, N.Y.: Doubleday, Doran, 1928. Sets Tweed against the background of the Democratic political machine.

Zink, Harold. *City Bosses in the United States: A Study of Twenty Municipal Bosses*. Durham, N.C.: Duke University Press, 1930. Excellent chapter on Tweed, with good references.

SEE ALSO: Horace Greeley; J. P. Morgan; Thomas Nast.

RELATED ARTICLES in *Great Events from History: The Nineteenth Century, 1801-1900:* September 24, 1869-1877: Scandals Rock the Grant Administration; May 24, 1883: Brooklyn Bridge Opens.

JOHN TYLER
President of the United States (1841-1845)

Upon the sudden death of President William Henry Harrison, Tyler became the first vice president to succeed to the presidency when the office was vacated. Many politicians wanted to regard his administration as a caretaker government until the next election, but he established the precedent that in such circumstances the new president holds the office in both fact and name.

BORN: March 29, 1790; Greenway Plantation, Charles
    City County, Virginia
DIED: January 18, 1862; Richmond, Virginia
AREA OF ACHIEVEMENT: Government and politics

EARLY LIFE

John Tyler was the son of a distinguished Virginian who served as governor, as speaker of the state House of Delegates, and as a judge. As a consequence, Tyler was reared in an atmosphere of aristocratic privilege and refinement and imbued with a sense of responsibility and commitment to public service. He attended the College of William and Mary and excelled academically, while his interest in political theory and practice grew. He shared the strict constructionist Jeffersonian Republican views of his father, under whom he began to read law at the age of seventeen. Tyler was admitted to the Virginia bar in 1809, and at the age of twenty-one, he was elected to the Virginia House of Delegates. After brief military service in the War of 1812, Tyler returned to civilian life as a public servant. His striking physical appearance was a considerable political asset. He was six feet tall, slender, with a high forehead, aquiline nose, fair complexion, brilliant eyes, and a ready smile.

LIFE'S WORK

Tyler first achieved national office with his election to the U.S. House of Representatives in 1816. As a congressman, Tyler was dedicated to the principles of his family and section. He was a strict constructionist in his view of the Constitution and favored limiting the powers of the federal government. These views led Tyler to oppose nationally financed internal improvements projects because they might extend the power of the federal government. He opposed creation of the first Bank of the United States for the same reason, as well as on constitutional grounds. Although Tyler was consistent in his opposition to the slave trade, he nevertheless voted against the Missouri Compromise in 1820, believing that the

"peculiar institution" would perish for lack of suitable geographical areas for its expansion. Tyler was defeated in a U.S. Senate race in 1820 and retired briefly from politics to serve as chancellor of the College of William and Mary. He was elected governor of Virginia in 1825, won a seat in the U.S. Senate in 1827, and began to move toward national prominence.

Tyler supported William H. Crawford for the presidency in 1824 and was elected to the Senate as an anti-Jacksonian. As the Republican Party split into factions and began the process of dividing into National Republicans and Democratic Republicans, Tyler was offended by the rising tide of mass politics that came to be known as "Jacksonian Democracy." Although the aristocratic Virginian was cordial and effective when dealing with members of his own class, the common folk and their heroes made him uncomfortable. Tyler was especially critical of what he termed the barking of newspapers and the brawling of demagogues. Nevertheless, in 1828, the Virginia senator supported Andrew Jackson's successful presidential bid as the candidate of the Democratic Republicans. Although Tyler agreed with Jackson's views on some matters, he was repulsed by what he perceived as the new president's authoritarianism, and soon his principles caused Tyler to split from the Tennessean and the Democratic Party.

Even when Tyler agreed with the president's positions on key issues, he often disapproved of his methods. Prime examples were nullification and the bank. Nullification became an issue during Jackson's presidency because of two developments affecting the South. The first was the tariff: In 1828, Congress passed a high protective tariff that southern planters, dependent on an export economy, strongly opposed. Tyler was among the southern senators who spoke and voted against this "Tariff of Abominations." The second development was the unification of the Northeast and Northwest into a national political force, relegating the South to minority status among the sections. Southern extremists were beginning to talk about separation from the Union in order to rescue the South from the tyranny of the majority. Vice President John C. Calhoun understood and empathized with the growing fear and frustration of the South yet wanted desperately to preserve the Union. Calhoun developed the theory of nullification as a means of protecting the interests of the minority section within the Union.

Nullification and the tariff were linked when South

Carolina threatened to declare the tariff null and void within its borders if it was not repealed by Congress. Despite an effort by Congress to avoid confrontation by passing a new compromise tariff, Calhoun decided the time had come to test his doctrine, and South Carolina began the process of nullification. President Jackson issued a strong proclamation rejecting South Carolina's constitutional position and threatened personally to lead a military force into the state to enforce the tariff and the will of the federal government.

Congress then passed the Force Act authorizing the president to use force to ensure that federal laws were obeyed. Tyler found himself in a troubling and ambiguous situation. On one hand, he shared South Carolina's opposition to high tariffs, but on the other, he did not accept the doctrine of nullification. He also considered, however, Jackson's nullification proclamation to be a violation of the Constitution, and he was the only senator to vote against the Force Act. Furthermore, Tyler objected to the forcefulness of Jackson's reaction to South Carolina's challenge.

The bank question created similar contradictions and ambivalence. Tyler opposed the attempt to recharter the Bank of the United States on economic and constitutional grounds. When President Jackson attempted to destroy the bank, however, by removing the government's deposits from its coffers, Tyler was among the senators supporting resolutions condemning Jackson's actions. When the Virginia legislature ordered him to recant and vote for a motion to expunge the resolutions, Tyler resigned from the Senate and left the Democratic Party.

The Virginian now found himself drifting into uncharted political territory. He was among those southerners who were moving toward the new Whig Party, which was emerging in opposition to the executive tyranny of "King Andrew." However, Tyler was somewhat out of step with his new political companions. His political and constitutional views were not consistent with those of most other Whigs. Tyler had left Jackson and the Democrats largely as a result of methodology rather than constitutional differences. He had remained true to his original views and philosophy, while the Whig Party seemed a loose coalition of diverse groups with room for considerable philosophical latitude. Nevertheless, although he was defeated in a Senate election in 1839, Tyler was nominated for the vice presidency on the William Henry Harrison ticket the following year as the Whigs attempted to win the votes of other former southern Democrats.

John Tyler. (Library of Congress)

By now the Virginia politician who featured in one of the most famous campaign slogans in American political history had matured into a dignified and appealing figure. He continued to be somewhat distant in dealing with the masses and was sometimes accused of vanity, but most considered him friendly and considerate. He was unfailingly good-humored and patient and scrupulously honest. Even Tyler's political enemies found him difficult to dislike, and they respected his ability as a campaigner, for he had become a polished and effective orator. Tyler was nominated not because of his character or abilities, however, but because he appealed to disaffected southern Democrats. Ironically, within a few short months the entire political structure was in turmoil, and Tyler was thrust onto center stage.

The Harrison and Tyler ticket won the election of 1840 easily, but within a month of his inauguration, Old Tippecanoe was dead. Supposedly, the dying chief executive's last words were a request that his vice president carry out the true principles of government. Ironically, the leaders of the Whig Party were soon to learn that Tyler did not share their concept of what constituted those true principles. Their chagrin and apparent amazement upon learning about the Virginian's views were somewhat surprising, for throughout his long political career, Tyler had demonstrated a philosophical and constitutional consistency that is unusual among politicians.

The marriage of Harrison and Tyler was strictly one of convenience. The Virginian had scarcely known, and was not favorably impressed by, Old Tippecanoe. The Whigs, however, expected that the actual leadership in a Harrison administration would emanate from Congress, and Tyler was a close friend of Senator Henry Clay of Kentucky. Clay probably believed that Tyler would support the Whig programs that the Kentuckian planned to introduce in Congress, including plans for a new national bank. Tyler's oratory in the presidential campaign was sufficiently vague to provide substance for such a view, but within a few months, Clay would be a bitter political enemy, attacking the Virginian as a traitor to the Whig Party.

The first question faced by Tyler and the nation was fundamental: What was his status upon Harrison's death? Was he president in fact or only in name? Whether he was simply to attempt to carry out Harrison's views and programs or operate just as though he had been elected to the office was unclear. This was the first time that a vice president had ascended to the presidency upon the death of a chief executive, and the Constitution is rather vague concerning the succession. It says simply that if the president is removed from office, dies, resigns, or is unable to discharge his duties, the office will devolve on the vice president. This phrase could imply that the vice president inherits the office itself or, equally plausible, that the vice president simply performs the duties of the office. Tyler, usually the strict constructionist, interpreted the Constitution broadly and claimed all the rights and privileges of the presidency. There was some contemporary criticism of his position, but the practice has been accepted and followed since that time.

Tyler retained the Harrison cabinet members, reinforcing the impression that he would follow in the dead president's footsteps. Clay and the Whig leadership quickly and confidently submitted their legislative program, which called for a higher tariff and the creation of a new Bank of the United States. Congress enacted legislation for both the bank and the tariff, but the Whigs soon discovered that they had misread the situation. Tyler vetoed both measures with language that was highly reminiscent of Andrew Jackson. Some Whigs angrily charged that Tyler was a traitor, others that he was jealous of Clay. In actuality, Tyler was neither. He was simply acting in accord with the strict constructionist, agrarian views that he had absorbed from his father and had held since his youth. He stood his ground in the face of tremendous pressure, which included recriminations from Clay, blandishments from majoritarian Whigs, and a rock-throwing mob that attacked the White House.

Tyler argued that the legislation creating the new bank was unconstitutional and that the proposed institu-

---

MEXICO'S WAR WITH TEXAS

In his December, 1843, state of the union address, President John Tyler spoke at length about the war between Mexico and the Republic of Texas. Although he attempted to phrase his remarks diplomatically, so as not to appear to take sides, the tone of his remarks in the extract below make it clear that his administration strongly sympathized with the Texans. Before he left the presidency, he would annex Texas to the United States.

The United States have an immediate interest in seeing an end put to the state of hostilities existing between Mexico and Texas. They are our neighbors, of the same continent, with whom we are not only desirous of cultivating the relations of amity, but of the most extended commercial intercourse, and to practice all the rites of a neighborhood hospitality. . . . Considering that Texas is separated from the United States by a mere geographical line; that her territory, in the opinion of many, down to a late period formed a portion of the territory of the United States; that it is homogeneous in its population and pursuits with adjoining States, makes contributions to the commerce of the world in the same articles with them, and that most of her inhabitants have been citizens of the United States, speak the same language, and live under similar political institutions with ourselves, this Government is bound by every consideration of interest as well as of sympathy to see that she shall be left free to act, especially in regard to her domestic affairs, unawed by force and unrestrained by the policy or views of other countries. In full view of all these considerations, the Executive has not hesitated to express to the Government of Mexico how deeply it deprecated a continuance of the war and how anxiously it desired to witness its termination.

Source: John Tyler, "State of the Union Address," December, 1843.

tion posed the threat of an economic monopoly. He suggested a modified "exchequer" system as a compromise, but the Whig leaders forged ahead and again attempted to created a new bank, this time thinly disguised as a "fiscal corporation." Tyler vetoed that too, and the situation deteriorated into open warfare between the Whig president and his party. Tyler also struck down Clay's distribution program and other Whig legislation, and the Kentuckian resigned from the Senate in frustration and disgust.

Clay's resignation was followed by those of most of Tyler's cabinet members. The president replaced them with men of his own stripe, former Democrats who shared his views. There were public demonstrations against Tyler, he was burned in effigy, and in January, 1843, the Whigs brought impeachment charges against the man they now called "His Accidency." He was not convicted, but the Whigs formally expelled him from the party, as it disintegrated into shambles.

Tyler was now a man without a party, but he continued to perform his duties in accordance with his principles and in apparent good humor. During his presidency, he signed the Preemption Act, which made land more accessible and stimulated settlement in the Northwest; he helped end the Seminole War; and he was involved in the resolution of the Canadian boundary dispute with Great Britain. By 1844, he hoped for election to the presidency as an independent candidate but failed to generate significant support. Tyler then withdrew from the race and endorsed the Democrat, James K. Polk of Tennessee, who ran and won on an expansionist platform. During his last days in the presidency, the Virginian signed measures annexing Texas and admitting Florida to statehood.

John Tyler retired to his James River plantation in Virginia, a man without a party. He continued to be interested in public affairs, and his graciousness, character, and obvious goodwill won the affection of his neighbors. He became an honored citizen and was an influential southern leader as sectional turmoil increased during the 1850's. Tyler remained loyal to the Union and attempted to promote compromise on sectional issues but finally voted in favor of secession as a delegate to the Virginia secession convention. He served in the provisional Congress of the Confederacy and was elected to the Confederate House of Representatives but died in January, 1862, before taking his seat. He was buried in Richmond.

SIGNIFICANCE

John Tyler was the first vice president to inherit the presidency upon the death of a chief executive, the first president to face impeachment charges, and the only one to be officially expelled from his party. He is remembered today primarily as a historical footnote, but he deserves better. He was a man of great integrity and considerable ability who remained steadfast in his views and true to his principles. Despite the turmoil of his presidency he achieved some positive accomplishments and significantly shaped the theory of vice presidential succession under the U.S. Constitution.

—*James E. Fickle*

FURTHER READING

Chitwood, Oliver Perry. *John Tyler: Champion of the Old South*. New York: D. Appleton-Century, 1939. Though dated, this book remains the standard biography of Tyler.

Fraser, Hugh Russell. *Democracy in the Making: The Jackson-Tyler Era*. Indianapolis: Bobbs-Merrill, 1938. A dated but useful account.

Gunderson, Robert G. *The Log-Cabin Campaign*. Lexington: University of Kentucky Press, 1957. Discusses Tyler's role in the 1840 presidential campaign.

Howe, Daniel Walker. *The Political Culture of the American Whigs*. Chicago: University of Chicago Press, 1980. Howe analyzes the anti-Jackson movement that helped to create the Whig Party.

Lambert, Oscar Doane. *Presidential Politics in the United States, 1841-1844*. Durham, N.C.: Duke University Press, 1936. A dated but useful treatment.

Monroe, Dan. *The Republican Vision of John Tyler*. College Station: Texas A&M University Press, 2003. Traces the origins of Tyler's political philosophy from his earliest years in the Virginia legislature through his presidency. Monroe seeks to determine the principles that led to Tyler to resign his U.S. Senate seat and to veto congressional measures.

Morgan, Robert J. *A Whig Embattled: The Presidency Under John Tyler*. Lincoln: University of Nebraska Press, 1954. Morgan's work focuses on Tyler's presidency.

Peterson, Norma Lois. *The Presidencies of William Henry Harrison and John Tyler*. Lawrence: University Press of Kansas, 1989. Peterson maintains Tyler was a strong executive who achieved his foreign policy objectives and fiercely guarded the power of the executive branch over Congress.

Seager, Robert. *And Tyler Too*. New York: McGraw-Hill, 1963. A joint biography of Tyler and his second wife, Julia Gardiner Tyler.

Walker, Jane C. *John Tyler: A President of Many Firsts.* Blacksburg, Va.: McDonald & Woodward, 2001. Concise, illustrated overview of Tyler's presidency, describing how he, and the future of the United States, were affected by the issues and conflicts during his term in office.

SEE ALSO: John C. Calhoun; Henry Clay; William Henry Harrison; Andrew Jackson; James K. Polk; Daniel Webster.

RELATED ARTICLES in *Great Events from History: The Nineteenth Century, 1801-1900:* September 16, 1810-September 28, 1821: Mexican War of Independence; April 14, 1834: Clay Begins American Whig Party; December 2, 1840: U.S. Election of 1840; September 4, 1841: Congress Passes Preemption Act of 1841; May 18, 1842: Rhode Island's Dorr Rebellion; August 9, 1842: Webster-Ashburton Treaty Settles Maine's Canadian Border; August 1, 1846: Establishment of Independent U.S. Treasury.

'UTHMAN DAN FODIO
Nigerian Islamic reformer

A Fulani teacher, 'Uthman began a holy war for Islamic renewal and reform that eventually led to the creation of northern Nigeria's Sokoto caliphate—the largest empire in West Africa since Songhai in the sixteenth century.

BORN: December, 1754; Maratta, Gobir, Hausaland (now in Nigeria)
DIED: April, 1817; Sokoto, Fulani Empire (now in Nigeria)
ALSO KNOWN AS: 'Uthman ibn Muḥammad Fūdī ibn 'Uthman ibn Salih (birth name); 'Uthman ibn Fūdī; Usuman dan Fodio; Usman dan Fodio; Shaihu 'Uthman dan Fodio; Shebu 'Uthman dan Fodio
AREAS OF ACHIEVEMENT: Religion and theology, warfare and conquest, government and politics

EARLY LIFE

'Uthman dan Fodio (UHTH-man dahn FOH-dee-oh) was born into an urbanized and scholarly Fulani family living within the Hausa city-state of Gobir in what is now northern Nigeria. His father, Muḥammad Fodio, was a member of the Torankawa Fulani tribe and was a respected Muslim scholar. From his early childhood through adolescent years, 'Uthman took Qur'ānic lessons from his father and several uncles—scholars with whom he studied hermeneutics and translations (*tafsīr*), the recorded sayings of the Prophet Muḥammad (*hadith*), biography of the Prophet (*sīrah*), jurisprudence (*fiqh*), mysticism (*taṣawwuf*), mathematics, astronomy, and Arabic.

In 1774, 'Uthman and his younger brother and loyal follower, Abdullahi, began a period that would last several years as wandering teachers and preachers, traveling throughout Hausaland. In 1786, they took additional lessons from their uncle Alhaji Jibrīl ibn 'Umar, a celebrated scholar from Gobir who was living at Agades after being expelled from Gobir because of his radical reformist ideas. 'Uthman and Abdullahi then started giving sermons and lectures that decried widespread syncretist practices and superstitions, while urging a return to the path of Islamic purity and righteousness. The brothers also took lessons from another scholar named Alhaji Muhammad ibn Raj. Meanwhile, 'Uthman wrote a number of religious treatises for the educated classes and poems for the ordinary people in an effort to reduce what he regarded as a general state of ignorance in the Hausa-Fulani community.

LIFE'S WORK

'Uthman soon earned a reputation for his scholarship and religious zeal and attracted a considerable following to his cause. At the same time, his call for reform and change incurred the ire of some scholars who contested many of the issues that he was addressing, such the education and role of women in society. Moreover, his indifference to the theological niceties of Islamic scholasticism in favor of his interest in what he regarded as more relevant issues of understanding the basics of Islam resulted in verbal and written recriminations from traditional scholars and clerics. Meanwhile, he composed nearly fifty essays denouncing scholars whom he regarded as venal.

Despite the opposition that he faced, 'Uthman emerged from the scholarly controversies unscathed. In 1783, he impressed the sultan of Gobir, Bawa, with his refusal of the royal largesse offered to him as a reward for his scholarship. He instead asked for these favors: reduction of taxes on the people, release of prisoners, freedom to preach, and suspension of government harassment of women wearing proper Islamic dress and of men wearing turbans.

In 1793, when he was approaching the age of forty, 'Uthman settled down in the town of Degel in the state of Gobir with a wide network of followers and students throughout Hausaland. By that time he had the honorific title of shehu (or shaikh), which was traditionally awarded to wise elders. Under his leadership, Degel was transformed into an autonomous town and developed as the site of a university that spearheaded a community movement (*Jama'a*). The movement's ever-widening and increasingly open denunciations of social and political corruption and its calls for reform and renewal of Islamic ideals and recognition of Shehu 'Uthman's messianic stature led to the movement's persecution by Hausa rulers of Hausaland, including the Gobir sultans Nafata (r. 1796-1803) and Yunfa (r. 1803-1808).

Fear of government reprisals further radicalized the *Jama'a*, and 'Uthman urged his followers to prepare for a *hijra*—recalling the Prophet Muḥammad's flight from Mecca to Medina—as a prelude to the impending holy war (jihad). Harassed by Sultan Yunfa, 'Uthman and his followers went from Degel to Gudu, some thirty miles to the northwest, in February, 1804. There 'Uthman was proclaimed by his followers to be the "commander of the faithful" of a jihad. The holy rebels repulsed attacks by the ruler of Gobir and created a permanent base at Birnin

Kebbi, the capital of Kebbi, in April, 1806. At Kebbi, ʿUthman finished writing *Bayān wujūb al-hijra ala'l-ibad*, which explained the necessity of *hijra* and *jihad* and provided a blueprint for an ideal Islamic polity.

ʿUthman endeared himself to his followers not only with the strength of his teachings but also by his personal example. His asceticism, self-discipline, and affable disposition laced with erudition brought him a massive following. His jihad spread throughout Hausaland and the neighboring state of Bornu, to the east. By 1808, the jihadists had conquered the Hausa states; however, members of the ruling dynasties retreated to the frontiers and built walled cities that remained independent.

ʿUthman's movement failed to subdue Bornu, where another cleric, Muḥammad al-Kanemi, overthrew the traditional ruling dynasty of the Sayfawa and established his own lineage as the new ruling house. By 1809, ʿUthman's jihad had created a large Fulani state known as the Sokoto caliphate—a loose confederation of emirates stretching nearly one thousand miles from east to west—that recognized ʿUthman's suzerainty. Shehu ʿUthman divided his newly created state into two parts, each with its own headquarters: Gwandu in the east and Sokoto in the west.

In 1810, ʿUthman retired from active life to the town of Sifawa. He continued his intellectual pursuits, while leaving his brother Abdullahi and his son Muḥammad Bello to administer the caliphate. In 1815, he returned to Sokoto, where he resided until his death in April, 1817.

SIGNIFICANCE

ʿUthman dan Fodio founded a large empire, and his jihad inspired many similar uprisings in other parts of West Africa's savanna and Sahel regions and even into North Africa. Later in the nineteenth century, Islamic states were founded in what are now Senegal, Mali, Côte d'Ivoire (Ivory Coast), Chad, the Central African Republic, and Sudan. Dan Fodio's holy war was more than a religious upheaval; it was at once a struggle for social, political, and cultural change, presaging West Africa's modern era.

ʿUthman's teachings contained in his *Wathiqat ahl al-Sudan* (dispatch to the people of the Sudan) inspired the rebel Muslim slave leader Muhammad Kaba of Manchester in distant Jamaica during the late 1820's. Kaba's jihad—regarded by the imperial government as a slave riot—against white plantation owners triggered similar upheavals on other Caribbean plantations.

When Great Britain colonized Nigeria at the end of the nineteenth century, it preserved the basic structure of ʿUthman's emirate system and accorded considerable autonomy to the local rulers under a principle that was articulated as "indirect rule." In the early twenty-first century, the reigning sultan of Sokoto was a descendant of ʿUthman dan Fodio and was still regarded as the primary religious leader of independent Nigeria's Muslim citizens.

—*Narasingha P. Sil*

FURTHER READING

Ballard, Martin. *Uthman dan Fodio: Commander of the Faithful.* London: Longman, 1977. A brief and readable but nonetheless comprehensive account of ʿUthman dan Fodio's life. A must for beginners.

Balogun, Ismail A. B. *The Life and Works of ʿUthman dan Fodio: The Muslim Reformer of West Africa.* Lagos, Nigeria: Islamic Publications Bureau, 1975. Originally a doctoral dissertation, this is a succinct account of ʿUthman's life and a critical analysis of his important work, *Ihya' al-Sunna wa-Ikhmad al-Bid'a.*

Bello, Muḥammad. *Infaku'l Maisuri.* Translated by C. E. J. Whitting. London: Luzac, 1957. An important source for the life and teachings of ʿUthman by his son, Muḥammad Bello, the sultan of Sokoto who died in 1837.

Hiskett, Mervyn. *The Sword of Truth: The Life and Times of the Shehu Usuman dan Fodio.* 2d ed. Evanston, Ill.: Northwestern University Press, 1994. Chronicles the revolutionary movement in Hausaland and ʿUthman dan Fodio's role in that movement.

Jameelah, Maryam. *Shehu Uthman dan Fodio: A Great Mujaddid of West Africa.* Lahore: Mohammed Usuf Khan, 1978. Brief but useful biographical sketch for beginners.

Metz, Helen C., ed. *Nigeria: A Country Study.* 5th ed. Washington, D.C.: Federal Research Division, Library of Congress, 1992. A reliable source for basic background information on ʿUthman dan Fodio's jihad and the Sokoto caliphate.

Sagari, Alhaji Shehu, and Jean Boyd. *Uthman dan Fodio: The Theory and Practice of His Leadership.* Lagos, Nigeria: Islamic Publications Bureau, 1978. An account of ʿUthman's life and teachings by a Hausa teacher who became president of Nigeria. Based on essays by ʿUthman's brother Waziri Abdullahi. An eminently readable work of sound scholarship.

SEE ALSO: Abdelkader; Muḥammad Bello; The Mahdi; Samory Touré; Shaka.

RELATED ARTICLE in *Great Events from History: The Nineteenth Century, 1801-1900:* May 4, 1805-1830: Exploration of West Africa.

MARTIN VAN BUREN
President of the United States (1837-1841)

Van Buren played a central role in the development of the modern American party system and, as president of the United States, he kept the peace, eased sectional tensions over slavery, and formally separated the U.S. Treasury from private banks.

BORN: December 5, 1782; Kinderhook, New York
DIED: July 24, 1862; Kinderhook, New York
AREA OF ACHIEVEMENT: Government and politics

EARLY LIFE

An early example of a self-made man, Martin Van Buren began his life in Kinderhook, a small village on the post road to New York City about twenty miles south of Albany. He was born into the family of Abraham and Hannah Van Buren, both of respectable if undistinguished Dutch stock, going back to early colonial days. After an apparently happy childhood, the young Van Buren ended formal schooling at fourteen and spent the next seven years in law offices, first at Kinderhook and then in New York.

Admitted to the bar in 1803, Van Buren began practice in his home village, soon moved to Hudson, and, in 1816, settled in Albany, where he continued practice for twelve more years. Each move marked a new level of success in the law and could be measured by the growing respect of his fellows and by an income, derived largely from small clients, which laid the basis for an estate later estimated at $200,000. In 1807, he married a childhood playmate and distant cousin, Hannah Hoes, and sired four sons—Abraham, John, Martin, and Smith Thompson—before Hannah's death in 1819. There were later flirtations and rumors of a second marriage, but Van Buren remained a widower.

Politics as well as the law engaged the ambitious Van Buren and opened a career leading from the state senate in 1812 to the White House twenty-five years later. Time spent in his father's tavern—a gathering place for Republicans in the exciting decade of the 1790's—had sparked his interest and had begun to draw out an uncommon aptitude that was to make him one of the first and best politicians in the nation's history.

Foes ascribed Van Buren's success to the arts of management and intrigue, calling him the Little Magician. Such epithets as "sly fox" and "noncommittalism" were also associated with his name. Friends, by contrast, appreciated his uncanny ability to "read men," to fathom the motives of opponents and conciliate the interests of followers. Moving into the political arena once dominated by upper-class gentlemen, Van Buren cultivated the needed qualities of prudence, compromise, and self-control. Elements of style also signaled the ambitions of a lower-class person in the period of transition to a more democratic society and found symbolic expression in the care that the young legal apprentice gave to his wardrobe. On borrowed funds, he replaced his simple Republican attire with the knee breeches, buckled shoes, and tricornered hat of his Federalist mentor. Along with fine clothes would come a taste for good wine, suavity of manners, and great conversational gifts.

Personal appearance enhanced Van Buren's style and image. Crowned with curly hair of sandy red and graced with ease of movement, the young Van Buren commanded attention in spite of his thin and smallish five-foot, six-inch frame. In later years, he gained a large amount of weight and lost most of his hair, but thick sideburns of reddish gray framed an imposing brow. Lending further distinction to his countenance were big, blue, penetrating eyes and the ever-present trace of a smile, suggesting benign contentment to some and calculating guile to others. Here was a man, one bemused Virginia aristocrat observed, who might row to his object with muffled oars.

LIFE'S WORK

Van Buren's career in public office was a mix of personal ambition and a statesman's sensitivity to the needs of a rapidly changing society. In 1812, he began an eight-year tenure in the state senate, and for four of those years he also held the office of attorney general. The first part of his senate service was distinguished by unswerving support of the War of 1812 at a time when Federalists voiced bitter opposition; by the end of the war he attracted national attention with his proposal for conscripting troops.

In 1817, Van Buren gave belated but indispensable support for digging the Erie Canal, a project closely linked to his political foe, DeWitt Clinton. At the same time, Van Buren opposed most applications for new bank charters, for he wished to moderate the forces of change that were transforming an agrarian society into one featuring manufacture, commerce, and the spirit of enterprise. He also played a central role in the state convention that made the old state constitution of 1777 more conformable to the new democratic age. More offices were opened to the elective principle, and the number of adult, white male voters was more than doubled.

It was also during his senate years that Van Buren and his associates developed a disciplined party organization along modern lines. Nurtured by spoils and animated with an ethic of loyalty to the will of the majority expressed in caucuses and conventions, the party apparatus reached out from Albany to all parts of the state. Techniques of mass appeal and a style of campaigning not unlike religious revivals generated excitement and drew the people into the political process. Although rank-and-file party workers were attracted to spoils, "new men" such as Van Buren saw the party as a means of access to the power of government once reserved for the elite. Through its democratic organization and appeal, Van Buren and his party were normally able to outmatch the old style of elite politics followed by Clinton and, by the mid-1820's, gained control of the state.

Supported by his party, Van Buren won election to the U.S. Senate in 1821 and remained in that post for the next seven years. His reputation had preceded him to the Senate, where he soon enjoyed great influence and claimed the chair of the Judiciary Committee. A central concern was to revive two-party competition, which had ended, with the rapid decline of the Federalists, in the so-called "era of good feelings." Van Buren saw it as an era of bad feelings: Political conflict did not cease but turned inward, shattering the unity of the Republican Party into personal and sectional factions.

The Missouri Controversy was one result; another was the disputed election of 1824, resolved at last by the House of Representatives in favor of John Quincy Adams—a neo-Federalist in Van Buren's eyes. Van Buren then assumed leadership of the opposition to the new administration with the object of reestablish-

ing the political base of the old Republican Party that had reposed in Virginia and New York. To attract southern support, he spoke out for states' rights against the idea of strong national government advocated by Adams. Working closely with others, he fashioned a North-South coalition behind Andrew Jackson in 1828, and he pictured the presidential contest with Adams as a rerun of the old battles between Republicans and Federalists. To aid the cause, Van Buren ran for governor of New York and, as he hoped, his election contributed to

---

SUPPRESSION OF THE SLAVE TRADE

A central issue that President Martin Van Buren faced during his presidency was suppression of the Atlantic slave trade—a subject that he commented on in all his state of the union addresses. He gave the subject his fullest attention in his final address in 1840.

The suppression of the African slave trade has received the continued attention of the Government. The brig *Dolphin* and schooner *Grampus* have been employed during the last season on the coast of Africa for the purpose of preventing such portions of that trade as were said to be prosecuted under the American flag. After cruising off those parts of the coast most usually resorted to by slavers until the commencement of the rainy season, these vessels returned to the United States for supplies, and have since been dispatched on a similar service.

From the reports of the commanding officers it appears that the trade is now principally carried on under Portuguese colors, and they express the opinion that the apprehension of their presence on the slave coast has in a great degree arrested the prostitution of the American flag to this inhuman purpose. It is hoped that by continuing to maintain this force in that quarter and by the exertions of the officers in command much will be done to put a stop to whatever portion of this traffic may have been carried on under the American flag and to prevent its use in a trade which, while it violates the laws, is equally an outrage on the rights of others and the feelings of humanity. The efforts of the several Governments who are anxiously seeking to suppress this traffic must, however, be directed against the facilities afforded by what are now recognized as legitimate commercial pursuits before that object can be fully accomplished.

Supplies of provisions, water casks, merchandise, and articles connected with the prosecution of the slave trade are, it is understood, freely carried by vessels of different nations to the slave factories, and the effects of the factors are transported openly from one slave station to another without interruption or punishment by either of the nations to which they belong engaged in the commerce of that region. I submit to your judgments whether this Government, having been the first to prohibit by adequate penalties the slave trade, the first to declare it piracy, should not be the first also to forbid to its citizens all trade with the slave factories on the coast of Africa, giving an example to all nations in this respect which if fairly followed can not fail to produce the most effective results in breaking up those dens of iniquity.

Source: Martin Van Buren, "State of the Union Address," December 5, 1840.

Jackson's triumph. After three months at Albany, Van Buren resigned as governor and joined Jackson in Washington.

During Jackson's presidency, from 1829 to 1837, Van Buren served in turn as secretary of state, minister to England, and vice president. At the State Department, he gained by treaty the long-standing goal of opening trade with the British West Indies. His tenure as minister in 1831-1832 was cut short when political foes in the Senate refused to confirm his recess appointment. Happily for his career, however, the Senate action created a backlash of sentiment that enabled Jackson to choose him, through the party's first national convention, as vice president for the second term.

In whatever position he held, Van Buren enjoyed great influence with Jackson. Except for the issue of internal improvements, he had little impact on the formulation of specific policies. His influence was of a more general kind, namely, that of helping shape Jackson's perception of the presidency in party terms. All earlier presidents, no matter how partisan their actions, had identified with the eighteenth century ideal of a "patriotic chief" above party. However, Jackson set a new pattern by acting both as a president of the party and a president of the whole country. With Jackson's support, Van Buren received the party's nomination for president and, thanks to the divided state of the Whig Party, he won the election of 1836.

During his own presidency, from 1837 to 1841, Van Buren addressed three key matters. First, as a party president, he worked to contain sectional tensions over slavery. He enlisted the support of northern Democrats to sustain the House "gag" on abolitionist petitions and to complete Jackson's timetable for removing Indians from the Old Southwest. In return for this support, he prevailed on southern Democrats to surrender for the time their desire for bringing slaveholding Texas into the Union. Second, Van Buren kept the peace with Great Britain.

The aid that many Americans gave to the rebels in Canada created great tensions, but Van Buren held firmly to the policy that citizens violating Canada's neutrality could expect no protection from the government. An even greater crisis arose over the disputed boundary with New Brunswick, leading by early 1839 to an impending confrontation between British forces and the Maine state militia. With bipartisan support, the president restrained further movements by the militia and worked out a truce arrangement with the British minister in Washington. The treaty resolving the boundary dis-

pute came in the following administration, but Van Buren rightly claimed a "peace with honor."

At great political cost, finally, Van Buren pushed through Congress his central domestic measure for an independent Treasury. As his basic response to the Panic of 1837, it would separate Treasury operations from all private banks. Jackson had severed the connection with the national bank and deposited government revenues in selected state banks.

Unhappily, the government funds added to the momentum of other forces that, by 1835, generated a speculative mania and then the collapse two years later. Van Buren's plan would have the Treasury keep and disburse its own funds and use only specie or government paper, but no bank notes, in all its operations. The effect on the general currency of the country would be deflationary to some degree, yet the clear need of a depressed economy would seem to be for some degree of currency inflation. Although fully aware of this fact, Van Buren held to the view that, over the long term, a deflationary policy would assure a sound recovery and work against any future cycle of boom and bust. Whig foes, by contrast, skillfully exploited the short-term need for some form of currency inflation, rightly sensing its popularity in a nation increasingly committed to enterprise.

The Whigs also put their political house in order as they looked to the election of 1840. Ending their earlier divisions, they nominated a military hero of sorts, General William Henry Harrison, and conducted a "log cabin" campaign that utilized to the fullest extent those techniques of mass appeal that Democrats had developed earlier. As a result, Van Buren was soundly defeated in his bid for reelection.

Van Buren was never able to avenge his stunning defeat. Principled opposition to the issue of Texas annexation four years later denied him the party nomination, which went instead to James K. Polk. For a number of reasons—among them a sense of betrayal by his party and a genuine concern for its increasingly prosouthern tilt—he agreed to stand as the candidate of the Free-Soil Party in 1848 on a platform of opposing the spread of slavery. Within two years, however, he returned to his old party. Even though it remained strongly prosouthern throughout the 1850's, he still believed that its states' rights doctrine and its appeal in both sections made it indispensable for preserving the Union. After the Civil War broke out, he supported President Abraham Lincoln, but before his death in July, 1862, it was clear that the war was in the process of transforming the federative Union of states into a more consolidated nation.

SIGNIFICANCE

Historians for the next half century generally tended to echo the epithets fashioned by Van Buren's foes and to underrate the Little Magician's contribution to the nation's history. His idea of disciplined party organization, two-party competition, and a party presidency survived the Civil War and helped shape political life ever since. As president, he served the nation well by keeping peace with Great Britain at a time when war might have brought disaster to the young country. To his credit, some other depression president might have welcomed war as a diversion from domestic problems.

Van Buren also merits good marks for his courage and consistency on the issue of an independent Treasury, for many expected him to follow a more popular course. His central measure also lasted a long time. Repealed by triumphant Whigs in 1841 and then restored by President Polk, the independent Treasury measure remained in operation until the Federal Reserve System was established in 1912. It did not end the cycle of boom and bust—as the panics of 1857, 1873, and 1893 show—but it is doubtful if any other plan would have worked much better in a country so fully committed to free enterprise. Along with his modest but real acts of statesmanship, in sum, Van Buren should also be remembered as an authentic expression of the American Dream, a genuine example of the self-made man.

—*Major L. Wilson*

FURTHER READING

Alexander, Holmes. *The American Talleyrand: The Career and Contemporaries of Martin Van Buren*. New York: Harper and Brothers, 1935. The most hostile biography of Van Buren. It elaborates Whig charges against the spoilsman politician, opportunist, and schemer but is lively and well written.

Cole, Donald B. *Martin Van Buren and the American Political System*. Princeton, N.J.: Princeton University Press, 1984. The best of the biographies. Thorough, balanced in assessment, and well researched, it does an especially good job placing Van Buren in the context of economic and political development.

Curtis, James C. *The Fox at Bay: Martin Van Buren and the Presidency, 1837-1841*. Lexington: University Press of Kentucky, 1970. The first full-length work on the presidential years. Light on analysis of the economic background but good on the intraparty politics in Van Buren's party.

Lynch, Denis Tilden. *An Epoch and a Man: Martin Van Buren and His Times*. New York: Horace Liveright, 1929. Dated but the most balanced of the older biographies. Contains much useful material on the personal life of Van Buren but fails to put his public career in context.

Niven, John. *Martin Van Buren: The Romantic Age of American Politics*. New York: Oxford University Press, 1983. The first biography on Van Buren in nearly fifty years. Well written, good on his private life, and good in synthesizing works that assess him in a favorable light. Too brief, however, on the presidential years.

Remini, Robert V. *Martin Van Buren and the Making of the Democratic Party*. New York: Columbia University Press, 1959. The best single volume on Van Buren's work in party organization. If he is pictured as a "politician," Van Buren is also pictured as a Jeffersonian ideologue and man of principle.

Shepard, Edward M. *Martin Van Buren*. Boston: Houghton Mifflin, 1889. Part of the American Statesman series and the most sympathetic of the older biographies. It shares the Whig judgment against spoils but praises Van Buren for his Jeffersonian ideals and hard-money policy.

Sibley, Joel H. *Martin Van Buren and the Emergence of American Popular Politics*. Lanham, Md.: Rowman & Littlefield, 2002. Describes the growing popular participation and sophistication of political parties in the years following the War of 1812, focusing on Van Buren's critical role in this development. Sibley dubs Van Buren "the founding father of systematic political organization and popular mobilization."

Widmer, Ted. *Martin Van Buren*. New York: Times Books, 2005. One in a series of books about the lives and careers of American presidents. Widmer, an advisor to former U.S. president Bill Clinton, concludes that Van Buren will always be considered one of the country's lesser leaders.

Wilson, Major L. *The Presidency of Martin Van Buren*. Lawrence: University Press of Kansas, 1984. Part of the Kansas presidential series. Thorough on the economic background of the Panic of 1837, the currency implications of the independent Treasury, and the party debate leading to Whig victory in 1840.

SEE ALSO: John Quincy Adams; George Bancroft; DeWitt Clinton; William Henry Harrison; Andrew Jackson; Abraham Lincoln; James K. Polk.

RELATED ARTICLES in *Great Events from History: The Nineteenth Century, 1801-1900:* December 1, 1824-February 9, 1825: U.S. Election of 1824; December 3,

1828: U.S. Election of 1828; July 10, 1832: Jackson Vetoes Rechartering of the Bank of the United States; April 14, 1834: Clay Begins American Whig Party; July 2, 1839: *Amistad* Slave Revolt; November, 1839: Stephens Begins Uncovering Mayan Antiquities; De-cember 2, 1840: U.S. Election of 1840; September 4, 1841: Congress Passes Preemption Act of 1841; August 1, 1846: Establishment of Independent U.S. Treasury.

CORNELIUS VANDERBILT
American industrialist

Vanderbilt was one of the great capitalist successes of all time, and his name has come to symbolize the possibilities of American free enterprise. He created a worldwide shipping and railroad business that was both efficient and profitable and endowed a university that was later named for him.

BORN: May 27, 1794; Port Richmond, Staten Island, New York
DIED: January 4, 1877; New York, New York
AREA OF ACHIEVEMENT: Business

EARLY LIFE

Cornelius Vanderbilt was one of nine children of Cornelius and Phebe Vanderbilt. His parents had difficulty supporting their huge household, yet managed, for the most part because of his mother's careful monitoring of family finances. His mother came from a family of New Jersey farmers. She tempered her husband's visionary schemes to get rich quick, and her strength and fortitude were the backbone of the family. Young Cornelius's father was of the third generation of a family that had migrated to America from Holland in search of the freedom to practice their Moravian religion; like the family of Mrs. Vanderbilt, they were farmers.

Thus, young Cornelius Vanderbilt was born into a situation that was not promising. Vanderbilt hated school, preferring to spend his time outside involved in sports and even work. He was tall and strong for his age and was an excellent swimmer, an unsurpassed climber, and a wrestler whom few could beat. Despite his distaste for school lessons, he had a vigorous mind and quickly learned to sail and to use tools.

Vanderbilt took to the water, and it became his substitute for the schoolhouse. He spent entire afternoons watching craft navigate upon the beauty of New York Bay. It was alleged that in time he knew by sight every ship that used the port, and that he had learned the rig and outline of every fishing boat or coaster that navigated on the rivers.

Vanderbilt became adept at sailing the clumsy family boat, and he became the one who was trusted to take farm produce into New York. At sixteen, his attraction for the sea became so strong that he announced to his mother he was running away from home to become a sailor. His mother intervened, and the two reached an agreement. Vanderbilt would be paid one hundred dollars to plough some hard, rough family land, and his earnings would be used to purchase a boat.

Vanderbilt quickly closed his first "contract." Like a crafty Tom Sawyer, he enlisted help from the neighborhood boys, promising his workers rides in his new boat. Vanderbilt put his new boat to work immediately and spent sixteen hours a day ferrying passengers for eighteen cents a trip. At the end of the first year, he repaid his mother the one hundred dollars and earned an additional one thousand dollars as well. At the end of the second year, he gave her one thousand dollars and bought partial interest in several other boats. Thus, he had devised on a small scale the system that would one day make him one of the wealthiest men in the world.

At nineteen, Vanderbilt fell in love with Sophia Johnson, the attractive daughter of his father's sister Eleanor. Both his parents objected, yet Vanderbilt married Sophia without their blessing on December 19, 1813.

LIFE'S WORK

To support his family, Vanderbilt set up a ferry system, and with his good reputation for delivery he obtained a contract to supply six forts around New York. The work was hard since it took a full day to supply one fort and that left Sunday as his only day off. However, profits were large, and new schooners were added to a growing fleet.

When Robert Fulton launched the *Clermont*, Vanderbilt was not alone in realizing that the steamboat was the future of sea travel. For several years, Vanderbilt worked for Thomas Gibbons, commanding boats and streamlining procedures. During this period, the two

Cornelius Vanderbilt. (Library of Congress)

men fought the state-granted monopoly Fulton enjoyed. The Supreme Court of the United States, after a wait of seven years, finally heard the case and declared that such monopolies were unconstitutional.

Because of his independent spirit and vision of the future, Vanderbilt resigned from his position with Gibbons and moved his family from New Brunswick back to New York in 1829. In the spring of 1830, with forty thousand dollars in savings, he entered the New York steamboat business. He constructed better boats than his competition and delivered services that were cheaper and more efficient. For the first five years, he made thirty thousand dollars a year and then his income in 1836 rose to sixty thousand. None of his more than one hundred vessels was ever burned, wrecked, or destroyed. He chose only the best captains and carried no insurance.

By age forty, Vanderbilt was worth $500,000. The Vanderbilts had twelve children (one son died in infancy) and lived at No. 10 Washington Place in New York City. Vanderbilt was all but brutal to his family, running it with more sternness than the captain of a vessel, and brooked no disobedience or contradiction. He educated all of his children, and George Washington Vanderbilt, his favorite, was sent to West Point. The sons were expected to earn their own living rather than count on their father's wealth. William Henry Vanderbilt, who

was especially distasteful to his father, married against Vanderbilt's wishes and lived with his wife on nineteen dollars a week.

It is ironic that this man, who will forever be associated with the railroad industry, was nearly killed in a train accident. In 1833, Vanderbilt was thrown from a train, dragged along the track, and flung down an embankment. He broke several ribs that punctured his lungs but survived despite archaic medical treatment.

As Vanderbilt aged, he looked more and more aristocratic, as if he had been born to be wealthy and handsome throughout his life. Time had caused the top of his head to go bald, but the sides of his head still sported the white, bushy sideburns that created a look of distinction.

By 1864, Vanderbilt had sold his steamships to Daniel B. Allen and Cornelius K. Garrison for three million dollars. He then began to shift his investments into the railroad industry. He was nearly seventy and was worth not less than twenty million dollars.

Vanderbilt's success in the railroad industry must be credited in some small part to his son William, whom Vanderbilt had treated so harshly in his youth. Without his father's help, William was soon quite wealthy himself, owning a house, a farm, and land, with the farm yielding twelve thousand dollars a year.

Vanderbilt, noticing William's success, decided to test him by placing him in charge of the failed Staten Island Railroad. William knew next to nothing about railroads but sold his farm and accepted the challenge. In two years, almost miraculously, he took the railroad from bankruptcy and no credit to solvency. His astonished father looked on in the background as William was made president of the Staten Island Railroad.

After some resistance, Vanderbilt entered the railroad industry on a larger scale in the winter of 1862-1863 by buying heavily the stock of the Harlem Railroad. The stock doubled and kept rising based on the magic name of the owner. Vanderbilt continued buying. The stock had sold for three dollars a share in 1857; on April 22, 1860, it sold for seventy-five dollars.

Vanderbilt was president of Harlem Railroad. His son William was made vice president and again implemented the procedures he had learned when he turned around the Staten Island Railroad. Within time, William created a second success.

Vanderbilt began adding more railroads to his empire, beginning with stock in the Hudson River Railroad. He was not interested in speculation but rather in making the railroads profitable. Soon he had full control of the Hudson and, as the Harlem Railroad began to show profits,

Vanderbilt rewarded William by naming him vice president of the Hudson.

Next, Vanderbilt began to buy the stock of the New York Central, using two million dollars he had made off Harlem, thus repeating his practices in the steamship business. At the age of seventy-three, he took over the New York Central, and the massive improvements that took place on the Harlem and the Hudson River railroads were repeated, this time with an even tougher overhauling, and the connections were multiplied.

Vanderbilt consolidated his New York railroads into the New York Central, thereby maximizing efficiency. He made William vice president, and the railroad profited quickly under his now experienced leadership.

On August 17, 1868, Sophia Vanderbilt died. Within a year, Vanderbilt married Miss Frank A. Crawford, a much younger woman who was a distant relative of Vanderbilt's mother.

Vanderbilt continued to add railroad lines to his holdings like so many toys in a child's closet. In time he owned Canada Southern, Michigan Central, and Great Western. The combined railroad was 978 miles long and worth $150 million, half of which he owned. However, this was the man who had fought against monopolies.

At eighty-one, Vanderbilt remained in good physical and mental health. He had accumulated one of the world's great fortunes, and, despite his tyranny and ruthlessness, he had created remarkable transportation systems for the United States. On January 4, 1877, Vanderbilt died at his home in New York.

SIGNIFICANCE

Cornelius Vanderbilt must be labeled one of the great capitalist successes of all time. Throughout his life, he fought for the principle of free enterprise as guaranteed by the Constitution. From his mother, he learned to be frugal and to save money; from his father, he learned that get-rich-quick schemes rarely worked and that, instead, one could make money through hard work and wise investment, delivering a good product for a fair price. Many of his business practices continue to be standards in the American trade world.

Vanderbilt was born with no privileges, yet his story could not exactly be called rags to riches. He did literally start with a one-hundred-dollar boat that in a lifetime of eighty-two years he turned into 100 million dollars. During his youth, he was an archetypal American child, a Huck Finn who loathed education and spent his time dreaming on the banks of New York's waterways learning obsessively all that he could about boating.

After his death, some of his heirs continued the family empire until its dissolution in the twentieth century. The family homes in Newport, Rhode Island, and Asheville, North Carolina, would become museums. The Vanderbilt name would be kept alive through its association with railroads no longer owned by the family and, with true irony, through Vanderbilt University.

—*John Harty*

FURTHER READING

Andrews, Wayne. *The Vanderbilt Legend: The Story of the Vanderbilt Family, 1794-1940*. New York: Harcourt, Brace, 1941. Only the first two chapters center on Cornelius Vanderbilt. Because of its span, the book fails to cover much in detail. Includes a family tree, photographs, footnotes, a bibliography, and an index.

Brands, H. W. *Masters of Enterprise: Giants of American Business from John Jacob Astor and J. P. Morgan to Bill Gates and Oprah Winfrey*. New York: Free Press, 1999. Includes a chapter on the business activities of Vanderbilt and Jay Gould.

Croffut, William A. *The Vanderbilts and the Story of Their Fortune*. Chicago: Belford, Clark, 1886. Reprint. New York: Arno Press, 1975. Croffut received help from the Vanderbilts until a disagreement severed the connection. A balanced analysis of the story, although the prose is turgid and the book is dated. Presents Vanderbilt with his rough edges.

Gordon, John Steele. *The Scarlet Woman of Wall Street: Jay Gould, Jim Fisk, Cornelius Vanderbilt, the Erie Railway Wars, and the Birth of Wall Street*. New York: Weidenfeld & Nicolson, 1988. Focuses on the cutthroat competition among railroad barons, describing how Vanderbilt instigated a rate war between his New York Central Railway and the competing Erie line.

Hoyt, Edwin P. *The Vanderbilts and Their Fortunes*. Garden City, N.Y.: Doubleday, 1962. Well-researched account, emphasizing money and power. Tells how the fourth generation lost the empire. Contains a bibliography.

Jennings, Walter Wilson. "Cornelius Vanderbilt: Illiterate Giant of Transportation." In *Twenty Giants of American Business*. New York: Exposition Press, 1952. Extracts from a variety of sources to summarize the high points of Vanderbilt's life. A good starting point.

Stoddard, William O. "Cornelius Vanderbilt: Competition." In *Men of Business*. New York: Charles Scribner's Sons, 1894. Short overview in dated language, written to inspire careers in business. Overly positive.

SEE ALSO: Andrew Carnegie; Robert Fulton; J. P. Morgan; John D. Rockefeller; Victoria Woodhull.

RELATED ARTICLES in *Great Events from History: The Nineteenth Century, 1801-1900:* June 16, 1855-May 1, 1857: Walker Invades Nicaragua; February 17-18, 1890: Women's Rights Associations Unite.

GIUSEPPE VERDI
Italian opera composer

One of the giants of nineteenth century opera, Verdi was an innovator who during a long career evolved his own form of music drama and contributed at least half a dozen of the most enduringly popular operas in the international repertory.

BORN: October 10, 1813; Le Roncole, Duchy of Parma (now in Italy)
DIED: January 27, 1901; Milan, Italy
ALSO KNOWN AS: Giuseppe Fortunino Francesco Verdi (full name)
AREA OF ACHIEVEMENT: Music

EARLY LIFE

Giuseppe Verdi (VAYR-dee) was the son of Carlo and Luigia Verdi, who eked out a modest living as owners of a wine and grocery store. Verdi's musical talent revealed itself early, and his father bought him an old spinet when he was eight. When he was ten, he played the organ at the village church. His talent was noticed by Antonio Barezzi, a wealthy merchant in nearby Busseto, who arranged for Verdi to be tutored by Ferdinando Provesi, the director of the music school in Busseto. Provesi taught him to play the flute, the bass clarinet, the horn, and the piano. After finishing high school in Busseto, Verdi became Provesi's assistant. In 1833, Verdi traveled to Milan, hoping to win a place at the conservatory, but his application was refused because he was over the age limit.

Barezzi provided for him to stay in Milan and take private lessons from Vincenzo Lavigna, a conductor at La Scala. Verdi proved to be a diligent student, sometimes working fourteen hours a day. In 1834, Verdi returned to Busseto, hoping to fill the vacancy left by the death of Provesi. The post, however, had already gone to another candidate, and the slight to Verdi caused a storm in the small town. Eventually, after a public competition, Verdi was appointed Busseto Master of Music. This was in April, 1836; the next month, Verdi married Margherita Barezzi, the daughter of his benefactor.

Verdi began teaching, composing, and conducting, and his first opera, *Oberto, conte di San Bonifacio*, was performed at La Scala in November, 1839. It ran for only fourteen performances, but Verdi received a contract for three more operas. He began working on *Un giorno di regno*, which was performed in September, 1840, but it was withdrawn after the premiere. Shocked by this failure and the death of his wife in the same year—as well as the loss of his infant son the previous year—Verdi decided never to compose again. After some months, the director of La Scala persuaded him to read a libretto based on the biblical story of Nebuchadnezzar. As a result, Verdi wrote *Nabucco*, his first major work. Premiered at La Scala in March, 1842, it was an immediate success, and Verdi found himself being hailed throughout Italy as the successor to his fellow countrymen, Vincenzo Bellini and Gaetano Donizetti.

LIFE'S WORK

Verdi often referred to the next nine years of his life, during which he wrote fourteen operas, as his period "in the galleys." The Italian operagoing public was accustomed to a regular supply of new works, and Verdi gave them what they wanted. After *Nabucco* came *I Lombardi alla prima crociata* (1843); audiences were quick to apply the story, about the struggle of the Lombards to free Jerusalem from the Saracens, to the contemporary Italian struggle to throw off Austrian rule, and Verdi's music became a symbol of Italian nationalism. *I Lombardi all prima crociata* was followed by *Ernani* (1844), *I due Foscari* (1844), and *Giovanna d' Arco* (1845). In 1845, dissatisfied with standards of production, Verdi broke his connection with La Scala and was not to return until 1869. His next two operas, *Alzira* (1845) and *Attila* (1846), were performed in Naples and Venice, respectively. Then came what is probably the best opera of his early period, *Macbeth*, based on William Shakespeare's tragedy. It premiered in Florence in March, 1847.

Verdi had by now gained an international reputation, and later in 1847 he was in London, producing *I masnadieri*. The successful premiere was attended by Queen Victoria. Verdi returned home via Paris, where he renewed his friendship with Giuseppina Strepponi, who had sung in the premiere of *Nabucco*. They began living together, in defiance of the rigid conventions of the period, and married twelve years later. In 1848, political events became more important than artistic ones in Verdi's life. It was a year of revolutions throughout Europe, and the Austrians were driven out of Milan. When Verdi, who was an enthusiastic patriot, heard the news in Paris, he left immediately for Milan. The freedom and unification of Italy was still in the future; republicans and monarchists quarreled among themselves, and in May Verdi returned to Paris. Milan was occupied by Austrian troops once more in August; the failure of the nationalist revolt depressed Verdi.

In 1849, Verdi and Strepponi moved back to Busseto, scandalizing the local people by their illicit liaison. Four

Giuseppe Verdi. (The Granger Collection, New York)

operas followed over the next four years, including the patriotic *La battaglia di Legnano* (1849) and *Luisa Miller* (1849). Then within two years came three masterpieces. *Rigoletto*, first performed in March, 1851, and based on a play by Victor Hugo, was Verdi's first worldwide success. The heartbreaking story of the hunchback Rigoletto and his beautiful daughter Gilda includes one of Verdi's most popular melodies, "La donna e mobile," and the brilliant quartet "Bella figlia dell' amore." Over the next four years, *Rigoletto* was performed all over Europe and in the United States.

After Verdi and Strepponi moved to a new home in Sant' Agata, close to Busseto, Verdi began working simultaneously on *Il trovatore* and *La traviata*. *Il trovatore*, based on a drama by the Spanish playwright Antonio Garcia Gutiérrez, premiered in January, 1853, in Rome. It was an immediate and brilliant success, its superb melodies weaving a compelling tale of passion and vengeance, tenderness and melancholy. Less than two months later came the premiere of *La traviata*, based on a novel by Alexandre Dumas, *père*. For several reasons, however, the first performance was a failure: Verdi had discarded some old conventions, and the opera was performed in contemporary dress; it also featured a courtesan as heroine, which offended public taste. In 1854, the opera was performed again, this time successfully, at a different theater in Venice.

Verdi was now famous and wealthy, although he was not immune to failure: *Simone Boccanegra* (1857), which followed *Les Vêpres siciliennes* (1855), was not well received. Verdi was to revise it twenty-four years later. His next opera, *Un ballo in maschera*, which concerns the assassination of Gustavus III Adolphus of Sweden, premiered in Rome in 1859. Like a number of Verdi's previous operas, it was subject to censorship—the authorities were wary of having an assassination depicted on the stage.

In 1859, political events once more came to the fore. To Verdi's delight, Milan was liberated, and after Parma voted to join neighboring Modena, Verdi was elected as deputy to the new assembly. He led a delegation to Vittorio Emanuele, king of Piedmont, to request the union of Parma with Piedmont. In 1861, Verdi was reluctantly persuaded to stand for election to Italy's new national parliament, and he remained a member until 1865. He did not care for the day-to-day business of politics. During the 1860's Verdi wrote only two operas: *La forza del destino* (1862), which was first performed in St. Petersburg in the presence of Czar Alexander II, and *Don Carlos* (1867). The latter was based on Friedrich

Schiller's verse drama of the same name, and the libretto was in French.

In the last twenty-two years of his life, Verdi entered yet another creative phase. *Aïda*, commissioned by the Khedive of Egypt to mark the opening of the Suez Canal, was first performed in Cairo in December, 1871. Verdi stayed in Italy preparing for the performance in Milan, which followed shortly afterward. Full of pageantry and spectacle, *Aïda* was his greatest success. It has been called the last grand opera, and yet in spite of its vastness—a performance can use up to five hundred extras—the tender emotions of the three main characters, caught in a love triangle, are intimately conveyed. After the success of *Aïda*, Verdi seemed to have reached the summit of his career. However, three great works were still to come. The first of these was the *Messa da requiem* (1874), in memory of the Italian poet and patriot Alessandro Manzoni, which is notable for the dramatic rather than devotional quality of the music.

For more than a decade following this work, Verdi lived in virtual retirement on his estate at Sant' Agata. He only reluctantly agreed to write *Otello* when he was shown the outstanding libretto, based on Shakespeare's play and written by the Italian poet Arrigo Boito. *Otello* was first performed at La Scala in February, 1887. It was another triumph: the musical event of the decade and Verdi's finest tragic opera. Verdi's final great work, *Falstaff* (1893), was an astonishing feat for a man in his eightieth year. It was his first comic opera in fifty years, and the libretto was again written by Arrigo Boito, based on Shakespeare's *The Merry Wives of Windsor* (1597), with some material from *Henry IV* (1598). Full of warm humor, fast-paced, and subtle, *Falstaff* was first performed at La Scala, in February, 1893. Verdi's last works were religious and included *Te Deum* (1896) and *Stabat mater* (1897). In 1897, his wife died, and in January, 1901, while in Milan, Verdi suffered a stroke. He died six days later, on January 27, at the age of eighty-seven.

SIGNIFICANCE

In spite of the fact that a large number of Giuseppe Verdi's twenty-six operas were hugely successful in his lifetime and that many of them quickly became part of the international repertory, full critical appreciation of his work was slow in coming. For some years after his death, only *Otello* and *Falstaff* were considered worthy of serious praise. The situation began to change first in Germany during the 1920's, with the Verdi Renaissance. This was partly a reaction against Verdi's great contemporary, Richard Wagner; indeed, during this period,

there were almost as many performances of Verdi's operas in Germany as there were of Wagner's and far more than those of any other composer. Since then Verdi's reputation has steadily grown throughout the world. At least six of his operas, *Rigoletto*, *Il trovatore*, *La traviata*, *Aïda*, *Otello*, and *Falstaff*, are universally acknowledged as masterpieces and are among the most frequently performed, and best loved, of all operas. In addition, the *Messa da requiem* has power to rouse those who do not normally respond to religious music.

Verdi revolutionized nineteenth century opera. As an innovator, he was second only to Wagner. He quickly outgrew the operatic conventions of the period, which valued beautiful melodies and demonstrations of vocal agility more than dramatic action. Particularly from *Aïda* onward, Verdi perfected a form of continuous music drama, quite distinct from that of Wagner, in which the music served as an expression of character and dramatic situation. In this he proved himself equal to the daunting task of putting Shakespeare, the dramatist he most revered, into operatic form. These final works of Verdi reveal his technical mastery, psychological insight, and that deep sympathy for humanity—its passions, sufferings, follies, and nobility—that pervades his work as a whole.

—Bryan Aubrey

FURTHER READING

Balthazar, Scott, ed. *The Cambridge Companion to Verdi*. New York: Cambridge University Press, 2004. Collection of essays, including discussions of Verdi's life, operas and other compositions, working methods, and Verdi criticism.

Budden, Julian. *The Operas of Verdi*. 3 vols. New York: Oxford University Press, 1973-1981. Three of the most impressive volumes ever written on Verdi. Volume 1 covers Verdi's first seventeen operas, including plot summaries and biographical background. Volume 2 covers *Il trovatore* to *La forza del destino* and includes details of Verdi's revisions and alterations. Volume 3 analyzes the composition, structure, and first performances of *Don Carlos*, *Aïda*, *Otello*, and *Falstaff*; the volume also discusses the creative process, the relationship between composer and librettist, and Verdi's relationship to contemporary Italian composers.

Conati, Marcello, ed. *Encounters with Verdi*. Translated by Richard Stokes. Ithaca, N.Y.: Cornell University Press, 1984. A major contribution to Verdi studies. Contains fifty eyewitness accounts written by Verdi's contemporaries who knew him between 1845 and 1900, including composers, artists, musicians, critics, and journalists. Conati's excellent introductions, and extensive notes further illuminate Verdi's life and music. Also includes bibliography and index.

Gatti, Carlo. *Verdi: The Man and His Music*. Translated by Elisabeth Abbott. New York: G. P. Putnam's Sons, 1955. One of the most important and enjoyable biographies, originally published in 1931. Gatti, who as a young man knew Verdi, writes tenderly and affectionately about the man he admired.

Rosselli, John. *The Life of Verdi*. New York: Cambridge University Press, 2000. A good introduction to Verdi's life and music for the general reader.

Sadie, Stanley, ed. *Verdi and His Operas*. Compiled by Roger Parker. New York: St. Martin's Press, 2000. The information about Verdi contained in the *New Grove Dictionary of Opera* has been extracted in this book. Includes a brief biography and detailed analyses of Verdi's operas.

Toye, Francis. *Giuseppe Verdi: His Life and Works*. London: William Heinemann, 1931. One of the first comprehensive studies of Verdi in English. Divided into two parts. The first is intended for the general reader and surveys Verdi's life and music; the second is more specialized, treating each opera in detail, including an account of the librettos and their origins.

Verdi, Giuseppe. *Letters of Giuseppe Verdi*. Edited, compiled, and translated by Charles Osborne. New York: Holt, Rinehart and Winston, 1972. Contains nearly three hundred letters written by Verdi between the ages of thirty and eighty-seven. Verdi did not expect these candid, down-to-earth, pithy letters to be published; they reveal his immense care for every detail of his craft and give insight into his dealings with theater directors, publishers, and librettists. Contains a biographical introduction.

Weaver, William, and Martin Chusid, eds. *The Verdi Companion*. New York: W. W. Norton, 1979. Ten short essays on various topics, including Verdi's relationship with the Risorgimento, with the city of Milan, and with librettists, as well as his attitude to operatic texts and his relationship to contemporary Italian opera. Includes a critical bibliography, a seventy-page chronological timetable of his life, and a list of major works by date of first performance.

SEE ALSO: Alexander II; Georges Bizet; Don Carlos; Gaetano Donizetti; Alexandre Dumas, *père*; Victor Hugo; Alessandro Manzoni; Gioacchino Rossini; Queen Victoria; Richard Wagner.

RELATED ARTICLES in *Great Events from History: The Nineteenth Century, 1801-1900:* February 20, 1816: Rossini's *The Barber of Seville* Debuts; March 3, 1830: Hugo's *Hernani* Incites Rioting; October 22, 1883: Metropolitan Opera House Opens in New York; January 14, 1900: Puccini's *Tosca* Premieres in Rome.

JULES VERNE
French novelist

Verne was a popular and prolific French novelist whose works were immediately translated into other major languages. He is credited with being the founder of the literary genre now known as science fiction, and his writings continue to be read and adapted to other media in the twenty-first century.

BORN: February 8, 1828; Nantes, France
DIED: March 24, 1905; Amiens, France
ALSO KNOWN AS: Jules Gabriel Verne (full name)
AREA OF ACHIEVEMENT: Literature

EARLY LIFE
One of five children, Jules Verne was the first son born to Pierre and Sophie Verne. Descended from a long line of merchants, seamen, and lawyers, it was expected that he would practice law. However, that expectation conflicted with his nature. The adventuresome Verne ran away from home at the age of eleven and attempted to set sail from Nantes on a departing ship. Caught and punished by his parents, Verne promised his mother that "from now on I'll travel only in my imagination." Only an average student, Verne was obedient to his father's hopes, studied law, and tried his luck as an attorney. For him it was a boring and frustrating profession.

While studying in Paris, Verne had met and befriended the famed writer Alexandre Dumas, *père*, author of *Les Trois Mousquetaires* (1844; *The Three Musketeers*, 1846) and the "father of the historical romance." Verne recalled his childhood fascination with "the literature of adventure," such as Daniel Defoe's *Robinson Crusoe* (1719) and Johann Wyss's *Der schwietzerische Robinson* (1812-1827; *The Swiss Family Robinson*, 1814, 1818, 1820). With the encouragement of Dumas, Verne left the security of his law practice to write. His initial play, *Les Pailles rompues* (1850; the broken straws), was successful at Dumas's Théâtre Historique. Between 1851 and 1861, Verne penned some fifteen plays, most of which were never produced. For a short time, however, he was the secretary of the Théâtre Lyrique.

In 1856, while attending a wedding, Verne met Honorine Fraysee, a rich young widow with two children. It was a case of love at first sight. They were married on January 10, 1857, in a simple ceremony. In 1861, their son, Michel, was born. A happy union, the marriage lasted for forty-eight years.

By 1860 Verne began to regard himself as a professional failure. His writings were not earning much income, and he was accused of living off the income of a wealthy wife. Attempts to supplement his income by selling stocks failed. Because he had written some scientific articles, Verne attempted a piece on aeronautics and exploration. Africa was a popular subject because of the discoveries of adventurers such as Sir Richard Francis Burton and John Hanning Speke. Verne proposed exploring the Dark Continent by balloon. This scientific text was repeatedly rejected by publishers. P. J. Hetzel (who wrote under the pseudonym P. J. Stahl) advised Verne to rewrite it as fiction, suggesting that Verne could do for science what Dumas had done for history. Verne acted on the advice, and the firm of Hetzel and Company published Verne's *voyages extraordinaires* (fantastic voyages) beginning with *Cinq Semaines en ballon* (1863; *Five Weeks in a Balloon*, 1876). The work was an immediate success, and Hetzel gave Verne a lifetime contract. His career as the creator of what would be called "science fiction" had begun.

LIFE'S WORK

At the age of thirty-five, Verne had found his life's work. In his remaining forty-two years, he would write more than sixty "scientific romances," averaging two books per year and winning the reputation of the founder of science fiction. Verne drew on two of his major loves in the writing of science fiction: geography and science.

Though he seldom traveled, Verne was an avid reader of travel books and was recognized as an accomplished amateur geographer. Early in his career, he wrote a popular history of geographical exploration from the Phoenicians to the nineteenth century, *La Decouverte de la*

Jules Verne. (Library of Congress)

terre (1878; *The Discovery of the Earth*, 1878), while he also collaborated on an illustrated geography of France. This fascination with a sense of place gave Verne the ability to provide intimate and convincing details in his novels, even those set in remote places in the Americas and the Pacific. Of seafaring stock and as an accomplished yachtsman, Verne filled his novels that were set on the oceans with compelling data that would normally be known only to a sailor. Verne's feeling for locale was consistently persuasive.

Although he was not an inventor, Verne was an avid reader of scientific literature and had the gift to see the technological application of many of the great discoveries of the nineteenth century. Verne's writing anticipated that of science fiction author Arthur C. Clarke in this respect, for there is always a hard core of scientific fact inside his fantastic tales. Late in his life, when someone dared to compare his writing to that of the British author H. G. Wells, Verne protested, insisting, "I do not see the possibility of comparison between his work and mine . . . his stories do not repose on very scientific bases. . . . I make use of physics. He invents."

Verne's novels predicted such twentieth century realities as helicopters in the skies, submarines under the seas, and space travel beyond the earth. In *Les Cinq Cents Millions de la Bégum* (1878; *The Begum's Fortune*, 1880), Verne foretold both poison gases and rocket-propelled missiles, while in *Face au drapeau* (1896; *For the Flag*, 1897), he anticipated the use of high explosives (atomic energy) to terrorize international trade. Verne, in fact, helped create what he described in fiction. Simon Lake, one of the developers of the modern submarine, stated in his autobiography that "Jules Verne was in a sense the director-general of my life." I. O. Evans, an authority on the history of science fiction, felt that "Verne and Wells may have done far more than to foretell such developments; they may actually have helped to bring them about."

To Verne's passion for geography and science, one must add his skill as a masterful storyteller. Though his

	VERNE'S NOVELS
1863	*Cinq Semaines en ballon* (*Five Weeks in a Balloon*, 1876)
1864	*Voyage au centre de la terre* (*A Journey to the Centre of the Earth*, 1872)
1864-1866	*Voyages et aventures du capitaine Hatteras* (2 volumes; includes *Les Anglais au pôle nord*, 1864 [*English at the North Pole*, 1874], and *Le Désert de glace*, 1866 [*Field of Ice*, 1876]; also as *Adventures of Captain Hatteras*, 1875)
1865	*De la terre à la lune* (*From the Earth to the Moon*, 1873)
1867-1868	*Les Enfants du capitaine Grant* (3 volumes; *Voyage Round the World*, 1876-1877; also as *Captain Grant's Children*, includes *The Mysterious Document*, *Among the Cannibals*, and *On the Track*)
1869-1870	*Vingt mille lieues sous les mers* (*Twenty Thousand Leagues Under the Sea*, 1873)
1870	*Autour de la lune* (*From the Earth to the Moon . . . and a Trip Around It*, 1873)
1871	*Une Ville flottante* (*A Floating City*, 1876)
1872	*Aventures de trois russes et de trois anglais* (*Meridiana: The Adventures of Three Englishmen and Three Russians in South Africa*, 1873)
1873	*Le Tour du monde en quatre-vingts jours* (*Around the World in Eighty Days*, 1873)
1874, 1876	*Docteur Ox* (in *Dr. Ox's Experiment and Master Zacharius*, 1876)
1874-1875	*L'Île mystérieuse* (3 volumes; includes *Les Naufrages de l'air*, *L'Abandonné*, and *Le Secret de l'île; The Mysterious Island*, 1875)
1875	*Le Chancellor* (*Survivors of the Chancellor*, 1875)
1876	*Michel Strogoff* (*Michael Strogoff*, 1876-1877)
1877	*Hector Servadac* (English translation, 1878)
1878	*Les Cinq Cents Millions de la Bégum* (*The Begum's Fortune*, 1880)
1880	*La Maison à vapeur* (*The Steam House*, 1881; includes *The Demon of Cawnpore* and *Tigers and Traitors*)
1881	*La Jangada* (2 volumes; *The Giant Raft*, 1881; includes *Down the Amazon* and *The Cryptogram*)
1885	*Mathias Sandorf* (English translation, 1886)
1886	*Robur le conquerant* (*The Clipper of the Clouds*, 1887)
1889	*Sans dessus dessous* (*The Purchase of the North Pole*, 1891)
1892	*Le Château des Carpathes* (*The Castle of the Carpathians*, 1893)
1895	*L'île à hélice* (*Floating Island*, 1896; also as *Propeller Island*, 1965)
1896	*Face au drapeau* (*For the Flag*, 1897)
1897	*Le Sphinx des glaces* (*An Antarctic Mystery*, 1898; also as *The Mystery of Arthur Gordon Pym*)
1898	*Le Superbe Orénoque* (*The Mighty Orinoco*, 2002)
1901	*Le Village aérien* (*The Village in the Treetops*, 1964)
1904	*Maître du monde* (*Master of the World*, 1914)
1905	*L'Invasion de la mer* (*Invasion of the Sea*, 2001)
1908	*La Chasse au météore* (*The Chase of the Golden Meteor*, 1909)
1909	*Les naufrages du "Jonathan,"* (*The Survivors of the "Jonathan,"* 1962)
1910	*Le Secret de Wilhelm Storitz* (*The Secret of Wilhelm Storitz*, 1965)
1920	*L'étonnante Aventure de la mission Barsac* (2 volumes; *Into the Niger Bend*, 1919; *The City in the Sahara*, 1965)
1994	*Paris au XXe siècle* (*Paris in the Twentieth Century*, 1996)

characters could sometimes lecture the readers on science, the excitement of the tale being told prevented one from feeling that the novel was pedantic. In an early story, Verne took his readers through an Icelandic volcano deep into the heart of the planet in *Voyage au centre de la terre* (1864; *A Journey to the Centre of the Earth*, 1872). That novel had a German hero, Professor Hardwigg, who encountered water-dwelling dinosaurs—the plesiosaurus and the ichthyosaurus—at the earth's core. Phileas Fogg, a proper English gentleman, was featured accomplishing a feat that many in the nineteenth century felt to be impossible, *Le Tour du monde en quatre-vingts jours* (1873; *Around the World in Eighty Days*, 1873). Fogg won his wager that he could circumnavigate the planet in less than two and one-half months, and soon Verne's fiction was being turned into fact by American and European reporters who attempted the task.

If one could go into the earth and around the earth, then why not leave the earth? An American hero designed a giant bullet-shaped projectile to be sent into space by the use of ordinary gunpowder from a site in Florida (coincidentally close to Cape Canaveral) in Verne's classic *De la terre à la lune* (1865; *From the Earth to the Moon*, 1873), which was followed by the sequel *Autour de la lune* (1870; *From the Earth to the Moon . . . and a Trip Around It*, 1873). From the depths of space, Verne took his fans to the depths of the ocean with the mysterious hero (whose nationality is still disputed) Captain Nemo (which means "No Name"), the captain of the *Nautilus*, earth's "first undersea ship," in *Vingt mille lieues sous les mers* (1869-1870; *Twenty Thousand Leagues Under the Sea*, 1873). This successful volume invited a sequel, *L'Île mystérieuse* (1874-1875; *The Mysterious Island*, 1875).

The influences on Verne's writing were many and complex. He was a devoted Roman Catholic and an avid reader of scientific literature, but he was especially indebted to the American author Edgar Allan Poe. Poe's short story "Hans Phfall," which described a balloon trip from the earth to the moon, inspired several of Verne's aerial adventures. Verne's novel *Le Sphinx des glaces* (1897; *An Antarctic Mystery*, 1898) was, in effect, an effort to try to complete Poe's unfinished *Narrative of Arthur Gordon Pym*. From Poe, Verne learned about the power of plot and the necessity of fascination in effective writing. His indebtedness to Dumas was obvious, for both encouragement and insight into the development of character. Verne, in turn, was to influence many of the major writers of science fiction in the twentieth century, from H. G. Wells to Isaac Asimov.

Though Verne wrote during Victorian times, his attitude toward the role of science in the human future was not one of uncritical optimism. At times science was viewed as a source of liberation. In *Twenty Thousand Leagues Under the Sea*, Captain Nemo informed Professor Aronnax that under the seas "there only is independence. . . . There I recognize no masters! There I am free." In *Maître du monde* (1904; *Master of the World*, 1914), Robur ("the conqueror") haunted the skies in his new machine, a combination helicopter-submarine called the Terror, which would enable him to rule the world. By poetic justice, Robur's Terror is destroyed by an act of nature, a thunderbolt. In later novels, Verne predicted that science would be used to produce instruments of mass destruction. As J. Kagarlitski noted, "Jules Verne, at the end of his life, arrived at the idea of the possible catastrophic consequences of the progress of science."

SIGNIFICANCE

As an author, Verne was a world celebrity within his own lifetime. As a French citizen, he was awarded the Légion d'Honneur in 1870. As a resident of Amiens, he was active in municipal government. As a lover of the sea, he was a skilled yachtsman who sailed to Britain, Scandinavia, the Baltic Sea, and the Mediterranean Sea until that activity was prevented in 1886 through a wound inflicted by a madman, his nephew Gaston, who shot Verne in the foot at point-blank range. Later in life, Verne, an authentic workaholic, suffered from arthritis, blindness in one eye caused by a cataract, and increasing struggles with depression. His death on March 24, 1905, deprived the planet of a prophet and master storyteller, but Verne's ability to entertain continued, for a number of successful motion pictures have been based on his movies, including *Twenty Thousand Leagues Under the Sea* (1916, 1954, and 1997), *The Mysterious Island* (1929 and 1961), *From the Earth to the Moon* (1958), *Journey to the Center of the Earth* (1959), and, perhaps the most popular of all, *Around the World in Eighty Days* (1956 and 2004).

—*C. George Fry*

FURTHER READING

Born, Franz. *Jules Verne: The Man Who Invented the Future*. Translated by Juliana Biro. Englewood Cliffs, N.J.: Prentice-Hall, 1964. This is a readable and reliable account of the novelist, presenting him as a "secular prophet" who anticipated the life-altering inventions of the twentieth century.
Costello, Peter. *Jules Verne: Inventor of Science Fiction*. New York: Scribner, 1978. This brief study relates

Verne to the literary genre that he is credited with inventing and perfecting, though Verne regarded himself simply as an author of "scientific romances," not "scientific fiction."

Evans, Arthur B., and Ron Miller. "Jules Verne, Misunderstood Visionary." *Scientific American* 276, no. 4 (April, 1997): 92. An overview of Verne's life and literary ambitions. Describes how a newly discovered novel, *Paris in the Twentieth Century*, expressed Verne's concerns about the dangers of technology.

Evans, Idrisyn Oliver. *Jules Verne and His Work*. New York: Twayne, 1966. This solid introduction to the "fictional futurist" and his writings by a respected Verne scholar of the post-World War II era is concise and nicely illustrated.

Lottman, Herbert R. *Jules Verne: An Exploratory Biography*. New York: St. Martin's Press, 1996. This scholarly examination of Verne is thoroughly researched and will remain definitive for some time. The exposition is lengthy and is enriched with an extensive bibliography.

Stewart, Doug. "Prescient and Accounted For." *Smithsonian* 35, no. 12 (March, 2005): 103. Describes how Verne's hometown planned to celebrate the centenary of his death. Analyzes Verne's writings, arguing they are more complex, skeptical, and political than is commonly believed.

Taves, Brian, Stephen Michaluk, Jr., and Edward Baxter. *The Jules Verne Encyclopedia*. Lanham, Md.: Scarecrow Press, 1996. This is a must. In spite of the brevity, the reader is introduced to the key facts, figures, and events of the Jules Verne corpus. It will prove invaluable when used in conjunction with a good biography while reading Verne's works.

Teeters, Peggy. *Jules Verne: The Man Who Invented Tomorrow*. New York: Walker, 1992. This work is popular, fast-paced, concise, and readable, and it provides a good starting point for the reader who needs a quick introduction to Verne.

Unwin, Timothy. "Jules Verne: Negotiating Change in the Nineteenth Century." *Science Fiction Studies* 32, no. 1 (March, 2005): 5. Examines how Verne's literature described the nineteenth century reaction to the positive and negative aspects of technology. This is one of several articles about Verne included in this issue of *Science Fiction Studies,* which commemorates the centenary of the author's death.

Verne, Jean Jules. *Jules Verne: A Biography*. Translated and abridged by Roger Greaves. New York: Taplinger, 1976. It is not often that one is afforded a view of an author from within his own family. Verne's grandson, a distinguished judge, insisted that his grandfather's philosophy was that "the world needed not new science, but new morals." Insightful and succinct.

SEE ALSO: Sir Richard Francis Burton; Alexandre Dumas, *père*; John Philip Holland; Edgar Allan Poe; Mary Wollstonecraft Shelley; John Hanning Speke; Mark Twain.

RELATED ARTICLES in *Great Events from History: The Nineteenth Century, 1801-1900:* July, 1881-1883: Stevenson Publishes *Treasure Island*; December, 1887: Conan Doyle Introduces Sherlock Holmes.

QUEEN VICTORIA
Queen of Great Britain (r. 1837-1901)

While striving to assert a greater role for the sovereign in British constitutional government, Queen Victoria accepted a gradually diminishing role. Her personal moral force lent such prestige to the Crown, however, that she made it possible for her successors to play a creative part in the continuity of government.

BORN: May 24, 1819; Kensington Palace, London, England
DIED: January 22, 1901; Osborne House, Isle of Wight, England
ALSO KNOWN AS: Alexandrina Victoria (birth name)
AREA OF ACHIEVEMENT: Government and politics

EARLY LIFE

Queen Victoria came to the British throne through a circuitous path that began on November 6, 1817, when Princess Charlotte, the only child of George, Prince of Wales, died in childbirth, and her infant son died with her. Their deaths meant that of the twelve surviving children of King George III, not one could claim legitimate offspring. Stained by debauchery, the monarchy had lost much of its prestige. Consequently, 1818 became the year in which three of King George III's unmarried sons were called upon to marry and beget royal progeny.

Leopold of Saxe Coburg Saalfeld, the widower husband of the late Princess Charlotte, served as matchmaker, presenting his sister Victoria as a bride for Edward, duke of Kent. Victoria was thirty years old, the widow of Prince Emich Charles of Leiningen, and unquestionably fertile, having borne her late husband a son, Charles, and a daughter, Feodore. The prospective parents of an heir to the British throne were married on July 11, 1818. On May 24, 1819, their daughter was born. The child was christened Alexandrina Victoria, the first name ultimately abandoned, being a tribute to Czar Alexander I of Russia, the infant's godfather. The duke of Kent died of pneumonia on January 23, 1820, but he had already served his country by producing the heir presumptive to the throne.

Princess Victoria grew to womanhood under the smothering watchfulness of her mother. Victoria of Leiningen shielded her daughter from too much contact with her uncles, King George IV and William IV, regarding their courts as hopelessly dissolute. Closeted at Kensington Palace, the two Princesses Victoria shared a chaste bedroom every night until the daughter became queen and could command her mother to give her some privacy. The young Victoria entered adolescence almost entirely deprived of the companionship of children her own age and surrounded by adults maneuvering to advance their own self-interest.

Under these abnormal conditions, observers may perceive the sources of three seemingly contradictory lifelong attitudes of Queen Victoria: She had a strong aversion to the physical aspect of sexuality, she overidealized male perfection, and she desperately needed a series of strong male figures whom she could dominate even as she was dominated by them. Understanding these elements is the key to grasping her complex relationship with her Uncle Leopold, who became king of the Belgians in 1831, with Baron Ernest Stockmar, with Prime Minister William Lamb, Viscount Melbourne, with her husband, Prince Consort Albert, with Prime Minister Benjamin Disraeli, and with her Scottish servant John Brown.

In reverse, those men who did not choose to master the fine art of simultaneously dominating and being dominated ended in stormy relationships with the queen. One need only remember Prime Ministers Henry Temple, Viscount Palmerston, Lord John Russell, William Ewart Gladstone, and most tragically, her son and heir the future King Edward VII.

LIFE'S WORK

At six o'clock on the morning of June 20, 1837, the eighteen-year-old Princess Victoria received word that she was queen, at the death of her uncle, William IV. She was fortunate in two ways. As she had passed her eighteenth birthday, no regency council was required. Her first prime minister, Lord Melbourne, established an excellent rapport with her from the start, training her unobtrusively in the delicate matter of understanding the limits placed on royal power under the unwritten British constitution.

Understanding British constitutional limits, always difficult, was particularly challenging in 1837. Until the onset of George III's final, nightmarish, ten-year illness in 1810, the old king had personally controlled patronage and appointments. This meant that through the disposition of thousands of lucrative posts and sinecures, Victoria's grandfather had been able to create a political machine that ensured that he could choose his own ministers. The king had no need to dirty his hands with the purchase of parliamentary seats. That task could be left

Queen Victoria. (Library of Congress)

tolerated it. A constitutional crisis would have resulted. In the low state of royal prestige following the reigns of three sick, debauched, or ineffective kings, the British might have toppled the throne itself, rather than allow an eighteen-year-old queen to assume powers last exercised by her grandfather in 1810.

Working to press Queen Victoria toward her proper constitutional role was her Uncle Leopold, king of the Belgians, and his confidential agent Baron Ernest Stockmar, a physician turned political philosopher. These two very able men began to inculcate in the young monarch their own view of the British constitution as seen through German binoculars. On February 10, 1840, a third and much more important Saxe Coburg ally entered Victoria's life. Her marriage to Prince Albert meant that a strong view of royal powers would prevail for the next twenty-one years, until the prince consort died in 1861. The match might never have been made if Uncle Leopold had not conspired to lead his brother's son and his sister's daughter to the altar. Nevertheless, the political alliance proved to be a love match.

While Albert lived, he was the gray eminence behind the throne. He read and made comments on all ministerial correspondence. It was Albert who saw to it that no important diplomatic dispatches left England until the queen had read and initialed them. Albert took care to allow Victoria to conduct interviews with ministers by herself, but she was the faithful conduit for his ideas and attitudes.

Even Albert, however, could not recover for Victoria what the royal uncles had thrown away. Parliament chose its own leaders. The chief of the majority party was almost always accepted as prime minister by the queen. As late as 1880, Queen Victoria tried to install a prime minister other than William Ewart Gladstone, whom she detested. However, she was beaten, had to accept Gladstone, and never attempted to assert her will in the choice of a prime minister again.

Precisely because the queen read all major foreign office correspondence, Lord John Russell and Lord

to borough mongers who owed the king their positions in society and government. Consequently, the king did not ordinarily have to fear a confrontation with his ministers, because nothing was likely to get through Parliament unless it had royal approval beforehand.

From 1810 to 1837, all that had changed. George IV and William IV, Queen Victoria's uncles, had allowed power to slip from their hands. Ambitious politicians had taken over the all-important power of patronage, though the sovereign was consulted, and usually heeded, if he chose to assert his will. The fact is that Victoria's two predecessors lacked the skill and the will to operate such a delicate mechanism. By the time that Victoria came to the throne, it would have taken such enormous strength to retrieve what had been squandered in the previous twenty-seven years that the politicians would not have

Palmerston sent controversial orders to envoys on their own personal stationery, without showing them to the queen. By that technique, Palmerston was able to recognize Napoleon III's seizure of power and to encourage the unification of Italy without gaining the royal assent. It was little wonder, then, that the queen referred to Lords Russell and Palmerston as "those terrible old men." Nevertheless, Albert, acting as royal watchdog, certainly placed restraints on the behavior of ministers acting irresponsibly. It is probable that the prince, by his editing of one of Lord Russell's ultimata to the United States in 1861, played a major role in preventing the Trent Affair from dragging Great Britain into the American Civil War.

The death of Prince Albert in 1861 brought the queen into the second phase of her sixty-three-year reign. At Albert's death, Victoria fell into such a pathologically deep mourning that her behavior bordered on psychotic. Two forces kept her in contact with reality. One was the obsessive need to control the lives of her nine children and, ultimately, her grandchildren and great-grandchildren. The enormous volume of her correspondence with her descendants reflects an energy that is essentially healthy.

The second element drawing Victoria to reality was her continued interest in all aspects of government. A prime minister such as Benjamin Disraeli, who needed a mother figure in his life as badly as the queen needed a father figure, enjoyed what can only be described as a perfect platonic love. Disraeli was always able to persuade the queen that a given measure would have pleased Prince Albert. Disraeli could dispense flattery with a neat blend of sincere devotion and theatrical art. Granting the queen the title empress of India in 1876 and staging a durbar at Windsor Castle, at which she wore the jewelry of the Moguls and received the homage of Indian princes, did not add one iota to royal power. It did, however, enhance Victoria's self-image to sign her letters, thenceforth, Victoria R[egina] and I[mperatrix]. The creation of an imperial monarchy encouraged the queen, to the end, to hold close to her heart every shred of the royal prerogative that had survived.

Nevertheless, the very fact that Victoria enjoyed the longest reign in British history meant that an eighty-one-year-old woman, at the end of her long career, could no longer keep her hand on all the strands of government. Even the railroad, the telegraph, and ultimately the telephone did not suffice to keep the queen entirely *au courant* on the fine details of events at London, when she was summering at Balmoral in Scotland, at Osborne on the south coast, or enjoying a winter visit to France or Germany. After every cabinet meeting, the queen's prime ministers dashed off reports of the minutes for the queen, but nothing replaced face-to-face discussions held at Buckingham Palace or Windsor Castle. The queen was too seldom in residence near London.

To almost the end, the queen remained free of serious illness. As late as January 15, 1901, she was prepared to go out for a drive at Osborne. Her final illness and confinement to bed lasted only six days. Surrounded by her family, she died peacefully on January 22.

SIGNIFICANCE

At the end of her life, Queen Victoria was the grandmother of an emperor of Germany, an empress of Russia, a queen of Spain, and of a vast concourse of lesser royal personages. In her person, she was the only link binding independent dominions such as Canada, Australia, and New Zealand to the United Kingdom of Great Britain. In 1837, she had inherited the throne of an oligarchic aristocracy dominated by a few hundred families. When she died in 1901, she found herself the beloved mother of a great industrial democracy in which any man of talent might rise in society and government. The early death of Prince Albert had been a great blow to the revival of royal power, but it may have been the greatest contribution possible to the survival of monarchy in Great Britain.

The historian Walter Bagehot defined the sovereign's rights as "to be consulted, to encourage and to warn." It is probable that Victoria never heard that definition. It is certain that she would not have accepted it as accurate. Nevertheless, the British monarchy has survived precisely because it is exactly what Bagehot said that it should be. Depending upon the intelligence and personality of individuals, British monarchs may still play a role in shaping policy, as King Edward VII certainly affected foreign affairs. Fundamentally, however, it was Victoria at the end of her career who captured the essence of a modern sovereign's role. She had become neutral in politics, elevated above national debates. She alone knew all the state secrets and could serve as a link, uniting all the administrations of her reign, a symbol of the eternity of the state itself.

—Arnold Blumberg

FURTHER READING

Arnstein, Walter L. *Queen Victoria*. New York: Palgrave Macmillan, 2003. Concise, balanced chronicle of Victoria's public and personal life.

Benson, Edward Frederic. *Queen Victoria*. New York: Longmans, Green, 1935. An excellent early study of the reign by one of the first scholars to have access to a full range of primary sources.

Bolitho, Hector. *The Reign of Queen Victoria*. New York: Macmillan, 1948. This treatment of the queen is more intimate than most, due to the author's experience as a biographer of several generations of the British royal family.

Cecil, Algernon. *Queen Victoria and Her Prime Ministers*. London: Eyre and Spottiswoode, 1953. A solid survey of the long series of ministers who shaped the course of the reign, 1837-1901.

De-la-Noy, Michael. *Queen Victoria at Home*. London: Constable, 2003. Focuses on Victoria's personal life, including her relationships with her husband, children, and other relatives; her household; and her various residences.

Eyck, Frank. *The Prince Consort: A Political Biography*. Boston: Houghton Mifflin, 1959. A particularly valuable book because it downplays the role of the prince as a husband and emphasizes his role as a royalist political leader interested in restoring the queen's prerogative rights.

Hibbert, Christopher. *Queen Victoria: A Personal History*. New York: Basic Books, 2000. Entertaining biography, focusing on Victoria's character and relationships with her husband, her children, and the politicians who ran her government. Describes how Great Britain evolved into a constitutional monarchy during her long reign.

Longford, Elizabeth. *Queen Victoria: Born to Succeed*. New York: Harper and Row, 1964. An exceptionally well-written, scholarly, and detailed account of the reign.

Marriott, Sir John Arthur Ransome. *Queen Victoria and Her Ministers*. New York: E. P. Dutton, 1934. This relatively short book cannot do full justice to all the prime ministers who served Victoria from 1837 to 1901. It is valuable, however, in two contexts. It emphasizes such noteworthy relationships as those of the queen with the great political rivals, Disraeli and Gladstone; it also offers particularly valuable insights drawn from analyses of the changing role of the monarchy.

Monypenny, William Flavelle, and George Earle Buckle, eds. *The Life of Benjamin Disraeli, Earl of Beaconsfield*. 6 vols. New York: Macmillan, 1913-1920. This six-volume work is rich in selections from the correspondence of Disraeli, containing candid references to the queen. As Disraeli enjoyed a more confidential relationship with Victoria than did any of her other ministers, his comments are revealing.

Victoria, Queen of Great Britain. *The Letters of Queen Victoria: A Selection from Her Majesty's Correspondence Between the Years 1837 and 1901*. Edited by Arthur C. Benson et al. 3 series in 9 vols. New York: Longmans, Green, 1907-1930. This is the largest published collection of the queen's correspondence, but there are numerous other collections of letters, particularly to and from her family. See Roger Fulford's *Dearest Child* (1964) and Sir Frederick Ponsonby's *Letters of the Empress Frederick* (1928).

_____. *Regina v. Palmerston: The Correspondence Between Queen Victoria and Her Foreign and Prime Minister, 1837-1865*. Edited by Brian Connell. London: Evans Brothers, 1962. Traces the gradually deteriorating relationship between the queen and one of her least liked ministers.

SEE ALSO: Alexander I; Benjamin Disraeli; George IV; William Ewart Gladstone; Second Viscount Melbourne; Napoleon III; Lord Palmerston; Baron John Russell; William IV.

RELATED ARTICLES in *Great Events from History: The Nineteenth Century, 1801-1900:* June 28, 1838: Queen Victoria's Coronation; November 5, 1850: Tennyson Becomes England's Poet Laureate; July 1, 1867: British North America Act.

ISWAR CHANDRA VIDYASAGAR
Indian educator and social reformer

Vidyasagar was a great Sanskrit scholar, educator, and social reformer who influenced almost every aspect of Indian life. He modernized the teaching of Sanskrit and Bengali, stressed the importance of learning English, and was a leader in Hindu social reform.

BORN: September 26, 1820; Birsinha, Bengal, British India (now West Bengal, India)

DIED: July 29, 1891; Calcutta, Bengal, British India (now Kolkata, West Bengal, India)

ALSO KNOWN AS: Iswar Chandra Bandopadhyay (birth name); Iswarchandra Vidyasagar; Isvar Chandra Vidyasagar; Isvarchandra Vidyasagar; Isvarcandra Vidyasagar; Iswar Chandra Surman; Ishwar Chandra Vidyasagar; Eshwar Chunder Vidyasagar

AREAS OF ACHIEVEMENT: Education, religion and theology, social reform, scholarship

EARLY LIFE

Iswar Chandra Vidyasagar (ee-shb-awr tch-awn-draw vidyah-shah-gawr) was born Iswar Chandra Bando-padhyay. He was a member of a poor Brahmin family known for the Sanskrit scholarship of some of its members. When he was nine years old, his father, Thakurdas, took him to Calcutta to give him a chance to learn Sanskrit. In June, 1829, he was admitted to the recently opened Sanskrit College, a government institution that required no fees. So poor that he could not afford a light under which to study at night, he studied under streetlights near his residence. Despite his poverty, Iswar Chandra had a brilliant academic career and won prizes, medals, and scholarships at every stage of his studies. Although some of his prizes and scholarships were quite valuable, he gave away much of his winnings.

Through twelve and one-half years, Iswar Chandra studied all branches of learning in Sanskrit including Hindu religious texts, philosophy, jurisprudence, and logic. In 1839, he passed an examination in Hindu law and because of his scholastic achievements was given the title of Vidyasagar (ocean of learning.) His formal studies at the Sanskrit College ended in December of 1841, when he was twenty-one years old.

LIFE'S WORK

Within a month of completing his formal studies, Vidyasagar took a job as the head of the Bengali Department of the Fort William College, which had been estab-lished to introduce young British expatriates to Indian history, languages, and culture. There, he taught Bengali and Hindi, while taking private courses for himself in English and Hindi. He met a number of civilians associated with the government who would help his later work.

In 1846, Vidyasagar resigned from Fort William College to join his alma mater, Sanskrit College. However, he had some differences of opinion with the secretary of that institution and resigned after only a brief stay. While he was at Fort William College, Vidyasagar had translated a well-known Hindi book, *Baital Paccisi*, into Bengali. He now started his own publishing firm, the Samskrta Jantra and Book Depository, to print and distribute his own books.

Although the Bengali language derives from ancient Sanskrit, it has certain consonants that are absent in Sanskrit, and a few Sanskrit letters are not used in Bengali. Through the publications from his press, Vidyasagar refined the Bengali alphabet that is still used today. He explained the changes he made in the introduction to one of his most famous books, *Baranaparichay* (introduction to letters). Some of the publications of the Fort William College were printed by his press.

In 1850, Vidyasagar was invited to return to Sanskrit College as professor of literature. Within two months, he was made principal, a position specially created for him. During the eight years that he held that position, he made critical changes in the school's educational system. When he started, only upper-caste Hindus were admitted to the college; under his administration, members of all castes were accepted. He also made the English language a compulsory subject. Because the texts used to teach Sanskrit grammar were ancient and difficult, Vidyasagar wrote several new textbooks on Sanskrit himself. Some of his books are still used today.

In 1859, a small group of Bengali Hindus started the Calcutta Training School. Vidyasagar took over the school's management in 1864. This first nongovernment-supported Indian school under independent management was later renamed the Metropolitan Institution, and it eventually became affiliated with Calcutta University, through which it awarded advanced degrees. In 1917, the institution was renamed Vidyasagar College.

Meanwhile, Vidyasagar continued to write and translated books from English, Hindi, and Sanskrit into Bengali to give Bengali-speaking students wider access to biography, history, astronomy, and world geography. Among his translations was William Shakespeare's *The Comedy of Errors* (1592-1594), which he published in Bengali as *Bhrantibilas* (1869). He was also actively involved in the publication two important Bengali journals, *Tattwabodhini* and *Somprakāsh*, and helped to keep going *The Hindu Patriot*, an influential liberal journal, after the death of its founder.

High among Vidyasagar's agenda for reforming Hindu society was female emancipation. In 1829, the British government had abolished suttee—the practice of widows' throwing themselves on the funeral pyres of their husbands. Since that time, Hindu widows—who were barred from remarrying—generally led menial and dismal lives and often depended on the charity of relatives. Through the pages of the journals he edited and tracts that he wrote, Vidyasagar fought for women's emancipation and especially for women's education. From his immense knowledge of Sanskrit religious and legal texts, he showed that remarriage had been permitted to widows in ancient India. In response to his publications and a signature campaign, the government finally passed the Hindu Widow Remarriage Act in 1856. Vidyasagar personally presided over many widow remarriage ceremonies and often provided financial support. His only son married a widow. His other efforts at Hindu female emancipation included proscribing polygamy in the Kulin sect of Brahmins and raising the age of consent for sexual intercourse for girls; however, neither objective was achieved during his lifetime.

Vidyasagar played a major role in making education available to Hindu women. He was the honorary secretary of the Bethune School (later College) for Women from 1850 to 1869. As a government inspector of schools, he opened a large number of schools for women in Bengal—usually at his own expense until he was later reimbursed by the government. To relieve the financial distress of Hindu women, especially widows, he was a prime mover in launching the Hindu Family Annuity Fund in 1872. That institution still exists as a part of the nationalized Life Insurance Corporation of India.

Vidyasagar was also interested in the dramatic arts. From 1865 to 1873, he was a member of the managing committee of the Bengali Theatre of Pathuriāghāta and regularly attended its stage performances. Because most women actors at that time were prostitutes, he did not allow the theater to employ them; he instead preferred to have men play female roles.

On July 29, 1891, Vidyasagar died in Calcutta. He was seventy years old at the time of his death.

SIGNIFICANCE

Iswar Chandra Vidyasagar remains a towering figure in modern Indian history. One of the greatest educators of India, he revolutionized the teaching of both Sanskrit and Bengali—which now ranks as the fifth most widely spoken language in the world. The great Hindu poet Sir Rabindranath Tagore credited Vidyasagar with effectively establishing the beauty of Bengali prose. Vidyasagar's Bengali textbook for children is still in use, as are his two textbooks on Sanskrit grammar. Vastly learned in Sanskrit religion, philosophy, and law, Vidyasagar used his knowledge to reduce caste distinctions in education, permit formal education for women, and encourage the teaching of English.

Vidyasagar always wore the simple Bengali dress of one piece of cloth for the lower body and another for the upper body, trimmed his hair in the fashion of Bengali Brahmins, and wore sandals instead of shoes. He was an atheist and did not himself perform the religious rites mandated for Brahmins. However, he permitted other members of his family to perform whatever religious rituals they wished. He considered the legalizing of widow remarriage to be his greatest achievement and was delighted that his own son married a widow of his own volition.

A generous person, Vidyasagar spent large parts of his considerable earnings in aiding the poor and the distressed—even when he had to incur debts to do so. During a famine, he fed the people of his birthplace at his own expense. Afterward, the villagers called him Dayār sāgar Vidyasagar (the Ocean of Learning is also the Ocean of Compassion)—a text that Bengali weavers wove into shirts and skirts. Over and above the respect of his countrymen, Vidyasagar was the recipient of many official honors. Portraits and statues of him are can be found throughout India. In 1970, the government issued a postage stamp with his portrait.

—*Ranès C. Chakravorty*

FURTHER READING

Bakshi, S. R., and Lipi Mahajan, eds. *Social Reformers of India*. Delhi, India: Deep & Deep, 2000. One of many books that discuss Vidyasagar's life and works within the broader context of Indian social reform.

Hatcher, Brian A. *Idioms of Improvement: Vidyasagar and Cultural Encounter in Bengal*. Calcutta, India: Oxford University Press, 1996. Hatcher focuses on Vidyasagar's association with the Brahmo Samaj, a contemporary quasi-religious movement that supported many of his ideas.

Mukhopadhyay, Manik, ed. *The Golden Book of Vidyasagar*. Calcutta, India: All Bengal Vidyasagar Death Centenary Committee, 1993. Published during the centenary of Vidyasagar's death, this is a collection of articles by selected authors who examine Vidyasagar's life and works. Also contains a good bibliography, a time line of his life, and some rare photographs.

Tripathi, Amales. *Vidyasagar, the Traditional Moderniser*. Calcutta, India: Punascha, 1998. Written in 1970 to commemorate the sesquicentennial of Vidyasagar's birth.

Vidyasagar, Iswar Chandra. *Vidyasagar Rachan Bali*. 3d ed. Calcutta, India: Tuli Kalam, 1997. A two-volume edition of Vidyasagar's collected works in the Bengali language. Includes his will and an incomplete memoir of his childhood.

SEE ALSO: Sir Sayyid Ahmad Khan; Annie Besant; Dadabhai Naoroji; Mahadev Govind Ranade; Vivekananda.

RELATED ARTICLE in *Great Events from History: The Nineteenth Century, 1801-1900:* 1885: Indian National Congress Is Founded.

RUDOLF VIRCHOW
German pathologist and statesman

Virchow received worldwide recognition for his contributions to medical science, anthropology, archaeology, and public health. His greatest contribution to medical science was in establishing the principles of cellular pathology.

BORN: October 13, 1821; Schivelbein, Pomerania, Prussia (now Swidwin, Poland)
DIED: September 5, 1902; Berlin, Germany
ALSO KNOWN AS: Rudolf Ludwig Karl Virchow (full name)
AREAS OF ACHIEVEMENT: Medicine, science and technology

EARLY LIFE
Born in a small eastern Pomeranian city, Rudolf Ludwig Karl Virchow (FIHR-koh) was the only child of a minor city official and farmer. He began his formal education in the gymnasium at Coslin, where he distinguished himself by his linguistic abilities; he soon mastered Latin; learned Greek, English, and French; and was a good Hebrew scholar. In October, 1839, he entered the medical school of the Friedrich-Wilhelms-Institut, in Berlin. Johannes Müller, a physiologist, anatomist, and pathologist, and Johann Lucas Schönlein, an outstanding German clinician, influenced Virchow as he began his research activities while still an undergraduate. In 1843, he presented his thesis "De rheumate praesertim corneae" (rheumatic disease, particularly of the cornea), received his doctorate in medicine, and was given the position of assistant at the Charité Hospital. In the following year, he obtained the post of prosector of anatomy to the Charité Hospital, acting as assistant to Robert Froriep,

whom he eventually succeeded only three years later, in 1846.

Froriep assigned to his young assistant, as a theme for independent investigation, the study of phlebitis. Virchow's thorough and brilliant studies outlining the principles of thrombosis and embolism formed a new chapter in pathology. In addition, his observations on leukemia opened new points of view on the origin and nature of white blood corpuscles. In 1847, at the age of twenty-six, with Benno Reinhardt he started the *Archiv für pathologische Anatomie und Physiologie, und für klinische Medizin* (archives for pathological anatomy and physiology and clinical medicine), a journal he continued to edit alone after his colleague's death in 1852.

In 1848, a singular event occurred that Virchow, in later life, regarded as the most decisive in his life. Sent on an official mission to study an epidemic of "hunger typhus" (relapsing fever) in famine-ridden Upper Silesia, a Prussian province occupied by a Polish minority, he published a scathing report indicting the government, insisting that the causes of the epidemic were social as much as—if not more than—medical. His antigovernment stance, coupled with the fact that, on his return, he had allied himself with the ultraradical party and founded a medico-political journal, *Die medizinische Reforme* (medical reform), resulted in his dismissal from all professional posts in Berlin. His fame as a pathologist had spread, and the University of Würzburg seized the opportunity and offered Virchow the professorship of pathology and the directorship of the newly founded Pathological Institute, where Virchow dedicated himself to research work.

As a young man, Virchow presented a small professorial figure. He was short, thin, blond, and dark-eyed, and was accorded the nickname *Der Kleine Doktor* (the little doctor). He was quick in mind and body, often transfixing inattention or incompetence with a flash of sarcasm. However, he was approachable, hospitable, and particularly warm and friendly to the sick and poor.

LIFE'S WORK

As professor of pathology at the University of Würzburg, Virchow entered the most creative period of his life. For the next seven years, his systematic and methodical research culminated in outlining the fundamental principles of cellular pathology. For centuries before Virchow, the origin of life and the seat of disease were the subjects of many theories and controversies. Medieval anatomists localized disease to one of the larger regions or cavities of the body, such as the head, chest, or abdomen. During the mid- to late eighteenth century, anatomists, led by Giovanni Battista Morgagni, attempted to find the actual diseased organ, and Marie François Xavier Bichat showed that in the same organ, sometimes one and sometimes another tissue might be the seat of disease.

In the third decade of the nineteenth century, the microscope had disclosed the existence of cells, and in the next decade the study of pathological anatomy was directed to their study. Research in this area was faced with two major hurdles: First, cells could not be demonstrated in several tissues, even in their most developed state; second, the origin of new cells was completely unknown. The answer to the latter question was heavily prejudiced by the so-called cell theory of Theodor Schwann, who asserted that new cells arose from unformed, amorphous matter, which he termed "cytoblastema."

When Virchow arrived at the University of Würzburg in 1849, he had already brought with him some ideas about the principles of cellular pathology. Here, he proceeded to demonstrate the existence of cells in bone and in connective tissue, where their existence had hitherto been doubtful. This discovery of cells of connective and other allied tissues offered him the possibility of finding a cellular matrix for many new growths. These studies led to his coining the aphorism *omnis cellula e cellula* (each cell stems from another cell), which became the recognized hallmark of the biological cell theory. Virchow's conception of disease rested on four main hypotheses: first, that all diseases are in essence active or passive disturbances of living cells; second, that all cells arise from parent cells; third, that functional capacities of the cells depended on intracellular physicochemical

Rudolf Virchow. (Library of Congress)

processes; and finally, that all pathological formations are degenerations, transformations, or repetitions of normal structures.

Internationally famous for his research and teaching at Würzburg, Virchow was called back to the University of Berlin in 1856. Virchow agreed to return on the condition that a pathological institute be founded. The government agreed, and Virchow arrived to continue work with indefatigable zeal and published his *Die cellular Pathologie in ihrer Begründung auf physiologische und pathologische Gewebelehre* (1858; *Cellular Pathology as Based upon Physiological and Pathological Histology*, 1860), describing his work on the subject. Virchow's own aphorism *omnis cellula e cellula* is the basis for his work on tumors during 1863-1867, which treats these formations as physiologically independent new growths of cellular structure.

Virchow continued to write and edit his medical journal and enjoyed the satisfaction of celebrating its jubilee in December, 1897. Under his direction, the department of pathology at the Charité Hospital became a model for other institutions. He personally supervised the establishment of one of the best pathology museums in the world. In addition, he delivered lectures regularly, which were attended by an international audience. He was not a great orator; his voice was weak and his speech simple, but once on the platform the small man with the sharp dark eyes commanded attention.

Virchow once again entered politics and was elected member of the municipal council; in 1862, he took his seat in the Prussian Diet, and by his sheer ability was recognized as leader of the opposition Radical Party. He led a desperate fight against Otto von Bismarck's dictatorship, and it is said that Bismarck became so annoyed with Virchow that he challenged him to a duel, which was averted by behind-the-scenes negotiations through Bismarck's intermediaries, who were determined to prevent it.

Virchow was also president of the German Geographical Society and the Society of Anthropology and Ethnology. He even had his own anthropological collection, mainly consisting of crania of the different human races. An accidental shelling of the Museum of Natural History in Paris during the war prompted the publication of an indignant pamphlet stating that the Prussians were not a Germanic but a barbaric race. That stirred Virchow's patriotism to the extent that he instigated a colossal public census of the color of the hair and eyes in six million German schoolchildren, concluding that there was no evidence of a predominant "German type" among them. He was interested in archaeology and worked in excavation sites of ancient Troy in Greece and Egypt; he also conducted his own fieldwork in the Caucasus in 1894.

Virchow remained at the forefront of international medicine and was showered with honors from scientific academies in Germany, France, and England. In 1891, his seventieth birthday was celebrated and a gold medal was presented to him by the emperor in recognition of the immense services Virchow had rendered to science. On January 5, 1902, he fell when exiting a tram car but, although he fractured a leg in the accident, he recovered and was able to move about on crutches. He then went to Harzburg to recuperate, but he became weaker. Three weeks prior to his death, his friends decided to take him back to Berlin; Virchow did not tolerate the journey well, lapsed into a coma from which he never recovered, and died on September 5, 1902. Virchow was given a public funeral with honors and laid to rest in the cemetery of St. Matthew.

SIGNIFICANCE

Rudolf Virchow, one of the founders of modern biomedicine, was also a proponent of social reform. According to Virchow, medicine was to be reformed on the basis of four principles: First, the health of the people is a matter of direct social concern; second, social and economic conditions have important effects on health and disease; third, the measures taken to promote health and to combat disease must be social as well as medical; and fourth, medical statistics should be the standard of measurement. Virchow's contribution to the improvement of public health was monumental; his discovery of the pathophysiology of the parasitic disease trichinosis led a successful ten-year campaign to establish compulsory meat inspection in Germany. At the request of the Berlin city council, he designed and supervised a sewage-disposal system that set the pattern for similar systems in Germany and elsewhere. He organized the ambulance service for the army and, recognizing the importance of nurses to medical care, he opened a nursing school.

Although Virchow made significant contributions in many fields, he became world-famous for his work in cellular pathology. The fundamental principles of cellular pathology outlined by him, particularly the dictum *omnis cellula e cellula*, forever closed the last loophole for opponents of this system and secured a position of great importance in physiology. Virchow was the first to systematize the theory of cellular pathology and to give medicine a common denominator for all diseases. Virchow's success may be attributed to the quality of his research, his prolific publications, his single-minded determination, and the growth of his influence on medicine. His work on cellular pathology had far-reaching consequences, contributing to progress in medicine and in surgery. It is therefore a fitting tribute that cellular pathology has been hailed as one of the great achievements in the history of medicine.

—*Anand Karnad*

FURTHER READING

Ackerknecht, Erwin H. *Rudolf Virchow: Doctor, Statesman, Anthropologist*. Madison: University of Wisconsin Press, 1953. The first full-length study of Virchow, covering 240 pages. Although the author introduces the book with a brief life history, this is primarily an analysis of Virchow's work in medicine, politics, and anthropology. An extensive bibliography, strictly confined to items quoted in the text, is supplemented by an exhaustive biographical glossary. This book contains one sketch and two portraits of Virchow, including the first published portrait of Virchow as a septuagenarian.

Boyd, Byron A. *Rudolf Virchow: The Scientist as Citizen*. New York: Garland, 1991. One of the few English-language biographies of Virchow, adapted from the author's doctoral thesis.

Carr, James G. *Rudolph Virchow*. Chicago, Ill.: Northwestern University Bulletin, 1938. This concise twenty-three-page biography of Virchow contains translated excerpts of letters from Virchow to his parents that shed light on his early years, family life, and customs. No bibliography or illustrations are provided.

Creedon, Jeremiah. "Dr. Virchow's Cure." *Utne Reader*, no. 111 (May, 2002): 79. An overview of Virchow's career, contributions to modern public health, and ideas about the link between poverty and disease.

Jacobi, Abraham. *Rudolf Virchow*. New York: Trow, 1881. This thirty-five-page booklet is packed with information. Emphasizes Virchow's work in pathology and the work leading to the establishment of the principles of cellular pathology. Bibliography is not provided.

Virchow, Rudolf. *Diseases, Life, and Man: Selected Essays*. Translated by Lelland Rather. Stanford, Calif.: Stanford University Press, 1958. Contains selected essays by Virchow on a range of subjects, including cellular pathology, scientific medicine, and philosophy. An excellent introduction by the translator covers Virchow's place in history and explores his role in the establishment of the principles of cellular pathology and the foundations of modern medicine. An appendix contains the German titles and sources of articles translated, including an extensive biographical glossary.

Welch, Henry. "Rudolph Virchow, Pathologist." *Boston Medical and Surgical Journal* 125 (1891): 453-457. An article written on the occasion of Virchow's seventieth birthday celebrations at Johns Hopkins University. This essay gives a thorough and scholarly review of Virchow's work in the field of pathology.

SEE ALSO: Otto von Bismarck; Ernst Haeckel; Robert Koch.

RELATED ARTICLES in *Great Events from History: The Nineteenth Century, 1801-1900:* August, 1856: Neanderthal Skull Is Found in Germany; March 24, 1882: Koch Announces His Discovery of the Tuberculosis Bacillus.

VIVEKANANDA
Indian philosopher and social reformer

Vivekananda made the original nondualistic form of Hinduism well known in India and the West. He preached the essential unity of all religions and the need to serve humanity.

BORN: January 12, 1863; Calcutta, Bengal, British India (now Kolkata, West Bengal, India)
DIED: July 4, 1902; Belur, Bengal, British India (now Belur, West Bengal, India)
ALSO KNOWN AS: Narendranath Datta (birth name); Narendranath Dutt; Narendra Nath Datta; Vividishananda; Swami Vivekananda
AREAS OF ACHIEVEMENT: Education, religion and theology, women's rights

EARLY LIFE
Vivekananda (Vi-vek-ah-nawn-daw) was born Narendranath Datta, a member of a high-caste Bengali family. He adopted the monastic name Vivekananda later in life.

His father, a successful attorney, was a linguist and a musician; his mother was a remarkable woman well versed in orthodox Hinduism. As a child, Naren—as he called—was a leader of his age group. He grew up proficient in several languages: Bengali, Sanskrit, Hindi, and English; later he also learned French. He also became a talented singer and dancer and could play several musical instruments well.

Along with an olive complexion and a sturdy body, he had remarkably impressive eyes. In his middle age he stood five feet, eight and one-half inches tall and weighed about 160 pounds.

In 1884, Naren passed the bachelor's examination of Calcutta University and entered the Metropolitan Law College to become a lawyer, as his father had done. Interested in religion and philosophy from an early age, he joined the Brahmo Samaj—a religious movement working to reestablish the original monistic form of Hinduism in place of the then-common Brahminical Hinduism, a polytheistic system of belief that ordered a strictly defined caste system and restricted rights for women. In 1884, he became a freemason like his father.

In 1881, Naren met Ramakrishna Paramhansa, a charismatic religious leader who believed in the equality of all religions and was deeply versed in nondualistic Hinduism. Naren became Ramakrishna's favorite disciple and was initiated by him into monisticity in July, 1886, shortly before Ramakrishna died. After Ramakrishna's death, Naren gathered together all Ramakrishna's disciples; as their new leader, he organized an order of monks based on Ramakrishna's Vedantic teachings.

LIFE'S WORK

During the late 1880's, Naren studied religion, philosophy, and monastic discipline and then set off on a journey throughout India as an itinerant mendicant. Carrying no money, he lived by begging and traveled the length and breadth of India, often on foot or in bullock carts, as railroads were then few and roads were poor. During his travels he met with many of the Indian intelligentsia and highly placed officers of both the British colonial government and the princely Indian states. Wherever he went, people were impressed by his knowledge and his many talents, including his singing. He gradually made himself known to the intelligentsia of the country—especially in the south—and to many of the people in power.

In 1893, organizers of the Columbian Exposition in Chicago arranged for the Parliament of Religions to be held in the newly built Art Institute in Chicago. Vivekananda wanted to attend that meeting, and people whom he met during his travels—commoners, students, and princes alike—raised the money to buy him passage to Chicago. In May, 1893, he left by ship from Bombay, sailing to Japan; then to Vancouver, British Columbia; and finally reached Chicago at the end of July. As the Parliament of Religions would not begin for another month and his funds were running short, he traveled to Boston, where living was cheaper. There he delivered eleven public talks that were well attended, and he soon became well known. John Henry Wright, a professor of Greek at Harvard University, entertained Vivekananda as his guest for four days and wrote him a letter of introduction to take to the organizers of the Parliament of Religions.

On Vivekananda's return to Chicago, he was accepted as a delegate to the parliament because of Wright's recommendation and was given a place to stay with other delegates. The parliament opened on September 11, and Vivekananda's speech had a tumultuous reception. He

Vivekananda.

was recognized as the most important speaker over the next two weeks of sessions. After this success, Vivekananda was invited to speak at many places, and he traveled all over the northeastern United States and throughout the Midwest. At every place where he spoke and gave classes on Vedanta philosophy, he was met with enthusiasm, and he made many disciples in all levels of society.

In 1895, Vivekananda visited France and England and then returned to New York, where his classes were again successful. In December of that same year, he organized a committee for the propagation of Vedanta in the United States. In October, 1898, the New York Vedanta Society was launched; that body expanded to sixteen Vedanta centers throughout the United States and Canada that still existed at the turn of the twenty-first century. Eventually, Vivekananda returned to India, by way of Western Europe and Ceylon. During his journey from Ceylon to Calcutta, he was greeted with magnificent receptions at every stop, and students and even some dignitaries helped pull his cart.

Vivekananda then again traveled and lectured extensively in northern India. By the late 1890's, his health was often poor, and he was starting to show symptoms of diabetes. During some of his travels he was accompanied by his disciples, including many from England and the United States. In May, 1897, he oversaw the creation of the Ramakrishna Mission in Calcutta. Over the succeeding years, the mission established many schools, colleges, and hospitals, and its members often assisted relief efforts during times of disasters.

Despite his failing health, Vivekananda began another journey to the West in June, 1899. He spent almost six months in California, where he established several Vedanta centers. On his return journey, he spent some time in France and England, then traveled through Europe and Egypt, before returning to Calcutta in July, 1900. On July 4, 1902, he died in Belur, Bengal.

SIGNIFICANCE

Vivekananda significantly changed life in India. During his travels through the country, he was deeply moved by the poverty of the people, by their general mistreatment by their British rulers, and by the rigidity and inequality imposed by the prevailing version of Hinduism. In his travels abroad, he was impressed by the industry, general honesty, and work ethics of the people whom he observed in Japan, Europe, and especially the United States.

Vivekananda widely disseminated the idea of monism among the Hindus, most of whom either had polytheistic beliefs or believed in individual Hindu deities. He inspired all Indians to ideas of equality of beings and religions and to the need for education and social reform. He encouraged Indians to accept the work ethic of the West before looking for personal salvation. His call for active participation in personal and social activism has deeply influenced Indian youths since his time and has helped to bring greater equality to women and members of the so-called lower Hindu castes.

Vivekananda worked to spread his master Ramakrishna's message of the equality of all beings and of all religions and of the nondualistic Vedanta philosophy. Through the Ramakrishna Mission, he helped organize schools, colleges, hospitals, and other socially beneficent organizations all over India. Vivekananda also carried the message of the equality of religions and human beings before the world outside India. The many Vedanta centers around the globe have continued to spread his message.

—*Ranès C. Chakravorty*

FURTHER READING

Burke, Marie L. *Swami Vivekananda in the West: New*

Discoveries. 3d ed. Hollywood, Calif.: Vedanta Press, 1985. This six-volume work chronicles Vivekananda's Western travels, focusing on his visits to the United States.

Datta, Bhupendranatha. *Swami Vivekananda, Patriot-Prophet: A Study.* Calcutta, India: Nababharat, 1954. An especially interesting biography written by Vivekananda's brother, a well-known intellectual in his own right.

Eastern and Western Disciples of Vivekananda. *The Life of Swami Vivekananda.* 5th ed. Calcutta, India: Advaita Ashrama, 1979- . A two-volume exhaustively detailed account of Vivekananda's life, describing how his teachings inspired others.

Mukherjee, Jayasree. *The Ramakrishna-Vivekananda Movement Impact on Indian Society and Politics (1893-1922): With Special Reference to Bengal.* Calcutta, India: Firma KLM, 1997. Vivekananda's message was not only about religious uplift; he also called for societal reform of the caste system, for female emancipation, and for independence from British rule. This book surveys the impact of his teachings on Indian society and politics.

Nikhilananda, Swami. *Vivekânanda: A Biography.* New York: Vivekananda Center, 1953. A chronicle of Vivekananda's life written by Swami Nikhilananda, a member of the same monastic order as Vivekananda. Nikhilananda also was the resident minister of the New York-based Center for many years and a well-known author and philosopher.

Noble, Margaret Elizabeth. *The Master as I Saw Him: Being Pages from the Life of the Swami Vivekananda [by] Sister Nivedita.* Calcutta, India: Udbodhan Office, 1977. Sister Nivedita, born Margaret Noble, was an Englishwoman who became a disciple of Vivekananda and went to Calcutta, where she started a school that remains in operation today.

Prabhu'sankara. *Swami Vivekananda Bibliography: A Descriptive Bibliography of Books and Articles by and on Swami Vivekananda.* Mysore, India: Prasanranga, University of Mysore, 1999. Comprehensive listing of books and articles written by, and about, Vivekananda.

Radice, William, ed. *Swami Vivekananda and the Modernisation of Hinduism.* Delhi, India: Oxford University Press, 1998. A series of articles analyzing the impact of Vivekananda's Vedantist teachings on classical Brahminical Hinduism.

Rolland, Romain. *The Life of Vivekananda and the Universal Gospel.* Hollywood, Calif.: Vedanta Press,

1987. English translation of a book by the French author who received the Nobel Prize in Literature in 1915. Rolland recounts Vivekananda's life and teachings, with the goal of teaching Western readers about Hindu philosophy.

Vivekananda, Swami. *The Complete Works of Swami Vivekananda.* 8 vols. Calcutta, India: Advaita Ashrama, 1987. A compilation of Vivekananda's writings, providing his comprehensive organization and consolidation of Hindu beliefs.

_____. *Teachings of Swami Vivekananda.* Calcutta, India: Advaita Ashrama, 1992. A collection of quotations culled from Vivekananda's numerous speeches and writings, tracing the evolution of his thought.

SEE ALSO: Sir Sayyid Ahmad Khan; Annie Besant; Dadabhai Naoroji; Mahadev Govind Ranade; Iswar Chandra Vidyasagar.

RELATED ARTICLE in *Great Events from History: The Nineteenth Century, 1801-1900:* May 1-October 30, 1893: Chicago World's Fair.

SIR JULIUS VOGEL
English-born prime minister of New Zealand (1873-1875, 1876)

Remembered for his innovative and daring fiscal policies, Vogel was the first New Zealand prime minister to set a serious agenda for the island nation. His policy of massive borrowing to build railroads was much debated in his own day but laid the modern foundations of New Zealand.

BORN: February 24, 1835; London, England
DIED: March 12, 1899; East Molesey, Surrey, England
AREAS OF ACHIEVEMENT: Government and politics, literature

EARLY LIFE

Julius Vogel (VOH-gel) was born the son of Leonard Vogel, a Protestant immigrant to England from Holland, and Phoebe Isaac Vogel, a member of a moderately prosperous Jewish family in London, where he was born. Religious differences between his parents may have contributed to the breakup of their marriage around the time he was six. Raised in the Jewish religion, Julius was educated in both London and Kent and prepared for a career in trade. As an adolescent he studied in the Government School of Mines.

In 1852, when Vogel was seventeen, he decided to emigrate to Australia, whose economy was booming after the discovery of gold. After arriving there, he tried to sell various goods to miners in Victoria. He met with little success over several years and then turned to journalism during the mid-1850's. He wrote for several western Victoria newspapers, advocating free trade policies with verve and flair. However, by 1861 the combination of a region economic downturn and his failure to win a seat in the Victoria legislative assembly led him to seek new opportunities across the Tasman Sea, in New Zealand.

Not long after settling in Dunedin, New Zealand, Vogel cofounded the *Otago Daily Times*, the first daily newspaper in all of New Zealand. He soon began accruing political influence in the South Island. He also became active in the region's community and cultural affairs. In 1863, he was elected to the Otago provincial council, on which he served until 1869.

LIFE'S WORK

In 1867, Vogel married Mary Clayton. He had already favored woman suffrage, but the influence of his wife strengthened his support of that goal. He also became known as a strong advocate of free trade and of increasing South Island's influence in New Zealand, which had traditionally been dominated by the more heavily populated North Island. Vogel and his wife moved to Auckland, New Zealand's largest city, where Vogel took up another newspaper editorship and got involved in national politics. He soon became the finance minister for the entire New Zealand colony, under premier William Fox.

Although Vogel held a subordinate portfolio, he quickly became the dominant figure in the colonial government. After a lifetime of theorizing, he was finally able to put his ideas into practice. He advocated expanding New Zealand's economy by any almost means possible. To do that, he needed more human resources and thus became an emphatic supporter of increased immigration to New Zealand. The Maori wars that had ravaged the North Island from 1840 to 1870 left disrupted Maori society, and Vogel purchased some of the lands that been allotted to the Maori by treaty and arrogated it for the use of new European immigrants. He also put some of the land to use for railroad construction. Having seen what the building of transcontinental railroads had done for the United States and Canadian economies, he applied a similar vision to the far smaller territory of New Zealand, working to improve the country's transportation infrastructure until it was one of the most extensive and efficient in the world.

New Zealand's economy remained primarily agricultural and was dependent on exports of wool, lamb, and grain to England. As Vogel's economic expansion schemes were not self-financing, he embarked on an extensive program of borrowing money, a plan that some deemed improvident but which quickly became popular as the islands' economy began to grow. To attract investment funds and to promote New Zealand's image abroad, Vogel traveled extensively in Australia, Great Britain, and the United States, where he not only secured needed financing but also saw how those more advanced economies operated.

Although Vogel had been an advocate of provincial autonomy when he lived in Dunedin, he quickly became frustrated by the way provincial safeguards prevented the implementation of his colony-wide fiscal policies. By 1875, he had maneuvered the abolition of the provinces. Another challenge that he faced was creating an efficient civil service with the type of trained bureaucracy that existed in the civil services of other English-speaking countries. He was hampered by the fact that implementation of his economic policies depended almost solely on his personal leadership. After Fox's government fell in 1872, he remained as treasurer and de facto premier.

In 1873, Vogel became prime minister of New Zealand himself. He held the post into 1875, when he was knighted by the British crown, and returned for another brief tenure as prime minister the following year. In that capacity, he became the first practicing Jew to lead a country in the English-speaking world. (Great Britain's Prime Minister Benjamin Disraeli was of Jewish descent, but his family had converted to Christianity.) As a Jew, Vogel encountered some anti-Semitism, but remarkably little, even though New Zealand differed from Australia, Canada, and the United States in not having substantial Jewish communities.

Vogel had a clear future vision of New Zealand as a power in the South Pacific Ocean and envisaged its expanding its influence into Polynesia. However, that dream was thwarted by growing American influence in the Pacific and lack of British support. After leaving the government in 1876, Vogel spent several years as New Zealand's agent-representative in London. When he returned to New Zealand and reentered local politics in

1885, he found the country in an economic recession for which he was blamed. In 1889, he resigned his seat in parliament.

In later years, Vogel turned to literature, writing a novel of the future, *Anno Domini 2000: Or, Woman's Destiny* (1889), which correctly predicted that in the year 2000 women would hold all major political offices in New Zealand but incorrectly predicted that Melbourne, Australia, would become the capital of a British Imperial Federation. In recognition of the novel's significance, the major award for science fiction writers in New Zealand was later named after Vogel, who died near London on March 12, 1899.

SIGNIFICANCE

Sir Julius Vogel appeared suddenly in New Zealand politics, and then vanished after a relative short period of intensive activity. Because New Zealand was not his lifelong home and because the Liberal-Radical government that took office in 1890, after he left politics, set the course for New Zealand's political future, his contributions are often overlooked in standard accounts of new Zealand history. However, his borrowing policies established the backbone of the modern New Zealand economy, and in their emphasis on deficit spending anticipated the Keynesian economics of the mid-twentieth century.

Vogel's abolition of the provinces made New Zealand the only English-seeking settler colony with neither states nor provinces—a fact that spared New Zealand the conflicts of federalism that played major roles in American, Canadian, and Australian history. Although abolishing the provinces seemed to override local rights, that action actually helped South Island, which then became part of a unitary state in which its interests were not neglected because of sectional rivalries.

—*Nicholas Birns*

FURTHER READING

Bassett, Michael. *The State in New Zealand, 1840-1984*. Auckland: Auckland University Press, 1998. Emphasizes the speculative elements of Vogel's economic policy but does not see him as a forerunner of the post-1984 New Zealand free market economic policy, which the author strongly endorses.
Belich, James. *Making Peoples: A History of New Zealanders from Polynesian Settlement to the End of the Nineteenth Century*. Honolulu: University of Hawai'i Press, 2002. The leading New Zealand historian of his generation, Belich sees Vogel's tenure as prime minister as both a time of economic growth for New

Zealand and—perhaps paradoxically—a period of increased dependence on Britain.

Brigg, Peter. "Sir Julius Vogel's *Anno Domini 2000: Or, Woman's Destiny:* On Mispredicting the Future." *Extrapolation: Journal of Science Fiction and Fantasy* 42 (2001): 357-361. This study of Vogel's science-fiction novel examines his attitudes toward women, colonial ties with Britain, and the organization of society. The brief article is useful, not merely for students of Vogel's literary output but also for those interested in his public career.

Dalziel, Raewyn. *Julius Vogel: Business Politician.* Auckland: Auckland University Press, 1986. The standard biography of Vogel focuses as much on his pre-prime ministerial career as his time in the land's highest office. Dalziel analyzes Vogel against the background of the early economic history of New Zealand. She also devotes considerable space to Vogel's overseas marketing of New Zealand, contending that his vision of social progress being tied to prosperity helped attract immigrantss from other parts of the English-speaking world.

Sinclair, Keith. *A History of New Zealand.* Harmondsworth: Penguin, 1969. Popular survey by New Zealand's most famous historian. Sinclair's sympathies are more with radical figures such as Vogel's successors Richard John Seddon and William Pember Reeves, and the improvident nature of Vogel's borrowing is given its due; however, Sinclair pays tribute to Vogel's dynamism, innovation, and genuinely felt aspirations for New Zealand.

SEE ALSO: Benjamin Disraeli; Sir George Grey; Meri Te Tai Mangakahia; Richard John Seddon; Edward Gibbon Wakefield.

RELATED ARTICLE in *Great Events from History: The Nineteenth Century, 1801-1900:* September 19, 1893: New Zealand Women Win Voting Rights.

RICHARD WAGNER
German composer

Wagner wrote the librettos and scores of some of the world's greatest operas, such as Tristan und Isolde *and* Der Ring des Nibelungen. *A conductor, musical director, and writer as well as a composer, he raised standards for musical performances and developed the aesthetic of the* Gesamkunstwerk *(total work of art), using compositional techniques based on chromaticism, variable meter, the leitmotif, and an "infinite melody" of continuous expressiveness and significance.*

BORN: May 22, 1813; Leipzig, Saxony (now in Germany)
DIED: February 13, 1883; Venice, Italy
ALSO KNOWN AS: Wilhelm Richard Wagner (full name)
AREA OF ACHIEVEMENT: Music

EARLY LIFE

Richard Wagner (VAHG-ner) was born in the German cultural and commercial center of Leipzig. Legally the son of police actuary Friedrich Wagner and his wife, Johanna, the young Wagner was never certain whether his father was actually Ludwig Geyer, the painter, actor, and poet whom his mother wed nine months after the death of Friedrich in November, 1813. Geyer died when Wagner was eight years old, but the child was called Richard Geyer until his middle teens.

Although Wagner never mastered score-reading or an instrument, he was an autodidact with ever-expanding interests in music, theater, and culture. His initial schooling took place during his family's stay in Dresden, where he took piano lessons and explored ancient Greek mythology. He spent his late adolescence in Leipzig, beginning lessons in harmonic theory in 1828 and briefly studying violin with a member of the Gewandhaus Orchestra in 1830. The following year, he dabbled in musical studies at the University of Leipzig and became a pupil of Christian Theodor Weinlig.

A survey of Wagner's earliest successes and failures during the ensuing years indicates the wide range of his ambitions. By the end of 1833, he had composed his Polonaise in D for Piano (1832), conducted his Concert Symphony in C Major (1832) in Prague and Leipzig, started and abandoned work on an opera, and secured employment at the Würzburg city theater. In 1834, he became music director of Heinrich Bethmann's theatrical company in Magdeburg, completed his opera *Die Feen* (the

fairies), published an essay for Robert Schumann's *Die Neue Zeitschrift für Musik*, made his debut as an opera conductor in Lauchstadt, and completed a libretto for *Das Liebesverbot* (1836; the ban on love). After first attempting to have this opera presented in Leipzig, Berlin, and Paris, Wagner conducted one performance of it in 1836 in Magdeburg, before the company there disbanded.

Also in 1836, Wagner wed Christine Wilhelmina ("Minna") Planer, an actor whom he first met in Lauchstadt. During the first years of this troubled marriage, Wagner experienced a decline in productivity. In 1837, he wrote an overture based on *Rule, Britannia!* (originally by Thomas Arne) and soon afterward assumed the post of music director of the city theater in Riga, where he sparked controversy (as he had in Magdeburg) by proposing numerous reforms, including plans for a subscription series.

When his contract in Riga was not renewed, Wagner traveled with Minna to Paris via the Norwegian coast, arriving in September, 1839. There he intensified his literary activity, received the support of Giacomo Meyerbeer, and became exposed to the work of Hector Berlioz. Initially occupying himself with such piecemeal work as composition for vaudevilles, he soon completed the first versions of the *Faust Overture* (1840), the grand tragic opera *Rienzi* (1840), and the Romantic opera *Der fliegende Holländer* (1841; the flying Dutchman). By early 1843, the premieres of the latter two works had established Wagner as a composer and conductor of note.

LIFE'S WORK

In February, 1843, Wagner assumed the position of royal *Kapellmeister* left vacant after the death of Francesco Morlacchi. During his stay in Dresden, Wagner again antagonized his colleagues. Rigorous rehearsal schedules, a rearrangement of the traditional seating arrangement, and the eradication of the seniority system were among the improvements suggested by Wagner, who rarely succeeded in having his ideas enacted.

Wagner's brilliant but unorthodox approach to conducting, eliciting an impressive range of dynamic nuance, called upon orchestra and audience members to follow an idiosyncratic series of tempo changes that fully indulged the maestro's subjectivism. To retain his office, Wagner was forced to promise to interpret only new operas in this manner and to conform to tradition in conducting the old ones.

Wagner's talent as a creative administrator enabled him to mount spectacles such as the 1843 choral festival, for which he hastily composed *Das Liebesmahl der Apostel* (1843; the love feast of the apostles) for more than thirteen hundred performers. He was, however, dissatisfied with this performance as well as with the premiere two years later of his grand Romantic opera *Tannhäuser* (1845), which he revised extensively over the years.

Wagner, who met the Russian anarchist Mikhail Bakunin in 1848, supported the Dresden Revolution of 1849. He fled Germany in the wake of its failure, staying briefly in Weimar, the home of his friend Franz Liszt, before settling in Zurich. Following a discouraging January, 1850, excursion to Paris, Wagner wrote the anti-Semitic essay "Das Judentum in der Musik" (1850; Jewishness and music). Wagner was also frustrated with circumstances surrounding the 1850 premiere of *Lohengrin*, directed by Liszt. In this Romantic opera, Elsa of Brabant loses the mysterious knight Lohengrin after the machinations of her enemies and her own curiosity compel her to ask him forbidden questions about his origin. Wagner's distance from the production (he did not hear a complete performance of the work until 1861) prompted him to ponder the creation of a theater designed to showcase his own works.

Richard Wagner. (Library of Congress)

While in exile, Wagner completed his aesthetic treatise *Oper und Drama* (1852; *Opera and Drama*, 1913) and finished *Das Rheingold* (1854; the Rhine gold) and *Die Walküre* (1856; the Valkyrie), the first half of *Der Ring des Nibelungen* (1874; the ring of the Nibelungs) cycle. Among his financial supporters in Zurich was his neighbor Otto Wesendonck, whose wife, Mathilde, was an object of Wagner's romantic interest; his settings of her poems are known as the *Wesendonck Lieder* (1858). When the tension between the Wesendoncks and the Wagners reached a point of crisis, Wagner left Zurich for Venice, where he finished the full score of the second act to *Tristan und Isolde* in 1859. Intervention of the Saxon police forced him to complete the work in Lucerne.

By the end of the year, Wagner had returned to Paris, where successful concerts in 1860 resulted in an order from Napoleon III for a production of *Tannhäuser* at the Opéra; this support from the French government helped Wagner secure a partial amnesty, allowing travel through any part of Germany except Saxony. The 1861 Opéra performances occasioned the famous anti-Austrian Jockey Club protests that forced *Tannhäuser* to close.

In 1862, a sickly Minna visited her husband in Biebrich before retiring to Dresden, where she died in 1866. Wagner, who soon received a full amnesty, dabbled in romantic affairs and conducted his own music throughout Europe, offering a profitable series of concerts in St. Petersburg and Moscow in 1863. Final relief from financial woes came in 1864 in the person of King Ludwig II of Bavaria, who provided the artist with generous political as well as monetary support. The mid-1860's also saw the intensification of Wagner's relationship with Cosima, the daughter of Liszt and the wife of conductor/pianist Hans von Bülow, for a time one of Wagner's staunchest supporters.

Supported by Ludwig, Wagner established a luxurious home in Munich, where *Tristan und Isolde* was first performed in 1865. A tragic love story colored by Wagner's relationship with Mathilde as well as his readings of Schopenhauerian and Buddhist philosophy, this opera is perhaps his most successful attempt at creating the sustained music drama that he proposed in his writings. Opening with the ambiguous "Tristan chord" (F-B-D-sharp-G-sharp), his score is characterized by an extreme chromaticism of melody and harmony that borders on atonality, and his verse is characterized by the deft employment of alliteration, rhyme, and assonance. Together with his sensuous phrasing and evocative manipulation of leitmotifs (musical phrases with dramatic

DEATH OF WAGNER'S FATHER

In his autobiography, Richard Wagner remembered the poignant circumstances of the death of the man he believed to be his father and recalled the impact his father's death had on his own education.

On the other hand, to show how seriously my father regarded my education, when I was six years old he took me to a clergyman in the country at Possendorf, near Dresden, where I was to be given a sound and healthy training with other boys of my own class. In the evening, the vicar, whose name was Wetzel, used to tell us the story of Robinson Crusoe, and discuss it with us in a highly instructive manner. I was, moreover, much impressed by a biography of Mozart which was read aloud; and the newspaper accounts and monthly reports of the events of the Greek War of Independence stirred my imagination deeply. My love for Greece, which afterwards made me turn with enthusiasm to the mythology and history of ancient Hellas, was thus the natural outcome of the intense and painful interest I took in the events of this period. In after years the story of the struggle of the Greeks against the Persians always revived my impressions of this modern revolt of Greece against the Turks.

One day, when I had been in this country home scarcely a year, a messenger came from town to ask the vicar to take me to my parents' house in Dresden, as my father was dying.

We did the three hours' journey on foot; and as I was very exhausted when I arrived, I scarcely understood why my mother was crying. The next day I was taken to my father's bedside; the extreme weakness with which he spoke to me, combined with all the precautions taken in the last desperate treatment of his complaint—acute hydrothorax—made the whole scene appear like a dream to me, and I think I was too frightened and surprised to cry.

In the next room my mother asked me to show her what I could play on the piano, wisely hoping to divert my father's thoughts by the sound. I played [Mozart's] *Üb' immer Treu und Redlichkeit*, and my father said to her, "Is it possible he has musical talent?"

In the early hours of the next morning my mother came into the great night nursery, and, standing by the bedside of each of us in turn, told us, with sobs, that our father was dead, and gave us each a message with his blessing. To me she said, "He hoped to make something of you."

Source: Richard Wagner, *My Life*, authorized translation (New York, 1911), part 1, chapter 1.

including an unbalanced Malvina—were as strenuously trying to point out to him. Cosima and Bülow finally dissolved their marriage in July, 1870; Cosima married Wagner the following month, by which time she was already the mother of Wagner's children Isolde, Eva, and Siegfried.

In 1868, Wagner saw the successful premiere of his most comic opera, *Die Meistersinger von Nürnberg* (1867; the mastersingers of Nuremberg). The story of an untrained singer who wins his beloved by outsinging members of a conservative songster's guild was in part a scarcely concealed attack on Eduard Hanslick, one of the composer's harshest critics. At the end of the year, Wagner met Friedrich Wilhelm Nietzsche, whose move from fervid support to chilly hostility can be traced through his writings.

Dominating Wagner's musical activities through the 1860's and the 1870's was his vision of mounting a full Ring cycle in a festival theater dedicated to his works. After plans to build such a house in Munich were abandoned in 1868, Wagner's discouragement turned to outrage when Ludwig commanded that performances of *Das Rheingold* and *Die Walküre* be given in 1869 and 1870, respectively; Wagner went so far as to deceive the king to forestall a similarly decreed performance of *Siegfried* (1871), the third part of the tetralogy.

import), these elements effectively evoke an atmosphere of intensifying yearning. The strenuous title roles were performed by Ludwig Schnorr von Carolsfeld (whose death three weeks after the fourth performance fueled rumors that the vocal parts were unperformable) and his wife, Malvina.

Later in 1865, local hostility toward Wagner led to his departure to Switzerland, where he and Cosima established their home, Tribschen. For the next two years, the two strenuously tried to hide their relationship from King Ludwig, who slowly awakened to what their enemies—

By 1872, Wagner had chosen the town of Bayreuth as the site of his festival. Leaving Tribschen, he spent the next four years supervising the construction of the Festspielhaus and engaging in fund-raising and the recruiting of personnel. He also completed the cycle's final installment, *Götterdämmerung* (1874; the twilight of the gods), and arranged the tetralogy's publication for performance.

The August, 1876, premiere of the Ring cycle in Bayreuth represented the triumphant culmination of twenty-eight years of labor. Prominent figures from around the world flocked to this four-day forerunner of modern festivals, where they were immersed in an epic of gods, Valkyries, and giants told through Wagner's alliterative *Stabreim* verse and massive orchestration. The only disappointments associated with the festival were its large deficit and Nietzsche's departure before its conclusion.

Wagner, however, was now secure enough to spend his later years riding the crest of his popularity, his operas receiving performances throughout Europe. He dedicated much of his time to writing essays on sundry topics, completing the fourth volume of his unreliable but revealing autobiography *Mein Leben* (1911; *My Life*, 1911). Months prior to his death of a heart attack, his final opera, *Parsifal* (1882), received its premiere under the direction of Hermann Levi at Bayreuth. Considered by Wagner and his followers as a sacred work, this tale of miraculous redemption is traditionally offered during the Christian holiday of Easter.

SIGNIFICANCE

Notwithstanding Richard Wagner's tremendous talent as a composer, conductor, and artistic manager, his sheer force of will seems to have permitted him to emerge triumphant from a career haunted by scandal and indebtedness. A combination of creativity, charisma, and controversy attracted followers to him, the cultish phenomenon of Wagnerism testifying to the magnetism of his personality. In the decades after his death, Wagner's stature as a musician mushroomed. Through the end of the nineteenth century, a significant portion of the creative world was influenced to some degree by his work, and composers past the turn of the century felt compelled to refer to his works in measuring the value of their own.

Considered in tandem with his musical achievements, Wagner's nationalism and anti-Semitism made him a cultural hero of the fascist regime of Adolf Hitler, who closely identified Wagner's thought with his own policies. As a result of this association, works by Wagner were not programmed in Israel until Zubin Mehta led the Israel Philharmonic in a 1974 concert that was disturbed by catcalls and fistfights.

Besides being performed regularly at the world's principal opera houses (Bayreuth remains a shrine for present-day Wagnerians and music lovers in general), Wagner's music has been preserved in numerous video and audio recordings. Outstanding among the latter is a 1965 recording of *Der Ring des Nibelungen*, a legendary performance by Sir Georg Solti and the Vienna Philharmonic Orchestra, featuring vocalists Dietrich Fischer-Dieskau, Kirsten Flagstad, Christa Ludwig, and Birgit

Nilsson. Wagner's music has penetrated into many aspects of popular culture, most notably as the familiar melody "Here Comes the Bride," which may be heard in act 3 of *Lohengrin*. Other settings in which excerpts from Wagner's works are heard outside their original context include Bugs Bunny cartoons, films by surrealist Luis Buñuel, works by composer John Cage, and Francis Ford Coppola's film *Apocalypse Now* (1979).

—*David Marc Fischer*

FURTHER READING

Burbridge, Peter, and Richard Sutton, eds. *The Wagner Companion*. New York: Cambridge University Press, 1979. This collection of essays covers a broad range of Wagner-related subjects.

Deathridge, John, and Carl Dahlhaus. *The New Grove Wagner*. Edited by Stanley Sadie. New York: W. W. Norton, 1984. Highly recommended as a supplement for serious research, this concise scholarly treatment of Wagner's life, thought, and music includes critical analyses of potentially misleading sources of information, particularly *My Life*.

Donington, Robert. *Wagner's "Ring" and Its Symbols*. New York: St. Martin's Press, 1974. An expert presents a thorough investigation of Wagner's most complex work.

Köhler, Joachim. *Richard Wagner: The Last of the Titans*. Translated by Stewart Spencer. New Haven, Conn.: Yale University Press, 2004. A psychological study of Wagner, using his compositions to gain a better understanding of the man and his life.

May, Thomas. *Decoding Wagner: An Invitation to His World of Music Drama*. Pompton Plains, N.J.: Amadeus Press, 2004. May analyzes Wagner's operas, maintaining they are richer and more artistically daring than commonly believed. Comes with two compact disc recordings of Wagner's music.

Millington, Barry. *Wagner*. Reprint. New York: Vintage Books, 1987. A brief and well-organized biography including a useful chronology and bibliography. Also includes guides to Wagner's musical compositions and a biographical listing of significant personalities in his life.

Newman, Ernest. *The Life of Richard Wagner*. New York: Alfred A. Knopf, 1933-1946. This four-volume biography remains the most comprehensive English-language account of Wagner's life.

Schonberg, Harold C. "Colossus of Germany." In *The Lives of the Great Composers*. New York: W. W. Norton, 1981. Schonberg , a major music critic of *The*

New York Times, surveys Wagner's life and most lasting contributions.

_____. "Richard Wagner." In *The Great Conductors*. New York: Simon & Schuster, 1967. Schonberg engagingly outlines Wagner's contributions to the art of conducting.

Shaw, George Bernard. *The Perfect Wagnerite*. Reprint. New York: Dover, 1967. The witty dramatist discusses the Ring cycle and other aspects of Wagner's legacy.

Shelton, Geoffrey. *Richard and Cosima Wagner*. London: Victor Gollanz, 1982. The translator of Cosima's diaries explores the famous couple's love affair and marriage.

Westernhagen, Curt von. *Wagner: A Biography*. New York: Cambridge University Press, 1979. This major study supplements Newman's biography with more recent scholarship.

SEE ALSO: Mikhail Bakunin; Hector Berlioz; Johannes Brahms; Anton Bruckner; Engelbert Humperdinck; Franz Liszt; Napoleon III; Friedrich Nietzsche; Robert Schumann; Theodore Thomas; Giuseppe Verdi.

RELATED ARTICLES in *Great Events from History: The Nineteenth Century, 1801-1900:* 1819: Schopenhauer Publishes *The World as Will and Idea*; January 2, 1843: Wagner's *Flying Dutchman* Debuts; August 13-17, 1876: First Performance of Wagner's Ring Cycle; October 22, 1883: Metropolitan Opera House Opens in New York; December 22, 1894: Debussy's *Prelude to the Afternoon of a Faun* Premieres.

EDWARD GIBBON WAKEFIELD
British imperialist

An acute observer of colonial affairs, Wakefield analyzed colonial practices and criticized the British government for its nonsystematic approach to settling Australia and New Zealand. His proposals helped prompt successful policy changes.

BORN: March 20, 1796; London, England
DIED: May 16, 1862; Wellington, New Zealand
AREA OF ACHIEVEMENT: Government and politics

EARLY LIFE
Edward Gibbon Wakefield was born into a Quaker family. He was the son of Edward Wakefield, the author of *Ireland, Statistical and Political* (1812) and a successful land agent. Edward studied in London and Edinburgh but was not successful in school. His father eventually despaired of his future, as Edward showed no promise of achieving anything noteworthy. Edward's arrogance and ill temper caused his expulsion from three institutions and would irritate his associates throughout his adult life.

Despite his poor academic record, Wakefield obtained a position as secretary to a British diplomat at Turin, Italy, where he served during 1814-1815. While he was on the Continent, he visited Paris and there wrote an impressive essay about the French capital, a piece that demonstrated his surprising talent as a thinker and author. Upon his return to London in 1815, he eloped with Eliza Susan Pattle, a seventeen-year-old heir. Although Eliza's family members were angry, they eventually accepted Wakefield, and he enjoyed a substantial income from his wife's inheritance. When Eliza died in 1820, Wakefield moved to Paris to assume a position in the British embassy. Their marriage had produced a daughter and a son.

In 1826, Wakefield entered a second marriage, one that revealed the dark side of his character, with Ellen Turner, the fifteen-year-old daughter of a wealthy industrialist. In collaboration with his brother William and his stepmother, Wakefield used a forged letter to abduct Ellen from her school by convincing her that her father was critically ill and needed her immediately. Later he told Ellen that the real reason for his action was that her family's prosperity was in jeopardy because of a bank failure, and that he, as her father's friend, had arranged a loan to sustain him. Wakefield then persuaded Ellen to marry him, although they shared no romantic feelings. The naïve girl seems actually to have believed that her family's welfare required her to marry Wakefield. Afterward, however, her outraged relatives persuaded her to leave Wakefield, and the marriage was not consummated. The Wakefield brothers' scheme to enrich themselves failed, and they both received three-year prison terms for fraud. An act of Parliament nullified Wakefield's marriage.

LIFE'S WORK

While incarcerated, Edward Gibbon Wakefield spent leisure time reading, writing, and composing proposals for social reforms and fundamental changes in his country's policies toward its colonies. His experience of prison life convinced him that severe punishment was not necessarily a deterrent to further crime but that the interval between commission of crimes and punishment was crucial to discourage recidivism. After his release, he testified before parliamentary committees seeking to reform penal laws. In 1831, he published *Facts Relating to the Punishment of Death in the Metropolis*, in which he decried the use of capital punishment for any but the most heinous offenses.

Wakefield's theory for colonial policy featured a plan for the development of Australia, where settlement had been haphazard, with small numbers of people being spread across too much land. Neither agriculture nor commerce was prospering, a condition due in part to the practice of using the country as a penal colony to which Britain dispatched undesirables. Disgruntled convicts were not productive laborers and made the colony unruly. Wakefield recommended giving free workers incentives by enabling them to become landowners. He wanted to stop grants of free land and to tax each acre. Careful supervision of emigration would ensure an adequate supply of reliable laborers, rather than convicts, and equal numbers of men and women would be permitted to go. He wanted to set prices for land so as to allow workers to purchase plots for themselves.

In 1829, Wakefield published a series of anonymous letters in *The Morning Chronicle*. The letters then appeared in a book titled *A Letter from Sydney*, which credited Robert Gouger, the colonial secretary of South Australia, as editor, but did not identify anyone as author. The book displayed such knowledge of Australia that many readers thought it must have been the work of a settler. Officials in places of authority found the book's proposals convincing, especially that income from the sale and taxation of land be used to fund transportation of free settlers, who should eventually be able to govern themselves. At that time, few people knew that the author of this theory was himself a convict in prison and one who had never even been to Australia.

Upon his release from prison in 1830, Wakefield created the National Colonization Society, which gained support from the noted political economists John Stuart Mill and Jeremy Bentham. Shortly afterward, the government adopted some of Wakefield's ideas, as he testified before committees of Parliament and suggested that

colonies could provide a means to relieve overpopulation at home. He elaborated his scheme in "The Art of Colonization," an appendix to *England and America*, which appeared in 1833, and his friendship with the publisher of *The Spectator* gave him an effective means to expound his views to the public.

In 1834, Wakefield took a leading role in the formation of the South Australia Association, a program to establish a new colony to demonstrate the feasibility of his theory. The duke of Wellington led Parliament in approving the scheme, which called for the settlement of no convicts and the granting of self-government when the colony's population reached fifty thousand. To Wakefield's chagrin, however, the government did not appoint him to the commission that administered this enterprise.

Between 1838 and 1843, Wakefield served in Canada as an aid to the governor-general, Lord Durham, whose recommendations to relieve tensions between British and French Canadians bear the impress of Wakefield's influence. In 1837, Wakefield become interested in New Zealand and formed the New Zealand Association, of which Durham was a member. However, the British government resisted calls for settlement of those islands because of warnings of the Colonial Office and the Church Missionary Society that the islands' Maori peoples would react violently to the arrival of many Europeans. Advocates of acquisition went ahead and formed the New Zealand Land Company and sent settlers to New Zealand without official permission, an action that forced the British government to claim New Zealand to avoid allowing France to do so. In 1840, Britain asserted its sovereignty over New Zealand.

Wakefield's brother William led the colonists in New Zealand, while Wakefield himself directed company affairs in England, often quarreling with officers of the Colonial Office and the Church Missionary Society. In 1841, the government chartered the New Zealand Company, as Wakefield continued to influence Parliament, which had come to respect his advice on colonial matters.

The year 1846 brought misfortune, as Wakefield suffered a stroke. While he was recuperating, he lost control of his company. After recovering from his stroke, he promoted creation of Canterbury, a project of the Church of England to establish an Anglican colony. By supporting this endeavor, Wakefield could pacify critics in the Church Missionary Society as well as demonstrate the practicality of his own ideas. In 1852, he went to New Zealand and participated in politics until 1854, when poor health forced him to withdraw from public life. He died in Wellington on May 16, 1862.

SIGNIFICANCE

Edward Gibbon Wakefield's influence upon British colonial policy was substantial. He was the first administrator to compose a comprehensive theory for the settlement and administration of the colonies and to propose ways to put it into practice. A tendency toward egotism and arrogance led him at times to employ dubious devices to gain his objectives, behavior that cost him some support. Nevertheless, despite his early criminal actions, he gained influence by forming friendships with people in high places. His recommendations generally worked well and enabled him to overcome the handicap of his shady reputation. His involvement in the domestic politics of New Zealand was contentious, as he quarreled with both the governor and the assembly of the colony. His skill as a parliamentarian ensured that he would not be ignored, but when New Zealand formed its first government, he was not invited to join the cabinet.

—*James E. McGoldrick*

FURTHER READING

Bloomfield, Paul. *Edward Gibbon Wakefield: Builder of the British Commonwealth.* London: Longmans, Green, 1961. A laudatory biography written in popular style with numerous illustrations and a large bibliography, this is a fine place to begin a study of Wakefield.

Simpson, Tony. *The Immigrants.* Auckland, New Zealand: Auckland University Press, 1997. A useful account of the entire phenomenon of emigration to New Zealand in which Wakefield was so influential.

Temple, Philip. *A Sort of Conscience: The Wakefields.* Auckland, New Zealand: Auckland University Press, 2002. A work of thorough and critical scholarship, this book examines the work of Wakefield and his associates and evaluates their achievements within the context of their times.

Wakefield, Edward Gibbon. *A Letter from Sydney and Other Writings on Colonization.* Edited by R. C. Mills. London: J. M. Dent & Sons, 1929. This is the primary source for a study of Wakefield's ideas.

Wakefield, Edward Jerningham. *Adventure in New Zealand.* London: Whitcombe and Tombs, 1955. New edition of a book first published in 1846 by Wakefield's son, who was with him in Canada and lived in New Zealand until 1844. Essentially the younger Wakefield's diary of those years, the book is a biased but primary source for the history of the settlement and his father's role in it. An abridged edition of the book was published in 1975.

SEE ALSO: First Earl of Durham; Sir George Grey; Meri Te Tai Mangakahia; John Stuart Mill; Richard John Seddon; Sir Julius Vogel.

RELATED ARTICLE in *Great Events from History: The Nineteenth Century, 1801-1900:* September 19, 1893: New Zealand Women Win Voting Rights.

JOHN WALTER II
English journalist

The son of the founder of The Times *of London, Walter fought to establish principles and practices that are fundamental to modern journalism, above all the freedom to report and interpret the news independent of financial sponsorship or government pressure. Under his leadership,* The Times *became the leading newspaper of Europe and created a body of informed public opinion that had the power to move government.*

BORN: February 23, 1776; London, England
DIED: July 28, 1847; London, England
AREA OF ACHIEVEMENT: Journalism

EARLY LIFE

John Walter II was the second son and fifth child of John Walter and his wife, Frances Landen. His father, a London businessperson who turned to printing in middle age after losing his shipping business in the American Revolution, had started *The Daily Universal Register* in 1784 as a way of publicizing a new printing technique, "logography." The newspaper prospered more than the process: By 1792, the paper—by then renamed *The Times*—had one of the largest circulations among English morning papers. "Logography" had been abandoned.

Walter attended Merchant Taylor's School in 1787. At the age of fourteen, he was apprenticed to the London printer Thomas Longman but soon transferred to work under his father in Printing House Square. In 1796, he went to Oxford with the intention, apparently, of studying for the church but was recalled by his father the following year to work in the printing house. Walter's father had handed over the management of his business and newspapers to his eldest son, William, in 1795, but this arrangement was evidently not a success. On Walter's return, he was made an equal partner with his father in the printing end of the business, while William remained editor of the papers. In 1801, at the age of twenty-five, Walter was given a sixteenth share of profits from *The Times* and from his father's other paper, *The Evening Mail*. From 1803, he became sole manager and editor of *The Times*. His father, though still principal shareholder, did not interfere with his management of the paper. Indeed, he had been contemplating closing it down because the circulation had again dropped.

LIFE'S WORK

Walter quickly put his stamp on *The Times*. At this time, newspapers were assumed to be venal, and journalism was considered hardly a respectable profession. It was customary for newspaper printers to cover some of their printing costs through political favors of one sort or another, whether to politicians or to customers. The elder Walter allied himself with William Pitt the Younger, newly in office, and sang his praises in the paper. He also sought and won the post of printer to the Customs Office in 1787, accepted from the Treasury three hundred pounds a year as "reward for the politics of the paper" from 1789 to 1799, routinely took payment for printing corrections and retractions to unflattering news reports, and as regularly accepted payment for theatrical puffs written by theater management (masquerading as impartial reviews).

Walter's son took every opportunity to break with this practice, struggling doggedly with the authorities and others whose interests were vested in the existing system. After some years, he succeeded in shaping a paper whose reputation for integrity brought it a circulation large enough to give financial independence, and thus political freedom. In a remarkable statement of principle in a leading article of *The Times* (February 11, 1810), Walter spelled out his objectives and his experience in trying to reach them.

An early opportunity to take a stand concerned the position of printer to the Customs, which his father had lost in 1799 after printing words critical of the House of Commons. In 1806, Walter was invited to petition for return of the post. It was understood that its return would be considered a favor of government, to be repaid in due course. Though Walter certainly had hoped to recover the position, he refused the terms on the grounds that he did not want *The Times* to carry an obligation to any office of government.

For most London newspapers foreign news was derived from foreign journals that were sent to the English Post Office, translated there, and distributed at a price to the newspaper offices. From 1805, Walter began building his own foreign news service. The apparatus included dispatch agents and foreign correspondents and translators, and was on a scale unheard of at that time. The service, however, was unacceptable to the postal officials, and Walter found that dispatches addressed to him were being held up at ports, on orders of the Home Office. He protested, but to no avail: He was told that the delays would cease if he wrote in support of the government. He had his mail sent undercover to other offices in London, and with the Napoleonic blockade of English ports Walter hired smugglers to bring his packages to Great Britain. At this point, however, the government had the same difficulties as Walter, so he made a deal: His own blockade-runners, unmolested, would supply foreign journals to the government also.

Walter himself was described as proud, reserved, and high-principled: an able businessperson who was hard on himself and strict with others. He believed in hard work, thrift, and self-reliance; thus, he never allowed "combinations" of his workmen and in 1810 broke a strike among his men by helping at the press and case himself. His friends contrasted him with his father, a man who "never did an honest act in his life." A family man, he had few close friends and little liking for social or political circles.

Walter established among the writers at *The Times* a system of anonymity in keeping with his own character, and that was said to have something of the quality of a secret society. Contributions to the paper were unsigned; positions on the staff of the paper were strictly confidential. Even within the organization writers might not know one another's names. The result was a degree of unity and protection that was important for a paper that had put itself at war with entrenched elements of authority. It also protected the reputation of writers who had some social standing, and who would not want their association with a newspaper to be known.

In 1812, John Walter I died. His will made John II sole owner of the premises at Printing House Square, sole and salaried manager and editor of *The Times*, and holder of a share in its ownership. This will has been interpreted variously as an expression of faith in his son's ability and as an act of revenge for the loss of the Customs Office.

With his father's death, Walter's work took a different direction. *The Times* had by now a reputation for serious news and comment, as well as a solid financial footing.

Walter gradually withdrew from direct management of the editorial side of the paper and turned his attention to running the printing business. His greatest contributions to journalism over the next decade were in two areas: pioneering the use of steam in the newspaper printing house, and separating the work of newspaper editing from management.

Walter's first encounter with improved printing presses was in 1804, when he underwrote the cost of developing a new "self-acting" printing system consisting of four presses driven by a single machine. After spending fourteen hundred pounds on the idea Walter abandoned it: He realized that, like his father's "logography," the invention would not work. In 1808, and again in 1812, he was approached by a German engineer, Friedrich Koenig, who was attempting to harness steam power to presses.

The demonstration of 1812 was convincing: Walter ordered two double cylinder presses and two steam engines at a total cost of twenty-eight hundred pounds. In 1814, the presses were assembled and installed in the printing office in complete secrecy, for fear that the regular employees would see them as a threat to their jobs and destroy them. The old presses were capable of printing about 240 sheets an hour; the new ones could print 1,100. There were also savings in composition costs, for with the old presses Walter had been obliged to set type in duplicate for any edition of over forty-five hundred in order to get the daily papers out in time. *The Times* (combined with Walter's thrice-weekly *The Evening Mail*) was for some years the only paper with a circulation large enough to justify the cost of Koenig's machines.

After the new machines were installed, Walter looked for someone to take over the responsibility of editing the papers. His first appointment was John Stoddart, but Stoddart proved too inflexibly Tory for either Walter or his readers. Later, he promoted one of his own writers, Thomas Barnes, and this choice was most successful. With Walter as editor *The Times* had been known for the high quality of its foreign, legal, and parliamentary reporting. Under Barnes, its domestic news and forceful leading articles became equally famous. During this period, the paper earned its popular name, "The Thunderer."

With Barnes in the editor's seat, Walter was developing a life for himself outside the newspaper business. His first wife died within a year; in 1818, he married again and his son John Walter III was born. He had bought land and built a house at Bear Wood in Berkshire. Over the next ten years, Walter gradually removed himself from direct responsibility for *The Times*. This retreat probably

had to do with his new ambition to sit in Parliament: Journalism was not yet considered a gentlemanly pursuit, and association with a particular paper would cast doubt on the impartiality of a man's judgment. Walter gave up the salary of one thousand pounds allowed him by his father's will and sold most of his shares in the paper to employees. In 1832, he was returned as the Whig member for Berkshire, a seat he held until 1837. He was known as a plain speaker and reluctant debater, but a vehement opponent of the Whig Party's oppressive Poor Laws: a better representative of the people than of his party. In 1841, changing to the Tory Party, Walter sat briefly as the member for Nottingham.

Walter did not interfere with Barnes's editorial policy, though he never gave up his ultimate responsibility for the management of *The Times* or for the hiring and firing of his staff. In 1841, Barnes died and Walter appointed John Thaddeus Delane his successor. Delane, the second great editor of the paper, held the position until 1879.

John Walter died of cancer in London on July 28, 1847. His son, John Walter III, who had worked alongside the father for the last years of his life, succeeded him as proprietor of *The Times*.

SIGNIFICANCE

John Walter II's outstanding achievement was to establish an honest daily paper at a time when such a thing was almost inconceivable. Not only was bribery commonplace, but also most printers assumed that there was no other way to cover costs. Walter met and overcame each aspect of venality in his trade and finally demonstrated that a truly independent newspaper could indeed be supported by no more than advertising and the subscriptions of its readers.

Walter was not alone in his beliefs. His success in building the paper's circulation showed that the public was ready to pay for serious reporting. When he refused to print theatrical puffs and printed candid theater reviews instead, Walter found allies among the young liberal writers of weekly and quarterly journals. When he found himself wrestling with the Post Office he published, on behalf of all newspapers, an account of the existing system whereby editors were obliged to pay the Post Office for foreign news. He was sued and lost the case, but the penalty was minimal and it was generally considered that *The Times*, and journalism, had won a moral victory.

The principle of editorial independence that Walter introduced is by no means invulnerable and has been tested again in many new circumstances. However, Walter demonstrated that a truly independent paper is a force with which government must reckon: a force that had not been seen before.

—Elizabeth Harris

FURTHER READING

The scarcity of published material dealing with the early years of *The Times* can be explained by Walter's own reserve and the rule of anonymity that he imposed on his writers. *The Times* has proved to be a tough nut for historians to crack. However, there are good original records of legal and financial transactions in the archives of *The Times*.

Evans, Harold. *Good Times, Bad Times*. New York: Atheneum Publishers, 1984. A personal and angry account of Evans's career as editor, first at *The Sunday Times* and then, for one stormy year, at *The Times*. Walter himself figures little, but the principles of editorial responsibility that he established become central to the tale and are reexamined in the modern context. Includes a bibliography, but it is mostly for the twentieth century.

Fulton, Richard D. "John Walter (1776-1847)." In *Oxford Dictionary of National Biography: In Association with the British Academy: From the Earliest Times to the Year 2000*. Edited by H. C. G. Matthew and Brian Harrison. New York: Oxford University Press, 2004. The recently revised, authoritative reference source contains biographies on each of the four proprietors of *The Times*: John Walter I, II, III, and IV. The *Dictionary* is also available in an online version.

The History of "The Times." 4 vols. London: The Times, 1935. A work in four volumes of which the first, subtitled "The 'Thunderer' in the Making, 1785-1841," deals extensively with Walter and his two great editors, Delane and Barnes. This, the "authorized" history, was written by staff of *The Times* (anonymously, in their own tradition). It is thoroughly researched, indexed, and documented and supplies a list of published and unpublished sources. Remains the best published source available on its subject.

A Newspaper History, 1785-1935: Reprinted from the 150th Anniversary Number of "The Times," January 1, 1935. London: The Times, 1935. A companion of sorts to *The History of "The Times"* and published on the same day, but by no means the same material. This book consists of a series of thirty-three studies of different aspects of *The Times* and journalism over 150 years: readership, reporting, the "agony" column, London newspapers, presses, type, and many other subjects. Walter has only a few pages to himself, but his work and era play a part in many of the essays. Illustrated and indexed but without bibliography or footnote references.

SEE ALSO: James Gordon Bennett; George Brown; Alexander Mackenzie; Joseph Pulitzer; Edward Wyllis Scripps.

RELATED ARTICLES in *Great Events from History: The Nineteenth Century, 1801-1900:* September 2, 1843: Wilson Launches *The Economist*; 1895: Rise of Yellow Journalism; 1895-1898: Hearst-Pulitzer Circulation War.

LESTER FRANK WARD
American sociologist

Ward's concern for the enduring features of social life led him to become one of the founders of the discipline of sociology. As a result of his contributions, the first systematic examinations of the complexities of the market economy, the social role of women, social and intrapersonal conflict, and social planning became core parts of social explanation.

BORN: June 18, 1841; Joliet, Illinois
DIED: April 18, 1913; Washington, D.C.
AREAS OF ACHIEVEMENT: Philosophy, scholarship

EARLY LIFE

Lester Frank Ward was the tenth and last child of Justus and Silence (Rolph) Ward. His father was an itinerant mechanic who worked at a host of jobs but never seemed to settle down into any one of them. He had been a fife major during the War of 1812 and received a warrant to 160 acres of virgin land in Iowa for his services. However, he did not take advantage of this grant until 1855, when the Wards homesteaded in Buchanan County, Iowa. There, Justus Ward died. Silence Ward outlived her husband by twenty-two years. The daughter of a clergyman, she was a refined and scholarly woman who had a flair for literature that ten children did not take away from her. Much of the physical strength Lester Ward possessed and most of his indomitable will were derived from his mother.

Of his early years, little is known. They were spent in relative hardship, poverty, and hard work. Quarrying rock, tending a sawmill, and breaking the virgin prairie are among the activities in which his family engaged. His much-traveled family and the frontier region where most of his adolescence was spent provided little opportunity for formal educational experience. He was briefly enrolled in elementary school in Cass, Illinois, until 1855, when the family moved to the rolling prairies of Iowa. No schools were near the Buchanan County farm. When Justus Ward died, Silence Ward returned to St. Charles, Illinois, with the two youngest children, Erastus and Lester. There, Lester Ward returned to school; to earn their tuition, he and his brother performed farm chores and assisted in the corn and wheat harvests of the area. Ward proved to be an avid and exceedingly able student. He read everything available, including what he would term "yellow covered literature"—the pulp books of that era. Indeed, so taken was he by them that he tried his own hand at writing romantic fiction; several of his pieces were published in the St. Charles *Argus*.

Ward's intellectual curiosity ranged well beyond the confines of the classroom into such areas as botany, zoology, and biology. He taught himself French, Latin, and Greek, and had a working knowledge of several other languages as well.

In 1858, Ward moved with his brother Erastus to Myersburg, Pennsylvania, to join another brother, Cyrenus Osborne Ward, in a wheel-hub factory. There, he met his future wife, Elizabeth (Lizzie) Caroline Vought, the daughter of a poor shoemaker. Ward enrolled at Susquehanna Collegiate Institute in Towanda, Pennsylvania, where he again excelled as a student. In 1862, he responded to the call for volunteers and enlisted at Myersburg in the 141st Regiment of Pennsylvania Volunteers. He married Elizabeth Vought on August 13 and reported for duty on August 26.

Ward saw action at Chancellorsville, where he was wounded three times and captured by Confederate forces. He was exchanged for a wounded Confederate lieutenant colonel and spent the remainder of his enlistment in the Veteran's Reserves Corps, which guarded Washington and handled army supply. Ever mindful of educational opportunities, Ward also tutored the wounded in French and Latin while he himself was convalescing. Ward was discharged in November, 1864, and early the following year he took a job as a clerk in the Treasury Department; he would remain a government employee for more than forty years. His wife joined him in early 1865. Their only child, Roy Fontaine, was born on June 14; the baby died in May, 1866.

While employed by the government, Ward enrolled in night school at Columbian College (now George Washington University), where he would be graduated with a bachelor of arts degree in 1869 and a master of arts in 1872; he also earned a law degree in 1871. His educational achievements led to several promotions and many added responsibilities. Quickly recognized for his expertise in the natural sciences, he undertook countless field trips into the West, eventually rising to the position of chief paleontologist in the United States Geological Survey. Ward was a prolific writer, and his scientific treatises range from *A Guide to the Flora of Washington, District of Columbia and Vicinity* (1882), *The Cretaceous Formation of the Black Hills as Indicated by the Fossil Plants* (1889), to *Status of the Mesozoic Floras of the United States* (1904), with many others in between. Ward resigned from governmental service in 1905. Following a summer in Europe, he took a professorship of sociology at Brown University. The remainder of his life was spent in higher education.

LIFE'S WORK

Lester Frank Ward is remembered in the twenty-first century as one of the primary founders of sociology as a distinct discipline. He helped create the American Sociology Society, of which he was president in 1906, and served as advisory editor of his fledgling *American Journal of Sociology* in 1896. Ward's intellectual significance and the justification for the study of his life and thought lie in his efforts to reconcile mid-nineteenth century democratic assumptions and ideas with late nineteenth century developments resulting from scientific work in biology and from the urban-industrial transformation of American life. This intellectual and social revolution began a period of rapid change—an era that, early in the twenty-first century, shows no signs of ending—and Ward's attempts to explain intellectual and social environments in transformation retain a profound relevance.

Ward championed a belief in the potential of the common person—a faith inspired by his own background and experiences. Early he became convinced that the differences between the upper and lower classes in American society were a matter of neither luck nor heredity but mainly one of education. He believed that universal public education operating within a framework of democratic political institutions could generate the human talent necessary for the exploitation of scientific knowledge for humanistic ends. As such, Ward believed that it was possible for the American public to remain true to its historical values in the midst of a world of rapid change—both physical and social. To Ward, humans were not the captives of deterministic natural laws, as many scientists and social philosophers of the late nineteenth century claimed. Humans, Ward taught, had the intellectual powers to control the forces of nature in the direction they chose.

Ward wrote that sociology is the science of human achievement. As such, he was not particularly concerned with method. He thought the main method of science was that of generalization—interpreting and reasoning about facts. Although Ward assumed that the social world was bound by the same scientific laws as all cosmic evolution, his work in botany, biology, and zoology forced him to argue that such forces were controllable by humans. He used intuition and keen observation to arrive at some of his sociological generalizations. He believed

that the social "laws" thus gained should be applied to improve human society. Ward held that humans, because of their intellect, had the ability to use social laws, if not change them. Ward offered a caution in this application. The tragedies of history, he believed, derived as much from false application as from false ideas. Thus, education must be universal, and government must become an agent of the people. The ideal government was a democratic one, which would channel its energies into producing the positive social changes benefiting the entire welfare of all classes.

Although sociological thought and modes of analysis have changed greatly since Ward's day, his concerns with the enduring features of social life are similar to the substantive interests of current sociologists. Such questions as the role of women in society; intellectual, scientific, and artistic creativity; social and intrapersonal conflicts; social welfare and social planning; the role of deception and ruse in social affairs and especially in political life; and the social consequences of professionalization, crime, and deviancy still provoke interest. Ward dealt with all of these issues.

Lester Ward's most significant writings are *Dynamic Sociology* (1883), on which he toiled for fourteen years, and *The Psychic Factors of Civilization* (1893). Those portions of his work that are most significant today reveal a passionate concern for social reform and the promotion of a liberal ideology. He believed that humans could shape their own destinies through the perfection of social mechanisms and institutions. Although he recognized evil and folly, he was not overawed by them. Reasoning humans, he said, could overcome them. Thus, he rejected the notions held by some sociologists that an authoritarian order needed to be imposed upon society. He denied Spencerian logic's conclusion that human beings can only react to the impersonal forces of nature. He provided the reasonable alternative to both.

Although Ward's professional career as a sociologist was relatively brief, his contributions to the discipline were significant. He died on April 18, 1913, in Washington, D.C.

SIGNIFICANCE

It is impossible to sum up in a brief fashion the thought of Lester Ward. His learning was vast, his interests broad, his impact upon American thought far-reaching. He was the first American sociologist to bring his learning and experiences in peace and war to bear upon the problems raised by Auguste Comte and Herbert Spencer. Ward destroyed forever the naïve Manchesterism that Spencer claimed represented the ultimate design of the universe and restored humanism to sociology. Ward recognized the role of women in civilization. He made a plea for humanity. Despite his vagaries, Ward stands among the giants of the nineteenth century.

—*Richard J. Amundson*

FURTHER READING
Chugerman, Samuel. *Lester F. Ward, the American Aristotle: A Summary and Interpretation of His Sociology.* Durham, N.C.: Duke University Press, 1939. The definitive biography of Ward. Must be consulted by anyone seeking to understand Lester Ward the man as well as his thought.
Rafferty, Edward C. *Apostle of Human Progress: Lester Frank Ward and American Political Thought, 1841-1913.* Lanham, Md.: Rowman & Littlefield, 2003. An intellectual portrait, describing the evolution of Ward's thought. Rafferty demonstrates how Ward's ideas laid the groundwork for the modern administrative state and contributed to the development of twentieth century liberalism.
Scott, Clifford H. *Lester Frank Ward.* Boston: Twayne, 1976. This introductory study combines a brief account of Ward's life with an analysis of his thought. Includes an assessment of Ward's impact on his contemporaries.
Timasheff, Nicholas S. *Sociological Theory: Its Nature and Growth.* New York: Random House, 1967. Places Ward in perspective as a social theorist.
Ward, Lester Frank. *Lester Frank Ward and the Welfare State.* Edited by Henry Steele Commager. Indianapolis: Bobbs-Merrill, 1967. Contains a brief autobiographical sketch that reveals much about Ward. Commager does a masterful job of explaining Ward's theories—especially those involving the need for governmental involvement. Indispensable for the serious student.
_____. *Lester Frank Ward: Selections from His Work.* Edited by Israel Gerver. New York: Thomas Y. Crowell, 1963. Excellent, brief presentation of key positions Ward espoused. Contains a good evaluation of Ward's impact upon the discipline of sociology.
_____. *Young Ward's Diary.* Edited by Berhard J. Stern. New York: G. P. Putnam's Sons, 1935. This diary, kept by Ward between 1860 and 1870, is a valuable source for discovering the origin of many of his explanations of social organization and social interaction.

SEE ALSO: Auguste Comte; Herbert Spencer.
RELATED ARTICLE in *Great Events from History: The Nineteenth Century, 1801-1900:* 1851-1854: Comte Advances His Theory of Positivism.

MONTGOMERY WARD
American merchant

Combining extraordinary business foresight with innovative technical methods and a genuine concern for his fellow citizens, Ward revolutionized the commercial trade by founding the first mail-order business and introduced the concept of environmental protection by beautifying the Chicago lakefront.

BORN: February 17, 1843; Chatham, New Jersey
DIED: December 7, 1913; Highland Park, Illinois
ALSO KNOWN AS: Aaron Montgomery Ward (full name)
AREA OF ACHIEVEMENT: Business

EARLY LIFE
Aaron Montgomery Ward was the son of Sylvester A. Ward and Julia Laura (Green) Ward. His great-grandfather, Israel Ward, served as a captain in the French and Indian War under George Washington at Springfield, New York, in 1772. His great-grandfather on his mother's side, Zeptha Squire, was an officer in the Revolutionary War. There were seven children in the Ward family, Aaron Montgomery being the third born. To his family and friends, he was known as Monty.

In 1853, when Ward was eight years old, his family was beset by financial difficulties and moved to Niles, Michigan. There, Ward attended public school until he was fourteen years old; at that time, he decided to abandon his studies in order to help his father support the family. His first job was that of an apprentice cobbler. After that, he did odd jobs for one year at a barrel factory. Next, he worked in a brickyard, where he loaded bricks on scows for shipment down the river; yet Ward had ambition, and he was unwilling to remain in an unskilled position such as that one for long. After two years, he was offered employment as a clerk in a general store in the port city of St. Joseph by the man who owned the scows that carried the bricks.

At the age of nineteen, Ward left Niles to begin his business training in St. Joseph. Within three years, Ward rose to head clerk and then general manager of the store. In 1861, the Civil War broke out. Ward decided to stay at the job, and he continued to send money home to help his family, thus abandoning any dreams of carrying on the family tradition of military service and glory. He learned about small-town retailing, became a first-rate book-keeper, and improved his writing of business letters and the grammatical accuracy of his everyday speech.

It was at this general store that Ward first became aware of the plight of the farmers and the discrimination they faced in the marketplace. The farm trade had always been an outlet for damaged or unfit stock. Through Ward's efforts, however, there was a notable change in the merchandise offered to the farmer. Ward insisted on receiving the perfect merchandise he ordered and was willing to pay for. The quality of merchandise did indeed improve, and the farmers grew to depend on it. Although the exchange of goods was done by barter, Ward insti-tuted the price tag system, whereby each farmer was given a due bill that stated the amount of money his goods were worth and with which he was, for the first time, given a choice of articles he could purchase from the store. The farmers were gratified to see a cash value equated with their hard labor.

Even at this young age, Ward always thought of his customers' convenience. For example, he made a picnic grove complete with tables and benches on the land adja-cent to the store so that the farm families could eat lunch and their children could play safely.

In 1865, at the age of twenty-one, Ward left the gen-eral store and Michigan to work as a clerk for two years in a wholesale house in Chicago called Field, Palmer and Leiter, the forerunner of Marshall Field and Company. Because there was no possibility for advancement, he took another job for another wholesale dry-goods house in Chicago. However, this firm failed, and he became a traveling salesperson for a similar firm based in St. Louis. Traveling and selling to the rural market, he ac-quired a deeper knowledge of the problems of the farm-ers and thus conceived the idea with which he would make his distinctive contribution to America.

The farmers had to pay extremely high prices for a small selection of inferior goods at retail prices com-pared with the money they earned in crop production at wholesale prices. Rural consumers wanted to enjoy the same comforts as city dwellers but were often the victims of monopolists and the numerous middlemen required to bring manufactured commodities to rural locations. Ward conceived a solution to the problem that revolu-tionized the business world: He envisioned a mail-order business to serve the rural trade, buying in large quanti-ties for cash direct from the manufacturers and selling for cash directly to the farmer at low markups. Eliminating the middlemen, Ward reasoned, would allow him to mar-ket merchandise directly to the farmers at reduced prices. Prices could be reduced even further by offering custom-ers additional savings accumulated through bulk orders from suppliers.

To execute his idea, Ward needed more experience in merchandising. Consequently, he found employment as a buyer for a wholesale dry-goods house in Chicago. This position introduced him to a new dimension of mer-chandising, for he was required to buy merchandise from the manufacturers for his firm to resell.

With his savings, Ward began to accumulate a small inventory with which he planned to launch his business. In 1871, he lost everything in the Great Chicago Fire, but this proved to be only a temporary setback, for he had ambition, tenacity, and a strong will to succeed. He low-ered his standard of living in order to begin saving again. Even during these times of personal misfortune, he was always sympathetic to the problems of the less fortunate and gave whatever he could to them. Also during this time, Ward—tall, slim and square-shouldered, with thick brown hair and a well-kept mustache—married Eliza-beth Cobb of Kalamazoo, Michigan, with whom he later had a daughter, Marjorie. In August of 1872, with the full support of the National Grange, he and his brother-in-law, George R. Thorne, founded Montgomery Ward and Company.

LIFE'S WORK

Ward and Thorne began their operations in the loft of a livery stable in Chicago. Ward chose the city of Chicago as the place to establish his business because he believed that it was the real capital of the United States, a country of farmers and ranchers who saw themselves as excluded from the commercial life and comforts of the prosperous and sophisticated East. There was a single desk among the stock, which was piled to the ceiling. The only em-ployee was a teenage boy who wrapped packages and carried them to the post office.

The partners sent the first Montgomery Ward and Company catalog out to National Grange members in the spring of 1872. It was a single eight-by-twelve-inch

Montgomery Ward.

printed sheet, with no pictures and little descriptive matter. It listed 163 articles, the most expensive of which was a lady's gold-plated watch selling for eight dollars. Nothing was priced below one dollar.

Ward was a keen judge of merchandise and bought at prices that enabled him to sell to the rural consumer at prices he could afford. He believed that his first duty was to his customers, and he sincerely wanted to meet the needs of the farmers. Thus, he often enclosed a friendly handwritten letter along with his catalog asking the farmer what his wishes and wants were. If their replies indicated that there was a large demand for an item, he would negotiate with the manufacturer; such was the case with the sewing machines. He concluded a deal with a sewing-machine manufacturer that enabled him to offer it at thirty dollars, twenty dollars under the retail price. If he received requests for isolated items, he bought them and sent them at only 5 percent over what it cost him, thus becoming the purchasing agent for rural America.

Ward's wife Elizabeth was invaluable in his endeavor. She suggested that he offer more variety in his catalog and that he expand to include gift items and other amenities. She also selected articles that were of interest to women and saw to it that only the most current fashions were listed in the catalog. As a result, the farm women were offered a selection of merchandise as stylish and modern as that of Marshall Field and Company.

In 1873-1874, the purchasing agencies of the National Grange bought merchandise through the Montgomery Ward and Company catalog to stock their cooperative retail stores, thus reinforcing the goodwill of the farmers and causing the line of merchandise to expand greatly. Because the business was conducted on a cash basis, it survived the Panic of 1873. By 1874, the firm had made several moves. The catalog was now a twenty-four-page booklet. In 1875, the catalog contained seventy-two pages and the first pictures of the articles. During that year, Ward adopted the first consumer protection policy: satisfaction guaranteed or your money back. This was a powerful inducement for distant customers. By 1876, the catalog had 150 pages with illustrations.

In 1878, the catalog created a sensation by offering ready-to-wear dresses for women. Previously, ready-to-wear merchandise was confined to men's suits and men's and women's overcoats. Orders from the National Grange ladies began to pour in.

During the first few years, Montgomery Ward and Company served only National Grange families. As more requests came in from outsiders, Ward consulted with Grange officials and, with their full approval, opened his field to the general public.

By 1888, annual sales had reached one million dollars. Local retail merchants felt threatened and reacted with hostile anti-Ward slogans and organized campaigns to burn Ward catalogs. The local newspapers, dependent upon the advertising of these town merchants, joined in attacking the mail-order houses. Ward and his company were often the butt of journalistic jokes, but Ward persevered and his firm expanded and flourished under his guidance and leadership, rooted in the conviction that business should be conducted for the benefit of the consumer. Ward believed that he was offering a service to farmers that local stores had failed to render; he left freedom of choice to the farmer.

The year 1899 was a peak for Montgomery Ward and Company. The catalog contained more than one thousand pages and featured a cover illustration of the new Ward Tower, the final headquarters of the company and the showplace of Michigan Avenue in Chicago. It had twenty-five stories, which made it the tallest commercial building in the world. It contained six steam elevators and a marble lobby. Sightseers were encouraged to visit and were given a tour of the warehouse, with its assortment of twenty-five thousand items, and the mailroom, where thirty clerks did nothing but open letters all day long.

Ward retired from active management of the company in 1901, although he still retained the title of president. At that time, it was the largest company in its field; it would eventually expand to include six hundred retail stores and enjoy many years of billion-dollar sales. Because Ward had no sons, the management of the business passed into the hands of his five nephews, the sons of his partner, Thorne. All became vice presidents in charge of various departments. At the time of Ward's death in 1913, annual sales amounted to forty billion dollars, customers were served in all parts of the world, and the staff of employees numbered six thousand.

Ward's conviction that business should be conducted for the benefit of the consumer was mirrored in his personal life. Court documents indicate that by 1890, long before pollution in lakes and parks was accorded any importance, Ward had begun a long legal battle that was to cost him a personal fortune and the friendship of some of Chicago's most influential citizens. It was in this year that he sued the city of Chicago for littering the lakefront with street debris, refuse, livery stables, and squatters' shacks. He fought against the erection of any human-made municipal structures on the lakefront, basing his suit on the original titles on maps of the area that prohibited buildings of any kind when it was acquired from the federal government.

Ward was severely criticized, accused of obstructing progress, and dubbed the Watchdog of the Water Front. He responded by saying that he was the one who was most concerned about Chicago's progress and that he would continue his fight in the name of the poor people of Chicago. He envisioned a park that would not be the heritage of the elite but of the masses, about whom he genuinely cared. It would be a place where they could repose and refresh their spirits during the noon hour. It took four court trials and twenty years of waiting before Ward would win the battle. By the late twentieth century, Grant Park, as it came to be called, was the envy of every waterside city.

SIGNIFICANCE

Aaron Montgomery Ward was single-handedly responsible for the most significant breakthrough in the history of trade. He made it possible for many people scattered over wide areas to buy a variety of high-quality goods at fixed and fair prices.

Ward's great success was the combination of three factors. First, he persevered until his firm was named the official supply house for the National Grange. He started his company with the intention of eradicating the economic and social discrimination directed at farmers, and he worked hard to cater to their interests and wants. Second, he introduced the idea of a money-back guarantee, which was one of the earliest landmarks in consumerism. This policy set a standard of excellence in consumer relations and conditioned the American public to expect high-quality merchandise and service as well as fair play from every business enterprise. Ward adamantly abided by his policy that the sacrifice of quality to the point of not giving satisfaction made an article worthless, however low the price. Finally, he developed the homey style of writing that became a trademark of his catalogs, contributing significantly to his success.

However, Ward contributed more than techniques to American business. He contributed a philosophy as well, an attitude of commitment and devotion to customer service that was just as revolutionary in its time as the idea of selling goods by mail.

As a result of the success of the new concept of mail-order business and the subsequent war that followed between the mail-order houses and the retail merchants, the town stores were forced to change their attitudes. They had no choice but to offer a larger variety of stock, improve the quality of their merchandise, and establish fair prices. Competition with Montgomery Ward and Company put an end to the previously accepted notion that anything is good enough for the farmer. The shopkeepers found, much to their astonishment, that the farm market was worth cultivating.

The creation of this new industry and its subsequent success was only part of the impact made by Ward. Material, social, and cultural aspects of American life were altered by catalog merchandising. The change was so evident that in 1946 the Montgomery Ward and Company catalog was selected among one hundred American books chosen for their bearing on the life and culture of the people.

Ward's interest in the American consumer was matched by his concern for the environment of his fellow citizens. For this reason, he undertook a lengthy battle with his personal resources so that the ordinary citizens of Chicago could one day enjoy the blue waters of Lake Michigan from a clean and beautiful park.

Ward had always been interested in the plight of the poor and the victimized. Even before he started his mail-order business, with which he sought to alleviate the problems of the farmers, he always gave of his time and whatever money he could to help the less fortunate. After he made his fortune, his philanthropic acts continued on a larger scale; he donated coal to heat homes and gave generously to hospitals. After his death, his wife carried on his spirit of generosity. Her largest donation was that of eight million dollars to Northwestern University to establish a medical and dental center in her husband's name.

—*Anne Laura Mattrella*

FURTHER READING

Baker, Nina Brown. *Big Catalog: The Life of Aaron Montgomery Ward*. New York: Harcourt, Brace, 1956. The story of the life and times of Aaron Montgomery Ward. Details the making of the company, Ward's views concerning consumerism, environmentalism, and philanthropy, and his methods and accomplishments.

Herndon, Booton. *Satisfaction Guaranteed: An Unconventional Report to Today's Consumers*. New York:

McGraw-Hill, 1972. Presents the problem of how to maintain the guarantee of satisfaction, first offered to consumers by Ward, in today's complex world.

Montgomery Ward and Company. *Aaron Montgomery Ward, Entrepreneur, Environmentalist, Consumerist*. Chicago: Author, 1971. A series of pamphlets and illustrations of the life of Aaron Montgomery Ward, pages of his catalog, and the Chicago lakefront.

Weil, Gordon L. *Sears Roebuck, USA: The Great American Store and How It Grew*. New York: Stein & Day, 1977. Discusses the American catalog business and how it grew. Some of the men most responsible for its success were former Montgomery Ward employees.

SEE ALSO: Marshall Field.

RELATED ARTICLE in *Great Events from History: The Nineteenth Century, 1801-1900:* 1869: First Modern Department Store Opens in Paris.

BOOKER T. WASHINGTON
American educator

One of the best-known and most widely respected African Americans of his time, Washington combined an optimistic outlook with a spirit of accommodation in race relations to provide leadership and a program to black Americans during an era of segregation.

BORN: April 5, 1856; near Hale's Ford, Virginia
DIED: November 14, 1915; Tuskegee, Alabama
ALSO KNOWN AS: Booker Taliaferro Washington (full name)
AREAS OF ACHIEVEMENT: Education, social reform

EARLY LIFE

Booker Taliaferro Washington was born into slavery on a Virginia farm. His mother, Jane Ferguson, was a slave and a cook for James Burroughs; his father was a white man whose identity is unknown. Washington had a brother John, four years his senior, also a mulatto, and a sister who died in infancy. When the family was emancipated, it settled in Malden, West Virginia, five miles from Charleston.

From 1865 to 1871, Booker worked in the local coal and salt mines, attending school between early morning and later afternoon stints of labor. For a year and a half, he was a houseboy for the wife of the mine owner; in this

capacity, he learned demanding standards of performance, attention to detail, and the virtues of hard work, cleanliness, and thrift.

Having heard of a new school in eastern Virginia where African Americans received vocational training, Washington entered Hampton Normal and Agricultural Institute in the fall of 1872. Founded by an idealistic Civil War general, Samuel C. Armstrong, the school reinforced the influences of his houseboy experience and pointed him toward his future. He later said,

> At Hampton, I found the opportunities . . . to learn thrift, economy and push. I was surrounded by an atmosphere of business, Christian influences, and the spirit of self-help, that seemed to have awakened every faculty in me.

With his emphasis on industrial education for African Americans and the virtues of hard work and self-discipline, Armstrong was perhaps the major influence in molding young Washington.

During the four years after his graduation in 1875, Washington taught school at Malden, West Virginia, and briefly attended Wayland Seminary in Washington, D.C. In 1879, he was called to Hampton Normal and Agricultural Institute to supervise instruction of Indian students whom Armstrong had recruited in the West. During his second year, he taught night classes for youths who worked for the institute during the day.

In 1881, Washington eagerly grasped the opportunity to start his own school at Tuskegee, Alabama. His model was Hampton, and he established in the Deep South an institution that expressed his by then mature social values. The Civil War and Reconstruction had brought freedom, citizenship, and suffrage to blacks, yet little had been done to prepare African Americans to live as citizens, voters, and independent workers. What was needed, Washington believed, was to give black people industrial education and moral training by which they could become economically self-sufficient and able to partake of the blessings of liberty and citizenship. The exercise of political rights and entrance into the professions could be deferred. "Let us give the black man so much skill and brains that he can cut oats like the white man; then he can compete with him," he affirmed. The liberal arts were not to be neglected, but they were not foremost.

LIFE'S WORK

At twenty-five years of age, Washington was in good health. A persuasive speaker, he stood tall, an energetic figure with striking features—gray eyes, full lips, broad nose, reddish hair, and brown skin. Throwing himself vigorously into his challenging responsibilities, he recruited students from the countryside and secured an abandoned plantation for a campus. In 1882, he married a childhood friend, Fannie N. Smith, who bore him a daughter and died in 1884. When the number of pupils grew to fifty, he employed another black teacher, Olivia A. Davidson, who became his second wife and gave birth to two sons. She died in 1889; a third marriage was to Margaret James Murray, "lady principal" at Tuskegee, who survived him.

Meager legislative appropriations and growing enrollments impelled Washington to solicit funds in the North and Midwest. Beginning in 1883, he secured assistance from the Slater and Peabody funds, the money from the first being used to build a carpenter shop and make other improvements. Fund-raising became a fixed part of his activities; in the course of time he was garnering $100,000 a year, gaining support from John D. Rockefeller, Andrew Carnegie, Julius Rosenwald, and others. By the end of his career, Tuskegee Institute owned an endowment of nearly two million dollars.

Washington quickly emerged as a national spokesperson for his race. In the summer of 1884, he was in-

vited to address the annual meeting of the National Education Association in Madison, Wisconsin. He spoke on "the broad question of the relations of the races," foretelling the views for which he became famous eleven years later. Meanwhile, the address won for him recognition among educators and helped his fund-raising efforts.

It was the address he delivered in 1895 at the Cotton States and International Exposition in Atlanta that made Washington a national figure and the leading spokesperson for black Americans. In this address, Washington rejected ideas of return to Africa or migration to the North. "Cast down your bucket where you are," he exhorted. Black people must begin at the bottom of life and not at the top, as Reconstruction policy had attempted; the leap from slavery to freedom had been too quick. Life at the bottom meant labor in agriculture, mechanics, commerce, and domestic service. Black people must "learn to dignify and glorify common labour and put brains and skill into the common occupations of life." Seeking to allay southern white apprehensions about the potential advance of African Americans within the region, Washington gave an assurance, "In all things that are purely social we can be as separate as the fingers, yet one as

Booker T. Washington. (Library of Congress)

the hand in all things essential to mutual progress." Progress, he went on, is inevitable, and nearly eight million blacks—one third of the South—would help in marching forward.

Black and white people listened while Washington warned against agitation on questions of social equality. Not artificial forces but production for the world's markets would bring black Americans the full privileges of the law. "The opportunity to earn a dollar in a factory just now is worth infinitely more than the opportunity to spend a dollar in an opera-house." Pledging the patient, sympathetic help of blacks, he looked forward to a time of material benefits to the South, followed by "a blotting out of sectional differences and racial animosities . . . and a willing obedience among all classes to the mandates of law."

Washington's Atlanta address came at a time of increasing discrimination against black people. The U.S. Supreme Court in the Civil Rights Cases had opened the door to segregation; a year after the Atlanta address, the Court gave positive sanction to separate but equal facilities for black Americans. A movement to strip black people of the right of suffrage had begun in Mississippi in 1890, and emboldened by Washington's subordination of political privileges to economic opportunity, southern white leaders pushed forward with segregation and disenfranchisement. Lynching of black men in the South, especially on the allegation of raping white women, was on the rise.

Pushing his idea of equal economic opportunity that he thought in time would blot out racial animosities, Washington advocated a policy of black accommodation to the oppressive climate. His policy won immediate favor with southern whites, who welcomed the renunciation of political privilege and equality as well as the prospect of a harmonious section prospering through the labor of skilled, contented blacks. Northern whites, who had turned away from notions of intervention in the South, applauded Washington's giant step down the road toward reunion and his vision of a southern economy where northern capital might profitably be invested.

African Americans, in the main, were proud of the recognition Washington won and looked to the Tuskegee educator as their principal leader for the next score of years. Washington's national influence grew quickly after the "Atlanta compromise." He had already made friends with powerful figures in the North, philanthropists who were contributing to Tuskegee; he came to exert control over giving to black colleges, and his favor was necessary to secure aid.

With the accession of Theodore Roosevelt to the presidency, Washington gained control of black appointments to federal office. His influence continued under William H. Taft, and Washington's secretary claimed

WASHINGTON'S ORIGINS

I was born a slave on a plantation in Franklin County, Virginia. I am not quite sure of the exact place or exact date of my birth, but at any rate I suspect I must have been born somewhere and at some time. As nearly as I have been able to learn, I was born near a crossroads post-office called Hale's Ford, and the year was 1858 or 1859. I do not know the month or the day. The earliest impressions I can now recall are of the plantation and the slave quarters—the latter being the part of the plantation where the slaves had their cabins.

My life had its beginning in the midst of the most miserable, desolate, and discouraging surroundings. This was so, however, not because my owners were especially cruel, for they were not, as compared with many others. I was born in a typical log cabin, about fourteen by sixteen feet square. In this cabin I lived with my mother and a brother and sister till after the Civil War, when we were all declared free.

Of my ancestry I know almost nothing. In the slave quarters, and even later, I heard whispered conversations among the coloured people of the tortures which the slaves, including, no doubt, my ancestors on my mother's side, suffered in the middle passage of the slave ship while being conveyed from Africa to America. I have been unsuccessful in securing any information that would throw any accurate light upon the history of my family beyond my mother. She, I remember, had a half-brother and a half-sister. In the days of slavery not very much attention was given to family history and family records—that is, black family records. My mother, I suppose, attracted the attention of a purchaser who was afterward my owner and hers. Her addition to the slave family attracted about as much attention as the purchase of a new horse or cow. Of my father I know even less than of my mother. I do not even know his name. I have heard reports to the effect that he was a white man who lived on one of the nearby plantations. Whoever he was, I never heard of his taking the least interest in me or providing in any way for my rearing. But I do not find especial fault with him. He was simply another unfortunate victim of the institution which the Nation unhappily had engrafted upon it at that time.

Source: Booker T. Washington, *Up from Slavery* (Boston, 1900), chapter 1.

that "During the administrations of both President Roosevelt and Taft hardly an office of consequence was conferred upon a Negro without first consulting Mr. Washington." He lost his influence in politics when Woodrow Wilson, a southern-born leader of a party with its base in the South, became president and ordered segregated facilities for black citizens in federal service.

Besides philanthropy and politics, Washington exerted influence in the black press. Backed by most of the black press in the nation, Washington dispatched reams of releases publicizing Tuskegee and his ideas. He fed unsigned editorials to receptive editors and on occasion made financial contributions to black editors. He secretly purchased the *New York Age*, which he believed to be "the strongest and most widely circulated Negro paper in the country," and after he sold it, continued to advise its editor.

It must not be supposed that Washington fully acquiesced in segregation and disfranchisement. His Atlanta speech was ambiguous, and if, for example, he declared that "the agitation of questions of social quality is the extremest folly," he did not intend racial inequality to be permanent. He believed in gradual evolutionary progress under which African Americans, enjoying material prosperity, would gain complete equality in the South. To this end and without fanfare, he exerted his influence to stem the tide of disenfranchisement. He wrote a public letter in 1895, urging the South Carolina convention to allow African Americans to qualify for the vote by education, and he made similar attempts to allow a degree of black voting and strengthen black education in other southern states.

Washington was less open and vocal in his opposition to segregation. Behind the scenes, he worked against the passage of laws segregating Pullman cars, though he himself was rarely accorded separate facilities. He also fought laws to segregate housing, usually in private letters and through other persons. Lynching, however, impelled him to be active; the burning alive of a Georgia black for alleged rape and murder elicited from him a letter appealing to both black and white people to maintain law and order. In later years, he continued to speak out against lynching and periodically compiled lists of lynchings in the United States that he cited in speeches and correspondence.

Washington's public stance of accommodation incurred criticism and opposition. The challenge sprang in part from a contrasting figure: a northern-born scholar who was the first black person to receive a doctoral degree from Harvard University. He was W. E. B. Du Bois,

historian and sociologist, who at first supported Washington's work and toyed with the notion of teaching at Tuskegee.

Du Bois held a set of ideas that stood in contrast to those of Washington. He believed that Washington's emphasis on industrial training was too narrow, his accommodation to segregation and disenfranchisement an acceptance of injustice, his protests too moderate, his faith in the white South's cooperation with black progress misplaced. Black people should acquire a broad education; the best minds, whom he called the Talented Tenth, should be prepared for leadership of the black race; caste distinctions found in segregation and disenfranchisement should be ended; black people should not allow their faith to repose in southern whites but feel free to migrate northward; and they should not rely heavily on self-help but seek external support. In keeping with this last idea, Du Bois helped organize a movement that in 1910 produced the National Association for the Advancement of Colored People (NAACP). A biracial movement, heavily dependent upon northern white support and leadership, the NAACP took up the fight for full legal and political rights for blacks, employing litigation as a principal weapon.

The NAACP presented a challenge that Washington met by stressing two alternatives. One was the National Negro Business League that Washington had founded in 1900, drawing together black business leaders from three hundred cities; the other was the Urban League, organized in 1911 to foster economic opportunities for African Americans in cities. These activities strengthened and complemented his strategy for achieving equality for blacks.

SIGNIFICANCE

Though he remained the preeminent leader of his race until his death on November 14, 1915, Washington saw his influence decline with the election of Wilson and the emergence of the NAACP. By 1915, his philosophy was becoming obsolete as the nation was rapidly urbanizing and industrializing, and black people were migrating to northern cities.

In many ways, Washington had caught the spirit of his age, with its stress on material advancement, faith in progress, self-help, and individualism. Living and working in the South, he probably necessarily accepted white-imposed restraints on black rights and favored white and black cooperation. Tuskegee Institute could not have existed under the administration of a militant black leader. For a generation of black Americans, Washington did much to inspire pride in race, point to a means of progress, and urge sharecroppers and tenants to become owners of farms and skilled workers.

—*James A. Rawley*

FURTHER READING

Baker, Houston A., Jr. *Turning South Again: Re-thinking Modernism/Re-reading Booker T. Washington*. Durham, N.C.: Duke University Press, 2001. A savage reassessment of Washington's ideas, in which the author criticizes Washington for his fear of offending whites, for founding Tuskegee Institute on the site of an abandoned plantation, and for training black people to work in servile occupations.

Brundage, Fitzhugh, ed. *Booker T. Washington and Black Progress: "Up from Slavery" One Hundred Years Later*. Gainesville: University Press of Florida, 2003. Collection of essays examining Washington's autobiography. Some of the essays discuss the book as biography, history, and legend, place Washington's thought in economic context, and explore the relevance of his autobiography to modern South Africans.

Du Bois, W. E. B. *The Souls of Black Folk: Essays and Sketches*. Chicago: A. C. McClurg, 1903. Written by Washington's leading critic, this book contains an early critique of the Tuskegee educator and his philosophy. It offers a useful contemporary perspective.

Harlan, Louis R. *Booker T. Washington: The Making of a Black Leader, 1856-1901*. New York: Oxford University Press, 1972. The first volume of the best biography, based upon profound scholarship, this work is written in a clear style and with good judgment.

_____. *Booker T. Washington: The Wizard of Tuskegee, 1901-1915*. New York: Oxford University Press, 1983. The second and final volume of the prize-winning definitive life, this work fulfills the promise of the first volume.

Harlan, Louis R., et al., eds. *The Booker T. Washington Papers*. 13 vols. Urbana: University of Illinois Press, 1972-1984. These volumes bring together the voluminous papers of Washington, encompassing his speeches, telegrams, letters, and miscellany. Edited with scholarly notes, the papers are invaluable for an understanding of the man and his activities.

Scott, Emmett, and Lyman Beecher Stowe. *Booker T. Washington: Builder of a Civilization*. Garden City, N.Y.: Doubleday, Page, 1916. Written by Washington's secretary and a descendant of abolitionists, this book is valuable for its inside vantage point. Sympathetic in tone, it is nevertheless frank and revealing.

Spencer, Samuel R., Jr. *Booker T. Washington and the Negro's Place in American Life*. Boston: Little, Brown, 1955. A short, reliable, and readable biography, with ample interpretation and balanced judgment.

Verney, Kevern. *The Art of the Possible: Booker T. Washington and Black Leadership in the United States, 1881-1925*. New York: Routledge, 2001. Examines Washington's ideas and achievements, explaining his responses to segregation and his opposition to black urban migration. Compares Washington to Frederick Douglass, W. E. B. Du Bois, and Marcus Garvey.

Washington, Booker T. *Up from Slavery: An Autobiography*. Garden City, N.Y.: Doubleday, Page, 1901. The author's account of his early years, this work also contains a straightforward description of Tuskegee Institute. It has enjoyed a wide readership and stands as a classic.

SEE ALSO: Andrew Carnegie; Frederick Douglass; John D. Rockefeller; Harriet Tubman.

RELATED ARTICLES in *Great Events from History: The Nineteenth Century, 1801-1900:* January 1, 1857: First African American University Opens; September 18, 1895: Washington's Atlanta Compromise Speech.

CARL MARIA VON WEBER
German composer

Best known as an opera composer, Weber was the principal founder of German Romantic music. He made many significant contributions to piano music and wrote some of the staples of the wind instrument player's repertoire.

BORN: November 18, 1786; Eutin, Holstein (now in Germany)
DIED: June 5, 1826; London, England
ALSO KNOWN AS: Carl Maria Friedrich Ernst, Baron von Weber (full name)
AREA OF ACHIEVEMENT: Music

EARLY LIFE

Carl Maria von Weber (VAY-ber) was the son of Franz Anton Weber, who directed a touring theatrical troupe, and Genovefa Brenner, an actor and singer. Weber's earliest memories were of playing among the theatrical scenery of his father's troupe. Sickly, and with a damaged right hipbone, he did not have an active childhood, and his early education was haphazard. Weber's father was the uncle of Wolfgang Amadeus Mozart's wife and hoped that the boy would become a musician.

When the theatrical company was trapped in Salzburg in 1797 by Napoleon I's invading army, Carl was enrolled in the choir school at the cathedral and received his first systematic instruction in music from Michael Haydn, the younger brother of the famous composer Franz Joseph Haydn. His first compositions, a set of six fughettas, were published in 1798 and favorably reviewed in the *Allgemeine musikalische Zeitung*, Germany's leading music periodical, for which Weber was later to write. After more travels, Weber returned to Salzburg to revise an early mass (now lost) and his first surviving opera, *Peter Schmoll und seine Nachbarn* (1803), of which the overture is still performed.

Weber then traveled extensively, and he studied most profitably with the composer-priest Georg Joseph Vogler in Vienna in 1803 and 1804. Vogler helped him obtain an appointment as music director in Breslau (modern Wrocław, Poland), where, at the age of seventeen, he was unable to cope with the intrigues of the musicians and singers and resigned. While in Breslau, he had a near-fatal accident, drinking by mistake engraving acid, which his father had carelessly stored in a wine bottle; though Weber recovered, his fine tenor singing voice was destroyed. After his resignation from Breslau, he stayed briefly in nearby Karlsruhe, where he wrote his

only two symphonies and the first version of his Concertino for French Horn for the orchestra of the duke of Württemberg-Öls.

LIFE'S WORK

The reasons for Weber's departure from Karlsruhe are unclear, but he left Breslau hurriedly when recognized by a creditor and, after a concert tour, accepted a post as secretary to the brother of the duke of Württemberg in Stuttgart in 1807. Weber went through a dissolute period when he was socially in great demand for his improvisations on the piano or guitar but was in disfavor with the tyrannical duke. Among his few Stuttgart works are piano pieces and his opera *Silvana* (1810).

Weber lost his position in Stuttgart in 1810. One account is that he was involved in selling a deferment from Napoleon's army; another is that the duke's brother entrusted Weber with money to buy horses but Weber's father, who was visiting at the time, used it to settle his own debts and left his son to get into financial trouble to cover the loss. In any case, Weber was imprisoned and banished from Württemberg.

Weber then embarked on a series of tours, including a visit to his teacher Vogler in Darmstadt, and resumed composing, with his first piano concerto, his first piano sonata with its perpetual-motion finale, and his sparkling one-act comic opera *Abu Hassan* (1811) as the main results. He began a fruitful association with the clarinetist Heinrich Baermann, for whom he wrote a successful clarinet concertino, which is still frequently performed. Weber later wrote a number of major works featuring the clarinet, including two concerti for that instrument and the *Grand Duo Concertant* for clarinet and piano. He also suffered several misadventures, including a string of unsuccessful love affairs and, while crossing Württemberg territory on his way to Switzerland, of being recognized, arrested, and briefly imprisoned before being allowed to proceed on his journey.

Weber's first really stable position was in Prague, where he accepted a three-year contract as director of the opera in 1813. He not only reorganized the musical establishment but also paid careful attention to the acting, to the scenic designs, and to the costumes in order to create a musical-dramatic whole. The repertoire was composed mainly of French operas of the time in German translation. One of the many new singers he engaged was Caroline Brandt, who was later to become his wife. During his stay in Prague, the first symptoms of the tuberculosis of which he was to die became evident. He resigned in 1816, ostensibly because of the damp winter weather, and, after visits to Berlin, accepted the post as director of the German opera in Dresden.

During the brief interval between Prague and Dresden, Weber wrote some of his most characteristic piano music, especially the second and third sonatas. Weber's piano music is quite unusual, because he had unusually long fingers and especially extended thumbs, which permitted him to execute extremely wide leaps or span large chords that are physically beyond the reach of most pianists. These characteristics account for the brilliant sonority of his piano music and for its neglect by most pianists, who lack the physical ability to do this music justice.

The capstones of Weber's piano works, the *Konzertstück* (concert piece) in F Minor (1821) and the fourth sonata (1819-1822), were written later. The freedom of form in the *Konzertstück* influenced Felix Mendelssohn and Robert Schumann in their piano concerti; the programmatic character and deep expression of the fourth

Carl Maria von Weber. (The Granger Collection, New York)

sonata influenced Schumann and Franz Liszt, who were champions of Weber's music.

Weber's position in Dresden, though it became permanent after 1818, was nevertheless difficult. He was director of the newly organized German opera (part of the movement of national consciousness that swept the German states during and after the wars with Napoleon), but the principal court opera was Italian, under the direction of Francesco Morlacchi. The Italian opera was able to hire the better singers and had the larger budget. Weber sought to resign to move to Berlin, but the opera house there was destroyed by fire. Weber's patron, Count Vitzthum, was able to obtain for Weber a permanent appointment in Dresden, enabling him to marry Caroline Brandt, whom he had courted for four years.

In Dresden, Weber extended his concern about producing operas in a manner that would ensure their dramatic as well as musical effect by insisting that the singers and chorus be able to act as well as sing, by strengthening the orchestra, and by improving the set designs. His ideal was to create a whole that would be greater than the sum of its individual parts and thus paved the way for such later reformers of operatic production as Richard Wagner and Gustav Mahler. He was a pioneer in the conducting of operas; instead of directing the performance from the piano, he stood in front of the stage, conducting with a thick baton, which he held in the middle, and rearranged the seating of the orchestra so that all the players could see his gestures. In addition, he published introductory summaries of the new operas before their performance in the local press to explain the works and thus educate his audience.

The work that occupied most of Weber's free time was the opera *Der Freischütz*, which was finished in 1820 and first performed in Berlin in the following year. The title is best translated as "the charmed bullet," although it is usually literally rendered as "the free shooter"; the libretto came from a popular ghost story adapted by Weber's poet friend in Dresden, Johann Friedrich Kind.

In the opera, the huntsman Max is unable to hit anything at which he shoots and thus is certain to lose the shooting contest at which the hand of his beloved Agathe is to be bestowed. In reality he is under a curse set by his colleague Caspar, who offers Max the chance to obtain charmed bullets from the devil Samiel. The climactic scene is the second act finale, laid in a desolate ravine in the forest, where Caspar and Max cast the magic bullets amid a host of various apparitions. Unknown to Max, the last bullet is Caspar's to direct; he plans to kill Agathe with it. At the shooting contest, however, the bullet kills

Caspar; Max then confesses what he has done and is sentenced to temporary banishment, but Agathe will wait for him. The work's popularity in German-speaking countries is owing not as much to the plot as to the musical numbers, the arsenal of Romantic horror effects in the Wolf's glen scene, the depictions of a smiling nature in the arias of the main protagonists, and the choruses composed in a popular vein.

Weber's opera was so popular so quickly that he was invited to write an opera for Vienna. He chose a medieval topic, *Euryanthe* (1823), for which Helmine von Chezy, a poet in Dresden, wrote an extremely convoluted libretto. The numerous inconsistencies of the plot and its stilted verse have been accused of having adversely affected an experimental opera with continuous music that contains some of Weber's best writing; attempts have been made to rewrite the libretto, but none has been successful.

During Weber's stay in Vienna, the symptoms of tuberculosis recurred, causing Weber to depart for Dresden. He had to abandon his writing about music (he had even drafted a semiautobiographical musical novel) and writing for piano in order to concentrate on a commission from London for a musical-dramatic work, which took shape as *Oberon* (1826), his last composition. With this work and his appearance as conductor in London, Weber hoped to amass enough money to support his wife and two sons after his death, which he sensed would be soon, because his illness was becoming worse. Weber even learned English in order to set the text appropriately.

Oberon can best be described as a multimedia work, a series of elaborate stage tableaux with vocal and instrumental music, as shown by the original playbill indicating the "order of the scenery," which includes Oberon's bower with an apparition of the Baghdad of Harun al-Rashid at the opening, and the hall of arms in the palace of Charlemagne at the end. Huon of Brabant is assigned the task of rescuing Rezia and her friends from the Emir of Tunis and bringing them before Charlemagne. Weber was thus given the opportunity to write in his chivalresque vein as well as to write exotic music for the Arabs and nature music in Rezia's grand air "Ocean, Thou Mighty Monster" and in the subsequent chorus of mermaids.

Weber had planned to rewrite *Oberon* as an opera with recitatives rather than spoken dialogue upon his return to Germany, but his death in London of tuberculosis and an ulcerated windpipe on June 5 brought an end to this project. Subsequent attempts have been made, mostly in Germany, to complete Weber's project or to perform the individual numbers linked together with spoken dialogue, as in the original production.

SIGNIFICANCE

Carl Maria von Weber is known in the twenty-first century chiefly through the overtures to his operas, his clarinet works, and Berlioz's arrangement for orchestra of his piano piece "Invitation to the Dance," a brilliant waltz. In German-speaking countries, the opera *Der Freischütz* is a national tradition, but it has resisted translation into other repertoires. Weber's extensive use of the orchestra to underscore the drama, his freedom of form, and his occasional use of leading motives and transforming their musical contexts influenced Wagner as well as several other composers.

In *Der Freischütz*, Weber had given a model of what a true national opera should be, with its use of popular idioms and with common people rather than kings and lords as principal characters. In this work and in *Oberon*, he furnished models for musically depicting both nature and the supernatural spirit world, as he provided examples for portraying the world of chivalry in *Euryanthe* and later in *Oberon*. Though Weber's reach often exceeded his grasp, and his development as a composer was cut short by an early death, he remains one of the most influential composers of the early nineteenth century.

—*Rey M. Longyear*

FURTHER READING

Finscher, Ludwig. "Weber's *Freischütz*: Conceptions and Misconceptions." *Proceedings of the Royal Musical Association* 40 (1983/1984): 79-90. The author examines the assumption that the first performance of Weber's *Der Freischütz* was the birthday of German Romantic opera. The libretto is based on the trivial aspects of "dark" Romanticism and has little to do with German Romantic poetry; the work owed its success not to folk melodies but to Weber's ability to compose in a popular vein.

Grout, Donald Jay, with Hermine Williams. "The Romantic Opera in Germany." In *A Short History of Opera*. 3d ed. New York: Columbia University Press, 1987. Presents the different characteristics of eighteenth and nineteenth century opera and the traits of German opera in particular before discussing Weber's last three operas. Weber was the real founder of German Romantic opera and the most important composer in that genre before Wagner.

Meyer, Stephen C. *Carl Maria von Weber and the Search for a German Opera*. Bloomington: Indiana University Press, 2003. During the late eighteenth and early nineteenth centuries, Germans sought a national opera that would create a vision for a new German nation. Meyer examines the aesthetic and political reception of four of Weber's operas, including *Der Freischütz* and *Euryanthe*, by contemporary German critics.

Tusa, Michael C. "Richard Wagner and Weber's *Euryanthe.*" *Nineteenth Century Music* 9 (Spring, 1986): 206-221. Many writers have commented on the strong influence and resemblances between Weber's *Euryanthe* of 1823 and Wagner's *Lohengrin* of 1847. The author identifies the various similarities between the two works in detail and shows the strong influence of Weber's opera on Wagner's *Tannhäuser* (1845).

Warrack, John. *Carl Maria von Weber.* New York: Macmillan, 1968. The standard biography of Weber in any language. The author presents careful discussion of the composer's life and music, with special attention to the operas. General readers will be grateful for the extensive plot summaries of each opera.

_____. "Carl Maria von Weber." In *The New Grove Dictionary of Music and Musicians*, edited by Stanley Sadie, vol. 20. London: Macmillan, 1980. A shorter version of the biography, with an updated bibliography, presented in a concise form but without the detail and operatic plot summaries of Warrack's full-length biography.

Weber, Carl Maria von. *Writings on Music.* Edited by John Warrack, translated by Martin Cooper. New York: Cambridge University Press, 1981. The vol-

ume contains Weber's fragmentary autobiographical novel as well as his reviews for various papers and journals and his introductions to the operas he conducted in Prague and Dresden. Each entry is given an extensive preface and is thoroughly annotated. The introduction shows that Weber's alleged attacks on Ludwig van Beethoven's music are unfounded; rather, he generally praised Beethoven's works. Weber's reviews illustrate the immense amount of music that was performed then but is completely forgotten in the twenty-first century.

Weber, Max Maria von. *Carl Maria von Weber: The Life of an Artist.* Translated by J. Palgrave Simpson. 2 vols. London: Chapman and Hall, 1865. Reprint. New York: Haskell House, 1968. Though this biography by Weber's son—based on the letters and documents saved by Weber's widow and the recollections of Weber's family—is extremely partisan and chauvinistic with reliance on obsolete information, it nevertheless presents a lively account of the petty intrigues and frustrations of court life, especially in Dresden, that Weber underwent.

SEE ALSO: Franz Liszt; Felix Mendelssohn; Napoleon I; Robert Schumann; Richard Wagner.

RELATED ARTICLE in *Great Events from History: The Nineteenth Century, 1801-1900:* January 2, 1843: Wagner's *Flying Dutchman* Debuts.

DANIEL WEBSTER
American politician and diplomat

Perhaps the greatest American orator of his time, Webster, more than any other individual, articulated a near-mystical devotion to the Union that would define Northern patriotism during the Civil War.

BORN: January 18, 1782; Salisbury, New Hampshire
DIED: October 24, 1852; Marshfield, Massachusetts
AREA OF ACHIEVEMENT: Government and politics

EARLY LIFE

Daniel Webster was the son of Ebenezer Webster. A veteran of the French and Indian War and of the American Revolution, his father was a tavern keeper, farmer, and local politician in New Hampshire. Webster's mother, Abigail Eastman, was a second wife, who, like her prede-

cessor, bore Ebenezer five children; Daniel was the youngest except for one girl. The teamsters who put up at his father's tavern nicknamed him "Black Dan" because of his dark complexion, jet-black hair, and black eyes.

Slight of stature for his age, although with an unusually large head, Daniel was often spared the heavier chores that his brothers and sisters shared on the farm. As a boy he cultivated his precocious mind and strongly emotional nature. Books were hard to come by, but he read everything he found and, blessed with almost total recall, remembered what he read. His father, with whom he had a close relationship, hoped Daniel would get the kind of education he had missed, and in May, 1796, enrolled him in the Phillips Academy in Exeter. The boy was shy and sensitive about his homespun clothing,

Daniel Webster. (Library of Congress)

clumsy cowhide boots, and awkward manners, but he made "tolerable progress" with his studies. Only in declamation was he unable to match his fellows; at the public exhibitions, despite careful preparation, he could never command sufficient resolution to rise from his seat and present his speeches.

In December, 1796, Webster returned to Salisbury without having completed his course. A brief period of country schoolteaching ended with an arrangement for him to study with a minister in the neighboring community of Boscawen, who had offered to prepare him for Dartmouth College. At Dartmouth, Webster pursued his studies with energy, was graduated near the top of his class, and was elected to Phi Beta Kappa. In contrast to his failure at Exeter, he was outstanding in his college literary society and developed a reputation as a public speaker. Although only a junior, he was invited to deliver a Fourth of July address at Hanover.

Following graduation, Webster spent several years in rather desultory preparation for a legal career. He read law with a Salisbury attorney, taught in the academy in

Fryeburg, Maine, and finally went to Boston, Massachusetts, in July, 1804, where he was accepted as a clerk in the law office of a leading New England Federalist, Christopher Gore. After completing his studies and being admitted to the bar in March, 1805, he began to practice law in Boscawen, where he could be near his family In September, 1807, his father having died the previous year, Webster moved to Portsmouth, New Hampshire, where he remained for nine happy years. In May, 1808, he married Grace Fletcher, a clergyman's daughter. In August, 1816, he moved with his wife and two children to Boston, a rising metropolis.

LIFE'S WORK

Webster entered politics as a strict constructionist and an antinationalist. During two terms in the House of Representatives as a Federalist, 1813-1817, Webster opposed the War of 1812. Although he did not advocate secession, he kept up his obstructionist activities in Congress, while the Republican administration grew increasingly desperate. As a spokesperson for the dominant merchants and shippers of New England, he vigorously opposed protective tariffs as probably unconstitutional and certainly inexpedient; in later years, as a protectionist, he was hard put to refute himself.

What national reputation Webster enjoyed prior to 1830 was largely derived from his appearances before the U.S. Supreme Court. He joined with Chief Justice John Marshall in giving a nationalistic, Hamiltonian interpretation to the Constitution. His skillful arguments in the *Dartmouth College* case (1819), *McCulloch v. Maryland* (1819), and *Gibbons v. Ogden* (1824) brought him recognition as the nation's leading constitutional lawyer.

In 1822, Webster won the Boston district seat in the House of Representatives. He shortly transcended his early sectionalism to become an outstanding nationalist, favoring a national bank, federal appropriations for internal improvements, and, reflecting New England's shift from commerce to manufacturing, a protective tariff. He became known as one of the chief exponents of the "cause of humanity" because of his advocacy of American support for Greek independence from the Ottoman Empire. In June, 1827, the Massachusetts legislature elected the ex-Federalist as a National Republican to the U.S. Senate. After the death of his wife, he was married in December, 1829, to Caroline Le Roy, the daughter of a wealthy New York merchant.

Webster's second reply to South Carolina senator Robert Y. Hayne, delivered in the Senate on January 26-27, 1830, answered Hayne's defense of John C. Calhoun's nullification doctrine with a powerful defense of national sovereignty. It gave Webster a reputation as one of the leading statesmen of the nation. His new stature made Webster a potential presidential candidate, and thereafter the hope of reaching the White House was constantly in the back of his mind and influenced many of his actions.

Webster's support for President Andrew Jackson during the nullification crisis of 1832-1833 brought rumors of a rapprochement between the two antagonists. Webster thought of uniting Jacksonians and Websterites in an anti-nullification "Constitution and Union" Party that would secure his own election to the presidency in 1836. He made overtures to Jackson, only to be rebuffed, and had no choice but to join the emerging Whig Party and to seek the presidency through that organization. His candidacy for 1836 ended when most northern Whigs and Anti-Masons supported General William Henry Harrison, a hero of the War of 1812. Webster received only the fourteen electoral votes of Massachusetts.

In the "log-cabin-hard cider" election of 1840, Webster campaigned for Harrison, and the victorious candidate made him secretary of state. The elderly Harrison died on April 4, 1841, only one month after his inauguration. Webster continued in office under Harrison's successor, John Tyler. His effort to settle the northeastern boundary dispute with Great Britain was successfully concluded with the signing of the Webster-Ashburton Treaty of 1842. Webster's decision to remain in the Tyler cabinet after all of his fellow Whigs had resigned severely strained his party ties and threatened his political future. Tyler's desire to annex Texas gave Webster the excuse he needed to give up his office in May, 1843.

IN DEFENSE OF THE CONSTITUTION

Daniel Webster made his reputation as an orator in 1830, when he responded to southern attacks on the U.S. Constitution with an eloquent defense of constitutionalism and the concept of national sovereignty over the right of states to nullify federal legislation. This excerpt from his speech touches on the core of his argument.

It is true, Sir, that the honorable member calls this a "constitutional" compact; but still he affirms it to be a compact between sovereign States. What precise meaning, then, does he attach to the term *constitutional*? When applied to compacts between sovereign States, the term *constitutional* affixes to the word *compact* no definite idea. Were we to hear of a constitutional league or treaty between England and France, or a constitutional convention between Austria and Russia, we should not understand what could be intended by such a league, such a treaty, or such a convention. In these connections, the word is void of all meaning; and yet, Sir, it is easy, quite easy, to see why the honorable gentleman has used it in these resolutions. He cannot open the book, and look upon our written frame of government, without seeing that it is called a *constitution*. This may well be appalling to him. It threatens his whole doctrine of compact, and its darling derivatives, nullification and secession, with instant confutation. Because, if he admits our instrument of government to be a *constitution*, then, for that very reason, it is not a compact between sovereigns; a constitution of government and a compact between sovereign powers being things essentially unlike in their very natures, and incapable of ever being the same. Yet the word *constitution* is on the very front of the instrument. He cannot overlook it. He seeks, therefore, to compromise the matter, and to sink all the substantial sense of the word, while he retains a resemblance of its sound. He introduces a new word of his own, viz. *compact*, as importing the principal idea, and designed to play the principal part, and degrades *constitution* into an insignificant, idle epithet, attached to *compact*. The whole then stands as a *"constitutional compact"*! And in this way he hopes to pass off a plausible gloss, as satisfying the words of the instrument. But he will find himself disappointed. Sir, I must say to the honorable gentleman, that, in our American political grammar, CONSTITUTION is a noun substantive; it imports a distinct and clear idea of itself; and it is not to lose its importance and dignity, it is not to be turned into a poor, ambiguous, senseless, unmeaning adjective, for the purpose of accommodating any new set of political notions. Sir, we reject his new rules of syntax altogether. We will not give up our forms of political speech to the grammarians of the school of nullification. By the Constitution, we mean, not a "constitutional compact," but, simply and directly, the Constitution, the fundamental law; and if there be one word in the language which the people of the United States understand, this is that word. We know no more of a constitutional compact between sovereign powers, than we know of a *constitutional* indenture of copartnership, a *constitutional* deed of conveyance, or a *constitutional* bill of exchange. But we know what the *Constitution* is; we know what the plainly written fundamental law is; we know what the bond of our Union and the security of our liberties is; and we mean to maintain and to defend it, in its plain sense and unsophisticated meaning. . . .

Source: Daniel Webster, "The Constitution Not a Compact Between Sovereign States," in *Select Speeches of Daniel Webster, 1817-1845*, edited by A. J. George (Boston, 1903).

Webster went back to the Senate in 1845. Mindful of the lasting harm that his opposition to the War of 1812 had done to his presidential ambitions, he reluctantly supported the Mexican War, but he never believed it to be justified. The election of 1848 brought him the usual fourth year frustration as the Whigs nominated General Zachary Taylor, the victor of Buena Vista, who was elected. Webster's seventh of March speech in support of the Compromise of 1850 was his final effort to eliminate the slavery issue from national politics; it enraged New England antislavery men, who likened him to a fallen angel.

After Taylor's death in July, 1850, Webster became secretary of state in Millard Fillmore's administration. His presidential ambitions were again revived in 1852, but the Whigs nominated General Winfield Scott. Sick in mind and body, Webster repudiated Scott's candidacy and correctly prophesied the downfall of the Whig Party. He died at his farm, Marshfield, on October 24, 1852, murmuring, "I still live!" Reflecting no more than his mental confusion about experiencing death, these final words would later take on a much broader symbolic meaning to many people.

SIGNIFICANCE

Webster was a highly flawed yet fascinating human being, the stuff of which legends are made. He drank and ate to excess, spent money recklessly, and was chronically dependent on powerful creditors such as the National Bank. Combined with his political ambition, these weaknesses in his character constituted the "Black Dan" alter ego of his patriotic, disinterested, "Godlike Daniel" self. The Democrats never tired of reminding the voters that the champion of the Constitution and the Union had been a partisan Federalist congressman during the War of 1812.

A perennial presidential candidate after 1830, Webster had to transcend New England's regional interests, while continuing to serve them. Intoning hymns to the Union was an obvious solution, and Webster's high point was his great debate with Hayne. Generations of northern schoolchildren would memorize his ringing appeal: "Liberty *and* Union, now and forever, one and inseparable!" Webster believed that the United States had a special destiny and that Americans had a unique character with which to fulfill it. The last hopes of humankind, he said at Bunker Hill in 1825, rested on the success of the Union, the American experiment in popular government.

Webster was less successful in trying to get the federal government to adopt a policy of economic national-

ism, helping business in an age of economic growth through high tariffs, bank charters, and transportation subsidies. In his various roles as constitutional lawyer, orator, politician, and diplomat, he strengthened the sense of American nationalism. President Abraham Lincoln would echo Webster's Union theme in his Civil War addresses, such as the one at Gettysburg on November 19, 1863.

—Norman D. Brown

FURTHER READING

Bartlett, Irving H. *Daniel Webster*. New York: W. W. Norton, 1978. This gracefully written, psychologically insightful biography is an attempt to understand the Black Dan-Godlike Man paradox along with the enigmatic inner man behind the dual images.

Baxter, Maurice G. *Daniel Webster and the Supreme Court*. Amherst: University of Massachusetts Press, 1966. Webster exerted a particularly strong influence on the bench in its application of the commerce and contract clauses. Baxter's handling of Webster's legal career, and especially his many appearances before the Supreme Court, is masterful.

_____. *One and Inseparable: Daniel Webster and the Union*. Cambridge, Mass.: Belknap Press of Harvard University Press, 1984. Benefiting from the Webster Papers project at Dartmouth College, this is the long-awaited full-scale scholarly biography. Webster is portrayed as an ardent patriot, an advocate of American nationality, and a champion of peace and Union—who was at the same time a self-promoting politician who changed his principles to meet the interests of his constituents and who was sometimes insensitive to the great moral issues of the day.

Brown, Norman D. *Daniel Webster and the Politics of Availability*. Athens: University of Georgia Press, 1969. An account of Webster's presidential ambitions during the years in which a second American party system of National Republican-Whig and Democratic parties emerged out of the superficial Republican unity of the so-called Era of Good Feelings. General Andrew Jackson's tremendous popular success influenced Whig strategists to pass over Webster in 1836, 1840, 1848, and 1852 in favor of military heroes for the presidency.

Current, Richard N. *Daniel Webster and the Rise of National Conservatism*. Boston: Little, Brown, 1955. This excellent brief biography emphasizes Webster's advocacy of a national conservatism for the United States as his response to the needs of the business community. The elements of his political philosophy were an expansive but peaceful Americanism, self-discipline, Constitution worship, beneficent technology, the harmony of group interests, and power tied to property.

Dalzell, Robert F., Jr. *Daniel Webster and the Trial of American Nationalism: 1843-1852*. Boston: Houghton Mifflin, 1973. Dalzell explains better than any previous study Webster's actions during his tragic last years, when the pressures on him to confirm, modify, or abandon his nationalism were the greatest.

Nathans, Sydney. *Daniel Webster and Jacksonian Democracy*. Baltimore: Johns Hopkins University Press, 1973. This study explores Webster's responses, as a man and as a type of political leader, to the organized, systematic, and continued party strife that took firm root in the era of Andrew Jackson.

Remini, Robert V. *Daniel Webster: The Man and His Time*. New York: W. W. Norton, 1997. Remini, biographer of Andrew Jackson and Henry Clay, explores the "Godlike Daniel-Black Dan" dichotomy evident in Webster's political career and personal life. The book provides a meticulously researched and balanced portrayal of Webster.

Smith, Craig R. *Daniel Webster and the Oratory of Civil Religion*. Columbia: University of Missouri Press, 2005. Biography focusing on Webster's legendary rhetorical ability. Smith examines Webster's career from the perspective of his greatest speeches, analyzing and placing the speeches into context, and describing how Webster's rhetoric created a civil religion of romantic patriotism.

SEE ALSO: John C. Calhoun; Caleb Cushing; Millard Fillmore; William Henry Harrison; Andrew Jackson; Abraham Lincoln; John Marshall; Winfield Scott; Samuel Slater; Joseph Story; Zachary Taylor; John Tyler.

RELATED ARTICLES in *Great Events from History: The Nineteenth Century, 1801-1900:* March 6, 1819: *McCulloch v. Maryland*; March 2, 1824: *Gibbons v. Ogden*; December 1, 1824-February 9, 1825: U.S. Election of 1824; January 19-27, 1830: Webster and Hayne Debate Slavery and Westward Expansion; March 18, 1831, and March 3, 1832: Cherokee Cases; July 10, 1832: Jackson Vetoes Rechartering of the Bank of the United States; April 14, 1834: Clay Begins American Whig Party; 1838-1839: Aroostook War; August 9, 1842: Webster-Ashburton Treaty Settles Maine's Canadian Border; June 15, 1846: United States Acquires Oregon Territory; January 29-September 20, 1850: Compromise of 1850; September 18, 1850: Second Fugitive Slave Law.

NOAH WEBSTER
American educator

A lexicographer whose very name has become almost synonymous with "dictionary," Webster helped to turn English into a universal language by compiling the first major dictionary of American usage. He was also a leader in bringing about the passage of copyright laws and was one of the founders of Amherst College.

BORN: October 16, 1758; West Hartford, Connecticut
DIED: May 28, 1843; New Haven, Connecticut
AREAS OF ACHIEVEMENT: Education, linguistics

EARLY LIFE

Noah Webster was the fourth of five children and the second son of Noah and Mercy Steele Webster. His father was a farmer who also served as justice of the peace; his mother was a great great-granddaughter of William Bradford, governor of the Plymouth Colony. Young Noah showed such unusual intellectual ability that, although he was not the first son, his father sacrificed to give him an education. The boy received his earliest tutelage from Nathan Perkins, a local clergyman, and from a Hartford schoolmaster, Mr. Wales.

At the age of sixteen, Webster entered Yale College, where his tutors were Ezra Stiles and Timothy Dwight. Upon graduation in 1778, he began to study law, but his father could give him no additional financial help, so the young Noah became a schoolmaster, an occupation to which he returned when, having passed the bar in 1781, he found that he could not make a dependable living as a beginning lawyer.

While he was teaching school in Sharon, Connecticut, in 1781, and in Goshen, New York, in 1782-1783, he began to question the wisdom of using British textbooks to teach American students. Convinced that the struggling new nation that had been created after the Revolutionary War had to divorce itself from the influence of the Old World, he began to write textbooks specifically for use in American schools. He expressed his credo in 1783 in a letter to John Canfield thus: "America must be as independent in *literature* as she is in *politics*, as famous for *arts* as for *arms*."

LIFE'S WORK

Webster set out with a vengeance to put his credo into effect. He first published part 1 of *A Grammatical Institute of the English Language* (1783), which presented a systematic method for education. It emphasized spelling and offered a new and accurate standard of pronunciation. A second part, focusing on grammar, followed in 1784, and in 1785, part 3, a reader designed to complete the study, was published.

Within Webster's lifetime, part 1 of his *A Grammatical Institute of the English Language*, which he revised twice and published under several titles, was reprinted almost four hundred times. From the first publication of this work, Webster's sphere of influence was considerable. His writings about the English language, particularly as it was used in the United States, helped to bring English to a position of worldwide prominence and to make it the international language that it is in the twenty-first century.

Webster's textbooks differed from their British counterparts, which had dominated American education, in recognizing the voice of common people as a legitimate voice, allowing general usage to determine correctness. His was a modern and radical view; as he became older and more conservative, he deviated from that viewpoint. It was not until the controversial *Webster's Third International Dictionary* (1961) was published, almost two centuries after the publication of his startling three-volume work on the English language, that a dictionary bearing his name was to include colloquial words as legitimate entries.

Webster's reader emphasized American subject matter and was a precursor of the McGuffey Eclectic Readers that began to appear in 1836 and that were second only to Webster's spelling books in the number of copies they sold up to 1900. Webster's *The Little Reader's Assistant* (1790), published the year after the U.S. Constitution was ratified, contained his "Federal Catechism," a simple and direct explanation of the Constitution, whose ratification he had supported vigorously.

Webster revised the widely used *New England Primer* under the title *The New England Primer, "Amended and*

Noah Webster. (Library of Congress)

Improved" (1789), which followed the publication of his *An Introduction to English Grammar* (1788). Something of a religious skeptic, Webster deleted from the *New England Primer* much of the didactic religious material that had been its hallmark. After personal losses during the early nineteenth century, however, Webster embraced the Calvinism that he had questioned in his youth and retained that faith until his death in 1843.

Before his thirtieth year, Webster, tall, sporting an unruly mop of red hair, chin jutting, brown eyes dancing, had gained considerable national prominence and was respected by the leaders of the new nation. In 1785 and 1786, he traveled extensively to promote his books and to lobby for the enactment of American copyright laws, which were finally passed in 1790. Prior to their passage, Webster was the plaintiff in many infringement suits because his work was extensively copied.

During his travels, Webster also did much to promote the ideas in his *Sketches of American Policy* (1785), a comprehensive political work that called for a strong central government in the United States and that urged a cultural and social unity that would keep the new nation from being the hodgepodge of cultures that the Old

World was. Many political scientists believe that Webster's *Sketches of American Policy*, which George Washington and James Madison are known to have read, had a profound and immediate effect upon the drafting of the Constitution.

In 1789, the year in which he married Rebecca Greenleaf, who bore him eight children, Webster, at the urging of Benjamin Franklin, published his lectures on language, *Dissertations on the English Language* (1789). This book, which called for a cultural nationalism, also set forth many of the lexicographical principles that Webster would incorporate into his dictionary. He called for a people's English rather than King's English and predicted that one day English, which was far from a dominant world language in Webster's early years, would be spoken by more than three hundred million people, a contention that seemed preposterous to many in his time.

While the Constitution was being framed, Webster was editor of the *American Magazine*, which he had founded. In its pages he argued strenuously in favor of the Constitution. When the magazine failed in 1788, Webster moved from New York City to Hartford, Connecticut, to practice law, a pursuit that lasted for four years, at which time he returned with his new wife to New York City to edit a daily newspaper, the *American Minerva*, which later became the *Commercial Advertiser*. In 1794, he became the editor, as well, of the *Herald*, later to become the *Spectator*.

Writing regular editorials for these two newspapers, Webster gained familiarity with many facets of society, and this broad range of knowledge was to be of inestimable help to him when he embarked seriously upon compiling his dictionary. His editorials in favor of the administration of George Washington also gained for him considerable public recognition, not all of it favorable.

Webster became increasingly concerned with matters of government, and he came to believe that a careless use of language in political discourse led to severe international misunderstandings that could escalate into all-out war. He became distrustful of popular rule and advocated that men not be permitted to vote until they were forty-five years old. Women did not vote in Webster's day.

Webster's far-ranging interests led him to write such diverse works as *Effects of Slavery, on Morals and Industry* (1793), *A Brief History of Epidemic and Pestilential Diseases* (1799), and *Peculiar Doctrines of the Gospel, Explained and Defended* (1809). His books and pamphlets numbered in the hundreds.

By 1803, Webster had severed his connection with the two newspapers he edited. He had returned to New Haven five years earlier and now, rapidly becoming a political conservative, he devoted much of his time to linguistic studies, a field in which he had no formal training but one that had always interested him.

Although he was not familiar with such major European philologists as Jacob Grimm, Franz Bopp, and Rasmus Rask, who were his contemporaries, Webster did heroic work in single-handedly compiling over a twenty-two-year period a dictionary of seventy thousand entries, twelve thousand more than Samuel Johnson's had. Webster's *An American Dictionary of the English Language* (1828) was the last comprehensive English dictionary to be compiled by one person.

A freethinker in his early years, Webster, as noted above, became a staunch Calvinist in 1808. His conversion was precipitated partly by the death of his second son, Henry Bradford, in 1806 and partly by the birth in 1808 of his daughter Louisa, who had a mental disability. His religious fervor led him to work on an authorized version of the English Bible, which he published in 1833.

Webster's first dictionary came off the presses more than three years after it had been completed, a two-thousand-page work in two quarto volumes that cost twenty dollars. The work sold fairly well in the United States but much better in England. Congress adopted this dictionary as its official arbiter of the English language, and many foreign governments adopted it as their official work on English.

In 1812, while he was working on his dictionary, Webster had moved his family to Amherst, Massachusetts, where he could live less expensively than in New Haven. In 1821, he was instrumental in founding Amherst College, an institution that he hoped would provide a stimulating intellectual and religiously conservative environment for young scholars.

Upon Webster's death in 1843, Charles and George Merriam bought the rights to his dictionary and all the copies of its 1841 edition for three thousand dollars. Merriam brought out a one-volume edition of the work in 1847, and it was such a resounding success that when the copyright came up for renewal, Merriam paid Webster's family $250,000 for it, an enormous sum at that time. Webster's dictionary has been the mainstay of the G. and C. Merriam Company since 1843.

SIGNIFICANCE

Webster's name will ever be associated with English lexicography. Indeed, his name means "dictionary" to many people. His broad range of interests, however, also prompted him to write essays and books that would affect how people looked upon slavery, how they interpreted the Gospel, and how they would deal with some diseases. His concern with education led him to be a strong motivating force behind the founding of Amherst College. Aside from his dictionary, Webster's greatest contribution to his country was probably his *Sketches of American Policy*, which had a direct influence upon the Constitution of the United States and upon the political direction that his fledgling nation would take.

—*R. Baird Shuman*

FURTHER READING

Baron, Dennis E. *Grammar and Good Taste: Reforming the American Language*. New Haven, Conn.: Yale University Press, 1982. Baron's chapter titled "Webster and Federal English" is detailed and provides interesting insights into Webster's changing notions about language and spelling.

Ford, Emily E. Fowler. *Notes on the Life of Noah Webster*. 2 vols. Privately printed, 1912. Reprint. New York: Burt Franklin, 1971. The new edition of this previously hard-to-find work has been carefully re-edited by Emily Ellsworth Ford Skeel, the daughter of the original compiler. It presents valuable, previously unpublished letters and essays.

Fuess, Claude Moore. *Amherst: The Story of a New England College*. Boston: Little, Brown, 1935. Presents important information about Webster's role in the founding of Amherst College as well as presenting suggestions as to his motivations.

Micklethwait, David. *Noah Webster and the American Dictionary*. Jefferson, N.C.: McFarland, 2000. Recounts Webster's life, describing the publications and methods that influenced his creation of a new American dictionary and examining his legacy.

Morgan, John S. *Noah Webster*. New York: Mason/Charter, 1975. One of the best books on Webster. Relates him to his times and gives extensive consideration to him as an educator, a patriot, and a lexicographer.

Scudder, Horace E. *Noah Webster*. Boston: Houghton Mifflin, 1882. This first important biography of Webster has been superseded, but it presents an accurate overview of its subject by a biographer who was initially not kindly disposed toward him. As part of the American Men of Letters series, it had gone into six editions by 1886.

Shoemaker, Ervin C. *Noah Webster: Pioneer of Learning*. New York: Columbia University Press, 1936. A detailed and appreciative doctoral dissertation on Webster that considers him broadly as an educator.

Unger, Harlow Giles. *Noah Webster: The Life and Times of an American Patriot*. New York: John Wiley & Sons, 1998. Comprehensive biography, recounting Webster's many accomplishments as a teacher, philosopher, orator, political leader, and editor as well as a lexicographer.

Warfel, Harry R. *Noah Webster: Schoolmaster to America*. New York: Macmillan, 1936. A full biography and critical assessment of Webster. By no means limited to him as an educator, as the title might suggest.

Webster, Noah. *Letters*. Edited by Harvey R. Warfel. New York: Library Publishers, 1953. Although this 562-page book barely touches the surface of Webster's voluminous correspondence, it does present the most significant letters. The editing is meticulous.

_____. *Noah Webster: On Being American*. Edited by Homer D. Babbidge, Jr. New York: Praeger, 1967. Babbidge's introduction to this well-selected edition of Webster's papers dealing with topics relating to the new nation is provocative and worthwhile.

SEE ALSO: Jacob and Wilhelm Grimm; William Holmes McGuffey.

RELATED ARTICLES in *Great Events from History: The Nineteenth Century, 1801-1900:* 1812-1815: Brothers Grimm Publish Fairy Tales; November, 1828: Webster Publishes the First American Dictionary of English.

AUGUST WEISMANN
German naturalist

Weismann is most noted for his development and refinement of the theory of the continuity of the germ plasm, for his devout support of Darwinism and the principle of natural selection, and for his discrediting the idea of the inheritance of acquired characteristics.

BORN: January 17, 1834; Frankfurt am Main (now in Germany)
DIED: November 5, 1914; Freiburg im Breisgau, Germany
ALSO KNOWN AS: August Friedrich Leopold Weismann (full name)
AREAS OF ACHIEVEMENT: Biology, science and technology

EARLY LIFE

August Friedrich Leopold Weismann (VIS-mahn) was the son of Johann Konrad August Weismann, a classics teacher at the gymnasium in Frankfurt, and Elise Eleanore Lübbren Weismann, a musician and painter. He was the eldest of four children, and his home life was simple and happy. As a young boy, Weismann showed an active interest in nature. He collected butterflies, caterpillars, beetles, and plants, and he assembled a herbarium. He was a lover of art, literature, and music (especially that of Ludwig van Beethoven). These interests continued throughout his life. He became an accomplished pianist. He attended and did well at the gymnasium where his father was a teacher.

Weismann was interested in chemistry and physics as a young adult and wanted to pursue studies in that direction. His father and friends of the family, however, suggested that he pursue medicine, because a career in medicine would be more lucrative. To this end, he entered the University of Göttingen in 1852, where he studied with Friedrich Henle and Friedrich Wöhler in an atmosphere that emphasized research rather than broader problems. He received his medical degree in 1856.

LIFE'S WORK

Following graduation, Weismann continued his research while working as an assistant in the medical clinic at Rostock. In 1857, he transferred to the Chemical Institute so that he could pursue his interest in chemistry. This was followed by a tour of four German universities and a more extensive stay in Vienna.

Weismann entered private medical practice in Frankfurt in 1858. His practice allowed him sufficient time to pursue studies on heart muscle fibers. His private practice was interrupted in 1859 by the war between Austria and Italy, at which time he entered the German army and served as a surgeon at the field hospital in Italy. He resumed private practice in 1860.

In 1861, Weismann abandoned medicine to pursue what had become his main interest, the biological sciences. He attended the University of Giessen for two months in 1861 and was profoundly influenced by Rudolf Leuckart, under whom he began his studies in insect embryology. He considered the two months he spent with Leuckart to be the most important and inspiring time of his career.

Following his stay at Giessen, Weismann became the private physician of Archduke Stephan of Austria. While in this position, from 1861 to 1863, Weismann had ample time to pursue his interest in insect development and completed his first major work, *Die Entwicklung der Dipteren* (on the development of the diptera in the egg), in 1864. He also had time to read Charles Darwin's *On the Origin of Species by Means of Natural Selection* (1859). Like so many scientists of the time, Weismann was profoundly influenced by Darwin's book. Along with Ernst Haeckel and Fritz Müller, Weismann became one of Germany's staunchest supporters of Darwinian theory.

In 1863, Weismann became a privatdocent at the University of Freiburg and taught zoology and comparative anatomy. In 1866, he was appointed extraordinary professor and, in 1874, professor. He was the first to occupy the chair of zoology at Freiburg. He soon became director of the Zoological Institute at the university. He was a well-respected teacher, who always attracted large numbers of students.

Weismann's first research papers examined insect histology and embryology. Several papers on these subjects were published between 1862 and 1866. One important discovery he made was that, during metamorphosis, tissues completely dedifferentiate and then redifferentiate during the formation of the adult. Weismann was also interested in the origin and fate of the germ cells of hydrozoans. The germ cells of multicellular organisms such as hydrozoans are set aside from the somatic cells early in development and provide for the continuity of the organism through the sperm and the egg. The somatic cells will eventually die, but the germ cells live on in a new individual. Only the reproductive cells have the capacity to form a complete, new individual. From these observations, Weismann developed the theory for which he is most noted, of the continuity of the germ plasm.

In 1864, Weismann's eyesight failed, and he had to cease work on the microscope. Although he turned to more general problems, his microscopic work was continued by his students, his assistants, and Marie Dorothea Gruber, whom he married in 1867. His wife read to him constantly so that he could keep abreast of the latest scientific developments. His eyesight became so poor that he took a leave of absence from his teaching position from 1869 to 1871. During that time, his eyesight improved, and he resumed lecturing in 1871 and active research in 1874. His eyesight again failed in 1884.

Work on the theory of the continuity of the germ plasm occupied the last thirty years of Weismann's life as an active scientist. The theory encompassed many areas but primarily focused on heredity and evolution. He first published on these topics in 1883. Although he was not the first to suggest the principle of the continuity of the germ plasm, he did develop the idea to its fullest. He contended that the germ plasm was to be found on the chromatin threads, the "idants" (chromosomes) in

August Weismann. (Library of Congress)

the nucleus of the cell. He hypothesized that the idants were composed of smaller units, the "ids," which in turn were composed of the "determinants," the individual hereditary units, which he correctly envisioned as being linearly arranged. The determinants, he thought, were composed of still smaller, more basic units, the "biophors."

Based only on a priori knowledge, Weismann reasoned that the chromosome number must be halved during the formation of the reproductive cells and hypothesized that a "reduction division" must occur during the process. This, he thought, was to prevent doubling of the germ plasm at each generation. This is considered by many to be his most significant and effective scientific contribution. Weismann believed that during fertilization individual ancestral germ plasms, each carrying variations, were combined. He thought that, as well as introducing new variations, this process created new combinations of variations.

Weismann's ideas on the continuity of the germ plasm put him in direct conflict with many other scientists of the time, because many had come to discredit natural selection as a mechanism of evolution and advocated Lamarckism, the inheritance of acquired traits, as an alternative. Even Charles Darwin proposed the theory of pangenesis, where each body part was thought to produce a gemmule, which could be modified by the environment and eventually passed to the germ cells. Weismann investigated many cases of reported inheritance of acquired characteristics and could find no authenticated instance of such inheritance. His own classic experiments, in which he cut off the tails of mice over several generations but found no tendency for the tail to shorten in succeeding generations, were instrumental in challenging Lamarckism. Weismann thought that the only way acquired characteristics could be passed to the offspring was if the germ cells were affected. He became more devoted to the theory of natural selection than did Darwin. Weismann did not believe that the environment in any way affected heredity.

Weismann extended Darwin's theory of natural selection to the germ cells in a new theory called germinal selection. He thought that the determinants struggled with one another for nutriment and that the stronger ones would triumph and eliminate the weaker ones. Thus, only the stronger ones would survive in the germ plasm and be passed to the offspring. This, he thought, could account for the loss of organs during evolution. Later work failed to support his idea of germinal selection. Weismann extended his germ plasm theory to development.

He correctly thought that the determinants directed differentiation in individual cells but incorrectly envisioned that this was a result of the distribution of different determinants to different cells during cell division. He therefore thought that mitosis could be qualitatively unequal while being quantitatively equal.

Weismann's main works on heredity and evolution were published in *Studien zur Descendenztheorie* (1875-1876; *Studies in the Theory of Descent*, 1882), *Essays upon Heredity and Kindred Biological Problems* (1889-1892), *Das Keimplasma: Eine Theorie der Vererbung* (1892; *The Germ-Plasm: A Theory of Heredity*, 1893), *On Germinal Selection as a Source of Definite Variation* (1896), and *Vorträge über Descendenztheorie* (1902; *The Evolution Theory*, 1904). *The Evolution Theory* became an important and widely read book. It has been said that since Weismann's theoretical contributions to science were so important, his experimental and observational work was often overshadowed.

Weismann retired from the faculty of the University of Freiburg in 1912. He died peacefully at Freiburg im Breisgau, Germany, on November 5, 1914, at the age of eighty.

SIGNIFICANCE

August Weismann was one of the most respected biologists of the latter part of the nineteenth century and the early part of the twentieth century. His ideas stimulated considerable discussion and research. His theories on heredity and development were far-reaching. He correctly recognized that the hereditary material was contained within the nucleus of the sperm and egg and that the hereditary material of the germ cells is reduced to one-half during the maturation of the sperm and egg. In a single theory, the germ plasm theory, he explained the meiotic reduction division, sexual reproduction, development, and natural selection. It has been said that Weismann's "ingenious synthesis helped prepare the way for twentieth-century genetics." Weismann was elected to the Bavarian Academy of Sciences and, as a foreign member, to the Linnean Society, the American Philosophical Society, and the Royal Society of London. He received numerous honorary degrees and medals, including the Darwin/Wallace Medal of the Linnean Society and the Darwin Medal of the Royal Society.

—*Charles L. Vigue*

FURTHER READING

Bowler, Peter J. *Evolution: The History of an Idea.* 3d ed. Berkeley: University of California Press, 2003. Chapter 7, "The Eclipse of Darwinism: Scientific Evolu-

tionism, 1875-1925," describes Weismann's germ plasm theories.

Churchill, Frederick B. "August Weismann and a Break from Tradition." *The Journal of the History of Biology* (1968): 91-112. This brief article discusses Weismann's most significant contribution, the theory of the continuity of the germ plasm. Also shows how his work related to that of Ernst Haeckel and others and how it influenced the development of modern biological thought.

Coleman, William. "The Cell, Nucleus and Inheritance: An Historical Study." *Proceedings of the American Philosophical Society* 109 (1965): 126, 149-154. Like the article by Churchill, this article analyzes the impact of the work of Weismann and others on modern biological thought. It is one of the few modern works that analyze Weismann in this light.

Conklin, Edwin. "August Weismann." *Proceedings of the American Philosophical Society* 54 (1915): iii-xii. This is a brief summary of Weismann's contribution to science, written by a friend on the occasion of Weismann's death.

Gottlieb, Gilbert. *Individual Development and Evolution: The Genesis of Novel Behavior.* New York: Oxford University Press, 1992. Reprint. Mahwah, N.J.: Lawrence Erlbaum Associates, 2002. Explores the interrelationship of heredity, individual development, and evolution by reviewing the ideas of Weismann and other scientists.

Steele, E. J., and Robert Blanden. "The Evidence of Lamarck." *Quadrant* 44, no. 3 (March, 2000): 47. Explores the hypotheses of Weismann and others that characteristics acquired during an individual's life time may be passed on genetically to offspring.

Weismann, August. *Essays upon Heredity and Kindred Biological Problems.* 2 vols. Oxford, England: Clarendon Press, 1891-1892. This collection contains some of Weismann's most important theoretical contributions on heredity, the continuity of the germ plasm, sexual reproduction, and evolution.

_____. *The Germ-Plasm: A Theory of Heredity.* London: Walter Scott, 1893. This is the most significant book written by Weismann. It addresses the most important theoretical contributions Weismann was to make to science.

SEE ALSO: Karl Ernst von Baer; Ludwig van Beethoven; Charles Darwin; Francis Galton; Ernst Haeckel; Louis Pasteur; Ignaz Philipp Semmelweis; Friedrich Wöhler.

RELATED ARTICLES in *Great Events from History: The Nineteenth Century, 1801-1900:* May, 1847: Semmelweis Develops Antiseptic Procedures; 1867: Lister Publishes His Theory on Antiseptic Surgery; March 24, 1882: Koch Announces His Discovery of the Tuberculosis Bacillus; August 20, 1897: Ross Establishes Malaria's Transmission Vector; 1898: Beijerinck Discovers Viruses.

DUKE OF WELLINGTON
British military leader and prime minister (1828-1830)

Remembered as the conqueror of Napoleon I, Wellington was one of Great Britain's finest military commanders. Through his victories in the Peninsular War and at Waterloo, he hastened the end of the Napoleonic Wars and was prime minister of his country.

BORN: May 1, 1769; Dublin, Ireland
DIED: September 14, 1852; Walmer Castle, near Dover, Kent, England
ALSO KNOWN AS: Arthur Wesley (birth name); Arthur Wellesley; Viscount Wellington of Talavera; Marquis of Douro; Marquis of Wellington; Earl of Wellington; Baron Douro; Baron Wellington; Iron Duke
AREAS OF ACHIEVEMENT: Military, government and politics

EARLY LIFE

The duke of Wellington was born Arthur Wesley (after 1798, Wellesley) to an Anglo-Irish family in Ireland. His father was Garret Wesley, first earl of Mornington, and his mother was Anne Hill, daughter of Viscount Dungannon. The family attached little importance to Arthur's education. He attended a preparatory school before going to Eton for two years. After his father's death in 1781, his mother decided that young Wellesley should pursue a military career and sent him to a French riding school at Angers, where he learned French tactics and language.

In 1787, Wellesley obtained a commission in the army but did little, if any, military duty as he was also an aide to the Lord Lieutenant of Ireland and a member of the Irish parliament. By his first military engagement in 1794 in Flanders, Wellesley was a lieutenant colonel in the Thirty-third Regiment of Foot.

LIFE'S WORK

In 1796, Wellesley went to India with his regiment. The appointment of his brother Richard, Lord Mornington (later Marquis Wellesley), as governor-general of India helped his prospects. After the fall of Seringapatam in

1799, he became governor of Mysore. He became chief political and military agent in the southern Maratha states and the Decan in 1803. War broke out, and Wellesley led his troops into a fierce battle near the village of Assaye. The British lost a third of their strength before the enemy broke. Wellesley would forever compare battle losses to those at Assaye. In December, 1803, the fortress of Gawilghur surrendered to his forces. For his Indian service, he received thanks from Parliament, a sword from the people of Calcutta, and the Order of the Bath. He resigned his Indian appointments early in 1805 and arrived in England on September 10, 1805, after eight years' service in India.

Sir Arthur Wellesley, as he was then known, was a handsome figure upon his return to England. He was of medium height and slim build, with closely cropped brown hair (defying both fashion and military regulations), piercing light-blue eyes, and an aquiline nose. He dressed simply and neatly, wearing military dress only when necessary. He was a man of honor and integrity and expected the same of others. He always did his duty regardless of his personal feelings.

Upon his return from India, Wellesley commanded an infantry brigade sent to reinforce British troops on the Elbe. There he learned of French emperor Napoleon I's victory at Austerlitz, which left Great Britain alone against France. Upon his return to England, Wellesley married the Honorable Catherine Dorothea Sarah (Kitty) Pakenham (daughter of Edward Pakenham, second Baron Longford) on April 10, 1806, in Dublin. They had two sons: Arthur Richard, born on February 3, 1807, and Charles, born on January 16, 1808. Wellesley became chief secretary of Ireland in 1807, a difficult and frustrating position that made him welcome the opportunity to join a military expedition to Denmark.

Foreign Secretary George Canning believed that Napoleon might use the fleet of neutral Denmark against England and demanded that it be placed in British custody until the end of the war. When Denmark refused, Canning sent the Royal Navy to Copenhagen in July, 1807, with a small land force including a brigade commanded by Wellesley. He played a small, but key, role in the successful British operation there.

In May, 1808, revolt broke out in Spain against Napoleon when he placed his brother, Joseph Bonaparte, on the Spanish throne. Delegations from Spain and Portugal urged English intervention in the Iberian Peninsula, and in July, Wellesley (now a lieutenant general) was given temporary command of an expeditionary force to Portugal. The British army landed in Mondego Bay and moved toward Lisbon. Wellesley's force fought the French on August 14 at Roliça, where he salvaged a desperate situation. Nevertheless, the French escaped. Wellesley moved to Vimeiro to cover British troop landings and was surprised by French forces. After heavy fighting, the French withdrew, leaving the road to Lisbon open. One senior officer prevented Wellesley from pursuing the French, while a second negotiated and persuaded him to sign an armistice. Published in London as the Convention of Sintra, it was extremely unpopular, and the three generals faced a Court of Inquiry, which approved the convention.

Meanwhile, Spanish resistance to the French collapsed and British forces were driven from Spain in De-

cember, 1808. By the end of March, 1809, the French were in Oporto and the Portuguese were demanding British aid. Wellesley, in command of a force to defend Portugal, arrived there April 22, 1809. On May 12, the British forces crossed the Douro River, captured Oporto, and then marched for Spain. On July 27 and 28, they defeated French forces in a fierce battle at Talavera. Wellesley (after September, 1809, Viscount Wellington of Talavera) retreated in the face of French reinforcements.

Because of inadequate supplies and transport, Wellington's army wintered in Portugal, where he ordered the secret construction of the Lines of Torres Vedras, defensive hill fortifications connected by natural escarpments. In 1810, the French took the key border fortresses of Ciudad-Rodrigo (Spain) and Almeida (Portugal). Wellington again withdrew his forces to Portugal, luring the French into the wasted countryside only to repel them on September 27 at Bussaco, where the French sustained heavy losses. By October, Wellington had the allied army inside the Lines of Torres Vedras.

Early in 1811, Wellington forced the French from Portugal, overextending his supply lines in the process. The French attempt to strengthen the garrison at Almeida ended with the Battle of Fuentes de Oñoro (May 3-5). Wellington's army took Almeida, but the garrison escaped. Increased French strength again caused Wellington's withdrawal to Portugal, where his army could be supplied by sea. In 1812, Wellington took the vital fortresses of Ciudad-Rodrigo (January 19) and Badajoz (April 16), liberated Salamanca (June 17), defeated the French at the Battle of Salamanca (July 22), and entered Madrid (August 12). Although the 1812 campaign had been his most successful to date, Wellington abandoned the siege of Burgos and retreated to Portugal to correct the deficiencies of the previous campaign.

In 1813, the French began withdrawing from Spain. Wellington's forces moved quickly north; a major victory at Vitoria (June 21) liberated Spain and opened France to invasion. On July 25, French forces crossed the Pyrenees but were stopped at Sorauren on July 28. On October 7, Wellington's forces were victorious at the Bidassoa and crossed into France. British victories followed at the Nivelle and the Nive. On February 27, 1814, Wellington bested the French at the Battle of Orthez. In April, he took Toulouse just before learning that the allies were in Paris and Napoleon had abdicated.

Wellington (now a duke) went to Paris and then to Madrid for twelve days, trying to prevent civil war. He bade farewell to his troops at Bordeaux and on June 23, after an absence of five years, arrived in England to a tu-

Duke of Wellington. (Library of Congress)

multuous reception. He served as British ambassador to France and then as delegate to the Congress of Vienna.

When news of Napoleon's escape from Elba reached Vienna, Wellington was given command of the joint allied force. He took command in Brussels on April 15, 1815, and began training his polyglot army. On June 15, Napoleon led the French army into Belgium. On June 18, Wellington deployed his forces near the village of Waterloo, where, in a hard-fought battle with heavy losses, the allies prevailed. Napoleon withdrew to France. Wellington led the allied armies in pursuit, crossing into France on June 21. Napoleon abdicated on June 22, the same day that Wellington became commander of the army of occupation. Wellington remained in France most of the time until the occupation ended in August, 1818.

Upon his return to England in 1818, Wellington's involvement in politics and public life seemed inevitable. After he joined the cabinet in December, he held several offices, including prime minister (January, 1828, to November, 1829). He was Lord High Constable at the coronations of George IV, William IV, and Victoria. He represented Great Britain at the Congress of Verona in 1822 and in Russia in 1826. He was commander in chief of the British army periodically from 1827 until his death. Though his career as a party politician ended in 1846, he was a close adviser to Queen Victoria and godfather to her third son. Wellington died at Walmer Castle on September 14, 1852, and was buried at St. Paul's, London, after a magnificent funeral.

SIGNIFICANCE

The duke of Wellington became for many the symbol of British success in the Napoleonic Wars. Ironically, during the war, his cautious military strategy drew much criticism. Wellington knew that his was the only army England had and that, if he lost it, it could not be replaced. He never lost a military battle, although he often retreated to avoid untenable situations. Until Waterloo, many people believed that he was unbeaten only because he had never faced Napoleon.

Wellington's success was based on learning from his mistakes. A disastrous night attack in India made him reluctant to attack at night without previous daylight reconnaissance. Problems with Spanish and Portuguese allies in the Peninsula made him distrust allies and avoid relying on them. The disasters of his first military engagement in Flanders made him realize the importance of keeping supply lines open and taking care of the men. Leaked information about his movements and plans appeared in British newspapers, making him reluctant to confide in anyone. Blunders by his staff officers made him attend to every detail himself.

Wellington was a gentleman and an officer. He always did his duty regardless of his personal feelings. As an officer he saw to the well-being of his men because it was his duty. His men had no affection for him, but they respected him because he took care of them. In battle he rode among them, calm and cool, always where fighting was thickest. He insisted upon strong discipline, using the lash and the gallows if necessary (and advocating corporal punishment for the army throughout his life). He recommended the Waterloo medal for all ranks, but he showed little gratitude to or interest in his men after the war.

Wellington was a die-hard aristocrat and fought change. In spite of difficulties with incompetent officers who bought commissions and promotions, he defended the system because it ensured that officers would come from the upper classes. He spent much of his early manhood outside England and never really understood the cares and concerns of the English people. He opposed reform in parliamentary representation despite gross inequities. His unwillingness to compromise on this made him the symbol of conservatism and the target of the mob. On several occasions, mobs surrounded Apsley House (his London home), throwing stones at the windows, which he had covered with iron shutters. He cared nothing for the opinions of his generation or of history.

Wellington's immediate legacy to the British military was a tragic one. In the years after Waterloo, the British army modeled itself on Wellington's army. It neglected training staff officers because Wellington considered the public school and the regiment the best training. Wellington did his own staff work, not trusting his officers. Later commanders did not have his ability or attention to detail. It took the British disasters in the Crimean War to change this system.

—Judith A. Parsons

FURTHER READING

Bryant, Arthur. *The Great Duke: Or, The Invincible General*. New York: William Morrow, 1972. Objective, thorough account of Wellington's military career. Gives attention to the often-neglected Indian period of his career.

Cooper, Leonard. *The Age of Wellington: The Life and Times of the Duke of Wellington, 1769-1852*. New York: Dodd, Mead, 1963. Popular treatment without documentation. Places Wellington's life in context with contemporaneous events.

Corrigan, Gordon. *Wellington: A Military Life*. London: Hambledon and London, 2001. Corrigan, a former soldier, examines Wellington's claims to military greatness, concluding he was the first modern general.

Davies, Godfrey. *Wellington and His Army*. Westport, Conn.: Greenwood Press, 1974. Brief account of the military aspects of Wellington's career (especially the Peninsula and Belgium). Generally uncritical of Wellington and harsh on his critics.

Guedalia, Philip. *The Duke*. Reprint. London: Hodder and Stoughton, 1974. Classic, literary biography. Guedalia believes that Wellington's later unpopularity with the British people came not from his opposition to reform but from his success as a soldier, as the British prefer heroes to be slightly unsuccessful.

Holmes, Richard. *Wellington: The Iron Duke*. London: HarperCollins, 2002. Holmes, a military historian, chronicles Wellington's career, depicting a man of great courage and sense of duty, who was idealistic in politics and cynical in love.

Jupp, Peter. *British Politics on the Eve of Reform: The Duke of Wellington's Administration, 1829-1830*. New York: St. Martin's Press, 1998. Analyzes the British monarchy, prime ministry, Parliament, and other political institutions before adoption of the Great Reform Act of 1832. Jupp concludes that pre-Reform politics was characterized by unpredictability and openness of parliamentary affairs.

Longford, Elizabeth. *Wellington: The Pillar of State*. New York: Harper and Row, 1972. Excellent and useful account of Wellington's life after Waterloo, a period often slighted.

_____. *Wellington: The Years of the Sword*. New York: Harper and Row, 1969. Detailed, factual account of Wellington's life from 1769 to 1815. The most useful and thorough of recent works.

Philips, C. H. *The Young Wellington in India*. London: Athlone Press, 1973. Originally given as the Creighton Lectures in History in 1972. Philips focuses on Wellington's years in India and how they contributed to his military leadership.

SEE ALSO: Sir Isaac Brock; George Canning; Viscount Castlereagh; George IV; Charles Grey; Napoleon I; Lord Nelson; Lord Palmerston; Queen Victoria; William IV.

RELATED ARTICLES in *Great Events from History: The Nineteenth Century, 1801-1900:* May 2, 1808-November, 1813: Peninsular War in Spain; July 22, 1812: Battle of Salamanca; June 18, 1815: Battle of Waterloo; November 20, 1815: Second Peace of Paris; October 20-30, 1822: Great Britain Withdraws from the Concert of Europe; May 9, 1828-April 13, 1829: Roman Catholic Emancipation; June 4, 1832: British Parliament Passes the Reform Act of 1832; June 15, 1846: British Parliament Repeals the Corn Laws.

W. C. WENTWORTH
Australian politician

One of the leading New South Wales politicians of the nineteenth century, Wentworth contributed both to egalitarian and conservative forces in Australian life and made major contributions to Australia's future educational system.

BORN: August 13, 1790; On board the *Surprize*, in harbor of Cascade Bay, Norfolk Island (now in Australia)

DIED: March 20, 1872; Merly House, near Wimborne, Dorset, England

ALSO KNOWN AS: William Charles Wentworth (full name)

AREA OF ACHIEVEMENT: Government and politics

EARLY LIFE

William Charles Wentworth was the son of Catherine (née Crowley) and D'Arcy Wentworth. His mother had been transported to Australia for seven years after being convicted at the Stafford assizes on July 30, 1788. She arrived at Sydney on June 28, 1790, and was then sent to Norfolk Island, where she arrived on August 7, 1790, six days before Wentworth was born. Wentworth's father was a medical practitioner who was charged with highway robbery on four occasions. He was acquitted each time, and before the last case was over he had obtained an appointment as an assistant surgeon on the Second Fleet. D'Arcy and Catherine sailed to Sydney on the same ship, and their son was probably born at sea as they sailed from Sydney to Norfolk Island.

For his first five years, Wentworth lived on Norfolk Island. The family returned to Sydney in February, 1796, and moved to Parramatta, where D'Arcy served in the medical center and where Catherine died in 1800.

Wentworth was educated in Great Britain. He returned to Sydney in 1810 but left for London in 1816, where he entered the Middle Temple in February, 1817, to prepare himself, as he wrote, to be "the instrument of procuring a free constitution for my country." He finished his legal studies in 1823, returning to Sydney in 1824, where he married Sarah Cox, the daughter of an emancipist blacksmith, in 1829. More than six feet tall, with auburn hair, Wentworth had a Roman head and massive form. He was also known for his slovenly dress and the disrespectful bearing he frequently adopted during his speeches. He had a harsh voice but was admired for his forceful speaking.

LIFE'S WORK

Upon returning from Great Britain in 1810, Wentworth was appointed acting provost marshal by Governor Lachlan Macquarie in October, 1811, and was granted 1,750 acres on the Nepean. Two years later, with William Lawson, Gregory Blaxland, and four servants, he set out to cross the Blue Mountains. After twenty-one days, as Wentworth wrote, "the boundless champaign burst upon our sight." They had found abundant pasture land and knew that animals could be transported to it on foot. Their discovery further stimulated the pastoral industry, and Wentworth was rewarded with an additional thousand acres.

Two years after this exploratory trip across the Blue Mountains, Wentworth went to Great Britain to continue his education. When he returned to Sydney in 1824, he brought with him a printing press and with it started a newspaper, *The Australian.* In that paper he took up the cause of the "emancipists," those persons who had served the sentence for which they had been transported. Before this time, he had reacted against the attempt by those with no convict heritage—the "exclusives"—to force the emancipists to remain inferior citizens. In *A Statistical, Historical, and Political Description of the Colony of New South Wales and Its Dependent Settlements in Van Dieman's Land* (1819), he commented that

> the covert aim of these men is to convert the ignominy of the great body of the people into a hereditary deformity. They would hand it down from father to son, and raise an eternal barrier of separation between their offspring, and the offspring of the unfortunate convict.

Wentworth used his newspaper to promote the rights of the emancipists and to advance his own political career. He criticized the pretensions of the exclusives and agitated for jury trial and political representation for both emancipists and the freeborn children of convicts. As free immigration increased and transportation to New South Wales ended, however, the emancipists decreased as a percentage of the population, with the result that by 1840 the emancipist issue was no longer as significant as it had been. In addition, trial by jury had been adopted in 1830, by which time Wentworth had sold his shares in the paper. He continued to agitate and to petition for self-government, and in 1835 he joined with others to found the Australian Patriotic Association to work for representative government in New South Wales.

During this period of agitation for self-government, his father died in 1827. Wentworth's inheritance added to his already considerable holdings, and he continued to acquire property. He purchased Vaucluse in 1827, where he proceeded to build a stately mansion that he made the center of his activities. The property was later increased to five hundred acres, making his home a substantial estate. He also acquired several sheep stations, possessing at least fifteen at one time. With these large holdings, his pastoral interests occupied much of his time, and he gave up his legal practice. At the time of his death, his properties in Australia were assessed at 96,000 pounds and those in London at 70,000 pounds.

Wentworth had prospered economically; politically, his success was slower. During the late 1820's and early 1830's, he was popular with the poorer people of Sydney and with the emancipists. Although he had deep feelings for the emancipists, he was no democrat. His own inclinations were to remove social barriers to advancement but to permit only people of wealth to have political rights. As he developed his pastoral holdings and acquired more and more wealth, these inclinations became more pronounced. When he defended the old land system, attempted to prevent the abolition of transportation, and gave his approval to the importation of Asiatic labor, many former supporters deserted him, and his former newspaper asserted that he had betrayed the native-born of New South Wales and that his day was over. In reality, while his day as the leader of the emancipists was indeed over, his day as the leader of the pastoralists was only beginning.

The pastoral industry was the leading one in Australia, but the change in land policy in 1831 had irritated the pastoralists. Now they must buy or lease their holdings, rather than receive free grants. Because this new policy came from London, pastoralists more than ever wanted the colony to be given more control over its own affairs. Already, there had been the gradual concession of rights

> ## AUSTRALIA'S ADVANTAGES OVER THE UNITED STATES
>
> *In an 1819 book written to promote the development of Australia, William Charles Wentworth outlined the advantages that the continent's colonies could offer prospective immigrants that were superior to those of the United States.*
>
> These various advantages which this colony and its dependencies offer for emigration, have many points of superiority over any to which the United States of America can lay claim; if we even admit the truth of all that the most enthusiastic admirers of that country have written, respecting its flourishing condition. Mr. [Morris] Birbeck, whose "Letters," if not "Notes," contain strong marks of an exaggerated anticipation of their resources and capabilities, has not, though evidently under the influence of feelings quite incompatible with a correct and disinterested judgment, ventured to rate his imaginary maximum of the profit to be derived from farming in the Illinois (which appears to be the principal magnet of attraction possessed by the United States) so high as I have proved by a calculation, to which I defy any one to attach the character of hyperbolical, that the investment of capital in the growth of fine wool in this colony will infallibly produce. This too, although certainly the most inviting and extensive channel of enterprize which it contains, is not its only ground of preference: it has many temptations besides for emigration, of which the United States are wholly destitute: among these the following are perhaps the most considerable.
>
> First, Any person of respectability upon emigrating to this colony, is given as much land as would cost him four hundred pounds in the United States.
>
> Secondly, He is allowed as many servants as he may require; and the wages which he is bound to pay them, are not one third the amount of the price of labour in America.
>
> Thirdly, He, his family and servants, are victualled at the expence of the government for six months.
>
> These are three considerations of great importance to the emigrant, and quite peculiar to this colony: added to which the value of the produce of this gratuitous land and labour is three times as great as in the Illinois. . . .
>
> *Source:* William Charles Wentworth, *Statistical, Historical, and Political Description of the Colony of New South Wales . . .* (London, 1819).

wealthy emancipists. In addition, the emancipists moderated their desire for a liberal franchise, recognizing that such a franchise might be a threat to their wealth. In other words, the emancipists and exclusives now found a common enemy in the Colonial Office, with James Macarthur and William Charles Wentworth leading the agitation for representative government and autonomy.

With the cessation of transportation to New South Wales in 1840, even more rights were conceded to the colony. The Constitution Act of 1842 enlarged the Legislative Council to thirty-six members, twenty-four of whom were elected. Wentworth became one of these twenty-four when he was elected to the council in 1843. In the council, Wentworth led the pastoralists in their struggle for a change in land policy. He and his fellow squatters wanted to protect their interests in the land, which they proposed to do by maintaining control of the Legislative Council and having control of crown lands transferred to the council.

The council remained Wentworth's forum of activity for the rest of his time in Australia. He remained popular with the pastoralists, but his standing with the majority of New South Welshmen declined. Determined to protect their economic interests, the pastoralists continued to control the Legislative Council. When the colony was authorized to draw up its own constitution during the early 1850's, Wentworth became the chairman of the select committee that drafted the constitution. In that document, the pastoralists attempted to maintain their control over affairs by a restrictive franchise and by requiring a two-thirds majority to amend the constitution.

Wentworth wanted to go even further and establish a hereditary peerage, which would serve as the upper house of the bicameral legislature. This proposed aristocracy did not survive the debates in the Legislative Council, and the British government struck out the two-thirds provision. Nevertheless, Wentworth and his col-

to the colony. An advisory legislative council of between five and seven official members had been established in 1823, and that council had been increased to fifteen members in 1828, with seven of the fifteen being unofficial members. With the diminution of the convict percentage of the population and the abolition of land grants, there was a reorientation from social and political concerns to economic and political matters.

This new focus brought Wentworth, the former emancipist leader, into alliance with his exclusivist antagonist, James Macarthur. The exclusives had previously desired a nominated Legislative Council but were willing to accept an elective one in order to win over the leagues had given to New South Wales a constitution that provided for control over their own domestic affairs. Wentworth had accomplished his goal of giving a free constitution to his country. Having done so, he retired from active affairs and spent the rest of his life in Great Britain, where he died in 1872. His body was returned to Australia, where it was interred on his estate at Vaucluse.

SIGNIFICANCE

On the surface, it appears that William Charles Wentworth changed his principles in mid-life; in reality, he was consistent. He was never a democrat, although his support of the emancipists caused many to look upon him as a believer in equality. He did not believe in distinctions made on the basis of birth, but he actively promoted distinctions made on the basis of ability. His support of the emancipists and then of the pastoralists is not, therefore, contradictory but rather consistent. The pastoralists had demonstrated their ability, and not all of them had come from the respectable class. The true measure of a person was not birth but what a person accomplished in life.

In keeping with Wentworth's support of ability was his commitment to education. If people were to develop to their fullest potential, and if New South Welshmen were to make free institutions work, education was essential. Wentworth was at least partly responsible for the establishment of the first real system of primary education in New South Wales. He was also a leader in the establishment of the University of Sydney and served on its original senate.

—*Albert A. Hayden*

FURTHER READING

Byrnes, John V. "William Charles Wentworth and the Continuity of Australian Literature." *Australian Letters*, April, 1963: 10-18. A discussion of Wentworth's role in the origin of Australian literature.

Clark, C. M. H. *A History of Australia*. 4 vols. Carlton, Vic.: Melbourne University Press, 1962-1978. Aside from being a detailed account of Australian history covering the period of Wentworth's political career, this volume provides almost the equivalent of a biography of Wentworth.

Green, H. M. "Wentworth as Orator." *Journal of the Royal Australian Historical Society* 21 (1935): 337-360. A sympathetic presentation of Wentworth as politician and speaker.

Hughes, Robert. *The Fatal Shore: The Epic of Australia's Founding*. New York: Alfred A. Knopf, 1987. A delightful book that gives a thorough account of convict life in Australia. Particularly useful for the discussion of the emancipist-exclusive controversy.

Jose, Arthur. *Builders and Pioneers of Australia*. London: J. M. Dent and Sons, 1928. Jose's sketch of Wentworth is a useful account of his life and work. Jose explicitly states that D'Arcy Wentworth was probably guilty of highway robbery and that friends arranged for him to leave Great Britain.

Melbourne, A. C. V. *Early Constitutional Development in Australia: New South Wales, 1788-1856*. 2d ed. London: Oxford University Press, 1963. The standard work dealing with constitutional agitation and the grant of responsible government.

_____. *William Charles Wentworth*. Brisbane, Qld.: Biggs, 1934. This is an expansion of the John Murtagh Macrossan Lectures for 1932. The book has to be used with caution, particularly with regard to Wentworth's birth. The interpretation of Wentworth presented by Melbourne is, however, the basis of all later interpretations.

Ritchie, John. *The Wentworths: Father and Son*. Carlton South, Vic.: Miegunyah Press, 1997. Chronicles the lives of W. C. Wentworth and his father, D'Arcy Wentworth, describing how D'Arcy reestablished himself to further his son's career.

Ward, John Manning. *James Macarthur: Colonial Conservative, 1798-1867*. Sydney: Sydney University Press, 1981. A biography by a sound scholar. Because of the relations, both unfriendly and friendly, between Macarthur and Wentworth, the references to Wentworth, which are based on research in the Wentworth papers, are extremely useful.

Wood, F. L. "Some Early Educational Problems, and W. C. Wentworth's Work for Higher Education." *Journal of Royal Australian Historical Society* 17 (1931): 368-394. A discussion of the impact of religion on education and of Wentworth's contribution to the founding of Sydney University.

SEE ALSO: Sir Edmund Barton; Alfred Deakin; Daniel Mannix; Sir Henry Parkes.

RELATED ARTICLES in *Great Events from History: The Nineteenth Century, 1801-1900:* 1851: Gold Is Discovered in New South Wales; 1868: Last Convicts Land in Western Australia.

GEORGE WESTINGHOUSE
American inventor

An ingenious inventor and a shrewd entrepreneur, Westinghouse developed mechanical and electrical inventions that permitted the United States to emerge as a major industrial nation during the late nineteenth century. His inventions include the air brake, signaling systems, and other important innovations for railroads, and as an entrepreneur he supported the creation of electric light and power systems, using alternating current.

BORN: October 6, 1846; Central Bridge, New York
DIED: March 12, 1914; New York, New York
AREA OF ACHIEVEMENT: Science and technology

EARLY LIFE

George Westinghouse was the eighth child in a family of ten. His mother, Emaline Vedder, was of Dutch-English stock, while his father, George Westinghouse, Sr., was German. A mechanic and an inventor, George, Sr., operated a machine shop in Schenectady, New York, where he manufactured agricultural equipment, mill machinery, and small steam engines. Along with his brothers, young George received most of his education by working in his father's shop. Although he briefly attended Union College in Schenectady in 1865, he soon decided that he preferred to learn by experimenting with machines rather than by reading books. Throughout his career, Westinghouse perfected his many inventions by drawing more on his mechanical skills than on any formal training in science or engineering.

At the outbreak of the Civil War, Westinghouse was anxious to set out on his own and win glory as a soldier. Though only fourteen, he attempted to run away and join the army, only to be stopped by his stern father. Two years later, he overcame his father's opposition and enlisted as a private. After passing a competitive examination in 1864, he transferred to the United States Navy and became an engineering officer. While serving on board ship, Westinghouse installed a small lathe, which he used to fashion various gadgets.

After the war, Westinghouse returned to work for his father but devoted his free time to invention. In 1865, he received his first patent, for a rotary steam engine that was an improvement over the common reciprocating (up and down) engines then in use. Rather than put this invention into production, however, Westinghouse was soon attracted by the challenges of improving railroad technology. Because of their scale of operations and importance to American business, railroads offered the greatest technological challenges and, consequently, attracted creative and ambitious Americans during the late nineteenth century.

After witnessing a train accident in which a number of cars were derailed, Westinghouse designed a car replacer that permitted repair crews to use a special set of rails to slide derailed cars back onto the main tracks. Joining with two local businesspeople, he began manufacturing his car replacer in Schenectady. Hoping that this new enterprise would succeed, Westinghouse married Marguerite Erskine Walker in 1867. However, Westinghouse did not prosper in Schenectady and his partners succeeded in pushing him out of the business. Disgusted, Westinghouse moved in 1868 to Pittsburgh, where he found a more cooperative group of business associates.

LIFE'S WORK

From the 1870's to the first decade of the twentieth century, Westinghouse was a major figure in Pittsburgh industry, designing numerous new products and establishing more than sixty different companies. Of his many inventions, perhaps the most original was the air brake. Shortly after he had perfected the car replacer, Westinghouse began giving serious thought to preventing accidents by developing better brakes for trains. At that time, trains were stopped by the engineer shutting off the locomotive and by brakemen in individual train cars applying mechanical brakes. With this arrangement, it was possible to bring a train to a scheduled stop at a station but it was impossible to stop in case of a sudden emergency. To remedy this, Westinghouse explored various mechanical and electrical schemes, all of which he found unreliable.

By chance, Westinghouse happened to read a magazine article about how compressed air was being used in boring the Mount Cenis tunnel in the Italian Alps. Inspired by this article, Westinghouse designed a brake system consisting of a series of brakes in each individual car, all of which were powered by an air compressor in the locomotive. By opening or closing a single valve, the engineer could apply the brakes throughout the train and bring the train to a quick stop. Westinghouse patented this device in 1869 and established the Westinghouse Air Brake Company. For the next two decades, Westinghouse continued to improve this invention, so that by

1890 it was the standard braking system used on all American trains. Not satisfied with the national market, Westinghouse went on to establish factories worldwide, and soon his air brakes were to be found on trains in Europe, Australia, and Russia.

Experience with the air brake led Westinghouse to develop other inventions for the railroad industry. To keep train cars from crashing into one another when the train was stopped, he perfected friction draft gear. To help coordinate the movement of numerous trains on railroad networks, Westinghouse designed an improved signaling system in which electricity and compressed air were used to control signals along the track. To manufacture his signaling system, Westinghouse organized the Union Switch and Signal Company in 1881 and hired a number of talented engineers.

Drawing on this team of engineers, Westinghouse decided in 1884 to plunge into the newly emerging field of electric lighting. At this time, the electrical industry was dominated by Thomas Alva Edison, who had perfected the incandescent lamp and a distribution system using direct current (DC). To compete with Edison, Westinghouse bought up the patents of other inventors and had his engineering staff convert the patents into successful products. Following this strategy, Westinghouse purchased the patents for an incandescent lamp and dynamo from William Stanley, an alternating current (AC) transformer from Lucien Gaulard and John Gibbs in Europe, and an AC motor from Nikola Tesla.

Working with Stanley and Tesla, Westinghouse engineers combined these individual inventions into a coherent system of light and power using AC. Perceiving this new system as a threat to his DC technology, Edison attacked the Westinghouse system, claiming that the high voltages used with AC would lead to unnecessary accidents and death by electrocution. In response to this attack, Westinghouse steadfastly maintained that his system was safe; to demonstrate its great potential, he undertook an impressive installation at the 1893 Chicago World's Fair.

At the fair, twenty-four giant AC generators delivered power safely to one hundred thousand lamps, which lit up the fair buildings in a spectacular fashion. Although the Chicago installation impressed the general public, Westinghouse convinced professional engineers of the value of his system by using AC to harness and transmit the tremendous power of Niagara Falls in 1896. Largely as a consequence of Westinghouse's entrepreneurial vision and the skill of his engineers, America came to enjoy the benefits of AC power.

The success of the Chicago and Niagara installations ensured that the Westinghouse Electric Company (organized in 1886) would grow and prosper. Rather than manufacture only AC equipment, however, Westinghouse encouraged this company to introduce new products. Drawing on his extensive experience with the railroads, he and his engineers developed both electric streetcars and locomotives. This work led the Westinghouse Company to build large-scale generating equipment and special motors for the New York subway system and to undertake the electrification of the New York, New Haven, and Hartford railroads in 1906.

Still fascinated by steam engines, Westinghouse purchased the patent rights to the steam turbine perfected by the English inventor Charles A. Parsons. Under his direction, the horizontal steam turbine was adapted first for use in electric generating stations in 1900 and then to power ships in 1912. Much more efficient than the reciprocating engine, the steam turbine has been used extensively in both nuclear power plants and steamships. Westinghouse acquired some 360 patents for these many inventions.

George Westinghouse. (National Archives)

In developing his inventions, Westinghouse moved easily from the machine shop, where he often worked with his hands, to the boardroom, where he met with financiers and businesspeople from around the world. In both contexts, his physical appearance and intellectual power commanded immediate attention. Photographs taken at the height of his career reveal a tall, portly man with a strong face and a walrus mustache. Generally soft-spoken and patient, he expressed dissatisfaction by raising his large right hand and quietly saying, "But you don't understand"; such an admonition from Westinghouse was usually enough to change the mind of any opponent.

From his earliest days as a manufacturer, Westinghouse took a special interest in the welfare of his employees. He was among the first major employers in the United States to give his men a half day off on Saturday. In 1889, when the Westinghouse Air Brake Company moved to Wilmerding, fourteen miles east of Pittsburgh, Westinghouse built a new town, complete with houses, churches, schools, and parks. With regard to his professional staff, Westinghouse advised his executive vice president, "I want you to employ none but gentlemen." In general, he succeeded in hiring only honest and hard-working young engineers, and many of the technical achievements of the Westinghouse organization can be attributed to Westinghouse's ability to hire, supervise, and motivate a strong engineering staff.

Although Westinghouse amassed a large fortune from his many inventions and enterprises, he generally regarded money as a resource for future projects and invested much of his money back into his companies. Throughout his career, he was always at work and seldom indulged in luxuries such as vacations. In 1913, however, at the first signs of a heart condition, his physician prescribed rest, and the great inventor reluctantly retired to his estate in Lenox, Massachusetts. To occupy himself, Westinghouse occasionally went fishing in a nearby pond. One day, his rowboat capsized and he was thrown into the chilly water. In the course of this accident, he strained his heart and caught a severe cold from which he never recovered. He died quietly in New York City on March 12, 1914. Curious and creative to the end, he spent his last days designing an electrically operated wheelchair, which he intended to use during his convalescence.

SIGNIFICANCE

As an inventor and entrepreneur, Westinghouse helped bring about a series of profound changes in American business and technology. When he began his career during the late 1860's, most American business firms were small-scale partnerships or family enterprises, employing at most a few hundred people. With the exception of the railroads, most technology was personal and familiar, developed and used by average Americans in small workshops and on family farms. By the time Westinghouse died in 1914, American industry was dominated by huge corporations with thousands of workers. By then, American technology was characterized by gigantic plants using complex machines and large amounts of electric power. Based on science, this new technology was essential yet incomprehensible to most Americans.

Westinghouse contributed to these fundamental changes in American business and technology by combining the strengths of the nineteenth century with the opportunities of the twentieth century. From his father's generation, he had learned about technology by working with his hands, and he used his skills as a machinist to perfect remarkable new devices such as the air brake and the steam turbine. From the past, he also carried forward a personal and fatherly concern for his workers, which translated into a policy of decent working conditions and which elicited deep respect from his employees. Finally, he was one of the last heroic entrepreneurs who insisted on presiding over all aspects of business. Westinghouse refused to specialize or delegate authority and took a lively interest not only in invention but also in finance, manufacture, and marketing.

However, Westinghouse was not simply a nineteenth century figure: He was also a visionary who vigorously shaped the business and technology of the twentieth century. He correctly perceived that as American industry expanded rapidly, it would require a better transportation network as well as new sources of power; consequently, he concentrated on improving railroad technology and introducing AC power. Although a craftsperson himself, he saw clearly that new technology would be continually improved through the application of science and he did not hesitate to hire college-trained engineers and scientists. Finally, like other twentieth century industrialists, Westinghouse realized that American business must serve both national and international markets, leading him to create several large, well-organized corporations with branches worldwide.

Thus, in the broadest sense, Westinghouse was a transitional figure in American business and technology. Through his personality and career, one can see how traditional nineteenth century values and practices were used to shape the modern industrial world of twentieth century America.

—W. Bernard Carlson

FURTHER READING

American Society of Mechanical Engineers. *George Westinghouse Commemoration*. New York: Author, 1937. Consists of papers given by leading engineers on the occasion of the ninetieth anniversary of the birth of Westinghouse. Although the papers are anecdotal, they provide valuable details about Westinghouse's personality and accomplishments.

Chandler, Alfred D., Jr. *The Visible Hand: The Managerial Revolution in American Business*. Cambridge, Mass.: Harvard University Press, 1977. Provides a broad overview of the changes occurring in American business and technology during the period in which Westinghouse was active.

Hughes, Thomas P. *Networks of Power: Electrification in Western Society, 1880-1930*. Baltimore: Johns Hopkins University Press, 1983. Discusses the role of Westinghouse in developing AC for use in electrical utilities.

Jonnes, Jill. *Empires of Light: Edison, Tesla, Westinghouse, and the Race to Electrify the World*. New York: Random House, 2003. Explains how the three inventors sought to create businesses that would provide safe, reliable electricity. Jonnes describes the inventions and careers of Westinghouse, Edison, and Tesla, and relates how they worked with bankers, lawyers, and financiers to create electrical "empires."

Leupp, Francis E. *George Westinghouse: His Life and Achievements*. Boston: Little, Brown, 1918. Though lively and entertaining, this biography contains many conversations made up by the author. Although accurate for general information, it should be used cautiously.

Moran, Richard. *Executioner's Current: Thomas Edison, George Westinghouse, and the Invention of the Electric Chair*. New York: A. A. Knopf, 2002. Chronicles the battle between Westinghouse and Edison over the source of power for the electric chair. After Edison suggested that Westinghouse's AC power this new form of execution, Westinghouse fought back, fearful of the negative stigma this would cause his business.

Passer, Harold C. *The Electrical Manufacturers: 1875-1900*. Cambridge, Mass.: Harvard University Press, 1953. Includes a full history of the Westinghouse Electric Company and its efforts to develop and promote AC.

Prout, Henry G. *A Life of George Westinghouse*. London: Benn Brothers, 1922. Reprint. New York: Arno Press, 1972. Commissioned by the American Society of Mechanical Engineers, this biography includes detailed descriptions of Westinghouse's inventions as well as a list of his patents. A business associate of Westinghouse, Prout provides insight into Westinghouse as financier and manufacturer. This is generally regarded as the standard biography of Westinghouse.

Usselman, Steven W. "Air Brakes for Freight Trains: Technological Innovation in the American Railroad Industry, 1869-1900." *Business History Review* 58 (Spring, 1984): 30-50. The best single source available on how Westinghouse developed and promoted the air brake.

Wilmerding and the Westinghouse Air Brake Company. Charleston, S.C.: Arcadia, 2002. A history of the company and its impact upon Wilmerding, the southwest Pennsylvania town where Westinghouse's air brake business was based.

SEE ALSO: Thomas Alva Edison; Étienne Lenoir; Charles Proteus Steinmetz; Joseph Wilson Swan; Nikola Tesla.

RELATED ARTICLES in *Great Events from History: The Nineteenth Century, 1801-1900:* May 1-October 30, 1893: Chicago World's Fair; December 15, 1900: General Electric Opens Research Laboratory.

JAMES MCNEILL WHISTLER
American painter

Aside from producing one of the most popular and best-known paintings in the world, Whistler developed an artistic style and ideas about the role of the artist that were to influence art and art criticism throughout the world.

BORN: July 10, 1834; Lowell, Massachusetts
DIED: July 17, 1903; London, England
ALSO KNOWN AS: James Abbott McNeill Whistler
(full name)
AREA OF ACHIEVEMENT: Art

EARLY LIFE

James Abbott McNeill Whistler was born in Massachusetts, but he claimed a variety of other birthplaces. For example, in a 1878 libel trial in London in which he sued the famous art critic John Ruskin, he thought to add glamour to his case by claiming that he had been born in St. Petersburg, Russia. On other occasions, because of his family ties to the American South, he claimed Baltimore as his birthplace. He was, however mundane it might have seemed to him, actually born in Lowell, Massachusetts, the son of George Whistler, a respected and successful engineer of Irish-English descent who had been educated at West Point and who built railroads in the United States and in Russia for the czar. Anna McNeill, George Whistler's second wife (his first died young), a member of a North Carolina family of Scottish lineage, was James's mother and was to be the subject of his famous painting.

It was while living in Russia with his family that young Whistler first showed artistic leanings; he took drawing lessons at the Imperial Academy of Science. The Whistler family, at the height of its prosperity, traveled well and extensively in Europe. For extended periods, most of the family lived in England, while George Whistler was occupied with his work in Russia, where he died in his late forties.

Whistler's family, now somewhat limited financially, returned to the United States, and Whistler, by then a young man, entered the United States Military Academy at West Point in 1851. A charming but willful and mischievous teenager, he made little attempt to conform to the disciplines of the academy and, in 1854, he was asked to leave. Through family connections, he was hired as a draftsman by the Winans Locomotive Works in Baltimore, but he was too eccentric in his working habits and had to withdraw. He moved on to a job with the United

States Coast Survey in Washington, where he again fell afoul of the system and was forced to resign. He did, however, gain valuable experience in etching at the survey office, and it was to be one of his strengths as an artist.

At the age of twenty-one, Whistler left the United States to study in Paris. He was supposed to study at the respectable, conservative École des Beaux-Arts, but he became a student in the more informal *atelier* system, in which pupils worked with individual artists. He entered the raucous, improper world of the Parisian art students with enthusiasm and was soon a close friend of Gustave Courbet and Henri Fantin-Latour. He met and associated with all the young painters who were to become the leaders in the Impressionist movement.

In 1859, having finished his education as a student artist, Whistler moved from Paris to London, where he was determined to make his career and where he was to live, save for occasional absences, for the rest his life.

LIFE'S WORK

In 1890, Whistler published a collection of his letters under the title *The Gentle Art of Making Enemies*. The title was no exaggeration, because his career had been one battle after another. England always had a difficult time with this upstart from the United States.

The English public had an established and confident taste for narrative pictures, usually of a high technical quality, when Whistler arrived in London. From the beginning, Whistler, influenced partly by his French experience and partly by his own natural gifts and inclinations, refused to paint moral tales of middle-class life or to follow the Pre-Raphaelites in creating an idealized medieval dreamworld, and he was not reluctant to make fun of painters who did so. Witty, acerbic, always saucily inclined to quarrel, he was not above punching his enemies. He fought in the streets, in the courts, and always in the newspapers and magazines, and he became one of the great "characters" of the world of English arts and letters.

What made him even more difficult to deal with, if one tried to do so, was his undependability as an artist, his maddening slowness, his too-common failure to deliver work, often long-since paid for. Smartly, if eccentrically, dressed, a neat slip of a man sporting a monocle, known for his series of mistresses and for never getting anything done, he had a difficult time financially. Influential figures such as Gabriel Rossetti befriended him, but he gained more enemies than friends.

If Whistler's personality was wildly improper, his art was quite the contrary. His work was low-keyed, lacking in definition, often unrealistically flat, and he tended to use few colors. In France, he might have had an easier time of it as he might have been seen in the context of his associations with Courbet, Edgar Degas, and Édouard Manet. He was not, however, really an Impressionist, because he was interested in rendering not reality but the artist's reaction to it. His paintings were, as the critics complained, meaningless, and Whistler happily agreed with that comment.

The French influence and Whistler's longtime interest in Japanese and Chinese art fused with his own talent for seeing a work of art as independent of its source, as an arrangement of mass and color. He was trying to achieve pattern, tonality, feeling. His landscapes, often night scenes, puzzled the British, who could not accept the lack of detail, the muzzy, muted colors, the seemingly sloppy draftsmanship. Even his portraits looked fuzzy, and he often quarreled with his sitters since he would not give them an idealized mirror image. What things really looked like, or ideally looked like, was irrelevant to Whistler.

Whistler's famous work, which everyone knows as "Whistler's Mother," was, in fact, called *Arrangement in Grey and Black, No. 1: The Artist's Mother*. As conservative as it seems, this painting was originally rejected by the Royal Academy in 1872, was accepted only by special arrangement, and was roundly derided by the critics. His titles for his paintings, which he called "nocturnes" and "arrangements" and numbered according to color groups, were original and confusing. When he did something well, he would do it in irritating ways. His famous *Harmony in Blue and Gold: The Peacock Room* (1867-1877) was a masterpiece of interior decoration, but Whistler produced it in a way that permanently alienated his patron. Savaged unfairly by Ruskin in print, Whistler sued the critic and won, but the jury would give him only a farthing, and the case forced him into bankruptcy.

The Ruskin case did produce one of Whistler's most famous comments upon the plight of the artist. He admitted that the painting commented upon by Ruskin had taken only a short time to paint. The lawyer questioning him suggested that the price that he had asked for it was high, given the time it took to produce. Whistler's rejoinder was to become famous: "I ask it for the knowledge of a lifetime."

This capacity to talk wittily about his art was to become an important part of Whistler's reputation, and he was to defend himself and his ideas of art and the artists in print as well. His pamphlet *Whistler v. Ruskin: Art and Art Critics* (1878), based in part on his experiences in the Ruskin trial, was a great success, and during the 1880's, still very much an outsider and still a magnet for financial and legal trouble, he gradually became accepted by the British intelligentsia. In 1881, the famous painting of his mother was shown in Philadelphia and New York, although no major gallery in the United States or Europe owned a Whistler.

A following of young British artists started to develop around the painter during the mid-1880's, and he often spoke in public in London with some considerable success. Even the students at the Royal Academy invited him to address them, and he was asked to speak at Cambridge University.

James McNeill Whistler. (Library of Congress)

In 1891, the tide turned. The Corporation of the City of Glasgow purchased his fine portrait of the Scottish man of letters Thomas Carlyle, and more telling, the Louvre purchased his *Arrangement in Grey and Black, No. 1*, and France made him an Officer of the Legion of Honor. For the first time in his life, there was a sustained demand for his work at prices that allowed him to settle his debts and buy a home in Paris. In Great Britain, there was criticism of the fact that Whistler, that most estimable representative of British contemporary art, was not represented in the major galleries; art society in the United States also started to take him seriously.

Charles Freer, the Detroit locomotive manufacturer, became a friend of Whistler during the 1890's and used his considerable fortune to collect slowly the works that were to be the basis for the finest collection of Whistler in the world, housed in an elegant gallery on the Mall in Washington and bearing Freer's name, but holding the treasures of Whistler's vision.

Financially secure, his reputation and popularity as a painter and as a spokesperson for the artist growing, Whistler continued to work sporadically through the decade, moving back and forth between London and Paris. He was no less inclined to quarrel than he had been when everyone rejected him in his youth, and he was continually in and out of the law courts and the gossip columns. For a time, he was involved, if only slightly, in an art school in Paris, and he never fully gave up working and sometimes finishing small portraits (sold at high prices). To the end, his charm and wit were in nervous balance with his zest for vindictive confrontation. He died in his studio in London one afternoon in 1903, while waiting for Charles Freer to take him for a drive.

SIGNIFICANCE

It is, perhaps, best to consider Whistler as a cultural phenomenon whose work and influence went far beyond his skills as a painter. His fierce independence and his determination to do things his way in the face of sometimes damaging artistic, financial, and personal consequences may be seen as an example of the American abroad, a man refusing to be either patronized or instructed by his European betters. It is, however, unwise to put too much emphasis upon his American personality, because he himself was so little interested in his native country and spent most of his life fighting his way into the European artistic community. He was proud of his American birth, his southern family connections, and even his West Point education (he seemed conveniently to forget that he had been virtually expelled), but his world was European.

In that world, however, he showed eventually that it was unwise to take him for granted intellectually or artistically as the poor American cousin, and he made major contributions to the way in which the public was to look at art, producing in his own work and in his public statements ideas that were to undermine the proposition that art's function was merely to mirror reality. He was, also, an important influence on the idea of "art for art's sake," and he showed that the artist had rights as well as obligations and was ready to fight for them.

Whistler's interest in and use of French and Asian influences in his own work were to lead many young English artists out of the insularity of the British tradition in art. In literature, the Symbolist poets, many of whom he knew personally, were influenced by him, and aspects of his style can be seen later in the work of T. S. Eliot and Ezra Pound, both American poets who chose to live and work in Europe in much the same way that Whistler had done. His use of musical terms as titles for his paintings came full circle in Claude Debussy, who admired him and whose style was in some ways a musical version of what Whistler was trying to achieve pictorially. The idea of "tone," the attempt to express the deepest, most delicate emotional ambiguities, a concept that became so common in art at the end of the nineteenth century, owed much to Whistler's quiet, dimly glowing paintings and to his combative declamations in the salons and law courts of London.

George du Maurier, an early friend, tried to include him as a character in the novel *Trilby* (1894), and Whistler enlisted the courts to get him out, but he lives on in novels by Henry James and Marcel Proust, who hardly had to fictionalize him.

—Charles H. Pullen

FURTHER READING

Anderson, Ronald, and Anne Koval. *James McNeill Whistler: Beyond the Myth*. London: J. Murray, 1994. Biography, recounting Whistler's life and work. The authors describe how Whistler's work was a bridge between British and French art and between traditional art and modernism.

Curry, David Park. *James McNeill Whistler: Uneasy Pieces*. New York: Quantuck Lane Press, 2004. Eight essays analyze Whistler's art, describing its influences and impact, and how Whistler combined his aesthetics with a flair for showmanship.

Fleming, Gordon. *The Young Whistler, 1834-66*. London: George Allen and Unwin, 1978. An exploration of the early years, with considerable use of French materials, letters, critiques, and journals. Whistler was a proficient linguist, and his letters to and from French friends, including Fantin-Latour, are used extensively.

Gregory, Horace. *The World of James McNeill Whistler.* New York: Thomas Nelson and Sons, 1959. Whistler is best understood in the labyrinthine context of his artistic and social connections. Gregory modestly eschews any attempt to be definitive, but he makes some sensitive points of connection between Whistler's art and his peculiar personality. A lively account.

Pennell, E. R., and Joseph Pennell. *The Life of James McNeill Whistler.* 2 vols. Philadelphia: J. B. Lippincott, 1908. The monumental biography by the husband and wife who became camp followers of Whistler in his last years. Essential reading, but highly prejudiced in Whistler's favor. Good selection of pictures in monochrome.

Spalding, Frances. *Whistler.* New York: E. P. Dutton and Phaidon, 1979. A short, handy study with good photographs and excellent reproductions.

Spencer, Robin. *James McNeill Whistler.* London: Tate, 2003. An examination of Whistler's art, describing how he was influenced by the poetry and literature of his time and by the British and French art scenes.

Sutton, Denys. *Nocturne: The Art of James McNeill Whistler.* Philadelphia: J. B. Lippincott, 1964. A good study of the development of his art, placing it and his ideas in the contemporary world.

Weintraub, Stanley. *Whistler: A Biography.* New York: Weybright and Talley, 1974. A graceful and entertaining retelling of the lunatic life of Whistler; as good as any novel.

SEE ALSO: Aubrey Beardsley; Thomas Carlyle; Gustave Courbet; Hiroshige; Henry James; Édouard Manet; John Ruskin; John Singer Sargent.

RELATED ARTICLES in *Great Events from History: The Nineteenth Century, 1801-1900:* Fall, 1848: Pre-Raphaelite Brotherhood Begins; May 15, 1863: Paris's Salon des Refusés Opens.

WALT WHITMAN
American poet

The first true poet of American English, Whitman created a language to express the spirit of American democracy and used that language to shape a vision of a new continent that still fires the American imagination.

BORN: May 31, 1819; West Hills, New York
DIED: March 26, 1892; Camden, New Jersey
ALSO KNOWN AS: Walter Whitman, Jr. (full name)
AREA OF ACHIEVEMENT: Literature

EARLY LIFE

Walt Whitman was born in a two-story, cedar-shingled house that his father had built about thirty miles east of New York City on Long Island. He was born in the same year as his fellow writers Herman Melville and James Russell Lowell. His father's family, as he recalled them, "appear to have been always of democratic and heretical tendencies." Walter Whitman, Sr., had been born on the day of the storming of the Bastille in France in 1789 and trained his sons as radical democrats, identifying with independent farmers and laborers and regarding financiers and power brokers as "the enemy." His mother's family

were of Dutch ancestry, inclined to the freethinking tradition of the Quakers, and Whitman ascribed his creative impulses to her nonbookish sense of practical learning. He felt that her combination of the "practical and the materialistic" with the "transcendental and cloudy" might be the source of his own contradictory instincts.

The family moved from the rural regions of Long Island to Brooklyn in 1823. Already a bustling market town, Brooklyn was the third largest city in the United States by 1855 with a population of 200,000. The elder Whitman hoped to make a fortune in real estate, but he lacked the shrewdness to prosper in a speculative arena, and the Whitman family moved about once every year for the next decade.

A mediocre student but an avid reader, young Walt went to work for the *Long Island Patriot*, a local newspaper, at the age of twelve in 1831. He became a journeyman printer, but a fire in the printing district forced him out of work, and a quarrel with his father ended the possibility of any work on the family farm. He took a series of jobs as a country schoolteacher between 1836 and 1841, but only a few of his quarter-year appointments were renewed. He established a warm relationship with many of his students, but his explosive temper and stubborn insistence on the validity of his ideas led to frequent clashes with the school authorities. Whitman moved back to New York City in 1841, but continued arguments with his father impelled him to take lodgings in a boardinghouse in lower Manhattan.

Between school assignments, Whitman had published his earliest known writing, an item entitled "Effects of Lightning," in the August 8, 1838, issue of the *Long Island Democrat*. The rather rough and motley group of people he met in the boardinghouse district became the models for some of the characters in his first novel, *Franklin Evans* (1842), the story of a farmer's apprentice from Long Island who comes to New York. Whitman also published about a dozen short stories—mostly in the manner of Edgar Allan Poe or Nathaniel Hawthorne—between 1841 and 1845, and while the stories are derivative and sentimental, his work during this time convinced him that he could be a writer.

Although Whitman continued to maintain close contact with his family, often acting as a third "parent" with his younger siblings, he was now an independent young man making his way in the world. He stood nearly six feet tall, weighed about 180 pounds, had large hands and feet, a broad nose, full lips, and in later life, a bristling beard.

Walt Whitman. (Library of Congress)

He walked with a confident stride, could leap easily aboard a moving Broadway stage, and appeared at ease with the rugged, masculine presence he projected. As his close friend John Burroughs observed, however, there was also "a curious feminine undertone in him which revealed itself in the quality of his voice, the delicate texture of his skin, the gentleness of his touch and ways."

By 1848, Whitman had worked for ten different newspapers, most prominently as the editor of the Brooklyn *Daily Eagle*, and was an active citizen in Brooklyn political affairs, even writing lumbering patriotic verse when the occasion required it. His involvement with the Democratic Party in Brooklyn drew him into the rapidly developing debate over slavery during the 1840's, and his stand on the explosive issue of free soil led to his firing in 1848 from the *Daily Eagle*. Through his contacts in the field of journalism, he was able to work briefly as an editor of the New Orleans *Crescent* while that paper was reorganized during the early part of 1848, his first trip to the South. Upon his return to New York, he rented a storefront in lower Manhattan with the plan of setting himself up as a kind of lecturer and "universal authority," a "Professor of Things in General" like the hero of Thomas Carlyle's *Sartor Resartus* (1833-1834), a book he found fascinating. Apparently, there was no public demand for his wisdom.

During the late 1840's and the early 1850's, Whitman continued with real estate work, renovating buildings with his family, including considerable carpentry work. He enjoyed the swirl of intellectual life in New York, counting young painters, actors, and writers among his friends. He attended numerous lectures (including Ralph Waldo Emerson's famous address "The Poet"), kept up with original theories in the sciences (phrenology, hydrology), studied archaeology as an interested layman and would-be Egyptologist, debated new philosophical constructs (Fourierism), and listened enthusiastically to music of all sorts, from American folk music to the celebrated "Swedish Nightingale" Jenny Lind. He recalled these times as "days of preparation; the gathering of the forces"; the preparation he referred to was for the creation and publication of his masterpiece, *Leaves of Grass* (1855-1892).

LIFE'S WORK

Whitman claimed that he had begun "elaborating the plan of my poems . . . experimenting much, writing and abandoning much" in 1847, but his assertion that he began "definitely" writing the poems down in 1854 seems closest to the actual facts. The first "notes" that Whitman made for the poems usually consisted of flashes of illumination, revelations of the self and its relationship to the world. He had no guide for the form of these poems, regarding most of the prominent poets of his day as negative examples. Henry Wadsworth Longfellow's enormously popular *The Song of Hiawatha* (1855) he thought had, at best, a "pleasing ripply" effect. Whitman invented a style that was appropriate for his subject, demonstrating that form is an extension of content or an expression of content, and proving the wisdom of Henry David Thoreau's contention that American poetry is nothing but "healthy speech."

On May 15, 1855, just before his thirty-sixth birthday, Whitman registered the title *Leaves of Grass* and brought the copyright notice to the printing office of Thomas and Joseph Rome. He had been working steadily there throughout that spring, continuing to write and revise while he helped to set type and read the proofs. He not only wrote but also designed, produced, published, and eventually promoted the book that, as Justin Kaplan says, "for nearly forty years [he] made the center of his life, the instrument of health and survival itself." There were 795 copies of the first edition, and two hundred were bound in cloth at a unit cost to Whitman of thirty-two cents, while the remaining copies were given a cheaper binding. The manuscript remained in the Rome brothers' print shop until it was burned accidently in 1858 "to kindle the fire" as Whitman remarked laconically. On the frontispiece, there was a portrait, uncaptioned, of a bearded man, hand on his hip, hat rakishly askew. Ten pages of prose were followed by eighty-three of poetry, and on page 29, the anonymous author revealed himself:

Walt Whitman, an American, one of the roughs, a kosmos
Disorderly, fleshy and sensual . . . eating and drinking
and breeding

No sentimentalist . . . no stander above men and women or
apart from them . . . no more modest than immodest.

"O CAPTAIN! MY CAPTAIN!"

O Captain! my Captain! our fearful trip is done,
The ship has weather'd every rack, the prize we sought is won,
The port is near, the bells I hear, the people all exulting,
While follow eyes the steady keel, the vessel grim and daring;
But O heart! heart! heart!
O the bleeding drops of red,
Where on the deck my Captain lies,
Fallen cold and dead.

O Captain! my Captain! rise up and hear the bells;
Rise up—for you the flag is flung—for you the bugle trills,
For you bouquets and ribbon'd wreaths—for you the shores a-crowding,
For you they call, the swaying mass, their eager faces turning;
Here Captain! dear father!
This arm beneath your head!
It is some dream that on the deck,
You've fallen cold and dead.

My Captain does not answer, his lips are pale and still,
My father does not feel my arm, he has no pulse nor will,
The ship is anchor'd safe and sound, its voyage closed and done,
From fearful trip the victor ship comes in with object won;
Exult O shores, and ring O bells!
But I with mournful tread,
Walk the deck my Captain lies,
Fallen cold and dead.

Source: Walt Whitman, *Leaves of Grass* (New York: H. M. Caldwell, 1900).

Whitman was a tireless champion of his own work, but of all of his acts of self-promotion, his most successful and in some senses his most audacious was his gift of *Leaves of Grass* to Ralph Waldo Emerson, the philosopher-poet king of American letters. Emerson replied from Concord, Massachusetts, on July 21, 1855, in a five-page tribute, in which he expressed his enthusiasm for the poetry and saluted the poet "at the beginning of a great career." Many other reviews were less generous, some extremely negative ("a mass of stupid filth"), but praise from people such as Henry David Thoreau, Charles Eliot Norton, and others was sufficient encouragement for the poet.

Whitman was already preparing the second edition of *Leaves of Grass* in 1855 and 1856, composing the first draft of his great poem "Crossing Brooklyn Ferry" (then known as "Sundown Poem") during this time. He continued to supply friendly journals with information about and anonymous reviews of his work, and supplemented his income by writing and selling articles to various newspapers. At Christmas, 1859, he published "Out of the Cradle Endlessly Rocking," then titled "A Child's Reminiscence," which was one of the new poems included in the 1860 edition.

Perhaps because of Emerson's compliments, a Boston publisher, Thayer and Eldridge, offered to produce the second edition of *Leaves of Grass*, and although Emerson cautioned Whitman about some of the sexually suggestive poetry (arguing that unimpeded sales of the book depended on public acceptance), Whitman felt that the book would have to stand as it was. "I have not lived to regret my Emerson no," he stated. He did discard the prose preface, retitled some of the poems, revised several and added 124 new ones, producing a thick volume of 456 pages, bound in orange cloth and stamped with symbolic devices. Now, he thought that *Leaves of Grass* was being "really published" for the first time. This time, the frontispiece was a portrait by a friend that presented Whitman wearing a coat, wide collar, expansive tie, and a grave, intent expression. The book's reception was important to Whitman, but events of a larger magnitude captured his attention.

In February, 1861, Whitman saw Abraham Lincoln, already a protoheroic image for him of the New Man of the West, when the president traveled up Broadway to stay at the Astor. In April of that year, 250,000 people filled the streets to welcome Major Robert Anderson, a soldier at Fort Sumter. The nation was moving toward civil war, and Whitman's admiration for Lincoln and his cause, plus his brother George's rather impetuous enlistment, tempted the poet himself momentarily to consider military service.

At the age of forty-two, Whitman recognized that he had neither the qualifications nor the disposition to be a soldier. Instead, his instinct for involvement in the great anguish of the Union, and his instinct to offer comfort to young men suffering, led him to New York hospitals, where he worked as a nurse (80 percent of the nurses were male). When his brother was wounded, he traveled to Virginia and shared mess and tent with George for a week. He was trying to earn a living by publishing occasional articles at this time, but when he returned to Washington, he wrote to Emerson that he had ended his "New York stagnation," and he began to try to find a government job. He spent the war years tending the wounded and casually seeking a political appointment, and in 1864, after a lifetime of exceptional health, he suffered a collapse as a result of stress, hypertension, and depression. He was never quite as vigorous again. He suc-

ceeded in obtaining a job as a government clerk in 1865, but after Lincoln's death, the new administration swept his friends out and he lost his job.

In October, 1865, Whitman published *Drum Taps*, including the poem "O Captain! My Captain!" his most successful poem during his lifetime, and the superb "When Lilacs Last in the Dooryard Bloom'd," the one poem not included in an anthology celebrating Lincoln a few years later. He was rehired by the government to work in the attorney general's office in 1866 and saw his good friend William O'Connor offer strong support for his work in a sixty-page pamphlet, *The Good Gray Poet* (1866), and in a positive review in *The New York Times*. His work was beginning to develop a favorable reputation in Europe that surpassed the public estimate of his accomplishments in the United States. As a kind of rejoinder to his old intellectual antagonist Carlyle, he published *Democratic Vistas* in 1871, agreeing with Carlyle's pessimistic view of the "present" but envisioning a positive future for his country. As a kind of poetic counterpart to *Democratic Vistas*, he also completed *Passage to India* (1871), in which he described materialistic concerns giving way to spiritual enlightenment.

Whitman suffered a stroke in January, 1873. His mother died in May of that year, a severe blow, and he was discharged from his government job in July. Another stroke occurred in February, 1875, but it did not keep Whitman from his enthusiastic plans for a centennial edition of *Leaves of Grass*, as well as readings and essays commemorating the event. His recollections of his wartime experiences were published in *Specimen Days and Collect* in 1882 and 1883, which also contained his thoughts on the natural world. In 1884, Whitman bought a house on Mickle Street in Camden, New Jersey, and slept under his own roof for the first time in his life. He lived there for eight years, remaining true to the emblem on his writing table, "Make the Works," through that time. In January, 1892, only two months before his death, he had prepared an announcement for what has become known as the "Death-Bed" edition of *Leaves of Grass*, and in his last years, he became, in the words of Allen Ginsberg, "lonely old courage teacher" to his friends and admirers.

SIGNIFICANCE

According to Justin Kaplan, *Leaves of Grass* contained "the most brilliant and original poetry yet written in the New World, at once the fulfillment of American literary romanticism and the beginnings of American literary modernism." As much as he contributed to American literature, however, Whitman's contributions to American cultural life were equally great. At a time when the arts in the United States were still held in a kind of patronizing thrall by European antecedents, Whitman claimed equality for American experience and demonstrated the dominion of singularly American creation. He liberated poetry from its narrow British inclination toward narrative and ode and closed the gap between poetry and its audience.

Similarly, Whitman resisted the tyranny of fashion by his insistence on the beauty of ordinary citizens of the republic and gave Americans a sense of the finest aspects of their own character through his definitive admiration for the open, easy, accepting nature of American life and social commerce. He celebrated the individual, saw the strength of the singular amid the surging crowds of American cities, and at the same time, caught the spirit of American pride in its growing industrial and technological might.

Whitman was reared a quasi-Quaker and followed no standard doctrine or specified religion, but his poetry is based on the best precepts of Christianity—a sympathy whose scope is universal and inclusive, stemming from a predisposition to love and understand. Nevertheless, he was also a kind of pagan, a lover of many gods, ecumenical and free of prejudice and bigotry in his writings, a feature all the more impressive for his personal struggle to overcome some of the more ingrained cultural assumptions of his day.

When the bridge near Camden was named for Whitman, objections from self-designated "Christians" and "Patriots" that Whitman's books were not properly moral echoed the criticism of his own time. Whitman's unabashed expressions of erotic ardor, especially the images of love emphasizing handsome young men, confounded the noxious Puritan strain still virulent in American life, but his sense of love, like his sense of religion, was not limited by any sectarian preference. Rather, his emphasis on social liberty, individual freedom, and artistic integrity, culminating in his archetypal image of the American nation always on the entrance of an open road, stands as a reminder of American strength as a country. As Guy Davenport says, Whitman has been woven into Americans' myth of themselves as their "greatest invention in literature" and as their "lyric voice." As his life and time fade into the glories of a heroic past, his poetry remains as an emblem of his country's beautiful innocence at the dawn of its creation.

—*Leon Lewis*

FURTHER READING

Allen, Gay Wilson. *The Solitary Singer: A Critical Biography of Walt Whitman*. New York: New York University Press, 1967. A good critical biography, the first one to connect the poet's life to his work. Comprehensive, if not exceptionally penetrating, it provides a sound overview of Whitman's life and his range as a poet.

Bloom, Harold, ed. *Walt Whitman*. Philadelphia: Chelsea House, 2003. One in a series of books aimed at literature students. Includes an introduction by Bloom, a brief biography of Whitman, and essays analyzing Whitman's poetry.

Brasher, Thomas L. *Whitman as Editor of the Brooklyn "Daily Eagle."* Detroit: Wayne State University Press, 1970. A thorough account of Whitman's work as a journalist, connecting his newspaper work to the social and political conditions of New York City and the country at large.

Davenport, Guy. "Whitman." In *The Geography of the Imagination*, edited by Guy Davenport. Berkeley, Calif.: North Point Press, 1981. An exceptionally imaginative and unusually empathetic essay that captures the sensibility of the poet and sets it amid the cultural context of Whitman's times.

Kaplan, Justin. *Walt Whitman: A Life*. New York: Simon & Schuster, 1980. An excellent biography, combining solid historic research with perceptive, revealing commentary, this is undoubtedly the definitive biography in the twentieth century. A Pulitzer Prize and National Book Award recipient, crucial for an understanding of Whitman's life and art.

Miller, James E., Jr., ed. *Walt Whitman's "Song of Myself": Origin, Growth, Meaning*. New York: Dodd, Mead, 1964. Detailed, competently academic interpretation of *Song of Myself*, demonstrating Whitman's interest in the development of the mystical tradition.

Reynolds, David S. *Walt Whitman*. New York: Oxford University Press, 2005. Brief overview of Whitman's life and his response to politics, theater, music, painting, photography, science, religion, sex, and other aspects of nineteenth century American culture.

Traubel, Horace. *With Walt Whitman in Camden*. Vol. 1. Boston: Small, Maynard, 1906.

_____. *With Walt Whitman in Camden*. Vol. 2. New York: D. Appleton, 1908.

_____. *With Walt Whitman in Camden*. Vol. 3. New York: M. Kennerly, 1914.

_____. *With Walt Whitman in Camden.* Vol. 4. Phila-delphia: University of Pennsylvania Press, 1953.

_____. *With Walt Whitman in Camden.* Vol. 5. Carbondale: Southern Illinois University Press, 1964. An account in five volumes (each published separately by a different company) by a close friend and companion of the poet's last years.

Whitman, Walt. *The Correspondence.* Edited by Edwin Haviland Miller. 6 vols. New York: New York University Press, 1961-1977. All the letters Whitman wrote that are available, plus solid scholarship that sets the context and explains the situation of their writing.

Zweig, Paul. *Walt Whitman: The Making of the Poet.* New York: Basic Books, 1984. Thoroughly researched and quite knowledgeable coverage of the period in Whitman's life between his employment with the Brooklyn *Daily Eagle* and the first publication of *Leaves of Grass.* An incisive tracing of the genesis of the poem.

SEE ALSO: Thomas Carlyle; Emily Dickinson; Charles William Eliot; Ralph Waldo Emerson; Nathaniel Hawthorne; Emma Lazarus; Abraham Lincoln; Jenny Lind; Henry Wadsworth Longfellow; Herman Melville; Edgar Allan Poe; Henry David Thoreau.

RELATED ARTICLES in *Great Events from History: The Nineteenth Century, 1801-1900:* November, 1828: Webster Publishes the First American Dictionary of English; November 5, 1850: Tennyson Becomes England's Poet Laureate.

JOHN GREENLEAF WHITTIER
American poet

Over a career spanning more than sixty years, Whittier produced a large body of poetry that was not only extremely popular in its own day but also reflected with remarkable clarity and consistency some of the cultural and social attitudes of nineteenth century America.

BORN: December 17, 1807; Haverhill, Massachusetts
DIED: September 7, 1892; Hampton Falls, New Hampshire
AREA OF ACHIEVEMENT: Literature

EARLY LIFE

The record of John Greenleaf Whittier's early life is almost a model of the American myth about the country boy who, through talent and diligence, comes to take his place among the leaders of his generation. The second of four children born to John and Abigail Whittier, John Greenleaf was reared on the family farm in northern Massachusetts. A secluded, lonely tract surrounded by low, rolling hills and forests, the farm sat amid the fertile Merrimack Valley, where the young poet spent his youth helping his father, uncle, and younger brother work the land.

Farm life had its moments of quiet, peaceful beauty, and, as the son of devout Quakers, young Whittier came to appreciate the emotional and religious security instilled by his rural surroundings. By fifteen, he was almost six feet tall and slender with dark, piercing eyes. A quiet boy, he enjoyed reading beside the kitchen fireplace, even dabbling in verses of his own. Besides the Bible, his favorite author was Robert Burns, the Scottish balladeer of the late eighteenth century.

The influence of Burns on Whittier's poetic taste and technique was to be indelible, from Whittier's early narrative and legendary poems of New England folklore to the later poetic reminiscences of his mature years. He later recalled, in numerous letters and essays, those early years on the farm when a Yankee peddler would arrive with dry goods for the family and a tale or two for the future poet.

In 1826, at the age of nineteen, Whittier published his first poem. "The Exile's Departure" appeared in *The Newberryport Free Press.* Generally regarded as a bad poem, it was Whittier's first venture into the two worlds that were to occupy him for most of his creative life: politics and poetry. The editor of *The Free Press* was William Lloyd Garrison, who was already establishing himself as an early opponent of slavery. Garrison recognized Whittier's literary talent and, in 1828, invited the young man to Boston, Massachusetts, to write for *The American Manufacturer.* These early efforts were mostly political editorials addressed to the laboring man and his fight for fair working conditions.

Over the next two years, Whittier produced a significant body of work—political editorials, book reviews, poems, sketches—and was gaining a reputation as an honest, fearless journalist. Whittier's Quaker heri-

John Greenleaf Whittier. (Library of Congress)

tage, in fact, played a crucial role in his development as a writer. Well liked, gentle, and dedicated, he was a lifelong pacifist and a conscientious supporter of social justice. By the early 1830's, the rumblings of the slavery issue were already being felt. Though he returned to the farm in 1829 and remained there to take care of the family after the death of his father in 1830, Whittier continued to write and work. His health, always brittle, broke down from the strain of overwork—he suffered continually from migraine headaches—but by 1832 he was writing regularly and had decided that politics were to be his serious calling, having concluded that political activity was the way to achieve moral and social reform.

LIFE'S WORK

Though Whittier's first book, *Legends of New-England*, was published in 1831, it was merely a hodgepodge of trite verse and light prose that added little to his reputation. Throughout the 1830's, Whittier's main focus was on the growing national concern with the issue of slavery. As early as 1833, he produced one of the earliest

manifestos on the cause of abolition. *Justice and Expediency*, a prose pamphlet, took the nation by storm, and Whittier became more famous as a propagandist in the cause of antislavery than as a poet. In December, 1833, he was elected to serve as a delegate to the National Anti-Slavery Convention in Philadelphia, Pennsylvania, a position that eventually led to his election to the Massachusetts legislature in 1835.

Amid his political life as a propagandist and legislator, he continued to produce poetry in support of his political ideals. The mid-1830's saw such antislavery poems as "Toussaint L'Ouverture," a brief account of a black revolutionary in Haiti who suffered treachery by Napoleon Bonaparte and died in chains. "The Slave Ships" of 1834 commemorated the drowning of dozens of African slaves who were thrown overboard from a French ship during an outbreak of contagion. "The Farewell of a Virginia Slave Mother" appeared in 1838 and anticipated, in some of its melodramatic images, the famous passages from Harriet Beecher Stowe's *Uncle Tom's Cabin* (1851).

The 1840's literally signaled a new era for Whittier. By faith (a Quaker), if not by disposition, he had been a zealous reformer and an active intellectual in the abolitionist cause, but with the growing "gentrification" of the country—a burgeoning middle class and a more literate public seeking "polite" literature—Whittier became more interested in celebrating the local and regional beauties of his own New England. However, he still wrote poems and essays in support of the antislavery movement. "Massachusetts to Virginia" (1843), for example, was a rebuke to "the Old Dominion" for coercing the state of Massachusetts to extradite an escaped slave.

Whittier's "The Christian Slave" (1843) was an angry denouncement of the hypocrisy involved in selling a slave who was considered more valuable for being a Christian. Alongside these indictments, whose bitter tone clearly shows the moral outrage of the poet, Whittier produced dozens of quiet, sunny poems of New England places, scenes, and characters. *Lays of My Home and Other Poems* appeared in 1843. A collection of ballads, New England legends, and nature poems, the book included the kind of work that was to establish Whittier as a major poet of his generation. "The Merrimack" was a reminiscence of the river that ran by his boyhood farm. "The Bridal of Pennacock" retold the American Indian legend about the fidelity of a wife, and "The New Wife and the Old" was a "Yankee Faust" tale that Whittier remembered being told as a boy.

Whittier continued to earn a living as an editor and major contributor to a number of newspapers and magazines, most notably *The National Era*, to which he contributed more than one hundred poems and hundreds of essays between 1847 and the late 1850's. This was a most prolific period in Whittier's career, during which many of his best-known poems appeared. One of his most famous, "Ichabod," was published in 1850. Whittier had read a speech by statesman Daniel Webster, who had called for a compromise on the slavery issue and who supported the Fugitive Slave Law, by which escaped slaves were to be returned to their masters. Surprised and infuriated, Whittier wrote about Webster as "Ichabod," a

forlorn, fallen creature who was spiritually dead because his faith and honor were gone. The poem is among his best, effectively fusing the reformer's fervid abolitionist ideals with the poet's restrained, allusive control of his material.

Another poem to catch the popular imagination was "The Barefoot Boy," which appeared in 1856. Often quoted in its day, the poem was an idyll of youth, a celebration of the country boy whose simple innocence was a source of joy to the poet, himself once a country boy. Though it echoed in sentiment some of the Romantic theories of childhood immortalized by the poet William Wordsworth, Whittier's poem was unashamedly senti-

"THE SLAVE SHIPS"

"ALL ready?" cried the captain;
"Ay, ay!" the seamen said;
"Heave up the worthless lubbers,—
The dying and the dead."
Up from the slave-ship's prison
Fierce, bearded heads were thrust:
"Now let the sharks look to it,—
Toss up the dead ones first!"

Corpse after corpse came up,
Death had been busy there;
Where every blow is mercy,
Why should the spoiler spare?
Corpse after corpse they cast
Sullenly from the ship,
Yet bloody with the traces
Of fetter-link and whip.

Gloomily stood the captain,
With his arms upon his breast,
With his cold brow sternly knotted,
And his iron lip compressed.

"Are all the dead dogs over?"
Growled through that matted lip;
"The blind ones are no better,
Let's lighten the good ship."

Hark! from the ship's dark bosom,
The very sounds of hell!
The ringing clank of iron,
The maniac's short, sharp yell!

The hoarse, low curse, throat-stifled;
The starving infant's moan,
The horror of a breaking heart
Poured through a mother's groan.

Up from that loathsome prison
The stricken blind ones came
Below, had all been darkness,
Above, was still the same.
Yet the holy breath of heaven
Was sweetly breathing there,
And the heated brow of fever
Cooled in the soft sea air.

"Overboard with them, shipmates!"
Cutlass and dirk were plied;
Fettered and blind, one after one,
Plunged down the vessel's side.
The sabre smote above,
Beneath, the lean shark lay,
Waiting with wide and bloody jaw
His quick and human prey.

God of the earth! what cries
Rang upward unto thee?
Voices of agony and blood,
From ship-deck and from sea.
The last dull plunge was heard,
The last wave caught its stain,
And the unsated shark looked up
For human hearts in vain.

Source: John Greenleaf Whittier, *Anti-slavery Poems: Songs of Labor and Reform* (Boston: Houghton, Mifflin, 1888).

mental, positive, and sunny. Its clarity and charm made it an instant success.

The founding of the *Atlantic Monthly* in 1857 opened a wider opportunity for Whittier as a poet. His reputation had already become secure with the publication of several volumes, including the so-called Blue and Gold edition of his work in the same year. Now, at the age of fifty, Whittier felt the financial security and creative freedom that his work as an editor and journalist had never afforded him. The years immediately before and after the Civil War saw the culmination of his achievement as a poet.

In "Skipper Ireson's Ride" (1857), Whittier produced a classic American ballad about the disgrace of Captain Floyd Ireson, who abandoned his sinking vessel and was tarred and feathered by the women of Marblehead. It was a poem of wit, irony, and narrative verve. In 1860, Whittier produced *Home Ballads and Other Poems*. "Telling the Bees," one of the thirty-six poems in the collection, was a notable example of the poet's mature work. Written to commemorate the death of his sister, Mary, this quiet elegy recorded the poet's feelings through the symbol of the beehives draped in black. It was controlled, concise, and moving.

Whittier's finest work was published in 1866. *Snow-Bound: A Winter Idyl* was a long reminiscence of the poet's boyhood. In sharply pictorial details, the poem recorded the Whittier family's physical and emotional security within the house while a snow storm raged. In a series of vignettes, the poet presented the half-dozen or so members of the household, including the visiting schoolmaster, who passed the time before the fire with stories and incidents of character. The poem was notable as well for its structure. Physical details of the approaching storm and its aftermath were contrasted with the warm, peaceful life inside. The poet skillfully expressed the theme of familial love, not through bald statement, but through contrasting and precise imagery. With *Snow-Bound*, Whittier achieved national recognition. His seventieth birthday in 1877 was celebrated in New England with a festive dinner in his honor. When he died in 1892, he was one of the most beloved American poets.

SIGNIFICANCE

John Greenleaf Whittier is an interesting poet for several reasons. He can be seen as an example of the kind of poet nineteenth century America considered important. His work was often dogmatic, trite, moralistic, even excessive; but in his use of native material such as New England history, legend, and landscape, Whittier made poetry accessible to the general reading public. Never obscure, he thus served as the poetic spokesman of his age. His work was a kind of cultural mirror that reflected the conventional middle-class attitudes of the period.

Whittier can also be appreciated on his own terms as a genuine poet. Over a span of sixty years, he evolved from a political versifier to a disciplined, learned artist who produced a handful of American ballads, moving elegies, and sensitive nature poems. His best work was honest and distinctively American.

—Edward Fiorelli

FURTHER READING

Blue, Frederick J. *No Taint of Compromise: Crusaders in Antislavery Politics*. Baton Rouge: Louisiana State University Press, 2005. Examines the work of Whittier and ten other antebellum activists who insisted that slavery would only be abolished through the political process.

Kribbs, Jayne K. *Critical Essays on John Greenleaf Whittier*. Boston: G. K. Hall, 1980. A collection of book reviews and critical assessments from Whittier's contemporaries, especially James Russell Lowell. Also includes articles by twentieth century critics and biographers.

Leary, Lewis. *John Greenleaf Whittier*. New York: Twayne, 1961. Good, short introduction to the poet's life and work that offers a brief review of Whittier's significant poetry in light of the poet's Quaker heritage.

Pickard, John. *John Greenleaf Whittier: An Introduction and Interpretation*. American Authors and Critics Series. New York: Holt, Rinehart and Winston, 1961. Pickard provides a largely sympathetic treatment of Whittier, whose best work is examined in light of the poet's religious humanism. The book emphasizes the evolution of the poet's work from the political and mundane to the sensitive and personal.

Pickard, Samuel T. *Life and Letters of John Greenleaf Whittier*. New York: Houghton Mifflin, 1894. This standard biography of the poet was written by his nephew. It is valuable for the contemporary accounts of the poet's life and work and presents Whittier as an honest reformer with genuine poetic gifts.

Stewart, Ralph. "'Barbara Frietchie' and the Civil War." *ANQ* 16, no. 2 (Spring, 2003): 32. A discussion of Whittier's poem, published in 1863, and its similarities to the Civil War. Analyzes the poem's symbolism, themes, and allegories.

Wagenknecht, Edward. *John Greenleaf Whittier: A Portrait in Paradox*. New York: Oxford University Press, 1967. Wagenknecht concentrates on the conflicts in Whittier's life, particularly the paradox between his celibate lifestyle and his attraction to women, between his moral conscience and his quest for fame.

SEE ALSO: Emily Dickinson; William Lloyd Garrison; Samuel Gridley Howe; Harriet Beecher Stowe; Daniel Webster; Walt Whitman; William Wordsworth.
RELATED ARTICLE in *Great Events from History: The Nineteenth Century, 1801-1900:* December, 1833: American Anti-Slavery Society Is Founded.

OSCAR WILDE
English playwright

Wilde's comedies, including such masterpieces as The Importance of Being Earnest, *were the finest seen on the British stage for many years and have endured as witty testaments to his artistic credo that art is superior to life.*

BORN: October 16, 1854; Dublin, Ireland
DIED: November 30, 1900; Paris, France
ALSO KNOWN AS: Oscar Fingal O'Flahertie Wills Wilde (full name)
AREAS OF ACHIEVEMENT: Literature, theater

EARLY LIFE

Oscar Fingal O'Flahertie Wills Wilde was the second son of Sir William Wilde, a prominent Irish surgeon, and Jane Wilde (née Elgee), a poet and Irish nationalist. He was raised in an affluent, successful, and intellectually stimulating home. From an early age, Oscar and his brother Willie were allowed to sit at the foot of the adults' dinner table and listen to the conversations of the Wildes and their guests, many of whom were prominent in Irish social and literary circles.

At ten, Oscar was sent to the Portora Royal School in Enniskillen. Physically, he was a tall and awkward boy, but he had already revealed signs of the sharp wit that would later fascinate the literary world. He was also noted for his fast reading, once claiming to have read a three-volume novel in thirty minutes. He excelled in Latin and Greek and won a scholarship to Trinity College, Dublin, which he entered in October, 1871.

At Trinity, Wilde won several academic prizes, including the Berkeley Gold Medal for Greek. Strongly influenced by his tutor, the Reverend John Mahaffy, a professor of ancient history, Wilde continued to excel at classics and won a scholarship worth ninety-five pounds per year at Magdalen College, Oxford, which he entered in October, 1874.

At Oxford Wilde encountered two men who were to influence his thought. The first was art critic and writer John Ruskin, who was at the time a professor of fine arts. Ruskin believed that art should have a moral component, and as Wilde worked with him on a road-building project, Wilde found the idea that art might promote the improvement of society to be an attractive one. Wilde was also exposed to a contrary, and more important, influence in the form of Walter Pater, fellow of Brasenose College. According to Pater, what mattered in life and art were not moral or social concerns, but the intense appreciation of sensual beauty, especially that produced by works of art. While under Pater's spell, Wilde took to referring to Pater's *Studies in the History of the Renaissance* (1873) as "my golden book."

Wilde flourished during his time at Oxford, living a flamboyant lifestyle and dressing as a dandy. He also excelled in academics, winning the Oxford Newdigate Prize for Poetry with "Ravenna," a poem that describes his response to his first sight of the Italian city. After receiving his bachelor of arts degree in November, 1878, Wilde went to London to pursue his career, unsure of what that career might be.

LIFE'S WORK

It did not take Wilde long to set himself up in London. He shared rooms off the Strand with his Oxford friend Frank Miles. Wilde cultivated a wide circle of acquaintances, and after his mother arrived in London, he was the chief attraction at the literary salon that she presided over at her Chelsea home. With his witty conversation, outrageous opinions, and outlandish, colorful taste in clothes, Wilde was soon the talk of London. He became the clear leader of the art-for-art's-sake school of aesthetics, a school of thought that had been introduced to England by Pater and emphasized that art need serve no utilitarian end; its mere existence as a thing of perfection and beauty was sufficient.

In 1881 Wilde published his first work, *Poems*, a collection of lyrical poems that are mainly derivative in style from poets such as John Keats, Alfred, Lord Tennyson, and Dante Gabriel Rossetti. The book quickly went through five editions but was badly reviewed by critics. However, such critical dismissal hardly made a dent in Wilde's growing celebrity, and the following year he visited the United States for a highly successful lecture tour. Upon arriving in New York on January 3, 1882, Wilde told a custom's officer, in one of his most famous bons mots, "I have nothing to declare but my genius." In the course of twelve months, Wilde delivered more than eighty lectures, and he arrived back in England more sought after than ever before. He promptly spent the next three months in Paris, where he made the acquaintance of many leading literary and artistic figures, including Stéphane Mallarmé, Paul Verlaine, and Edgar Degas.

In the fall of 1883, Wilde became engaged to Constance Lloyd, the daughter of an Irish barrister, whom he had met two years earlier. They married in May of the following year and, within just over two years, gave birth to two sons, Cyril and Vyvyan. The growth of his family put Wilde under financial strain; although he was well known and celebrated, he was without a reliable income. After another lecture tour and taking on some literary journalism, he became editor of *The Woman's World* in 1887, a position he retained until 1889.

In 1888, Wilde entered the seven-year period of his greatest success, during which he published almost all the work—as novelist, short-story writer, dramatist, and social and literary critic—on which his reputation rests. The first such work was *The Happy Prince and Other Tales* (1888), a collection of fairy tales that one reviewer compared to those of Hans Christian Andersen.

In 1890, the abbreviated serial version of Wilde's novel *The Picture of Dorian Gray* appeared in *Lippincott's Monthly Magazine*; it was published in book form the following year and made an immediate impact on the reading public. The story tells of a young man of great beauty who pursues a selfish, hedonistic life, apparently without any consequences. However, a mysterious portrait of him slowly changes in a way that reveals how his soul has been corrupted. When he finally decides to reform his life, he stabs the portrait in a rage; when others arrive on the scene, they find the portrait restored to one of youth and beauty, while Dorian Gray himself lies dead—old, wrinkled, and disgusting.

In 1891, Wilde also published *Intentions*, a collection of essays that expressed his ideas about the relationship between life and art; two more collections of short stories; and an essay called "The Soul of Man Under Socialism," a somewhat misleading title to a piece that is mainly about individualism and art. In addition, Wilde's play *The Duchess of Padua* was produced in New York under the title *Guido Ferranti*.

From 1892 to 1895, Wilde's career reached its zenith with London and New York productions of his witty comedies *Lady Windermere's Fan* (1892), *A Woman of No Importance* (1893), *An Ideal Husband* (1895), and his masterpiece, *The Importance of Being Earnest* (1895),

LECTURE TO ART STUDENTS

In the lecture which it is my privilege to deliver before you to-night I do not desire to give you any abstract definition of beauty at all. For we who are working in art cannot accept any theory of beauty in exchange for beauty itself, and, so far from desiring to isolate it in a formula appealing to the intellect, we, on the contrary, seek to materialise it in a form that gives joy to the soul through the senses. We want to create it, not to define it. The definition should follow the work: the work should not adapt itself to the definition.

Nothing, indeed, is more dangerous to the young artist than any conception of ideal beauty: he is constantly led by it either into weak prettiness or lifeless abstraction: whereas to touch the ideal at all you must not strip it of vitality. You must find it in life and re-create it in art.

While, then, on the one hand I do not desire to give you any philosophy of beauty—for, what I want to-night is to investigate how we can create art, not how we can talk of it—on the other hand, I do not wish to deal with anything like a history of English art.

To begin with, such an expression as English art is a meaningless expression. One might just as well talk of English mathematics. Art is the science of beauty, and Mathematics the science of truth: there is no national school of either. Indeed, a national school is a provincial school, merely. Nor is there any such thing as a school of art even. There are merely artists, that is all.

And as regards histories of art, they are quite valueless to you unless you are seeking the ostentatious oblivion of an art professorship. It is of no use to you to know the date of Perugino or the birthplace of Salvator Rosa: all that you should learn about art is to know a good picture when you see it, and a bad picture when you see it. . . .

Source: Oscar Wilde, "Lecture to Art Students," in *Essays and Lectures* (London, 1911).

which ran for eighty-six performances to popular and critical acclaim. With its brilliant wordplay (including extensive use of paradoxes and epigrams) and its farcical plot (which includes such stock devices as intercepted letters and mistaken identities), the play embodies a perfect fantasy world that has little relation to life as it is really lived. Describing his overall aim in the play, Wilde explained that he wished to treat all the trivial things of life seriously and the serious things with a studied triviality.

However, the year of Wilde's greatest success, during which three of his plays were playing simultaneously in London, was also the year of his downfall. In May, 1895, Wilde was tried and found guilty of "gross indecency," a euphemism for homosexual activity, which at the time was a criminal offense. He was sentenced to two years in prison with hard labor. The seeds of Wilde's tragic fall had been sown in 1891 when he had met Lord Alfred Douglas, a young poet with whom he formed an intimate friendship. Douglas's father, the marquis of Queensberry, accused Wilde of homosexuality. In March, 1895, Wilde recklessly sued Queensberry for criminal libel, but he lost the case and was immediately arrested and put on trial. The trial ended with the jury unable to reach a verdict, but Wilde was retried almost immediately, and this time there was to be no reprieve.

Wilde was imprisoned under harsh conditions. Confined to his cell for twenty-three hours per day, he was at first denied all books except a Bible, a prayer book, and a hymn book. His hard labor consisted of picking oakum in his cell. Conditions improved later, and he was able to obtain more books. While in prison, Wilde wrote a confessional letter to Douglas called *De Profundis* (1905) and a collection of poetry titled *The Ballad of Reading Gaol* (1898). On his release from prison in May, 1897, Wilde emigrated to France, never to return to England. Divorced and financially ruined, he had to rely on friends for support. His health deteriorated, and he died in 1900 in the Hotel d'Alsace in Paris.

SIGNIFICANCE

Oscar Wilde's greatest achievement was the way he used language to create what has been called a form of comedy as pure as the music of Wolfgang Amadeus Mozart. Demolishing the complacency of Victorian social, moral, and artistic assumptions with the weapons of wit, Wilde delighted in turning stuffy platitudes upside down and then turning to the audience for applause. It was a brilliant performance that ensured that during his life, Wilde would be both greatly admired and maliciously mocked.

Although Wilde's enemies eventually found satisfaction in his disgrace, it is Wilde, if literary history is the judge, who has had the last laugh. This is not only because he was an important influence on a variety of twentieth century writers and literary forms—from the Symbolist dramas of William Butler Yeats to the stylish comedies of W. Somerset Maugham and Noël Coward, and perhaps even the absurdist plays of Eugène Ionesco and Samuel Beckett—but also because of the fact that of those artists during the 1890's who worked in the literary forms known as aestheticism and Decadence, it is Wilde who has remained enduringly popular.

During the late 1990's, as the centenary of Wilde's death approached, interest in Wilde underwent a kind of renaissance. There was an outpouring of scholarly studies, and plays such as the Off-Broadway *Gross Indecency: The Three Trials of Oscar Wilde* (1997), by Moisés Kaufman, and David Hare's *The Judas Kiss* (1997), which played in London and New York, further imprinted Wilde's name on the popular imagination.

—*Bryan Aubrey*

FURTHER READING

Belford, Barbara. *Oscar Wilde: A Certain Genius*. New York: Random House, 2000. Focuses on Wilde's life and work within the context of 1890's London society, portraying Wilde as a clever self-promoter and provocateur.

Ellmann, Richard. *Oscar Wilde*. New York: Knopf, 1988. This is the definitive biography, a prodigious work of scholarship that is elegantly written and sympathetic to Wilde. Ellmann argues from circumstantial evidence that Wilde died of complications from syphilis that he picked up while at Oxford and also disputes the commonly held notion that Wilde converted to Catholicism on his deathbed.

Ericksen, Donald H. *Oscar Wilde*. Boston: Twayne, 1977. This useful, concise introduction to Wilde's life and career emphasizes the analysis of individual works and includes an annotated bibliography.

Foldy, Michael S. *The Trials of Oscar Wilde: Deviance, Morality, and Late-Victorian Society*. New Haven, Conn.: Yale University Press, 1997. By analyzing the trial testimony and press coverage, Foldy argues cogently that the prosecution of Wilde was not solely based on matters of morality but was directly linked to wider social, cultural, and political issues.

Harris, Frank. *Oscar Wilde: Including My Memories of Oscar Wilde by George Bernard Shaw*. 2d ed. New York: Carroll & Graf, 1997. Harris was one of the few friends who remained loyal to Wilde after his downfall. His biography, although highly readable and full of interesting anecdotes, is not always reliable. Shaw's afterward is a shrewd assessment of Wilde.

Holland, Merlin. *The Wilde Album*. New York: Henry Holt, 1998. This is a useful complement to the weightier biography by Ellmann. Holland, Wilde's grandson, supplements his biographical narrative with various artifacts—including photographs, press clippings, and political cartoons—that document Wilde's emergence as a media celebrity and show how Wilde consciously created his own fame. The book includes rare family photos and all twenty-eight publicity portraits made for Wilde's 1882 U.S. tour.

Pearson, Hesketh. *Oscar Wilde: His Life and Wit*. New York: Harper Bros., 1946. Although superseded by

the massive research and detail contained in Ellmann, this remains a full and engaging account of Wilde's life.

Sloan, John. *Oscar Wilde*. New York: Oxford University Press, 2003. Places Wilde's work within the context of late nineteenth century London society. Examines how his work has been adapted to film, stage, and other media since his death.

SEE ALSO: Hans Christian Andersen; Aubrey Beardsley; Sarah Bernhardt; Edgar Degas; John Keats; Lillie Langtry; Walter Pater; John Ruskin; Ellen Terry.

RELATED ARTICLES in *Great Events from History: The Nineteenth Century, 1801-1900:* October 10, 1881: London's Savoy Theatre Opens; c. 1884-1924: Decadent Movement Flourishes.

CHARLES WILKES
American explorer

Wilkes's determination and leadership as commander of the United States Exploring Expedition of 1838-1842 ensured the success of this major step in the emergence of the United States as a naval and scientific power.

BORN: April 3, 1798; New York, New York
DIED: February 8, 1877; Washington, D.C.
AREA OF ACHIEVEMENT: Exploration

EARLY LIFE

Charles Wilkes was the youngest child of John Deponthieu Wilkes, who had immigrated to the United States from Great Britain during the Revolutionary War, and Mary Seton, whose father was her husband's business partner. Because of John D. Wilkes's success in business, the family was relatively affluent. Wilkes's life was disrupted before his third birthday by the death of his mother. Thereafter, he was reared by various female relatives and friends, including his aunt, Elizabeth Seton (the first American saint, canonized in 1974). Subsequently educated at boarding and preparatory schools, Wilkes rejected Columbia College or a career in business for a life in the army. After three cruises on merchant ships during the years 1815-1817, Wilkes obtained his commission as a midshipman in the United States Navy in 1818.

Wilkes's decision to pursue a naval career despite the objections of his father may have been an early in-

dication of two of his most enduring characteristics; his determination to do things his way and his self-assuredness. After he decided that a particular course of action was correct, he never wavered, no matter who criticized or objected. Add to this a bluntness in word and manner and a self-righteous attitude, and the result was a man in constant conflict with superiors, peers, and subordinates.

LIFE'S WORK

Wilkes served on a number of ships during the early years of his career. There were also extensive stretches of land duty and periods of leave while awaiting orders. The time during which he was not at sea was spent studying mathematics and the naval sciences: hydrography, geodesy, and astronomy. He studied with Ferdinand Hassler, the first superintendent of the United States Coast Survey, and gained experience in surveying. (During one of these periods on land, in April, 1826, just prior to his promotion to lieutenant, Wilkes married Jane Renwick, whom he had known since childhood.) In February, 1833, he became superintendent of the Depot of Charts and Instruments (the forerunner of the Navy Hydrographic Office and the Naval Observatory). By the mid-1830's, it was clear that he was one of the leading scientific minds in the United States Navy.

It was his scientific reputation, relatively minor among civilian scientists but outstanding compared to his fellow naval officers, which led to Wilkes's orders in March, 1838, to command the United States Exploring Expedition, despite his junior rank (he was thirty-ninth of forty lieutenants). It was not Wilkes's first contact with the expedition, which would occupy more than two decades of his life. When the expedition was first authorized in 1828, Wilkes had volunteered for duty with it; the idea of such an expedition was shelved a year later. In 1836, it was again authorized, and Wilkes was selected to travel to Europe to purchase the necessary scientific apparatus. When he returned in January, 1837, he found the expedition in disarray and still far from ready for sailing. After rejecting subordinate positions with the expedition, he accepted the responsibility as commander.

On August 18, 1838, the United States Exploring Expedition, usually known as the Wilkes Expedition, set sail from Norfolk, Virginia. Among its objectives were the surveying and charting of portions of the Pacific Ocean for the benefit of the American shipping industry, the establishment of good relations with the native populations of the region, and scientific observations and collecting in a number of disciplines. There were six ships, five hundred sailors, and nine civilian scientists under the command of the clean-shaven lieutenant whose hair always appeared disobedient. In a typical act of audacity, Wilkes assumed the rank of acting captain upon leaving port, despite the fact that the secretary of the navy had denied him that appointment.

The expedition returned to New York in the summer of 1842, having circumnavigated the earth and cruised more than eighty-seven thousand miles. Only two of the original ships survived the entire cruise; two had sunk, one was sent back early, and one was sold, while another ship had been added in 1841 to replace one of the lost ships. The expedition had explored, surveyed, charted, and mapped the Pacific Ocean basin from Oregon to Australia. Its exploration of the coast of Antarctica confirmed that the great ice mass was in fact a continent. More than four thousand zoological, fifty thousand botanical, and thousands of ethnographical specimens were brought back by the explorers. Most of these scientific specimens were eventually deposited in the Smithsonian Institution in 1858.

The first order of business, however, was courts-martial. Wilkes brought charges against a number of his junior officers, and in turn, a number were brought against him. He was found guilty on only one charge, excessive punishment of sailors, and sentenced to a public reprimand. Characteristically, in his autobiography

Charles Wilkes. (Library of Congress)

Wilkes dismisses his court-martial as a vendetta on the part of the secretary of the navy.

With the courts-martial out of the way, Wilkes focused his energy on ensuring that the fruits of the expedition would not be lost. In the summer of 1843, he was promoted to commander and given the responsibility for the expedition's collections and reports. Except for survey duty in 1858, the expedition remained his only official concern until the outbreak of the Civil War (he was promoted to captain in 1855). He published the five-volume *Narrative of the United States Exploring Expedition* in 1844, taking credit for authorship, although in fact he functioned more as an editor. He lobbied Congress for the funding for, and oversaw the publication of, nineteen scientific reports, authoring those on meteorology and hydrography himself.

Wilkes's personal life changed during these years. In 1848, his wife, Jane, who had borne him four children, died. Six years later, he married Mary Lynch Bolton, who bore him two additional children, although one, born when Wilkes was sixty-seven, did not survive infancy.

During the Civil War, Wilkes held a number of successful commands and was promoted to commodore. There was, however, controversy during this time as well. While captain of the *San Jacinto* in November, 1861, he removed two Confederate agents from the British mail packet *Trent*. Although he was hailed as a hero by the American public and government, members of the latter changed their attitude when it was realized that Wilkes's action could precipitate a war with Great Britain. The agents were freed. A subsequent clash with Secretary of the Navy Gideon Welles led to a second court-martial of Wilkes in 1864 for disobedience of orders, a finding of guilty, and suspension from the navy.

In 1866, Wilkes was promoted to rear admiral on the retired list. He continued working for the publication of the final volumes of the expedition reports, although Congress ceased their funding in 1873 with a number of reports unpublished. Wilkes died in his home in Washington on February 8, 1877. In 1909, his remains were placed in Arlington National Cemetery.

SIGNIFICANCE

During the 1830's, American science was just beginning to step upon the international stage. Although scientific exploration, a common enough activity among the great European powers, had been attempted with some success by the United States Army, the United States Exploring Expedition represented an effort on a scale far larger than the republic had ever attempted. The possibility of failure was high.

Despite the odds, the expedition succeeded. Not only did the expedition meet its military objectives, but also its scientific achievements placed the United States in a position of intellectual respectability. A model was provided for subsequent naval exploratory expeditions. To a very large extent, credit for that success must go to Wilkes. He was a difficult man to get along with, could not tolerate opposition or criticism, and knew far less about the world, especially science, than he thought he did. However, when energy, drive, and determination were needed, whether aboard ship or in the halls of Congress, Wilkes met the challenge. James Dwight Dana, the young geologist on the expedition, thought that no other naval officer could have done better. Combining a dedi-

cation to duty with a sympathy for science, Wilkes left the world a legacy of scientific and geographical knowledge.

—*Marc Rothenberg*

FURTHER READING

Philbrick, Nathaniel. *Sea of Glory: America's Voyage of Discovery, the U.S. Exploring Expedition, 1838-1842.* New York: Viking Press, 2003. A well-researched chronicle of the expedition and a portrait of its commander. Portrays Wilkes as passionate, brash, enthusiastic, but also petty, mean-spirited and egotistical.

Ponko, Vincent, Jr. *Ships, Seas, and Scientists: U.S. Naval Exploration and Discovery in the Nineteenth Century.* Annapolis, Md.: Naval Institute Press, 1974. Surveys the naval exploring expeditions of the antebellum period. Places the Wilkes Expedition in its larger context.

Reynolds, William. *The Private Journal of William Reynolds: United States Exploring Expedition, 1838-1842.* Edited with an introduction and notes by Nathaniel Philbrick and Thomas Philbrick. New York: Penguin Books, 2004. A first-person narrative of the four-year expedition by Reynolds, a junior officer who served under Wilkes. Describes how Wilkes lost the support of his crew.

Stanton, William. *The Great United States Exploring Expedition of 1838-1842.* Berkeley: University of California Press, 1975. Provides an analysis of the scientific contributions of the Wilkes Expedition. Stanton argues that the expedition gained international respect for the American scientific community.

Tyler, David B. *The Wilkes Expedition: The First United States Exploring Expedition, 1838-1842.* Philadelphia: American Philosophical Society, 1968. Concentrates on the exploring and surveying aspects of the expedition rather than the scientific. This history focuses on the performance of Wilkes as a commander and his relationship with his officer corps and civilian scientists.

Viola, Herman J., and Carolyn Margolis, eds. *Magnificent Voyagers: The U.S. Exploring Expedition, 1838-1842.* Washington, D.C.: Smithsonian Institution Press, 1985. A collection of articles by scientists and historians. This represents a later and more balanced account of Wilkes and his expedition.

Wilkes, Charles. *Autobiography of Rear Admiral Charles Wilkes, U.S. Navy: 1798-1877.* Edited by William James Morgan, David B. Tyler, Joye L.

Leonhart, and Mary F. Loughlin. Washington, D.C.: Naval History Division, 1979. A massive defense of his career, this autobiography provides unique insight into the mind of the man. Both the positive and the negative aspects of his character shine through.

SEE ALSO: John C. Frémont; Matthew C. Perry.
RELATED ARTICLES in *Great Events from History: The Nineteenth Century, 1801-1900:* 1820-early 1840's: Europeans Explore the Antarctic; May, 1842-1854: Frémont Explores the American West.

EMMA WILLARD
American educator

Willard's contribution to the education of women helped prompt the development of women's colleges and coeducational universities in the United States. Her strong belief in the need for women to be properly educated moved her to develop new methods of training teachers and to work for the professionalization of teaching.

BORN: February 23, 1787; Berlin, Connecticut
DIED: April 15, 1870; Troy, New York
ALSO KNOWN AS: Emma Hart (birth name)
AREAS OF ACHIEVEMENT: Education, women's rights

EARLY LIFE

Emma Hart Willard was the ninth of the ten children her mother, née Lydia Hinsdale, bore as Samuel Hart's second wife. Her paternal forefathers included Stephen Hart and Thomas Hooker, a clergyman who left England in 1633 and founded the towns of Hartford and Farmington, Connecticut. Robert Hinsdale, a maternal forefather, settled in Dedham, Massachusetts, in 1637 and later became a founder of Deerfield, Massachusetts.

Life in the simple farmhouse where Willard was born was anything but routine. Her home was a center of intellectual curiosity that encouraged learning. Evenings were spent listening to Samuel Hart speak of the founding of the republic, or discussing John Locke, Bishop George Berkeley, and other philosophers. Lydia Hart frequently read aloud and taught the children about Geoffrey Chaucer, John Milton, and William Shakespeare.

Willard, eager for learning and a voracious reader, taught herself geometry at the age of thirteen. At fifteen she enrolled at the Berlin Academy. Two years later, she began teaching the younger children of Berlin in the district school. When Willard taught, she made her subjects interesting, allowed recreation periods, and gave much deserved praise to her students. In 1805 she conducted

classes for older boys and girls in her father's house. A year later she took charge of the Berlin Academy during the winter term. During the spring and fall of these years, she also attended classes at two private female schools in Hartford.

Willard's reputation as a teacher grew. She was offered positions at three schools: in Middlebury, Vermont; Westfield, Massachusetts; and Hudson, New York. Willard accepted the position as an assistant at the academy in Westfield because it was close to her parents' home. She was not, however, given full authority to direct the school. Disappointed with her limited duties, she left after only a few months, to take charge of the girls' academy in Middlebury, Vermont.

A pretty blue-eyed girl with fair hair and a well-proportioned figure, Willard spent her free time studying science, writing poetry, and visiting friends. While in Middlebury she fell in love with Dr. John Willard, a twice-widowed physician, who had given up medical practice to accept the position of Marshal of Vermont offered by President Jefferson. They were married on August 10, 1809, when Emma was twenty-two and Dr. Willard, fifty. John Hart Willard, their only child, was born a year later.

With her husband's encouragement, Willard began to study his medical books. His nephew, John Willard, lived with them while attending Middlebury College. John freely shared his class notes and texts with Emma and patiently answered all questions as she taught herself the knowledge that formal education had denied her. This experience opened Willard's eyes to the inequities between male and female education. Never before had she fully realized that women were deprived of educational opportunities.

Dr. Willard was on the board of directors when the State Bank of Vermont was robbed in 1812. The board members were suspected and made to pay restitution. To aid her husband and ease his financial burdens, Willard opened the Middlebury Female Seminary in her own home during the spring of 1814. Her second goal was to create a better school than those in existence.

Willard pioneered new fields of study for women. She was careful, however, also to satisfy those of conventional mind. Gradually adding mathematics, history, and modern languages to the curriculum, Willard showed that women could pursue subjects traditionally reserved for men. From the outset, she encouraged her students to consider teaching. Those interested became assistant teachers while continuing their studies. She personally conducted examinations of students and invited Middlebury College teachers to attend and witness the strength and development of the students' minds.

Willard knew she needed more teachers to teach additional subjects, but she had no money. When negotiations with Vermont officials failed to result in the establishment of a female seminary located at Burlington, she chose to seek the support of Governor DeWitt Clinton and the New York legislature for a program of state-aided schools for girls. In February, 1818, she sent Clinton a completed copy of *An Address to the Public; Particularly to the Members of the Legislature of New-York, Proposing a Plan for Improving Female Education* (1819).

The plan contained four sections detailing the existing inadequacies in female education, outlining both the

Emma Willard. (Library of Congress)

proper facilities and the curriculum needed, and carefully listing the benefits of such an education to society. Emphasized were the facts that there would be better trained teachers for the common schools and that women would be willing to work for less pay. This last statement would come to haunt Emma. The following year, a determined Emma went to Albany to lobby for her plan. Almost fearless in the face of prejudice against female education, she personally met with, and presented her proposal to, members of the New York legislature. The legislature chartered the Waterford Academy for Young Ladies and passed legislation authorizing a share of the Literary Fund to be given to female seminaries.

LIFE'S WORK

In anticipation of state funding, the seminary was relocated to Waterford, New York, where Willard could make her work more visible to the legislature. No money was allocated, however, and none was received for sixteen years. Within a short time, she received an offer of financial aid from the Common Council of Troy, New York. The Council agreed to raise four thousand dollars by means of a special tax to purchase a female academy. In September, 1821, the Troy Female Seminary opened. The city was an ideal location. Because the seminary was situated in an inland port on the Hudson, students from distant areas could easily come to the school, and its newly trained teachers could easily travel westward. At her new school, Willard continued to develop the methods she had initiated at Middlebury. Workdays of twelve to fifteen hours were not uncommon for her. To illustrate and supplement her teaching methods, she began to write the first of numerous textbooks on geography and history. A collection of her poems was also published.

The seminary was successful; within ten years it had an enrollment of more than three hundred, including more than one hundred boarding students. The school was designed to prepare students for life. Willard initiated a system of self-government with monitors and demerits. She emphasized good manners and personal appearance, not fancy dress. To make the girls feel more at home, Willard offered each student a small room with a roommate. Willard held weekly talks with the girls stressing manners and behavior. She was their role model, just as the school became a model for future American boarding schools.

The seminary's curriculum included classical and domestic subjects and introduced advanced science courses. Willard held public examinations of individual students at the end of each term. She gave financial aid to those students interested in teaching, providing free tuition, board, and even clothes, if needed. Repayment was to be made after graduation when the student secured a teaching position. Willard did not believe in the same education for boys and girls. She adhered to the ideology of woman's domestic role, and she discouraged any interest in politics.

As her students began careers in teaching across the United States, Willard founded the Willard Association for Mutual Improvement of Female Teachers. She kept in touch with her former students, providing news about alumnae, constantly advising them about teaching methods, and exhorting them to continue to learn new subjects throughout life.

When Dr. Willard, who had been school physician and business manager, died in 1825, Willard took full charge of the school. Thirteen years later, royalties from her numerous books made it possible for Willard to give control of the seminary to her son John and his wife, Sara Lucretia (née Hudson). Following retirement, she married Christopher Yates, an Albany physician, on September 17, 1838. The marriage was a disaster, and after nine months she left him to live in Berlin, Connecticut, with her sister Mary. (A divorce was granted in 1843 by the legislature of Connecticut.) While she lived there, Willard began to assist Henry Barnard, secretary of the State Board of Commissioners, in his campaign to improve the common schools, and later that same year, 1840, she was elected superintendent of four district schools for Kensington, Connecticut.

Four years later, at her son's urging, she returned to Troy and lived in a small house on the school grounds. Willard continued to write and publish poems, as well as *A Treatise on the Motive Powers which Produce the Circulation of the Blood* (1846). She gained recognition for her work in physiology and was one of the few women admitted to the Association for the Advancement of Science.

In 1845-1846, Willard conducted a series of teacher institutes throughout southern New York State and southern and Western states as far as Texas. In her later years, in addition to revising her textbooks, Willard studied both Greek and Hebrew because she wanted to read books in their original language. Willard also began to work for different causes. She exhorted the French government to consult women as it drafted a new constitution. She worked to preserve the Union and peace. She published *Universal Peace* (1864), which proposed an international organization, similar to what later became the League of Nations, to settle international problems.

Willard remained active until her death in 1870, at eighty-three. She was buried in Oakwood Cemetery outside Troy, New York. The Troy Female Seminary was renamed the Emma Willard School in 1895.

SIGNIFICANCE

Before 1820, women's place was in the home. All intellectual pursuit was discouraged because it was thought that it would harm the female. The little education available to females was obtained either at "dame" schools, usually conducted by poorly trained women in their own homes, or during summer months when some district schools would admit girls. After 1790, female seminaries began to develop. Because of tuition and other costs, poor girls were automatically excluded.

As Willard grew to adulthood and developed into a teacher, she began to realize how limited female education was. Later, when she established her own school, she worked vigorously to free women from ignorance. Willard was interested in developing thinkers, scholarship, and high ideals and encouraged self-respect and self-support.

Willard's aim had been to advance the cause of female education as the only base that could support the advancement of women. She believed that women had much to give to their country. Willard proved that women could do serious study without harm to themselves. Although Willard did not work for women's rights as such, she served as a bridge between traditional supportive women and the Victorian suffragists by being willing and able to challenge conservative notions.

The Troy Female Seminary predated the establishment of girls' schools in Boston and New York. It was a pioneer normal school established some eighteen years before the founding of Horace Mann's normal school. Willard was the first to think seriously about the problems and methods of teaching, the first to encourage the professionalization of teaching. She was the first woman to write textbooks on advanced subjects and may have been the first female lobbyist. She recognized the virtue of continuing education throughout one's life. Willard's contribution to female education was a major element in the development of women's colleges and coeducational universities into a permanent part of national life in the United States.

—*Rita E. Loos*

FURTHER READING

Anticaglia, Elizabeth. *Twelve American Women.* Chicago: Nelson-Hall, 1975. Presents good biographical sketches of twelve women, ranging from Anne

Hutchinson to Margaret Mead, selected for their significant contributions to American civilization. One chapter is devoted to Willard.

Cott, Nancy F. *The Bonds of Womanhood: "Woman's Sphere" in New England, 1780-1835*. New Haven, Conn.: Yale University Press, 1977. Tries to explain the duality of the "bond" that tied New England women together as well as to their station in life. Of particular interest is the third chapter, which offers a cohesive rationale for schooling women beyond the level of minimal literacy.

Crevin, Lawrence A., and R. Freeman Butts. *A History of Education in American Culture*. New York: Holt, Rinehart and Winston, 1953. Provides a sound historical background of the development of American education.

Flexner, Eleanor. *Century of Struggle: The Woman's Rights Movement in the United States*. Cambridge, Mass.: Harvard University Press, 1959. Covers the women's rights movement from the Mayflower Compact to 1920, when women won the vote. Flexner provides significant information about the many smaller movements within the larger one. The first two chapters cover the position of women up to 1800 and the early steps taken to secure equal education.

Goodsell, Willystine, ed. *Pioneers of Women's Education in the U.S.: E. Willard, C. Beecher, M. Lyon*. New York: AMS Press, 1970. Following a brief introduction to women's education, part 1 presents a brief biography of Willard. Excerpts from her *Plan* and three selections from the prefaces of her texts are included.

Hoffman, Nancy. *Women's "True" Profession: Voices from the History of Teaching*. Old Westbury, N.Y.: Feminist Press, 1981. Presents the experience of teaching from the viewpoint of the teacher and highlights critical themes that defined teaching as woman's work. Representative teachers are chosen, Willard among

them. A brief biography of Willard is included along with a facsimile of the handwritten letter she sent to Governor Clinton.

Lutz, Alma. *Emma Willard: Daughter of Democracy*. Boston: Houghton Mifflin, 1929. Written in the style of Willard's *Letters and Journals*, this dated portrait, written by an alumna of the school, remains the definitive work on Willard. All subsequent biographers have drawn from it.

_____. *Emma Willard, Pioneer Educator of Women*. Boston: Beacon Press, 1964. Written in honor of the sesquicentennial of the Emma Willard School, it borrows much from Lutz's earlier work, which contains more complete information.

Scott, Anne Firor. "The Ever Widening Circle: The Diffusion of Feminist Values from the Troy Female Seminary, 1822-1872." *History of Education Quarterly* 19 (Spring, 1979): 3-25. Presents an analysis of the alumnae of the Troy Female Seminary and attempts to show the decisive influence Willard had not only on the students but also on every part of the country to which they went. Valuable, well-documented study that concludes that higher education played an important part in the diffusion of feminist values.

Seller, Maxine Schwartz, ed. *Women Educators in the United States, 1820-1993*. Westport, Conn.: Greenwood Press, 1994. Willard is one of the sixty-six women who are profiled in this book. The profile contains information about her life, goals, influences, and achievements, and lists works by and about her.

SEE ALSO: Henry Barnard; DeWitt Clinton; Horace Mann.

RELATED ARTICLES in *Great Events from History: The Nineteenth Century, 1801-1900:* May, 1823: Hartford Female Seminary Is Founded; July 19-20, 1848: Seneca Falls Convention.

FRANCES WILLARD
American educator and social reformer

Advocating a "do everything" policy for reformers during the late nineteenth century, Willard helped advance the causes of temperance and women's rights as president and the most famous and symbolic leader of the Woman's Christian Temperance Union.

BORN: September 28, 1839; Churchville, New York
DIED: February 18, 1898; New York, New York
ALSO KNOWN AS: Frances Elizabeth Caroline Willard (full name)
AREAS OF ACHIEVEMENT: Social reform, women's rights

EARLY LIFE

Frances Elizabeth Caroline Willard was the fourth of five children, three of whom survived infancy. Her mother, Mary Thompson (Hill) Willard, traced her ancestry back to early New Englanders of English origin. Her father, Josiah Flint Willard, came from a long line of New England and New York farmers.

When Frances was two, her family moved to Ohio and then migrated to the Janesville, Wisconsin, area, where she grew up. Her mother provided her first schooling. A young tutor and a visiting aunt continued her schooling until Frances was fifteen. After attending a district school and a school for girls, she enrolled in the Milwaukee Female College and thereafter transferred to Northwestern Female College in Evanston, Illinois. Frances was graduated in 1859 with a laureate of science degree. She held a number of teaching positions in Illinois during the next few years and moved to Genesee Wesleyan Seminary in Lima, New York, to hold a job as a preceptress during the 1866-1867 academic year. Frances returned to Evanston in the winter of 1867-1868 and nursed her father until he died in January, 1868.

Shortly after her father's death, Willard departed for two years of travel throughout Europe, including Russia and Greece, and to Egypt, Palestine, and Turkey, with her friend Kate Jackson. Jackson's wealthy father paid for the travel. Willard attended lectures and studied languages, art, and music in Berlin, Paris, and Rome, thus expanding her intellectual capacity and heightening her desire to achieve.

In 1871, Willard was appointed president of Evanston College for Ladies. In 1873, when Northwestern University totally absorbed Evanston College, she was made dean of women and professor of English and art at Northwestern. During that same year, Willard helped found the

Association for the Advancement of Women. In 1874, after suffering academic frustration and experiencing personal difficulties with Charles Fowler, the president of Northwestern and her former fiancé, she resigned, never again to hold a formal academic position. Her stately physical presence, kindly face, and penetrating eyes belied the fact that this attractive and highly motivated thirty-five-year-old woman was unhappy and, at that point in her life, lacking clear direction.

LIFE'S WORK

In the midst of rising temperance fervor and expanding antisaloon activity throughout the country, Willard was soon able to realize her ambitions. In October, 1874, she was chosen secretary of a newly formed women's temperance organization in Chicago. The next month, she attended the organizing convention of the National Woman's Christian Temperance Union (WCTU) and was chosen national corresponding secretary. She immediately advocated that the WCTU should dedicate itself to numerous other reforms. Annie Wittenmyer, the first president of the WCTU, opposed broadening the organization's perspective beyond temperance and was shocked by Willard's 1876 national convention speech in support of a women's suffrage resolution.

In early 1877, Willard resigned her Chicago WCTU position to become the director of women's meetings for the evangelist Dwight L. Moody. Moody's orthodoxy, however, was too restraining; hence, she resigned in September and returned to Evanston with Anna A. Gordon, whom she had met in the Boston Moody Crusade and who thereafter became her lifelong secretary, aide, and confidante. In 1877, when her relationship with Wittenmyer became even more strained, Willard resigned as WCTU national corresponding secretary and began lecturing nationwide on women's rights and suffrage.

After being elected president of the Illinois WCTU in 1878, Willard campaigned vigorously for new temperance laws. She initiated and directed a petition campaign to induce state legislators to pass a law allowing women in Illinois to vote on the liquor question. Although the petition died in committee, its effect was evident in the state's spring election as a majority of Illinois towns adopted local option. This petition campaign served as a model for subsequent and similar actions for the WCTU in other states.

Although the internal organizational fight over political activity continued, Willard steadily won new adherents. In 1879, she was elected president of the National WCTU and held that position for the remaining years of her life. Under her leadership, the WCTU expanded from a religious group primarily dedicated to temperance to a strong women's organization. She effected many internal changes in the organization and molded the annual conventions into well-publicized, smooth-running, and inspiring affairs. She sought and acquired for the WCTU working relationships with other religious and reform groups.

As National WCTU president, Willard, already highly regarded, became a well-traveled and effective speaker who could and did move audiences. Her speaking fees were her only source of income until 1886, when the WCTU presented her with an annual salary of eighteen hundred dollars, later raised to twenty-four hundred dollars. Supporting herself, her mother, and Gordon, Willard remained in constant financial need throughout the 1880's. The sales of her autobiography, *Glimpses of Fifty Years: An Autobiography of an American Woman*, published in 1889, provided sufficient additional income to allow her barely to meet her needs.

After becoming national president, Willard continued to speak out for woman suffrage. Responding to her urging, delegates to the national convention in 1880 endorsed the ballot for women; in 1882, a new WCTU department of franchise was established to distribute suffrage literature and to encourage members to work for the vote. A member of the American Woman Suffrage Association, Willard worked closely with numerous suffrage organizations and introduced leading suffrage leaders to WCTU national conventions.

Willard carefully led the WCTU and her followers into various other reform causes. She pinpointed her strategy well in her handbook *Do Everything*, published in 1895. She argued that almost all reforms had temperance aspects. By 1889, thirty-nine WCTU departments of work existed, each of which was designed to educate the public and be a group to bring pressure in order to secure reform legislation. The areas of reform, in addition to temperance, included prostitution, health and hygiene, city welfare, prison reform, labor reform, and rights for blacks. Attempting to do so much meant that at times the work was superficial. Many WCTU members, moreover, continued to concern themselves only with the liquor problem.

Beginning in 1883, Willard led the WCTU into international work. She persuaded the WCTU to send temper-

Frances Willard. (Library of Congress)

ance missionaries abroad to establish unions and to persuade women in other countries to oppose the traffic in alcohol and narcotic drugs. The World's WCTU was established in 1891; Willard was elected president. By 1897, the World's WCTU represented more than two million women.

In attempting to bring the WCTU into party politics, Willard encountered her greatest internal organizational difficulties. After endorsing James A. Garfield for the presidency in 1880 and then being disappointed by his repudiation of his pledge to support prohibition and woman suffrage, Willard established the Home Protection Party and attempted in 1882 to combine it with the Prohibition Party. Many members opposed involving their organization in party politics. During the early 1890's, Willard tried to get prohibition and woman suffrage planks inserted into the 1892 Populist Party platform and attempted to bring the Prohibition Party into the Populist Party. She regarded her failure to accomplish these results as a personal defeat.

Affected by her political failure and by the death of her mother, Willard went to England in the summer of 1892 to rest and to spend time with a friend, Lady Henry Somerset. From then until the end of 1896, she stayed mostly in England, spending only sixteen months in the

United States. During this time, she attempted with but little success to garner support from British women for her "do everything" policy. She also changed both her thinking and advocacy. She espoused socialism, argued that poverty was the major cause of intemperance, and spoke out on her belief that education rather than prohibition was the best way to solve the liquor problem.

Dissatisfaction with Willard among WCTU leaders grew between 1892 and 1896. Her unorthodox views, continued emphasis upon politics, extended absences, and lack of attention to developing organizational problems finally caused an eruption of opposition at the 1897 national convention. Her rank-and-file followers held the line, however, reelecting her by an overwhelming vote of 387 to 19. Chronic anemia took its toll the next year as Willard's health declined dramatically. She died in New York City on February 18, 1898.

SIGNIFICANCE

Although she did not wholly realize her dream of creating an all-inclusive women's reform organization, Willard, stressing the familiar themes of home, family, and temperance, successfully persuaded many women, who had previously been indifferent to reforms, to broaden their perspective and to engage in numerous reform activities. During her twenty years as national WCTU president, she retained the backing of the great majority of WCTU members. After her death, the WCTU moved away from the "do everything" policy and emphasized the issues of prohibition and total abstinence. Willard nevertheless remained the most illustrious and idealized symbol of the WCTU woman.

In many ways, Willard's story is the story of the WCTU, the largest organization of women in nineteenth century America. Led by Willard, the WCTU fought not only for temperance but also for woman suffrage, prison reform, facilities for dependent and neglected children, federal aid to education, and legislation to help laborers. During the Willard presidency, 1879 to 1898, the WCTU dominated the entire woman movement in the United States. In addition to molding the WCTU into the model for future women's organizations, Willard, more than any of her contemporaries, instilled the vision of feminist goals in the consciousness of great numbers of American women.

—*Norton Mezvinsky*

FURTHER READING

Borden, Ruth. *Women and Temperance*. Philadelphia: Temple University Press, 1981. The best book on the WCTU and one of the best analyses of Willard. A well-documented, well-written, and careful study that places both the WCTU and Willard in historical perspective.

Earhart, Mary. *Frances Willard: From Prayers to Politics*. Chicago: University of Chicago, 1944. The best overall biography and one of the best analyses of Willard. Well documented and objective. Lists all of Willard's writings.

Gordon, Anna A. *The Beautiful Life of Frances Willard*. Chicago: Woman's Temperance Publishing Association, 1898. Uncritical, but typifies those books that have produced an idealized myth of the life and work of Willard.

Gordon, Elizabeth Putnam. *Women Torch Bearers: The Story of the Woman's Christian Temperance Union*. Evanston, Ill.: National Woman's Christian Temperance Union Publishing House, 1924. Although mostly uncritical and apologetic, this history of the WCTU presents a unified sketch of activity influenced by Willard. Not nearly as good as, but should be compared to, Borden.

Gusfield, Joseph. *Symbolic Crusade: Status Politics and the American Temperance Movement*. Urbana: University of Illinois Press, 1963, 1986. A sociological study of what the author calls status politics and the American temperance movement. The book contains some insights into the leadership of Willard and data on the WCTU and the temperance movement.

Leeman, Richard W. *"Do Everything" Reform: The Oratory of Frances E. Willard*. Foreword by Bernard K. Duffy. New York: Greenwood Press, 1992. An examination of Willard's oratory, including a critical analysis of her speaking style and texts of her representative speeches. Also includes a chronology and bibliography of primary and secondary sources.

Willard, Frances. *Glimpses of Fifty Years: An Autobiography of an American Woman*. Chicago: Woman's Temperance Publishing Association, 1889. Reprint. New York: Source Book Press, 1970. Contains details about Willard and other WCTU leaders. Tends to be apologetic and spotty in coverage but does give a flavor of Willard.

_____. *Woman and Temperance: Or, The Work and Wonders of the Woman's Christian Temperance Union*. Hartford, Conn.: Park, 1883. Contains "field notes" of Willard but is badly organized and apologetic. Has considerable information about some WCTU leaders and their activities. First biographical sketch, praiseworthy but uncritical, is of Willard and is written by Mary A. Lathbury.

_____. *Writing Out My Heart: Selections from the Journal of Frances E. Willard, 1855-96.* Edited by Carolyn De Swarte Gifford. Urbana: University of Illinois Press, 1995. These selections from Willard's journal trace the development of her religious and reform commitments and describe her struggle to reconcile the conflicting demands of family, society, and self.

SEE ALSO: Amelia Bloomer; Lydia Folger Fowler; James A. Garfield; Dwight L. Moody; Carry Nation; Anna Howard Shaw.
RELATED ARTICLE in *Great Events from History: The Nineteenth Century, 1801-1900:* February 17-18, 1890: Women's Rights Associations Unite.

WILLIAM IV
King of Great Britain (r. 1830-1837) and Hanover (r. 1830-1837)

William IV's reign as king of Great Britain was relatively brief, but he oversaw some of the most fundamental changes in British government of the nineteenth century. The Reform Bill of 1832, which may well have averted a revolution, could not have been passed without his support, and his reign also witnessed the continued increase of the power of the House of Commons and the continued erosion of the power of the Crown.

BORN: August 21, 1765; Buckingham House, London, England
DIED: June 20, 1837; Windsor Castle, near London, England
ALSO KNOWN AS: William Henry (birth name); Prince William Henry; Duke of Clarence; Wilhelm Heinrich; Sailor King
AREA OF ACHIEVEMENT: Government and politics

EARLY LIFE

The third son of King George III and his queen, Charlotte of Mecklenberg-Streilitz, Prince William Henry was born in what was then known as Buckingham House (Buckingham Palace after its expansion during the 1820's) in London. His eldest brother, George, Prince of Wales, was to be educated as heir to the throne; his older brother Frederick, later the duke of York, was slated for an army career. George III decided that William should have a naval career. Accordingly, after being tutored at Kew Palace from 1772, William, accompanied by his tutor, joined the Royal Navy in June, 1779. He was on active service for nine of the next eleven years and served on vessels that cruised to America and the West Indies; his voyages were punctuated by brief visits to Kew or Windsor.

When William was in New York in the last year of the American Revolution, he was the subject of an abortive kidnapping plot. He was on the Continent from 1783 to 1785, primarily in the family court of Hanover. Elevated to the rank of captain in 1786, William was given command of his own ship and posted to the maritime provinces of Canada. Summoned home by the Prince of Wales during their father's fit of madness in 1788, he returned to England via the West Indies. To his surprise and perhaps to his disappointment, he found that the king had recovered and resumed authority. Some months thereafter, in May, 1789, William was created duke of Clarence.

The duke had few apparent talents and lacked a commanding presence. Even flattering portraits reveal the pear-shaped head that provided an irresistible feature for caricaturists. Moreover, he was often boorish, insensitive, and vulgar and offended the strict king by leading a profligate life, having engaged in a series of affairs. A capable junior officer and captain, he was judged by both the Admiralty and the king to be lacking the abilities necessary for command of a fleet. Denied that promotion, his naval career was effectively ended. For decades, William remained unemployed, subsisting on the parliamentary grant provided him as a royal duke. Given his situation, perhaps it was inevitable that he drift into the filial opposition that characterized royal relations in eighteenth century England and associate himself, briefly, with the social circle that formed around the Prince of Wales.

LIFE'S WORK

In 1790, the duke of Clarence established a liaison with the actor Dorothea Jordan. The relationship lasted some two decades. The couple had ten illegitimate children, all surnamed FitzClarence, and lived with their brood near Hampton Court, the duke having been appointed Ranger of Bushy Park, which gave him the use of that property. Mrs. Jordan continued her acting career, thereby supplementing the duke's parliamentary grant. Most likely it was boredom as well as mounting debts that impelled Clarence to end their connection and search for a younger and more well-endowed consort who would meet with the approval of the monarch as required by the Royal Marriages Act of 1772.

That quest soon became an affair of state, all the more important after Princess Charlotte, the Prince Regent's only child, died in 1817. After his overtures had been spurned by several English heirs and foreign princesses, William finally secured the engagement of Adelaide, princess of Saxe-Meiningen. The prospective marriage allowed the duke to negotiate a significantly larger parliamentary grant, and the couple was married in July, 1818. Each of their two children, both girls, died in infancy.

When George III died in 1820, the Prince of Wales, Prince Regent since 1812, succeeded to the throne in his own right as George IV. In 1827, the duke of York died, which made the duke of Clarence heir presumptive. The new prime minister, George Canning, thereupon appointed him Lord High Admiral, an office that had been unfilled for more than a century. The duke launched into naval business with alacrity. He soon overstepped the bounds of the restored but restricted office, however, and was compelled to resign in August, 1828. He had, however, emerged from a lifetime of relative obscurity.

The duke of Clarence succeeded to the throne as William IV in June, 1830, at the age of sixty-four. The unpopularity of his predecessor coupled with William's breezy informality resulted in his succession being welcomed by the populace. He also had ample opportunity to indulge an idiosyncratic penchant for speechmaking during the early months of his reign. The elections of July, 1830, resulted in no immediate change of government, but the duke of Wellington some months later remained intransigent about parliamentary reform, lost the confidence of the House of Commons, and resigned. William called upon the second Earl Grey, leader of the Whig Party now pledged to reform, to form a government.

In his capacity as a peer since 1789, William had publicly discussed only a few issues. He had unabashedly denounced the evils of adultery; he cited his West Indian experience in supporting the slave trade and slavery; he supported his brother's divorce from Queen Caroline; and he supported the Wellington government's bill for Catholic emancipation. Despite little political involvement, he had been imbued with traditional ideas about the English constitution that he thought validated a government comprising kings, lords, and commons; presumably there was an equilibrium or balance among these three estates of the realm. William recognized, however, that the powers of the House of Commons had increased and that the monarch's powers were not as great as they once had been, but certain functions, he knew, still belonged to the king as part of the royal prerogative. Above all, he retained the increasingly anachronistic view that the ministers were still the king's ministers in fact as well as in theory.

Although he consented to Grey's selection of each minister, William reposed his confidence in Lord Grey personally, not in the cabinet collectively. Grey, moreover, was most responsible for reassuring the king about the essentially conservative intentions of the government and in persuading him that the alternative to parliamentary reform was a revolution that would destroy both the monarchy and the aristocracy. Impressing the king with these views, Grey had to counter the overwhelmingly Tory sentiments of Queen Adelaide, the FitzClarences, and the duke of Cumberland, the king's younger brother. The court's opposition to reform was all the more shrill given the looting and riots that occurred in the countryside and the agitation of political unions in some of the towns.

William IV. (Library of Congress)

The government's Reform Bill was far more extensive than had been anticipated, but the king's reservations were overcome by Lord Grey. When the government was reversed on an amendment in the House of Commons, however, it called upon the king to dissolve Parliament and hold new elections. Despite his fear of violence accompanying elections, William agreed, persuading himself that the Lords' imminent address requesting that he refuse a dissolution constituted an infringement on the royal prerogative. The elections of 1831, virtually a plebiscite on reform, resulted in securing the House of Commons for the Reform Bill. The king became enormously popular, because his name was associated with the reform cause, a development he resented. The Lords, however, rejected the bill on its second reading in October, 1831.

The months that followed witnessed a few concessions to the peers, but none on what ministers considered to constitute the principles of the bill—abolition of rotten boroughs, a uniform franchise in the boroughs, and extension of parliamentary representation to the unrepresented towns. William sought to have the government make some concession on the last point, but to no avail. He could do little more than encourage Grey to negotiate with a few moderate peers, but those negotiations were fruitless. It became increasingly evident even to the most conservative ministers that the Reform Bill could only be passed if the government were armed with the king's promise to create sufficient new peers to force the bill through the House of Lords.

The king first consented to a token creation and then to sufficient peers to carry the bill, but the prospect of a mass creation of peers—even if preference were given, as he stipulated, to eldest sons of existing peers, collateral heirs, and Scottish and Irish peers—caused him to renege. Consequently, when the government resigned in May, 1832, the king recruited Wellington to form a coalition administration that could produce a bill acceptable to the Lords. Wellington was unable to do so. William, therefore, had to recall Grey and formally submit to his government's demand for a creation of peers if necessary. It proved to be unnecessary only when William's pledge became known. The Reform Bill became law in June, 1832, though the king declined a personal appearance in Parliament to give the royal assent.

Other important legislation was promulgated by the Whig governments of the 1830's, much of it distasteful to the king. Such was the case with the abolition of slavery in 1833, to which he consented but which he still considered objectionable. He was most upset with the ministers' treatment of the Irish question, which occupied much of Parliament's time during the remainder of his reign. In particular, he opposed the intended appropriation of Irish church revenues to secular purposes, considering it an erosion of established institutions.

The controversy about the matter resulted in the resignation of four conservative ministers in 1834. William accepted their resignations only on condition that Grey accept them, once again demonstrating his reliance upon his prime minister. He construed the subsequent resignation of Lords Grey and Althorp in July, 1834, on a related Irish matter, to be tantamount to the resignation of the entire cabinet. Once again, he attempted to establish a coalition government of all parties, which he thought was necessary to stem encroachment upon the powers of both the Crown and the House of Lords by the newly reformed House of Commons. Again, none of the leading politicians seriously considered a coalition practical or desirable. William then selected the Whig second Viscount Melbourne as his prime minister.

William's most dramatic attempt to restore the Crown's power was his dismissal of the Whig government in November, 1834, ostensibly because Lord Althorp had to leave the Commons for the Lords to succeed his father. It proved to be the last time that a king dismissed a ministry that had the support of a majority of the House of Commons. Although the constitutionality of the king's action was not seriously questioned at the time, it was ineffective politically. The House of Commons refused to support the succeeding Tory government. When Grey declined a plea that he abandon retirement and lead a coalition, the king was forced to submit again to Melbourne and the Whigs in April, 1835. His suggestion that Melbourne submit the matter of appropriation of Irish church revenues to a board of judges as a judicial question was rejected out of hand. Melbourne would not formally accept the king's right to exclude specific politicians from his cabinet.

William continued to feel besieged during the last two years of his reign. He was dismayed by some legislation, such as the Municipal Corporations Bill of 1835, but was relieved that the government was unable to enact the legislation for diverting surplus Irish church revenues to secular purposes. He died at Windsor Castle on June 20, 1837, and was succeeded by his niece, Victoria.

SIGNIFICANCE

William IV's brief reign remains of considerable importance in English constitutional history. Although the power of the Crown had been declining steadily for decades, during the early nineteenth century the king to some extent still ruled as well as reigned. Far more than a figurehead, the monarch had real power. In William IV's reign, that was most evident in the need to have the king's support to pass the Reform Bill. William's views on foreign affairs also had to be considered, especially since he was the last king of England who was also king of Hanover. The Reform Bill that required the king's support to pass, however, further eroded the Crown's power. It gave even greater power to the electorate, now augmented in numbers, and thereby reinforced the House of Commons as the dominant part of government as defined by the English constitution.

William IV's old-fashioned views about a balance of power between King, Lords, and Commons were no longer appropriate. He was compelled in 1835 to recall the Whigs after dismissing them because the cabinet was far more responsible to the House of Commons than to the king. The cabinet may have remained the king's ministers in theory, but they were no longer the king's ministers in fact. William IV had also expressed concern about the erosion of the House of Lords' power and the conflict between the two houses of Parliament. That conflict would continue throughout the nineteenth century, until the power of the Lords was drastically reduced by the Parliament Act of 1911.

—Abraham D. Kriegel

FURTHER READING

Brock, Michael. *The Great Reform Act*. London: Hutchinson, 1973. Now the standard account of the struggle for the Reform Bill. William's dependence on Grey is emphasized.

Butler, J. R. M. *The Passing of the Great Reform Bill*. London: Frank Cass, 1964. A reprint of the 1914 edition, this book is an old but still valuable account in which the king is somewhat more at center stage than in Brock (above).

Fulford, Roger. *From Hanover to Windsor*. London: Batsford, 1960. The first chapter of this volume on the monarchy contains an elegant essay on William IV, who is favorably evaluated.

Gash, Norman. *Reaction and Reconstruction in English Politics, 1832-1852*. Oxford, England: Clarendon Press, 1965. A judicious interpretation of the constitution and political parties by a distinguished scholar. The first chapter discusses the decline of the Crown's power during William IV's reign.

Kriegel, Abraham D., ed. *The Holland House Diaries, 1831-1840*. London: Routledge & Kegan Paul, 1977. The introductory essay discusses the legislation of the Whig governments of the 1830's, the functions of the cabinet, and its relations with the king.

Pocock, Tom. *Sailor King: The Life of King William IV*. London: Sinclair-Stevenson, 1991. Biography of William, describing his life in the Royal Navy as well as his subsequent monarchy. In Pocock's opinion, William saw himself as a naval officer who happened to become king—not a king who used to be a naval officer.

Somerset, Anne. *The Life and Times of William IV*. London: Weidenfeld and Nicolson, 1980. A popular biography, recommended mainly for the lavish reproductions of contemporary paintings and political cartoons.

Thompson, Grace E. *The Patriot King: The Life of William IV*. New York: E. P. Dutton, 1932. An older, well-written, popular biography, out of date in its interpretation of politics but good in its portrait of William.

Tomalin, Claire. *Mrs. Jordan's Profession: The Actress and the Prince*. New York: Alfred A. Knopf, 1995. Biography of actor Dorothea Jordan, chronicling her twenty-year relationship as William's surrogate spouse and the mother of the couple's ten children.

Ziegler, Philip. *King William IV*. London: Collins, 1971. The best biography. Ziegler goes a bit too far in claiming that William was England's first constitutional monarch.

SEE ALSO: George Canning; George IV; Charles Grey; Second Viscount Melbourne; John Nash; Queen Victoria; Duke of Wellington.

RELATED ARTICLES in *Great Events from History: The Nineteenth Century, 1801-1900:* June 4, 1832: British Parliament Passes the Reform Act of 1832; June 28, 1838: Queen Victoria's Coronation.

GEORGE WASHINGTON WILLIAMS
American historian

As the author of the first reliable history of African Americans and as a prominent political spokesman and observer, Williams contributed to the development of African American identity and racial pride.

BORN: October 16, 1849; Bedford Springs, Pennsylvania
DIED: August 2, 1891; Blackpool, England
AREA OF ACHIEVEMENT: Historiography

EARLY LIFE

George Washington Williams was the son of a free black man named Thomas Williams, who is believed to have been the son of a white Virginia planter and a slave woman. Sometime during the 1840's, the elder Williams moved to Bedford Springs, where he met and married Ellen Rouse, a light-skinned local black woman. George was the second of five children born to the couple. His childhood was a difficult one, plagued by frequent moves, family instability, a scant education, and Thomas Williams's heavy drinking. Although the elder Williams eventually tempered his lifestyle enough to serve as the minister of a black church in Newcastle, Pennsylvania, George became incorrigible and was placed in a refuge house for delinquent juveniles. There, he discovered literature and religion, interests that were to permeate his adult life.

Drawn by a sense of adventure, Williams went off to fight in the Civil War at the age of fourteen. By falsifying his age and using an assumed name, he was able to enlist in a black Union army regiment in August, 1864. He saw action in the closing battles in Virginia, including the campaigns against Petersburg and Richmond. After the war, his unit was transferred to Texas, but he soon left it and joined the revolutionary forces that were fighting to overthrow Emperor Maximilian, an Austrian interloper on the Mexican throne. Shortly before Maximilian's capture and execution in 1867, Williams returned to the United States and reenlisted. He served for more than a year as a cavalry sergeant at military posts in Kansas and Indian Territory (modern Oklahoma) until discharged in 1868.

Although untrained and barely literate, Williams was licensed as a Baptist preacher shortly after his military career ended. In September, 1870, he enrolled at the Newton Theological Institution, a Baptist school and seminary near Boston, Massachusetts. Williams completed both his general studies and his theological training in an astonishingly brief four years and was recognized as a good student. In June, 1874, he was graduated from Newton, was ordained in the Baptist clergy, and married Sarah A. Sterrett. A prominent member of Boston's black community during his Newton years, Williams was named pastor of the city's historic, black Twelfth Baptist Church in 1873. While in that position, he joined other black leaders in working for passage of a national civil rights bill, publicly voiced his concerns about the course of Reconstruction, and penned a history of the local congregation. When he resigned his pastorate in October, 1875, it was to pursue these two emerging interests—politics and history.

LIFE'S WORK

One month before resigning his Boston pastorate, Williams went with his wife and infant son to Washington, D.C., which had become a gathering place for many of the nation's black leaders. With their assistance, he soon inaugurated a new weekly newspaper called *The Commoner*, which he hoped would reach beyond the "chilling shadow of slavery" and become "a powerful agent for reorganizing the race." Although he believed that it would attract a national audience, few subscribed and he was unable to sustain it beyond eight issues. The brevity of his encounter with the national political scene merely heightened Williams's interest in politics.

In February, 1876, Williams was called to the pastorate of the Union Baptist Church in Cincinnati, Ohio. He quickly made his mark on the local black community as an energetic pastor, an articulate spokesperson and imaginative leader in racial affairs, and a regular contributor to the *Commercial*—a leading local newspaper—on a variety of local and national issues. He also became active in local Republican Party circles, rapidly gaining control of the party machinery in the city's black precincts. Nominated as a candidate for the Ohio legislature in 1877, Williams proved a strong campaigner, but he was overwhelmingly defeated as many white voters openly refused to cast their ballot for a black man. After this taste of politics, he left the ministry and briefly published a newspaper called *The Southwestern Review* (1877-1878). When it folded, the peripatetic Williams embarked upon the study of law with Alphonso Taft, the father of President William Howard Taft and a politician of national prominence in his own right. He later attended lectures at the Cincinnati Law School.

Continuing to campaign extensively for Republican candidates, Williams proved to be particularly adept at "waving the bloody shirt"—linking the Democratic Party with the Confederacy, slavery, and responsibility for starting the Civil War. In 1879, he was again nominated as a candidate for the Ohio legislature. Despite widespread criticism, he campaigned hard, openly courted white support, and was narrowly elected. Williams distinguished himself as an active legislator, sponsoring several reform measures, including legislation to control the use of alcoholic beverages. On occasion he became the center of controversy, as when he called for a civil rights resolution after encountering racist treatment in Columbus restaurants, hotels, and newspapers. He also unsuccessfully sought the repeal of a state law prohibiting interracial marriages.

In 1881, Williams refused to seek a second term in the Ohio legislature. His announced reason was the desire to devote his time to historical research and writing. The centennial celebrations of American independence in 1876 had heightened his early interest in history. Moving to Columbus, he began work on a general history of African Americans. A diligent and thorough researcher, he succeeded in completing a massive, two-volume study of his race from its African origins through the end of Re-

George Washington Williams. (The Associated Publishers, Inc.)

construction. This work, entitled *History of the Negro Race in America from 1619 to 1880* (1883), established Williams as a capable historian and was well received by leading eastern magazines and newspapers. The New York *Independent* called it "an epoch-making book."

Although sales of his first book were disappointing, Williams began work on a second, which was eventually published as *History of the Negro Troops in the War of the Rebellion, 1861-1865* (1888). The work proved to be much broader than the title, examining the role of black soldiers in the American Revolution, the War of 1812, the Haitian Revolution, and other conflicts. This work was widely heralded, but the subsequent appearance of Joseph T. Wilson's *Black Phalanx* (1888), another history of black participation in the Civil War, limited sales and publicity for the volume. Williams also researched a two-volume history of Reconstruction, but it was never published. He experimented with other literary forms, penning a play on the African slave trade and a novel on the subject of interracial marriage. Although the novel was rejected by numerous publishers, its first eight chapters were eventually published in the Indianapolis *World* (1888), a black newspaper.

Shortly after the publication of his *History*, Williams returned to Massachusetts to live. Although he practiced law and stumped the state for Republican candidates, he derived most of his income from lecturing on black history, Africa, and general literature. Delivering hundreds of lectures throughout the Northeast, he soon gained a reputation as an eloquent speaker, and the handsome, mustached Williams must have cut a striking figure for his audiences.

Williams maintained his interest in politics. On March 2, 1885, two days before leaving office, President Chester A. Arthur, a Republican, nominated him to serve as minister resident and consul general to Haiti. Although the Senate immediately confirmed him, and he was sworn in, the incoming Democratic administration of President Grover Cleveland refused him the post. He challenged the action in federal court but was denied redress. He abandoned the effort in 1889 after the newly inaugurated Republican president, Benjamin Harrison, appointed black leader Frederick Douglass to the post.

Depressed by his inability to obtain a diplomatic position, Williams turned his attention to Africa. In 1884, he had written articles on African geography, and, in testimony before the Senate Committee on Foreign Relations, he had urged American recognition of the Congo Free State. In the years that followed, he visited Eu-

---

"DEGRADATION" OF THE AFRICAN RACE

In his monumental History of the Negro Race in America, *George Washington Williams sought explanations for what he regarded as the "degradation of the African races." He found one explanation in "idolatry," for which he saw Christianity as the solution.*

Is it asked what caused the decline of all this glory of the primitive Negro? why this people lost their position in the world's history? Idolatry! Sin!

Centuries have flown apace, tribes have perished, cities have risen and fallen, and even empires, whose boast was their duration, have crumbled, while Thebes and Meroe stood. And it is a remarkable fact, that the people who built those cities are less mortal than their handiwork. Notwithstanding their degradation, their woes and wrongs, the perils of the forest and dangers of the desert, this remarkable people have not been blotted out. They still live, and are multiplying in the earth. Certainly they have been preserved for some wise purpose, in the future to be unfolded.

But, again, what was the cause of the Negro's fall from his high state of civilization? It was forgetfulness of God, idolatry! "Righteousness exalteth a nation; but sin is a reproach to any people."

Source: George Washington Williams, *History of the Negro Race in America* (New York, 1883), chapter 3.

---

rope several times to attend conferences on the African slave trade and African missions. In 1889, he interviewed King Leopold II of Belgium about his efforts to bring commerce and Christianity to Africa's Congo basin. When S. S. McClure of the Associated Literary Press commissioned him to write a series of articles on the Congo, and railroad magnate Collis P. Huntington asked him to report on the progress of the Congo railway being built by the Belgians, he visited the African continent.

Although King Leopold attempted to discourage him, Williams sailed for Africa in January, 1890. He spent four months exploring the Congo from the mouth of the Congo River to its headwaters at Stanley Falls. The trip revealed the Belgians' inhuman exploitation of black Africans. Williams responded by publishing *An Open Letter to His Serene Majesty, Leopold II, King of the Belgians* (1890), which extensively criticized Belgian colonial policy in the Congo. After visiting Portuguese and British possessions in East Africa, Williams went to Egypt, where he contracted tuberculosis. By the spring of 1891, he had improved enough to return to England, where he intended to write a full report of the European colonial impact on Africa. Concerned for his health, he hurried to the coastal city of Blackpool, where he hoped that the Irish Sea air and the curative powers of a local spa

would restore his health. They did not. Williams died of tuberculosis and pleurisy on August 2, 1891.

SIGNIFICANCE

George Washington Williams contributed many "firsts" to the African American experience. He was one of only a few African Americans outside the South to serve in a state legislature during the nineteenth century. Representing Hamilton County, Ohio, he distinguished himself during a single term in the Ohio legislature.

Williams is best remembered for his contributions to the writing of African American history. His books were the first reliable studies of the black role in America's past. On the cutting edge of historical research, Williams gathered information from thousands of volumes, but also employed church minutes, school statistics, newspapers, and oral interviews in compiling his works. This took him on an extensive tour of Western military posts, where he interviewed numerous black veterans of the Civil War.

Williams explored beyond the stereotypes and prejudices in his research on the war and thus reclaimed a place for black Americans in the history of the American Revolution, the antislavery movement, and the Civil War. He also delved into African history and was among the first historians to provide a realistic portrayal of the African kingdoms of Benin, Dahomey, Yoruba, and Ashanti. The epic quality of his work brought it attention in major magazines and newspapers, which was highly unusual for black research at that time. In researching his history of black soldiers in the Civil War, Williams became one of the first students of that conflict to use the official records of the Union and Confederate armies. Although he eventually moved away from historical studies, he left his mark on future investigations of the African American experience. Twentieth century black leader W. E. B. Du Bois called Williams "the greatest historian of the race."

Williams was the first African American to investigate extensively European colonialism in Africa. His criticism at first stirred controversy in the United States and abroad, but later colonial observers substantiated his claims. As a result, the Congo Reform Association was founded in 1904 to crusade against conditions in the Congo Free State. In 1890, these accomplishments prompted readers of the *Indianapolis Freeman* to vote Williams one of the ten greatest African Americans in history.

—Roy E. Finkenbine

FURTHER READING

Franklin, John Hope. *George Washington Williams: A Biography*. Chicago: University of Chicago Press, 1985. The only reliable biography of Williams, this well-documented and balanced study is based on years of extensive research in a wide variety of obscure sources.

Gerber, David A. *Black Ohio and the Color Line: 1860-1915*. Urbana: University of Illinois Press, 1976. This valuable, well-documented work provides a context for understanding Williams's Ohio years. It includes a lengthy discussion of black institutions, politics, and race relations in Ohio during the 1870's and 1880's.

Hochschild, Adam. *King Leopold's Ghost: A Story of Greed, Terror, and Heroism in Colonial Africa*. Boston: Houghton Mifflin, 1998. Hochschild's chronicle of Belgium's tyrannical rule of the Congo includes information about Williams's interview with King Leopold II, his visit to the colony, and his indictment of Leopold's regime.

Sanoff, A. P. "Tracking a Pioneer: Forgotten Case." *U.S. News & World Report* 109, no. 11 (September 17, 1990): 53. Briefly describes how historian John Hope Franklin spent almost forty years conducting research and preparing his biography of Williams.

Slade, Ruth. *King Leopold's Congo: Aspects of the Development of Race Relations in the Congo Independent State*. London: Oxford University Press, 1962. Examines King Leopold II's policies in the Congo Free State. It credits Williams as one of the first critics of colonialism to demonstrate that Belgian officials in the Congo violated international trading practices established by European diplomats.

Thorpe, Earl E. *Black Historians: A Critique*. New York: William Morrow, 1971. A general overview of African American historians from 1836 to the present. It critically analyzes Williams's historical writings and compares him with Joseph T. Wilson and other black historians of his time.

Williams, George Washington. *History of the Negro Race in America from 1619 to 1880*. 2 vols. New York: G. P. Putnam's Sons, 1883. Reprint. New York: Arno Press, 1968. The best way to understand Williams's historical contribution is to pursue this massive, two-volume study of African Americans from colonial days through Reconstruction. It has been conveniently reprinted in a single volume by Arno Press and *The New York Times*.

SEE ALSO: Chester A. Arthur; Grover Cleveland; Frederick Douglass; Benjamin Harrison; Leopold II; Maximilian; Booker T. Washington.

RELATED ARTICLE in *Great Events from History: The Nineteenth Century, 1801-1900:* 1824: Ranke Develops Systematic History.

ISAAC MAYER WISE
American religious leader

As a pioneering Reform rabbi with the avowed goal of uniting American Jewry, Wise became the greatest organizer of Reform Jewish institutions. He was the architect of and prime mover in the establishment of the Union of American Hebrew Congregations, Hebrew Union College, and the Central Conference of American Rabbis, and he served as the first president of each of those three organizations.

BORN: March 29, 1819; Steingrub, Bohemia, Austrian Empire (now Lomnice, Czech Republic)
DIED: March 26, 1900; Cincinnati, Ohio
AREAS OF ACHIEVEMENT: Education, religion and theology

EARLY LIFE

Isaac Mayer Wise was the oldest surviving son of Regina and Leo Weiss. At the age of four, he began his studies under the direction of his father, an impoverished teacher who had his own primary school. By the age of six, it was clear that he was a prodigy; he was studying the Bible and the Talmud. By the age of nine, after having learned everything his father could teach him, he went to study with his grandfather, a physician well steeped in Jewish learning. In 1831, when twelve and after the death of his grandfather, he went to Prague to study in a school famous for instruction in the Talmud. He then became an outstanding student in Prague. In 1835, Wise journeyed to Jenikau and enrolled in Bohemia's most famous rabbinical school, headed by Rabbi Aaron Kornfield. At Kornfield's school, Isaac Mayer studied secular as well as religious topics. He completed his formal education by attending the University of Prague for two years and the University of Vienna for one year, during which time he also worked as a tutor.

After officially becoming a rabbi in 1842, at the age of twenty-three, Wise accepted a rabbinical position in Radnitz, Bohemia. In May, 1844, he married Theresa Bloch, a former student, with whom he had ten children during thirty years of happy marriage. Continuing to study and to advance intellectually, he was greatly influenced by Gabriel Kiesser, the great jurist and parliamentarian, who heightened his awareness of nature and the need for political liberalism. He was also greatly influenced in religious liberalism by Samuel Hirsch. Attending a rabbinical conference in Frankfurt in 1845, Wise met, spoke with, and listened to four noted religious thinkers, Abraham Geiger, Samuel Adler, Zacharias Frankel, and David Einhorn, all of whom severely questioned many aspects of traditional Judaism and laid the basis for Reform.

Wise soon realized that Radnitz was too small and isolated for him. Believing the United States to be a place where Jews would be receptive to the idea of Judaism as an evolving faith open to liberal and rational thinking consistent with the Enlightenment, he decided to emigrate to the New World. With his wife and young daughters, he began a sixty-three-day voyage in May, 1846, arriving in New York on July 23.

LIFE'S WORK

Isaac Mayer Wise served as rabbi of Congregation Beth-El in Albany, New York, for four years. In his desire to improve public worship, he introduced numerous reforms, including mixed pews for men and women, the full inclusion of women in the synagogue, choral singing, and confirmation as a replacement for the Bar Mitzvah. Although continually facing opposition from the more traditionally oriented, Orthodox element in his congregation, Wise continued to advocate and pursue changes and reforms in both faith and practice. In 1847, he originated the idea of a single ritual for the American Jewish community. In 1848, he called for a rabbinical meeting the next year to establish a union of congregations; this first call for a meeting failed. Having become a regular contributor to two American Jewish publications, Wise continued writing as well as arguing orally the merits of this union proposal.

Wise, in 1850, accepted an offer to become the rabbi of Beth Elohim in Charleston, South Carolina, an avowedly Reform congregation. He changed his mind, however, and finally refused the offer. Opposition to his Reform ideas increased at Congregation Beth-El. On the morning of the eve of Rosh Hashanah (the beginning of the High Holy Days) in 1850, he was dismissed as rabbi at a rump meeting of the board of directors. At services the next day, a riot broke out. Shortly thereafter, a minority of the Beth-El congregation left with Wise and established a new synagogue, Anshe Emet (men of truth). Anshe Emet was a congregation committed to Reform, the fourth such in the United States; the other Reform congregations were in Charleston, Baltimore, and New York.

In 1854, Wise accepted the post of rabbi of Congregation B'nai Jeshuran in Cincinnati and stayed there the rest of his life. Soon after arriving in Cincinnati, he began to publish a weekly, *The Israelite*, which was later renamed *The American Israelite*, and a German supplement, *Die Deborah*. In both publications, he advocated the centralization of Jewish institutions. He also established Zion College, which combined Judaic and secular studies. In 1855, Wise called for a rabbinical synod that, he hoped, would unite American Jewry by developing an overall authority for Judaism in the United States.

Wise's call prompted the convening of a rabbinical conference in Cleveland, at which an intense debate between Orthodox and Reform rabbis erupted. Desiring to avoid conference failure, Wise sought agreement for a public declaration that would meet the minimal requirements of Orthodoxy but not violate the spirit of Reform. Wise's carefully worded declaration was finally accepted by the Orthodox and moderate Reform representatives in attendance. In the declaration, Wise stated that the Bible was "of immediate divine origin and the standard of our religion." He referred to the Talmud as containing the traditional, legal, and logical exposition of the biblical laws that must be expounded upon and practiced "according to the comments of the Talmud."

Wise, who presided at the conference, was overjoyed with the affirmative vote for the declaration. For him, this signaled a forthcoming union of all congregations in the United States. He believed that Orthodoxy would ultimately bow to a Reform emphasis attached to Jewish tradition. Wise's joy, however, was short-lived. Orthodox rabbis, at first satisfied, became suspicious of Wise's intentions. Radical Reform rabbis, led by David Einhorn in Baltimore, violently attacked the declaration as betraying Reform. Wise engaged in vigorous debate with both sides, but the synod idea quickly collapsed from lack of support.

Despite numerous setbacks, Wise continued to advocate a union of congregations, a common prayer book, and a college to train American rabbis. In 1856, he published *Minhag America*, a modified curtailment of the traditional Hebrew ritual. He wrote extensively and discussed his ideas orally in repeated visits to Jewish communities throughout the United States.

The coming of the Civil War not only deferred Wise's activities somewhat but also seemed to spark within him a desire to seek a career in national politics. He showed little sympathy for the abolitionist agitation preceding the Civil War and was willing to tolerate slavery rather than risk dissolution of the Union. During the Civil War, he joined the so-called Copperhead Democrats; in 1863, he accepted nomination for election to the Ohio State Senate, but he withdrew from the race because of his congregation's opposition to his candidacy.

After the Civil War, Wise agitated again for a union of congregations. He attended the 1869 Reform rabbinical conference in Philadelphia and assented to the resolutions adopted there. Soon thereafter, however, he moved away from the substance of those resolutions, realizing that his identifying with too radical a stand would put him beyond his own dream for a comprehensive union of American synagogues under his leadership. During the next few years, Wise carried on spirited debates with the more radical Reform rabbis in the East. He called rabbinic conferences in Cleveland, Cincinnati, and New York, which were boycotted by the radical Reform rabbis he opposed. He also reissued his *Minhag America*.

In 1873, a part of Wise's dream became a reality. Delegates from thirty-four Reform congregations convened in Cincinnati on July 8 and organized the Union of American Hebrew Congregations (1873). Wise had wanted a union of all congregations in the United States; this was a union only of Reform congregations, mostly from the South and Midwest. Realizing the impossibility of bringing the Orthodox and Reform together at that time, Wise was happy with this development. He had contributed immensely; he was chosen the union's first president.

For Wise, the most important task for the union was the establishment of a college to train rabbis. In July, 1875, the union established Hebrew Union College (1875), the first Jewish seminary in the United States; the formal opening occurred in October. Wise became president and taught as a member of the faculty. He spent the remainder of his life working at and on behalf of the college. He shaped its curriculum and supervised its administration; he ordained more than sixty rabbis. He was an excellent teacher. His classroom presentations were substantive and analytical. His kindly face, scholarly appearance, penetrating eyes, and spectacles, often balanced on his forehead, commanded attention. During his years as college president, he was also able to write some of his more scholarly works.

Although Wise preferred one national organization for all American rabbis, he more realistically became the major advocate of a national organization for Reform rabbis. The Central Conference of American Rabbis (CCAR) was formally established in 1889. Wise was elected president and served in that post until he died.

In the last years of his life, Wise, who believed in the universal mission of Judaism, emerged as a great opponent of Zionism and the establishment of a Jewish state in Palestine. In his 1897 presidential address at the CCAR conference in Montreal, he stated his case and won unanimous endorsement of a resolution proclaiming Reform's rejection of Zionism as being incompatible on many grounds with Judaism.

Having lived a lengthy and productive life, Wise, who remained alert to the end, died quietly in Cincinnati on March 26, 1900.

SIGNIFICANCE

Isaac Mayer Wise was the outstanding American Jew and the leading rabbi of his day. Although he failed to achieve his primary goal of uniting all American Jews, he contributed mightily to developing unanimity among Reform Jews and succeeded in adapting Reform Judaism to the society of the New World. He advocated religious reforms in Jewish thought and practice consistent with the democratic liberalism of the nineteenth century, of which he was a product. This often placed him at the center of controversy but, more important, earned for him a place of distinction in Jewish history.

Wise had a worldview, the major aspect of which was that God had established the United States as the symbolic model of nation-state freedom, equality, and brotherhood. Jews and Judaism, he believed, should conform to this divine new order. He felt obligated to point them in that direction. In this concept, Isaac Mayer Wise was an American reformer as well as a Jewish reformer.

—*Norton Mezvinsky*

FURTHER READING

Heller, James Gutheim. *Isaac M. Wise: His Life, Work and Thought*. New York: Union of American Hebrew Congregations, 1965. The most complete biography and critical analysis of Wise. Contains an extensive bibliography.

Knox, Israel. *Rabbi in America: The Story of Isaac M. Wise*. Boston: Little, Brown, 1957. A good biographical sketch and a thoughtful, incisive analysis of Wise's ideas and activities within the context of Reform Judaism in the United States.

May, Max Benjamin. *Isaac Mayer Wise: The Founder of American Judaism*. New York: G. P. Putnam's Sons, 1916. Factual chronicle of Wise's boyhood in Bohemia and his major accomplishments in the United States. Written by Wise's grandson, this book attempts limited analysis and contains little judgment.

Sachar, Howard M. *A History of the Jews in America*. New York: Knopf, 1992. Chapter III, "The Americanization of German Jewry," includes information on Wise's ideas and contributions to Reform Jewry. Additional references to Wise are listed in the index.

Temkin, Sefton D. *Creating American Reform Judaism: The Life and Times of Isaac Mayer Wise*. New York: Oxford University Press for the Littman Library, 1992. Reprint. Portland, Oreg.: Littman Library of Jewish Civilization, 1998. Biography examining Wise's role in creating a new form of Judaism for American Jews.

Wise, Isaac Mayer. *Judaism: Its Doctrines and Duties*. Rev. ed. Cincinnati, Ohio: L. Wise, 1872. Along with *Pronaos to Holy Writ* (below), this book is representative of Wise's best writing about theology and practice. A popularized, better-written revision of his earlier work, *Essence of Judaism*, published in Cincinnati in 1861 by O. Bloch and Company.

_____. *Pronaos to Holy Writ*. Cincinnati, Ohio: Robert Clarke, 1891. A scholarly analysis of the Old Testament, providing good insight into Wise's thought.

_____. *Reminiscences*. Translated and edited by David Philipson. Cincinnati, Ohio: L. Wise, 1901. Originally written by Wise and published in German in *Die Deborah*, these reminiscences were translated and published in English after his death. Highly personal and partial, they are nevertheless rich in detail and useful in understanding Wise.

_____. *Selected Writings of Isaac M. Wise*. Edited by David Philipson and Louis Grossmann. Cincinnati, Ohio: Robert Clarke, 1900. Contains a short biographical essay of varying quality representing aspects of Wise's thought.

SEE ALSO: Emma Lazarus.

RELATED ARTICLE in *Great Events from History: The Nineteenth Century, 1801-1900:* February, 1896-August, 1897: Herzl Founds the Zionist Movement.

FRIEDRICH WÖHLER
German chemist

In synthesizing urea, Wöhler was the first scientist to demonstrate that organic materials—which had previously been believed to possess a vital force—need not be made exclusively within living organisms. He also isolated aluminum metal and discovered the elements beryllium and yttrium.

BORN: July 31, 1800; Eschersheim, near Frankfurt am Main (now in Germany)
DIED: September 23, 1882; Göttingen, Germany
AREA OF ACHIEVEMENT: Chemistry

EARLY LIFE

Friedrich Wöhler (VEW-ler) was the son of Anton August Wöhler and his wife, Anna Katharina Schröder. He received his early education from his father, who had been Master of the Horse to the Prince of Hesse Kassel and subsequently one of Frankfurt's leading citizens. As a child Wöhler pursued both mineralogy and chemistry as hobbies and, in addition to public school, received tutoring in Latin, French, and music.

Wöhler's early years imbued him with the Romantic spirit of the day. He studied music and poetry, and the well-known landscape painter Christopher Morgenstern encouraged him in artistic endeavors. However, Wöhler also showed an early interest in science, as he built voltaic piles from zinc plates and some old Russian coins and experimented with the reactive elements phosphorus and chlorine. Between 1814 and 1820, Wöhler attended the gymnasium to prepare himself for the University of Marburg, where he began to study medicine and won a prize for his work on the transformation of waste substances into urine. It became obvious to him, at this early stage of his career, that his interests lay more in chemistry than in medicine, and thus he went to Heidelberg, where he studied under the well-known Leopold Gmelin. At Heidelberg, Wöhler earned his medical degree in 1823; rather than seek employment as a physician, however, he received permission to work in Stockholm with Jöns Jakob Berzelius, perhaps the greatest figure in chemistry of the day.

It was in Stockholm that Wöhler gained the scientific and technical skills that were crucial to his future career, as he was carefully trained in exact chemical analysis using such simple tools as a platinum crucible, a balance, and a blow pipe. This expertise, coupled with his interest in cyanic acid and the cyanates, ultimately led to investi-

gations that transformed the fundamental nature of modern chemistry.

LIFE'S WORK

At the beginning of the nineteenth century, organic chemistry was normally associated with the extraction, isolation, and identification of animal and vegetable matter for medicinal purposes. It was thought that only in the animal and vegetable kingdom could organic molecules be synthesized and form organized bodies. The presence of a vital force was attributed to this unique chemistry found only in living systems.

Organic chemistry was a science concerned primarily with understanding the nature of life and creation—not merely a study of isolated reactions of carbon-containing compounds. The concept of vitalism discouraged the use of the theory of chemical affinities associated with mineral or inorganic chemistry in explanations related to the organic branch of the discipline. Thus Berzelius wrote in 1819 that his electrochemical theory could not be applied to organic matter, because, in his opinion, the influence of a vital force led to entirely different electrochemical properties. Wöhler's researches would subsequently refute this idea and thus unify the animal and mineral branches of chemistry.

Upon returning from Berzelius's laboratory in 1825, Wöhler began his teaching career at an industrial school in Berlin. He soon began communicating with University of Giessen professor Justus von Liebig, who had learned exact chemical analysis from Joseph-Louis Gay-Lussac in Paris. The two quickly formed a lifelong friendship and began collaborating on problems of mutual interest. For some time, Liebig had been working on explosive fulminates, and, during the course of these investigations, he prepared a compound that was similar in composition to silver cyanate, a compound Wöhler had prepared in 1823. Despite the fact that silver cyanate and silver fulminate had the same empirical formula, $AgCNO$, they had different chemical and physical properties; it remained for Berzelius in 1830 to call the new phenomenon isomerism.

Wöhler's studies on the cyanates directed him to reexamine reactions that he had initially undertaken while a student in Berzelius's laboratory, thus setting the stage for his artificial synthesis of urea, which stands as a milestone in the history of science. Wöhler prepared urea by first reacting lead cyanate with ammonia. Beautiful

Friedrich Wöhler. (Library of Congress)

white crystals appeared that, when treated with nitric acid, were transformed into lustrous flakes of a substance he quickly recognized as urea. In February of 1828, Wöhler boasted to Berzelius that he had prepared urea without the kidney of a human or a dog.

Wöhler's synthesis marked the beginning of a new chemistry in which distinctions between inorganic and organic fields were blurred. Wöhler's career was now on the rise, and in 1831 he left Berlin for Kassel, where he held a similar position. Tragedy struck amid his early scientific triumphs, however, for a year later his young wife and cousin, Franziska Wöhler, died. For consolation, Wöhler went to Liebig's laboratory, where they collaborated on an important paper dealing with oil of bitter almonds (benzaldehyde). In their investigations they demonstrated that a group of atoms remained unchanged through a series of chemical operations, and to this fundamental unit they gave the name benzoyl. This discovery played a major role in debates of the 1830's dealing with radical theory.

Liebig and Wöhler continued to work together during the 1830's, even though Wöhler returned to Kassel, where he remarried. In 1836, Wöhler succeeded Frie-

drich Strohmeyer at Göttingen and filled this chair for almost half a century until his death in 1882. Although Wöhler worked on various problems related to organic chemistry during his first few years at Göttingen, by 1840 he increasingly turned to the study of inorganic and mineralogical chemistry. Perhaps his reorientation was the result of the frustration of working in the field of organic chemistry at that time. The field was experiencing a kind of chaos because of internal reorientation in terms of nomenclature and central concepts related to molecular structure.

Wöhler's previous background in inorganic and mineralogical chemistry had been a solid one, the result of his studies with his former mentor Berzelius on silicon, selenium, and zirconium. Indeed, in 1827 he had been the first scientist to isolate metallic aluminum by reacting a small quantity of potassium with an excess of aluminum chloride. By 1850, Wöhler was active in preparing a large number of metallic salts, and later in 1862 he was the first to synthesize calcium carbide from acetylene. Other important contributions included the preparation of silicon hydride, silicon chloroform, iodoform, and bromoform.

Unlike his close friend Liebig, Wöhler remained interested and active in chemical research until his death. Friedrich Wöhler's professional accomplishments encompassed broad areas within chemistry, and he stands out in an era in which the discipline was transformed in terms of both theoretical knowledge and technical methods.

SIGNIFICANCE

During the past four decades, historians of science have debated the significance of Friedrich Wöhler's synthesis of urea. The importance of Wöhler's investigation lay not in his refutation of the concept of vitalism but in the development of ideas related to structural chemistry. His demonstration of the isomeric relationship between urea and ammonium cyanate further exposed previously little-known chemical complexities that could be best understood in terms of molecular structure. For chemists such as Wöhler, Berzelius, and Liebig, the vital force apparently remained a scientific concept even after 1828.

The experimental synthesis of acetic acid by Hermann Kolbe in 1844 and the synthesis of methane and acetylene by Marcelin Berthelot in 1855 and 1856 contributed to the decline in popularity of the vitalistic theory. More significant, however, as Timothy Lipman has suggested, is that vitalism's importance in organic chemistry declined by the mid-nineteenth century, when the life sciences became increasingly specialized. Organic chemistry dealt with compounds of carbon atoms; physiology focused on organic functions; but neither subdiscipline examined the creation of life. Thus, for the organic chemist, vitalism was no longer a necessary concept.

—John A. Heitmann

FURTHER READING

Buckingham, John. *Chasing the Molecule*. Stroud, Gloucestershire, England: Sutton, 2004. Describes how scientists during the mid-nineteenth century made significant discoveries about molecules. Includes information about Wöhler's synthesis of an organic from an inorganic compound, and how this accomplishment challenged previous theories of vitalism.

Ihde, Aaron. *The Development of Modern Chemistry*. New York: Harper & Row, 1964. This general survey in the history of chemistry includes a thorough discussion of Wöhler's chief contributions to both organic and inorganic chemistry. It is essential in placing Wöhler's work within its proper intellectual context.

Keen, Robin. "Friedrich Wöhler and His Lifelong Interest in the Platinum Metals." *Platinum Metals Review* 29 (1985): 81-85. A well-researched and clearly written article that not only provides an overview of Wöhler's life and professional career but also focuses upon his work in the isolation of aluminum and the separation of iridium and osmium. In addition, Keen links the careers of two of Wöhler's students, Wilhelm Carl Heraeus and Heinrich Rössler, to the development of the platinum industry.

Lipman, Timothy O. "Wöhler's Preparation of Urea and the Fate of Vitalism." *Journal of Chemical Education* 41 (1964): 452-458. Lipman's essay on vitalism and Wöhler provides a model of careful research and critical thinking for scholars working in the field of the history of chemistry. Lipman's purpose is to settle the issue of whether Wöhler's 1828 synthesis of urea overturned vitalistic notions in organic chemistry. In the process of demonstrating that Wöhler's experiment was one of a number of facts that accumulated during the first half of the nineteenth century to make

vitalism untenable, the author thoroughly characterizes the place of vitalism in chemistry both before and after 1828.

McKie, Douglas. "Wöhler's Preparation of Urea and the Fate of Vitalism: A Chemical Legend." *Nature* 153 (1944): 608-610. This work strongly argues that Wöhler's 1828 synthesis of urea had far less influence in refuting the doctrine of vitalism than previously believed. Indeed, McKie attempts to shatter a legend that emerged long after Wöhler's early experiments, a legend perpetuated by successive generations of chemists.

Smith, Edgar F. "Some Experiences of Dr. Edgar F. Smith as a Student Under Wöhler." *Journal of Chemical Education* 5 (1928): 1554-1557. In 1928, Edgar Fah Smith of the University of Pennsylvania, one of the leading figures in the development of chemistry in nineteenth century America, reminisced to a small group of chemists, one of whom recorded the conversation. Smith's recollections are a delightful account of one student's experiences in Göttingen and provide an interesting view of Wöhler as a mentor of graduate students.

Warren, W. H. "Contemporary Reception of Wöhler's Discovery of the Synthesis of Urea." *Journal of Chemical Education* 5 (1928): 1539-1553. Although somewhat dated in terms of scholarship, this essay traces the response of several important chemists to Wöhler's 1828 synthesis of urea. By carefully examining contemporary correspondence, periodical literature, and books, the author argues that by 1840 a number of chemists were convinced of the significance of Wöhler's work in the changing views concerning vitalism and thus of the boundaries between organic and inorganic chemistry.

SEE ALSO: Amedeo Avogadro; Joseph-Louis Gay-Lussac; Justus von Liebig; Dmitry Ivanovich Mendeleyev; August Weismann.

RELATED ARTICLES in *Great Events from History: The Nineteenth Century, 1801-1900:* 1803-1808: Dalton Formulates the Atomic Theory of Matter; 1869-1871: Mendeleyev Develops the Periodic Table of Elements.

VICTORIA WOODHULL
American social reformer

An impassioned advocate of woman suffrage, racial and sexual equality, and spiritualism, Woodhull ran for the office of United States president, established a New York brokerage firm, and edited a radical newspaper.

BORN: September 23, 1838; Homer, Ohio
DIED: June 10, 1927; Bredon's Norton, Worcestershire, England
ALSO KNOWN AS: Victoria Claflin (birth name)
AREAS OF ACHIEVEMENT: Women's rights, social reform, government and politics

EARLY LIFE

Victoria Woodhull was born Victoria Claflin and was one of nine surviving children of Roxanna (Anna) Hummel Claflin, a religious fanatic, and Reuben Buckman "Buck" Claflin, an unsuccessful Ohio businessperson and criminal. Woodhull had only three years of formal education, but from childhood thought that she was a vehicle for spirit voices and believed herself to be a faith healer. To exploit her apparent gift, her father set up her and her sister Tennessee (later Tennie C.) as faith healers. The sisters became and long remained the primary source of their large family's income.

To escape the life into which her abusive father was driving her, Victoria married a physician, Canning Woodhull, on November 20, 1853, when she was fifteen years old. However, her husband proved to be an alcoholic and morphine addict. When their first child, Byron, was born in 1854, Victoria blamed her husband's alcoholism for the infant's severe brain damage. For some years, the family traveled widely, ranging as far as California. Victoria gave birth to a daughter, Zulu (later Zula) in 1861. Delivered under her husband's drunken care, the baby almost died, and Victoria decided to divorce her husband.

By 1863, Victoria's father, Buck Claflin, was advertising himself as a curer of cancer and was operating an infirmary in Ottawa, Illinois. Conditions in the place were squalid, and after a patient's death in 1864, Victoria's sister Tennie C. was indicted for manslaughter.

In 1864, Victoria was in St. Louis, Missouri, where she met Colonel James Harvey Blood, a wounded Union Army veteran who was working as the St. Louis city auditor and serving as organizer of the St. Louis Society of Spiritualists. Blood left his wife and reputation behind to leave St. Louis with Victoria and her children. Victoria married Blood on July 12, 1866, in Dayton, Ohio. Blood also took Tennie C. under his protection, earning the undying hatred of Victoria and Tennie's parents. After Victoria's departure at fifteen, Tennie C. had supported the extended family.

LIFE'S WORK

Victoria, Tennie C., and Blood moved to New York in 1868, taking with them their extended family of fifteen, including Woodhull's parents. There Victoria and Tennie C. met Cornelius Vanderbilt, a seventy-three-year-old railroad pioneer who was probably the richest man in America. Fascinated by clairvoyants, Vanderbilt was so charmed by Tennie C. that he established Victoria and her as the first women stockbrokers under the company name "Woodhull, Claflin & Company."

With Vanderbilt's backing, the sisters' firm was highly successful and earned Victoria the fortune she needed for her political goals. Although woman suffrage leaders did not generally support her efforts, Victoria wanted to be numbered among the reformers. She was a powerful speaker and became a popular lecturer. Her experiences as a medium and faith healer had exposed her to the misery underlying many marriages in which women had no control over their money, children, sex lives, or childbearing. Victoria wanted more than the vote for women; she wanted full equality between men and women and—as she later added—full equality among all races and religions. After surveying the badly fragmented woman suffrage movement, she chose a new direction. On April 2, 1870, she announced her candidacy for president of the United States, explaining that her business success demonstrated both her ability, and that of other women, to succeed in public life. For a brief time, she was, indeed, partially successful.

To support her political candidacy, Victoria began publishing *Woodhull & Claflin's Weekly* on May 14, 1870. Much of the writing for the paper was done by Blood and Stephen Pearl Andrews, a left-wing reformer whose extreme radicalism caused the papers' editors to run occasional disclaimers indicating that they did not stand behind every opinion they printed. Andrews occasionally even attacked the popular Protestant preacher Henry Ward Beecher, whose Brooklyn church was an important center of political power. At a time when the corruptness of President Ulysses S. Grant's administration was becoming known, the laboring classes increasingly saw corporate America as their enemy, and *Woodhull & Claflin's Weekly* and its editors became associated with the socialist movement. On December 30, 1871, the paper published the first United States publication of Karl Marx and Friedrich Engels' *Communist Manifesto* (1848). These publications and the paper's support of radical proposals such as a woman's right to divorce and free love, as well as attacks on fraudulent corporate practices, all made enemies.

By late 1870, *Woodhull & Claflin's Weekly* had a circulation of twenty thousand, and Victoria and Tennie C. were the subjects of positive stories in other papers. With the woman suffrage movement split and devoid of ideas, radical leaders such as Susan B. Anthony briefly welcomed Victoria's ideas and financial support. Influenced by Benjamin Butler, a retired Civil War general and former congressman, Victoria based her political candidacy on the idea that women did not need special legislation to win suffrage, as they already possessed it because the Fourteenth and Fifteenth Amendments to the Constitution, which defined voting rights and citizenship, referred to "persons" and "citizens," not to "men" or "women." Victoria took the position that if all Americans were citizens, then they all had the right to vote. She

Victoria Woodhull. (Courtesy, Harvard University Library)

wrote a memorandum on that subject that was printed and sent to the U.S. Congress's House and Senate Judiciary Committees for consideration. In 1871, she became the first woman to testify before a congressional committee.

Woodhull began to fall from fame into scandal on May 15, 1871, when her mother instituted court proceedings against James Harvey Blood, claiming that he had tried to kill her. She eventually lost her case, but the trial focused on Victoria's domestic life, not the attempted murder charge. Reporters learned that Victoria's former husband, Canning Woodhull, was now a helpless drug addict whom Victoria supported. Every aspect of Victoria's domestic life was sensationalized in the press, which implied that she shared herself with two men. Victoria explained that she was supporting a large extended family, but the public focused on scandal.

Despite the growing scandal, in 1872 Victoria became the presidential nominee of the Equal Rights Party, a party of working-class people. Frederick Douglass, a former slave, was the party's vice presidential candidate. Although the party's ticket was destined to failure, Victoria's candidacy nonetheless marked a new step toward sexual equality in the United States.

Increasingly under siege for her controversial views and apparently scandalous life, Victoria realized that, despite her successes, she was still victim of a double standard of morality, and she began an attack on the sexual hypocrisy of the womanizing preacher Henry Ward Beecher. However, Beecher was so powerful that Victoria's support faded away, and Harriet Beecher Stowe, Beecher's sister, joined Victoria's enemies. The famed author of *Uncle Tom's Cabin* (1852), Stowe satirized Victoria as Audacia Dangyereyes in *My Wife and I*, a novel that she serialized in *The Christian Year* in 1871. Among the forces of conventional morality arrayed against Victoria, one of the most influential was Anthony Comstock, the self-appointed censor for the United States Post Office. He initiated a series of arrests on trumped-up charges that eventually bankrupted Victoria. Victoria's brokerage firm was gone, her newspaper limped to a halt, and her money was exhausted on legal fees.

After Victoria divorced Blood in 1877, she fled to England—probably financed with Vanderbilt's money—with Tennie C., her children, and part of her extended family. There she met John Biddulph Martin, an heir to a banking fortune. Martin defied his family and polite society by marrying Victoria on October 31, 1883. Letters published by Mary Gabriel in 1998 suggest this union was a genuinely affectionate marriage until Martin died on March 20, 1897. Meanwhile, Tennie C. married Francis Cook, a successful businessperson who possessed the title of viscount of Monserrat and a castle in Portugal. Tennie C. thus became Lady Cook, the viscountess of Monserrat.

While attempting to rewrite part of the past for the sake of her new marriage, Victoria retained her old vigor. With her daughter Zula, she edited *The Humanitarian* (1892-1901). She also took up bicycling, became the first woman motorist to drive through the English countryside, and was among organizers of the Ladies Automobile Club. With her daughter, she turned the manor house in which she lived in Bredon's Norton, Worcestershire, into a woman's agricultural college and established a private model school in the village in 1907. She sponsored youth groups. After the outbreak of World War I, she actively engaged in fund-raising and the entertainment of wounded soldiers. After a full and busy life, she died in Bredon's Norton on June 10, 1927.

SIGNIFICANCE

Despite her poverty-stricken and unsavory background and lack of education, Victoria Woodhull became a key figure in the spiritualist, women's rights, and racial and sexual equality movements of her time. However, after scandal overtook her, she was essentially written out of histories of those movements, and her contributions were largely forgotten.

During the nineteenth century, spiritualism was a widespread movement that was especially important to women. Denied public utterance in conventional churches, spiritualist women were encouraged to demonstrate their abilities in public. Denied self-confidence because of conventional notions of female inferiority, they found self-assurance in the faith that voices other than their own were speaking through them. Victoria also brought wealth and new vitality to the badly fractured woman suffrage movement.

Woodhull's nomination, with Frederick Douglass as her vice presidential nominee, marked the first time that either a woman or an African American was a candidate for high political office. Her public speeches on the need

for women to gain rights over their own bodies and her public denunciations of marital rape and the exhaustion inflicted on many women by repeated childbearing placed her far in advance of her time.

—*Betty Richardson*

FURTHER READING

Frisken, Amanda. *Victoria Woodhull's Sexual Revolution: Political Theater and the Popular Press in Nineteenth-Century America*. Philadelphia: University of Pennsylvania Press, 2004. Describes how Woodhull engaged in political theatrics to manipulate the popular press and culture and accomplish her political goals.

Gabriel, Mary. *Notorious Victoria: The Life of Victoria Woodhull, Uncensored*. Chapel Hill, N.C.: Algonquin Books of Chapel Hill, 1998. Straightforward biography that contains a lengthy account of Woodhull's life in England.

Goldsmith, Barbara. *Other Powers: The Age of Suffrage, Spiritualism, and the Scandalous Victoria Woodhull*. New York: Alfred A. Knopf, 1998. Although accepting the most scandalous interpretations of Woodhull's activities, Goldsmith also offers a comprehensive view of post-Civil War racial, political and religious problems and scandals that affected her.

Underhill, Lois Beachy. *The Woman Who Ran for President: The Many Lives of Victoria Woodhull*. Bridgehampton, N.Y.: Bridge Works, 1995. Emphasizes American conflicts and has an introduction by the modern feminist Gloria Steinem.

SEE ALSO: Susan B. Anthony; Henry Ward Beecher; Frederick Douglass; Ulysses S. Grant; Belva A. Lockwood; Karl Marx; Harriet Beecher Stowe; Cornelius Vanderbilt; Frances Wright.

RELATED ARTICLES in *Great Events from History: The Nineteenth Century, 1801-1900:* June 17-18, 1873: Anthony Is Tried for Voting; March 9, 1875: *Minor v. Happersett*; February 17-18, 1890: Women's Rights Associations Unite.

WILLIAM WORDSWORTH
English poet

As one of the first and probably the greatest of the English Romantic poets, Wordsworth redirected the literary trends of the time. His most important poems present a vision of the expanded human mind in creative interplay with the external world.

BORN: April 7, 1770; Cockermouth, Cumberland, England

DIED: April 23, 1850; Rydal Mount, Westmorland, England

AREA OF ACHIEVEMENT: Literature

EARLY LIFE

Born on the borders of the Lake District in northwest England, William Wordsworth was the second of five children born to John and Ann Wordsworth. His mother died when he was eight, and when he was nine he was sent to Hawkshead Grammar School, thirty-five miles to the south, on the shores of Esthwaite Lake. Wordsworth loved the Lakeland countryside, where he was free to roam for long periods, as he was later to record in *The Prelude: Or, The Growth of a Poet's Mind* (1850). He was an adventurous, imaginative, strong-minded, and rebellious boy, who was also given to periods of solitude. His was a happy childhood, though his father also died when Wordsworth was young.

In 1787, Wordsworth entered St. John's College, Cambridge, but the tall, lean, and dour northerner, his long face usually serious in expression, his clothes plain and unsophisticated, and his manner awkward, neither excelled as a scholar nor fitted smoothly into fashionable social circles. He later wrote in *The Prelude* that he believed that he was "not for that hour,/ Nor for that place," but at the time he had no clear idea of his vocation.

During his summer vacation in 1790, Wordsworth went on a walking tour with his friend Robert Jones through France and the Alps. The following year, after receiving his degree from Cambridge, he climbed Mount Snowdon, the highest peak in Great Britain. It was an important event because he would later incorporate the story of the climb, giving it great symbolic importance, in the final book of *The Prelude*.

In November, 1791, Wordsworth returned to France, where the French Revolution was at its height. Stimulated by his friendship with the Republican soldier Michel Beaupuy, Wordsworth enthusiastically embraced the revolutionary cause, later writing of "France standing on the top of golden hours/ And human nature seeming born again."

Wordsworth also had a love affair with a Frenchwoman, Annette Vallon, from Orleans, who later gave birth to his child, Caroline. He returned to England in December, 1792, and one month later his first published poetry, *An Evening Walk* and *Descriptive Sketches*, appeared. For the next two years, he lived mainly in London and was involved in radical politics. Wordsworth was appalled that England had gone to war against revolutionary France, but over the next few years, as he watched the revolution turn into tyranny and wars of conquest, he was thrown into a state of moral confusion.

In 1795, Wordsworth's financial position eased when a young friend, Raisley Calvert, died and left him a legacy of nine hundred pounds. He and his devoted sister, Dorothy, rented a cottage in Racedown, in the southwest county of Dorset, where Wordsworth recovered his peace of mind. He also met two young poets, Robert Southey and Samuel Taylor Coleridge. The friendship with Coleridge, which became fully established in 1797, coincided with the beginning of a golden decade in which Wordsworth was to write most of his greatest poems.

LIFE'S WORK

Coleridge, a great poet in his own right, worshipped Wordsworth, and Wordsworth, in his turn, was stimulated by the range of Coleridge's learning and the depth of his critical insight. It was Coleridge who helped to shape Wordsworth's conception of his own poetic vocation. For several years, the two were almost daily in each other's company, and in 1798 they published anonymously a joint collection (although Wordsworth was the chief contributor) entitled *Lyrical Ballads*. It did not win favorable reviews and did not sell many copies, but it later came to be recognized as one of the landmarks in the history of English literature. Wordsworth had developed a new idea of what poetry could be about. He wrote about ordinary events in the lives of ordinary people: simple country folk and children mainly, but also social outcasts and misfits. Not only did this break all the neoclassical rules about the proper subject matter of poetry, but, in using simple, nonliterary language, what he called the common language of men, Wordsworth also challenged the conventional wisdom regarding poetic diction.

In December, 1799, following a brief visit to Germany with Coleridge, Wordsworth and Dorothy moved to Dove Cottage, in the Lake District village of Grasmere. Coleridge and his wife followed them to nearby Keswick. The Wordsworths were to live in Dove Cottage for nearly ten years; it was to be the most creative period of the poet's life. This was in part a result of the serenity and happiness of domestic life at Dove Cottage; Dorothy was a devoted helper, and Wordsworth's marriage to his childhood friend Mary Hutchinson in 1802 increased his tranquillity. It was an ideal environment for writing. During this period, Wordsworth completed an early version of *The Prelude*, planned a long poem titled *The Recluse* (1888), and wrote most of *Home at Grasmere* (published in 1888 as part of *The Recluse*), as well as *Michael* (1800) and a preface to *Lyrical Ballads*, which was published in a new and expanded edition in 1801. The following year, he wrote the first four stanzas of the magnificent *Ode: Intimations of Immortality* (1807).

In the same year, tragedy struck the close-knit family when Wordsworth's brother, John, a naval captain, was drowned when his ship was wrecked in a storm. Wordsworth and Dorothy were grief-stricken; the 1807 "Ele-

giac Stanzas Suggested by a Picture of Peele Castle" records Wordsworth's feelings at the time. In 1805, the second version of *The Prelude* was completed, although Wordsworth never gave the poem a title, referring to it only as the poem about his life.

Now in midlife, Wordsworth was undergoing a profound change of outlook. Formerly a supporter of the French Revolution and a political radical, he now began to lean heavily toward conservatism in politics and religion, giving his support to the governing Tory Party, the landed aristocracy, as well as the Church of England. As an established man with family responsibilities (by 1810, he had become the father of five children), he felt safer with the status quo. "Ode to Duty" is a sign of the stern, unbending Wordsworth that the Victorian age was to admire. In addition, Wordsworth was aware that he had lost the visionary power with which, as a youth, he had communed with nature, and which had inspired so much of his best poetry. The effects of the loss, as well as the renewed strength that he had found, is recorded in *Ode: Intimations of Immortality* and the "Elegiac Stanzas."

In 1808, Dove Cottage was becoming overcrowded, and the Wordsworths moved to larger accommodations at Allan Bank in the same town, where Coleridge stayed with them for long periods. The famous friendship, however, was showing signs of strain. Coleridge's health was deteriorating, largely through his dependence on opium, and he seemed incapable of sustained and productive work. In 1810 came an open quarrel, when some critical remarks made by Wordsworth about his friend got back to Coleridge. The quarrel was patched up eighteen months later, but the two were never to regain their former intimacy.

Tragedy struck the family again in 1812, when two of the Wordsworths' children died in infancy. The following year, the family left Allan Bank for nearby Rydal Mount, where they were to stay for the remainder of their lives. Their financial security improved when Wordsworth accepted a government position as Distributor of Stamps for the county of Westmoreland, a post that confirmed the conservative trend in his life that had been apparent for at least a decade.

In 1814, Wordsworth published *The Excursion*, his first publication in seven years. Like *Lyrical Ballads*, however, it did not find favor with professional reviewers. In spite of their reservations about some aspects of his work, however, there was a growing recognition in literary circles that Wordsworth was one of the leading poets of the age and that some of his work was indeed the

William Wordsworth. (Library of Congress)

work of genius. When, in 1820, he published a series of sonnets, *The River Duddon*, he was, for the first time, universally acclaimed. Ironically, however, his golden years as a poet were behind him. Although he continued to write a large number of poems, little of the work of his later years retained the freshness, the visionary quality, of his early poems.

APOLOGY FOR THE FRENCH REVOLUTION

During his youth, William Wordsworth was sympathetic toward the aims of the French Revolution. In this letter that he wrote in 1793, he defends the revolutionaries' execution of King Louis XVI.

At a period big with the fate of the human race I am sorry that you attach so much importance to the personal sufferings of the late royal martyr, and that an anxiety for the issue of the present convulsions should not have prevented you from joining in the idle cry of modish lamentation which has resounded from the Court to the cottage. You wish it to be supposed you are one of those who are unpersuaded of the guilt of Louis XVI. If you had attended to the history of the French Revolution as minutely as its importance demands, so far from stopping to bewail his death, you would rather have regretted that the blind fondness of his people had placed a human being in that monstrous situation which rendered him unaccountable before a human tribunal. A bishop [Abbé Grégoire], a man of philosophy and humanity as distinguished as your Lordship, declared at the opening of the National Convention—and twenty-five millions of men were convinced of the truth of the assertion—that there was not a citizen on the tenth of August who, if he could have dragged before the eyes of Louis the corpse of one of his murdered brothers, might not have exclaimed to him: "Tyran, voilà ton ouvrage." Think of this, and you will not want consolation under any depression your spirits may feel at the contrast exhibited by Louis on the most splendid throne of the universe, and Louis alone in the tower of the Temple or on the scaffold. But there is a class of men who received the news of the late execution with much more heartfelt sorrow than that which you, among such a multitude, so officiously express. The passion of pity is one of which, above all others, a Christian teacher should be cautious of cherishing the abuse when, under the influence of reason, it is regulated by the disproportion of the pain suffered to the guilt incurred. It is from the passion thus directed that the men of whom I have just spoken are afflicted by the catastrophe of the fallen monarch. They are sorry that the prejudice and weakness of mankind have made it necessary to force an individual into an unnatural situation, which requires more than human talents and human virtues, and at the same time precludes him from attaining even a moderate knowledge of common life, and from feeling a particular share in the interests of mankind. But, above all, these men lament that any combination of circumstances should have rendered it necessary or advisable to veil for a moment the statues of the laws, and that by such emergency the cause of twenty-five millions of people, I may say of the whole human race, should have been so materially injured. Any other sorrow for the death of Louis is irrational and weak.

Source: William Wordsworth, "Apology for the French Revolution," in *The Prose Works of William Wordsworth* (London, 1876), vol. 1.

The remaining years of Wordsworth's life were years of fame. There was a constant stream of distinguished visitors to Rydal Mount, as well as tourists hoping to catch a glimpse of the great man. In 1843, as the elder statesman of the British literary scene, he was appointed poet laureate. Four years later came a devastating personal blow when his daughter Dora died. Another tragedy was with Wordsworth constantly. Twelve years previously, his beloved sister Dorothy had become seriously ill, and she lived the last twenty years of her life as a physical invalid and mental child. Wordsworth nursed her devotedly until his death on April 23, 1850. *The Prelude*, which he had been revising on and off for forty years, was published posthumously, as he had wished. It is his greatest achievement as a poet.

SIGNIFICANCE
William Wordsworth was at the forefront of the revolution in literature that took place when the neoclassicism of the eighteenth century gave way to the Romanticism of the early nineteenth. There were several major areas in which change took place. First, the Romantic age reestablished the importance of the imagination in the creative process, in contrast to neoclassicism, which had exalted the rational intellect. The power of the imagination gives the poet the ability to see the external world from a higher perspective. It reunites the perceiver and the perceived, subject and object, and creates a unity in diversity, in contrast to the tendency of the intellect to separate and compartmentalize. The imagination is central to Wordsworth's design in *The Prelude*.

The Romantics also emphasized the importance of feeling and emotion and the spontaneity of the creative act. Poetry arises from the "spontaneous overflow of powerful feelings," wrote Wordsworth in the preface to *Lyrical Ballads*, one of the central documents of English Romanticism. Emotional and intellectual crises became legitimate subjects for poetry (Wordsworth's *The Prelude* is an excellent example). In part, this was a result of the highly exalted view of poetry and the poet. The poet is viewed as a seer ("I was a chosen son," wrote Wordsworth in *The Prelude*), and poetry itself, according to Wordsworth, is "the first and last of all knowledge—it is as immortal as the heart of man."

Other Romantics, younger men such as Percy Bysshe Shelley and John Keats, were profoundly influenced by Wordsworth's poetry and ideas. Although Wordsworth's reputation went into a slight decline after his death, the Victorian poet and critic Matthew Arnold emerged to champion his cause. Since then, he has not lost his high rank among the English poets, standing behind only John Milton and William Shakespeare. Although much of his later work is undistinguished, the serene and solemn majesty of the best portions of *The Prelude* remains unmatched in the language, and the great *Ode: Intimations of Immortality*, as many generations of readers have found, has enormous power to inspire, uplift, and console.

—Bryan Aubrey

FURTHER READING

Bloom, Harold, ed. *William Wordsworth*. Philadelphia: Chelsea House, 2003. One in a series of books aimed at literature students. Contains an introductory essay by Bloom, a biography of Wordsworth, and essays aimed at introducing Wordsworth's poetry to readers.

Darbishire, Helen. *The Poet Wordsworth*. Oxford, England: Clarendon Press, 1950. Lucid, concise, and eloquent introduction to the poetry by a senior Wordsworth scholar.

Davies, Hunter. *William Wordsworth: A Biography*. New York: Atheneum Publishers, 1980. Written in an informal style for the general reader. Davies avoids discussion of the poetry, but the result is that his biography, although readable and accurate, fails to convey any sense of Wordsworth's greatness.

Gill, Stephen, ed. *The Cambridge Companion to Wordsworth*. New York: Cambridge University Press, 2003. The fifteen essays in this compilation provide an excellent introduction to Wordsworth's poetry. The essays include explorations of Wordsworth's literary career, poetic craft, Wordsworth and Romanticism, and Wordsworth and America.

_____. *Wordsworth and the Victorians*. New York: Oxford University Press, 1998. Examines how Wordsworth's reputation flourished during the Victorian Era, and how his work influenced Matthew Arnold, George Eliot, and other nineteenth century writers.

Hebron, Stephen. *William Wordsworth*. New York: Oxford University Press, 2000. Concise 120-page overview of Wordsworth's life, aimed at the general reader and student.

Moorman, Mary. *William Wordsworth: A Biography*. 2 vols. Oxford, England: Clarendon Press, 1957, 1965. Moorman's meticulous scholarship, and her sympathetic understanding of the poet, make this the standard biography.

Wordsworth, William. *Letters of William Wordsworth: A New Selection*. Edited by Alan G. Hill. Oxford, England: Clarendon Press, 1984. Contains more than 160 of Wordsworth's direct, matter-of-fact letters, revealing much about himself as man and poet, and about his relations with family and friends.

_____. *The Poetical Works*. Edited by Ernest de Selincourt and Helen Darbishire. 5 vols. Oxford, England: Oxford University Press, 1940-1949. The complete poetry. Classified according to Wordsworth's own arrangement.

_____. *The Prelude, 1799, 1805, 1850*. Edited by Jonathan Wordsworth, M. H. Abrams, and Stephen Gill. New York: W. W. Norton, 1979. Definitive edition of Wordsworth's masterpiece. Format allows easy comparison of the 1805 version with the 1850 version. Includes contemporary responses to *The Prelude* and a selection of recent critical essays.

Wu, Duncan. *Wordsworth: An Inner Life*. Malden, Mass.: Blackwell, 2002. Traces how Wordsworth's art developed between 1787 and 1813. Wu examines the impact of Wordsworth's early childhood, particularly the delayed mourning of his parents' deaths, on Wordsworth's later poetry.

SEE ALSO: Matthew Arnold; Thomas Arnold; Elizabeth Barrett Browning; Samuel Taylor Coleridge; John Keats; Percy Bysshe Shelley; Catharine Parr Traill.

RELATED ARTICLES in *Great Events from History: The Nineteenth Century, 1801-1900:* December, 1816: Rise of the Cockney School; 1842: Tennyson Publishes "Morte d'Arthur"; November 5, 1850: Tennyson Becomes England's Poet Laureate.

FANNY BULLOCK WORKMAN
American explorer and social reformer

A tireless explorer and geographer, writer, linguist, feminist, and suffragist, Workman set international mountain-climbing records for women. Her enormous contribution to the body of geographical knowledge was acknowledged by numerous geographical societies around the world.

BORN: January 8, 1859; Worcester, Massachusetts
DIED: January 22, 1925; Cannes, France
ALSO KNOWN AS: Fanny Bullock (birth name)
AREAS OF ACHIEVEMENT: Exploration, geography, sports

EARLY LIFE

Fanny Bullock was born into a wealthy Massachusetts family. Her mother was Elvira Hazard Bullock. Fanny's maternal grandfather was Augustus George Hazard, a merchant and gunpowder manufacturer based in Connecticut, where he built up the family fortune. Fanny's father, Alexander Hamilton Bullock, was a politician who served as the Republican governor of Massachusetts from 1866 to 1868. Fanny had an older sister and brother. Her early education came from private tutors. After completing Miss Graham's Finishing School in New York, she spent two years in Dresden and Paris, where she became fluent in German and French.

Fanny returned to Massachusetts when she was twenty. At the age of twenty-two, on June 16, 1881, she married William Hunter Workman, a physician. He was twelve years older than she was, had done his postgraduate studies in Munich, and had already traveled extensively in Europe. They had one daughter, Rachel, in 1884. Fanny began hiking with her husband in the White Mountains of New Hampshire. It was there that she climbed her first mountain, Mount Washington (6,293 feet), an unusual accomplishment for a woman of that time. In 1886, they began taking trips to Scandinavia and Germany. William Workman became ill in 1888, and since they were independently wealthy, he retired from his medical practice without causing them any economic hardship. The Workmans spent the next nine years in Europe, using Germany as their home base while they traveled, leaving their child in the care of nurses or at boarding school. It was during these years that Fanny did her first serious climbing.

LIFE'S WORK

Fanny Bullock Workman, who preferred to be called

Mrs. Bullock Workman, began her adventurous career when her husband took her hiking in the White Mountains of New Hampshire. She climbed Mount Washington several times. After her husband retired and they moved to Europe, she began to make her first serious ascents.

Most of the climbing that Fanny did during their early years in Europe was in the Alps. With the help of guides, she scaled Zinal Rothorn (4,221 feet), the Matterhorn (14,780 feet), and Mont Blanc (15,781 feet). These were exceptional accomplishments, because it was unacceptable during the 1890's for women to do mountain climbing.

Amazingly, she made these climbs wearing the long skirts that were considered proper for women of that era. In fact, throughout the years of her exploring and climbing, she continued to wear skirts as a part of her outfit, though in later years she did begin to wear them shortened up to her boot tops.

Wearing skirts was Fanny Workman's only concession to the feminine role that was considered appropriate in the Victorian age. She and her husband were adamant in their belief in the equality of women with men. As their excursions grew longer and more complex, they began trading roles from year to year. One would organize the expedition, arranging for all the necessary supplies, pack animals, permits, workers, and guides. The other would be responsible for all the photography and record keeping. Both tasks were enormous. Their expedition parties grew to include more than a hundred people, and many arrangements had to be made long distance via mail and telegraph. The records that they kept during these expeditions included precise scientific readings of geographic location and altitude, mapping, and geological descriptions of the terrain. Hundreds of photos were taken with the best equipment then available—bulky, heavy cameras and tripods that had to be carried in cumbersome wooden cases.

During the early 1890's, Fanny and her husband began going on bicycle tours, first in Europe and then in North Africa. These journeys were not mere sightseeing trips; they were adventures. The Workmans faced attacks by wild dogs, journalists eager for interviews, bandits, extremes of weather, poor food and water supplies, epidemics of malaria and the plague, and other problems that would have stopped less determined travelers. They began writing collaborative accounts of their adventures, and the first book they published was *Algerian Memories: A Bicycle Tour over the Atlas Mountains to the Sahara* (1895).

During that same year, the couple took with them the recently invented Kodak camera to the Iberian Peninsula. The book that followed was *Sketches Awheel in Modern Iberia* (1897). The book recording their longest journey, which they took from 1897 through 1899, was *Through Town and Jungle: Fourteen Thousand Miles Awheel Among the Temples and People of the Indian Plain* (1904). This trip also involved traveling 1,800 miles in Ceylon and 1,500 miles in Java, Sumatra, and Cochin China (South Vietnam). These books all had many good reviews and were well received by a wide audience.

The part of this longest journey that had the most impact on them was a side trip that they took to escape the intense summer heat while in India in 1898. In Kashmir, they put aside their bicycles for a few weeks and proceeded on foot to see the Karakoram and Himalayan mountain ranges up close. They were so enchanted that they put together an expedition the next year, planning to return to Sikkim to spend two months hiking and climbing there.

The venture in Sikkim was beset by problems from the beginning. The Workmans had never arranged such a major venture before, were unaccustomed to the terrain and the climate, and were unfamiliar with the local customs and language. It had taken so long to arrange the expedition that, by the time they got started, the weather—which had already been unseasonably bad for some weeks—was worsening with the approaching winter, and the days were growing short. They were determined, however, and they set off with their large caravan and staff in October. The couple's eagerness and spirit of adventure were not shared by the porters and bearers. These workers were used to less-determined mountaineers who did not insist on risking the arduous journey under such dangerous weather conditions or traveling at such a fast pace.

Despite their convictions regarding the equality of women, the Workmans treated their hired workers with astonishing insensitivity. In the Workmans' account of this expedition, *In the Ice World of the Himálaya* (1900), they showed that they had not risen above the American social model of the time—racism. Not recognizing the impact of their lack of experience and the environmental conditions, let alone the devastating effects of their leadership style, they placed the blame for the nearly overwhelming problems of this expedition on their percep-

Fanny Bullock Workman. (Library of Congress)

tion that the Asian workers were uncooperative and unmanageable.

The Workmans never modified their approach when working with their porters and bearers in any of their further ventures in the Karakoram or Himalayan ranges, and they suffered many enormous hardships because of it. In one expedition in the Karakoram, 150 of their workers deserted, taking huge amounts of staple foods with them.

The work that Fanny and her husband did in their seven expeditions in the Himalayas and Karakoram ranges was remarkable and invaluable, and it included many firsts. Fanny set altitude records—as high as 23,00 feet—for women that went unmet for decades. They mapped uncharted areas, including some of the largest nonpolar glaciers in the world. Their observations were essential to geological knowledge of glacial processes. Their maps were the first records of the watersheds for several rivers in the areas bordering Nepal and Tibet. They wrote five books recording these expeditions—the one previously mentioned and *Ice-Bound Heights of the Mustagh* (1908), *Peaks and Glaciers of Nun Kun* (1909), *The Call of the Snowy Hispar* (1910), and *Two Summers in the Ice-wilds of Eastern Karakoram* (1917). They also wrote articles for magazines such as *The National Geographic* and *Alpine Journal*.

Fanny's professional recognition by scholars and boards of geographical societies came slowly. It was not an era when women were accepted as knowledgeable or capable of such undertakings. It was not only the sheer volume of precise data that she had collected but also the documentation of the care that had been taken to collect it that won them over. They may have been swayed also by the length of her career in such daunting expeditions. The peak recognition that she received was from the Royal Geographical Society, where she lectured in 1905, becoming only the second woman to have done so.

After World War I, the Workmans retired for good in the South of France. Fanny was ill for several years before she died at the age of sixty-six in Cannes, France.

SIGNIFICANCE

Fanny Bullock Workman excelled as an explorer, climber, and geographer at a time when women were expected to be fragile and helpless. Her accomplishments were recognized by geographic societies and academic institutions around the world.

Because Bullock Workman spoke several languages, she could usually communicate directly with people in many of the places she traveled. She delivered lectures in several countries in their national language. She was the first American woman to speak at the Sorbonne.

Honors from ten European nations' geographical societies were bestowed on Fanny. She was a member of the Royal Asiatic Society and was a fellow of the Royal Geographical Society and the Royal Scottish Geographical Society. In the United States, she was a corresponding member of the National Geographic Society and the Brooklyn Institution of Arts and Science. She was a charter member of the American Alpine Club and an honorary member of the Appalachian Mountain Club.

Fanny was an ardent feminist. In 1912, she was photographed at an altitude of 21,000 feet on the Silver Throne plateau in the Himalayas, reading a newspaper. Its headline proclaims "Votes for Women." She believed

strongly in higher education for women, and to that end she willed a total of $125,000 to Bryn Mawr, Radcliffe, Smith, and Wellesley, which were then exclusively women's colleges. She believed that women should be granted equal status with men in the scientific, social, literary, and political fields.

In her private life, she and her husband were patrons of the arts. They were great fans of the music of Richard Wagner, literature, and art. The two were devoted to each other, and their marriage was a partnership in both their personal and professional lives.

—*Marcella Joy*

FURTHER READING

Hamalian, Leo, ed. *Ladies on the Loose: Women Travellers of the Eighteenth and Nineteenth Centuries*. New York: Dodd, Mead, 1981. The chapter on Fanny Bullock Workman in this book provides limited biographical information and then an excerpt from *Through Town and Jungle*, which is about bicycling in India. It is the only book that Bullock Workman wrote without her husband. Her comments regarding the native peoples are careful, detailed, and objective.

McHenry, Robert, ed. *Liberty's Women*. Springfield, Mass.: G. and C. Merriam, 1980. This volume includes brief but detailed biographical information. No photos or maps are included, and no specific information on any specific expedition is given.

Miller, Luree. *On Top of the World: Five Women Explorers in Tibet*. New York: Paddington Press, 1976. A balanced, very readable account. Discusses some of the controversy that surrounded the couple's treatment of the hired workers and guides during the 1898 expedition in Sikkim. Includes studio photos of Fanny Bullock Workman.

Tinling, Marion. *Women Into the Unknown: A Source Book on Women Explorers and Travelers*. New York: Greenwood Press, 1989. Includes a chapter on Bullock Workman's Himalayan climbs.

Waterman, Laura, and Guy Waterman. *A Fine Kind of Madness: Mountaineering Adventures, Tall and True*. Seattle, Wash.: Mountaineers Books, 2000. Includes a fictionalized exchange of letters between mountaineers Bullock Workman and Annie Peck, demonstrating the women's competitiveness.

Workman, Fanny Bullock, and William Hunter Workman. *In the Ice World of Himálaya: Among the Peaks and Passes of Ladakh, Nubra, Suru, and Baltistan*. New York: Cassell, 1900. Their first book about the Workmans' Himalayan expeditions. The narration is uneven in content, though it is interesting. In it are harsh comments about the workers they hired. Many photos and illustrations are provided. Includes a chapter in two parts, one by each author, detailing physiological responses to high altitudes.

_____. *Two Summers in the Ice-wilds of Eastern Karakoram: The Exploration of Nineteen Hundred Square Miles of Mountain and Glacier.* New York: E. P. Dutton, 1917. The body of this book was written by Fanny, which may account for its warm, personal tone. It includes fine geologic and geographic observations and detailed descriptions. There are also numerous photographs, many of which are fold-out panoramas, of the expedition in progress. Also includes several scientific tables.

SEE ALSO: Ferdinand Vandeveer Hayden; Mary Kingsley; John Muir; Zebulon Pike; Richard Wagner.
RELATED ARTICLES in *Great Events from History: The Nineteenth Century, 1801-1900:* July 15, 1806-July 1, 1807: Pike Explores the American Southwest; 1822-1831: Jedediah Smith Explores the Far West; May, 1842-1854: Frémont Explores the American West.

FRANCES WRIGHT
Scottish-born American social reformer

Wright was the first American woman to speak publicly against the institution of slavery and in favor of women's rights. She also championed the cause of organized labor, was a pioneer of social reform, and paved the way for others to follow and to fight for the rights of the traditionally marginalized members of society.

BORN: September 6, 1795; Dundee, Scotland
DIED: December 13, 1852; Cincinnati, Ohio
ALSO KNOWN AS: Fanny Wright; Frances d'Arusmont
AREAS OF ACHIEVEMENT: Social reform, women's rights

EARLY LIFE

Frances Wright was the second of three children born to James and Camilla Campbell Wright. When she was two years old, both her parents died, and she and her sister Camilla were sent to live with their mother's sister, Frances Campbell. In her aunt's aristocratic home, Frances was exposed to a conservative and rigid upbringing. Nevertheless, in spite of her aunt's strict tutelage, she became fascinated with and inspired by the ideals of the American Revolution after stumbling upon a book on the subject.

For reasons that are not now entirely clear, Frances and her sister abruptly left their aunt's home after only a few years and settled with Professor James Milne, their father's maternal uncle and a professor of moral philosophy at Glasgow College. In her uncle's home, Frances had access to a vast library and spent her days reading books on Epicurean philosophy and American revolutionary ideals. She also began doing her first writing, which included a play she titled *Altorf*. She also wrote *A Few Days in Athens*, a novelistic sketch modeled on Plato's dialogues that outlined the materialistic philosophy to which she adhered throughout her life.

LIFE'S WORK

During her years in Glasgow, Wright befriended Mrs. Craig Millar, a woman who had lived for two years in the United States during George Washington's presidency. Mrs. Millar served not only as a mother figure for the young and impressionable Wright but also as a crucial source of information about the United States. With letters of introduction from the Millars to several important people in New York, Frances and Camilla set sail for a long visit to the United States in August, 1818. During their two-year stay there, Wright managed to get her play *Altorf* produced in New York City. By traveling extensively throughout New York State and Pennsylvania, she also was able to gather keen observations of American life, which she developed in her first major work, *Views of Society and Manners in America* (1820).

Views of Society and Manners in America was sharply critical of England and highly laudatory about most aspects of the United States. One of Wright's central themes was education, which she found to be exemplary in America. Recognizing that education was the key to individual liberty and freedom, she especially praised the public school system in New England, which she claimed provided a common education to every young citizen regardless of sex or race. She was particularly enthusiastic about the opportunities for female education in

America. In contrast to European women, she claimed that women in the United States did not waste time studying such frivolous subjects as language and literature, but instead concentrated on philosophy, history, economics, and science. Therefore, she argued, American women seemed to enjoy more freedom than their European counterparts.

Wright's book won her widespread critical praise, most notably from the marquis de Lafayette, whom she later befriended during a visit to his French country estate in 1821. She timed her second trip to the United States to coincide with Lafayette's tour of the nation on a personal invitation from U.S. president James Monroe. The highlight of her second trip was a two-week visit with former president Thomas Jefferson at his Monticello home that was arranged by Lafayette.

While she was at Monticello, Wright had the opportunity to discuss with Jefferson the issue of slavery, which she had come to believe was a glaring contradiction to the freedoms and liberties of the America she loved. Influenced by Jefferson's views on gradual emancipation and Robert Owen's utopian cooperatives, she conceived of a plan to purchase, educate, and then emancipate slaves and to help them start colonies outside the United States. In December, 1825, she put her plan into practice by personally purchasing eight slaves and a 640-acre plot of land in western Tennessee that she called Nashoba.

After leaving her sister and a director to handle the day-to-day operations of Nashoba, Wright embarked on a series of lectures in which she greatly exaggerated the success of her experimental colony, criticized organized religion, and argued in favor of women's rights, miscegenation, and free love. She also criticized the widespread poverty and ignorance of urban America and fought for limited working hours and free education for American workers.

During this period, Wright helped to edit Robert Owen's *New Harmony Gazette*. In 1829, she settled with Owen in New York City. There, they published a radical newspaper called the *Free Enquirer*, which called for liberalized divorce laws, birth control, state-funded public education, and the political organization of the working classes. Wright's public lectures and writings eventually resulted in widespread public criticism and accusations that Nashoba was nothing more than a free-love colony. On her return to Nashoba, Wright was shocked to find her sister Camilla both pregnant and ill and her experimental colony in ruins. In 1830, she finally arranged for the emancipation of the Nashoba slaves and had them

sent to the black-ruled island nation of Haiti. A year later, Camilla died in England at the age of thirty.

Deeply grieved over her sister's death, Wright turned for comfort to Guillaume Sylvan Casimir Phiquepal d'Arusmont, a physician whom she had first met at New Harmony. After living with d'Arusmont in Paris, she married him in 1831 after she had become pregnant. Her first child died shortly after it was born, and she had a second child, Frances Sylva, in 1832.

Through the next decade, Wright supported her family by going on lecture tours in the United States and England, while d'Arusmont assumed most of the domestic and child-rearing responsibilities. Around 1835, she and her family settled in Philadelphia, where she began to publish a new paper, *Manual of American Principles*. In 1844, she learned that she had inherited the sizeable Wright holdings in Scotland. However, her desire to retain sole control over her newfound wealth led to an irreconcilable split with her husband and a bitter divorce in 1850.

On December 13, 1852, Frances Wright died in Cincinnati, Ohio, from complications resulting from a broken hip. She left all of her possessions to her only daughter, Frances Sylva d'Arusmont. The headstone on her grave reads, "I have wedded the cause of human improvement, staked on it my fortune, my reputation and my life."

SIGNIFICANCE

Frances Wright was a woman ahead of her time. Throughout her very public life, she was both praised and criticized for her radical positions on a number of contested issues. Twenty years before women began speaking publicly about women's rights and before the advent of the organized abolitionist movement, Wright was calling for female liberation through education and free love and the freeing of slaves through gradual emancipation and colonization. In her ideas, one can see the forerunners of community action programs, free public education, and labor laws that emerged years after her death.

—*Jan Doolittle Wilson*

FURTHER READING

Bartlett, Elizabeth Ann. *Liberty, Equality, Sorority: The Origins and Interpretation of American Feminist Thought: Frances Wright, Sarah Grimké, and Margaret Fuller*. Brooklyn, N.Y.: Carlson Publishers, 1994. This work traces the origins of feminism in the writings of three notable American women.
Eckhardt, Celia Morris. *Fanny Wright: Rebel in America*. Cambridge, Mass.: Harvard University Press,

1984. This work remains the definitive biography of Wright.

Perkins, A. J., and Theresa Wolfson. *Frances Wright: Free Enquirer—A Study of a Temperament*. New York: Harper and Brothers, 1939. One of the first scholarly studies of Frances Wright, this book remains one of the best and most insightful examinations of her private life.

Wright, Frances. *Reason, Religion, and Morals*. Foreword by Susan S. Adams. Amherst, N.Y.: Humanity Books, 2004. Most of Wright's public lectures make up this volume.

_____. *Views of Society and Manners in America, in a Series of Letters from That Country to a Friend in England, During the Years 1818, 1819, 1820*. London: Longman, 1821. Wright's first major publication, this work resulted from her first visit to the United States. In it, Wright is very critical of English society and highly laudatory of most aspects of American life.

SEE ALSO: Frederick Douglass; Sarah and Angelina Grimké; James Monroe; Robert Owen; Harriet Beecher Stowe; Frances Trollope; Victoria Woodhull.

RELATED ARTICLE in *Great Events from History: The Nineteenth Century, 1801-1900:* Spring, 1814-1830: Communitarian Experiments at New Harmony.

CHARLOTTE MARY YONGE
English novelist

One of the most popular English novelists of her time, Yonge wrote more than one hundred books and was the editor of a girls' magazine through four decades. Although she is best remembered for her juvenile novels, she is regarded as the leading female voice of the Oxford Movement, and her adult novel The Heir of Redclyffe *ranked alongside the works of Jane Austen and the Brontë sisters during her time.*

BORN: August 11, 1823; Otterborne, Hampshire,
   England
DIED: March 24, 1901; Elderfield, Hampshire,
   England
ALSO KNOWN AS: Charlotte M. Yonge
AREA OF ACHIEVEMENT: Literature

EARLY LIFE

Born into a landed English country family, Charlotte Mary Yonge (yahng) was the first child of William Yonge and Fanny Bagus. She was educated by both parents, with her father taking a leading role after the birth of her brother, Julian, in 1830. As a young girl, Charlotte was devoted to reading William Shakespeare, the novels of Sir Walter Scott, and Maria Edgeworth's children's tales that carried specific moral messages. She was seven when she learned to write; her father postponed teaching her to write until he believed her hand was strong enough to hold, chalk, slates, and pens.

Charlotte had a happy childhood, playing with her dolls, wandering in nature, and enjoying a quiet life with her parents. She would later return to her childhood in her fiction and children's stories. The entire Yonge family was distinguished, and Charlotte would also later draw on the careers of her relatives for the families in her fiction. Yonge was later described as possessing an expressive face with lively brown eyes and hair that turned white as she aged. Although a private person who never married, she enjoyed being around large families with children.

In 1833, Yonge visited London. She did not make another significant trip until 1869, when she joined her brother and his wife on a trip to France. Meanwhile, the year 1835 was a turning point in her life as John Keble (1792-1865) was installed as the vicar of Hursely, her family's home parish. Yonge had had little religious instruction during her childhood, but under Keble's tutelage, she prepared for confirmation in 1838. She also developed a close friendship with Keble, who worked with her father in church building, for which Charlotte developed a passion. Around that same time, Charlotte became a parish teacher in a school that her mother founded.

In 1839, Yonge published her first fiction—children's stories in French. Her first novel, *Abbeychurch*, was published in 1844 over the objections of her grandmother, Mary Kingman Bargus, who lived with Yonge's family and forced Charlotte to donate her earnings to charity. From the time of her publication of *Henrietta's Wish; Or, Domineering* (1850), the story of a disobedient son with an overly protective mother, Yonge continued to produce a steady stream of popular novels and shared the literary marketplace with Charles Dickens and Anthony Trollope, through 1900.

LIFE'S WORK

Later known as the "novelist of the Oxford Movement," Yonge was devoted to writing fiction that displayed the positive virtues of family, hard work, and devotion to the Christian faith. She was passionate about education for both sexes and had a special interest in educating girls. She believed in missionary work and put twelve thousand pounds of her earnings from *The Daisy Chain* (1856) into the building of a religious school in the Melanesian Islands. She was also responsive to the "crisis of faith" of her era and used it as a theme in *The Two Guardians* (1852), *Hopes and Fears* (1860), *Magnum Bonum* (1876), and *The Long Vacation* (1895).

Yonge extended her interest in church building into *Abbeychurch*, *Heartease* (1854), *The Daisy Chain*, and *The Pillars of the House* (1873). She was also drawn to theme of service to the poor, using *The Three Brides* (1876) and *Modern Broods* (1900) to create characters who strive to be unselfish in their charitable acts. Shortly before her death, she was writing *The Making of a Missionary*, a novel designed to present missionaries as respectable characters in an effort to redress such characters as Mrs. Jellyby, whom Charles Dickens had used in *Bleak House* (1852-1853) to satirize missionary efforts.

Yonge's career as a novelist spanned 1844 to 1900, during which time she published more than one hundred books. She was also the editor of *The Monthly Packet* from 1851 to 1890. Her primary interests in both her novels and her magazine were the lives of women and women's places in the family. Her women characters consistently show resourcefulness and loyalty to their

YONGE AND MARK TWAIN

The best known of Charlotte Mary Yonge's many juvenile novels is *The Little Duke* (1854). Less well known is the fact that her book helped inspire one of the most famous children's books of all time—Mark Twain's *The Prince and the Pauper* (1881). In 1908, Twain admitted to having gotten the idea for his book from *The Little Duke*.

Twain's famous book is about Edward VI, who became king of England at the age of nine when his father, King Henry VIII, died in 1547. In *The Prince and the Pauper*, a somewhat older Edward accidentally switches places with a pauper boy named Tom Canty, who looks exactly like him, is expelled from his palace, and then cannot persuade anyone to accept who he really is. The bulk of the story concerns Edward's and Tom's struggles to resume their rightful places. After Edward is finally restored to his throne, he institutes reforms to relieve the suffering he has observed among his subjects.

Set in tenth-century France, Yonge's *The Little Duke* (1854) is a similarly moralistic tale showing how the youthful duke of Normandy—the grandfather of William the Conqueror—becomes a more merciful ruler after escaping from the confines of political imprisonment and struggling to claim his rightful throne with the aid of an older protector—a character similar to Miles Hendon in Twain's novel.

Another Yonge novel that may have influenced the title of *The Prince and the Pauper* is *The Prince and the Page* (1865). In that story, a cousin of England's late thirteenth century King Edward I spends several years disguised as a blind beggar.

families, without ever sacrificing their tightly prescribed behaviors as respectable women. Yonge charted the evolution of the family and its many tensions through her fictional May family in books such as *The Daisy Chain* and *The Trial* and through the Underwood family of *The Pillars of the House*. Of all Yonge's novels, those titles and her adult novel *The Heir of Redclyffe* (1853) are her best known.

The Daisy Chain introduces Ethel May, a character drawn after Yonge herself, as a child, while *The Trial* shows her as the pillar of the May family after the death of Mrs. May. Ethel is a retiring, but wise and stable, character who sacrifices her own happiness for that of others and who is devoted to her own family and the families close to her, as Yonge herself was. *The Heir of Redclyffe* has been credited with introducing several innovations to Victorian novels, particularly the expert manner in which Yonge handles her male characters, Guy Morville and Philip Edmonstone, as they struggle against their own human natures to live up to social expectations of manhood. *The Pillars of the House* presents the Underwood family at work for the good of the neighborhood in their church building and other social activities.

As a stylist, Yonge made greater use of dialogue than description. Her plots are intricate but not complicated, and evidence of her reading of Shakespeare and Scott abounds in the multiple layers of the plot and their seamless integration. Major and minor characters are equally developed, and Yonge shows skill in the treatment of strains and tests of will. For example, the female protagonist in *Hopes and Fears* makes choices that ultimately leave her unmarried.

In 1876, Yonge lost much of her income when she paid off the debts of her brother Julian, who faced bankruptcy after his coal mining venture failed. In 1884, Julian sold the family's Otterborne House. However, Charlotte had earlier moved to a smaller house on the same property in 1862 and lived there throughout the rest of her life.

In her later years, Yonge returned to her own past to write *Old Times at Otterbourne* (1891), *An Old Woman's Outlook* (1892), and *John Keble's Parishes* (1898). In 1899, Sir Walter Besant arranged a scholarship for a Winchester High School girl called the Charlotte Mary Yonge Scholarship to be awarded to fund a young worthy girl's college education. On March 24, 1901, Yonge died in her home. At the time of her death, she was working on three other books, mainly memoirs about her childhood.

SIGNIFICANCE

Charlotte Yonge's novels continue to attract critical attention, especially in the arena of feminist criticism. Her main themes are family, education, service, and challenges of achieving adulthood. She wrote nostalgically of an innocent world of childhood in which moral choices are clear and life paths appear to be well defined. She appreciated the details of ordinary life and created a fictional world in which her characters, although tested, remain confident that happy outcomes are within reach.

—Beverly Schneller

FURTHER READING

Battiscombe, Georgina. *Charlotte Mary Yonge: The Story of an Uneventful Life*. London: Constable, 1943.

Provides a succinct account of Yonge's life and major works; includes portraits of Yonge in watercolor and photographs.

Coleridge, Christabel Rose. *Charlotte Mary Yonge: Her Life and Letters.* London: Macmillan, 1903. The first biography by her friend Coleridge is written in the tradition of Victorian biographies; includes extracts from her letters.

Dennis, Barbara. *Charlotte Yonge, 1823-1901: Novelist of the Oxford Movement.* Lewiston: Edwin Mellen Press, 1992. Presents Yonge in the context of the main ideas of the Oxford Movement.

Jordan, Ellen, et al. "'A Handmaid to the Church': How John Keble Shaped the Life and Work of Charlotte Yonge, the 'Novelist of the Oxford Movement.'" In *John Keble in Context,* edited by Kirstie Blair. London: Anthem Press, 2004. Charts the ways Keble influenced Yonge's career, including her work as a parish teacher, as editor of *The Monthly Packet,* organizer of parish social events, and manager of the parish library. Examines Keble's role in Yonge's selection of

themes and approaches, including that of showing characters humbled by forces beyond their control.

Sturrock, June. *"Heaven and Home": Charlotte Mary Yonge's Domestic Fiction and the Victorian Debate over Women.* Victoria, B.C.: University of Victoria, 1995. Focuses on *The Daisy Chain, The Clever Woman of the Family,* and *The Three Brides* to illustrate how they exemplify Yonge's depiction of the heroine and the ideal woman.

Thompson, Nicola D., ed. *Victorian Women Writers and the Woman Question.* Cambridge, England: Cambridge University Press, 1999. Collects essays on the theme of Victorian womanhood in general and on Yonge, in Sturrock's chapter 7 essay on Dyvenor Terrace.

SEE ALSO: Mary Elizabeth Braddon; Charles Dickens; Maria Edgeworth; Sir Walter Scott; Anthony Trollope; Mark Twain.

RELATED ARTICLE in *Great Events from History: The Nineteenth Century, 1801-1900:* July 14, 1833: Oxford Movement Begins.

BRIGHAM YOUNG
American religious leader

Young's leadership of the Church of Jesus Christ of Latter-day Saints in the Utah territory influenced both the religious and the secular development of the American West. After the murder of the church's founder, Joseph Smith, Young held the church together, led its members from Illinois to Utah, and oversaw its development into a mature institution that has continued to expand into the twenty-first century.

BORN: June 1, 1801; Whitingham, Vermont
DIED: August 29, 1877; Salt Lake City, Utah
AREAS OF ACHIEVEMENT: Religion and theology, church government

EARLY LIFE

Born shortly after his parents moved from Hopkinton, Massachusetts, to Whitingham, Vermont, Brigham Young was the last of four sons of the nine children whom his consumptive mother, Abigail (Nabby) Young, bore her husband, John Young. His father was probably a tenant farmer, and the life of the Young family was harsh. After moving several times, the family settled in Sherburne, New York, at the junction of the Chenango

and Susquehanna Rivers. When Brigham was thirteen, the family moved to Aurelius, where Nabby finally lost her battle against consumption in June, 1815. Accounts of the early life of Brigham are based largely on anecdotes, because accurate factual information concerning this period of his life is scarce.

Because of the family's poor circumstances, Young received no formal education, and he worked beside his father from an early age. In 1824, when he was twenty-three, he married eighteen-year-old Miriam Angeline Works, the second child of Asa and Abigail Works. Both her father and John Young were Revolutionary War veterans. Brigham and Miriam were married on October 5, 1824. Gilbert Weed, the justice of the peace of Aurelius, married them at the James Pine tavern. At the time of the marriage, Brigham worked in a factory. They joined the Methodist Church shortly after their marriage. Elizabeth, their first child, was born on September 19, 1825. Several years later, Miriam contracted chronic tuberculosis, becoming a semi-invalid. In order to make a living, Young did a variety of odd jobs: building homes; putting in window panes, doorways, staircases, and fireplace mantels; and making and repairing furniture.

Young was not a stern religious type like his father; it was not until he and his entire immediate family joined Joseph Smith's Church of Jesus Christ of Latter-day Saints in April, 1832, that he embraced a religious doctrine. This conversion was the turning point in Young's life. He had not joined a church earlier because he could not accept many of the religious doctrines that were prevalent. He believed that most clergymen dwelt only on the way to get to Heaven, but none of them ever told him anything about Heaven, God, or salvation. He desired a more positive approach in his search for religious truth.

During this period, Young familiarized himself with Baptist, Freewill Baptist, Wesleyan and Reformed Methodist, Episcopalian, and Presbyterian theologies. Because of the intensity and emotionalism of the evangelists in western New York, Young became cynical about professors of religion. This cynicism was extended to many social, business, and other customs in society and on the frontier.

After his conversion to Mormonism, Young had no immediate contact with the people in his new church. He spent much time reading and examining the Book of Mormon, which he admired for its simple biblical style and its clear explanations of many passages in the Old and the New Testaments. Young was greatly impressed by the Mormon missionaries he met, but it was not until January, 1832, at Bradford County, Pennsylvania, that he actually attended a Mormon meeting.

LIFE'S WORK

One week after being baptized in his new faith, Young preached his first sermon, without using notes or a text. This practice was followed in all of his future sermons. In order to propagate Mormonism, Young placed his wife Miriam in the care of Vilate Kimball and spent the summer of 1832 traveling and preaching. He returned home in time to attend Miriam during her last days. She died in his arms on September 8, 1832. He now devoted himself completely to his new church.

Young's first meeting with the Mormon prophet, Joseph Smith, was in the summer of 1832, in Kirtland. He was impressed tremendously, and at one of the meetings spoke in tongues, a gift he seldom used after 1832. After having a vision in February, 1835, Joseph Smith held a meeting, which resulted in twelve men being chosen as apostles; these twelve became the Council of Twelve. Young was the second selected and only two were older than he. In his ordination, Young's future was thus predicted: He would do great things in the name of Jesus; he

would behold heavenly messages; and he would have influence among heathen nations.

The entire Mormon community was shattered on October 27, 1838, when Lilburn W. Boggs, governor of the state of Missouri, reacted to religious pressures and prejudices and issued his "Exterminating Order." This order stated that the Mormons were to be treated as enemies and were to be exterminated or driven from Missouri and made legal the pillage, killing, and burning that followed. Young was active in helping Mormons to escape from Missouri.

After returning from a mission in Great Britain, Young joined his family in Nauvoo, Illinois, in August, 1841. From Nauvoo, the Council of Twelve directed the proselytizing activities in the United States, in Canada, in Great Britain, in continental Europe, and in the South Pacific. Young became the most important of the Twelve and was its president.

Joseph Smith introduced to the Council of Twelve four new doctrines in the fall and winter of 1841-1842. The first was the performance of baptism for the dead. The second and most controversial of the four was plural marriage. The council became convinced that it was a biblical injunction, and Young accepted the doctrine.

Brigham Young. (Library of Congress)

With the consent of Mary Ann, his second wife, he married his first plural wife, Lucy Ann Decker Seeley, in June, 1842. At that time, all plural marriages were performed secretly. The actual writing down of the practice did not take place until July, 1843. The word "polygamy," meaning plural mates (husband or wife) was used rather than the word "polygyny," meaning more than one wife. Despite the choice of words, the Mormons never accepted the idea that a woman could have more than one husband.

The third and fourth doctrines were not as controversial as the second. The third doctrine was the full endowment, a ritualistic religious ceremony. The fourth doctrine was sealing—the binding of children to parents, and persons with unbelieving or worldly parents to faithful families. Young had several young men sealed to him as his spiritual sons.

Joseph Smith's decision to run for the presidency of the United States in 1844 in order to propagate his faith infuriated his opponents. Young carried the message of church and politics throughout the nation, as did the other apostles. Meanwhile, in Nauvoo, a group of Mormons opposed the revelation on plural marriages and the ecclesiastical control that had become complete. Smith and his followers destroyed their newspaper, whereupon Smith and his City Council were charged with inciting a riot and suppressing a free press. This charge was actually an excuse for which many citizens and politicians of Illinois had been waiting. Smith and some of his followers were jailed in Carthage. On June 27, a mob broke into the jail and killed Joseph and his brother, Hyrum Smith. With the murder of Joseph Smith, Young became head of the Mormons. The church needed a strong, capable, and devoted leader; Young was more than able to fulfill that need.

At that time Emma Smith, the wife of the prophet Joseph Smith, split with Young over control of the church.

RICHARD F. BURTON ON BRIGHAM YOUNG

In 1860, the famous British explorer Richard Francis Burton traveled across the United States and its western territories. During his journey, he had an extended stay in Salt Lake City, where he interviewed Brigham Young. As an experienced observer of Middle Eastern and Asian cultures, Burton had a particular interest in meeting a modern American prophet and practitioner of polygamy and was able to describe Young with unusual objectivity.

I had expected to see a venerable-looking old man. Scarcely a grey thread appears in his hair, which is parted on the side, light coloured, rather thick, and reaches below the ears with a half curl. He formerly wore it long after the Western style, now it is cut level with the ear lobes. The forehead is somewhat narrow, the eyebrows are thin, the eyes between grey and blue, with a calm, composed, and somewhat reserved expression: a slight droop in the left lid made me think he had suffered from paralysis, I afterwards heard that the ptosis is the result of a neuralgia which has long tormented him. For this reason he usually covers his head—except in his own house or in the tabernacle. . . . The nose, which is fine and somewhat sharp pointed, is bent a little to the left. The lips are close like the New Englander's, and the teeth, especially those of the under jaw, are imperfect. The cheeks are rather fleshy, and the line between the alæ of the nose and the mouth is broken; the chin is somewhat peaked, and the face clean shaven, except under the jaws, where the beard is allowed to grow. The hands are well made, and not disfigured by rings. The figure is somewhat large, broad-shouldered, and stooping a little when standing.

The Prophet's dress was neat and plain as a Quaker's, all grey homespun, except the cravat and waistcoat. His coat was of antique cut, and, like the pantaloons, baggy, and the buttons were black. A necktie of dark silk, with a large bow, was loosely passed round a starchless collar, which turned down of its own accord. The waistcoat was of black satin . . . single-breasted and buttoned nearly to the neck, and a plain gold chain was passed into the pocket. The boots were Wellingtons, apparently of American make.

Altogether the Prophet's appearance was that of a gentleman farmer in New England—in fact such as he is . . . His manner is at once affable and impressive, simple and courteous: his want of pretension contrasts favorably with certain pseudo-prophets that I have seen. . . . He shows no signs of dogmatism, bigotry, or fanaticism, and never once entered—with me at least—upon the subject of religion. He impresses a stranger with a certain sense of power. . . .

Source: Richard F. Burton, *The City of the Saints*, edited by Fawn M. Brodie (New York, 1963), pp. 263-264.

Emma wanted the control of the church to pass to her son, Joseph Smith III. Young opposed this succession, and the Mormons split into Young and Emma Smith camps. The Smith group eventually formed the Reorganized Church of Jesus Christ of Latter-day Saints. Neither Emma nor the Reorganized Church ever accepted the practice of plural wives.

After this split in the Mormon Church, Young led the majority of Mormons from Nauvoo to Utah. With the extremely difficult march to Salt Lake City and the reestablishment of the church in Utah, Young stamped his mark on the future of Mormonism. It took a strong-willed, devoted, capable, and energetic man to establish a new settlement in the isolated West—to organize new political, economic, social, and religious structures that would accommodate and protect his followers and their descendants as well as the constant influx of settlers.

The Mormons were now outside the fundamentalism of the United States' religious climate. Young's great organizing skill, as well as his overall leadership, combined with the hard work of the Mormon people who followed him, resulted in the growth and prosperity of the area. The westward movement of the citizens of the United States greatly aided their prosperity. It was only natural that Young would become the first governor of the federal territory of Utah in 1857. The Treaty of Guadalupe Hidalgo had brought the area back into the United States after the Mexican War. In 1871, Young was tried on charges of polygamy but was not convicted.

Young was a deeply religious as well as a practical man who was also a great leader. He died in his city on August 29, 1877, leaving behind at least seventeen wives and fifty-six children.

SIGNIFICANCE

Without a doubt, Brigham Young was at the right place at the right time. However, had he not been a devoted and practical individual with visions of what he and his followers could create, the Mormons and the state of Utah would not be what they are in the twenty-first century. A lesser man would have failed miserably. Born in an age and an area of the United States known for its deep religious convictions and activity, Young focused his energy, belief, and ability to create one of the most rapidly growing churches in the United States.

—*C. E. Frazier*

FURTHER READING

Anderson, Edward Henry. *The Life of Brigham Young.* Salt Lake City, Utah: G. Q. Cannon and Sons, 1893. Anderson had some access to materials in the church archives in Salt Lake City. To a degree, the book is an expanded rewrite of earlier Mormon publications on Young.

Anderson, Nels. *Desert Saints: The Mormon Frontier in Utah.* Chicago: University of Chicago Press, 1942. A favorable account, most useful for the general reader.

Arrington, Leonard J. *Brigham Young: American Moses.* New York: Alfred A. Knopf, 1985. Written by a histo-

rian who used extensive materials in the church archives. This is probably the best biography of Young. Pro-Mormon, but basically objective.

Bagley, Will. *Blood of the Prophets: Brigham Young and the Massacre at Mountain Meadows.* Norman: University of Oklahoma Press, 2002. In 1857, local settlers and Paiutes in southern Utah murdered about 100 people who were traveling via wagon train from Arkansas. Bagley recounts the incident, providing evidence to confirm an earlier account of Young's involvement in the massacre and subsequent cover-up.

Bergera, Gary James. *Conflict in the Quorum: Orson Platt, Brigham Young, Joseph Smith.* Salt Lake City, Utah: Signature Books, 2002. Critical study that chronicles the dissension between Pratt, who preached a controversial brand of Mormonism, and rival church leaders Young and Smith. Describes how Young outmaneuvered Smith to control church doctrine and practice.

Brodie, Fawn M. *No Man Knows My History: The Life of Joseph Smith, the Mormon Prophet.* Rev. ed. New York: Alfred A. Knopf, 1971. First published in 1946, the first major critical study of Smith's life by a professional historian. An essential starting point for any study of the Mormon prophet, this book proved so challenging to the Mormon Church that its author was excommunicated.

Newell, Linda King, and Valeen Tippetts Avery. *Mormon Enigma: Emma Hale Smith, Prophet's Wife, Elect Lady, Polygamy's Foe.* Garden City, N.Y.: Doubleday, 1984. Both authors are Mormons; Avery is a professor of history. This is the most complete examination of Emma Hale Smith, a remarkable woman who was torn between her love for the church founded by her husband and her opposition to Brigham Young's attempts to lead it.

Werner, Morris R. *Brigham Young.* New York: Harcourt Brace, 1925. Written by a New York sportswriter, who based his research upon published materials. Although Werner pokes fun at his subject, for years this was one of the best biographies of Young.

SEE ALSO: Sir Richard Francis Burton; John C. Frémont; Joseph Smith.

RELATED ARTICLES in *Great Events from History: The Nineteenth Century, 1801-1900:* April 6, 1830: Smith Founds the Mormon Church; February 4, 1846: Mormons Begin Migration to Utah; June 30, 1846-January 13, 1847: United States Occupies California and the Southwest; December, 1869: Wyoming Gives Women the Vote.

ALEXANDER AND DEMETRIOS YPSILANTIS
Greek revolutionaries

In their individual ways, the Ypsilantis brothers, idealistic aristocratic Greek revolutionaries of the Byzantine Phanariote class, demonstrated the problems as well as the possibilities of the Greek movement toward national autonomy and independence.

ALEXANDER YPSILANTIS

BORN: 1792; place unknown
DIED: January 31, 1828; Vienna, Austria
ALSO KNOWN AS: Alexander Ipsilantis; Alexander Hypsilantis; Alexander Hpyselantes; Alexander Ypsilanti; Alexandros Ypsilantis

DEMETRIOS YPSILANTIS

BORN: December 25, 1793; place unknown
DIED: 1832; place unknown
ALSO KNOWN AS: Demetrios Ipsilantis; Demetrios Hypsilantis; Demetrios Hypselantes; Demetrios Ypsilanti
AREA OF ACHIEVEMENT: Government and politics

EARLY LIVES

In the narrow, winding alleys of Constantinople was a district that became notable as a seat of power for the Christian communities of the Ottoman Empire. This district, called the Phanar after the lighthouse that was one of its principle landmarks, formed the seat of the Patriarchate of the Orthodox millet of the Ottoman Empire and the center of Eastern Orthodox Christendom. It was populated primarily by Greeks and included a number of ancient and noble Greek families dating back to the Byzantine Empire before it was conquered by the Ottoman Turks in 1453. One such family, ostensibly related to the Greek imperial dynasty of the Comneni, was the Ypsilantis (sometimes spelled Ipsilantis or Hypsilantis). This aristocratic Phanariote family originally came from Trebizond (Trabzon) on the Black Sea coast of Asia Minor and became active in the movement for Greek independence that gradually emerged in the eighteenth and nineteenth centuries, although the history of the family dates back many centuries earlier.

The Ypsilantis had, for many years, been active in the administration of the Ottoman Empire (the Turks preferred to turn this aspect of the running of their state over to the multilingual and well-educated Greeks). Members of the Ypsilanti family not only attained the important post of grand dragoman to the Sublime Porte in Constantinople but also obtained the lucrative and politically advantageous position of *hospodar* of the Romanian principalities of Wallachia and Moldavia. Because Russia at this time also had an interest in this region as protectors of the Orthodox Christian subjects and because the Ypsilantis were coreligionists with the Russians, members of the family also became noteworthy for their Russian attachments. The growing nationalist aspirations of the Greeks of the diaspora at the end of the eighteenth century, fed by hopes aroused by earlier Serb insurrections and by anticipation of Russian support against their Turkish overlords, were naturally centered on their Phanariote Greek fellow countrymen.

Constantine Ypsilanti, *hospodar* of Wallachia and the father of the brothers Alexander Constantine and Demetrios Ypsilanti, had become actively engaged in conspiratorial activity with Russia against the Ottomans during the latter half of the eighteenth century, had served as liaison between the Serbs and Russians during the Serb revolt of 1804, and had fought on the side of the Russians in the Russo-Turkish War of 1806 to 1812. Constantine finally defected to Russia in 1806 and died there in 1816.

LIVES' WORK

Constantine's eldest son, Alexander, who was raised in an atmosphere of nationalist fervor aroused by the changes brought about by the French Revolution, made an early successful career in the Russian army. He participated in the 1812 war against Napoleon Bonaparte and became an aide-de-camp and major general of the army of Russian czar Alexander I. He was decorated for heroism and was one of the youngest generals of the Russian army.

Around 1820 Alexander became embroiled in the activities of the Philiki Hetairia, a Greek secret society founded by undistinguished Greek merchants in Odessa in 1814 devoted to achieving the liberation of the Greeks from Ottoman domination. This society had the aim of creating an independent Greek state in southeastern Europe, perhaps even reviving the Byzantine Empire.

In 1818, the headquarters of the society moved from Odessa to Constantinople, the center of the Greek diaspora, and began to increase its membership. It was rumored that the designs of the society were supported by the Russian czar and his Greek foreign minister, John Capodistrias, although in actuality Capodistrias had, in 1816, refused an invitation to join the society as its leader. Alexander became its leader in 1820. He used this position and its secret membership as a springboard to plan insurrections against the Turks from the Danubian principalities as well as Greece. His plan was to involve the Serbian royal dynasty of Obrenović, the Bulgarians, the Romanians, and the Greeks in an all-Balkan insurrection against the Ottoman Empire, which, in late 1820 and early 1821, was occupied with putting down the revolt of the Albanian despot Ali Pasha of Yannina. Alexander felt that the time was ripe for revolt.

This period of history represents a convergence of the histories of several nations and intellectual movements. First, it was a period of nationalistic and Romantic striving of the Balkan nations, in particular the Serbs, Greeks, Bulgarians, and the Romanians of the Danubian principalities, for liberation from the oppression of the declining Turkish, or Ottoman, Empire. These Eastern Orthodox people looked to Russia, at this time a powerful czarist empire, to come to their assistance since they shared the same religion and, in several cases, the same Slavic blood.

The Russian Empire also had imperial ambitions on this region and maintained a continued interest in it. The Ottoman Empire, although it had suffered militarily, especially from the depredations of its own Janissary corps, had made attempts at reform and was at the same time in collision with the imperial aspirations of the British and Russian Empires. At this time the Ottomans had not only lost many of their possessions in Anatolia and North Africa but were also in the throes of opposition from their Balkan subjects. One of the more serious of these was the rebellion of Ali Pasha Tepelenë, the Albanian warlord and brigand who had become the despot of Yannina in Epirus. He had created a small state for himself in Epirus and was quickly becoming a powerful force to be reckoned with. In 1804 the Serbs, under their leader Karadjordje Petrović, had revolted against the intolerable conditions created by the Turkish Janissaries and were, by 1807, demanding independence from Turkey itself.

The question as to the ultimate fate of the Ottoman Empire was at this time a complex foreign policy issue, because the allocation of power in Europe hung in the balance. It was an age of intrigue, secret societies, freemasonry, and committed revolutionaries whose patriotic aspirations did not always spring from strategic calculation or common sense. It was an age of incipient national-

ism and quest for freedom inspired by the ideas of the French Revolution and the Enlightenment.

In 1820 the Turks turned their forces against the troublesome Ali Pasha of Yannina. The Greeks saw this as an opportunity to make their own bid for autonomy. Alexander had been waiting for just such an opportunity. He planned to personally lead a revolt that would restore to the Greeks their state and the freedom to recover the great empire of the Byzantines. Although there were a number of Hetairists in the principalities who might support him, he felt that he needed to act expeditiously before the Turks could raise a counterrevolutionary force.

The first Greek insurrection broke out in the Romanian principalities when Alexander led a group of Greek officers of the Russian army and other supporters into Moldavia in March of 1821. He issued a call for Greek and Romanian popular support, intimating that he already had the support of the Russian czar. He did not succeed in gaining peasant adherence, however, or that of fellow Romanian insurrectionists, in particular that of Tudor Vladimirescu, mainly because of mistrust of the Phanariotes because of their past injustices. He also appealed to the czar to come to his aid, but to no avail.

The czar disclaimed any responsibility for the insurrection, expressed his extreme displeasure, and dismissed Alexander and his brothers from the Russian army henceforth. In June, 1821, Alexander and his Sacred Battalion were thoroughly defeated by the Turks at the Battle of Dragasani. Alexander, his brother Nicholas, and a few supporters escaped into Austria only to be captured later. Alexander was tried and imprisoned in Bohemia, only to be released shortly before his death in 1828.

Although the movement was initially unsuccessful, this marked the beginning of the pathway to the independence of Greece, because Alexander's ill-fated attempt coincided with another uprising that was taking place in the Peloponnese with the involvement of his brother Demetrios, and with better fortune. Demetrios had also joined the Russian army and in 1821 fought in the Peloponnese on the side of the Greeks. He later achieved a career in Greek politics. He had been appointed by his brother Alexander as the representative of the revolutionary secret society, the Philiki Hetairia, in Greece.

Demetrios first attempted to organize the Greek islanders from Hydra and then went to the Peloponnese, where he put forth his plan for organizing the Greek Morea into a sort of parliament. He encountered opposition, however, from the more entrenched local notables, most of whom did not wish to submit to a central authority. He became president of the national assembly that met at Argos in December, 1821, partly because he, too, was presumed to have Russian support. However, he became disillusioned by the internal squabbling of the Greeks and instead went to Corinth to organize its siege against the Turks.

This insurrection captured the popular imagination, attracting philhellenes from all over Europe along with material and financial support. Although beset with internal factionalism, the Greek revolt was saved through foreign intervention after Great Britain, France, and Russia combined against the Ottoman Empire at the Battle of Navarino on October 20, 1827. This victory was followed by the Russo-Turkish War of 1828-1829. By 1832 the sultan had acknowledged the independence of Greece. As later dissension arose among the Greeks, Demetrios withdrew from politics. His ideas were in advance of his time since he envisioned a rule of law in which Greeks and Turks could live together.

SIGNIFICANCE

Alexander and Demetrios Ypsilanti both continued the revolutionary tradition begun by their illustrious family, including the attainment of high office, attachment and loyalty to Russia, distinguished military service, and active involvement in revolts against the forces of oppression. They both put misguided faith in secret societies and intrigue and misled their followers concerning the level of their support from Russia, but both were natural leaders who were able to find a following. Although both saw their dreams and aspirations fail during their lifetimes, the ultimate goals of both brothers were vindicated by history.

—*Gloria Fulton*

FURTHER READING

Campbell, John, and Philip Sherrard. *Modern Greece.* New York: Praeger, 1968. Contains considerable discussion of the Philiki Hetairia and its import.

Clogg, Richard, ed. *The Struggle for Greek Independence: Essays to Mark the 150th Anniversary of the Greek War of Independence.* London: Archon, 1973. Covers the Phanariotes, Philiki Hetairia, the independence movement, insurrections, and the philhellenic movement.

Dakin, Douglas. *The Unification of Greece, 1770-1923.* London: Ernest Benn, 1972. Dakin focuses on the constitutional and state formation questions that followed the independence movement.

Djordjevic, Dimitrije, and Stephen Fischer-Galati. *The Balkan Revolutionary Tradition.* New York: Columbia University Press, 1981. Djordjevic discusses the revolutionary movements of the seventeenth through the nineteenth centuries and the formation of states in the Balkans.

Woodhouse, C. M. *The Greek War of Independence: Its Historical Setting.* London: Hutchinson's University Library, 1952. Woodhouse discusses the effect of Ypsilanti's abortive insurrection and its effect of the *megali idea* of a greater Greece.

_____. *Modern Greece: A Short History.* 5th ed., rev. London: Faber and Faber, 1991. Includes information about the Philiki Hetairia and about the Ypsilantis's participation in the Greek War of Independence.

Zakynthos, D. A. *The Making of Modern Greece: From Byzantium to Independence.* Totowa, N.J.: Rowman & Littlefield, 1976. Zakynthos discusses the social and political background of Greece and the Greeks during the Ottoman period.

SEE ALSO: Alexander I; Lord Byron.
RELATED ARTICLES in *Great Events from History: The Nineteenth Century, 1801-1900:* March 7, 1821-September 29, 1829: Greeks Fight for Independence from the Ottoman Empire; September 24, 1829: Treaty of Adrianople; 1863-1913: Greece Unifies Under the Glücksburg Dynasty.

MARIE ELIZABETH ZAKRZEWSKA
German-born American physician and social reformer

Zakrzewska brought to medicine a scientific rigor and demanding spirit that elevated the status of women in the medical professions. She was also an enthusiastic socialist and feminist, and both her life and her writing vividly illustrated the need for social and professional reform.

BORN: September 6, 1829; Berlin, Prussia (now in Germany)
DIED: May 12, 1902; Boston, Massachusetts
ALSO KNOWN AS: Dr. Zak
AREAS OF ACHIEVEMENT: Medicine, social reform, women's rights

EARLY LIFE

Marie Elizabeth Zakrzewska (zak-SHEHF-skah) was the daughter of Ludwig Martin Zakrzewska, a German civil servant who had been dismissed from the Prussian army for being too liberal, and Caroline Fredericke Wilhelmina Urban, a trained professional midwife. Her family was from the Polish nobility but had lost everything to Russia in 1793.

As a teenager, Marie accompanied her mother on her midwife's rounds. In 1849, she enrolled as a midwifery student at Berlin's Hospital Charité, where her mother had trained. Her mentor and champion there was Joseph Hermann Schmidt, a professor of obstetrics at the University of Berlin and the director of the school of midwifery at Charité. In 1850, Zakrzewska was appointed a teaching assistant and during the following year graduated with highest honors. Shortly before Schmidt died on May 15, 1852, he named Zakrzewska chief midwife at Charité. However, Zakrzewska's youth and the fact that she was a woman turned the rest of the faculty and staff against her, despite her qualifications. After six months she resigned her prestigious position. In March, 1853, she emigrated to the United States.

Through much of 1853 and 1854, Zakrzewska and two of her four sisters eked out their livings in New York City by making and selling clothes and accessories. On May 15, 1854, Zakrzewska met Elizabeth Blackwell, who had become the world's first professionally certified woman physician in 1849. Blackwell's sister Emily had also recently earned a medical degree from Western Reserve University in Cleveland, Ohio. The Blackwell sisters encouraged Zakrzewska to become a physician and helped secure her admission to Western Reserve. Zakrzewska entered the medical school in October, 1854. In March, 1856, she graduated with a medical degree, after writing a thesis on the uterus.

LIFE'S WORK

After obtaining her medical degree, Zakrzewska returned to New York City to begin a small practice under Elizabeth Blackwell's roof. There she acquired the nickname "Dr. Zak" because few could pronounce her full name. Meanwhile Blackwell was working on her dream of opening a women's hospital, and Zakrzewska soon proved to be adept at raising funds to support that project. With Emily Blackwell as chief of surgery and Zakrzewska as chief resident physician, Elizabeth Blackwell founded the New York Infirmary for Women and Children in 1857. It was the first institution of its kind run entirely by women. Over the next two years, Zakrzewska worked there without pay, while continuing her fund-raising efforts.

In March, 1859, Zakrzewska accepted an invitation to teach obstetrics, gynecology, and pediatrics at Boston's New England Female Medical College, which Samuel Gregory had founded eleven years earlier as the world's first medical school for women only. Zakrzewska began her work there with high hopes to expand the prospects for women in medicine but was soon disappointed. With the exception of obstetrical cases, the school provided no clinical training for its students. Its offerings in anatomy, histology, microscopy, physiology, and other basic medical sciences were far below the standards of contemporary men's medical schools. Gregory saw nothing wrong with this discrepancy, but Zakrzewska disagreed. She published the lecture she delivered at the opening of the school's 1859-1860 term; its articulation of her views on the need for higher standards for the medical school instantly created a conflict between her and Gregory.

One irony of Zakrzewska's situation was that she received a better medical education as a midwifery student in Germany than the New England Female Medical College offered to its students in America. At Charité, she had learned how to use a microscope, but her American medical college refused her request to purchase one. Its administrators told her that American physicians should be capable of diagnosing and treating patients properly without having to use microscopes and other "newfangled European" gadgets. The college's founder, Gregory, was not a physician, and he resented Zakrzewska's attempt to elevate female medical practitioners beyond the level of midwives. His own goal was ideological: to train female obstetricians and thus prevent what he called "man-midwives" from offending the modesty of women in childbirth. The differences between Zakrzewska's and Gregory's standards were irreconcilable. Zakrzewska resigned in 1862.

Immediately after Zakrzewska left Gregory's school, she used the New York Infirmary as her model to found the New England Hospital for Women and Children in Boston. It was the world's second such institution. She demanded the maximum in clinical competence and managed her hospital's training facilities with the utmost regard for patients, staff, and trainees. She insisted that all staff members be women, that no alternative practitioners be allowed, and that the recommendations of the emerging science of sanitation be strictly followed. Her hospital flourished and soon became one of the main teaching hospitals in Boston. Among the first generation of women physicians who interned there was Mary Putnam Jacobi.

After starting with only ten beds, Zakrzewska's New England Hospital grew steadily. In 1872, she moved it to Columbus Avenue in Roxbury, Massachusetts. It then became the first American hospital with a nursing school. In 1873, it graduated Linda Richards as America's first fully credentialed nurse and in 1879 Mary Eliza Mahoney as the first African American nurse.

Zakrzewska was intensely political and was involved in many other reform causes in addition to medicine. Soon after arriving in Massachusetts, she bought a house in Roxbury, where she became a friend and landlord of Karl Heinzen, a notorious refugee from Germany's 1848 revolution. Heinzen was an advocate of political assassination, a socialist firebrand, and the publisher of *Der Pionier*, a radical weekly newspaper, which Zakrzewska supported.

In 1890, Zakrzewska moved to Jamaica Plain, Massachusetts, where her home became a frequent meeting place for radicals of all sorts, especially feminists. She retired from medicine in 1899 and died in Boston on May 12, 1902, at the age of seventy-two.

SIGNIFICANCE

Marie Elizabeth Zakrzewska was among the first truly scientific women physicians. She had a dedication to the most challenging aspects of science that was without any trace of sentimentality. An atheist, feminist, radical socialist, and physicalist, she promoted egalitarianism and her chosen political causes boldly and straightforwardly. Nevertheless, she was a compassionate and broadminded clinician who came to be beloved in Boston.

Zakrzewska's New England Hospital for Women and Children grew to eight buildings by the 1930's. After World War II it was still a major institution in Boston medicine, but by then its mission had changed. In 1969, to reflect its new role, it was renamed the Dimock Community Health Center after Susan Dimock, a surgeon who had been on Zakrzewska's staff from 1872 until her untimely death by shipwreck in 1875. The hospital's modern mission is no longer clinical training for women physicians and nurses, but rather health care for the urban poor. Its campus includes the Zakrzewska Medical Building, first built in 1872 and restored during the 1980's by Historic Boston Incorporated.

—*Eric v. d. Luft*

Marie Elizabeth Zakrzewska. (Courtesy, Harvard University Library)

FURTHER READING

Goldstein, Linda Lehmann. "Without Compromising in

Any Particular: The Success of Medical Coeducation in Cleveland, 1850-1856." *Caduceus* 10, no. 2 (Autumn, 1994): 101-115. Contains information about Zakrzewska's experience as one of the earliest women medical students.

Seller, Maxine, ed. *Women Educators in the United States, 1820-1993: A Bio-Bibliographical Sourcebook.* Westport, Conn.: Greenwood Press, 1994. Includes an article by Maureen A. Kingston on Zakrzewska.

Tuchman, Arleen Marcia. "'Only in a Republic Can It Be Proved That Science Has No Sex': Marie Elizabeth Zakrzewska (1829-1902) and the Multiple Meanings of Science in the Nineteenth-Century United States." *Journal of Women's History* 11, no. 1 (Spring, 1999): 121-142. A scholarly analysis of the impact of Zakrzewska's career on political reform.

_____. "Situating Gender: Marie E. Zakrzewska and the Place of Science in Women's Medical Education." *Isis* 95, no. 1 (March, 2004): 34-57. An extension of Tuchman's 1999 article, focusing on Zakrzewska's opposition to Samuel Gregory at Boston's New England Female Medical College.

Zakrzewska, Marie Elizabeth. "Fifty Years Ago: A Retrospect." *Woman's Medical Journal (Toledo)* 1 (1893): 193-195. A brief reminiscence of the era in medicine before women physicians.

_____. *A Practical Illustration of "Woman's Right to Labor"; Or, A Letter from Marie E. Zakrzewska, M.D., Late of Berlin, Prussia.* Edited by Caroline H. Dall. Boston: Walker, Wise, 1860. The earliest of Zakrzewska's several autobiographies. The full text is on the Web at www.fullbooks.com/a-practical-illustration-of-woman-s-right-to.html.

_____. *A Woman's Quest: The Life of Marie E. Zakrzewska, M.D.* Edited by Agnes C. Vietor. 1924. New York: D. Appleton, Arno, 1972. A compelling autobiography.

SEE ALSO: Elizabeth Blackwell; Marie Anne Victorine Boivin; Dorothea Dix.

RELATED ARTICLE in *Great Events from History: The Nineteenth Century, 1801-1900:* May 12, 1857: New York Infirmary for Indigent Women and Children Opens.

ZENG GUOFAN
Chinese statesman and military leader

By suppressing China's Taiping Rebellion, Zeng Guofan contributed materially to the survival of the imperial Qing Dynasty, and he and his protégés were responsible for a remarkable Confucian restoration that sought to modernize China technologically while keeping its traditional philosophical and moral basis.

BORN: November 26, 1811; Xiang Xiang, Hunan Province, China
DIED: March 12, 1872; Nanjing, China
ALSO KNOWN AS: Tseng Kuo-fan (Wade-Giles)
AREAS OF ACHIEVEMENT: Warfare and conquest, government and politics

EARLY LIFE

Zeng Guofan (tsehng GOO-oh-fahn) was born into an impoverished but well-educated aristocratic landowning family whose members claimed to be descendants of a disciple of the ancient philosopher Confucius. They lived in China's central province of Hunan. Zeng's grandfather bestowed a strong sense of realism on the young boy. His father, Zeng Linshu, struggled hard with his own education. His mother devoted herself to her husband and her son, who started to study at age four.

At the age of eight, Zeng Guofan started studying the Chinese classics and began to write compositions. At thirteen, his family arranged for him to marry a young girl from the Ou Yang family of Hunan. Zeng and his wife eventually had three sons and six daughters. Two boys and five girls survived to adulthood, and his oldest son became a diplomat.

Meanwhile, Zeng passed his first examination in 1826. In 1833, he earned his first degree during the same year that his father finally earned his own degree. On June 23, 1838, when he was twenty-seven, he earned the *jinshi* degree, which is comparable to a doctorate, and became a member of the prestigious Han Lin Academy in Beijing. As was typical for a scholar in imperial China, Zeng held a variety of government positions and steadily rose in rank. In 1843, he became examiner for Sichuan Province, a position that allowed him to pay off the debts he had accumulated during his studies, and help his family and fellow Hunanese.

Zeng was elevated to cabinet rank on July 29, 1847, and became acting vice president of the Board of Ceremonies in Beijing in 1849. It was a remarkable accomplishment for someone only thirty-eight years old. When his mother died on July 28, 1852, Zeng took temporary leave. Custom demanded he mourn her for twenty-seven months at his home in Hunan.

LIFE'S WORK

In December, 1852, while Zeng was still in mourning, imperial orders to fight the Taiping rebels reached him. The Taiping Rebellion had begun in 1850 in the remote mountains west of Guangxi Province, bordering Vietnam. Under the leadership of Hong Xiuquan, who proclaimed himself the younger brother of Jesus Christ and Heavenly King, the Taiping rebels sought to erect a quasi-religious empire. Their stunning military successes led them north into Hunan in 1852. Shocked by the defeats of his armies, Emperor Xianfeng commissioned Zeng Guofan to raise a defense force in his home province. His order required an astonishing violation of the Qing law prohibiting leading government officials from commanding military forces within their home provinces.

In early 1853, Zeng recruited and built his Xiang (or Hunan) army, named for the river running through his province. To finance his forces, Zeng used the special Lijin tax. While the rebels captured Nanjing in March, 1853, and made that city the capital of their pseudo-Christian sect, Zeng had to learn how to be a military general—a task for which his classical education had scarcely prepared him. Meanwhile, he devoted his energies to raising his militia.

Zeng's initial force of 540 boats, 5,000 marines, and a large number of infantry troops were unsuccessful against the Taiping, so frustrating Zeng that he attempted suicide. In 1854, however, two of his generals won a major victory against the Taiping and checked their advance into Hunan. Nevertheless, by the spring of 1855, Zeng was being outmaneuvered and was left isolated. He was encircled by a small force of troops and a few ships in neighboring Jianxi Province. He was relieved only in the summer of 1856. His counteroffensive in Jianxi was aided by internal dissent among the rebels that saw the murder of two of their subordinate kings and nearly saw the collapse of its leadership in May, 1857. When Zeng's father died in early 1857, he resigned his command and returned home to mourn.

In 1858, Zeng was recalled from retirement by an imperial edict ordering him to halt the Taiping invasion of coastal Zhejiang Province. One of his most gifted protégés, Li Hongzhang, then joined his staff. Later that same year, Zeng's Xiang army was defeated, however, and his brother Zeng Guo Hua was killed. In July, 1859, Zeng finally cleared Hunan Province of rebels. After the defeat of a large Qing army by the Taiping in May, 1860, Zeng was made imperial commissioner for suppressing the Taiping on June 8, 1860. Indicative of his trust in his subordinate commanders, who exceeded his own military capabilities, Zeng placed Zuo Zongfang in command of his forces south of Nanjing. Encircled again, this time at Qimen north of Hunan, Zeng was saved by Zuo's victory in April, 1861. On September 5, 1861, Anqing, the provincial capital of Anhui, fell to his younger brother Zeng Guo Quan.

Zeng's position was aided in November, 1861, when Prince Gong and the empress dowager Cixi assumed power in the name of Cixi's six-year-old son, the new emperor Tongzhi. Both leaders trusted Zeng. Meanwhile, his generals Li Hongzhang and Zuo Zongtang continued to defeat the Taiping. Zeng reached Nanjing in June, 1862, and completed its encirclement in February, 1894, aided by his brother Guo Quan. The Taiping leader Hong Xiuquan died on June 1, 1864, and Zeng captured Nanjing on July 19, killing more than ten thousand Taiping soldiers. When Hong's grave was discovered on July 30, Zeng ordered Hong's body to be exhumed, beheaded, and burned.

While mopping-up operations against surviving Taiping continued, Zeng demobilized 120,000 troops of his victorious Xiang army in late 1864 as a display of loyalty. He was then made a marquis of the first class, the first civilian ever so honored, and was also made the governor of three provinces.

On May 27, 1865, Zeng became imperial commissioner for the suppression of the Nian rebels raiding the area between Shanghai and Beijing. He organized a static defense against the highly mobile rebels that failed to contain them. Sick and frustrated, Zeng recommended that he be replaced by Li Hongzhang, who was given his task. He was made grand secretary in 1867 and became governor of Zhili Province—the region around Beijing—in 1868, the same year in which Li defeated the Nian.

In 1870, Zeng was asked to negotiate with France in a difficult situation arising from the massacre of French missionaries in Tianjin (Tientsin). The following year, he was again named governor of the three Liangjiang provinces. Exhausted and seriously ill, he refused Western medical treatment but allowed his wife to be saved by Western medicine. In early 1872, he sent off the first mission of Chinese students to study in the United States. On March 12, 1872, Zeng Guofan died in Nanjing, at the age of sixty.

SIGNIFICANCE

Beyond the triumph he won overseeing a military victory over the Taiping, Zeng Guofan excelled as a conservative reformer who significantly contributed to the unexpected restoration of the Qing Dynasty. Guided by the highest moral principles and ethical standards, Zeng exemplified the ideal of the Confucian scholar-statesman. His pragmatism and ability to support people of talent yielded remarkable results.

Zeng witnessed the superiority of Western weaponry and the scientific and industrial advances that made possible their production and ceaselessly promoted Chinese emulation of Western military science. He supported Chinese production of steamships, cannons, and other Western weapons. He established military arsenals at Anqing and Shanghai and helped Li Hongzhang develop the Nanjing arsenal and Zuo Zongtang develop the Fuzhou dockyards, imperial China's most modern industrial complex. Zeng's decision to promote the education of Chinese in America and his support for buying American manufacturing machinery for the Shanghai arsenal were visionary. Indeed, his vision was especially unusual, as his philosophy was quintessentially Confucian, nationalist, and conservative.

In twentieth century China, Zeng Guofan was most widely praised by the nationalist leader Chiang Kai-shek, who promoted Zeng's legacy as a model for anti-communist modernism and progress. Similarly, Mao Zedong's communists vilified Zeng as a feudalist reactionary who failed to be aggressive against Western powers. Nevertheless, Zeng Guofan served both the imperial government and the Chinese nation with the utmost loyalty, devotion, and creativity. His leadership prevented China from breaking apart, and he promoted a balance between modern military and traditional values.

—*R. C. Lutz*

FURTHER READING

Hall, William James. *Tsêng Kuo-fan and the Taiping Rebellion: With a Short Sketch of His Later Career*. New Haven, Conn.: Yale University Press, 1927. Still the only book-length biography of Zeng in English, this work gives a thorough and sympathetic account of his life, focusing on his struggle with the Taiping. It also summarizes his neo-Confucian philosophy and outlines his achievements.

Porter, Jonathan. *Tseng Kuo-fan's Private Bureaucracy*. Berkeley: University of California Press, 1972. Study of the institutions through which Zeng sought to organize and finance his war against the Taiping; argues that Zeng created a rational government that anticipated twentieth century technocratic bureaucracy.

Spence, Jonathan. *God's Chinese Son: The Taiping Heavenly Kingdom of Hong Xiuquan*. New York: W. W. Norton, 1996. Although this book focuses on Zeng's great adversary, Spence discusses his contribution to fighting and defeating the Taiping and explains how Zeng's capable subordinates helped destroy the rebels.

_____. *The Search for Modern China*. 2d ed. New York: W. W. Norton, 1999. The most widely available book on modern Chinese history in English. Chapter 8 deals with Zeng's achievements in the war against Taiping and Nian rebels. Chapter 9 describes his contributions to the Confucian reform movement and shows his portrait.

Wright, Mary Clabaugh. *The Last Stand of Chinese Conservatism: The T'ung Chich Restoration, 1862-1874*. Stanford, Calif.: Stanford University Press, 1957. Discusses Zeng's significant contributions to the remarkable recovery of the fortunes of the Qing Dynasty, his war against the rebels, and his work for the self-strengthening movement; especially valuable for the concluding discussion of Chiang Kai-shek's propagandistic use of Zeng in his own twentieth century war against communists.

Yingjie Guo, and Baogang He. "Reimagining the Chinese Nation." *Modern China* 25, no. 2 (April, 1999): 142. Examines the historical writings of Zeng and how these writings have spurred debate about the politics of Chinese identity.

SEE ALSO: Cixi; Hong Xiuquan; Li Hongzhang.

RELATED ARTICLE in *Great Events from History: The Nineteenth Century, 1801-1900:* January 11, 1851-late summer, 1864: China's Taiping Rebellion.

2485

ZHANG ZHIDONG
Chinese scholar and administrator

Zhang Zhidong was a leading scholar-official in China during the last half-century of the Qing Dynasty. His educational, military, and economic reforms contributed greatly to the survival of China's last imperial dynasty.

BORN: September 2, 1837; Nanpi, Chihli (now Hebei), China
DIED: October 4, 1909; Beijing, Chihli, China
ALSO KNOWN AS: Chang Chih-tung (Wade-Giles)
AREA OF ACHIEVEMENT: Government and politics

EARLY LIFE

Zhang Zhidong (tshang TSHEE-dahng) came from a gentry family of modest means. His father, Zhang Ying, provided him with a rigorous classical education, and Zhidong responded with diligence and precocity. At the age of thirteen, he passed the prefectural exam, becoming a *sheng-yüan*. At fifteen, Zhidong, in competition with almost ten thousand scholars, led the list of about one hundred who received the *chü-jen* degree in Chihli (Hebei) Province.

Zhang Zhidong delayed taking the metropolitan exam, deterred in part by his father's death in 1855. In 1863, however, he passed the Beijing exam, becoming a *chin-shih* degree-holder and member of China's upper gentry. His palace examination, though somewhat controversial, apparently pleased Cixi (Tz'u-hsi), the empress dowager, who appointed him to the Hanlin Academy in Beijing.

From 1867 to 1881, Zhang alternated between provincial posts in education in Hubei (Hupeh) and Sichuan (Szechwan), and positions at the Hanlin Academy. At the capital, he associated with a group of conservative Confucian scholars who called themselves the Qingliu, or purists. The Qingliu demanded that China adopt a militant stand against foreign encroachment and characterized the policies of moderating as constituting cowardly appeasement. Zhang was no better than any of the purists, however, in his constant efforts to please Cixi. He condoned her decision, in 1875, to defy Confucian tradition by breaking the normal line of succession and securing the throne for her nephew, Emperor Guangxu (Kuang-hsü). When a censor, Wu Kedu (Wu K'o-tu), committed suicide in 1879 to protest Cixi's policies, Zhang wrote a lengthy memorial criticizing Wu and justifying the empress dowager's actions.

Zhang's memorials were usually less sycophantic and usually concerned foreign policy. He and the purists called for military action against Russia over the I-li and against France over the status of Annam. In the first instance, their bellicose posturing appeared to be effective, and Russia agreed to replace the earlier Treaty of Livadia (October, 1789) with the less favorable Treaty of St. Petersburg (February, 1881). Unfortunately, the purists, encouraged by their apparent success in I-li, prodded the throne into applying the same kind of threatening approach to France, which precipitated the Sino-French War (1883-1885). The fighting resulted in France's destruction of the Chinese fleet and shipyards at Fuzhou (Foochow), and China reluctantly agreed to the unfavorable terms of the Li-Fournier Agreement (May, 1884).

Most of the purists were discredited for having pushed China into a losing war, and Zhang might have suffered a similar fate. Fortunately for him, he had already embarked upon a more substantive career than that of warmonger. The bitter experience of witnessing China's ignominy during the Sino-French fiasco had radically altered Zhang's perspectives on the West and on change, and he had become an energetic reformer.

LIFE'S WORK

Earlier, while still basking in the success at I-li, Zhang received several rapid promotions and became governor of Shanxi (Shansi) Province in 1881. As governor, Zhang initiated numerous industrial and educational projects to help reduce the deplorable economic conditions in Shanxi. In 1884, during the Sino-French hostilities, the throne appointed Zhang viceroy of Liangkwang (Guangdong and Guangxi). At the conclusion of the war, the throne not only criticized Zhang for his earlier bellicosity but also praised him for having undertaken several positive measures, including the defense of Guangdong (Kwangtung). Zhang began to adopt the ideas of Feng Guifen (Feng Kuei-fen), who during the early 1860's had popularized the concept of *ziqiang*, or self-strengthening.

To Zhang, strengthening China required the adoption of Western technology. He was, however, deeply concerned with the relationship between modernization and Westernization—the dilemma facing all Chinese reformers. His interest was not to alter China in a radical way but rather to save it by entertaining certain modifications. Thus, he insisted upon preserving Confucianism as the central core of Chinese culture. To this end, Zhang promoted the slogan that translates as "Chinese studies as the foundation, Western studies for their practicality." This signified that modernization should not entail Westernization, because Chinese values were superior to those of the West.

Among Zhang's many proposals was the construction of a railway line between Beijing and Hankou. The throne appointed Zhang viceroy of Hunan-Hubei in 1889, with instructions to oversee this project. Having earlier constructed a foundry in Guangdong. Zhang also undertook to establish the Hanyeping Iron and Steel works in Hanyang. Though small and wiry, Zhang was apparently tireless in his efforts to seek funds for these and other projects. His zeal, however, did not mean that he understood either the mechanics or the financial underpinnings of successful industrialization. When it became evident that he could not obtain the necessary capital for either of these projects, he turned them over to private corporations.

During the Sino-Japanese War of 1894-1895, when the viceroy of the Anhui-Jiangsu-Jiangsi area, Liu Kuni, was commanding troops, Zhang took over at Nanjing on an interim basis. In his efforts to prepare China for continued war, Zhang undertook the creation of a self-strengthening army, with German advisers and foreign weapons. Zhang turned over this modern force to Liu upon the latter's return to Nanjing, but he re-created essentially the same type of units on his resumption of the viceroyalty post at Hanyang.

During 1895-1898, Zhang associated with many young zealous reformers, who ultimately became involved in the famous Hundred Days' Reform during the summer of 1898. Prior to this abortive movement, Zhang published his famous *Quan xue pian* (exhortation to study). The reformers, reading their own convictions into this work, construed it as a rallying platform. For his part, Zhang, who had originally financed and sponsored many of the reformers, became alarmed by their misrepresentation of his ideas. He also disliked their leader, Kang Youwei (K'ang Yu-wei) for his constant representation of Confucius as a radical reformer.

As the reformers moved toward constitutional monarchy, Zhang, who distrusted participatory democracy, began to distance himself from them. When Cixi's coup ended the Hundred Days' Reform, Zhang was one of the first to call for the severe punishment of the reform leaders. He even refused to join Liu Kuni in memorializing the throne against the threatened deposition of the young emperor. Zhang emerged from this movement the object

of suspicion and hatred, both by court conservatives and young reformers. Whatever remaining ties existed between Zhang and the new reformers ended in 1900, when Zhang arrested and executed twenty conspirators who had been plotting the overthrow of Cixi.

During the Boxer Rebellion (1899-1900), Zhang joined a few other provincial leaders in guaranteeing the safety and property of foreigners in southern China. While he complied with orders from the court to send troops to the north, he kept his strongest units at home and sent untrained recruits to the capital. At the conclusion of the Boxer Rebellion, he and other moderate provincial officials requested that foreign powers not hold Cixi accountable for Boxer outrages. Zhang thus consolidated his position at the court and also endeared himself to many foreigners in China. He eventually made use of his ties to British representatives, asking them repeatedly to intercede on his behalf at the imperial court.

With the deaths of Li Hongzhang and Liu Kuni, in 1901 and 1902, respectively, Zhang became China's senior statesman. Among many reform activities, he spearheaded a commission to study the future of the civil service examination system. Calling at first for their gradual abolition, Zhang suddenly suggested an immediate end to the exams and the creation of a national Confucian school system. Cixi complied with alacrity and on September 2, 1905, abolished the examination system, ending what was probably the most salient feature of China's Confucian imperial system.

In the summer of 1907, Zhang came to the capital as a grand secretary, but the court also made him a grand councillor and directed him to head the Ministry of Education. By this time, however, he was beset both by infirmity and considerable doubts about the Qing Dynasty's ability to survive. The death of Cixi in November, 1908, did little to improve his outlook. Zhang had come to accept the idea of a constitutional monarchy but was frustrated by what he construed as moral decay in China. On October 4, 1909, the same day he submitted a memorial eulogizing Cixi, he died, surrounded by friends and family.

SIGNIFICANCE

An educational innovator who founded dozens of academies and modern schools and an initiator of numerous industrial and communications ventures, Zhang Zhidong unquestionably helped arrest the continued decline of the Qing Dynasty. Nevertheless, he embodied both the best and worst features of China's traditional elite class. Honest to a fault, Zhang died a relatively poor man. However, his loyalty to a dynasty led him to tolerate the venality and corruption of Cixi, the empress dowager. He understood that China was weak and needed reform, but he also remained firmly convinced that China's traditional value system should remain virtually intact.

In essence, Zhang failed to grasp the relationship between technological modernity and the sociocultural foundations that were necessary for such modernization. His formulas for self-strengthening proved to be bankrupt rationalizations that failed to acknowledge inherent weaknesses in China's cultural tradition itself. His occasional opportunism was a reflection of the corrupt state of the Qing Dynasty, and, in the end, most of his projects served only to retard the process of dynastic deterioration. Zhang could neither save the dynasty nor conserve the Confucian tradition that he cherished. He died a famous and respected man but ultimately was a failed leader of a country that had become weaker during his own lifetime. Although he did not bear the principal responsibility for this decline, the empress dowager, the Qing Dynasty, and, in large measure, the unaltered Confucian tradition that he supported, all contributed to China's decay.

—*Hilel B. Salomon*

FURTHER READING

Ayers, William. *Chang Chih-tung and Educational Reform in China.* Cambridge, Mass.: Harvard University Press, 1971. Although concentrating on Zhang's role as an educational reformer, this well-documented work can serve as a biography of his life as well.

Bays, Daniel H. *China Enters the Twentieth Century: Chang Chih-tung and the Issues of a New Age, 1895-1909.* Ann Arbor: University of Michigan Press, 1978. A thorough and analytical account of Zhang's career during the last fifteen years of his life.

Cohen, Paul A., and John E. Schrecker, eds. *Reform in Nineteenth Century China.* Cambridge, Mass.: Harvard University Press, 1976. Numerous articles discuss Zhang's association with the Qingliu reformers and his other activities. Most of the articles provide an excellent background for a study of Zhang.

Eastman, Lloyd E. *Throne and Mandarins: China's Search for a Policy During the Sino-French Controversy, 1880-1885.* Cambridge, Mass.: Harvard University Press, 1967. An excellent review of this period, with much discussion of Zhang and the purists.

Hummel, Arthur W., ed. *Eminent Chinese of the Ch'ing Period, 1644-1912.* 2 vols. Washington, D.C.: Government Printing Office, 1943-1944. Volume 1 contains a fairly detailed biography of Zhang that is still accurate and useful.

Levenson, Joseph R. *Confucian China and Its Modern Fate.* 3 vols. Berkeley: University of California Press, 1958-1965. In volume 1, the author discusses the conflict between continuity and change during the Qing Dynasty. Referring frequently to Zhang, the author gives a superb analysis of the dilemma facing Confucian reformers.

Powell, Ralph L. *The Rise of Chinese Military Power, 1895-1912.* Princeton, N.J.: Princeton University Press, 1955. Offers substantial coverage of Zhang's military reforms and his efforts involving the self-strengthening army.

Wright, Mary C. *The Last Stand of Chinese Conservatism: The T'ung-Chih Restoration, 1862-1874.* Stanford, Calif.: Stanford University Press, 1957. Although concentrating on the period prior to Zhang's prominence, this classic is essential to understanding the struggle between conservatism and modernization in the late Qing Dynasty. The author frequently refers to Zhang's ideas and actions.

SEE ALSO: Cixi; Kang Youwei; Li Hongzhang.

RELATED ARTICLES in *Great Events from History: The Nineteenth Century, 1801-1900:* 1860's: China's Self-Strengthening Movement Arises; September 6, 1899-July 3, 1900: Hay Articulates "Open Door" Policy Toward China; May, 1900-September 7, 1901: Boxer Rebellion.

ÉMILE ZOLA
French novelist

Zola's major contributions were in three areas: literature, as a writer of poetry, drama, novels, and essays; literary theory, as one of the major forces in defining naturalism as a literary school; and human rights, as a defender of Alfred Dreyfus, who was falsely accused of treason and sentenced to Devil's Island.

BORN: April 2, 1840; Paris, France
DIED: September 28, 1902; Paris, France
ALSO KNOWN AS: Émile-Édouard-Charles-Antoine Zola (full name)
AREA OF ACHIEVEMENT: Literature

EARLY LIFE

Born in Paris, Émile Zola spent his first eighteen years in Aix-en-Provence. His father, Francesco Zola, was a high-spirited Venetian, bursting with grandiose ideas for engineering projects. With a doctorate in engineering from the University of Padua, Francesco helped plan the first public railway in Europe, served in the French foreign legion, and, in 1839, married Émilie-Aurélie Aubert. Twenty thousand francs in debt, he nevertheless installed Émilie in an expensive Paris apartment, where Émile, their only child, was born.

Francesco's fortunes improved when Aix accepted his plan to build a canal to bring water to the municipality. The family moved to Provence, where work on the canal proceeded. During construction, Francesco caught cold and succumbed to pneumonia, leaving his family not only destitute but also ninety thousand francs in debt. Émilie moved with her son to smaller quarters, bringing her parents to live with them. Émilie's parents looked after the grieving Émile while Émilie did housework for other people, supplementing that modest income by gradually selling most of her furniture.

The family tried to protect the delicate Émile. Dark-haired and dark-eyed, he had his father's broad face and protruding brow, on which worry lines, lines of conscience, developed early. A speech defect caused Émile's classmates to taunt him. His mother used her dead husband's connections to obtain for the boy a scholarship to Collège Bourbon, where he emphasized scientific studies but developed his passion for literature. Here began his friendship with his classmate Paul Cézanne.

When he was eighteen, Zola moved to Paris, where his mother had relocated to increase her earnings. Isolated and lonely, he lived in squalid surroundings, first with his mother, then alone. Poverty was ever-present. Émile enrolled in the Lycée Saint-Louis, but twice he failed the baccalaureate examinations, partly because his use of French was judged limited and defective. He took menial jobs and at twenty-four published his first collection of stories, *Contes à Ninon* (1864; *Stories for Ninon*, 1895), which was encouragingly reviewed but brought him little money.

LIFE'S WORK

Stories for Ninon, although a promising beginning for a young author, shows little of the combination of careful observation, practiced objectivity, and scientific method that characterized Zola's most celebrated works. The stories are modeled on medieval fables, quite a different focus from that of the naturalistic themes for which Zola is best known. Zola's first novel, *La Confession de Claude* (1865; *Claude's Confession*, 1882), failed to employ the close, objective techniques of observation Zola demanded in his naturalistic credo, *Le Roman expérimental* (1880; *The Experimental Novel*, 1893), a theoretical work that significantly changed the course of writing in Europe, Great Britain, and the United States. His second and third novels, *Thérèse Raquin* (1867; English translation, 1881) and *Madeleine Férat* (1868; English translation, 1880), moved toward the realism practiced by Honoré de Balzac, Gustave Flaubert, and the brothers Edmond de Goncourt and Jules de Goncourt, whose writings attracted Zola, a voracious reader.

When Zola was writing these novels, however, he had not yet been exposed to Claude Bernard's *Introduction à l'étude de la médecine expérimentale* (1865; *An Introduction to the Study of Experimental Medicine*, 1927), a book from a nonliterary field on which Zola was to model his formal approach to literature, which catapulted him to the forefront of an emerging school of literature that took writing well beyond the realism then prevalent in French literature.

Almost a decade before Zola read Bernard's influential book in 1878, the year of its author's death, he had begun the daunting literary task of writing *Les Rougon-Macquart* (1871-1893; *The Rougon-Macquart Novels*, 1885-1907), designed to examine in minute detail two generations of a family, considering especially the roles that both heredity and environment played in the lives of its members. This work is an interconnected series of twenty novels. Three books of the ambitious cy-

Émile Zola. (Library of Congress)

cle, *L'Assommoir* (1877; English translation, 1879), *Nana* (1880; English translation, 1880), and *Germinal* (1885; English translation, 1885), are considered Zola's finest.

Before Zola began work on this cycle, however, he had stirred controversy in literary circles with *Claude's Confession*, in which his forthright and nonjudgmental presentation of a prostitute created legal problems for him in a France that strongly controlled language and the arts. If his early work was considered notorious, by the time he was writing the Rougon-Macquart cycle, the bourgeoisie viewed him as completely outrageous, a threat to public decency.

Not until *L'Assommoir*, the seventh book of the Rougon-Macquart series, was published in 1877 did Zola's writing bring him much money. He had eked out a living before that time writing essays and doing a variety of journalistic jobs. Income from *L'Assommoir*, however, enabled him to buy a summer home at Médan. He had already attracted an enthusiastic following, especially among notable writers and artists who took seriously Zola's writing in defense of the Impressionistic artists of his day.

A significant turning point in Zola's life came in 1880, the year in which his mother died and in which *Nana* and

The Experimental Novel were published. In this year, also, Zola's theory of literary naturalism was exemplified with the publication of the anthology *Les Soirées de Médan* (1880). This work grew out of regular weekly soirées Zola held in both Médan and Paris. In these soirées, the participants, under Zola's staunch guidance, defined literary naturalism categorically, and the regular attendees, including Guy de Maupassant, Joris-Karl Huysmans, and Henri Céard, each contributed a story to the anthology.

If *The Experimental Novel* was the handbook for literary naturalists, *Les Soirées de Médan* became their manifesto. The naturalism Zola espoused moved beyond realism in that realism attempts to present life as it really is, whereas naturalism applies a scientific method to presenting reality, with the intention of identifying social ills and, through experimentation, reaching an understanding of those ills in ways that will enable society to remedy them.

Bernard wrote of the "vital circulus," the symbiosis between the muscular and nervous activities that preserve the blood-producing organs and the blood that nourishes the organs manufacturing it. Zola transformed this concept into his "social circulus." When an organ of society becomes infected, novelists, according to Zola, must proceed scientifically as physicians do. They must discover the simple initial cause that explains the indisposition. By exposing the cause, they then make it amenable to remedy.

Naturalistic writers, then, observe, record faithfully and in detail as a laboratory scientist would, and present their findings in literary form. Naturalistic authors remain detached from their material, presenting consistently exact records of their observations rather than observations colored by personal predilections. They show how heredity and environment act upon the human organism in the social setting to create human behavior. Few literary naturalist, including Zola, remained wholly faithful to the tenets of naturalism. Nevertheless, these tenets profoundly affected the writings of future generations of authors. The positive aspects of society were treated only as they contributed to causes of social ills. Just as medicine deals with physical pathologies, so did Zola's naturalism explore social pathologies.

From his earliest days, Zola had a great zeal for reform. He sought to change a society he considered imperfect. He was fearless and, when necessary, autocratic in working to bring about social changes he deemed imperative. He was incredibly hardworking, ever planning literary projects huge in scope, not unlike the grandiose engineering projects his father had planned a generation earlier. By 1893, Zola had, quite remarkably, completed the twenty novels of the Rougon-Macquart cycle and in the same year began work on the trilogy *Les Trois Villes* (1894-1898; *The Three Cities*, 1894-1898), consisting of *Lourdes* (1894; English translation, 1894), *Rome* (1896; English translation, 1896), and *Paris* (1898; English translation, 1898).

As his work on the trilogy neared its end, Zola, incensed at what he considered the wrongful conviction for treason and sentencing to Devil's Island of Captain Alfred Dreyfus in 1894, took a public stand in support of Dreyfus and published his stirring letter "J'accuse"

(1898; "The Dreyfus Case," 1898), which led to a reopening of the case and to the eventual acquittal of the defendant. Zola, however, as a result of his stand, was found guilty on two charges of libel, fined three thousand francs, and sentenced to a year in prison.

Before the execution of his sentence, Zola fled to England, where he remained until France's president, Émile-François Loubet, pardoned him in 1899, whereupon Zola returned to France. There, he continued work on another massive project, *Les Quatre Évangiles* (1899-1903; English translation, 1900-1903), to consist of four novels, three of which, *Fécondité* (1899; *Fruitfulness*, 1900), *Travail* (1901; *Work*, 1901), and *Vérité* (1903; *Truth*, 1903), he completed before his death by coal gas

ZOLA'S NOVELS	
1865	*La Confession de Claude* (*Claude's Confession*, 1882)
1866	*Le Vœu d'une morte* (*A Dead Woman's Wish*, 1902)
1867	*Les Mystères de Marseille* (*The Flower Girls of Marseilles*, 1888; also as *The Mysteries of Marseilles*, 1895)
1867	*Thérèse Raquin* (English translation, 1881)
1868	*Madeleine Férat* (English translation, 1880)
1871	*La Fortune des Rougon* (*The Rougon-Macquart Novels*, 1879; also as *The Fortune of the Rougons*, 1886)
1872	*La Curée* (*The Rush for the Spoil*, 1886; also as *The Kill*, 1895)
1873	*Le Ventre de Paris* (*The Markets of Paris*, 1879; also as *Savage Paris*, 1955)
1874	*La Conquête de Plassans* (*The Conquest of Plassans*, 1887; also as *A Priest in the House*, 1957)
1875	*La Faute de l'abbé Mouret* (*Albine: Or, The Abbé's Temptation*, 1882; also as *Abbé Mouret's Transgression*, 1886)
1876	*Son Excellence Eugène Rougon* (*Clorinda: Or, The Rise and Reign of His Excellency Eugène Rougon*, 1880; also as *His Excellency*, 1897)
1877	*L'Assommoir* (English translation, 1879; also as *The Dram-Shop*, 1897)
1878	*Une Page d'amour* (*Hélène: A Love Episode*, 1878, also as *A Love Affair*, 1957)
1880	*Nana* (English translation, 1880)
1882	*Pot-Bouille* (*Piping Hot*, 1924)
1883	*Au bonheur des dames* (*The Bonheur des Dames*, 1883; also as *The Ladies' Paradise*, 1883)
1884	*La Joie de vivre* (*Life's Joys*, 1884; also as *Zest for Life*, 1955)
1885	*Germinal* (English translation, 1885)
1886	*L'Œuvre* (*His Masterpiece*, 1886; also as *The Masterpiece*, 1946)
1887	*La Terre* (*The Soil*, 1888; also as *Earth*, 1954)
1888	*Le Rêve* (*The Dream*, 1888)
1890	*La Bête humaine* (*Human Brutes*, 1890; also as *The Human Beast*, 1891)
1891	*L'Argent* (*Money*, 1891)
1892	*La Débâcle* (*The Downfall*, 1892)
1893	*Le Docteur Pascal* (*Doctor Pascal*, 1893; previous 20 novels (*La Fortune des Rougon* through *Docteur Pascal* collectively known as *Les Rougon-Macquart* [*The Rougon-Macquart Novels*])
1894	*Lourdes* (English translation, 1894)
1896	*Rome* (English translation, 1896)
1898	*Paris* (English translation, 1897, 1898; previous 3 novels collectively known as *Les Trois Villes*)
1899	*Fécondité* (*Fruitfulness*, 1900)
1901	*Travail* (*Work*, 1901)
1903	*Vérité* (*Truth*, 1903; previous 3 novels collectively known as *Les Quatre Évangiles*)

asphyxiation in his Paris apartment on September 28, 1902. The death, first thought to be accidental, was likely a murder committed by elements who opposed his participation in the Dreyfus case.

SIGNIFICANCE

Émile Zola was a man with exuberant plans, a man of enormous energy and courage. He lived a life guided by principles he arrived at consciously and intelligently. In addition to his prolific literary career, Zola's involvement in public affairs, always guided by his intellect and his immutable conscience, distinguished him throughout his life.

Zola's support of Impressionist artists during the 1860's forced him into an unpopular public stand well before his own future was assured. He supported what he believed without regard to personal consequences. He was equally stalwart during the 1870's and 1880's, as he was developing his own literary credo, which, in its final formulation as literary naturalism, became a publicly unpopular movement. Zola spent the last years of his life preoccupied with the Dreyfus affair, and on his death it was this stand that seemed best to exemplify to his countrymen his spirit of social reform, as Anatole France noted in his oration at Zola's funeral.

Zola's literary theories directly affected scores of authors, among whom some direct inheritors were Gerhart Hauptmann, Hermann Sudermann, Arthur Schnitzler, August Strindberg, Henrik Ibsen, Thomas Hardy, D. H. Lawrence, Eugene O'Neill, Frank Norris, Upton Sinclair, and Thomas Mann. Indirectly, his literary theories affected even those authors who rebelled against naturalism and went on to found such important countermovements as literary expressionism.

—R. Baird Shuman

FURTHER READING

Baguley, David. *Critical Essays on Émile Zola*. Boston: G. K. Hall, 1986. The twenty essays in this book, some written especially for this volume, others drawn from previously published sources, present a balanced view of Zola criticism, ranging from such early critics as Algernon Swinburne, Henry Havelock Ellis, and Heinrich Mann to such later ones as Roland Barthes, Irving Howe, and Naomi Schor.

Bloom, Harold, ed. *Emile Zola*. Philadelphia: Chelsea House, 2004. One in a series of books aimed at literature students. Features an introductory essay by Bloom, a brief biography of Zola, a chronology, and essays describing Zola's works.

Brown, Frederick. *Zola: A Life*. New York: Farrar, Strauss, Giroux, 1995. Massive, meticulously researched account of Zola's life, with analyses of all of his novels, set within the context of Second Empire France. According to Brown, Zola viewed each of his novels as a personal triumph over impotence, death, and guilt.

Knapp, Bettina L. *Émile Zola*. New York: Frederick Ungar, 1980. A brief, direct presentation, accurate and highly appropriate for those just beginning to explore Zola. The chronological table is especially useful.

Richardson, Joanna. *Zola*. New York: St. Martin's Press, 1978. Richardson argues that Zola was contentious, and this quality relates to the impact of his work, which overall is excellent more as a reflection of a well-defined literary credo than as an artistic contribution. Especially valuable for its clear exposition of the Dreyfus affair.

Schom, Alan. *Émile Zola: A Biography*. New York: Henry Holt, 1987. The excellence of its prose style and the carefully chosen illustrations make this book a reading delight. The research is exhaustive, and the revelations that point to Zola's death's being a well-planned assassination made to look like an accident raise fascinating questions for the modern reader.

Schor, Naomi. *Zola's Crowds*. Baltimore: Johns Hopkins University Press, 1978. Schor is concerned with Zola's remarkable ability to control the huge numbers of people who populate a work as massive as the Rougon-Macquart series, in which each novel is at once independent from but interconnected with the others. An interesting thesis in the light of Gustave Le Bon's theory of the crowd.

Walker, Philip. *Zola*. London: Routledge & Kegan Paul, 1985. This thoughtful book is meticulous in its research although somewhat pedestrian in its organization. The most valuable chapter in it is "Full Summer," which explores fruitfully Zola's necrophobia, a matter that had significant bearing on his writing.

SEE ALSO: Honoré de Balzac; Claude Bernard; Paul Cézanne; Gustave Flaubert; Anatole France; Thomas Hardy; Henrik Ibsen; Guy de Maupassant; Pierre-Auguste Renoir.

RELATED ARTICLES in *Great Events from History: The Nineteenth Century, 1801-1900:* c. 1865: Naturalist Movement Begins; October, 1894-July, 1906: Dreyfus Affair; January 14, 1900: Puccini's *Tosca* Premieres in Rome.

Appendixes

RULERS AND HEADS OF STATE

Major world leaders during and beyond the period covered in *Great Lives from History: The Nineteenth Century, 1801-1900* are listed below, beginning with the Roman Catholic popes and followed by rulers of major nations or dynasties, alphabetically by country. Within each country section, rulers are listed chronologically. It is important to note that name spellings and regnal dates vary among sources, and that variations do not necessarily suggest inaccuracy. For example, dates when leaders took power may not match dates of coronation, and the names by which leaders have been recorded in history may represent birth names, epithets, or regnal names. Date ranges and geographical borders of nations and dynasties vary, given the complexities of politics and warfare, and the mere fact that "nations" evolved over time from competing and allied principalities. Hence, not every civilization, dynasty, principality, or region can be covered here; we have, however, attempted to provide lists of rulers for those countries most likely to be addressed in general history and area studies courses.

CONTENTS

POPES AND ANTIPOPES

Asterisked (*) names indicate popes who have been sainted by the Church. Names appearing in square brackets [ ] are antipopes.

Term	Pope
440-461	*Leo I the Great
461-468	*Hilarius
468-483	*Simplicius
483-492	*Felix III
492-496	*Gelasius I
496-498	Anastasius II
498-514	*Symmachus
498-505	[Laurentius]
514-523	*Hormisdas
523-526	*John I
526-530	*Felix IV

Term	Pope	Term	Pope
530-532	Boniface II	827-844	Gregory IV
530	[Dioscursus]	844	[John VIII]
533-535	John II	844-847	Sergius II
535-536	*Agapetus I	847-855	*Leo IV
536-537	*Silverius	855-858	Benedict III
537-555	Vigilius	855	[Anastasius III]
556-561	Pelagius I	858-867	*Nicholas I the Great
561-574	John III	867-872	Adrian II
575-579	Benedict I	872-882	John VIII
579-590	Pelagius II	882-884	Marinus I
590-604	*Gregory I the Great	884-885	*Adrian III
604-606	Sabinian	885-891	Stephen V
607	Boniface III	891-896	Formosus
608-615	*Boniface IV (Adeodatus I)	896	Boniface VI
615-618	*Deusdedit	896-897	Stephen VI
619-625	Boniface V	897	Romanus
625-638	Honorius I	897	Theodore II
638-640	Vacant	898-900	John IX
640	Severinus	900-903	Benedict IV
640-642	John IV	903	Leo V
642-649	Theodore I	903-904	Christopher
649-655	*Martin I	904-911	Sergius III
655-657	*Eugene I	911-913	Anastasius III
657-672	*Vitalian	913-914	Lando
672-676	Adeodatus II	914-928	John X
676-678	Donus	928	Leo VI
678-681	*Agatho	929-931	Stephen VII
682-683	*Leo II	931-935	John XI
684-685	*Benedict II	936-939	Leo VII
685-686	John V	939-942	Stephen IX (VIII)
686-687	Conon	942-946	Marinus II
687	[Theodore II]	946-955	Agapetus II
687-692	[Paschal I]	955-963	John XII
687-701	*Saint Sergius I	963-964	Leo VIII
701-705	John VI	964	Benedict V
705-707	John VII	965-972	John XIII
708	Sisinnius	973-974	Benedict VI
708-715	Constantine	974-983	Benedict VII
715-731	*Gregory II	983-984	John XIV
731-741	*Gregory III	984-985	[Boniface VII]
741-752	*Zachary	985-996	John XV
752-757	Stephen II	996-999	Gregory V
757-767	*Paul I	996-998	[John XVI]
767	[Constantine]	999-1003	Sylvester II
767	[Philip]	1003	John XVII
767-772	Stephen III	1003-1009	John XVIII
772-795	Adrian I	1009-1012	Sergius IV
795-816	*Leo III	1012-1024	Benedict VIII
816-817	Stephen IV	1012	[Gregory VI]
817-824	*Paschal I	1024-1033	John XIX
824-827	Eugene II	1033-1045	Benedict IX
827	Valentine	1045	Sylvester III

Term	Pope
1045-1046	Gregory VI (John Gratian Pierleoni)
1046-1047	Clement II (Suitgar, count of Morslegen)
1048	Damasus II (Count Poppo)
1049-1054	*Leo IX (Bruno of Egisheim)
1055-1057	Victor II (Gebhard, count of Hirschberg)
1057-1058	Stephen IX (Frederick of Lorraine)
1058	Benedict X (John, count of Tusculum)
1058-1061	Nicholas II (Gerhard of Burgundy)
1061-1073	Alexander II (Anselmo da Baggio)
1061-1064	[Honorius II]
1073-1085	*Gregory VII (Hildebrand)
1080-1100	[Clement III]
1086-1087	Victor III (Desiderius, prince of Beneventum)
1088-1099	Urban II (Odo of Lagery)
1099-1118	Paschal II (Ranieri da Bieda)
1100-1102	[Theodoric]
1102	[Albert]
1105	[Sylvester IV]
1118-1119	Gelasius II (John Coniolo)
1118-1121	[Gregory VIII]
1119-1124	Callixtus II (Guido, count of Burgundy)
1124-1130	Honorius II (Lamberto dei Fagnani)
1124-1130	[Celestine II]
1130-1143	Innocent II (Gregorio Papareschi)
1130-1138	[Anacletus II (Cardinal Pierleone)]
1138	[Victor IV]
1143-1144	Celestine II (Guido di Castello)
1144-1145	Lucius II (Gherardo Caccianemici)
1145-1153	Eugene III (Bernardo Paganelli)
1153-1154	Anastasius IV (Corrado della Subarra)
1154-1159	Adrian IV (Nicolas Breakspear)
1159-1181	Alexander III (Roland Bandinelli)
1159-1164	[Victor IV]
1164-1168	[Paschal III]
1168-1178	[Calixtus III]
1179-1180	[Innocent III (Lando da Sessa)]
1181-1185	Lucius III (Ubaldo Allucingoli)
1185-1187	Urban III (Uberto Crivelli)
1187	Gregory VIII (Alberto del Morra)
1187-1191	Clement III (Paolo Scolari)
1191-1198	Celestine III (Giacinto Boboni-Orsini)
1198-1216	Innocent III (Lothario of Segni)
1216-1227	Honorius III (Cencio Savelli)
1227-1241	Gregory IX (Ugo of Segni)
1241	Celestine IV (Goffredo Castiglione)
1243-1254	Innocent IV (Sinibaldo Fieschi)
1254-1261	Alexander IV (Rinaldo di Segni)
1261-1264	Urban IV (Jacques Pantaléon)
1265-1268	Clement IV (Guy le Gros Foulques)
1268-1271	Vacant
1271-1276	Gregory X (Tebaldo Visconti)
1276	Innocent V (Pierre de Champagni)

Term	Pope
1276	Adrian V (Ottobono Fieschi)
1276-1277	John XXI (Pietro Rebuli-Giuliani)
1277-1280	Nicholas III (Giovanni Gaetano Orsini)
1281-1285	Martin IV (Simon Mompitie)
1285-1287	Honorius IV (Giacomo Savelli)
1288-1292	Nicholas IV (Girolamo Masci)
1294	*Celestine V (Pietro Angelari da Murrone)
1294-1303	Boniface VIII (Benedict Caetani)
1303-1304	Benedict XI (Niccolò Boccasini)
1305-1314	Clement V (Raimond Bertrand de Got)
1316-1334	John XXII (Jacques Duèse)
1328-1330	[Nicholas V (Pietro di Corbara)]
1334-1342	Benedict XII (Jacques Fournier)
1342-1352	Clement VI (Pierre Roger de Beaufort)
1352-1362	Innocent VI (Étienne Aubert)
1362-1370	Urban V (Guillaume de Grimord)
1370-1378	Gregory XI (Pierre Roger de Beaufort, the Younger)
1378-1389	Urban VI (Bartolomeo Prignano)
1378-1394	[Clement VII (Robert of Geneva)]
1389-1404	Boniface IX (Pietro Tomacelli)
1394-1423	[Benedict XIII (Pedro de Luna)]
1404-1406	Innocent VII (Cosmto de' Migliorati)
1406-1415	Gregory XII (Angelo Correr)
1409-1410	[Alexander V (Petros Philargi)]
1410-1415	[John XXIII (Baldassare Cossa)]
1415-1417	Vacant
1417-1431	Martin V (Ottone Colonna)
1423-1429	[Clement VIII]
1424	[Benedict XIV]
1431-1447	Eugene IV (Gabriele Condulmero)
1439-1449	[Felix V (Amadeus of Savoy)]
1447-1455	Nicholas V (Tommaso Parentucelli)
1455-1458	Calixtus III (Alfonso de Borgia)
1458-1464	Pius II (Enea Silvio Piccolomini)
1464-1471	Paul II (Pietro Barbo)
1471-1484	Sixtus IV (Francesco della Rovere)
1484-1492	Innocent VIII (Giovanni Battista Cibò)
1492-1503	Alexander VI (Rodrigo Borgia)
1503	Pius III (Francesco Todeschini Piccolomini)
1503-1513	Julius II (Giuliano della Rovere)
1513-1521	Leo X (Giovanni de' Medici)
1522-1523	Adrian VI (Adrian Florensz Boeyens)
1523-1534	Clement VII (Giulio de' Medici)
1534-1549	Paul III (Alessandro Farnese)
1550-1555	Julius III (Giovanni Maria Ciocchi del Monte)
1555	Marcellus II (Marcello Cervini)
1555-1559	Paul IV (Gian Pietro Carafa)
1559-1565	Pius IV (Giovanni Angelo de' Medici)
1566-1572	Pius V (Antonio Ghislieri)
1572-1585	Gregory XIII (Ugo Buoncompagni)
1585-1590	Sixtus V (Felice Peretti)

Term	Pope
1590	Urban VII (Giambattista Castagna)
1590-1591	Gregory XIV (Niccolò Sfondrato)
1591	Innocent IX (Giovanni Antonio Facchinetti)
1592-1605	Clement VIII (Ippolito Aldobrandini)
1605	Leo XI (Alessandro de' Medici)
1605-1621	Paul V (Camillo Borghese)
1621-1623	Gregory XV (Alessandro Ludovisi)
1623-1644	Urban VIII (Maffeo Barberini)
1644-1655	Innocent X (Giovanni Battista Pamphili)
1655-1667	Alexander VII (Fabio Chigi)
1667-1669	Clement IX (Giulio Rospigliosi)
1670-1676	Clement X (Emilio Altieri)
1676-1689	Innocent XI (Benedetto Odescalchi)
1689-1691	Alexander VIII (Pietro Ottoboni)
1691-1700	Innocent XII (Antonio Pignatelli)
1700-1721	Clement XI (Giovanni Francesco Albani)
1721-1724	Innocent XIII (Michelangelo Conti)
1724-1730	Benedict XIII (Pierfrancesco Orsini)
1730-1740	Clement XII (Lorenzo Corsini)hh
1740-1758	Benedict XIV (Prospero Lambertini)
1758-1769	Clement XIII (Carlo Rezzonico)
1769-1774	Clement XIV (Giovanni Ganganelli)
1775-1799	Pius VI (Giovanni Angelo Braschi)
1800-1823	Pius VII (Barnaba Gregorio Chiaramonti)
1823-1829	Leo XII (Annibale della Genga)
1829-1830	Pius VIII (Francesco Saverio Castiglioni)
1831-1846	Gregory XVI (Bartolomeo Cappellari)
1846-1878	Pius IX (Giovanni Mastai-Ferretti)
1878-1903	Leo XIII (Gioacchino Pecci)
1903-1914	Pius X (Giuseppe Sarto)
1914-1922	Benedict XV (Giacomo della Chiesa)
1922-1939	Pius XI (Achille Ratti)
1939-1958	Pius XII (Eugenio Pacelli)
1958-1963	John XXIII (Angelo Roncalli)
1963-1978	Paul VI (Giovanni Battista Montini)
1978	John Paul I (Albino Luciani)
1978-2005	John Paul II (Karol Wojtyla)
2005-	Benedict XVI (Joseph Ratzinger)

AFRICA. *See also* EGYPT

BENIN

Reign	Ruler
1200-1235	Eweke I
1235-1243	Uwakhuanhen
1243-1255	Ehenmihen
1255-1280	Ewedo
1280-1295	Oguola
1295-1299	Edoni
1299-1334	Udagbedo
1334-1370	Ohen

Reign	Ruler
1370-1400	Egbeka
1400-1430	Orobiru
1430-1440	Uwaifiokun
c. 1440-1473	Ewuare the Great
1473	Ezoti (14 days)
1473-1480	Olua
1481-1504	Ozolua
c. 1504-1550	Esigie
1550-1578	Orhogbua
1578-1606	Ehengbuda
1606-1641	Ohuan
1641-1661	Ahenzae
1661-1669	Ahenzae
1669-1675	Akengboi
1675-1684	Akenkpaye
1684-1689	Akengbedo
1689-1700	Oroghene
1700-1712	Ewuakpe
1712-1713	Ozuaere
1713-1735	Akenzua I
1735-1750	Eresonyen
1750-1804	Akengbuda
1804-1816	Obanosa
1816	Ogbebo (8 months)
1816-1848	Osomwende
1848-1888	Adolo
1888-1914	Ovonramwen
1914-1933	Eweka II
1933-1978	Akenzua II
1978-	Erediauwa

ETHIOPIA

The evidence for the succession of Ethiopian rulers is debated by scholars; here, the regnal dates reflect primarily the order of succession and vary widely among sources.

Early Kings

Reign	Ruler
c. 320-350	Ezana
c. 328-370	Shizana
c. 356	Ella Abreha
?	Ella Asfeha
?	Ella Shahel
474-475	Agabe
474-475	Levi
475-486	Ella Amida (IV?)
486-489	Jacob I
486-489	David
489-504	Armah I
504-505	Zitana
505-514	Jacob II
c. 500-542	Ella Asbeha (Caled)
542-c. 550	Beta Israel

Reign	Ruler
c. 550-564	Gabra Masqal
?	Anaeb
?	Alamiris
?	Joel
?	Israel
?	Gersem I
?	Ella Gabaz
?	Ella Saham
c. 625	Armah II
?	Iathlia
?	Hataz I
?	Wazena
?	Za Ya'abiyo
?	Armah III
?	Hataz II
?	Gersem II
?	Hataz III

Zagwe Dynasty

Reign	Ruler
c. 1137-1152	Mara Tekle Haimanot
c. 1152-1181	Yimrehane-Kristos
c. 1181-1221	Lalibela
c. 1221-1260	Na 'akuto La 'ab
c. 1260-1270	Yitbarek (Yetbarek)
1270	Solomonid Dynasty begins; reign of Yekuno Amlak

Solomonid Dynasty

Reign	Ruler
1270-1285	Yekuno Amlak
1285-1294	Solomon I
1294-1297	Bahr Asgad
1294-1297	Senfa Asgad
1297-1299	Qedma Asgad
1297-1299	Jin Asgad
1297-1299	Saba Asgad
1299-1314	Wedem Arad
1314-1344	Amade Tseyon I
1344-1372	Newaya Krestos
1372-1382	Newaya Maryam
1382-1411	Dawit (David) I
1411-1414	Tewodros (Theodore) I
1414-1429	Isaac
1429-1430	Andrew
1430-1433	Takla Maryam
1433	Sarwe Iyasus
1433-1434	Amda Iyasus
1434-1468	Zara Yacob (Constantine I)
1468-1478	Baeda Mariam I
1478-1484	Constantine II
1494	Amade Tseyon II
1494-1508	Naod

Reign	Ruler
1508-1540	Lebna Dengel (David II)
1529	Battle of Shimbre-Kune
1540-1559	Galawedos (Claudius)
1543	Battle of Lake Tana (defeat of Muslims)

Later Rulers

Reign	Ruler
1560-1564	Menas
1564-1597	Sarsa Dengel
1597-1603	Jacob
1603-1604	Za Dengel
1604-1607	Jacob
1607-1632	Susneyos (Sissinios)
1632-1667	Fasilidas (Basilides)
1667-1682	Yohannes (John) I
1682-1706	Iyasu (Jesus) I the Great
1706-1708	Tekle Haimanot I
1708-1711	Tewoflos (Theophilus)
1711-1716	Yostos (Justus)
1716-1721	Dawit (David) III
1721-1730	Bekaffa
1730-1755	Iyasu II
1755-1769	Iyoas (Joas) I
1769	Yohannes II
1769-1777	Tekle Haimanot II
1777-1779	Salomon (Solomon) II
1779-1784	Tekle Giorgis I (first)
1784-1788	Jesus III
1788	Ba'eda Maryam I
1788-1789	Tekle Giorgis I (second)
1789-1794	Hezekiah
1794-1795	Tekle Giorgis I (third)
1795	Ba'eda Maryam II
1795-1796	Tekle Giorgis I (fourth)
1796-1797	Solomon III
1797-1799	Tekle Giorgis I (fifth)
1799	Solomon III
1799-1800	Demetrius
1800	Tekle Giorgis I (sixth)
1800-1801	Demetrius
1801-1818	Egwala Seyon
1818-1821	Joas II
1821-1826	Gigar
1826	Ba'eda Maryam III
1826-1830	Gigar
1830-1832	Jesus IV
1832	Gabra Krestos
1832-1840	Sahla Dengel (first)
1840-1841	Yohannes III
1841-1855	Sahla Dengel (second)
1855-1868	Tewodros II
1868-1872	Tekle Giorgis II
1872-1889	Yohannes IV

Reign	Ruler
1875-1876	Egyptians defeated
1889-1913	Menelik II
1896	Italians defeated
1909-1916	Lij Iyasu (regent)
1916-1930	Empress Zawditu
1916-1930	Haile Sellassie
1930-1936	Italian occupation
1936-1941	Victor Emmanuel (III of Italy)
1941-1974	Haile Sellassie (restored)
1974	Aman Mikael Andom
1974-1977	Tafari Benti
1977-1991	Mengistu Haile Mariam
1991-1995	Meles Zenawi
1995-	Negasso Gidada

KONGO

Reign	Ruler
Before 1482-1506	João I (Nzinga Nkuwu)
1506-1543	Afonso I (Nzinga Mbemba)
1543-1545	Peter I
1545-1545	Francis I
1545-1561	Diogo I
1561-1561	Affonso II
1561-1566	Bernard I
1566-1567	Henry I
1568-1587	Alvare I
1587-1614	Alvare II
1614-1615	Bernard II
1615-1622	Alvare III
1622-1624	Peter II
1624-1626	Garcia I
1626-1631	Ambrosio
1631-1636	Alvaro IV
1636-1636	Alvaro V
1636-1642	Alvaro VI
1642-1661	Garcia II
1661-1665	Antonio I
1665	Battle of Mbwila, decline of independent Kingdom of Kongo

MOROCCO

Almoravids

Reign	Ruler
1061-1106	Yūsuf ibn Tāshufīn
1107-1142	ʿAlī ibn Yūsuf
1142-1146	Tāshufīn ibn ʿAlī
1146	Ibrāhīm ibn Tāshufīn
1146-1147	Isḥāq ibn ʿAlī

Almohads

Reign	Ruler
To 1130	Ibn Tūmart
1130-1163	ʿAbd al-Muʾmin
1163-1184	Yūsuf I Abū Yaʿqūb
1184-1199	Yaʿqūb Yūsuf al-Manṣūr
1199-1213	Muḥammad ibn Yaʿqūb
1213-1224	Yūsuf II Abū Yaʿqūb
1224	ʿAbdul Wāḥid I
1224-1227	ʿAbdallah Abū Muḥammad
1227-1235	Yaḥyā Abū Zakariyyāʾ
1227-1232	Idrīs I ibn Yaʿqūb
1232-1242	ʿAbd al-Wāḥid ibn Idrīs I
1242-1248	ʿAlī ibn Idrīs I
1248-1266	ʿUmar ibn Isḥāq
1266-1269	Idrīs II ibn Muḥammad
After 1269	Dissolution; power divided among Marīnids, Ḥafṣids, and Zayyānids

Marīnids

Reign	Ruler
1269-1286	Abū Yūsuf Yaʿqūb
1286-1307	Abū Yaʿqūb Yūsuf al-Nasīr
1307-1308	Abū Tabit
1308-1310	Abū Rabia
1310-1331	Abū Said Othman (Osman ibn Yaʿqūb)
1331-1348	Abū al-Hasan
1348-1358	Abū Inan Faris
1358-1361	Vacant
1361-1366	Moḥammad ibn Yaʿqūb
1366-1372	ʿAbd al-Aziz I
1372-1384	Vacant
1384-1387	Mūsā ibn al-Fers
1387-1393	ʿAbu al-ʿAbbās
1393-1396	ʿAbd al-Aziz II
1396-1398	Abdallah
1398-1421	Osman III
1421-1465	ʿAbd al-Haqq

Wattasides

Reign	Ruler
1472-1504	Moḥammad al-Saih al-Mahdi
1505-1524	Abū Abdallah Moḥammad
1524-1550	Abul ʿAbbās Aḥmad

Saʿdīs (Cherifians)

Reign	Ruler
1510-1517	Muḥammad al-Qāʿim
1517-1544	Aḥmad al-Aʿraj
1544-1557	Muḥammad I al-Shaykh
1557-1574	Abdallah al-Ghālib
1574-1576	Muḥammad al-Mutawakkil
1576-1578	ʿAbd al-Malik
1578	Battle of the Three Kings
1578-1603	Aḥmad al-Manṣūr

Reign	Ruler
1603-1607	ʿAbd al ʿAbd Allah Moḥammad III
1607-1628	Zaidan al-Nāṣir
1628-1631	Abū Marwan ʿAbd al-Malik II
1631-1636	al-Walīd
1636-1654	Moḥammad IV
1654-1659	Aḥmad II
1659-1665	War

Alawis

Reign	Ruler
1666-1672	Rashid ben Ali Cherif (founder)
1672-1727	Ismael ben Ali Cherif
1727-1729	Civil war
1729-1757	Abdallah
1757-1790	Mohamed III
1790-1792	Yazid
1792-1822	Suleiman
1822-1859	Abdelrahman
1859-1873	Mohamed IV
1873-1894	Hassan I
1894-1908	Aziz
1908-1912	Hafid

SONGHAI

Reign	Ruler
c. 1464-1492	Sonni ʿAlī
1493	Sonni Baru
1493-1528	Mohammed I Askia (Mohammed Ture)
1528-1531	Askia Mūsā
1549-1582	Askia Daud
1588-1591	Askia Ishak II

AMERICAS. *See also* **ARGENTINA, BOLIVIA, BRAZIL, CHILE, MEXICO, PERU, THE UNITED STATES, AND VENEZUELA**

MAYA KINGS OF TIKAL

The Maya, who occupied the region of Central America from the Yucatán to Guatemala, maintained several centers in the region, but one, Tikal, recorded in Mayan glyphs a line of kings for nearly eight hundred years, roughly corresponding to the Classic Period now considered by scholars to be the height of Mayan civilization. The list below is from Chronicle of the Maya Kings and Queens, *by Simon Martin and Nikolai Grube (New York: Thames and Hudson, 2000).*

Reign	Ruler
c. 90-150	Yax Ehb Xook (First Step Shark)
c. 307	Siyaj Chan K'awiil I
d. 317	Ix Une Balam (Baby Jaguar)
d. 359	K'inich Muwaan Jol
360-378	Chak Tok Ich'aak I (Great Jaguar Paw)

Reign	Ruler
378-404	Nuun Yax Ayiin I (Curl Snout)
411-456	Siyaj Chan K'awiil II (Stormy Sky)
458-c. 486	K'an Chitam
c. 486-508	Chak Tok Ich'aak II
c. 511-527	Kaloomte' B'alam
537-562	Wak Chan Ka'awiil
c. 593-628	Animal Skull
c. 657-679	Nuun Ujol Chaak
682-734	Jasaw Chan K'awiil I
734-746	Yik'in Chan K'awiil
768-794	Yax Nuun Ayiin II
c. 800	Nuun Ujol K'inich
c. 810	Dark Sun
c. 849	Jewel K'awiil
c. 869	Jasaw Chan K'awiil II
c. 900	End of Mayan Classic Period

AZTEC KINGS OF TENOCHTITLÁN (MEXICO)

Reign	Ruler
Legendary	Ténoch (founder)
1375-1395	Acamapichtili
1395-1417	Huitzilíhuitl
1417-1427	Chimalpopoca
1427-1440	Itzcóatl
1440-1469	Montezuma (Moctezuma) I
1469-1481	Axayacatl
1481-1486	Tízoc
1486-1502	Ahuitzotl (Auítzotl)
1502-1520	Montezuma (Moctezuma) II
1520	Cuitláhuac
1520-1521	Cuauhtémoc

INCAS (PERU)

Reign	Ruler
c. 1200	Manco Capac I
?	Sinchi Roca
?	Lloque Yupanqui
?	Mayta Capac
?	Capac Yupanqui
?	Inca Roca
?	Yahuar Huacac
?	Viracocha
1438-1471	Pachacuti
1471-1493	Topa
1493-1525	Huayna Capac
1525-1532	Huáscar
1525-1533	Atahualpa
1532-1533	Spanish conquest (Pizarro)
1533	Manco Capac II
1544-1561	Sayri Tupac
1561-1571	Titu Cusi
1571	Tupac Amaru I

ARGENTINA

Term	President
1854-1860	Justo José de Urquiza
1860-1862	Santiago Derqui
1862-1868	Bartolomé Mitre
1868-1874	Domingo Faustino Sarmiento
1874-1880	Nicolás Avellaneda
1880-1886	Julio Argentino Roca
1886-1890	Miguel Juárez Celman
1890-1892	Carlos Pellegrini
1892-1895	Luis Sáenz Peña
1895-1898	José Evaristo Uriburu
1898-1904	Julio Argentino Roca
1904-1906	Manuel A. Quintana
1906-1910	José Figueroa Alcorta
1910-1914	Roque Sáenz Peña
1914-1916	Victorino de la Plaza
1916-1922	Hipólito Irigoyen
1922-1928	Marcelo Torcuato de Alvear
1928-1930	Hipólito Irigoyen
1930-1932	José Félix Uriburu
1932-1938	Agustín Pedro Justo
1938-1942	Roberto M. Ortiz
1940-1943	Ramón S. Castillo
1943	Arturo Rawson Corvalán
1943-1944	Pedro Pablo Ramírez Machuca
1944-1946	Edelmiro J. Farrell
1946-1955	Juan Domingo Perón
1955	José Domingo Molina Gómez (military junta)
1955	Eduardo A. Lonardi (provisional president)
1955-1958	Pedro Eugenio Aramburu
1958-1962	Arturo Frondizi
1962-1963	José María Guido (acting president)
1963-1966	Arturo Illia
1966	Revolutionary junta
1966-1970	Juan Carlos Onganía
1970	Pedro Alberto José Gnavi (chairman of Junta of Commanders)
1970-1971	Roberto Marcelo Levingston
1971-1973	Alejandro Agustín Lanusse
1973	Héctor José Cámpora
1973-1974	Juan Domingo Perón
1974-1976	Isabel Perón
1976	Military junta
1976-1981	Jorge Rafael Videla
1981	Roberto Eduardo Viola
1981	Carlos Alberto Lacoste (acting president)
1981-1982	Leopoldo Fortunato Galtieri
1982	Alfredo Óscar Saint Jean (acting president)
1982-1983	Reynaldo Bignone
1983-1989	Raúl Alfonsín

Term	President
1989-1999	Carlos Saul Menem
1999-2001	Fernando de la Rúa
2001	Ramón Puerta (interim president)
2001-2002	Adolfo Rodríguez Saá (interim president)
2002	Eduardo Camaño (interim president)
2002-2003	Eduardo Duhalde (interim president)
2003-	Néstor Kirchner

AUSTRIA. *See* HOLY ROMAN EMPIRE

BELGIUM

Term	Minister
1830-1831	Charles Rogier
1831	E. L. Baron Surlet de Chokier
1832-1834	Charles Rogier
1834-1840	Joseph Lebeau
1841-1845	Jean Baptiste de Nothomb
1845-1846	Sylvain van de Weyer
1847-1852	Charles Rogier
1852-1855	Henri de Brouckére
1855-1857	Pierre Jacques François de Decker
1857-1867	Charles Rogier
1868-1870	Hubert Frére-Orban
1870-1871	Jules Joseph d'Anethan
1871-1874	B. T. Comte de Theux de Merlandt
1874-1878	Comte de Aspremont-Linden
1878-1884	Hubert Frére-Orban
1884	Jules Malou
1884-1894	Auguste Beernaert
1894-1896	Jules P. Marie de Burlet
1896-1899	Paul Comte de Smet de Naeyer
1899	Julius Vandenpeereboom
1899-1907	Paul Comte de Smet de Naeyer
1907	Jules de Trooz
1908-1911	Frans Schollaert
1911-1918	Charles de Broqueville
1918	Gerhard Looreman
1918-1920	Leon Delacroix
1920-1921	Henri de Carton de Wiart
1921-1926	George Theunis
1925	Alois van de Vyvere
1925-1926	Prosper Vicomte Poullet
1926-1931	Henri Jaspar
1931-1932	Jules Reikin
1932-1934	Charles de Broqueville
1934-1935	George Theunis
1935-1937	Paul van Zeeland
1937-1938	Paul Emil Janson
1938-1939	Paul Henri Spaak

Term	Minister
1939-1945	Hubert Pierlot
1945-1946	Achille van Acker
1946	Paul Henri Spaak
1946	Achille van Acker
1946-1947	Camille Huysmans
1947-1949	Paul Henri Spaak
1949-1950	Gaston Eyskens
1950	Jean Duvieusart
1950-1952	Joseph Pholien
1952-1954	Jan van Houtte
1954-1958	Achille van Acker
1958-1961	Gaston Eyskens
1961-1965	Théo Levèvre
1965-1966	Pierre Harmel
1966-1968	Paul Vanden Boyenants
1968-1972	Gaston Eyskens
1973-1974	Edmond Leburton
1974-1978	Leo Tindemans
1978-1979	Vanden Boyenants
1979-1981	Wilfried Martens
1981	Mark Eyskens
1981-1992	Wilfried Martens
1992-1999	Jean-Luc Dehaene
1999-	Guy Verhofstadt

BOHEMIA. *See also* HUNGARY, POLAND

PŘEMYSLIDS

Reign	Ruler
c. 870-888/889	Borivoj I
894/895-915	Spytihnev I
915-921	Vratislav I
921-935	Duke Wenceslaus I
935-972	Boleslaus I the Cruel
972-999	Boleslaus II the Pious
999-1002	Boleslaus III
1002-1003	Vladivoj
1003	Boleslaus III
1003	Jaromir
1003	Boleslaus III
1003-1004	Boleslaus I (nondynastic Piast)
1004-1012	Jaromir
1012-1033	Oldrich
1033-1034	Jaromir
1034	Oldrich
1035-1055	Bretislav I
1055-1061	Spytihnev II
1061-1092	Vratislav II
1092	Konrad I
1092-1100	Bretislav II
1101-1107	Borivoj II

Reign	Ruler
1107-1109	Svatopluk
1109-1117	Vladislav I
1117-1120	Borivoj II
1120-1125	Vladislav I
1125-1140	Sobeslav I
1140-1172	Vladislav II
1172-1173	Bedrich
1173-1178	Sobeslav II
1178-1189	Bedrich
1189-1191	Konrad II Ota
1191-1192	Duke Wenceslaus II
1192-1193	Ottokar I
1193-1197	Jindrich Bretislav
1197	Vladislav Jindrich
1197-1230	Ottokar I
1230-1253	King Wenceslaus I
1253-1278	Ottokar II
1278-1305	King Wenceslaus II
1305-1306	King Wenceslaus III
1306	Henry of Carinthia (nondynastic)
1306-1307	Rudolph I of Habsburg (nondynastic)
1307-1310	Henry of Carinthia (nondynastic)

LUXEMBOURGS

Reign	Ruler
1310-1346	John of Luxembourg
1346-1378	Charles I
1378-1419	Wenceslaus IV
1419-1420	Sigismund
1420-1436	Hussite wars
1436-1437	Sigismund

HABSBURGS

Reign	Ruler
1437-1439	Albert of Habsburg
1439-1457	Ladislas I (V of Hungary)
1458-1471	George of Podebrady (nondynastic)
1469-1490	Matthias Corvinus (antiking)

JAGIEŁŁOS

Reign	Ruler
1471-1516	Vladislav (Ladislaus) II
1516-1526	Louis

HABSBURGS

Reign	Ruler
1526-1564	Ferdinand I
1564-1575	Maximilian
1575-1611	Rudolf II
1612-1619	Matthias
1619	Ferdinand II

Reign	Ruler
1619-1620	Frederick, Elector Palatine (Wittelsbach)
1620-1637	Ferdinand II
1627-1657	Ferdinand III
1646-1654	Ferdinand IV
1656-1705	Leopold I
1705-1711	Joseph I
1711-1740	Charles II
1740-1780	Maria Theresa

HABSBURG-LOTHRINGENS

Reign	Ruler
1780-1790	Joseph II
1790-1792	Leopold II
1792-1835	Francis
1835-1848	Ferdinand V
1848-1916	Francis Joseph
1916-1918	Charles III

BOLIVIA

Term	President
1825	Simón Bolívar
1825-1828	Antonio José de Sucre Alcalá
1828	José María Pérez de Urdininea
1828	José Miguel de Velasco Franco
1828-1829	Pedro Blanco Soto
1829	José Miguel de Velasco Franco
1829-1839	Andrés de Santa Cruz y Calahumana
1839-1841	José Miguel de Velasco Franco
1841	Sebastián Ágreda
1841	Mariano Enrique Calvo Cuellar
1841-1847	José Ballivián Segurola
1847-1848	Eusebio Guilarte Vera
1848	José Miguel de Velasco Franco
1848-1855	Manuel Isidoro Belzu Humerez
1855-1857	Jorge Córdova
1857-1861	José María Linares Lizarazu
1861-1864	José María Achá Valiente
1864-1871	Mariano Melgarejo Valencia
1871-1872	Agustín Morales Hernández
1872-1873	Tomás Frías Ametller
1873-1874	Adolfo Ballivián Coll
1874-1876	Tomás Frías Ametller
1876-1879	Hilarión Daza Groselle
1880-1884	Narciso Campero Leyes
1884-1888	Gregorio Pacheco Leyes
1888-1892	Aniceto Arce Ruiz
1892-1896	Mariano Baptista Caserta

Term	President
1896-1899	Severo Fernández Alonso Caballero
1899-1904	José Manuel Pando Solares
1904-1909	Ismael Montes Gamboa
1909-1913	Eliodoro Villazón Montaño
1913-1917	Ismael Montes Gamboa
1917-1920	José Gutiérrez Guerra
1921-1925	Bautista Saavedra Mallea
1925-1926	Felipe Segundo Guzmán
1926-1930	Hernando Siles Reyes
1930-1931	Carlos Blanco Galindo
1931-1934	Daniel Salamanca Urey
1934-1936	José Luis Tejada Sorzano
1936-1937	David Toro Ruilova
1937-1939	Germán Busch Becerra
1939-1940	Carlos Quintanilla Quiroga
1940-1943	Enrique Peñaranda del Castillo
1943-1946	Gualberto Villarroel López
1946	Néstor Guillén Olmos
1946-1947	Tomás Monje Gutiérrez
1947-1949	Enrique Hertzog Garaizabal
1949-1951	Mamerto Urriolagoitia Harriague
1951-1952	Hugo Ballivián Rojas
1952-1956	Víctor Paz Estenssoro
1956-1960	Hernán Siles Zuazo
1960-1964	Víctor Paz Estenssoro
1964-1965	René Barrientos Ortuño
1965-1966	René Barrientos Ortuño
1965-1966	Alfredo Ovando Candía
1966-1969	René Barrientos Ortuño
1969	Luis Adolfo Siles Salinas
1969-1970	Alfredo Ovando Candía
1970-1971	Juan José Torres Gonzáles
1971-1978	Hugo Banzer Suárez
1978	Juan Pereda Asbún
1978-1979	David Padilla Arancibia
1979	Wálter Guevara Arze
1979	Alberto Natusch Busch
1979-1980	Lidia Gueiler Tejada
1980-1981	Luis García Meza Tejada
1981-1982	Celso Torrelio Villa
1982	Guido Vildoso Calderón
1982-1985	Hernán Siles Zuazo
1985-1989	Víctor Paz Estenssoro
1989-1993	Jaime Paz Zamora
1993-1997	Gonzalo Sánchez de Lozada
1997-2001	Hugo Banzer Suárez
2001-2002	Jorge Quiroga Ramírez
2002-2003	Gonzalo Sánchez de Lozada
2003-2005	Carlos D. Mesa Gisbert
2005-2006	Eduardo Rodríguez Veltzé
2006-	Juan Evo Morales Aima

BRAZIL

Reign	Emperor
1822-1831	Pedro I
1831-1889	Pedro II

Term	President
1889-1891	Manuel Deodoro da Fonseca
1891-1894	Floriano Peixoto (acting president)
1894-1898	Prudente de Morais
1898-1902	Manuel Ferraz de Campos Sales
1902-1906	Francisco de Paula Rodrigues Alves
1906-1909	Afonso Augusto Moreira Pena
1909-1910	Nilo Peçanha
1910-1914	Hermes Rodrigues da Fonseca
1914-1918	Venceslau Brás Pereira Gomes
1918-1919	Delfim Moreira (acting president)
1919-1922	Epitâcio da Silva Pessoa
1922-1926	Artur da Silva Bernardes
1926-1930	Washington Luís Pereira de Sousa
1930	Augusto Tasso Fragoso (junta chairman)
1930-1945	Getúlio Vargas
1945-1946	José Linhares
1946-1951	Eurico Gaspar Dutra
1951-1954	Getúlio Vargas
1954-1956	João Café Filho
1956-1961	Juscelino Kubitschek de Oliveira
1961	Jânio da Silva Quadros
1961-1964	João Belchior Marques Goulart
1964-1967	Humberto de Alencar Castelo Branco
1967-1969	Artur da Costa e Silva
1969	Military junta
1969-1974	Emílio Garrastazú Médici
1974-1979	Ernesto Geisel
1979-1985	João Baptista de Oliveira Figueiredo
1985-1990	José Sarney
1990-1992	Fernando Collor de Mello
1992-1995	Itamar Franco (acting president for Collor)
1995-2002	Fernando Henrique Cardoso
2003-	Luís Inácio Lula da Silva

BULGARIA

EARLY BULGARIA

Reign	Czar
c. 681-701	Asparukh
c. 701-c. 718	Tervel
c. 718-750	Sevar
750-762	Kormesios

Reign	Czar
762-763	Vinekh
762-763	Teletz
763	Umar
763-765	Baian
765	Tokt
c. 765-777	Telerig
c. 777-c. 803	Kardam
c. 803-814	Krum
814-815	Dukum
814-816	Ditzveg
814-831	Omurtag
831-836	Malamir (Malomir)
836-852	Presijan
852-889	Boris I
865	Boris converts to Christianity
889-893	Vladimir
893-927	Simeon I the Great
927-969	Peter I
969-972	Boris II
971	Bulgaria conquered by John I Tzimisces
971-1018	Dissolution, instability
1018	Basil II annexes Bulgaria to Macedonia

ASEN LINE

Reign	Czar
1186	Bulgarian Independence
1186-1196	John I Asen
1196-1197	Peter II Asen
1197-1207	Kalojan Asen
1207-1218	Boril
1218-1241	John II Asen
1242	Mongol invasion
1242-1246	Kaloman I
1246-1257	Michael II Asen
1257-1258	Kaloman II
1257-1277	Constantine Tich
1277-1279	Ivalio
1278-c. 1264	Ivan Mytzes
1279-1284?	John III Asen
c. 1280	Terter takeover

TERTER LINE

Reign	Czar
1280-1292	George I Terter
1285	Mongol vassal
1292-1295/8	Smilech
1295/8-1298/9	Caka (Tshaka)
1298/9-1322	Theodore Svetoslav
1322-1323	George II

SHISHMANS

Reign	Czar
1323-1330	Michael III Shishman
1330-1331	John IV Stephan
1331-1371	John V Alexander
1355-1371	John Sracimir
1360-1393	John VI Shishman
1385-1396	Decline
1396-1879	Ottoman rule

MODERN ERA

Reign	Ruler
1879-1886	Alexander I Joseph
1887-1918	Ferdinand of Bulgaria (Saxe-Coburg-Gotha)
1918-1943	Boris III
1943-1946	Simeon II

BYZANTINE EMPIRE

Reign	Emperor or Empress
330-337	Constantine I the Great
337-361	Constantius
361-363	Julian the Apostate
363-364	Jovian
364-378	Valens
379-395	Theodosius I the Great
395-408	Arcadius
408-450	Theodosius II
450-457	Marcian
457-474	Leo I the Great
474	Leo II
474-475	Zeno
475-476	Basiliscus
476-491	Zeno (restored)
491-518	Anastasius I
518-527	Justin I
527-548	Theodora
527-565	Justinian I the Great
565-578	Justin II
578-582	Tiberius II Constantinus
582-602	Maurice
602-610	Phocas
610-641	Heraclius
641	Constantine III and Heracleonas
641-668	Constans II Pogonatus
668-685	Constantine IV
685-695	Justinian II Rhinotmetus
695-698	Leontius
698-705	Tiberius III
705-711	Justinian II (restored)
711-713	Philippicus Bardanes
713-715	Anastasius II
716-717	Theodosius III

Reign	Emperor or Empress
717-741	Leo III the Isaurian (the Syrian)
741-775	Constantine V Copronymus
775-780	Leo IV the Khazar
780-797	Constantine VI
797-802	Saint Irene
802-811	Nicephorus I
811	Stauracius
811-813	Michael I
813-820	Leo V the Armenian
820-829	Michael II the Stammerer
829-842	Theophilus
842-867	Michael III the Drunkard
867-886	Basil I the Macedonian
886-912	Leo VI the Wise (the Philosopher)
912-913	Alexander
913-919	Constantine VII Porphyrogenitus (Macedonian)
919-944	Romanus I Lecapenus (Macedonian)
944-959	Constantine VII (restored)
959-963	Romanus II (Macedonian)
963	Basil II Bulgaroktonos (Macedonian)
963-969	Nicephorus II Phocas (Macedonian)
969-976	John I Tzimisces
976-1025	Basil II (restored)
1025-1028	Constantine VIII (Macedonian)
1028-1034	Zoë and Romanus III Argyrus (Macedonian)
1034-1041	Zoë and Michael IV the Paphlagonian (Macedonian)
1041-1042	Zoë and Michael V Calaphates (Macedonian)
1042	Zoë and Theodora (Macedonian)
1042-1050	Zoë, Theodora, and Constantine IX Monomachus (Macedonian)
1050-1055	Theodora and Constantine IX (Macedonian)
1055-1056	Theodora (Macedonian)
1056-1057	Michael VI Stratioticus
1057-1059	Isaac I Comnenus
1059-1067	Constantine X Ducas
1067-1068	Michael VII Ducas (Parapinaces)
1068-1071	Romanus IV Diogenes
1071-1078	Michael VII Ducas (restored)
1078-1081	Nicephorus III Botaniates
1081-1118	Alexius I Comnenus
1118-1143	John II Comnenus
1143-1180	Manuel I Comnenus
1180-1183	Alexius II Comnenus
1183-1185	Andronicus I Comnenus
1185-1195	Isaac II Angelus
1195-1203	Alexius III Angelus
1203-1204	Isaac II (restored) and Alexius IV Angelus
1204	Alexius V Ducas
1204-1205	Baldwin I
1206-1222	Theodore I Lascaris

Reign	Emperor or Empress
1222-1254	John III Vatatzes or Ducas
1254-1258	Theodore II Lascaris
1258-1261	John IV Lascaris
1259-1282	Michael VIII Palaeologus
1282-1328	Andronicus II Palaeologus
1328-1341	Andronicus III Palaeologus
1341-1376	John V Palaeologus
1347-1355	John VI Cantacuzenus (usurper)
1376-1379	Andronicus IV Palaeologus
1379-1391	John V Palaeologus (restored)
1390	John VII Palaeologus (usurper)
1391-1425	Manuel II Palaeologus
1399-1412	John VII Palaeologus (restored as coemperor)
1425-1448	John VIII Palaeologus
1449-1453	Constantine XI Palaeologus
1453	Fall of Constantinople to the Ottomans

CANADA

Term	Prime Minister
1867-1873	Sir John A. Macdonald
1873-1878	Alexander Mackenzie
1878-1891	Sir John A. Macdonald
1891-1892	Sir John J. C. Abbott
1892-1894	Sir John S. D. Thompson
1894-1896	Sir Mackenzie Bowell
1896	Sir Charles Tupper
1896-1911	Sir Wilfrid Laurier
1911-1917	Sir Robert L. Borden
1917-1920	Sir Robert L. Borden
1920-1921	Arthur Meighen
1921-1926	William Lyon Mackenzie King
1926	Arthur Meighen
1926-1930	William Lyon Mackenzie King
1930-1935	Richard B. Bennett
1935-1948	William Lyon Mackenzie King
1948-1957	Louis S. St. Laurent
1957-1963	John G. Diefenbaker
1963-1968	Lester B. Pearson
1969-1979	Pierre Elliott Trudeau
1979-1980	Charles Joseph Clark
1980-1984	Pierre Elliott Trudeau
1984	John Turner
1984-1993	Brian Mulroney
1993	Kim Campbell
1993-2003	Jean Chrétien
2003-2006	Paul Martin
2006-	Stephen Harper

CHILE

Term	President
1818-1823	Bernardo O'Higgins (dictator)
1823-1826	Ramón Freire
1826	Manuel Blanco Encalada
1827-1829	Francisco Antonio Pinto
1831-1841	Joaquín Prieto
1841-1851	Manuel Bulnes
1851-1861	Manuel Montt
1861-1871	José Joaquín Pérez
1871-1876	Federico Errázuriz Zañartu
1876-1881	Anibal Pinto
1881-1886	Domingo Santa María
1886-1891	José Manuel Balmaceda
1891-1896	Jorge Montt
1896-1901	Federico Errázuriz Echaurren
1901	Aníbal Zañartu Zañartu (acting president)
1901-1906	Germán Riesco
1906-1910	Pedro Montt
1910	Elías Fernández Albano (acting president)
1910	Emiliano Figueroa Larraín
1910-1915	Ramón Barros Luco
1915-1920	Juan Luis Sanfuentes
1920-1924	Arturo Alessandri Palma
1924-1925	Luis Altamirano Talavera (junta chairman)
1925	Pedro Pablo Dartnell Encina (junta chairman)
1925	Arturo Alessandri Palma
1925	Luis Barros Borgoño (acting president)
1925-1927	Emiliano Figueroa Larraín
1927-1931	Carlos Ibáñez del Campo
1931-1932	Juan Esteban Montero Rodríguez
1932	Arturo Puga Osorio (junta chairman)
1932	Carlos Gregorio Dávila Espinosa (junta chairman)
1932	Bartolomé Blanche Espejo (provisional president)
1932	Abraham Oyanedel Urrutia (acting president)
1932-1938	Arturo Alessandri Palma
1938-1941	Pedro Aguirre Cerda
1941-1942	Jerónimo Méndez Arancibia (acting president)
1942-1946	Juan Antonio Ríos Morales
1946	Alfredo Duhalde Vásquez (acting president)
1946	Vicente Merino Bielich (acting president)
1946	Juan Antonio Iribarren Cabezas (acting president)
1946-1952	Gabriel González Videla
1952-1958	Carlos Ibáñez del Campo
1958-1964	Jorge Alessandri Rodríguez
1964-1970	Eduardo Frei Montalva

Term	President
1970-1973	Salvador Allende
1973-1974	Augusto Pinochet Ugarte (junta leader)
1973-1974	José Toribio Merino Castro (junta leader)
1973-1974	César Mendoza Durán (junta leader)
1973-1974	Gustavo Leigh Guzmán (junta leader)
1974-1990	Augusto Pinochet Ugarte
1990-1994	Patricio Aylwin Azócar
1994-2000	Eduardo Frei Ruiz-Tagle
2000-2006	Ricardo Lagos Escobar
2006-	Michelle Bachelet

CHINA

SUI DYNASTY

Reign	Ruler
581-604	Wendi
604-617	Yangdi
618	Gongdi

TANG DYNASTY

Reign	Ruler
618-626	Gaozu (Li Yuan)
627-649	Taizong
650-683	Gaozong
684	Zhonggong
684-690	Ruizong
690-705	Wu Hou
705-710	Zhongzong
710-712	Ruizong
712-756	Xuanzong
756-762	Suzong
762-779	Daizong
779-805	Dezong
805	Shunzong
805-820	Xianzong
820-824	Muzong
824-827	Jingzong
827-840	Wenzong
840-846	Wuzong
846-859	Xuanzong
859-873	Yizong
873-888	Xizong
888-904	Zhaozong
904-907	Aizong

LIAO DYNASTY

Reign	Ruler
907-926	Abaoji (Taizu)
926-947	Deguang (Taizong)
947-951	Shizong

Reign	Ruler
951-969	Muzong
969-982	Jingzong
982-1031	Shengzong
1031-1055	Xingzong
1055-1101	Daozong
1101-1125	Tianzuodi

WESTERN LIAO DYNASTY

Reign	Ruler
1125-1144	Dezong
1144-1151	Empress Gantian
1151-1164	Renzong
1164-1178	Empress Chengtian
1178-1211	The Last Ruler

JIN DYNASTY

Reign	Ruler
1115-1123	Aguda (Wanyan Min; Taizu)
1123-1135	Taizong (Wanyan Sheng)
1135-1149	Xizong
1150-1161	Wanyan Liang, king of Hailing
1161-1190	Shizong
1190-1209	Zhangzong
1209-1213	Wanyan Yongji, king of Weishao
1213-1224	Xuanzong
1224-1234	Aizong
1234	The Last Emperor

NORTHERN SONG DYNASTY

Reign	Ruler
960-976	Taizu (Zhao Kuangyin)
976-997	Taizong
998-1022	Zhenzong
1022-1063	Renzong
1064-1067	Yingzong
1068-1085	Shenzong
1086-1101	Zhezong
1101-1125	Huizong
1125-1126	Qinzong

SOUTHERN SONG DYNASTY

Reign	Ruler
1127-1162	Gaozong
1163-1190	Xiaozong
1190-1194	Guangzong
1195-1224	Ningzong
1225-1264	Lizong
1265-1274	Duzong
1275-1275	Gongdi
1276-1278	Duanzong
1279	Bing Di

YUAN DYNASTY. *See also* MONGOLS

Reign	Ruler
1279-1294	Kublai Khan (Shizu)
1294-1307	Temür Oljeitu (Chengzong)
1308-1311	Khaishan (Wuzong)
1311-1320	Ayurbarwada (Renzong)
1321-1323	Shidelbala (Yingzong)
1323-1328	Yesun Temür (Taiding)
1328-1329	Tugh Temür (Wenzong Tianshundi)
1329	Tugh Khoshila (Mingzong)
1329-1332	Tugh Temür (Wenzong)
1333-1368	Toghon Temür (Shundi)
1368	Ming Dynasty begins: Hongwu

MING DYNASTY

Reign	Ruler
1368-1398	Hongwu (Zhu Yuanzhang)
1399-1402	Jianwen (Zhu Yunwen)
1402-1424	Yonglo (Zhu Di)
1424-1425	Hongxi
1426-1435	Xuande
1436-1449	Zhengtong
1449-1457	Jingtai
1457-1464	Tianshun
1465-1487	Chenghua (Xianzong)
1488-1505	Hongzhi (Xiaozong)
1505-1521	Zhengde
1522-1567	Jiajing
1567-1572	Longqing
1573-1620	Wanli
1620	Taichang
1621-1627	Tianqi
1628-1644	Chongzhen

SOUTHERN MING DYNASTY

Reign	Ruler
1644-1645	Fu (Hongguang)
1645-1646	Tang (Longwu)
1645	Lu (Luh)
1645-1653	Lu (Lou)
1646	Tang (Shaowu)
1646-1662	Gui (Yongli)

QING (MANCHU) DYNASTY

Reign	Ruler
1616-1626	Nurhachi
1626-1643	Hong Taiji
1643-1661	Shunzi
1644	Occupation of China; defeat of the Ming
1661-1722	Kangxi
1722-1735	Yongzheng
1735-1796	Qianlong
1796-1820	Jiaqing

Reign	Ruler
1820-1850	Daoguang
1850-1861	Xianfeng
1861-1875	Tongzhi
1875-1908	Guangxu
1908-1924	Puyi

REPUBLIC OF CHINA: PRESIDENTS

Reign	Ruler
1911-1912	Sun Yat-sen
1912-1916	Yüan Shih-k'ai
1916-1917	Li Yüan-hung
1917-1918	Feng Kuo-chang
1918-1922	Hsü Shih-ch'ang
1922-1923	Li Yüan-hung
1923	Tsao Kun
1924	Tuan Chi-jui
1923-1925	Sun Yat-sen (Nanking government)
1948-1975	Chiang Kai-shek
1975-1988	Chiang Ching-kuo
1988-2000	Lee Teng-hui
2000-	Chen Shui-bian

PEOPLE'S REPUBLIC OF CHINA (COMMUNIST CHINA)

Term	Prime Minister
1949-1976	Zhou Enlai (Mao Zedong, Communist Party chair)
1976-1980	Hua Guofeng
1980-1987	Zhao Ziyang
1987-1998	Li Peng
1998-2003	Zhu Rongji
2003-	Wen Jiabao

Term	President
1959-1968	Liu Shaoqi
1968-1975	Dong Biwu
1975-1976	Zhu De
1976-1978	Song Qingling
1978-1983	Ye Jianying
1983-1988	Li Xiannian
1988-1993	Yang Shangkun
1989-2003	Jian Zemin
2003-	Hu Jintao

DENMARK. *See also* NORWAY, SWEDEN

Reign	Ruler
588-647	Ivar Vidfamne
647-735?	Harald I Hildetand
735-750?	Sigurd I Ring (poss. 770-812)
c. 750	Randver
850-854	Horik I
c. 854-?	Horik II

Reign	Ruler
c. 860-865	Ragnar Lobrok
865-873	Sigurd II Snogoje
873-884	Hardeknut I
884-885	Frodo
885-889	Harald II
c. 900-950	Gorm
c. 950-985	Harald III Bluetooth
985-1014	Sweyn I Forkbeard
1014-1019	Harald IV
1019-1035	Canute I (III) the Great
1035-1042	Hardeknut
1042-1047	Magnus the Good
1047-1074	Sweyn II
1074-1080	Harald V Hen
1080-1086	Canute II (IV) the Holy
1086-1095	Olaf IV the Hungry
1095-1103	Eric I the Evergood
1103-1134	Niels Elder
1134-1137	Eric II
1137-1146	Eric III
1146-1157	Sweyn III
1147-1157	Canute III (V) Magnussen
1157-1182	Valdemar I the Great
1182-1202	Canute IV (VI) the Pious
1202-1241	Valdemar II the Victorious
1241-1250	Eric IV
1250-1252	Abel
1252-1259	Christopher I
1259-1286	Eric V
1286-1319	Eric VI
1320-1326	Christopher II
1326-1330	Instability
1330-1332	Christopher II (restored)
1332-1340	Instability
1340-1375	Valdemar III
1376-1387	Olaf V (or II; IV of Norway)
1380	Unification of Denmark and Norway
1376-1412	Margaret I of Denmark, Norway, and Sweden
1397	Unification of Norway, Denmark, and Sweden
1412-1439	Eric VII (III of Norway, XIII of Sweden)
1439-1448	Christopher III

HOUSE OF OLDENBURG

Reign	Ruler
1448-1481	Christian I
1481-1513	John (Hans)
1523	Sweden leaves Kalmar Union
1523-1533	Frederick I
1523-1536	Union with Norway
1534-1559	Christian III
1559-1588	Frederick II

Reign	Ruler
1588-1648	Christian IV
1648-1670	Frederick III
1670-1699	Christian V
1699-1730	Frederick IV
1730-1746	Christian VI
1746-1766	Frederick V
1766-1808	Christian VII
1808-1839	Frederick VI
1839-1848	Christian VIII
1848-1863	Frederick VII

SCHLESWIG-HOLSTEIN-SONDERBURG-GLÜCKSBURG

Reign	Ruler
1863-1906	Christian IX
1906-1912	Frederik VIII
1912-1947	Christian X
1947-1972	Frederik IX
1972	Margrethe II

EGYPT

After the rise of Islam in the seventh century, Egypt was Islamicized and came under the control of a succession of emirs and caliphs.

ṬULUNID EMIRS

Reign	Ruler
868-884	Aḥmad ibn Ṭūlūn
884-896	Khumārawayh
896	Jaysh
896-904	Hārūn
904-905	Shaybān
905	Recovered by Abbasids

IKHSHIDID EMIRS

Reign	Ruler
935-946	Muḥammad ibn Ṭughj al-Ikhshīd
946-961	Unūjūr
961-966	ʿAlī
966-968	Kāfūr al-Lābī (regent)
968-969	Aḥmad
969	Fāṭimid conquest

FĀṬIMID CALIPHS IN EGYPT

Reign	Ruler
975-996	al-ʿAzīz
996-1021	al-Ḥākim
1021-1036	al-Zahīr
1036-1094	al-Mustanṣir
1094-1101	al-Mustadī
1101-1130	al-Amīr
1130-1149	al-Ḥāfiz

Reign	Ruler
1149-1154	al-Zafīr
1154-1160	al-Fāʾiz
1160-1171	al-ʿAdīd

AYYŪBID SULTANS

Reign	Ruler
1169-1193	Saladin
1193-1198	al-ʿAzīz Imad al-Dīn
1198-1200	al-Mansūr Naṣīr al-Dīn
1200-1218	al-ʿAdil I Sayf al-Dīn
1202-1204	Fourth Crusade
1217-1221	Fifth Crusade
1218-1238	al-Kāmil I Nāṣir al-Dīn
1227-1230	Sixth Crusade
1238-1240	al-ʿAdil II Sayf al-Dīn
1240-1249	al-Ṣāliḥ II Najm al-Dīn
1249-1250	al-Muʿazzam Tūrān-Shāh Ghiyāt al-Dīn
1248-1254	Seventh (or Eighth) Crusade
1252	Cairo seized by Mamlūks

MAMLŪK SULTANS

Baḥrī Line (Mongol, then Turkish)

Reign	Ruler
1252-1257	Aybak al-Turkumānī
1257-1259	ʿAlī I
1259-1260	Quṭuz al-Muʿizzī
1260-1277	Baybars I (defeats Mongols 1260)
1277-1279	Baraka (Berke) Khān
1279	Salāmish (Süleymish)
1279-1290	Qalāʾūn al-Alfī
1290-1293	Khalīl
1291	Fall of Acre
1293	Baydarā (?)
1293-1294	Muḥammad I
1294-1296	Kitbughā
1296-1299	Lāchīn (Lājīn) al-Ashqar
1299-1309	Muḥammad I
1303	Earthquake destroys Pharos lighthouse
1309-1310	Baybars II al-Jāshnakīr (Burjī)
1310-1341	Muḥammad I
1341	Abū Bakr
1341-1342	Kūjūk (Küchük)
1342	Aḥmad I
1342-1345	Ismāʿīl
1345-1346	Shaʿbān I
1346-1347	Ḥājjī I
1347-1351	al-Ḥasan
1351-1354	Ṣāliḥ
1354-1361	al-Ḥasan
1361-1363	Muḥammad II
1363-1377	Shaʿbān II
1377-1382	ʿAlī II

Reign	Ruler
1382	Ḥājjī II
1389-1390	Ḥājjī II

Burjī (Circassian) line

Reign	Ruler
1382-1398	Barqūq al-Yalburghāwī
1399-1405	Faraj
1405	ʿAbd al-ʿAzīz
1405-1412	Faraj (second rule)
1412	al-Mustaʿīn
1412-1421	Shaykh al-Maḥmūdī al-Ẓāhirī
1421	Aḥmad II
1421	Ṭāṭār
1421-1422	Muḥammad III
1422-1438	Barsbay
1438	Yūsuf
1438-1453	Chaqmaq (Jaqmaq)
1453	ʿUthmān
1453-1461	Ināl al-ʿAlāʾī al-Ẓāhirī
1461	Aḥmad III
1461-1467	Khushqadam
1467	Yalbay
1467-1468	Timurbughā
1468-1496	Qāyit Bay (Qāytbāy) al-Ẓāhirī
1496-1498	Muḥammad IV
1498-1500	Qānṣawh I
1500-1501	Jānbulāṭ
1501	Ṭūmān Bay I
1501-1516	Qānṣawh II al-Ghawrī
1516-1517	Ṭūmān Bay II
1517	Ottoman conquest

ʿABBĀSID CALIPHS OF EGYPT

Unlike the earlier ʿAbbāsid line (see Islamic Caliphs, below), these were ʿAbbāsid figureheads in place under the Mamlūks.

Reign	Ruler
1261	Aḥmad al-Mustanṣir
1261-1302	Aḥmad al-Ḥākim I (Aleppo 1261-1262, Cairo, 1262-1302)
1302-1340	Sulaymān al-Mustakfī I
1340-1341	Ibrāhīm al-Wāthiq I
1341-1352	Aḥmad al-Ḥakīm II
1352-1362	Abū Bakr al-Muʿtadid I
1362-1377	Muḥammad al-Mutawakkil I
1377	Zakariyyāʾ al-Muʿtaṣim
1377-1383	Muḥammad al-Mutawakkil I
1383-1386	ʿUmar al-Wāthiq II
1386-1389	Zakariyyāʾ al-Muʿtaṣim
1389-1406	Muḥammad al-Mutawakkil I
1406-1414	Sulṭān
1412	ʿAbbās or Yaʿqūb al-Mustaʿīn
1414-1441	Dāwūd al-Muʿtadid II
1441-1451	Sulaymān al-Mustakfī II

Reign	Ruler
1451-1455	Ḥamza al-Qāʾim
1455-1479	Yūsuf al-Mustanjid
1479-1497	ʿAbd al-ʿAzīz al-Mutawakkil II
1497-1508	Yaʿqūb al-Mustamsik
1508-1516	al-Mutawakkil III
1516-1517	Yaʿqūb al-Mustamsik
1517	Ottoman conquest

ENGLAND

ANGLO-SAXONS (HOUSE OF WESSEX)

Reign	Ruler
802-839	Egbert
839-856	Æthelwulf
856-860	Æthelbald
860-866	Æthelbert
866-871	Ethelred (Æthelred) I
871-899	Alfred the Great
899-924	Edward the Elder (with sister Æthelflæd)
924-939	Æthelstan
939-946	Edmund the Magnificent
946-955	Eadred
955-959	Eadwig (Edwy) All-Fair
959-975	Edgar the Peaceable
975-978	Edward the Martyr
978-1016	Ethelred (Æthelred) II the Unready
1016	Edmund II Ironside

DANES

Reign	Ruler
1016-1035	Canute (Knud) the Great
1035-1040	Harold I Harefoot
1040-1042	Harthacnut

WESSEX (RESTORED)

Reign	Ruler
1043-1066	Edward the Confessor
1066	Harold II

NORMANS

Reign	Ruler
1066-1087	William I the Conqueror
1087-1100	William II Rufus
1100-1135	Henry I Beauclerc
1135-1154	Stephen

PLANTAGENETS: ANGEVINS

Reign	Ruler
1154-1189	Henry II (with Eleanor of Aquitaine, r. 1154-1189)
1189-1199	Richard I the Lion-Hearted

Reign	Ruler
1199-1216	John I Lackland
1216-1272	Henry III
1272-1307	Edward I Longshanks
1307-1327	Edward II (with Isabella of France, r. 1308-1330)
1327-1377	Edward III (with Philippa of Hainaut, r. 1327-1369)
1377-1399	Richard II

PLANTAGENETS: LANCASTRIANS

Reign	Ruler
1399-1413	Henry IV
1413-1422	Henry V
1422-1461	Henry VI

PLANTAGENETS: YORKISTS

Reign	Ruler
1461-1470	Edward IV
1470-1471	Henry VI (Lancaster)
1471-1483	Edward IV (York, restored)
1483	Edward V (York)
1483-1485	Richard III Hunchback (York)

TUDORS

Reign	Ruler
1485-1509	Henry VII
1509-1547	Henry VIII
1547-1553	Edward VI
1553	Lady Jane Grey
1553-1558	Mary I
1558-1603	Elizabeth I

STUARTS

Reign	Ruler
1603-1625	James I (VI of Scotland)
1625-1649	Charles I

COMMONWEALTH (LORD PROTECTORS)

Reign	Ruler
1653-1658	Oliver Cromwell
1658-1659	Richard Cromwell

STUARTS (RESTORED)

Reign	Ruler
1660-1685	Charles II
1685-1689	James II (VII of Scotland)
1689-1702	William of Orange (III of England, II of Scotland) and Mary II
1702-1707	Anne
1707	Act of Union (Great Britain and Ireland)
1707-1714	Anne

HANOVERS

Reign	Ruler
1714-1727	George I
1727-1760	George II
1760-1801	George III
1801	Act of Union creates United Kingdom
1801-1820	George III
1820-1830	George IV
1830-1837	William IV

SAXE-COBURG-GOTHA

Reign	Ruler
1837-1901	Victoria
1901-1910	Edward VII
1910-1936	George V

WINDSOR

Reign	Ruler
1910-1936	George V
1936	Edward VIII
1936-1952	George VI
1952-	Elizabeth II

FRANKISH KINGDOM AND FRANCE

The Merovingians and Carolingians ruled different parts of the Frankish kingdom, which accounts for overlapping regnal dates in these tables. The term "emperor" refers to rule over what eventually came to be known as the Holy Roman Empire.

THE MEROVINGIANS

Reign	Ruler (Principality)
447-458	Merovech
458-481	Childeric I
481-511	Clovis I (with Clotilda, r. 493-511)
511	Kingdom split among Clovis's sons
511-524	Chlodomer (Orléans)
511-534	Theodoric I (Metz)
511-558	Childebert I (Paris)
511-561	Lothair I (Soissons 511-561, all Franks 558-561)
534-548	Theudebert I (Metz)
548-555	Theudebald (Metz)
561	Kingdom split among Lothair's sons
561-567	Charibert I (Paris)
561-575	Sigebert I (Austrasia)
561-584	Chilperic I (Soissons)
561-592	Guntram (Burgundy)
575-595	Childebert II (Austrasia 575-595, Burgundy 593-595)
584-629	Lothair II (Neustria 584, all Franks 613-629)

Reign	Ruler (Principality)
595-612	Theudebert II (Austrasia)
595-613	Theodoric II (Burgundy 595-612, Austrasia 612-613)
613	Sigebert II (Austrasia, Burgundy)
623-639	Dagobert I (Austrasia 623-628, all Franks 629-639)
629-632	Charibert II (Aquitaine)
632-656	Sigebert III (Austrasia)
639-657	Clovis II (Neustria and Burgundy)
656-673	Lothair III (Neustria 657-673, all Franks 656-660)
662-675	Childeric (Austrasia 662-675, all Franks 673-675)
673-698	Theodoric III (Neustria 673-698, all Franks 678-691)
674-678	Dagobert II (Austrasia)
691-695	Clovis III (all Franks)
695-711	Childebert III (all Franks)
711-716	Dagobert III (all Franks)
715-721	Chilperic II (Neustria 715-721, all Franks 719-720)
717-719	Lothair IV (Austrasia)
721-737	Theodoric IV (all Franks)
743-751	Childeric III (all Franks)

THE CAROLINGIANS

Reign	Ruler
687-714	Pépin II of Heristal (mayor of Austrasia/Neustria)
714-719	Plectrude (regent for Theudoald)
719-741	Charles Martel (the Hammer; mayor of Austrasia/Neustria)
747-768	Pépin III the Short (mayor of Neustria 741, king of all Franks 747)
768-814	Charlemagne (king of Franks 768, emperor 800)
814-840	Louis the Pious (king of Aquitaine, emperor)
840-855	Lothair I (emperor)
843	Treaty of Verdun divides Carolingian Empire into East Franks (Germany), West Franks (essentially France), and a Middle Kingdom (roughly corresponding to Provence, Burgundy, and Lorraine)
843-876	Louis II the German (king of Germany)
843-877	Charles II the Bald (king of Neustria 843, emperor 875)
855-875	Louis II (emperor)
877-879	Louis II (king of France)
879-882	Louis III (king of France)
879-884	Carloman (king of France)
884-887	Charles III the Fat (king of France, emperor 881)
887-898	Odo (Eudes; king of France)
887-899	Arnulf (king of Germany 887, emperor 896)
891-894	Guy of Spoleto (Wido, Guido; emperor)

Reign	Ruler
892-898	Lambert of Spoleto (emperor)
893-923	Charles III the Simple (king of France)
915-923	Berengar I of Friuli (emperor)
923-929?	Robert I (king of France)
929-936	Rudolf (king of France)
936-954	Louis IV (king of France; Hugh the Great in power)
954-986	Lothair (king of France; Hugh Capet in power 956)
986-987	Louis V (king of France)

THE CAPETIANS

Reign	Ruler
987-996	Hugh Capet
996-1031	Robert II the Pious
1031-1060	Henry I
1060-1108	Philip I the Fair
1108-1137	Louis VI the Fat
1137-1179	Louis VII the Younger (with Eleanor of Aquitaine, r. 1137-1180)
1179-1223	Philip II Augustus
1223-1226	Louis VIII the Lion
1223-1252	Blanche of Castile (both queen and regent)
1226-1270	Louis IX (Saint Louis)
1271-1285	Philip III the Bold
1285-1314	Philip IV the Fair
1314-1316	Louis X the Stubborn
1316	Philip, brother of Louis X (regent before birth of John I and during his short life)
1316	John I the Posthumous
1316-1322	Philip V the Tall
1322-1328	Charles IV the Fair

Valois Dynasty, Main Branch

Reign	Ruler
1328-1350	Philip VI the Fortunate
1350-1364	John II the Good
1364-1380	Charles V the Wise
1380-1382	Louis I of Anjou (regent for Charles VI)
1380-1422	Charles VI the Well-Beloved
1422-1461	Charles VII the Victorious
1461-1483	Louis XI
1483-1484	Anne de Beaujeu (regent for Charles VIII)
1483-1498	Charles VIII the Affable

Valois-Orléans Branch

Reign	Ruler
1498-1515	Louis XII, the Father of His People

Valois-Angoulême Branch

Reign	Ruler
1515-1547	Francis I
1547-1559	Henry II (with Catherine de Médicis)

Reign	Ruler
1559-1560	Francis II
1560-1563	Catherine de Médicis (regent for Charles IX)
1560-1574	Charles IX
1574-1589	Henry III (King of Poland, 1573-1574)

BOURBON DYNASTY

Reign	Ruler
1589-1610	Henry IV (Henry III of Navarre, 1572-1610)
1610-1614	Marie de Médici (regent for Louis XIII)
1610-1643	Louis XIII the Well-Beloved
1643-1651	Anne of Austria (regent for Louis XIV)
1643-1715	Louis XIV the Sun King
1715-1723	Philip II of Orléans (regent for Louis XV)
1715-1774	Louis XV the Well-Beloved
1774-1792	Louis XVI the Beloved
1792-1804	First Republic
1804-1814	First Empire (Napoleon I Bonaparte)
1814-1824	Louis XVIII
1824-1830	Charles X
1830-1848	Louis-Philippe of Orléans

MODERN ERA

Term	Government/President
1848-1852	Second Republic
1852-1870	Second Empire (Napoleon III)
1871-1940	Third Republic
1940-1944	Vichy State (German occupation)
1944-1947	Provisional government
1944-1946	Charles de Gaulle
1947-1958	Fourth Republic
1947-1954	Vincent Auriol
1954-1958	René Coty
After 1958	Fifth Republic
1958-1969	Charles de Gaulle
1969-1974	Georges Pompidou
1974-1981	Valéry Giscard d'Estaing
1981-1995	François Mitterrand
1995-	Jacques Chirac

GERMANIC TRIBES. *See also* **HOLY ROMAN EMPIRE**
In the fifth and sixth centuries, Europe was invaded from the east by several "barbarian" tribes from eastern Europe and Central Asia, including the Visigoths, who inflicted the earliest damage on Rome in the late fourth and early fifth centuries; the Burgundians, from central and northeastern Europe; the Vandals, who eventually settled in Spain and North Africa; the Suevi, who made their way to the north of Spain and finally fell to the Visigoths; the Alans, a non-Germanic steppe tribe from Iran who, along with the Suevi and the Visigoths, overran Gaul

(France) and the Iberian Peninsula; and the Franks (see Frankish Kingdom and France, above), who occupied most of Gaul during the later Roman Empire and were the only of these early tribes to survive. The Franks would evolve into the Merovingian and Carolingian lines, and by the ninth century they dominated Europe. Below is a list of some of the Germanic tribes and tribal leaders before and during the Frankish period. The region known today as Germany was initially occupied by these tribes and then came under the subjugation of the Frankish Merovingians and Carolingians. In 962, the Holy Roman Empire came into existence and held sway over Germany for nearly a millennium (see Holy Roman Empire, below). Not until the late nineteenth century did the nation-state of Germany come into existence.

ALEMANNI (OR ALAMANNI)

The Alemanni occupied Swabia.

Reign	Ruler
c. 536-554	Leuthari
c. 536-554	Butilin
d. c. 539	Haming
c. 570-587	Leutfred I
588-613	Uncilen
d. 613	Gunzo
c. 615-639	Chrodebert
c. 640-673/95	Leutfred II
c. 700-709	Godefred
d. c. 712	Huocin
d. c. 712	Willehari
c. 720-730	Lanfred I
c. 737-744	Theodobald
d. 746	Nebi
746-749	Lanfred II
791-799	Gerold
799-806	Isenbard
After 806	Annexed by the Franks

BAVARIANS

The Bavarians occupied a region approximating present-day Bavaria.

Reign	Ruler
508-512	Theodo I
512-537	Theodo II
537-565	Theodo III
537-567	Theodobald I
550-590	Garibald I
590-595	Grimwald I
591-609	Tassilo I
609-630	Agilulf
609-640	Garibald II
640-680	Theodo IV

Reign	Ruler
680-702	Theodo V
702-715	Theodobald II
702-723	Grimwald II
702-725	Theodobert
702-730	Tassilo II
725-737	Hubert
737-748	Odilo
748-788	Tassilo III
After 788	Annexed by Franks

BURGUNDIANS

The Burgundians occupied central and southeastern France.

Reign	Ruler
c. 407	Gebicca
407-434	Gundahar/Gondikar/Gunther
434-473	Gundioc/Gunderic
443-c. 480	Chilperic I
473-486	Gundomar I
473-493	Chilperic II
473-501	Godegisel
473-516	Gundobad
516-524	Sigismund
524-532	Gudomar II
532	Frankish conquest

FRANKS

The Franks initially occupied the area now known as the Netherlands and northern France, and they eventually dominated Europe. See Frankish Kingdom and France, above.

LOMBARDS

The Lombards occupied northern Italy.

Reign	Ruler
565-572	Alboin
573-575	Celph
575-584	Unstable
584-590	Authari
590-591	Theodelinda
591-615	Agilulf
615-625	Adaloald
625-636	Arioald
636-652	Rotharis
652-661	Aribert I
661-662	Godipert
662-671	Grimoald
671-674	Garibald
674-688	Bertharit
688-700	Cunibert
700-701	Liutpert
701	Raginpert
701-712	Aribert II
712-744	Liutprand

Reign	Ruler
744-749	Rachis of Friuli
749-756	Aistulf of Friuli
756-774	Desiderius
774	Frankish conquest

OSTROGOTHS

The Ostrogoths migrated from the east into the Balkans and Italian peninsula.

Reign	Ruler
474-526	Theodoric the Great
526-534	Athalaric
534-536	Theodahad (with Amalasuntha)
536-540	Vitiges (Witiges)
540	Theodobald (Heldebadus)
541	Eraric
541-552	Totila (Baduila)
552-553	Teias
553-568	Roman domination (Byzantine emperor Justinian I)
568-774	Lombard domination
774	Frankish conquest

SUEVI

The Suevi migrated from the east into northern Spain.

Reign	Ruler
409-438	Hermeric
428-448	Rechila
439	Mérida
441	Seville
448-456	Rechiar
452	Peace with Romans
456	Visigoths defeat Rechiar
456-457	Aioulf
457-460	Maldras
460-c. 463	Richimund
460-c. 465	Frumar
c. 463-?	Remisund
c. 500-550	Unknown kings
c. 550-559	Carriaric
559-570	Theodemar
561	Catholic
570-582	Miro
582-584	Eboric
584-585	Andeca
After 585	Visigoth conquest

VANDALS

The Vandals migrated west into southern Spain and northern Africa.

Reign	Ruler
c. 406-428	Gunderic
428-477	Gaiseric
477-484	Huneric
484-496	Gunthamund
496-523	Thrasamund
523-530	Hilderic
530-534	Gelimer
After 534	Roman overthrow

VISIGOTHS

The Visigoths migrated west into southwestern France.

Reign	Ruler
395-410	Alaric I
410-415	Athaulf (Ataulfo)
415	Sigeric
415-417	Wallia
417-451	Theodoric I
451-453	Thorismund
453-466	Theodoric II
466-484	Euric I
484-507	Alaric II
508-511	Amalaric
511-526	Theodoric the Great
526-531	Amalaric
531-548	Theudes
548-549	Theudegisel
549-554	Agila
554-567	Athanagild
567-571	Theodomir
571-572	Leuva (Leova) I
572-586	Leuvigild
586-601	Reccared I
601-603	Leova II
603-610	Witterich
610-612	Gundemar
612-621	Sisebut (Sisebur)
621	Reccared II
621-631	Swintilla (Suinthila)
631-636	Sisenand
636-640	Chintila
640-642	Tulga
642-653	Chindaswind
653-672	Recdeswinth
672-680	Wamba
680-687	Euric (Erwig) II
687-702	Egica (Ergica)
702-709	Witiza
709-711	Roderic (Rodrigo)
711	Overthrown by Umayyads
718	Christian Kingdom of Asturias

GERMANY

FIRST REICH. SEE HOLY ROMAN EMPIRE

SECOND REICH

Term	Leader
1862-1890	Otto von Bismark (chancellor)
1871-1888	Wilhelm I (emperor)
1888	Frederick (emperor)
1888-1918	Wilhelm II (emperor)
1890-1894	Count Leo von Caprivi (chancellor)
1894-1900	Chlodwig von Hohenzollern-Schillingsfürst (chancellor)
1900-1909	Bernhard von Bülow (chancellor)
1909-1917	Theobald von Bethmann-Hollweg (chancellor)
1917	George Michaelis (chancellor)
1917-1918	George von Hertling (chancellor)
1918	Maximilian of Baden (chancellor)
1918	Friedrich Ebert (chancellor)

WEIMAR REPUBLIC

Term	Leader
1919-1925	Friedrich Ebert (president)
1919	Philip Scheidemann (chancellor)
1919-1920	Gustav Bauer (chancellor)
1920	Hermann Müller (chancellor)
1920-1921	Konstantin Fehrenbach (chancellor)
1921-1922	Joseph Wirth (chancellor)
1922-1923	Wilhelm Cuno (chancellor)
1923	Gustav Stresemann (chancellor)
1923-1925	Wilhelm Marx (chancellor)
1925-1934	Paul von Hindenberg (president)
1925-1926	Hans Luther (chancellor)
1926-1928	Wilhelm Marx (chancellor)
1928-1930	Hermann Müller (chancellor)
1930-1932	Heinrich Brüning (chancellor)
1932	Franz von Papen (chancellor)
1932-1933	Kurt von Schleider (chancellor)
1933-1934	Adolf Hilter (chancellor)

THIRD REICH

Term	Führer
1934-1945	Adolf Hitler
1945	Karl Dönitz
1945-1949	Allied occupation
1949	Germany divided into Federal Republic of Germany (West Germany) and German Democratic Republic (East Germany)
1990	Reunification

FEDERAL REPUBLIC OF GERMANY

Term	Office
1949-1959	Theodor Heuss (president)
1949-1963	Konrad Adenauer (chancellor)
1959-1969	Heinrich Lübke (president)
1963-1966	Ludwig Erhard (chancellor)
1966-1969	Kurt Georg Kiesinger (chancellor)
1969-1974	Gustav Heinemann (president)
1969-1974	Willy Brandt (chancellor)
1974-1979	Walter Scheel (president)
1974-1982	Helmut Schmidt (chancellor)
1979-1984	Karl Carstens (president)
1982-1998	Helmut Kohl (chancellor)
1984-1994	Richard von Weizsäcker (president)
1990	Reunification of East and West Germany
1994-1999	Roman Herzog (president)
1998-2005	Gerhard Schröder (chancellor)
1999-2004	Johannes Rau (president)
2004-	Horst Köhler (president)
2005-	Angela Merkel (chancellor)

HOLY ROMAN EMPIRE

Although some sources consider the Holy Roman Empire to have begun with Otto I's coronation in 962, others date the Empire's beginning as early as Charlemagne's consolidation of the Franks and his coronation as emperor of the Frankish Empire in 800. The term "Sacrum Romanum Imperium" (Holy Roman Empire) dates to 1254, the use of the term "Holy Empire" to 1157, and the term "Roman Empire" to 1034 (reign of Conrad II). "Roman emperor" was applied to Otto I during his reign; however, Charlemagne also used the term to refer to his own reign. The concept of a "Holy" Roman Empire goes back to the beginning of the Byzantine Empire and the reign of the first Christian Roman emperor, Constantine the Great. Hence, the concept of this political entity can be considered to have evolved incrementally over time. The practice of papal coronation to legitimate the emperor began with Otto I. Regnal dates are therefore often listed as beginning with the date of coronation. However, the German kings who became Holy Roman Emperors frequently asserted their de facto power earlier as rulers of West Frankia (France), East Frankia (essentially Germany), and/or Italy (roughly the northern portion of modern Italy). In the table below, where a date of ascension to the West Frankish (French), East Frankish (German), Middle Frankish (Lorraine south to Italy), or other throne is different from that to Emperor, the former date is set before a slash and the date of assuming the rule of the Empire falls after the slash. Asterisks indicate that the monarch was not formally crowned at Rome by the pope, a practice that officially ended with Frederick II, although Charles V was last to be crowned outside Rome.

Reign	Emperor (House)
768/800-814	Charlemagne (Carolingian)
814/813-840	Louis I the Pious (Carolingian)
840/817-855	Lothair I (Carolingian)
840-876	Louis II the German (Carolingian; first king of East Franks only)
840/875-877	Charles II the Bald (Carolingian)
855/850-875	Louis II of Italy (Carolingian)
877-881	Empire unstable
876/881-888	Charles III the Fat (Carolingian)
888-891	Viking and Arab incursions
891	Italian line begins
888/891-894	Guy (Guido, Wido) of Spoleto (Italian)
894/892-898	Lambert of Spoleto (Italian, co-emperor)
888/896-899	Arnulf (East Frankish)
899/901-905	Louis III of Provence (Carolingian, deposed)
905/915-924	Berengar I of Friuli (Italian)
911-918	*Conrad
919	Saxon line begins
919-936	*Henry I the Fowler (Saxon)
936/962-973	Otto I (Saxon): crowned in 962 by Pope John XII; the Empire no longer lays claim to West Frankish lands (essentially France), but now is basically a union of Germany and northern Italy
973/967-983	Otto II (Saxon)
983/996-1002	Otto III (Saxon)
1002/14-1024	Henry II the Saint (Saxon)
1024	Franconian/Salian line begins
1024/27-1039	Conrad II (Franconian/Salian)
1039/46-1056	Henry III (Franconian/Salian)
1056/84-1106	Henry IV (Franconian/Salian)
1077-1080	*Rudolf of Swabia
1081-1093	*Hermann (of Luxemburg)
1093-1101	*Conrad (of Franconia)
1106/11-1125	Henry V (Franconian/Salian)
1125	Franconian/Salian line ends
1125/33-1137	Lothair II (duke of Saxony)
1138	Hohenstaufen line begins
1138-1152	*Conrad III (Hohenstaufen)
1152/55-1190	Frederick I Barbarossa (Hohenstaufen)
1190/91-1197	Henry VI (Hohenstaufen)
1198-1208	*Philip of Swabia (Hohenstaufen)
1208/09-1215	Otto IV (married into Hohenstaufens)
1215/20-1250	Frederick II (Hohenstaufen): Last emperor crowned at Rome
1246-1247	*Henry Raspe
1247-1256	*William of Holland

Reign	Emperor (House)
1250-1254	*Conrad IV
1254-1273	Great Interregnum
1257-1272	*Richard of Cornwall (rival, Plantagenet)
1257-1273	*Alfonso X of Castile (rival)
1273-1291	*Rudolf I (Habsburg)
1292-1298	*Adolf of Nassau
1298-1308	*Albert (Albrecht) I (Habsburg)
1308/11-1313	Henry VII (Luxembourg)
1314/28-1347	Louis IV of Bavaria (Wittelsbach)
1314-1325	*Frederick of Habsburg (co-regent)
1346/55-1378	Charles IV (Luxembourg): Changes the name to the Holy Roman Empire of the German Nation as France begins to assert power; Charles abandons the Empire's French and Italian claims, and the history of the Holy Roman Empire and Germany are now basically the same
1349	*Günther of Schwarzburg
1378-1400	*Wenceslaus (Luxembourg; deposed)
1400	*Frederick III (of Brunswick)
1400-1410	*Rupert of the Palatinate (Wittelsbach)
1410-1411	*John (of Moravia)
1410/33-1437	Sigismund (Luxembourg)
1438-1439	*Albert II (Habsburg)
1440/52-1493	Frederick III (Habsburg)
1486/93-1519	*Maximilian I (Habsburg)
1499	Peace of Basle; Swiss independence
1513	Swiss Confederation of the Thirteen Cantons
1519-1558	*Charles V (Habsburg, last emperor crowned)
1555	Peace of Augsburg
1558-1564	*Ferdinand I (Habsburg)
1559	Peace of Cateau-Cambrésis
1564-1576	*Maximilian II (Habsburg)
1576-1612	*Rudolf II (Habsburg)
1612-1619	*Matthias (Habsburg)
1619-1637	*Ferdinand II (Habsburg)
1637-1657	*Ferdinand III (Habsburg)
1648	Peace of Westphalia
1658-1705	*Leopold I (Habsburg)
1686-1697	War of the League of Augsburg, conquest of Hungary, Nine Years' War (1688-1697)
1705-1711	*Joseph I (Habsburg)
1711-1740	*Charles VI (Habsburg)
1713	Peace of Utrecht
1740-1742	Interregnum
1742-1745	*Charles VII (Wittelsbach-Habsburg)
1745-1765	*Francis I (Lorraine)
1745-1780	*Maria Theresa (empress consort; queen of Hungary, 1740; empress dowager, 1765)
1756-1763	Seven Years' War
1765-1790	*Joseph II (Habsburg-Lorraine)

Reign	Emperor (House)
1790-1792	*Leopold II (Habsburg-Lorraine)
1792-1806	*Francis II (Habsburg-Lorraine; abdicated)
1806	Holy Roman Empire falls to Napoleon I of France

HUNGARY. *See also* BOHEMIA, POLAND

Reign	Ruler
c. 896-907	Árpád
d. 947	Zsolt
d. 972	Taksony
997	Géza
997-1038	Saint Stephen (István) I
1038-1041	Peter Orseleo
1041-1044	Samuel
1044-1046	Peter (second rule)
1047-1060	Andrew I
1060-1063	Béla I
1063-1074	Salamon
1074-1077	Géza I
1077-1095	Saint László (Ladislas) I
1095-1116	Kalman
1116-1131	Stephen II
1131-1141	Béla II
1141-1162	Géza II
1162-1163	László II
1163-1172	Stephen III
1163-1165	Stephen IV
1172-1196	Béla III
1196-1204	Imre
1204-1205	László III
1205-1235	Andrew II
1235-1270	Béla IV
1270-1272	Stephen V
1272-1290	László IV
1290-1301	Andrew III (end of the Árpád line)
1301-1304	Wenceslaus (Václav) II
1304-1308	Otto I of Bavaria
1305-1306	Wenceslaus (Václav) III
1306	End of the Přemlysid line
1306-1310	Instability
1310-1342	Károly (Charles Robert) I
1342-1382	Lajos (Louis) I
1382-1395	Maria
1387-1437	Sigismund
1438-1439	Albert II of Habsburg
1440-1444	Ulászló I (Władysław III, Poland)
1444-1457	László (Ladislas) V
1458-1490	Matthias (Matyas) I Corvinus
1490-1516	Ulászló II (Vladislav or Władisław Jagiełło)
1516-1526	Louis II
1526-1564	Ferdinand I (Habsburg claims suzerainty)

Reign	Ruler
1526-1540	John I Zápolya (simultaneous claimant)
1540-1571	John II Sigismund
1556-1559	Isabel
1562	Split between Habsburgs, Ottomans, and Ottoman principality Transylvania
1563-1576	Maximilian II (Holy Roman Emperor)
1571-1575	Stephen Báthory
1572-1608	Rudolf II (Holy Roman Emperor)
1575-1581	Christopher (Kristóf) Báthory
1581-1599	Sigismund Báthory
1599	Andrew Cardinal Báthory
1599-1602	Sigismund Báthory
1604-1606	Stephen Bocskay
1607-1608	Sigismund Rákóczy
1608-1619	Matthias (Holy Roman Emperor)
1608-1613	Gabriel (Gábor) Báthory
1613-1629	Gábor Bethlen
1618-1637	Ferdinand II
1625-1657	Ferdinand III
1630-1648	George (György) I Rákóczy
1647-1654	Ferdinand IV
1648-1657	George II Rákóczy
1655-1705	Leopold I
1660-1682	Emeric Thököly (Tökölli)
1687-1711	Joseph I
1703-1711	Francis II Rákóczy leads liberation movement
1711-1740	Charles III
1740-1780	Maria Theresa
1780-1790	Joseph II
1790-1792	Leopold II
1792-1835	Francis
1835-1848	Ferdinand V
1848	Revolutions of 1848
1848-1916	Francis Joseph I (Ferenc József)
1916-1918	Charles IV
1918	Hungary declares independence, forms First Republic

INDIA

FIRST CĀLUKYA DYNASTY

Reign	Ruler
543-566	Pulakeśin I
c. 566-597	Kīrtivarman I
598-610	Maṅgaleśa
610-642	Pulakeśin II
655-680	Vikramāditya I
680-696	Vinayāditya
696-733	Vijayāditya
733-746	Vikramāditya II
747-757	Kīrtivarman II

PALLAVAS

Reign	Ruler
c. 550-575	Simhavarman (some sources give c. 436)
c. 575-600	Simhavishnu
c. 600-630	Mahendravarman I
c. 630-668	Narasiṃhavarman I Mahāmalla
c. 668-670	Mahendravarman II
c. 670-700	Paramesvaravarman I
c. 695-728	Narasiṃhavarman II
c. 728-731	Paramesvaravarman II
c. 731-796	Nandivarman
750-770	Gopāla
770-810	Dharmapāla
810-850	Devapāla
854-908	Narayanpāla
c. 988-1038	Māhipāla I
c. 1077-1120	Rāmapāla
1143-1161	Madanpāla

SECOND WESTERN CĀLUKYA DYNASTY

Reign	Ruler
973-997	Taila II
997-1008	Saṭyaśraya
1008-1014	Vikramāditya I
1014-1015	Ayyana
1015-1042	Jayasimha I
1043-1068	Someśvara I
1068-1076	Someśvara II
1076-1126	Vikramāditya VI
1127-1135	Someśvara III
1135-1151	Jagadhekamalla II
1151-1154	Taila III
1155-1168	Bijjala
1168-1177	Someśvara IV
1177-1180	Saṅkama II
1180-1183	Āhavamalla
1183-1184	Singhana
1184-1189/90	Someśvara IV

GURJARA-PRATIHĀRA DYNASTY

Reign	Ruler
c. 730-c. 756	Nāgabhaṭa I
n.d.	Devaraja
c. 778-c. 794	Vatsarāja
c. 794-c. 833	Nāgabhaṭa II
c. 836-c. 885	Mihira Bhoja I
c. 890-c. 910	Mahendrapāla I
c. 914-?	Mahipāla
n.d.	Mihira Bhoja II
n.d.	Vinayakapāla
c. 946-c. 948	Mahendrapāla II
c. 948-c. 960	Devapāla
c. 960-?	Vijayapāla

Reign	Ruler
n.d.	Rājyapāla
c. 1018-c. 1027	Trilocanapāla

THE CŌLAS

Reign	Ruler
c. 850-c. 870	Vijayālaya
871-907	Āditya I
907-955	Parāntaka I
956	Arinjayā
956	Parāntaka II
956-969	Āditya II
969-985	Madhurantaka Uttama
985-1014	Rājarāja I
1014-1044	Rājendracōla Deva I
1044-1052	Rājadhirāja I
1052-1060	Rājendracōla Deva II
1060-1063	Ramamahendra
1063-1067	Virarājendra
1067-1070	Adhirājendra
1070-1122	Rājendra III
1122-1135	Vikrama Cōla
1135-1150	Kulottuṅga II Cōla
1150-1173	Rājarāja II
1173-1179	Rājadhirāja II
1179-1218	Kulottuṅga III
1218-1246	Rājarāja III
1246-1279	Rājendra IV

DELHI SULTANATE

Muʿizzī Slave Sultans

Reign	Ruler
1206-1210	Quṭ al-Dīn Aybak
1210-1211	Ārām Shāh
1211-1236	Iltutmish
1236	Ruknuddin Firūz Shāh
1236-1240	Raziya
1240-1242	Bahrām Shāh
1242-1246	Masʿūd Shāh
1246-1266	Maḥmūd Shāh
1266-1287	Balban Ulugh Khān
1287-1290	Kay Qubādh
1290	Kayūmarth

Khaljī Dynasty

Reign	Ruler
1290-1296	Jalāl-ud-Dīn Fīrūz Khaljī
1296-1316	ʿAlāʾ-ud-Dīn Muḥammad Khaljī
1316	ʿUmar Shāh
1316-1320	Mubārak Shāh
1320	Khusraw Khān Barwārī

Tughluq Dynasty

Reign	Ruler
1320-1325	Tughluq I (Ghiyās-ud-Dīn)
1325-1351	Muḥammad ibn Tughluq
1351-1388	Fīrūz III
1388-1389	Tughluq II (Ghiyās-ud-Dīn)
1389-1390	Abū Bakr
1390-1394	Nāṣir-ud-Dīn
1394	Sikandar I (Humayun Khān)
1394-1395	Maḥmūd II
1395-1399	Nuṣrat
1401-1412	Maḥmūd II (second rule)
1412-1414	Dawlat Khān Lōdī

Sayyid Dynasty

Reign	Ruler
1414-1421	Khiḍr
1421-1434	Mubārak II
1434-1443	Muḥammad IV
1443-1451	ʿĀlām

Lodī Dynasty

Reign	Ruler
1451-1489	Bahlūl
1489-1517	Sikandar II
1517-1526	Ibrāhīm II

MUGHAL EMPERORS

Reign	Ruler
1526-1530	Bābur
1530-1540	Humāyūn
1540-1545	Shīr Shāh Sūr
1545-1553	Islām Shāh Sūr
1554	Muḥammad V Mubāriz Khān
1554-1555	Ibrāhām III Khān
1555	Aḥmad Khān Sikandar Shāh III
1555-1556	Humāyūn (second rule)
1556-1605	Akbar I
1605-1627	Jahāngīr
1627-1628	Dāwar Bakhsh
1628-1657	Jahān I Khusraw
1658-1707	Aurangzeb (Awrangzīb ʿĀlamgīr I)
1707-1712	ʿĀlam I Bahādur
1712-1713	Jahāndār Muʿizz al-Dīn
1713-1719	Farrukh-siyar
1719	Shams al-Dīn Rāfʿ al-Darajāt
1719	Jahān II Rāfiʿ al-Dawla
1719	Nīkūsiyar Muḥammad
1719-1720	Muḥammad Shāh Nāṣir al-Dīn
1720	Mohammed Ibrahim
1720-1748	Muḥammad Shāh Nāṣir al-Dīn
1739	Nādir Shāh sacks Delhi
1748-1754	Aḥmad Shāh Bahadur
1754-1779	Alamgir II

Reign	Ruler
1760?	Shāh Jahān III
1779-1806	Shāh Alam II
1806-1837	Akbar Shāh II
1837-1857	Bahadur Shāh II (Bahadur Shāh Zafar)

IRAN (PERSIA). *See also* ISLAMIC CALIPHS, OTTOMAN EMPIRE, SELJUK EMPIRE

LATER SĀSĀNIAN EMPIRE

Reign	Ruler
309-379	Shāpūr II
379-383	Ardashīr II
383-388	Shāpūr III
388-399	Barham (Varahran) IV
399-421	Yazdegerd (Yazdgard) I
421-439	Barham (Varahran) V
439-457	Yazdegerd (Yazdgard) II
457-459	Hormizd III
459-484	Peroz
484-488	Valash
488-496	Kavadh I
496-498	Zamasp
499-531	Kavadh I (restored)
531-579	Khosrow (Khusro or Chosroes) I
579-590	Hormizd IV
590-628	Khosrow (Khusro or Chosroes) II
628	Kavadh II
628-629	Ardashīr III
629-630	Boran
630-632	Hormizd V and Khosrow III
633-651	Yazdegerd (Yazdgard) III
651	Islamic conquest
651-656	ʿUthmān ibn ʿAffān
656-661	Alī ibn Abī Ṭālib
661-750	Umayyad caliphs (*see* Islamic Caliphs)
750-821	ʿAbbāsid caliphs (*see* Islamic Caliphs)

LATER IRANIAN DYNASTIES

Dates	Dynasty
821-873	Tāhirid Dynasty (in Khorāsān, northeastern Persia)
c. 866-c. 900	Ṣafārrid Dynasty
c. 940-1000	Sīmjūrid Dynasty (in Khorāsān)
945-1055	Būyid Dynasty (western Iran)
977-1186	Ghaznavid Dynasty (in Khorāsān, Afghanistan, northern India)
999-1211	Qarakhanid Dynasty (Transoxania)
c. 1038	Seljuks take power (*see* Seljuk Empire)
1153-1231	Khwārezm-Shāh Dynasty (in Khwārezm, northeastern Iran)

Dates	Dynasty
c. 1231	Mongol invasion
1256-1353	Il-Khanid (Mongol) Dynasty
1353-1393	Mozaffarid Dynasty
1393-c. 1467	Timurid Dynasty
c. 1467-1500	Turkmen/Ottoman incursions

ṢAFAVID DYNASTY

Reign	Ruler
1501-1524	Ismāʿīl I
1524-1576	Ṭahmāsp I
1576-1578	Ismāʿīl II
1578-1587	Muḥammad Khudabanda
1587-1629	ʿAbbās I
1629-1642	Safi
1642-1667	ʿAbbās II
1667-1694	Süleyman I
1694-1722	Ḥoseyn I
1722-1732	Ṭahmāsp II
1732-1736	ʿAbbās III
1736-1750	Afshāid shahs
1750	Süleyman II in Mashad
1750-1765	Ismāʿīl III (Karim Khān, regent 1751-1765)

AFSHĀR DYNASTY

Reign	Ruler
1736-1747	Nāder Shāh (regent)
1747	ʿĀdel Shāh
1748	Ibrāhim
1748-1750	Shāh Rukh
1755-1796	Shāh Rukh in Khorāsān
1796-1803	Nāder Mīrza in Mashad

ZAND DYNASTY (WESTERN IRAN)

Reign	Ruler
1750-1779	Karim Khān
1779	Abu'l Fath (Shirāz)
1779	Moḥammad ʿAlī (Shirāz)
1779-1781	Moḥammad Ṣādiq (Shirāz)
1781-1785	ʿAlī Morād (Eṣfahān)
1785-1789	Ja'far (Eṣfahān, later Shirāz)
1789-1794	Luṭf ʿAlī (Shirāz)
1796	Qajar Dynasty begins

QAJAR DYNASTY

Reign	Ruler
1796-1797	Agha Moḥammad (1794, southern Persia; 1796, Khorāsān)
1797-1834	Fatḥ ʿAlī
1834-1848	Moḥammad
1848-1896	Nāser ad-Din
1896-1907	Muẓaffar ad-Din

Reign	Ruler
1907-1909	Moḥammad ʿAlī
1909-1925	Aḥmad

PAHLAVI DYNASTY

Reign	Ruler
1925-1941	Reẓā Shāh
1941-1979	Moḥammad Reẓā
1979	Exile of Moḥammad Reẓā
1979	Ayatollāh Khomeini declares Islamic Republic of Iran

PRESIDENTS OF IRAN

Term	President
1980-1981	Abolhassan Banisadr (impeached)
1981	Mohammad Ali Rajai (assassinated)
1981-1989	Ali Khamenei (Supreme Leader as of June 4, 1989)
1989-1997	Ali Akbar Hashemi Rafsanjani
1997-2005	Mohammad Khatami
2005-	Mahmoud Ahmadinejad

IRELAND

THE HIGH-KINGS

Reign	Ruler
379-405	Niall Noígillach of the Nine Hostages
405-428	Dathi (Nath) I
429-463	Lóeguire MacNéill
456-493	Saint Patrick converts Irish
463-483	Ailill Motl MacNath I
483-507	Lugaid MacLóeguiri O'Néill
507-534	Muirchertach MacErcae O'Néill (Muiredach)
534-544	Tuathal Máelgarb MacCorpri Cáech O'Néill
544-565	Diarmait MacCerbaill O'Néill
565-566	Domnall MacMuirchertaig O'Néill and Forggus MacMuirchertaig O'Néill
566-569	Ainmere MacSátnai O'Néill
569-572	Báetán MacMuirchertaig O'Néill and Eochaid MacDomnaill O'Néill
572-581	Báetán MacNinnedo O'Néill
581-598	Aed MacAinmerech O'Néill
598-604	Aed Sláine MacDiarmato O'Néill
598-604	Colmán Rímid MacBáetáin O'Néill (rival)
604-612	Aed Uaridnach MacDomnaill O'Néill
612-615	Máel Cobo MacAedo O'Néill
615-628	Suibne Menn MacFiachnai O'Néill
628-642	Domnall MacAedo O'Néill
642-658	Conall Cóel MacMáele Cobo O'Néill and Cellach MacMáele Cobo O'Néill
656-665	Diarmait MacAedo Sláine O'Néill and Blathmac MacAedo Sláine O'Néill

Reign	Ruler
665-671	Sechnussach MacBlathmaic O'Néill
671-675	Cenn Fáelad MacBlathmaic O'Néill
675-695	Finsnechtae Fledach MacDúnchada O'Néill
695-704	Loingsech MacOengus O'Néill
704-710	Congal Cinn Magir MacFergus Fánat O'Néill
710-722	Fergal MacMáele Dúin O'Néill
722-724	Fogartach MacNéill O'Néill
724-728	Cináed MacIrgalaig
724-734	Flaithbbertach MacLoingsig O'Néill
734-743	Aed Allán MacFergal O'Néill
743-763	Domnall Midi O'Néill
763-770	Niall Frossach MacFergal O'Néill
770-797	Donnchad Midi MacDomnaill Midi O'Néill
797-819	Aed Oirdnide MacNéill Frossach O'Néill
819-833	Conchobar MacDonnchado Midi O'Néill
833-846	Niall Caille MacAedo Oirdnide O'Néill
846-862	Máel Sechnaill MacMáele Ruanaid O'Néill
862-879	Aed Findliath MacNéill Caille O'Néill
879-916	Flann Sionna MacMáele Sechnaill O'Néill
916-919	Niall Glúndubh MacAedo Findliath O'Néill
919-944	Donnchad Donn MacFlann O'Néill
944-950	Ruaidrí ua Canannáin (rival)
944-956	Congalach Cnogba MacMáel Mithig O'Néill
956-980	Domnall MacMuirchertaig O'Néill
980-1002	Máel Sechnaill MacDomnaill O'Néill
1002-1014	Brian Bóruma MacCennétig and Brian Boru
1014-1022	Máel Sechnaill MacDomnaill O'Néill (restored)
1022-1064	Donnchad MacBrian
1064-1072	Diarmait MacMáil na mBó
1072-1086	Toirdelbach O'Brien
1090-1121	Domnall MacArdgar O'Lochlainn O'Néill
1121-1135	Toirrdelbach MacRuaidrí na Saide Buide ua Conchobair (Turlogh)
1141-1150	Toirrdelbach MacRuaidrí na Saide Buide ua Conchobair (Turlogh)
1150-1166	Muirchertach MacNéill MacLochlainn (Murtagh)
1166-1175	Ruaidrí MacToirrdelbaig (Rory O'Connor)
1175-1258	Henry II of England claims title Lord of Ireland
1258-1260	Brian Catha an Duin
1260-1316	English rule restored
1316-1318	Edward de Bruce
1318	English rule restored
1801	Act of Union: Ireland is joined with Britain

KINGDOM OF IRELAND (WITH ENGLAND/GREAT BRITAIN)

Reign	Ruler
1509-1547	Henry VIII
1547-1553	Edward VI

Reign	Ruler
1553-1558	Mary I
1558-1603	Elizabeth I
1603-1625	James (I of England, VI of Scotland)
1625-1649	Charles I
1649-1660	Commonwealth and Restoration
1660-1685	Charles II
1685-1689	James (II of England, VII of Scotland)
1689-1702	William and Mary
1702-1707	Anne
1707	Act of Union (Great Britain and Ireland)
1707-1714	Anne
1714-1727	George I
1727-1760	George II
1760-1801	George III
1801	Act of Union creates United Kingdom

UNITED KINGDOM OF GREAT BRITAIN AND IRELAND

Reign	Ruler
1801-1820	George III
1820-1830	George IV
1830-1837	William IV
1837-1901	Victoria
1901-1910	Edward VII
1910-1936	George V
1922	Irish Free State leaves United Kingdom

IRISH FREE STATE (ÉIRE)

Reign	Ruler
1922-1936	George V
1936	Edward VIII
1936-1949	George VI

REPUBLIC OF IRELAND, NORTHERN IRELAND

Reign	Ruler
1949-1952	George VI
1952-	Elizabeth II

ISLAMIC CALIPHS. *See also* IRAN, OTTOMAN EMPIRE, SELJUK EMPIRE, SPAIN

ORTHODOX (SUNNI) CALIPHS, 632-661

Reign	Caliph
632-634	Abū Bakr
634-644	ʿUmar I
644-656	ʿUthmān ibn ʿAffān
656-661	Alī ibn Abī Ṭālib

UMAYYAD CALIPHS, 661-750

Reign	Caliph
661-680	Muʾāwiyah I (Muʾāwiyah ibn Abī Sufyna)
680-683	Yazīd I

Reign	Caliph
683	Mu³āwiyah II
684-685	Marwān I
685-705	ʿAbd al-Malik
705-715	al-Walīd I
715-717	Sulaimān
717-720	ʿUmar II
720-724	Yazīd II
724-743	Hishām
743-744	al-Walīd II
744	Yazīd III
744	Ibrāhīm
744-750	Marwān II

ʿABBĀSID CALIPHS, 750-1256

Reign	Caliph
750-754	Abū al-ʿAbbās al-Saffāḥ
754-775	al-Manṣūr
775-785	al-Mahdī
785-786	al-Hādī
786-809	Hārūn al-Rashīd
809-813	al-Amīn
813-833	al-Maʾmūn (Maʾmūn the Great)
833-842	al-Muʿtaṣim
842-847	al-Wathīq
847-861	al-Mutawakkil
861-862	al-Muntaṣir
862-866	al-Mustaʿin
866-869	al-Muʿtazz
869-870	al-Muqtadī
870-892	al-Muʿtamid
892-902	al-Muʿtaḍid
902-908	al-Muktafī
908-932	al-Muqtadir
932-934	al-Qāhir
934-940	al-Rāḍī
940-944	al-Mustaqfī
946-974	al-Mutī
974-991	al-Ṭāʾiʿ
991-1031	al-Qadir
1031-1075	al-Qāʾim
1075-1094	al-Muqtadī
1094-1118	al-Mustazhir
1118-1135	al-Mustarshid
1135-1136	al-Rashīd
1136-1160	al-Muqtafī
1160-1170	al-Mustanjid
1170-1180	al-Mustadī
1180-1225	al-Nāṣir
1225-1226	al-Zāhir
1226-1242	al-Mustanṣir
1242-1256	al-Mustaʿṣim

FĀṬIMID CALIPHS, 909-1171

Reign	Caliph
909-934	al-Mahdī
934-945	al-Qāʾim
945-952	al-Manṣūr
952-975	al-Muʿizz
975-996	al-ʿAzīz
996-1021	al-Ḥākim
1021-1036	al-Zahīr
1036-1094	al-Mustanṣir
1094-1101	al-Mustadī
1101-1130	al-Amīr
1130-1149	al-Ḥāfiz
1149-1154	al-Zafīr
1154-1160	al-Fāʾiz
1160-1171	al-ʿAdīd

ITALY

The Italian peninsula was occupied by a number of fiefs and principalities during the better part of the millennium that made up the Middle Ages. These included Lombardy in the north, the Papal States in the center, and various duchies, margavates, and republics, including Sardinia, Benevento, Spoleto, Modena, Milan, Tuscany, Parma, Montferrat, and independent centers of trade such as Venice and Genoa. Only those early rulers who dominated the area are listed below; thereafter, the northern part of the peninsula was primarily under the power of the Carolingians (see Frankish Kingdom and France), the Holy Roman Emperors (see Holy Roman Empire, above), and the Papacy (see Popes and Antipopes, above). In the south, Naples and Sicily dominated. Thus, during the millennium 476-1453, the Italian Peninsula was a complex of ever-shifting jurisdictions, of which only the more prominent rulers are listed below.

BARBARIAN RULERS

Reign	Ruler
476-493	Odoacer
493-526	Theodoric
526-534	Athalaric
534-536	Theodatus (Theodahad)
536-540	Vitiges (Witiges)
540-541	Theodobald (Heldebadus)
541	Eraric
541-552	Totila
552-553	Teias

BYZANTINE (EAST ROMAN) RULE

Reign	Ruler
518-527	Justin I
527-565	Justinian I

LOMBARDS (NORTHERN ITALY)

Reign	Ruler
565-572	Alboin
573-575	Celph
575-584	Unstable
584-590	Authari
590-591	Theodelinda
591-615	Agilulf
615-625	Adaloald
625-636	Arioald
636-652	Rotharis
652-661	Aribert I
661-662	Godipert
662-671	Grimoald
671-674	Garibald
674-688	Bertharit
688-700	Cunibert
700-701	Liutpert
701	Raginpert
701-712	Aribert II
712-744	Liutprand
744-749	Rachis of Friuli
749-756	Aistulf of Friuli
756-774	Desiderius
774-888	Frankish conquest, subsumed under Carolingian Empire

KINGDOM OF ITALY

Reign	Ruler
888-891	Berengar I of Friuli
891-894	Guy of Spoleto (Guido, Wido)
894-896	Lambert of Spoleto
896-899	Arnulf, King of Germany
899-905	Louis III
905-922	Berengar I of Friuli (restored)
922-933	Rudolf II
933-947	Hugh of Arles
947-950	Lothair II of Arles
950-961	Berengar II of Ivrea
961	Conquest by Otto I; Italian peninsula divided among Holy Roman Empire, Papacy, and other principalities until unification in 1861

NAPLES AND SICILY

Reign	Ruler (Line)
1042-1046	William Iron Arm (Norman)
1046-1051	Drogo (Norman)
1051-1057	Humphrey (Norman)

Reign	Ruler (Line)
1057-1085	Robert Guiscard (Norman)
1071-1101	Roger I (Norman)
1101-1154	Roger II of Sicily (Norman; king in 1130)
1154-1166	William I (Norman)
1166-1189	William II the Good (Norman)
1190-1194	Tancred of Lecce (Norman)
1194	William III (Norman)
1194-1197	Henry VI (Hohenstaufen)
1197-1250	Frederick II (Hohenstaufen)
1250-1254	Conrad IV (Hohenstaufen)
1250-1266	Manfred (Hohenstaufen)
1267-1268	Conradin (rival)
1266-1285	Charles I of Anjou (Angevin)
1282	Sicily and Naples split

SICILY

Reign	Ruler
1282-1285	Pedro III of Aragón
1285-1296	James II of Aragón
1296-1337	Frederick II (or I)
1337-1342	Peter II
1342-1355	Louis
1355-1377	Frederick III (or II) the Simple
1377-1401	Mary
1390-1409	Martin the Younger
1395-1410	Martin (I) the Older of Aragón
1412-1416	Ferdinand I of Sicily & Aragón
1416-1458	Alfonso (V of Aragón)
1458-1468	John II
1468-1516	Ferdinand II (III of Naples)
1516-1713	United with Spain
1713-1720	Victor Amadeus II (duke of Savoy)
1720	Returned to Spain as part of Kingdom of the Two Sicilies
1720-1735	Austrian rule
1735-1759	Charles (Bourbon king of Spain)
1759-1825	Ferdinand I/IV
1825-1830	Francis I
1830-1859	Ferdinand II/V
1859-1860	Francis II
1861	Annexed to Italy

NAPLES

Reign	Ruler
1285-1309	Charles II (Angevin)
1309-1343	Robert Ladislas (Angevin)
1343-1382	Joanna I (Angevin)
1382-1386	Charles III (Angevin)
1386-1414	Ladislas (Angevin)
1414-1435	Joanna II (Angevin)
1435-1442	René of Anjou
1442-1458	Alfonso I (V of Aragón)

Reign	Ruler
1458-1494	Ferdinand I
1494-1495	Alfonso II (Naples only)
1495-1496	Ferdinand II (Ferrandino)
1496-1501	Frederick IV (III)
1501-1503	French occupation
1504-1516	Ferdinand III (II of Sicily)
1516-1713	United with Spain
1713	Ceded to Austria
1720	Returned to Spain as part of the Kingdom of the Two Sicilies
1799	Parthenopean Republic
1805	Bourbons deposed
1806-1808	Joseph Bonaparte
1808-1815	Joachim Murat
1815	Bourbon restoration
1825-1830	Francis I
1830-1859	Ferdinand II/V
1859-1860	Francis II
1861	Annexed to Italy

VISCONTIS (GENOA)

Reign	Ruler
1310-1322	Matteo Visconti
1322-1328	Galeazzo I
1328-1339	Azzo
1339-1349	Lucchino
1349-1354	Giovanni
1354-1355	Matteo II and Bernabò
1354-1378	Galeazzo II
1378-1402	Gian Galeazzo II
1402-1447	Filippo Maria

SFORZAS (GENOA)

Reign	Ruler
1450-1466	Francesco Sforza
1466-1476	Galeazzo Maria
1476-1481	Gian Galeazzo
1481-1499	Ludovico
1500-1512	[Louis XII of France]
1512-1515	Massimiliano
1521-1535	Francesco Maria

DOGES OF VENICE

Reign	Doge
727-738	Orso (Ursus) Ipato
742, 744-736	Teodato (Deusdedit) Ipato
756	Galla Gaulo
756-765	Domenico Monegaurio
765-787	Maurizio I Galbaio
787-802	Giovanni and Maurizio II Galbaio
802-811	Obelerio Antenorio
808-811	Beato

Reign	Doge
811-827	Angello Partecipazio
827-829	Giustiniano Partecipazio
829-836	Giovanni I Partecipazio
836-864	Pietro Tradonico
864-881	Orso I Badoer (I Partecipazio)
881-888	Giovanni Badoer (II Partecipazio)
887	Pietro I Candiano
888-912	Pietro Tribuno
912-932	Orso II Badoer (II Partecipazio)
932-939	Pietro II Candiano
939-942	Pietro Badoer (Partecipazio)
942-959	Pietro III Candiano
959-976	Pietro IV Candiano
976-978	Pietro I Orseolo
978-979	Vitale Candiano
979-991	Tribuno Menio (Memmo)
991-1009	Pietro II Orseolo
1009-1026	Ottone Orseolo
1026-1030	Pietro Centranico (Barbolano)
1030-1032	Ottone Orseolo (second rule)
1032-1043	Domenico Flabianico
1043-1070	Domenico Contarini
1070-1084	Domenico Silvio (Selvo)
1084-1096	Vitale Falier
1096-1101	Vitale I Michiel (Michel)
1101-1118	Ordelafo Falier
1118-1129	Domenico Michiel
1129-1148	Pietro Polani
1148-1155	Domenico Morosini
1155-1172	Vitale II Michiel
1172-1178	Sebastiano Ziani
1178-1192	Orio Mastropiero (Malipiero)
1192-1205	Enrico Dandolo
1205-1229	Pietro Ziani
1229-1249	Giacomo Tiepolo
1249-1253	Marino Morosini
1253-1268	Reniero Zeno
1268-1275	Lorenzo Tiepolo
1275-1280	Jacopo Contarini
1280-1289	Giovanni Dandolo
1289-1311	Pietro Gradenigo
1311-1312	Marino Zorzi
1312-1328	Giovanni Soranzo
1328-1339	Francesco Dandolo
1339-1342	Bartolomeo Gradenigo
1343-1354	Andrea Dandolo
1354-1355	Marino Falier
1355-1356	Giovanni Gradenigo
1356-1361	Giovanni Dolfin
1361-1365	Lorenzo Celsi
1365-1368	Marco Corner
1368-1382	Andrea Contarini

Reign	Doge
1382	Michele Morosini
1382-1400	Antonio Venier
1400-1413	Michele Steno
1414-1423	Tommaso Mocenigo
1423-1457	Francesco Foscari
1462-1471	Cristoforo Moro
1471-1473	Nicolò Tron
1473-1474	Nicolò Marcello
1474-1476	Pietro Mocenigo
1476-1478	Andrea Vendramin
1478-1485	Giovanni Mocenigo
1485-1486	Marco Barbarigo
1486-1501	Agostino Barbarigo
1501-1521	Leonardo Loredan
1521-1523	Antonio Grimani
1523-1538	Andrea Gritti
1539-1545	Pietro Lando
1545-1553	Francesco Donato
1553-1554	Marcantonio Trevisan
1554-1556	Francesco Venier
1556-1559	Lorenzo Priuli
1559-1567	Girolamo Priuli
1567-1570	Pietro Loredan
1570-1577	Alvise I Mocenigo
1577-1578	Sebastiano Venier
1578-1585	Nicolò da Ponte
1585-1595	Pasquale Cicogna
1595-1605	Marino Grimani
1606-1612	Leonardo Donato
1612-1615	Marcantonio Memmo
1615-1618	Giovanni Bembo
1618	Nicolò Donato
1618-1623	Antonio Priuli
1623-1624	Francesco Contarini
1625-1629	Giovanni Corner
1630-1631	Nicolò Contarini
1631-1646	Francesco Erizzo
1646-1655	Francesco Molin
1655-1656	Carlo Contarini
1656	Francesco Corner
1656-1658	Bertucci (Albertuccio) Valier
1658-1659	Giovanni Pesaro
1659-1675	Domenico Contarini
1675-1676	Nicolò Sagredo
1676-1684	Luigi Contarini
1684-1688	Marcantonio Giustinian
1688-1694	Francesco Morosini
1694-1700	Silvestro Valier
1700-1709	Alvise II Mocenigo
1709-1722	Giovanni II Corner
1722-1732	Alvise III Mocenigo
1732-1735	Carlo Ruzzini

Reign	Doge
1735-1741	Alvise Pisani
1741-1752	Pietro Grimani
1752-1762	Francesco Loredan
1762-1763	Marco Foscarini
1763-1778	Alvise IV Mocenigo
1779-1789	Paolo Renier
1789-1797	Lodovico Manin
1797	Venice Falls to Napoleon Bonaparte

FLORENCE (MEDICIS)

Reign	Ruler
1434-1464	Cosimo the Elder
1464-1469	Piero I
1469-1478	Giuliano
1469-1492	Lorenzo I the Magnificent
1492-1494	Piero II
1494-1512	Charles VIII expels the Medici
1512-1519	Lorenzo II
1519-1527	Giulio (Pope Clement VII)
1527	Sack of Rome
1527-1530	Second expulsion
1530-1537	Alessandro
1537-1574	Cosimo I
1574-1587	Francesco I
1587-1609	Ferdinand I
1609-1621	Cosimo II
1621-1670	Ferdinand II
1670-1723	Cosimo III
1723-1737	Gian Gastone

TUSCANY (AFTER THE MEDICIS)

Reign	Ruler
1738-1745	Francis
1745-1790	Leopold I
1790-1801	Ferdinand III
1801-1803	Louis of Parma (king of Etruria)
1803-1807	Charles Louis of Parma
1803-1807	Maria Louisa of Parma (regent)
1807-1814	Annexed to France
1824-1859	Leopold II
1859-1860	Ferdinand IV
1860	Annexed to Italy

PARMA

Farneses

Reign	Ruler
1545-1547	Pier Luigi
1547-1586	Ottavio
1586-1592	Alessandro
1592-1622	Ranuccio I
1622-1646	Odoardo I

Reign	Ruler
1646-1694	Ranuccio II
1694-1727	Francesco
1727-1731	Antonio

Bourbons

Reign	Ruler
1731-1736	Charles
1738-1748	Habsburg rule
1748-1765	Philip
1765-1802	Ferdinand
1805-1814	French rule
1814-1847	Marie Louise (Habsburg)
1848-1849	Charles II Louis
1849-1854	Charles III
1854-1859	Robert
1859	Annexed to Italy

SARDINIA

Reign	Ruler
1720-1730	Victor Amadeus II (duke of Savoy)
1730-1773	Charles Emanuel III
1773-1796	Victor Amadeus III
1796-1802	Charles Emanuel IV
1802-1821	Victor Emanuel I
1821-1831	Charles Felix
1831-1849	Charles Albert
1849-1861	Victor Emanuel II
1861	Annexed to Italy

KINGDOM OF ITALY

Reign	Ruler
1861-1878	Victor Emanuel II
1878-1900	Umberto I
1900-1946	Victor Emanuel III
1922-1943	Benito Mussolini (dictator)
1943-1945	German occupation
1946	Umberto II

MODERN ITALY: PRIME MINISTERS

Term	Prime Minister
1860-1861	Count Camillo Benso di Cavour
1861-1862	Baron Bettino Ricasoli
1862	Urbano Ratazzi
1862-1864	Marco Minghetti
1864-1866	General Alfonso La Marmora
1866-1867	Baron Bettino Ricasoli
1867	Urbano Ratazzi
1867-1869	Federigo Menabrea
1869-1873	Domenico Lanza
1873-1876	Marco Minghetti
1876-1878	Agostino Depretis
1878	Benedetto Cairoli

Term	Prime Minister
1878-1879	Agostino Depretis
1879-1881	Benedetto Cairoli
1881-1887	Agostino Depretis
1887-1891	Francesco Crispi
1891-1892	Marquis di Rudini
1892-1893	Giovanni Giolitti
1893-1896	Francesco Crispi
1896-1898	Marquis de Rudini
1898-1900	General Luigi Pelloux
1900-1901	Giuseppe Saracco
1901-1903	Giuseppe Zanardelli
1903-1906	Giovanni Giolitti
1906	Baron Sidney Sonnino
1906-1909	Giovanni Giolitti
1909-1910	Baron Sidney Sonnino
1910-1911	Luigi Luzzatti
1911-1914	Giovanni Giolitti
1914-1916	Antonio Salandra
1916-1917	Paolo Boselli
1917-1919	Vittorio Orlando
1919-1920	Francesco Nitti
1920-1921	Giovanni Giolitti
1921-1922	Ivanoe Bonomi
1922	Luigi Facta
1922-1943	Benito Mussolini
1943-1944	Marshal Pietro Badoglio
1944-1945	Ivanoe Bonomi
1945	Ferruccio Parri
1945-1953	Alcide De Gasperi
1953-1954	Giuseppe Pella
1954-1955	Mario Scelba
1955-1957	Antonio Segni
1957-1958	Adone Zoli
1958-1959	Amintore Fanfani
1959-1960	Antonio Segni
1960	Fernando Tambroni-Armaroli
1960-1963	Amintore Fanfani
1963	Giovanni Leone
1963-1968	Aldo Moro
1968	Giovanni Leone
1968-1970	Mariano Rumor
1970-1972	Emilio Colombo
1972-1973	Giulio Andreotti
1973-1974	Mariano Rumor
1974-1976	Aldo Moro
1976-1979	Giulio Andreotti
1979-1980	Francesco Cossiga
1980-1981	Arnaldo Forlani
1981-1982	Giovanni Spadolini
1982-1983	Amintore Fanfani
1983-1987	Bettino Craxi
1987	Amintore Fanfani

Term	Prime Minister
1987-1988	Giovanni Goria
1988-1989	Ciriaco De Mita
1989-1992	Giulio Andreotti
1992-1993	Giuliano Amato
1993-1994	Carlo Azeglio Ciampi
1994-1995	Silvio Berlusconi
1995-1996	Lamberto Dini
1996-1998	Romano Prodi
1998-2000	Massimo D'Alema
2000-2001	Giuliano Amato
2001-2006	Silvio Berlusconi
2006-	Romano Prodi

MODERN ITALY: PRESIDENTS

Term	President
1946-1948	Enrico de Nicola
1948-1955	Luigi Einaudi
1955-1962	Giovanni Gronchi
1962-1964	Antonio Segni
1964-1971	Giuseppe Saragat
1971-1978	Giovanni Leone
1978-1985	Alessandro Pertini
1985-1992	Francesco Cossiga
1992	Giovanni Spadolini
1992-1999	Oscar Luigi Scalfaro
1999	Nicola Mancino
1999-2006	Carlo Azeglio Ciampi
2006-	Giorgio Napolitano

JAPAN

ASUKA PERIOD

Reign	Ruler
539-571	Kimmei
572-585	Bidatsu
585-587	Yōmei
587-592	Sushun
593-628	Suiko (empress)
629-641	Jomei
642-645	Kōgyoku (empress)
645-654	Kōtoku
655-661	Saimei (empress)
661-672	Tenji
672	Kōbun
673-686	Temmu
686-697	Jitō (empress)
697-707	Mommu
707-715	Gemmei (empress)

NARA PERIOD

Reign	Ruler
707-715	Gemmei (empress)
715-724	Genshō (empress)
724-749	Shōmu
749-758	Kōken (empress)
758-764	Junnin
764-770	Shōtoku (Kōken, empress)
770-781	Kōnin

HEIAN PERIOD

Reign	Ruler
781-806	Kammu
806-809	Heizei
809-823	Saga
823-833	Junna
833-850	Nimmyō
850-858	Montoku
858-876	Seiwa
876-884	Yōzei
884-887	Kōkō
887-897	Uda
897-930	Daigo
930-946	Suzaku
946-967	Murakami
967-969	Reizei
969-984	En'yu
984-986	Kazan
986-1011	Ichijō
1011-1016	Sanjō
1016-1036	Go-Ichijō
1036-1045	Go-Suzaku
1045-1068	Go-Reizei
1068-1073	Go-Sanjō
1073-1087	Shirakawa (cloistered, 1086-1129)
1087-1107	Horikawa
1107-1123	Toba (cloistered, 1129-1156)
1123-1142	Sutoku
1142-1155	Konoe
1155-1158	Go-Shirakawa (cloistered, 1158-1192)
1158-1165	Nijō
1165-1168	Rokujō
1168-1180	Takakura
1180-1185	Antoku

KAMAKURA PERIOD AND KEMMU RESTORATION

Reign	Ruler
1183-1198	Go-Toba
1198-1210	Tsuchimikado
1210-1221	Jintoku
1221	Chukyo
1221-1232	Go-Horikawa
1232-1242	Shijō

Reign	Ruler
1242-1246	Go-Saga
1246-1260	Go-Fukakusa
1260-1274	Kameyama
1274-1287	Go-Uda
1287-1298	Fushimi
1298-1301	Go-Fushimi
1301-1308	Go-Nijō
1308-1318	Hanazonō
1318-1339	Go-Daigo

KAMAKURA SHOGUNATE

Reign	Shogun
1192-1199	Minamoto Yoritomo
1202-1203	Minamoto Yoriie
1203-1219	Minamoto Sanetomo
1226-1244	Kujo Yoritsune
1244-1252	Kujo Yoritsugu
1252-1266	Prince Munetaka
1266-1289	Prince Koreyasu
1289-1308	Prince Hisaaki
1308-1333	Prince Morikuni

HŌJŌ REGENTS

Reign	Regent
1203-1205	Hōjō Tokimasa
1205-1224	Hōjō Yoshitoki
1224-1242	Hōjō Yasutoki
1242-1246	Hōjō Tsunetoki
1246-1256	Hōjō Tokiyori
1256-1264	Hōjō Nagatoki
1264-1268	Hōjō Masamura
1268-1284	Hōjō Tokimune
1284-1301	Hōjō Sadatoki
1301-1311	Hōjō Morotoki
1311-1312	Hōjō Munenobu
1312-1315	Hōjō Hirotoki
1315	Hōjō Mototoki
1316-1326	Hōjō Takatoki
1326	Hōjō Sadaaki
1327-1333	Hōjō Moritoki

NAMBOKUCHŌ PERIOD

Emperors: Southern Court

Reign	Ruler
1318-1339	Go-Daigo
1339-1368	Go-Murakami
1368-1383	Chōkei
1383-1392	Go-Kameyama

Ashikaga Pretenders: Northern Court

Reign	Ruler
1336-1348	Komyō
1348-1351	Sukō
1351-1371	Go-Kogon
1371-1382	Go-En'yu

MUROMACHI PERIOD

Reign	Ruler
1382-1412	Go-Komatsu
1412-1428	Shōkō
1428-1464	Go-Hanazono
1464-1500	Go-Tsuchimikado
1500-1526	Go-Kashiwabara
1526-1557	Go-Nara
1557-1586	Ōgimachi

ASHIKAGA SHOGUNATE

Reign	Shogun
1338-1358	Ashikaga Takauji
1359-1368	Ashikaga Yoshiakira
1368-1394	Ashikaga Yoshimitsu
1395-1423	Ashikaga Yoshimochi
1423-1425	Ashikaga Yoshikazu
1429-1441	Ashikaga Yoshinori
1442-1443	Ashikaga Yoshikatsu
1449-1473	Ashikaga Yoshimasa
1474-1489	Ashikaga Yoshihisa
1490-1493	Ashikaga Yoshitane
1495-1508	Ashikaga Yoshizumi
1508-1521	Ashikaga Yoshitane (second rule)
1522-1547	Ashikaga Yoshiharu
1547-1565	Ashikaga Yoshiteru
1568	Ashikaga Yoshihide
1568-1573	Ashikaga Yoshiaki

AZUCHI-MOMOYAMA PERIOD

Reign	Ruler
1573-1582	Oda Nobunaga (dictator)
1586-1611	Go-Yōzei (emperor)

EDO PERIOD

Emperors

Reign	Emperor
1612-1629	Go-Mi-no-o
1630-1643	Meishō (Myōshō)
1644-1654	Go-Kōmyō
1655-1662	Go-Saiin
1663-1686	Reigen
1687-1709	Higashiyama
1710-1735	Nakamikado
1736-1746	Sakuramachi
1746-1762	Momozono

Reign	Emperor
1763-1770	Go-Sakuramachi
1771-1779	Go-Momozono
1780-1816	Kōkaku
1817-1846	Ninkō
1847-1866	Kōmei

Tokugawa Shogunate

Reign	Shogun
1603-1605	Tokugawa Ieyasu
1605-1623	Tokugawa Hidetada
1623-1651	Tokugawa Iemitsu
1651-1680	Tokugawa Ietsuna
1680-1709	Tokugawa Tsunayoshi
1709-1712	Tokugawa Ienobu
1713-1716	Tokugawa Ietsugu
1716-1745	Tokugawa Yoshimune
1745-1760	Tokugawa Ieshige
1760-1786	Tokugawa Ieharu
1787-1837	Tokugawa Ienari
1837-1853	Tokugawa Ieyoshi
1853-1858	Tokugawa Iesada
1858-1866	Tokugawa Iemochi
1867-1868	Tokugawa Yoshinobu

MODERN PERIOD

Emperors

Reign	Emperor
1867-1912	Mutsuhito (crowned 1868; Meiji era)
1912-1926	Yoshihito (Taishō era)
1926-1989	Hirohito (Shōwa era)
1989	Akihito (Heisei era)

Prime Ministers

Term	Prime Minister
1885-1888	Itō Hirobumi
1888-1889	Kuroda Kiyotaka
1889-1891	Yamagata Aritomo
1891-1892	Matsukata Masayoshi
1892-1896	Itō Hirobumi
1896-1898	Matsukata Masayoshi
1898-1898	Itō Hirobumi
1898-1898	Okuma Shigenobu
1898-1900	Yamagata Aritomo
1900-1901	Itō Hirobumi
1901-1906	Katsura Tarō
1906-1908	Saionji Kimmochi
1908-1911	Katsura Tarō
1911-1912	Saionji Kimmochi
1912-1913	Katsura Tarō
1913-1914	Yamamoto Gonnohyōe
1914-1916	Okuma Shigenobu
1916-1918	Terauchi Masatake

Term	Prime Minister
1918-1921	Hara Takashi (assassinated)
1921-1922	Takahashi Korekiyo
1922-1923	Katō Tomosaburō
1923-1924	Yamamoto Gonnohyoe
1924-1924	Kiyoura Keigo
1924-1926	Katō Takaaki
1926-1927	Wakatsuki Reijirō
1927-1929	Tanaka Giichi
1929-1931	Hamaguchi Osachi (assassinated)
1931-1931	Wakatsuki Reijiro
1931-1932	Inukai Tsuyoshi (assassinated)
1932-1934	Saitō Makoto
1934-1936	Okada Keisuke
1936-1937	Hirota Kōki
1937-1937	Hayashi Senjūrō
1937-1939	Konoe Fumimaro
1939-1939	Hiranuma Kiichirō
1939-1940	Abe Nobuyuki
1940-1940	Yonai Mitsumasa
1940-1941	Konoe Fumimaro
1941-1944	Tōjō Hideki
1944-1945	Koiso Kuniaki
1945-1945	Suzuki Kantarō
1945-1945	Higashikuni Naruhiko
1945-1946	Shidehara Kijūrō
1946-1947	Yoshida Shigeru
1947-1948	Katayama Tetsu
1948-1948	Ashida Hitoshi
1948-1954	Yoshida Shigeru
1954-1956	Hatoyama Ichirō
1956-1957	Ishibashi Tanzan
1957-1960	Kishi Nobusuke
1960-1964	Ikeda Hayato
1964-1972	Satō Eisaku
1972-1974	Tanaka Kakuei
1974-1976	Miki Takeo
1976-1978	Fukuda Takeo
1978-1980	Ohira Masayoshi
1980-1982	Suzuki Zenko
1982-1987	Nakasone Yasuhiro
1987-1989	Takeshita Noboru
1989-1989	Uno Sosuke
1989-1991	Kaifu Toshiki
1991-1993	Miyazawa Kiichi
1993-1994	Hosokawa Morihiro
1994-1994	Hata Tsutomu
1994-1996	Murayama Tomiichi
1996-1998	Hashimoto Ryūtarō
1998-2000	Obuchi Keizō
2000-2001	Mori Yoshirō
2001-	Koizumi Junichiro

KINGDOM OF JERUSALEM

The Christian rulers of Jerusalem were ushered in by the First Crusade and essentially were ushered out after the last Crusade.

Reign	King
1095-1099	First Crusade
1099-1100	Godfrey of Boulogne (or Bouillon)
1100-1118	Baldwin I of Boulogne
1118-1131	Baldwin II of Le Bourg
1131-1153	Melisende
1131-1143	Fulk V of Anjou
1143-1162	Baldwin III
1147-1149	Second Crusade
1162-1174	Amalric I
1174-1183	Baldwin IV the Leper
1183-1186	Baldwin V
1185-1190	Sibylla
1186-1192	Guy of Lusignan
1189-1192	Third Crusade
1190-1192	Conrad of Montferrat
1192-1197	Henry of Champagne
1192-1205	Isabella I
1197-1205	Amalric II
1202-1204	Fourth Crusade
1205-1210	Maria of Montferrat (regent)
1210-1225	John of Brienne
1210-1228	Isabella (Yolanda) II
1217-1221	Fifth Crusade
1225-1228	Frederick II
1227-1230	Sixth Crusade
1228-1254	Conrad IV Hohenstaufen
1244	Fall of Jerusalem
1248-1254	Seventh (or Sixth) Crusade
1254-1268	Conradin Hohenstaufen
1268-1284	Hugh III
1268-1284	Charles of Anjou (rival)
1270	Eighth (or Seventh) Crusade
1284-1285	John I
1285-1306	Henry I of Jerusalem (II of Cyprus)
1291	Fall of Acre to the Mamluks

KOREA

UNIFIED SILLA DYNASTY

Reign	Ruler
661-681	Munmu Wang
681-692	Sinmun Wang
692-702	Hyoso Wang
702-737	Sŏngdŏk Wang
737-742	Hyosŏng Wang
742-765	Kyŏngdŏk Wang
765-780	Hyesong Wang
780-785	Sŏndŏk Wang
785-798	Wŏnsŏng Wang
798-800	Sosŏng Wang
800-809	Aejang Wang
809-826	Hŏndŏk Wang
826-836	Hŭngdŏk Wang
836-838	Hŭigang Wang
838-839	Minae Wang
839	Sinmu Wang
839-857	Munsŏng Wang
857-861	Hŏnan Wang
861-875	Kyŏngmun Wang
875-886	Hŏn'gang Wang
886-887	Chŏnggang Wang
887-896	Queen Chinsŏng
897-912	Hyogong Wang
912-917	Pak Sindŏ Wang
917-924	Kyŏngmyŏng Wang
924-927	Kyŏngae Wang
927-935	Kyŏngsun Wang

KORYŎ DYNASTY

Reign	Ruler
918-943	T'aejo (Wang Kŏn)
944-945	Hyejong
946-949	Chŏngjong
949-975	Kwangjong (Wang So)
975-981	Kyŏngjong (Wang Yu)
981-997	Sŏngjong (Wang Ch'i)
997-1009	Mokshong
1009-1031	Hyŏnjong
1031-1034	Tokjong
1034-1046	Chŏngjong
1046-1083	Munjong (Wang Hwi)
1083	Sunjong
1083-1094	Sŏnjong
1094-1095	Hŏnjong
1095-1105	Sukjong
1105-1122	Yejong I
1122-1146	Injong I (Wang Hae)
1146-1170	Ŭijong
1170-1197	Myŏngjong
1197-1204	Sinjong
1204-1211	Hŭijong
1211-1213	Kangjong
1214-1259	Kojong I
1260-1274	Wŏnjong
1274-1308	Ch'unguyŏl Wang
1308-1313	Ch'ungsŏn Wang
1313-1330	Ch'ungsuk Wang
1330-1332	Ch'unghye Wang

Reign	Ruler
1332-1339	Ch'angsuk Wang
1339-1344	Ch'unghye Wang
1344-1348	Ch'ungmok Wang
1348-1351	Ch'ungjŏng Wang
1351-1374	Kongmin Wang
1374-1388	U (Sin-u)
1389	Sinch'ang
1389-1392	Kongyang Wang

YI DYNASTY

Reign	Ruler
1392-1398	Yi T'aejo
1398-1400	Chŏngjong
1400-1418	T'aejong
1418-1450	Sejong
1450-1452	Munjong
1452-1455	Tanjong
1455-1468	Sejo
1468-1469	Yejong
1469-1494	Sŏngjong
1494-1506	Yŏnsan Gun
1506-1544	Chungjong
1544-1545	Injong
1546-1567	Myŏngjong
1567-1608	Sŏnjo
1608-1623	Kwanghae-gun
1623-1649	Injo
1649-1659	Hyojong
1659-1674	Hyŏnjong
1674-1720	Sukchong
1720-1724	Kyŏngjong
1724-1776	Yŏngjo
1776-1800	Chŏngjo
1800-1834	Sonjo
1834-1849	Hŏnjong
1849-1864	Ch'ŏljong
1864-1897	Kojong
1907-1910	Sunjong
1905-1910	Japanese protectorate
1910-1945	Annexed to Japan
1945-1948	Allied military occupation
1948	Division into North and South Korea

DEMOCRATIC PEOPLE'S REPUBLIC OF KOREA (NORTH KOREA)

Term	President
1948-1993	Kim Il-sung
1993-	Kim Jong-il

REPUBLIC OF KOREA (SOUTH KOREA)

Term	President
1948-1960	Syngman Rhee
1960-1962	Yun Boseon
1963-1979	Park Chunghee
1979-1980	Choi Kyuha
1980-1988	Chun Doo-hwan
1988-1993	Roh Tae-woo
1993-1998	Kim Young-sam
1998-2003	Kim Dae-jung
2003-	Roh Moo-hyun

MEXICO

Term	President
1824-1829	Guadalupe Victoria
1829	Vicente Ramón Guerrero
1829-1830	Pedro Velez and Lucas Alamán Luis de Quintana (acting presidents)
1830-1832	Anastasio Bustamante
1832-1833	Manuel Gómez Pedraza
1833	Valentín Gómez Farías
1833-1837	Antonio López de Santa Anna
1837-1841	Anastasio Bustamante
1841-1844	Antonio López de Santa Anna
1844	Valentín Canalizo
1844-1845	Antonio López de Santa Anna
1845	José Joaquín de Herrera
1846	Gabriel Valencia
1846	Mariano Paredes
1846	José Mariano de Salas
1846-1847	Valentín Gómez Farías
1847	Antonio López de Santa Anna
1847	José Manuel de la Peña y Peña
1847-1848	Pedro María de Anaya
1848	José Manuel de la Peña y Peña
1848-1851	José Joaquín de Herrera
1851-1853	Mariano Arista
1853-1855	Antonio López de Santa Anna
1855	Rómulo Díaz de la Vega
1856	Juan Álvarez
1856-1858	Ignacio Comonfort
1858	Félix María Zuloaga
1858-1859	Manuel Robles Pezuela
1859	José Mariano de Salas
1859	Miguel Miramón
1859-1860	Félix María Zuloaga
1861-1863	Benito Juárez
1863	Juan Nepomuceno Almonte
1863	Teodosio Lares
1863-1864	Supreme Provisional Executive Power
1864-1867	Maximilian I (emperor)
1867-1872	Benito Juárez

Term	President
1872-1876	Sebastián Lerdo de Tejada
1876	José María Iglesias
1876-1880	Porfirio Díaz
1880-1884	Manuel González
1884-1911	Porfirio Díaz
1911	Francisco León de la Barra
1911-1913	Francisco Indalécio Madero
1913-1914	Victoriano Huerta
1914	Francisco S. Carvajal
1914	Venustiano Carranza
1914	Antonio I. Villarreal González
1914-1915	Eulalio Martín Gutiérrez Ortiz
1915	Roque González Garza
1915	Francisco Lagos Cházaro
1915-1920	Venustiano Carranza
1920	Adolfo de la Huerta
1920-1924	Álvaro Obregón
1924-1928	Plutarco Elías Calles
1928-1930	Emilio Portes Gil
1930-1932	Pascual Ortiz Rubio
1932-1934	Abelardo L. Rodríguez
1934-1940	Lázaro Cárdenas
1940-1946	Manuel Ávila Camacho
1946-1952	Miguel Alemán
1952-1958	Adolfo Ruíz Cortines
1958-1964	Adolfo López Mateos
1964-1970	Gustavo Díaz Ordaz
1970-1976	Luis Echeverría Álvarez
1976-1982	José López Portillo
1982-1988	Miguel de la Madrid Hurtado
1988-1994	Carlos Salinas de Gortari
1994-2000	Ernesto Zedillo
2000-2006	Vicente Fox Quesada
2006-	Felipe Calderón

MONGOLS. *See also* CHINA: YUAN DYNASTY

From his base in Mongolia, founder Genghis Khan conquered a large and diverse region covering much of Asia from the Far East to the steppes of Russia, Turkey and the Middle East, Central Asia, and even parts of Southeast Asia. Although the individual leaders of those who inherited this empire remain unfamiliar to most, Genghis's heirs, among whom are the "great khans" of the immediate generations to follow, would indelibly change and shape the world from Russia to China, the Mideast to India. Genghis divided his empire among four sons. Jochi, the eldest, received the northwestern quadrant of this expanse, and his sons would found the "hordes" (armies) the would become known as the Blue, White, and eventually Golden Hordes; the latter would not meet its match until Russia's founder, Ivan the Great, refused to pay

tribute in 1476 and thereafter would dissolve into the various khanates of Kazan, Astrakhan, and the Crimea. Genghis's second son, Chaghatai, would receive the area of Central Asia lying north of India and east of the Caspian and Aral seas, sometimes called Moghulistan or Mughulistan. Genghis's third son, Ogatai, oversaw the southeastern and far east coastal "quadrant" or swathe, which would eventually become part of the huge realm of his nephew Kublai Khan, who in turn was the son of Genghis's youngest, Tolui, heir to the Mongolian homeland. It was Tolui's sons, beginning with Kublai, who would spawn the Chinese emperors of the Yuan Dynasty in the east and, beginning with Hulegu, the great Ilkhans who conquered the Middle East. The Ilkhans' successors, the Jalāyirids, Black Sheep Turks, White Sheep Turks, and ultimately the Timurids (founded by the part-Mongol Timur or Tamerlane), would dominate the Mideast and also give rise to the Mughal Dynasty in India.

GREAT KHANS

Reign	Ruler
1206-1227	Genghis Khan (founder)
1227-1229	Tolui
1229-1241	Ogatai Khan
1241-1246	Toregene (regent, wife of Ogatai)
1246-1248	Güyük
1248-1251	Oghul Qaimish (regent, wife of Güyük)
1251-1259	Mongu
1259-1260	Arigböge (regent, brother of Mongu and Kublai)
1260-1294	Kublai Khan

KHANS OF CHINA'S YUAN DYNASTY

Reign	Ruler
1267-1279	Mongols conquer Southern Song
1294-1307	Temür Öljeitü (Chengzong)
1307-1311	Kaishan (Wuzong)
1311-1320	Ayurbarwada (Renzong)
1321-1323	Shidebala (Yingzong)
1323-1328	Yesün Temür (Taiding)
1328	Arigaba (Aragibag)
1328-1329	Tugh Temür (Wenzong)1
1329	Tugh Koshila (Mingzong)
1329-1332	Tugh Temür (restored)
1333-1368	Toghon Temür (Shundi)
1368	Chinese expel Mongols

LATER MONGOLIAN KHANS

Reign	Ruler
1370-1388	Togus-Temür
1370-1379	Biliktu
1379-1389	Usaqal

Reign	Ruler
1389-1393	Engke Soriktu
1393-1400	Elbek
1400-1403	Gun Timur
1403-1411	Oljei Timur
1411-1415	Delbeg
1415-1425	Eseku
1425-1438	Adai Qa'an
1438-1440	Esen Toghan Tayisi
1440-1452	Tayisung Qa'an
1452-1455	Esen Tayisi
1452-1454	Molon Khan Togus
1454-1463?	Maqa Kurkis
1463?-1467	Mandughuli
1467-1470	Bayan Mongke
1470-c.1485	Civil war
1479-1543	Dayan Khan
1543-1582	Altan Khan
1547-1557	Kudeng Darayisun
1557-1592	Tumen Jasaghtu
1592-1604	Sechen Khan
1604-1634	Ligdan Khan
1628-1759	Manchurian conquest

MIDDLE EAST (IRAQ, IRAN, EASTERN TURKEY, ARABIA)

Il Khāns

Reign	Ruler
1255-1260	Invasion of Middle East
1256-1265	Hülegü (Hülägü)
1260	Battle of ʿAin Jalut (defeat by Mamlūks)
1265-1282	Abaqa
1282-1284	Aḥmad Tegüder
1284-1291	Arghūn
1291-1295	Gaykhatu
1295	Baydu
1295-1304	Maḥmūd Ghāzān
1304-1316	Muḥammad Khudābanda Öljeytü
1316-1335	Abū Saʿīd ʿAlāʾ ad-Dunyā wa ad-Dīn
1335-1336	Arpa Ke'ün
1336-1337	Mūsā
1337-1338	Muḥammad
1338-1353	Conflict among successor states

Jalāyirids

Reign	Ruler
1340-1356	Shaykh Ḥasan-i Buzurg Tāj ad-Dīn
1356-1374	Shaykh Uways
1374-1382	Ḥusayn I Jalāl ad-Dīn
1382-1410	Sulṭān Aḥmad Ghiyāth ad-Dīn
1410-1411	Shāh Walad
1411	Maḥmūd
1411-1421	Uways II
1421-1425	Maḥmūd

Reign	Ruler
1421	Muḥammad
1425-1532	Ḥusayn II
1432	Conquest by Kara Koyunlu

Kara Koyunlu (Black Sheep Turks)

Reign	Ruler
1351-1380	Bayram Khōja (Jalāyirid vassal)
1380-1389	Kara Muḥammad
1382	Independent
c. 1390-1400	Kara Yūsuf
1400-1406	Occupation by Tamerlane
1406-1420	Kara Yūsuf
1420-1438	Iskandar
1439-1467	Jahān Shāh
1467-1469	Ḥasan ʿAlī
1469	Abū Yūsuf
1469	Conquest by Ak Koyunlu

Ak Koyunlu (White Sheep Turks)

Reign	Ruler
1403-1435	Kara Osman (Qara Yoluq ʿUthmān Fakhr ad-Dīn)
1435-1438	ʿAlī Jalāl ad-Dīn
1438-1444	Ḥamza Nūr ad-Dīn
1444-1453	Jahāngīr Mu'izz ad-Dīn
1453-1478	Uzun Ḥasan
1478	Sulṭān Khalīl
1478-1490	Yaʿqūb
1490-1493	Baysonqur
1493-1497	Rustam
1497	Aḥmad Gövde
1497-1502	Alwand (Diyār Bakr and Azerbaijan)
1497-1500	Muḥammad (Iraq and Persia)
1500-1508	Sulṭān Murād (Persia)
1504-1508	Zayn al-ʿAbidīn (Diyār Bakr)
1508	Ṣafawid conquest

SOUTH CENTRAL ASIA

Chaghatayid or Jagataiid (Turkistan and the Tarim Basin)

Reign	Ruler
1227-1244	Chaghatay (Jagatai)
1244-1246	Kara Hülegü
1246-1251	Yesü Möngke
1251-1252	Kara Hülegü
1252-1260	Orqina Khātūn
1260-1266	Alughu
1266	Mubārak Shāh
c. 1266-1271	Baraq Ghiyāth ad-Dīn
1271-1272	Negübey
1272-1282	Buqa/Toqa Temür
c. 1282-1306	Du'a
1306-1308	Könchek

Reign	Ruler
1308-1309	Taliqu
1309	Kebek
1309-1320	Esen Buqa
c. 1320-1326	Kebek
1326	Eljigedey
1326	Du'a Temür
1326-1334	Tarmashīrīn ʿAlāʾ ad-Dīn
1334	Buzan
1334-1338	Changshi
c. 1338-1342	Yesün Temür
c. 1342-1343	Muḥammad
1343-1346	Kazan
1346-1358	Danishmendji
1358	Buyan Kuli
1359	Shāh Temür
1359-1363	Tughluq Temür
c. 1363	Timurids rule Mughulistan

Timurids

Reign	Ruler
1370-1405	Tamerlane (Timur)
1402	Capture of Bayezid, Battle of Ankara
1405-1407	Pīr Muḥammad (Kandahar)
1405-1409	Khalīl Sulṭān (Samarqand)
1405-1409	Shāh Rukh (Khorāsān)
1409-1447	Shāh Rukh (Transoxania, Iran)
1447-1449	Ulugh Beg (Transoxania, Khorāsān)
1449-1450	ʿAbd al-Laṭīf (Transoxania)
1450-1451	ʿAbdallāh
1451-1469	Abū Saʿīd (Transoxania, Iran)
1469-1494	Sulṭān Aḥmad (Transoxania)
1494-1495	Maḥmūd
1495-1500	Baysonqur, Masʾūd, ʿAlī (Transoxania)
1500	Özbeg conquest of Transoxania

WESTERN ASIA, RUSSIA, NORTH CENTRAL ASIA

Blue Horde

Reign	Ruler
1227-1256	Batu
1236-1239	Russia conquered
1239-1242	Europe invaded
1256-1257	Sartaq
1257	Ulaghchi
1257-1267	Berke
1267-1280	Möngke Temür
1280-1287	Töde Möngke
1287-1291	Töle Buqa
1291-1313	Toqta
1313-1341	Muḥammad Özbeg

Reign	Ruler
1341-1342	Tīnī Beg
1342-1357	Jānī Beg
1357-1359	Berdi Beg
1357-1380	Period of anarchy
1378	Union with White Horde

White Horde

Reign	Ruler
1226-1280	Orda
1280-1302	Köchü
1302-1309	Buyan
1309-1315	Sāsibuqa?
c. 1315-1320	Ilbasan
1320-1344	Mubārak Khwāja
1344-1374	Chimtay
1374-1376	Urus
1376-1377	Toqtaqiya
1377	Temür Malik
1377-1395	Toqtamïsh
1378	White and Blue Hordes form Golden Horde

Golden Horde

Reign	Ruler
1378-1395	Toqtamïsh
1395-1419	Edigü (vizir)
1395-1401	Temür Qutlugh
1401-1407	Shādī Beg
1407-1410	Pūlād Khān
1410-1412	Temür
1412	Jalāl ad-Dīn
1412-1414	Karīm Berdi
1414-1417	Kebek
1417-1419	Yeremferden?
1419-1422	Ulugh Muḥammad/Dawlat Berdi (rivals)
1422-1433	Baraq
c. 1433-1435	Sayyid Aḥmad I
c. 1435-1465	Küchük Muḥammad
c. 1465-1481	Aḥmad
1476	Ivan refuses to pay tribute
1480	Russian independence
1481-1498	Shaykh Aḥmad
1481-1499	Murtaḍā
1499-1502	Shaykh Aḥmad
1502	Annexed to Crimean khanate

Remnants of the Golden Horde

Reign	Rulers
1437-1552	Kazan khans
1449-1783	Crimean khans
1466-1554	Astrakhan khans

THE NETHERLANDS

Date	Ruler/Government/Event
1559-1567	William I, the Silent, Prince of Orange, Count of Nassau (stadtholder)
1568	Dutch Revolt
1568-1648	Eighty Years' War
1572-1584	William the Silent
1579	Union of Utrecht
1581	Dutch independence declared
1585-1625	Maurice (Maurits)
1609-1621	Twelve Years' Truce
1618-1648	Thirty Years' War
1625-1647	Frederik Hendrik
1647-1650	William II
1648	Peace of Westphalia, Spanish recognition of Dutch independence
1652-1654	First Anglo-Dutch War
1664-1667	Second Anglo-Dutch War
1672-1702	William III
1672-1678	Dutch War with France
1672-1674	Third Anglo-Dutch War
1688-1697	War of the League of Augsburg
1689-1702	England rules
1701-1713	War of the Spanish Succession
1702-1747	Republic
1747-1751	William IV Friso
1751-1795	William V
1780-1784	Fourth Anglo-Dutch War
1795-1806	Batavian Republic
1806-1810	Louis Bonaparte (king)
1810-1813	Annexed by France
1813-1840	William I (VI) King of the Netherlands
1840-1849	William II
1849-1890	William III
1890-1948	Wilhelmina (in exile 1940-1945)
1940-1945	German ccupation (World War II)
1948-1980	Juliana (abdicated)
1980-	Beatrix

NORWAY. *See also* DENMARK, SWEDEN

Reign	Ruler
680-710	Olaf the Tree Hewer
710-750	Halfdan I
750-780	Oystein (Eystein) I
780-800	Halfdan II White Legs
800-810	Gudrod the Magnificent
810-840	Olaf Geirstade
840-863	Halfdan III the Black
863-872	Civil war
872-930/33	Harald I Fairhair

Reign	Ruler
933-934	Erik I Bloodaxe
934-961	Hákon I the Good
961-970	Harald II Grayfell
970-995	Earl (Jarl) Hákon
995-1000	Olaf I Tryggvason
1000-1015	Erik I
1016-1028	Saint Olaf II Haraldsson
1028-1035	Canute the Great
1035-1047	Magnus I the Good
1047-1066	Harald III Hardrada
1066-1069	Magnus II
1069-1093	Olaf III the Peaceful
1093-1103	Magnus III the Barefoot
1103-1122	Oystein (Eystein) II
1103-1130	Sigurd I the Crusader
1130-1135	Magnus IV the Blinded
1130-1136	Harald IV Gillechrist
1136-1155	Sigurd II
1136-1161	Inge I
1142-1157	Oystein (Eystein) III
1161-1162	Hákon II
1163-1184	Magnus V
1184-1202	Sverre Sigurdsson
1202-1204	Hákon III
1204-1217	Inge II
1217-1263	Hákon IV
1263-1281	Magnus VI
1281-1299	Erik II Magnusson
1299-1319	Hákon V
1320-1343	Magnus VII (II of Sweden)
1343-1380	Hákon VI
1376-1387	Olaf IV (V of Denmark)
1380	Unification of Norway and Denmark
1380-1410	Margaret I of Denmark, Norway, and Sweden
1397	Unification of Norway, Denmark, and Sweden
1412-1439	Erik III (VII of Denmark, XIII of Sweden)
1439-1448	Christopher (III of Denmark)
1448-1481	Christian I of Oldenburg
1481-1513	Hans/John (II of Sweden)
1513-1523	Christian II
1523-1533	Frederick I
1534-1559	Christian III
1536-1814	Union with Denmark
1559-1588	Frederick II
1588-1648	Christian IV
1648-1670	Frederick III
1670-1699	Christian V
1699-1730	Frederick IV
1730-1746	Christian VI
1746-1766	Frederick V
1766-1808	Christian VII
1808-1814	Frederick VI

Reign	Ruler
1814	Christian Frederik
1814-1818	Carl II
1814-1905	Union with Sweden
1905-1957	Haakon VII
1957-1991	Olav V
1991-	Harald V

OTTOMAN EMPIRE. *See also* IRAN, ISLAMIC CALIPHS, SELJUK EMPIRE, SPAIN

Reign	Sultan
1281/88-1326	Osman I
1326-1360	Orhan I
1360-1389	Murad I
1389-1402	Bayezid I
1402-1421	Mehmed I
1421-1444	Murad II
1444-1446	Mehmed II
1446-1451	Murad II (second rule)
1451-1481	Mehmed II (second rule)
1453	Ottomans take Constantinople
1481	Djem I
1481-1512	Bayezid II
1512-1520	Selim I
1520-1566	Süleyman I the Magnificent
1566-1574	Selim II
1574-1595	Murad III
1595-1603	Mehmed III
1603-1617	Ahmed I
1617-1618	Mustafa I
1618-1622	Osman II
1622-1623	Mustafa I
1623-1640	Murad IV
1640-1648	Ibrahim I
1648-1687	Mehmed IV
1687-1691	Süleyman II
1691-1695	Ahmed II
1695-1703	Mustafa II
1703-1730	Ahmed III
1730-1754	Mahmud I
1754-1757	Osman III
1757-1774	Mustafa III
1774-1789	Abd-ul-Hamid I
1789-1807	Selim III
1807-1808	Mustafa IV
1808-1839	Mahmud II
1839-1861	Abd-ul-Mejid
1861-1876	Abd-ul-Aziz
1876	Murad V
1876-1909	Abd-ul-Hamid II
1909-1918	Mehmed V
1918-1922	Mehmed VI

PERU

Term	President
1821-1822	José de San Martín (Protector of Peru)
1822-1823	José La Mar
1823	Manuel Salazar y Baquíjano (provisional president)
1823	José de la Riva Agüero
1823-1824	José Bernardo de Tagle (Supreme Delegate)
1824-1826	Simón Bolívar (liberator of Peru)
1826-1827	Andrés de Santa Cruz
1827-1829	José La Mar
1829-1833	Agustín Gamarra
1834	Pedro Pablo Bermúdez (provisional Supreme Ruler)
1834-1835	Luis José de Orbegoso
1835-1836	Felipe Santiago Salaverry (Supreme Ruler)
1836-1838	Andrés de Santa Cruz (Supreme Protector)
1838-1841	Agustín Gamarra
1841	Manuel Menéndez
1842	Juan Crisóstomo Torrico (provisional president)
1842-1843	Francisco Vidal (provisional president)
1843	Domingo Elías (provisional president)
1843-1844	Domingo Nieto
1844	Justo Figueroa (acting president)
1844	Manuel Ignacio de Vivanco (Supreme Director)
1845-1851	Ramón Castilla
1851-1855	José Rufino Echenique
1855-1862	Ramón Castilla
1862-1863	Miguel de San Román
1863-1865	Juan Antonio Pezet
1865-1868	Mariano Ignacio Prado
1868	Pedro Diez Canseco (provisional president)
1868-1872	José Balta
1872	Tomás Gutiérrez (dictator)
1872	Mariano Herencia Zevallos (provisional)
1872-1876	Manuel Pardo
1876-1879	Mariano Ignacio Prado
1879	Luis La Puerta (provisional president)
1879-1881	Nicolás de Piérola
1881	Francisco García Calderón (provisional president)
1881-1883	Lizardo Montero (provisional president)
1883-1886	Miguel Iglesias
1886	Antonio Arenas (provisional president)
1886-1890	Andrés Avelino Cáceres
1890-1894	Remigio Morales Bermúdez
1894	Justiniano Borgoño (provisional president)
1894-1895	Andrés Avelino Cáceres
1895-1899	Nicolás de Piérola
1899-1903	Eduardo López de Romaña

Term	President
1903-1904	Manuel Candamo
1904	Serapio Calderón (provisional president)
1904-1908	José Pardo y Barreda
1908-1912	Augusto B. Leguía y Salcedo
1912-1914	Guillermo Billinghurst
1914-1915	Óscar Benavides
1915-1919	José Pardo y Barreda
1919-1930	Augusto B. Leguía y Salcedo
1930	Manuel María Ponce Brousset
1930-1931	Luis Miguel Sánchez Cerro
1931	Ricardo Leoncio Elías Arias
1931	Gustavo Jiménez
1931	David Samanez Ocampo
1931-1933	Luis Miguel Sánchez Cerro
1933-1939	Óscar Benavides
1939-1945	Manuel Prado y Ugarteche
1945-1948	José Luis Bustamante y Rivero
1948-1950	Manuel Odría
1950	Zenón Noriega Agüero
1950-1956	Manuel Odría
1956-1962	Manuel Prado y Ugarteche
1962-1963	Ricardo Pérez Godoy (first President of the Military Junta)
1963	Nicolás Lindley (second President of the Military Junta)
1963-1968	Fernando Belaúnde Terry
1968-1975	Juan Velasco Alvarado (first President of the Government of the Armed Forces)
1975-1980	Francisco Morales Bermúdez (second President of the Government of the Armed Forces)
1980-1985	Fernando Belaúnde Terry
1985-1990	Alan García
1990-2001	Alberto Fujimori
2001	Valentín Paniagua
2001-2006	Alejandro Toledo
2006-	Alan García

POLAND

Reign	Ruler
962-992	Mieszko I
992-1025	Bolesław I the Brave
1025-1034	Mieszko II
1034-1037	Instability
1037-1058	Casimir I the Restorer Instability
1058-1079	Bolesław II
1079-1102	Władysław (Vladislav or Ladislas) I
1102-1106	Zbigniev (rival to brother Bolesław III)
1102-1138	Bolesław III

Reign	Ruler
1138-1146	Instability following Bolesław III's division of Poland into five principalities
1146-1173	Bolesław IV
1173-1177	Mieszko III
1177-1194	Casimir II
1194-1227	Leszek I
1227-1279	Bolesław V
1228-1288	Instability: arrival of Teutonic Knights followed by Mongol incursions
1288-1290	Henry Probus
1290-1296	Przemyslav II (crowned 1295)
1297-1300	Instability
1300-1305	Wenceslaus (Vacław) I
1306-1333	Władysław I (Vladislav IV, Lokietek)
1333-1370	Casimir III the Great
1370	End of the Piast Dynasty
1370-1382	Ludvik I the Great (Louis of Anjou)
1382-1384	Confederation of Radom and civil war
1384-1399	Queen Jadwiga
1386-1434	Władysław II Jagiełło
1410-1411	Battle of Tannenberg and Peace of Thorn
1434-1444	Władysław (Vladislav) III
1444-1447	Instability; Poland united with Lithuania
1447-1492	Casimir IV
1454-1466	Poles defeat Teutonic Order, gain access to the Baltic in the Second Peace of Thorn
1471-1516	Vladislav Jagiełło (son of Casimir IV) king of Bohemia and then Hungary
1492-1501	John I Albert
1496	Statute of Piotrkow (Poland's Magna Carta)
1501-1506	Alexander Jagiełło
1506-1548	Sigismund I, the Old
1548-1572	Sigismund II Augustus
1573-1574	Henry Valois (Henry III)
1575-1586	Stephen Báthory

VASA KINGS OF SWEDEN AND POLAND

Reign	Ruler
1587-1632	Sigismund III Vasa
1632-1648	Vladislaus IV Vasa
1648-1668	Jan Kazimierz Vasa
1669-1673	Michael Korybut Wisniowiecki
1674-1696	John III Sobieski

WETTIN ELECTORS OF SAXONY OF HOLY ROMAN EMPIRE

Reign	Ruler
1697-1706	Augustus II, the Strong (Wettin)
1706-1709	Stanisław Leszczynski
1709-1733	Augustus II, the Strong (Wettin)
1733-1736	Stanisław Leszczynski
1733-1763	August III Wettin
1764-1795	Stanisław August Poniatowski

DUCHY OF WARSAW

Reign	Ruler
1807-1815	Ksiestwo Warszawskie (dependent from France)
1807-1815	Frederick Augustus I of Saxony Wettin

CONGRESS KINGDOM, KINGDOM OF POLAND

Reign	Ruler
1815-1825	Alexander I of Russia
1825-1831	Nicholas I of Russia (dismissed during November uprising)

SECOND POLISH REPUBLIC

Term	President
1918-1922	Józef Pilsudski
1922	Gabriel Narutowicz (assassinated)
1922-1926	Stanisław Wojciechowski (ousted)
1926-1939	Ignacy Moscicki

POLISH GOVERNMENT IN EXILE

Term	President
1939-1947	Władysław Raczkiewicz
1947-1972	August Zaleski
1972-1979	Stanisław Ostrowski
1979-1986	Edward Raczyński
1986-1989	Kazimierz Sabbat
1989-1990	Ryszard Kaczorowski (resigned after election of Lech Wałęsa)

COMMUNIST POLAND

Term	Leader
1944-1952	Bolesław Bierut

PEOPLE'S REPUBLIC OF POLAND

Chairmen of Council of State

Term	Chair
1952-1964	Aleksander Zawadzki
1964-1968	Edward Ochab
1968-1970	Marian Spychalski
1970-1972	Józef Cyrankiewicz
1972-1985	Henryk Jablonski
1985-1989	Wojciech Jaruzelski

First Secretaries of the Central Committee

Term	Secretary
1948-1956	Bolesław Bierut
1956	Edward Ochab
1956-1970	Władysław Gomułka
1970-1980	Edward Gierek
1980-1981	Stanisław Kania
1981-1989	Wojciech Jaruzelski

THIRD POLISH REPUBLIC

Term	President
1989-1990	Wojciech Jaruzelski
1990-1995	Lech Wałęsa
1995-2005	Aleksander Kwaśniewski
2005-	Lech Kaczyński

PORTUGAL

Reign	Ruler
1093-1112	Henry of Burgundy, count of Portugal
1112-1185	Afonso I (count of Portugal 1112-1139, king 1139-1185)
1185-1211	Sancho I
1211-1223	Afonso II
1223-1245	Sancho II
1245-1279	Afonso III
1279-1325	Diniz (Denis)
1325-1357	Afonso IV
1357-1367	Peter I
1367-1383	Ferdinand I
1385-1433	John I of Avis
1433-1438	Edward I
1438-1481	Afonso V
1481-1495	John II
1495-1521	Manuel I
1521-1557	John III
1557-1578	Sebastian I
1578-1580	Cardinal Henry
1580-1598	Philip I of Portugal (Philip II of Spain)
1598-1621	Philip II of Portugal (Philip III of Spain)
1621-1640	Philip III of Portugal (Philip IV of Spain)
1640	Revolt of Portugal
1640-1656	John IV (duke of Braganza)
1656-1667	Afonso VI
1667-1706	Pedro II
1706-1750	John V
1750-1777	José I
1777-1786	Pedro III
1777-1816	Maria I Francisca
1799-1816	John VI (regent)
1816-1826	John VI
1826	Pedro IV (I of Brazil)
1826-1828	Maria II da Glória
1828-1834	Miguel I (exiled)
1834-1853	Maria II da Glória
1853-1861	Pedro V
1861-1889	Luis I
1889-1908	Carlos I
1908	Manuel II
Oct. 5, 1910	Republic declared

RUSSIA

PRINCES OF KIEVAN RUS

Reign	Ruler
c. 862-879	Rurik
879-912	Oleg
912-945	Igor
945-964	Saint Olga (regent)
964-972	Svyatoslav I
972-980	Yaropolk
980-1015	Vladimir I (with Anna, Princess of the Byzantine Empire)
1015-1019	Sviatopolk I
1019-1054	Yaroslav
1054-1073	Iziaslav
1073-1076	Svyatoslav II
1076-1078	Iziaslav (restored)
1078-1093	Vsevolod
1093-1113	Sviatopolk II
1113-1125	Vladimir II Monomakh
1125-1132	Mstislav
1132-1139	Yaropolk
1139-1146	Vyacheslav
1146-1154	Iziaslav
1149-1157	Yuri I Dolgoruky
1154-1167	Rostislav

PRINCES OF VLADIMIR

Reign	Ruler
1169-1174	Andrei I Bogolyubsky
1175-1176	Michael
1176-1212	Vsevolod III
1212-1217	Yuri II
1217-1218	Constantin
1218-1238	Yuri II (restored)
1238-1246	Yaroslav II
1240	Mongol conquest
1246-1247	Svyatoslav III
1248-1249	Michael
1249-1252	Andrei II
1252-1263	Saint Alexander Nevsky
1264-1271	Yaroslav III of Tver
1272-1276	Vasily
1276-1281	Dmitry
1281-1283	Andrei III
1283-1294	Dmitry (restored)
1294-1304	Andrei III (restored)
1304-1319	Saint Michael of Tver
1319-1326	Yuri III of Moscow
1326-1327	Alexander II of Tver
1328-1331	Alexander III

PRINCES OF MOSCOW

Reign	Ruler
1263-1303	Daniel
1303-1325	Yuri III
1328-1341	Ivan I
1341-1353	Simeon
1353-1359	Ivan II
1359-1389	Dmitry Donskoy
1389-1425	Vasily I
1425-1462	Vasily II
1462-1505	Ivan III the Great
1480	Fall of the Golden Horde
1505-1533	Vasily III

CZARS OF ALL RUSSIA

Reign	Ruler
1547-1584	Ivan IV the Terrible
1584-1613	Time of Troubles
1584-1598	Fyodor I
1598-1605	Boris Godunov
1605	Fyodor II
1605-1606	False Dmitri I
1606-1610	Vasily IV Shuysky
1610-1613	Ladislaus IV of Poland
1613-1645	Michael I (first Romanov)
1645-1676	Aleksey I
1676-1682	Fyodor III
1682-1696	Ivan V (with Peter I)
1682-1721	Peter I (with Ivan V)

EMPERORS OF ALL RUSSIA

Reign	Ruler
1721-1725	Peter I
1725-1727	Catherine I the Great
1727-1730	Peter II
1730-1740	Anne
1740-1741	Ivan VI
1741-1762	Elizabeth
1762	Peter III
1762-1796	Catherine II
1796-1801	Paul
1801-1825	Alexander I
1825-1855	Nicholas I
1855-1881	Alexander II
1881-1894	Alexander III
1894-1917	Nicholas II
1917	Michael II (exiled)
1917-1921	Revolution
1918	Execution of Romanovs

SCOTLAND

Reign	Ruler
404-420	Fergus
420-451	Eugenius II
451-457	Dongardus
457-479	Constantine I
479-501	Congallus
569-606	Aldan
606-621	Eugenius III
646-664	Ferchard II
664-684	Mulduinns
684-688	Eugenius V
688-699	Eugenius VI
699-715	Eugenius VII
715-730	Mordachus
730-761	Etfinus
761-767	Interregnum
767-787	Solvatius
787-819	Achaius
819-824	Dongallus III
824-831	Dongal
831-834	Alpine
834-854	Kenneth
854-858	Donald V
858-874	Constantine II
874-893	Gregory
893-904	Donald VI
904-944	Constantine III
944-953	Malcolm I
953-961	Gondulph
961-965	Duff
965-970	Cullen
970-995	Kenneth II
995-1005	Grimus
1005-1034	Malcolm II
1034-1040	Duncan I
1040-1057	Macbeth
1057-1058	Lulach
1058-1093	Malcolm III
1093-1094	Donaldbane
1094	Duncan II
1094-1097	Donaldbane (second rule)
1097-1107	Edgar
1107-1124	Alexander I
1124-1153	David I
1153-1165	Malcolm IV
1165-1214	William I the Lion
1214-1249	Alexander II
1249-1286	Alexander III
1286-1290	Margaret
1290-1292	Interregnum
1292-1296	John Baliol

Reign	Ruler
1296-1306	Interregnum
1306-1329	Robert I the Bruce
1329-1371	David II
1371	Ascendancy of Robert II, House of Stuart
1371-1390	Robert II
1390-1406	Robert III
1406-1437	James I
1437-1460	James II
1460-1488	James III
1488-1513	James IV
1513-1542	James V
1542-1567	Mary
1567-1625	James VI
1625	Joined with England

SELJUK EMPIRE. *See also* IRAN, ISLAMIC CALIPHS, OTTOMAN EMPIRE

GREAT SULTANS

Reign	Sultan
1037-1063	Toghrïl Beg
1063-1072/73	Alp Arslan
1073-1092	Malik Shāh I
1092-1093	Maḥmūd I
1093-1104	Berk Yaruq (Barkyaruk, Barkiyarok)
1104-1105	Malik Shāh II
1105-1117	Muḥammad Tapar
1117-1157	Aḥmad Sanjar (Sinjar)

SULTANS OF IRAQ

Reign	Sultan
1105-1118	Maḥmūd Tapar
1118-1131	Maḥmūd
1131-1132	Dāʿūd (Dawd)
1132-1135	Toghrïl I
1135-1152	Masʿūd
1152-1153	Malik Shāh
1153-1159	Muḥammad
1159-1161	Sulaimān Shāh
1161-1177	Arslan Shāh
1177-1194	Toghrïl II

SELJUK SULTANS OF ANATOLIA/RUM

Reign	Sultan
1077-1066	Sulaimān Shāh
1092-1107?	Qïlïch (Kilij) Arslan I
1107?-1116	Malik Shāh I

Reign	Sultan
1116-1156	Masʿūd I
1156-1192	Qïlïch (Kilij) Arslan II
1192	Malik Shāh II
1192-1196	Kai Khusrau (Khosrow, Khosru, Khusraw) I
1196-1204	Suleiman II
1203-1204	Qïlïch (Kilij) Arslan III
1204-1210	Kai Khusrau I (second rule)
1210-1219	Kai Kāʾūs I
1219-1236	Kai Qubād (Kobadh) I
1236-1246	Kai Khusrau II
1246-1259	Kai Kāʾūs II
1248-1264	Qïlïch (Kilij) Arslan IV
1249-1257	Kai Qubād (Kobadh) II
1264-1283	Kai Khusrau III
1283-1298	Masʿūd II
1298-1301?	Kai Qubād (Kobadh) III
1303-1308	Masʿūd II (second rule)

Seljuk Sultans of Syria

Reign	Sultan
1078-1094	Tutush
1095-1113	Riḍwān (Damascus)
1098-1113	Duqaq (Aleppo)
1113-1114	Alp Arslan
1114-1117	Sultan Shāh

Sultans of Kirmān (Kerman)

Reign	Sultan
1041-1073	Qāvurt (Qawurd)
1073-1074	Kirmān (Kerman) Shāh
1074-1085	Sultan Shāh
1085-1097	Turān Shāh I
1097-1101	Īrān Shāh
1101-1142	Arslan Shāh I
1142-1156	Muḥammad I
1156-1170	Toghrïl Shāh
1170-1175	Bahrām Shāh
1170-1177	Arslan Shāh II
1175-1186	Muḥammad Shāh II
1177-1183	Turān Shāh II

SPAIN. *See also* PORTUGAL

The Iberian Peninsula now occupied by Spain and Portugal was a turbulent region during the Middle Ages, a place where numerous cultures clashed, notably Christianity and Islam but also a broad and ethnically diverse group of peoples, from the Suevi and Visigoths of the seventh century through the Berbers and Islamic peoples in the south. Through most of the Middle Ages the region saw a succession of fluctuating principalities in the north—primarily Asturias, Galicia, Aragón, Navarre, León, and Castile, while in the south Islam held sway from the eighth century to the time of Columbus's voyage to the Americas in 1492. In that year the Reconquista concluded with the Fall of Granada, and Christianity claimed the peninsula. In 1516, the Kingdom of Spain united all former kingdoms, with the exception of Portugal, into one Kingdom of Spain.

Major Islamic Rulers

Córdoba's Umayyad Caliphs (emirs until 929)

Reign	Ruler
756-788	ʿAbd al-Raḥmān I (emir)
788-796	Hishām I (emir)
796-822	al-Hakam I (emir)
822-852	ʿAbd al-Raḥmān II (emir)
852-886	Muḥammad I (emir)
886-888	al-Mundhir (emir)
888-912	ʿAbd Allāh (emir)
912-961	ʿAbd al-Raḥmān III al-Nāṣir
961-976	al-Hakam II al-Mustanṣir
976-1008	Hishām II al-Muayyad
1008-1009	Muḥammad II al-Mahdī
1009	Sulaimān al-Mustaʿīn
1010-1013	Hishām II (restored)
1013-1016	Sulaimān (restored)
1016-1018	Alī ben Hammud
1018	ʿAbd al-Raḥmān IV
1018-1021	al-Qasim
1021-1022	Yaḥyā
1022-1023	al-Qasim (restored)
1023-1024	ʿAbd al-Raḥmān V
1024-1025	Muḥammad III
1025-1027	Yaḥyā (restored)
1027-1031	Hishām III
1031	End of Umayyads; dissolution of Umayyad Spain into small states

After the Umayyads, Turbulence: Some Major Rulers

Reign	Ruler
1031-1043	Jahwar ibn Muḥammad ibn Jahwar
1043-1058	Muḥammad ar-Rashīd
1058-1069	ʿAbd al-Malik Dhu's-Siyādat al-Manṣur
1069	ʿAbbādid conquest
1085	Toledo falls to León and Castile; Christian Reconquista begins

Almoravid Sultans (Spain and North Africa)

Reign	Ruler
1061-1107	Yūsuf ibn Tāshufīn
1086	Entry into Spain; Alfonso VI defeated at Zallāqa

Reign	Ruler
1107-1142	ʿAlīx ibn Yūsuf
1142-1146	Tāshufīn ibn ʿAlī
1146	Ibrāhīm ibn Tāshufīn
1146-1147	Isḥāq ibn ʿAlī
1147	Almohad conquest

Almohad Caliphs (Spain and North Africa)

Reign	Ruler
1130-1163	ʿAbd al-Muʾmin
1163-1184	Abū Yaʿqūb Yūsuf
1184-1199	Abū Yūsuf Yaʿqūb al-Manṣūr
1199-1213	Muḥammad ibn Yaʿqūb
1212	Christians defeat Almohads at Las Navas de Tolosa
1213-1224	Yūsuf II Abū Yaqūb
1224	ʿAbd al-Wāḥid Abū Muḥammad
1224-1227	ʿAbd Allāh Abū Muḥammad
1227-1232	Idrīs I ibn Yaʿqūb
1227-1235	Yaḥyā Abū Zakariyyāʿ
1228-1229	Retreat from Spain
1232-1242	ʿAbdul-Wāḥid ibn Idrīs I
1242-1248	ʿAlī ibn Idrīs I
1248-1266	ʿUmar ibn Isḥāq
1266-1269	Idrīs II ibn Muḥammad
1269	End of Almohad domination in North Africa

Naṣrid Sultans of Granada

Reign	Ruler
1232-1273	Muḥammad I al-Ghālib (Ibn al-Aḥmar)
1273-1302	Muḥammad II al-Faqīh
1302-1309	Muḥammad III al-Makhlūʿ
1309-1314	Naṣr
1314-1325	Ismāʿīl I
1325-1333	Muḥammad IV
1333-1354	Yūsuf I al-Muʾayyad
1354-1359	Muḥammad V al-Ghani
1359-1360	Ismāʿīl II
1360-1362	Muḥammad VI al-Ghālib (El Bermejo)
1362-1391	Muḥammad V al-Ghani (restored)
1391-1392	Yūsuf II al-Mustahgnī
1392-1408	Muḥammad VII al-Mustaʿīn
1408-1417	Yūsuf III an-Nāṣir
1417-1419	Muḥammad VIII al-Mustamassik (al-Ṣaghīr, El Pequeño)
1419-1427	Muḥammad IX al-Ghālib (al-Aysar, El Zurdo)
1427-1429	Muḥammad VIII al-Mustamassik
1429-1432	Muḥammad IX al-Ghālib
1432	Yūsuf IV, Abenalmao
1432-1445	Muḥammad IX al-Ghālib
1445	Muḥammad X al-Aḥnaf (El Cojo)
1445-1446	Yūsuf V (Aben Ismael)
1446-1447	Muḥammad X al-Aḥnaf
1447-1453	Muḥammad IX al-Ghālib

Reign	Ruler
1451-1455	Muḥammad XI (El Chiquito)
1454-1464	Saʿd al-Mustaʿīn (Ciriza, Muley Zad)
1462	Yūsuf V (Aben Ismael)
1464-1482	ʿAlī (Muley Hácen)
1482-1492	Muḥammad XII al-Zughūbī (Boabdil, El Chico)
1483-1485	ʿAlī (Muley Hácen)
1485-1490	Muḥammad ibn Saʿd al-Zaghal
1492	Conquest by Castile and Aragón, end of Islamic Spain

NON-ISLAMIC AND CHRISTIAN RULERS

Asturias and Galicia

Reign	Ruler
718-737	Pelayo
737-739	Favila
739-757	Alfonso I the Catholic
757-768	Fruela I
768-774	Aurelio
774-783	Silo
783-788	Mauregato
788-791	Vermundo I
791-842	Alfonso II the Chaste
842-850	Ramiro I
850-866	Ordoño I
866-910	Alfonso III the Great
910	Subsumed by León

Navarre

Reign	Ruler
840-851	Inigo Arista
905-925	Sancho Garces
925-970	Garcia Sanchez I
970-994	Sancho Abarca
994-1000	Garcia Sanchez II
1000-1035	Sancho III the Great
1035-1054	Garcia IV
1054-1076	Sancho IV
1076-1094	Sancho Ramirez
1094-1134	Subsumed under Aragón, Castile, León; reemerges with reduced territory
1134-1150	Garcia V Ramirez
1150-1194	Sancho VI
1194-1234	Sancho VII
1234-1253	Teobaldo I of Champagne
1253-1270	Teobaldo II
1270-1274	Henry I
1274-1305	Juana I
1305-1316	Luis (Louis)
1316-1322	Philip V the Tall
1322-1328	Charles I
1328-1349	Juana II

Reign	Ruler
1349-1387	Charles II the Bad
1387-1425	Charles III the Noble
1425-1479	Blanca & John
1479	Leonora
1479-1483	Francis Febo
1483-1517	Catalina
1516	Part of Navarre annexed to Spain
1517-1555	Henry II
1555-1572	Jeanne d'Albret
1572-1589	Henry III (IV of France); French rule

León

Reign	Ruler
910-914	Garcia
914-924	Ordoño II
924-925	Fruela II
925-930	Alfonso IV the Monk
930-950	Ramiro II
950-956	Ordoño III
956-967	Sancho I the Fat
967-982	Ramiro III
982-999	Vermundo II
999-1028	Alfonso V the Noble
1028-1037	Vermundo III
1038-1065	Fernando
1065-1070	Sancho II
1070-1072	Sancho III
1072-1109	Alfonso VI (king of Castile)
1109-1126	Urraca (married to Alfonso I of Aragón)
1126-1157	Alfonso VII
1157-1188	Ferdinand II
1188-1230	Alfonso IX
1230-1252	Saint Fernando III
1252	Subsumed under Castile

Castile

Reign	Ruler
1035-1065	Ferdinand I
1065-1072	Sancho II
1072-1109	Alfonso VI
1109-1157	Castile joins with León
1157	Castile restored as separate principality
1157-1158	Sancho III
1158-1214	Alfonso VIII
1214-1217	Henry I
1217-1252	Saint Ferdinand III
1252	Castile rejoins with León
1252-1284	Alfonso X (emperor)
1284-1295	Sancho IV
1295-1312	Ferdinand IV
1312-1350	Alfonso XI
1350-1369	Peter the Cruel
1369-1379	Henry II

Reign	Ruler
1379-1390	John I
1390-1406	Henry III
1406-1454	John II
1454-1474	Henry IV
1474-1504	Ferdinand V (II of Aragon) and Isabella I
1492	Fall of Granada, end of Reconquista
1504-1516	Joan (Juana) the Mad and Philip I of Habsburg
1516	Formation of Kingdom of Spain

Aragon

Reign	Ruler
1035-1063	Ramiro I
1063-1094	Sancho Ramirez
1094-1104	Pedro I
1104-1134	Alfonso I (co-ruled León and Castile, 1109-1126)
1134-1137	Ramiro II
1137	Union with County of Barcelona
1137-1162	Petronilla
1162-1196	Alfonso II
1196-1213	Pedro II
1213-1276	James I the Conqueror (under regency to 1217)
1276-1285	Pedro III
1285-1291	Alfonso III
1291-1327	James II
1327-1336	Alfonso IV
1336-1387	Peter IV
1387-1395	John I
1395-1410	Martin I
1412-1416	Ferdinand I
1416-1458	Alfonso V
1458-1479	John II
1479-1516	Ferdinand II and Isabella I (d. 1504)

KINGDOM OF SPAIN

Reign	Ruler
1516-1556	Carlos (Charles) I (V as Holy Roman Emperor)
1556-1598	Philip (Felipe) II
1598-1621	Philip III
1621-1665	Philip IV
1665-1700	Carlos II

BOURBONS

Reign	Ruler
1700-1724	Philip V
1724	Luis I
1724-1746	Philip V (restored)
1746-1759	Fernando VI
1759-1788	Carlos III
1788-1808	Carlos IV

Reign	Ruler
1808	Fernando VII
1808	Carlos IV (restored)

BONAPARTES

Reign	Ruler
1808-1813	José I Napoleón

BOURBONS (RESTORED)

Reign	Ruler
1813-1833	Fernando VII
1833-1868	Isabel II

SAVOY

Reign	Ruler
1871-1873	Amadeo I

FIRST SPANISH REPUBLIC

Reign	Ruler
1874-1887	Alfonso XII
1886-1931	Alfonso XIII

SECOND SPANISH REPUBLIC

Reign	Ruler
1939-1975	Francisco Franco

BOURBONS (RESTORED)

Reign	Ruler
1975-	Juan Carlos I

SWEDEN. *See also* **DENMARK, NORWAY**

Reign	Ruler
647-735?	Harald Hildetand
735-750?	Sigurd Ring
750-794?	Ragnar Lodbrok
?	Eystein Beli
794-804	Björn Järnsida
804-808	Erik II (to 870?)
808-820	Erik III
820-859	Edmund I
860?-870	Erik I (poss. Erik II)
870-920	Björn
920-930	Olaf I Ring
?	Erik IV
930-950	Erik V
950-965	Edmund II
965-970	Olaf II
970-995	Erik VI the Victorious
995-1022	Olaf III Skötkonung
1022-1050	Anund Jakob Kolbrenner
1050-1060	Edmund III

Reign	Ruler
1066-1067	Erik VII (VIII)
1066-1070	Halsten
1066-1080	Inge I Elder
1080-1083	Blot-Sven
1083-1110	Inge I Elder
1110-1118	Filip Halstensson
1118-1125	Inge II Younger
1125-1130	Magnus Nielsson
1130-1156	Sverker I Elder
1156-1160	Sain Erik IX
1161-1167	Charles VII
1167-1196	Knut I
1196-1208	Sverker II Younger
1208-1216	Erik X
1216-1222	John I
1222-1229	Erik XI
1229-1234	Knut II the Long
1234-1250	Erik XI
1250-1275	Valdemar
1275-1290	Magnus I
1290-1320	Berger
1320-1365	Magnus II (VII of Norway)
1356-1359	Erik XII
1364-1389	Albert
1389-1412	Margaret I of Denmark, Norway, and Sweden
1397	Unification of Norway, Denmark, and Sweden
1412-1439	Erik XIII (VII of Denmark, III of Norway)
1439-1448	Christopher (III of Denmark)
1448-1481	Christian I of Oldenburg
1481-1513	Hans/John II
1513-1523	Christian II
1523-1560	Gustav I Vasa
1560-1568	Erik XIV
1568-1592	Johan/John III
1592-1604	Sigismund
1604-1611	Carl/Charles IX
1611-1632	Gustav II Adolf
1632-1654	Christina
1654-1660	Charles X
1660-1697	Charles XI
1697-1718	Charles XII (Madman of the North)
1718-1720	Ulrika
1730-1751	Frederick (landgrave of Hesse)
1751-1771	Adolphus Frederick
1771-1792	Gustav III
1792-1809	Gustav IV Adolf
1809-1818	Charles XIII
1814	Sweden and Norway joined
1818-1844	Charles XIV
1844-1859	Oscar I
1859-1872	Charles XI
1872-1907	Oscar II

Reign	Ruler
1905	Norway separates
1907-1950	Gustav V
1950-1973	Gustav VI Adolf
1973-	Karl/Charles XVI Gustaf

UNITED STATES

Term	President
1789-1797	George Washington
1797-1801	John Adams
1801-1809	Thomas Jefferson
1809-1817	James Madison
1817-1825	James Monroe
1825-1829	John Quincy Adams
1829-1837	Andrew Jackson
1837-1841	Martin Van Buren
1841	William Henry Harrison
1841-1845	John Tyler
1845-1849	James K. Polk
1849-1850	Zachary Taylor
1850-1853	Millard Fillmore
1853-1857	Franklin Pierce
1857-1861	James Buchanan
1861-1865	Abraham Lincoln
1865-1869	Andrew Johnson
1869-1877	Ulysses S. Grant
1877-1881	Rutherford B. Hayes
1881	James A. Garfield
1881-1885	Chester A. Arthur
1885-1889	Grover Cleveland
1889-1893	Benjamin Harrison
1893-1897	Grover Cleveland
1897-1901	William McKinley
1901-1909	Theodore Roosevelt
1909-1913	William Howard Taft
1913-1921	Woodrow Wilson
1921-1923	Warren G. Harding
1923-1929	Calvin Coolidge
1929-1933	Herbert Hoover
1933-1945	Franklin D. Roosevelt
1945-1953	Harry S. Truman
1953-1961	Dwight D. Eisenhower
1961-1963	John F. Kennedy
1963-1968	Lyndon B. Johnson
1969-1974	Richard M. Nixon
1974-1977	Gerald R. Ford
1977-1981	Jimmy Carter
1981-1989	Ronald Reagan
1989-1993	George H. W. Bush
1993-2001	Bill Clinton
2001-	George W. Bush

VENEZUELA

Term	President
1819	Francisco Antonio Zea (acting president)
1819	Simón Bolívar
1830-1835	José Antonio Páez
1835	Andrés Narvarte (acting president)
1835	José María Vargas
1835	Pedro Briceño (provisional president)
1835	Santiago Mariño (Superior Chief of State)
1835	José María Carreño (acting president)
1836	José María Vargas
1836-1837	Andrés Narvarte (acting president)
1837	José María Carreño (acting president)
1837-1839	Carlos Soublette (acting president)
1839-1843	José Antonio Páez
1843	Santos Michelena (acting president)
1843-1847	Carlos Soublette (acting president)
1847	Diego Bautista Urbaneja (acting president)
1847-1851	José Tadeo Monagas
1851	Antonio Leocadio Guzmán (acting president)
1851-1855	José Gregorio Monaga
1855	Joaquín Herrera (acting president)
1855-1858	José Gregorio Monaga
1858	Pedro Gual (president of provisional government)
1858-1859	Julián Castro
1859	Juan Crisóstomo Falcón
1859	Pedro Gual (acting president)
1859-1861	Manuel Felipe de Tovar (acting president)
1861	Pedro Gual (acting president)
1861-1863	José Antonio Páez
1863	Antonio Guzmán Blanco
1863-1865	Juan Crisóstomo Falcón (provisional president)
1865	Antonio Guzmán Blanco
1865-1868	Juan Crisóstomo Falcón
1868-1869	Guillermo Tell Villegas
1869-1870	José Ruperto Monagas (acting president)
1870	Juan Vicente González (acting president)
1870	Esteban Palacios (acting president)
1870-1877	Antonio Guzmán Blanco
1877	Jacinto Gutiérrez Martínez (acting president)
1877-1878	Francisco Linares Alcántara
1878-1879	Jacinto Gutiérrez Martínez (acting president)
1879	José Gregorio Valera (acting president)
1879	Gregorio Cedeño
1879	José Rafael Pacheco
1879-1884	Antonio Guzmán Blanco
1884-1886	Joaquín Crespo

Term	President
1886	Manuel Antonio Diez (acting president)
1886-1888	Antonio Guzmán Blanco
1888-1890	Juan Pablo Rojas Paúl
1890-1892	Raimundo Andueza Palacio
1892	Guillermo Tell Villegas
1892-1894	Joaquín Crespo
1894	Manuel Guzmán Álvarez (acting president)
1894-1898	Joaquín Crespo
1898	Manuel Guzmán Álvarez (acting president)
1898-1899	Ignacio Andrade
1899	Víctor Rodríguez Párraga (acting president)
1899-1909	Cipriano Castro
1909-1910	Juan Vicente Gómez
1910	Emilio Constantino Guerrero (acting president)
1910	Jesús Ramón Ayala (acting president)
1910-1914	Juan Vicente Gómez
1914-1922	Victorino Márquez Bustillos (provisional president)
1922-1929	Juan Vicente Gómez
1929-1931	Juan Bautista Pérez
1931	Pedro Itriago Chacín (acting president)
1931-1935	Juan Vicente Gómez
1935-1936	Eleazar López Contreras
1936	Arminio Borjas (acting president)
1936-1941	Eleazar López Contreras
1941-1945	Isaías Medina Angarita
1945-1948	Rómulo Betancourt (chairman of revolutionary junta)
1948	Rómulo Gallegos
1948-1950	Carlos Delgado Chalbaud (chairman of military junta)
1950-1952	Germán Suárez Flamerich (chairman of military junta)
1952-1958	Marcos Pérez Jiménez
1958	Wolfgang Larrazábal (chairman of government junta)
1958-1959	Edgar Sanabria Arcia (chairman of government junta)
1959-1964	Rómulo Betancourt
1964-1969	Raúl Leoni
1969-1974	Rafael Caldera
1974-1979	Carlos Andrés Pérez
1979-1984	Luis Herrera Campins
1984-1989	Jaime Lusinchi
1989-1993	Carlos Andrés Pérez
1993	Octavio Lepage (acting president)
1993-1994	Ramón José Velásquez (interim president)
1994-1999	Rafael Caldera
1999-	Hugo Chávez

VIETNAM

NGO DYNASTY
Reign	Ruler
939-945	Kuyen
945-951	Duong Tam Kha
951-954	Suong Ngap
951-965	Suong Van

DINH DYNASTY
Reign	Ruler
968-979	Dinh Tien
979-981	Dinh De Toan

EARLY LE DYNASTY
Reign	Ruler
981-1005	Hoan
1005-1009	Trung Tong

LATER LI (LY) DYNASTY
Reign	Ruler
1010-1028	Thai To
1028-1054	Thai Tong
1054-1072	Thanh Tong

LATER LE DYNASTY
Reign	Ruler
1072-1127	Nan Ton
1127-1138	Than Tong
1138-1175	Anh Tong
1175-1210	Kao Tong
1210-1224	Hue Tong
1224-1225	Tieu Hoang

EARLY TRAN DYNASTY
Reign	Ruler
1225-1258	Thai Tong
1258-1277	Thanh Tong
1278-1293	Nan Tong
1293-1314	Anh Tong
1314-1329	Minh Tong
1329-1341	Hien Tong
1341-1369	Du Tong
1370-1372	Nghe Tong
1372-1377	Due Tong
1377-1388	De Hien
1388-1398	Tran Thuan Tong
1398-1400	Tran Thieu De

HO DYNASTY

Reign	Ruler
1400	Kui Li
1400-1407	Han Thuong
1407-1428	Ming Chinese occupation

LATER TRAN DYNASTY

Reign	Ruler
1407-1409	Hau Tran Jian Dinh De
1409-1413	Hau Tran
1413-1428	vacant

CHAMPA

Reign	Ruler
1390-1400	Ko Cheng
1400-1441	Jaya Sinhavarman v
1441-1446	Maija Vijaya
1446-1449	Qui Lai
1449-1458	Qui Do (Bi Do)
1458-1460	Ban La Tra Nguyet (Tra Duyet)
1460-1471	Ban La Tra Toan
1471-1478	Bo Tri Tri

LATER LE DYNASTY

Reign	Ruler
1428-1433	Thai To
1433-1442	Thai Tong
1442-1459	Nan Tong
1460-1497	Thanh Tong
1497-1504	Hien Tong
1504-1509	Vi Muc De
1509-1516	Tuong Duc De
1516-1522	Tieu Tong
1522-1527	Kung Hoang
1533-1548	Le Trang Tong (restored)

MAC DYNASTY

Reign	Ruler
1527-1530	Dang Dung
1530-1540	Dang Doanh
1533	Kingdom divides

NGUYEN DYNASTY

Reign	Ruler
1533-1545	Kim
1545-1558	Civil war
1558-1613	Hoang
1613-1635	Phuc Nguyen
1635-1648	Phuc Lan
1648-1687	Phuc Tan
1687-1691	Phuc Tran
1691-1725	Phuc Chu I
1725-1738	Phuc Chu II
1738-1765	Phuc Khoat
1765-1778	Phuc Thuan
1778-1802	Anh
1802	Absorbs other Vietnamese kingdoms
1802-1820	Gia Long
1820-1841	Minh Mang
1841-1848	Thieu Tri
1848-1883	Tu Duc
1883-1940	French protectorate
1883	Duc Duc
1883	Hiep Hoa
1883-1884	Kien Phuc
1884-1885	Ham Nghi
1885-1889	Dong Khanh
1889-1907	Thanh Thai
1907-1916	Duy Tan
1916-1925	Khai Dinh
1925-1945	Bao Dai
1940-1945	Japanese occupation
1945-1954	French occupation
1949-1955	Bao Dai
1954-1975	Republic of Vietnam
1954	Communist government

Chronological List of Entries

The arrangement of personages in this list is chronological on the basis of birth years. All personages appearing in this list are the subjects of articles in *Great Lives from History: The Nineteenth Century, 1801-1900*. Subjects of multiperson essays include The Becquerel Family, The Brontë Sisters, William Fothergill Cooke and Charles Wheatstone, W. S. Gilbert and Arthur Sullivan, Sarah and Angelina Grimké, Jacob and Wilhelm Grimm, Jesse and Frank James, Meriwether Lewis and William Clark, Daniel and Alexander Macmillan, The Rothschild Family, The Siemens Family, and Alexander and Demetrios Ypsilantis.

1741-1750

Gebhard Leberecht von Blücher (December 16, 1742-September 12, 1819)

Ali Paşa Tepelenë (c. 1744-February 5, 1822)

Mayer Amschel Rothschild (February 23, 1744-September 19, 1812)

Johann Heinrich Pestalozzi (January 12, 1746-February 17, 1827)

Jacques-Louis David (August 30, 1748-December 29, 1825)

Pierre-Simon Laplace (March 23, 1749-March 5, 1827)

Karl von Hardenberg (May 31, 1750-November 26, 1822)

1751-1760

John Nash (September 1752-May 13, 1835)

Miguel Hidalgo y Costilla (May 8, 1753-July 30, 1811)

Jean-Jacques-Régis de Cambacérès (October 18, 1753-March 8, 1824)

Talleyrand (February 2, 1754-May 17, 1838)

ʿUthman dan Fodio (December, 1754-April, 1817)

Samuel Hahnemann (April 10, 1755-July 2, 1843)

John Marshall (September 24, 1755-July 6, 1835)

Gerhard Johann David von Scharnhorst (November 12, 1755-June 28, 1813)

Aaron Burr (February 6, 1756-September 14, 1836)

Sir Henry Raeburn (March 4, 1756-July 8, 1823)

Thomas Telford (August 9, 1757-September 2, 1834)

Freiherr vom Stein (October 26, 1757-June 29, 1831)

Antonio Canova (November 1, 1757-October 13, 1822)

Kamehameha I (c. 1758-May 8, 1819)

James Monroe (April 28, 1758-July 4, 1831)

Lord Nelson (September 29, 1758-October 21, 1805)

Noah Webster (October 16, 1758-May 28, 1843)

Paul Cuffe (January 17, 1759-September 7, 1817)

Henri de Saint-Simon (October 17, 1760-May 19, 1825)

August von Gneisenau (October 27, 1760-August 23, 1831)

1761-1770

Albert Gallatin (January 29, 1761-August 12, 1849)

William Carey (August 17, 1761-June 9, 1834)

Gia Long (February 8, 1762-January 25 or February 3, 1820)

George IV (August 12, 1762-June 26, 1830)

Tadano Makuzu (1763-July 26, 1825)

Charles XIV John (January 26, 1763-March 8, 1844)

William Cobbett (March 9, 1763-June 18, 1835)

Joséphine (June 23, 1763-May 29, 1814)

John Jacob Astor (July 17, 1763-March 29, 1848)

James Kent (July 31, 1763-December 12, 1847)

Charles Bulfinch (August 8, 1763-April 4, 1844)

Charles Grey (March 13, 1764-July 17, 1845)

Benjamin Henry Latrobe (May 1, 1764-September 3, 1820)

Nicéphore Niépce (March 7, 1765-July 5, 1833)

Chronological List of Entries

William IV (August 21, 1765-June 20, 1837)
Robert Fulton (November 14, 1765-February 24, 1815)
Thomas Robert Malthus (February 13, 1766-December 23, 1834)
John MacArthur (August 18, 1766-April 11, 1834)
John Dalton (September 6, 1766-July 27, 1844)
Black Hawk (1767-October 3, 1838)
Andrew Jackson (March 15, 1767-June 8, 1845)
John Quincy Adams (July 11, 1767-February 23, 1848)
Henri Christophe (October 6, 1767-October 8, 1820)
Maria Edgeworth (January 1, 1768-May 22, 1849)
Tecumseh (March, 1768-October 5, 1813)
Joseph Fourier (March 21, 1768-May 16, 1830)
Dolley Madison (May 20, 1768-July 12, 1849)
Samuel Slater (June 9, 1768-April 21, 1835)
François-René de Chateaubriand (September 4, 1768-July 4, 1848)
Friedrich Schleiermacher (November 21, 1768-February 12, 1834)
Muḥammad ʿAlī Pasha (1769-August 2, 1849)
Michel Ney (January 10, 1769-December 7, 1815)

DeWitt Clinton (March 2, 1769-February 11, 1828)
Marc Isambard Brunel (April 25, 1769-December 12, 1849)
Duke of Wellington (May 1, 1769-September 14, 1852)
Viscount Castlereagh (June 18, 1769-August 12, 1822)
Napoleon I (August 15, 1769-May 5, 1821)
Georges Cuvier (August 23, 1769-May 13, 1832)
Alexander von Humboldt (September 14, 1769-May 6, 1859)
Sir Isaac Brock (October 6, 1769-October 13, 1812)
Sequoyah (c. 1770-August, 1843)
William Wordsworth (April 7, 1770-April 23, 1850)
George Canning (April 11, 1770-August 8, 1827)
Second Earl of Liverpool (June 7, 1770-December 4, 1828)
William Clark (August 1, 1770-September 1, 1838)
Georg Wilhelm Friedrich Hegel (August 27, 1770-November 14, 1831)
Ludwig van Beethoven (baptized December 17, 1770-March 26, 1827)

1771-1780

Richard Trevithick (April 13, 1771-April 22, 1833)
Robert Owen (May 14, 1771-November 17, 1858)
Eleuthère Irénée du Pont (June 24, 1771-October 31, 1834)
Thomas Talbot (July 19, 1771-February 5, 1853)
Sir Walter Scott (August 15, 1771-September 21, 1832)
Francis Place (November 3, 1771-January 1, 1854)
Mikhail Mikhaylovich Speransky (January 12, 1772-February 23, 1839)
Charles Fourier (April 7, 1772-October 10, 1837)
David Ricardo (April 18, 1772-September 11, 1823)
Rammohan Ray (May 22, 1772-September 27, 1833)
Samuel Taylor Coleridge (October 21, 1772-July 25, 1834)
William Henry Harrison (February 9, 1773-April 4, 1841)
James Mill (April 6, 1773-June 23, 1836)
Marie Anne Victorine Boivin (April 9, 1773-May 16, 1841)
Metternich (May 15, 1773-June 11, 1859)
Amschel Mayer Rothschild (June 12, 1773-December 6, 1855)
Lord Jeffrey (October 23, 1773-January 26, 1850)

George Cayley (December 27, 1773-December 15, 1857)
Meriwether Lewis (August 18, 1774-October 11, 1809)
Saint Elizabeth Seton (August 28, 1774-January 4, 1821)
Salomon Mayer Rothschild (September 9, 1774-July 27, 1855)
Johnny Appleseed (September 26, 1774-March 18?, 1845)
Friedrich Wilhelm Joseph von Schelling (January 27, 1775-August 20, 1854)
J. M. W. Turner (April 23, 1775-December 19, 1851)
Daniel O'Connell (August 6, 1775-May 15, 1847)
Jane Austen (December 16, 1775-July 18, 1817)
Ho Xuan Huong (c. 1776-1820?)
John Walter II (February 23, 1776-July 28, 1847)
Sophie Germain (April 1, 1776-June 27, 1831)
John Constable (June 11, 1776-March 31, 1837)
Amedeo Avogadro (August 9, 1776-July 9, 1856)
Barthold Georg Niebuhr (August 27, 1776-January 2, 1831)
Roger Brooke Taney (March 17, 1777-October 12, 1864)
Henry Clay (April 12, 1777-June 29, 1852)

Carl Friedrich Gauss (April 30, 1777-February 23, 1855)

Nathan Mayer Rothschild (September 16, 1777-July 28, 1836)

Heinrich von Kleist (October 18, 1777-November 21, 1811)

Francis Greenway (November 20, 1777-September 26, 1837)

Alexander I (December 23, 1777-December 1, 1825)

José de San Martín (February 25, 1778-August 17, 1850)

Henry Brougham (September 19, 1778-May 7, 1868)

Joseph Lancaster (November 25, 1778-October 24, 1838)

Joseph-Louis Gay-Lussac (December 6, 1778-May 9, 1850)

Sir Humphry Davy (December 17, 1778-May 29, 1829)

Zebulon Pike (January 5, 1779-April 27, 1813)

Stephen Decatur (January 5, 1779-March 22, 1820)

Friedrich Karl von Savigny (February 21, 1779-October 25, 1861)

Frances Trollope (March 10, 1779-October 6, 1863)

Second Viscount Melbourne (March 15, 1779-November 24, 1848)

Francis Scott Key (August 1, 1779-January 11, 1843)

Joseph Story (September 18, 1779-September 10, 1845)

William Ellery Channing (April 7, 1780-October 2, 1842)

Elizabeth Fry (May 21, 1780-October 12, 1845)

Carl von Clausewitz (June 1, 1780-November 16, 1831)

Jean-Auguste-Dominique Ingres (August 29, 1780-January 14, 1867)

Ranjit Singh (November 13, 1780-June 27, 1839)

Mary Somerville (December 26, 1780-November 29, 1872)

1781-1790

Muḥammad Bello (1781-October 26, 1837)

George Stephenson (June 9, 1781-August 12, 1848)

Daniel Webster (January 18, 1782-October 24, 1852)

Thomas Hart Benton (March 14, 1782-April 10, 1858)

John C. Calhoun (March 18, 1782-March 31, 1850)

Friedrich Froebel (April 21, 1782-June 21, 1852)

Niccolò Paganini (October 27, 1782-May 27, 1840)

Martin Van Buren (December 5, 1782-July 24, 1862)

Stendhal (January 23, 1783-March 23, 1842)

Washington Irving (April 3, 1783-November 28, 1859)

Simón Bolívar (July 24, 1783-December 17, 1830)

Friedrich Wilhelm Bessel (July 22, 1784-March 17, 1846)

Lord Palmerston (October 20, 1784-October 18, 1865)

Zachary Taylor (November 24, 1784-July 9, 1850)

Jacob Grimm (January 4, 1785-September 30, 1863)

Alessandro Manzoni (March 7, 1785-May 22, 1873)

John James Audubon (April 26, 1785-January 27, 1851)

Sylvanus Thayer (June 9, 1785-September 7, 1872)

Oliver Hazard Perry (August 20, 1785-August 23, 1819)

Lin Zexu (August 30, 1785-November 22, 1850)

La Saragossa (1786-1857)

Nicholas Biddle (January 8, 1786-February 27, 1844)

Wilhelm Grimm (February 24, 1786-December 16, 1859)

Sir Thomas Fowell Buxton (April 1, 1786-February 19, 1845)

Sir John Franklin (April 16, 1786-June 11, 1847)

Winfield Scott (June 13, 1786-May 29, 1866)

David Crockett (August 17, 1786-March 6, 1836)

Carl Maria von Weber (November 18, 1786-June 5, 1826)

Shaka (c. 1787-September 22, 1828)

Emma Willard (February 23, 1787-April 15, 1870)

Edmund Kean (November 4, 1787-May 15, 1833)

Jacques Daguerre (November 18, 1787-July 10, 1851)

Sacagawea (c. 1788-December 20, 1812)

Lord Byron (January 22, 1788-April 19, 1824)

Sir Robert Peel (February 5, 1788-July 2, 1850)

Arthur Schopenhauer (February 22, 1788-September 21, 1860)

Antoine-César Becquerel (March 8, 1788-January 18, 1878)

Don Carlos (March 29, 1788-March 10, 1855)

Carl Mayer Rothschild (April 24, 1788-March 10, 1855)

James Gadsden (May 15, 1788-December 26, 1858)

Alexander Campbell (September 12, 1788-March 4, 1866)

Sarah Josepha Hale (October 24, 1788-April 30, 1879)
Jules Michelet (August 21, 1789-February 9, 1874)
James Fenimore Cooper (September 15, 1789-
September 14, 1851)

John Tyler (March 29, 1790-January 18, 1862)
W. C. Wentworth (August 13, 1790-March 20, 1872)
John Ross (October 3, 1790-August 1, 1866)

1791-1800

Saʿīd ibn Sulṭān (1791-October 19, 1856)
James Buchanan (April 23, 1791-June 1, 1868)
Samuel F. B. Morse (April 27, 1791-April 2, 1872)
Michael Faraday (September 22, 1791-August 25, 1867)
Théodore Géricault (September 26, 1791-January 26, 1824)
Charles Babbage (December 26, 1791-October 18, 1871)
Alexander Ypsilantis (1792-January 31, 1828)
Gioacchino Rossini (February 29, 1792-November 13, 1868)
Karl Ernst von Baer (February 29, 1792-November 28, 1876)
Thaddeus Stevens (April 4, 1792-August 11, 1868)
First Earl of Durham (April 12, 1792-July 28, 1840)
Pius IX (May 13, 1792-February 7, 1878)
James Mayer Rothschild (May 15, 1792-November 15, 1868)
Percy Bysshe Shelley (August 4, 1792-July 8, 1822)
John Russell (August 18, 1792-May 28, 1878)
Sarah Grimké (November 26, 1792-December 23, 1873)
Nikolay Ivanovich Lobachevsky (December 1, 1792-February 24, 1856)
Lucretia Mott (January 3, 1793-November 11, 1880)
Sam Houston (March 2, 1793-July 26, 1863)
William Charles Macready (March 3, 1793-April 27, 1873)
Felicia Dorothea Hemans (September 25, 1793-May 16, 1835)
Stephen Fuller Austin (November 3, 1793-December 27, 1836)
Demetrios Ypsilantis (December 25, 1793-1832)
Antonio López de Santa Anna (February 21, 1794-June 21, 1876)
Matthew C. Perry (April 10, 1794-March 4, 1858)
Anna Jameson (May 19, 1794-March 17, 1860)
Cornelius Vanderbilt (May 27, 1794-January 4, 1877)
William Cullen Bryant (November 3, 1794-June 12, 1878)

Dred Scott (c. 1795-September 17, 1858)
Antonio José de Sucre (February 3, 1795-June 4, 1830)
William Lyon Mackenzie (March 12, 1795-August 28, 1861)
Sir Charles Barry (May 23, 1795-May 12, 1860)
Thomas Arnold (June 13, 1795-June 12, 1842)
James Gordon Bennett (September 1, 1795-June 1, 1872)
Frances Wright (September 6, 1795-December 13, 1852)
John Keats (October 31, 1795-February 23, 1821)
James K. Polk (November 2, 1795-June 15, 1849)
Thomas Carlyle (December 4, 1795-February 5, 1881)
Leopold von Ranke (December 21, 1795-May 23, 1886)
Jakob Steiner (March 18, 1796-April 1, 1863)
Edward Gibbon Wakefield (March 20, 1796-May 16, 1862)
William Hickling Prescott (May 4, 1796-January 28, 1859)
Horace Mann (May 4, 1796-August 2, 1859)
Nicholas I (July 6, 1796-March 2, 1855)
George Catlin (July 26, 1796-December 23, 1872)
Hiroshige (1797-October 12, 1858)
Sojourner Truth (c. 1797-November 26, 1883)
Franz Schubert (January 31, 1797-November 19, 1828)
Mary Lyon (February 28, 1797-March 5, 1849)
Adolphe Thiers (April 15, 1797-September 3, 1877)
Mary Wollstonecraft Shelley (August 30, 1797-February 1, 1851)
Sir Charles Lyell (November 14, 1797-February 22, 1875)
Gaetano Donizetti (November 29, 1797-April 8, 1848)
Heinrich Heine (December 13, 1797-February 17, 1856)
Joseph Henry (December 17, 1797-May 13, 1878)
Auguste Comte (January 19, 1798-September 5, 1857)
Charles Wilkes (April 3, 1798-February 8, 1877)
Eugène Delacroix (April 26, 1798-August 13, 1863)
Pedro I (October 12, 1798-September 24, 1834)
Jedediah Smith (January 6, 1799-May 27, 1831)

Fourteenth Earl of Derby (March 29, 1799-October 23, 1869)

Honoré de Balzac (May 20, 1799-August 18, 1850)

Alexander Pushkin (June 6, 1799-February 10, 1837)

Bronson Alcott (November 29, 1799-March 4, 1888)

Millard Fillmore (January 7, 1800-March 8, 1874)

Caleb Cushing (January 17, 1800-January 2, 1879)

Edwin Chadwick (January 24, 1800-July 6, 1890)

Sir James Clark Ross (April 15, 1800-April 3, 1862)

John Brown (May 9, 1800-December 2, 1859)

Friedrich Wöhler (July 31, 1800-September 23, 1882)

E. B. Pusey (August 22, 1800-September 16, 1882)

Catharine Beecher (September 6, 1800-May 12, 1878)

William Holmes McGuffey (September 23, 1800-May 4, 1873)

Nat Turner (October 2, 1800-November 11, 1831)

George Bancroft (October 3, 1800-January 17, 1891)

Thomas Babington Macaulay (October 25, 1800-December 28, 1859)

Charles Goodyear (December 29, 1800-July 1, 1860)

1801-1810

John Henry Newman (February 21, 1801-August 11, 1890)

Vincenzo Gioberti (April 5, 1801-October 26, 1852)

Gustav Theodor Fechner (April 19, 1801-November 18, 1887)

William H. Seward (May 16, 1801-October 10, 1872)

Brigham Young (June 1, 1801-August 29, 1877)

David G. Farragut (July 5, 1801-August 14, 1870)

Samuel Gridley Howe (November 10, 1801-January 9, 1876)

Catharine Parr Traill (January 9, 1802-August 28, 1899)

Sir Charles Wheatstone (February 6, 1802-October 19, 1875)

Lydia Maria Child (February 11, 1802-October 20, 1880)

Victor Hugo (February 26, 1802-May 22, 1885)

Dorothea Dix (April 4, 1802-July 17, 1887)

Harriet Martineau (June 12, 1802-June 27, 1876)

Alexandre Dumas, *père* (July 24, 1802-December 5, 1870)

Niels Henrik Abel (August 5, 1802-April 6, 1829)

Sir James Outram (January 29, 1803-March 11, 1863)

Flora Tristan (April 7, 1803-November 14, 1844)

Justus von Liebig (May 12, 1803-April 18, 1873)

Ralph Waldo Emerson (May 25, 1803-April 27, 1882)

Ferenc Deák (October 17, 1803-January 28, 1876)

Susanna Moodie (December 6, 1803-April 8, 1885)

Hector Berlioz (December 11, 1803-March 8, 1869)

Osceola (c. 1804-January 30, 1838)

Robert Baldwin (May 12, 1804-December 9, 1858)

Elizabeth Palmer Peabody (May 16, 1804-January 3, 1894)

Richard Cobden (June 3, 1804-April 2, 1865)

George Sand (July 1, 1804-June 8, 1876)

Nathaniel Hawthorne (July 4, 1804-May 19, 1864)

Franklin Pierce (November 23, 1804-October 8, 1869)

Benjamin Disraeli (December 21, 1804-April 19, 1881)

Fanny Calderón de la Barca (December 23, 1804-February 3, 1882)

Angelina Grimké (February 20, 1805-October 26, 1879)

Hans Christian Andersen (April 2, 1805-August 4, 1875)

Frederick Denison Maurice (April 29, 1805-April 1, 1872)

Giuseppe Mazzini (June 22, 1805-March 10, 1872)

Alexis de Tocqueville (July 29, 1805-April 16, 1859)

Sir William Rowan Hamilton (August 3/4, 1805-September 2, 1865)

Ferdinand de Lesseps (November 19, 1805-December 7, 1894)

William Lloyd Garrison (December 10, 1805-May 24, 1879)

Joseph Smith (December 23, 1805-June 27, 1844)

Samuel Ajayi Crowther (c. 1806-December 31, 1891)

Matthew Fontaine Maury (January 14, 1806-February 1, 1873)

Elizabeth Barrett Browning (March 6, 1806-June 29, 1861)

Edwin Forrest (March 9, 1806-December 12, 1872)

Benito Juárez (March 21, 1806-July 19, 1872)

Isambard Kingdom Brunel (April 9, 1806-September 15, 1859)

William Fothergill Cooke (May 4, 1806-June 25, 1879)

John Stuart Mill (May 20, 1806-May 7, 1873)

John Augustus Roebling (June 12, 1806-July 22, 1869)

Robert E. Lee (January 19, 1807-October 12, 1870)

Henry Wadsworth Longfellow (February 27, 1807-March 24, 1882)

Louis Agassiz (May 28, 1807-December 14, 1873)

Giuseppe Garibaldi (July 4, 1807-June 2, 1882)

John Greenleaf Whittier (December 17, 1807-September 7, 1892)

Salmon P. Chase (January 13, 1808-May 7, 1873)

Napoleon III (April 20, 1808-January 9, 1873)

Jefferson Davis (June 3, 1808-December 6, 1889)

Henry Edward Manning (July 15, 1808-January 14, 1892)

James Nasmyth (August 19, 1808-May 7, 1890)

Abdelkader (September 6, 1808-May 25/26, 1883)

Andrew Johnson (December 29, 1808-July 31, 1875)

Louis Braille (January 4, 1809-January 6, 1852)

Friedrich von Beust (January 13, 1809-October 24, 1886)

Pierre-Joseph Proudhon (January 15, 1809-January 19, 1865)

Edgar Allan Poe (January 19, 1809-October 7, 1849)

Felix Mendelssohn (February 3, 1809-November 4, 1847)

Abraham Lincoln (February 12, 1809-April 15, 1865)

Charles Darwin (February 12, 1809-April 19, 1882)

Cyrus Hall McCormick (February 15, 1809-May 13, 1884)

Nikolai Gogol (March 31, 1809-March 4, 1852)

Alfred, Lord Tennyson (August 6, 1809-October 6, 1892)

Oliver Wendell Holmes (August 29, 1809-October 7, 1894)

Fanny Kemble (November 27, 1809-January 15, 1893)

Kit Carson (December 24, 1809-May 23, 1868)

William Ewart Gladstone (December 29, 1809-May 19, 1898)

Abby Kelley Foster (January 15, 1810-January 14, 1887)

Frédéric Chopin (March 1, 1810-October 17, 1849)

Leo XIII (March 2, 1810-July 20, 1903)

Theodore Parker (April 24, 1810-May 10, 1860)

Margaret Fuller (May 23, 1810-July 19, 1850)

Robert Schumann (June 8, 1810-July 29, 1856)

Fanny Elssler (June 23, 1810-November 27, 1884)

P. T. Barnum (July 5, 1810-April 7, 1891)

Count Cavour (August 10, 1810-June 6, 1861)

Asa Gray (November 18, 1810-January 30, 1888)

1811-1820

Charles Sumner (January 6, 1811-March 11, 1874)

Henry Barnard (January 24, 1811-July 5, 1900)

Horace Greeley (February 3, 1811-November 29, 1872)

Domingo Faustino Sarmiento (February 14, 1811-September 11, 1888)

John Laird Mair Lawrence (March 4, 1811-June 27, 1879)

George Caleb Bingham (March 20, 1811-July 7, 1879)

Harriet Beecher Stowe (June 14, 1811-July 1, 1896)

Sir William Robert Grove (July 11, 1811-August 1, 1896)

Sir George Gilbert Scott (July 13, 1811-March 27, 1878)

William Makepeace Thackeray (July 18, 1811-December 24, 1863)

Franz Liszt (October 22, 1811-July 31, 1886)

Évariste Galois (October 25, 1811-May 31, 1832)

Louis Blanc (October 29, 1811-December 6, 1882)

John Bright (November 16, 1811-March 27, 1889)

Zeng Guofan (November 26, 1811-March 12, 1872)

Wendell Phillips (November 29, 1811-February 2, 1884)

Charles Dickens (February 7, 1812-June 9, 1870)

Alexander H. Stephens (February 11, 1812-March 4, 1883)

Augustus Welby Northmore Pugin (March 1, 1812-September 14, 1852)

Aleksandr Herzen (April 6, 1812-January 21, 1870)

Sir George Grey (April 14, 1812-September 19, 1898)

First Marquis of Dalhousie (April 22, 1812-December 19, 1860)

Alfred Krupp (April 26, 1812-July 14, 1887)

Sir Henry Bessemer (January 19, 1813-March 15, 1898)

John C. Frémont (January 21, 1813-July 13, 1890)

David Livingstone (March 19, 1813-May 1, 1873)

Stephen A. Douglas (April 23, 1813-June 3, 1861)

Søren Kierkegaard (May 5, 1813-November 11, 1855)

Richard Wagner (May 22, 1813-February 13, 1883)

Henry Ward Beecher (June 24, 1813-March 8, 1887)

Claude Bernard (July 12, 1813-February 10, 1878)

Daniel Macmillan (September 13, 1813-June 27, 1857)

Giuseppe Verdi (October 10, 1813-January 27, 1901)

Táhirih (1814/1820-1852)

Hong Xiuquan (January 1, 1814-June 1, 1864)

Mikhail Bakunin (May 30, 1814-July 1, 1876)

Samuel Colt (July 19, 1814-January 10, 1862)

Anaïs Ségalas (September 21, 1814-August 31, 1893)

Mikhail Lermontov (October 15, 1814-July 27, 1841)

Luise Aston (November 26, 1814-December 21, 1871)

Edwin M. Stanton (December 19, 1814-December 24, 1869)

Sir John Alexander Macdonald (January 11, 1815-June 6, 1891)

Otto von Bismarck (April 1, 1815-July 30, 1898)

Anthony Trollope (April 24, 1815-December 6, 1882)

Sir Henry Parkes (May 27, 1815-April 27, 1896)

Elizabeth Cady Stanton (November 12, 1815-October 26, 1902)

Ii Naosuke (November 29, 1815-March 24, 1860)

Countess of Lovelace (December 10, 1815-November 27, 1852)

Charlotte Brontë (April 21, 1816-March 31, 1855)

Stephen J. Field (November 4, 1816-April 9, 1899)

Werner Siemens (December 13, 1816-December 6, 1892)

Frederick Douglass (February, 1817?-February 20, 1895)

Henry David Thoreau (July 12, 1817-May 6, 1862)

Sir Sayyid Ahmad Khan (October 17, 1817-March 27, 1898)

Bahā'ullāh (November 12, 1817-May 29, 1892)

Theodor Mommsen (November 30, 1817-November 1, 1903)

Tewodros II (c. 1818-April 13, 1868)

Alexander II (April 29, 1818-March 13, 1881)

Karl Marx (May 5, 1818-March 14, 1883)

Jacob Burckhardt (May 25, 1818-August 8, 1897)

Amelia Bloomer (May 27, 1818-December 30, 1894)

Louis Faidherbe (June 3, 1818-September 29, 1889)

Charles Gounod (June 17, 1818-October 18, 1893)

Ignaz Philipp Semmelweis (July 1, 1818-August 13, 1865)

William Edward Forster (July 11, 1818-April 5, 1886)

Emily Brontë (July 30, 1818-December 19, 1848)

Maria Mitchell (August 1, 1818-June 28, 1889)

Lucy Stone (August 13, 1818-October 18, 1893)

Alexander Macmillan (October 3, 1818-January 26, 1896)

Ivan Turgenev (November 9, 1818-September 3, 1883)

Lewis Henry Morgan (November 21, 1818-December 17, 1881)

George Brown (November 29, 1818-May 9, 1880)

Mary Todd Lincoln (December 13, 1818-July 16, 1882)

John Ruskin (February 8, 1819-January 20, 1900)

Lydia E. Pinkham (February 9, 1819-May 17, 1883)

Isaac Mayer Wise (March 29, 1819-March 26, 1900)

Queen Victoria (May 24, 1819-January 22, 1901)

Julia Ward Howe (May 27, 1819-October 17, 1910)

Walt Whitman (May 31, 1819-March 26, 1892)

Gustave Courbet (June 10, 1819-December 31, 1877)

Jacques Offenbach (June 20, 1819-October 5, 1880)

Elias Howe (July 9, 1819-October 3, 1867)

Herman Melville (August 1, 1819-September 28, 1891)

William Thomas Green Morton (August 9, 1819-July 15, 1868)

Clara Schumann (September 13, 1819-May 20, 1896)

The Bāb (October 20, 1819-July 9, 1850)

George Eliot (November 22, 1819-December 22, 1880)

Harriet Tubman (c. 1820-March 10, 1913)

Anne Brontë (January 17, 1820-May 28, 1849)

William Tecumseh Sherman (February 8, 1820-February 14, 1891)

Susan B. Anthony (February 15, 1820-March 13, 1906)

Alexandre-Edmond Becquerel (March 24, 1820-May 11, 1891)

Herbert Spencer (April 27, 1820-December 8, 1903)

Florence Nightingale (May 12, 1820-August 13, 1910)

James Buchanan Eads (May 23, 1820-March 8, 1887)

Iswar Chandra Vidyasagar (September 26, 1820-July 29, 1891)

Jenny Lind (October 6, 1820-November 2, 1887)

Friedrich Engels (November 28, 1820-August 5, 1895)

Carolina Coronado (December 12, 1820-January 15, 1911)

1821-1830

Elizabeth Blackwell (February 3, 1821-May 31, 1910)

Lola Montez (February 17, 1821-January 17, 1861)

Sir Richard Francis Burton (March 19, 1821-October 20, 1890)

Charles Baudelaire (April 9, 1821-August 31, 1867)

Sir Charles Tupper (July 2, 1821-October, 30, 1915)

Mary Baker Eddy (July 16, 1821-December 3, 1910)

Jay Cooke (August 10, 1821-February 18, 1905)

Hermann von Helmholtz (August 31, 1821-September 8, 1894)

Rudolf Virchow (October 13, 1821-September 5, 1902)

Fyodor Dostoevski (November 11, 1821-February 9, 1881)

Gustave Flaubert (December 12, 1821-May 8, 1880)

Clara Barton (December 25, 1821-April 12, 1912)

Red Cloud (1822-December 10, 1909)

Heinrich Schliemann (January 6, 1822-December 26, 1890)

Étienne Lenoir (January 12, 1822-August 4, 1900)

Alexander Mackenzie (January 28, 1822-April 17, 1892)

Francis Galton (February 16, 1822-January 17, 1911)

Albrecht Ritschl (March 25, 1822-March 20, 1889)

Frederick Law Olmsted (April 26, 1822-August 28, 1903)

Ulysses S. Grant (April 27, 1822-July 23, 1885)

Lydia Folger Fowler (May 5, 1822-January 26, 1879)

Gregor Mendel (July 22, 1822-January 6, 1884)

Rutherford B. Hayes (October 4, 1822-January 17, 1893)

Elizabeth Cabot Agassiz (December 5, 1822-June 27, 1907)

César Franck (December 10, 1822-November 8, 1890)

Matthew Arnold (December 24, 1822-April 15, 1888)

Louis Pasteur (December 27, 1822-September 28, 1895)

Mathew B. Brady (c. 1823-January 15, 1896)

Li Hongzhang (February 15, 1823-November 7, 1901)

Ernest Renan (February 28, 1823-October 2, 1892)

William Marcy Tweed (April 3, 1823-April 12, 1878)

William Siemens (April 4, 1823-November 19, 1883)

Charlotte Mary Yonge (August 11, 1823-March 24, 1901)

Francis Parkman (September 16, 1823-November 8, 1893)

Mary Ann Shadd Cary (October 9, 1823-June 5, 1893)

Thomas Wentworth Higginson (December 22, 1823-May 9, 1911)

Stonewall Jackson (January 21, 1824-May 10, 1863)

Leland Stanford (March 9, 1824-June 20, 1893)

George Edmund Street (June 20, 1824-December 18, 1881)

Baron Kelvin (June 26, 1824-December 17, 1907)

Anton Bruckner (September 4, 1824-October 11, 1896)

Ferdinand Lassalle (April 11, 1825-August 31, 1864)

Thomas Henry Huxley (May 4, 1825-June 29, 1895)

Dadabhai Naoroji (September 4, 1825-June 30, 1917)

Paul Kruger (October 10, 1825-July 14, 1904)

Johann Strauss (October 25, 1825-June 3, 1899)

Pedro II (December 2, 1825-December 5, 1891)

Cetshwayo (c. 1826-February 8, 1884)

Matilda Joslyn Gage (March 24, 1826-March 18, 1898)

Wilhelm Liebknecht (March 29, 1826-August 7, 1900)

Stephen Collins Foster (July 4, 1826-January 13, 1864)

Friedrich Siemens (December 8, 1826-May 24, 1904)

Saigō Takamori (1827/1828-September 24, 1877)

William Holman Hunt (April 2, 1827-September 7, 1910)

Joseph Lister (April 5, 1827-February 10, 1912)

Barbara Leigh Smith Bodichon (April 8, 1827-June 11, 1891)

John Hanning Speke (May 4, 1827-September 15, 1864)

Konstantin Petrovich Pobedonostsev (May 21, 1827-March 23, 1907)

Ferdinand Julius Cohn (January 24, 1828-June 25, 1898)

Jules Verne (February 8, 1828-March 24, 1905)

Henrik Ibsen (March 20, 1828-May 23, 1906)

Josephine Butler (April 13, 1828-December 30, 1906)

Hippolyte Taine (April 21, 1828-March 5, 1893)

Jean-Henri Dunant (May 8, 1828-October, 30, 1910)

Leo Tolstoy (September 9, 1828-November 20, 1910)

Joseph Wilson Swan (October 31, 1828-May 27, 1914)

Carl Schurz (March 2, 1829-May 14, 1906)

Karl Siemens (March 3, 1829-March 21, 1906)

William Booth (April 10, 1829-August 20, 1912)

Geronimo (June, 1829-February 17, 1909)

Marie Elizabeth Zakrzewska (September 6, 1829-May 12, 1902)

Ferdinand Vandeveer Hayden (September 7, 1829-December 22, 1887)

Tu Duc (September 22, 1829-July 9, 1883)

Chester A. Arthur (October 5, 1829-November 18, 1886)

Samory Touré (c. 1830-June 2, 1900)

Albert Bierstadt (January 7, 1830-February 18, 1902)

James G. Blaine (January 31, 1830-January 27, 1893)

Third Marquis of Salisbury (February 3, 1830-August 22, 1903)

Camille Pissarro (July 10, 1830-November 13, 1903)

Francis Joseph I (August 18, 1830-November 21, 1916)

Porfirio Díaz (September 15, 1830-July 2, 1915)

Isabella II (October 10, 1830-April 10, 1904)

Helen Hunt Jackson (October 15, 1830-August 12, 1885)

Belva A. Lockwood (October 24, 1830-May 19, 1917)

Christina Rossetti (December 5, 1830-December 29, 1894)

Emily Dickinson (December 10, 1830-May 15, 1886)

1831-1840

Sitting Bull (March, 1831-December 15, 1890)

Dorothea Beale (March 21, 1831-November 9, 1906)

James Clerk Maxwell (June 13, 1831-November 5, 1879)

Richard Dedekind (October 6, 1831-February 12, 1916)

Frederic Harrison (October 18, 1831-January 14, 1923)

Anna Leonowens (November 6, 1831-January 19, 1915)

James A. Garfield (November 19, 1831-September 19, 1881)

Horatio Alger (January 13, 1832-July 18, 1899)

Édouard Manet (January 23, 1832-April 30, 1883)

Lewis Carroll (January 27, 1832-January 14, 1898)

Nikolaus August Otto (June 10, 1832-January 26, 1891)

Maximilian (July 6, 1832-June 19, 1867)

Louisa May Alcott (November 29, 1832-March 6, 1888)

Gustave Eiffel (December 15, 1832-December 27, 1923)

Charles George Gordon (January 28, 1833-January 26, 1885)

Johannes Brahms (May 7, 1833-April 3, 1897)

Benjamin Harrison (August 20, 1833-March 13, 1901)

Alfred Nobel (October 21, 1833-December 10, 1896)

Aleksandr Borodin (November 12, 1833-February 27, 1887)

Edwin Booth (November 13, 1833-June 7, 1893)

Lord Acton (January 10, 1834-June 19, 1902)

August Weismann (January 17, 1834-November 5, 1914)

Dmitry Ivanovich Mendeleyev (February 8, 1834-February 2, 1907)

Ernst Haeckel (February 16, 1834-August 9, 1919)

Gottlieb Daimler (March 17, 1834-March 6, 1900)

Charles William Eliot (March 20, 1834-August 22, 1926)

William Morris (March 24, 1834-October 3, 1896)

John Wesley Powell (March 24, 1834-September 23, 1902)

James McNeill Whistler (July 10, 1834-July 17, 1903)

Edgar Degas (July 19, 1834-September 27, 1917)

James Gibbons (July 23, 1834-March 24, 1921)

Marshall Field (August 18, 1834-January 16, 1906)

Samuel Pierpont Langley (August 22, 1834-February 27, 1906)

Olympia Brown (January 5, 1835-October 23, 1926)

Sir Julius Vogel (February 24, 1835-March 12, 1899)

Simon Newcomb (March 12, 1835-July 11, 1909)

Leopold II (April 9, 1835-December 17, 1909)

Adah Isaacs Menken (June 15, 1835-August 10, 1868)

Mary Elizabeth Braddon (October 4, 1835-February 4, 1915)

Theodore Thomas (October 11, 1835-January 4, 1905)

Andrew Carnegie (November 25, 1835-August 11, 1919)

Cixi (November 29, 1835-November 15, 1908)

Mark Twain (November 30, 1835-April 21, 1910)

Samuel Butler (December 4, 1835-June 18, 1902)

Lobengula (c. 1836-January, 1894)

Léo Delibes (February 21, 1836-January 16, 1891)

Winslow Homer (February 24, 1836-September 29, 1910)

Thomas Hill Green (April 7, 1836-March 26, 1882)

Sir Joseph Norman Lockyer (May 17, 1836-August 16, 1920)

Joseph Chamberlain (July 8, 1836-July 2, 1914)

W. S. Gilbert (November 18, 1836-May 29, 1911)

Tippu Tib (c. 1837-June 14, 1905)

Dwight L. Moody (February 5, 1837-December 22, 1899)

Grover Cleveland (March 18, 1837-June 24, 1908)

J. P. Morgan (April 17, 1837-March 31, 1913)

Friedrich von Holstein (April 24, 1837-May 8, 1909)

Wild Bill Hickok (May 27, 1837-August 2, 1876)

Charlotte Forten (August 17, 1837-July 22, 1914)

Zhang Zhidong (September 2, 1837-October 4, 1909)

Marcus A. Hanna (September 24, 1837-February 15, 1904)

Abby Sage Richardson (October 14, 1837-December 5, 1900)

George Dewey (December 26, 1837-January 16, 1917)

Jamāl al-Dīn al-Afghānī (1838-March 9, 1897)

André Rebouças (January 13, 1838-May 9, 1898)

Henry Irving (February 6, 1838-October 13, 1905)

Henry Adams (February 16, 1838-March 27, 1918)

Léon Gambetta (April 2, 1838-December 31, 1882)

John Muir (April 21, 1838-December 24, 1914)

Henry Sidgwick (May 31, 1838-August 28, 1900)

Liliuokalani (September 2, 1838-November 11, 1917)

James Jerome Hill (September 16, 1838-May 29, 1916)

Victoria Woodhull (September 23, 1838-June 10, 1927)

Henry Hobson Richardson (September 29, 1838-April 27, 1886)

John Hay (October 8, 1838-July 1, 1905)

Georges Bizet (October 25, 1838-June 3, 1875)

Octavia Hill (December 3, 1838-August 13, 1912)

Paul Cézanne (January 19, 1839-October 22, 1906)

Josiah Willard Gibbs (February 11, 1839-April 28, 1903)

Modest Mussorgsky (March 21, 1839-March 28, 1881)

Joaquim Maria Machado de Assis (June 21, 1839-September 29, 1908)

John D. Rockefeller (July 8, 1839-May 23, 1937)

Walter Pater (August 4, 1839-July 30, 1894)

Henry George (September 2, 1839-October 29, 1897)

Charles Sanders Peirce (September 10, 1839-April 19, 1914)

Frances Willard (September 28, 1839-February 18, 1898)

George A. Custer (December 5, 1839-June 25, 1876)

Chief Joseph (c. 1840-September 21, 1904)

Émile Zola (April 2, 1840-September 28, 1902)

Odilon Redon (April 20, 1840-July 6, 1916)

Peter Ilich Tchaikovsky (May 7, 1840-November 6, 1893)

Thomas Hardy (June 2, 1840-January 11, 1928)

Thomas Nast (September 27, 1840-December 7, 1902)

Auguste Rodin (November 12, 1840-November 17, 1917)

1841-1850

Henry Morton Stanley (January 28, 1841-May 10, 1904)

Pierre-Auguste Renoir (February 25, 1841-December 3, 1919)

John Philip Holland (February 29, 1841-August 12, 1914)

Lester Frank Ward (June 18, 1841-April 18, 1913)

Antonín Dvořák (September 8, 1841-May 1, 1904)

Itō Hirobumi (October 14, 1841-October 26, 1909)

Crazy Horse (1842?-September 5, 1877)

William James (January 11, 1842-August 26, 1910)

Mahadev Govind Ranade (January 18, 1842-January 16, 1901)

Arthur Sullivan (May 13, 1842-November 22, 1900)

Ambrose Bierce (June 24, 1842-January, 1914?)

Mary Putnam Jacobi (August 31, 1842-June 10, 1906)

Abdülhamid II (September 21, 1842-February 10, 1918)

Ellen Swallow Richards (December 3, 1842-March 30, 1911)

Frank James (January 10, 1843-February 18, 1915)

William McKinley (January 29, 1843-September 14, 1901)

Montgomery Ward (February 17, 1843-December 7, 1913)

Henry James (April 15, 1843-February 28, 1916)

Bertha von Suttner (June 9, 1843-June 21, 1914)

Edvard Grieg (June 15, 1843-September 4, 1907)

Robert Koch (December 11, 1843-May 27, 1910)

Nikolay Rimsky-Korsakov (March 18, 1844-June 21, 1908)

Anatole France (April 16, 1844-October 12, 1924)

Henri Rousseau (May 21, 1844-September 2, 1910)

Mary Cassatt (May 22, 1844-June 14, 1926)
Thomas Eakins (July 25, 1844-June 25, 1916)
The Mahdi (August 12, 1844-June 22, 1885)
Menelik II (August 17, 1844-December 12, 1913)
Friedrich Nietzsche (October 15, 1844-August 25, 1900)
Louis Riel (October 22, 1844-November 16, 1885)
Sarah Bernhardt (October 22, 1844-March 26, 1923)
Carl Benz (November 25, 1844-April 4, 1929)
Wilhelm Conrad Röntgen (March 27, 1845-February 10, 1923)
Richard John Seddon (June 22, 1845-June 10, 1906)
F. H. Bradley (January 30, 1846-September 18, 1924)
William Cody (February 26, 1846-January 10, 1917)
Sir George Goldie (May 20, 1846-August 20, 1925)
Charles Stewart Parnell (June 27, 1846-October 6, 1891)
Daniel Hudson Burnham (September 4, 1846-June 1, 1912)
George Westinghouse (October 6, 1846-March 12, 1914)
Carry Nation (November 25, 1846-June 9, 1911)
Thomas Alva Edison (February 11, 1847-October 18, 1931)
Anna Howard Shaw (February 14, 1847-July 2, 1919)
Ellen Terry (February 27, 1847-July 21, 1928)
Alexander Graham Bell (March 3, 1847-August 2, 1922)
Joseph Pulitzer (April 10, 1847-October 29, 1911)
Sir Edwin Ray Lankester (May 15, 1847-August 15, 1929)
Dame Millicent Garrett Fawcett (June 11, 1847-August 5, 1929)
Jesse James (September 5, 1847-April 3, 1882)
Annie Besant (October 1, 1847-September 20, 1933)

John Peter Altgeld (December 30, 1847-March 12, 1902)
Augustus Saint-Gaudens (March 1, 1848-August 3, 1907)
Wyatt Earp (March 19, 1848-January 13, 1929)
Helene Lange (April 9, 1848-May 13, 1930)
Hubertine Auclert (April 10, 1848-April 4, 1914)
Paul Gauguin (June 7, 1848-May 8, 1903)
William Gilbert Grace (July 18, 1848-October 23, 1915)
Margaret Lindsay Huggins (August 14, 1848-May 24, 1915)
Gottlob Frege (November 8, 1848-July 26, 1925)
Joel Chandler Harris (December 9, 1848-July 3, 1908)
Muḥammad ʿAbduh (c. 1849-July 11, 1905)
Sir Edmund Barton (January 18, 1849-January 7, 1920)
Luther Burbank (March 7, 1849-April 11, 1926)
Sir William Osler (July 12, 1849-December 29, 1919)
Emma Lazarus (July 22, 1849-November 19, 1887)
Sarah Orne Jewett (September 3, 1849-June 24, 1909)
George Washington Williams (October 16, 1849-August 2, 1891)
Frances Hodgson Burnett (November 24, 1849-October 29, 1924)
Sofya Kovalevskaya (January 15, 1850-February 10, 1891)
Samuel Gompers (January 27, 1850-December 13, 1924)
Frances Xavier Cabrini (July 15, 1850-December 22, 1917)
Guy de Maupassant (August 5, 1850-July 6, 1893)
Robert Louis Stevenson (November 13, 1850-December 3, 1894)

1851-1860

Kate Chopin (February 8, 1851-August 22, 1904)
Sir Arthur Evans (July 8, 1851-July 11, 1941)
Felix Adler (August 13, 1851-April 24, 1933)
Walter Reed (September 13, 1851-November 22, 1902)
Melvil Dewey (December 10, 1851-December 26, 1931)
Calamity Jane (May 1, 1852?-August 1, 1903)
Mutsuhito (November 3, 1852-July 30, 1912)

Clorinda Matto de Turner (November 11, 1852-October 25, 1909)
Antoine-Henri Becquerel (December 15, 1852-August 25, 1908)
Albert A. Michelson (December 19, 1852-May 9, 1931)
José Martí (January 28, 1853-May 19, 1895)
Vincent van Gogh (March 30, 1853-July 29, 1890)
Cecil Rhodes (July 5, 1853-March 26, 1902)

Lillie Langtry (October 13, 1853-February 12, 1929)

Emil von Behring (March 15, 1854-March 31, 1917)

Henri Poincaré (April 29, 1854-July 17, 1912)

Ottmar Mergenthaler (May 11, 1854-October 28, 1899)

Edward Wyllis Scripps (June 18, 1854-March 12, 1926)

Engelbert Humperdinck (September 1, 1854-September 27, 1921)

Oscar Wilde (October 16, 1854-November 30, 1900)

Arthur Rimbaud (October 20, 1854-November 10, 1891)

Alice Freeman Palmer (February 21, 1855-December 6, 1902)

Olive Schreiner (March 24, 1855-December 10, 1920)

John Singer Sargent (January 12, 1856-April 15, 1925)

Booker T. Washington (April 5, 1856-November 14, 1915)

L. Frank Baum (May 15, 1856-May 6, 1919)

H. Rider Haggard (June 22, 1856-May 14, 1925)

Nikola Tesla (July 9, 1856-January 7, 1943)

William Rainey Harper (July 26, 1856-January 10, 1906)

Alfred Deakin (August 3, 1856-October 7, 1919)

Keir Hardie (August 15, 1856-September 26, 1915)

Louis Sullivan (September 3, 1856-April 14, 1924)

James Buchanan Duke (December 23, 1856-October 10, 1925)

Sir Robert Stephenson Smyth Baden-Powell (February 22, 1857-January 8, 1941)

Williamina Paton Stevens Fleming (May 15, 1857-May 21, 1911)

Rudolf Diesel (March 18, 1858-September 29, 1913)

Kang Youwei (March 19, 1858-March 31, 1927)

Charlotte Angas Scott (June 8, 1858-November 10, 1931)

Sir Robert Abbott Hadfield (November 28, 1858-September 30, 1940)

Fanny Bullock Workman (January 8, 1859-January 22, 1925)

Aleksandr Stepanovich Popov (March 16, 1859-January 13, 1906)

Sir Arthur Conan Doyle (May 22, 1859-July 7, 1930)

Jean Jaurès (September 3, 1859-July 31, 1914)

Georges Seurat (December 2, 1859-March 29, 1891)

Anton Chekhov (January 29, 1860-July 15, 1904)

Theodor Herzl (May 2, 1860-July 3, 1904)

Lizzie Borden (July 19, 1860-June 1, 1927)

Annie Oakley (August 13, 1860-November 3, 1926)

1861-1870

Frederic Remington (October 4, 1861-December 26, 1909)

O. Henry (September 11, 1862-June 5, 1910)

Mary Kingsley (October 13, 1862-June 3, 1900)

Vivekananda (January 12, 1863-July 4, 1902)

A. B. Paterson (February 17, 1864-February 2, 1941)

Daniel Mannix (March 4, 1864-November 6, 1963)

Henri de Toulouse-Lautrec (November 24, 1864-September 9, 1901)

Charles Proteus Steinmetz (April 9, 1865-October 26, 1923)

Rudyard Kipling (December 30, 1865-January 18, 1936)

Rubén Darío (January 18, 1867-February 6, 1916)

Meri Te Tai Mangakahia (May 22, 1868-October 10, 1920)

Scott Joplin (November 24, 1868-April 1, 1917)

Grigori Yefimovich Rasputin (c. 1870-December 30, 1916)

1871-1880

Stephen Crane (November 1, 1871-June 5, 1900)

Paul Laurence Dunbar (June 27, 1872-February 9, 1906)

Aubrey Beardsley (August 21, 1872-March 16, 1898)

CATEGORY INDEX

LIST OF CATEGORIES

AGRICULTURE

Johnny Appleseed, 68
Luther Burbank, 350
Justus von Liebig, 1366
Cyrus Hall McCormick, 1438
Thomas Robert Malthus, 1475

ARCHITECTURE

Sir Charles Barry, 142
Charles Bulfinch, 346
Daniel Hudson Burnham, 360
Gustave Eiffel, 734
Francis Greenway, 974
Benjamin Henry Latrobe, 1325
William Morris, 1606
John Nash, 1642
Frederick Law Olmsted, 1706
Augustus Welby Northmore
    Pugin, 1838
Henry Hobson Richardson, 1905
Sir George Gilbert Scott, 2044
George Edmund Street, 2191
Louis Sullivan, 2198

ART

John James Audubon, 91
Aubrey Beardsley, 162
Sarah Bernhardt, 208
Albert Bierstadt, 232
George Caleb Bingham, 234
Barbara Leigh Smith Bodichon,
    263
Samuel Butler, 374
Antonio Canova, 406
Mary Cassatt, 433
George Catlin, 441
Paul Cézanne, 453
John Constable, 540
Gustave Courbet, 559
Jacques-Louis David, 607
Edgar Degas, 632
Eugène Delacroix, 635
Thomas Eakins, 717
Paul Gauguin, 879
Théodore Géricault, 898
Vincent van Gogh, 932
Hiroshige, 1107

Winslow Homer, 1122
William Holman Hunt, 1157
Jean-Auguste-Dominique Ingres,
    1171
Édouard Manet, 1479
William Morris, 1606
Thomas Nast, 1649
Walter Pater, 1755
Camille Pissarro, 1799
Sir Henry Raeburn, 1852
Odilon Redon, 1875
Frederic Remington, 1881
Pierre-Auguste Renoir, 1888
Auguste Rodin, 1925
Henri Rousseau, 1951
John Ruskin, 1954
Augustus Saint-Gaudens, 1972
John Singer Sargent, 1996
Georges Seurat, 2074
Hippolyte Taine, 2216
Henri de Toulouse-Lautrec, 2287
J. M. W. Turner, 2322
James McNeill Whistler, 2420

ASTRONOMY

BIOLOGY

BUSINESS

CHEMISTRY

CHURCH GOVERNMENT

COMMUNICATIONS

CRIME

DIPLOMACY

ECONOMICS

EDUCATION

Geographical Index

HUNGARY
Ferenc Deák, 619
Franz Liszt, 1393
Ignaz Philipp Semmelweis, 2064

INDIA
Sir Sayyid Ahmad Khan, 35
Sir Richard Francis Burton, 368
Rudyard Kipling, 1284
Dadabhai Naoroji, 1634
Mahadev Govind Ranade, 1855
Ranjit Singh, 1857
Rammohan Ray, 1866
Iswar Chandra Vidyasagar, 2363
Vivekananda, 2368

IRAN
The Bāb, 105
Bahā'ullāh, 117
Jamāl al-Dīn al-Afghānī, 1203
Táhirih, 2214

IRELAND
Alexander Campbell, 399
Viscount Castlereagh, 437
Sir William Rowan Hamilton,
   1015
John Philip Holland, 1113
Anna Jameson, 1217
Baron Kelvin, 1264
Daniel Mannix, 1492
Lola Montez, 1590
Daniel O'Connell, 1695
Charles Stewart Parnell, 1747
Thomas Talbot, 2219
Duke of Wellington, 2409
Oscar Wilde, 2432

ITALY
Amedeo Avogadro, 101
Antonio Canova, 406
Count Cavour, 444
Gaetano Donizetti, 674
Giuseppe Garibaldi, 871
Vincenzo Gioberti, 921
Leo XIII, 1342
Alessandro Manzoni, 1495
Giuseppe Mazzini, 1531
Niccolò Paganini, 1724
Pius IX, 1802

Gioacchino Rossini, 1944
Giuseppe Verdi, 2351

JAPAN
Hiroshige, 1107
Ii Naosuke, 1168
Itō Hirobumi, 1185
Mutsuhito, 1631
Matthew C. Perry, 1776
Saigō Takamori, 1968
Tadano Makuzu, 2212

MEXICO
Fanny Calderón de la Barca, 389
Porfirio Díaz, 652
Miguel Hidalgo y Costilla, 1094
Benito Juárez, 1245
Maximilian, 1525
Antonio López de Santa Anna,
   1990

MIDDLE EAST
The Bāb, 105
Bahā'ullāh, 117
Sir Richard Francis Burton, 368
Jamāl al-Dīn al-Afghānī, 1203
Táhirih, 2214

NETHERLANDS
Vincent van Gogh, 932

NEW ZEALAND
Sir George Grey, 981
Meri Te Tai Mangakahia, 1483
Richard John Seddon, 2058
Sir Julius Vogel, 2371
Edward Gibbon Wakefield, 2378

NICARAGUA
Rubén Darío, 601

NIGERIA
Muḥammad Bello, 186
Samuel Ajayi Crowther, 574
'Uthman dan Fodio, 2342

NORTH AFRICA
Abdelkader, 1
Muḥammad 'Abduh, 4
Muḥammad 'Alī Pasha, 1620

NORWAY
Niels Henrik Abel, 9
Edvard Grieg, 984
Henrik Ibsen, 1165

OMAN
Sa'īd ibn Sulṭān, 1965

OTTOMAN EMPIRE
Abdelkader, 1
Abdülhamid II, 7
Ali Paşa Tepelenë, 55
Jamāl al-Dīn al-Afghānī, 1203
Muḥammad 'Alī Pasha, 1620

PERU
Simón Bolívar, 267
Clorinda Matto de Turner, 1512

POLAND
Frédéric Chopin, 486
Carl von Clausewitz, 499

PORTUGAL
Pedro I, 1763

RUSSIA
Alexander I, 45
Alexander II, 48
Mikhail Bakunin, 119
Aleksandr Borodin, 280
Anton Chekhov, 478
Fyodor Dostoevski, 677
Nikolai Gogol, 937
Aleksandr Herzen, 1085
Sofya Kovalevskaya, 1295
Mikhail Lermontov, 1352
Nikolay Ivanovich Lobachevsky,
   1403
Dmitry Ivanovich Mendeleyev,
   1544
Modest Mussorgsky, 1626
Nicholas I, 1670
Konstantin Petrovich
   Pobedonostsev, 1810
Aleksandr Stepanovich Popov,
   1824
Alexander Pushkin, 1848
Grigori Yefimovich Rasputin,
   1863

Nikolay Rimsky-Korsakov, 1915
Mikhail Mikhaylovich Speransky, 2129
Peter Ilich Tchaikovsky, 2233
Leo Tolstoy, 2283
Ivan Turgenev, 2319

SCOTLAND
Alexander Graham Bell, 182
James Gordon Bennett, 188
Henry Brougham, 312
Fanny Calderón de la Barca, 389
First Marquis of Dalhousie, 595
Sir Arthur Conan Doyle, 688
Williamina Paton Stevens Fleming, 788
Keir Hardie, 1025
Lord Jeffrey, 1223
Baron Kelvin, 1264
David Livingstone, 1400
William Lyon Mackenzie, 1454
Daniel and Alexander Macmillan, 1464
James Clerk Maxwell, 1528
James Mill, 1571
James Nasmyth, 1646
Sir Henry Raeburn, 1852
Sir Walter Scott, 2047
Mary Somerville, 2121
Robert Louis Stevenson, 2173
Thomas Telford, 2240
Frances Wright, 2469

SIERRA LEONE
Samuel Ajayi Crowther, 574

SOUTH AFRICA
Sir Robert Stephenson Smyth Baden-Powell, 110
Cetshwayo, 450
Sir George Grey, 981
H. Rider Haggard, 1006
Paul Kruger, 1298
David Livingstone, 1400
Cecil Rhodes, 1891
Olive Schreiner, 2023
Shaka, 2081

SOUTH AMERICA
Simón Bolívar, 267
Joaquim Maria Machado de Assis, 1449
Clorinda Matto de Turner, 1512
Bernardo O'Higgins, 1703
Pedro I, 1763
Pedro II, 1766
André Rebouças, 1869
José de San Martín, 1984
Domingo Faustino Sarmiento, 2000
Antonio José de Sucre, 2195

SPAIN
Fanny Calderón de la Barca, 389
Don Carlos, 412
Carolina Coronado, 556
Isabella II, 1183
La Saragossa, 1993

SUDAN
The Mahdi, 1473

SWEDEN
Charles XIV John, 468
Jenny Lind, 1387
Alfred Nobel, 1689

SWITZERLAND
Jacob Burckhardt, 354
Jean-Henri Dunant, 699
Johann Heinrich Pestalozzi, 1782
Jakob Steiner, 2154

TANZANIA
Sa'īd ibn Sulṭān, 1965
Tippu Tib, 2277

THAILAND
Anna Leonowens, 1346

UNITED STATES
Henry Adams, 16
John Quincy Adams, 20
Felix Adler, 26
Elizabeth Cabot Agassiz, 29
Louis Agassiz, 31
Bronson Alcott, 38
Louisa May Alcott, 41

Horatio Alger, 51
John Peter Altgeld, 57
Susan B. Anthony, 65
Johnny Appleseed, 68
Chester A. Arthur, 79
John Jacob Astor, 86
John James Audubon, 91
Stephen Fuller Austin, 98
George Bancroft, 130
Henry Barnard, 135
P. T. Barnum, 138
Clara Barton, 145
L. Frank Baum, 155
Catharine Beecher, 168
Henry Ward Beecher, 172
Alexander Graham Bell, 182
James Gordon Bennett, 188
Thomas Hart Benton, 192
Nicholas Biddle, 225
Ambrose Bierce, 228
Albert Bierstadt, 232
George Caleb Bingham, 234
Black Hawk, 244
Elizabeth Blackwell, 247
James G. Blaine, 251
Amelia Bloomer, 257
Edwin Booth, 271
Lizzie Borden, 277
Mathew B. Brady, 291
John Brown, 319
Olympia Brown, 323
William Cullen Bryant, 340
James Buchanan, 343
Charles Bulfinch, 346
Luther Burbank, 350
Frances Hodgson Burnett, 357
Daniel Hudson Burnham, 360
Aaron Burr, 363
Frances Xavier Cabrini, 383
Calamity Jane, 386
John C. Calhoun, 392
Alexander Campbell, 399
Andrew Carnegie, 419
Kit Carson, 426
Mary Ann Shadd Cary, 431
Mary Cassatt, 433
George Catlin, 441
William Ellery Channing, 464
Salmon P. Chase, 470
Lydia Maria Child, 482

Great Lives from History

Indexes

PERSONAGES INDEX

Melbourne of Melbourne, Baron.
  See Melbourne, Second
  Viscount
Melville, Herman, 1052, 1537-
  1541
Ménard, Anne-Caroline. *See*
  Ségalas, Anaïs
Mendel, Gregor, 1541-1544
Mendeleyev, Dmitry Ivanovich,
  1544-1549
Mendelssohn, Felix, 952, 1549-
  1551, 2033
Mendelssohn-Bartholdy, Jacob
  Ludwig Felix. *See*
  Mendelssohn, Felix
Menelik II, 1552-1554, 2256
Menken, Adah Isaacs, 1555-1557;
  Mark Twain, 1556
Mergenthaler, Ottmar, 1558-1560
Mérimée, Prosper, 242
Merriam, Charles, 2404
Merriam, George, 2404
Merryman, John, 2228
Metcalfe, Sir Charles, 124, 1858
Metternich, 222, 404, 440, 818,
  1023, 1561-1564
Mey, Lev, 1915
Meyer, Lothar, 103, 1547
Mhlangane, 2082
Michelet, Jules, 1564-1566
Michelson, Albert A., 1567-1571
Mickiewicz, Adam, 487
Middleton, Frederick D., 1911
Miguel, Dom, 413, 1764
Miles, Nelson, 525, 568, 906,
  1240
Mill, James, 1571-1574, 1576,
  1807
Mill, John Stuart, 264, 1572,
  1574-1579, 2103; Dame
  Millicent Garrett Fawcett, 768
Millais, John Everett, 1755, 1940
Millennial Harbinger, 400
Miller, Alfred Jacob, 232
Miller, William Allen, 1145
Milner, Henry M., 1555
Milton, Frances. *See* Trollope,
  Frances
Minh Mang, 908
Minkus, Ludwig, 639

Miranda, Francisco de, 268
Mīrzā ʿalī. *See* Bāb, the
Mīrzā Ḥoseynʿalī Nūrī. *See*
  Bahāʾullāh
Mīrzā Ḥusaynʿalī Nūrī. *See*
  Bahāʾullāh
Mīrzā Rezā Kermānī, 1205
Mitchell, Maria, 812, 1580-1582
Mitre, Bartolomé, 2001
Moffat, John Smith, 1407
Moffat, Robert, 1402
Moffat, W. B., 2044
Mohammed Ahmed, 950, 1553
Moll, Gerrit, 1079
Moltke, Helmuth Karl Bernhard
  von, 501
Mommsen, Christian Matthias
  Theodor. *See* Mommsen,
  Theodor
Mommsen, Theodor, 1582-1585
Monet, Claude, 453, 632, 1800,
  1888
Monge, Gaspard, 809
Mongkut, 1346; invitation to Anna
  Leonowens, 1347
Monroe, James, 21, 348, 404,
  1586-1590; Monroe Doctrine,
  1588
Montez, Lola, 1590-1592
Montojo, Patricio, 646
Moodie, Susanna, 1593-1595,
  2292; *Roughing It in the Bush*,
  1594
Moody, Dwight L., 1596-1599
Moore, Carry Amelia. *See* Nation,
  Carry
Moore, Thomas, 1224
Moran, Thomas, 233
Morelli, Felice, 384
Morelos, José María, 1096
Morgan, J. P., 421, 510, 1102,
  1599-1603, 2253
Morgan, Lewis Henry, 1603-1606
Morgenthau, Henry, 27
Morisot, Berthe, 1800
Morley, Edward Williams, 1568
Morris, Charles A., 1114
Morris, William, 1606-1609
Morse, Samuel F. B., 292, 535,
  557, 1080, 1610-1613

Morton, William Thomas Green,
  1613-1616
Moscozo, Flore-Célestine-
  Thérèse-Henriette Tristan y.
  See Tristan, Flora
Moses, Phoebe Anne. *See* Oakley,
  Annie
Moskowa, Prince de la. *See* Ney,
  Michel
Mott, Lucretia, 257, 1616-1619
Moulton, Elizabeth Barrett. *See*
  Browning, Elizabeth Barrett
Mount, William Sidney, 235
Moynier, Gustave, 699
Mpande, 450
Muḥammad. *See* Bāb, the
Muḥammad ʿAbduh, 1204
Muḥammad Aḥmad ibn as-Sayyid
  ʿAbd-Allāh. *See* Mahdi, the
Muḥammad ʿAlī Pasha, 1620-
  1623, 1733, 2265
Muḥammad Ballo. *See* Bello,
  Muḥammad
Muḥammad Bello ibn Uthman.
  See Bello, Muḥammad
Muḥammad Rʾuf Pasha, 1474
Muḥammad Tawfīq Pasha, 1204
Muḥammad ʿUthmān Abu Qarja,
  1474
Muhammed Ahmed, 2140
Muhammed Bin Hamid. *See*
  Tippu Tib
Muir, John, 748, 1623-1626; *The
  Yosemite*, 1625
Mullā Ḥūsayn, 105
Müller, Johannes, 1003
Muncke, Georg Wilhelm, 547
Murad V, 7
Murat, Joachim, 2224
Murchison, Sir Roderick Impey,
  369, 1423, 2125
Murphy, Anna Brownell. *See*
  Jameson, Anna
Murray, Margaret Lindsay. *See*
  Huggins, Margaret Lindsay
Musset, Alfred de, 1988
Mussorgsky, Modest, 281, 1626-
  1630, 1915
Mutsuhito, 1631-1633
Mzilikazi, 1406

Paul, Oom. *See* Kruger, Paul
Pavlovich, Aleksandr. *See* Alexander I
Pavlovich, Nikolay. *See* Nicholas I
Peabody, Elizabeth Palmer, 1761-1763
Peale, Titian Ramsay, 232
Pecci, Vincenzo Gioacchino. *See* Leo XIII
Pedro I, 1763-1766
Pedro II, 1766-1768, 1870
Peel, Sir Robert, 303, 521, 643, 667, 840, 924, 1696, 1768-1771, 2122
Peirce, Charles Sanders, 1215, 1772-1775
Pérez, José Julián Martí y. *See* Martí, José
Perrault, Charles, 1155
Perry, Carolina Coronado. *See* Coronado, Carolina
Perry, Horatio Justus, 557
Perry, Matthew C., 1109, 1169, 1776-1779, 1969
Perry, Oliver Hazard, 1776, 1779-1781
Pestalozzi, Johann Heinrich, 1782-1785
Peter Porcupine. *See* Cobbett, William
Pétion, Alexandre, 268, 495
Petrović, Karadjordje, 2479
Pettigrew, Richard F., 1019
Phillips, Wendell, 1231, 1785-1788
Piazzi, Giuseppi, 884
Pierce, Edward L., 472
Pierce, Franklin, 344, 612, 682, 1789-1793; state of the union address, 1791
Piérola, Nicolás, 1513
Pigneau de Béhaine, Pierre Joseph Georges, 908
Pike, Zebulon, 1793-1796
Pinkham, Lydia E., 1796-1799
Pinkney, William, 1587
Pissarro, Camille, 453, 879, 934, 1799-1802
Pissarro, Jacob-Abraham-Camille. *See* Pissarro, Camille

Pitt, William, the Younger, 437, 1397
Pius IX, 13, 872, 922, 1532, 1802-1805
Place, Francis, 1769, 1806-1809
Planck, Max, 1818
Pobedonostsev, Konstantin Petrovich, 1810-1813
Poe, Edgar Allan, 153, 1813-1816
Poincaré, Henri, 1816-1819
Poincaré, Jules Henri. *See* Poincaré, Henri
Poinsett, Joel, 831
Poisson, Siméon-Denis, 858, 903
Polignac, Jules de, 477
Polk, James K., 132, 194, 344, 505, 1819-1824; state of the union address, 1821
Pope, John, 1199
Popov, Aleksandr Stepanovich, 1824-1827
Porcupine, Peter. *See* Cobbett, William
Porter, David, 762, 764
Porter, John, 763
Porter, William Sydney. *See* Henry, O.
Pottinger, Henry, 1379
Powell, John Wesley, 1827-1831
Prescott, William Hickling, 390, 1831-1834
Pretorius, Andries, 1298
Pretorius, Marthinus, 1299
Price, Stephen, 1257
Price, Uvedale, 1643
Proudhon, Pierre-Joseph, 119, 1321, 1834-1837
Proust, Antonin, 1479
Puccini, Giacomo, 1155
Pueyrredón, Juan Martín, 1985
Pugin, Augustus Welby Northmore, 143, 1838-1841, 2044
Pulitzer, Joseph, 1841-1844, 2056
Pusey, E. B., 77, 1844-1848
Pushkin, Alexander, 937, 1848-1851
Putnam, Mary Corinna. *See* Jacobi, Mary Putnam
Puyi, 498

Qazwini, Fāṭima Khanum Baragani. *See* Táhirih
Quang Trung, 1110
Quantrill, William Clarke, 1211
Quimby, Phineas P., 723
Quiroga, Juan Facundo, 2000
Qurrat al-ʿAyn. *See* Táhirih

Raeburn, Sir Henry, 1852-1855
Ramakrishna Paramhansa, 2369
Ramsay, James Andrew Broun. *See* Dalhousie, first marquis of
Ranade, Mahadev Govind, 1855-1857
Ranjit Singh, 1857-1859
Ranke, Leopold von, 354, 1860-1862
Rashid Bey Ayman, 1474
Rasputin, Grigori Yefimovich, 1863-1866
Rattazzi, Urbando, 446
Raʾuf Pahsa, 1474
Rawnsley, Canon Hardwicke, 1105
Ray, Rammohan, 1866-1869
Reade, Charles, 2250
Rebouças, André, 1869-1871
Red Cloud, 567, 1871-1874
Redon, Bertrand-Jean. *See* Redon, Odilon
Redon, Odilon, 1875-1877
Rée, Paul, 1682
Reed, Walter, 1877-1880
Reeves, William Pember, 982, 2059
Reid, Sir George, 624
Reményi, Eduard, 296
Remington, Frederic, 1881-1884
Renan, Ernest, 1204, 1884-1888
Renan, Joseph-Ernest. *See* Renan, Ernest
Renoir, Pierre-Auguste, 453, 632, 1800, 1888-1891
Reynolds, John Hamilton, 1260
Rhodes, Cecil, 462, 1286, 1299, 1406, 1891-1895
Ricardo, David, 1896-1898
Ricardo, John Lewis, 549
Rice, Thomas "Daddy," 802
Richards, Ellen Swallow, 1899-1901

SUBJECT INDEX

All personages whose names appear in **boldface type** in this index are the subjects of articles in *Great Lives from History: The Nineteenth Century, 1801-1900*. Note that some articles cover more than one person.

Meistersinger von Nürnberg, Die
(Wagner), 2376
Melbourne, Second Viscount,
709, 1534-1536, 2447
Melbourne of Melbourne, Baron.
See Melbourne, Second
Viscount
Melville, Herman, 1052, 1537-
1541
Memoir (Davis, V.), 614
*Mémoire sur une propriété
générale d'une classe très-
étendue de fonctions
transcendantes* (Abel), 11
Memoirs of a Tourist (Stendhal),
2163
Memoirs of an Egotist (Stendhal),
2160
Memoirs of Rossini (Stendhal),
2162
Memoirs of Sherlock Holmes, The
(Doyle), 689
Memorial de Ayres. See *Counselor
Ayres' Memorial* (Machado)
*Memorial de l'art
d'accouchements* (Boivin), 266
*Memórias póstumas de Bráz
Cubas*. See *Epitaph of a Small
Winner* (Machado)
Memories of My Life (Galton),
860
Memory of Solferino, A (Dunant),
699
Ménard, Anne-Caroline. *See*
Ségalas, Anaïs
Mendel, Gregor, 1541-1544
Mendeleyev, Dmitry Ivanovich,
1544-1549
Mendelssohn, Felix, 952, 1549-
1551, 2033
Mendelssohn-Bartholdy, Jacob
Ludwig Felix. *See*
Mendelssohn, Felix
Menelik II, 1552-1554, 2256
Menken, Adah Isaacs, 1555-
1557; Mark Twain, 1556
Menschenerziehung, Die. See
Education of Man, The
(Froebel)
Menschliches, Allzumenschliches.

See *Human, All Too Human*
(Nietzsche)
Mental illness, treatment of, 671,
1486
Méphis (Tristan), 2298
Mercedes automobile, 594
Merchant Shipping Act of 1876,
669
Mercy Philbrick's Choice
(Jackson), 1195
Mergenthaler, Ottmar, 1558-1560
Mergenthaler Linotype Company,
1559
Mérimée, Prosper, 242
Merriam, Charles, 2404
Merriam, George, 2404
*Merrie Tales of Jacques
Tournebroche, The* (France),
816
*Merry Men and Other Tales and
Fables, The* (Stevenson), 2176
Merryman, John, 2228
Mes Mémoires. See *My Memoirs*
(Dumas, A.)
Messa da requiem (Verdi), 2353
Message (newspaper), 1459
Messe de morts. See *Requiem*
(Berlioz)
Messe solennelle de Sainte Cécile
(Gounod), 953
Metallurgy; England, 218;
Germany, 1301; United States,
1000
Metamora (Stone), 792
Metaphysical Club, 1773
Metcalfe, Sir Charles, 124, 1858
Meteoritic Hypothesis, The
(Lockyer), 1414
*Méthodes nouvelles de la
mécanique céleste, Les*
(Poincaré), 1817
Methods of Ethics, The
(Sidgwick), 2103
*Methods of Study in Natural
History* (Agassiz, L.), 34
Metis, 1909
Metternich, 222, 404, 440, 818,
1023, 1561-1564
Meunier d'Angibault, Le. See
Miller of Angibault, The (Sand)

Mexican-American War. *See*
Mexican War (1846-1848)
Mexican Revolution of 1910, 654
Mexican War (1846-1848), 25,
194, 1821-1822, 1991; Kit
Carson, 428; Jefferson Davis,
611; David G. Farragut, 764;
Ulysses S. Grant, 958; guns,
535; Matthew C. Perry, 1777;
Franklin Pierce, 1790; Winfield
Scott, 2053; Zachary Taylor,
2231
Mexico, 820; French intervention
in, 1246; independence of,
1095, 1991. *See also*
Geographical Index
Mey, Lev, 1915
Meyer, Lothar, 103, 1547
Mhlangane, 2082
Michael (Wordsworth), 2463
Michael Kohlhaas (Kleist), 1290
Michelet, Jules, 1564-1566
Michelson, Albert A., 1567-1571
Michelson interferometer, 1568
Mickiewicz, Adam, 487
Microbiology, 1752, 2407
Midas (Shelley, M.), 2088
Middle East; *map*, xlvii, lxxxv,
cxxiii, clxi. *See also* Ottoman
Empire; Geographical Index
under Ottoman Empire
Middlemarch (Eliot), 741
Middleton, Frederick D., 1911
Midsummer Night's Dream, A
(Mendelssohn), 1549
Mighty Handful, 1915
Miguel, Dom, 413, 1764
Mikado, The (Gilbert and
Sullivan), 919
Milan Commission, 892
Miles, Nelson, 525, 568, 906,
1240
Military; Prussia, 930; United
States, 962. *See also* Category
Index
Military Academy, U.S., 2261
Military Reorganization
Commission, 929
Mill, James, 1571-1574, 1576,
1807

Pettigrew, Richard F., 1019
Peuple, Le. See *People, The* (Michelet)
Peveril of the Peak (Scott), 2048
Pflanze, Die (Cohn), 528
Phalanstère, Le, 807
Phänomenologie des Geistes, Die. See *Phenomenology of Spirit, The* (Hegel)
Phantasmagoria (Carroll), 424
Phenomenology of Spirit, The (Hegel), 1066
Philadelphia Anti-Slavery Society, 989
Philadelphia Functionalists, 2198
Philanthrophy; Andrew Carnegie, 421; James Buchanan Duke, 694; Marshall Field, 775; J. P. Morgan, 1602; Alfred Nobel, 1691; Robert Owen, 1721; Joseph Pulitzer, 1843; Cecil Rhodes, 1894; John D. Rockefeller, 1924; Leland Stanford, 2134; Montgomery Ward, 2389. *See also* Category Index
Philanthropist (newspaper), 471
Philémon et Baucis (Gounod), 953
Philharmonic Society, 2268
Philiki Hetairia, 2478
Philippines, 647, 1462
Phillips, Wendell, 1231, 1785-1788
Philosopher or Dog? (Machado), 1451
Philosophical Essay on Probabilities, A (Laplace), 1318
Philosophical Fragments (Kierkegaard), 1280
Philosophical Radicalism, 456, 1576
Philosophie der Mythologie (Schelling), 2011
Philosophie des Unbewussten. See *Philosophy of the Unconscious* (Hartmann)
Philosophische Untersuchungen über das Wesen der menschlichen Freiheit. See *Of Human Freedom* (Schelling)

Philosophiske Smuler. See *Philosophical Fragments* (Kierkegaard)
Philosophy; Denmark, 1278; England, 289, 1045, 1572, 1574, 2103, 2127; France, 255, 806, 1836, 1976; Germany, 837, 1066, 1682, 2009, 2020; Great Britain, 971; Japan, 2213; Russia, 120, 1811; United States, 746, 1215, 1773. *See also* Category Index
Philosophy of Right (Hegel), 1067
Philosophy of the Unconscious (Hartmann), 2021
Philothea (Child), 483
Phineas Redux (Trollope, A.), 2302
Phoenix Park murders, 1749
Phonograph, 731
Photography, 590; American West, 1058; development of, 1678; England, 423; United States, 293. *See also* Category Index
Photometric Researches (Peirce), 1772
Phrenology, 812, 1143
Physical Geography (Somerville), 2122
Physical Geography of the Sea (Maury), 1523
Physics; atomic theory, 599, 887; celestial mechanics, 1817; conical refraction, 1016; conservation of energy, 997; dynamos, 760; electric cell, 996; electrodynamics, 1074; electromagnetism, 1079, 1529, 1825; England, 2122; France, 166; gases, 598, 617, 886; Germany, 1931; heat diffusion, 810; optics, 1074; radioactivity, 166; relativity theory, 1818; thermodynamics, 914, 1265; velocity of light, 1568; X rays, 1932. *See also* Category Index
Physiologie als Erfahrungswissenschaft, Die (Burdach), 114

Physiology; France, 206; Germany, 1073
Piano Concerto in A Minor (Grieg), 986
Piano Concerto in A Minor (Schumann, R.), 2033-2034
Piano Concerto No. 2 in B-flat, Op. 83 (Brahms), 298
Piano Concerto, Op. 7 (Schumann, C.), 2029
Piano Quintet in A Major (Schubert), 2026
Piano Quintet in F Minor, Op. 34 (Brahms), 297
Piano Trio in A Minor (Tchaikovsky), 2234
Piano Trio in B Major, Op. 8 (Brahms), 297
Piazza Tales, The (Melville), 1539
Piazzi, Giuseppi, 884
Pickering-Fleming system, 789
Pickett's charge (1863), 1336
Pickwick Papers (Dickens), 655
Picture of Dorian Gray, The (Wilde), 2433
Pictures from an Exhibition (Mussorgsky), 1628
Pictures of Travel (Heine), 1070
Pièges et charlatanisme des deux sectes Saint-Simon et Owen, qui promettent l'association et le progrès (Fourier, C.), 805
Pierce, Edward L., 472
Pierce, Franklin, 344, 612, 682, 1789-1793; state of the union address, 1791
Piérola, Nicolás, 1513
Pierre (Melville), 1539
Pierre and Jean (Maupassant), 1516
Pierre Nozière (France), 815
Pigneau de Béhaine, Pierre Joseph Georges, 908
Pike, Zebulon, 1793-1796
Pike County Ballads and Other Pieces (Hay), 1054
Pikes Peak, 1794
Pikovaya dama. See *Queen of Spades, The* (Pushkin); *Queen of Spades, The* (Tchaikovsky)

Truth (Zola), 2491

Tsar's Bride, The (Rimsky-Korsakov), 1916

Tshaka. *See* Shaka

Tsygany. See *Gypsies, The* (Pushkin)

Tu Duc, 2310-2312

Tuberculosis, 1293

Tübingen school, 1918

Tubman, Harriet, 2312-2316

Tulipe Noire, La. See *Black Tulip, The* (Dumas, A.)

Tupper, Sir Charles, 2316-2318

Tupper, First Baronet. *See* Tupper, Sir Charles

Turgenev, Ivan, 2319-2321

Turkey, 1732. *See also* Ottoman Empire; Geographical Index under Ottoman Empire

Turkish Bath, The (Ingres), 1173

Turn of the Screw, The (James), 1207

Turner, Clorinda Matto de. *See* Matto de Turner, Clorinda

Turner, J. M. W., 1954, 2322-2325

Turner, Nat, 876, 2326-2329; motives for rebellion, 2327

Turpin, John, 1236

Turton, Thomas, 709

Tuskegee Institute, 2391

TUV. *See* Trades Union Congress

Twain, Mark, 961, 1039, 2329-2333; autobiography, 2331; on Alexander Campbell, 401; on Leopold II, 1351; on Adah Isaacs Menken, 1556; Charlotte Mary Yonge, 2473

Tweed, William Marcy, 1650, 2333-2336

Tweed Ring, 1650

Twenty-eighth Congregational Society, 1736

Twenty Thousand Leagues Under the Sea (Verne), 2357

Twenty Years After (Dumas, A.), 697

Twice-Told Tales (Hawthorne), 1051, 1814

Two Admirals, The (Cooper), 555

Two Guardians, The (Yonge), 2472

Two Summers in the Ice-wilds of Eastern Karakoram (Workman, F., and Workman, W.), 2468

Two Years Before the Mast (Melville), 1538

Tyler, John, 505, 579, 2337-2341; state of the union address, 2339

Typee (Melville), 1537

Tz'u-hsi. *See* Cixi

Über Bacterien. See *Bacteria* (Cohn)

Über den Willen in der Natur. See *On the Will in Nature* (Schopenhauer)

Über die Möglichkeit einer Form der Philosophie überhaupt (Schelling), 2009

Über die Religion. See *On Religion* (Schleiermacher)

Über die vierfache Wurzel des Satzes vom zureichende Grunde. See *On the Fourfold Root of the Principle of Sufficient Reason* (Schopenhauer)

Über Entwickelungsgeschichte der Thiere (Baer), 114

Übermensch, 1682

Uccialli, Treaty of (1889), 1553

Uchenye zapiski, 1404

Ukiyo-e, 1107

Ulster rebellion (1798), 438

Ultra-Conservatives, 1442

Ultramontanism, 13

Umar Tal, al-Hājj, 756

Uncalled, The (Dunbar), 703

Uncle Remus (Harris), 1036

Uncle Tom's Cabin (Stowe, H.), 990, 2184, 2186

Uncle Vanya (Chekhov), 480

Unconscious Memory (Butler), 375

Under the Greenwood Tree (Hardy), 1028

Underground Railroad, 2313

Undine (Schreiner), 2024

Unges forbund. See *League of Youth, The* (Ibsen)

Uniformitarianism, 1424

Union, Act of (1801, Ireland), 439

Union, Act of (1839, Oklahoma), 1938

Union, Act of (1840, Canada), 317, 1441, 1452

Union of American Hebrew Congregations, 2454

Union of South Africa, 1299

Union ouvrière, L'. See *Worker's Union, The* (Tristan)

Union Pacific Railroad, 2134

Union Switch and Signal Company, 2417

Union to Combat Anti-Semitism, 2207

Unions; coal strike, 1020; England, 669; France, 2298; Samuel Gompers, 943; Knights of Labor, 910; Alfred Krupp, 1302; mine strikes, 1043; newspaper, 2057; Scotland, 1025; technological innovation, 1559; United States, 895; women, 212

Unitarian Controversy, 464

Unitarianism, 465, 1735, 1868

United African Company, 941

United Irishmen, 438

United Kingdom; creation of, 439. *See also* Geographical Index under England; Ireland; Scotland; Wales

United Press, 2057

U.S. election of 1824, 22, 1190; dispute surrounding, 2345

U.S. election of 1840, 579; Henry Clay, 505; Martin Van Buren, 2346

U.S. election of 1844, 579; Henry Clay, 505

U.S. election of 1856; Millard Fillmore, 783

U.S. election of 1860; Abraham Lincoln, 612

U.S. election of 1872; Susan B. Anthony, 67; Horace Greeley, 969; Victoria Woodhull, 2460

U.S. election of 1876; controversy, 869; Rutherford B. Hayes, 869